Client-Server Programming with OS/2 Extended Edition

Robert Orfali · Dan Harkey

VNR VAN NOSTRAND REINHOLD
New York

Library of Congress Catalog Card Number 90-28345
ISBN 0-442-00826-0

Manufactured in the United States of America

Published by Van Nostrand Reinhold
115 Fifth Avenue
New York, N.Y. 10003

Chapman and Hall
2-6 Boundary Row
London, SE1 8HN

Thomas Nelson Australia
102 Dodds Street
South Melbourne 3205
Victoria, Australia

Nelson Canada
1120 Birchmount Road
Scarborough, Ontario M1K 5G4, Canada

16 15 14 13 12 10 9 8 7 6 5 4 3 2

Library of Congress Cataloging-in-Publication Data

Orfali, Robert
Client-server programming with OS/2 / by Robert Orfali, Dan Harkey
—Extended ed.
p. cm.
Includes index.
"October 17, 1990."
ISBN 0-442-00826-0
1. OS/2 (Computer operating system) 2. Local Area Networks
(Computer networks) I. Harkey, Dan. II. Title.
QA76.76.063074 1990
004.6'8—dc20 90-28345
CIP

Dedication

This book is dedicated to my wife and daughter, Michiko and Tomomi, and to my parents, Howard and Barbara. Their support and encouragement were invaluable.

Dan Harkey

This book is dedicated with love to my wife Jeri and my mother Mimi.

Robert Orfali

Trademarks

Preface

The new generation of *client-server* business solutions combines the intuitive user interface of the PC with multiuser server capabilities for transaction processing previously found only on superminis or mainframes. Client-Server makes it possible to create industrial strength software solutions on low cost network-attached PCs. These solutions promise to maintain the PC's traditional autonomy and ease of use and at the same time overcome the "stand-alone" isolation of PC software.

To create these new solutions, you must learn how to use and integrate the *extended* services provided by a new breed of PC operating systems. The services that "extend" the PC include: preemptive multitasking, interprocess communication, peer-to-peer LAN protocols, SQL database, and an advanced graphical user interface (GUI). This book teaches you how to develop client-server solutions using OS/2 Extended Edition (OS/2 EE) as the extended operating system platform.

Why OS/2 EE? Because it is a modern operating system that was designed from the ground up for personal computer technology and client-server environments. OS/2 EE provides a very complete platform on which you can build working software.

What You Will Learn

In this book we will go beyond merely telling you about client-server architecture; we will create working client-server systems that demonstrate *how the pieces play together*. These working systems will give you a practical understanding of how to exploit the synergy (and avoid the pitfalls) inherent in distributed applications. OS/2 EE is the operating system package that comes closest to providing all the necessary platform ingredients needed to create these systems.

In learning how to program OS/2 EE, you will cover almost the entire curriculum of applied computer science. By the time you get through this book you will be able to use the C-language to create multitasking applications that communicate with other applications over a Local Area Network (LAN). Your applications will be able to use the full power of the Standard Query Language (SQL) to interface to a database. Your graphics will be created using Presentation Manager's object-oriented interface.

Client-Server is primarily a relationship between programs running on separate machines. The separation of the client and server tasks became cost-justifiable with the advent of low-cost and robust peer-to-peer communications over LANs and Wide Area Networks (WANs). We assume that you will want existing MS-DOS machines to communicate with your new OS/2 EE application code over the network. With that in mind, we will explore how to write OS/2 EE applications that service MS-DOS machines over a LAN. You will be able to create hybrid networks of low-cost MS-DOS clients that work in conjunction with powerful OS/2 EE "super servers." Your OS/2 EE servers will use the most advanced form of communications such as Named Pipes and remote SQL to synchronize their services. At the other end of the spectrum you may want to communicate with your mainframes. You will learn how to write peer-to-peer applications using Advanced Program to Program Communications (APPC). With APPC you can treat the mainframe as just another server. You'll see that OS/2 EE was born to network.

Once you master communications, you will have the capability to provide useful services to remote clients. In this book, you will learn to combine this capability with the power of a network-based relational database. Since OS/2 EE breaks the 640 KByte memory limitation of DOS, you will have plenty of memory space available to write powerful transaction processing applications. These applications will provide a variety of services to remote clients. You will find that OS/2 EE provides a powerful platform for creating intelligent network objects. These objects may be combined into "ensembles" that cooperate to provide increasingly more sophisticated functions.

How hard will it be for you to learn all these technologies and build working systems out of them? We wrote this book with the intention of getting you there by the shortest route possible. We also want you to enjoy the process. We believe that studying working code is probably the most effortless way to demystify the arcane terminology of Operating Systems, Database, Data Communications, and Presentation Manager Programming.

We will start you off with simple C programs that eventually become building blocks in creating industrial-strength applications. You will see ensembles come together from diverse elements. Most importantly, you will understand which of the different techniques provides the best fit for a job. In many instances, we will program the same function using different OS/2 EE Application Programming Interfaces (APIs) and then compare the cost benefits of each approach. The programming examples will be accompanied by in-depth tutorials that provide you with the necessary background on a particular topic.

Who Is This Book For?

This book is for anyone interested in creating client-server software solutions and in the process learn how to program OS/2 EE. If you are a novice, the book will serve as a crash course in computer science in addition to teaching OS/2 EE. If you are a seasoned professional programmer, then you can dive straight into the examples where you will find a wealth of working code that may save you hundreds of hours of debugging and wading through a pile of manuals. If you are a manager, system architect, or planner, this book will address issues such as:

- When to use processes and when to use threads.
- What are the relative merits of the different peer-to-peer communication protocols?
- What to look for in a Graphical User Interface (GUI) for On-line Transaction Processing (OLTP).
- How hard is it to put together a graphic application using GUI tools?
- What is the most effective way to provide network services?
- What is the best strategy for developing client-server software using an SQL database as a platform?

To get the most out of this book, you should have a working knowledge of the C language and be somewhat familiar with PCs. Prior experience with networks and databases would be nice to have, but we will help you get by without it.

How the Information Is Organized

Part I introduces the client-server model and presents a detailed overview of OS/2 and its extensions. You get to see the whole thing in one place before plunging into the details.

Part II covers the important core services which are needed for the creation of multitasking clients and servers. Many of OS/2's kernel strengths such as preemptive multitasking, multithreading and the hardware enforced protection between applications are invisible to the end-user. Nevertheless, these are the strengths that are critical to building LAN-based, mission critical, client-server applications. When you combine these elements with the OS/2 EE Database and Communications Manager, you are very close to having a world-class server platform on a PC. We will develop a benchmark program that demonstrates how to effectively use multitasking and multithreading. OS/2 is the first commonly available operating system to provide threads which allow you to multitask very effectively from within a process. You will use the program to learn how to use processes and threads effectively and fine tune their performance using OS/2's priority levels. We will then explore Named Pipes, OS/2's most powerful and elegant method for interprocess communication. The expertise you develop with processes, threads, semaphores, and Named Pipes will serve you well with the programs in the book.

Part III covers protocols for LAN-based client-server communications. We will develop a client-server repository for files using a layered software approach. The client-server implementation uses a generic file transfer program that runs on top of APPC, NetBIOS, Named Pipes, and the LAN Server. We will run benchmarks that compare the performance of these four protocols and the ease of programming them. We will show you how to package these communications programs as Dynamic Link Libraries (DLLs). This is an area that should be of great interest to providers of commercial software.

Part IV covers the Database Manager. This component constitutes the heart of the *Database Server* platform. We will show you how to use SQL to program the Database Manager. You will learn how to invoke the Database Manager's environment, configuration, and system utilities directly through the C language API. We will use this knowledge to create an all-in-one utility that runs scripts of SQL and Database Administration commands. This utility teaches you how to use SQL effectively and measure the performance of the various commands.

Part V introduces benchmarks which compare the performance of *Database Servers* and *Transaction Servers*. We will develop a standard TP1 benchmark toolkit which measures raw OLTP performance in units of transactions per second (tps). We will use the TP1 benchmark to measure the performance of different client-server architectures. We will answer questions like: How slow is Dynamic SQL? How much faster are Transaction Servers than Database Servers? What is the effect of CPU speed on server performance? What is the effect of the network?

Part VI is about creating interactive front-end clients using the Presentation Manager and Dialog Manager window services. The screens will use IBM's Common User Access (CUA) Object/Action model. This is not a book about programming the Presentation Manager. Our aim is to use a graphical user interface (GUI) tool to create the bulk of the client code. GUI tools provide you some level of platform independence allowing your clients to work with either PM or Windows 3.0. We will use the Dialog Manager, a tool which comes with every OS/2 toolkit, to create the bulk of our Presentation Manager applications (a Windows 3.0 version of Dialog Manager is available from Arcadia Technologies Inc.). We will program directly to the Presentation Manager from a Dialog Manager shell when we need to produce specialized graphic effects. We will demonstrate how this graphic environment can be used as a front-end for networked database transactions. In the process, we discuss what is needed from GUI tools in client-server environments.

Part VII is the grand finale that brings together all the client-server elements developed in this book. We will develop a fun client-server application called Club Med. In this adventurous example, the multithreaded Club Med clients use a PM-based graphical user interface. The clients communicate with a Club Med *Transcation Server* via Named Pipes.

Acknowledgements

- To Dick Conklin, Editor of the IBM Personal Systems Developer. He was there when we needed him and was instrumental in making this book happen.
- To Jeri Edwards, who created the illustrations for this book. She taught us a lot about client-server computing.
- To our managers at IBM; Ken Ouchi, Dick Luedtke, Jim Eldridge, and Yean-Ming Huang. They gave us four challenging years to learn client-server technology as it is used in the "real world."
- To the team of IBM programmers in San Jose and Seattle who helped us make TxE into a world-class client-server platform. This book was inspired by the TxE effort.
- To Reese Ferry and Claire Foster of the IBM Seattle branch office, who taught us how client-server systems work in production environments.
- To the OS/2 EE developers in IBM and Microsoft, who created a first-class operating system for PCs.
- To Beth McAuliffe and Joan Dunkin of IBM Yorktown, who helped us create this book with Bookmaster.
- To Jim Stuart and Art Schmidt in IBM San Jose who helped us prepare this book for Postscript printing.
- To Dianne Littwin, the Senior Editor at Van Nostrand Reinhold. She is a pleasure to work with. We also thank the members of Dianne's staff.
- We thank our copy editor George Chipman. He spent his Christmas and New Year's vacation reading our book.

Contents

Part I

The Big Picture

The OS/2 platform provides the raw building blocks we will use to develop working examples of client-server business solutions. So the first order of the day will be to understand these building blocks and their functions. We will then examine what business solutions can be provided using these building blocks as our platform. Finally, we will develop an architectural framework that helps us better understand how the building blocks and the business solutions come together. Here is the road map for Part I:

- In Chapter 1, "Welcome To Client-Server Computing", we introduce the concept of client-server. We explain what client-server computing is and what makes a product "client-server." We also explain the importance of client-server software for the next generation of PC applications.
- In Chapter 2, "Why OS/2 Extended Edition", we introduce OS/2 EE in a very general manner. Among other things we explain where OS/2 EE fits into the scheme of things and why we chose it for our client-server platform base. The platform you choose will directly influence what software systems you can build, how fast can you build them, and at what cost. Yes, a platform is like a long-term marriage; think through it carefully before you jump into it.
- In Chapter 3, "OS/2 EE: A Grand Tour", we provide an extensive overview of the building blocks OS/2 EE provides. This is a long chapter because OS/2 EE is a well endowed operating system. A first encounter with OS/2 EE is like looking at a very long buffet table filled with hundreds of exotic food dishes, most of which you do not recognize. Where do you start? Ideally you should take a quick tour of the buffet and then return to make your choice of dishes at a more leisurely pace. In this chapter, we will take that tour around OS/2 EE in fifty pages or less. As you will see in later chapters, much of what OS/2 EE provides can be used in the development of client-server systems.
- In Chapter 4, "Architectures for Client-Server Computing", we introduce a set of distributed architecture models which should help you make sense out of the seemingly overabundant software technology introduced in Chapter 3, "OS/2 EE:

A Grand Tour". These models will also help you identify the technology components that provide the best fit for a particular business solution. If the last chapter provided an overview of hundreds of exotic dishes, then this chapter teaches the principles of good dieting and how to be selective in the food you eat. Architecture provides a framework in which we can organize our thinking. It teaches us how to create systems from individual components. The client-server model is an example of an architectural construct that can be used to create cost-efficient business solutions using the OS/2 EE platform. However, architecture is also used to develop a vision of future systems. We will first look at what OS/2 EE can do for us today as a super-server for low cost (skinny) clients on a network. We will then look at how OS/2 EE allows us to play in the distributed world of SAA and cooperative software architecture.

Chapter 1

Welcome To Client-Server Computing

So much has been said about client-server computing that it has come to mean "all things to all people." The purpose of this chapter is, of course, to provide our own view of what this all means. So let's start out this chapter by defining the emerging world of client-server computing.

THE EMERGING CLIENT-SERVER MARKET

Client-Server is the culmination of an irresistible trend toward *downsizing* business applications to PCs, PS/2s, Macintosh, and Unix workstations. Downsizing is a process which breaks up large supermini-type applications into program modules which run on one or more network servers. The user-interface functions are moved to the client workstations with the intention of replacing the "green screen uglies" with state-of-the-art graphical user interfaces.

Client-Server software solutions on low-cost standard hardware are the driving force behind downsizing. Client-Server allows us to create a coherent environment out of autonomous desktop workstations. It combines the best of two worlds: the cost effective and almost addictive power of desktop computers with multiuser access to shared resources and data. Client-Server solutions almost always result in lower development and maintenance costs. They also provide an *open* flexible environment where mix and match is the rule. Through the SAA architectural context, client-server may also provide the seamless integration of PCs and mainframes.

It's no wonder that Forrester Research Inc., a market researcher, projects that the client-server market will account for $29 billion worth of sales by 1993 with the big losers from these sales being minicomputer-based solutions.

WHAT IS CLIENT-SERVER?

Even though "client-server" is a leading industry buzzword, there is no agreed upon definition of what that term means. This provides us with the opportunity to come up with our own definition. As the name implies, clients and servers are separate logical entities that work together over a network to accomplish a task. So what makes client-server different from other forms of distributed software? We propose that all client-server systems have the following distinguishing characteristics:

- ***Service:*** Client-Server is primarily a relationship between processes running on separate machines. The server process is a provider of services. The client is a consumer of services. In essence, client-server provides a clean separation of function based on the idea of service.

- ***Shared Resources:*** A server can service many clients at the same time and regulate their access to shared resources.

- ***Asymmetrical protocols:*** There is a many-to-one relationship between clients and server. Clients always *initiate* the dialog by requesting a service. Servers are passively waiting on requests from the clients.

- ***Transparency of location:*** The server is a process which can reside on the same machine as the client or on a different machine across a network. Client-Server software usually masks the location of the server from the clients by redirecting the service calls when needed.

- ***Mix and match:*** The ideal client-server software is independent of hardware or operating system software platforms. You should be able to mix and match client and server platforms.

- ***Message-based exchanges:*** Clients and servers are loosely coupled systems which interact through a message-passing mechanism. The message is the delivery mechanism for the service requests and replies.

- ***Encapsulation of services:*** The server is a "specialist." A message tells a server what service is requested and it is then up to the server to determine how to get the job done. Servers can be upgraded without affecting the clients as long as the published message interface is not changed.

- ***Scalability:*** Client-Server systems can be scaled horizontally or vertically. Horizontal scaling means adding or removing client workstations with only a slight performance impact. Vertical scaling means migrating to a larger and faster server machine or multiservers.

- ***Integrity:*** The server code and server data is centrally maintained, which results in cheaper maintenance and the guarding of shared data integrity. At the same time, the clients remain personal and independent.

The client-server characteristics described above allow intelligence to be easily distributed across a network and provide a framework for the design of loosely coupled network based applications.

WILL THE REAL CLIENT-SERVER PLEASE STAND UP?

Many systems with very different architectures have been called "client-server." System vendors often use "client-server" as if the term can only be applied to their specific packages. For example: file server vendors swear they first invented the term, and database server vendors are known in some circles solely as *the* client-server vendors. To add to the confusion, we make the claim that this book teaches you how to write client-server applications. So who is right? Which of these packages is the real client-server? The answer is all of the above.

The idea of splitting an application along client-server lines has been used over the last ten years to create various forms of Local Area Network software solutions. Typically these solutions sell as shrink-wrapped software packages, and many are sold by more than one vendor. However, each of these solutions is distinguished by the nature of the service it provides to its clients as shown in the examples which follow.

File Servers

With a file server, the client (typically a PC) passes requests for file records over a network to the file server (Figure 1-1). This is a very primitive form of data service that necessitates many message exchanges over the network to find the requested data.

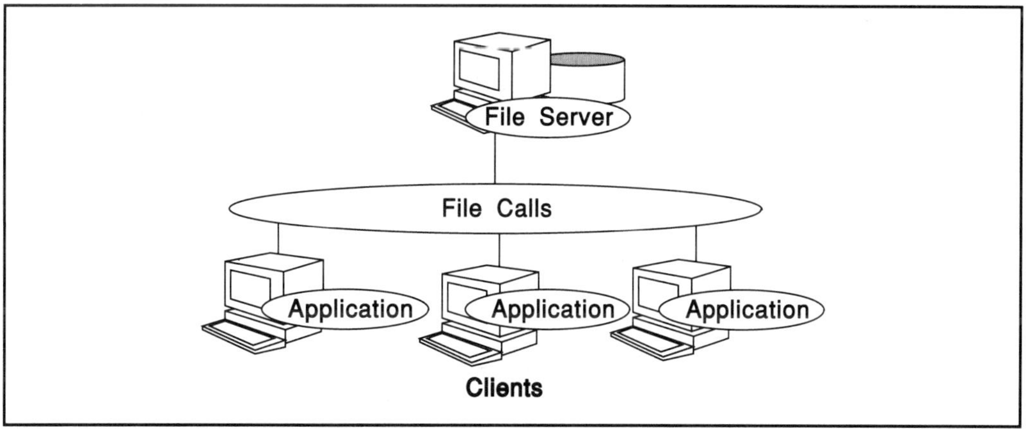

Figure 1-1. Client-Server with File Servers.

Database Servers

With a database server, the client passes SQL requests as messages to the database server (Figure 1-2). Only the final results of the data search are returned over the network. The code that processes the SQL request and the data reside on the same machine. This allows the server to use its own processing power to find the requested data, rather than pass all the records back to a client and let it find its own data as was the case for the file server. The result is a much more efficient use of distributed processing power. With this approach, the server code is shrink-wrapped by the vendor; but you often need to write code for the client application (or you can buy shrink-wrapped clients like Query Manager or Paradox).

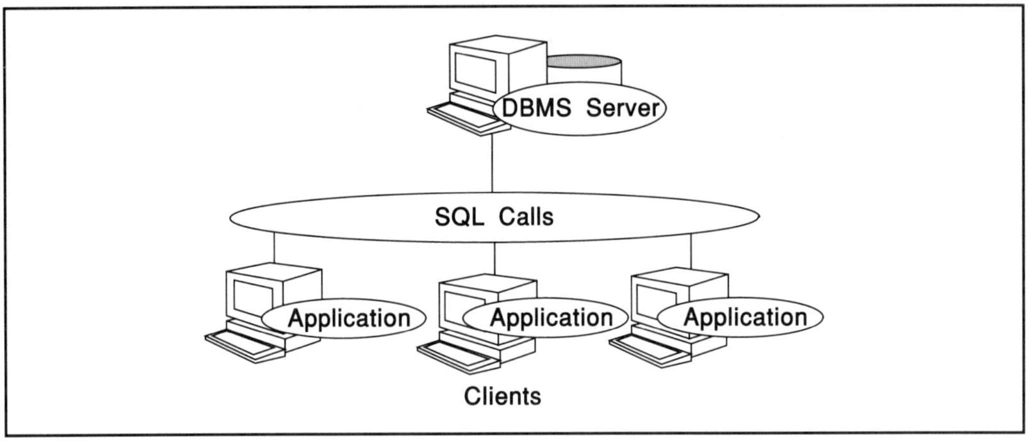

Figure 1-2. Client-Server with Database Servers.

Transaction Servers

With a transaction server, the client invokes *remote procedures* that reside on a server which also contains an SQL database engine (Figure 1-3). These remote procedures on the server execute a group of SQL statements. The SQL statements either all succeed or fail as a unit. These grouped SQL statements are called *transactions*.

You create client-server applications by writing the code for both the client component which usually includes a graphical user interface and the server transactions. These applications are called "On-line Transaction Processing" or *OLTP*. They tend to be mission-critical applications which require a 1-3 second response time 100% of the time. These applications also require tight controls over the security and integrity of the database. The communication overhead in this approach is kept to a minimum. The exchange consists of a single request/reply (as opposed to multiple SQL statements). You will need to use a peer-to-peer protocol to issue the call to the remote procedure and obtain the results.

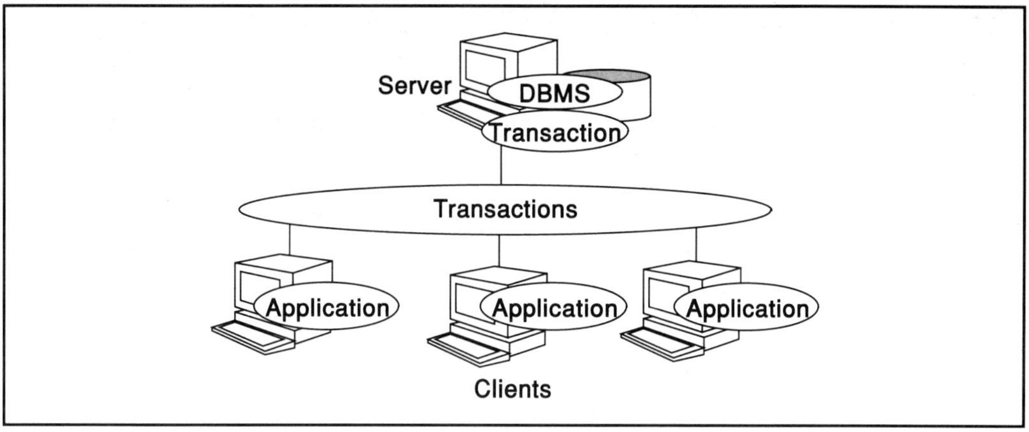

Figure 1-3. Client-Server with Transaction Servers.

Application Servers

With an application server, you also supply the code for both the client and the server (Figure 1-4). However, unlike transaction servers, application servers are not necessarily database centered. For example, an application server can control a device such as an optical jukebox or serve as an inference engine with download capabilities from Dow Jones. It is a general purpose roll-your-own network application using the client-server model.

Application and transaction servers represent the new growth area for PC-based client-server computing. They both require people like us creating *custom* applications that use the client-server model and build on top of "shrink-wrapped" system components. The idea is to create vertical packages that provide total business solutions using low-cost commodity type hardware and Local Area Networks.

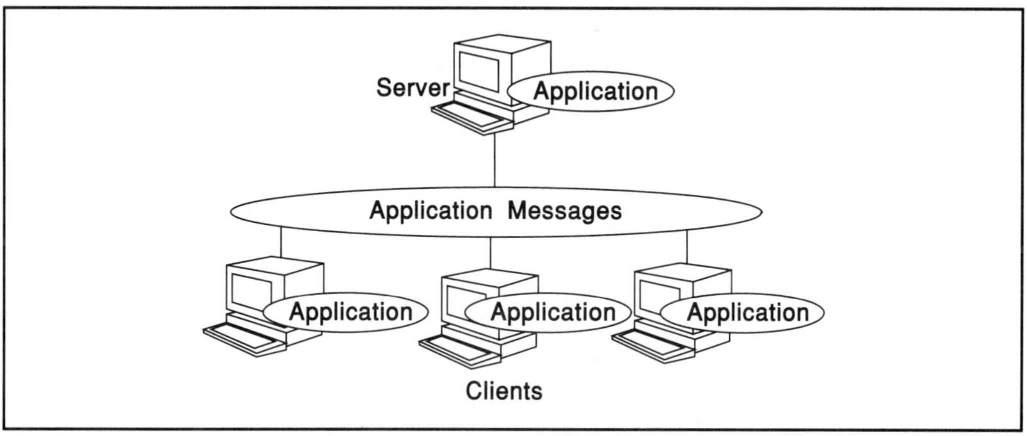

Figure 1-4. Client-Server with Application Servers.

WHAT OS/2 EE BRINGS TO CLIENT-SERVER

Client-Server solutions on a PC platform require the services of a robust operating system which provides multitasking, a multiuser database engine, LAN communications, and a graphical user interface. The server should be able to handle concurrent requests from clients with minimal performance degradations. Client-Server solutions on PCs must provide the same level of service as multiuser superminis while maintaining the autonomy of the client PCs. This is where OS/2 EE comes into the picture:

- OS/2 EE servers provide minicomputer power at PC prices. OS/2 EE running on a PC with an 80486 processor has the power of a minicomputer both in terms of brute processor speed and system software sophistication, such as its built-in SQL Database Manager. OS/2's preemptive multitasking and multithreading services, and its memory protection make it possible to create "mission-critical" systems around personal computers.

- OS/2 is an "open" commercial platform. An open platform provides a choice of vendor products and services at competitive prices. These translate into enormous savings in hardware and software system costs, when compared to an equivalent supermini solution.

- OS/2 EE servers, unlike minicomputers, were designed from the ground up to communicate "seamlessly" with MS-DOS and OS/2 clients. The client and server use the same file, commands, and internal data representations. Operating system calls can be transparently "redirected" to the server via a network operating system.

- OS/2 EE eliminates the need for minicomputers to act as the middle tier between PC clients and hosts in three-tiered networks. OS/2 EE is fully equipped to seamlessly communicate with SAA mainframes.

In short, OS/2 EE is a commercially available operating system that comes fully loaded with the hooks that make it possible to design client-server systems around personal computers. Any discussion of client-server architecture which goes beyond the "armchair design" phase will need working programs to demonstrate the design trade-offs involved. In the chapters that follow we will explain the hooks OS/2 provides and how they can be used to effectively create working client-server solutions.

Chapter 2

Why OS/2 Extended Edition

This chapter examines OS/2 EE's credentials and helps situate it as a client-server platform. You'll want to pass this chapter to someone who asks, "What is OS/2 EE, and why should I care?" We answer this question by providing a short history of OS/2 and OS/2 EE. We then explain where OS/2 and OS/2 EE each fit into the scheme of things. We will show you why OS/2 is more than just a "fatter" version of DOS, and why OS/2 EE is more than just a "super fat" version of OS/2.

A SHORT HISTORY OF OS/2 EXTENDED EDITION

In spite of its recent introduction, OS/2 has already gone through several major versions and two editions. OS/2 is transforming the stand-alone PC of the MS-DOS world into a powerful multitasking workstation endowed with an advanced graphic subsystem, a distributed database engine, and a very rich set of communications capabilities. The various OS/2 components collectively provide the most advanced operating system platform in existence for the creation of client-server solutions while retaining the much cherished stand-alone autonomy of the PC.

Figure 2-1 on page 10 shows the progression of OS/2 editions and versions and the new features they bring to the operating system. Referring to the figure, there is an OS/2 Standard Edition and there is an OS/2 Extended Edition both of which have gone through four versions. The OS/2 Standard Edition, developed jointly by Microsoft and IBM, is readily available from IBM and Microsoft as well as from many manufacturers of IBM PC compatibles. The OS/2 Extended Edition includes all the features of the Standard Edition and also provides a Database Manager and an integrated Communications subsystem. This enhanced OS/2, called the *Extended Edition* or *OS/2 EE* is available only from IBM. Unlike OS/2 Standard Edition, which is licensed to non-IBM vendors through Microsoft, IBM directly handles the licensing of OS/2 EE. Microsoft in conjunction with several database and communications vendors provides a functionally equivalent extension of OS/2.

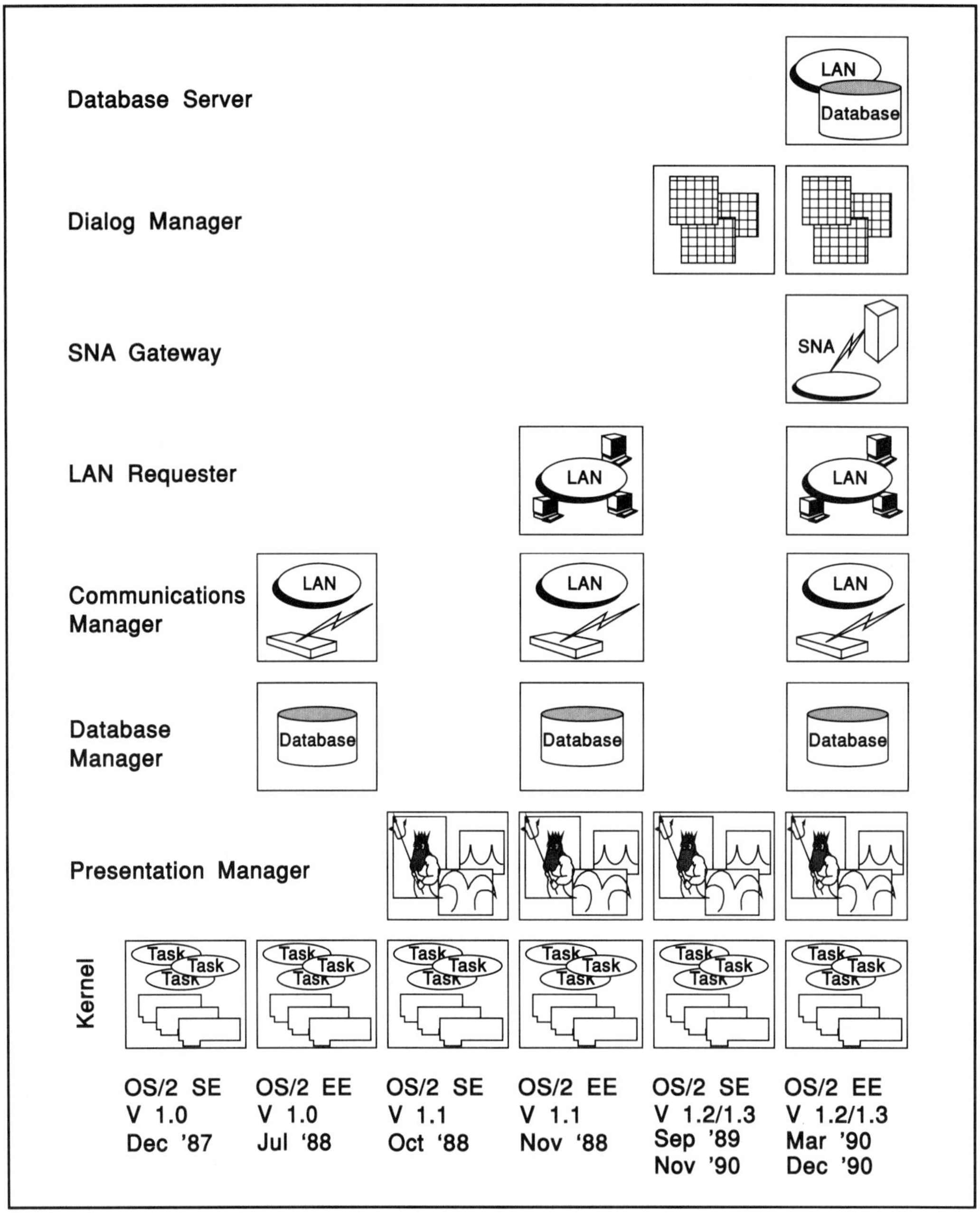

Figure 2-1. The Evolution of OS/2 EE.

OS/2 **Standard Edition** version 1.0 unveiled by IBM and Microsoft in December 1987, provides the base operating system functions such as multitasking, file services, memory management, keyboard services, and character-mode output. This base system, consisting of over 250 system calls, is commonly called the OS/2 "kernel." In October 1988, IBM and Microsoft released OS/2 Standard Edition version 1.1, which enhanced OS/2 with the Presentation Manager, an advanced windowing and graphic subsystem with a repertoire of approximately 500 new system calls. The OS/2 Standard Edition version 1.2, introduced in September 1989, introduced the Dialog Manager subsystem which greatly simplifies the writing of Presentation Manager applications and automatically creates screen dialogs that conform to IBM's **Common User Access (CUA)** standard for user interfaces. Version 1.2 also introduced a new High Performance File System. The OS/2 Standard Edition version 1.3, introduced in November 1990, is a slimmer and faster version of OS/2. The OS/2 Standard Edition has a list price of $325.

OS/2 **Extended Edition** Version 1.0 introduced by IBM in July 1988, enhances OS/2 with two additional subsystems: the Communications Manager and the Database Manager. Extended Edition Version 1.1, shipped in November 1988, added support for Local Area Network (LAN) protocols including NetBIOS, 802.2, and the LAN Requester. OS/2 EE version 1.2, which shipped in March 1990, enhanced the Communications Manager with X.25 support for packet switching data networks (PSDN), and added an SNA LAN gateway server. The Database Manager was also enhanced with remote SQL access. This enables an OS/2 EE workstation to become a networked database server for OS/2 or MS-DOS clients. OS/2 EE version 1.3, which shipped in December 1990, fixes many of the bugs of the previous release but adds no significant new features. The OS/2 EE version 1.3 product from IBM, which includes the OS/2 Kernel, the Presentation Manager, the Database Manager, and the Communications Manager, sells for $795.

We will also be covering the **IBM OS/2 LAN Server**, a related product from IBM, that extends OS/2 EE's file, printer, and Named Pipes services over networks. IBM sells the OS/2 LAN Server separately from OS/2 EE for $1,040. The good news is that you only need one LAN Server per network. IBM's LAN Server offering is largely compatible with a similar offering from Microsoft: the LAN Manager 2.0. The LAN Manager is readily available from manufacturers of PC-compatibles and from some LAN vendors.

The term OS/2 EE will be used for the remainder of this book to refer to IBM's OS/2 Extended Edition Version 1.2 and above. The term LAN Server will be used to refer to the IBM OS/2 LAN Server Version 1.2 and above. You will need these two products to run most of the software developed in this book.

WHAT IS OS/2 AND WHAT IS EXTENDED?

OS/2 was designed to be "piecemeal extensible out in the field." This means a user can add new functions to the operating system or upgrade and replace existing system components without a new release from IBM or Microsoft. Each component of OS/2 was designed so that it does not restrict new features and can be supported by a new version of OS/2 even if the internals are dramatically changed. OS/2's modular operating system design is a radical departure from MS-DOS's monolithic COMMAND.COM. In MS-DOS, almost any change or improvement to the operating system requires a modification of COMMAND.COM, as shown in the top half of Figure 2-2 on page 13. This is an impediment to MS-DOS's ability to grow or change as an operating system.

In contrast, extensions are a way of life for OS/2. Indeed, OS/2 EE is as much a departure from Standard Edition as OS/2 was from DOS. The key to understanding OS/2's extensions is in the layered approach to OS/2's design as shown in the bottom half of Figure 2-2 on page 13. Between the application and the hardware, OS/2 provides three interacting yet modular layers: the Dynamic Link Library (DLL) layer, the resident kernel, and the device drivers.

The Dynamic Link Libraries provide a call-based interface to the operating system services in place of the MS-DOS number-based interrupts. When a program runs under OS/2, the resident portion of the operating system kernel determines which dynamic libraries are required and loads them into memory at run-time or at load-time. Now your program can call any of the functions provided by the DLLs. Most of OS/2, including much of the file I/O, keyboard, mouse and screen systems, and all of the Presentation Manager consists of a collection of DLLs supplied jointly by Microsoft and IBM. In the case of Extended Edition, IBM added another collection of DLLs to the base OS/2 and documented their calls in several technical reference manuals.

Independent software and hardware vendors have the following options in providing their "extended" OS/2 versions:

- They may add their own DLLs and functions. For example, hardware vendors may want to extend the operating system to work with an optical jukebox. Software vendors may want to add operating system calls for an expert system inference engine. These new functions would then have to be documented and may need to become part of an industry "standard" before they become de facto extensions.

- They may choose to go with the DLL interface published by IBM but extend it with some new features. As an example, a database vendor may want to replace IBM's Database Manager with their own database engine while retaining the IBM supplied SQL interface. To make their product more attractive those vendors could presumably add new functionality to the existing DLLs such as triggers or rules-based referential integrity.

Under the IBM/Microsoft Joint Development Agreement, third parties may configure the base components of OS/2 for their hardware and sell the product through their own channels. Microsoft with the help of Ashton-Tate, Sybase, 3Com, and others provides extended components of OS/2 such as SQL Server and the LAN Manager to third parties. IBM, of course, also provides OS/2 EE to third parties.

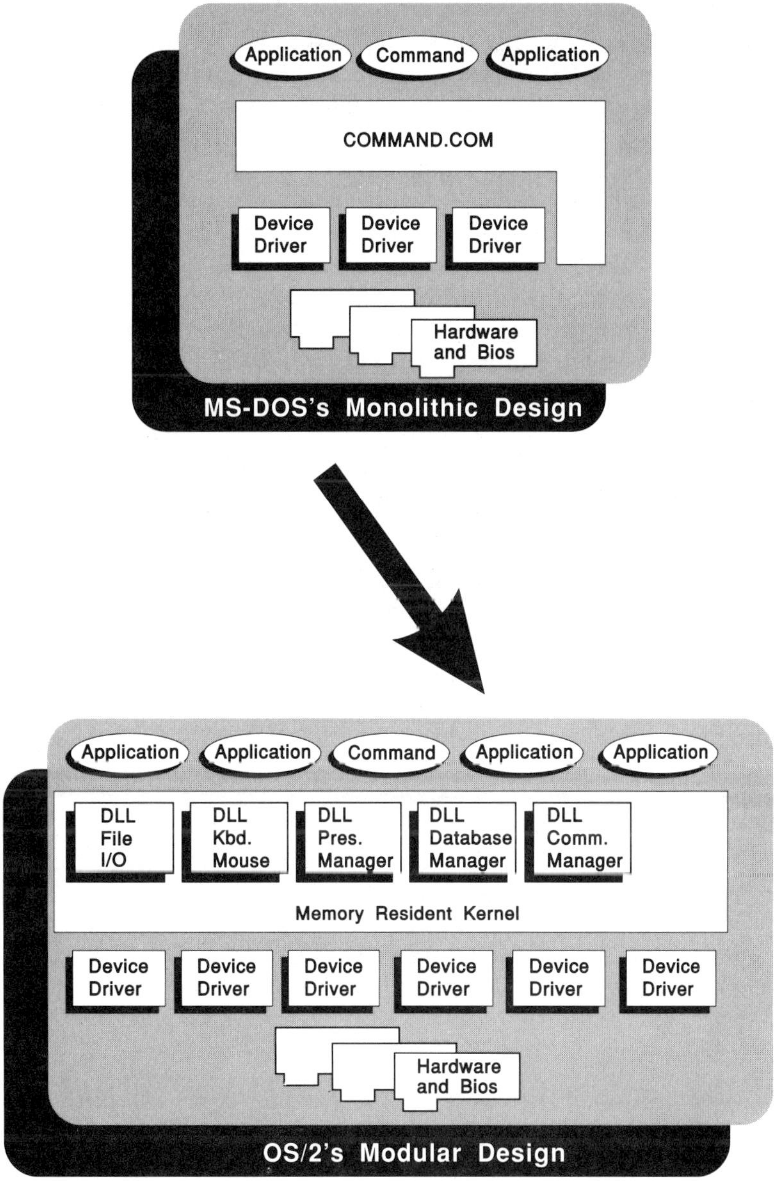

Figure 2-2. From Monolithic To Modular.

OS/2 EE AND IBM'S SAA

OS/2 EE is an integral part of Systems Application Architecture (*SAA*), IBM's strategic plan to provide seamless connectivity and interfaces across the spectrum of its major product lines. To comply with SAA a database running under OS/2 will provide the same functionality as IBM's best-selling mainframe-based DB2 offering. OS/2 EE Database Manager does that quite successfully by incorporating 95% of DB2's function. The OS/2 EE database Query Manager is very similar to its mainframe counterpart. OS/2 EE's Presentation Manager is the first IBM product to fully demonstrate the new window-based Common User Access (CUA). OS/2 EE's Communications Manager incorporates IBM's latest communications technology. It was designed to meet IBM's large customers' expectations of a *total network solution* that includes connectivity between products, peer-to-peer protocols between PCs and mainframes, centralized network management, SNA compliance, Token Ring support, and distributed database.

In view of OS/2 EE's special show-case role in the context of SAA it is not surprising that IBM has created a "fully loaded" extension of OS/2 which it will replenish with new extensions for a long time to come. OS/2 EE will be used as the leading-edge platform for the majority of IBM's new software introductions throughout the 1990s. The incorporation of OS/2 EE into SAA provides software developers with a stable set of API services which allows their code to run on a multiplicity of operating systems and hardware platforms. In theory, you should be able to port the code developed in this book to IBM's SAA family of computers by just recompiling (we're not quite there yet!). This means your application is upwardly scalable; and when you consider that IBM's product line ranges from an IBM PC to the ES/9000, you are talking of a factor of about 1000 in performance.

C is an SAA language and many of the C library calls, and most of the OS/2 EE API are part of what IBM calls the Common Programming Interface (CPI) standard of SAA. You can think of the CPI as the operating system interface to a generic SAA machine that has a full range of network, database and graphic capabilities. IBM has pledged to enhance this generic SAA platform, over the long-haul, with additional application-enabling interfaces.

COMPARING IBM'S OS/2 EE WITH MICROSOFT'S

IBM's and Microsoft's OS/2 extensions are to a large degree functionally equivalent. The differences occur in the following areas:

- PC/Host communications is an area where IBM's OS/2 EE offers a variety of additional APIs and services.
- The database engine IBM offers is *DB2 on OS/2*. Microsoft teamed up with Ashton-Tate and Sybase to offer SQL Server. However, both database engines run SQL and provide the same set of core functions.

- The database front-end tool offerings are different. IBM offers Query Manager which is functionally a replica of its host-based Query Management Facility (QMF). Microsoft offers Ashton-Tate and Sybase tools. Third party tools like Borland's Paradox can front-end either database.
- Product packaging from Microsoft and IBM differs. IBM offers a bundled OS/2 EE product that will work on IBM PCs and PS/2s with IBM communications hardware. Microsoft's offering will vary depending on how it gets packaged by manufacturers of PC compatibles.

In November 1989, IBM and Microsoft broadened the scope of their development partnership and agreed that *"they will work together to ensure that the Database Manager, Communications Manager, and LAN Requester and Server functions of IBM's OS/2 Extended Edition are available to all OS/2 users"*. They also stated that IBM's LAN Server and Microsoft's LAN Manager *"will be converged into identical products"*.

In September 1990, IBM and Microsoft rewrote the terms of their development agreement. Under the new agreement, IBM will take responsibility for OS/2 versions 1.X and 2.X. Microsoft will oversee the development of the "portable" OS/2 which will support, among other things, RISC and multiprocessors. Microsoft will also take charge of the development of MS-DOS and Windows. The agreement is supposed to eliminate the coordination problems that were caused by the multisite/multiorganizational development of OS/2. The agreement is also supposed to ensure compatibility between the IBM and Microsoft OS/2 releases and speed up the delivery of new versions of OS/2.

WHICH EXTENDED OS/2 SHOULD I USE?

It may be easier for you to start learning OS/2 EE with IBM's "all-in-one" package, simply because all the pieces are guaranteed to work together. This is no small feat in a system environment as complex as OS/2 EE. IBM also provides an automatic 90 day warranty and 12-month service with the purchase of OS/2 EE. Most importantly, IBM will fix any bug you find in the product and send you a corrective service diskette with the fixes within days. IBM's single package solution also provides a common focus for OS/2 EE support, installation, configuration, documentation, administration, and education.

However, once you obtain a firm handle on the subject and understand the various trade-offs, then you may want to look at other vendor offerings for missing components or for extensions that suit your particular needs. The IBM solution is the *de facto* standard for extensions and is an excellent base for comparison shopping and for establishing your framework for OS/2 extensions. For example, once you have mastered SQL using OS/2 EE and the examples in this book, you may decide to switch database engines to SQL Server, Oracle, or Gupta's SQLBase. For database front-end tools you may prefer to use Borland, Sybase, or Ingres tools. You may want to develop your own graphic interface using Gupta's SQLWindows. Regardless of the preferences in your "mix and match," you can still use IBM's OS/2 EE as your reference point.

MS-DOS AND OS/2: A FAMILY AFFAIR

It is our belief that MS-DOS is here to stay. We also believe that OS/2 provides the server platform of choice for MS-DOS machines and that MS-DOS machines running Windows 3.0 can be treated as a low-end version of PM clients (or PM may be called "Windows Plus"). MS-DOS with Windows and OS/2 with PM are all part of the same family of operating systems. What is important is the client-server architecture that allows us to create software solutions that "mix and match" operating system elements.

Is Windows 3.0 a Trojan Horse for PM?

Microsoft's May 1990 introduction of Windows 3.0 sparked a debate which pitted Windows against OS/2. The phenomenal acceptance of Windows and the continued popularity of MS-DOS was seen by some as a rebuff of OS/2. Far from being a rival to OS/2, we see Windows 3.0 as providing the foundation for the mass acceptance of OS/2. Here's why:

- Since Windows 3.0 runs on DOS it will help introduce a sizeable portion of the 40-million DOS community to the wonders of a graphical user interface and multitasking.
- Once the DOS community adopts Windows 3.0 they will have effectively adopted the OS/2 Presentation Manager, which was designed from the ground-up by Microsoft as a compatible superset of Windows. Microsoft provides a Software Migration Kit (SMK), which allows developers to migrate Windows applications into OS/2 1.X PM. In addition, OS/2 2.X will run Windows programs directly using a 400K Dynamic Link Library that will translate Windows calls into PM calls. This strategy ensures that most of the popular Windows programs will be made available under OS/2.
- Windows 3.0 will prompt users to add an additional two to three MBytes of memory to their PCs, making the transition to OS/2 easier.
- Presentation Manager versions of Windows programs can be made more reactive by using OS/2's powerful multithreaded capabilities. A PM application designer can schedule computational or I/O bound activities as separate threads to ensure crisp user interaction at all times. The multithread PM versions of Windows applications may entice power users to migrate to OS/2.
- Windows will serve as a training ground for many developers of graphical user interface (GUI) programs. They will start by learning the roughly 400 API calls within Windows. These GUI implementation skills can then be applied to PM's 900 plus API calls.

In short, we see Windows as a low-end version of the OS/2 operating system. It's still "all in the family." We see OS/2's competition as coming from Unix and the

Macintosh not from DOS or Windows. The migration to Windows will, in the long run, strengthen OS/2's position as the top contender for the replacement of DOS on personal computers.

MS-DOS: The Operating System That Won't Go Away

It will take a long time before OS/2 supplants MS-DOS in the business environment for the following reasons:

- MS-DOS machines, when not running Windows 3.0, are significantly less expensive than OS/2 machines. They require a lot less memory, a lot less disk, and may run on low-cost 8086-type machines.
- MS-DOS is an acceptable operating system for many applications that do not require multitasking or large amounts of memory.
- There is a large inventory of 8086 type machines that cannot run OS/2.
- There is a huge investment in MS-DOS application software.
- MS-DOS is familiar to large numbers of users and there may be a reluctance to migrate away from a familiar base.
- MS-DOS is constantly being improved. Windows 3.0, for example, allows DOS applications to run in extended memory and provides a powerful graphical user interface.

Paradoxically, the reservations listed above do not carry over to OS/2 as a server in a networked environment. In such an environment, OS/2 EE machines can cost effectively provide shared services to DOS client machines on a network. Networks give DOS clients access to thc advantagcs of OS/2 servers without requiring an all-at-once switch from DOS. The same organizations that find it too costly to put OS/2 on every workstation will find that OS/2 EE servers can help them leverage their existing MS-DOS machine base. Such organizations will accept OS/2 in network servers long before putting OS/2 on every machine.

OS/2 EE as a Super Server for DOS Machines

As we explained in "What OS/2 EE Brings To Client-Server" on page 8, OS/2 EE is a natural server for MS-DOS machines. OS/2 EE servers blend well with the MS-DOS environment, and at the same time provide minicomputer power at PC prices. The OS/2 server can replace both the overworked DOS server machines and the minicomputers in the PC environment.

The real change in personal computing will be brought about by the new breed of client-server applications on LANs. As you will discover later in this book, the action is in the networked *Transaction Servers* and the client-server model that ties it all together. Anyone putting together a client-server application on a PC LAN will almost have to run OS/2 on the server machine. So, it appears that OS/2's primary niche will

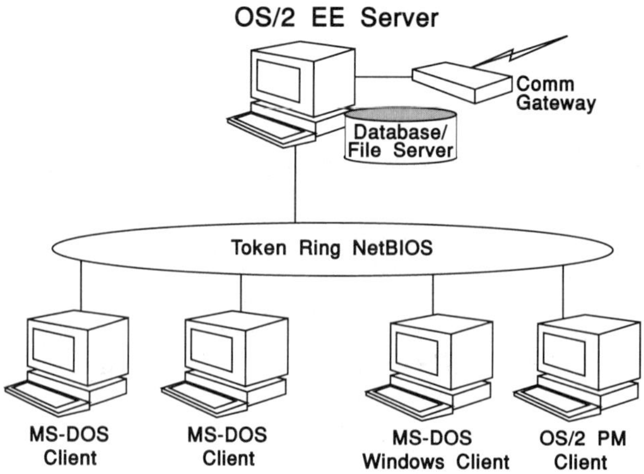

Figure 2-3. OS/2 EE as a Super Server for Mixed Clients.

be to provide a robust platform for the creation of the next generation of LAN-based personal software.

The client-server platform allows us to "mix and match" clients and servers almost seamlessly. Figure 2-3 shows a mixed operating system network environment where an application is split between "skinny" clients running the application front-end and an OS/2 EE Super Server, which runs the application's back-end. We anticipate that the bulk of clients may initially be DOS and Windows machines and that these will be gradually replaced with PM clients running OS/2. We will need to design software solutions for an environment that will remain "mixed" for a long time. The client-server platform we develop in this book fully takes into account this mixed client reality. We will be using standard peer-to-peer protocols such as NetBIOS, Named Pipes, and APPC which allow servers to communicate with practically every form of client.

THE FUTURE VERSIONS OF OS/2

Yes, there will always be a "newer" version of OS/2, and as usual it will be followed shortly after by a "newer" version of OS/2 EE. And, yes, these new versions will always have something "newer and better" to offer. There will be a 32-bit OS/2, followed by a RISC-engine OS/2, followed by multiprocessor OS/2, followed by an object-oriented OS/2, etc. This is the nature of the business: a bigger and better mouse-trap is always on the horizon. Should you wait for the ultimate OS/2? Only if you enjoy a perpetual chase for Nirvana. It's like continually delaying your purchase until the fastest and cheapest PC hits the market. A better strategy is to bite the bullet now and convert your server platform to OS/2, since sooner or later you will be using OS/2.

If you're buying new workstations, start with a 80386-based machine and lots of disk and memory. This decision is a no-brainer. The only thing involved is money changing hands. But what should software developers do? Luckily for us, OS/2 migrations have become "a family affair." The current OS/2 provides an upgrade path into future OS/2s. *All future OS/2s will be backwardly compatible with their predecessors.*

As a case study, let's look at what a conversion to the 32-bit OS/2 means to current developers of OS/2 1.X software. The first piece of good news is that the conversion will not put you into "API shock." You will find that the shift in programming models is for the most part "graceful." The 32-bit OS/2 programming platform offers a variety of application models to facilitate the migration of applications from the current OS/2. For example, the architecture allows 16-bit and 32-bit modules to coexist simultaneously. This means that you can run all the code in this book *as is* under the new OS/2 using its *pure* 16-bit model or using its *mixed* (16-bit with 32-bit) model. This is the good news. However, there are some existing applications that will greatly benefit from the gains in performance to be had by converting to the pure 32-bit model. A good example is a database server application. So, what will this 32-bit conversion cost? The impact will depend on the language the program was written in and the functions used:

- A 16-bit application that uses the standard C run-time library, the large memory model and PM calls for interacting with the user can be recompiled almost *as is* into the 32-bit model.
- The vast majority of the kernel and Presentation Manager API calls stay the same. This compatibility is provided by an operating system layer that takes 16-bit API requests, converts them into 32-bit requests, and completes the call using 16-bit API semantics. The programs should have been written in C using the header files provided with the IBM or Microsoft Programmer's Toolkit.
- The bulk of OS/2 EE is expected to stay the same.
- The 32-bit OS/2 abandons memory segments, in favor of a more efficient 32-bit flat model with demand-paged virtual memory. This means the 32-bit API does not include calls that manipulate segment selectors. This is a small price most of us will gladly pay for saying good-bye forever to 64-k segments.
- The 32-bit OS/2 supports 4096 threads and processes as opposed to the current limits of 511. It also allows you to have 64,000 semaphores per process. The semaphore model is also improved. The semaphores now come in three flavors: event, mutual exclusion, and multiple wait. This also means the 32-bit API introduces new semaphore functions that are not present in the 16-bit version.
- The VIO/KBD/MOU functions do not have analogous 32-bit APIs. This is Microsoft's and IBM's not too gentle way of telling programmers to go to Presentation Manager to enforce a common *look and feel.* For those of us who can't stay away

from the direct control of the keyboard, mouse, and screen, the 16-bit versions of these APIs may still be used by 32-bit mixed applications.

You can see that the 16- to 32-bit conversion, while major in terms of new and improved function, is not too drastic in terms of its impact on our code. Let's be philosophical about it; these migrations are inevitable. But we've already had our "big one," the migration from DOS to OS/2. Now that we've paid that traumatic price, we can look forward to "graceful" migrations, at least until the turn of the century.

Chapter 3

OS/2 EE: A Grand Tour

This chapter reads like a giant feature, function, and benefit list of what OS/2 EE offers programmers. This is the chapter you'll want to pass to someone who says, "tell me all OS/2 EE does in 50 pages or less." It may be hard to believe, but the OS/2 and OS/2 EE projects are so massive, that the size of this chapter is probably the minimum size for an "architectural overview" that goes one step beyond the marketing literature.

THE COMPONENTS OF OS/2 EE

The OS/2 EE program diskettes contain the following components:

- The Base Operating System: Kernel
- The Base Operating System: Presentation Manager
- The Database Manager
- The Communications Manager
- The LAN Requester

To extend OS/2 into a *Network Operating System* and to develop OS/2 software professionally you also will need the following two software products:

1. The **IBM OS/2 LAN Server**, which in conjunction with the OS/2 EE provided LAN Requester, transforms OS/2 into a Network Operating System. The LAN Server is also needed for Named Pipes to work over a network.

2. The OS/2 Software Development Toolkit, which is required to develop Presentation Manager and Dialog Manager applications. This Toolkit, now called the **OS/2 Programming Tools and Information V 1.3**, is available for $650.00. The Dialog Manager's development and runtime environments are shipped with the Programming Tools. The Dialog Manager runtime, unlike the Presentation Manager runtime, is not shipped with the OS/2 base. However, developers can ship the Dialog Manager runtime DLLs with their applications without requiring a runtime license fee.

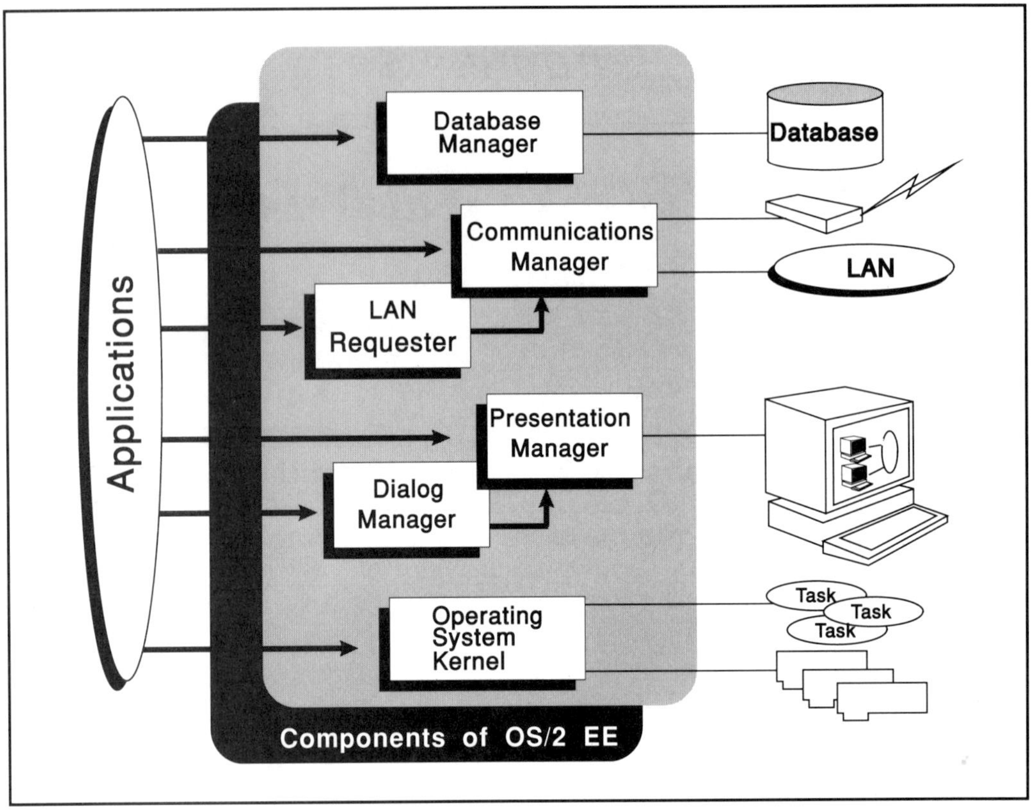

Figure 3-1. OS/2 EE Functional Components.

IBM uses the term *Base Operating System* to refer to the OS/2 kernel and Presentation Manager. We separate the two components for the purposes of this book into: Kernel and Presentation Manager. Figure 3-1 on page 22 shows the OS/2 EE components. Your application can obtain the services of any of those subsystems as well as those of the OS/2 kernel through API calls. In the case of the Database Manager, the API is supplemented with a SQL precompiler that allows you to embed SQL statements directly into a C program. We will start building our common vocabulary by explaining the functions and features of the various OS/2 EE components from a programmer's perspective.

THE BASE OPERATING SYSTEM: KERNEL

The OS/2 kernel is the first major single-user, multitasking operating system kernel developed specifically for personal computers. Unix for example, runs on personal computers and provides multitasking but it does this by creating a time-share multiuser environment that is not optimized for single-user situations.

OS/2, like MS-DOS, was designed from the ground up for Intel's family of microprocessors. MS-DOS was designed for the Intel 8086 processors which have a limited address space of 1 megabyte of which 360 KBytes are reserved for the ROM and video RAM, which leaves only 640 KBytes for your applications and the operating system itself. OS/2, on the other hand, was designed to take advantage of the Intel 80286 processor's protected mode. In this mode, the processor can directly access 16 megabytes of physical memory and up to one gigabyte per process of virtual memory.

OS/2 is the embodiment of multitasking for Intel's 80286 family. It is the most complex and complete system code ever written for a microcomputer (the kernel took three years to develop by a joint IBM/Microsoft team and it is mostly written in assembler). This section presents the major features and functions provided by the kernel.

Multitasking

Multitasking, or the ability to run multiple programs concurrently, is OS/2's most powerful new feature. OS/2 provides a very granular level of multitasking which is optimized for concurrency on a single-user machine. The architecture builds on a three-tiered tasking model: the thread, the process, and the session (or screen group). Threads run within processes which in turn run within screen groups. Figure 3-2 shows the relationships in the hierarchy. The *thread* is the basic unit of concurrency and CPU allocation in OS/2. The *process* in OS/2 provides a level of multitasking which roughly corresponds to a running program. A process consists of one or more threads. This means that in addition to having multiple programs execute at the same time, a single program may have multiple threads that are executing concurrently. OS/2 controls multitasking by using a preemptive priority-based scheduler. Starting with OS/2 version 1.1, a thread can be assigned to one of four priority classes, and within each class the scheduler recognizes 32 priority levels. The *priority classes* are:

- *Time-critical* for threads that require immediate attention. Such threads will be used in communications and real-time systems.
- *Fixed-high* for threads that require good responsiveness without being critical.
- *Regular* for normally executing threads.
- *Idle-time* for very low priority threads.

OS/2 uses time-slicing to ensure that threads of equal priority are given equal chances to execute. OS/2 can preempt a thread when its time slice expires if a thread with a higher or equal priority is ready to execute. If not defined otherwise, the default minimum time-slice is 250 milliseconds. The elaborate OS/2 scheduling capabilities make it possible to create realtime applications that have almost deterministic response times.

In addition, OS/2 makes available an even higher level of multitasking: the *session* or *screen-group*. The session represents a logically separate unit of screen, keyboard, and mouse, and the group of processes associated with those resources. You can think of the session as providing a virtual personal computer. You can move between sessions using the Alt/Esc keys. OS/2 also provides the capability to start a process in the background. A *background process* will not have its own screen and it will continue executing in the background even if you exit from your OS/2 screen group (background processes should be self-terminating). You can start a background process using the DETACH command.

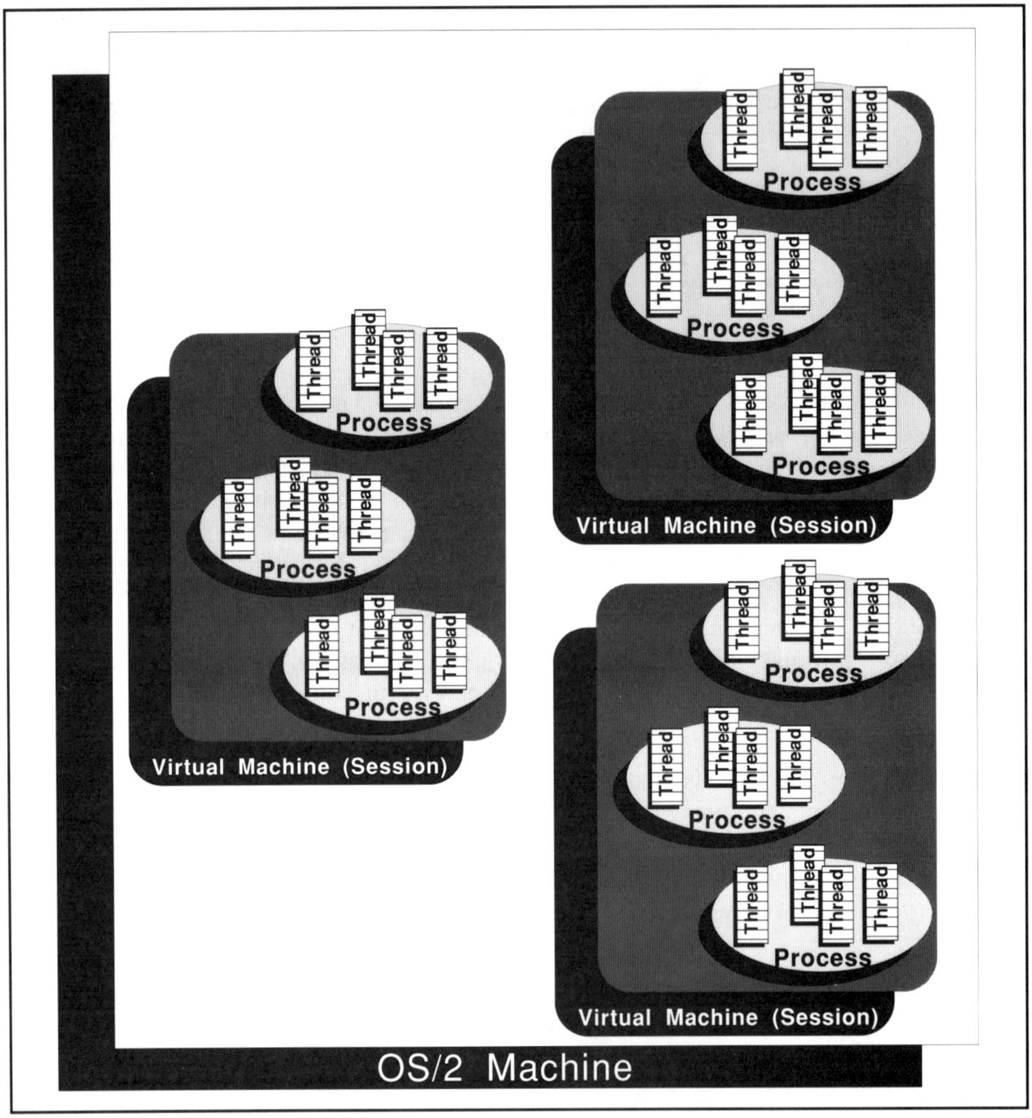

Figure 3-2. OS/2's Multitasking.

This three-level hierarchy of multitasking control: sessions, processes, and threads addresses the user's need to control concurrent execution and the developer's need to design applications whose activities can be controlled at a very granular level. We will look at OS/2's multitasking capabilities in great detail by developing a program that compares the overheads of processes and threads. This program will help us develop a framework for how best to exploit OS/2's powerful concurrency features in the design of modular system components and network server software.

Virtual Resources

The basis for multitasking is to manage the physical resources of the computer in such a way that multiple programs can run at the same time without bumping into each other as they use the PC's resources. This is where the OS/2 kernel comes in; it sits between the programs and the hardware and regulates the access to memory, disks, printers, screens, and modems. Applications interact with virtual memory and devices which OS/2 then maps to the real device. OS/2 maintains order when many programs go after the same resource. It also serializes access from the virtual device to the actual physical device automatically without user intervention. This ability of OS/2 to *redirect* output (without the application knowing it) is essential for networked environments. Resources can be mapped across a LAN to remote machines, thus extending OS/2's *virtual* reach.

Interprocess Communication

Interprocess Communication is a corollary of multitasking. Now that PCs can have more than one program running at the same time, there will most likely be a need for those programs to exchange information and commands. OS/2 provides the facilities for separate programs, each running in their own address space, to communicate information through system supported interprocess communication protocols (*IPCs*). Some of the IPCs can operate across machine boundaries and are key to the development of LAN-based client-server applications. OS/2 provides a rich set of IPCs. These include: Anonymous Pipes, Named Pipes, Queues, and Shared Memory.

An **Anonymous Pipe** is a fixed length circular buffer in memory that can be accessed like a file of serial characters through a write handle and a read handle (handles are pointers into the file). Anonymous pipes are used mostly by a parent process to communicate with its descendants by passing the pipe handles through inheritance.

Named Pipes provide two-way communications among unrelated processes either locally or remotely. The server side of an OS/2 process creates the pipe and waits for the clients to access it. Clients use the standard OS/2 file services to gain access to the Named Pipe. Multiple clients can be serviced concurrently over the same pipe. The elegance of Named Pipes and their support for *remote* interprocess communication makes them the IPC of choice for client-server software development.

A **Queue** allows byte stream packets written by multiple processes to be read by a single process. The exchange does not have to be synchronized. The receiving process can order the access to the packets or messages in one of three modes: first-in/first-out (FIFO), last-in/first-out (LIFO), or priority. Items can be retrieved from the queue either sequentially or by random access. The OS/2 queues contain pointers to messages, as opposed to a copy of the data itself.

Shared Memory is another interprocess communication protocol. OS/2 provides facilities for the creation of named shared segments. Any process that knows the named segment has automatic shared access to it. Processes must coordinate their access to shared memory through the use of synchronization techniques.

Interprocess Synchronization

Interprocess Synchronization is another corollary of multitasking. It consists of the mechanisms for keeping concurrent processes or threads from interfering with one another when accessing shared resources. The idea is to serialize the access to the shared resource by using a protocol that all parties agree to follow. OS/2, like most operating systems, provides an atomic service called the *semaphore* which applications may use to synchronize their actions. OS/2 provides three types of semaphores: System, RAM, and Fail-Safe RAM semaphores. We will learn how to use semaphores to synchronize processes and threads.

Dynamic Linking

Dynamic Linking is an OS/2 feature that allows applications to be linked with library routines at load time (or at run time), instead of at compile time. Dynamic linking solves two problems:

1. It allows functions to be added to a program without having to relink the entire program. This makes it easier to add new extensions to a system. As described earlier, OS/2 uses Dynamic Linking to provide its system extensions.

2. It removes the need to store on disk and load in memory multiple copies of the same code. This is especially important in a multiprogram environment where each application may require the same library code. Without dynamic linking, each program would have to load its own copy of the system library in memory, even if some other executable program has already loaded a copy of the library in memory.

You should be aware of the benefits of DLLs and how they are used to extend system code. You may want to consider the benefits of packaging your programs as DLLs for commercial distribution.

Managing Subsystem I/O

OS/2 provides a rich set of API calls through which an application can request the services of the video, keyboard, and mouse subsystems. The performance of the OS/2 video API rivals the efficiency and flexibility of code that directly manipulates the video hardware under DOS. For each session (virtual machine), OS/2 maintains: a logical video buffer which is a shadow of the screen contents, a keyboard input queue, and a mouse event queue. The session manager is responsible for coordinating the subsystems, so that I/O flows to the correct applications. An application sees a dedicated keyboard, video buffer, and mouse to which API calls can be issued at any time.

Managing File I/O

The OS/2 file system is compatible with that of MS-DOS. Both file systems represent a hierarchy of files on physical disk. The disk can also be subdivided into logical disks or partitions, each with its own hierarchy. Using the CONFIG.SYS file OS/2 allows you to specify the number of KBytes allocated to a cache in RAM. The system then uses a Least Recently Used (LRU) algorithm to manage the cache. Starting with OS/2 version 1.2, the file system can now accommodate 64,000 file handles, with a maximum of 32,000 handles per process.

OS/2 provides *locking and sharing* facilities to support concurrent file access in a multitasking environment. A process can open a file in exclusive mode (not allowing other processes access), or it can provide read access while denying write, or it can opt to share the file for read/write access with other processes. A process can lock any contiguous range of bytes within a shared file. These services allow multiple processes to share information at the byte level on a single file.

OS/2 also supports a **High Performance File System (HPFS)** to manage large disk media. The HPFS supports disk partitions with capacities of up to 2199 Gigabytes. The maximum file size supported is 2 Gigabytes. This new file system maintains compatibility with the old File Allocation Table (FAT) based file system at the API level. However, it is less performance sensitive as file sizes or directories get very large. The HPFS also supports new long file names (up to 254 characters), but can still work with the traditional eleven character file names (the infamous 8.3 format). Fully qualified path names can be up to 260 characters as opposed to the FAT limit of 64. The HPFS makes it possible for OS/2 to support very large databases on personal computers.

The HPFS introduces an important new concept, the *Extended Attributes*, which allow each file to have up to 64 KBytes of file-related descriptive information. This information can be used to create object-oriented file systems.

Device Monitors

Device Monitors allow a program to intercept data intended for various I/O devices. You can install a device monitor program, which then acts as an extension of a device driver. You can use it to trap "hot-keys" without having to deal with the keyboard driver. Device monitors make it easy to create daemons, which are programs installed in memory that remain inactive until certain conditions are met. Daemons are also known as *Terminate-Stay-Resident* programs in MS-DOS. Device monitors can only be applied to character-oriented devices such as the keyboard, mouse, or printer.

Memory Management

In addition to breaking the DOS 640 KByte barrier, the following services are provided by the OS/2 memory management subsystem:

- OS/2 provides one gigabyte of virtual memory which allows you to *overcommit* the memory of the system knowing that if a segment of data or code is not in memory, OS/2 will automatically swap to the disk some of the least-used segments to make room for the newly requested segments. The overflow memory goes to a swap file on disk. The sum of the space required by all your applications must not exceed the available RAM plus the disk space available for the swap file. Figure 3-3 on page 29 shows the swappable areas of the OS/2 memory map.
- OS/2 provides an extensive collection of services for creating, using, and freeing memory segments. You should be able to use your C library to obtain most of those services independently of the OS/2 API. You will need OS/2 for allocating shared memory segments. We will look at this in more detail in the chapter on interprocess communication.
- OS/2 provides protection against memory inter-segment violations by misbehaved programs. The goal is to prevent concurrent programs from inadvertently affecting each other. OS/2 also protects a program from executing instructions from a data segment or from writing into a code segment. The processor always checks the offset portion of an address, and does not allow a process to reference a memory address beyond the segment's limits. If a program attempts to access memory outside its currently defined segments, a general protection fault is generated by the hardware. OS/2 is notified of the fault and terminates the process that caused it.
- OS/2 in conjunction with the 80286 hardware uses the segmented address space to enforce privilege and access rights. The 80286 makes sure that less privileged code stays within its address boundaries and uses a carefully restricted *call gate* to police access to more privileged code. Likewise the 80286 controls access to input/output and interrupt instructions via a program's I/O privilege level (IOPL for short). The privilege level mechanisms prevent a program from accessing any part of OS/2 in an uncontrolled manner. The 80286 supports four privilege levels which are arranged hierarchically, from level 0 (maximum protection) to level 3

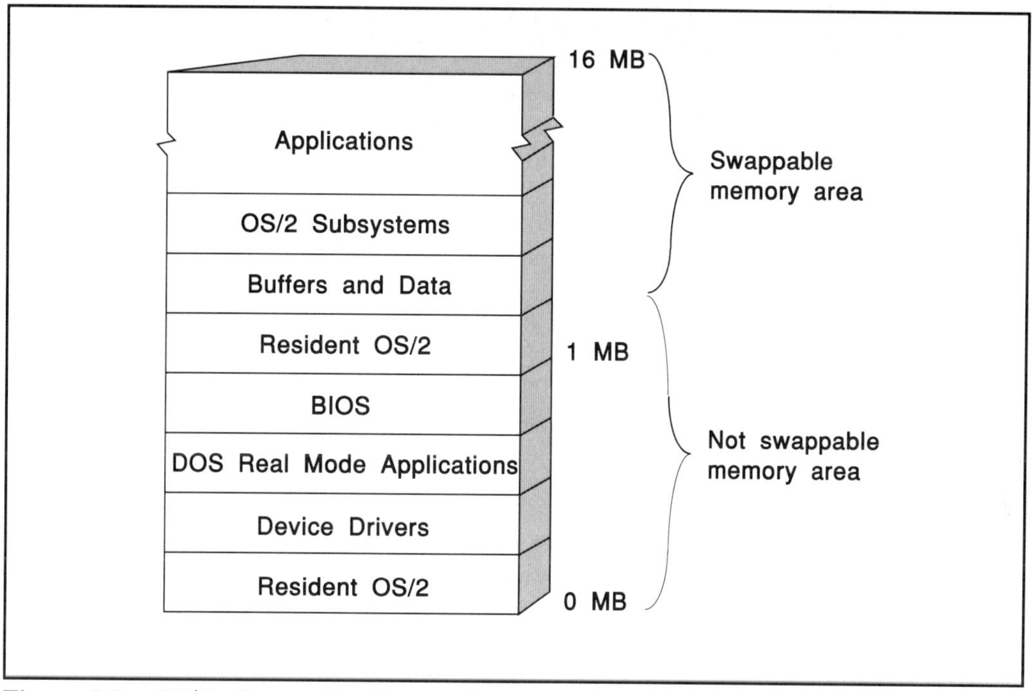

Figure 3-3. OS/2's Swappable Memory Map.

(minimum protection). The OS/2 core runs in level 0, level 1 is unused, level 2 is used by programs that directly manipulate I/O devices (have IOPL privilege level), and level 3 is where your normal OS/2 programs run.

PRESENTATION MANAGER (PM)

The OS/2 Presentation Manager (PM) provides a powerful graphics subsystem which you can use to create applications with a consistent *look and feel* (see Figure 3-4 on page 30). The PM subsystem includes a full set of two-dimensional graphic APIs, a window management API, and a protocol for data exchange among applications. The PM API is totally device independent which makes it very portable across machines which have highly differentiated display capabilities.

PM's Origins

The Presentation Manager window services are similar to the Microsoft Windows environment under DOS. This is not surprising since much of PM's windowing technology, user interface, raster graphics and bitmap support comes directly from Microsoft Windows. IBM's contribution to PM is the powerful vector-graphics draw commands called the Graphic Programming Interface (GPI). The GPI is largely derived form the Graphical Data Display Manager (GDDM) mainframe graphics

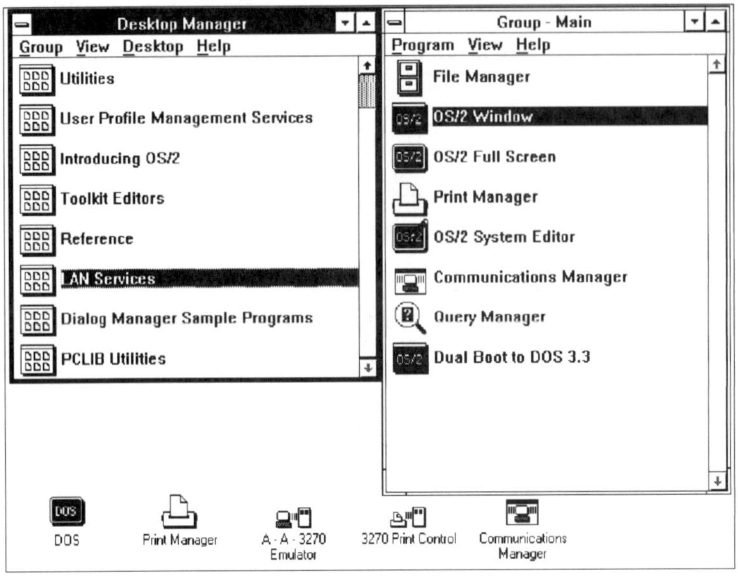

Figure 3-4. The OS/2 Desktop.

system. The software technology of Presentation Manager combines the best that IBM and Microsoft have to offer and it has resulted into one of the most powerful graphic subsystems ever brought to a personal computer.

Messages and Object-Orientation

PM enforces an *object-oriented* message-based style of programming. The core of a Presentation Manager program is a set of window procedures that you write to process outside events such as the mouse or keyboard input associated with a particular window. Presentation Manager will call the appropriate window procedure and pass it parameters in the form of a message (see Figure 3-5). An application becomes, in effect, a set of window procedures that react to user input. This paradigm forces application designers to think in terms of windows reacting to user input.

PM and SAA

PM fully conforms to the SAA programming guidelines for structuring a graphic application. This includes how the application's data is displayed on the screen, how messages are handled, and how pictures are exchanged. The Presentation Manager's pre-registered window classes (standard window, menus, scroll bars, and dialog boxes) comply with the Common User Access standard of IBM's SAA architecture. The PM API fully conforms to the Common Programming Interface (CPI) of SAA which facilitates the portability of your applications to other IBM platforms.

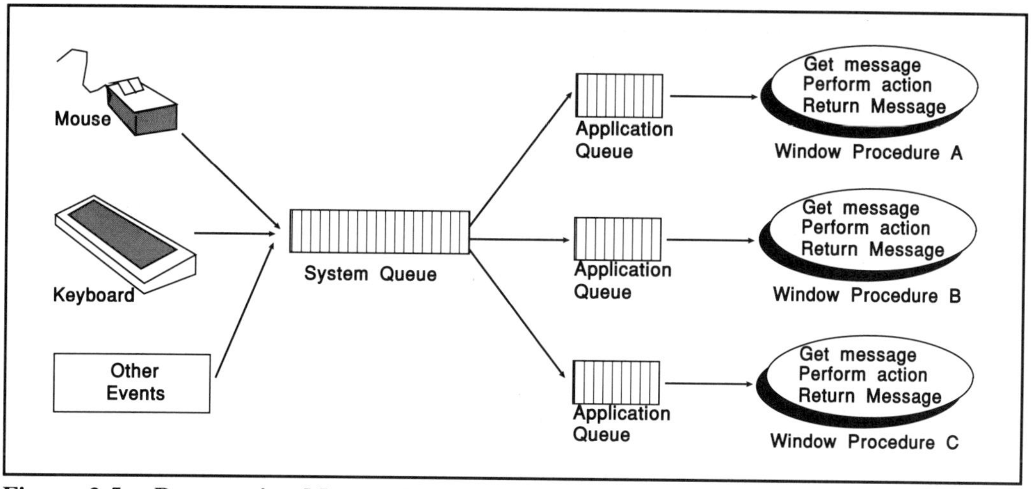

Figure 3-5. Presentation Manager's System and Window Procedure Queues.

PM's Programming Services

The following is a list of PM's most important API services:

- ***Managing windows***: PM provides a large set of API calls for controlling windows. This includes calls to allow an application to create, size, move, and control windows and their contents.

- ***Graphic primitives***: The PM GPI primitives allow you to create lines, markers, areas, arcs, and character fonts. Using these primitives you can construct complete graphic objects which can then be displayed, printed, or stored. You can invoke the primitive set with specific attributes such as color, type of line, shape to fill, or shading levels.

- ***Graphic object management***: PM provides a set of API calls to manage graphic objects. The PM API allows you to place the graphic objects you construct (known as graphic segments) in libraries. It allows you to reuse your stored segments by drawing the same segment repeatedly into a single picture or on many graphic devices.

- ***Graphic object manipulation***: PM provides a set of API calls through which you can transform a graphic object by scaling it in size, rotating it, translating its position, or changing its slant. PM will also clip the parts of an object that lie outside a specified boundary.

- ***Presentation spaces***: PM provides a set of API calls to manage the presentation space while assembling an object from world coordinates to the coordinates of your display device or printer. PM allows you to draw in a virtual space and then associate your drawing with a device context. You can then switch your associations to a different device context. For example, you assemble your drawing in a virtual space, then you can choose to associate that space with a printer, display, or plotter. Thus PM provides a device-independent graphic system. The presentation drivers virtualize the display environment (screen, printer, plotter). Your API calls interact with the virtual driver (a device independent interface) which then translates the request into commands for a specific device driver when you request an association.

- ***Metafiles***: PM provides a set of API calls to import or export an image object. Pictures created with the PM API can be packaged in a metafile that conforms to IBM's Mixed Object Document Content Architecture (MODCA) interchange standard. This allows another application to run the metafile and recreate the picture. The metafile contains all the PM API instructions to create the final version of the picture.

- ***Bitmaps***: PM provides a set of API calls for bitmap manipulation. Bitmap operations are very useful for animation and when areas of a screen need to be filled, moved, or restored. The PM API supports high speed operations on bitmap representations of a screen.

- ***Clipboard***: PM provides a set of API calls that enable the user-initiated exchange of data between applications using the clipboard. A user first copies selected data into the clipboard, deletes (cut) it from the source application, and then inserts it (paste) into the target application from the clipboard. The cut, copy, and paste commands must be supported by an application. They are implemented as a set of PM API calls.

- ***Dynamic Data Exchange (DDE)***: PM provides a set of API calls that support the DDE protocol for message-based exchanges of data among applications. DDE can be used to construct *hot links* between applications where data can be fed from window to window without operator intervention. As an example, the changes in an inventory table in a database window can be fed directly into another window where a spreadsheet is dynamically displaying inventory in graphical bar-chart format. As the inventory changes in the database, the changes get automatically reflected on the bar-charts. Hot links provide a level of integration between PM applications that goes beyond the Clipboard's "Cut and Paste." The hot link ties the data in an application to its source. When the source data changes, the pasted data is updated automatically via the hot link. DDE defines the data format and control sequences of the message exchange. The data is exchanged using the OS/2's shared memory services. Through a DDE API call, an application can automatically be advised by way of a message if some data of interest has changed. Two DDE compliant applications having no prior knowledge of each other can negotiate (in theory) an interchange format and exchange details such as the length of each message.

PM Resources

PM allows you to create resources that are defined apart from your source code in a resource script (.RC) file. You may place in the resource files existing PM resources or create your own using the OS/2 Programmer's Toolkit (purchased separately from OS/2). The Toolkit supplies font, icon, and dialog box editors together with the RC utility which allows you to compile and bind resources to your applications. Resources can also be put in a DLL and accessed by your application at run-time.

PM Application Generators and GUI Tools

In the next section, we present OS/2's Dialog Manager, a tool that greatly facilitates the creation of PM applications. The Dialog Manager's program development facility is also part of the OS/2 Programmer's Toolkit. The Dialog Manager's runtime library can be distributed with your code free of charge. In addition to Dialog Manager, there is a wide selection of PM application development tools on the market. Most of these tools allow your applications to also run on Windows 3.0. Here's a sample of what tools are available:

- **EASEL** from Interactive Images, Inc.
- **Choreographer** from GUIdance Technologies, Inc.
- **CASE:PM** from CASEWORKS, Inc.
- **Object/1** from mdbs, Inc.
- **Extensible Virtual Toolkit** from XVT Software, Inc.
- **Applications Manager** from Intelligent Environments, Inc.
- **Arcadia CUA Workbench** from Arcadia Technologies, Inc.
- **VZ Programmer** from VZCorp, Inc.

Even with this excellent choice of tools, you will need to program the Presentation Manager for applications that require animation or need to take full advantage of multimedia. In addition, most tools cannot handle the direct manipulation of objects through mouse "drag and drop" techniques. Many of the tools do not even provide support for multiple fonts, bitmaps, metafiles, and DDE.

The bottom line: If you're producing the normal window type of PM graphics, then a tool will greatly increase your productivity. However, if you're producing leading-edge graphic applications, then you'll have to learn PM at an intimate level.

THE DIALOG MANAGER (DM)

The Dialog Manager, which comes with the OS/2 Programmer's Toolkit, provides programmers with a powerful GUI tool for creating Presentation Manager (PM) applications quickly and easily. It is especially well suited for creating and maintaining form-fill applications that have a CUA *look and feel.*

DM: The API Services

The Dialog Manager consists of twelve runtime API calls and a *tag language* that describes the structure of the screens. The Dialog Manager handles the presentation of window panels and the interaction between the user and an application. Your application would use the Dialog Manager services to request that a specific window panel be displayed. After a window panel is displayed, all navigation, selection, and text entry is handled by the Dialog Manager. You regain control of your application after the user enters the data and submits a request for processing the information.

DM: The Tag Language

The Dialog tag language is based on the **Standard Generalized Mark-up Language** (SGML), a recently adopted ISO standard. SGML is used extensively for document preparation and desk-top publishing. By using the tag mark-up language you can concentrate on the role of the objects you want to place on the screen and their interrelationships with other objects. You leave the actual formatting of the panel elements to the Dialog Manager. The Dialog Manager will then create a consistent user interface that fully conforms to SAA's Common User Access (CUA) standard. Thus, the Dialog Manager frees you from having to learn CUA's hundreds of rules and lets you concentrate instead on the contents and flow of your application. Other tag language benefits are:

- It enforces an object/action approach to dialog definition.
- It makes it easy to translate screens into different national languages.
- It may be used by an information developer as a specification language.
- It separates screens and messages from the application's procedural logic.

DM and PM

The Dialog Manager builds on top of the graphic capabilities of PM. For example, when you start an application the Dialog Manager uses PM to display the primary window. PM takes care of adding the borders, the maximize/minimize icons, the system icons, and the scroll bars. Finally, Dialog Manager takes over from PM and completes the window by displaying the user-defined panel in the body area. The user-defined panels consist of the objects that appear in the client area of a window such as: action bar choices, pull-downs, scroll bars, radio buttons, check boxes, list boxes, push buttons, data entry areas, and output areas. The client area is the area that you define through the tag language.

Dialog Manager applications (unlike the event-driven PM applications) are procedural in nature. Referring to Figure 3-6 Dialog Manager applications use the services of the Dialog Manager *layer*, which in turn uses the services of the Presentation Manager *layer*. Dialog Manager applications are thus one layer removed from the Presentation

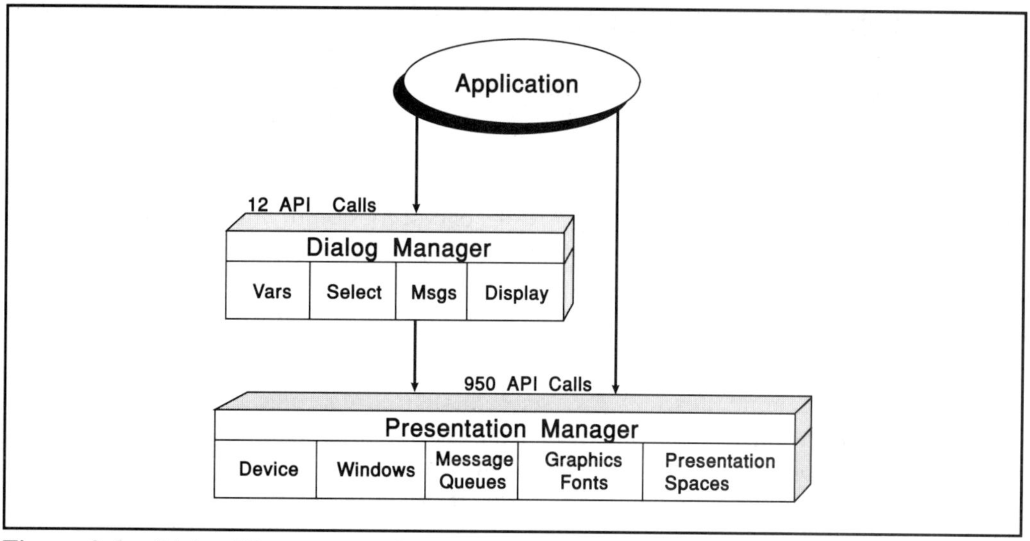

Figure 3-6. Dialog Manager and Presentation Manager Interaction.

Manager's message queues and polling loop mechanisms. The Dialog Manager service layer handles all the user interaction and does not return control to your application until users have completed all their interactions. Your application does not need to monitor the mouse and keystroke events as they occur.

You cannot mix Presentation Manager and Dialog Manager calls in the same application. However, Dialog Manager provides two constructs that allow you to add Presentation Manager code to extend or customize your Dialog Manager applications: user controls and user exits.

- **User controls** allow you to create your own fields within a Dialog Manager panel. You can then create your own graphics, track the mouse, and display metafiles using the Presentation Manager services.
- **User exits** are points of control in the Dialog Manager where your application can provide customized processing options that can be applied to a displayed field. Exits are carried out before the Dialog Manager returns from DISPLAY processing.

THE COMMUNICATIONS MANAGER

This section focuses on the Communications Manager, OS/2 EE's *all-in-one* subsystem for communicating with almost everything, from PCs to mainframes. The intent was to provide a fully integrated and tested product that provides a "superset" of communications functions, which can then be *scaled downwards* to meet a particular machine's communications needs. The Communications Manager, effectively, turns the PC into a powerful, low-cost communication processor that can handle both local and remote networking.

"All-In-One" Communications

The Communications Manager supports a variety of communication protocols and communication hardware which can all run concurrently on the same machine. The product is made up of modular building blocks with well defined APIs to many of the popular protocols. The APIs are reentrant, meaning that they can be used simultaneously by more than one user. The support of concurrent communications and the reentrant APIs is a marked improvement over comparable protocols in the MS-DOS environment. In addition, network management support is built into all the elements of Communications Manager, providing another major improvement over similar MS-DOS packages.

The packaging of Communication Manager as a single subsystem ensures that the constituent subcomponents will not interfere with one another, as was so common in the MS-DOS environment. The single package also offers a consistent PM user interface for installation, configuration, network management, and common services. Using a set of windows and panels, you can: start or stop a communication service, send and receive files, display status and messages, remap your keyboard, and look at traces and alert messages for problem determination.

When to Unbundle

The bundled Communications Manager package provides a large amount of function at a price significantly lower than a comparable system of separately purchased applications. However, these improvements incur a price in terms of hardware. The communication software alone requires 5 MBytes of hard-disk space. The run-time requires 200 KBytes of RAM for the Communication Manager base and 100 KBytes to 400 KBytes for each of the protocols. Most probably, you will only need a small subset of the communication offerings. Make sure to exclude the functions that you do not need in order to save memory. One of your minor challenges when using Communications Manager will be learning how to configure your machines to fit your particular mix of communication needs.

Layers and Communication APIs

One glance at Figure 3-7 should help convince you that Communications Manager makes available a kaleidoscope of Application Programming Interfaces (APIs). These APIs sit on top of layers of communication protocols and services. Each layer builds on top of the services provided by the layers below it. The APIs allow you to tap into the system at selective interfaces. To understand the layers of Communications Manager, we will start at the bottom of Figure 3-7 and work our way upwards.

The lowest layer of software belongs to the device drivers that provide an interface to several types of communication hardware adapters. The OS/2 kernel sits on top of the device drivers. On top of the OS/2 kernel, there are several layers of protocol functions implemented as Dynamic Link Libraries (DLLs). The DLLs provide protocol stacks for SNA, NetBIOS, Asynchronous communications, and X.25. The functions provided by some of the protocol stacks are roughly equivalent to the OSI Link, Network, Transport, Session, and to some degree Presentation layers. Some of the protocol stacks are far more complete than others; X.25 for example only partially covers the OSI Physical, Link, and Network layers, while SNA covers all the OSI layers.

The terminal emulators provide user level presentation services that allow you to run your OS/2 machine as a dumb terminal attached to a multiuser host. The screen-driven common services enable you to interactively manage the communications environment. The Network Management functions that are necessary to monitor and control a communication network are present in all the layers. The LAN Requester and ECF components redirect requests to remote servers that extend the local operating system into a network operating system. The top layer of Figure 3-7 provides a callable interface (API) through which a user program may gain access to the communication resources it requires.

Connectivity Options

The first requirement of a communication subsystem is to be able to physically link up with other machines. This rudimentary link-up, or *connectivity*, is the prerequisite for all communications, and forms the platform on which more meaningful forms of information exchange are constructed. Communication Manager provides connectivity through its device drivers and the link layer protocols shown at the bottom of Figure 3-7 on page 38. The large selection of connectivity options provided by Communications Manager can be divided into three categories: LAN attachment, remote connectivity, and direct attachment to IBM mainframes.

LAN Attachments

LAN attachments provide high-speed local connectivity over a shared LAN cable which serves as the broadcast medium. The media access link layer, which is built into the hardware, arbitrates the access to the cable and allows packets of information to be exchanged reliably over the medium. The Communications Manager provides built-in driver support for the IEEE 802.5 Media Access Control protocol, otherwise known as Token Ring, and the IEEE 802.3 Media Access Control, otherwise known as Ethernet. In terms of connectivity hardware, the following networks are supported:

1. IBM Token Ring (IEEE 802.5).
2. IBM PC Network broadband (a low cost variation of IEEE 802.3).
3. IBM PC Network baseband (a very low cost variation of IEEE 802.3).
4. The original Ethernet V2 protocol (a variation of IEEE 802.3).
5. The new Ethernet protocol (IEEE 802.3).

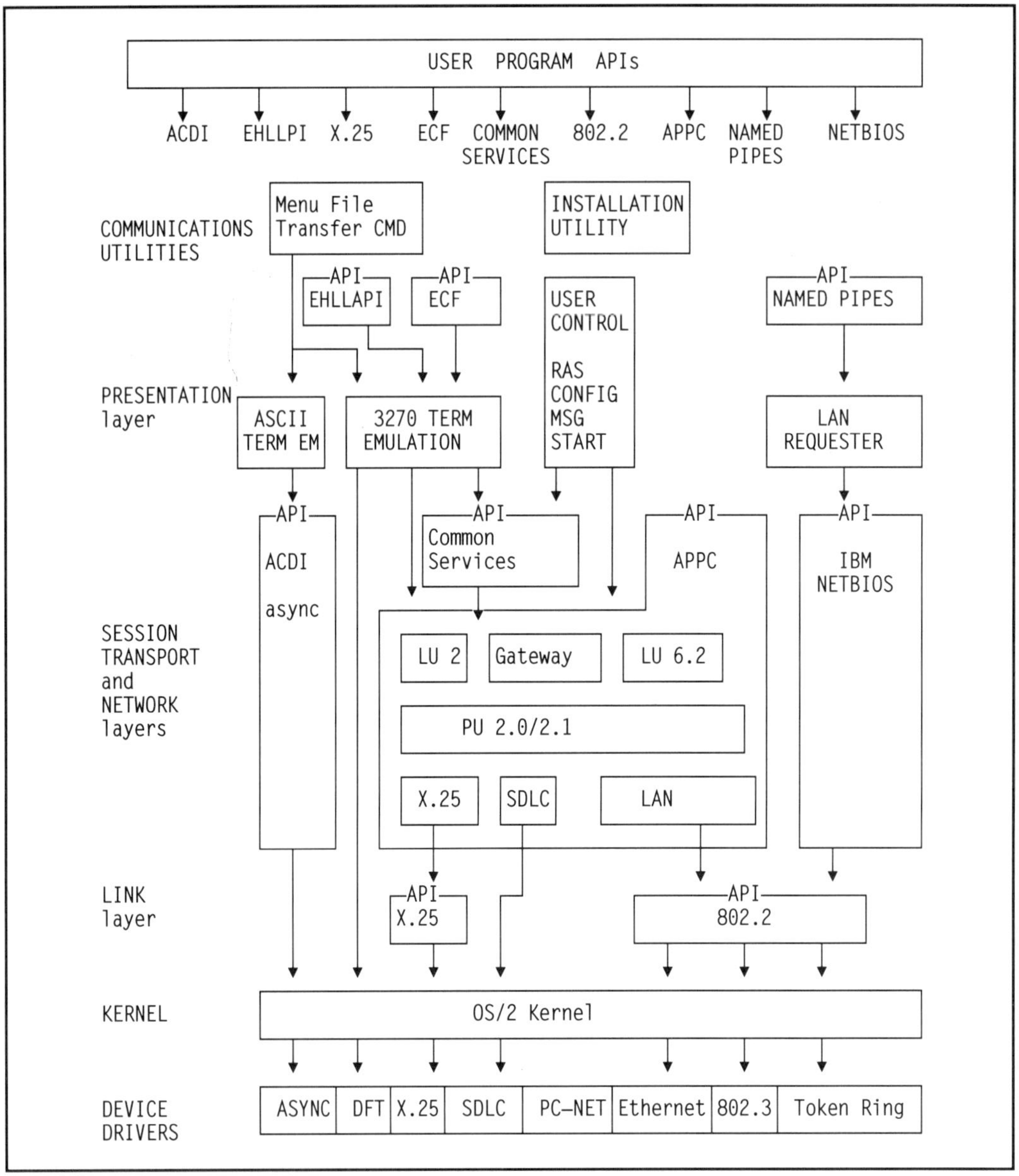

Figure 3-7. Communications Manager Functional Layers and Programming Interfaces.

To support Ethernet, IBM extended its PCNETDD driver to map to the Network Driver Interface Spec (NDIS). NDIS is the Microsoft/3Com standard for interfacing protocol stacks to IEEE 802.3 device drivers. Communications Manager can thus support Ethernet adapters from vendors such as: Ungermann-Bass, 3Com, and Western Digital. Figure 3-8 shows the Communications Manager LAN driver support options.

The various LAN adapters provide a wide choice of physical layer cabling options. The Token Ring LAN adapter, from IBM, supports low-cost telephone twisted-pair

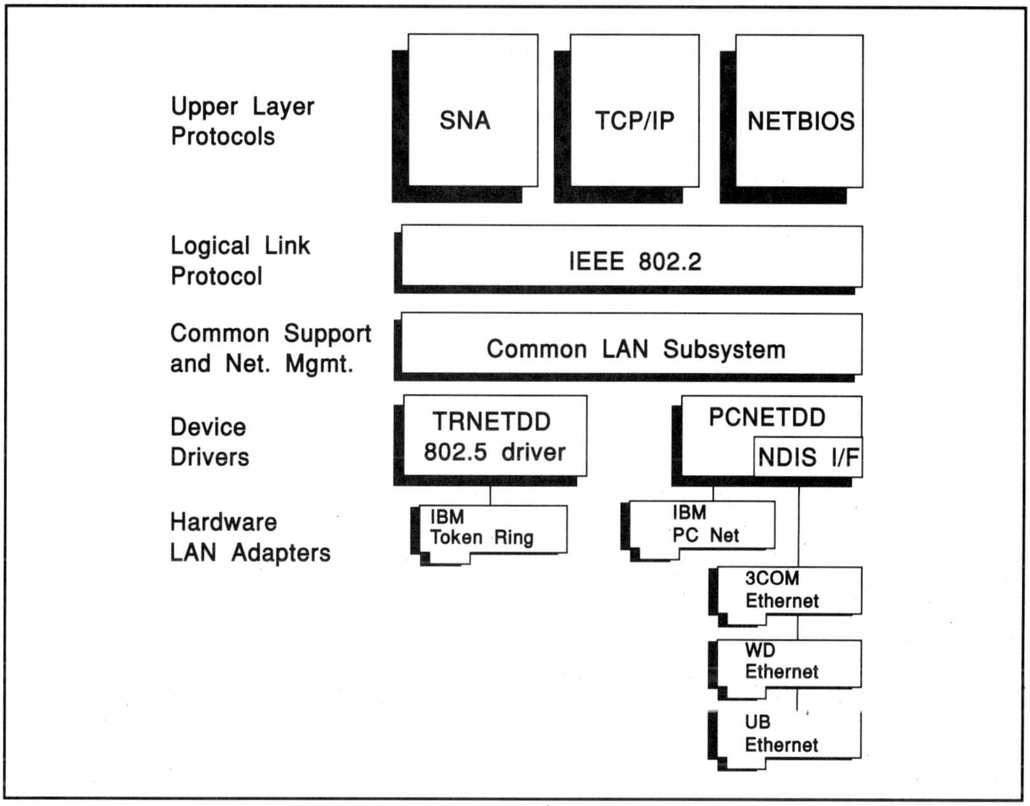

Figure 3-8. LAN Connectivity Options.

cable at 4Mb/s bandwidth. The more reliable shielded twisted-pair cable supports 16Mb/s bandwidth, and the fiber-optic cable can be used for wiring long segments (up to 2 KM). The PC Network Broadband LAN adapter, from IBM, works with cable-TV technology and in theory can support multiple (2 Mb/s) LAN channels over the same cable. The PC Network Baseband LAN adapter, also from IBM, provides low cost, low bandwidth communication over ordinary telephone cables. The various OEM Ethernet adapters usually work with baseband coax cable that come in a variety of cable thickness and prices.

Remote Connectivity

The remote connectivity options enable your machine to communicate with the world-at-large. Communications Manager supports remote connectivity over telephone lines through public or private networks using a variety of link protocols, including: Asynchronous (ASYNC), Synchronous Data Link Control (SDLC), and CCITT's X.25 standard for packet switching. Figure 3-9 shows the various options provided by Communication Manager for programs to "reach out and talk" to other programs over long distance carriers.

The term *DTE* stands for Data Terminal Equipment in data communication jargon. DTE's are your OS/2 EE machine, including the adapter hardware. DTE's connect to the Data Communications Equipment (or *DCE*) which provides the long distance connectivity service through communication carriers. The DCE consists of the modem and the carrier facilities. ASYNC adapters require asynchronous modems. SDLC and X.25 require synchronous modems. The long distance carrier may be your ordinary telephone service (switched lines) or it can be a dedicated leased line (where speed, connection availability, and noise immunity are requirements), or it can be an X.25 Packet Switched Data Network (PSDN).

*PSDN*s provide reliable long distance service over a shared network of connected computers and provide an alternative to networks made up of lines dedicated to pairs of users. Packet switching technology allows multiple users to use the same network paths by breaking the information transmitted into intelligent packets that are routed through a network and re-assembled at the destination. PSDNs create permanent or switched virtual circuits between network subscribers and offer various ways of paying for network bandwidth, including schemes where you can literally *pay by the packet.* The term "virtual" in the X.25 context means that you can have multiple logical connections (virtual circuits) over a single physical link. OS/2 EE supports up to 128 virtual circuits which can be used by up to 40 concurrent X.25 applications. To use a PSDN you connect your equipment (the DTE) to the network through a modem (the DCE) as shown in Figure 3-9 on page 41. The OS/2 EE X.25 driver works with up to eight concurrent Micro-Channel IBM X.25 Coprocessor/2 adapters which provide bit-synchronous attachment to the DCE.

Direct Attachment to IBM Mainframes

Direct attachment to IBM mainframes is another form of connectivity that is supported by Communications Manager. In fact, Communications Manager transforms a PC into a "great communicator" in the world of IBM host networks. This is accomplished by supporting the old terminal networks as well as the new *peer-to-peer* host/PC connectivity strategies, which are typically LAN based.

A PC can attach directly through point-to-point coax cable to System/370 terminal controllers (the 3174, 3274, 3X74 series) and the 9370 workstation controller. This type of attachment is called *Distributed Function Terminal (DFT).* Most IBM customer shops have miles of coax cables on their premises. OS/2 EE's DFT support can help leverage some of that coax base. Note that you can also connect to most IBM hosts and their Front End Processors (the 3705, 3725, 37XX series) through Token Ring LANs, ASYNC, SDLC, and X.25.

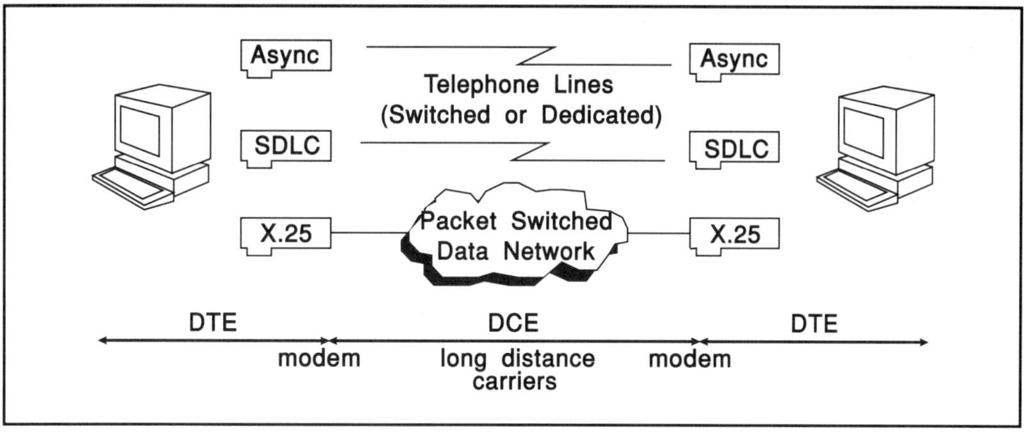

Figure 3-9. Reaching Out Long Distance the Communications Manager Way.

Upper Layer Protocol Support

It takes more than link layer connectivity for two entities to communicate. Additional layers of protocol are required on top of the link. An upper-layer protocol should provide:

- Reliable end-to-end service across multiple networks.
- Logical names for network entities.
- Session-based rules of exchange. This is the protocol which is followed after a session is established. It includes agreements on who talks first, on how to gracefully end conversations, and who does what in case of error. It also includes some convention for establishing checkpoints during a conversation.
- Common data structures for the representation of information that gets exchanged over a network. This includes protocols for mail, documents, folders, images, etc.
- Common network services such as: file transfers, terminal emulation, network management, network authentication and security, network directory services, network time, electronic mail, etc.

As you can see, the list of upper layer services is extensive and open-ended. Communications software vendors have tackled the problem by offering the upper-layer protocols as a *stack* of offerings that is architected to work together to provide system solutions. Some of the protocol stacks are more complete than others. Examples of the more complete protocol stacks are: SNA, TCP/IP, and OSI.

Communications Manager supports a variety of upper-layer protocol stacks over the connectivity links that were described above. Each of OS/2 EE's protocol stacks opens up a communication universe in which your programs can participate. A very complete implementation of the TCP/IP stack on OS/2 is offered by IBM as a *separate* product.

At present, the main deficiency in the Communications Manager protocol stack offering is the lack of support for the OSI stack. However, IBM has stated that SAA will support ISO (support for X.25 is a first installment of that support). In spite of the noted limitation, Communications Manager comes close to providing more connectivity, at the upper and lower layers, than any single product ever offered. The upper layer protocol stacks provided by Communications Manager are: SNA, X.25, and LAN peer-to-peer protocols. TCP/IP is a separate product.

System Network Architecture (SNA)

The Communications Manager implements IBM's System Network Architecture (SNA) in both its old and new forms. The *old SNA* is a hierarchical terminal controller network. This is a network in which hosts reside at the center of the universe and are surrounded by dumb terminals. All the processing power in the network resides at the top of the hierarchy, in mainframes running VTAM (in SNA parlance a Physical Unit 5 or PU 5 node). Mainframes are *front-ended* by communication controllers running the NCP program (a PU 4 node) which in turn is *front-ended* by terminal cluster controllers (PU 2 nodes). Terminals talk to the host through terminal controllers. Communication Manager allows the PC to look like a dumb terminal, that is, act as a Logical Unit type 2 or LU 2 in SNA terminology. A logical unit type describes the characteristics of an SNA session. In an LU 2 session, the entire application runs in the host. The PC can attach to hosts by looking like a terminal through a coax cable or Token Ring. Another option is to have the PC look like a terminal combined with a terminal controller (a PU 2 node) and talk to the host through SDLC.

The *new SNA* is a network of peers, where PC programs can talk to the host programs at a program-to-program level through the use of well defined *verb* commands (this type of session is called an LU 6.2 type in SNA terminology). Physically, the PCs are endowed with local intelligence to provide parallel session initiation services without VTAM host involvement. A node with those attributes is an SNA PU 2.1 node.

As part of SAA's architectural goals, IBM intends to evolve the new SNA into a true distributed operating system that supports: cross network directory services, transparent network access to resources (such as servers, applications, displays, printers, and data), common data streams, and integrated network management. The network that will make a lot of this happen is called an SNA Low Entry Network or *LEN*. OS/2 EE is already providing many of the pieces of this distributed platform. Beginning with VTAM version 3.2, LEN nodes can operate in peer-to-peer mode over large SNA multiple-hop backbone networks with VTAM providing the backbone routing of sessions across multiple SNA networks. Netview can provide central network management by monitoring and controlling such sessions.

X.25

X.25 is an international standard that defines how to connect computers to either public or private packet switching data networks (PSDNs). X.25 support is provided by IBM to primarily extend SNA communications across packet switched networks and to communicate with equipment from other vendors. X.25 is an SAA supported protocol that provides an alternative network service to SNA's VTAM/NCP. There are no indications, however, that X.25 will replace SNA's VTAM/NCP backbone networks.

LAN Protocols

The Communications Manager supports Local Area Network Protocol stacks such as NetBIOS, Named Pipes, and the LAN requester/server. These protocols provide an excellent platform for the creation of network operating systems and client-server applications. We defer the in-depth discussion of the LAN Upper Layer protocols to a later section.

TCP/IP

IBM offers a TCP/IP protocol stack as a separate product under the name **TCP/IP for OS/2**. This product, shipped in March 1990, provides a very complete TCP/IP protocol suite over Ethernet or Token Ring LANs. It interoperates with IBM's TCP/IP products for VM, MVS, MS-DOS, AS/400 and the AIX family. It costs between $675 and $1675, depending on the additional source material you require. Figure 3-10 shows the TCP/IP stack components that are offered with that product. It's a very respectable offering that allows an OS/2 machine to fully participate in a TCP/IP network.

Terminal Emulation and File Transfers

The Communications Manager includes the following terminal emulation programs:

- IBM 3270 terminal emulation
- IBM 3101 and DEC VT100 Terminal Emulation
- IBM 5250 terminal emulation

IBM 3270 Terminal Emulation

IBM 3270 terminal emulation provides interactive access to IBM System/370 host computers. The IBM 3270 terminal models that are emulated include: the 3178, 3278 and 3279. As many as ten 3270 terminal emulation sessions can be active at any one time. This includes up to five sessions multiplexed over a single DFT coaxial cable link and up to five more sessions multiplexed over either an SDLC or a Token Ring network. Each logical terminal appears in a separate Presentation Manager window. You can start and stop sessions and move the session windows using the Presentation Manager controls. Multiple sessions can be viewed simultaneously on the screen and

The Application Layer:
The following protocols are supported in both client and server modes:

TELNET	FTP, TFTP	MAIL/SMTP	REXEC and REXECD	Remote Procedures:
This is a full screen terminal emulation for VT100, 3270 and ANSITERM	(File Transfer Protocol and Trivial File Transfer Protocol)	(Electronic Mail using Simple Mail Transfer Protocol)	(Remote Command and Daemon Execution)	1.SUN's RPC 2.Apollo's NCS 3.Berkeley Sockets 4.Kerberos Interface

Network Management Services:

SNMP	Security and Authentication	NETSTAT	LPR/LPD	DNS
(Simple Network Management Protocol) Used to gather network statistics	(Kerberos Library for Encryption and security)	Used to obtain machine statistics and routing status	Used to print on remote printers or as a print server for clients	(Domain Name Resolver) client only

Transport Layer Services:

TCP	UDP
(Transmission Control Protocol) This is a session-based connection service for reliable transmission	(User Datagram Protocol) This is a connectionless, unacknowledged transmission service

Network Layer Services:

IP	RIP	ICMP
(Internet Protocol) Provides internet datagram delivery	(Routing Information Protocol) This service provides internet routing support	(Internet Control Messaging Protocol) Used to for internet status exchanges

Physical and Link Layers:

Hardware LAN adapters	IBM Token Ring	IEEE 802.3	Ethernet Version 2

→ To IBM's TCP/IP products for VM, MVS, MS-DOS, AS/400 and AIX.

Figure 3-10. IBM's TCP/IP Protocol Suite for OS/2 (sold separately from OS/2 EE).

PM functions such as Mark, Cut, Paste, Copy can be used to transfer simple text or bitmaps between windows.

Terminal emulation sessions are represented by unique Presentation Manager icons when they get minimized. The icon gets modified if a host session is updated. As a convenience for the user, each session window may have its colors and font sizes individually configured.

In addition to terminal emulation, an active 3270 session can be used to move files to and from an IBM/370 host on which the 3270-PC file transfer program (IND$FILE) is installed. File transfer to and from IBM hosts running MVS/TSO, VM/CMS, or CICS is supported over any active 3270 session. You can initiate a file transfer from the OS/2 command line with the SEND or RECEIVE command. An OS/2 workstation can also access and display during a 3270 emulation session host GDDM graphics (the GDDM-OS/2 link program must be installed on the host). This support allows a host GDDM picture to be downloaded to an OS/2 EE PC where it can be displayed, printed, or plotted. The GDDM picture may also be saved as a Presentation Manager or PIF Metafile.

IBM 3101 and DEC VT100 Terminal Emulation

The IBM 3101 and DEC VT100 terminal emulation options provide interactive access to hosts that support ASCII terminals via an asynchronous link. Multiple ASCII terminal emulations may be configured but only one may be active at any time. With the asynchronous services a user can access a range of data services such as Dow Jones News, Compuserve, MCI Mail and the Source. Three kinds of file transfers are supported over an asynchronous link:

- With an IBM host (VM/CMS or MVS/TSO) using the 3270-PC File Transfer Program (IND$FILE).
- With any host that supports the XMODEM file transfer protocol.
- With any partner that supports a simple Send ASCII Text File function. This works well with systems like MCI Mail.

IBM 5250 Terminal Emulation

The IBM 5250 terminal emulation option provides interactive access to IBM AS/400 hosts via SDLC, X.25, Twinax or Token Ring connections. Up to five concurrent 5250 sessions can be supported; each 5250 session being a separate APPC session.

SNA Gateway

The SNA Gateway is a PS/2 machine which provides to multiple workstations on a LAN a shared link to an IBM System/370 host. Each workstation thinks it is directly connected to the host, while the host thinks it is communicating with a single terminal controller. The gateway uses a single host communication link to get data from the host and route it to the appropriate workstation. In the other direction, it accepts data from workstations, appends the appropriate control headers and routes the data to the host. The gateway code emulates the SNA cluster controller 3X74 family with the gateway PC made to appear to the host as a single PU 2 in SNA terminology. A PU 2 can support up to 254 users or what SNA calls LUs. Only 64 users can be active at any one time. The gateway can transparently extend a 3270 emulation (LU 2) or an APPC (LU6.2) session.

The gateway communicates with the host using SNA/SDLC, SNA/X.25 or APPC on an IBM Token Ring. The users may attach to the gateway via an IBM Token Ring LAN, an IBM PC Network LAN, an Ethernet LAN, an SDLC switched link, or an X.25 network. Figure 3-11 shows some of the connectivity options the gateway makes available to workstations. You should note that the gateway makes it possible for PC Network and Ethernet attached workstations to connect to an IBM host (IBM hosts do not normally directly attach to Ethernet or PC Network). The gateway also offers useful remote services via SDLC or X.25 to all LAN-attached workstations.

In addition to OS/2 the gateway can support DOS workstations running any of the following programs:

- IBM 3270 Emulation Program Version 3.0
- IBM 3270 Workstation Program
- IBM APPC/PC

Communications and System Management (C&SM)

Network Management features are built into all the levels of Communication Manager (see Figure 3-12). Errors are detected, logged and can be forwarded as network alerts to an IBM host running Netview. Netview allows a network to be remotely managed from a central location and provides tools that allow an operator to stay current on error conditions and monitor network performance. Communications Manager supports the TRANSFER_MS_DATA API call that allows an application to send its own alerts and messages to Netview. Hardware-related errors from SDLC, ASYNC, IBM Token Ring, PC Network, Ethernet and the X.25 co-processor can be recorded in a local error log and also sent to Netview as a generic alert if a host connection is provided. The generic alert contains information about the type of error detected, probable causes of failure and recommended action.

Communications Manager also supports the receipt of remote commands from Netview. The commands are passed to the program that requests them. For example, a command may be sent to run remote diagnostics on a device and to send back the results to Netview.

In addition Communications Manager provides local utilities for problem determination, running traces of the flow of commands and data across interfaces, and for displaying and printing error information. The utilities can be run under program control allowing user written programs to monitor error incidents selectively, and take appropriate action. Message pop-ups on the screen can be suppressed making it easy to run un-attended diagnostics.

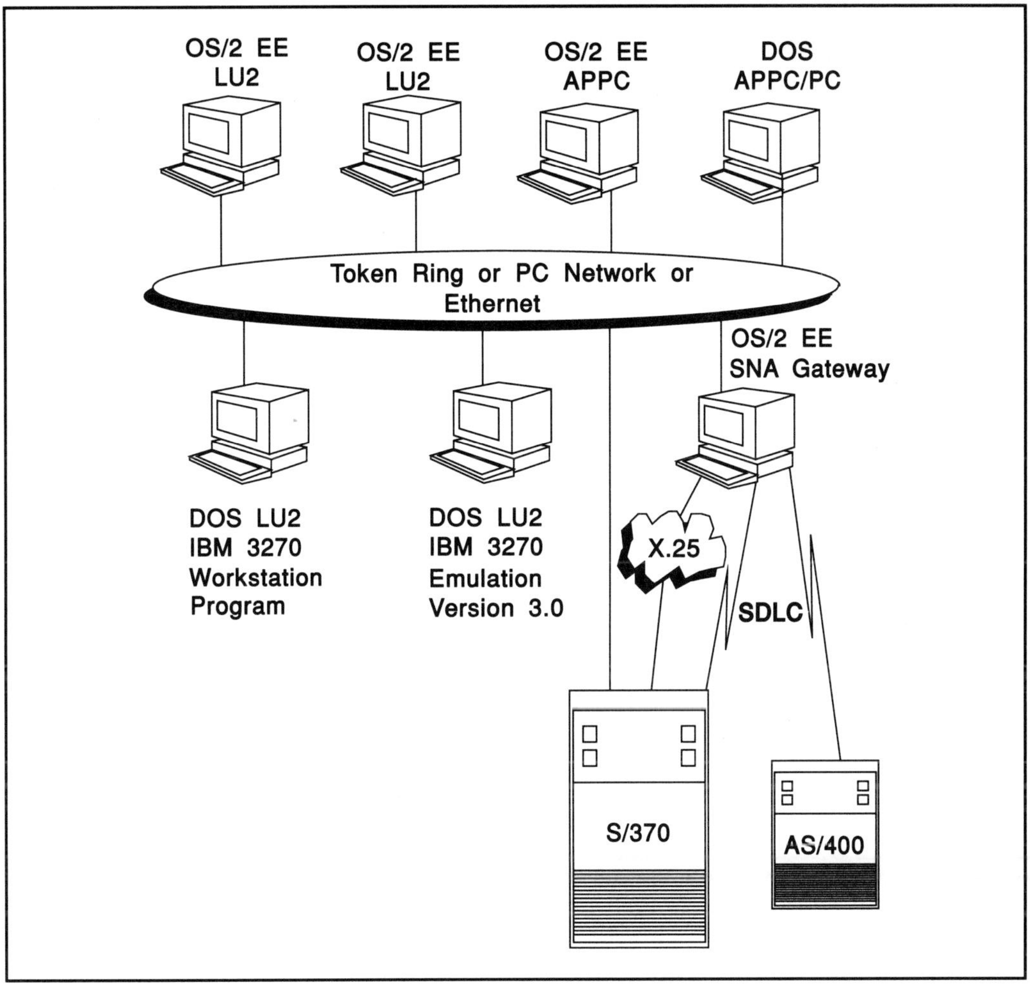

Figure 3-11. SNA Gateway: Host Connectivity Options.

Programming Interfaces (APIs)

In this section we describe the programming interfaces Communications Manager brings to the C programmer. The Communications Manager makes its whole repertoire of network services and protocols available to the C programmer through API sets. Each of the API sets has a specific purpose making it possible to create programs that can communicate with many host and PC environments across Local Area Networks, Wide Area Networks and telephone lines. The APIs are accessible from C applications running concurrently under OS/2 user sessions or within the windows of a Presentation Manager session.

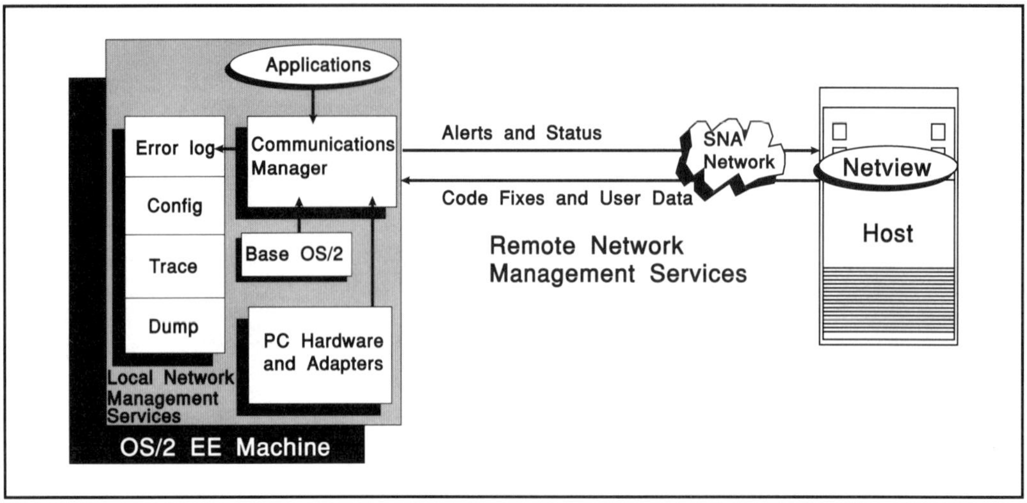

Figure 3-12. OS/2 EE's Local and Remote Network Management Facilities.

Communication API Types

The Communications Manager provides eight sets of protocol APIs in addition to an API set to obtain common services. The protocol APIs can be classified into three categories:

- **Program-to-Program APIs** which you can use to create cooperative and client-server applications. The term "program-to-program" indicates that the two sides of a communication link use the same protocol interface to conduct a networked conversation. Any computer can initiate a conversation with any other computer. The protocol tends to be quite symmetric and is sometimes called "peer-to-peer." The program-to-program APIs fall into two categories:

  1. Higher level APIs that mask the communications and provide associations between two logical programs. The APIs that fall into this category include NetBIOS, Named Pipes, and APPC.
  2. Lower level APIs that do not quite mask the communications and require that you get more involved with the mechanics of networking, message buffer allocation, session management, and sometimes the direct control of the communication adapter. Protocols that fall into this category include IEEE 802.2, Asynchronous Communications Device Interface (ACDI) and X.25. Both ACDI and X.25 are interface protocols, as opposed to end-to-end protocols. This means that a portion of the API has only local significance and is involved with interfacing to the communications equipment, as opposed to the remote partner.

- **Requester/Server APIs** provide protocols and message structures for the remote invocation of services. An application (a requester) is provided with a data structure for requesting a service. The provider of the service (the server) interprets the incoming structure and fulfills the request. The fulfilled request comes back to the requester in the reply. OS/2 EE provides an API for remote host services through the Server-Requester Programming Interface (SRPI), which makes it easier for a PC to share resources on S/370 hosts. The LAN requester/server makes use of a different remote service protocol that uses Microsoft's Server Message Block (SMB) architecture. The remote database services are also an example of a requester/server API which uses SQL over the network (more on that in the sections on OS/2 EE's database services).

- **Emulation service APIs** help to automate and simplify the interaction between a PC user and a terminal-based mainframe application. Unlike the more modern application-to-application protocols (like APPC), emulation service APIs do not require any changes to the numerous mainframe programs designed to work with terminals. APPC, on the other hand, is a more general protocol that provides communications among cooperating programs, but it requires writing new software on the mainframe. Communications Manager supports the Emulator High-Level Language Application Interface (EHLLAPI).

The Communications Manager APIs

In this section, we provide a brief overview of the Communications Manager APIs and common services. Refer to Figure 3-7 on page 38 to understand the make-up of the underlying protocols on which the APIs build their services.

- **NetBIOS** is currently the premier protocol for LAN-based program-to-program communications. Introduced by IBM and Sytek in 1984 for the IBM PC Network, NetBIOS now runs with almost no changes on Ethernet, Token Ring, ARCnet, StarLAN, and even low-cost serial-port LANs. NetBIOS interfaces to TCP/IP, XNS, OSI, and IEEE 802.2 protocol stacks. Support for a NetBIOS platform exists on many operating systems including MS-DOS, OS/2, UNIX, and some host environments such as Tandem Computers. NetBIOS is currently the de facto portable standard for network application providers.

  One of the many reasons for NetBIOS's success is its intuitive simplicity, which makes it easy to master. NetBIOS provides a naming service that allows a LAN adapter card to have multiple logical names. Through NetBIOS, you can write LAN applications that can exchange information between named entities on the network. NetBIOS provides two classes of network transmission services: sessions and datagrams.

  Sessions provide a reliable two-way connection service in which each packet is tracked and acknowledged in sequenced message exchanges. *Datagrams* provide a simple, but unreliable, service with powerful broadcast capabilities. You can send datagrams to a named entity, or to a select group of entities (multicast), or to all entities on a network (broadcast). Datagrams are unreliable in the sense that they are not acknowledged or tracked through a sequence number. You "transmit and pray" that your datagram gets received.

The NetBIOS API consists of about 20 commands which are grouped into four categories: general purpose (such as reset, cancel, adapter status), name support (such as add name, add group name), datagram support (such as send datagram, send broadcast datagram), and session support (such as call, listen, hang up, send, receive). NetBIOS does have some weaknesses; it does not support an internetwork naming convention, and it does not provide authentication and security mechanisms.

- **APPC** is IBM's architected solution for program-to-program communication, distributed transaction processing, and remote database access across the entire IBM product line. An application program, called a Transaction Program (TP) using the APPC API, can communicate with other TPs on systems that support APPC/SNA. This includes MS-DOS/APPC, OS/400s, System/370 (MVS/XA, TSO-E, VM/APPC, and CICS/MVS environments). APPC is also supported by many non-IBM host vendors.

  APPC supplies a variety of advanced communication functions such as: password validation, starting a remote program and sending it Program Initialization Parameters (PIP), and distributed checkpoints. The checkpoint function can be used to synchronize distributed applications, and in the future will synchronize distributed databases using a 2-phase commit protocol.

  APPC's weaknesses include the lack of support for datagrams, broadcast, and multicast services. The APPC model is inherently conversational. In addition, the APPC protocol is half-duplex over a session, which means that it requires two sessions for full-duplex operation. These sessions like everything else associated with APPC, are resource hogs. The OS/2 EE version of APPC is a great improvement over DOS's APPC/PC. OS/2 EE now handles the creation of the application subsystem, the activation and deactivation of links, and the handling of incoming allocates.

- **Named Pipes** extend the OS/2 Interprocess Communication (IPC) mechanism across the network. Most LAN vendors now support Named Pipes on MS-DOS and OS/2. This includes Novell's Netware, Banyan's Vines, and the LAN Manager/LAN Server family of products from IBM, Microsoft and 3Com. Unix support for Named Pipes is provided by LAN Manager/X.

  Named Pipes are an abstraction of a full-duplex session. Processes can read and write streams of messages as well as byte-streams. Named Pipes employ a file naming convention as well as file-like semantics (such as open, close, read, write). Named Pipes offer transaction services through the powerful **DosCallNmPipe** call which combines a connect, send, receive, disconnect. Another feature of Named Pipes is that they allow messages to queue in the pipe. When a process reads from a Named Pipe, it gets one completed message per read. This is a useful implementation of a buffered transmission queue facility. Named Pipes build their services using NetBIOS primitives. They provide *value-added* by making it easy to code communication functions using file-like metaphors to obtain network services. The main drawback of Named Pipes is that you must have the LAN Server program installed in order to use the service over the network.

- **SRPI** provides an API which allows an OS/2 EE application to request host services through an active 3270 session (LU 2) with a System/370 host server running VM/CMS or MVS/TSO. The calling application first specifies a server name, a function ID, request parameters, and data, and then issues a SEND_REQUEST API call. OS/2 EE ensures that the request is routed to the appropriate 3270 session according to the profile you configured. You also must logon to the appropriate 3270 session, and start the host router programs (CMSSERV and/or MVSSERV), prior to using SRPI. Multiple applications can use SRPI concurrently; however, each 3270 session can handle only one call at a time. Calls are queued if a session is busy; however, if SRPI is active you cannot use the session for interactive work or file transfers.

  SRPI's first limitation is that, under OS/2, it does not support the host-based Enhanced Connectivity Function (ECF) which allows a PC to share S/370 host-based printers, disks and files. It does, however, support ECF under DOS. SRPI's other limitation is that it communicates using 3270 terminal emulation, rather than a program-to-program interface such as APPC. Terminal emulation is a very clumsy protocol in unattended client-server environments (that do not have a human sitting at a terminal). The reason for this clumsiness is that your application has to anticipate all the hung-terminal conditions and recover from them without human intervention. IBM made a statement of direction that SRPI will eventually run on APPC. When this happens, SRPI will become a very useful, cooperative processing requester function (SRPI's design is protocol independent).

- **IEEE 802.2** API provides a low-level interface to the 802.2 Local Area Network Logical Link Control (LLC) layer. 802.2 is the ISO standard which defines the protocol for accessing LAN link layer services in a media-access independent manner. The LLC interfaces to the Media Access Control (MAC) link protocols such as: Token Ring (IEEE 802.5) and CSMA/CD (IEEE 802.3). Communications Manager provides built-in drivers for IBM Token Ring, Ethernet V 2.0 (also known as Ethernet DIX for DEC, Intel, and Xerox), IEEE 802.3 (the new Ethernet), and the IBM PC Network.

  The 802.2 API provides a set of commands for directly controlling the LAN adapters, such as Open and Close. The API supports two types of service: *Connectionless* and *Connection-oriented.* The Connectionless service provides datagram-like "unreliable" frame transmissions between Service Access Points (SAPs). The Connection-oriented service provides reliable sequenced packet exchanges over a session between link station interfaces. The number of link stations that can be supported is adapter dependent. For example, an IBM Token Ring Adapter/A supports 64 link stations.

  You should program to the IEEE 802.2 API only if you have serious memory constraints and cannot afford NetBIOS or APPC, or if you need to provide special network utilities that require an intimate control of the communication facilities (it's like programming in assembler versus a high-level language).

- **ACDI** provides a low-level programming interface to asynchronous serial ports. ACDI can perform concurrent communications over multiple serial ports (three on a PS/2). ACDI supports modem commands including AutoDial and AutoAnswer which you can use to customize and automate dialing procedures, such as redialing a busy number. ACDI provides device-independent services for setting line parameters and for device connection control. For example, ACDI allows you to set and read the following parameters: bit rate, word length, flow control, parity, time-outs, stop bits, modem command strings, and AutoAnswer controls. An application can send and receive data through a buffered (block I/O) interface.

The main benefit of ACDI is that it makes it easy to develop an asynchronous communications program without requiring detailed knowledge of the hardware, device drivers, or the multitasking environment. Hopefully, an ACDI application will work without requiring modification if the hardware or device drivers are changed.

ACDI's main weakness is that it does not provide a reliable session service, such as that provided by NetBIOS, APPC, and 802.2. You will have to code your own packet sequencing and control protocol if you need such a service. However, ACDI does provide some limited error-detection services. It can detect the following error conditions: parity errors, framing errors, overflow and overrun errors, device errors, and line errors.

- **X.25**'s API service provides a low-level interface to packet switched networks. Much of the X.25 interface is concerned with interfacing the local data communication equipment to the packet switched network. Through the API service you request a virtual-circuit and, from then on, you can send and receive information on your virtual circuit. The virtual circuit can be permanent or switched. X.25 allows you to multiplex virtual circuits over the same communication interface (OS/2 EE limits you to 128 virtual circuits, the X.25 standard supports 4095). The virtual circuits provide a reliable end-to-end service. X.25 provides two facilities for recovering from errors: reset and restart. Reset is used to re-initialize a virtual circuit (the sequence counts are reset). Restart causes all virtual circuits to be cleared.

  Communications Manager's implementation of X.25 conforms to CCITT's 1980 and 1984 recommendations. Two complementary types of X.25 are provided by Communication Manager:

  1. For SNA applications, the Qualified Link Level Control (QLLC) allows up to 128 SNA switched or virtual circuits. A virtual circuit has a maximum bandwidth of 64 Kb/s.
  2. For non-SNA applications, the API can be used to support multiple concurrent applications across X.25 virtual network sessions.

  Both the SNA and non-SNA applications require, and may share, the same IBM X.25 Interface Co-Processor/2 adapter (the C2X adapter card) to attach to one or more X.25 packet-switched networks. The C2X outboard adapter code is loaded onto the co-processor when X.25 is started as a Communications Manager task. The X.25 DLL can control and manage multiple adapter cards, and it routes incoming calls to the target programs and outgoing calls to the appropriate X.25 virtual circuit.

- **EHLLAPI** was introduced by IBM in 1986 as a generic API for accessing terminal emulation functions. EHLLAPI (pronounced "ee-ha-lap-pee") is mainly used by PCs to communicate with existing mainframe applications without altering the code on the mainframe side. It is a cost-effective way to extend the capabilities and lifetimes of the huge inventory of existing IBM 3270 applications. EHLLAPI was designed to be terminal emulator independent. The Communications Manager implementation of EHLLAPI works with 3270 terminal emulators for S/370 mainframes, and with the 5250 terminal emulators for AS/400 minicomputers. Prior to EHLLAPI, programs had to be tediously written in assembler to manipulate the host data streams, and a program written for a particular terminal emulator would not work with another terminal emulator.

  Generally speaking, EHLLAPI applications are not difficult to develop. The API consists of over 30 API calls that handle an assortment of terminal operator functions, from simple automatic host logon to the complexities of starting and monitoring an unattended host task. Developers can create OS/2 applications to take on tasks formerly performed by a human operator, such as sending keystrokes to the host or capturing information from a 3270 or 5250 "screen." When writing an EHLLAPI program, you should think of yourself as an operator interacting with a host through a 3270 or 5250 terminal emulation session. Your program should be able to automate tasks performed by an operator, such as: sending keystrokes to the host, requesting host update information, and copying to and from a screen. EHLLAPI API provides calls that perform the above mentioned functions. This should allow you to write applications which automate console operations, filter host messages, and monitor host response time and availability. You can use EHLLAPI to customize PC screens to display only certain fields from a host screen, or you can make a single screen from many screens. You can also run multiple host sessions and display the results on a single composite screen. The data received from the host by EHLLAPI is in the PC memory and is not necessarily displayed on the screen.

  The EHLLAPI API verbs can be categorized as follows:

  1. Operator Services that provide you with controls such as: query the system and session status, set session parameters, send_key, wait, pause, reset system, query host update, and start/stop host notification.
  2. Presentation Services that allow you to manipulate a block of memory on the PC (the *presentation space*) which represents what the host displays on a terminal screen. It is up to your application to display any, all, or none of the received data. You can use the presentation services to query and set the cursor location, query field attributes, position, and length. You can copy field contents or the presentation space to/from a string. You can search fields or the entire presentation space for string matches or updates.
  3. Device Services that allow you to intercept key strokes and to reserve or release a device.

4. Communication Services that allow you to send and receive files.

You should consider EHLLAPI as a useful tool that allows you to work with existing host applications. It is by no means a reliable peer-to-peer protocol which could be used by serious cooperative or client-server applications.

- **Common Services** API provides general services that can be used with any of the above APIs. You can, for example, use the CONVERT API verb to translate a character string from/to ASCII and EBCDIC. The DEFINE_TRACE verb turns on or off the Communications Manager trace. The LOG_MESSAGE verb allows you to append a message to the Communications Manager's system log file. The message can be displayed through the message services. The TRANSFER_MS_DATA verb allows you to send alerts to a System/370 host running Netview or you could have the alert stored in the Communications Manager error log for local display.

THE DATABASE MANAGER

The *Database Manager* component of OS/2 EE, is more than just a multiuser Database Management System (DBMS) package on a PC. It is a DBMS on a network, a member of a new breed of PC software, popularly referred to as *SQL Database Servers*. But this is only the tip of the iceberg. The Database Manager is also being groomed for playing a "kingpin" role in IBM's SAA platfonn for distributed databases. It is the designated front-end to IBM's SAA databases, which means that most of IBM's database tools will run on the OS/2 EE platform.

Because what is offered today is really an embryonic form of what is yet to come, we will start this section by positioning the Database Manager in the dual contexts of IBM's SAA architecture and that of an SQL LAN Database Server. Having done this, we can then proceed with the description of the three major sub-components of the system: *Database Services*, *Query Manager*, and *Remote Data Services*.

The Database Manager as a SQL Server

Perhaps the most important trend among database servers of any size is the emergence of **SQL** as the standard Lingua Franca for the manipulation, definition, and control of data. SQL, originally developed at IBM's San Jose Research Lab and now an ANSI standard, is a powerful set-oriented language consisting of 12 commands. SQL was created as a language for databases that adhere to the *relational model*. Relational Databases have a strong foundation in set theory and predicate logic; the model calls for a clear separation of the physical aspects of data from their logical representation. Data is made to appear as simple tables that mask the complexity of the storage access mechanisms. The SQL language can then be used to perform complex data operations with a few simple commands in situations that would have required hundreds of lines of conventional code. Physicists might call SQL "the grand unified theory of database" because of the many-faceted roles it plays. Here is a partial list of roles:

- SQL is an interactive Query Language for ad hoc database queries.
- SQL is a database programming language. It can be embedded in languages such as C and Cobol to access data.
- SQL is a data definition and data administration language. It is used for security and access control and for defining complex data integrity constraints and rules.
- SQL is the language of networked database servers.

SQL is the predominant database language of mainframes and minicomputers, where it provides the focus for a market-share battleground. The emergence of SQL on OS/2, offers many of the advantages of mainframe and minicomputer Database Management Systems (DBMSs) at PC prices, and with intuitive PC front-ends.

The Database Manager in the SAA Context

The OS/2 EE Database Manager is a vital part of IBM's long-term distributed database strategy and SAA direction. IBM is in the process of creating uniform SQL programming interfaces across four strategic product platforms:

1. Database Manager for OS/2 EE workstations
2. SQL/400 for the AS/400 mid-range processors
3. SQL/DS for the S/370 VM Operating System
4. DB2 for IBM's high end S/370 MVS Operating System

While the implementation of each product is tuned for its environment, the commonality of the interfaces is key in realizing the SAA distributed database goal. This goal is to make it possible for the end user to access any SAA database from an OS/2 EE machine as if it were a local OS/2 EE database. To realize this goal, IBM has stated it will provide the following:

- The OS/2 EE environment "will serve as the primary window" for end users to access any of the IBM SAA databases, including those on the S/370s and the AS/400s.
- The OS/2 EE Database Manager will be cognizant of multisite data and provide a logical view of the distributed data that makes the location transparent.
- The OS/2 EE Database Manager will handle the multisite synchronization, security, and data integrity functions on behalf of its users and in cooperation with other SAA Database Managers. This means locating the remote data sites and coordinating requests (including the update of data) at several locations in a single transaction. It also means servicing of single requests that span multiple sites, such as a *multisite JOIN*.

The current implementation of the OS/2 EE Database Manager is an embryonic version of the fully distributed SAA goal described above. IBM calls this embryonic level the *Remote Unit of Work*. This means that an application can connect to a remote OS/2 EE Database Manager and process multiple SQL statements against that database, issue a commit to make the work permanent, and then switch to another OS/2 EE Database Manager to start a subsequent unit of work. In the Remote Unit Of Work model offered today, transactional integrity is only provided on a per site basis. It is up to the application to coordinate the multisite integrity and access of data. However, with the Remote Unit of Work capability, an OS/2 EE machine can be used as a *Database Server* that can provide centralized data storage services to multiple users. These multiuser services include security and data integrity.

Why Should I Care?

In summary, the OS/2 EE Database Manager uses SQL, the language of choice for DBMSs on mainframes, superminis, and the high end of the PC market. The Database Manager is an integral part of IBM's SAA strategy, both as a database front-end tool and as a Database Server. IBM customers will eventually be able to scale up their server applications with OS/2 EE at the entry level, and DB2 at the high end. Thus, the SQL code you develop on the OS/2 EE Database Manager should eventually be able to talk to DB2 without requiring changes to your application. More importantly, OS/2 EE and other SAA machines will eventually all be able to coexist on a network and provide a single logical view of distributed data, with all the necessary integrity and controls that this entails.

The Components of Database Manager

The Database Manager consists of three components: Database Services, Query Manager and Remote Data Services (see Figure 3-13 on page 57).

Database Services

The heart of OS/2 EE's Database Manager is *Database Services*, which in industry jargon is typically referred to as an *SQL Engine*. This is the component that controls all accesses to the database, manages the logical and physical views of the data, generates optimized access plans to the data, and provides the transaction management, data integrity, data security, and concurrency support that allow multiple applications to access the same database at the same time. The Referential Integrity feature provides a consistent level of data integrity similar to DB2. The Database Services is a multiuser database that can be configured either in *stand-alone* mode or as a network *Database Server* machine. A user application can access multiple local or remote SQL Engines serially.

The Database Services also includes a wide repertoire of service calls for maintaining and fine-tuning a database. These services include: import and export of bulk data, backup and restore a database, table reorganization, statistics for query optimization,

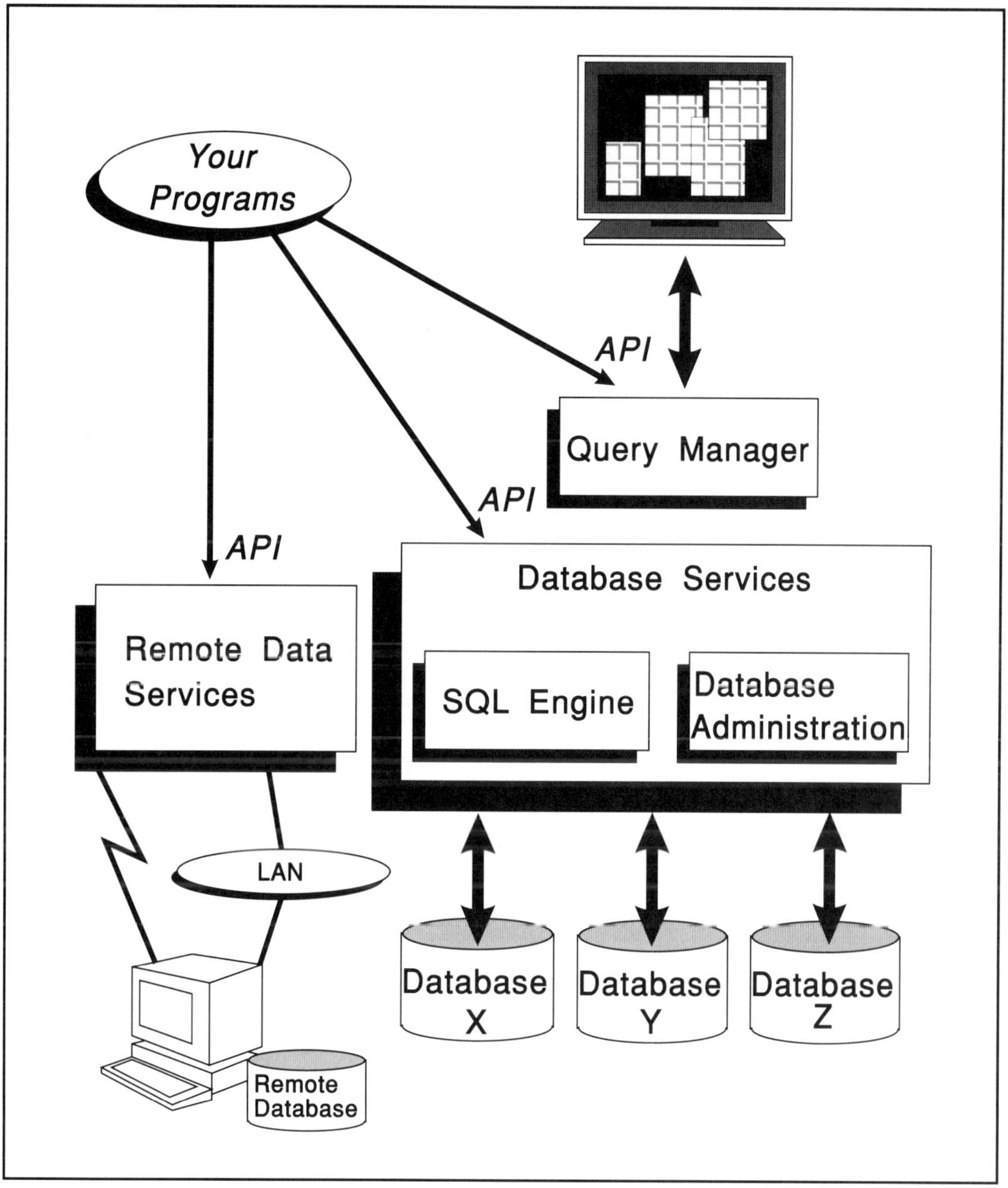

Figure 3-13. The Components of the OS/2 EE Database Manager.

and operations on database directories. Service calls are also provided to create and delete databases and for connecting to databases on local or remote machines. IBM includes a precompiler with the Database Services that allows applications written in IBM C/2 to invoke the Database Manager API. Through the API, you can submit SQL statements, invoke the database utilities, or trigger the execution of stored procedures. IBM also includes the REXX procedures language with OS/2, which requires no precompiler to access the database services available to the programmer. The REXX interpreter can be used in prototyping situations.

Query Manager

Complementing the SQL engine is *Query Manager*, an interactive end-user tool, used to execute database functions and utilities. The Query Manager uses Presentation Manager (see Figure 3-14) to provide a front-end for creating database elements, submitting SQL queries, editing and entering table data, and for generating reports and procedures. The Query Manager can also be used to create customized applications with forms, menus, queries, reports, and procedures. The customized application can then be executed without the user ever knowing of Query Manager's involvement. Query Manager is the most direct route between an end user and the Database Manager. Via the Remote Data Services, it can serve as a window on either local or remote databases. The Query Manager also provides an API which enables you to call Query Manager functions and commands from within your C programs.

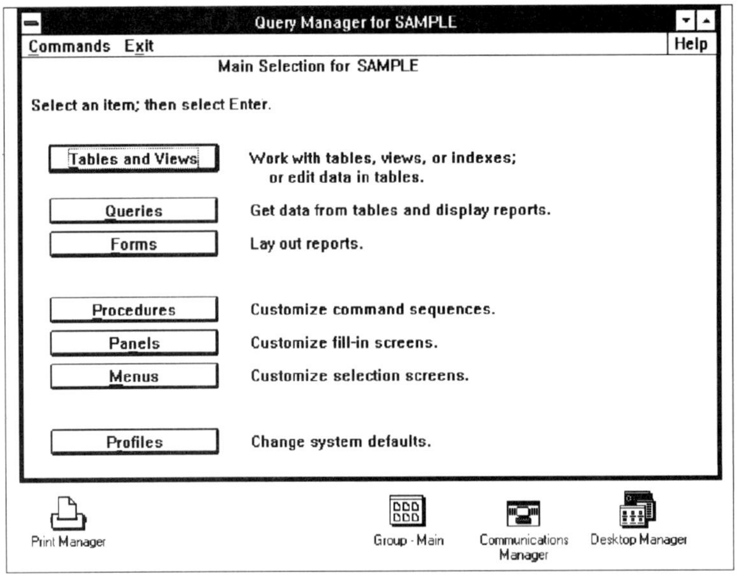

Figure 3-14. The Query Manager Main Panel.

Remote Data Services (RDS)

This is the component of the Database Manager that provides distributed database capabilities to OS/2 EE or MS-DOS clients on a LAN. Here's what these capabilities currently include:

- ***Transparent SQL access:*** This means that your SQL call is automatically routed to either a local or remote database (see Figure 3-15). This form of remote access is useful for ad hoc SQL calls over networks.

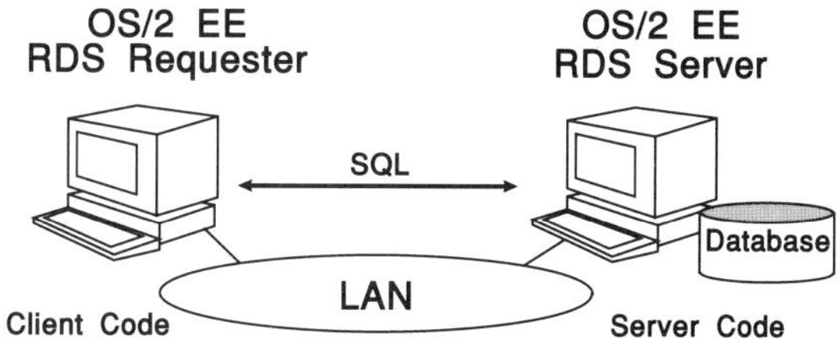

Figure 3-15. Remote Data Services: SQL Client-Server.

- ***Remote Procedure Calls:*** This capability allows you to invoke remote procedures (DLLs) that are stored on the database machine (see Figure 3-16). This form of remote invocation cuts down on network traffic and is typically used for transaction processing.

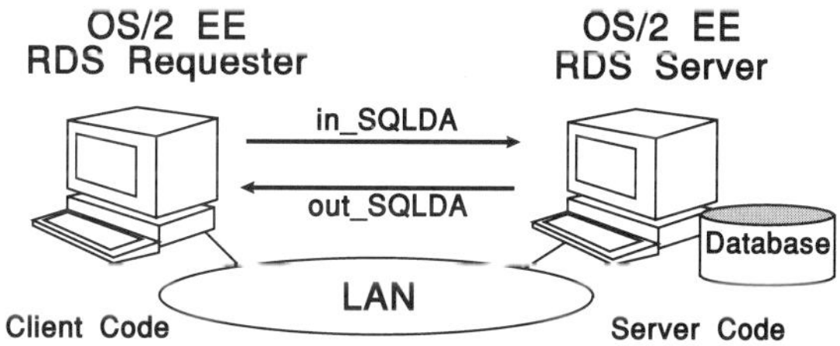

Figure 3-16. Remote Data Services: Remote Procedure Call Client-Server.

- ***Database consistency across the network:*** This means that if a remote site fails, the transaction for that application is rolled back and the database is returned to its last consistent state.

- ***Network directory services:*** The current method for achieving local/remote transparency consists of manually adding information about the physical location of the databases to the system directories. These directories are consulted when an application first connects to the database. The RDS requester routes the non-local database calls to the RDS server where the database resides. The application is not cognizant whether the database being accessed is local or remote, and the same code can be run in both situations.

- ***Multiple configuration support:*** This means that an application can run in either a stand-alone configuration or in a client-server configuration without requiring any changes to the code:

- The *stand-alone* application runs in a single workstation with no Remote Data Services (RDS).
- The *client-server* application requires two components: an RDS requester (on either an MS-DOS or OS/2 workstation) and an RDS server (on an OS/2 EE workstation). The server can be configured as an RDS requester/server if it needs access to remote databases.

The RDS requester component allows a DOS or OS/2 EE workstation, that does not have a full SQL Engine, to access a remote SQL Server as if it were on the local machine. A good piece of news is that the Remote Data Services component consumes less than 64 KBytes of the requesting workstation's RAM. Remote Data Services also require the communication services of NetBIOS for DOS requesters, and APPC for OS/2 EE requesters.

OS/2 EE LAN REQUESTER AND THE IBM LAN SERVER

The IBM LAN Server program transforms OS/2 EE into a full-fledged *Network Operating System.* This allows applications to become "networked" without being rewritten. The beauty of a Network Operating System is that it lets you get all this network power through your standard OS/2 commands and APIs. The reach of the application programmer is now extended beyond the physical boundaries of a single machine, while the network is transparent to the application. The OS/2 LAN Server is packaged as two complementary IBM products:

- ***The LAN Requester:*** This component is included as part of IBM's OS/2 EE.
- ***The IBM OS/2 LAN Server Version 1.2:*** This program is packaged and sold separately. With a purchase of the OS/2 LAN Server, you are authorized by IBM to make up to 128 copies of the DOS LAN Requester and the LAN Support Program at no additional charge. The DOS Requester makes available to applications an additional 30 KBytes of RAM by using the first 64 KByte segment above the 1 MByte address in 80286 and 80386 machines with Extended or Expanded memory.

The IBM LAN Server is based on the Microsoft LAN Manager platform. This platform has become a de facto Network Operating System standard for OS/2. It makes the network an integral part of OS/2. The LAN Manager platform also provides interoperability with MS-NET and PC-LAN workstations running MS-DOS. LAN Manager/X extends the platform to UNIX System V (the first release provides fairly complete support for Named Pipes interoperability).

The LAN Server is a classic implementation of client-server architecture. The server machine acts as a *central hub* that fulfills work requests from requesters (i.e., clients) all over the network (see Figure 3-17 on page 61). The server forms the core of the LAN Server application. At least one machine on the network must run the server function before requesters can perform anything useful. Network Servers can be added

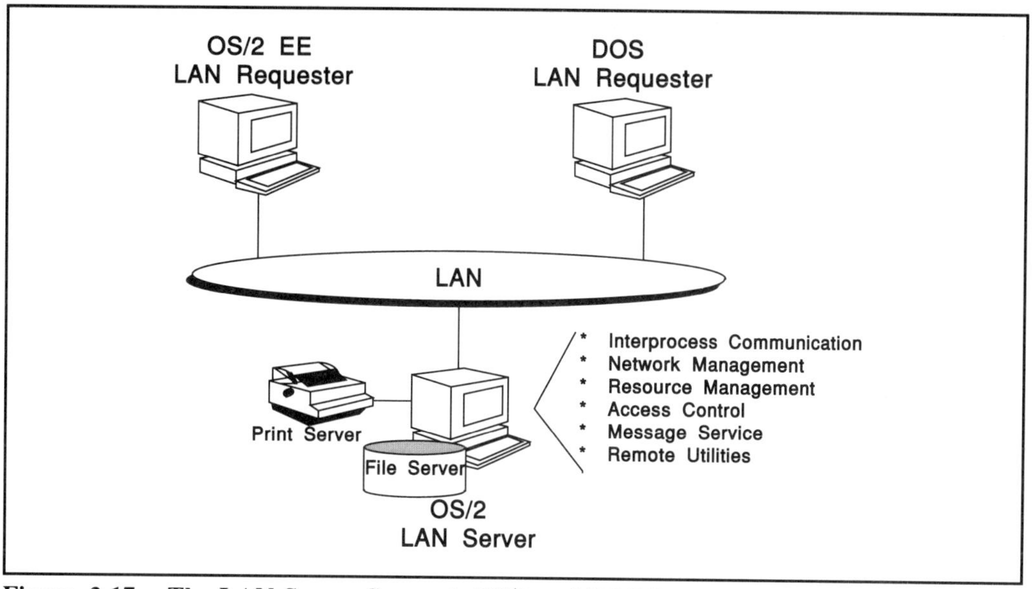

Figure 3-17. The LAN Server Supports OS/2 and DOS Requesters.

to the network to provide more resources, remove bottlenecks, and scale an application upward (or downward). Network devices, programs, and data can be centralized on a single server or distributed on multiple servers as the environment dictates. Your LAN Server machines can be dedicated or they can be running other programs concurrently with the server function. The modular capabilities of LAN Server appear to be limited only by checkbook constraints.

From a programmer's viewpoint, LAN Server offers flexibility and the capability to distribute an application easily and without having to learn a communication API. In essence it transforms OS/2 EE into a powerful Network Operating System. This augmented OS/2 EE opens up a universe of network services. The repertoire of network functions falls into the following categories:

- Transparent access to remote resources
- Network device/queue management
- Remote network applications
- Single Systems Image
- Network services
- Network Management and Administration
- Network Security and access controls
- An open network API of over 100 functions most of which are also supported by the DOS Requester

Together these functions provide a very complete Network Operating System offering based on Microsoft's LAN Manager platform. We explain the Network Operating System enhancements in the sections that follow.

Local/Remote Transparency

A requester workstation can access the resources of an OS/2 LAN Server workstation as if they were locally attached. This feature makes the physical location of resources (over a network) transparent to an application. Resources that can be shared on a LAN Server include: disk directories, disk files, printers and printer queues, serially attached devices and queues, application programs, and Named Pipes. The LAN Requester *redirects* (over the network) API calls for resources that reside on an OS/2 LAN Server and it passes back the response to the application just as if the call was locally serviced. The LAN Server thus extends OS/2's virtual device support across the network. Practically anything that can be done on a local OS/2 PC can be done remotely in a transparent fashion. Basic file sharing is done using logical drives. Users map their own virtual drives to drives and directories on various file servers. Printer sharing is done with virtual printer ports. Users can redirect their serial or parallel printer ports to logical ports on various servers.

Network Device and Queue Management

The OS/2 LAN Server allows an application to send its network job to a printer when it is busy. The jobs get queued at the printer and executed in the order received, or in the order set by the network administrator.

Remote Network Application Support

The LAN Server program allows workstations to execute programs that reside on the server. Such programs include standard OS/2 commands, utilities supplied with the LAN Manager, or user supplied programs. You could, for instance, offload compiles, backups, and other processor or disk intensive tasks to the LAN Server machines on the network. The remote program runs on the server with the standard input, output, and error streams redirected back to the requester station that invoked the program. This makes it possible to interactively control a remote program and to receive its output.

Single System Image

The LAN Server program extends OS/2's logical device management capabilities by allowing multiple OS/2 LAN Servers to be managed as a single logical system. This capability allows users and administrators to view the network as a single server instead of as a collection of separate resources attached to specific servers. A *domain* consists of the set of servers whose resources are configured as a single logical system. There may be one or more servers per domain. One server within a domain is designated as the domain controller; this is the machine that provides the view of the OS/2

LAN Server domain to the users. Multiple OS/2 LAN Server domains may coexist on the same LAN. User and machine names can be defined in several domains as long as they maintain unique names.

Network Services

The bulk of the LAN Server code consists of configurable *services.* These are programs that can be started (installed), stopped (uninstalled), paused, or resumed through LAN Server commands. You can also create your own services by writing programs to a set of simple specifications. This makes it possible to extend the core of LAN Server. You can also individually configure the functional components to provide a certain level of service. Here's a brief description of the standard LAN Server services:

- The ***Workstation Service*** enables the redirection of system calls. This service and the operating system work closely together. The redirector packages and passes system calls from the operating system and sends them to a remote server. The server software reissues the call against a local resource, packages the results, and returns them to the redirector. This basic service must be started before any other services can be installed on a client workstation.

- The ***Server Service*** handles network requests for disk, printer and serially attached device services. These primary services can only be provided by servers.

- The ***Message Service*** supports the sending and receiving of synchronous messages.

- The ***Netpopup Service*** displays received messages as pop-up panels on a user's screen.

- The ***Alerter Service*** runs in the server and sends alert notifications to designated users.

- The ***Netrun Service*** lets a workstation execute a program on a remote server. This service must also be installed on the servers where the programs execute.

- The ***Remoteboot Service*** runs in the server and supports the remote IPL of MS-DOS machines (this service is particularly important to users, such as financial institutions, who require diskless PCs).

- The ***PCLP130 Service*** runs in the server and supports DOS users running the IBM PC LAN Program V 1.30.

Other Network services include the network copy and move utilities and extensive network help.

Network Management and Administration

The administrative and network management facilities of LAN Server are extensive. An administrator can *logon* to LAN Server from any OS/2 requester workstation. An intuitive interface allows the administrator to control installation and configuration facilities, and to support daily operations such as: Startup, Shutdown, Audit Control, and LAN Usage monitoring. An administrator may browse or update user, group, or resource profiles. The administrator can also manage server print queues, close files, and terminate user sessions. Additionally, the OS/2 LAN Server allows administrators to see at a glance who is using a server, how long they have been connected, what resources they are using, and when they were last active.

In a network environment it is important to track who has used or misused what resource and when. The LAN Server can capture in an audit trail almost everything that is happening on a network: every file accessed, every attempted access, every connection made, every resource used, every logon and logoff, changes in server states (start, pauses, continued, stopped), and violations in sharing limits or access permission. The network administrator can configure the audit system to only track exceptional events. Audit information may be displayed by the administrator.

The LAN Server maintains a log of statistics on network traffic and response time indicators. These statistics can help an administrator configure and tune the network. LAN Server also provides a network error log which includes comprehensive diagnostic information of errors that have occurred. A LAN Server can send automatic administrative alert messages to designated users or groups of users when errors that require immediate attention are encountered. Such alerts are generated in case of disk or printer problems, and when bad passwords or excessive error occurrences exceed a threshold.

The OS/2 LAN Server provides time scheduled execution through an **AT** command for automating scheduled functions under time controls. The AT command can run any OS/2 command periodically at a specified date/time. The schedule for periodically executed commands is saved on disk and loaded when the server starts. An AT command may be used for example to run a utility command such as a disk backup on a time-scheduled basis.

Network Security: Who Can Do What?

The network security and access controls provided by LAN Server allow practically every aspect of a user's network activity to be defined by the network administrator. The network administrator defines a user's login script and privileges, the files they may use, the resources they may share, the programs they may execute, and the mode in which they perform these activities. Users may belong to groups and are assigned various privilege levels.

OS/2 LAN Server provides two facets of system access controls: logon control and resource protection. A system administrator controls whether a password is required at logon for a specific user and the interval of password expiration. LAN Server is smart when it comes to passwords. All passwords are doubly encrypted. Passwords are encrypted at the workstation before being sent to the server for validation. Resources are controlled by identifying the relationship between the user and the resource. For example files and directories may be made accessible to a particular user, group of users, or all users. Access authority may be granted to the user or group of users in conjunction with a single resource or with a generic resource profile. Access authorities include: None, Read, Update, Alter, and Execute. Execute privileges prevent users from copying a program while allowing them to run it. An administrator can specify the maximum number of users that can concurrently execute a program to enforce network license agreements.

The category of resources that can be protected through the access control system includes: disk directories, individual files, groups of files (specified via wild cards), application programs, print queues, and serial device queues.

The Network API

The publication of the OS/2 LAN API creates an open architecture for OS/2 and DOS LAN applications. With the network API, a C programmer can now explicitly control many of the above described Network Operating System functions through programming interfaces. Through the DOS Requester component, the API also allows MS-DOS programmers to use the interprocess communication facilities to exchange data and event signals with OS/2 servers. The DOS Requesters support a subset of the API calls in all the categories except Alerts and Error Logging. We will present a quick summary of what these calls do by functional category.

Interprocess Communication Services

This group of APIs includes:

- **Named Pipes:** These are the same 23 Named Pipe API calls that are part of the native OS/2 interprocess communication. They are included here because you must have a running copy of the LAN Server to use Named Pipes remotely. Most of the OS/2 Named Pipe API calls are extended to DOS Requesters through the LAN Server.

- **MailSlots:** This new service consists of 6 API calls which provide one-way interprocess communication. Mailslots can come in handy for remote data collection and "I'm alive" heartbeats. Mailslots use NetBIOS datagrams to provide their services. The server side of the communication creates a mailslot for receiving messages (NetBIOS *add name*). The client writes messages to the mailslot. The server side can block waiting for messages to arrive. Mailslots are inherently fast because they do not need to be opened or closed. A process can write to a remote Mailslot with a class and priority attribute. Priority controls the order in which messages are read. *First-class messages* on Mailslots are abstractions of acknowledged datagrams. A sending process blocks (or waits) until its first-class message is delivered and acknowledged or an error occurs. *Second-class messages* are simple datagrams of the "transmit-and-pray" variety. An important feature of second class messages is that they can be broadcast to all workstations in a domain. The full repertoire of Mailslot API calls is available to DOS Requesters.

- **Alerts:** This service consists of three API calls that notify applications of the occurrence of certain network events.

Network Management Services

There are 23 new API calls in this category that do the following:

- Control the server's Audit log file.
- Control the Error log.
- Collect and reset network statistics on both servers and requesters.
- Control network sessions, requesters, and servers.
- Read remote configuration information from the IBMLAN.INI file.

Resource Management Services

There are 23 new API calls in this category that do the following:

- Control the sharing of server resources.
- Establish controls and connections between requesters and servers.
- Control the sharing of serial devices and their associated queues.
- Monitor the open file, device, and pipe resources on a server.
- Set or obtain information on a per-handle basis.

Access Control Services

There are 27 new API calls in this category that do the following:

- Examine or modify user or group access permissions for server resources.
- Control user and group accounts.

Network Services

There are 19 new API calls in this category that do the following:

- Send, forward, and log messages.
- Copy and move files.
- Execute remote programs.
- Obtain time-of-day from a server.
- Start and control network service programs.

This concludes our "brief" overview of the services OS/2 EE provides. In the chapters that follow we will show you these services are used to create client-server solutions.

Chapter 4

Architectures for Client-Server Computing

In this chapter we examine the architectural principles that can be used to create powerful system solutions on low-cost hardware. We will start with the client-server model and show how it can be extended to play in the distributed world of SAA and cooperative software. OS/2 EE brings to the personal computer the power of network communications and SQL databases and makes it possible to write highly robust applications that can control huge amounts of data. OS/2's preemptive multitasking allows you to modularize your code based on processes and to add services where needed, when needed. When we add the graphics environment of Presentation Manager, we have all the major ingredients to create powerful new distributed systems on low-cost hardware.

THE POWER OF ARCHITECTURE

What are you able to build with your blocks?
Castles and palaces, temples and docks.

R. L. Stevenson
A Child's Garden of Verses

We are all familiar with the concept of *architecture* as applied in the construction of buildings. Architectures help us identify structural elements that may be used as building blocks in the construction of ever more complex systems. The purpose of this chapter is to identify some durable architectural concepts and structures which can be used in the design of distributed systems.

We will discuss system building using OS/2 EE in the following architectural contexts:

- ***Client-Server:*** where we examine OS/2 EE as a server for networked DOS machines and other *skinny* clients. We then introduce the concept of OS/2 EE multiservers.
- ***Cooperative processing:*** where we examine OS/2 EE's role in a post-scarcity computing environment. We will look at the concept of the network agent and the personal agent.
- ***SAA cooperative environment:*** where we examine OS/2 EE's role in a heterogeneous host-PC environment. We also define what SAA means to distributed processing.

In the sections that follow, we explain each architectural model. These models will help guide our software development strategy. They also help us identify what system provides the best fit for a particular business solution.

THE CLIENT-SERVER ARCHITECTURE MODEL

We will start this section with a design of servers which are front-ended by *skinny clients*. A *skinny client* is a low-cost client machine which runs MS-DOS (with or without Windows) or a *bare bones* base OS/2-PM machine. We then introduce a multiserver architecture which demonstrates the upward scalability of the client-server model.

How to Create Servers for "Skinny" Clients

Generally, users do not buy architectures; they buy solutions to business problems. The million dollar question is: how is the application split between the client and the server? What function goes in the client and what function goes in the server? Here's a set of "rules of thumb" for the design of client-server applications that use an OS/2 EE server platform to service skinny clients:

1. Run the bulk of your application code on the OS/2 EE server. This is where all the system extensions, such as the OS/2 EE Database Manager and the Communications Manager, reside. A well-endowed server can provide the following to its clients: database services, gateway services, and shared file access through the LAN Server Program. Since the OS/2 EE server is not memory-bound, you can also use it to "roll-your-own" server applications.

2. The client machines, also known as the *front-end*, manage the user interface portion of a distributed application. The server machine provides the *back-end* of an application. The back-end typically provides shared services to the front-end clients.

3. Use a transaction discipline to code your back-end database services. A *transaction* is an *all or nothing* set of operations. Either all the operations succeed and the transaction gets recorded on the database, or the entire transaction gets rolled-back if any step fails. A failed transaction leaves the database in its pre-transaction state.

4. Partition and fine-tune your server applications to take advantage of OS/2 EE's multitasking.

5. Lightly load your client machines and fully load your OS/2 EE server. Buy a *super-server* machine if you can afford it. A single OS/2 EE server helps you leverage dozens of lower cost client machines. So it makes business sense that your server should be the fastest machine you can afford (load the machine with extra memory for caching, an extra disk for backup, and all the communication boards you may need for gateway services).

6. Provide the highest level of interface possible to the server's services. The client should be shielded from the inner workings of the resources a server controls. For example, if a server controls a database, then it should not surface the table structures to the clients. Instead, the interface should consist of requests for actions to be applied against the database.

7. Use a LAN for local communications between the clients and the server. LANs provide high speed, low-cost, reliable communications.

8. Use NetBIOS or Named Pipes as your LAN protocol. NetBIOS requires less than 30 KBytes of memory address space on the MS-DOS PC. This is close to ideal for a low-cost front-end node.

9. Publish the message protocol for requesting services. Use it as the requester interface to your network services.

10. Invest in maintenance and configuration tools. Client-Server products, being inherently distributed, are complex to install and maintain. You will need tools to distribute new versions of the client code over the network and to add new services as required. Where possible build your tools on top of the server's OS/2 EE database. For example, a configuration management tool could maintain a list of client workstations and their attributes in the OS/2 EE database. A workstation's attributes may include: the version of code it is running, its network address, its hardware components, the logon IDs of its users, etc. A maintenance tool should periodically fine-tune the database, log errors, maintain statistics, and *call home* (to some central maintenance organization) when a machine starts to act funny.

11. Buy off-the-shelf "shrink wrapped" solutions wherever they exist.

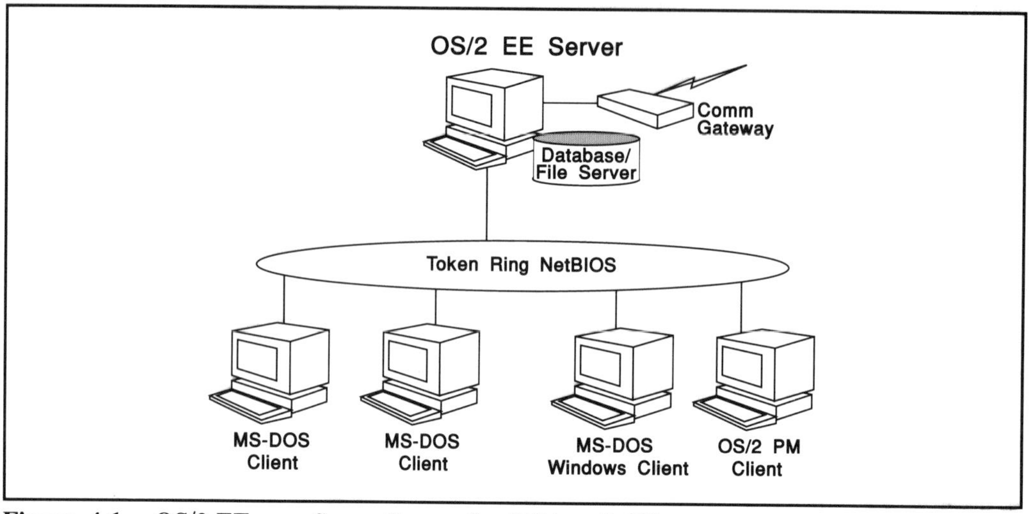

Figure 4-1. OS/2 EE as a Super Server for "Skinny" Clients.

Example: A "Widget" Server

An example should help clarify the anatomy of a *Transaction Server* application and will introduce some common terminology that will be used throughout this book. Figure 4-1 on page 72 shows a mixed operating system network environment where an application is split between skinny clients running the application front-end and an OS/2 EE server running the application's back-end. The back-end manages a hypothetical object-type called "widgets." It provides "widget retrieval and filing" services to its front-end clients. The back-end OS/2 EE server controls a database consisting of multiple tables that are used to represent an application-created object type: "widget." The details of the database implementation of the widget object are hidden from the clients.

A client only needs to know the set of commands that can be issued to manipulate widget objects. The commands are issued over a network in the form of messages. A widget object is only known to its clients by its behavior. For example, the widget object type is defined by such higher level actions as *move to another operation*, *rework*, *scrap from inventory*, and *ship to customer*. The set of actions a server is capable of performing on object types get published in the form of network request and reply message formats. These are the messages eligible clients can send to a network server to request remote services. For example, the receipt of a *scrap from inventory* request message may trigger a procedure (or transaction) on the server that performs the following operations:

1. Checks the authority of the client against a table of authorized users of widgets. This is to make sure the client has the authority to scrap widgets.
2. Sends a copy of the widget record to archive.
3. Deletes the widget from the active database.
4. Removes the entry for this widget from a directory table.

5. Executes any *triggers* or *alerters* that may be associated with this transaction.
6. Commits the transaction to the database.
7. Sends an "OK" reply to the client.

In essence, widgets are database-centered creations. Real world examples of widgets are: parts on a manufacturing floor, CAD folders, bank accounts, airline seats, or plain old widgets. What these entities have in common is that they can be implemented on servers as encapsulated database object types that respond to certain messages. Servers become a collection of persistent data objects and the programs that control them.

Extending Client-Server with OS/2 EE Multiservers

Multiservers are used in environments that require more processing power than that provided by a single OS/2 EE server. The client-server model is upwardly scalable. When more processing power is needed, more servers can be added (thus creating a pool of servers), or the existing server machine can be traded up to the latest generation of PC super-server machine. In this section we focus on multiservers, an area that's becoming a hot topic in the industry as solutions are moving from a few large computers to LAN-based servers. The applications in this "downsizing" process are broken up into program modules that run on one or more network servers. The mainframe or supermini in this environment is relegated to providing enterprise level information.

How to Mix and Match?

We can partition servers based on the function they provide, the resource they control, or the database they own. In addition, we may choose to replicate servers for fault tolerance or for performance considerations. There can be as many servers combinations as your budget will tolerate. Multiserver capability when properly used, can provide an awesome amount of computing power and flexibility, in many cases rivaling that of mainframes. A topology of OS/2 EE multiservers front-ended by MS-DOS machines and skinny OS/2 clients is depicted in Figure 4-2.

What New Functions are Needed?

To exploit the full power of OS/2 EE multiservers, we will have to supplement our architecture with the following repertoire:

- We need a *network resource locator* so that clients can find their servers wherever they may be. One way to accomplish that is through a "network yellow pages" service. In this approach, a server process whose network address is well-known to all will provide the yellow page service. We will call that server the "location

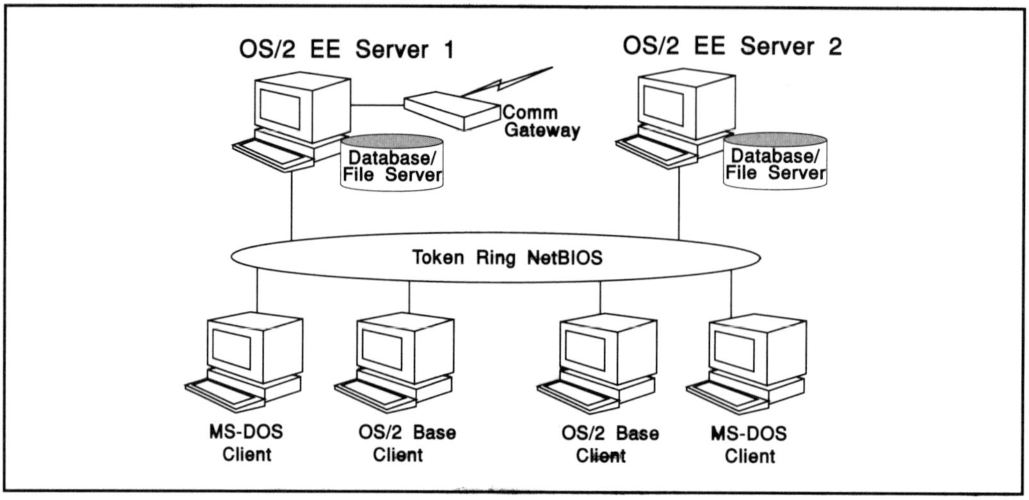

Figure 4-2. Multiple OS/2 EE Servers.

broker." The location broker maintains a yellow pages database of known services and will supply service related information to network subscribers when they ask for it. Providers of services will advertise their services through the location broker.

- We need a method for *partitioning work among the servers*. One such method is to partition work based on object managers. A server can act as an object manager, and accept message based requests to perform actions against the object it controls. Objects can be files, databases, transactions, communication lines, printers, inference engines, video libraries etc. A particular machine may provide more than one service using OS/2 EE's multitasking facilities.

- We need to design our servers so that they can *delegate work* to their fellow object managers. We shouldn't always have to re-invent the wheel. A complex request may involve a *task-force* of object servers working together on the request. Preferably, the client should not be made aware of this *behind-the-scenes* collaboration. The object server that the client first made contact with, should be in charge of orchestrating the object manager task-force and returning its findings to the client. This last constraint should be balanced against the need to keep interfaces generic and modular, in which case the client may be required to act as the integrator.

Creating system "ensembles" out of modular building blocks is what good software architecture is all about. With some practice, you may develop creative skills akin to those of a composer in the articulation of OS/2 EE servers.

BEYOND CLIENT-SERVER: COOPERATIVE SOFTWARE

In this section we up the ante. We will investigate what new systems can be created on a distributed PC platform when memory and hardware become *super cheap*? A network of OS/2 EE machines opens the door to a whole new class of cooperative software. Each OS/2 EE machine contains (as standard equipment) a preemptive multitasking operating system, a Communications Manager, a Database Manager, and a Presentation Manager. This creates a new set of opportunities in the design of distributed software. This new environment, which presents us with a set of architectural opportunities in the design of systems, may be aptly named *post-scarcity personal computing*.

Programming Your Way to Tahiti

The post scarcity paradigm of OS/2 EE opens new vistas for network-based transactions. For example, OS/2 EE may be used in a small business environment or in branch offices of large companies to create a new generation of business software packages. The best way to describe the capabilities of the technology is to work our way through an imaginary application; *the Automated Travel Agent*. The following scenario will explain the features of this imaginary application.

You walk into travel agency **"Paradise OS/2 EE"** to discuss your vacation plans. You are greeted by the Automated Travel Agent, a computer with a Presentation Manager *look and feel*. You start a friendly conversation with the Automated Agent and a few dialog windows later the Automated Agent knows that you have ten days of vacation coming in March, you want to spend them on a nice beach, and you have at most $2000 to spend on your vacation.

The Automated Agent searches its local database for a vacation strategy that fits your needs and offers you a set of alternative choices in the form of icons placed on a map. The choices for this time of the year are Tahiti, Hawai, Cancun, etc. You click your mouse on Tahiti and the Automated Travel Agent displays a set of resort choices that include the Club Meds at Bora Bora and Morea. You choose to explore the Club Med alternative and ask for more information about the Club Med Villages in Tahiti, and you are now placed in a Hypermedia-like environment that allows you to explore the sports offered, the beaches, the room accommodations, etc. Embedded in the Hypermedia displays are *links* that allow you to view and zoom in on pictures of beaches, lagoons, huts on the water, romantic restaurants with views of the sunset, water sports, and tennis. After spending a delightful 30 minutes or so browsing through screens of dreamland and imagining what your vacation will be like, you decide to book your vacation now!

The Automated Agent presents you with more choices, and by the time you are finished you've decided you want to spend six days in Bora Bora and four in Morea. You want a hut on the lagoon with a double bed and you opt for low-cholesterol dinners. You may even decide to make table reservations in the romantic restaurant with the view of the sunset.

The Automated Agent now has all the information it needs from you to carry out the transaction so it starts a background process that places a call to Club Med's mainframe computer. It also starts another background process that calls your credit card company's mainframe computer. While all this activity is happening in the background, the Automated Agent keeps you occupied by listing information in a window that may be relevant to your trip, like what kind of clothes to bring, etc.

A few seconds elapse and now all the parties are ready to carry out the transaction. We have established a rendezvous between the Club Med computer, the credit card company's computer, and the Automated Agent who is your broker. The transaction is electronically prepared. You have your reservation, Club Med has your money, the Automated Agent has the commission, and you are set for a wonderful vacation. You are asked one last time if you want to confirm the transaction. Click OK and you will be in Morea next March.

Implementing Paradise OS/2 EE

The Hardware Base

Figure 4-3 shows a possible implementation of the "Paradise OS/2 EE." First, notice that all the machines in the system run OS/2 EE. The machines in the bottom-half of the figure run the *Automated Travel Agent* application and those in the top-half are dedicated file servers that run the off-the-shelf LAN Server Program. The first file server in our hypothetical implementation controls two 500 MByte drives that are designated as network drives E: and F: on which small objects, such as text files and graphic metafiles, are stored. The second server controls eight optical disk drives that are each 1000 MBytes in size. These will be known as drives G: through N:. We will store large objects, such image bitmaps, on the optical disks. We now have 9 Gigabytes of shared storage on the LAN which is used to store travel brochures, airline-schedules, images of distant sunsets, etc. You also have private hard disks on the OS/2 EE machines. If you run out of storage, or if your servers are too slow, add more machines and storage.

The Software Base

The "Automated Travel Agent" application maintains, in its private database cache, the list of available files (viewing objects) and a reference to the network drive on which they reside. The application may maintain a local copy of some of the files using its own hard disk as a cache. The network files are, of course, viewed through the Presentation Manager's display services which allow you to manipulate both vector and bitmap graphics.

In the implementation, the "Automated Travel Agent" may access remote mainframes through either an SDLC card or through an Asynchronous RS232 port (with their respective modems). These two gateways to the outside world allow us to talk to service providers such as the airlines, Club Med, and the credit card services. The protocol on top of SDLC could be APPC, and that on top of the Async line could be X-Modem. The handshake with the mainframe may range from a simple file download or upload, to a series of requests and replies that lead to the commitment of a transaction. Authentication and network security are essential in this environment.

The "Automated Travel Agent" and the mainframes cooperate to perform business transactions. During non-peak hours, the Automated Travel Agent, having a ravenous appetite for information, downloads price lists and other related information from the mainframes and caches it on its local database server. This allows the Automated Travel Agent to provide extensive searches against local data to find the best rates for a given function. The Automated Travel Agent is an example of a cooperative type of application that makes full use of OS/2 EE's advanced features. The transactions involved several parties with the OS/2 EE machine (the Automated Travel Agent) acting as the transaction coordinator.

From an architectural viewpoint, we've gone past the concept of client server where every event is generated by the client. We've augmented this architectural paradigm with the concept of *autonomous agents* which reside in the network machines and perform background tasks. In our example, an agent downloads the price-lists from the hosts during non-peak hours. These agents can be augmented to analyze data and perform some actions based on a set of rules. In other words, the agents are always on *fact-finding* missions working on your behalf.

A More Personal Version of Paradise

It is easy to imagine that the next step is to have a personal version the Automated Agent run on your own OS/2 EE PC. You will have your own personal agent to take care of your vacations. Your agent will know your vacation schedule and preferences and has kept a history of your previous vacations in the database and has learned from them your likes and dislikes. Your personal agent knows you like to take your vacations in March, so it started a search sometime in December to find you the best bargains. Your agent is of course always negotiating with other agents all over the world, always "wheeling and dealing" on your behalf. The best part is that you do not have to babysit your agent while it's out there doing all this work on your behalf. You get the picture?

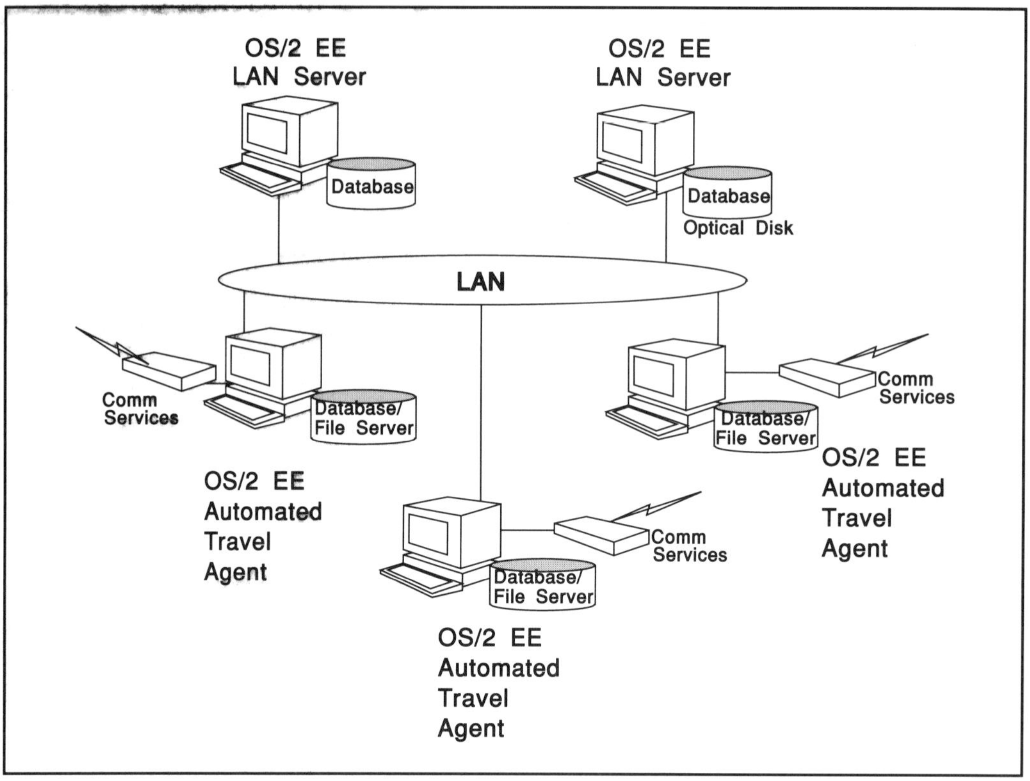

Figure 4-3. The Configuration of "Paradise OS/2 EE" Travel Agency.

Distributed Data: Client-Server Agents vs. Distributed Database

What does "post-scarcity" mean to database servers? With disk prices coming down every day and with the database software bundled with every operating system (OS/2 EE), data storage is no longer a scarce resource. We can now enjoy the luxury of storing large amounts of data in our personal databases. This will make life very pleasant for personal software providers; however, the question which cries for an answer is: *how is shared data handled in a post-scarcity data storage world?* There are two strategies to shared data:

- Keep all shared data on servers using the technology developed for servers and multiservers. This is the straight client-server model we previously discussed.
- Allow outsiders to access the public parts of your shared data and obtain, when you require it, access to other people's data. There are two ways of providing this type of service in a distributed data sharing environment:
  1. Through a standard *distributed database package.*
  2. Through a *network of agents.* These agents use the client-server model to exchange services and data.

We will now compare the distributed database and network agent approaches to shared data.

The Distributed Database Model

Standard *off the shelf* commercial distributed database packages will provide, when they fully blossom, transparent access to data on a network. The distributed database keeps track of the location of data on the network, and will route your requests to the right database nodes and make their location transparent. OS/2 EE's remote SQL provides a rudimentary distributed database function. To be fully distributed, a database should allow you to join data from tables that reside on several machines. It should also *atomically* update data in tables that reside on several machines.

Distributed databases make it easy to write distributed applications without having to first decompose your applications (as we had to do for client-server). With *true* distributed database, the location of the data is completely transparent to the application. The chief advantage of a distributed database is that it makes it possible to access remote data transparently, while keeping most of the data local to the locations that actually use it. The disadvantages are:

1. Distributed databases do not work in heterogeneous database environments. This locks you into a single vendor SQL server solution.
2. Poor modularity. You cannot change a local database table if it is being used by other nodes.
3. Poor message performance. Your network interface is more primitive than that of the client-server, thus requiring more message exchanges per unit of work.

Network Agents

In this approach, each machine on the network contains an agent that runs in the background and performs useful tasks such as dealing with requests for remote information both outgoing and incoming. The agents communicate with one another using the client-server message based interface described in the previous sections. The Named Pipe *Remote Procedure Call* mechanism that OS/2 provides may be used for communicating requests between the client and the server. APPC and NetBIOS also provide this capability.

Agents are better suited than distributed database management systems to handle heterogeneous databases from multiple vendors. The local agent acts as a client to a remote agent server when it needs data from the server's database and vise versa. The agent client-server paradigm provides better local autonomy. A node can change its database designs without affecting clients. The database design and structure does not have to be known to the outside world. The only thing that cannot easily change are the request and reply message formats.

The network shown in Figure 4-4 on page 80 is totally made up of OS/2 EE machines. The **Personal Agents** are an application that run on OS/2 EE. These agents are more than just background tasks, they have to cooperate with other agents on the network through the client-server interface to get their work done. They also

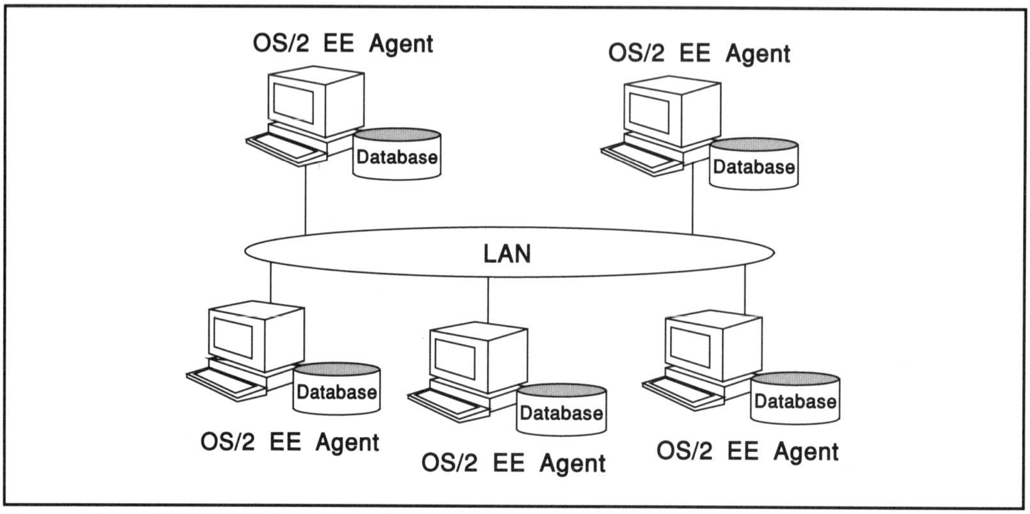

Figure 4-4. OS/2 EE Network with Personal Agents.

need to be programmed to understand their user's personal information needs. In other words, we're creating a brave new world of *agents* which are programmed to have a ravenous appetite for information on a list of topics. These agents control the private information on your machine. Your machine's agent is always operating on your behalf in the background accumulating and sorting information on topics which interest you. It does that by conducting constant negotiations and fact-finding missions with fellow information agents on remote machines. The background agent is always ready to immediately service any request for information from either a foreground process on your machine or from a *cooperative* network agent.

OS/2 EE IN AN SAA ENVIRONMENT

SAA, as you recall, is the architecture that promises to seamlessly integrate IBM's four mainstream, commercial operating-system platforms (OS/2 EE, OS/400, MVS, and VM). SAA addresses three specific needs: 1) to migrate an application across SAA machine platforms, 2) to split up an application across SAA machines, and 3) to communicate data between different SAA machine types independent of location.

If it succeeds, IBM's SAA will remove the present distinction between mainframes, minicomputers, and PCs, with everyone writing to a common programming interface (CPI) and no one knowing (or caring) about target machines, about where data comes from, or how information gets passed over networks. SAA is IBM's most strategic architectural blueprint since the unveiling of the System/360 in 1964. It promises to have an immense impact on how PCs are used in commercial environments. SAA defines a "standard" operating environment for executing cooperative software solutions.

In this section, we will first outline the architecture of a virtual distributed SAA machine. Since OS/2 EE is so fundamentally linked to SAA, you will need to understand SAA architecturally in order to understand OS/2 EE's present and future distributed processing capabilities. We will then demonstrate, through two scenarios, how OS/2 EE can be used in a distributed SAA architecture context.

What Does an SAA Machine Look Like?

In order for you to navigate in the world of SAA, you will need to familiarize yourself with its many acronyms. This section will serve as a "gentle" guide to SAA. We will create the architectural framework for an idealized SAA machine. This machine will look very much like an OS/2 EE machine. This is not too surprising, since IBM has chosen to support SAA across three major systems: System/370, AS/400, and Personal System/2 (PS/2). OS/2 EE is the embodiment of SAA for the PS/2s. You will note that the System/370 supports two SAA operating systems: VM and MVS.

SAA is a collection of selected software interfaces, conventions and protocols that collectively provide the framework for the development and execution of consistent distributed applications. Figure 4-5 on page 82 presents a layered representation of the SAA components from a programmer's perspective. We will start from the top of the figure and introduce the various SAA components

- **Common User Access (CUA)** is a set of rules and guidelines for providing a consistent user *look and feel* across all SAA machines. CUA is a window-based point and select interface. Dialogs with the user are conducted through windows that provide a concurrent display of information using an object-action model. Graphics and icons are used to make the controls visible and concrete. We will have a lot more to say about CUA in the chapters on OS/2 EE's Dialog and Presentation Managers.

- **SAA applications** have the following attributes:

  1. They provide a CUA look and feel to the user.
  2. They use SAA languages, system interfaces, and protocols. This makes it easy to port applications across SAA machines.
  3. They store data in SQL databases.
  4. They should be able to share function and data with related SAA applications.
  5. They preferably use a PC to provide the user interface (ideally the workstation would run OS/2's Presentation Manager).

- **SAA languages** provide the interface to the SAA Common Programming Interface (CPI) through run-time libraries of SAA services and precompilers (where applicable). SAA supports Fourth Generation Languages (4GLs) and IBM is making its CSP application generator SAA compatible. IBM's Query Manager may also be considered to be an SAA-supported 4GL. The third generation languages (3GLs) SAA supports are: Cobol, C, Fortran, and PL/1. Finally, the command

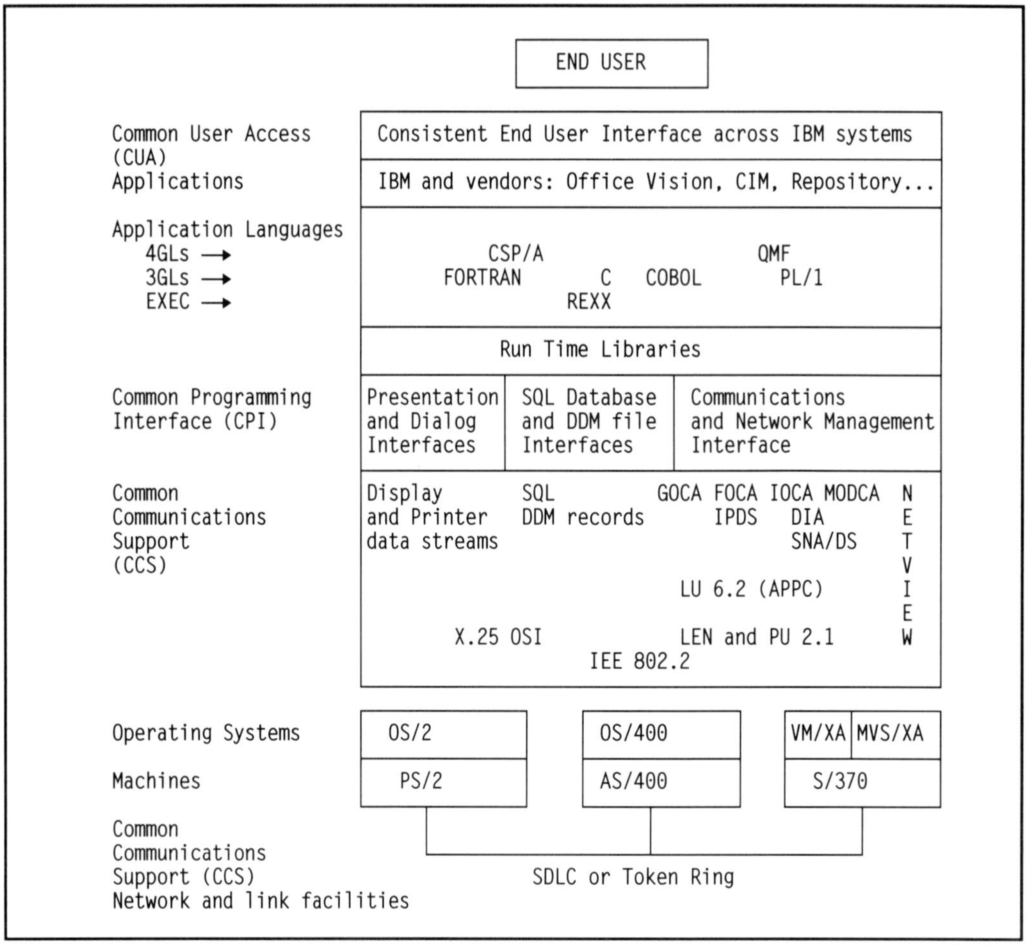

Figure 4-5. The Anatomy of an SAA Machine.

language of choice for SAA environments is REXX. The SAA languages run on all of IBM's SAA compliant operating systems.

- **Common Programming Interface (CPI)** specifies the programming interfaces (APIs) to the key "enablers" that allow you to write portable SAA applications. This is the part of SAA that is most relevant to programmers. Through the CPI, you have access to the SAA's major services in an operating system-independent manner. Currently SAA specifies the CPI to the following services:

1. **SAA Data Services** are provided through a Relational Databases and network file systems. The SAA Relational Database Manager's CPI is SQL. The remote SQL CPI will provide a single view of the database throughout a network of SAA machines. The SAA network file system's CPI is based on the Distributed Data Manager (DDM) architecture which allows an application to access file records transparently over an SAA network. DDM provides a network directory of files and takes care of format translation of records

between dissimilar file systems. DDM is based on a record model of data (as opposed to a byte stream).

2. **SAA Presentation Services** are provided through an SAA Dialog Manager CPI and an SAA Presentation Manager CPI. The Dialog Manager CPI provides a high-level programming capability for defining and displaying CUA compliant screens and windows. The Presentation Manager CPI interface provides lower-level graphic controls of screens and printers.
3. **SAA Communication Services** provide a consistent high-level programming interface to the SAA communication and network facilities, referred to as the Common Communication Support (CCS) services. The communication services primarily provide an interface to the SNA LU Type 6.2 protocol for program-to-program communications (also known as APPC). The Communications CPI may be architecturally extended to include the API to network management services (IBM's Netview) and APIs to generic remote services such as the Document Interchange Architecture (DIA) for the retrieval, processing, and distribution of documents.

- **Common Communication Support (CCS)** specifies the protocols for the interconnection and data interchange among the SAA systems. Over time, CCS will allow applications to be executed cooperatively across SAA systems and will provide transparent access to distributed data. CCS specifies the following communications' related areas:

1. It defines the *contents and structure* of network objects. The Mixed Object Document Content Architecture (MODCA) specifies the structure of multimedia documents. The Image Object Content Architecture (IOCA) specifies image interchanges. The Graphics Object Content Architecture (GOCA) specifies graphic interchanges. The Font Object Content Architecture (FOCA) specifies font interchanges. DDM specifies the format of logical records and files. The SAA 3270 data stream specifies a virtual screen protocol. The SAA Intelligent Printer Data Stream (IPDS) specifies a protocol for all-points-addressable printing.
2. It defines *Remote Services*, such as remote SQL and a network file directory. In an SAA office system, DCA-structured documents may be interchanged with other SAA office systems using the Document Interchange Architecture (DIA), which in turn uses SNA Distribution Services, a store-and-forward SNA service.
3. It defines *Network Management Services* which facilitate the process of planning, organizing, and controlling a network. The SAA network management architecture is part of SNA Management Services which is embodied in IBM's Netview product.
4. It defines *Peer-to-Peer* services for establishing sessions and conversations between SAA programs. The SAA architecture specifies the use of SNA Logical Unit Type 6.2 (LU 6.2) which specifies the handshakes and message formats used during a peer-to-peer SNA session. LU 6.2 roughly corresponds to the International Standard's Organization's (ISO's) Open System Interconnection (OSI) framework for the Presentation, Session, and Transport layers.

5. It defines an *Internet Packet Service* based on SNA's Low Entry Network (LEN) architecture and SNA's PU 2.1 protocol for node control. This corresponds roughly to OSI's network Layer
6. It defines the *Data Link and Physical layers* for the interconnection of SAA machines. SAA systems may be interconnected using LANs, telecommunication links, or packet-switched networks. SAA specifies three data-link protocols, namely X.25, SDLC, and Token Ring.

It should be apparent to you by now that the SAA virtual machine we just described is, by design, almost fully compatible in function and feature to an OS/2 EE machine. In fact, OS/2 EE is being built from the ground-up as an SAA machine. So if you are still not comfortable with SAA after this concentrated and acronym-intensive explanation, do not despair. Most of this book is about SAA in one form or another. The code we develop is mostly SAA-compatible. You will have every opportunity to explore the CUA, the CPI, and the CCS in great depth supplemented with a lot of "hands-on" examples.

OS/2 EE in a Distributed SAA World

Now that we know what constitutes an SAA machine, we will put together two somewhat futuristic scenarios that help situate OS/2 EE architecturally in the distributed world of SAA. The scenarios should help you understand the total system solution that SAA will provide across the IBM product line and beyond. In fact, if you think about it, SAA is a de facto standard that specifies in abundant detail how any set of *heterogeneous* computer systems from IBM or any other vendor may interoperate architecturally.

It was pointed out in the previous section that a distributed SAA environment provides:

- Distributed database
- Distributed application management
- Cooperative processing
- Network management
- Location-transparent application run-time environment
- A single system image to the application programmer

When it comes to building SAA system solutions, the OS/2 EE workstation lies at the *center of the universe*. The OS/2 EE workstation is not only SAA's primary user interface device, it is also the primary gateway between SAA environments and provides a single image of the SAA system.

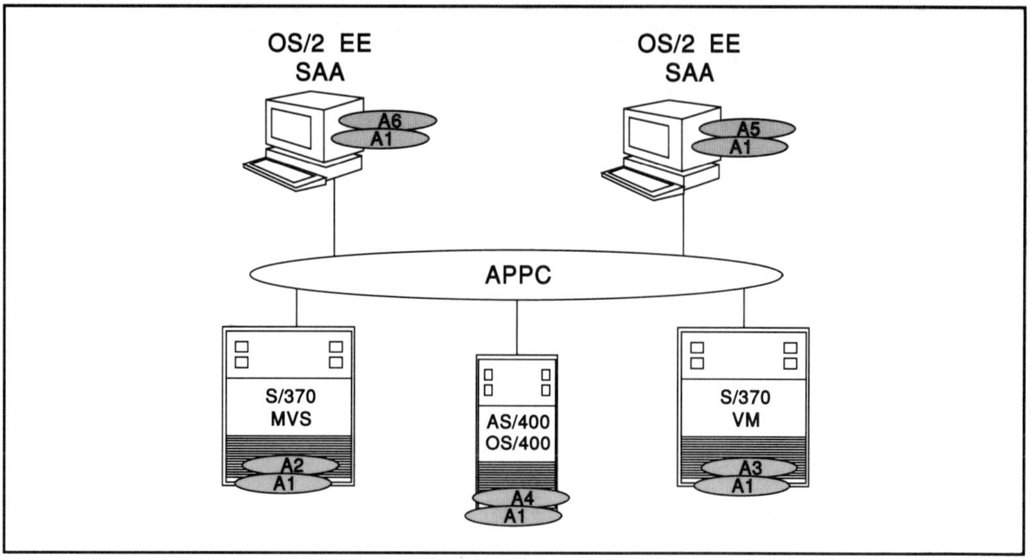

Figure 4-6. OS/2 EE in a Distributed SAA Environment.

Futuristic Scenario 1: An SAA Cooperative Environment

The scenario will help clarify the workings of SAA and more specifically will clarify the key role OS/2 EE will play in that environment. Figure 4-6 on page 85 shows a network of distributed applications running on a variety of SAA machines.

Application *A1* runs on all the machines in the network. *A1* is an example of a cooperative SAA application parts of which run on various SAA machines. In our scenario, *A1* could be accessing data from various SAA machines and then pre-process the data before it gets delivered to the end user. *A2* is an application that runs on an IBM S/370 under MVS. *A3* is an application that runs on an IBM S/370 under VM. *A4* is an application that runs on an IBM AS/400 under OS/400. Finally, *A5* and *A6* are applications that run on OS/2 EE machines.

We assume that the OS/2 EE machine with *A6* provides a front-end to all the applications. In this futuristic scenario, this front-end may be similar to the Desktop Manager currently provided by IBM's Office Vision (see Figure 4-7 on page 86). When users first sign on to the *A6* OS/2 EE machine, they will be asked for a logon id; this single id will be used under-the-covers to connect to a variety of remote applications. This implies a common authentication service across SAA machines. The Desktop presents an iconic view of the programs that are available to the user (in this case, the iconic representation of *A1* through *A6*). The fact that *A1* through *A5* are remote or have remote elements is totally transparent to the user who only sees a single image of the entire system.

The user clicks on an icon to start a particular application. This causes a frenzy of under-the-covers network activity as APPC sessions get established with the remote applications. Since all the applications are SAA-compliant, each application will have

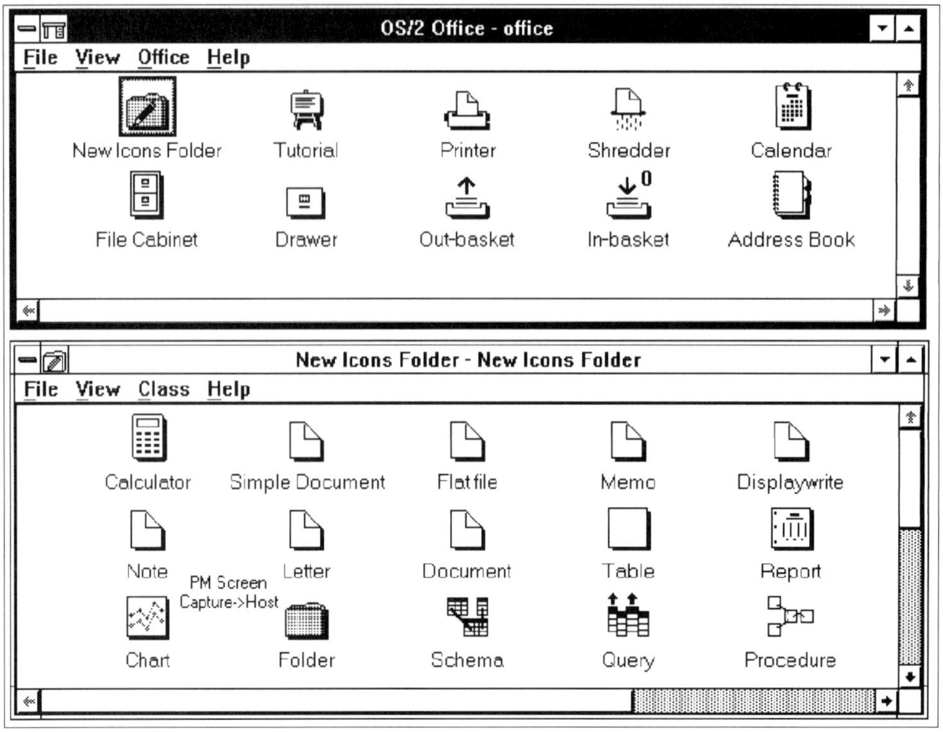

Figure 4-7. The Office Vision Desktop.

its window and the user can move from application to application by clicking the mouse. More interestingly, the user can use the clipboard or *drag and drop objects* with a mouse between windows to exchange data between applications. Thus, a user can move data from an AS/400 to a S/370 and vice versa through cut-and-paste window operations.

This scenario shows that through the OS/2 EE front-end, the user is at the control of a vast universe of SAA applications all of which appear to run locally under a Presentation Manager Desktop. The user is totally oblivious as to where those applications actually reside or on which machines they are running. If application *A4* is too slow when it runs on an AS/400 machine, there is no architectural reason why it cannot be moved to an IBM S/370. From the user's perspective, when the application gets moved to the S/370, nothing changes except the response time, which should improve substantially.

Futuristic Scenario 2: An SAA Life-cycle Repository

Future SAA applications will be managed through their entire life-cycle from conception to run-time. We will explain the implications of this by introducing the concept of a *network repository*. The *repository* in our scenario is an application that supports network applications from build-time to run-time. It does this by controlling objects in a repository database. The repository is used in the creation, distribution, and management of networked SAA applications.

The scenario starts with business planners and modelers who use an Upper CASE tool on a repository to design an enterprise-wide distributed application. A Lower CASE tool then uses the specifications stored by the Upper CASE tool in the repository to build the panels, tables, and transactions that will make up the application. Once built, the transactions, tables, and panels will be versioned and stored in the repository.

A runtime manager application then uses the repository to download the transaction code, the tables, and the panels to the network machines that will do the actual work. A runtime network manager uses the repository to control the code versions and to provide security and configuration services. It will measure application performance and, if necessary, migrate the applications to faster SAA machines or it may simply redirect client requests to faster servers. All this is done by consulting the repository for topological information. The repository is also kept informed of changes on the network and of significant events.

As you can see, this is a "brave new world" that operates without programmers like us. The business planners are at the controls. Don't panic, it will require millions of hours of programmer time to create the intelligent repository tools that will make this scenario a reality. So plan your retirement accordingly.

Moving Through Virtual SAA Space

These two examples are architectural renditions of what an SAA foundation should be able to provide in the not too distant future. The first scenario demonstrates the SAA runtime. You should get the picture that SAA provides a machine-independent and location-transparent environment to its applications and users. Think of it as a *virtual SAA space* in which applications float. The front-end and entry-point to this brave new universe is our friendly OS/2 EE workstation. The second scenario demonstrates how future SAA applications can be created and managed. Applications will live in repositories and move back and forth between repositories and virtual SAA space.

SAA is a foundation for the creation of distributed architectures on heterogeneous computer systems. The good news is that SAA is an *open* architecture. This means that any computer vendor that adheres to the SAA virtual machine standard can play in this game. Personal computers using OS/2 EE are fully equipped to become major players in the SAA scheme of things. Most importantly, the software you create is what brings "life" to this architectural space. You can see an embryonic form of that life in IBM's Office Vision.

How to Profit from SAA?

Brave new architectural possibilities are opening up for PCs in the MIS shops of the future. There are no limits to the possible system ensembles that can be built on top of an architectural base, such as the one SAA provides. The winners in the software development game will be those who learn how to harness that architectural power and use it to create exciting new software packages. Just think of all the personal agents and network gnomes that can roam through the SAA universe and do all kinds of interesting stuff. Keep in mind that the launching pad into this cooperative post client-server universe is an OS/2 EE caliber machine.

Part II

Multitasking Fundamentals

The chapters in Part II teach you how to effectively make use of multitasking in your programs. Using multitasking effectively will enable you to develop increasingly sophisticated client-server programs that are limited only by your imagination. OS/2's processes, threads, and interprocess communications services provide a state-of-the-art platform for understanding what multitasking can do for you. You will need to acquire a working knowledge of these fundamental OS/2 services before you can write programs that use OS/2 EE's Database, Communications, and Presentation Managers.

In client-server applications, the server uses multitasking to service multiple clients concurrently. The clients use multitasking to provide highly responsive and non-modal user interfaces. Multitasking is the natural way to simplify the coding of complex applications that can be divided into a collection of discrete and logically distinct, concurrent tasks. Multitasking can increase the performance, throughput, and responsiveness of your programs. However, there is no "free lunch." To use multitasking *effectively*, it is not enough just to learn how to use the OS/2 kernel services. You will also need to develop some good design techniques that enable you to:

- Decompose a program effectively into tasks and threads.
- Control the access to critical shared resources.
- Synchronize the execution of independent threads and processes.
- Create protocols for passing data and information between processes.
- Avoid deadlocks by programming defensively.
- Use priorities effectively to enhance performance.
- Write event-driven code that avoids *busy looping* by suspending execution (i.e., blocking) while waiting on events.
- Debug programs in a concurrent non-sequential environment.

We will develop a framework that will help you understand these concepts. The time that you invest in learning OS/2's multitasking is time well spent. The payoff is sharpened programming skills and better performing programs.

The approach we'll take in presenting the OS/2 multitasking services is to avoid simply rehashing the OS/2 Programmer's Manual. What we do instead is provide the necessary background information in tutorial form, and then develop a set of useful program examples that bring together the most important OS/2 API calls in a realistic setting. In addition to serving as production-quality OS/2 template programs, the examples also serve as learning tools that you can use to understand and measure the performance trade-offs of the OS/2 kernel services. In short, the program examples teach you how to program OS/2 and at the same time serve as tools that you can use to better understand OS/2's real-time performance attributes.

To provide realistic programs, we chose to write our code using standard C library calls where possible. The OS/2 API calls are *only* used where they can provide added function and performance, or in situations where the equivalent C library function is not available. You will find that this approach lets you explore OS/2 from a familiar C base, and that when you see an OS/2 call in the program it provides a new or improved service over what is already available in C. With your C background, you are already in a position to put together some working OS/2 programs that make use of the kernel's services. Your C programs only need to call the OS/2 kernel to obtain multitasking services, to write to the screen, and to invoke new services that are not in the C library. Here is the road map we will follow in Part II:

- In Chapter 5, "Processes, Threads and Semaphores", we provide a tutorial on the kernel's tasking services for threads and processes. We also explain the use of semaphores for task control and inter-task coordination.

- In Chapter 6, "Daemons and Killers", we introduce our first OS/2 programs, DAEMON.C and KILLER.C, which serve as a gentle introduction to the C/2 compiler and the MAKE utility.

- In Chapter 7, "MULTI.C - Multitasking Can Be Fun", we introduce a longer program, MULTI.C, whose effect is to give a visual demonstration of multithread and multiprocess performance. The user is able to interactively change the running priorities and levels of the executing threads or processes, as well as control their execution dynamically by setting or clearing semaphores. The MULTI.C program is a tool that lets you learn, through experimentation and immediate feedback, how to fine-tune an OS/2 multitasking program. MULTI is used again in Part V to study the effects of multitasking on the performance of client-server architectures for OLTP.

- In Chapter 8, "Named Pipes", we present a tutorial on Named Pipes, OS/2's *top-of-the-line* Interprocess Communication (IPC) mechanism. IPCs are mostly used for managing the exchange of data between processes. OS/2 offers a rich set of IPC mechanisms that include: Named Pipes, Anonymous Pipes, Queues, Shared Memory, and PM's Dynamic Data Exchange (DDE). Each IPC protocol has some strengths and weaknesses and appropriate uses. These IPC protocols were briefly covered in Chapter 3, "OS/2 EE: A Grand Tour". This book focuses exclusively on Named Pipes because it is the only IPC that provides communications between processes running on the same computer or on different computers. This inter-computer IPC is used to create multiprocess applications that can be configured to work over networks. The tutorial provides the prerequisite background information on Named Pipes you will need to understand the programs in this book.

- In Chapter 9, "A Generic Client-Server File Transfer Service", we introduce the concept of "layering" as it applies in the design of distributed programs. We then create the topmost layer of an application that is used to measure the performance of various interprocess communication techniques. This topmost layer provides a generic file transfer protocol that is used to move data or files between two processes. The protocol is generic in the sense that it is independent of the underlying IPC or LAN communication protocol service. The same calls will execute on top of Named Pipes, NetBIOS, and APPC. The generic file transfer is performed by two programs, FXREQ.C and FXSVR.C, which respectively implement the client and server portions of the client-server application. This application also measures the performance of the file transfer and displays the results. The actual file transfer is done using the underlying IPC and LAN protocols. In Part II, the underlying IPC is provided by local Named Pipes. In Part III, the underlying IPC is provided by the LAN protocols: APPC, NetBIOS, remote Named Pipes, and the LAN Requester/Server.

- In Chapter 10, "FX Using Named Pipes", we develop FXNPIPE.DLL. This is a Dynamic Link Library package that we provide to execute data movement commands using Named Pipes. The Dynamic Link Library is linked at runtime to the FXREQ and FXSVR processes, which in this chapter, run on the same machine. In Part III, the FXREQ and FXSVR will execute on separate machines and will be used to measure the comparative performance of file transfers using: Named Pipes, NetBIOS, APPC, and the LAN Requester/Server. You will then be in the remarkable position of having in front of you a consistent set of benchmarks that compare local and remote process-to-process communications using OS/2 EE's most popular communication protocols. In the process, you will also have gained valuable knowledge on the mechanics of implementing those protocols. This is the in-depth comparative knowledge you will need to help you make decisions such as which protocol provides the best fit for a particular application? Most importantly, you will have some good code skeletons on which to build your future applications.

Chapter 5

Processes, Threads, and Semaphores

The term *tasks* is used in this book to include both processes and threads. This chapter starts us in our exploration of OS/2's tasking repertoire with a tutorial on processes, threads, and the basic semaphore service used for synchronizing them.

ABOUT PROCESSES AND THREADS

We'll start out the tutorial on processes and threads with a sanity check: do you really need multitasking? We then provide a definition of what is a thread and what is a process? We then offer some guidelines for determining when to use threads and when to use processes in your multitasking programs. We conclude with a brief exposition on how to use OS/2's tasking API services.

Do You Really Need Multitasking?

So when do you need multitasking? It would be tempting to answer "you'll know when you need it." In general, you need multitasking if you have interspersed code throughout the main body of your application that waits on events to happen. Multitasking can also help you maintain context for multiple users in a LAN Server type of application. You can also benefit from multitasking if your code can be divided into logically distinct simultaneous tasks.

There are many applications that do not fall into the above categories. This is not too surprising since the predominant thinking paradigm is sequential. We usually do not think in parallel; our spoken languages are "sequential" and most of our computer architectures and computer languages are sequential. The result is that few of our programs are written to exploit concurrency. If your application does not need multitasking and can be coded easily using sequential code, then the KISS principle (Keep It Simple and Stupid) dictates *not* using multitasking. Don't be tempted to introduce processes and threads over sequential code purely because it provides a more elegant structure or style. You should be aware that multitasking is no panacea. Concurrent programs are difficult to design and debug. Multitasking introduces side effects such as "deadlocks." In some cases, multitasking may slow down an application that is highly sequential in nature. If these dire warnings have not persuaded you otherwise, then read on because multitasking may be what you really need. If nothing else, it's a lot of fun.

What Type of Multitasking?

Once you've determined to go with a multitasking solution, then the rule of thumb is to use processes to implement functions that are loosely coupled, require a minimum amount of shared resources and can be packaged to run independently as well as concurrently. Processes should be used to implement independent programs that can run concurrently. The size of the multitasking unit is the program itself.

On the other hand, use threads to implement functions that are closely coupled, require the use of shared resources, and are the size of a typical C procedure. You are generally better off under OS/2 if you can allocate tasks (i.e., concurrently executing units of code) to parts of the same program rather than allocate them to separate programs. You use threads when you want to run many functions at the same time within a single program. Threads can be thought of as separate procedures within the same program, except that they are procedures that execute concurrently. The term *coroutines* is synonymous with threads, if that means something to you. Threads have also been called *lightweight processes*.

OS/2 can handle a theoretical maximum of 511 threads and 511 processes for the entire system. The number of threads that can be started by one process is 53. You will need to learn how to manage these resources effectively to obtain a reasonable level of performance. To work successfully with multitasking, you clearly need to understand the differences between processes and threads.

What is a Process?

A process is simply an OS/2 program that has been loaded into memory and prepared for execution. A process consists of code, data, and other resources such as open files and open queues. The OS/2 kernel considers every program that gets loaded through **CMD.EXE**, **DosExecProcess**, and **DosStartSession** to be a process. Creating a new process is relatively slow and requires a substantial amount of overhead, since the program files must be read from disk and loaded into memory. How do processes that are self-contained programs, each in its own isolated address space, communicate with each other? This is done through the Interprocess Communication services provided by OS/2 such as Named Pipes, Queues, and Shared Memory.

What is a Thread?

A thread provides a unique way of sharing the processor within an application, as opposed to between applications. OS/2 is one of the few commercial operating systems that provides the power of multithreading. So what is a thread? A thread is a dispatchable piece of code which merely owns a stack, registers, and its priority. It shares everything else with all the other active threads in a process. The OS/2 multitasking model is thread-based, which means that the scheduler allocates CPU time to threads, not processes. Every process must have at least one thread. A program executes when the system scheduler gives the thread execution control.

Creating a thread requires much less system overhead than creating a process. The overhead is comparable to calling a C function, where the function is in the same file as the calling program. Threads, like functions, are loaded into memory as part of the calling program; so no disk access is necessary when a thread is invoked by another thread. It is much easier to share data between threads than it is between processes. Threads use variables the same way C functions do, and any thread in a process can access global variables. Threads, therefore, can communicate easily using global variables. On the negative side, threads require elaborate protocols based on semaphores to protect all shared resources. You must design these protocols carefully to avoid deadlocks. Debugging threads can be quite tricky.

Processes or Threads?

So, which is the preferred multitasking method? The answer to this question is of course, "all of the above." The choice of method will depend on the nature of your application. It will depend on how much time you can afford between task switches, how long it takes to create a task, and how easy it is for tasks to share information. Other factors that may affect your choice are the ease of debugging and the required level of intertask isolation and protection.

Use *processes* if your application:

- Is to be packaged as independent cooperating processes which can be sold as separate and even interchangeable modules. An example would be a Computer Integrated Manufacturing (CIM) offering.
- Is oversized and needs to make more efficient use of memory. A process then becomes the unit of memory swapping which gives you a lot more control then relying on OS/2 to do the swapping on your behalf.
- Needs to protect its resources from indiscriminate access. Processes provide better encapsulation than threads and should be used as object managers.
- Needs to be ported to other operating systems. Threads are a leading-edge OS/2 construct.

Use *threads* if your application:

- Manipulates a lot of devices at the same time. The handling of each device should be assigned to a separate thread.
- Requires background tasks that get put on timers to perform chores that are unrelated to the main program's thrust. As an example, you could have a background thread wake up every 24 hours and backup a database.
- Spends a lot of time waiting on things to happen. You can assign each waiting event to a thread that blocks until the event occurs. In the meantime, other threads can use the CPU's cycles productively to perform useful work. The use of threads can considerably improve the performance and responsiveness of such applications.
- Requires an interactive user interface which supports CPU intensive background processing. By using separate threads for the user interface and background processing you can keep the program responsive to user input.
- Requires a high-level of concurrency within a single program.

HOW TO MULTITASK WITH PROCESSES

The Life of a Process

OS/2 allows you to start a process using **DosExecPgm**, self-terminate a process using **DosExit**, kill a child process using **DosKillProcess**, synchronize with a child process using **DosCWait**, and prepare a process for premature death using **DosExitList**. Processes can query and set their priority using **DosGetPrty** and **DosSetPrty**. A process can obtain its process ID (**PID**) and that of its parent process through **DosGetPid**. The parent process ID can be obtained for any specified process through **DosGetPPid**. Processes can find out information about themselves and a wealth of useful system information using **DosGetInfoSeg**.

Processes and Their Children

Processes form close parental bonds with their child processes. Typically, a child process will inherit all the resources owned by the parent process unless the parent specifies otherwise, through the inheritance flag, when it creates the resource. When a thread or child process is created, it is initially dispatched with the same priority as the thread of the parent that created it. Child processes typically execute in the same Virtual Screen group (or session) as the parent. An interesting part of the relationship between a parent and its child processes is how they will manage this common session without corrupting the display.

A parent can choose to pass command line arguments to its child process at invocation time. The child process also inherits the parent's environment, with the parent having the option to enhance or change this legacy at invocation time. Environment strings contain values for system variables such as PATH and any variables defined using the SET command. These variables reside in the environment segment of an application and can be retrieved using the **DosGetEnv** call.

When a parent process is terminated, all its children are terminated as well, unless the parent specifies otherwise (as a parameter of **DosExit**). A parent can also abort a child's execution through **DosKillProcess**, or it can wait for the child to terminate through **DosCWait**. The parent also has the option of blocking its execution until the child process completes, or it can run in parallel with its child processes. The blocking option, called the *synchronous* execution mode, is provided mainly for compatibility with MS-DOS's EXEC function (interrupt 21, function 4BH), and it does not particularly take advantage of OS/2's multitasking. The parallel execution option, officially called *asynchronous* execution, is what you will need in order to develop cooperative multiprocess applications.

The Children Are Not All Equal

Under OS/2, not all the child processes are created equal. With OS/2, not unlike the real world, a child process can be born *ordinary*, *deprived*, or *spoiled rotten*. We've already discussed the parental bonds with the ordinary children, we now present how the process deals with its deprived and spoiled rotten children.

The *deprived* children, officially called *background* processes, are detached asynchronous processes, that are disinherited by the parent. Thus, the background processes do not inherit resources from the parent, and are not allowed access to the parent's virtual screen group. To interact with the outside world, they use special constructs called **VioPopUps** that overlay information on the parent's screen temporarily. To receive keyboard input, they need another special construct, *Device Monitors*, which monitor the input stream. Thus when the appropriate sequence of keys is entered, the monitor can activate the background process, which can then pop-up into the foreground and momentarily take control of the screen and keyboard.

Background processes do not terminate when their parents *die*, instead they continue to run forever long after the parent is gone. You cannot stop them by issuing Control-C or Control-Break, either. The parent has to explicitly kill its background children, if the application dictates it, as part of the clean up it performs before termination. Creating a background process has the same effect as issuing the **DETACH** command at the OS/2 prompt. Background processes are used to implement Daemon programs under OS/2 and provide a very useful construct in the design of multitasking applications.

The *spoiled rotten* children processes are created and given their own session, i.e., virtual screen group, through **DosStartSession**. The new session can be run in either a controlled *related* mode or in an autonomous *unrelated* mode. If the session is run in a controlled mode, then the creating process can select, set or stop the child session using **DosSelectSession, DosSetSession, or DosStopSession**, respectively. Developers will mainly use threads and processes as opposed to session services. When you want one process to cause the execution of another, related process, you will use **DosExecPgm**, as opposed to **DosStartSession**, and cause the child to be run in the parent's session. It should be noted that even Presentation Manager, with its rich window environment, only consumes one OS/2 session. The session services are used mostly by unrelated processes and applications like the OS/2 Program Selector (which allows users to create, delete, and switch between multiple sessions).

HOW TO MULTITASK WITH THREADS

The Life of a Thread

OS/2 provides a rich set of tasking functions for working with threads. The first thread of execution, the *primary thread* of a process, gets created automatically by OS/2 when a process is first executed. This primary thread can create other threads, which in turn can create threads of their own, etc. To create a new thread, you need to allocate a stack for the new thread and then issue **DosCreateThread** or preferably use the more powerful new C library call: **_beginthread**. The creation of threads should be as easy and error-free as the invocation of a procedure.

The **DosCreateThread** function contains many stack-oriented "gotchas" and it cannot easily be used to pass parameters to a child thread. The **_beginthread** C function does eventually call **DosCreateThread** on your behalf. We recommend you use it because it provides a cleaner API. It is good programming practice to have each thread in the application terminate itself explicitly by issuing a **DosExit** call. The C library includes a special thread termination API, **_endthread**; however, we recommend you use **DosExit** instead since it returns a termination code which may be useful to your application.

Once created, each thread is assigned a thread ID which is used as a handle for identifying the particular thread. A thread can obtain the current thread ID (TID), the current PID and the PID of the parent through **DosGetPid**.

Controlling Threads

OS/2 allows a thread to suspend other threads in a program (i.e., within the same process) by issuing the **DosSuspendThread** call. The suspended thread will stop execution until a **DosResumeThread** call is issued. OS/2 provides an even more drastic thread control mechanism, the **DosEnterCritSec** call, whose effect is to suspend all running threads in the current process, except for the thread that issued the call. The calling thread must issue **DosExitCritSec** very soon after, or you will not have any kind of working system left. Interestingly, OS/2 does not provide a function equivalent to the **DosKillProcess**, for threads. There is no way for one thread to explicitly kill another thread in OS/2.

In general, the thread control mechanisms just discussed are too blunt to provide a fine level of control. For example, **DosEnterCritSec**, is overkill in most situations and its effect of suspending all threads is quite arbitrary. In the next section we will introduce semaphores; you will find that they provide a much finer scalpel-like level of control for thread execution and for the coordination of interthread activity.

OS/2 provides a full range of very handy interval timers that can be used for timing a thread's execution. The **DosSleep** API call causes a thread to suspend its execution for a specified time interval (a thread cannot use **DosSuspendThread** to suspend itself). The **DosTimerAsync** call will notify a running thread, through the clearing of a semaphore, when a specified time interval elapses. The **DosTimerStart** call creates a repeatable timer that can be used by threads to perform an operation on a regular basis.

Thread Priorities

Threads, like processes, can query and set their execution priority (i.e., how often they get a CPU execution time-slice) using **DosGetPrty** and **DosSetPrty**. A thread may run in one of four priority classes: Idle-time, Regular, Fixed-high, and Time-critical. *Idle-time* threads have the lowest priority and receive the least amount of scheduling attention. *Time-critical* threads have the highest and get scheduled ahead of other threads. *Regular* priority is the default priority OS/2 assigns to a new process (and primary thread). The *Fixed-high* priority assists in the synchronization of a background thread that is expected to run at a certain priority in relation to a foreground thread.

Within each priority class, OS/2 supports 32 distinct priority levels. When a thread is created, it is initially dispatched with the same priority as the creating thread. Your code will then adjust the priorities of the various threads in a program using **DosSetPriority** to meet the variety in demand for performance. For example, to satisfy a time-critical requirement, you can raise the priority of a thread temporarily during its critical processing, or you can assign the critical processing to a separate dedicated thread. The best use of high priority, in general, is to assign it to threads in a program that are part of the critical-path that other threads depend on for their execution.

Thread Coexistence

Each thread inherits all the common resources of the process of which it is a part. Thus, all threads that are part of the same process share the same code and data segments, environmental strings, open file and semaphore handles, and global data. This common environment is both a blessing and a curse. The blessing is that threads can easily communicate with each other, invoke common procedures, and have unlimited access to global data. The curse is that the unrestricted access can cause threads to interfere with each other and corrupt common data. Of course, OS/2's rich semaphore service is there to solve this problem and turn threads (and processes) into blessings you can count on.

ABOUT SEMAPHORES

This section provides a tutorial on OS/2's elaborate set of semaphore services. We start by explaining what a semaphore is and what semaphores can do for your programs. We then introduce OS/2's semaphore types. You will need to understand what each type does best. Following that, we go over the semaphore API calls with an emphasis on how to combine API calls to perform different services. We end the section with some scenarios that explain how semaphores are used in typical multi-tasking situations.

What is a Semaphore?

Semaphores are OS/2-managed software flags, used to coordinate the actions of concurrent threads and processes. You can think of semaphores as "stop and go" traffic lights, that synchronize the flow of independently executing pieces of software. Without traffic lights, our roads would look more like non-intersecting straight lines or circles, instead of the complex street-grids we are used to. Presumably, without traffic-lights and driving conventions, anarchy would prevail on the roads, leading to traffic accidents and more traffic jams. For traffic conventions to work, motorists need to abide by the traffic laws and voluntarily "stop on red" and "go on green" and respect the various signals and signs. In a similar vein, the use of semaphores in programs implies some form of voluntary cooperation between processes and threads. The trick is to write "law-abiding," yet highly autonomous, programs that strictly adhere to a set of mutually agreed upon semaphore rules that enable the different pieces to work together when necessary while staying out of each other's way.

The Mutual Exclusion Semaphore Protocol

A semaphore can be in one of two states: **set** or **clear**. The setting and clearing of semaphores are atomic operations performed through OS/2 API calls. A thread owns (*holds*) the semaphore by *setting* it, and relinquishes control by *clearing* it. For example, to gain exclusive access to a critical resource that must be serially used, a thread must perform the following:

1. It first requests the semaphore that guards the resource and waits, if necessary, until it becomes available.

2. When the request is granted, the semaphore is automatically set to *busy*, which means any requests for the semaphore by other threads are blocked.
3. It operates on the resource.
4. Finally, it clears the semaphore to free it when done.

The effect of this protocol is to enforce the serial access to a resource. Using this protocol, tasks wait for their turn to use a *critical* resource, with only one task unblocking when a semaphore clears. The protocol enforces a "this is mine, stay out" agreement while a task is in the critical region. The semaphore is considered to be *owned* until the task exits the critical region. When the task exits the critical region, it relinquishes its ownership of the semaphore by clearing it.

The Event Signaling Semaphore Protocol

A thread can set or clear a semaphore to represent the occurrence of an event: "your timer popped." The clearing of a semaphore in this case signals the occurrence of an event. All the interested tasks *block* their execution waiting for the event to take place (i.e., for the semaphore to clear). The semaphore is cleared by a separate event-handling task.

The Multiple-Wait Semaphore Protocol

A thread can block waiting on multiple events to occur: "an incoming message" or "a timer pop." The thread is actually blocked waiting for one of several semaphores in a list to clear. Each semaphore in the list represents an event. This kind of signaling is extremely useful in real-time event-driven systems where a task may be monitoring hundreds of asynchronous events. The alternative is to go into a polling loop looking for things to happen. Polling loops use up CPU cycles *busy-waiting* which is not very good practice in multitasking systems. A multiple-wait semaphore scheme must be able to identify which of the various multiplexed semaphores cleared. OS/2 does that by returning an index number to indicate which semaphore on the list cleared.

USING SEMAPHORES

DosSemSet is issued to acquire ownership of a semaphore, while **DosSemClear** is issued to relinquish ownership and restart a process that is blocked waiting on a semaphore to clear. Many threads can wait on a single semaphore to clear by issuing **DosSemWait**. The API call, **DosSemRequest**, waits for a sempaphore to clear and then sets the semaphore in one single atomic operation. The atomic *wait and set* service provided by **DosSemRequest** makes it the ideal semaphore for serializing access to shared resources. The API call, **DosSemSetWait**, lets you set a semaphore and then wait for some thread to clear it, making it very useful if you have to run two threads in lock-step with one thread doing something and then blocking until the other thread signals that it has caught up.

Edge-triggered Versus Level-triggered Semaphores

OS/2 provides a very useful API call, **DosMuxSemWait**, that can be used by a thread to wait on multiple events. The clearing of any of any semaphore (up to 16) will unblock the waiting thread. **DosMuxSemWait** is an *edge-triggered* semaphore, meaning that all waiting threads are immediately enabled when a semaphore clears. The edge triggered semaphore is ideal for broadcasting events to waiting threads. In contrast, the rest of OS/2's wait-on-semaphore calls are *level triggered*, meaning that a semaphore may go through many iterations of being set-and-cleared by other waiting threads before a particular waiting thread gets released. A level trigger may be thought of as a key that gets passed by the operating system from one owning thread to the next, with only one thread owning the key at any one time. Level triggered semaphores are used for serializing access to shared resources, since they guarantee the release of only one waiting thread at a time.

A Semaphore for Each Season

OS/2 supports three types of semaphores: *System*, *RAM* and *Fast-safe RAM*.

The System Semaphore: This is the slowest, safest, and most versatile type of semaphore OS/2 provides. It is mainly used between processes. Unlike, RAM and FS-RAM semaphores, system semaphores need to be created through the API call **DosCreateSem**. System semaphores are named using a file naming convention. OS/2 maintains a pseudo directory called **\SEM** in RAM to keep track of system semaphores. Whenever a thread refers to a system semaphore by name it must include the **\SEM** subdirectory prefix as part of the name. Thus, the full format for a system semaphore name is, **\SEM\name**, where each name must be unique. Even though the semaphore name must conform to OS/2 file naming conventions, no actual file is created for the semaphore. Instead, OS/2 simply returns a handle for the semaphore. The creating process and all its threads can subsequently use the handle to set, clear, and wait for the semaphore.

If any other process wants to use the system semaphore, it must issue a **DosOpenSem** with the same name that was previously used for creating the semaphore. When a process is finished using a system semaphore, it should close it by issuing a **DosCloseSem** call. When all threads that use a system semaphore close it, OS/2 automatically deletes the semaphore. System semaphores are made "safe" by OS/2, in the following sense:

- If a process "dies" or exits while still owning a system semaphore, OS/2 will notify any threads in other processes that are waiting on that semaphore by waking them and returning an error code indicating the loss of the owner.

- A thread that owns a system semaphore can issue a request for that semaphore again without first clearing the semaphore. This helps in the writing of reentrant threads. If this is done with a RAM semaphore, it will result in a deadlock with the thread blocking on the second request for the semaphore waiting for itself to clear the semaphore. OS/2 counts how many times the owning thread has requested the semaphore without a corresponding clear. The semaphore is not cleared until the count is zero.
- At the time of creation, a system semaphore can be specified as being for the *exclusive* use of the creating process and its descendants. If a system semaphore is exclusive, it can be read by other processes but it can only be modified by threads within the creating process.

The RAM Semaphore: This is simply a four-byte (unsigned long) global variable and the pointer to that variable which serves as the semaphore handle. Both variables must be defined by your application. The global variable should be initialized to zero to indicate that it is clear and can be claimed by a thread issuing the standard OS/2 semaphore API calls using the address of global variable for the semaphore handle. RAM semaphores do not use OS/2's calls for creating or opening a semaphore. Since a RAM semaphore is a global variable, you must be extra careful to prevent its value from being changed in any way other than by using the OS/2 semaphore API calls. OS/2 will not clean up after threads that terminate while still owning a RAM semaphore. RAM semaphores do not protect reentrant threads that issue **DosSemRequest** and **DosSemClear** calls recursively. On the other hand, RAM semaphores are considerably faster than system semaphores since they require much less system overhead. You can use RAM semaphores very effectively and safely if you limit yourself to non-recursive threads that belong to the same process.

The Fast-Safe RAM (FS-RAM) Semaphore: This semaphore combines the safety features of a system semaphore with the performance of a RAM semaphore. FS-RAM semaphores, like RAM semaphores, are global variables; but unlike RAM semaphores the variable is a **DOSFSRSEM** structure that contains information about the process and thread that have set the semaphore. It also contains a count of the number of times a semaphore has been set. The structure must be initialized before using an FS-RAM semaphore for the first time.

OS/2 provides only two API calls in support of FS-RAM semaphores: **DosFSRamSemRequest** and **DosFSRamSemClear**. These two calls are analogous to the **DosSemRequest** and **DosSemClear** calls used by system and RAM semaphores. FS-RAM semaphores can be safely used between processes or between threads in the same process. If you use them between processes, be sure to place your FS-RAM semaphores in an allocated shared memory segment. If a process dies while owning an FS-RAM semaphore, an associated exit list procedure can issue a **DosFSRamRequest** call to override the owning thread ID and perform normal cleanup. The exit list procedure should then read the count field in the **DOSFSRSEM** structure and issue a corresponding number of **DosFSRamSemClear** clear calls to release the resource. Like the system semaphore, an FS-RAM semaphore can be used re-entrantly with OS/2 keeping track of the number of outstanding requests.

How the Semaphores Compare

Table 5-1 compares and summarizes the features of OS/2's three semaphore services:

Table 5-1. Comparing OS/2's Three Semaphore Services.

Feature	System Semaphores	RAM Semaphores	FS-RAM Semaphores
Creating and initializing a semaphore	DosCreateSem DosOpenSem	Assign and clear a 4-byte variable pointer in RAM.	Assign and initialize a variable of type DOSFSRSEM in shared memory.
Using a semaphore	DosSemRequest DosSemClear DosSemSet DosSemSetWait DosSemWait DosMuxSemWait	DosSemRequest DosSemClear DosSemSet DosSemSetWait DosSemWait DosMuxSemWait	DosFSRamSemRequest DosFSRamSemClear
Closing a semaphore	DosCloseSem		
Safe exit	Yes	Only within one process with non-recursive threads	Yes, with Exit List procedure
Support for recursive calls	Yes	No	Yes
Performance	Slow	Fast	Fast

Semaphore Scenarios

We now present some scenarios that choreograph the use of semaphores in typical multitasking environments. Once you grasp the mechanics of semaphore usage, you can create your own repertoire of API sequences using our scenarios as a starting point.

Scenario 1: Mutual Exclusion

Scenario 1 demonstrates how semaphores can be used to provide mutual exclusive access to shared resources. For demonstrative purposes, we implement the same mutual exclusion scenario using: RAM, FS-RAM, and system semaphores (Figure 5-1). Notice that only the system semaphore can be used across processes, and only the system semaphore requires API calls for creating and closing a semaphore. Notice too that both the RAM and system semaphores use the same API calls for manipulating semaphores. All three semaphores guarantee that only one thread at a time will obtain access to the shared resource.

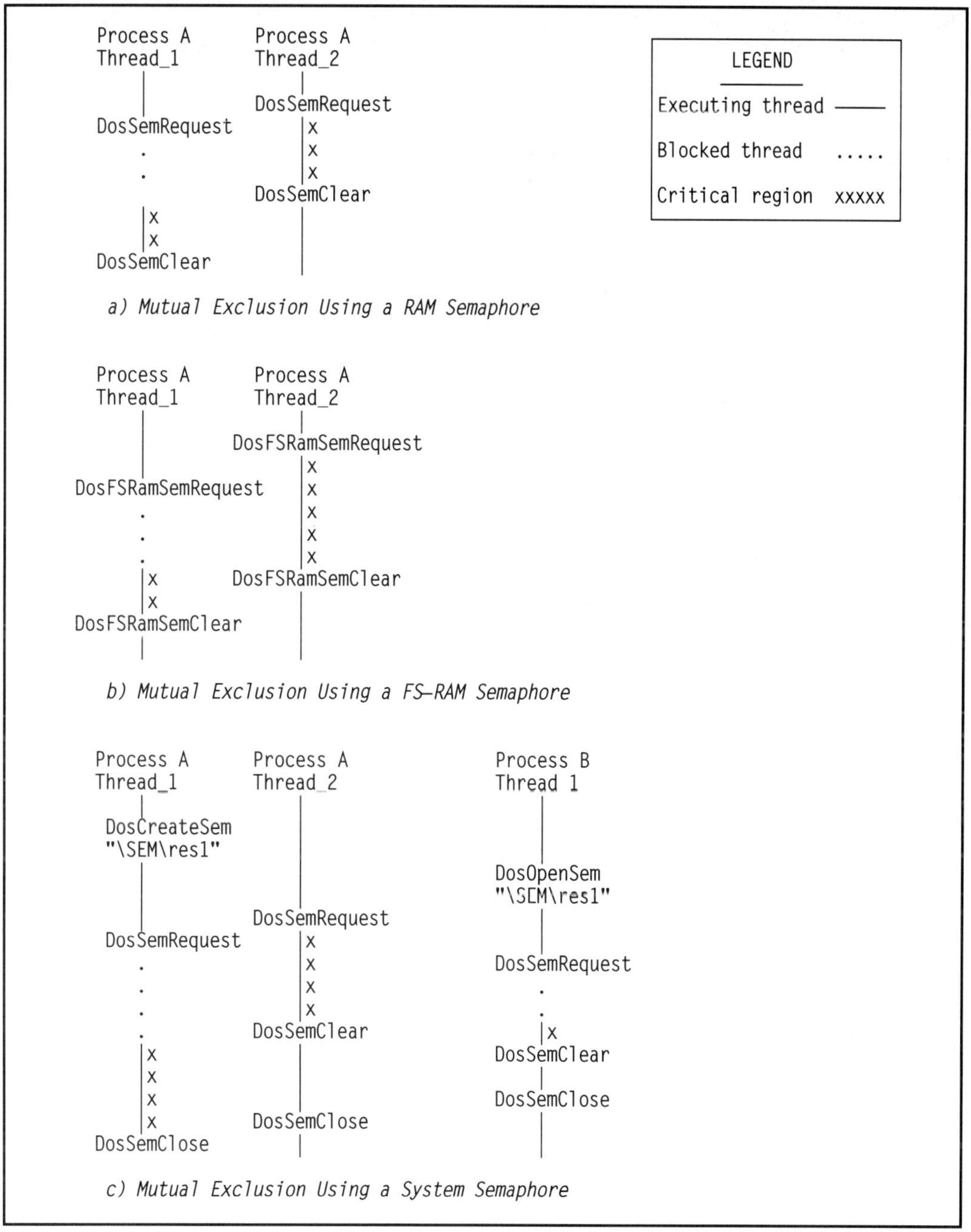

Figure 5-1. Scenario 1: Serializing Access with RAM, FS-RAM and System Semaphores.

Scenario 2: Signaling Events

Scenario 2 demonstrates the use of semaphores to signal events between tasks (Figure 5-2). The scenario shows how a semaphore is used to organize a race between threads. Such a race could be used to measure the performance of a set of threads (or processes). The start-of-execution is synchronized by clearing a semaphore.

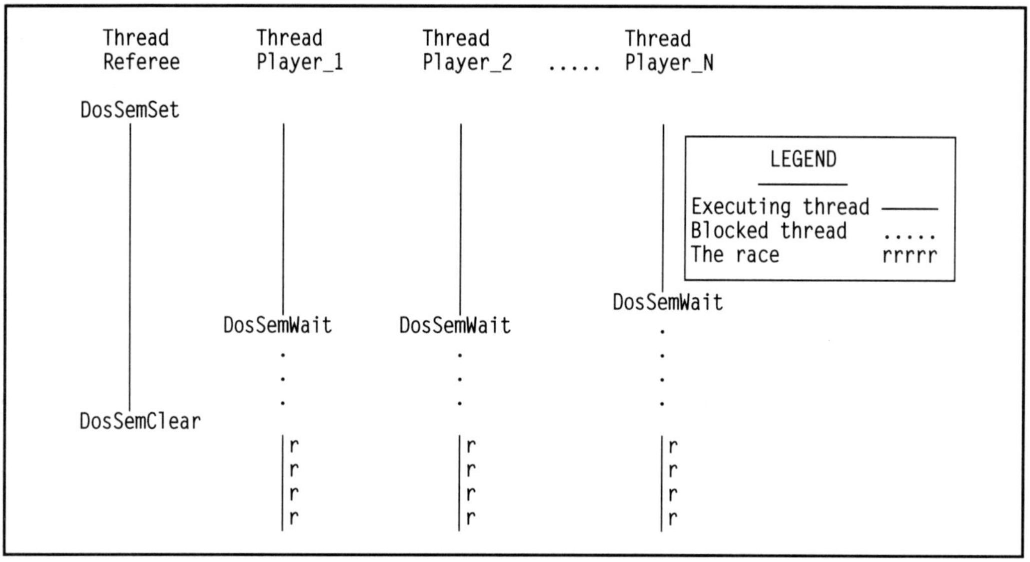

Figure 5-2. Scenario 2: Using a Semaphore to Broadcast an Event, START Running!

Scenario 3: Synchronizing Activities

Scenario 3 demonstrates how semaphores can be used to synchronize the activity of two threads (Figure 5-3). The scenario shows two threads: obtain_input() and store_in_db(). The obtain_input() thread interacts with a user and prompts for input, while store_in_db() stores the data. The synchronization between the two threads is through a semaphore which store_in_db() sets and then waits for it to clear, using **DosSemSetWait**. The semaphore is cleared by obtain_input() when the user inputs data. Only the store_in_db() waits on a semaphore. Why? This is because our scenario assumes that the data gets put away in the database before the user gets a chance to interactively enter the next piece of information.

```
Thread               Thread
store_in_db()        obtain_input()

    |                   |x
    |                   |x                 LEGEND
DosSemSetWait           |x               ---------
    .                   |x          Executing thread ----
    .                   |x          Blocked thread   .....
    .                   |x          Obtain input     xxxxx
    |y               DosSemClear    Store in DB      yyyyy
    |y                  |x
DosSemSetWait           |x
    .                   |x
    .                   |x
    .                DosSemClear
    |y                  |x
    |y                  |x
DosSemSetWait           |x
    .                   |x
    .                   |x
```

Figure 5-3. Scenario 3: Synchronizing the Execution of Two Threads Using Semaphores.

Scenario 4: Producer/Consumer

Scenario 4 demonstrates how semaphores can be used to synchronize two threads into lock-step for producer/consumer types of situations (Figure 5-4). The scenario imposes more stringent synchronization requirements than any of the methods discussed so far. It imposes an ordered alternating access to the shared resource with the producer always going first. The producer and consumer also need to wait for each other when the resource is busy. This kind of lock-step is used in situations where tasks are assigned different functional responsibilities but still have a need to synchronize their production in the style of an assembly line.

To accomplish this, we will use two semaphores, *buff_full_sem* and *buff_empty_sem*, each of which indicate the beginning of a particular state. The clearing of *buff_full_sem* indicates that the buffer is full and the clearing of *buff_empty_sem* indicates that the buffer is empty. Why do we need two semaphores? Because all the OS/2 semaphore API functions wait for semaphores to clear as opposed to waiting for them to set. So we need to have one semaphore for each event we're waiting on.

```
Thread                  Thread
producer                consumer
    |                       |
DosSemSet                   |                  LEGEND
"buff_full_sem"             |               ----------
    |                       |          Executing thread  ----
DosSemClear                 |          Blocked thread    .....
"buff_empty_sem"            |          Produce           ppppp
    |                   DosSemRequest  Consume           ccccc
DosSemRequest           "buff_full_sem"
"buff_empty_sem"            .
    |p                      .
    |p                      .
DosSemClear                 .
"buff_full_sem"             |c
    |                       |c
DosSemRequest               |c
"buff_empty_sem"            |c
    .                   DosSemClear
    .                   "buff_empty_sem"
    |p                      |
    |p                  DosSemRequest
    |p                  "buff_full_sem"
    |p                      .
DosSemClear                 .
"buff_full_sem"             |c
    |                       |c
DosSemRequest               |c
"buff_empty_sem"            |c
    .                       |c
    .                   DosSemClear
    .                   "buff_empty_sem"
    |                       |
```

Figure 5-4. Scenario 4: Producer/Consumer Lock-Step Synchronization of Two Threads.

Scenario 5: A Multiple-Event Handler

Scenario 5 demonstrates how semaphores can be used in creating event-driven systems (Figure 5-5). The multiple-event scenario shows an event-dispatcher task blocked waiting for any of the several semaphores on its list to clear. Eventually, some event clears a semaphore and the event-dispatcher task comes to life and does its thing!

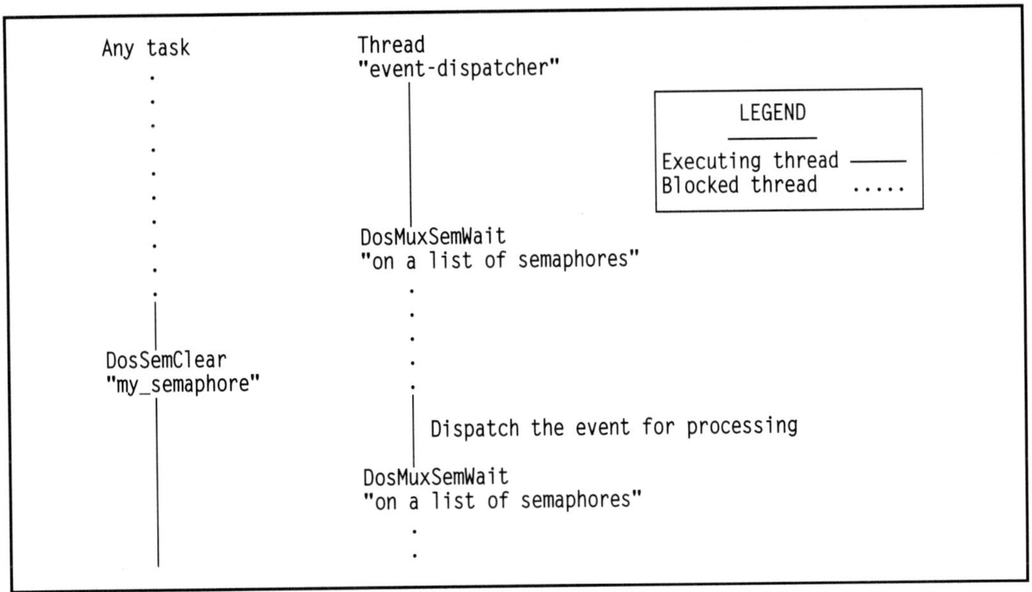

Figure 5-5. Scenario 5: The Event-Dispatcher Thread Blocks Waiting for Any Event.

Chapter 6

Daemons and Killers

This chapter provides a gentle introduction to writing, compiling, and debugging an OS/2 program. It has become customary for programming books to start with a *do nothing* program, that just writes "Hello World" to the screen. The purpose of such programs is to introduce the compiler, the MAKE utility, and the operating system's programming interface. Our version of the "Hello World" is a Daemon program that wakes up every day at a set time and says hello to the world.

A *Daemon* is an ominous-sounding name for a parentless background process that sleeps inside a machine waiting for some event to trigger it. When a Daemon comes to life, it does whatever it was programmed to do and may then put itself back to sleep waiting for the next event to trigger it. Clearly, a Daemon may be put to good uses such as backing up your database, notifying you of your next appointment with the dentist, or executing a batch file of commands at a set time. We also provide as a public service, KILLER, a daemon-killer program. If you get a chance to run DAEMON, you may be thankful to have KILLER, which gets rid of the Daemons without forcing you to reboot your machine.

The plan for this chapter is to take you through a panoramic grand tour that starts out with what you'll need in terms of software to program in OS/2 EE. We'll then walk you through the code listings of DAEMON.C and KILLER.C, your "gentle" introductions to program-writing under OS/2. Once we have a program in hand, we'll want to compile and run it. This will serve as our chance to introduce you to the joys of *making* programs using the OS/2 **MAKE** utility. We'll walk through a *make* file that automates the production of DAEMON and KILLER. This takes us to the last leg of our grand tour in which we briefly touch on the topic of debugging, multitasking, and multithreaded programs using **CodeView**, the symbolic debugger that comes with IBM and Microsoft C compilers.

WHAT YOU NEED TO GET STARTED

This is a good time to create the environment on your machines for running the programs in this book. Even though most programs will run on a single machine what you really need to get the most benefit are two machines connected via a Token Ring or Ethernet LAN.

Installing OS/2 EE and the LAN Server

We found that the easiest way to prepare a system is by using the **Basic Configuration Services Installation** that comes with OS/2. Just follow the cookbook style instruction provided in the "OS/2 EE: Getting Started" documentation. An interactive installation program will guide you step-by-step through installation. Context-specific help is available by hitting F1 anywhere in the process. Configure one of your machines as a "server" and the other one as a "requester" (or, you can configure a single machine as a requester/server). Here's what you install on the "server" machine:

- The Base Operating System (OS/2).
- The LAN Requester (OS/2).
- The Communications Manager (OS/2 EE).
- The Database Manager configured as a Remote Data Services server machine (OS/2 EE).
- The Query Manager (OS/2 EE).
- The LAN Server Program (IBM OS/2 LAN Server).

Here's what you install on the "requester" machine:

- The Base Operating System (OS/2).
- The LAN Requester (OS/2).
- The Communications Manager (OS/2 EE).
- The Database Manager configured as a Remote Data Services requester machine (OS/2 EE).
- The Query Manager (OS/2 EE). This is optional.

Now you're all set up to run the programs in this book in a luxurious style.

Installing The Software Development Toolkit

If you plan to modify and compile the programs, you'll need the Software Development Toolkit, now known as the **Programming Information and Tools Package**. The Toolkit includes all the OS/2 C-language header files which contain: the function prototypes, data types, and the structures and constants needed to program the OS/2 and Dialog Manager APIs. Use the **INSTAID** utility to install the package. While you're at it, make sure to install the C language sample programs and the online documentation for the OS/2 API calls.

IBM C/2

If you plan to modify and recompile the programs, you'll also need a C compiler. Our programs were compiled using the IBM C/2 compiler and the C/2 MAKE utility. As of this writing the INSTAID utility does not work reliably with OS/2 1.2. We found that the easiest way to install C/2 is to use the **SETUP** command from the DOS box.

OS/2 EE Memory Requirements

The table below gives you a feeling for OS/2 and OS/2 EE's memory requirements. You can start out with a 3 MByte system in stand-alone Base Edition mode, and quickly work your way to a 10 MByte fully loaded Database and LAN Server machine. It all depends on your requirements. Make sure you refer to IBM's **Information and Planning Guide** for the latest official numbers.

Table 6-1. Memory Requirements for OS/2 EE Version 1.3.

OS/2 or OS/2 EE Function	Recommended Memory (MByte)
Operating System	
Base (Required)	1.5
Active Spooling (while printing)	0.3
High Performance File System	0.3
DOS compatibility box	0.5
System Performance Buffer	0.5
Communications Manager	
Base (required for all communications)	0.1
3270 terminal emulation	0.3
3270 host print	0.3
SNA gateway	0.1
ASCII terminal emulation	0.3
APPC	0.4
Host File Transfer	0.3
Database Manager	
Database Services (stand-alone)	1.3
Database Requester	0.5
Database Server	1.5
add for each concurrent process	0.15
Query Manager	1.6
LAN Requester	
LAN Requester	0.4
OS/2 LAN Server V 1.3 (separate product)	2.3

OS/2 EE Fixed Disk Requirements

The table below gives you a feeling for OS/2 and OS/2 EE's hard disk requirements. You can start out with a 20 MByte disk in stand-alone Base Edition mode and quickly work your way to a 100 MByte fully loaded Database and LAN Server machine. It all depends on your requirements. Make sure you refer to IBM's **Information and Planning Guide** for the latest official numbers.

Table 6-2. Disk Requirements for OS/2 EE Version 1.3.

OS/2 or OS/2 EE Function	Required Fixed Disk (MByte)
Operating System	
Base (required)	9.5
Base (optional)	3.5
Disk swapping (normal)	2.5
Communications Manager	
Base (required for all communications)	2.7
3270 terminal emulation	0.6
SNA gateway	0.2
ASCII terminal emulation	0.4
APPC	0.3
For each LAN adapter	0.3
Configuration Services	2.9
Terminal emulator keyboard remap	0.3
Programming Interfaces APIs	1.3
Database Manager	
Database Services (stand-alone)	3.0
Database Requester	2.4
Database Server	3.2
for each additional database	1.1
Query Manager	3.2
LAN Requester	
LAN Requester	4.6
OS/2 LAN Server V 1.3 (separate product)	6.2 (minimum)

Your Roadmap for Reading the Programs in this Book

Due to size limitations, there will be little opportunity in this book to explain C language programming basics. To understand the program listings, you should be reasonably familiar with C. On the other hand, we do not assume that you are familiar with OS/2 EE, so we will explain each new function when it is first encountered in a program and then reference it from there on.

Our explanation of the API will focus on the *essential* elements in each function. A book has the advantage over a technical reference, of not having the burden of presenting every last feature in a function. Because of the broad nature of OS/2 EE and our emphasis on client-server systems, we do not always have the luxury of grouping related API functions. An API function will be introduced at the point where it is first encountered in the development of a program. The advantage of this approach is that each function will be explained within the context where it is first used. The disadvantage, of course, is that not all related functions are grouped in one place. We compensate for this inconvenience by indexing all API references which, in itself, is a convenient way of reminding you of where you first encountered a function. The tutorials, however, cover the APIs by related area and, in many cases, present scenarios that show the interrelationships between the calls.

In most cases we will present you with the complete set of listings you will need to compile the programs. We also include the *make* file that is used to build the program. To follow a program, first take a quick look at the *make* file to understand what set of modules make up the code. Then, move straight to the **main()** procedure, which we've written in the form of an outline for the program. From the outline, you can follow the top-level functions that are usually listed in the order in which they appear within **main()**. Common functions that provide an underlying service are usually grouped together under a **helper** function sub-heading.

We are the first to admit that some chapters have listings that seem to go on forever. Much of those listings consist of header files, error recovery code, and the normal stuff that makes "real life" production programs fat. Remember, that this is a book about OS/2 EE as it gets used in production-level code. The tab you may have to pay for obtaining this level of code completeness is an occasional lengthy program listing. When you encounter one of those programs, you can avoid letting the "fat" get in your way by setting your focus on the overall workings of the program, while taking an occasional dip into the detail where you think you may need it. The programs were designed to provide you this kind of two-tier navigation into the code; so make sure you use it!

The OS/2 EE Application Programming Interface (API)

From the programmer's point of view OS/2 EE should be looked at as one giant, massively documented toolkit with a well designed programming interface. OS/2 EE's interface is much more consistent than MS-DOS's. For example, to obtain MS-DOS's services you had to place your parameters in registers and then issue an interrupt to the operating system. Error status from MS-DOS was returned through a variety of irregular schemes. In the place of the chaotic DOS interface, OS/2 offers an Application Programming Interface (API for short) written to work seamlessly with high-level languages like C. You invoke OS/2 services much the same way you call your procedures or functions. In both cases, parameters are passed through the stack and the error status is returned by the function call (OS/2 uses the 80286's AX register uniformly for error returns).

The base OS/2 API functions begin with a three letter prefix that identifies the general operating system category to which the function belongs. The OS/2 kernel functions have prefixes of **DOS** (OS/2 system), **VIO** (video I/O), **KBD** (keyboard), and **MOU** (mouse). The Presentation Manager adds new prefixes such as **WIN** (Windows) and **GPI** (Graphics Program Interface), etc.

In general, you will not have to concern yourself with OS/2 function declarations. Both IBM and Microsoft supply C header files with their toolkits. Including the appropriate header files with your programs will take care of your OS/2 function prototype definitions, as well as the definitions of constants, data types, structures, and macros.

You may, however, decide to write your own header files incorporating the structures and API functions you commonly use. This approach allows you to define your own data types (which may improve readability and portability) and you may save money by not having to purchase the toolkit. The example below will serve to demonstrate the convention you must follow if you decide to pre-declare your operating system calls. The OS/2 API prototype call to obtain the date and time would look like:

```
extern unsigned far pascal DosGetDateTime(struct DATETIME far *);
```

We will now explain what each of these keywords does:

- The **extern** directive specifies the use of the external storage class.
- The **unsigned** keyword denotes that the function returns an unsigned integer. Most of the OS/2 API functions are of type unsigned since they return the error code as an unsigned integer. Those functions that do not return error codes are of type void.
- The **far** directive is specified because the OS/2 API requires that all pointers passed as parameters be 32 bit addresses. Of course, if you are compiling your code using one of the large code memory models, then all your addresses will be far by default.
- The **pascal** keyword tells the C compiler to use the pascal calling convention instead of the C default when calling DosGetDateTime. The pascal calling convention requires that function parameters be placed on the stack starting from left to right. It also places the burden of removing the parameters from the stack to the function that got called; in this case, DosGetDateTime removes the function parameters from the stack before returning control to the calling procedure. Note that the C default does exactly the opposite.
- The **DATETIME** structure is already pre-defined by Microsoft and IBM in a header file. If you provide your own header files, you will have to match the type definitions for all the required data structures.

In this book we will generally include header files that come with the IBM Programmer's Toolkit. Occasionally we will introduce our own types to improve readability while referring you to the IBM originals.

The OS/2 Data Types

After a lot of deliberation, we decided to bite the bullet and follow the IBM-Microsoft data type conventions for OS/2. These are derived data types that replace the standard C types as shown in Table 6-3. So why are we introducing these new types instead of sticking to the familiar C types? Here's the benefits of using the OS/2 types:

- They are consistent with the OS/2 technical documentation and, more importantly, the OS/2 supplied header files.
- They provide more information regarding the purpose of an item than the C data type. This is especially the case for the Presentation Manager APIs.
- They make your programs more portable across system platforms: for example, your data types will remain valid with 32-bit OS/2 or a RISC version of OS/2.
- They shorten the function descriptions.
- They sometimes begin with letters that identify what the type is used for. For example, **P** identifies a far pointer; **U**, an unsigned variable; and **H**, a handle.

Table 6-3. A Sample of the Most Commonly Used OS/2 Data Types.

OS/2 Type	C Language Equivalent	Meaning
BOOL	unsigned short	16-bit Boolean value
BYTE	unsigned char	8-bit unsigned value
CHAR	char	8-bit signed value
UCHAR	unsigned char	8-bit unsigned value
INT	int	16-bit signed value
UINT	unsigned int	16-bit unsigned value
LONG	long	32-bit signed value
ULONG	unsigned long	32-bit unsigned value
PBYTE	unsigned byte far *	32-bit pointer to a BYTE value
PSZ	unsigned char far *	32-bit pointer to a null-terminated string
PCHAR	char far *	32-bit pointer to a string
PINT	int far *	32-bit pointer to an INT value
PLONG	long *	32-bit pointer to a LONG value
PVOID	void far *	32-bit pointer to a void value
TRUE	1	Predefined constant set to one
FALSE	0	Predefined constant set to zero
NULL	0	Predefined pointer set to zero
APIENTRY	pascal far	This is a type identifier for OS/2 API functions.

The "Official" DosGetDateTime

Here's the revised (and official toolkit version) of the API prototype call to obtain the date and time using the OS/2 data types:

```
USHORT APIENTRY DosGetDateTime(PDATETIME pdatetime);
```

If this looks strange and unfamiliar don't despair: you'll soon get used to it. You may find it easier to simply use the OS/2 types without paying attention to the equivalent basic C types.

DAEMON: OUR FIRST OS/2 PROGRAM

Now that we have spelled out the rules we're going to code by, let's move on and work our way through some live OS/2 program examples. We will start by exploring **DAEMON.C**, followed by **KILLER.C**. DAEMON.C is a simple OS/2 program that illustrates the workings of a time of day activated background task. It also illustrates the **VioPopUp** mechanism that it uses to communicate information to the foreground screen.

DAEMON.C: main()

DAEMON's **main**() function, listed in Figure 6-1, will serve as the outline for the program. Like any good C program, DAEMON starts out by including the various C library header files. Like any good OS/2 program DAEMON needs to include header material from **OS2.H**, which serves as the *master file* for a set of IBM (and Microsoft) provided include files that contain definitions for specific groups of OS/2 functions. These definitions include the OS/2 API declarations and OS/2 defined data types and structures.

To minimize the time required to process some of the header files, each function group can be *conditionally* included on the basis of whether a corresponding constant is defined within the program source file. To use a function within your program, you simply define the corresponding include constant using the **#define** directive before you include OS2.H. In DAEMON.C, we define the following include constants, before including OS2.H:

```
#define INCL_VIO                    /* include VIO api calls       */
#define INCL_KBD                    /* include KBD api calls       */
#define INCL_DOSDATETIME            /* include timer api calls     */
#define INCL_DOSPROCESS             /* for DosSleep, DosExitList   */
```

The final file to be included is **daemon.h**, listed in Figure 6-2. This file contains DAEMON's forward function declarations, the definitions of constants and data types, and the program's global variables.

The **main**() DAEMON procedure follows. You can see from reading it that DAEMON is a rather simple program:

1. It starts out by invoking **get_args**(), listed in Figure 6-3, which obtains the time of day when "Hello" is to be displayed.

2. It then calls **initialize_daemon()**, listed in Figure 6-4, to perform some initialization chores.
3. This is followed by a do forever loop that does the following:
   a. It calculates how long to wait before saying hello.
   b. It takes a nap for that duration of time. The function **wait_to_display_hello()**, listed in Figure 6-5, calculates how long DAEMON is to sleep and then puts the program to sleep for that time duration.
   c. It says "Hello World" whenever the time is right to do so. When the time is right, **tell_the_world_hello()**, listed in Figure 6-6, announces "Hello World" on the foreground screen via a pop-up.

Aside from the top level functions just mentioned, the DAEMON program also contains a set of common helper routines. The **print_error()** helper function, listed in Figure 6-7, is a pop-up adaptation of a generic print error function. The **daemon_exit()**, listed in Figure 6-8, is an illustration of the use of OS/2's **Exit Lists** for program termination.

```
/*****************************************************************************/
/*  PROGRAM NAME: DAEMON - a background task example                         */
/*                                                                           */
/*  PROGRAM DESCRIPTION:  This program demonstrates the use of a background  */
/*    task to tell the world Hello!                                          */
/*                                                                           */
/*  PROGRAM INVOCATION:    DAEMON time                                       */
/*****************************************************************************/
#include <process.h>                      /* For exit()                      */
#include <stdio.h>                        /* For sprintf()                   */
#include <string.h>                       /* For string functions            */

#define INCL_VIO                          /* include VIO api calls           */
#define INCL_KBD                          /* include KBD api calls           */
#define INCL_DOSDATETIME                  /* include timer api calls         */
#define INCL_DOSPROCESS                   /* for DosSleep, DosExitList       */
#include <os2.h>
#include "daemon.h"

/*-------------------------------------------------------------------------*/
/* Main routine.                                                             */
/*-------------------------------------------------------------------------*/
VOID main(USHORT argc, PCHAR argv[], PCHAR envp[])
{
  get_args(argc, argv);        /* read time information from command line    */

  initialize_daemon();

  do
    {
     wait_to_display_hello();  /* calculate time to wait, then sleep          */

     tell_the_world_hello();   /* show a pop-up, tell the world hello         */
    } while (TRUE); /* enddo */
} /* end main */
```

Figure 6-1. DAEMON.C: main().

DAEMON.H: The daemon.h Include File

The **daemon.h** include file is your garden variety C include file that contains the declarations of constants, forward declarations of procedures, and the global variables used in the program. The only strange encounter in **daemon.h** may be the special OS/2 type **PIDINFO**. The OS/2 types will be explained when we encounter the functions that use them.

```
/******************************************************************************/
/*  INCLUDE NAME: DAEMON - declarations for DAEMON program                    */
/******************************************************************************/
/*----------------------------------------------------------------------------*/
/* defines                                                                    */
/*----------------------------------------------------------------------------*/
                   /*-----------------------------------*/
                   /* function return values            */
                   /*-----------------------------------*/
#define GOOD              0
#define WARNING           1
#define FAILED           -1
/*----------------------------------------------------------------------------*/
/* Forward declarations of procedures in this module                          */
/*----------------------------------------------------------------------------*/
                   /*-----------------------------------*/
                   /* top level routines                */
                   /*-----------------------------------*/
VOID   get_args(USHORT, PCHAR []);
VOID   initialize_daemon(VOID);
VOID   wait_to_display_hello(VOID);
VOID   tell_the_world_hello(VOID);
                     /*-----------------------------------*/
                     /* Miscellaneous helper routines     */
                     /*-----------------------------------*/
VOID   print_error(USHORT, PCHAR , PCHAR , USHORT);
VOID   FAR daemon_exit(USHORT);
/*----------------------------------------------------------------------------*/
/* Global variables/type definitions for this module                          */
/*----------------------------------------------------------------------------*/
ULONG    hello_hours,
         hello_minutes,
         hello_seconds;               /* time to display hello              */

PIDINFO  daemon_pid;

USHORT   rc;                          /* return code variable               */
USHORT   i;                           /* loop counter variable              */
```

Figure 6-2. Daemon Program Include File.

DAEMON.C: get_args()

The **get_args()** procedure listed below uses the C library **sscanf** function to format and set the time of day variables based on the command line argument that is passed when the DAEMON program is invoked.

```
/*--------------------------------------------------------------------------*/
/* read time from command line                                              */
/*--------------------------------------------------------------------------*/
VOID get_args(USHORT argc, PCHAR argv[])
{
  if ((argc != 2) ||
      (sscanf(argv[1]," %lu:%lu:%lu ",
       &hello_hours, &hello_minutes, &hello_seconds) != 3))
     { printf("Enter command as follows: DAEMON hh:mm:ss \n");
       exit(FAILED);
     }
} /* end get_args */
```

Figure 6-3. The get_args() Procedure.

DAEMON.C: initialize_daemon()

The **initialize_daemon()** function, listed in Figure 6-4, introduces our first two OS/2 API calls: **DosExitList** and **DosGetPID**. The **DosExitList** function is used here to add the **daemon_exit()** function to the exit list. DAEMON, being an independent background task, is acutely aware that it can be killed at any time by a DAEMON killer or through natural causes. By registering **daemon_exit()** with OS/2, DAEMON will be notified of its pending death and will be given a chance to run one last procedure **daemon_exit()** before it is put to eternal rest. Obviously, exit functions can be put to good uses, such as program clean-up. We recommend that you make it a practice, under OS/2, to register a "last will" at the start of every program. We explain the workings of **DosExitList** API in detail in the section below.

The **DosGetPID** API call is used by DAEMON to obtain its process ID or **PID**. The **PID** is like a "passport number" that is used to uniquely identify a process. In the next chapter, we will show how **DosGetInfoSeg** can also be used for obtaining the **PID**, as well as a mass of other OS/2 information. The **DosGetPID** API service is described in "DosGetPID" on page 122. We recommend you read the API descriptions carefully *before and after* you've gone through the code, because this is where you'll find the detailed information on how to use OS/2's programming services.

DosExitList

The **DosExitList** API specifies a list of exit routines used for process clean-up. Exit lists allow you to set up routines that are run just before a process terminates (either normally or abnormally). You could set up exit lists to: clear semaphores, deallocate memory, write to a trace log, reset hardware, etc. Exit lists will run even if your process gets killed unexpectedly. They are part of the *defensive* programming you should provide in a multitasking environment where you need to protect yourself from others. The prototype for this call is:

```
DosExitList(USHORT       action_flag,                /* 1=add, 2=delete, 3=exit*/
            PVOID        proc(USHORT   term_code)); /* Exit routine address   */
```

A description of the parameters follows:

- The ***action_flag*** parameter specifies the action to perform on the exit list. This parameter can be one of the following values:

Value	Meaning
1	Add procedure to exit list
2	Remove procedure from exit list
3	Current exit procedure executed, move on to the next exit list procedure or terminate program if none are left.

- The ***proc*** parameter points to an exit list procedure, which has one input parameter, no return value, and must be declared with the *far* attribute. The input parameter to the procedure contains a termination code that indicates the reason why the process terminated. The termination code values have the same meanings as those for **DosExecPgm** and **DosCWait** and can be any of the following: normal exit, hard error, trap, and process killed. The exit list procedure should carry out its tasks and then call **DosExitList** with the action_flag parameter set to the value 3. This directs OS/2 to call the next procedure on the list. When all procedures are executed the process terminates. Here are some ground-rules for writing exit list procedures:
  1. Keep your procedures short and fail-safe and take into account that OS/2 has already terminated all the other threads in the process except for your current thread.
  2. An incorrectly constructed exit procedure will not necessarily crash the operating system; but you may not be able to exit from the process, thereby causing a degradation in performance.
  3. Do not issue a return or call **DosExit** from your exit procedure. You should always end your procedure by issuing a call to **DosExitList** with the action_flag set to 3, so that OS/2 can transfer control to the next exit list procedure.
  4. Do not issue calls from an exit procedure to **DosExecPgm** or to **DosCreateThread**.

DosGetPID

The **DosGetPID** API call is used to obtain the current process ID, thread ID, and the process ID of the parent process. The prototype for this call is:

```
DosGetPID(PIDINFO far  *pidinfo);    /* pointer to a struct receiving ids */
```

A description of the parameters follows:

- The ***pidinfo*** parameter points to the **PIDINFO** structure that receives the process identifiers. The PIDINFO structure has the following form:

```
typedef struct _PIDINFO {
    PID pid;                    /* current process' process ID */
    TID tid;                    /* current process' thread ID  */
    PID pidParent;              /* process ID of the parent    */
} PIDINFO;
```

```
/*------------------------------------------------------------------*/
/* initialize daemon program                                        */
/*------------------------------------------------------------------*/
VOID initialize_daemon(VOID)
{
  rc = DosExitList(1,(PFNEXITLIST) daemon_exit);
  if (rc)
     { print_error(rc,"establishing DosExitList",__FILE__,__LINE__);
       exit(FAILED);
     }

  rc = DosGetPID(&daemon_pid);
  if (rc)
     { print_error(rc,"getting DosGetPID",__FILE__,__LINE__);
       exit(FAILED);
     }
} /* end initialize_daemon */
```

Figure 6-4. The initialize_daemon() Procedure.

DAEMON.C: wait_to_display_hello()

The **wait_to_display_hello()** function, listed in Figure 6-5, first calculates the difference in milliseconds between the time when DAEMON is to make its "Hello" statement to the world and the current time. It then puts DAEMON to sleep for that entire time duration. Two new OS/2 API calls are introduced: **DosGetDateTime** and **DosSleep**. The **DosGetDateTime** API call, described below, is used to obtain the current date and time. We will show, in the next chapter, how **DosGetInfoSeg** can also be used for obtaining the date and time as well as a mass of other system information. The **DosSleep** API call, also described below, is used to suspend the execution of DAEMON until the time comes to say "Hello."

DosGetDateTime

The **DosGetDateTime** API call, returns the current date and time maintained by the operating system. The prototype for this call is:

```
DosGetDateTime(DATETIME far  *datetime);  /* pointer to structure     */
```

A description of the parameters follows:

- The ***datetime*** parameter points to the **DATETIME** structure that receives the date and time information. The DATETIME structure has the following form:

```
typedef struct _DATETIME {
    UCHAR   hours;                      /* current hour                */
    UCHAR   minutes;                    /* current minute              */
    UCHAR   seconds;                    /* current second              */
    UCHAR   hundredths;                 /* current hundredths of a second */
    UCHAR   day;                        /* current day                 */
    UCHAR   month;                      /* current month               */
    USHORT  year;                       /* current year                */
    SHORT   timezone;                   /* minutes of time west of GMT */
    UCHAR   weekday;                    /* current day of week         */
} DATETIME;
```

The day of week value is based on Sunday being zero.

Note: These variables may also be obtained by calling DosGetInfoSeg instead of this function. We will introduce DosGetInfoSeg in the next chapter.

DosSleep

The **DosSleep** API call suspends the current thread for the specified time period. The actual sleep time may be off by a clock tick or two, depending on the execution status of other threads running in the system. The prototype for this call is:

```
DosSleep(ULONG          delay);        /* delay time in milliseconds */
```

A description of the parameters follows:

- The ***delay*** parameter specifies the sleep interval in milliseconds. If the time is set to zero, the thread gives up the remainder of its current time slice allowing other ready threads of equal priority to run.

DAEMON.C: tell_the_world_hello()

The **tell_the_world_hello()** procedure, listed in Figure 6-6, uses OS/2's highly efficient **VIO** subsystem to write to the screen. The efficiency of **VIO** services are such that they have removed the need for an application to manipulate the video hardware directly as was the case with MS-DOS. In the present situation, we are faced with the problem of finding a way to allow DAEMON, (a background task that does not have its own screen-group) to gain access to a screen and keyboard to say "hello." Fortu-

```
/*-----------------------------------------------------------------------*/
/* calculate time to wait before Hello is to appear, wait that time       */
/*-----------------------------------------------------------------------*/
VOID wait_to_display_hello(VOID)
{
  DATETIME date_time;                    /* structure for DosGetDateTime   */
  ULONG    current_time_seconds;         /* current time in seconds        */
  ULONG    hello_time_seconds;           /* time to display hello in seconds*/
  ULONG    wait_time_seconds;            /* time to wait in seconds        */
  ULONG    wait_time_msecs;              /* time to wait in milliseconds   */

  DosGetDateTime(&date_time);
  current_time_seconds = date_time.hours * 3600 + date_time.minutes * 60
                       + date_time.seconds;
  hello_time_seconds = hello_hours * 3600 + hello_minutes * 60 + hello_seconds;

  if (hello_time_seconds > current_time_seconds)
     wait_time_seconds  = hello_time_seconds - current_time_seconds;
  else
     {  wait_time_seconds = 24 * 3600     /* seconds in 1 day                */
                          - (hello_time_seconds - current_time_seconds);
     } /* endif */

  wait_time_msecs = wait_time_seconds * 1000;

  rc = DosSleep(wait_time_msecs);
  if (rc)
     { print_error(rc,"during DosSleep", __FILE__,__LINE__);
       exit(FAILED);
     }
} /* end wait_to_display_hello */
```

Figure 6-5. The wait_to_display_hello() Procedure.

nately, **VIO**, offers a means by which the background process can temporarily pop up in the foreground using the VIO API calls **VioPopUp** and **VioEndPopUp**, for activating a pop-up program. The two API calls are described in "VioPopUp" on page 126 and "VioEndPopUp" on page 127. Once the pop-up mode is activated, **tell_the_world_hello()** uses the **VioWrtCharStrAtt** API call to write to the screen. This call, which is described in "VioWrtCharStrAtt" on page 127, offers considerable control over how text is written to the screen, including control over the color attribute and the position.

While we're on the subject of pop-ups, you may be tempted to think of a pop-up as being comparable to an MS-DOS terminate-stay-resident program or *TSR*. This is not quite the case. Under MS-DOS, TSRs provide a multitasking element in a single-tasking environment. Under OS/2 you don't need TSRs, since you can run applications in different screen groups and switch between screen groups whenever you like. This is even more the case under PM where a single screen group can simultaneously display and run multiple windows. In this sense, every OS/2 program can be thought of as a TSR. Pop-ups, on the other hand, should be used only in exceptional conditions, since other OS/2 processes cannot be switched into the foreground during the pop-up. The pop-up must be designed to perform its action and relinquish control of the screen as quickly as possible. The best use of pop-ups is for displaying error alerts and for DETACHED daemon programs, that otherwise make very little use of the screen and keyboard facilities.

The **KbdCharIn** API call used by **tell_the_world_hello()** is a good example of the power OS/2 packs into its **KBD** subsystem. Not only does this function return the ASCII code of the character, it also tells you the status of the shift keys and the time the key was pressed. The **KbdCharIn** API call is described in "KbdCharIn" on page 128. The **tell_the_world_hello()** procedure calls the **DosExit** OS/2 API for terminating DAEMON. This exit function can be used to return information to a parent process. The capabilities of **DosExit**, are explained in "DosExit" on page 129.

VioPopUp

The **VioPopUp** API call allocates a pop-up display screen. It is used primarily by background processes to temporarily take over the screen and keyboard. When the interaction is complete, the previous screen is restored by issuing **VioEndPopUp**. While a video pop-up is in effect, all video calls from the previous foreground session are blocked until the process that issued VioPopUp issues VioEndPopUp. If you're thinking of using pop-ups, don't forget to take into account the disrupting effect frequent interruptions may have on the foreground application. The prototype for this call is:

```
VioPopUp(USHORT        *wait_flags,     /* pointer to flag word        */
         USHORT         handle);        /* video handle                */
```

A description of the parameters follows:

- The ***wait_flags*** parameter points to a flag variable. The flag contents specify whether the pop-up is to be opaque or transparent, and whether the function should wait for an open pop-up to close or return immediately with an error code if a pop-up screen already exists. There can be only one pop-up in existence at any time. The flag word bits are defined as follows:

```
Bits   Description
----   -----------
0      0 = No-wait- return with an error code if pop-up already exists.
       1 = Wait- if a pop-up screen already exists.

1      0 = Opaque Mode.  Sets the screen to 25 lines by 80 columns of
       text, clears the screen, and positions the cursor at the upper-
       left corner.
       1 = Transparent Mode.  If the video mode of the outgoing fore-
       ground session is text the screen remains unchanged.
       Otherwise the pop-up request is refused.

       OS/2 is responsible for saving and restoring the display buffer
       of the foreground session.  This is true for both modes.

2-15   Reserved, set to zero.
```

- The ***handle*** parameter is a presentation handle used by PM applications. It is NULL otherwise.

Note: DosExecPgm cannot be issued by a process during a pop-up, and the process must not access or modify the physical video buffer.

VioEndPopUp

The **VioEndPopUp** API call, closes a pop-up screen and restores the physical video buffer to its previous contents. The pop-up may only be closed by the process that opened it. The prototype for this call is:

```
VioEndPopUp(USHORT          handle);        /* video handle                */
```

A description of the parameters follows:

- The ***handle*** parameter is a presentation handle used by PM applications. It is NULL otherwise.

VioWrtCharStrAtt

The **VioWrtCharStrAtt** call writes a character string to a screen location using the specified attribute. The prototype for this call is:

```
VioWrtCharStrAtt(PCHAR    charstr,       /* character string            */
                 USHORT   length,        /* length of string            */
                 USHORT   row_x,         /* row to start writing        */
                 USHORT   column_y,      /* column to start writing     */
                 PCHAR    attr,          /* pointer to attribute byte   */
                 USHORT   handle);       /* video handle                */
```

A description of the parameters follows:

- The ***charstr*** parameter points to the character string you want to write. If the string is longer than the current line, the function continues writing at the start of the next line, but it does not go past the end of the screen.
- The ***length*** parameter specifies the length of the string in bytes.
- The ***row_x*** parameter specifies the row at which to start writing the string.
- The ***column_y*** parameter specifies the column at which to start writing the string.
- The ***attr*** parameter points to the display attribute of the string. Here's the structure of the attribute byte:

```
Key to bits: B = Blinking bit
             I = Intensify bit

             fff = foreground color
             bbb = background color

              7   6   5   4   3   2   1   0
             +---+---+---+---+---+---+---+---+
             | B | b | b | b | I | f | f | f |
             +---+---+---+---+---+---+---+---+
                  0   0   0       0   0   0      No display
                  0   0   0       0   0   1      Underline
                  0   0   0       1   1   1      Normal
                  1   1   1       0   0   0      Reverse Video
                  x   x   x       x   x   x      Colors
```

- The ***handle*** parameter is a presentation handle used by PM applications. It is NULL otherwise.

KbdCharIn

The **KbdCharIn** API call reads the character and scan-code information from a logical keyboard. The keystroke information includes the ASCII value of the key, the scan code, the state of the various shift keys, and the system time when the key was pressed. The function does not echo the characters it reads. The prototype for this call is:

```
KbdCharIn(KBDKEYINFO far  *kbdinfo,    /* pointer to KBDKEYINFO structure */
          USHORT           wait_flag,  /* 0=wait for character, 1=no wait */
          USHORT           hkbd);      /* keyboard handle, usually 0      */
```

A description of the parameters follows:

- The ***kbdinfo*** parameter points to a **KBDKEYINFO** structure where the keyboard information is placed. Here's what the structure looks like:

```
typedef struct _KBDKEYINFO {
        UCHAR    chChar;     /* ASCII character code                     */
        UCHAR    chScan;     /* Scan Code                                */
        UCHAR    fbStatus;   /* State of the character for NLS           */
        UCHAR    bNlsShift;  /* Reserved (must equal 0)                  */
        USHORT   fsState;    /* state of the shift keys                  */
        ULONG    time;       /* time stamp of key stroke (ms since ipl)  */
        }KBDKEYINFO;
```

The *chChar* field returns the ASCII value of the key pressed by translating the *chScan* field. The field is set to zero when it retrieves an extended ASCII code, such as when the ALT key and a character key are pressed simultaneously or when a non-shift special key (such as a function key) is pressed. In such situations, the scan code should be read to get the extended ASCII or special key value. The *chScan* field returns the scan code provides an unambiguous indication of the key that was pressed based on its position on the keyboard. But it does not report the state of the shift keys. The *fbStatus* field is used in National Languages. The *fsState* field returns the status of the various shift keys. The *time* field returns the time in milliseconds when a key was pressed and can be used to measure the time duration between characters typed.

- The ***wait_flag*** parameter specifies if the API is to wait for keystroke information if there is no character information. Wait suspends the thread until a key is pressed. The *no wait* option causes the API call to return immediately with whatever keystroke information is present. The value of the *fbstatus* field returns zero if no keystroke is received in the no wait option. Warning: A thread in the foreground session that repeatedly polls the keyboard with KbdCharIn (with no wait) can prevent all regular priority class threads from executing. If polling must be used and a minimal amount of other processing is being performed, the thread should periodically yield to the CPU by issuing a DosSleep call.
- The ***hkbd*** parameter identifies the logical keyboard. It is usually set to zero unless your application makes use of the **KbdOpen** function.

DosExit

The **DosExit** API call ends a thread or a process and all its threads. The prototype for this call is:

```
DosExit(USHORT   terminate_action,    /* Current thread or process  */
        USHORT   exit_code);          /* Any exit code for parent   */
```

A description of the parameters follows:

- The ***terminate_action*** parameter specifies what to terminate. It is set to zero to terminate the current thread only. It is set to one to terminate the current process and all its threads.
- The ***exit_code*** parameter specifies the program's exit code. This is an arbitrary number sent to the parent process. If there is any interest, the parent process can retrieve the exit code through **DosCWait**. By convention, use zero to indicate an OK return. Use positive numbers to indicate an error type. If you really want to get fancy, use negative numbers to indicate warnings!

```
/*--------------------------------------------------------------------------*/
/* Create popup, display hello message, wait for user key press, then end.   */
/*--------------------------------------------------------------------------*/
VOID tell_the_world_hello(VOID)
{
  USHORT wait_flags = 0;
  BYTE   attribute  = 0x71;            /* blue on grey                      */
  USHORT row        =  7;
  USHORT column     = 27;
  static CHAR   *hello_msg[] =  {"┌─────────────────────────┐",
                                 "│      Hello World!!      │",
                                 "│                         │",
                                 "│ The time is             │",
                                 "│                         │",
                                 "│ Daemon PID =            │",
                                 "│                         │",
                                 "│ Press Q/q to quit.      │",
                                 "│ Press any other key to  │",
                                 "│ enable Daemon again.    │",
                                 "└─────────────────────────┘",
                                 ""};
  CHAR   hello_time[10];
  CHAR   pid[6];
  KBDKEYINFO key;

  /*----------------------------*/
  /* create the popup           */
  /*----------------------------*/
  rc = VioPopUp(&wait_flags, 0L);

  /*----------------------------*/
  /* display the message        */
  /*----------------------------*/
  i = 0;
  do
   {
    VioWrtCharStrAtt(hello_msg[i], strlen(hello_msg[i]),
                     row+i, column, &attribute, 0);
    ++i;
   } while ( strcmp(hello_msg[i],"") != 0  ); /* enddo */
  sprintf(hello_time,"%lu:%lu:%lu",hello_hours, hello_minutes, hello_seconds);
  VioWrtCharStrAtt(hello_time, strlen(hello_time),
                   row + 3, column + 15, &attribute, 0);
  sprintf(pid,"%u",daemon_pid.pid);
  VioWrtCharStrAtt(pid, strlen(pid), row + 5, column + 15, &attribute, 0);

  /*----------------------------*/
  /* wait for a key press       */
  /*----------------------------*/
  KbdCharIn(&key,0,0);

  /*----------------------------*/
  /* end the popup              */
  /*----------------------------*/
  VioEndPopUp(0);
```

Figure 6-6 (Part 1 of 2). The tell_the_world_hello() Procedure.

```
    /*-------------------------------------*/
    /* re-enable or not?                   */
    /*-------------------------------------*/
    if ((key.chChar == 'Q') || (key.chChar == 'q'))
       DosExit(1,1);                    /* kill all threads, return code=1 */

  } /* end tell_the_world_hello */
```

Figure 6-6 (Part 2 of 2). The tell_the_world_hello() Procedure.

DAEMON.C: print_error()

The **print_error()** helper function, listed in Figure 6-7, records useful debug information such as the error number, the error description, and the name and line number of the source code file where the error occurred. Both the IBM and Microsoft C compilers maintain two predefined preprocessor symbols, **__FILE__** and **__LINE__**, which refer to the current input file name and the current line number being processed by the compiler. A failing procedure uses the preprocessor symbols to obtain the source code file and line number where the error occurs; it then passes these numbers to **print_error()** as parameters.

We introduce a new OS/2 API call that extends our **VIO** repertoire, **VioWrtTTY**. Since error messages are variable in length, the **VioWrtTTY** is a better fit in this situation than the previously encountered **VioWrtCharStrAtt** call which requires a row/column location. The **VioWrtTTY** uses the cursor as its starting point and carries the cursor along with it. This leaves the cursor in the correct position for the next screen call. The description of **VioWrtTTY** is given below

VioWrtTTY

The **VioWrtTTY** call writes a character string to a screen starting at the current cursor position. At the completion of the write, the cursor is at the first position beyond the end of the string. The prototype for this call is:

```
VioWrtTTY(PCHAR     string,              /* pointer to string     */
          USHORT    length,              /* length of string      */
          USHORT    handle);             /* video handle          */
```

A description of the parameters follows:

- The ***string*** parameter points to the character string that will be written to the screen.
- The ***length*** parameter specifies the length in bytes of the character string.
- The ***handle*** parameter is a presentation handle used by PM applications. It is NULL otherwise.

```
/*---------------------------------------------------------------------------*/
/* Error Display Routine                                                     */
/*---------------------------------------------------------------------------*/
VOID print_error(USHORT Error, PCHAR msg, PCHAR file, USHORT line)
{
  CHAR   error_msg[80];
  USHORT wait_flags = 0;
  BYTE   attribute  = 0x47;          /* grey on red                         */
  USHORT row        = 0;
  USHORT column     = 0;
  KBDKEYINFO key;

  /*--------------------------*/
  /* display the error message  */
  /*--------------------------*/
  VioPopUp(&wait_flags, 0);
  sprintf(error_msg, "Error %d detected while %s at line %d in file %s.\n",
        Error, msg, line, file);
  VioWrtTTY(error_msg, strlen(error_msg), 0);

  /*--------------------------*/
  /* wait for a key press       */
  /*--------------------------*/
  KbdCharIn(&key,0,0);

  /*--------------------------*/
  /* end the popup              */
  /*--------------------------*/
  VioEndPopUp(0);

} /* end print_error */
```

Figure 6-7. The print_error() Helper Routine.

DAEMON.C: daemon_exit()

The **daemon_exit()** function, listed below, gets executed as part of the previously setup **DosExitList**. This is DAEMON's "last will" that gets executed by OS/2 just before it terminates DAEMON. Not unexpectedly, this is a sentimental occasion for which DAEMON uses most of the **VIO** calls we have just learned to say "Good bye World." The grand exit gets performed by issuing a **DosExitList** (as described in "DosExitList" on page 121) with the action_flag set to 3. This tells OS/2 that it can now transfer control to the next exit list procedure, which in this case is non-existent, so in effect DAEMON gets terminated.

```
/*-------------------------------------------------------------------*/
/* Exit Routine                                                      */
/*-------------------------------------------------------------------*/
VOID FAR daemon_exit(USHORT exit_type)
{
  USHORT wait_flags = 0;
  BYTE   attribute  = 0x71;          /* blue on grey                 */
  USHORT row        = 10;
  USHORT column     = 27;
  static CHAR   *exit_msg[] =   {"┌─────────────────────┐",
                                 "│ Good-bye world!     │",
                                 "│                     │",
                                 "│  Press any key...   │",
                                 "└─────────────────────┘",
                                 ""};
  KBDKEYINFO key;

  /*-----------------------------*/
  /* display the error message   */
  /*-----------------------------*/
  VioPopUp(&wait_flags, 0);

  /*-----------------------------*/
  /* display the exit message    */
  /*-----------------------------*/
  i = 0;
  do
   {
    VioWrtCharStrAtt(exit_msg[i], strlen(exit_msg[i]),
                     row+i, column, &attribute, 0);
    ++i;
   } while ( strcmp(exit_msg[i],"") != 0  ); /* enddo */

  /*-----------------------------*/
  /* wait for a key press        */
  /*-----------------------------*/
  KbdCharIn(&key,0,0);

  /*-----------------------------*/
  /* end the popup               */
  /*-----------------------------*/
  VioEndPopUp(0);

  DosExitList(3, (void far *) 0);
} /* end daemon_exit */
```

Figure 6-8. The daemon_exit() Helper Routine.

KILLER: OUR SECOND OS/2 PROGRAM

We are now ready for our second OS/2 program, **KILLER.C**, a program whose sole purpose in life is to kill daemon programs. DAEMON by now is an old and intimate friend, so you may ask why are we introducing this killer? Well, we too like DAEMON and are not too fond of homicidal maniac program-killers, but there may come a time when you may want to clear your machine of some unwanted DETACHED daemons and so we offer you KILLER. The good news is that killer is a very short program, which should take less than five minutes of your reading time.

KILLER.C: main()

As usual we start with the **main()** program listing, see Figure 6-9. At the top we have the usual C and OS/2 include files. Notice that we've introduced a new *include flag*:

```
#define INCL_DOSPROCESS          /* for DosSleep, DosExitList          */
```

As is to be expected, we have a **killer.h** include file, which is listed in Figure 6-10, and which does not contain any startling new information.

The KILLER **main()** procedure, which serves as our program outline consists of two functions: **get_args()** listed in Figure 6-11 and **kill_the_process()** listed in Figure 6-12. The first function, **get_args()**, simply obtains the **PID** of the process we're trying to kill. The actual killing gets done by **kill_the_process()**, which introduces the one new OS/2 call in the program. Finally, KILLER makes use of a new **print_error()**, listed in Figure 6-13, which uses the **printf()** C library function. This is because KILLER executes as a foreground task and has the screen to itself, and the need for pop-ups has been removed. We said it would take less than five minutes of reading and we're almost there!

```
/*****************************************************************************/
/*  PROGRAM NAME: KILLER - a kill process example                            */
/*                                                                           */
/*  PROGRAM DESCRIPTION:  This program demonstrates the use of               */
/*    DosKillProcess to kill a process.                                      */
/*                                                                           */
/*  PROGRAM INVOCATION:    KILLER process-id                                 */
/*****************************************************************************/
#include <process.h>                 /* For exit()                           */
#include <stdio.h>                   /* For sprintf()                        */
#include <string.h>                  /* For string functions                 */

#define INCL_DOSPROCESS              /* for DosSleep, DosExitList            */
#include <os2.h>
#include "killer.h"

/*---------------------------------------------------------------------------*/
/* Main routine.                                                             */
/*---------------------------------------------------------------------------*/
VOID main(USHORT argc, PCHAR argv[], PCHAR envp[])
{
  get_args(argc, argv);         /* read process id from command line        */

  kill_the_process();           /* kill the process                         */

} /* end main */
```

Figure 6-9. KILLER.C main().

KILLER.C: The killer.h Include File

```
/*************************************************************************/
/*  INCLUDE NAME: KILLER - declarations for KILLER program              */
/*************************************************************************/
/*______________________________________________________________________*/
/* defines                                                              */
/*______________________________________________________________________*/
                   /*_____________________________*/
                   /* function return values      */
                   /*_____________________________*/
#define GOOD                0
#define WARNING             1
#define FAILED             -1
/*______________________________________________________________________*/
/* Forward declarations of procedures in this module                    */
/*______________________________________________________________________*/
                   /*_____________________________*/
                   /* top level routines          */
                   /*_____________________________*/
VOID   get_args(USHORT, PCHAR []);
VOID   kill_the_process(VOID);
                     /*_____________________________*/
                     /* Miscellaneous helper routines */
                     /*_____________________________*/
VOID   print error(USHORT, PCHAR , PCHAR , USHORT);
/*______________________________________________________________________*/
/* Global variables/type definitions for this module                    */
/*______________________________________________________________________*/
                   /*_____________________________*/
                   /* process variable            */
                   /*_____________________________*/
USHORT      process_id;             /* time to display hello       */
RESULTCODES term_result;            /* termination result code     */
PID         term_processid;         /* terminating process id      */
                   /*_____________________________*/
                   /* misc. variables             */
                   /*_____________________________*/
USHORT   rc;                       /* return code variable         */
USHORT   i;                        /* loop counter variable        */
```

Figure 6-10. KILLER.H Include File.

KILLER.C: get_args()

```
/*--------------------------------------------------------------------*/
/* read process ID from command line                                   */
/*--------------------------------------------------------------------*/
VOID get_args(USHORT argc, PCHAR argv[])
{
  if (argc != 2)
     { printf("Enter command as follows: KILLER process-id \n");
       exit(FAILED);
     }

  process_id = atoi(argv[1]);

} /* end get_args */
```

Figure 6-11. KILLER.C: get_args().

KILLER.C: kill_the_process()

This is the function that contains the new OS/2 API call that KILLER introduces. Not too surprising given the context, it is called **DosKillProcess**. A full explanation of its workings is given below.

DosKillProcess

The **DosKillProcess** API call kills the specified process with the option of terminating all of its descendants. The prototype for this call is:

```
DosKillProcess(USHORT   scope_flag,      /* Scope of killing      */
               USHORT   processID);      /* ID of process to kill */
```

A description of the parameters follows:

- The ***scope_flag*** parameter specifies what to kill. Setting it to zero kills the specified process and all of its descendants. Setting it to one only kills the specified process.
- The ***processID*** parameter specifies the ID of the process to be killed.

```
/*----------------------------------------------------------------*/
/* kill the process number indicated by the user.                 */
/*----------------------------------------------------------------*/
VOID kill_the_process(VOID)
{
  rc = DosKillProcess(1,            /* only this process          */
                      process_id);  /* process id number          */
  if (rc)
     { print_error(rc,"killing a process",__FILE__,__LINE__);
       exit(FAILED);
     }

} /* end kill_the_process */
```

Figure 6-12. KILLER.C: kill_the_process().

KILLER.C: print_error()

```
/*----------------------------------------------------------------*/
/* Error Display Routine                                          */
/*----------------------------------------------------------------*/
VOID
print_error(USHORT Error, PCHAR msg, PCHAR file, USHORT line)
{
 printf("Error %u (0x%x) detected while %s at line %u in file %s.\n",
         Error, Error, msg, line, file);
} /* end print_error */
```

Figure 6-13. KILLER.C: print_error().

MAKE: A BRIEF TUTORIAL

This short tutorial covers the majority of the MAKE language constructs that will be used by the *make* files in this book. The IBM C/2 compiler provides a MAKE utility that is used to automate the code production process. You will discover MAKE to be a great time saver for programs that consist of several source files. This is because the utility only performs those steps that are necessary to produce an up-to-date version of a program. MAKE is smart enough to build the program using only the components that changed since the last time the program was compiled. MAKE takes a text file as its input. The input file contains a series of commands, rules, and macros. MAKE's goal is to create one or more executable files from one or more source code files using the rules it was given.

Target Rule Blocks

The heart of the *make* file are the target rule blocks that specify the conditions for something to happen, followed by what is to happen. The syntax for these target rule blocks is:

```
target-list: dependent-list
  [command]
  [command]
```

The first line consists of a list of *target* file names, followed by a colon, followed by a list of dependent files. If one of the dependent files is older than any of the target files, the rule fires and the associated commands get executed. A command usually specifies an action to be taken to generate the target. An action is the execution of an operating system command or a program.

Inference Rules

If you do not specify any commands, MAKE searches for an *inference rule* to build the target files. An inference rule is a way of telling MAKE how to produce a file with one type of extension from a file with the same name and a second type of extension. It's a lazy way out of having to specify explicit commands for each target list. The following format is used to specify an inference rule:

```
.dependent-ext.target_ext:
  command
  [command]
```

Inference rules start with a period in column one, followed by the dependent extension, followed by a period, followed by the target extension, followed by a colon, followed by the command to be executed on the dependent files to produce the "target" file. More than one command can be given, but each must be listed on a separate line. Commands cannot start in the first column.

Comments

You can place **comments** in a *make* file by starting them with the comment character #. The following samples show how to use comments:

```
daemon.exe:  daemon.obj        #valid comment
# valid comment starts in first column
  link daemon.obj;             # invalid, comments cannot be in command line
```

Macros

MAKE supports *macro definitions* which associate a symbolic name on the left side of an equal sign with the value on the right side of the equal sign. Macros can be used to change values in a *make* file without editing every line that uses the particular value. A macro is invoked by preceding the macro name with a $ sign. Macro names that are longer than one character, require parentheses around them. The following is an example of the use of macro called **program**:

```
program = daemon
$(program).obj = $(program).c
 CC $(program),$(program),$(program),$(program)
```

MAKE recognizes some special macros, two of which we use extensively in our *make* files. The first macro symbol (you'll see a lot of symbols) is **$***, which means "substitute the target file name without an extension." The second ubiquitous macro symbol is, **$****, which means "substitute the complete list of dependents."

Build Goals

The IBM C/2 MAKE utility, starting with Versions 1.1, uses new forms of meta-rules for determining what needs to be built. In the old days, MAKE would search through the *make* file sequentially and evaluate each target rule-block in order. With the new version, when you invoke MAKE, the targets you specify in the command line are updated regardless of their positions in the file. If you do not specify a target, MAKE updates or builds the first target in the file. If you need to build multiple targets, then you must either pass the name of each target in the command line, or you can make your first target rule block a pseudo target with all the other targets as its dependents list. The following is an example of a pseudo target rule:

```
all: daemon.exe killer.exe
```

Here, **all** is the name of a dummy file that does not exist, and daemon.exe and killer.exe are the names of the two separate programs that we want to build with this one *make* file. This is how MAKE goes about executing this rule: in order to build **all**, MAKE has to first instantiate the build rules for daemon.exe and killer.exe, which is exactly what we want it to do for us. In this manner, you can specify all the files you want to build and the order in which you want them built.

MAKE as a Documentation Tool

We find that *make* files serve as an excellent source of program documentation. A good practice when looking at a new program, is to start with its *make* file, and use it to understand the relationship between the different modules that make up a program. We will encourage this practice by starting all our programming chapters with the *make* file for that particular program. Our *make* files have the same name as the program they create, with the extension (.MAK). If more than one program is produced, the name will be that of the first program created.

DAEMON.MAK

DAEMON.MAK, see Figure 6-14, is the *make* file used to create DAEMON.EXE and KILLER.EXE. You can invoke the MAKE program from the OS/2 command line by entering:

```
MAKE DAEMON.MAK
```

DAEMON.MAK contains many of the constructs you will encounter in the *make* files presented in this book. We will walk very carefully through this *make* file in the next section. The idea is to take an exhaustive look at MAKE, so as not to have to explain it again in subsequent chapters.

```
#*****************************************************************************
# Make File for DAEMON program
#*****************************************************************************

#** MACROS *******************************************************************
cflags=-c -AL -G2 -Zp -W3 -Od -Zi -nologo
lflags=/ST:10000/CO/NOD
linklibs=llibcep.lib doscalls.lib

#** INFERENCE RULES **********************************************************
.obj.exe:
      echo LINKING   $*.exe
      link $(lflags) $**,$*.exe,,$(linklibs),;

.c.obj:
      echo COMPILING $*.c
      cl $(cflags) $*.c

#** BUILD STATEMENTS *********************************************************
all: daemon.exe killer.exe

daemon.exe:             daemon.obj
daemon.obj:             daemon.c      daemon.h

killer.exe:             killer.obj
killer.obj:             killer.c      killer.h
```

Figure 6-14. Daemon Make File.

DAEMON.MAK: WALKING THROUGH A MAKE FILE

We will walk through the *make* file in Figure 6-14 in great detail with the idea of having it serve as the "Rosetta Stone" for deciphering all the *make* files in this book.

DAEMON.MAK starts off with some comment lines, that are followed by macro definitions for three symbols: **cflags**, **lflags**, and **linklibs**. The contents of the three macros provide some insight into how to compile and link in the OS/2 environment. We will take a short detour in our exploration of DAEMON.MAK to understand what these symbols mean:

- The **cflags** macro defines the compiler flags which are used to control and modify the operation of the compiler. The flags are preceded by a hyphen. The following is a "flag by flag" description of what it all means:

  c This flag suppresses linking during compilation. We will link the program in a separate link step.
  AL This flag specifies the large memory model. The OS/2 API calls use **far** pointers.
  G2 This flag specifies the use of the 80286 and later model processor instruction sets. OS/2 requires the use of an 80286 processor or above, so you might as well give yourself a performance boost by enabling this flag.
  Zp This flag packs structures by placing each structure field on the next available byte address. This is important because some OS/2 API calls assume that the structures passed are packed.
  W3 This flag enables the highest level of compiler warnings. Why not find out about your type mismatches at compile time?
  Od This flag disables code optimization. We do this because optimized code sometimes causes confusion when running CodeView. You can disable this flag once you have stable code.
  Zi This flag produces an object file that allows you to debug under CodeView. You definitely will need to keep this flag enabled until you have stable code!
  nologo This flag suppresses writing the logo and copyright lines in the compiler output stream.

- The **lflags** macro defines the link flags or options which are used to control and modify the operation of the linker. The flags or options are preceded by a "/" symbol. The following is a "flag by flag" description of what it all means:

  ST This option specifies the size of the stack. We are assigning a stack of 10,000 bytes to the program.
  CO This flag directs LINK to include symbolic debug information for CodeView.
  NOD This flag directs LINK to bypass the default libraries and lets us name the libraries as a parameter to the LINK command. We will be specifying the special C library for multithreaded applications.

- The **linklibs** macro defines the libraries we need to link with. The **llibcep.lib** library is the protected mode version of the C library for the large memory model. The **doscalls.lib** resolves all references to OS/2 Dynamic Link Library calls, without supplying the actual code. Instead, it provides the name of a DLL library and the entry point of the function within this library.

Continuing with our walk through DAEMON.MAK, we encounter our first inference rule, **obj.exe**, whose effect is to produce an "**.exe**" file from an "**.obj**" file of the same name. MAKE does not execute the inference rule at this point because it still does not know what is to be built. So, MAKE skips over the next two lines and encounters a second inference rule, **c.obj**, whose effect is to produce an "**.obj**" file from a "**.c**" file of the same name. But since MAKE still has no idea of what needs to be built, it also skips over this inference rule and the two lines that follow it.

Finally, MAKE finds something it can build when it encounters the "dummy" condition list statement:

```
all: daemon.exe killer.exe
```

Here's how it works:

1. When MAKE encounters the dummy, it says, "Aha! they want me to build **all**." So off it goes looking for **all**, which it will not find, because it's just a dummy name which we are using to get it to build the other two programs.
2. MAKE eventually gives up looking for **all** and decides to build it from scratch. So it looks at the right side and says, "In order to build **all**, I will need the most recent versions of daemon.exe and killer.exe. So let me start with daemon.exe, and then I'll come back and do killer.exe."
3. Before MAKE can determine that daemon.exe is up-to-date, it must first check for a target-dependent rule where daemon.exe appears as a target. Any rule with daemon.exe as a target could potentially update daemon.exe, so it needs to be executed first. In fact, the MAKE utility builds a tree of interrelated target-dependent rules before it executes any commands. The bottom part of the tree contains rules where the dependents are existing files and have no references as targets in any target-dependent rule in the *make* file. The following shows the tree for daemon.exe:

```
all: daemon.exe killer.exe
     ----------
     |
     v
daemon.exe:          daemon.obj
                     ----------
     |
     v
daemon.obj:          daemon.c     daemon.h
```

4. Once the tree has been determined, the build process begins starting from the bottom of the tree and working upward. If any of the dependents have a later time-stamp than the targets for the rule, the commands or the inference rule commands for the target-dependent rule are executed. In our example, the rule

```
daemon.obj:          daemon.c     daemon.h
```

is checked first. If daemon.c or daemon.h is of a later time-stamp than daemon.obj or daemon.obj doesn't exist, then the **.obj.c** inference rule commands are executed. In our example

```
cl -c -AL -G2 -Zp -W3 -Od -Zi -nologo daemon.c
```

is executed. This line should also be very familiar to any C programmer that has used a Microsoft compiler. You are essentially compiling daemon.c using the **cl** (i.e., compile-link command) with the specified compiler flags. Remember, that we've disabled the link part of compile-link by using the **c flag**. We do that because we want the much finer level of link control which is obtained by invoking the **link** command separately.

5. So now, MAKE has an up-to-date **daemon.obj**, and it is ready to examine the next higher target-dependent rule in the tree:

```
daemon.exe:   daemon.obj
```

Again, if daemon.obj has a later time-stamp than daemon.exe or if daemon.exe doesn't exist, then the commands or inference rule commands associated with the rule are executed. In our example the inference rule commands are executed. Before producing the "**.exe**" file. The inference rule then echoes **LINKING daemon.exe**. The name, of course, is obtained through the **$*** macro.

6. The real action, once more, takes place in the next line which after all the macro substitutions reads:

```
LINK /ST:10000/CO/NOD daemon.obj, daemon.exe,, llibcep.lib doscalls.lib,;
```

This line should be familiar to any C programmer that has used a Microsoft linker. You are essentially linking daemon.obj with the specified libraries and creating daemon.exe (using the specified link option flags). No LISTING or MAP output is required.

7. The MAKE has now successfully either created or found an up-to-date version of daemon.exe.
8. The MAKE now works on the second goal which is create or find an up-to-date version of killer.exe. The last two lines of DAEMON.MAK are, thankfully, the rules for creating killer.exe, which leads to the execution of the following two commands associated with our inference rules:

```
cl -c -AL -G2 -Zp -W3 -Od -Zi -nologo killer.c
LINK /ST:10000/CO/NOD daemon.obj, killer.exe,, llibcep.lib doscalls.lib,;
```

9. At this point, MAKE has up-to-date versions of both daemon.exe and killer.exe, so it can go about building **all**, its primary goal for this *make* file. Unfortunately for MAKE and fortunately for us, there are no further rules that apply to **all**, so MAKE terminates and we've got what we were looking for.

The key then to reading any of our *make* files is to first look for the dummy rule for building **all**. The left side of the rule tells you what it is that we're trying to build and in which order. From there you can follow the various dependency lists, and get a good understanding of how the programs are put together.

RUNNING DAEMON AND KILLER

You can run DAEMON by either invoking it from the command line, or running it as a background process using the DETACH command. If you run it from the command line, your screen will remain frozen until DAEMON comes to life, so you may want to consider running the program in a separate screen group. If you run DAEMON using the DETACH command, OS/2 will display the program's **process ID** and then return control to you while DAEMON executes in the background. In all cases, DAEMON will interrupt whatever screen group you are in and tell you "Hello" when the right time comes. To invoke DAEMON from the command line type:

```
C>DAEMON hh:mm:ss
```

To invoke it as a background process type:

```
C>DETACH DAEMON hh:mm:ss
```

where hh:mm:ss is the time in hours, minutes, and seconds when you want DAEMON to wake-up and say Hello on a daily basis. As an example, if you were to enter:

```
C>DETACH DAEMON 15:30:30
```

You should expect to see on your screen, every day, at three-thirty in the afternoon, the following greeting:

```
      Hello World!!

The time is 15:30:30

Daemon PID = 8

Press Q/q to quit.
Press any other key to
enable Daemon again.
```

You can kill DAEMON by pressing **Q** to quit at the time the greeting appears on the screen, or you can invoke from the command line, at any time:

```
KILLER 8
```

where **8** is the process ID that OS/2 returned when DAEMON was first created. DAEMON also tells you its process ID when it displays Hello!

DEBUGGING MULTITASKING PROGRAMS WITH CODEVIEW

IBM C/2 provides a powerful symbolic debugger utility, **CodeView**, which is identical to its Microsoft counterpart. When you run your programs under CodeView, you can set break-points, single-step through the code, view variables, evaluate expressions, and do all the things that are expected from a world-class debugger. In this section, we briefly touch on how to use CodeView for debugging multitasking programs.

Debugging Child Processes

CodeView gives you the ability to debug child processes. You do that by specifying the **/O** switch when you start CodeView. Thus, you would start CodeView in the OS/2 protected mode with the multitasking mode enabled by entering:

```
CVP /O PROGRAM
```

where PROGRAM is the name of the program you want to debug. When your application starts another process, CodeView will display the following prompt:

```
Pid n started.  Do you wish to debug (y/n)?
```

where **n** is the id assigned to the newly created process. If you answer yes, then CodeView will start another copy of itself to debug process **n**. The two debugging sessions are completely independent of each other and you can move between them using the Presentation Manager. If process **n** starts another process, CodeView will repeat the above scenario.

Debugging Threads

Multiple threads can occur within the same program and are slightly harder to debug under CodeView. You have to tell CodeView which source line and which thread, you are interested in. To help you do that, CodeView provides a new prompt which is preceded by a three-digit number indicating the current thread. Codeview also provides a set of new thread commands:

BP Break point for thread.
E Run thread in slow motion.
F Freeze the thread(s).
G Run current thread freeze all others.
S The code for the selected thread is displayed.
U Unfreeze thread(s).
P Run one instruction, stepping over any function calls.

T Run one instruction.

Here are the objects you can apply a thread command to:

(blank) The current thread.
***** All threads.
# The last thread that ran.
n The indicated thread.

The purpose of this brief introduction is to make you aware that tools do exist to help you debug programs in a multitasking environment. To obtain more details on how to use them, you should consult the documentation that comes with the C compiler.

This concludes our panoramic grand tour of the C programming environment under OS/2.

Chapter 7

MULTI.C - Multitasking Can Be Fun

This chapter is about MULTI.C, a program that lets you organize "races" between tasks. In this chapter, we make use of MULTI's facilities to run races between four threads, or four processes. The processes and threads will perform the same counting function. This will give us a chance to compare threads vs processes from two angles: ease of programming, and execution speeds. After going through the program, you should be able to get a good feel for the relative merits of OS/2's two multitasking approaches. MULTI.C also lets you experiment with multitasking performance. For example, you can vary the number of concurrently executing tasks or change the priority level of individual tasks and get immediate feedback on how these effect system performance.

MULTI.C is easy to follow and understand. A good portion of MULTI's bulk comes from familiar C function calls whose sole purpose is to provide us with a working set of dialog tools to be used until we get to the fancy graphics and windowing pizzaz of the Presentation Manager. You can skip over MULTI's screen and keyboard interaction code, if you choose to, without detracting from your understanding MULTI's treatment of multitasking. The "long walk" through MULTI.C code and the time you spend playing with the program will count heavily towards your "accreditation" as an OS/2 multitasking guru.

OFF TO THE RACES WITH MULTI THREADS

To run MULTI, first edit MULTI.CFG, a configuration file that specifies what threads or processes you want MULTI to run. Then invoke the program by entering MULTI at the command line and off you go into the world of multitasking. Once MULTI is up and running, you are at the controls.

Creating a Config File for Threads

We will first run MULTI in **THREADS** mode by creating the entries in the MULTI.CFG file shown in Figure 7-1.

```
PROGRAM_TYPE    = THREADS
STOP_TIME_MS    = 20000
TASK_NAME       = THREAD_1
TASK_NAME       = THREAD_2
TASK_NAME       = THREAD_3
TASK_NAME       = THREAD_4
```

Figure 7-1. A MULTI.CFG File for Running Four Threads.

Let's take a look at what the entries in this file mean:

- The PROGRAM_TYPE entry tells MULTI that it will be racing threads as opposed to processes.
- The STOP_TIME_MS entry specifies the duration of the race in units of milliseconds. In this example, we've specified that our races will be 20 seconds long.
- The TASK_NAME entries contain the names of the contending tasks. In the case of processes, these are the names of separately compiled programs that will be run. Threads, on the other hand, are compiled as part of the MULTI program. So in effect, we're telling MULTI to run in THREADS mode for 20 seconds after we say GO.

How to Read a MULTI Screen

We will now go through some screen capture sequences of MULTI races that were obtained on an IBM PS/2 Mod 70. Figure 7-2 shows the MULTI screen that gets displayed when the program first comes up. You can think of the MULTI screen as a control panel for running races between tasks.

The MULTI control panel is organized into several window areas:

- We start with the top window, whose current title indicates that MULTI is running threads as opposed to processes. Remember, this is exactly what we told MULTI to do in the MULTI.CFG file for this run. Below the title are the instructions you will need to manipulate MULTI's control knobs.
- In the middle of the screen are four windows, one for each of the tasks (in this case threads) that we told MULTI to run in MULTI.CFG. Notice that all four tasks first come up with their task semaphore in the CLEAR state, indicating that they are ready to run. You can START or STOP a particular task by moving the cursor to the semaphore knob in the task's window, and then use the + or - keys to CLEAR or SET the task's control semaphore. Even with the semaphore CLEAR, the task will not run so long as MULTI itself is STOPPED.

```
                      Multithread Execution Example

 Use arrow keys to move the cursor.  Use + and - keys to change field values.
 Press R to start running, S to stop, or C to clear the count.
 Press ESC to terminate the program.

┌THREAD_1──────────┐┌THREAD_2──────────┐┌THREAD_3──────────┐┌THREAD_4──────────┐
│ Count =          ││ Count =          ││ Count =          ││ Count =          │
│                  ││                  ││                  ││                  │
│ Priority  = RG   ││ Priority  = RG   ││ Priority  = RG   ││ Priority  = RG   │
│ Level     = 0    ││ Level     = 0    ││ Level     = 0    ││ Level     = 0    │
│ Semaphore = CLEAR││ Semaphore = CLEAR││ Semaphore = CLEAR││ Semaphore = CLEAR│
│                  ││                  ││                  ││                  │
│ Ready            ││ Ready            ││ Ready            ││ Ready            │
└──────────────────┘└──────────────────┘└──────────────────┘└──────────────────┘
┌EXECUTION STATUS─────────────────────┐┌SYSTEM INFORMATION──────────────────────┐
│ Stop Time     = 20.0           sec  ││ Maximum Wait       = 3            sec  │
│ Elapsed Time  =                sec  ││ Minimum Time Slice = 32           ms   │
│ Total Count   =                     ││ Maximum Time Slice = 248          ms   │
│ Run Status    = STOPPED             ││ Dynamic Variation  = ACTIVE            │
└─────────────────────────────────────┘└────────────────────────────────────────┘
```

Figure 7-2. MULTI: When it First Comes Up.

- Currently, MULTI is in a STOPPED state as shown in the bottom left window. You can start MULTI by pressing **R** for RUN.
- The parameters displayed in the lower right hand window display the maximum and minimum **time-slices** of CPU time allocated to a running thread before it gets preempted. The other two parameters *Max Wait* and *Dynamic Variation* specify the maximum wait interval that a thread waits without being executed. OS/2 automatically boosts the priority of a thread that has waited longer than maxwait seconds when the Dynamic Variation parameter is enabled. This is to prevent a low priority task from starving when it shares the CPU with higher priority tasks. You specify all four of these parameters in your *config.sys* file.

Our First Race: One Thread Running Solo

We will now bring MULTI to life, by first running a race with a single task contender. We do this by moving the cursor to the windows of THREAD_2 and THREAD_3, and SET their respective semaphores. Having set up the conditions for the race, we are now ready to hit **R**, our signal to start the race. When we do so, MULTI will run for 20 seconds, at the end of which our display looks like Figure 7-3. The display shows that THREAD_1 accumulated a count of 14,923 during the 20 second run interval. The other three threads didn't budge since their semaphores were in the SET state.

```
                    Multithread Execution Example

Use arrow keys to move the cursor.  Use + and - keys to change field values.
Press R to start running, S to stop, or C to clear the count.
Press ESC to terminate the program.

THREAD_1               THREAD_2               THREAD_3               THREAD_4

Count = 14923          Count =                Count =                Count =

Priority  = RG         Priority  = RG         Priority  = RG         Priority  = RG
Level     = 0          Level     = 0          Level     = 0          Level     = 0
Semaphore = CLEAR      Semaphore = SET        Semaphore = SET        Semaphore = SET

Ready                  Ready                  Ready                  Ready

EXECUTION STATUS                              SYSTEM INFORMATION

Stop Time     = 20.0        sec               Maximum Wait       = 3       sec
Elapsed Time  = 20.0        sec               Minimum Time Slice = 32      ms
Total Count   = 14923                         Maximum Time Slice = 248     ms
Run Status    = STOPPED                       Dynamic Variation  = ACTIVE
```

Figure 7-3. One Regular Priority Thread.

Our Second Race: Four Regular Threads

Here's what you do to organize a race between all four threads:

1. Clear all four thread semaphores. CLEAR should appear in all four thread windows.
2. Clear all the counters by entering **C**.
3. Give the Go signal to start the race by entering **R** to run MULTI.

Observing MULTI run during this 20 second race is interesting in its own right. You get to see different tasks come to life during short time durations. Unfortunately, providing animated output is beyond the display capabilities of this book's pages. So we're counting on you to run the program to observe all the special effects.

What we can do is show you a screen capture of the MULTI display at the end of the 20 seconds (see Figure 7-4 on page 151). What the screen shows is that all four threads produced a cumulative count of 15,007. We also observe a sizeable deviation in the counts produced by *equal priority* threads. The first and third thread ran a better race. In theory, all four threads should have produced the same count since they were all set to run at the same priority. Should we expect a closer race by making the STOP_TIME_MS parameter longer than 20 seconds?

```
                    Multithread Execution Example

 Use arrow keys to move the cursor.  Use + and - keys to change field values.
 Press R to start running, S to stop, or C to clear the count.
 Press ESC to terminate the program.

-THREAD_1-------------  -THREAD_2-------------  -THREAD_3-------------  -THREAD_4-------------
 Count = 4861            Count = 3013            Count = 4307            Count = 2826

 Priority  = RG          Priority  = RG          Priority  = RG          Priority  = RG
 Level     = 0           Level     = 0           Level     = 0           Level     = 0
 Semaphore = CLEAR       Semaphore = CLEAR       Semaphore = CLEAR       Semaphore = CLEAR

 Ready                   Ready                   Ready                   Ready

-EXECUTION STATUS-----------------------------  -SYSTEM INFORMATION---------------------------
 Stop Time     = 20.0          sec               Maximum Wait       = 3        sec
 Elapsed Time  = 20.0          sec               Minimum Time Slice = 32       ms
 Total Count   = 15007                           Maximum Time Slice = 248      ms
 Run Status    = STOPPED                         Dynamic Variation  = ACTIVE
```

Figure 7-4. Four Regular 0 Threads.

Our Third Race: Introducing Extreme Priorities

Now, let's try to make this race more uneven by varying the priority levels. Priorities determine how often a task gets assigned a CPU execution time-slice by the OS/2 scheduler. As a review, under OS/2 a thread may run in one of four priority classes: *Idle-time, Regular, Fixed-high,* and *Time-critical.* Idle-time threads have the lowest priority and receive the least amount of scheduling attention. Time-critical threads have the highest priority and get scheduled ahead of all others. OS/2 assigns regular priority to a new process (and its primary thread) as the default. You can assign any of OS/2's four priority levels to a MULTI task by moving the cursor to the task's Priority field, and then use the + or - keys to "sequence" to the priority class you want to assign. You'll see the field change from BG (for background or idle-time) to RG (for regular) to FH (for fixed-high) to TC for (time-critical).

Within each priority class, OS/2 supports 32 distinct priority levels. When a thread is created, it is initially dispatched with the same priority as the creating thread. MULTI starts you out at level 0, but you can sequence through 32 levels by placing your cursor on a task's level field and then hitting + or - keys to increment or decrement the level, until you're at the level you want to assign to a task.

So now that we know something about priorities, let's apply this new knowledge to some practical undertaking, like rigging the race between our four tasks. We can do that by placing the cursor on Thread_1's Priority field and hitting + twice. The display indicates **TC** for time-critical. Having done this, we hit **C** to clear the counters, and

```
                     Multithread Execution Example

 Use arrow keys to move the cursor.  Use + and - keys to change field values.
 Press R to start running, S to stop, or C to clear the count.
 Press ESC to terminate the program.

-THREAD_1-----------  -THREAD_2-----------  -THREAD_3-----------  -THREAD_4-----------

 Count = 14915         Count =               Count =               Count =

 Priority  = TC        Priority  = RG        Priority  = RG        Priority  = RG
 Level     = 0         Level     = 0         Level     = 0         Level     = 0
 Semaphore = CLEAR     Semaphore = CLEAR     Semaphore = CLEAR     Semaphore = CLEAR

 Ready                 Ready                 Ready                 Ready

-EXECUTION STATUS---------------------------  -SYSTEM INFORMATION-------------------------

 Stop Time     = 20.0            sec           Maximum Wait       = 3          sec
 Elapsed Time  = 20.0            sec           Minimum Time Slice = 32         ms
 Total Count   = 14915                         Maximum Time Slice = 248        ms
 Run Status    = STOPPED                       Dynamic Variation  = ACTIVE
```

Figure 7-5. One Time Critical 0 Thread, Three Regular 0 Threads.

enter **R** our signal to start a new race. Once more, the race will last 20 seconds, at the end of which the MULTI screen would look like Figure 7-5 on page 152.

The results displayed in Figure 7-5 show that our race rigging was an absolute success! Thread_1, our time-critical winner, was able to starve out the competition and deliver all 14,915 counts. The OS/2 *Dynamic Variation* feature did not help because it cannot boost a thread past its current priority level.

Our Fourth Race: Introducing the Smallest Priority

In our next variation of a rigged race, we will apply the smallest level of rigging and see what OS/2 can do with its automatic boosts of priority to help out the starving tasks. The plan for this new race is to demote Thread_1 to the Regular Priority class, but raise its level by a notch to 1 (of 32). In so doing, we are applying the smallest increment of priority that OS/2 provides. The display indicates **RG** for all threads and Level 1 for Thread_1.

Once again, we hit **C** to clear the counters and enter **R** to start the minimally rigged race. The race lasts 20 seconds at the end of which the MULTI screen looks like Figure 7-6 on page 153. The results shown in Figure 7-6 on page 153 are worthy of note. Once again, Thread_1, is the undisputed winner. However, this time the OS/2 *Dynamic Variation* feature was able to throw a few crumbs of CPU time-slices at the other starving contenders, and they were able to do much better than in the previous

```
                    Multithread Execution Example

Use arrow keys to move the cursor.  Use + and - keys to change field values.
Press R to start running, S to stop, or C to clear the count.
Press ESC to terminate the program.

-THREAD_1-           -THREAD_2-           -THREAD_3-           -THREAD_4-
Count = 14822        Count = 98           Count = 2            Count = 2

Priority  = RG       Priority  = RG       Priority  = RG       Priority  = RG
Level     = 1        Level     = 0        Level     = 0        Level     = 0
Semaphore = CLEAR    Semaphore = CLEAR    Semaphore = CLEAR    Semaphore = CLEAR

Ready                Ready                Ready                Ready

-EXECUTION STATUS-                        -SYSTEM INFORMATION-
Stop Time     = 20.0         sec          Maximum Wait       = 3       sec
Elapsed Time  = 20.0         sec          Minimum Time Slice = 32      ms
Total Count   = 14924                     Maximum Time Slice = 248     ms
Run Status    = STOPPED                   Dynamic Variation  = ACTIVE
```

Figure 7-6. One Regular 1 Thread, Three Regular 0 Threads.

race. The question is what made OS/2 manifest so much generosity this time around? The answer is that after 3 seconds (the Maximum Wait), OS/2 was able to raise the priority of some threads to level 1 where they were able to get some CPU time-slices.

OFF TO THE RACES WITH MULTI PROCESSES

In this section, we organize a race between four processes. We do this by running MULTI in the **PROCESS** mode. This is easily done by creating the new MULTI.CFG file shown in Figure 7-7.

```
PROGRAM_TYPE     = PROCESS
STOP_TIME_MS     = 20000
TASK_NAME        = COUNT.EXE 0
TASK_NAME        = COUNT.EXE 1
TASK_NAME        = COUNT.EXE 2
TASK_NAME        = COUNT.EXE 3
```

Figure 7-7. A MULTI.CFG File for Running Four Processes.

The first line entry tells MULTI that it will be dealing with processes as opposed to threads. The STOP_TIME_MS parameter, specified in the second line, tells MULTI to run the races in 20 second intervals. The last four lines are the names of the processes to run. Since processes are separately compiled programs, we need to specify the name of the executable file. The example in Figure 7-7 will be running four instances of the same program, COUNT.EXE, each of which is a separate process. The number following COUNT.EXE in the MULTI.CFG file gives each process a unique identifier.

The COUNT.EXE program, which is described later in this chapter, is designed to provide the same COUNT function as the threads we've been running. The idea is to get a feel for the relative performance of threads vs processes, and more importantly, we want to demonstrate how to code the same function using either method.

Our Fifth Race: Four Regular Processes

We will run this race between four REGULAR processes. Once again, we hit **C** to clear the counters and enter **R** to give the Go signal to start the new race. At the end of 20 seconds the MULTI screen looks like Figure 7-8

```
                    Multiprocess Execution Example

Use arrow keys to move the cursor.  Use + and - keys to change field values.
Press R to start running, S to stop, or C to clear the count.
Press ESC to terminate the program.

COUNT.EXE            COUNT.EXE            COUNT.EXE            COUNT.EXE

Count = 3816         Count = 3458         Count = 3813         Count = 3457

Priority  = RG       Priority  = RG       Priority  = RG       Priority  = RG
Level     = 0        Level     = 0        Level     = 0        Level     = 0
Semaphore = CLEAR    Semaphore = CLEAR    Semaphore = CLEAR    Semaphore = CLEAR

Ready                Ready                Ready                Ready

EXECUTION STATUS                          SYSTEM INFORMATION

Stop Time     = 20.0          sec         Maximum Wait       = 3        sec
Elapsed Time  = 20.0          sec         Minimum Time Slice = 32       ms
Total Count   = 14542                     Maximum Time Slice = 248      ms
Run Status    = STOPPED                   Dynamic Variation  = ACTIVE
```

Figure 7-8. Four Regular Processes.

Not too surprisingly, we observe in Figure 7-8 that, all things being equal, there are still some minor variations in the performance of "equal" processes. More importantly, if we compare the results of Figure 7-8 with the corresponding run for threads shown in Figure 7-4 on page 151, we show 14,542 counts for processes vs 15,007 counts for threads. This may mean that there is more operating system overhead involved in the running of processes. Does the overhead get larger or smaller with time?

Run Your Own Races

MULTI is a tool for running empirical experiments. It is up to you to set up the experiments and draw the appropriate conclusions. The numbers we've shown so far were for demonstrative purposes only. We caution you to run your own experiments before you start quoting them. You should also be getting the idea, by now, that in addition to running benchmarks, MULTI can be a useful learning tool. We will be returning to MULTI in future chapters to run some database benchmark tests.

DISSECTING THE MULTI.C PROGRAM

The purpose of MULTI in the context of the current chapters is to learn how to write multitasking programs using the OS/2 kernel. Now that we know what MULTI does, we are ready to dive into the code and find out how it gets done.

MULTI.C: main()

The **main()** function, listed in Figure 7-9, will serve as the MULTI.C program outline. This means that whenever you feel you're getting lost in the detail of the code, you should come back to **main()** to refresh your top-down perspective on what the program does. This section also provides a good index into the different code listings. We will walk through MULTI's code components with the idea of demonstrating OS/2's kernel functions in the context of a fairly realistic program setting. We are especially interested in how the different multitasking elements come together in programming ensembles. So, stay alert during this long exposition on how the new OS/2 kernel services can be put to work, and avoid getting hung up on the more mundanc aspccts of MULTI, likc **get_user_input()** or **update_screen_fields()**.

Like most C programs, MULTI starts out by including the various header files. Starting from the top, we include headers for the C library functions. This is followed by a list of **#define** directives whose purpose is to define the OS/2 header material that gets included through **OS2.H**. The OS/2 API functions we include with this program are: VIO display, shared memory, process control, semaphores, date/time, and the information segment. Following the OS/2 include files are two MULTI specific header files: const.h and multi.h. The first file, **const.h**, listed in Figure 7-10, contains the declarations of constants used by both the MULTI.C and COUNT.C programs. The second file, **multi.h**, listed in Figure 7-11, contains the forward declarations of the procedures and global variables used in the MULTI.C program.

The main program starts right after the include files and is mostly self explanatory. The first seven functions are involved in setting up the environment for running the task "races." This is followed by the code that starts the four tasks. From then on the program is under interactive user controls and consists of running the races and displaying results. Eventually, the user gets tired of watching threads and processes chase each other, and terminates the program. Let's first take a look at the seven functions involved in setting up the races:

1. The first of the set up functions is **read_config()**, listed in Figure 7-12. This function simply obtains the race setup information and the list of task contenders from MULTI.CFG.
2. The **read_system_info()** function listed in Figure 7-13, is invoked next. Its sole purpose is to obtain information from OS/2's *global information segment.* We are particularly interested in the information that concerns tasks and timing.
3. The **create_semaphores()** function listed in Figure 7-15, sets up the control mechanisms for the races.
4. The, **create_timer_thread()** function listed in Figure 7-16 creates the **elapsed_time_thread()** which serves as the referee for the race and keeps track of elapsed time. The **elapsed_time_thread()** is listed in Figure 7-17.
5. The next function, **set_thread_priorities()**, listed in Figure 7-18, assigns time-critical priority class to **main()** and the **elapsed_time_thread()**, so that the organizers of the race and the referee can remain in control at all times.
6. The **create_counter_segment()** function listed in Figure 7-19, creates a global memory area where all the task contenders record their output counts.
7. Finally, **paint_screen()** function listed in Figure 7-20, displays the control panel from which the races are run.

Having set up the conditions for the races, **main()** now lines up and starts four task contenders. If the contenders are processes, **main()** invokes **create_processes()**, listed in Figure 7-22, and starts four processes specified in MULTI.CFG. Otherwise, **main()** invokes **create_threads()**, listed in Figure 7-21, and starts four threads. For the purposes of this chapter, the four processes started are four instances of **COUNT.EXE** and the four threads are four instances of the **thread_count()** thread. For comparison purposes, both the threads and the processes perform the same *counting* function. The source code listing for the **COUNT** process is given in Figure 7-32 and Figure 7-33. The code for the **thread_count()** thread, is listed in Figure 7-31. **Main()** updates the screen to reflect the state of the contenders by invoking **update_screen_fields()**, listed in Figure 7-23.

From this point on, the races are run under user control and **main()** obtains its input through **get_user_input()**, listed in Figure 7-24, and performs the requested actions through **perform_field_action()**, listed in Figure 7-25. Eventually, the user puts out a TERMINATE request which causes **main()** to invoke **terminate_program()**, listed in Figure 7-30. The MULTI program also contains four sets of helper routines:

1. The screen helper functions listed in Figure 7-26.
2. The OS/2 **DOS** helper functions listed in Figure 7-27.
3. The **VIO** helper functions listed in Figure 7-28.
4. The miscellaneous helper functions listed in Figure 7-29.

```
/*****************************************************************************/
/*  PROGRAM NAME: MULTI - a multitasking execution example                   */
/*                                                                           */
/*  PROGRAM DESCRIPTION:  This program gives a visual demonstration of      */
/*    the execution of 4 processes or 4 threads.   The user can             */
/*    interactively control the task execution environment.                 */
/*****************************************************************************/
#include <process.h>                    /* For exit()                        */
#include <conio.h>                      /* For getch()                       */
#include <stdio.h>                      /* For printf() & NULL               */
#include <stdlib.h>                     /* For printf                        */
#include <stddef.h>                     /* For _beginthread                  */
#include <string.h>                     /* For printf                        */
#define INCL_VIO                        /* include VIO calls                 */
#define INCL_DOSMEMMGR                  /* for shared segment functions      */
#define INCL_DOSPROCESS                 /* include priority api calls        */
#define INCL_DOSSEMAPHORES              /* include semaphore api calls       */
#define INCL_DOSDATETIME                /* include timer     api calls       */
#define INCL_DOSINFOSEG                 /* include getinfoseg api calls      */
#include <os2.h>
#include "const.h"
#include "multi.h"
/*---------------------------------------------------------------------------*/
/* Main routine.                                                             */
/*---------------------------------------------------------------------------*/
VOID main(USHORT argc, PCHAR argv[], PCHAR envp[])
{
  read_config(argc, argv);  /* read configuration information from MULTI.CFG */
  read_system_info();       /* get system info from global info segment      */

  create_semaphores();      /* Create semaphores for task control            */

  create_timer_thread();    /* Start a time critical referee thread          */

  set_thread_priorities();  /* Increase timer and main thread priorities     */

  create_counter_segment(); /* Create shared memory segment for count values */

  paint_screen();           /* Draw screen with title, task status etc..     */

  if (program_type == PROCESSES)
       create_processes();  /* Start processes                               */
  else create_threads();    /* Start threads                                 */

  update_screen_fields();   /* display current values of screen fields       */

  while (get_user_input() != TERMINATE)
     perform_field_action(last_field_x, last_field_y);

  terminate_program();      /* At user request, kill tasks and clean up      */
} /* end main */
```

Figure 7-9. MULTI main() Function.

MULTI.C: Include Files

MULTI.C is packaged with two separate include files: CONST.H and MULTI.H. The **CONST.H** file, listed in Figure 7-10, contains the symbolic names of constants that are used by the MULTI.C and COUNT.C programs. The main purpose of the constant **#defines** is to make the programs easier to read, especially in the sections that deal with screen display attributes and task priorities.

The **MULTI.H** include file, listed in Figure 7-11, is your garden variety C include file. We first pre-declare all the procedures that will be used by the program to make the compiler happy. We then declare, and in many cases initialize, the program's global variables. One look at the include file variables shows a heavy usage of 4-element arrays. We have 4-element arrays of: task_names, task_status, thread_stack, thread_id, fields, etc. This magic number *four* comes from the fact that MULTI keeps track at all times of four tasks. The arrays maintain the necessary information on those tasks.

The most formidable looking of these arrays, **field**, uses a home-made **FIELD** structure to keep track of information pertinent to each screen field such as: screen location, length, minimum and maximum values, and current field value. Notice that the MULTI control panel shown in Figure 7-2 on page 149 contains four task windows, each consisting of multiple fields such as PRIORITY, LEVEL, and SEMAPHORE. An array of arrays of structures is used for this occasion.

The only other "unfamiliar" occurrences in MULTI.H are the OS/2-defined types such as: **VIOCURSORINFO**, **PID**, **GINFOSEG**, and **LINFOSEG**. These types are defined in **OS2.H** and should be used for OS/2 program portability. We will be explaining the new OS/2 types when we get to the OS/2 calls that use them. Likewise, we explain a new OS/2 function the first time we encounter it in a program.

```
/*****************************************************************************/
/*  INCLUDE NAME: CONST.H - constants for MULTI and related programs        */
/*****************************************************************************/
/*───────────────────────────────────────────────────────────────────────────*/
/* defines                                                                   */
/*───────────────────────────────────────────────────────────────────────────*/
                   /*──────────────────────────────────*/
                   /* box characters                   */
                   /*──────────────────────────────────*/
#define HORIZONTAL_LINE "─"
#define VERTICAL_LINE   "│"
#define BOX_UL_CORNER   "┌"
#define BOX_UR_CORNER   "┐"
#define BOX_LL_CORNER   "└"
#define BOX_LR_CORNER   "┘"
#define BLANK           " "

                   /*──────────────────────────────────*/
                   /* foreground color values          */
                   /*──────────────────────────────────*/
#define BLACK               0x00
#define BLUE                0x01
#define GREEN               0x02
#define CYAN                0x03
#define RED                 0x04
```

Figure 7-10 (Part 1 of 4). CONST.H Include File.

```
#define MAGENTA             0x05
#define BROWN               0x06
#define LT_GRAY             0x07
#define GRAY                0x08
#define LT_BLUE             0x09
#define LT_GREEN            0x0A
#define LT_CYAN             0x0B
#define LT_RED              0x0C
#define LT_MAGENTA          0x0D
#define YELLOW              0x0E
#define WHITE               0x0F

                    /*------------------------------------*/
                    /* background color values            */
                    /*------------------------------------*/
#define BGND_BLACK          0x00
#define BGND_BLUE           0x10
#define BGND_GREEN          0x20
#define BGND_TURQ           0x30
#define BGND_RED            0x40
#define BGND_MAGENTA        0x50
#define BGND_BROWN          0x60
#define BGND_LT_GRAY        0x70
#define BGND_GRAY           0x80
#define BGND_LT_BLUE        0x90
#define BGND_LT_GREEN       0xA0
#define BGND_LT_CYAN        0xB0
#define BGND_LT_RED         0xC0
#define BGND_LT_MAGENTA     0xD0
#define BGND_YELLOW         0xE0
#define BGND_WHITE          0xF0

                    /*------------------------------------*/
                    /* panel color attributes             */
                    /*------------------------------------*/
#define BOX_ATTR            ((CHAR)CYAN     | BGND_BLACK)
#define BOX_TITLE_ATTR      ((CHAR)GREEN    | BGND_BLACK)
#define FIELD_TEXT_ATTR     ((CHAR)BROWN    | BGND_BLACK)
#define IO_FIELD_ATTR       ((CHAR)LT_GRAY  | BGND_BLACK)
#define OUTPUT_FIELD_ATTR   ((CHAR)WHITE    | BGND_BLACK)
#define CURSOR_FIELD_ATTR   ((CHAR)BLACK    | BGND_LT_GRAY)
#define PANEL_TITLE_ATTR    ((CHAR)YELLOW   | BGND_BLACK)
#define PANEL_HELP_ATTR     ((CHAR)LT_RED   | BGND_BLACK)
#define PANEL_STATUS_ATTR   ((CHAR)RED      | BGND_BLACK)

                    /*------------------------------------*/
                    /* key definitions                    */
                    /*------------------------------------*/
#define UP_ARROW            (256 + 72)
#define DOWN_ARROW          (256 + 80)
#define LEFT_ARROW          (256 + 75)
#define RIGHT_ARROW         (256 + 77)
#define PLUS_KEY            '+'
#define MINUS_KEY           '-'
#define ESC_KEY             27
```

Figure 7-10 (Part 2 of 4). CONST.H Include File.

```
                    /*_____________________________________*/
                    /* panel field limits                  */
                    /*_____________________________________*/
#define FIELD_X_MAX         3
#define FIELD_Y_MAX         2

                    /*_____________________________________*/
                    /* task field values                   */
                    /*_____________________________________*/
#define PRIORITY            0
#define LEVEL               1
#define SEMAPHORE           2

                    /*_____________________________________*/
                    /* function return values              */
                    /*_____________________________________*/
#define GOOD                0
#define WARNING             1
#define FAILED             -1

                    /*_____________________________________*/
                    /* program terminate flag              */
                    /*_____________________________________*/
#define CONTINUE            0
#define TERMINATE           1

                    /*_____________________________________*/
                    /* program types                       */
                    /*_____________________________________*/
#define THREADS             0
#define PROCESSES           1

                    /*_____________________________________*/
                    /* semaphore types                     */
                    /*_____________________________________*/
#define EXCLUSIVE           0
#define NONEXCLUSIVE        1

                    /*_____________________________________*/
                    /* update_value direction flags        */
                    /*_____________________________________*/
#define DECREMENT           0
#define INCREMENT           1

                    /*_____________________________________*/
                    /* task execution states               */
                    /*_____________________________________*/
#define SUSPENDED           0
#define RUNNING             1

                    /*_____________________________________*/
                    /* semaphore states                    */
                    /*_____________________________________*/
#define CLEAR               0
#define SET                 1
```

Figure 7-10 (Part 3 of 4). CONST.H Include File.

```
                  /*-----------------------------------------*/
                  /* thread priorities                       */
                  /*-----------------------------------------*/
#define BACKGROUND          1
#define REGULAR             2
#define TIME_CRITICAL       3
#define FIXED_HIGH          4
```

Figure 7-10 (Part 4 of 4). CONST.H Include File.

```
/*********************************************************************************/
/*  INCLUDE NAME: MULTI.H  - declarations for MULTI program                      */
/*********************************************************************************/
/*-------------------------------------------------------------------------------*/
/* Forward declarations of procedures in this module                             */
/*-------------------------------------------------------------------------------*/
                  /*-----------------------------------------*/
                  /* top level routines                      */
                  /*-----------------------------------------*/
VOID   read_config(USHORT argc, PCHAR argv[]);
VOID   read_system_info(VOID);
VOID   create_semaphores(VOID);
VOID   create_timer_thread(VOID);
VOID   set_thread_priorities(VOID);
VOID   create_counter_segment(VOID);
VOID   paint_screen(VOID);
VOID   create_processes(VOID);
VOID   create_threads(VOID);
VOID   update_screen_fields(VOID);
USHORT get_user_input(VOID);
VOID   perform_field_action(USHORT, USHORT);
VOID   terminate_program(VOID);

                  /*-----------------------------------------*/
                  /* thread routines                         */
                  /*-----------------------------------------*/
VOID   thread_count(PUSHORT);
VOID   elapsed_time_thread(PUSHORT);

                  /*-----------------------------------------*/
                  /* screen helper routines                  */
                  /*-----------------------------------------*/
VOID   move_cursor(USHORT);
VOID   update_value(PUSHORT, USHORT, USHORT, USHORT);

                  /*-----------------------------------------*/
                  /* DOS call helper routines                */
                  /*-----------------------------------------*/
VOID   request_semaphore(HSEM, PUSHORT);
VOID   clear_semaphore(HSEM, PUSHORT);
VOID   set_semaphore(HSEM, PUSHORT);
VOID   set_priority(USHORT);
```

Figure 7-11 (Part 1 of 4). MULTI.H Include File.

```
                /*-------------------------------*/
                /* VIO call helper routines      */
                /*-------------------------------*/
VOID   clear_screen(VOID);
VOID   draw_title_box(USHORT, USHORT);
VOID   draw_task_box(PCHAR, USHORT, USHORT);
VOID   display_sys_info(USHORT, USHORT);
VOID   display_exec_status(USHORT, USHORT);
VOID   draw_box(PCHAR, CHAR, USHORT, USHORT, USHORT, USHORT, CHAR);
VOID   hide_cursor(VOID);
VOID   restore_cursor(VOID);
VOID   draw_cursor(BYTE, USHORT, USHORT, USHORT);
VOID   write_str(PCHAR, CHAR, USHORT, USHORT);
VOID   fill_area(PCHAR, CHAR, USHORT, USHORT, USHORT, USHORT);
VOID   draw_horizontal_line(USHORT, USHORT, USHORT, CHAR);
VOID   draw_vertical_line(USHORT, USHORT, USHORT, CHAR);

                /*-------------------------------*/
                /* Miscellaneous helper routines */
                /*-------------------------------*/
VOID   print_error(USHORT, PCHAR , PCHAR , USHORT);
VOID   FAR multi_exit(USHORT);

/*--------------------------------------------------------------------*/
/* Global variables/type definitions for this module                  */
/*--------------------------------------------------------------------*/
                /*-------------------------------*/
                /* configuration variables       */
                /*-------------------------------*/
USHORT   program_type;                /* threads or processes?        */
ULONG    stop_time_msecs;             /* number of ms to run a test   */
CHAR     task_names[4][15] =
      {"              ",              /* program names go in this     */
       "              ",              /* array and are used for       */
       "              ",              /* DosExecPgm                   */
       "              "};

                /*-------------------------------*/
                /* variables for DosGetInfoSeg   */
                /*-------------------------------*/
GINFOSEG *global_info;           /* global information pointer        */
LINFOSEG *local_info;            /* local  information pointer        */

                /*-------------------------------*/
                /* variables for run all semaphore */
                /*-------------------------------*/
HSEM   runall_sem_handle;           /* semaphore handle               */
USHORT runall_sem_status;           /* is the semaphore set or clear  */
```

Figure 7-11 (Part 2 of 4). MULTI.H Include File.

```
                    /*------------------------------------*/
                    /* variables and typedefs for task    */
                    /*  execution control.                */
                    /*------------------------------------*/
typedef struct STATUS { USHORT active;
                        USHORT semaphore;} STATUS;

STATUS task_status[4] = {{RUNNING, CLEAR},
                         {RUNNING, CLEAR},
                         {RUNNING, CLEAR},
                         {RUNNING, CLEAR}};

HSEM     run_sem_handle[4];
BYTE     thread_stack[4][4096];       /* thread stacks                    */
USHORT   threadid[4];                 /* thread IDs                       */
SHORT    thread_parm[4]               /* array of parameters, one for each */
                = {0, 1, 2, 3};       /*  executing thread                */

                    /*------------------------------------*/
                    /* variables for stop time/elapsed    */
                    /* time update and control            */
                    /*------------------------------------*/
ULONG  elapsed_time_msecs;            /* ms elapsed from beginning of test */
ULONG  current_msecs;                 /* current ms counter value from     */
                                      /* DosGetInfoSeg                     */
ULONG  start_msecs;                   /* beginning of current time interval*/
ULONG  delta_msecs;                   /* current time interval             */
USHORT test_running;                  /* flag to indicate a test is running*/

TID    elapsed_time_threadid;         /* id of timer thread                */
BYTE   elapsed_time_thread_stack[4096]; /* timer thread stack              */

                    /*------------------------------------*/
                    /* count variable definition          */
                    /*------------------------------------*/
typedef struct
        { ULONG count[8];
        } COUNT;
COUNT   *count ptr;
ULONG   total_count = 0;

                    /*------------------------------------*/
                    /* variables and typedefs for screen  */
                    /*  paint and cursor control.         */
                    /*------------------------------------*/
typedef struct FIELD { USHORT x;      /* column location                   */
                       USHORT y;      /* row location                      */
                       USHORT cx;     /* field length                      */
                       USHORT min;    /* field minimum value               */
                       USHORT max;    /* field maximum value               */
                       USHORT value;  /* current field value               */
                     } FIELD;
```

Figure 7-11 (Part 3 of 4). MULTI.H Include File.

```
     /* x    y  cx  min  max   value */
FIELD field[4][3] =
   {{{14, 11 , 2,  1,   4,    2},  /* task 1, PRIORITY field          */
     {14, 12 , 2,  0,  31,    0},  /* task 1, LEVEL field             */
     {14, 13 , 5,  0,   1,    0}   /* task 1, SEMAPHORE field         */
    },
    {{34, 11 , 2,  1,   4,    2},  /* task 2, PRIORITY field          */
     {34, 12 , 2,  0,  31,    0},  /* task 2, LEVEL field             */
     {34, 13 , 5,  0,   1,    0}   /* task 2, SEMAPHORE field         */
    },
    {{54, 11 , 2,  1,   4,    2},  /* task 3, PRIORITY field          */
     {54, 12 , 2,  0,  31,    0},  /* task 3, LEVEL field             */
     {54, 13 , 5,  0,   1,    0}   /* task 3, SEMAPHORE field         */
    },
    { {74, 11 , 2,  1,   4,    2},  /* task 4, PRIORITY field          */
     {74, 12 , 2,  0,  31,    0},  /* task 4, LEVEL field             */
     {74, 13 , 5,  0,   1,    0},  /* task 4, SEMAPHORE field         */
    }};
VIOCURSORINFO cursor_data;         /* used for hiding cursor          */
VIOCURSORINFO save_cursor_data;    /* used for restoring the cursor   */

USHORT field_x      = 0;           /* variables                       */
USHORT field_y      = 0;           /*   for tracking                  */
USHORT last_field_x = 0;           /*     cursor                      */
USHORT last_field_y = 0;           /*       movement                  */

                  /*------------------------------------*/
                  /* variables for child processes      */
                  /*------------------------------------*/
USHORT processid[4];                /* thread IDs                      */
CHAR object_name[13];               /* buffer for failure name         */
RESULTCODES ExecResult;             /* structure for child proc. results */
CHAR programs[4][80] =
     {"          0",                /* program names go in this        */
      "          1",                /*   array and are used for        */
      "          2",                /*   DosExecPgm                    */
      "          3"};

RESULTCODES term_result;            /* termination result code         */
PID         term_processid;         /* terminating process id          */

                  /*------------------------------------*/
                  /* misc. variables                    */
                  /*------------------------------------*/
USHORT   i,x,y;                    /* for loop indices                */
USHORT   rc;                       /* return code variable            */
```

Figure 7-11 (Part 4 of 4). MULTI.H Include File.

MULTI.C: read_config()

The **read_config**() code, listed in Figure 7-12, is straightforward C code that consists of reading a MULTI.CFG file and obtaining from it the parameters that govern the running of a race. Figure 7-1 contains an example of MULTI.CFG for running a race between threads, while Figure 7-7 provides an example of a MULTI.CFG file for processes.

```
/*---------------------------------------------------------------------------*/
/* read configuration information from MULTI.CFG                            */
/*---------------------------------------------------------------------------*/
VOID read_config(USHORT argc, PCHAR argv[])
{
  CHAR config_file_name[80];
  CHAR program_parms[80];
                   /*-------------------------------------*/
                   /* configuration file variables        */
                   /*-------------------------------------*/
  FILE    *config_file;              /* Input file control block          */
  CHAR     line[80];                 /* one line of config file           */
  CHAR     name[80];                 /* variable for building ascii names */
  CHAR     prog_type[15];

  /*-------------------------------------*/
  /* determine config file name          */
  /*-------------------------------------*/
  if (argc == 2)
     strcpy(config_file_name, argv[1]);
  else
     strcpy(config_file_name, "multi.cfg");

  /*-------------------------------------*/
  /* open the configuration file         */
  /*-------------------------------------*/
  if (NULL == (config_file = fopen(config_file_name,"r")))
     { print_error(rc,"opening configuration file",__FILE__,__LINE__);
       exit(FAILED);
     }

  /*-------------------------------------*/
  /* read program type                   */
  /*-------------------------------------*/
  fgets(line, sizeof(line), config_file);
  if (sscanf(line,"PROGRAM_TYPE     = %s ", prog_type) != 1)
     { print_error(rc,"reading program type from configuration file",
                   __FILE__,__LINE__);
       exit(FAILED);
     }
  if  (strcmp(strupr(prog_type),"THREADS") == 0)
      program_type = THREADS;
  else
      program_type = PROCESSES;

  /*-------------------------------------*/
  /* read stop time                      */
  /*-------------------------------------*/
  fgets(line, sizeof(line), config_file);
  if (sscanf(line,"STOP_TIME_MS     = %lu ", &stop_time_msecs) != 1)
     { print_error(rc,"reading stop time from configuration file",
                   __FILE__,__LINE__);
       exit(FAILED);
     }
```

Figure 7-12 (Part 1 of 2). The read_config() Function.

```
/*─────────────────────────────────────*/
/* read task names for 4 tasks         */
/*─────────────────────────────────────*/
for (i=0; i < 4; ++i)
   {
    /*─────────────────────────────────────*/
    /* read a line from config file        */
    /*─────────────────────────────────────*/
    fgets(line, sizeof(line), config_file);
    if (sscanf(line,"TASK_NAME        = %s %[^;] ",
                &task_names[i][0], program_parms) == 0)
       { print_error(rc,"reading program name from configuration file",
                     __FILE__,__LINE__);
         exit(FAILED);
       }
    sprintf(programs[i],"%s%c%s", task_names[i], '\0', program_parms);
   }
/*─────────────────────────────────────*/
/* all done with the config file       */
/*─────────────────────────────────────*/
fclose(config_file);

} /* end read_config */
```

Figure 7-12 (Part 2 of 2). The read_config() Function.

MULTI.C: read_system_info()

OS/2 maintains some rather useful system information in a data structure called the **Global Information Segment**. This structure contains "global" information that concerns all processes. OS/2 separately maintains a set of structures called the **Local Information Segments**, which contain information relevant to a particular process. The Local Information Segment for a particular process is only accessible from that process.

DosGetInfoSeg

The **DosGetInfoSeg** API call is used to obtain the segment selectors for both the *local* and *global* information structures. This function returns two segment selectors which must be converted to an address pointer by shifting each selector left 16 bits. To do that, we use the OS/2 supplied macro **MAKEP(sel, off)** which combines a segment selector and an address offset to create a far (32-bit) pointer to a memory address. The prototype for this call is:

```
DosGetInfoSeg(PUSHORT        GlobalSeg,  /* global segment selector */
              PUSHORT        LocalSeg);  /* local segment selectors */
```

A description of the parameters follows:

- The ***GlobalSeg*** parameter points to the segment selector of the *global* information segment.

- The ***LocalSeg*** parameter points to the segment selector of the *local* information segment.

Once you get into the info segments, you will be rewarded with a wealth of information. Here's what the **GINFOSEG** global info structure looks like:

```
typedef struct _GINFOSEG {
    ULONG   time;               /* time in seconds                          */
    ULONG   msecs;              /* milliseconds                             */
    UCHAR   hour;               /* hours                                    */
    UCHAR   minutes;            /* minutes                                  */
    UCHAR   seconds;            /* seconds                                  */
    UCHAR   hundredths;         /* hundredths                               */
    USHORT  timezone;           /* minutes from UTC                         */
    USHORT  cusecTimerInterval; /* timer interval (units = 0.0001 seconds)  */
    UCHAR   day;                /* day                                      */
    UCHAR   month;              /* month                                    */
    USHORT  year;               /* year                                     */
    UCHAR   weekday;            /* day of week                              */
    UCHAR   uchMajorVersion;    /* major version number                     */
    UCHAR   uchMinorVersion;    /* minor version number                     */
    UCHAR   chRevisionLetter;   /* revision letter                          */
    UCHAR   sgCurrent;          /* current foreground session               */
    UCHAR   sgMax;              /* maximum number of sessions               */
    UCHAR   cHugeShift;         /* shift count for huge elements            */
    UCHAR   fProtectModeOnly;   /* protect mode only indicator              */
    USHORT  pidForeground;      /* pid of last process in forground session */
    UCHAR   fDynamicSched;      /* dynamic variation flag                   */
    UCHAR   csecMaxWait;        /* max wait in seconds                      */
    USHORT  cmsecMinSlice;      /* minimum timeslice (milliseconds)         */
    USHORT  cmsecMaxSlice;      /* maximum timeslice (milliseconds)         */
    USHORT  bootdrive;          /* drive from which the system was booted   */
    UCHAR   amecRAS[32];        /* system trace major code flag bits        */
    UCHAR   csgWindowableVioMax;/* maximum number of VIO windowable sessions */
    UCHAR   csgPMMax;           /* maximum number of pres. services sessions */
} GINFOSEG;
```

We will be interested in the MULTI example in the fields that provide the current time, and in the fields which contain information relevant to task races such as: csecMaxWait, cmsecMinSlice, and cmsecMaxSlice.

Here's what the **LINFOSEG** the local info structure looks like:

```
typedef struct _LINFOSEG {
    PID     pidCurrent;        /* current process id                 */
    PID     pidParent;         /* process id of parent               */
    USHORT  prtyCurrent;       /* priority of current thread         */
    TID     tidCurrent;        /* thread ID of current thread        */
    USHORT  sgCurrent;         /* session                            */
    UCHAR   rfProcStatus;      /* process status                     */
    UCHAR   dummy1;
    BOOL    fForeground;       /* current process has keyboard focus */
    UCHAR   typeProcess;       /* process type                       */
    UCHAR   dummy2;
    SEL     selEnvironment;    /* environment selector               */
    USHORT  offCmdLine;        /* command line offset                */
    USHORT  cbDataSegment;     /* length of data segment             */
    USHORT  cbStack;           /* stack size                         */
    USHORT  cbHeap;            /* heap size                          */
    HMODULE hmod;              /* module handle of the application   */
    SEL     selDS;             /* data segment handle of the application */
} LINFOSEG;
```

You will notice that the local info segment contains a wealth of information on the current process and task.

We introduce the use of **DosGetInfoSeg** in **read_system_info()** (see listing in Figure 7-13). As part of the system initialization, **read_system_info()** sets up the **global_info** variable as a pointer to the global info segment, and the **local_info** variable as a pointer to the local info segment. Since both these variables were declared as global in multi.h, they make the information segments available to any function that needs to reference them. We encourage you to make it a programming practice to invoke, early in your programs, a setup function like **read_system_info()** that points you to the wealth of information available in the info segments.

MULTI.C: create_semaphores()

Semaphores provide the controls for MULTI's races. The semaphore, \SEM\RUNALL, is used as the referee's signal to start the race. In addition, each task's execution is individually controlled through the task semaphores: \SEM\RUN1 through \SEM\RUN4. Figure 7-14, provides a pictorial view of how MULTI uses its semaphores.

The program initially starts with the **main()** thread running. As part of its setup, **main()** calls **create_semaphores()**, listed in Figure 7-15, which creates the system semaphore, \SEM\RUNALL, and then sets it. The **create_semaphores()** function also creates and clears the four system semaphores that provide individual task control: \SEM\RUN1 through \SEM\RUN4.

Main() then creates the **elapsed_time_thread()**, the referee and broadcasting thread. Since the race has not yet started, **elapsed_time_thread()** blocks its execution and

```
/*--------------------------------------------------------------------------*/
/* get system information from global information segment                   */
/*--------------------------------------------------------------------------*/
VOID read_system_info(VOID)
{
  SEL     global_info_sel;             /* global information seg selector   */
  SEL     local_info_sel;              /* local  information seg selector   */

  /*-----------------------------------*/
  /* get the info segment selectors    */
  /*-----------------------------------*/
  if (rc = DosGetInfoSeg(&global_info_sel,/* global information              */
                         &local_info_sel))/* local information               */
     { print_error(rc,"during DosGetInfoSeg",__FILE__,__LINE__);
       exit(FAILED);
     }

  /*-----------------------------------*/
  /* make pointers to the segments     */
  /*-----------------------------------*/
  global_info = MAKEP(global_info_sel,0);
  local_info  = MAKEP(local_info_sel,0);

} /* end read_system_info */
```

Figure 7-13. The read_system_info() Function.

waits on \SEM\RUNALL to clear. Following that, **main()** starts the four race contenders which may be either threads or processes, and they too are blocked waiting for \SEM\RUNALL to clear. In the case where the four tasks are processes, they need to first issue a **DosOpenSem** before using the semaphores.

At this point, everybody is blocked waiting for \SEM\RUNALL to clear while **main()** itself is blocked waiting for keyboard input. MULTI is in a state, like that shown in Figure 7-2 on page 149, waiting for you to give the GO! signal to start the race. You, of course, do that by hitting **R** which brings **main()** back to life long enough to issue a **DosSemClear** on \SEM\RUNALL.

This time, **main()** itself goes back to sleep waiting for your next keyboard input, but all the other active tasks are still running. The **elapsed_time_thread()** starts the countdown and periodically updates the elapsed_time and total_count values. When the elapsed time is equal to the race stop_time, the **elapsed_time_thread()**, like any good referee, stops the race by setting \SEM\RUNALL. As for our racing contenders, as long as both their semaphores are clear they will keep on racing, incrementing their COUNTs as fast as the CPU will let them do so. The race abruptly stops when either semaphore gets set. Note that the loop in the code is linearly represented in Figure 7-14 on page 170.

The user, in the example of Figure 7-14 on page 170, now decides to start another race with only one task contending. The user does that by moving the cursor to the different task windows and setting their respective semaphores. All the semaphores are now set, except for \SEM\RUN1. When the user hits **R** to start a second race, all the tasks come to life because \SEM\RUNALL is CLEAR. However, for most this life

```
 Thread       Thread       Task       Task       Task
 main()    elapsed_time()  1          2 ...      4

DosCreateSem                                         LEGEND
"runall"                                             --------
    |                                                Executing thread  ——
DosSemSet                                            Blocked thread    .....
"runall"                                             The race          ccccc
    |
DosCreateSem
"run1".."run4"
    |
DosSemClear
"run1".."run4"    |
    |        DosSemWait    |          |          |
    |         "runall"  DosSemWait DosSemWait DosSemWait
    .             .      "runall"   "runall"   "runall"
DosSemClear       .         .          .          .        ←User hits "R"
"runall"          |         |          |          |          Start of 1st race
    .             .     DosSemWait DosSemWait DosSemWait
    .             .       "run1"     "run2"     "run4"
    .             .         |c         |c         |c
    .             |         |c         |c         |c
    .             .     DosSemWait DosSemWait DosSemWait
    .             .      "runall"   "runall"   "runall"
    .             .         |          |          |
    .             |     DosSemWait DosSemWait DosSemWait
    .             .       "run1"     "run2"     "run4"
    .             .         |c         |c         |c
    .             .         |c         |c         |c
    .             |     DosSemWait DosSemWait DosSemWait
    .             .      "runall"   "runall"   "runall"
    .             .         |          |          |
    .             .     DosSemWait DosSemWait DosSemWait
    .             |       "run1"     "run2"     "run4"
    .                       |c         |c         |c
    .        DosSemSet      |c         |c         |c
    .         "runall"  DosSemWait DosSemWait DosSemWait   ←End of 1st race
    .        DosSemWait  "runall"   "runall"   "runall"
    .         "runall"      .          .          .
DosSemSet         .         .          .          .
"run2".."run4"    .         .          .          .
    .             .         .          .          .
DosSemClear                                                User hits "C" then "R"
"runall"          |         |          |          |        ←Start of 2nd race
    .             |     DosSemWait DosSemWait DosSemWait
    .             |       "run1"     "run2"     "run4"
    .             |         |c         .          .
    .             |         |c         .          .
    .             |     DosSemWait     .          .
    .             |      "runall"      .          .
```

Figure 7-14. MULTI's Semaphore Structure.

is short, and except for task1, they all go back to sleep after discovering that the run semaphore that controls them is in the "set" state. Task 1, the sole contender in the race, runs until the **elapsed_time_thread()** stops the race by setting \SEM\RUNALL.

The **create_semaphores()**, function listed in Figure 7-15 on page 172, introduces the use of three OS/2 calls: **DosCreateSem**, **DosSemSet**, and **DosSemClear**. A description of these calls follows.

DosCreateSem

The **DosCreateSem** API call is used to create a system semaphore. The effect of the call is to establish the semaphore, initialize it, and return a handle to it. The prototype for this call is:

```
DosCreateSem(USHORT   ownership_flag,/* 0=exclusive 1=non-exclusive */
             PVOID    sem_handle,    /* semaphore handle            */
             PCHAR    sem_name);     /* pointer to semaphore name   */
```

A description of the parameters follows:

- The ***ownership_flag*** parameter specifies ownership. If set to 0, the creating process claims an exclusive right to the semaphore; if set to 1, the semaphore ownership is non-exclusive. **Exclusive** ownership means that only the creating process can change the status of the semaphore; other processes can only test the semaphore and wait for it to change. Exclusive semaphores provide one-way communications and are used for controlling the execution of tasks. **Non-exclusive** semaphores provide two-way communications and can be used to control access to shared resources.
- The ***sem_handle*** parameter is the semaphore handle that points to a semaphore variable. The handle returned is only available to threads that are part of the calling process.
- The ***sem_name*** parameter points to a null-terminated string where you provide the semaphore name. The format of the string is, **\SEM\name**, where the name must be unique and follow OS/2 file-naming conventions. The SEM pathname is fictitious and does not exist on disk.

DosSemSet

The **DosSemSet** API call sets a system or RAM semaphore. The prototype for this call is:

```
DosSemSet(PVOID     sem_handle);/*  semaphore handle      */
```

A description of the parameters follows:

- The ***sem_handle*** parameter points to a variable where you provide the semaphore handle. In the case of system semaphores, this handle must have been previously created using **DosCreateSem** or **DosOpenSem**

DosSemClear

The **DosSemClear** API call clears a system or RAM semaphore that has been set using **DosSemRequest**, **DosSemSet**, or **DosSemSetWait**. The prototype for this call is:

```
DosSemClear(PVOID     sem_handle);/*  semaphore handle     */
```

A description of the parameters follows:

- The ***sem_handle*** parameter points to a variable where you provide the semaphore handle. In the case of system semaphores, this handle must have been previously created using **DosCreateSem** or **DosOpenSem**.

```
/*------------------------------------------------------------------------*/
/* Create semaphores for task control                                     */
/*------------------------------------------------------------------------*/
VOID create_semaphores(VOID)
{
  CHAR sem_name[30];

  /*----------------------------------*/
  /* create the run all semaphore     */
  /*----------------------------------*/
  sprintf(sem_name,"\\SEM\\RUNALL");
  if (rc = DosCreateSem(NONEXCLUSIVE,      /* nonexclusive ownership        */
                        &runall_sem_handle,
                                           /* handle to semaphore returned  */
                        sem_name))         /* ASCIIZ name of semaphore      */
     { print_error(rc,"during DosCreateSem", __FILE__,__LINE__);
       exit(FAILED);
     }

  /*----------------------------------*/
  /* set the semaphore to stop        */
  /* execution                        */
  /*----------------------------------*/
  if (rc = DosSemSet(runall_sem_handle))
     { print_error(rc,"during DosSemSet", __FILE__,__LINE__);
       exit(FAILED);
     }
  runall_sem_status = SET;
```

Figure 7-15 (Part 1 of 2). The create_semaphores() Function.

```
        /*------------------------------------*/
        /* create task specific semaphore     */
        /*------------------------------------*/
        for (i=0; i < 4; ++i)
           {
             sprintf(sem_name,"\\SEM\\RUN%d",i);
             if (rc = DosCreateSem(EXCLUSIVE,          /* must own exclusively     */
                                  &run_sem_handle[i], /* sem handle returned      */
                                  sem_name))          /* ASCIIZ name of semaphore */
                { print_error(rc,"during DosCreateSem", __FILE__,__LINE__);
                  exit(FAILED);
                }

             /*------------------------------------*/
             /* clear the semaphore to allow       */
             /* execution                          */
             /*------------------------------------*/
             if (rc = DosSemClear(run_sem_handle[i]))
                { print_error(rc,"during DosSemClear", __FILE__,__LINE__);
                  exit(FAILED);
                }
           }
     } /* end create_semaphores */
```

Figure 7-15 (Part 2 of 2). The create_semaphores() Function.

MULTI.C: create_timer_thread()

The **create_timer_thread()** function listed in Figure 7-16 creates the **elapsed_time_thread**. This is the famous race referee thread you've already heard so much about. The listing for the thread itself can be found in Figure 7-17. Notice that a thread looks like any ordinary procedure. However, you just can't call a thread the way you do an ordinary procedure. Instead you create the thread and from then on it runs concurrently with your code. The newly created thread begins to execute immediately after it is successfully created.

Your program is also responsible for allocating space for the thread's stack. IBM and Microsoft recommend at least 4 KBytes, to play it safe. You may need to provide even more stack space if your thread uses lots of local storage or makes C library calls. For example, the C function **printf** requires more than 500 bytes of stack space. To create the thread we'll be using the C-language **_beginthread()** function. This function is recommended over OS/2's **DosCreateThread** for the following reasons:

- It lets you pass a parameter to the thread in an explicit fashion.
- It will let you run your program without false stack overflow errors.
- It makes your code more portable.

_beginthread()

The **_beginthread()** C-language function creates and starts the execution of a new thread. The function returns a thread's identifier number if it is successful. If it fails, it returns -1. The prototype for this function is:

```
_beginthread(VOID (FAR *thread)(VOID FAR *),/* thread name            */
             PVOID    stack_bottom,         /* pointer to end of stack */
             USHORT   stack_size,           /* stack size              */
             PVOID    args);                /* arguments to be passed  */
```

A description of the parameters follows:

- The ***thread*** parameter points to the starting address of a far routine the newly created thread will execute. This is the name of the thread you want to execute. The thread does not return a parameter and must be declared as **VOID FAR**
- The ***stack_bottom*** parameter points to an area in memory to be used as the new thread's stack. It must be on a word boundary. Remember, that stacks grow downward, so this is in effect the first element in a global array of bytes you provide for the thread's stack.
- The ***stack_size*** parameter is the length in bytes of the stack you're providing. It must be both even and non-zero.
- The ***args*** parameter points to an argument you want passed to the newly created thread. It is usually the address of a data item, such as a **char** string. It may be NULL if not needed.

```
/*------------------------------------------------------------------------*/
/* Create a time critical thread for maintaining elapsed time             */
/*------------------------------------------------------------------------*/
VOID create_timer_thread(VOID)
{
  /*-------------------------------*/
  /* start the elapsed timer thread  */
  /*-------------------------------*/
  if ((elapsed_time_threadid =
       _beginthread(elapsed_time_thread,        /* name of function     */
                    elapsed_time_thread_stack,  /* thread stack         */
                    sizeof(elapsed_time_thread_stack), /* size of stack */
                    NULL) ) == -1)              /* no parms             */
    { print_error(elapsed_time_threadid,"creating a thread", __FILE__,__LINE__);
      exit(FAILED);
    }

} /* end create_timer_thread */
```

Figure 7-16. The create_timer_thread() Function.

MULTI.C: elapsed_time_thread()

We now get a chance to explore the code that makes our famous referee thread tick. The listing for the thread in Figure 7-17 looks like any ordinary procedure. No parameters were passed to the thread by **_beginthread()**, even though the thread is capable of accepting one. The thread code consists of a do-forever loop that blocks itself waiting until the semaphore \SEM\RUNALL clears. This happens when the **R** key is pressed to indicate the start of a given race. As soon as the thread comes to life, it obtains the current time from a field in the **Global Info Segment**, and then it goes into another loop which executes throughout the duration of the race. So, what does the referee do while looping?

Well, first it takes a short 100 millisecond nap! Now, before you jump to conclusions and imply that our referee is lazy, you should be made aware that the "nap" is really an act of great generosity! By going to sleep and doing nothing for a while, our referee gives up its share of machine time. This means that the actual contenders for the race can run a little faster! At the end of the nap; however, the referee goes back to work and performs the following:

- It calculates the current elapsed time for the race and displays it on the MULTI control panel.
- It calculates the running total count by adding the counts produced by each contender. It then displays the current total on the MULTI control panel.
- It checks to see if the time for the race is up, in which case it stops the race by setting the semaphore \SEM\RUNALL. Otherwise, its time for another round through the loop. Which means another well deserved nap and a repeat performance of the work items described above.

So what is new and exciting in this code? Well, we have one new OS/2 function: **DosSemWait** which we will shortly explore. We have an example of getting some information out of the Global Info Segment, described in “DosGetInfoSeg” on page 166. Notice how the code handles timer roll-over. Another interesting tid-bit is how the referee adds counts, which in the case of processes are produced by four separate programs. This is done through the use of shared memory which the referee can access through the use of the pointer: **count_ptr->**.

Also new, but certainly not as exciting, is the use of two of our helper routines: set_semaphore() and write_str(). The helper routine set_semaphore(), listed in Figure 7-27, sets semaphores. The write_str() helper, listed with the other VIO helper routines in Figure 7-28, writes a string with a display attribute to an x,y location on the screen. The OS/2 API call, **DosSleep**, was previously encountered and explained in “DosSleep” on page 124. However, this is our first encounter with **DosSemWait**, so an explanation follows:

DosSemWait

The **DosSemWait** API call is used in "wait-until-semaphore-clears" situations for synchronizing the execution of processes or threads. The thread blocks until a RAM or system semaphore clears, or until a time-out occurs. The API is level-triggered, meaning that a thread may have to wait through multiple changes of the semaphore before it continues. This may happen if another waiting thread grabs the semaphore before it. The prototype for this call is:

```
DosSemWait(PVOID    sem_handle,  /* semaphore handle            */
           LONG     timeout);    /* -1L= wait, 0=nowait, >0=msecs*/
```

A description of the parameters follows:

- The ***sem_handle*** parameter is the semaphore handle which points to a semaphore variable. This handle must have been previously created using **DosCreateSem** or **DosOpenSem**.
- The ***timeout*** parameter specifies how long to wait. Setting the value to zero causes the call to return immediately. A return code of 121 in this case lets you know that the semaphore is already owned. Setting the value to -1L will cause the call to wait indefinitely until the semaphore clears. Otherwise, a positive value specifies the number of milliseconds to wait before returning.

```
/*-----------------------------------------------------------------------*/
/* thread to keep elapsed timer up to date, and determine when to stop   */
/*-----------------------------------------------------------------------*/
VOID elapsed_time_thread(PUSHORT parm)
{
  CHAR time_str[20];
  CHAR value_str[20];

  while (TRUE)
    {
     /*-------------------------------*/
     /* wait for execution control semaphore*/
     /* to clear                         */
     /*-------------------------------*/
     rc = DosSemWait(runall_sem_handle,               /* semaphore handle */
                     -1L);                            /* infinite timeout */
     if (rc)
        { print_error(rc,"during DosSemWait", __FILE__,__LINE__);
          exit(FAILED);
        }

     /*-------------------------------*/
     /* get ms value from DosInfoSeg, save  */
     /* for later use                    */
     /*-------------------------------*/
     start_msecs = global_info->msecs;

     while (test_running)
       {
       /*-------------------------------*/
       /* sleep for a while                */
       /*-------------------------------*/
       DosSleep(100L);
```

Figure 7-17 (Part 1 of 2). The elapsed_time_thread() Thread.

```
        /*─────────────────────────────────────*/
        /* get ms value from DosInfoSeg        */
        /*─────────────────────────────────────*/
        current_msecs = global_info->msecs;
        if (current_msecs >= start_msecs)    /* was there a timer rollover?   */
           delta_msecs   = current_msecs - start_msecs;
        else
           {
            delta_msecs = delta_msecs +     /* compensate for rollover        */
                 (0xFFFFFFFF - start_msecs)
                 + current_msecs;
           }
        start_msecs    = current_msecs;

        /*─────────────────────────────────────*/
        /* update elapsed time value           */
        /*─────────────────────────────────────*/
        elapsed_time_msecs = elapsed_time_msecs + delta_msecs;
        if (elapsed_time_msecs >= stop_time_msecs)
           {
            set_semaphore(runall_sem_handle, &runall_sem_status);
            elapsed_time_msecs = stop_time_msecs;
            write_str("STOPPED", OUTPUT_FIELD_ATTR,
                       18, 22);
            test_running = FALSE;
           }

        sprintf(time_str,"%lu.%-4lu",
                elapsed_time_msecs / 1000, elapsed_time_msecs % 1000);
        write_str(time_str, OUTPUT_FIELD_ATTR, 18, 20);

        /*─────────────────────────────────────*/
        /* update total count value            */
        /*─────────────────────────────────────*/
        total_count = 0;
        for (i=0; i < 4; ++i)
            total_count = total_count + count_ptr->count[i];
        sprintf(value_str,"%lu", total_count);
        write_str(value_str, OUTPUT_FIELD_ATTR, 18, 21);

        } /* end while */

     } /* end while */

 } /* elapsed_time_thread */
```

Figure 7-17 (Part 2 of 2). The elapsed_time_thread() Thread.

MULTI.C: set_thread_priorities()

The set_thread_priorities() function, listed in Figure 7-18, sets the priority of **main()** and all of its threads to *time-critical.* As the comment in the listing points out, we want the referee and the race organizers to be in control and responsive to user input at all times. This function, introduces the OS/2 API call **DosSetPrty** described below:

DosSetPrty

The **DosSetPrty** API call is used to change the priority level and the priority class of the specified process or thread. You may recall, that OS/2 supports 4 priority classes and 32 distinct priority levels within each class. Most programs are regular class and they start out at level 0. These are default values that can be changed using DosSetPrty. The prototype for this call is:

```
DosSetPrty(USHORT   scope_flag,     /* change process or thread?  */
           USHORT   prty_class,     /* class to be set  0-4       */
           USHORT   prty_lvl_delta,/* add to level (-31 to +31)  */
           USHORT   id);            /* process or thread ID       */
```

A description of the parameters follows:

- The ***scope_flag*** parameter specifies the scope of the request. This parameter can be one of the following values:

Value	Meaning
0	The specified process (including all its threads)
1	The specified process and all its descendants
2	A single thread in the current process

- The ***prty_class*** parameter specifies the requested priority class of the process or thread. This parameter can have one of the following values:

Value	Meaning
0	No change to priority class
1	Idle-time priority class (lowest priority)
2	Regular priority class (default)
3	Time-critical priority class (highest priority)
4	Fixed-high priority class (second highest priority)

  Most threads should run at regular priority. Time-critical priority is reserved for those threads that cannot tolerate interruption. The fixed-high priority assists in the synchronization of a background thread that is expected to run at a certain priority in relation to a foreground thread. You have to be careful not to arbitrarily use the higher-level priorities, if you have to share the system with other tasks that may have time-critical requirements of their own.
- The ***prty_lvl_delta*** parameter specifies the delta change to the current priority level. Since there are 32 priority levels, numbered from 0 through 31, delta can range from -31 to +31 to accommodate a change in either direction.
- The ***id*** parameter is the PID if the scope_flag is set to 0 or 1, or is a thread_ID if the scope_flag is 2. If you set the this parameter to 0, it indicates the current thread or process.

```
/*-------------------------------------------------------------------------*/
/* Set timer and main thread priority to time critical                     */
/*-------------------------------------------------------------------------*/
VOID set_thread_priorities(VOID)
{
  /*---------------------------------*/
  /* Make threads in this process time   */
  /* critical.  We want user input and   */
  /* timer management to be done         */
  /* responsively regardless of what the */
  /* user sets in the other tasks.       */
  /*---------------------------------*/
  if (rc = DosSetPrty(0,              /* this process, all threads        */
                      3,              /* time critical                    */
                      10,             /* level                            */
                      0))             /* this thread                      */
     {print_error(rc,"during DosSetPriority",__FILE__,__LINE__);
      exit(FAILED);
     }

} /* end set_thread_priorities */
```

Figure 7-18. The set_thread_priorities() Function.

MULTI.C: create_counter_segment()

The **create_counter_segment()** function, listed in Figure 7-19, creates a shared area in memory where different tasks can output their counts to. If MULTI was only involved in running races between threads, then a regular global variable, would have been used instead. However, MULTI is also in the business of organizing races between processes, which tend to be far more isolated from one another. One of the means OS/2 provides for interprocess communication is **shared memory segments**, where any process can randomly access any location in the entire segment.

The **create_counter_segment()** function, uses the OS/2 API call **DosAllocShrSeg** to allocate a shared segment named **\SHAREMEM\TASK**. Once this named segment is created any process that knows its name can access it. The **create_counter_segment()** function uses the OS/2 supplied macro **MAKEP(sel, off)** to create, count_ptr->, which points to the start of the shared area. Remember, this is the same pointer the referee thread used to add the counts. We now introduce the OS/2 API call **DosAllocShrSeg**.

DosAllocShrSeg

The **DosAllocShrSeg** API call allocates a shared memory segment and provides a copy of the segment selector. Shared memory is a form of OS/2 inter-process communications. The prototype for this call is:

```
DosAllocShrSeg(USHORT      size,  /* number of bytes requested */
               PCHAR       name,  /* pointer to segment name   */
               PUSHORT     psel); /* returned segment selector */
```

A description of the parameters follows:

- The ***size*** parameter specifies the number of bytes to be allocated. You can specify a number between 0 and 65,535. If you specify zero the API allocates 65,536 bytes.
- The ***names*** parameter points to a null-terminated string, which is the name to be given to the segment. The string must include the fictitious subdirectory name **\SHAREMEM**, and the name must be unique.
- The ***psel*** parameter points to a variable that receives the segment selector returned by OS/2.

```
/*-------------------------------------------------------------------------*/
/* Create shared memory segment for count values                          */
/*-------------------------------------------------------------------------*/
VOID create_counter_segment(VOID)
{
  CHAR     shared_seg_name[40];        /* variable for building ascii names  */
  USHORT   selector;                   /* variable for selector values       */

  /*----------------------------------*/
  /* allocate a shareable segment for   */
  /*   the count arrays and make pointer */
  /*----------------------------------*/
  sprintf(shared_seg_name,"\\SHAREMEM\\TASK");
  rc = DosAllocShrSeg(sizeof(COUNT),      /* size of count structure         */
                      shared_seg_name,    /* name of shared segment          */
                      &selector);         /* returned segment selector       */
  if (rc)
     { print_error(rc,"allocating count buffer",__FILE__,__LINE__);
       exit(FAILED);
     }
  count_ptr = MAKEP(selector,0);          /* make pointer out of selector     */

  /*----------------------------------*/
  /* initialize the count array         */
  /*----------------------------------*/
  for (i=0; i<8; ++i)
      count_ptr->count[i] = 0;

} /* end create_counter_segment */
```

Figure 7-19. The create_counter_segment() Function.

MULTI.C: paint_screen()

The **paint_screen()** function paints and fills in the information for the different windows that make up MULTI's control panel. The procedures used in **paint_screen()** are part of the VIO helper routines, listed in Figure 7-28. These are the helper routines that provide value-added services, such as drawing boxes and centering titles, using OS/2's powerful VIO API calls for writing to the screen, and controlling the cursor.

Thus, **paint_screen()**, through the use of its helpers clears the screen, hides the cursor, draws the top window that contains MULTI's instructions, draws the four task windows, and finally draws the bottom two windows that display the status of the race and the system information.

```
/*----------------------------------------------------------------------*/
/* Draw screen with title, task, execution status, and system blocks   */
/*----------------------------------------------------------------------*/
VOID paint_screen(VOID)
{
  clear_screen();
  hide_cursor();

  /*--------------------------------------------------------------------*/
  /* paint the title at column  0, row  0                               */
  /*--------------------------------------------------------------------*/
  draw_title_box(0,0);

  /*--------------------------------------------------------------------*/
  /* draw 4 task boxes with titles read from configuration file         */
  /*--------------------------------------------------------------------*/
  for (i=0; i < 4; ++i)
      draw_task_box(task_names[i], i*20, 7);

  /*--------------------------------------------------------------------*/
  /* display execution status at column 0, row 17                       */
  /*--------------------------------------------------------------------*/
  display_exec_status(0,17);

  /*--------------------------------------------------------------------*/
  /* display system info box at column 40, row 17                       */
  /*--------------------------------------------------------------------*/
  display_sys_info(40,17);

} /* end paint_screen */
```

Figure 7-20. The paint_screen() Function.

MULTI.C: create_threads() and create_processes()

This is the section where we create our four task contenders. We do that by calling either **create_threads()** or **create_processes()**, depending on whether the contenders are threads or processes. The **create_threads()** function, listed in Figure 7-21, uses the **_beginthread** C library function, previously described in "_beginthread()" on page 174. We want to use the same thread, **thread_count** (see listing in Figure 7-31) to run as Thread 1 through Thread 4. But how does a thread know its race contender number? An argument is passed to it specifying its contender number. This number is then used by the thread to index into the global arrays and to identify the task window it will interact with.

The **create_processes()** function, listed in Figure 7-22, uses the OS/2 **DosExecPgm** call to create the four processes that were specified in MULTI.CFG. The parameter passed to each process is its process name, which in this case is very helpful since we are running four instances of the program COUNT.C, listed in Figure 7-32. We do not have to worry about re-entrancy with processes or providing them with a stack. Processes are independent entities and do not share global variables, except through the shared segment. Each instance of COUNT.EXE will know where to write its output based on the contender number that was passed to each process at creation time.

DosExecPgm

The **DosExecPgm** API call starts a process from a currently running program. The prototype for this call is:

```
DosExecPgm(PCHAR        object_name,         /* Name of failing object */
           USHORT       sizeof_object_name,  /* Size of object buffer  */
           USHORT       exec_mode,           /* Sync or async or trace */
           PCHAR        args,                /* Command line string    */
           PCHAR        env,                 /* Environment string     */
           RESULTCODES  *results,            /* PID or termination code*/
           PCHAR        child_program_name); /* Name of program to run */
```

A description of the parameters follows:

- The ***object_name*** parameter is the address of a buffer that receives the name of an object that contributed to the failure of the API call. The named object could be a nonexistent program file or a missing dynamic link library module.
- The ***sizeof_object_name*** parameter is the length (in bytes) of the buffer that contains the object_name.
- The ***exec_mode*** parameter specifies how the child program should execute and can be one of the following values:

Value	Meaning
0	Child executes synchronously to the parent process. The parent waits for child to terminate, and obtains the child's result code in the structure pointed to by the results parameter.
1	Child executes asynchronously to parent, no result code.
2	Child executes asynchronously to parent, the result code is saved for DosCWait.
3	Child executes under conditions for tracing used by parent to debug the child. An example of such a parent is CodeView.
4	Child executes as a background process.

The asynchronous processes in exec_modes 1 or 2 can be brought back into synchronization with the caller process when the latter issues a **DosCWait** . This has the effect of suspending the parent thread until the child process terminates. When the exec_mode is set to 2, it directs OS/2 to save a copy of the child process's termination code and result codes. The result code is supplied by the terminating process using **DosExit** and can contain any mutually agreed upon values. The OS/2 termination codes can have the following values:

Value	Meaning
0	Normal exit
1	Unrecoverable or hard error
2	System trap error
3	Process killed

These values can be obtained by the parent process using **DosCWait**.

- The ***args*** parameter points to the string of command line arguments that get passed to the child process. The string can be NULL (no command line arguments passed) or can have any format but must end with two NULL characters. A conventional format is the program name, a NULL, the program arguments (separated by spaces), followed by a double NULL termination. A command line string may look like this:

```
"parent.exe\0arg1 arg2 arg3 argN\0\0"
```

- The ***env*** parameter points to the environment double NULL terminated string. If left NULL, the child inherits the parent process's environment "as is." The parent has the option of augmenting or modifying the environment it passes to the child through the environment string. An environment string has the following format:

```
"variable1=value1\0variable2=value2\0variable3=value3\0\0"
```

An example of an environment variable is the PATH and the value can be any string, which then gets copied into the process's environment segment. A C-language program can access both the environment and the command line arguments through the familiar **main()** function prototype declaration:

```
main(argc, argv, envp)
```

- The ***results*** parameter points to the **RESULTCODES** structure which has the following form:

```
struct  _RESULTCODES
    {USHORT   codeTerminate;  /* Term code for SYNC or PID for ASYNC */
     USHORT   codeResult;     /* Exit code for SYNC or 0 for ASYNC   */
    } RESULTCODES;
```

The *codeTerminate* field returns the OS/2 process termination code if the child executes synchronously, or it returns the child's process identifier (PID) if the child executes asynchronously. The PID can be used to control the child and change its priority. The *codeResult* field returns the child's exit code for synchronous operation and is not used otherwise.

- The ***child_program_name*** parameter points to a NULL terminated string that specifies the file name and extension of the program (process) to start.

```
/*-------------------------------------------------------------------------*/
/* Start processes based on configuration information                      */
/*-------------------------------------------------------------------------*/
VOID create_threads(VOID)
{
  for (i=0; i<4; ++i)
      {
       /*-------------------------------*/
       /* start the threads             */
       /*-------------------------------*/
       if ((threadid[i] =
            _beginthread(thread_count,             /* name of function      */
                         thread_stack[i],          /* thread stack          */
                         sizeof(thread_stack[i]),  /* size of stack         */
                         &thread_parm[i]) ) == -1) /* pointer to parm       */
                                                   /*  passed to thread     */
                                                   /*  function             */
         { print_error(threadid[i],"creating a thread", __FILE__,__LINE__);
           exit(FAILED);
         }
      }
} /* end create_threads */
```

Figure 7-21. The create_threads() Function.

```
/*-------------------------------------------------------------------------*/
/* Start processes based on configuration information                      */
/*-------------------------------------------------------------------------*/
VOID create_processes(VOID)
{
  /*-------------------------------*/
  /* start the process             */
  /*-------------------------------*/
  for (i=0; i<4; ++i)
      {
       rc = DosExecPgm(object_name,         /* failing object if progam fails*/
                       sizeof(object_name), /* the object size               */
                       2,                   /* async. program execution      */
                       programs[i],         /* program parameters            */
                       NULL,                /* inherit environment           */
                       &ExecResult,         /* termination reason code       */
                       programs[i]);        /* program name                  */
       if (rc)
          { print_error(rc,"creating a process", __FILE__,__LINE__);
            exit(FAILED);
          }
        processid[i] = ExecResult.codeTerminate;   /* save process id        */
      }
} /* end create_processes */
```

Figure 7-22. The create_processes() Function.

MULTI.C: User Interaction Functions

The functions described in this section perform the user interaction and field update portions of the MULTI program. The **update_screen_fields()** function, listed in Figure 7-23, is used to display information in the four task windows when the MULTI control panel first comes up. The function simply invokes **perform_field_action()** twelve times, since we have four task windows each containing a PRIORITY field, a LEVEL field, and a SEMAPHORE field.

The **perform_field_action()** function, listed in Figure 7-25, specializes in performing the operations specified in the fields located in the four task windows. It knows which field to update by the task/task_field parameter pair that gets passed to it. The function maintains information on each of the task fields in the **field** array which we introduced in Figure 7-11 on page 161. It will display a string on the control panel which is derived from the current field value.

The **get_user_input()** function, listed in Figure 7-24, blocks on **getch()** waiting for the user to enter something. When this happens, the function comes to life, and with the assistance of its helper routines, it performs some work. Here's what the different keys do:

- The ARROW keys result in moving the cursor to an adjacent task window field and updating the field focus.
- The + and - keys, increment and decrement the value of the field with the focus. The action itself gets executed when **perform_field_action()** is invoked.
- The ESC key terminates MULTI.
- The **R** and **S** keys, are used to start or terminate a race.
- The **C** key is used to reset the race counters.

No new OS/2 API calls are introduced here; we will encounter new calls when we get into the helper routine listings.

```
/*----------------------------------------------------------------------*/
/* Update fields on the screen that the user can modify                 */
/*----------------------------------------------------------------------*/
VOID update_screen_fields(VOID)
{
  for (x = 0; x <= FIELD_X_MAX; ++x)
    {for (y = 0; y <= FIELD_Y_MAX; ++y)
       perform_field_action(x, y);
    }
} /* end update_screen_fields */
```

Figure 7-23. The update_screen_fields() Function.

```
/*---------------------------------------------------------------------*/
/* get keystrokes from user, act on input                              */
/*---------------------------------------------------------------------*/
USHORT get_user_input()
{
  USHORT ch;                            /* input char from keyboard        */
  CHAR   time_str[10];                  /* for formulating a time  to display*/

  /*------------------------------------*/
  /* get the user key strokes and        */
  /* process them.                       */
  /*------------------------------------*/
  draw_cursor(CURSOR_FIELD_ATTR, field[field_x][field_y].x,
                                 field[field_x][field_y].y,
                                 field[field_x][field_y].cx);


  ch = getch();
  if (ch == 0)
     ch = getch() + 256;

  last_field_x = field_x;               /* set the current task field focus */
  last_field_y = field_y;               /*    ,,                            */

  switch (ch)
   {
    case LEFT_ARROW :
    case RIGHT_ARROW:
    case UP_ARROW   :
    case DOWN_ARROW : move_cursor(ch);
                      break;

    case PLUS_KEY   : update_value(&field[field_x][field_y].value,
                                   INCREMENT,
                                   field[field_x][field_y].min,
                                   field[field_x][field_y].max);
                      break;

    case MINUS_KEY  : update_value(&field[field_x][field_y].value,
                                   DECREMENT,
                                   field[field_x][field_y].min,
                                   field[field_x][field_y].max);
                      break;

    case ESC_KEY    : return(TERMINATE);

    case 'c'        : /*-------------------------------------*/
    case 'C'        : /* reset and redisplay the count fields*/
                      /*-------------------------------------*/
                      for (i=0; i<4; ++i)
                          {
                           count_ptr->count[i] = 0;
                           count_ptr->count[i+4] = 0;
                           write_str("       ", OUTPUT_FIELD_ATTR,
                                     (i * 20) + 10, 9);
                           write_str("       ", OUTPUT_FIELD_ATTR,
                                     (i * 20) + 10,10);
                          }
```

Figure 7-24 (Part 1 of 2). The get_user_input() Function.

```
                        /*-----------------------------------*/
                        /* reset elapsed time msecs          */
                        /*-----------------------------------*/
                        elapsed_time_msecs = 0;
                        sprintf(time_str,"%lu.%-4lu",
                                elapsed_time_msecs / 1000,
                                elapsed_time_msecs % 1000);
                        write_str(time_str, OUTPUT_FIELD_ATTR, 18, 20);

                        /*-----------------------------------*/
                        /* reset total count                 */
                        /*-----------------------------------*/
                        write_str("         ", OUTPUT_FIELD_ATTR, 18, 21);
                        break;

      case 'r'        : /*-----------------------------------*/
      case 'R'        : /* start execution                   */
                        /*-----------------------------------*/
                        clear_semaphore(runall_sem_handle, &runall_sem_status);
                        test_running = TRUE;
                        write_str("RUNNING", OUTPUT_FIELD_ATTR, 18, 22);
                        break;

      case 's'        : /*-----------------------------------*/
      case 'S'        : /* stop execution                    */
                        /*-----------------------------------*/
                        set_semaphore(runall_sem_handle, &runall_sem_status);
                        test_running = FALSE;
                        write_str("STOPPED", OUTPUT_FIELD_ATTR, 18, 22);
                        break;

      default         :
                        break;
    } /* end switch */

    return(CONTINUE);
} /* end get_user_input */
```

Figure 7-24 (Part 2 of 2). The get_user_input() Function.

```
/*------------------------------------------------------------------------*/
/* write IO field value to screen, perform action                         */
/*------------------------------------------------------------------------*/
VOID perform_field_action(USHORT task, USHORT task_field)
{
  CHAR     field_str[20];

  switch(task_field)
    {
     case PRIORITY  : switch(field[task][task_field].value)
                       {case BACKGROUND   : strcpy(field_str,"BG");
                                            break;
                        case REGULAR      : strcpy(field_str,"RG");
                                            break;
                        case TIME_CRITICAL: strcpy(field_str,"TC");
                                            break;
                        case FIXED_HIGH   : strcpy(field_str,"FH");
                                            break;
                       }
                      set_priority(task);
                      break;

     case LEVEL     : sprintf(field_str, "%-2d", field[task][task_field].value);
                      set_priority(task);
                      break;

     case SEMAPHORE : if (field[task][task_field].value == 0)
                         {strcpy(field_str,"CLEAR");
                          clear_semaphore(run_sem_handle[task],
                                          &task_status[task].semaphore);
                         }
                      else
                         {strcpy(field_str,"SET  ");
                          request_semaphore(run_sem_handle[task],
                                            &task_status[task].semaphore);
                         }
                      break;

     default             : break;
    }

  write_str(field_str, IO_FIELD_ATTR,
            field[task][task_field].x,
            field[task][task_field].y);

} /* end perform_field_action */
```

Figure 7-25. The perform_field_action() Function.

MULTI.C: Screen Helper Routines

The two screen helper routines listed below are used primarily by **get_user_input()**. They consist of straight C code that does not introduce new OS/2 functions.

```
/*****************************************************************************/
/* Screen helper routines                                                    */
/*****************************************************************************/
/*---------------------------------------------------------------------------*/
/* Update cursor location                                                    */
/*---------------------------------------------------------------------------*/
VOID move_cursor(USHORT key)
{
  switch (key)
    {
      case DOWN_ARROW : update_value(&field_y, INCREMENT, 0, FIELD_Y_MAX);
                        break;

      case UP_ARROW   : update_value(&field_y, DECREMENT, 0, FIELD_Y_MAX);
                        break;

      case RIGHT_ARROW: update_value(&field_x, INCREMENT, 0, FIELD_X_MAX);
                        break;

      case LEFT_ARROW : update_value(&field_x, DECREMENT, 0, FIELD_X_MAX);
                        break;
    } /* endswitch */

} /* end move_cursor */

/*---------------------------------------------------------------------------*/
/* Update value of a variable                                                */
/*---------------------------------------------------------------------------*/
VOID update_value(PUSHORT value,     USHORT direction,
                  USHORT  min_value, USHORT max_value)
{
  if (direction == INCREMENT)
      if (*value == max_value)
          *value = min_value;
       else
          ++*value;
  else
      if (*value == min_value)
          *value = max_value;
       else
          --*value;
} /* end update_value */
```

Figure 7-26. The Screen Helper Routines.

MULTI.C: DOS Helper Routines

The helper functions, listed in Figure 7-27 invoke some of the more frequently used OS/2 calls and take care of the error handling associated with them. We've already encountered most of the OS/2 calls used in this section. The **DosSetPrty** call was described in "DosSetPrty" on page 178. The **DosSemClear** call was described in "DosSemClear" on page 172, and the **DosSemSet** call was described in "DosSemSet" on page 171. The only new OS/2 call in this code section is **DosSemRequest**. A description of **DosSemRequest** follows.

DosSemRequest

The **DosSemRequest** API call is used in "wait until the semaphore clears then grab it" mutual exclusion situations. The call waits on a system or RAM semaphore to clear, then sets it in one uninterruptible *atomic* operation. The calling thread blocks until the semaphore clears or a time-out occurs. If multiple calls to **DosSemRequest** are issued, they must be matched by a corresponding number of **DosSemClear** calls to clear the semaphore. The API is level-triggered, meaning that a thread may have to wait through multiple changes of the semaphore before it continues. This may happen if another waiting thread grabs the semaphore before it. The prototype for this call is:

```
DosSemRequest(PVOID    sem_handle,  /* semaphore handle            */
              LONG     timeout);    /* -1L= wait, 0=nowait, >0=msecs*/
```

A description of the parameters follows:

- The ***sem_handle*** parameter is the handle which points to a semaphore variable. This handle must have been previously created using **DosCreateSem** or **DosOpenSem**
- The ***timeout*** parameter specifies how long to wait on the semaphore to clear. If you set this parameter to zero, the call returns immediately. A return code of 121 will let you know that the semaphore is already owned. A positive value specifies the number of milliseconds to wait before returning. Most probably, you will be setting this value to -1L, which means "wait indefinitely until the semaphore clears."

```
/****************************************************************************/
/* DOS call helper routines                                                 */
/****************************************************************************/
/*------------------------------------------------------------------------*/
/* request a semaphore which controls a thread's execution                  */
/*------------------------------------------------------------------------*/
VOID request_semaphore(HSEM sem_handle, PUSHORT status)
{
 if (*status == CLEAR)
    {if (rc = DosSemRequest(sem_handle,-1L))
        { print_error(rc,"during DosSemRequest", __FILE__,__LINE__);
          exit(FAILED);
        }
     *status = SET;
    }
} /* end request_semaphore */
```

Figure 7-27 (Part 1 of 2). The DOS Call Helper Routines.

```
/*-----------------------------------------------------------------*/
/* clear a semaphore which controls a thread's execution           */
/*-----------------------------------------------------------------*/
VOID clear_semaphore(HSEM sem_handle, PUSHORT status)
{
 if (*status == SET)
    {if (rc = DosSemClear(sem_handle))
        { print_error(rc,"during DosSemClear", __FILE__,__LINE__);
          exit(FAILED);
        }
     *status = CLEAR;
    }
} /* end clear_semaphore */

/*-----------------------------------------------------------------*/
/* set a semaphore which controls a thread's execution             */
/*-----------------------------------------------------------------*/
VOID set_semaphore(HSEM sem_handle, PUSHORT status)
{
 if (*status == CLEAR)
    {if (rc = DosSemSet(sem_handle))
        { print_error(rc,"during DosSemSet", __FILE__,__LINE__);
          exit(FAILED);
        }
     *status = SET;
    }
}  /* end set_semaphore */

/*-----------------------------------------------------------------*/
/* set the priority of a task                                      */
/*-----------------------------------------------------------------*/
VOID set_priority(USHORT task_number)
{
  /*------------------------------*/
  /* set the  priority, level     */
  /*------------------------------*/
  if (program_type == PROCESSES)
      rc = DosSetPrty(0,                    /* id is a process id     */
                field[task_number][PRIORITY].value,      /* priority*/
                field[task_number][LEVEL   ].value,      /* level   */
                processid[task_number]);                 /* thread  */
  else
      rc = DosSetPrty(2,                    /* id is a thread id      */
                field[task_number][PRIORITY].value,      /* priority*/
                field[task_number][LEVEL   ].value,      /* level   */
                threadid[task_number]);                  /* thread  */

  if (rc)
     {print_error(rc,"during DosSetPriority",__FILE__,__LINE__);
      exit(FAILED);
     }
}  /* end set_priority */
```

Figure 7-27 (Part 2 of 2). The DOS Call Helper Routines.

MULTI.C: VIO Helper Routines

In this section, we introduce a number of screen helper routines that build on top of the OS/2 **VIO** API calls. The helper routines, listed in Figure 7-28, fall into two categories:

- Application specific helper routines that are used to paint the MULTI control panel windows.
- Generic helper routines which provide a set of screen primitives which you may want to use in future programs.

Application Specific Helper Routines

These are the helper routines which paint the MULTI control panel window. They use the generic help routines to provide their services; and since they are written using ordinary C code and should be easy to follow:

- The **draw_title_box()** routine draws the top window.
- The **draw_task_box()** routine is used to draw the four task windows.
- The **display_exec_status()** routine draws the lower left window that displays the execution status.
- The **display_sys_info()** routine displays the lower right window that contains system information.

Generic Helper Routines

These helper routines provide a set of reusable screen primitives. You can tell by their names what they do:

- clear_screen()
- write_str()
- fill_area()
- draw_box()
- draw_horizontal_line(), draw_vertical_line()
- draw_cursor(), hide_cursor(), restore_cursor()

The generic routines use the OS/2 VIO services. This service provides a very fast set of API functions for writing text to the screen and for controlling the cursor. You will find that these API functions can be used quite effectively to supplement the standard C library functions you are familiar with. You should still use C functions, such as **sprintf()**, to format complex string output. However, you can now supplement those functions with the OS/2 VIO API calls to add color, manipulate display attributes, control the cursor, or write to a particular location on the screen.

The generic helper routines make use of a total of five OS/2 VIO calls, on top of which they create their services:

VioWrtCharStrAtt: This API call is used for placing a character string at a specified screen location, with video attributes such as: bold, color, reverse video, blinking, and underline. It is used by **write_str()**. We previously encountered this API in "VioWrtCharStrAtt" on page 127.

VioWrtNAttr: This API call is issued to change the color or display attributes of portions of the screen. It is used by **draw_cursor()** to create a custom cursor. This API call is described in "VioWrtNAttr."

VioScrollDn: This API call is the preferred method for clearing the screen and may be used, of course, for scrolling down the screen. It is used by **fill_area()**. This API call is described in "VioScrollDn" on page 194.

VioGetCurType and VioSetCurType: These API calls are used to change the cursor format interactively. We can for example, choose to hide the cursor entirely when we do not expect any user input, and this is precisely how it is used by **hide_cursor()**. These API calls are described in "VioGetCurType" on page 194 and in "VioSetCurType" on page 195.

A description of the newly introduced VIO calls follows

VioWrtNAttr

The **VioWrtNAttr** API call writes a character attribute string to a screen a specified number of times. The prototype for this call is:

```
VioWrtNAttr(PCHAR      attr,          /* pointer to fill char/attrib  */
            USHORT     times,         /* number of times to write     */
            USHORT     row_x,         /* row to start writing         */
            USHORT     column_y,      /* column to start writing      */
            USHORT     handle);       /* video handle                 */
```

A description of the parameters follows:

- The ***attr*** parameter points to the display attribute that will be used to write to the screen. The description of the character attribute is in "VioWrtCharStrAtt" on page 127.
- The ***times*** parameter specifies the number of times to write the character attribute. If the number is larger than the current line, the function continues writing at the start of the next line but does go past the end of the screen.
- The ***row_x*** parameter specifies the row at which to start writing attributes.
- The ***column_y*** parameter specifies the column at which to start writing attributes.
- The ***handle*** parameter is the presentation handle used by PM applications, and is otherwise NULL.

VioScrollDn

The **VioScrollDn** API call scrolls an area of the screen downward a specified number of lines. The prototype for this call is:

```
VioScrollDn(USHORT    top_x,          /* top row of scrolled area      */
            USHORT    left_y,         /* left column of scrolled area */
            USHORT    bottom_x,       /* bottom row of scrolled area  */
            USHORT    right_y,        /* right column of scrolled area*/
            USHORT    lines,          /* number of lines              */
            PCHAR     fill,           /* pointer to fill char/attrib  */
            USHORT    handle);        /* video handle                 */
```

A description of the parameters follows:

- The ***top_x*** parameter specifies the top row of the scroll area.
- The ***left_y*** parameter specifies the leftmost column of the scroll area.
- The ***bottom_x*** parameter specifies the bottom row of the scroll area.
- The ***right_y*** parameter specifies the rightmost column of the scroll area.
- The ***lines*** parameter specifies the number of blank lines to be inserted at the top of the screen area which gets scrolled.
- The ***fill*** parameter points to a character/attribute array, also called a cell, that fills the screen area left blank by scrolling. The first array element contains the character. The second array element contains an attribute byte such as that described in "VioWrtCharStrAtt" on page 127.
- The **handle** parameter is the presentation handle used by PM applications, and is otherwise NULL.

VioGetCurType

The **VioGetCurType** API call retrieves information about the cursor, such as the height and width, and whether it is currently visible. The prototype for this call is:

```
VioGetCurType(VIOCURSORINFO      *curdata,      /* pointer to cur info struct*/
              USHORT             handle);       /* video handle              */
```

A description of the parameters follows:

- The ***curdata*** parameter points to the **VIOCURSORINFO** structure which receives the information about the cursor. The structure has the following form:

```
struct _VIOCURSORINFO
   {USHORT   yStart;      /* Top scan line in cursor 0=top                 */
    USHORT   cEnd;        /* Bottom scan line in cursor max=cell height    */
    USHORT   cx;          /* Width of cursor columns in pels or chars
                             0 =default i.e., 1 char or cell width in pels*/
    USHORT   attr;        /* 0xFFFF = hides the cursor                     */
   } VIOCURSORINFO;
```

- The ***handle*** parameter is a presentation handle used by PM applications. It is set to NULL by non-PM applications..

VioSetCurType

The **VioSetCurType** API call sets the cursor type for all processes in a screen group. The prototype for this call is:

```
VioSetCurType(VIOCURSORINFO far *curdata,      /* pointer to cur info struct*/
              USHORT            handle);       /* video handle              */
```

A description of the parameters follows:

- The ***curdata*** parameter points to the **VIOCURSORINFO** structure which specifies the characteristics of the cursor. The structure is defined in "VioGetCurType" on page 194.
- The ***handle*** parameter is a presentation handle used by PM applications. It is set to NULL by non-PM applications.

Now that we have a description of the VIO calls, it becomes easy to follow the code for the generic helper functions. Note that the **hide_cursor()** helper routine uses **DosExitList** (see "DosExitList" on page 121) with the action_flag set to 1 to add the function **multi_exit()** to the exit list. The **multi_exit()** function, among other things, invokes **restore_cursor()** which re-enables the cursor for the screen group when MULTI terminates.

```
/*************************************************************************/
/* VIO call helper routines                                              */
/*************************************************************************/
/*-----------------------------------------------------------------------*/
/* draw a MULTI panel title box window                                   */
/*-----------------------------------------------------------------------*/
VOID draw_title_box(USHORT x, USHORT y)
{
  #define TITLE_BOX_CX 80
  #define TITLE_BOX_CY 7

  draw_box("", BOX_TITLE_ATTR, x, y,
           TITLE_BOX_CX, TITLE_BOX_CY, BOX_ATTR);
  if (program_type == THREADS)
     write_str("Multithread Execution Example", PANEL_TITLE_ATTR, x+25, y+1);
  else
     write_str("Multiprocess Execution Example", PANEL_TITLE_ATTR, x+25, y+1);
  write_str("Use arrow keys to move the cursor.  "
            "Use + and - keys to change field values.",
            PANEL_HELP_ATTR, x+2, y+3);
  write_str("Press R to start running, S to stop, or C to clear the count.",
            PANEL_HELP_ATTR, x+2, y+4);
  write_str("Press ESC to terminate the program.",
            PANEL_HELP_ATTR, x+2, y+5);
}  /* end draw_title_box */

/*-----------------------------------------------------------------------*/
/* draw MULTI task display window                                        */
/*-----------------------------------------------------------------------*/
VOID draw_task_box(PCHAR title, USHORT x, USHORT y)
{
  #define TASK_BOX_CX 20
  #define TASK_BOX_CY 10

  draw_box(title, BOX_TITLE_ATTR,
           x, y, TASK_BOX_CX, TASK_BOX_CY, BOX_ATTR);

  write_str("Count = ",     FIELD_TEXT_ATTR, x+2, y+2);
  write_str("Priority  = ", FIELD_TEXT_ATTR, x+2, y+4);
  write_str("Level     = ", FIELD_TEXT_ATTR, x+2, y+5);
  write_str("Semaphore = ", FIELD_TEXT_ATTR, x+2, y+6);

  /*----------------------------------*/
  /* display task status              */
  /*----------------------------------*/
  write_str("Initializing", PANEL_STATUS_ATTR,
            x+2, y+8);                 /* calculate display location    */
                                       /*  based on thread number       */
}  /* end draw_task_box */
```

Figure 7-28 (Part 1 of 5). The VIO Call Helper Functions.

```
/*--------------------------------------------------------------------------*/
/* display MULTI system configuration window                                */
/*--------------------------------------------------------------------------*/
VOID display_sys_info(USHORT x, USHORT y)
{
  #define SYSTEM_BOX_CX 40
  #define SYSTEM_BOX_CY  8

  CHAR value_str[20];                  /* format string for displaying values*/

  /*-------------------------------*/
  /* draw the box, display the info */
  /*-------------------------------*/
  draw_box("SYSTEM INFORMATION", BOX_TITLE_ATTR,
           x, y, SYSTEM_BOX_CX, SYSTEM_BOX_CY, BOX_ATTR);

  write_str("Maximum Wait      =              sec", FIELD_TEXT_ATTR, x+2, y+2);
  sprintf(value_str, "%u", global_info->csecMaxWait);
  write_str(value_str, OUTPUT_FIELD_ATTR, x+23, y+2);

  sprintf(value_str, "%u", global_info->cmsecMinSlice);
  write_str("Minimum Time Slice =             ms ", FIELD_TEXT_ATTR, x+2, y+3);
  write_str(value_str, OUTPUT_FIELD_ATTR, x+23, y+3);

  sprintf(value_str, "%u", global_info->cmsecMaxSlice);
  write_str("Maximum Time Slice =             ms ", FIELD_TEXT_ATTR, x+2, y+4);
  write_str(value_str, OUTPUT_FIELD_ATTR, x+23, y+4);

  write_str("Dynamic Variation  =                ", FIELD_TEXT_ATTR, x+2, y+5);
  if (global_info->fDynamicSched)
     write_str("ACTIVE", OUTPUT_FIELD_ATTR, x+23, y+5);
  else
     write_str("INACTIVE", OUTPUT_FIELD_ATTR, x+23, y+5);

} /* end display_sys_info */

/*--------------------------------------------------------------------------*/
/* display MULTI execution status data window                               */
/*--------------------------------------------------------------------------*/
VOID display_exec_status(USHORT x, USHORT y)
{
  #define SYSTEM_BOX_CX 40
  #define SYSTEM_BOX_CY  8

  CHAR value_str[20];                  /* format string for displaying values*/

  /*-------------------------------*/
  /* draw the box, display the info */
  /*-------------------------------*/
  draw_box("EXECUTION STATUS", BOX_TITLE_ATTR,
           x, y, SYSTEM_BOX_CX, SYSTEM_BOX_CY, BOX_ATTR);

  write_str("Stop Time     =                  sec", FIELD_TEXT_ATTR, x+2, y+2);
  sprintf(value_str,"%lu.%-4lu", stop_time_msecs/1000, stop_time_msecs % 1000);
  write_str(value_str, OUTPUT_FIELD_ATTR, x+18, y+2);
```

Figure 7-28 (Part 2 of 5). The VIO Call Helper Functions.

```
  write_str("Elapsed Time  =                    sec", FIELD_TEXT_ATTR, x+2, y+3);
  sprintf(value_str,"%lu.%-4lu", elapsed_time_msecs/1000,
          elapsed_time_msecs % 1000);
  write_str(value_str, OUTPUT_FIELD_ATTR, x+18, y+3);

  write_str("Total Count   =                       ", FIELD_TEXT_ATTR, x+2, y+4);

  write_str("Run Status    =                       ", FIELD_TEXT_ATTR, x+2, y+5);
  write_str("STOPPED", OUTPUT_FIELD_ATTR, x+18, y+5);
} /* end display_exec_status */

/*----------------------------------------------------------------------*/
/* draw a generic box with a title.                                     */
/*----------------------------------------------------------------------*/
VOID draw_box(PCHAR title, CHAR title_attribute,
         USHORT x, USHORT y, USHORT cx, USHORT cy, CHAR box_attribute)
{
  draw_horizontal_line(x+1   , y     , cx-2  , box_attribute); /* top        */
  draw_horizontal_line(x+1   , y+cy-1, cx-2  , box_attribute); /* bottom     */
  draw_vertical_line  (x     , y+1   , cy-2  , box_attribute); /* left side  */
  draw_vertical_line  (x+cx-1, y+1   , cy-2  , box_attribute); /* right side */

  write_str(BOX_UL_CORNER, box_attribute,   x     , y     );   /* update     */
  write_str(BOX_UR_CORNER, box_attribute,   x+cx-1, y     );   /*   the      */
  write_str(BOX_LL_CORNER, box_attribute,   x     , y+cy-1);   /*    corners */
  write_str(BOX_LR_CORNER, box_attribute,   x+cx-1, y+cy-1);   /*            */

  write_str(title, title_attribute,  x+2, y);                  /* box title  */
}  /* end draw_box */

/*----------------------------------------------------------------------*/
/* hide the cursor                                                      */
/*----------------------------------------------------------------------*/
VOID hide_cursor(VOID)
{

  if (rc = VioGetCurType(&save_cursor_data,      /* cursor definition      */
                         0))                     /* reserved               */
     print_error(rc,"during VioGetCurType",__FILE__,__LINE__);

  cursor_data.yStart = 0;
  cursor_data.cEnd   = 0;
  cursor_data.cx     = 0;
  cursor_data.attr   = -1;

  if (rc = VioSetCurType(&cursor_data, /* cursor definition                */
                         0))          /* reserved                          */
     print_error(rc,"during VioSetCurType",__FILE__,__LINE__);

  /*--------------------------------*/
  /* exit routine to restore cursor */
  /*   when program ends            */
  /*--------------------------------*/
  if (rc = DosExitList(1,(PFNEXITLIST) multi_exit))
     { printf("Error establishing error exit routine.\n");
       exit(FAILED);
     }
} /* end hide_cursor */
```

Figure 7-28 (Part 3 of 5). The VIO Call Helper Functions.

```
/*--------------------------------------------------------------------------*/
/* restore the cursor                                                       */
/*--------------------------------------------------------------------------*/
VOID restore_cursor(VOID)
{

  if (rc = VioSetCurType(&save_cursor_data,      /* cursor definition       */
                         0))                     /* reserved                */
     print_error(rc,"during VioSetCurType",__FILE__,__LINE__);
} /* end restore_cursor */

/*--------------------------------------------------------------------------*/
/* draw field cursor                                                        */
/*--------------------------------------------------------------------------*/
VOID draw_cursor(BYTE attribute, USHORT x, USHORT y, USHORT cx)
{
  if (rc = VioWrtNAttr(&attribute,     /* attribute                         */
                       cx,             /* number of times                   */
                       y, x,           /* screen position                   */
                       0))             /* reserved                          */
     print_error(rc,"during VioWrtNAttr",__FILE__,__LINE__);

} /* end draw_cursor */

/*--------------------------------------------------------------------------*/
/* write a character string to the screen.                                  */
/*--------------------------------------------------------------------------*/
VOID write_str(PCHAR charstr, CHAR attribute, USHORT x, USHORT y)
{
  CHAR cell[2];
  BYTE attr;

  if (rc = VioWrtCharStrAtt(charstr,   /* character string                  */
                       strlen(charstr),/* number of times                   */
                       y, x,           /* screen position                   */
                       &attribute,     /* attribute                         */
                       0))             /* reserved                          */
     print_error(rc,"during VioWrtCharStrAtt",__FILE__,__LINE__);
} /* end write_str */

/*--------------------------------------------------------------------------*/
/* fill an area with a specified char and attribute                         */
/*--------------------------------------------------------------------------*/
VOID fill_area(PCHAR ch, CHAR attribute, USHORT x, USHORT y, USHORT cx, USHORT cy)
{
  CHAR fill[2];

  fill[0] = ch[0];
  fill[1] = attribute;
  /*------------------------------------------------------------------------*/
  /* Scroll cy lines to fill an area                                        */
  /*------------------------------------------------------------------------*/
  if (rc = VioScrollDn(y, x,                   /* upper left of scroll area  */
                       y+cy-1, x+cx-1,         /* lower right of scroll area */
                       cy,                     /* lines to scroll            */
                       fill,                   /* fill char/attrib pair      */
                       0))                     /* reserved word of 0's       */
     print_error(rc,"during VioScrollDn",__FILE__,__LINE__);
} /* end fill_area */
```

Figure 7-28 (Part 4 of 5). The VIO Call Helper Functions.

```
/*---------------------------------------------------------------------------*/
/* clear the screen                                                          */
/*---------------------------------------------------------------------------*/
VOID clear_screen()
{
  fill_area(BLANK, FIELD_TEXT_ATTR, 0, 0, 999, 999);
}  /* end clear_screen */

/*---------------------------------------------------------------------------*/
/* draw a horizontal line.                                                   */
/*---------------------------------------------------------------------------*/
VOID draw_horizontal_line(USHORT x, USHORT y, USHORT cx, CHAR attribute)
{
  fill_area(HORIZONTAL_LINE, attribute, x, y, cx, 1);
} /* end draw_horizontal_line */

/*---------------------------------------------------------------------------*/
/* draw a vertical line.                                                     */
/*---------------------------------------------------------------------------*/
VOID draw_vertical_line(USHORT x, USHORT y, USHORT cy, CHAR attribute)
{
  fill_area(VERTICAL_LINE, attribute, x, y, 1, cy);
} /* end draw_vertical_line */
```

Figure 7-28 (Part 5 of 5). The VIO Call Helper Functions.

MULTI.C: Miscellaneous Helper Routines

The miscellaneous helper routines, **print_error()** and **multi_exit()**, are listed in Figure 7-29. The **print_error()** function records useful debug information such as the error number, the error description, and the source code file and line number where the error occurred. Both the IBM and Microsoft C compilers maintain two predefined preprocessor symbols, **__FILE__** and **__LINE__**, which refer to the current input file name and the current line number being processed by the compiler. A failing uses the preprocessor macros to obtain the source code file and line number where the error occurs. It then passes these numbers to **print_error()** as parameters.

The **multi_exit()** function simply restores the cursor and issues a **DosExitList**, (see "DosExitList" on page 121) with the action_flag set to 3. This indicates that OS/2 can transfer control to the next exit list procedure.

```
/*****************************************************************************/
/* miscellaneous helper routines                                             */
/*****************************************************************************/
/*--------------------------------------------------------------------------*/
/* Error Display Routine                                                    */
/*--------------------------------------------------------------------------*/
VOID print_error(USHORT Error, PCHAR msg, PCHAR file, USHORT line)
{
 printf("Error %d detected while %s at line %d in file %s.\n",
        Error, msg, line, file);
} /* end print_error */

/*--------------------------------------------------------------------------*/
/* Exit Routine                                                             */
/*--------------------------------------------------------------------------*/
VOID FAR multi_exit(USHORT exit_type)
{
  restore_cursor();
  DosExitList(3, (PVOID)0);
} /* end multi_exit */
```

Figure 7-29. Miscellaneous Helper Routines.

MULTI.C: terminate_program()

The **terminate_program()** function, listed in Figure 7-30, kills the four process contenders, clears the screen, and returns to OS/2. Notice that we only kill processes; threads terminate automatically with the program. Killing processes is a two-step affair. First, the OS/2 **DosKillProcess** call (see "DosKillProcess" on page 136) is issued to kill the process, followed by a **DosCWait** call which performs a post-mortem. The following is a description of **DosCWait**.

DosCWait

The **DosCWait** API call, blocks the calling process until a specified child process (or processes) terminate. It is used when the parent is asynchronously executing with a child process and the parent has to wait at some point in the program for the child to finish processing. The prototype for this call is:

```
DosCWait(USHORT       scope_flag,     /* Process or descendants too*/
         USHORT       wait_flag,      /* Wait or no wait          */
         RESULTCODES  far *results,   /* Result codes             */
         PUSHORT      processID,      /* Pointer to returned PID  */
         USHORT       waitprocessID);/* 0 = any or PID to wait for*/
```

A description of the parameters follows:

- The ***scope_flag*** parameter specifies how many processes to wait for. If it is 0, the parent waits only for the specified process. If it is 1, the function waits for the specified process and all its child processes to end.

- The ***wait_flag*** parameter specifies whether or not to wait for processes to end. If it is 0, the function waits for a process to terminate. If it is 1, the function returns immediately with the resultcodes of the most recent process to end; however, an error message is returned if the specified process is still running.
- The ***results*** parameter points to the RESULTCODES structure, previously described for **DosExecProgram**, see "DosExecPgm" on page 182. The structure is filled with a termination code supplied by OS/2 and the result code supplied by the terminating process when it invokes **DosExit**
- The ***processID*** parameter is a pointer to the PID returned by OS/2 for the terminating process. This is used to identify which of the descendants just terminated.
- The ***waitprocessID*** parameter specifies the PID of the process to wait for. If it is NULL and the scope flag specifies all descendants, then the first child to terminate causes the function to return. This option requires **DosCWait** to be called repeatedly for each child process of the specified PID.

The **DosExit** API is used to end a thread or a process and all its threads. When a process terminates, all its resources are closed and its buffers are flushed. If no other invocation of the process is active, OS/2 frees the code and data segments as well. When a thread or process terminate their execution, they do not return to a caller, they just stop running.

```
/*-------------------------------------------------------------------------*/
/* User requested program terminate, kill tasks and clean up              */
/*-------------------------------------------------------------------------*/
VOID terminate_program(VOID)
{
  if (program_type == PROCESSES)
     {
      for (i=0; i<4; ++i)
          {
           /*------------------------------*/
           /* display process status       */
           /*------------------------------*/
           write_str("Terminating ", PANEL_STATUS_ATTR,
                     (i * 20) + 2, 15);      /* calculate display location   */
                                             /*  based on process number     */
```

Figure 7-30 (Part 1 of 2). The terminate_program() Function.

```
            rc = DosKillProcess(1, /* only kill one process */
                        processid[i]);
            if (rc)
               { print_error(rc,"killing a process",
                        __FILE__,__LINE__);
                 exit(FAILED);
               }

            rc = DosCwait(1, /* wait for child and descendants*/
                        0, /* wait for child termination    */
                        &term_result,
                        &term_processid,
                        processid[i]);/* id to wait for  */
            if (rc)
               { print_error(rc,"waiting for a process to end",
                        __FILE__,__LINE__);
                 exit(FAILED);
               }

            write_str("Terminated  ", PANEL_STATUS_ATTR,
                  (i * 20) + 2, 15);       /* calculate display location    */
                                           /*  based on process number      */
            }
       }
    clear_screen();
    exit(GOOD);
 } /* end terminate_program */
```

Figure 7-30 (Part 2 of 2). The terminate_program() Function.

MULTI.C: thread_count

Up until this point, the MULTI program was involved with setting up the infrastructure for running races. In the remaining sections of this chapter, we examine the code that gets executed by the race contenders. The listing in Figure 7-31, is that of our representative thread champion, **thread_count**. Remember that we will be running races between four thread instances of the code listed here, which we do by passing a thread_number parameter. A thread first clears its counter in the shared segment area of memory and then goes into a do forever loop. Before getting into the details of the loop, you should refer to Figure 7-14 on page 170, for a quick refresher on the semaphore structure that was put in place by MULTI to control the races.

This is how a racing thread champion loops through life:

- The champ first waits on \SEM\RUNALL to clear indicating a race just started.
- The champ then waits on \SEM\RUNn to clear (where "n" is the particular champ's number). If the semaphore is clear, this means that this champ was asked to participate in the race. The champ then sets the semaphore and starts racing.
- The champ then increments its race counter by 1, and updates the task window on MULTI's control panel, with the new count.
- The champ then clears \SEM\RUNn.
- The champ is now ready for another round through the loop...

Our champion's life, as you see, literally revolves around updating its counters. In later chapters, we will introduce other champions that perform more interesting types of additional activity that we will want to measure in a race setting.

The **thread_count**, does not introduce any new OS/2 functions. The **DosSemWait** call is described in "DosSemWait" on page 175, the **DosSemRequest** call is described in "DosSemRequest" on page 190, and **DosSemClear** call, is described in "DosSemClear" on page 172.

```
/*-----------------------------------------------------------------------*/
/* Thread routine. This routine continuously 1) requests a semaphore,    */
/*   2) increments and displays a count, 3) clears the semaphore. The user */
/*   can disable counting by setting the semaphore from the display panel. */
/*-----------------------------------------------------------------------*/
VOID thread_count(PUSHORT thread_number)
{
  CHAR   count_str[10];
  USHORT rc;

  count_ptr->count[*thread_number] = 0;

  /*-----------------------------------*/
  /* display thread status             */
  /*-----------------------------------*/
  write_str("Ready       ", PANEL_STATUS_ATTR,
          (*thread_number * 20) + 2, 15); /* calculate display location   */
                                          /*  based on thread number      */

  /*-----------------------------------*/
  /* continuous count loop             */
  /*-----------------------------------*/
  while (TRUE)
    {
      /*-----------------------------------*/
      /* wait for control sem to clear     */
      /*-----------------------------------*/
      if (rc = DosSemWait(runall_sem_handle,               /* semaphore handle */
                         -1L))                              /* infinite timeout */
        { print_error(rc,"during DosSemWait",
                       __FILE__,__LINE__);
          exit(FAILED);
        }

      /*-----------------------------------*/
      /* request the semaphore             */
      /*-----------------------------------*/
      if (rc = DosSemRequest(run_sem_handle[*thread_number], /* sem handle   */
                            -1L))                           /* infinite timeout */
        { print_error(rc,"during DosSemRequest",
                       __FILE__,__LINE__);
          exit(FAILED);
        }
```

Figure 7-31 (Part 1 of 2). The thread_count() Thread.

```
        /*-----------------------------------*/
        /* increment the count               */
        /*-----------------------------------*/
        ++(count_ptr->count[*thread_number]);

        /*-----------------------------------*/
        /* display the count value           */
        /*-----------------------------------*/
        sprintf(count_str, "%-7lu", count_ptr->count[*thread_number]);
        write_str(count_str, OUTPUT_FIELD_ATTR,
                  (*thread_number * 20) + 10,  9);/* calculate display loction */
                                                  /*  based on thread number   */
        /*-----------------------------------*/
        /* clear the semaphore               */
        /*-----------------------------------*/
        if (rc = DosSemClear(run_sem_handle[*thread_number]))
           { print_error(rc,"during DosSemClear", __FILE__,__LINE__);
             exit(FAILED);
           }
     }/* end while */
  } /* end thread_count */
```

Figure 7-31 (Part 2 of 2). The thread_count() Thread.

COUNT.C: THE PROCESS CHAMPION

This section describes **COUNT.C**, our representative process champion. As you can see from the listing in Figure 7-32, a process is just a separate program. This program performs the same counting function as the representative **thread_count** thread (see listing in Figure 7-31). The purpose of this exercise is to compare OS/2's thread and process tasking services. So, we'll run races, using MULTI's racing infrastructure, between four process champions that all execute the same **COUNT.EXE** code.

Dissecting the COUNT.C Program

The **main()** program starts with the OS/2 and C library include files. The **const.h** include file is identical to the one used in MULTI.C and is listed in Figure 7-10 on page 158. The **count.h** include file, contains the forward procedure declarations and global variables for **COUNT.C** and is listed in Figure 7-33.

The first piece of code **main()** executes is to decode the champion number it will run the race under. This is needed, of course, because we will be using the same code for the four process contenders. The next pieces of code in **main()** are very important because they distinguish the way processes do things from threads:

- A process needs to issue a **DosSemOpen** to access the two global semaphores: **\SEM\RUNALL** and **\SEM\RUNn** (where "n" is the champion's number for the race). Threads don't have to issue this call because they run in the same address space as MULTI and have direct access to the semaphore handles. For processes, the following semaphore protocol is followed:

```
MULTI.C                         COUNT.C
-------                         -------
DosSemCreate                       .
"\SEM\RUNALL"                      .
DosSemCreate                       .
"\SEM\RUNn"                        .
     .                          DosSemOpen
     .                          "\SEM\RUNALL"
     .                          DosSemOpen
     .                          "\SEM\RUNn"
                                   .
     .                             .
```

- A process issues **DosGetShrSeg** to obtain a selector to the shared memory segment **\SHAREMEM\TASK**, which was previously allocated by MULTI. This is the area in memory where each champion writes its count. The protocol between MULTI.C and COUNT.C for sharing memory is as follows:

```
MULTI.C                         COUNT.C
-------                         -------
DosAllocShrSeg                     .
"\SHAREMEM\TASK"                   .
     .                          DosGetShrSeg
     .                          "\SHAREMEM\TASK"
     .                             .
     .                             .
```

With the exceptions noted, the **main**() process champion code is identical to its thread champion. You can convince yourself of this by noting, that the last thing **main**() does is invoke **thread_count**(), a procedure that runs code that is functionally identical to the **thread_count** champion thread code we presented in Figure 7-31 on page 204 You should consult the explanation given in that section to find out what a champion process does as it loops through life.

The two new OS/2 API calls introduced in this section are **DosOpenSem** and **DosGetShrSeg**; their description follows.

DosOpenSem

The **DosOpenSem** API call allows a process to obtain access to a system semaphore that was created by another process. The effect of the call is to return the handle to the semaphore; it does not test or change the status of the semaphore. The prototype for this call is:

```
DosOpenSem(PVOID     sem_handle,  /* semaphore handle          */
           PCHAR     sem_name);   /* pointer to semaphore name */
```

A description of the parameters follows:

- The ***sem_handle*** parameter is a handle that points to a semaphore variable. This is the same handle as that received by the process that issued **DosCreateSem**.
- The ***sem_name*** parameter points to a null-terminated string that provides the semaphore name. This is the same name that was provided originally by the process that issued **DosCreateSem**.

DosGetShrSeg

The **DosGetShrSeg** API call obtains a selector to a shared memory segment, which was previously allocated by another process. The call increments the segment's reference count by one to indicate that the segment is in use. The prototype for this call is:

```
DosGetShrSeg(PCHAR          name,   /* pointer to segment name   */
             PUSHORT        psel);  /* returned segment selector */
```

A description of the parameters follows:

- The ***name*** parameter points to a null-terminated string, which is the name to be given to the segment. The string must include the fictitious subdirectory name **\SHAREMEM**, and the name must be unique.
- The ***psel*** parameter points to a variable that receives the segment selector returned by OS/2.

```
/****************************************************************************/
/*  PROGRAM NAME: COUNT - A process program that MULTI starts              */
/*                                                                          */
/*  PROGRAM DESCRIPTION:  This program is run as a child task of the MULTI */
/*    program to illustrate multiprocess interaction.                      */
/****************************************************************************/
#include <process.h>                /* For exit()                          */
#include <string.h>                 /* For printf                          */
#include <stdlib.h>                 /* For atoi                            */
#include <stdio.h>                  /* For sprintf, printf                 */

#define INCL_VIO                    /* include VIO calls                   */
#define INCL_DOSMEMMGR              /* for shared segment functions        */
#define INCL_DOSSEMAPHORES          /* include semaphore api calls         */
#include <os2.h>
#include "const.h"
#include "count.h"
```

Figure 7-32 (Part 1 of 4). COUNT Program Listing.

```
/*------------------------------------------------------------------*/
/* Main routine.                                                    */
/*------------------------------------------------------------------*/
SHORT
main(USHORT argc, PCHAR argv[], PCHAR envp[])
{
  USHORT i;
  CHAR sem_name[30];

  /*--------------------------------*/
  /* validate and get arguments     */
  /*--------------------------------*/
  if (argc <= 1)
     { printf("Incorrect number of arguments (argc = %u).\n", argc);
       exit(FAILED);
     }

  process_number = atoi(argv[1]);
  if ((process_number < 0) || (process_number > 3))
     { printf("Process Number out of range.\n");
       exit(FAILED);
     }

  /*--------------------------------*/
  /* open the semaphores            */
  /*--------------------------------*/
  sprintf(sem_name,"\\SEM\\RUN%d", process_number);
  if (rc = DosOpenSem(&sem_handle,     /* handle to semaphore returned*/
                      sem_name))      /* ASCIIZ name of semaphore    */
     { print_error(rc,"during DosCreateSem", __FILE__,__LINE__);
       exit(FAILED);
     }

  sprintf(sem_name,"\\SEM\\RUNALL");
  if (rc = DosOpenSem(&control_sem_handle, /* handle to semaphore returned*/
                      sem_name))           /* ASCIIZ name of semaphore    */
     { print_error(rc,"during DosCreateSem", __FILE__,__LINE__);
       exit(FAILED);
     }

  /*--------------------------------*/
  /* get a shared segment for the count */
  /*   values                       */
  /*--------------------------------*/
  sprintf(name,"\\SHAREMEM\\TASK");
  rc = DosGetShrSeg( name, &selector);
  if (rc)
     {print_error(rc,"allocating count buffer",__FILE__,__LINE__);
      return(FAILED);
     }
  count_ptr = MAKEP(selector,0);   /* create a pointer to file buffer    */

  thread_count(process_number);
} /* end main */
```

Figure 7-32 (Part 2 of 4). COUNT Program Listing.

```
/*-------------------------------------------------------------------------*/
/* Thread routine. This routine continuously 1) requests a semaphore,        */
/*   2) increments and displays a count, 3) clears the semaphore.  The user */
/*   can disable counting by setting the semaphore from the display panel.   */
/*-------------------------------------------------------------------------*/
VOID
thread_count(USHORT process_number)
{
  CHAR   count_str[10];
  USHORT rc;

  count_ptr->count[process_number] = 0;

  /*-----------------------------------*/
  /* display process status            */
  /*-----------------------------------*/
  write_str("Ready       ", PANEL_STATUS_ATTR,
            (process_number * 20) + 2, 15); /* calculate display location    */
                                            /*  based on thread number       */

  /*-----------------------------------*/
  /* continuous count loop             */
  /*-----------------------------------*/
  while (TRUE)
    {
      /*-----------------------------------*/
      /* wait for control sem to clear     */
      /*-----------------------------------*/
      if (rc = DosSemWait(control_sem_handle,           /* semaphore handle */
                         -1L))                          /* infinite timeout */
         { print_error(rc,"during DosSemWait",
                       __FILE__,__LINE__);
           exit(FAILED);
         }

      /*-----------------------------------*/
      /* request the semaphore             */
      /*-----------------------------------*/
      if (rc = DosSemRequest(sem_handle,                /* semaphore handle */
                             -1L))                      /* infinite timeout */
         { print_error(rc,"during DosSemRequest",
                       __FILE__,__LINE__);
           exit(FAILED);
         }
      /*-----------------------------------*/
      /* increment the count               */
      /*-----------------------------------*/
      ++(count_ptr->count[process_number]);
```

Figure 7-32 (Part 3 of 4). COUNT Program Listing.

```
        /*-----------------------------------*/
        /* display the count value           */
        /*-----------------------------------*/
        sprintf(count_str, "%-7lu", count_ptr->count[process_number]);
        write_str(count_str, OUTPUT_FIELD_ATTR,
                  (process_number * 20) + 10,  9);/* calculate display location*/
                                                   /*  based on thread number   */
        /*-----------------------------------*/
        /* clear the semaphore               */
        /*-----------------------------------*/
        if (rc = DosSemClear(sem_handle))
           { print_error(rc,"during DosSemClear", __FILE__,__LINE__);
             exit(FAILED);
           }
     }/* end while */
}

/*---------------------------------------------------------------------------*/
/* write a character string to the screen.                                   */
/*---------------------------------------------------------------------------*/
VOID
write_str(PCHAR charstr, CHAR attribute, USHORT x, USHORT y)
{
  CHAR cell[2];
  BYTE attr;

  if (rc = VioWrtCharStrAtt(charstr,    /* character string                  */
                      strlen(charstr),/* number of times                   */
                      y, x,           /* screen position                   */
                      &attribute,     /* attribute                         */
                      0))             /* reserved                          */
     print_error(rc,"during VioWrtCharStrAtt",__FILE__,__LINE__);
}

/*---------------------------------------------------------------------------*/
/* Error Display Routine                                                     */
/*---------------------------------------------------------------------------*/
VOID
print_error(USHORT Error, PCHAR msg, PCHAR file, USHORT line)
{
 printf("Error %d detected while %s at line %d in file %s.\n",
        Error, msg, line, file);
} /* end print_error */
```

Figure 7-32 (Part 4 of 4). COUNT Program Listing.

```
/****************************************************************************/
/*  INCLUDE NAME: COUNT - declarations for COUNT program                    */
/****************************************************************************/
/*--------------------------------------------------------------------------*/
/* Forward declarations of procedures in this module                        */
/*--------------------------------------------------------------------------*/
                    /*-----------------------------*/
                    /* top level routines          */
                    /*-----------------------------*/
VOID thread_count(USHORT);
                    /*-----------------------------*/
                    /* VIO call helper routines    */
                    /*-----------------------------*/
VOID write_str(PCHAR, CHAR, USHORT, USHORT);
                    /*-----------------------------*/
                    /* Error display routine       */
                    /*-----------------------------*/
VOID print_error(USHORT, PCHAR, PCHAR, USHORT);

/*--------------------------------------------------------------------------*/
/* Global variables/type definitions for this module                        */
/*--------------------------------------------------------------------------*/
USHORT process_number;                /* number of this process             */
HSEM   sem_handle;                    /* semaphore handle                   */
HSEM   control_sem_handle;            /* semaphore handle                   */
USHORT rc;                            /* return code variable               */

                    /*-----------------------------*/
                    /* count variable definition   */
                    /*-----------------------------*/
typedef struct
       { ULONG count[4];
       } COUNT;
COUNT   *count_ptr;

CHAR     name[80];                   /* variable for building ascii names */
USHORT   selector;                   /* variable for selector values      */
```

Figure 7-33. COUNT Include File.

Chapter 8

Named Pipes

This chapter presents a tutorial on *Named Pipes*, OS/2's most complete service for interprocess communications (*IPC*). In previous chapters we covered the *semaphore services* which are OS/2's most primitive IPC service. Semaphores are used to synchronize the actions of independent processes and regulate their access to shared resources. The information carried in semaphores consists, at most, of simple signals and flags. Clearly, a form of IPC is needed that goes beyond semaphores and allows independent processes to exchange and share data. This function is provided by OS/2's advanced IPC services for interprocess data transfer.

The interprocess data transfer services are the most complex and sophisticated form of IPC provided by an operating system. OS/2, being a late-model operating system, is endowed with several state-of-the-art IPC data exchange mechanisms namely: Named Pipes, Shared Memory, Anonymous Pipes, Queues, and PM's Dynamic Data Exchange.

In this book, we focus on Named Pipes because it is the most powerful and complete IPC OS/2 offers. It is also the only IPC that allows communicating processes to be distributed on different computers on a network. The communicating processes can even be MS-DOS or UNIX (through LAN Manager/X) applications on the network.

The plan for this chapter is to first define the "ideal" interprocess data transfer IPC. We then explore how Named Pipes measure-up against the check-list of "ideal" IPC features by way of the tutorial. We conclude the tutorial with scenarios that demonstrate the use of the Named Pipes IPC protocol in typical application environments. The tutorials provide the prerequisite background information on IPCs for the programming examples in the chapters that follow.

WHAT SHOULD THE "IDEAL" IPC PROVIDE?

The "ideal" IPC for interprocess data transfer should provide the following services:

- A built-in protocol for coordinating the sending and receiving of data between processes.

- A mechanism for pacing the data interchange, so that new data does not overwrite old data before it gets consumed. An example of such a mechanism is a queue.
- Support for data transfers that may involve many-to-one exchanges. An example of a many-to-one exchange is a server process that concurrently services several client processes.
- Support for the interprocess exchange of data over a network. The location of processes should be made transparent to the programmer. Network security and network recovery should be integrated into the protocol.
- A Remote Procedure Call-like mechanism to facilitate the creation of transaction-based applications between processes.
- Support for the exchange of data using a variety of data structures.
- A familiar programming interface that does not require learning a large number of new commands or a new programming metaphor.
- A protocol that can be implemented using a minimum amount of code. Interprocess communications in a multitasking environment should be "natural" and easy to use.
- A protocol that does not introduce a heavy performance overhead.

The above is a checklist of what to expect from a well designed interprocess data transfer protocol. In the tutorial that follows, we evaluate how Named Pipes, OS/2's *best of breed* IPC protocol, measures up to this "ideal" wish list.

NAMED PIPES: THE "IDEAL" IPC?

Named Pipes are the OS/2 IPC mechanism that comes closest to providing the "ideal" interprocess data transfer protocol. For starters, Named Pipes are the only OS/2 IPC mechanism that can transfer data across a network. They provide a file-like programming API for the two-way exchange of data. Using Named Pipes, processes can exchange data as if they were writing to, or reading from, a sequential file.

Named Pipes are especially suitable for implementing server programs which require many-to-one pipelines. A server application can set up a pipeline where the receiving end of the pipe can exchange data with several client processes and have OS/2 handle all the scheduling and synchronization issues. Named Pipes also provide a very strong platform for the development of client-server applications. Here is what they offer:

- They provide a method for exchanging data and control information between processes running on different computers.
- They hide the interface to the network.
- They provide API calls that are optimized for the implementation of *Remote Procedure Calls* which are request/reply message pairs that can be used for building client-server applications using procedure-like calls. The invocation of a remote procedure will result in a request/reply exchange over the Named Pipe. The incoming request may be used to trigger a procedure on a server and pass it the

required parameters. The results will be returned by the server in a reply message over the same pipe.

USING NAMED PIPES

Creating a Named Pipe: What's in a Name?

To establish a Named Pipe, a server process has to first create the pipe using **DosMakeNmPipe** which returns a handle that identifies the pipe. A Named Pipe is identified by a unique name that conforms to the OS/2 file naming convention, although no actual file is created. Pipes are named: **\PIPE\name**, and local pipes are referenced by that name. Remote pipes are referenced as **\\server\PIPE\name**, where "server" is the network name of a server machine. A local pipe can only be used by processes on the same machine; whereas a remote pipe can be used by processes connected over a local area network. This network-naming capability is one of Named Pipes' most important features. It means a client application can communicate with a Named Pipe from any machine on the network.

How Do You Like Your Pipe?

When a server process first creates a Named Pipe, it specifies several parameters that will determine the nature of that Named Pipe and how it can be used. Here is a list of what can be specified:

Which direction? Although Named Pipes are bidirectional, you have the option of putting constraints on the direction of data through the pipe. You can specify that a pipe be *in-bound*, *out-bound*, or *duplex*. An *in-bound* pipe can only read data from a client process. An *out-bound* pipe can only write data to a client process. A *duplex* pipe supports bidirectional data exchanges between clients and the server.

Byte stream or message stream? You can specify whether the pipe will be used in byte stream or message stream mode. In byte stream mode, the processes read and write bytes; whereas in message stream mode, they read and write messages with OS/2 providing a system-supplied length header. The size and content of the individual messages is determined by the application.

How many concurrent clients? What happens when many clients all want to open the same Named Pipe? You can specify through an *instance count* the number of times a Named Pipe can be opened by clients at the same time. Each instance of the pipe has its own handle and file buffer. When multiple clients connect to the same pipe, each connection is assigned its own instance (handle) of the pipe. Of course, the data from simultaneous clients is multiplexed through a single pipe by OS/2.

Will the pipe be inherited? You can specify whether the Named Pipe handle is to be inherited by child processes.

Flushing versus blocking? You can specify for remote pipes whether the data is to be sent over the remote pipe immediately (flushed) as it is written or whether it gets blocked and then sent when an internal buffer fills up. Blocking reduces the message traffic over a network and improves performance. The cost, however, is the loss of the immediate acknowledgement that the data arrived at its destination.

Wait or immediate return? You can specify whether all subsequent operations on a pipe will block waiting when no data is available or will return immediately.

Making the Connection

Once the pipe is created on the server, it must be in a listening state before a client can connect to it. The server does that by issuing **DosConnectNmPipe**. The pipe is now in a *LISTENING* state waiting for a client process to open it. At this point, any client process that knows the fully qualified path name of a Named Pipe can open the pipe by issuing a **DosOpen**. This is the same OS/2 call that is used for opening a regular file. If **DosOpen** succeeds, it returns a handle and the pipe is then in the *CONNECTED* state.

If the call fails and returns ERROR_PIPE_BUSY, the client may issue **DosWaitNmPipe** which will block the process until the first pipe instance becomes available. What happens when many clients are waiting on the same pipe? OS/2 will wake up the process that has waited the longest, when an instance of the pipe becomes available. The *unblocked* process should then reissue **DosOpen** to connect to the pipe.

Information Exchange Using File Semantics

Once a pipe is in the *CONNECTED* state, server and client processes can use the regular OS/2 file-subsystem calls to communicate over it as follows:

- **DosWrite** or **DosWriteAsync** are issued to write data to a pipe.
- **DosRead** or **DosReadAsync** are issued to read data from a pipe.
- **DosBufReset** is used to synchronize read and write dialogs. It does this by blocking the calling process at one end of the pipe until all the data it has written has been read at the other end of a pipe.

Transaction Processing with Named Pipes

Named Pipes support two API calls that are ideally suited for transaction processing: **DosTransactNmPipe** and **DosCallNmPipe**. These two calls can only be issued on a duplex message pipe that is setup for the message-stream mode.

DosTransactNmPipe: This API call writes a message and receives a reply in one single operation. The request/reply pair can be used to trigger a transaction or a Remote Procedure Call. This call is typically issued over "persistent" connections. In this type of connection, several transactions are usually issued over an open pipe before the connection is terminated. The persistent connection is appropriate for remote pipes because their overhead for establishing connections is high.

DosCallNmPipe: This API call combines a **DosOpen**, **DosTransactNmPipe**, and a **DosClose** in a single operation. It is used in "non-persistent" connections that get established and terminated just to issue a single Remote Procedure Call. Non-persistent connections are ideal for simple request/reply transactions.

Terminating a Named Pipe Dialog

When a client process is through using a Named Pipe, it closes the pipe by issuing a **DosClose**. This is the same OS/2 call that is used for closing regular files. The pipe is now in the *CLOSING* state. The server process can then issue a **DosDisConnectNmPipe**, which puts the pipe in a *DISCONNECTED* state. The server can then issue another **DosConnectNmPipe** and wait for the next client. Or, it can close the Named Pipe for good by using issuing **DosClose**. A server may also issue a **DosClose** without a preceding **DosDisconnectNmPipe**. This will free the pipe handle and still enable the client to read any data remaining in the buffer. However, a closed pipe cannot be reused again without reissuing **DosMakeNmPipe**.

If the client end of the pipe is open when **DosDisConnectNmPipe** is issued, it is forced to close and the client gets an error code on its next operation. Forcing the client end to close prematurely may cause data to be discarded that has not yet been read by the client. A client that gets forced off a pipe by a **DosDisConnectNmPipe** must issue **DosClose** to free the handle resource.

Although **DosDisConnectNmPipe** makes the client's handle invalid, it does not free the resource. Any threads that are blocked on the pipe are awakened by **DosDisConnectNmPipe**. A thread blocked on the pipe by a **DosWrite** returns ERROR_BROKEN_PIPE. A thread blocked on the pipe by a **DosRead** returns an **EOF** indicator. In general, forced disconnects should be avoided. You can do that by providing a user enforced protocol for gracefully shutting down a pipe.

Using Semaphores with Named Pipes

System semaphores can be used in conjunction with a local Named Pipe to control access to that pipe. A reading process can use **DosSemWait** or **DosMuxSemWait** to wait for data to arrive on one or more pipes. This avoids more costly methods, such as dedicating a thread for each incoming pipe or polling each pipe with no-wait mode. The **DosSetNmPipeSem** call is used to associate a system semaphore with an instance of a local Named Pipe. If an attempt is made to attach a semaphore to a remote Named Pipe, ERROR_INVALID_FUNCTION is returned. Up to two semaphores may be attached to a pipe, one for the server and one for the client. If there is already a semaphore associated with one end of the pipe, the old semaphore is replaced. OS/2 will clear the semaphore whenever new data is available, whenever buffer space is available for a write, or whenever either side closes the pipe. An application is notified of this event through the regular semaphore calls (Example: DosSemRequest or DosMuxSemWait). You can associate a semaphore with more than one pipe handle. A parameter identifies which pipe handle cleared.

A process can check the state of the Named Pipe semaphores by issuing **DosQNmPipeSemState**. This call returns information about local Named Pipes attached to a specific system semaphore, as well as additional information about the I/O that can be performed on the set of pipes. This information can be scanned to determine which pipes can be read or written. In addition, this call provides all the information about the event that triggered the clearing of a semaphore associated with a particular pipe handle (through DosSetNmPipeSem).

Obtaining and Modifying Pipe Information

A process can peek at data from a Named Pipe without removing the data by issuing **DosPeekNmPipe**. This call also returns the state of the pipe. A process can obtain general information about a pipe by issuing **DosQNmPipeInfo**. The information returned includes: the input and output buffer sizes, the maximum number of allowed pipe instances, the current number of pipe instances, and the name of the pipe including the server's computer name if the pipe is remote.

By issuing **DosQNmPHandState**, a process can obtain information on the current state of the pipe, the current number of pipe instances, the pipe's direction, and what type of pipe it is.

A process can modify the state of a pipe through the **DosSetNmPHandState** call. This call is issued to change the mode of a pipe from byte stream to message stream or vise versa, and to change the wait/no-wait mode. This call will be used mostly by clients to modify the default **DosOpen** which always opens Named Pipes with the wait mode enabled and sets the pipe to read the pipe in byte stream mode.

Table 8-1. The Named Pipes State Transition Table.

Current State	Action		Next State
	From:	API Call	
none	server	DosMakeNmPipe	DISCONNECTED
DISCONNECTED	server	DosConnectNmPipe	LISTENING
LISTENING	client	DosOpen	CONNECTED
CONNECTED	server	DosDisConnectNmPipe	DISCONNECTED
CONNECTED	client	DosClose	CLOSING
CLOSING	server	DosDisconnectNmPipe	DISCONNECTED
CONNECTED	server	DosClose	CLOSING

Named Pipes State Transitions

Named Pipes may be in one of several states depending on the actions that have been taken on it by the server and client ends. The state/action diagram in Table 8-1 summarizes the valid state transitions.

THE ANATOMY OF A NAMED PIPES PROGRAM

This section summarizes how Named Pipes are used by describing the anatomy of a typical Named Pipe program:

1. ***Create the Named Pipe.*** The server side of an application creates a Named Pipe by issuing DosMakeNmPipe. The instances parameter specifies how many clients can use this pipe concurrently.

2. ***Wait for the clients to connect.*** The server application creates as many threads as the number of simultaneous clients it wants to service. Each "server" thread issues a DosConnectNmPipe and blocks waiting for a client to connect to the other end of the pipe instance.

3. ***Establish the connection with the clients.*** The clients connect to their end of the pipe by issuing a DosOpen or DosCallNmPipe (which performs the DosOpen automatically). Each successful DosOpen returns a unique handle to the pipe. On the server side, the DosConnectNmPipe succeeds.

4. ***Conduct your business.*** After both sides of a pipe are connected, they can begin to conduct their business using one of two dialog styles:

   - By maintaining a *persistent* pipe connection. Here the client and the server conduct multiple message exchanges over the pipe. This is like carrying out a long conversation over the telephone. A *conversational dialog* typically uses calls like DosWrite, DosRead and DosTransactNmPipe.
   - By maintaining a *non-persistent* pipe connection. Here the client and the server conduct a *transactional dialog*, which typically consists of a single

request/reply exchange after which both parties disconnect from their end of the pipe. A transactional dialog is conducted by issuing calls such as DosCallNmPipe on the client side and DosTransactNmPipe on the server side. Non-persistent pipes cost you setup time, but the benefit is that the pipe instance can be serially reused by other clients. This is useful in situations where one server may be required to talk to hundreds of clients.

5. ***Disconnect and take the next call.*** When the business is completed, the server side of the pipe issues a DosDisconnectNmPipe and the client issues a DosClose (DosCallNmPipe performs a DosClose automatically). The server can then execute another DosConnectNmPipe and wait on the next client to call.

6. ***Terminate the pipe.*** When the server thread wants to stop accepting calls from clients it issues a DosClose to delete that instance of the Named Pipe. When the last instance is closed, the pipe no longer exists.

NAMED PIPES SCENARIOS

The scenarios that follow will help demonstrate the use of Named Pipes in environments that require interprocess data exchanges. Once you grasp the mechanics of Named Pipe usage, you can create your own repertoire of API sequences using our scenarios as a starting point.

Scenario 1: A Simple Transaction Involving Two Processes

Scenario 1 consists of a simple transaction which results in a single request/reply data exchange. A typical example is a simple banking transaction to query an account, such as:

```
What is Bob's Balance?  ------->

                        <-------    $300
```

We implement this simple transaction three different ways:

- The first implementation of Scenario 1 uses file-oriented Named Pipe calls exclusively (see Figure 8-1).
- The second implementation of Scenario 1 refines the client by introducing the use of **DosTransactNmPipe** (see Figure 8-2).
- The third implementation of Scenario 1 further refines the client by introducing the use of **DosCallNmPipe** (see Figure 8-3).

Clearly, the third implementation of scenario 1 is the most elegant and economical way to design simple *transactional dialogs*. The **DosCallNmPipe** was designed specifically for a single request/reply exchange over a non-persistent connection. This call is sometimes referred to in the OS/2 literature as the *Remote Procedure Call.* What this means is that DosCallNmPipe can be used to implement a request/reply exchange using the semantics of a procedure call. To get Bob's account, you would call a local procedure stub with "Bob" as the argument. The local stub, in turn, creates a message and issues DosCallNmPipe. On the server side, the arrival of the message results in the invocation of a server procedure that calculates Bob's balance and returns the result: $300. The result is returned to the client stub over the Named Pipe. The client stub *unblocks* and returns the result to its caller.

The effect of this Remote Procedure Call is to introduce procedure-like semantics for interprocess communications. From the point of view of Named Pipes, however, it does not really matter how the interface is presented to the user or what data gets passed on the pipe. The pipe is simply a super-efficient delivery mechanism which can be used either "raw" or through a presentation forms such as the Remote Procedure Call.

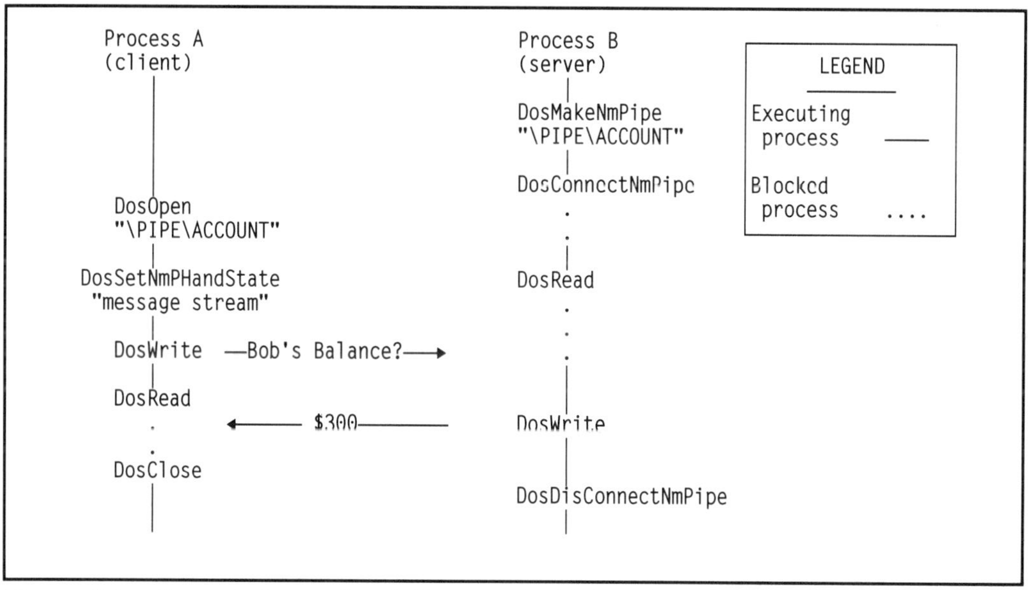

Figure 8-1. Scenario 1a: A Simple Transaction Using File Service Named Pipe Calls.

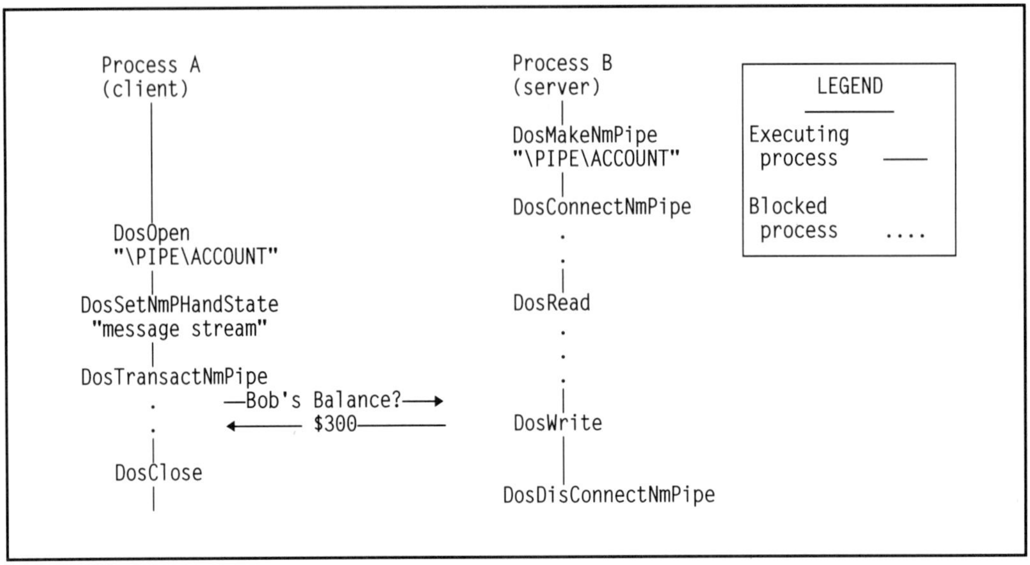

Figure 8-2. Scenario 1b: A Simple Transaction Using DosTransactNmPipe.

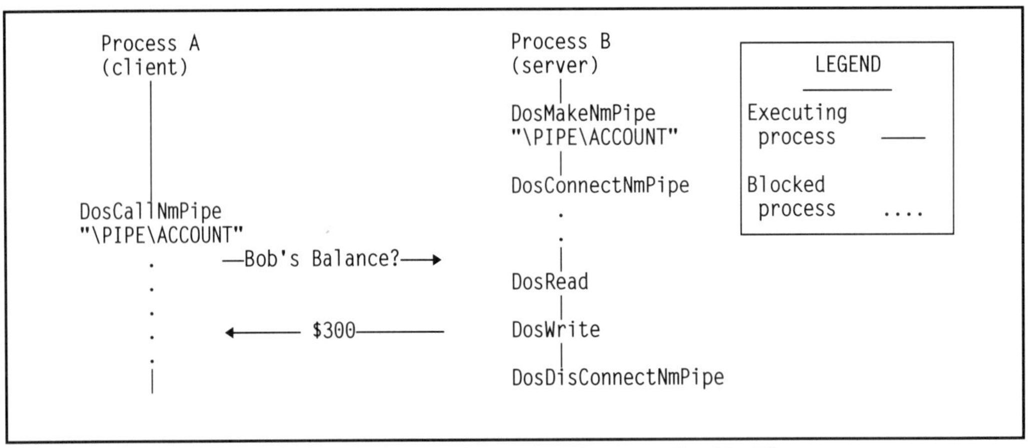

Figure 8-3. Scenario 1c: A Simple Transaction Using DosCallNmPipe.

Scenario 2: One Server Multiple Clients Using a Single Pipe Instance

Scenario 2, shows how a single pipe instance may be used to serially service two clients (see Figure 8-4). The scenario can easily be expanded to "n" clients. We assume that all the clients will be executing simple transactions, such as the one described in Scenario 1. The key point to notice in the scenario is how the server reconnects the Named Pipe to allow other clients to use it. In Scenario 2, the server services Process 1 followed by Process 2. We assume that the time-out values on **DosCallNmPipe** are large enough to keep a process blocked until the server frees up.

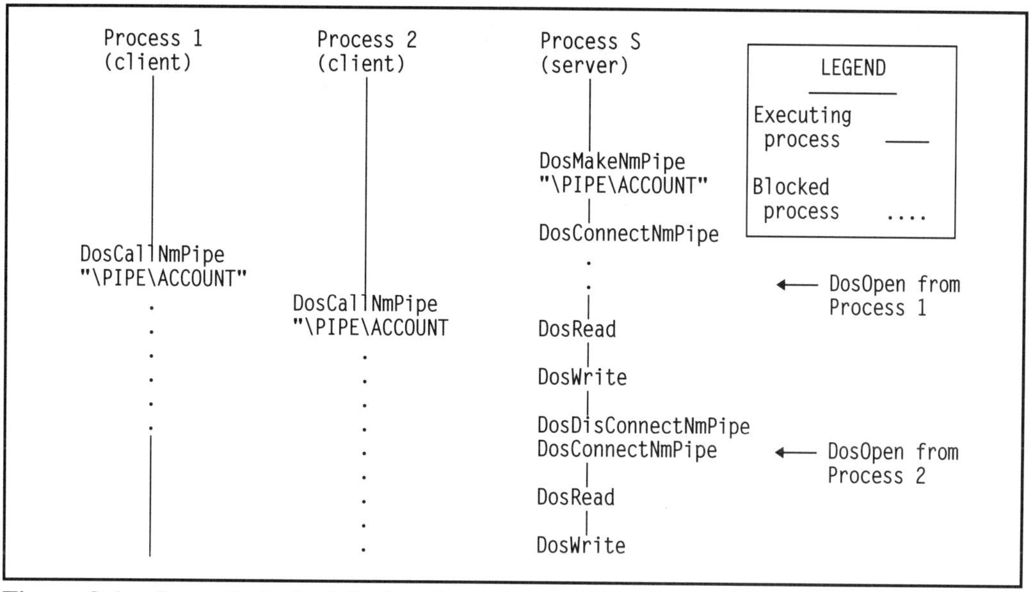

Figure 8-4. Scenario 2: Serially Reusing a Named Pipe Instance.

Scenario 3: A Multithreaded Server Using Multiple Pipe Instances

Scenario 3, shows how a single pipe with multiple instances can be used to accommodate two clients (see Figure 8-5). The scenario can easily be extended to "n" clients. We will assume in the scenario that the client transactions are persistent, meaning that multiple simple transactions will be issued over a single pipe connection. The server must also be capable of providing simultaneous service for up to two clients over the well-known pipe: \PIPE\ACCOUNT. Here are some observations that are pertinent to how this scenario plays out:

1. The scenario starts out with the server process creating two server threads, each of which will handle an instance of the pipe. Each pipe instance will be used to service a client process, meaning that up to two clients can open \PIPE\ACCOUNT simultaneously.

2. Each server thread issues a **DosMakeNmPipe** to create the pipe: \PIPE\ACCOUNT with two instances specified. OS/2 returns a separate handle for each pipe instance. The server thread will then use the returned handle to manage its instance of the pipe and connect to a client through **DosConnectNmPipe**.

3. In Scenario 3, all the threads execute concurrently. At any one time, only one thread is running and only one message is going through the pipe. OS/2 will make sure that all messages get to their appropriate thread. A thread need not be aware that it is sharing the pipe with other threads. If there are more clients than there are server threads, then the additional clients will get a busy return when

they try to do a **DosOpen**. However, take note that OS/2 will only support up to 53 threads per process. For systems that need to support large number of clients, you may want to implement a non-persistent server thread pool in addition to the persistent server thread pool shown in Scenario 3.

4. A non-persistent thread is similar to the server thread in Scenario 2. It conducts its business with a client and disconnects as soon as it is able to do so.

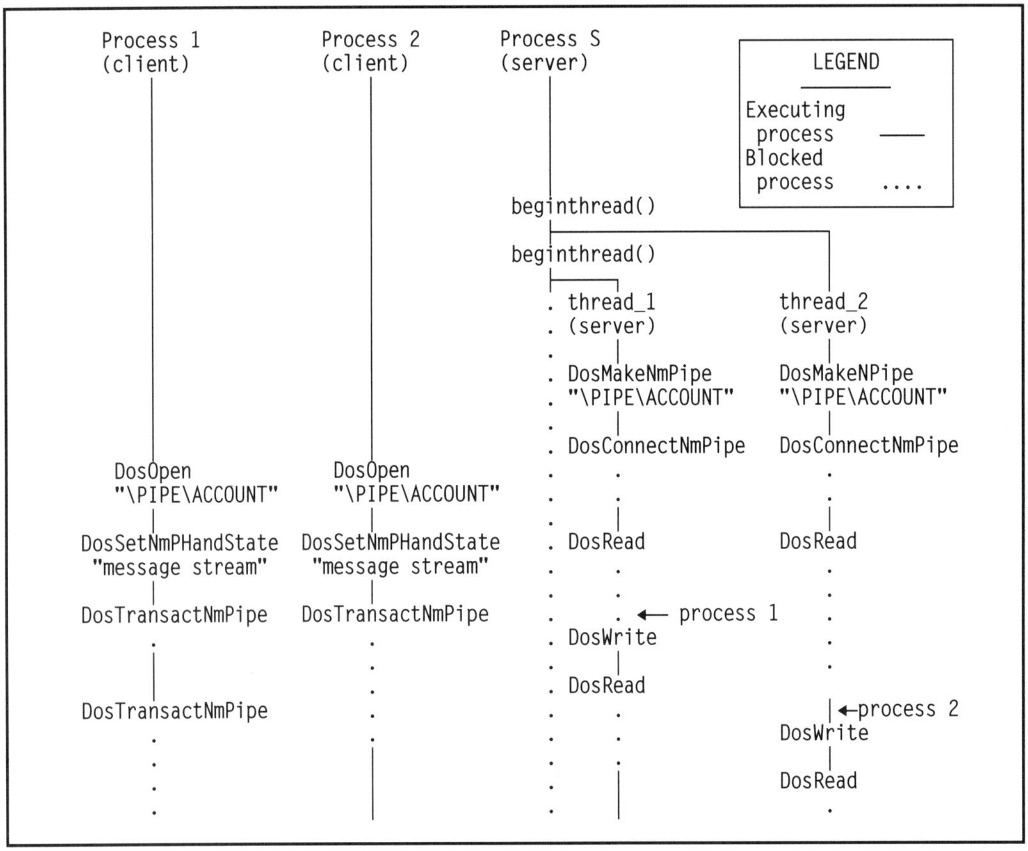

Figure 8-5. Scenario 3: A MultiThreaded Server Using a Named Pipe with 2 Instances.

Scenario 4: Sending Bulk Data Over a Named Pipe

Scenario 4, shows how moving bulk data, such as a file transfer, can be implemented over a Named Pipe (see Figure 8-6). Initially, the server is blocked waiting for the client. The client starts the file transfer by telling the server, through a **DosTransactNmPipe** transaction that it is about to receive a file and gives it the name of the file and its size. The server says "OK" and issues a **DosRead** waiting on the first file segment to arrive. The file copy gets done through a series of exchanges. Eventually, the server finishes consuming the file and sends a message to the client saying the file got there OK after which both sides break their end of the pipe.

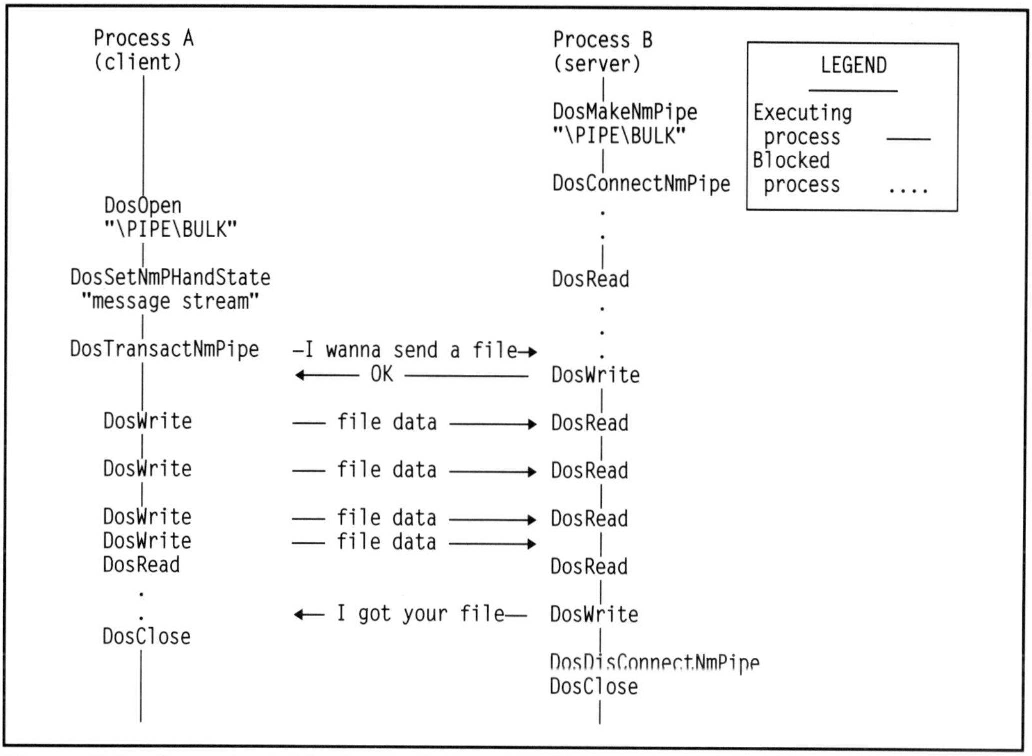

Figure 8-6. Scenario 4: Moving Bulk Data Over a Named Pipe.

Chapter 9

A Generic Client-Server File Transfer Service

By the time you finish this chapter, you will have accomplished five things:

1. You will have learned how to design and build communicating programs using layered software techniques.
2. You will have learned how to create a server program that provides a file repository service to its clients. Clients will be able to store and retrieve files using the server.
3. You will have learned how to use Dynamic Link Libraries (DLLs) to provide flexible runtime services and operating system extensions.
4. You will have walked through the design of a *protocol independent interface* to the service layer that moves the data between processes.
5. You will have walked through **FXREQ.C** and **FXSVR.C**, the code for the protocol-independent client (or requester) and server components of a generic file transfer service. These two programs will be used to benchmark the performance of IPC and LAN protocols.

In this chapter, we create the topmost layers of an application that is used to measure the performance of various interprocess communication techniques. These topmost layers provide a generic file transfer protocol that can be used to move data or files between two processes. The protocol is *generic* in the sense that it is independent of the underlying IPC or LAN communication service. The same calls will execute on top of Named Pipes, NetBIOS, and APPC.

The generic file transfer is performed by two programs, **FXREQ.C** and **FXSVR.C**, which respectively implement the client and server portions of the distributed application. These programs also measure the performance of the file transfer and display the results. The actual file transfer is done using the underlying IPC and LAN protocols. In Part II, the underlying IPC is provided by local Named Pipes. In Part III, the underlying IPC is provided by the LAN protocols: APPC, NetBIOS, remote Named Pipes, and the LAN Requester/Server.

LAYERING AND CLIENT-SERVER SOFTWARE DESIGN

Layering is a software design technique used to break down complex programs into a hierarchy of services. Powerful new services can be provided by adding new layers on top of more primitive service layers. A service interface defines the services provided by an underlying layer to the layers above it.

Layering also provides an ideal framework for explaining and organizing the communications between two independent programs. Program-to-program communications is broken down into exchanges between the corresponding peer layers in each program. The following three concepts form the basis for the layered approach:

1. At each layer, client and server peers cooperate jointly to provide a service. Of course, one peer can end up doing all of the work, but the service is still considered to be a joint effort by the peers for that layer. The *protocol* is the contract the peers abide by. It specifies how the work is divided among the peers, the semantics of the message exchanges for that layer, and the handshake sequences.
2. Each layer builds on top of the services provided by the layers beneath it. A *service interface* specifies how a layer can obtain access to the services of the layer directly below it. The interface should hide all the nasty details of the workings of the underlying layer while providing a complete set of services.
3. Services become more abstract the higher the layer. For example, the lower layers may be concerned with the interfaces to the hardware or the operating system, while the higher layers may provide a more application-specific type of service, such as a file transfer.

We will apply layering techniques to the design of a client-server file repository. The server can be used to store all kinds of large data objects such as: documents, images, video, voice, metafiles, and database snapshots. We will use the file transfer service to compare how the IPC and LAN protocols perform when it comes to moving large data objects.

Our layered model of the file transfer service breaks the client and server programs into three layers (see Figure 9-1 on page 229). We now discuss the function each layer provides starting with the top layer.

The Application Layer

This layer calculates and displays the performance of the file transfer service. It displays the overhead for establishing a connection between the client and server, the total number of bytes transferred, the average transfer rate in KBytes per second, and the overhead for closing a connection. The application layer function is provided jointly by **FXREQ.C** on the client side and **FXSVR.C** on the server side.

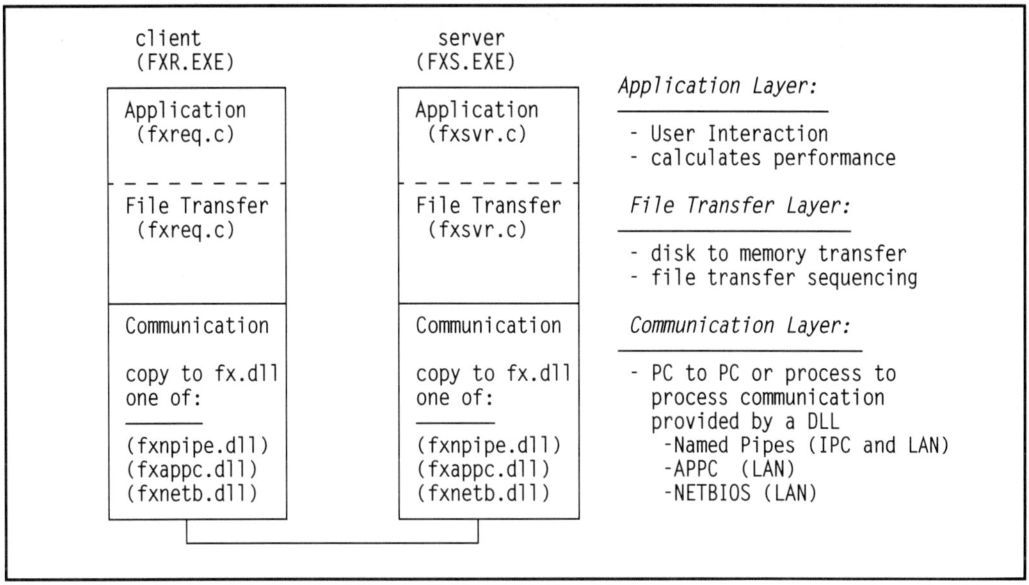

Figure 9-1. A Layered Model of the File Transfer Client and Server Programs.

The File Transfer Layer

This layer provides a logical file transfer protocol for moving the file from a client to the server and vice versa. The protocol includes a method for requesting a remote service as well as an implementation of the requested service. Of course, the only services we currently provide are *Send* and *Receive* a file, both of which use the same interprocess file transfer protocol. The file transfer protocol specifies how a service is requested, the handshaking for transferring the file, and the message structures used. The file transfer layer only provides the logical protocol. It *delegates* the actual moving of the data to the layers below it. The requests to the layer below are communicated through a generic service interface which we will define later in this chapter. The file transfer layer function is provided jointly by **FXREQ.C** on the client side and **FXSVR.C** on the server side.

The Communication Layer

This layer performs the actual movement of data between processes. If the client and server processes are in the same machine, the communications is provided by the Named Pipes IPC. If the client and server processes are on separate machines, the communications is provided using one of OS/2 EE's LAN-based protocols. The communication layer implements the generic interface calls using either **Named Pipes**, **NetBIOS**, **APPC**, remote **Named Pipes**, or the **LAN Requester/Server**. Each of these implementations will be packaged as a Dynamic Link Library (DLL). Before running a benchmark test, the appropriate (.DLL) file gets copied into FX.DLL. Both FXREQ.EXE and FXSVR.EXE will be linked dynamically to FX.DLL to create the client process and server processes of the benchmark program. The code that implements the DLLs will be introduced as follows:

- In Chapter 10, "FX Using Named Pipes", we develop **FXNPIPE.DLL** which will move the data using Named Pipes.
- In Part III we introduce: **FXAPPC.DLL** and **FXNETB.DLL**, to move the data across the network. We will also be re-introducing **FXNPIPE.DLL** to perform the remote Named Pipe service. Each of these programs will be linked dynamically with FXSVR.EXE and FXREQ.EXE to produce the respective server and client versions of the program.

A PROTOCOL-INDEPENDENT GENERIC INTERFACE

This section defines the service level interface between the File Transfer layer and the Communications Layer (see Figure 9-2). This interface will drive the different IPC and LAN protocols and will be used to measure and compare the performance of the various protocols. This interface should mask the details of the underlying layer while providing the required service. We also have an additional design challenge: how to package this interface so that it can work with the different underlying protocols? As you can see in Figure 9-2, we face quite a challenge. The generic interface should work for Named Pipes, APPC, and NetBIOS. This means the same set of calls can be issued from the upper layer and still work transparently on any of those protocols. So where do we start with our design?

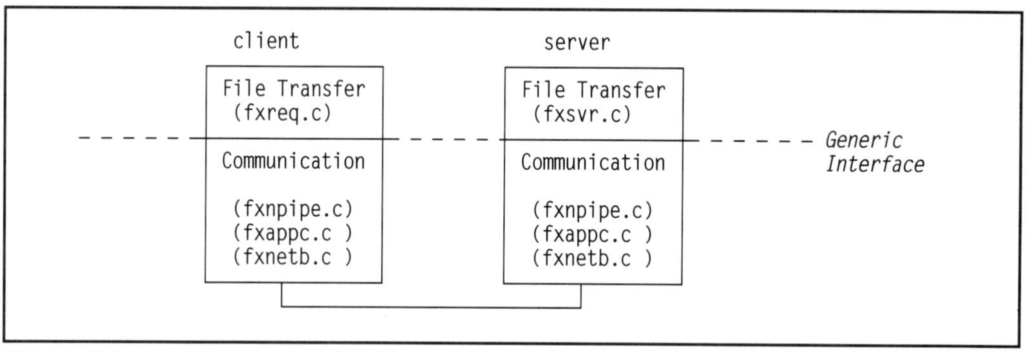

Figure 9-2. A Generic Interface Layer for Moving Data.

The Art of Defining a Service Level Interface

We first have to decide which services will be offered by the communication layer, while keeping in mind that:

1. The communication layer is there to service the file transfer layer.
2. The services required should be supported by the underlying IPCs or LAN protocols.

The approach we take is to look at the interface from both a top-down and bottom-up perspective and then balance the set of requirements. The top-down perspective defines the set of services required by a generic file transfer layer to do its job. The bottom-up perspective introduces the constraints that are specific to IPCs or LAN protocols.

What is Required From the Top Down?

Looking at the service requirements top-down, the file transfer layer consists of two communicating peers: a client and a server. The client and server peers first need to establish some kind of a connection or "rendezvous." The client needs to indicate to the server what type of service it needs performed. Then the two sides need to send and receive the file data. Finally, there should be some way to break a connection.

What is Required Bottom-Up?

Looking at the service requirements bottom-up, the IPC or LAN protocol needs to be initialized with parameters that are going to be different for each LAN protocol or IPC. In addition, the LAN protocol or IPC has to be told what to connect to and when. The implementation of a connection will be different for each of the protocols. Servers need to be told to listen for incoming requests. Data needs to be exchanged. Finally, the IPC or LAN protocol has to be told when to break the connection.

Choosing The "Right" Interface Calls

You do not have the necessary background, at this point, to determine the specifics of what each IPC and LAN protocol needs to do its job. This means you will have to trust us to come up with a solution. We get to specify the interface without having to justify all "the wisdom" that went behind our choice! So after many aborted efforts at combining the top-down and bottom-up requirements, we propose the following generic interface which we name **FX**:

- fx_Initialize(buffer_pointer, size)
- fx_MakePipe()*
- fx_ConnectPipe()*
- fx_DisconnectPipe()*
- fx_Open()**
- fx_Write(Buffer, Bufferlength, BytesWritten)
- fx_Read(Buffer, Bufferlength, BytesRead)
- fx_Transact(InBuffer, InBufferLength, OutBuffer, OutBufferLength, BytesRead)
- fx_Close()

Note: Calls with an "*" are server-specific. Calls with "**" are client-specific. The remaining calls can be issued by either servers or clients.

How Does the FX Interface Compare with Named Pipes?

The FX interface consists of general purpose service calls which *emulate* the functions of the very flexible and state-of-the-art Named Pipes API. The FX interface can support almost any form of interprocess data transfer. It can be used for transaction processing as well as for the bulk movement of data required by file transfer protocols. You should already be familiar with the FX calls; if not, please take a few minutes to review the Named Pipes tutorial in Chapter 8, "Named Pipes". We borrowed the *flavor and function* of the Named Pipes protocol. But make no mistake, this is our own private FX service call interface. Our calls look like the Named Pipes API, but in fact, they all start with **fx_**, meaning that they are special procedures that we've implemented.

Notice that many of the FX calls do not pass parameters, while their Named Pipes counterparts do. This is because most of the required parameters are specific to the underlying protocols. Rather than over-complicate the interface, we will pass the required information through a protocol-specific configuration file when we issue **fx_Initialize**. The Named Pipes API does not support a counterpart of **fx_Initialize**. We introduced **fx_Initialize** to initialize the various protocols by having them read a protocol-specific configuration. Each protocol will then do whatever it takes to obtain its required resources based on the user-specified configuration parameters. The service layer will also allocate a communication buffer of a size specified in the configuration file as part of **fx_Initialize**. A pointer to that buffer, as well as the buffer size, is returned to the caller.

The FX interface will be implemented in subsequent chapters using Named Pipes and the OS/2 EE LAN protocols. Does this choice of interface give Named Pipes a competitive advantage over the other protocols? Perhaps a very slight one, and we may have to take that into account when we come up with our final verdict on which protocol wins.

How to Package a Service Layer?

We have to determine how the program layers are going to be packaged, for it will influence the method by which the services get invoked. We made the choice to package the various implementations of the FX functions in DLLs, which get linked to **FXREQ.EXE** and **FXSVR.EXE** at runtime. It may be instructive, however, to walk through the thought process that got us there. We had three packaging options to choose from:

1. The communication layer could be packaged as a *separate process*. In this case, the communications between layers would take place through an IPC.

2. The communication layer could be packaged as a *module of code* that gets combined with the other modules that form the program through static linking. The invocation of services in this case is through calls to external procedures that get resolved at link time.
3. The communication layer could be packaged as a *Dynamic Link Library*. With standard libraries, such as the C-language runtime library, the code is combined with the program code when the program is created. With DLLs the code is not combined. Instead, the program contains an import record of the function and the name of the DLL which implements it. The function is not linked until the program needs it. The invocation of services would work very much like OS/2's API. We could even advertise our "added services" as an operating system extension!

Packaging FX Using Dynamic Link Libraries

The choice was made to go with the third option for the following reasons:

- DLLs provide new opportunities for packaging and distributing software. Our project will serve as an excellent example on how DLLs can be used to package OS/2 programs.
- Dynamic Link Libraries permit library functions to be changed without recompiling or relinking the programs that call them. This is very important to us, because our project requires us to run **FXREQ** and **FXSVR** on a multiplicity of IPC and LAN platforms. One easy way to provide that is to link to the different libraries that implement the protocols at runtime. We can then change the underlying protocol or IPC by just using a different DLL.
- Dynamic Link Libraries make it possible for common functions to be shared by different programs while maintaining a single copy of the function in memory. This means that both **FXREQ** and **FXSVR** can use the same copy of the DLL when their code runs in the same machine.
- The operation of dynamic linking is largely transparent to the user. A procedure in a Dynamic Link Library is declared like any other external call. You call a DLL function like you would call any ordinary procedure in a statically linked library. The only immediate visible difference is smaller (.EXE) files since the procedure is not copied to your executable file as in static linking.

A TUTORIAL ON DYNAMIC LINK LIBRARIES

What is a DLL?

Dynamic linking lets a program gain access to functions at runtime that are not part of its executable code. DLLs make it possible for you to use the same code without making it part of any single application. DLLs can be bound to an (.EXE) file when the application loads, or later on demand, during the execution of an application. Once a DLL is loaded, it can be shared with any other program that needs it. A function in a DLL library is called like any statically linked procedure in your code. The DLL code executes as part of the calling thread or process and the DLL function gets its arguments from the calling program's stack. Dynamic Linking has become the standardized mechanism for attaching add-ins to OS/2.

The Module-Definition File

Each DLL library must provide some mechanism to make its functions directly available to other modules. The vehicle provided by OS/2 to do that is a module-definition (.DEF) file, which describes the name of the DLL the functions it exports and other attributes.

The IMPLIB Utility

Once you've created the (.DEF) file, the **IMPLIB** utility is used to create a (.LIB) file which can be added to the list of library files a module can link to. The (.LIB) file does not contain the code for the library functions. However, it does contain the information that tells the (.EXE) file which (.DLL) is to be invoked to perform a function.

Creating the DLL

The source code for the function that provides the DLL is first compiled normally into an (.OBJ) file. The link utility is then used to create the (.DLL) file from the (.OBJ). The C-Language **LLIBCDLL** library is used to create (.DLL) files.

Loading and Executing an Application That Uses DLLs

OS/2 examines an application's (.EXE) file at loadtime for the special records that indicate references to DLLs. If such records are found, the operating system finds the (.DLL) file on disk and loads it into memory *if it is not already there.* It also puts the addresses for the DLL functions in the special records, so that the application can place its calls. The DLLs will stay in memory until all the applications that use its services are terminated.

DLLs that are Managed by an Application at Runtime

The tutorial has so far focused on DLLs that are loaded by OS/2 and made available to the application at runtime. The whole DLL process is totally invisible to your programs. A DLL function is called just like any other function. It is OS/2's responsibility to make sure the function is there when you need it. All this is very convenient, but what happens if you want to add a new function to the system at runtime? This is where OS/2's super flexible *runtime dynamic linking* service comes to play.

Here's what this service allows you to do:

1. Your application can be created without any prior knowledge of the DLL.
2. At runtime, your application can issue a **DosLoadModule** call to tell OS/2 to load a DLL module.
3. Your application then issues a **DosGetProcAddr** call to obtain the address of a DLL function in that module.
4. Your application then invokes the DLL function.
5. Your application can then unload from memory the DLL module by issuing a **DosFreeModule** call. Or, you can choose not to do that and leave the DLL in memory for performance reasons.

What this means is that you can have it both ways. You can let OS/2 manage DLLs on your behalf; or, you can do it all yourself. If you know ahead of time which functions are going to execute, then you're better off letting OS/2 manage the DLLs for you. If you need maximum flexibility (for example you may be adding new commands at runtime), then you're better off managing the DLLs yourself.

HOW THE FX DLLS ARE BUILT

The plan is to build each of our IPC and LAN implementations of FX as a separate (.DLL) file. Thus, in future chapters, we will build the following (.DLL) files out of corresponding (.C) files: fxnpipe.dll, fxnetb.dll and fxappc.dll. The **FXREQ.EXE** and **FXSVR.EXE** programs we create in this chapter dynamically link to **FX.DLL** at runtime to obtain the FX services. Since we know ahead of time what our FX functions look like, we'll let OS/2 load and manage the FX DLLs.

The **FX.DLL** file will contain a copy of the IPC or LAN protocol (.DLL) file needed to run a particular benchmark. So here's what we need to do to build our system:

1. The first thing we need to create is the **FX.DEF** file, which describes provides the name of the DLL and the functions it exports. This file is shown in Figure 9-3. The first line says that this a DLL library named FX and that we want it to be initialized each time it is called by a different application. The next nine lines specify the name of the FX functions which will be exported by FX to other applications. The last line specifies that a different data segment needs to be loaded for each application that uses FX. We do this in order to maintain separate copies of the FX variables and stack for each running program that uses FX.DLL.

2. We then run FX.DLL through the IMPLIB utility to create FX.LIB. We do this through the **FX.MAK** make file shown in Figure 9-4. Notice the order of what "ALL" is going to build:

```
all:    fx.lib fxsvr.exe fxreq.exe fxlsvr.exe \
        fxnpipe.dll fxnetb.dll fxappc.dll
```

   The "ALL" statement specifies that FX.LIB is the first thing to be built. MAKE obliges by applying the **.def.lib** inference rule.

3. The next thing on the "ALL" agenda is to build FXREQ.EXE and FXSVR.EXE. MAKE does that by compiling the (.C) files for FXREQ and FXSVR into (.EXE) files. Note that the FX.LIB which was built in the previous step is now included with the link libraries for creating (.EXE) files. Remember from the tutorial that FX.LIB does not contain any code, it just provides the stubs to access the services of a FX.DLL.

4. The next thing on the "ALL" agenda is to build our (.DLL) files for the various protocols and IPCs. Of course, we first have to develop the (.C) code in the coming chapters before anything can be built. The only strange thing about building (.DLL) files is that they have their own link libraries (see the **dll_libs** macro definition in Figure 9-4). The **ACS** library is needed by the NetBIOS LAN protocol.

The FX.DEF Import Library

```
LIBRARY FX INITINSTANCE
EXPORTS _fx_Initialize
EXPORTS _fx_MakePipe
EXPORTS _fx_ConnectPipe
EXPORTS _fx_DisconnectPipe
EXPORTS _fx_Open
EXPORTS _fx_Write
EXPORTS _fx_Read
EXPORTS _fx_Transact
EXPORTS _fx_Close
DATA MULTIPLE
```

Figure 9-3. The FX.DEF Import Library.

The FX.MAK Make File

```
# Make File for FXREQ, FXSVR and the DLLs that implement FX
#** MACROS ********
cflags=-c -Alfu -G2s -Zp -W3 -Od -Zi -nologo
lflags=/ST:15000/SE:1024/A:16/CO/NOD/NOI/L/PACKCODE
exe_libs=llibcep  doscalls fx
dll_libs=llibcdll doscalls acs         # acs is used by NetBIOS

#** INFERENCE RULES *****
FFIXES: .lib .def                   # non-default extensions need definition

.obj.exe:
      echo linking   $** to create $*.exe
      link $**,,nul, $(exe_libs) $(lflags),;

.obj.dll:
      echo linking   $** to create $*.dll
      link $**,$*.dll,nul, $(dll_libs) $(lflags),fx.def;

.c.obj:
      echo COMPILING $*.c
      cl $(cflags) $*.c

.def.lib:
      echo CREATING  $*.lib import library
      implib $*.lib $*.def            # used for the imports

#** BUILD STATEMENTS ****
all:       fx.lib fxsvr.exe fxreq.exe fxlsvr.exe \
           fxnpipe.dll fxnetb.dll fxappc.dll

fx.lib:      fx.def                   # create library for fx dll

fxsvr.exe:   fxsvr.obj                # create server executable module
fxsvr.obj:   fxsvr.c
fxreq.exe:   fxreq.obj                # create requester executable module
fxreq.obj:   fxreq.c

fxnpipe.dll: fxnpipe.obj              # create named pipe dll
fxnpipe.obj: fxnpipe.c
fxnetb.dll:  fxnetb.obj               # create NETBIOS dll
fxnetb.obj:  fxnetb.c
fxappc.dll:  fxappc.obj               # create APPC dll
fxappc.obj:  fxappc.c
fxlsvr.exe:  fxlsvr.obj               # create LAN Server file transfer
fxlsvr.obj:  fxlsvr.c                 #  program
```

Figure 9-4. The FX.MAK Make File.

THE GENERIC FILE TRANSFER PROTOCOL

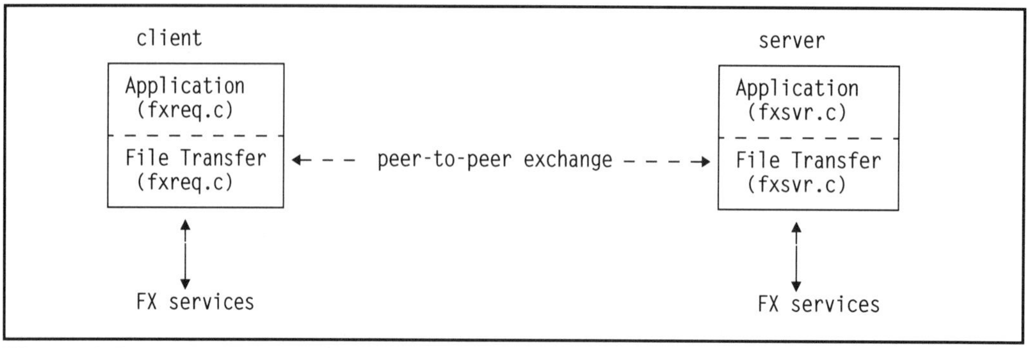

Figure 9-5. The File Transfer Protocol Exchange as Seen by the File Transfer Layer.

The best way to explain the workings of the file transfer layer is by demonstrating through two scenarios how a file gets sent to the server (see Figure 9-6) and how a file gets retrieved from the server (see Figure 9-7). The scenarios depict the exchange from the perspective of file transfer layer (see Figure 9-5), and do not deal with the mechanics of how the data gets moved between processes. We leave that for later chapters. The scenarios describe the handshake part of the protocol: "who does what and when." Protocols also specify the structure and meaning (or semantics) of the messages exchanged. So, we provide the message specifications for FX in the sections that follow the scenarios.

Walking through the File Send Scenario

1. When the server first comes, up it issues **fx_Initialize** which initializes the underlying service layer (see Figure 9-6). It then calls **fx_MakePipe** to create an **FX PIPE**, followed by an **fx_ConnectPipe** which waits for a client to connect to this instance of the pipe.
2. A client program is started by a user and told to send the file "test.txt" to the server.
3. The client program issues **fx_Initialize** to initialize its underlying service layer, followed by **fx_Open** to start a connection with the server.
4. Once the connection is made, the client prepares a FILE_SEND_TO_SERVER request packet, whose format is shown in Figure 9-8, and then issues **fx_Transact** which sends the request packet and obtains the reply from the server all in one operation. The reply packet format is shown in Figure 9-9. This request/reply exchange is an example of how FX may be used for simple transaction processing.
5. The server accepts the request for a file transfer and issues a **fx_Read** which waits for the first packet of file data to arrive.

6. The client reads the file from disk and prepares a data packet which it sends to the server using **fx_Write**. This operation will be repeated until the entire file has been read from the disk and sent to the server. The data packet format is shown in Figure 9-10.
7. After the entire file is sent, the client prepares a DISCONNECT request packet (see Figure 9-8) and sends it to the server using **fx_Write**.
8. After receiving the DISCONNECT packet, the server issues **fx_DisconnectPipe** which frees the pipe for the next client.
9. The client issues **fx_Close** to close its end of the pipe. It then displays the file transfer performance statistics on the screen.

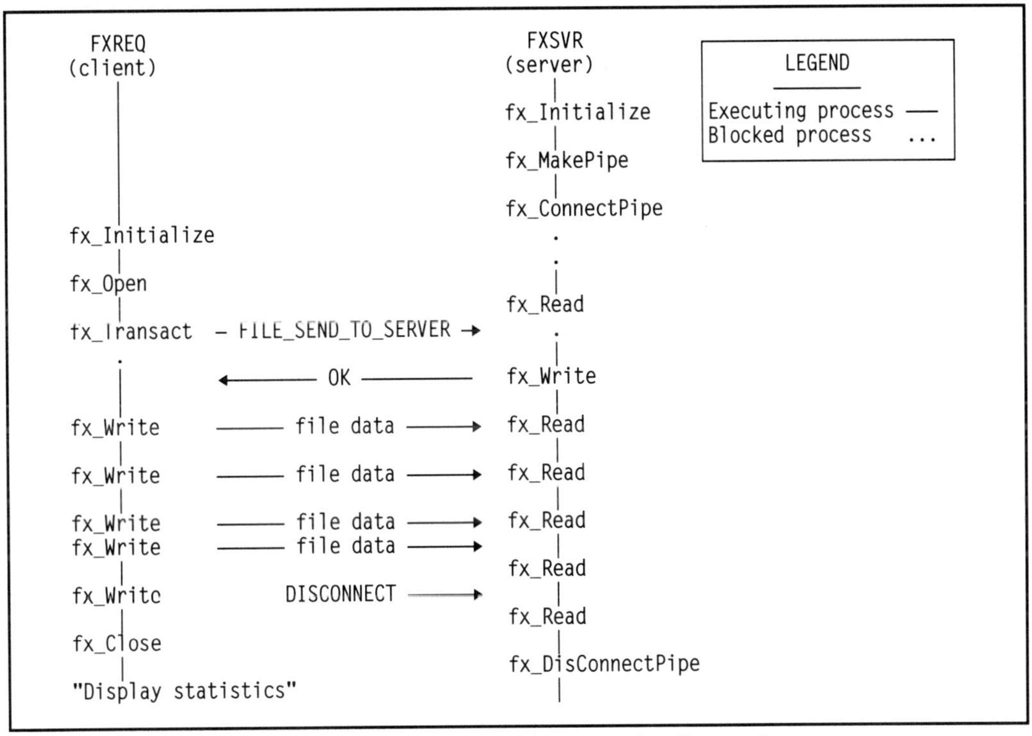

Figure 9-6. Sending a File Using the "FX" File Transfer Protocol.

Walking through the File Receive Scenario

This scenario is very similar to the file send scenario, with the following exceptions:

1. A client program is started by a user and told to *receive* the file "test.txt" from the server.
2. After the connection the client sends a FILE_RECEIVE_FROM_SERVER request packet, whose format is shown in Figure 9-8, and then issues **fx_Transact**.
3. The direction of the file transfer is reversed.

The File Receive Scenario

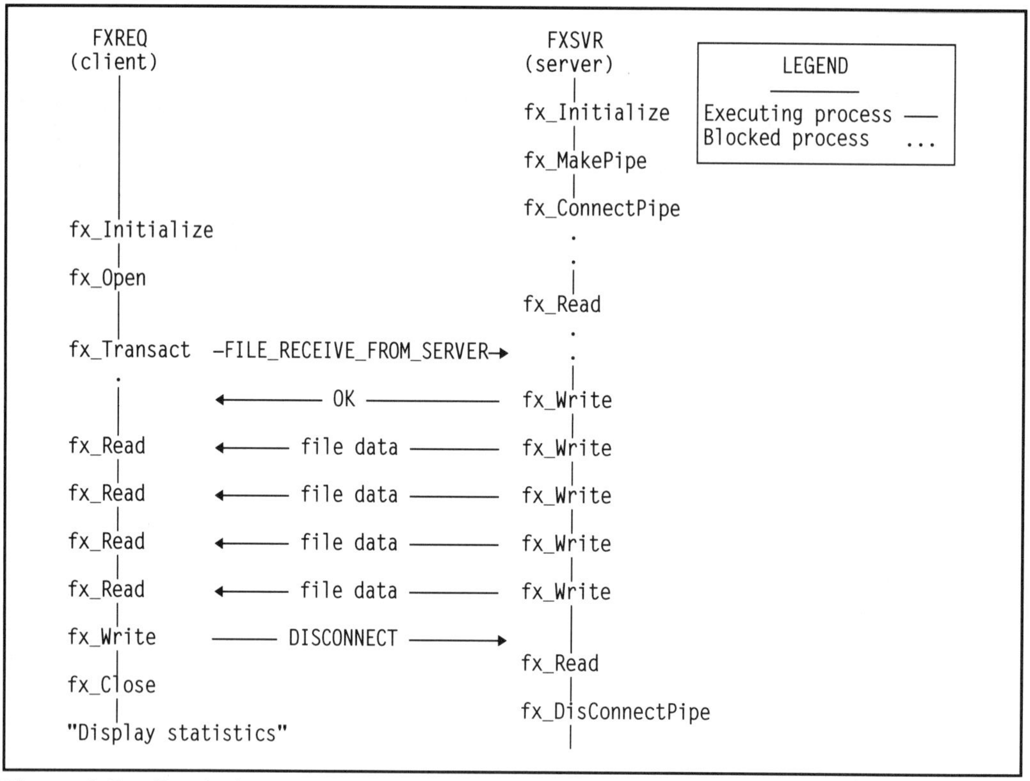

Figure 9-7. Retrieving a File From the Server Using the "FX" File Transfer Protocol.

REQUEST_PACKET Format

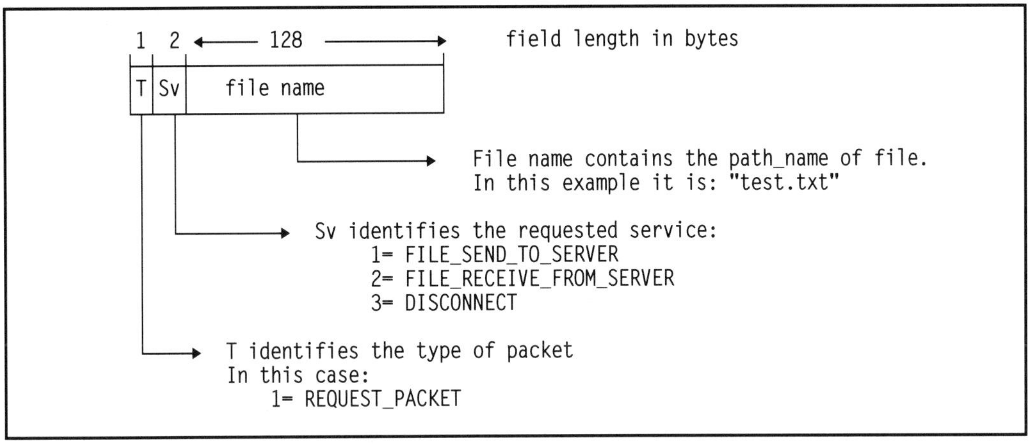

Figure 9-8. Format of the Request Packet.

RESPONSE_PACKET Format

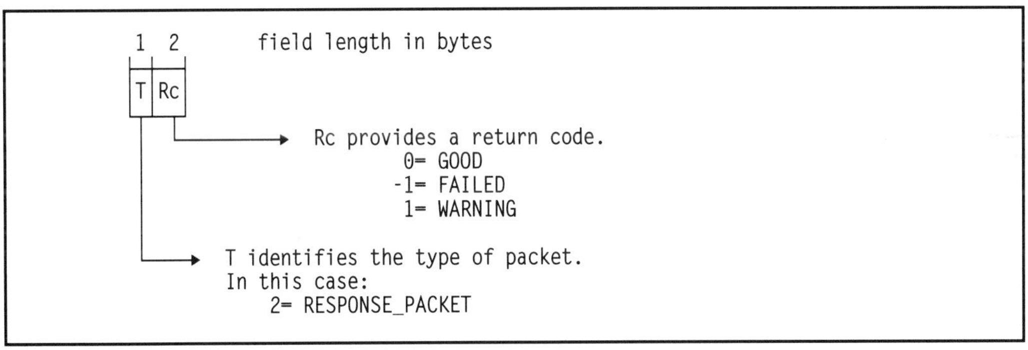

Figure 9-9. Format of a Response Packet.

FILEDATA_PACKET Format

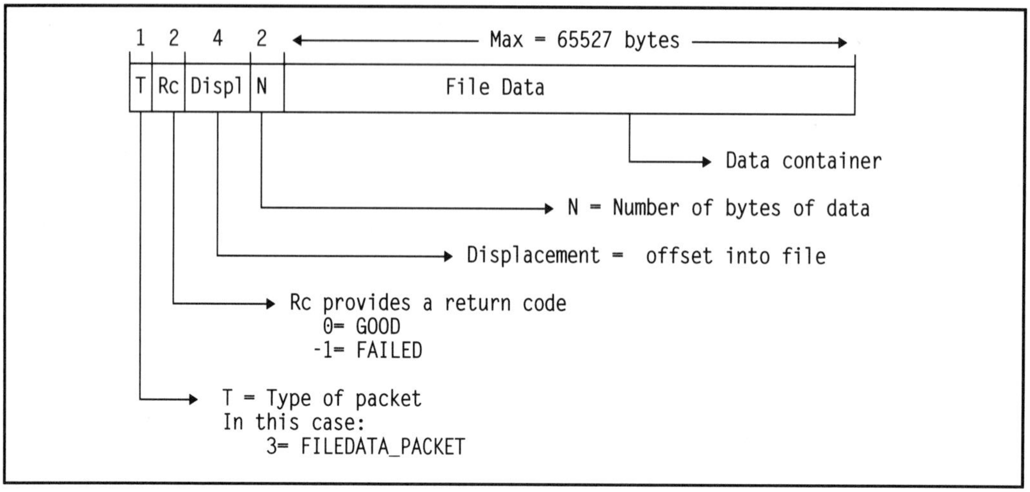

Figure 9-10. Format of a File Data Packet.

The fields in the FILEDATA_PACKET (see Figure 9-10) require further explanation:

T The **type** field specifies the format of the message (or packet). Our protocol supports 3 types of packets: request, response and filedata. The type field acts as a signature that identifies the type of packet received.

Rc This field contains the **return code**. You may wonder why a return code is sent with a data packet. The answer is that it provides an easy way to abort a file transfer. If, for example, the sender reads bad data from the file in the middle of a file transfer, it sends a FILEDATA_PACKET with a FAILED return code. This will cause the receiver to discontinue the file transfer. If we didn't have this field, we would need to add a new type of packet that provides an ABORT function.

Displ The **displacement** field specifies the offset in bytes inside a file where the receiver is to write the data. Having the sender specify explicitly where to write the data, protects against corrupting the received file. This can happen, for example, if a packet gets inadvertently retransmitted and the duplication is not recognized by the underlying protocol. Without the displacement field, the duplicate data gets written in the file starting at the current location. On the other hand, if the sender specifies the displacement, the worse that can happen is that the same information gets rewritten in the same file locations.

N This field specifies the actual *number* of bytes of file data sent. This number will depend on how many bytes of data are read from the disk, which in turn is dependent on the disk read *block size*. The block size is specified by the user in the configuration file (see next chapters). The file transfer layer obtains this block size when it calls **fx_Initialize**.

File Data This field can contain up to 65,527 bytes of *file data*. The actual number of bytes sent is specified'by the **N** parameter.

HOW TO READ FXREQ.C

FXREQ.C, listed in Figure 9-11, is an implementation of the application and file transfer layers (see Figure 9-1 on page 229) of a file client program. The file client program in conjunction with a file server program will be used for benchmarking the OS/2 EE LAN and IPC protocols.

FXREQ.C shares, with **FXSVR.C**, the use of the common include file: **FXFER.H**, listed in Figure 9-12. It also uses **FXREQ.H** a custom include file, listed in Figure 9-13.

The following is a list of general observations about the code:

- No OS/2 calls are used in this module. We have included **OS2.H** only to obtain the OS/2 data type definitions.
- The FX calls are not implemented in this module. They get implemented in the DLLs. The FX calls make extensive use of OS/2 EE.
- Since there is no new OS/2 material to introduce, we assume that walking through the code will be a straightforward exercise in reading C listings. However, here are some simple directions that can help you in your reading:
  1. Start with **main()**, which serves as the outline for the program.
  2. Use the scenarios (see Figure 9-6 on page 239 and Figure 9-7 on page 240) as your protocol guide. The code is no more than the implementation of the scenarios.
  3. Use the message structures (see Figure 9-8 on page 241 through Figure 9-10 on page 242) as your guide to the data structures used in the program.
- Make sure you read the sections of the code that implement the gathering and display of file transfer performance statistics. The end goal of this project is to come up with an equitable benchmark, and it's your job to keep us honest!
- Make sure you understand how the FX calls are used. It is important to develop a user's perspective of FX to better understand the implementations of FX in the chapters that follow.

FXREQ.C LISTING

```
/*****************************************************************************/
/*  PROGRAM NAME: FXREQ - File Transfer example,  requester module (client)  */
/*                                                                           */
/*  PROGRAM DESCRIPTION:  This module is the requester portion of a file     */
/*    transfer program.  This module uses communication functions modeled    */
/*    after named pipe functions to perform the file transfer.  The services */
/*    are implemented in separate modules using NETBIOS, APPC, or named pipe */
/*    communication for PC-PC communication.  Named pipes is used to         */
/*    implement a local file transfer between two processes.                 */
/*    A summary report is displayed showing how long it took to transfer     */
/*    the file.                                                              */
/*                                                                           */
/*  PROGRAM INVOCATION:                                                      */
/*                                                                           */
/*  FXREQ direction file-name                                                */
/*                                                                           */
/*     where:                                                                */
/*         direction is either SEND or RECV.                                 */
/*                                                                           */
/*         file-name is the name of the file to transfer.  If a path is      */
/*                   specified the path must exist on the client  and        */
/*                   server machines.                                        */
/*                                                                           */
/*         NOTE: The DLL for the protocol you wish to test must be copied    */
/*               to PROTOCOL.DLL in a subdirectory in your LIBPATH.          */
/*                                                                           */
/*  EXAMPLE INVOCATIONS:                                                     */
/*                                                                           */
/*    FXREQ SEND MYFILE.TMP                                                  */
/*    FXREQ RECV MYFILE.TMP                                                  */
/*****************************************************************************/
#include <process.h>                    /* For exit()                        */
#include <stdio.h>                      /* For printf() & NULL               */
#include <stdlib.h>                     /* For printf                        */
#include <string.h>                     /* For printf                        */
#include <sys\types.h>                  /* For time()                        */
#include <sys\timeb.h>                  /* For time()                        */
#include <sys\stat.h>                   /* For stat()                        */
#include <io.h>                         /* For file I/O                      */
#include <fcntl.h>                      /* For file I/O                      */
#include <sys\types.h>                  /* For file I/O                      */

#include <os2.h>                        /* for types only                    */

#include "fxfer.h"
#include "fxreq.h"
```

Figure 9-11 (Part 1 of 8). File Transfer Requester Program.

```
/*-------------------------------------------------------------------------*/
/* Main routine. Performs a file transfer and calculates statistics.       */
/*-------------------------------------------------------------------------*/
VOID main(SHORT argc, PCHAR argv[], PCHAR envp[])
{
   /*------------------------------------*/
   /* get command line arguments         */
   /*------------------------------------*/
   if (get_args(argc, argv))
      { print_help();
        exit(FAILED);
      }

   /*------------------------------------*/
   /* initialize requester               */
   /*------------------------------------*/
   initialize_requester();

   /*------------------------------------*/
   /* request service                    */
   /*------------------------------------*/
   switch (service)
     {
      case FILE_SEND_TO_SERVER:      open_file();
                                     request_file_transfer();
                                     send_file();
                                     break;
      case FILE_RECEIVE_FROM_SERVER: open_file();
                                     request_file_transfer();
                                     receive_file();
                                     break;
     } /* end switch */

   /*------------------------------------*/
   /* end the service request            */
   /*------------------------------------*/
   terminate_service_request();

   /*------------------------------------*/
   /* print the statistics               */
   /*------------------------------------*/
   printf("File transfer completed.\n");
   file_size = get_file_size(file_name);
   print_statistics();

   exit(GOOD);

} /* end main */
```

Figure 9-11 (Part 2 of 8). File Transfer Requester Program.

```
/*-------------------------------------------------------------------*/
/* Initialize program variables from command line.                   */
/*-------------------------------------------------------------------*/
USHORT get_args(SHORT argc, PCHAR argv[])
{
   /*-----------------------------------*/
   /* are there the right number of args? */
   /*-----------------------------------*/
   if (argc != 3)
     return(FAILED);

   /*-----------------------------------*/
   /* send or receive??                 */
   /*-----------------------------------*/
   if (strcmp("SEND", strupr(argv[1])) == 0)
     service = FILE_SEND_TO_SERVER;
   else
     if (strcmp("RECV", strupr(argv[1])) == 0)
       service = FILE_RECEIVE_FROM_SERVER;
     else return(FAILED);

   /*-----------------------------------*/
   /* get the file name                 */
   /*-----------------------------------*/
   strcpy(file_name, argv[2]);

   /*-----------------------------------*/
   /* everything is OK!                 */
   /*-----------------------------------*/
   return(GOOD);
} /* end get_args */

/*-------------------------------------------------------------------*/
/* Initialize requester from config file data.                       */
/*-------------------------------------------------------------------*/
VOID initialize_requester(VOID)
{
  /*-----------------------------------*/
  /* perform initialization            */
  /*   -get configuration data         */
  /*   -allocate a buffer for          */
  /*     communication (pointer to buffer*/
  /*     and size are returned)        */
  /*-----------------------------------*/
  printf("Initializing...\n");
  open_bgn_time = save_time();
  if (fx_Initialize(&packet_ptr, &filedata_packet_size))
     { printf("Error Initializing.\n");
       exit(FAILED);
     }
  /*-----------------------------------*/
  /* calculate header and data sizes of */
  /* packet used for file transfer     */
  /*-----------------------------------*/
  filedata_header_size = (sizeof(packet_ptr->filedata) -
                          sizeof(packet_ptr->filedata.Data));

  filedata_data_size = filedata_packet_size - filedata_header_size;
```

Figure 9-11 (Part 3 of 8). **File Transfer Requester Program.**

```
  /*-----------------------------------*/
  /* open the pipe                     */
  /*-----------------------------------*/
  if (fx_Open())
     { printf("Error Opening Communication Pipe.\n");
       exit(FAILED);
     }

  printf("Initialization complete.\n\n");
} /* end initialize_requester */

/*---------------------------------------------------------------------------*/
/* Function to open an existing file or create a new file.                   */
/*---------------------------------------------------------------------------*/
VOID open_file(VOID)
{
  /*-----------------------------------*/
  /* open the file                     */
  /*-----------------------------------*/
  printf("Starting file transfer...\n");
  if (service == FILE_SEND_TO_SERVER)
     {if (-1 == (FileHandle = open(file_name, O_BINARY | O_RDONLY )))
         {print_error(errno,"opening a file",__FILE__,__LINE__);
          exit(FAILED);
         }
     }
  else
     {if (-1 == (FileHandle = open(file_name,
                      O_BINARY | O_WRONLY | O_CREAT, S_IREAD | S_IWRITE)))
         {print_error(errno,"opening a file",__FILE__,__LINE__);
          exit(FAILED);
         }
     }
} /* end open_file */
/*---------------------------------------------------------------------------*/
/* Function to request the file transfer service.                            */
/*---------------------------------------------------------------------------*/
VOID request_file_transfer(VOID)
{
  /*-----------------------------------*/
  /* send file transfer parms to server */
  /* and get response                  */
  /*-----------------------------------*/
  xfer_bgn_time = save_time();
  packet_ptr->request.packet_type = REQUEST_PACKET;
  packet_ptr->request.service     = service;
  strcpy(packet_ptr->request.file_name, file_name);
```

Figure 9-11 (Part 4 of 8). File Transfer Requester Program.

```
    if (fx_Transact(packet_ptr,                      /* packet to be sent         */
                    sizeof(packet_ptr->request),  /* packet size               */
                    packet_ptr,                      /* packet to be received     */
                    sizeof(packet_ptr->response),/* packet size               */
                    &PipeBytesRead))                 /* number of bytes received  */
       {printf("Error starting file transfer.\n");
        exit(FAILED);
       }

    if (packet_ptr->response.rc != 0)
       {printf("Server Error when starting file transfer.\n");
        exit(FAILED);
       }
  } /* end request_file_transfer */

  /*------------------------------------------------------------------------*/
  /* Function to receive a file from the server.                            */
  /*------------------------------------------------------------------------*/
  VOID receive_file(VOID)
  {
    /*------------------------------------*/
    /* receive file data from requester   */
    /*------------------------------------*/
    do {
        /*------------------------------------*/
        /* receive a block of file data       */
        /*------------------------------------*/
        if (fx_Read(packet_ptr,
                    filedata_packet_size,
                    &PipeBytesRead))
            break;

        /*------------------------------------*/
        /* seek to file location for the block */
        /*------------------------------------*/
        if (-1L == lseek(FileHandle,
                         packet_ptr->filedata.offset,
                         SEEK_SET))
           {print_error(errno,"performing a LSEEK",__FILE__,__LINE__);
            break;
           }
        /*------------------------------------*/
        /* write the block to the file        */
        /*------------------------------------*/
        if (-1 == write(FileHandle,
                        packet_ptr->filedata.Data,
                        packet_ptr->filedata.length))
           {print_error(errno,"writing to a file",__FILE__,__LINE__);
            break;
           }

       } while ((packet_ptr->filedata.rc == 0)
              && (packet_ptr->filedata.length != 0));/*enddo*/
```

Figure 9-11 (Part 5 of 8). File Transfer Requester Program.

```
  /*________________________________________*/
  /* end the file transfer                  */
  /*________________________________________*/
  close(FileHandle);                /* close the file                */

} /* end receive_file */

/*______________________________________________________________________________*/
/* Function to send a file to the server.                                       */
/*______________________________________________________________________________*/
VOID send_file(VOID)
{
  /*________________________________________*/
  /* send file data to server               */
  /*________________________________________*/
  packet_ptr->filedata.offset = 0;
  do {
      /*________________________________________*/
      /* read a block of file data              */
      /*________________________________________*/
      packet_ptr->filedata.length = read(FileHandle,
                                         packet_ptr->filedata.Data,
                                         filedata_data_size);
      if (packet_ptr->filedata.length == -1)
         {print_error(errno,"reading file data",__FILE__,__LINE__);
          packet_ptr->filedata.rc = FAILED;
          packet_ptr->filedata.length = 0;
         }
      /*________________________________________*/
      /* send the block of file data, drop      */
      /*   out of loop if send error or file    */
      /*   error.                               */
      /*________________________________________*/
      packet_ptr->filedata.packet type = FILEDATA PACKET;
      if (fx_Write(packet_ptr,
                   filedata_header_size +
                   packet_ptr->filedata.length,
                   &PipeBytesWritten)
         | packet_ptr >filedata.rc)
         break;
      packet_ptr->filedata.offset = packet_ptr->filedata.offset +
                                    packet_ptr->filedata.length;

    } while ((packet_ptr->filedata.rc == 0) &&
             (packet_ptr->filedata.length != 0)); /* enddo */

  /*________________________________________*/
  /* end the file transfer                  */
  /*________________________________________*/
  close(FileHandle);                /* close the file                */

} /* end send_file */
```

Figure 9-11 (Part 6 of 8). File Transfer Requester Program.

```
/*------------------------------------------------------------------------*/
/* close the file, terminate service request, close the comm. pipe        */
/*------------------------------------------------------------------------*/
VOID terminate_service_request(VOID)
{
  /*-------------------------------------*/
  /* Send disconnect request             */
  /*-------------------------------------*/
  packet_ptr->request.packet_type = REQUEST_PACKET;
  packet_ptr->request.service     = DISCONNECT;
  if (fx_Write(packet_ptr,
               sizeof(packet_ptr->request),
               &PipeBytesRead))
     { printf("Error terminating service.",__FILE__,__LINE__);
       exit(FAILED);
     }

  /*-------------------------------------*/
  /* end the pipe session                */
  /*-------------------------------------*/
  close_bgn_time = save_time();
  if (fx_Close())
     {printf("Error Closing communication pipe.");
      exit(FAILED);
     }
  end_time = save_time();
} /* end terminate_service_request */
/*------------------------------------------------------------------------*/
/* Start timing an event.                                                 */
/*------------------------------------------------------------------------*/
double save_time(VOID)
{
  ftime(&timebuff);
  return((double)timebuff.time+((double)timebuff.millitm)/(double)1000);
} /* end save_time */

/*------------------------------------------------------------------------*/
/* Print Statistics.                                                      */
/*------------------------------------------------------------------------*/
VOID print_statistics(VOID)
{
  if (service == FILE_SEND_TO_SERVER)
     printf("\n%s sent to the server.\n", file_name);
  else
     printf("\n%s received from the server.\n",file_name);

  printf("Communication link open time was %f seconds.\n",
         xfer_bgn_time-open_bgn_time);
  printf("%ld bytes transferred in %f seconds.\n",
         file_size, close_bgn_time-xfer_bgn_time);
  printf("The average transfer rate was %.2f kilobytes/second.\n",
         file_size/((close_bgn_time-xfer_bgn_time)*1000));
  printf("Communication link close time was %f seconds.\n",
         end_time-close_bgn_time);
} /* end print_statistics */
```

Figure 9-11 (Part 7 of 8). File Transfer Requester Program.

```
/*--------------------------------------------------------------------------*/
/* Print Help.                                                              */
/*--------------------------------------------------------------------------*/
VOID print_help(VOID)
{
  printf("\nIncorrect command invocation.  Enter as follows:\n");
  printf("\n");
  printf("FXR  direction file-name                                        \n");
  printf("                                                                \n");
  printf(" where:                                                         \n");
  printf("     direction is either SEND or RECV.                          \n");
  printf("                                                                \n");
  printf("     file-name is the name of the file to transfer.  If a      \n");
  printf("               path is specified the path must exist on the    \n");
  printf("               requester and server machines.                  \n");
  printf("                                                                \n");
  printf("     NOTE: The DLL for the protocol you wish to test must      \n");
  printf("           be copied to PROTOCOL.DLL in a subdirectory in      \n");
  printf("           your LIBPATH.                                        \n");
  printf("\n\n");
} /* end print_help */
/*--------------------------------------------------------------------------*/
/* Get File Size                                                            */
/*--------------------------------------------------------------------------*/
ULONG get_file_size(PCHAR name)
{
  SHORT fhandle;
  ULONG size;

  if (-1 == (fhandle = open(name, O_BINARY | O_RDONLY )))
     {print_error(errno,"opening a file",__FILE__,__LINE__);
      return(FAILED);
     }
  size = filelength(fhandle);
  close(fhandle);

  return(size);
} /* end get_file_size */

/*--------------------------------------------------------------------------*/
/* Error Display Routine                                                    */
/*--------------------------------------------------------------------------*/
VOID print_error(USHORT Error, PCHAR msg, PCHAR file, USHORT line)
{
 printf("Error %u (0x%x) detected while %s at line %u in file %s.\n",
        Error, Error, msg, line, file);
} /* end print_error */
```

Figure 9-11 (Part 8 of 8). File Transfer Requester Program.

FXFER.H INCLUDE FILE

```
/*******************************************************************************/
/*  INCLUDE NAME: FXFER - declarations for FXFER programs                      */
/*******************************************************************************/
/*-----------------------------------------------------------------------------*/
/* defines                                                                     */
/*-----------------------------------------------------------------------------*/
                   /*------------------------------------*/
                   /* file transfer direction defines    */
                   /*------------------------------------*/
#define RECEIVE    0
#define SEND       1
                   /*------------------------------------*/
                   /* return code defines                */
                   /*------------------------------------*/
#define FAILED     -1
#define GOOD       0
#define WARNING    1
                   /*------------------------------------*/
                   /* thread must perform the following  */
                   /*------------------------------------*/
#define REQUEST_PACKET      1
#define RESPONSE_PACKET     2
#define FILEDATA_PACKET     3
                   /*------------------------------------*/
                   /* service request codes              */
                   /*------------------------------------*/
#define FILE_SEND_TO_SERVER          1
#define FILE_RECEIVE_FROM_SERVER     2
#define DISCONNECT                   3
/*-----------------------------------------------------------------------------*/
/* Structure declarations                                                      */
/*-----------------------------------------------------------------------------*/
                   /*------------------------------------*/
                   /* service request packet             */
                   /*------------------------------------*/
typedef struct
   { BYTE   packet_type;              /* packet type = REQUEST_PACKET      */
     USHORT service;                  /* service being requested           */
                                      /*   FILE_SEND                       */
                                      /*   FILE_RECEIVE                    */
                                      /*   DISCONNECT                      */
     CHAR   file_name[128];           /* file name for file transfer       */
   } REQUEST;
                   /*------------------------------------*/
                   /* response packet                    */
                   /*------------------------------------*/
typedef struct
   { BYTE   packet_type;              /* packet type = RESPONSE_PACKET     */
     USHORT rc;                       /* service being requested           */
   } RESPONSE;
```

Figure 9-12 (Part 1 of 2). FXFER.H Include File.

```
                    /*-----------------------------------*/
                    /* filedata packet                   */
                    /*-----------------------------------*/
typedef struct
   { BYTE   packet_type;                 /* packet type = FILEDATA_PACKET     */
     USHORT rc;                          /* return code                       */
     ULONG  offset;                      /* filedata offset                   */
     USHORT length;                      /* filedata length                   */
     BYTE   Data[65527];                 /* file data                         */
   } FILEDATA;
                    /*-----------------------------------*/
                    /* union of all packet types         */
                    /*-----------------------------------*/
typedef union PACKET
   { REQUEST  request;                  /* request  packet                    */
     RESPONSE response;                 /* response packet                    */
     FILEDATA filedata;                 /* filedata packet                    */
   } PACKET;

/*---------------------------------------------------------------------------*/
/* Forward declarations of communication functions                           */
/*---------------------------------------------------------------------------*/
USHORT fx_Initialize(PVOID *, PUSHORT);
USHORT fx_MakePipe(VOID);
USHORT fx_ConnectPipe(VOID);
USHORT fx_DisconnectPipe(VOID);
USHORT fx_Open(VOID);
USHORT fx_Write(PVOID, USHORT, PUSHORT);
USHORT fx_Read(PVOID,  USHORT, PUSHORT);
USHORT fx_Transact(PVOID, USHORT, PVOID, USHORT, PVOID);
USHORT fx_Close(VOID);
```

Figure 9-12 (Part 2 of 2). FXFER.H Include File.

FXREQ.H INCLUDE FILE

```
/***************************************************************************/
/*  INCLUDE NAME: FXREQ - declarations for FXREQ program                  */
/***************************************************************************/
/*-----------------------------------------------------------------------*/
/* Forward declarations of functions in this module                      */
/*-----------------------------------------------------------------------*/
USHORT get_args(SHORT, PCHAR *);
VOID   initialize_requester(VOID);
VOID   open_file(VOID);
VOID   request_file_transfer(VOID);
VOID   receive_file(VOID);
VOID   send_file(VOID);
VOID   terminate_service_request(VOID);
double save_time(VOID);
VOID   print_statistics(VOID);
VOID   print_help(VOID);
ULONG  get_file_size(PCHAR);
VOID   print_error(USHORT, PCHAR, PCHAR, USHORT);

/*-----------------------------------------------------------------------*/
/* Global variables for this module                                      */
/*-----------------------------------------------------------------------*/
                   /*--------------------------------*/
                   /* command line argument variables */
                   /*--------------------------------*/
USHORT  service;
CHAR    file_name[128];
                   /*--------------------------------*/
                   /* timing variables               */
                   /*--------------------------------*/
double  open_bgn_time   = 0.0;       /* Begin fx_Open                    */
double  xfer_bgn_time   = 0.0;       /* Begin start of data transfer     */
double  close_bgn_time  = 0.0;       /* Begin fx_Close                   */
double  end_time        = 0.0;       /* fx_Close complete                */
struct  timeb  timebuff;             /* Timer buffer                     */
                   /*--------------------------------*/
                   /* file size variable             */
                   /*--------------------------------*/
ULONG   file_size;
                   /*--------------------------------*/
                   /* file transfer variables        */
                   /*--------------------------------*/
PACKET   *packet_ptr;                /* pointer to packet                */
USHORT    filedata_packet_size;      /* size of packet for file transfer */
USHORT    filedata_data_size;        /* size of data area for file transfer*/
USHORT    filedata_header_size;      /* size of header area for file xfer */
USHORT    PipeBytesRead;             /* number of bytes read from pipe   */
USHORT    PipeBytesWritten;          /* number of bytes written to pipe  */
USHORT    FileHandle;                /* handle for File                  */

USHORT    rc;                        /* variable to receive return codes */
```

Figure 9-13. FXREQ.H Include File.

HOW TO READ FXSVR.C

FXSRV.C, listed in Figure 9-14; is an implementation of the application and file transfer layers (see Figure 9-1 on page 229) of a file server program. The file server program, in conjunction with a file requester program, will be used for benchmarking the OS/2 EE LAN and IPC protocols. **FXSVR.C** shares, with **FXREQ.C**, the use of the common include file: **FXFER.H** listed in Figure 9-12 on page 252. It also uses **FXSVR.H**, a custom include file, listed in Figure 9-15. The following is list of general observations about the code:

- The only OS/2 call used in this module is **DosExitList** which you've already encountered in "DosExitList" on page 121. The call is used to set up a routine which is run just before the server terminates. We use it for file cleanup.
- The FX calls are not implemented in this module. They get implemented in the DLLs. The FX calls make extensive use of OS/2 EE.
- Since there is no new OS/2 material to introduce, we assume that walking through the code will be a straightforward exercise in reading C listings. The same directions we recommended for **FXREQ.C** apply here:
  1. Start with **main()**, which serves as the outline for the program.
  2. Use the scenarios (see Figure 9-6 on page 239 and Figure 9-7 on page 240) as your protocol guide. The code is no more than the implementation of the scenarios.
  3. Use the message structures (see Figure 9-8 on page 241 through Figure 9-10 on page 242) as your guide to the data structures used in the program.
- The file transfer itself, as implemented by **send_file()** and **receive_file()**, is identical to its counterpart in **FXREQ.C**. After all, this part of the protocol is totally symmetrical.
- Make sure you understand how the FX calls are used. It is important to develop a user's perspective of FX to better understand the implementations of FX in the chapters that follow.

If you've already gone through the **FXREQ.C** code, you're almost at the finishing line for this chapter. What remains is the implementation of the other side of the protocol. It should be quick and easy reading!

FXSVR.C LISTING

```
/****************************************************************************/
/*  PROGRAM NAME: FXSVR - A File Transfer example, server module           */
/*                                                                          */
/*  PROGRAM DESCRIPTION:  This module is the server portion of a file      */
/*    transfer program.  This module uses communication functions modeled  */
/*    after named pipe functions to perform the file transfer. The services */
/*    are implemented in separate modules using IEEE 802.2, NETBIOS,        */
/*    APPC, or named pipe communication for PC-PC communication.  Named    */
/*    pipes, queues, and shared segments are used to implement a local file */
/*    transfer between two processes.                                       */
/*                                                                          */
/*    Refer to the FXREQ module for a more detailed description of the file */
/*    transfer programs.                                                    */
/*                                                                          */
/*  PROGRAM INVOCATION:    FXSVR                                            */
/****************************************************************************/
#include <process.h>                    /* For exit()                       */
#include <stdio.h>                      /* For printf() & NULL              */
#include <stdlib.h>                     /* For printf                       */
#include <string.h>                     /* For printf                       */
#include <io.h>                         /* For file I/O                     */
#include <fcntl.h>                      /* For file I/O                     */
#include <sys\types.h>                  /* For time()                       */
#include <sys\timeb.h>                  /* For time()                       */
#include <sys\stat.h>                   /* For stat()                       */

#define INCL_DOSPROCESS                 /* for DosExit function call        */
#include <os2.h>

#include "fxfer.h"
#include "fxsvr.h"
```

Figure 9-14 (Part 1 of 7). File Transfer Server Program.

```
/*------------------------------------------------------------------*/
/* Main routine. Performs file transfer.                            */
/*------------------------------------------------------------------*/
VOID main(VOID)
{
   initialize_server();

   /*-----------------------------------------*/
   /* loop which continuously services requests  */
   /*-----------------------------------------*/
   do
   {
     if (get_service_request() == GOOD)
        {
         switch (packet_ptr->request.service)
           {
            case FILE_SEND_TO_SERVER:      receive_file();
                                           break;
            case FILE_RECEIVE_FROM_SERVER: send_file();
                                           break;
            default : printf("Request for unknown service received.\n");
           } /* end switch */

         terminate_service_request();
        }
   } while (TRUE); /* enddo */
} /* end main */

/*------------------------------------------------------------------*/
/* Initialize server from config file data                          */
/*------------------------------------------------------------------*/
VOID initialize_server(VOID)
{
  printf("Initializing Server...\n");

  /*-----------------------------------*/
  /* exit routine to close pipe if      */
  /*   server terminates                */
  /*-----------------------------------*/
  if (rc = DosExitList(1,(PFNEXITLIST) fxsvr_exit))
     { print_error(rc,"establishing DosExitList",__FILE__,__LINE__);
       exit(FAILED);
     }

  /*-----------------------------------*/
  /* perform initialization             */
  /*   -get configuration data          */
  /*   -allocate a buffer for           */
  /*     communication (pointer to buffer*/
  /*     and size are returned)         */
  /*-----------------------------------*/
  if (rc = fx_Initialize(&packet_ptr, &filedata_packet_size))
     { print_error(rc,"during fx_Initialize",__FILE__,__LINE__);
       exit(FAILED);
     }
```

Figure 9-14 (Part 2 of 7). File Transfer Server Program.

```
    /*--------------------------------------*/
    /* calculate header and data sizes of  */
    /* packet used for file transfer        */
    /*--------------------------------------*/
    filedata_header_size = (sizeof(packet_ptr->filedata) -
                            sizeof(packet_ptr->filedata.Data));
    filedata_data_size = filedata_packet_size - filedata_header_size;

    /*--------------------------------------*/
    /* Establish the server                 */
    /*--------------------------------------*/
    if (rc = fx_MakePipe())
       { print_error(rc,"during fx_MakePipe",__FILE__,__LINE__);
         exit(FAILED);
       }

    printf("Server Initialization complete.\n\n");
  } /* end initialize_server */

  /*------------------------------------------------------------------------*/
  /* receive client request                                                  */
  /*------------------------------------------------------------------------*/
  USHORT get_service_request(VOID)
  {
    /*--------------------------------------*/
    /* Wait for requester to open the pipe */
    /*--------------------------------------*/
    printf("\nWaiting for service request...\n");
    if (fx_ConnectPipe())
       return(FAILED);

    /*--------------------------------------*/
    /* Receive the file transfer parameters*/
    /*--------------------------------------*/
    if (fx_Read(packet_ptr,            /* read file xfer parms              */
                sizeof(packet_ptr->request),
                &PipeBytesRead))
       return(FAILED);

  } /* end get_service_request */
```

Figure 9-14 (Part 3 of 7). File Transfer Server Program.

```
/*------------------------------------------------------------------------*/
/* Server program function which receives a file using the following steps: */
/*   1) create file,  2) respond to request, 3) receive file data          */
/*------------------------------------------------------------------------*/
VOID receive_file(VOID)
{
  printf("File Send Request received.\n");
 /*-----------------------------------*/
 /* create file                       */
 /*-----------------------------------*/
 FileHandle = open(packet_ptr->request.file_name,
                   O_BINARY | O_WRONLY | O_CREAT,
                   S_IREAD | S_IWRITE);
 if (FileHandle == -1)
    {print_error(errno,"opening a file",__FILE__,__LINE__);
     packet_ptr->response.rc = FAILED;
    }
 else packet_ptr->response.rc = GOOD;
 packet_ptr->filedata.packet_type = RESPONSE_PACKET;

 /*-----------------------------------*/
 /* respond to request                */
 /*-----------------------------------*/
 if ( (fx_Write(packet_ptr,
               sizeof(packet_ptr->response),
               &PipeBytesWritten) == 0)
     && (packet_ptr->response.rc == 0))

 /*-----------------------------------*/
 /* receive file data from requester  */
 /*-----------------------------------*/
 do {
     /*-----------------------------------*/
     /* Receive a block of data           */
     /*-----------------------------------*/
     if (fx_Read(packet_ptr,
                 filedata_packet_size,
                 &PipeBytesRead))
         break;

     /*-----------------------------------*/
     /* seek to file location for the block */
     /*-----------------------------------*/
     if (-1L == lseek(FileHandle,
                      packet_ptr->filedata.offset,
                      SEEK_SET))
        {print_error(errno,"performing a LSEEK",__FILE__,__LINE__);
         break;
        }
```

Figure 9-14 (Part 4 of 7). File Transfer Server Program.

```
      /*------------------------------------*/
      /* write the block to the file        */
      /*------------------------------------*/
      if (-1 == write(FileHandle,
                     packet_ptr->filedata.Data,
                     packet_ptr->filedata.length))
         {print_error(errno,"writing to a file",__FILE__,__LINE__);
          break;
         }

     } while ((packet_ptr->filedata.rc == 0)
            && (packet_ptr->filedata.length != 0));/*enddo*/

  /*------------------------------------*/
  /* close the file                     */
  /*------------------------------------*/
  close(FileHandle);
} /*end receive_file */

/*-------------------------------------------------------------------------*/
/* Server program function which sends a file using the following steps:  */
/*   1) open file,  2) respond to request, 3) send file data               */
/*-------------------------------------------------------------------------*/
VOID send_file(VOID)
{
  printf("File Receive request received.\n");

  /*------------------------------------*/
  /* open existing file                 */
  /*------------------------------------*/
  FileHandle = open(packet_ptr->request.file_name,
                    O_BINARY | O_RDONLY );
  if (FileHandle == -1)
     {print_error(errno,"opening a file",__FILE__,__LINE__);
      packet_ptr->response.rc = FAILED;
     }
  else packet_ptr->response.rc = GOOD;
  packet_ptr->filedata.packet_type = RESPONSE_PACKET;

  /*------------------------------------*/
  /* respond to request                 */
  /*------------------------------------*/
  if ( (fx_Write(packet_ptr,
                 sizeof(packet_ptr->response),
                 &PipeBytesWritten) == 0)
       && (packet_ptr->response.rc == 0))
     {packet_ptr->filedata.offset = 0L;
```

Figure 9-14 (Part 5 of 7). File Transfer Server Program.

```
      /*--------------------------------------*/
      /* send file data to requester          */
      /*--------------------------------------*/
      do {
          packet_ptr->filedata.packet_type = FILEDATA_PACKET;
          packet_ptr->filedata.length = 0L;
          /*--------------------------------------*/
          /* read a block of data from the file  */
          /*--------------------------------------*/
          packet_ptr->filedata.length = read(FileHandle,
                                        packet_ptr->filedata.Data,
                                        filedata_data_size);
          if (packet_ptr->filedata.length == -1)
             {print_error(errno,"reading file data",__FILE__,__LINE__);
              packet_ptr->filedata.rc = -1;
              packet_ptr->filedata.length = 0;
             }

          /*--------------------------------------*/
          /* send the block of file data          */
          /*--------------------------------------*/
          if (fx_Write(packet_ptr,
                       filedata_header_size +
                       packet_ptr->filedata.length,
                       &PipeBytesWritten)
              | packet_ptr->filedata.rc)
              break;
          packet_ptr->filedata.offset =
                      packet_ptr->filedata.offset +
                      packet_ptr->filedata.length;

        } while ((packet_ptr->filedata.rc == 0) &&
                (packet_ptr->filedata.length != 0)); /* enddo */

    } /* end if */
  /*--------------------------------------*/
  /* close the file                       */
  /*--------------------------------------*/
  close(FileHandle);
} /* end send_file */

/*-----------------------------------------------------------------------------*/
/* function to end a service request                                           */
/*-----------------------------------------------------------------------------*/
USHORT terminate_service_request(VOID)
{
  /*--------------------------------------*/
  /* Receive disconnect request           */
  /*--------------------------------------*/
  if (fx_Read(packet_ptr,
              filedata_packet_size,
              &PipeBytesRead))
    { print_error(rc,"receiving request disconnect",__FILE__,__LINE__);
      return(FAILED);
    }

  if (!((packet_ptr->request.packet_type == REQUEST_PACKET) &&
      (packet_ptr->request.service     == DISCONNECT)))
     printf("Incorrect protocol. Disconnect request expected.\n");
```

Figure 9-14 (Part 6 of 7). File Transfer Server Program.

```
    /*-------------------------------------*/
    /* end the pipe session                */
    /*-------------------------------------*/
    if (fx_DisconnectPipe())          /* prepare for next request          */
       { print_error(rc, "during fx_DisconnectPipe",__FILE__,__LINE__);
         return(FAILED);
       }

    printf("Service Request completed.\n");

  } /* end server_send_receive_file */

  /*--------------------------------------------------------------------*/
  /* Error Display Routine                                              */
  /*--------------------------------------------------------------------*/
  VOID print_error(USHORT Error, PCHAR msg, PCHAR file, USHORT line)
  {
   printf("Error %u (0x%x) detected while %s at line %u in file %s.\n",
          Error, Error, msg, line, file);
  } /* end print_error */

  /*--------------------------------------------------------------------*/
  /* Exit Routine                                                       */
  /*--------------------------------------------------------------------*/
  VOID FAR
  fxsvr_exit(USHORT exit_type)
  {
    if (fx_Close())
       printf("Error encountered will terminating the file transfer server.");
    else
       printf("File transfer server terminated normally.\n");

    DosExitList(3, (void far *) 0);
  } /* end fxsvr_exit */
```

Figure 9-14 (Part 7 of 7). File Transfer Server Program.

FXSVR.H INCLUDE FILE

```
/******************************************************************************/
/*  INCLUDE NAME: FXSVR - declarations for FXSVR program                      */
/******************************************************************************/
/*--------------------------------------------------------------------------*/
/* Forward declarations of functions in this module                         */
/*--------------------------------------------------------------------------*/
VOID   initialize_server(VOID);
USHORT get_service_request(VOID);
USHORT terminate_service_request(VOID);
VOID   send_file(VOID);
VOID   receive_file(VOID);
VOID   print_error(USHORT, PCHAR, PCHAR, USHORT);
VOID   FAR fxsvr_exit(USHORT);

/*--------------------------------------------------------------------------*/
/* Global variables for this module                                         */
/*--------------------------------------------------------------------------*/
                   /*--------------------------------------*/
                   /* file transfer variables              */
                   /*--------------------------------------*/
PACKET   *packet_ptr;                /* pointer to packet                   */
USHORT    filedata_packet_size;      /* size of packet for file transfer    */
USHORT    filedata_data_size;        /* size of data area for file transfer*/
USHORT    filedata_header_size;      /* size of header area for file xfer   */

USHORT    PipeBytesRead;             /* number of bytes read from pipe      */
USHORT    PipeBytesWritten;          /* number of bytes written to pipe     */
USHORT    FileHandle;                /* handle for File                     */
                   /*--------------------------------------*/
                   /* miscellaneous variables              */
                   /*--------------------------------------*/
USHORT    rc;
```

Figure 9-15. FXSVR.H Include File.

Chapter 10

FX Using Named Pipes

This chapter presents an implementation of the communication layer of the FX protocol using OS/2's *Named Pipes* Interprocess Communication (IPC) protocol. The interface will be packaged as a Dynamic Link Library (FXNPIPE.DLL). The DLL is created from **FXNPIPE.C** using the FX make file introduced in Chapter 9.

The Named Pipes communication DLL makes it possible to transfer files using FXREQ and FXSVR, the client-server programs developed in Chapter 9. Figure 10-1 shows how this all comes together. We will use this setup to collect benchmark numbers on the performance of Named Pipes. We do this by measuring the time it takes to exchange files between the client and the server programs.

The plan for this chapter is to make use of whatever mechanisms are provided by the Named Pipes IPC to implement the nine **FX** interface calls shown in Figure 10-1 on page 266. Figure 10-2 demonstrates how each of the FX calls is implemented by the FXNPIPE.DLL using OS/2's Named Pipes services. It also shows the effect each call has on the partner transaction.

HOW THE FXNPIPE.DLL USES NAMED PIPES

Figure 10-2 on page 267 demonstrates how *send file* gets implemented at the DLL level. Notice that, with two exceptions, there is a one-to-one correspondence between the FX calls and their Named Pipes counterparts. The two exceptions are **fx_initialize**, for which there is no counterpart, and **fx_open**, which gets implemented using two Named Pipes API calls: **DosOpen** and **DosSetNmPHandState**.

Since the FX protocol is an emulation of Named Pipes, the implementation of **FXNPIPE.C** should be a "piece of cake." The C code is certainly the most straightforward (almost one-for-one) implementation of any of the FX DLLs. However, we will not let you get off the hook that easily; in this chapter, we introduce nine new OS/2 API calls. Some of these new API calls are "feature-packed" and can be applied to files and devices as well as Named Pipes. This all leads to some lengthy API

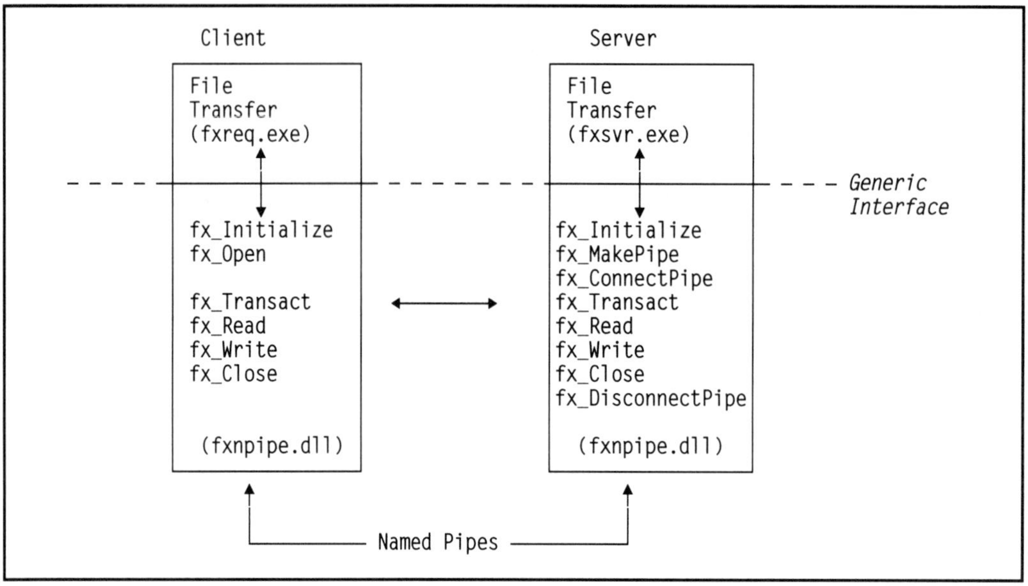

Figure 10-1. Implementing the FX Interface Using the Named Pipes DLL.

descriptions. So, once again, please make sure you understand the material in the Named Pipes tutorial in Chapter 8, before you immerse yourself into the details of this chapter.

By the end of this chapter, you will know both OS/2's Named Pipe and file service APIs and you will probably notice the similarities between these two services. One of the design goals of Named Pipes was to extend the familiar file service paradigm to the LAN and IPC services. You'll find that obtaining LAN and IPC services is just as easy as issuing calls to the file system. Remember that Named Pipes provide a very complete set of IPC and peer-to-peer LAN services. By the time you get through this straightforward chapter you will have a greatly expanded programming repertoire.

FXNPIPE.C: THE NAMED PIPE FX DLLS

The code we present in this section does *not* contain a **main()** procedure. The FX DLLs are simply functions that get linked to a (.EXE) file at runtime. The **main()** procedure is provided by the program that calls the DLL functions. This means **FXNPIPE.C** is not a separate program; it contains a list of functions that get packaged in a DLL.

FXNPIPE.C: General Stuff

The listing (see Figure 10-3) contains all the miscellaneous header "stuff" that will be used by the FX procedures. The first thing to notice is the enabled

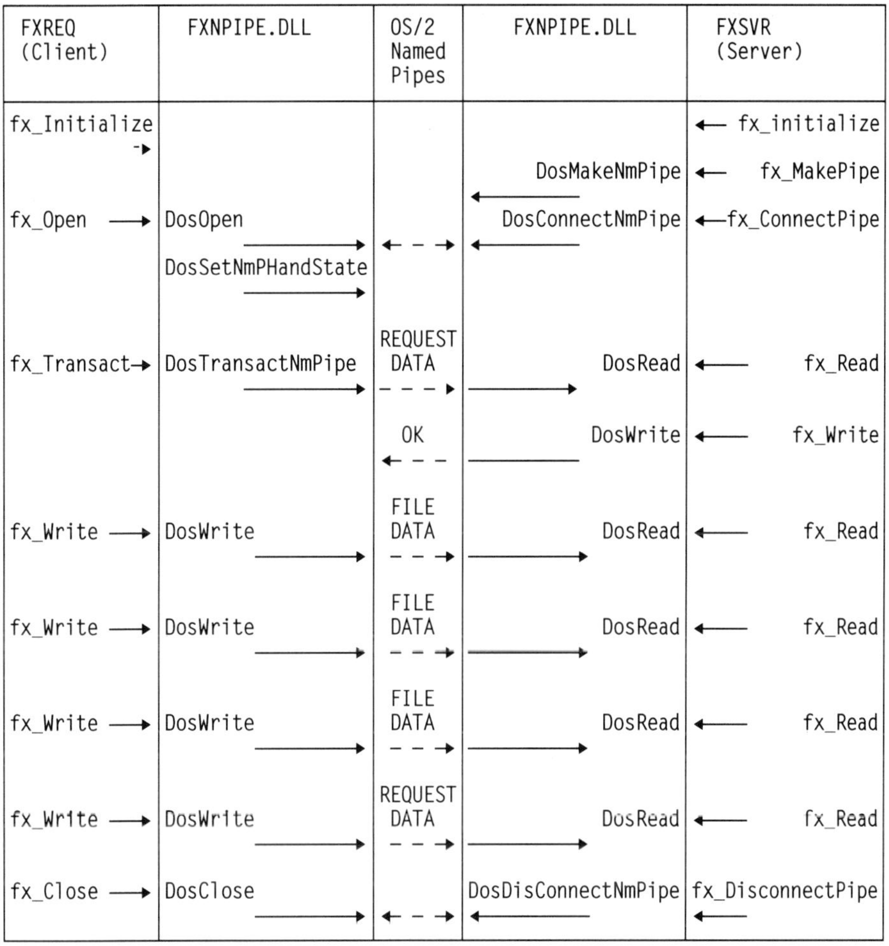

Figure 10-2. Sending a File Using the FXNPIPE.DLL.

INCL_DOSNMPIPES flag. By enabling this flag, we include the Named Pipes services from **OS2.H**. We follow that with the usual declarations of constants, global variables, and forward declarations of functions. Notice that with the exception of **print_error()**, the nine new functions we introduce are all one-for-one implementations of the **FX** interface services. The **print_error()** helper function is similar to the functions with the same name that were introduced in previous chapters.

```
/*******************************************************************************/
/*  MODULE NAME: FXNPIPE - Named pipe communication.                            */
/*                                                                             */
/*  PROGRAM DESCRIPTION:                                                       */
/*    This module implements the FX services using OS/2 EE named pipes.       */
/*    The FXNPIPE.C code will be packaged as the FXNPIPE.DLL Dynamic link     */
/*    library.                                                                 */
/*******************************************************************************/
#include <stdio.h>                    /* For printf() & NULL                  */
#include <stdlib.h>                   /* For conversion routines              */
#include <string.h>                   /* For string functions                 */

#define INCL_DOSNMPIPES               /* for named pipe function declares     */
#include <os2.h>

/*---------------------------------------------------------------------------*/
/* defines                                                                     */
/*---------------------------------------------------------------------------*/
#define FAILED     -1                 /* return code                          */
#define GOOD        0                 /* return code                          */
#define WARNING     1                 /* return code                          */

/*---------------------------------------------------------------------------*/
/* forward declaration for functions in this module                            */
/*---------------------------------------------------------------------------*/
VOID   print_error(USHORT, PCHAR, PCHAR, USHORT);

USHORT fx_Initialize(PVOID *, PUSHORT);
USHORT fx_MakePipe(VOID);
USHORT fx_ConnectPipe(VOID);
USHORT fx_DisconnectPipe(VOID);
USHORT fx_Open(VOID);
USHORT fx_Write(PVOID, USHORT, PUSHORT);
USHORT fx_Read(PVOID,  USHORT, PUSHORT);
USHORT fx_Transact(PVOID, USHORT, PVOID, USHORT, PVOID);
USHORT fx_Close(VOID);

/*---------------------------------------------------------------------------*/
/* Configuration variables, initialized after fx_Initialize()                  */
/* function call.                                                              */
/*---------------------------------------------------------------------------*/
CHAR   PipeName[128];
CHAR   ComputerName[128];
USHORT OutBufSize;                   /* out buffer size for DosMakeNmPipe    */
USHORT InBufSize;                    /* in buffer  ,,     ,,     ,,          */
USHORT FileBufferSize;               /* file and message buffer              */

/*---------------------------------------------------------------------------*/
/* global variables for this module.                                           */
/*---------------------------------------------------------------------------*/
USHORT PipeHandle;                   /* handle from DosOpen or DosMakeNmPipe*/
USHORT rc;                           /* return code                          */
USHORT ActionTaken;                  /* DosOpen action                       */
```

Figure 10-3 (Part 1 of 2). FXNPIPE.C: General Header Stuff and print_error().

```
/*---------------------------------------------------------------------*/
/* Error Display Routine                                               */
/*---------------------------------------------------------------------*/
VOID print_error(USHORT Error, PCHAR msg, PCHAR file, USHORT line)
{
 printf("Named pipe error %u (0x%x) detected while %s at line %u in file %s.\n",
        Error, Error, msg, line, file);
} /* end print_error */
```

Figure 10-3 (Part 2 of 2). FXNPIPE.C: General Header Stuff and print_error().

FXNPIPE.C: fx_Initialize()

The **fx_Initialize()** function (see Figure 10-5) reads a protocol-specific configuration file to obtain the parameters required to initialize the system. The name of the user-specified configuration file for Named Pipes is **fxnpipe.cfg**. Here is an example of a such a file:

```
PIPE_NAME          = \PIPE\filesvr
COMPUTER_NAME      =
OUT_BUFFER_SIZE    = 4096
IN_BUFFER_SIZE     = 4096
FILE_BUFFER_SIZE   = 16384
```

Figure 10-4. FXNPIPE.CFG: The Configuration File for the FX Named Pipes DLL.

PIPE_NAME This parameter defines the pipe name. \PIPE\ refers to a pseudo subdirectory name.

COMPUTER_NAME This parameter defines the network name of the server computer. It is used for remote Named Pipes. We left it blank because we are using Named Pipes as a local IPC in this chapter.

OUT_BUFFER_SIZE This parameter defines the output buffer size (in bytes) and is used in DosMakeNmPipe.

IN_BUFFER_SIZE This parameter defines the input buffer size (in bytes) and is used in DosMakeNmPipe.

FILE_BUFFER_SIZE This parameter defines the size (in bytes) of the message buffer. This is the buffer we will use for reading and writing data to the disk and for exchanging messages across the LAN or the IPC. The memory space for this parameter will be dynamically allocated. The **fx_Initialize** function returns a pointer to this buffer and its size to the application. One of the factors we will measure in our benchmarks is the effect of the message buffer size on performance.

No new OS/2 calls are introduced in the implementation of this function. This should come as no surprise, since the OS/2 Named Pipes service does not provide an "initialize" API call. We introduced this call in the FX protocol as a "catch-all" for performing protocol-specific start-up actions.

```
/*--------------------------------------------------------------------------*/
/* function to read communication specific parameters and allocate a buffer */
/* for communication.  A pointer to the buffer and the buffer size is       */
/* returned.                                                                */
/*--------------------------------------------------------------------------*/
USHORT fx_Initialize(PVOID *buffer_p , PUSHORT size)
{
  FILE    *config_file;                /* Input file control block          */
  CHAR     line[80];                   /* one line of config file           */

  printf("Reading configuration parameters.\n");
  /*--------------------------------*/
  /* open the configuration file    */
  /*--------------------------------*/
  if (NULL == (config_file = fopen("fxnpipe.cfg","r")))
     {print_error(rc,"opening configuration file",__FILE__,__LINE__);
      return(FAILED);
     }
  else
     /*------------------------------------*/
     /* read the configuration parameters.  */
     /* The parameters are expected to be:  */
     /*    - in the form <name = value>     */
     /*    - in the order read below        */
     /*------------------------------------*/
     {
      fgets(line, sizeof(line), config_file);
      if (sscanf(line,"PIPE_NAME = %s ", PipeName) != 1)
         {print_error(rc,"reading PipeName from configuration",
                      __FILE__,__LINE__);
          return(FAILED);
         }
      printf("PIPE_NAME = %s \n", PipeName);

      fgets(line, sizeof(line), config_file);
      if (sscanf(line,"COMPUTER_NAME = %s ", ComputerName) == EOF)
         strcpy(ComputerName,"");
      printf("COMPUTER_NAME = %s \n", ComputerName);

      fgets(line, sizeof(line), config_file);
      if (sscanf(line,"OUT_BUFFER_SIZE = %u ", &OutBufSize) != 1)
         {print_error(rc,"reading OutBufSize from configuration",
                      __FILE__,__LINE__);
          return(FAILED);
         }
      printf("OUT_BUFFER_SIZE = %u \n", OutBufSize);

      fgets(line, sizeof(line), config_file);
      if (sscanf(line,"IN_BUFFER_SIZE = %u ", &InBufSize) != 1)
         {print_error(rc,"reading InBufSize from configuration",
                      __FILE__,__LINE__);
          return(FAILED);
         }
      printf("IN_BUFFER_SIZE = %u \n", InBufSize);
```

Figure 10-5 (Part 1 of 2). FXNPIPE.C: fx_Initialize().

```
        fgets(line, sizeof(line), config_file);
        if (sscanf(line,"FILE_BUFFER_SIZE = %u ", &FileBufferSize) != 1)
           {print_error(rc,"reading FileBufferSize from configuration",
                        __FILE__,__LINE__);
            return(FAILED);
           }
        printf("FILE_BUFFER_SIZE = %u \n", FileBufferSize);
      } /* end if */

    fclose(config_file);

    /*--------------------------------------*/
    /* allocate buffer, return pointer      */
    /* and size                             */
    /*--------------------------------------*/
    if ((*buffer_p = (void *)malloc(FileBufferSize)) == NULL)
       {print_error(rc,"allocating file buffer",__FILE__,__LINE__);
        return(FAILED);
       }
    *size = FileBufferSize;

    return(GOOD);
  } /* end fx_Initialize */
```

Figure 10-5 (Part 2 of 2). FXNPIPE.C: fx_Initialize().

FXNPIPE.C: fx_MakePipe()

The **fx_MakePipe()** function (see Figure 10-6) is as straightforward as things get. All it does is turn around and issue the equivalent OS/2 **DosMakeNmPipe** IPC call described below:

DosMakeNmPipe

The **DosMakeNmPipe** API call creates a Named Pipe and returns its handle. If the Named Pipe is to be used over a network, it must be created by a server process running on the IBM LAN Server product. The prototype for this call is:

```
DosMakeNmPipe(PSZ       name,       /* Pipe Name                      */
              PHPIPE    handle,     /* Pointer to returned pipe handle */
              USHORT    OpenMode,   /* Open mode of pipe              */
              USHORT    PipeMode,   /* Pipe-specific mode             */
              USHORT    OutBuf,     /* Output buffer size in bytes    */
              USHORT    InBuf,      /* Number of bytes in input buffer */
              ULONG     TimeOut);   /* Timeout value                  */
```

A description of the parameters follows:

- The ***name*** parameter points to a null-terminated string that contains the name of the pipe. Pipes are named **\PIPE\PipeName**, where **\PIPE** is the name of a virtual subdirectory in memory. The rest of the name can use any valid file system characters including a backslash.

- The ***handle*** parameter points to a variable that receives the Named Pipe identifier (a file system handle). If multiple instances of the pipe are created, each DosMakeNmPipe call returns a different handle.
- The ***OpenMode*** parameter consists of a set of bits which specify the mode with which to open the Named Pipe. More specifically, this parameter specifies: when to flush the data, inheritance, and the direction of the pipe. The OpenMode parameter contains the following bit fields:

```
Bits     Value
----     -----
15       must be zero.
14       Flush buffer flag (for remote pipes):
         0 = Multiple-writes may be blocked before data is sent over LAN.
         1 = Send data over LAN after each write.
13-8     Reserved, must be zero.
7        Inheritance Flag:
         0 = Pipe handle is inherited by child process
         1 = Pipe handle is private to the current process.
6-2      Reserved, must be zero.
1-0      Access mode flags:
         00 = In-bound Pipe, from client to server
         01 = Out-bound Pipe, from server to client
         10 = Duplex Pipe, server to/from client
         Any other value is invalid.
```

- The ***PipeMode*** parameter is a set of bits which specify: wait/nowait, the message type and the instance count. Here is a more detailed description of the bit fields:

```
Bits     Value
----     -----
15       Wait flag:
         0 = Wait (i.e.block) if no data available.
         1 = Return immediately if no data available.
14-11    Reserved, must be zero.
10       Type flag:
         0 = Pipe is a byte stream pipe.
         1 = Pipe is a message stream pipe.
         All writes to message stream pipes record the length of the write
         along with the Message Data.  In message stream mode the first
         two bytes of each message represents the length of that message
         is called the message header.
9        Reserved, must be zero.
8        Read-Mode Flag:
         0 = Read pipe as a byte stream.
         1 = Read pipe as a message stream.
         Message pipes can be read as byte or message streams,
         Byte pipes can only be read as byte streams.
7-0      Instance count:  Byte wide (8-bit) count to which specifies how
         many instances of the pipe can be created.  A value of 1 through
         254 can be specified.  A -1 value specifies unlimited instances,
         0 is reserved. Attempts to make a pipe fail if the maximum
         instances already exists.  This parameter is ignored when making
         any other than the first instance of a pipe.  When multiple
         instances are allowed, multiple clients can simultaneously
         issue the same pipe name and get handles to distinct pipe
         instances.
```

- The ***OutBuf*** parameter specifies the number of bytes to allocate for the outgoing buffer. This is a hint to the operating system.
- The ***InBuf*** parameter specifies the number of bytes to allocate for the incoming buffer. This is a hint to the operating system.
- The ***TimeOut*** parameter specifies how long DosWaitNmPipe should wait (in milliseconds) for the next available instance of a Named Pipe. This value may be set only at the creation of the first instance of the pipe name. If the value is set to zero, a default value of 50 milliseconds is chosen. Your programs will be more readable if you specify the timeout directly when issuing a DosWaitNmPipe, instead of relying on the default timeout value from DosMakeNmPipe.

FXNPIPE.C: fx_ConnectPipe()

The **fx_ConnectPipe()** function (see Figure 10-7) is also very straightforward. All it does is turn around and issue the equivalent OS/2 **DosConnectNmPipe** IPC call described below:

DosConnectNmPipe

The **DosConnectNmPipe** API call is issued by a server process to wait on a client to open a Named Pipe. If the client end is already open, this call returns immediately and has no effect. If the client end is not open, the behavior of this call depends on the pipe's blocking mode:

- If the blocking mode is active, the call "blocks" until the client issues a DosOpen.
- If blocking is not set, the call returns immediately with an error value and the pipe enters a listening state, permitting a client to issue a successful DosOpen. A DosOpen to a pipe that is not in a listening state fails.

The prototype for this call is:

```
DosConnectNmPipe(HPIPE   handle);       /* Pipe Handle            */
```

A description of the parameters follows:

- The ***handle*** parameter is the pipe instance identifier returned by DosMakeNmPipe.

FXNPIPE.C: fx_DisconnectPipe()

The **fx_DisconnectPipe()** function (see Figure 10-8) is also very straightforward. All it does is turn around and issue the equivalent OS/2 **DosDisConnectNmPipe** IPC call described below:

```
/*-------------------------------------------------------------------------*/
/* function to establish the server end of the communication pipe.         */
/*-------------------------------------------------------------------------*/
USHORT fx_MakePipe(VOID)
{
                    /*------------------------------------*/
                    /* defines for DosMakeNmPipe          */
                    /*------------------------------------*/
  #define PIPE_OPENMODE      0x4002    /* no write-behind allowed, duplex    */
  #define PIPEMODE           0x0501    /* message pipe, one instance only    */
  #define TIMEOUT            0L        /* wait forever timeout value         */

  rc = DosMakeNmPipe(PipeName,         /* PipeName from fx_Initialize       */
                     &PipeHandle,      /* pipe handle returned              */
                     PIPE_OPENMODE,
                     PIPEMODE,
                     OutBufSize,       /* OutBufSize set during fx_Initialize*/
                     InBufSize,        /* InBufSize set during fx_Initialize */
                     TIMEOUT);
  if (rc)
     {print_error(rc,"Making a named pipe",__FILE__,__LINE__);
      return(FAILED);
     }

  return(GOOD);
} /* end fx_MakePipe */
```

Figure 10-6. FXNPIPE.C: MakePipe().

DosDisConnectNmPipe

The **DosDisConnectNmPipe** API call is issued by the server side of a Named Pipe to close a Named Pipe instance. This call will force the client end off the pipe. This forced closure may cause data to be discarded, in which case the client will get an error code on the next operation. The DosDisConnectNmPipe must be issued before a new client is allowed to connect to the pipe. The prototype for this call is:

```
DosDisConnectNmPipe(HPIPE   handle);      /* Pipe Handle              */
```

A description of the parameters follows:

- The ***handle*** parameter is the pipe's instance identifier returned by a DosMakeNmPipe.

```
/*-----------------------------------------------------------------------*/
/* function to enable the server end of the communication pipe.          */
/*-----------------------------------------------------------------------*/
USHORT fx_ConnectPipe(VOID)
{
  rc = DosConnectNmPipe(PipeHandle);   /* handle from DosMakeNmPipe      */
  if (rc)
     {print_error(rc,"Connect to a named pipe",__FILE__,__LINE__);
      return(FAILED);
     }
  return(GOOD);
} /* end fx_ConnectPipe */
```

Figure 10-7. FXNPIPE.C: fx_ConnectPipe().

```
/*-----------------------------------------------------------------------*/
/* function to disable the server end of the communication pipe.         */
/*-----------------------------------------------------------------------*/
USHORT fx_DisconnectPipe(VOID)
{
  rc = DosDisConnectNmPipe(PipeHandle);
  if (rc)
     {print_error(rc,"Disconnecting from a named pipe",__FILE__,__LINE__);
      return(FAILED);
     }
  return(GOOD);
} /* end fx_DisconnectPipe */
```

Figure 10-8. FXNPIPE.C: fx_DisconnectPipe().

FXNPIPE.C: fx_Open()

The **fx_Open**() function (see Figure 10-9) does a little bit more work than its predecessors. First, it appends the computer network name to the pipe name (for cases where the pipe is remote). It then issues the OS/2 **DosOpen** API call. In addition to Named Pipes, this important function is used for opening files and devices. It is described in "DosOpen." It may seem like the description of this function goes on forever. This is because the function contains many of the sharing hooks required by a file system to operate in a multitasking environment. The **fx_Open**() function does a little more than just issue **DosOpen**, it follows the open with a **DosSetNmPHandState**, which changes the pipe from a byte-stream pipe (the default for open) to a message-pipe. The **DosSetNmPHandState** API call is described in "DosSetNmPHandState" on page 278.

DosOpen

The **DosOpen** API call opens an existing file, device, or Named Pipe. It can also create a new file. The call returns a handle which can be used to read from and write to a file, device, or Named Pipe. The prototype for this call is:

```
DosOpen(PSZ         Name,          /* path name of file, pipe, device*/
        PHFILE      Handle,        /* handle (returned )             */
        PUSHORT     Action,        /* action taken (returned)        */
        ULONG       Size,          /* file's new size                */
        USHORT      Attr,          /* attributes                     */
        USHORT      OpenFlags,     /* action take if file exists     */
        USHORT      OpenMode,      /* open shared/access mode        */
        ULONG       Reserved);     /* reserved (must be 0)           */
```

A description of the parameters follows:

- The ***Name*** parameter points to a null-terminated string that contains the name of the file, device, or Named Pipe to be opened. Named Pipes are named **\PIPE\PipeName**, where **\PIPE** is the name of a virtual subdirectory in memory.
- The ***Handle*** parameter points to a variable that receives the Named Pipe, device or file handle.
- The ***Action*** parameter points to a variable that specifies the action taken by the API if successful. It is one of the following three values:

Value	Action Taken
0001H	File, device or Named Pipe already exists
0002H	File, device or Named Pipe created
0003H	File existed and was replaced (truncated)

- The ***Size*** parameter specifies the file's new size in bytes. It is significant only when creating a new file or replacing an existing file and is otherwise ignored. This is only a recommended size for the file. The file system makes a reasonable attempt to allocate the new size in as nearly contiguous an area as possible on the medium.
- The ***Attr*** parameter specifies the file attributes. It can be a combination of the following values:

Value	Meaning
FILE_NORMAL	File is read/write
FILE_READONLY	File is read only
FILE_HIDDEN	File does not appear in directories
FILE_SYSTEM	System file
FILE_ARCHIVED	File should be archived

```
The following are the defines for the file attributes:
#define FILE_NORMAL     0x0000
#define FILE_READONLY   0x0001
#define FILE_HIDDEN     0x0002
#define FILE_SYSTEM     0x0004
#define FILE_DIRECTORY  0x0010
#define FILE_ARCHIVED   0x0020
```

- The ***OpenFlags*** parameter specifies what to do when opening a file which exists or does not exist. Choices of actions are:

Value	Meaning
FILE_CREATE	Create new file; fail if file exists
FILE_OPEN	Open existing file; fail if file does not exist
FILE_OPEN | FILE_CREATE	Open existing file; create if does not exist
FILE_TRUNCATE	Open existing file and change to given size
FILE_TRUNCATE | FILE_CREATE	Open existing file and truncate it or create file if it does not exist

The following are the define statements:

```
#define FILE_OPEN       0x0001
#define FILE_TRUNCATE   0x0002
#define FILE_CREATE     0x0010
```

- The ***OpenMode*** parameter specifies, among other things, how file sharing is enforced in a multiprocess environment. File sharing requires interprocess cooperation, which gets communicated through the sharing and access modes. Any sharing restrictions placed on a file opened by a process are removed when the process closes the file with a DosClose request. The *Sharing Mode* specifies the type of access other processes may have to the file. For example, if you will allow other processes to read the file after your process opened it, then specify Deny Write. This sharing mode prevents other processes from writing to the file, but still allows them to read it. The *Access Mode* specifies the type of access to the file needed by your process. For example, if your process requires Read/Write access, and another process has already opened the file with a sharing mode of Deny None, your DosOpen request succeeds. However, if the file is open with a sharing mode of Deny Write, your process is denied access. All the sharing and access restrictions are inherited. They will also apply to duplicated handles. The *OpenMode* parameter must contain one access mode choice and one shared mode choice. The other options can be given in any combination:

Value	Meaning
OPEN_ACCESS_READONLY	Caller will only read from file
OPEN_ACCESS_READWRITE	Caller will read/write
OPEN_ACCESS_WRITEONLY	Caller will write only
OPEN_SHARE_DENYNONE	Other processes can open file for any access
OPEN_SHARE_DENYREAD	Other processes can open file for write only
OPEN_SHARE_DENYWRITE	Other processes can open file for read only
OPEN_SHARE_DENYREADWRITE	Caller has exclusive access to file.
OPEN_FLAGS_DASD	FileName is "Drive:" and represents a mounted disk or diskette volume to be opened for direct access.
OPEN_FLAGS_FAIL_ON_ERROR	Report media errors to caller via return code. Don't display error popup
OPEN_FLAGS_NOINHERIT	File is not to be inherited by child processes.
OPEN_FLAGS_WRITE_THROUGH	Write data to actual device before returning. No file buffering.
OPEN_FLAGS_NO_CACHE	Write the data to actual device before returning. No file caching.

```
The following is the list of defines for the open mode parameter:

#define OPEN_ACCESS_READONLY        0x0000  /* ---- ---- ---- -000 */
#define OPEN_ACCESS_WRITEONLY       0x0001  /* ---- ---- ---- -001 */
#define OPEN_ACCESS_READWRITE       0x0002  /* ---- ---- ---- -010 */
#define OPEN_SHARE_DENYREADWRITE    0x0010  /* ---- ---- -001 ---- */
#define OPEN_SHARE_DENYWRITE        0x0020  /* ---- ---- -010 ---- */
#define OPEN_SHARE_DENYREAD         0x0030  /* ---- ---- -011 ---- */
#define OPEN_SHARE_DENYNONE         0x0040  /* ---- ---- -100 ---- */
#define OPEN_FLAGS_NOINHERIT        0x0080  /* ---- ---- 1--- ---- */
#define OPEN_FLAGS_NO_CACHE         0x1000  /* ---1 ---- ---- ---- */
#define OPEN_FLAGS_FAIL_ON_ERROR    0x2000  /* --1- ---- ---- ---- */
#define OPEN_FLAGS_WRITE_THROUGH    0x4000  /* -1-- ---- ---- ---- */
#define OPEN_FLAGS_DASD             0x8000  /* 1--- ---- ---- ---- */
```

- The ***reserved*** parameter must be set to zero.

Named Pipe Considerations

- DosOpen opens the client end of a pipe by name and returns a handle. The open succeeds only if the pipe is in a listening state.
- Once a given instance has been opened by a client, that same instance cannot be opened by another client at the same time.
- Pipes can only be two-ended; however, the opening process can duplicate the open handle as many times as desired.
- The access and sharing modes specified on the open must be consistent with those specified by the DosMakeNmPipe.

DosSetNmPHandState

The **DosSetNmPHandState** API call is issued to change the read or wait modes of a Named Pipe handle. This call will be used mostly by clients to modify the default DosOpen. The default always opens the Named Pipe with the wait and byte stream message modes activated. The client can change these modes by calling **DosSetNmPHandState** if desired. The prototype for this call is:

```
DosSetNmPHandState(HPIPE   handle,          /* Pipe Handle       */
                   USHORT  state_flag);     /* State flag        */
```

A description of the parameters follows:

- The ***handle*** parameter is the Named Pipe instance identifier returned by DosMakeNmPipe or DosOpen.
- The ***state_flag*** parameter specifies the updated mode of the Named Pipe handle, and consists of the following bit fields:

```
Bits      Value
____      _____
15        Wait flag:
          0 = Wait (i.e block) if no data available.
          1 = Return immediately if no data available.
14-10     Reserved, must be zero.
9         Reserved, must be zero.
8         Read-Mode Flag:
          0 = Read pipe as a byte stream.
          1 = Read pipe as a message stream.
          Message pipes can be read as byte or message streams,
          Byte pipes can only be read as byte streams.
7-0       Reserved, must be zero.
```

```
/*------------------------------------------------------------------------------*/
/* function a requester uses to prepare a pipe for communication.               */
/*------------------------------------------------------------------------------*/
USHORT fx_Open(VOID)
{ CHAR RemotePipeName[128];

                    /*------------------------------*/
                    /* defines for DosOpen          */
                    /*------------------------------*/
#define PIPE_HANDLE_STATE  0x0100   /* blocking, message stream                 */

  /*-------------------------------*/
  /* create a remote pipe name from */
  /*   parameters read during       */
  /*   fx_Initialize                */
  /*-------------------------------*/
  strcpy(RemotePipeName, ComputerName);
  strcat(RemotePipeName, PipeName);

  rc = DosOpen(RemotePipeName,      /* name of pipe to open, may include    */
                                    /*   the name of a remote computer      */
         &PipeHandle,               /* handle returned                      */
         &ActionTaken,              /* open action returned                 */
         0L,                        /* File size for name pipe              */
         FILE_NORMAL,               /* File is read/write                   */
         FILE_OPEN,                 /* open if pipe exists, otherwise fail  */
         OPEN_FLAGS_FAIL_ON_ERROR |
         OPEN_SHARE_DENYNONE      |
         OPEN_ACCESS_READWRITE,     /* open mode flags                      */
         0L);
  if (rc)
     {print_error(rc,"Opening a named pipe",__FILE__,__LINE__);
      return(FAILED);
     }
```

Figure 10-9 (Part 1 of 2). FXNPIPE.C: fx_Open().

```
    /*-------------------------------------*/
    /* change to a message pipe            */
    /*-------------------------------------*/
    rc = DosSetNmPHandState(PipeHandle,  /* pipe handle returned from DosOpen  */
                            PIPE_HANDLE_STATE);
    if (rc)
       {print_error(rc,"setting a named pipe handle state",__FILE__,__LINE__);
        return(FAILED);
       }

    return(GOOD);
  } /* end fx_Open */
```

Figure 10-9 (Part 2 of 2). FXNPIPE.C: fx_Open().

FXNPIPE.C: fx_Write()

The **fx_Write()** function (see Figure 10-10) falls in the very straightforward category. All it does is turn around and issue the equivalent OS/2 **DosWrite** IPC call described below:

DosWrite

The **DosWrite** API call transfers the specified number of bytes from a buffer to the specified file, pipe, or device. The prototype for this call is:

```
DosWrite(HFILE    handle,          /* file, device or pipe handle       */
         PVOID    OutBuf,          /* output buffer                     */
         USHORT   count,           /* number of bytes to be written     */
         PUSHORT  BytesWritten);   /* number of bytes written (returned) */
```

A description of the parameters follows:

- The ***handle*** parameter identifies the file, device, or Named Pipe instance to be read. The handle must have been previously created using DosOpen.
- The ***OutBuf*** parameter points to the buffer that contains the data to be written.
- The ***count*** parameter specifies the number of bytes to write.
- The ***BytesWritten*** parameter points to a variable that receives the count of the number of bytes written. If BytesWritten is different from count, this usually indicates insufficient disk space.

Named Pipe Considerations

- Each write to a *message* pipe writes a message whose size is the length of the write. DosWrite automatically encodes message lengths in the pipe, so applications need not encode this information in the buffer being written.
- In the case of a *byte* pipe, if the number of bytes to be written exceeds the space available in the pipe, DosWrite writes as many bytes as it can and returns with the number of bytes actually written.

- Writes in blocking mode always write all the requested bytes before returning. If the pipe buffer can't hold all the data, this call will block until the other end reads the data off the pipe and makes room in the buffer. Message mode pipes will block if the pipe can't hold the entire message.
- In non-blocking mode, if the message size is bigger than the buffer size, the write blocks. If the message size is smaller than the pipe but not enough space is left in the pipe, the write returns immediately with a value of zero, indicating no bytes were written.
- An attempt to write to a pipe whose other end has been closed returns ERROR_BROKEN_PIPE.

```
/*-------------------------------------------------------------------------*/
/* function both requester and server use to write to a pipe.              */
/*-------------------------------------------------------------------------*/
USHORT fx_Write(PVOID BufferArea, USHORT BufferLength, PUSHORT BytesWritten)
{
  rc = DosWrite(PipeHandle,           /* handle returned from DosOpen or   */
                                      /* DosMakeNmPipe                     */
                BufferArea,
                BufferLength,
                BytesWritten);
  if (rc)
     {print_error(rc,"Writing to a named pipe",__FILE__,__LINE__);
      return(FAILED);
     }
  else return(GOOD);
} /* end fx_Write */
```

Figure 10-10. FXNPIPE.C: fx_Write().

FXNPIPE.C: fx_Read()

The **fx_Read()** function (see Figure 10-11) is also in the very straightforward category. All it does is turn around and issue the equivalent OS/2 **DosRead** IPC call described below:

DosRead

The **DosRead** API call reads the specified number of bytes from a file, pipe, or device to a buffer location. The function may read fewer than the specified number of bytes if it reaches the end of the file or if it is in Named Pipe message mode. The prototype for this call is:

```
DosRead(HFILE   handle,        /* file, device or pipe handle     */
        PVOID   InBuf,         /* input buffer                    */
        USHORT  count,         /* number of bytes to be read      */
        PUSHORT BytesRead);    /* number of bytes read (returned) */
```

A description of the parameters follows:

- The ***handle*** parameter identifies the file, device, or Named Pipe instance to be read. The handle must have been previously created using DosOpen.
- The ***InBuf*** parameter points to the buffer that receives the data.
- The ***count*** parameter specifies the number of bytes to read.
- The ***BytesRead*** parameter points to a variable that receives the count of the number of bytes actually read. This parameter is 0 if the file pointer is positioned at the end of the file prior to the DosRead call.

Named Pipe Considerations

- A Named Pipe in *byte* read mode reads all currently available data, up to the size requested.
- A message pipe in *message* read mode, returns only the next available message even if more bytes are requested than are in the message (the BytesRead argument will be set appropriately). If the read request is for fewer bytes than the size of the message, the bytes requested are read into the buffer and an ERROR_MORE_DATA is also returned. Subsequent DosRead calls will continue to read the message where the last call left off, but without crossing over to the next message.
- A message pipe is read as if it were a byte stream, skipping over message headers. This is like reading a byte pipe in byte read mode. A read size that is smaller than the next available message returns with the number of bytes requested and an ERROR_MORE_DATA return code. When resuming the reading of a message after ERROR_MORE_DATA is returned, a read always blocks until the next piece (or the rest) of the message can be received. DosPeekNmPipe may be used to determine how many bytes are left in the message.
- When blocking mode is set for a Named Pipe, a read blocks until data is available. The read never returns with BytesRead = 0 except at EOF. In message read mode, messages are always read in their entirety, except in the case where the message is bigger than the size of the read.
- When non-blocking mode is set, BytesRead = 0 is returned when no data is available at the time of the read.

```
/*---------------------------------------------------------------------------*/
/* function both requester and server use to read from a pipe.              */
/*---------------------------------------------------------------------------*/
USHORT fx_Read(PVOID BufferArea, USHORT BufferLength, PUSHORT BytesRead)
{
  rc = DosRead(PipeHandle,            /* handle returned from DosOpen or    */
                                      /* DosMakeNmPipe                      */
               BufferArea,
               BufferLength,
               BytesRead);
  if (rc)
     {print_error(rc,"Reading from a named pipe",__FILE__,__LINE__);
      return(FAILED);
     }
  else return(GOOD);
} /* end fx_Read */
```

Figure 10-11. FXNPIPE.C: fx_Read().

FXNPIPE.C: fx_Transact()

The **fx_Transact()** function (see Figure 10-12) is also very straightforward. All it does is turn around and issue the equivalent OS/2 **DosTransactNmPipe** IPC call described below:

DosTransactNmPipe

The **DosTransactNmPipe** API call performs, in one step, a write followed by a read. This call can only be used on duplex message pipes and allows you to implement transaction-oriented dialogs. **DosTransactNmPipe** writes the entire InBuffer to the pipe and then reads a response from the pipe into the OutBuffer and does not return until a message has been read into the OutBuffer. The transaction fails if the Named Pipe contains any unread data. The prototype for this call is:

```
DosTransactNmPipe(HPIPE     handle,       /* Pipe handle                 */
                  PBYTE     OutBuf,       /* Write buffer address        */
                  USHORT    OutLength,    /* Write buffer length         */
                  PBYTE     InBuf,        /* Read buffer address         */
                  USHORT    InLen,        /* Read buffer length          */
                  PUSHORT   BytesRead);   /* Actual number of Bytes read */
```

A description of the parameters follows:

- The ***handle*** parameter identifies a the Named Pipe instance. It is the handle returned by DosMakeNmPipe or DosOpen.
- The ***OutBuf*** parameter points to the buffer containing the data to be written to the pipe.
- The ***OutLength*** parameter specifies the size in bytes of the output buffer.
- The ***InBuf*** parameter points to the input buffer.
- The ***InLen*** parameter specifies the size in bytes of the input buffer.

- The ***BytesRead*** parameter points to a variable that receives the actual number of bytes read into the input buffer.

```
/*-------------------------------------------------------------------------*/
/* function requester uses to request a service.                           */
/*-------------------------------------------------------------------------*/
USHORT fx_Transact(PVOID InBufferArea,  USHORT InBufferLength,
                   PVOID OutBufferArea, USHORT OutBufferLength,
                   PUSHORT BytesRead)
{
  rc = DosTransactNmPipe(PipeHandle,    /* handle returned from DosOpen      */
                         InBufferArea,
                         InBufferLength,
                         OutBufferArea,
                         OutBufferLength,
                         BytesRead);
  if (rc)
     {print_error(rc,"executing a pipe transaction",__FILE__,__LINE__);
      return(FAILED);
     }
  else return(GOOD);
} /* end fx_Transact */
```

Figure 10-12. FXNPIPE.C: fx_Transact().

FXNPIPE.C: fx_Close()

The **fx_Close()** function (see Figure 10-13) is the last of a streak of very straightforward to implement functions. All it does is turn around and issue the equivalent OS/2 **DosClose** IPC call described below:

DosClose

The **DosClose** API call closes a handle to a file, pipe, or device. The call causes the system to write the contents of the file's internal buffers to the device, and to update directory information where applicable. If one or more additional handles to a file have been created with DosDupHandle, the directory is not updated and all internal buffers are not written to the medium until DosClose has been issued for the duplicated handles. The prototype for this call is:

```
DosClose(HFILE    handle);          /* file handle                    */
```

A description of the parameters follows:

- The first ***handle*** parameter identifies the file, device, or Named Pipe instance to be closed. The handle must have been previously created using DosOpen.

Named Pipe Considerations

- When all handles referencing one end of a pipe are closed, the pipe is considered broken.
- If the client end closes, no other process can reopen the pipe until the serving end issues a DosDisConnectNmPipe followed by a DosConnectNmPipe.
- If the server end closes when the pipe is already broken, it is deallocated immediately; otherwise, the pipe is not deallocated until the last client handle is closed.

```
/*-----------------------------------------------------------------------*/
/* function reqester uses to end communication with a server.            */
/*-----------------------------------------------------------------------*/
USHORT fx_Close(VOID)
{
  rc = DosClose(PipeHandle);         /* handle from DosOpen or DosMakeNmPipe */
  if (rc)
     {print_error(rc,"Closing a named pipe",__FILE__,__LINE__);
      return(FAILED);
     }
  else return(GOOD);

} /* end fx_Close */
```

Figure 10-13. FXNPIPE.C: fx_Close().

Part III

Protocols for Client-Server Communications

Part III covers peer-to-peer protocols for client-server exchanges over Local Area Networks (LANs). We will develop programs that use the OS/2 EE Communications Manager's LAN protocols. As was explained in Part I, Communications Manager provides a gigantic offering of communication services. We will focus our attention on those offerings that are of interest to a client-server programming platform. These are primarily the *peer-to-peer* facilities required for the exchange of data and services between clients and servers. Peer-to-peer protocols allow you to create your *own* intercomputer message exchanges. As you will soon discover, message exchanges provide the life-blood of client-server systems.

We also cover in Part III the LAN Requester/Server types of "canned" exchanges which transform OS/2 EE into a "Network Operating System". The LAN Server provides a powerful repertoire of services which includes: file server, print server, remote Named Pipes, and network management. In Part IV, we will add to our repertoire of canned client-server services, the power of a network database server. This is when you'll have at your disposal all the distributed software ingredients needed to provide your client-server applications access to data and services wherever they are.

The approach we take in Part III is to provide you with the necessary background information in the form of tutorials and then focus on developing a set of peer-to-peer program examples that use the OS/2 EE LAN protocols: **NetBIOS** and **APPC**. We will also cover **Named Pipes** as a peer-to-peer LAN protocol. Named Pipes extend OS/2's Interprocess Communication (IPC) services across the network without your programs ever being aware of it (the network is made transparent). We will also be covering the important **LAN Requester/Server** service, even though it does not fall into the category of a peer-to-peer LAN protocol. We will look at this service from the viewpoint of how it performs, compared to the "do-it-yourself" types of communications schemes we will be introducing.

The programming examples that are introduced in Part III extend the **FX DLL** services to work across machines using the OS/2 EE LAN protocols. In addition to serving as production-quality OS/2 EE template programs, the examples double as learning tools that can be used to understand and measure the performance trade-offs of the LAN protocols.

Here is the "road map" we will follow in Part III:

- In Chapter 11, "A Tutorial on NetBIOS" we cover all you need to know about the NetBIOS LAN protocol.
- In Chapter 12, "A Tutorial on APPC", we cover all you need to know about APPC and SNA.
- In Chapter 13, "FX Using NetBIOS", we develop FXNETB.C which implements the **FX DLL** interface for file transfer using NetBIOS.
- In Chapter 14, "FX with APPC", we develop FXAPPC.C which implements the **FX DLL** interface for file transfer using APPC.
- In Chapter 15, "FX Using the LAN Server and Remote Named Pipes", we perform the file transfers using *remote* Named Pipes and the LAN Requester/Server.
- In Chapter 16, "The Great FX LAN Derby", we compare the performance of the LAN protocols. We are in the remarkable position of having in front of us a consistent set of benchmarks that compare local and remote process-to-process communications using the wide range of standard protocols.

Chapter 11

A Tutorial on NetBIOS

This chapter presents a tutorial on NetBIOS, a *peer-to-peer* LAN protocol. We start by defining peer-to-peer protocols. We then examine what makes distributed software so different and in the process develop a set of requirements for an "ideal" peer-to-peer protocol. This should provide us with a framework for evaluating the LAN protocols that OS/2 EE provides. It tells us what to look for when we do our comparison shopping for protocols. We then look in some detail at NetBIOS and the services it provides. We conclude the tutorial with scenarios that demonstrate how NetBIOS is used in typical network applications.

PEER-TO-PEER PROTOCOLS

In this section, we will answer questions such as: What is a peer-to-peer protocol? When do I need to use one? What are the pitfalls of network software? What should I be looking for in an "ideal" peer-to-peer protocol?

What is a Peer-to-Peer Protocol?

A *Peer-to-peer* protocol, as the name implies, is the communication between equals. This is in contrast to the older hierarchical *master-slave* type of network protocols where all the communications is initiated by the master. A peer-to-peer protocol provides the primitives to perform process-to-process communications across network nodes. This kind of communication is required to synchronize the nodes involved in a client-server network application and to pass work requests back and forth. You would typically use the peer-to-peer protocols to create your own LAN exchanges, with message structures and semantics that are customized to your application's needs.

Do I Need a Peer-to-Peer Protocol?

Typically, a large percentage of your network services can be provided by an "off-the-shelf" client-server package with built-in network communications. Here are some examples:

- The OS/2 EE **LAN Requester/Server**, which can be used "as is" to obtain remote file and printer services that extend the operating system.
- The OS/2 EE Database Manager's **Remote Data Services** provide transparent access to remote tables and stored procedures.
- Off-the-shelf products with built-in communications services and the APIs to access them. An example is IBM's **Office Vision**, which provides access electronic mail and document distribution services.

However, there are times when "off-the-shelf" solutions may not do a job. This is when you will need to program a peer-to-peer protocol. The peer-to-peer protocol is the general purpose communication toolkit that you can always rely on to perform almost any "network job."

OS/2 EE's Peer-to-Peer Protocols

There are four peer-to-peer protocol offerings bundled in the OS/2 EE Communications Manager: NetBIOS, APPC, Named Pipes, and IEEE 802.2. These protocols are, in a sense, competing for the endorsement of network application developers. One of the purposes of the material in Part III is to give you a clear idea of how the first three protocols (IEEE 802.2 is too low-level and should be avoided) stack up in the following areas:

- The systems they connect to.
- The communications features they provide.
- Performance.
- Ease of programming.

It is imperative that you understand the trade-offs involved before we go too far down the path of software development. Ideally, you will want to invest time and energy understanding and keeping up with, at most, one LAN protocol. It should be there ready to be used when needed, very much like a hammer or a screwdriver in a toolbox.

Cooperative Network Software

As we said in the introduction to Part III, OS/2 EE provides the platform to create software that goes beyond the "stand-alone put it on your desk" type of application. We can now create the tools to develop new categories of distributed software that can access data and services wherever they are. Data in particular tends to start its life in many strange locations, and eventually may need to be collected and assembled from different sources and repositories. Local Area Networks are making it possible to use PCs in shared applications while retaining their autonomy for personal computing. The number of different ways applications and data can come together over networks is only limited by the imagination. So, how can we talk meaningfully about network software?

Client-Server Transaction Processing

The approach we'll take is to concentrate on a particular kind of *cooperative* network software and use it as a generic model for establishing a common framework. Applications in distributed environments can be partitioned in several different ways. One of the more popular partitions is the *client-server* model where applications are broken into front-end and back-end entities. We will use the client-server model as our network software paradigm because most of the distributed software developed in this book falls into that category. This book is on applications where the front-end clients and the back-end servers work together on executing a *cooperative transaction.* These applications are characterized as real-time, multiuser, shared database applications that alter the state of a business entity. *Transactions* are business activities that transform a database from one state to another (e.g., monitor the movement of a part on a shop floor, make an airline reservation, or custom order an automobile).

The Front-End Client

Front-end client nodes provide the following functions:

- Screen display and management.
- Error reporting
- Data validation.
- Interactive dialog with the user.
- Varying amounts of local computation.
- Message communication with the back-end nodes that provide shared services.
- Graphics.

The Back-End Server

Back-end server nodes provide shared services to the front-ends. Back-end servers may be PCs, hosts, clusters of hosts, or combinations of the above. Back-end nodes either singly or in some form of cooperative arrangement, provide the following services:

- Shared database access

- Shared services such as: wide-area communications, electronic-mail, printer services, file services etc.
- Batch computing facilities (including report generation and running large background jobs that run against the database).

The Cooperative Transaction

The cooperative synergy between the back-end and front-end nodes over the LAN introduces a new form of architecture that replaces the traditional terminal/host paradigm of computing with a new form of *cooperative computing*.

The fundamental building block of cooperative applications is the *cooperative transaction*. Unlike transactions in traditional host/terminal environments, cooperative transactions span multiple nodes. As an example, a cooperative transaction may start when the end user first enters or selects data on the screen of the front-end node, and ends when all nodes have completed all of the work for the transaction and control is back to the front-end node. This time span may be short, with a simple request resulting in a single response. Or it may be long and complex, and require many front-end interactions with the user and several exchanges between the front-end and back-end nodes. Transaction management is a distributed task in which the front-end and back-end processes must cooperate to provide the services and synchronization necessary for success or recovery in the case of a failure.

LAN technology is a requirement for these kinds of applications. LANs not only provide low-error high-bandwidth communications, but also provide new functionality such as broadcast facilities, group names, and multiple sessions per PC. These facilities enable new types of applications that are far richer and more cost effective than their "stand-alone" counterparts.

The Pitfalls of Distributed Software

However, all these gains come at a price. The distributed software introduces some new levels of complexity in application design. For example, consider the following design implications introduced by the client-server category of software:

- The front-end and back-end processes are autonomous entities connected via a network. They must be able to fail and recover independently. Each must be robust despite failures of the other.
- Communication failures may look like hardware or software failures. The communicating processes must be able to detect the error and resynchronize after a network failure, regardless of the cause.
- The number of messages to maintain global state across a network must be mini mized to enhance performance.
- Peer-to-peer symmetrical protocols create more complex situations and more subtle errors than the centralized master/slave protocols of host/terminals.

Is it still worth pursuing? The answer is absolutely yes; the potential benefits far outweigh the costs.

So What Should the "Ideal" Peer-to-Peer Protocol Do?

From a network application programmer's perspective, an "ideal" peer-to-peer protocols should at the very least, provide the same list of functions as the "ideal" IPC (see Chapter 8). We add to the IPC list the following "wish list" of network-specific functions:

- Any-to-any protocols that provide program-to-program communications, independent of operating systems, hardware, programming languages, transport and link protocols, data representation, etc.. In short, provide a wide choice of connectivity options. If nothing else, the protocol should connect whatever your application requires to have connected.
- Logical naming of network entities. There should be a mechanism to provide unique names and group names or "aliases."
- Broadcast of messages to all nodes on a network.
- Multicast of messages to named groups.
- Reliable end-to-end sequenced transmissions between two named entities. We will refer to this form of reliable transmission as a session-based service.
- Concurrent multiple-session support on a given node. This allows for multiple conversations to take place at the same time.
- Support multiple conversations on a single session. A conversation provides a way for applications to take turns using a shared session.
- Datagram commands for low overhead short messages. Datagram is required for broadcast and multicast transmissions.
- Execution of the network commands in "wait" or "no-wait" modes so that processing may continue while communication occurs.
- Cancelling a network command.
- Stacking multiple network commands for execution in order to do several LAN-related tasks at the same time.
- Remote invocation of procedures by network events. A network event may be the receipt of a message, a datagram alert, a session connect request, the abnormal termination of a session, a high priority message, or a communication from a particular named entity. Support for conditional event triggering should be provided as a feature, allowing us to trigger on the receipt of a combination of events. At the least, the recipient program should be started if it is not already running by the arrival of a request to start a session.
- An authentication mechanism such as encrypted passwords for secure sessions.
- Support for *transaction processing* which includes the following:

  1. ***Recoverable sessions*** which support the logging of messages on fixed media. A recoverable message queue can be used to reconstitute the system after a network crash.

2. ***Sync-points*** that allow programs to establish mutually agreed upon points at which programs or data can be verified. In case of error, work can be backed up to the last sync-point rather than starting all over from scratch. Sync-point commands may be useful to delineate units of recovery provided work can be rolled back at the application level up to the last communication sync-point. This means a network sync-point and a database commit should be simultaneously issued. If the database commit will be surfaced at the peer-to-peer level, then it requires additional primitives, such as abort and prepare-to-commit (i.e., the full implementation of a two-phase commit protocol).

NETBIOS: A PEER-TO-PEER LAN PROTOCOL

In this section of the tutorial, we answer the following questions: Where does NetBIOS fit in the scheme of things? What services are provided by NetBIOS? How is NetBIOS used? The intimate details on how to program NetBIOS will appear in a later chapter.

Situating NetBIOS

As you may recall from the introduction to Communications Manager in Part I, NetBIOS is the premier protocol for LAN-based program-to-program communications. Introduced by IBM and Sytek in 1984 for the IBM PC Network, NetBIOS now runs with almost no changes on Ethernets, Token Rings, ARCnets, StarLANs, and even low-cost serial-port LANs. NetBIOS interfaces to IBM, TCP/IP, XNS, OSI, and IEEE 802.2 protocol stacks. Support for a NetBIOS platform exists on a multiplicity of operating system environments including MS-DOS, OS/2, UNIX, and some mainframe environments. NetBIOS is currently the de facto portable standard for network application providers. One of the many reasons for NetBIOS's success is its intuitive simplicity which makes it easy to master.

Providing Services: The NetBIOS way

The NetBIOS services are provided through a set of **commands**, specified in a structure called the Network Control Block or **NCB**. The structure also contains the parameters associated with the command and the fields in which NetBIOS will return information to the program. The NCB can be viewed as a general purpose command container which gets passed to a NetBIOS DLL by invoking the **NETBIOS()** OS/2 EE API call. So technically speaking, the NetBIOS API consists of a single OS/2 call.

The NetBIOS DLL can handle multiple commands concurrently. A command can be issued in either wait or no-wait mode. In the *wait* mode, the requesting thread is blocked until the command completes. In the *no-wait* mode, control is returned to the calling thread "at the earliest time possible, usually before the command completes." When the command completes, the NetBIOS DLL places a return code in the NCB. You may request, through the NCB, to have a "post-routine" executed when a command completes. An NCB is owned by the NetBIOS DLL until the command completes. The NetBIOS DLL creates a thread for each active no-wait command; so if you have too many outstanding commands, you may eventually run out of system resources.

NetBIOS's Four Command Categories

The NetBIOS commands (see Table 11-1) can be placed into the following four categories:

- General services commands.
- Name support commands.
- Session support commands.
- Datagram support commands.

Table 11-1. NetBIOS's Four Command Categories.

General Services	Name Services	Session Services	Datagram Services
Reset Status Cancel Alert Unlink	Add Name Add Group Name Delete Name Find Name	Call Listen Send Chain Send Send No-Ack Chain Send No-Ack Receive Receive Any Hang Up Session Status	Send Datagram Send-Broadcast Datagram Receive Datagram Receive-Broadcast Datagram

NetBIOS: General Purpose Commands

The general purpose commands provide miscellaneous types of networking services. Table 11-2 presents a quick summary of the function each general service command provides, as well as the command codes for both wait and no-wait modes where applicable.

Table 11-2. NetBIOS: General Purpose Commands.

Command Name	Command Code		Function Description
	Wait (Hex)	No-Wait (Hex)	
Reset	32		Under OS/2 a process issues Reset to request resources for its use from the NetBIOS resource pool. A process should also issue a Reset to deallocate its resources and return them to the NetBIOS pool for subsequent use by other processes. When a process terminates, OS/2 EE implicitly issues a NetBIOS Reset to deallocate the resources the process owns. The resources that can be requested include: the number of sessions, number of commands, names, etc..
Status	33	B3	This command is used to obtain information on the status of a local or remote network adapter. A wealth of information gets returned including: the adapter's burned-in address, the NetBIOS version, how long the adapter was up, the number of soft errors, the packet size, the NetBIOS resource consumption, traffic statistics. It's a great source of network management info!
Cancel	35		This command is used to cancel a pending command. This is useful when you are using no-wait commands. Cancellation always ends a session.
Alert		F3	This command is used by applications that want to be notified of soft error conditions at the adapter level that last over one minute.
Unlink	70		This command is provided for compatibilty with previous NetBIOS versions. Under OS/2 it is treated as a "no-operation."

NetBIOS: Name Support Commands

Why Logical Naming?

Through NetBIOS's name services a LAN adapter card can have multiple logical names each consisting of 16 bytes. Logical naming is a way to make your programs independent from burned-in adapter numbers. Not having to rely on a stream of digits makes communications programs clearer and less error-prone. It is much more convenient (and more personal) to call a remote adapter by a logical nickname such as "Bob"; instead of a burned-in address such as X'444221113355'.

NetBIOS Naming Services

The following is a list of the naming services NetBIOS provides:

- It maintains a list of logical names assigned to an adapter in a local name table. This table is volatile and needs to be recreated dynamically when an application program is started.

- It supports both unique names and group names. If a name is unique, NetBIOS will make sure no such name already exists on the network before it gets added to the name table. If the name is a group name, NetBIOS will make sure that nobody else on the LAN is claiming that name as unique. Group names are used for sending messages to a group of workstations.
- It returns a name handle that identifies successfully registered names.
- It allows you to deregister a name when it is no longer needed.

Table 11-3 provides a quick summary of the function each NetBIOS name support command provides as well as the command codes for both wait and no-wait modes.

Table 11-3. NetBIOS: Name Support Commands.

Command Name	Command Code		Function Description
	Wait (Hex)	No-Wait (Hex)	
Add Name	**30**	**B0**	This command allows you to add a unique name to the local name table. This is the name an application on this machine will be known by.
Add Group Name	**36**	**B6**	This command allows you to add a group name to the local name table. This is the name this application and other applications are known by.
Delete Name	**31**	**B1**	This command deletes a name from the local name table. This name must not be associated with active sessions when the command is issued.
Find Name	**78**	**F8**	This command is issued to find the location on the network of a given name. NetBIOS broadcasts a query and returns whether the name is a unique name or group name, and the list of adapters that responded to the query.

NetBIOS: Session Support Commands

What is a Session?

NetBIOS sessions provide a reliable logical connection service over which a pair of network applications can exchange information. Each packet of information that gets exchanged over a session is given a sequence number through which it gets tracked and individually acknowledged. The packets are received in the order sent and blocked into user messages. Duplicate packets are detected and discarded by the session services. The price you pay for this reliable class of service is the overhead associated with creating and managing the session.

NetBIOS's Session Services

Here is what NetBIOS provides to help you get this class of service:

- Applications can create sessions between two adapter names. You tell NetBIOS through a listen command who you want to talk to, and NetBIOS will inform you when you've been called. Through an asterisk (*) you can specify that you will accept a connection from *any* adapter that calls you. Once the two applications are *matched*; NetBIOS will provide a handle number that is used to identify this session.
- Once a session is in place applications can receive information from a particular partner or from any partner that is in session with a specified name, or from any partner to any name for which a session was created.
- Applications can send messages, up to 64 KBytes (contiguous in memory) with a single send command. If this is not enough, the Chain Send command can be used to send two buffers of user data for up to 128 KBytes. On the receiver end, the receive command will treat the two buffers as a contiguous single message if the combined size of the two messages does not exceed 64 KBytes. Otherwise, a second receive is issued to accept the remaining data.
- Applications can find out the status of a session and discover if it is still active or if it got cancelled. In addition, a wealth of other information is provided for a particular session or for all sessions including: the number of sessions with this local name, the name of the remote partners, the number of NCBs outstanding, etc.

Table 11-4 provides a quick summary of the function each NetBIOS session support command provides, as well as the command codes for both wait and no-wait modes.

Table 11-4. NetBIOS: Session Support Commands.

Command Name	Command Code		Function Description
	Wait (Hex)	No-Wait (Hex)	
Call	10	90	This command attempts to open a session with another name. The caller's name and the partner's name are both specified in the NCB. The destination station must have an outstanding Listen in order for the session to be established. Multiple sessions may be established with the same pair of names.
Listen	11	91	This command allows you to accept a session call. You can specify whether you will accept calls from a named partner or from any name that calls.
Send	14	94	This command sends data to the session partner as defined in the lsn NCB field. You will supply the data to send in a separate buffer pointed to by the buffer_address field in the NCB. You must supply the message size length, which can be between 0 and 65,535 bytes long.

Table 11-4. NetBIOS: Session Support Commands.

Command Name	Command Code		Function Description
	Wait (Hex)	No-Wait (Hex)	
Chain Send	17	97	This command is like the Send command except that you can point to two data buffers that get sent as a single message. The message size must be between 0 and 131,070 bytes long.
Send Ack	71	F1	This command is like the Send command except that no data acknowledgement is required at the NetBIOS level. This will speed up the send and you'll still get some reliability from the link layer sequencing.
Chain Send No-Ack	72	F2	This command is like the Chain Send except that no data acknowledgement is required at the NetBIOS level.
Receive	15	95	This command receives data from a session partner which sends data using any of the session send commands. A return code will tell you if the receive buffer you specified is not large enough for the incoming message. Issue another Receive to read the rest of the message.
Receive Any	16	96	This command is like the Receive command except that data can be received from any partner that is in session with the specified name.
Hang Up	12	92	This command closes an open session identified by the lsn field in the NCB.
Session Status	34	B4	This command obtains information about all the sessions with a local name or for all local names

NetBIOS: Datagram Support Commands

What is a Datagram?

NetBIOS's datagrams provide a simple but unreliable transmission service with powerful broadcast capabilities. You can send datagrams to a named entity, or to a select group of entities (multicast), or to all entities on a network (broadcast). Datagrams are unreliable in the sense that their information packets are not acknowledged or tracked through a sequence number. You "transmit and pray" that your datagram gets received. The recipient may not be there or may not be expecting a datagram, and you will never know. You may, of course, design your own acknowledgement schemes on top of the datagram service.

Creating Electronic Bazaars with Datagrams

Datagrams are very useful to have in "discovery" types of situations. These are situations where you "discover" things about your network environment by broadcasting queries and learning who is out there from the responses. Broadcast can be used to obtain bids for services or to advertise the availability of new services. Broadcast datagrams provide the capability of creating electronic "bazaars." They support the creation of very dynamic types of environments where things can happen spontaneously. In situations where the name of the recipient is not known, broadcast datagrams are the only way to get the message out. The cost of broadcast datagrams is that, in some cases, recipients may get overloaded with "junk mail" that they have to sift through. The multicast facility helps alleviate that somehow, since broadcast mail can then be sent only to "special interest" groups. The alternative to broadcast is the network "yellow pages." These are well-known names on the network that specialize in giving out information.

Sending Control Information with Datagrams

Datagrams are very useful in situations where there is a need to send a quick message, without the world coming to an end if the message is not received. The typical situation is sending control-like information, such as telling a network manager "I'm alive." It doesn't make sense to go through all the overhead of creating a session with the network manager just to say "I'm alive," and what if there are 500 nodes on the network? The manager will need 500 permanent sessions, an exorbitant cost in resources. This is where the datagram alternative comes in. With datagrams you can send your "I'm alive" message, and if the manager misses your message once, it will get another one when you next send your next heartbeat (provided you're still alive).

NetBIOS's Datagram Services

Here is what NetBIOS provides in terms of datagram services:

- Datagrams are very fast small messages. They consume much less time and system overhead resources than the session service.
- Simple datagrams are sent to a recipient name. This may either be a unique name or a group name (multicast).
- Broadcast datagrams are sent to all adapters including the sending machine's adapter.
- Applications can receive simple datagrams or broadcast datagrams for a specific name or for any name.
- The default size of a datagram is 512 bytes. The maximum size of the datagram is based on the size of the LAN adapter's transmit buffer.
- Datagrams cannot be received and filtered based on specific sender names.

Table 11-5 provides a quick summary of the function each NetBIOS datagram support command provides, as well as the command codes for both wait and no-wait modes.

Table 11-5. NetBIOS: Datagram Support Commands.			
Command Name	**Command Code**		**Function Description**
	Wait Hex	**No-Wait Hex**	
Send Datagram	**20**	**A0**	This command sends a datagram message to any unique name or group name on the network.
Send Broad-cast Datagram	**22**	**A2**	This command sends a datagram to every station on the network that has an outstanding Receive Broadcast Datagram command.
Receive Datagram	**21**	**A1**	This command receives a datagram from any name on the network that issues a send datagram to the local name. You can also specify by putting X'FF' in the NCB num field that you'll accept datagrams directed to any local adapter name. This command will not receive a broadcast datagram. If the receive buffer is not large enough you will get notified but the overflow data is lost.
Receive Broadcast Datagram	**23**	**A3**	This command receives a datagram from any name that issues a Send Broadcast Datagram. If the receive buffer is not large enough you will get notified but the overflow data is lost.

The Anatomy of a NetBIOS Program

A NetBIOS program goes through the following sequence of operations:

1. ***Allocate the Resources.*** Every process must issue a *Reset* as its first NetBIOS command. The *Reset* is used to allocate resources for the process's exclusive use from the NetBIOS environment. The three important resources you need to allocate on a per process basis are: sessions, names, and commands. You can specify the NetBIOS environment's resource pool through the Communications Manager configuration services. The following figure should give you an idea of the valid range of parameters that constitute the NetBIOS pool:

```
Load Parameter          Default    Valid Values
  SESSIONS                32         0 - 254
  COMMANDS                32         0 - 255
  NAMES                   17         0 - 254
```

Figure 11-1. NetBIOS: Load Parameters System Defaults and Valid Ranges.

You can change the NetBIOS defaults through the Communications Manager's Installation and Configuration facilities. You will also need to check on the maximum numbers of sessions, commands, and names supported by your LAN adapter hardware. (Note: you will be sharing the resource pool with other processes that are running concurrently on your PC. So make sure that NetBIOS has enough resources to satisfy all of the concurrent process needs).

2. ***Add the adapter names***. The next thing a process does is issue *Add Name* and *Add Group Name* commands to create the unique and group logical names that identify an adapter to the network.

3. ***Start the persistent sessions***. The process then issues a *Listen* command for each session which will be initiated by an incoming *Call*. The application can accept a *Call* from a particular name; or by specifying (*) it can accept calls from any name on the network. The application will also issue a *Call* for each session it needs to initiate. The sessions are persistent in the sense that they will persist for the duration of an application or until they are explicitly terminated through a *Hang Up* command.

4. ***Conduct network business***. The network business can be conducted in the following NetBIOS environments:

   - Using **persistent sessions**. Here the sender and receiver exchange messages over existing sessions using NetBIOS's session-based send and receive commands (see Table 11-4 on page 298).
   - Using **non-persistent sessions**. Here the sender and receiver first establish a session and then exchange messages using NetBIOS's session-based send and receive commands (see Table 11-4 on page 298). When they're through conducting their business, each party issues a *Hang Up* command. Non-persistent sessions cost you setup time, but the benefit is that they get around the limitation placed on the number of sessions. Non-persistent sessions are especially useful in situations where one server may be required to talk to hundreds of clients.
   - Using **Datagrams**. Here the sender and receiver exchange messages using datagrams (see Table 11-5 on page 301). The sender and receiver may create their own protocol for acknowledging the datagrams.

5. ***Log off the Network***. A well-behaved network citizen "logs off the network" by issuing a NetBIOS *Reset* with the deallocate option (a non-zero in the lsn NCB field). This returns all the processes's resources to the NetBIOS pool. A deallocating *Reset* also performs the following terminating actions on behalf of the process:

   - All current NetBIOS names are deleted.
   - All current sessions are aborted.
   - All pending commands are cancelled.
   - All outstanding NCBs are purged.

   If your process terminates at the same time as it stops using the network, then it need not issue an explicit *Reset*; OS/2 automatically issues a *Reset* on behalf of a terminating process that has open NetBIOS resources.

NETBIOS SCENARIOS

The scenarios that follow will help demonstrate the use of NetBIOS in typical peer-to-peer exchanges.

Scenario 1: A Simple Transaction Involving Two Processes

Scenario 1 is the NetBIOS version of the simple transaction:

```
What is Bob's Balance?  ------->
                        <-------   $300
```

We show two implementations of this simple transaction (or Remote Procedure Call):

1. Using a NetBIOS session (see Figure 11-2 on page 304).
2. Using a NetBIOS datagram exchange (see Figure 11-3 on page 304).

Notice that in both implementations we issued receive commands before issuing the sends. We can do that because NetBIOS allows us to issue multiple outstanding commands in no-wait mode. Issuing a receive before the send is a way to make sure that the reply will not get lost. This may happen, for example, if the server code runs on a very fast machine and the client runs on a very slow machine.

So which implementation is better? It's a tossup. The session may be overkill for a two-message exchange. It does, however, provide all the built-in sequencing and error recovery. The datagram requires a lower setup overhead, but you have to include information with the data that uniquely identifies each message.

Scenario 2: One Server with a Serially Reusable Session

Scenario 2 shows how a single NetBIOS session is used to serially service two clients (see Figure 11-4 on page 305). The scenario can easily be expanded to "n" clients. We assume that all the clients will be executing simple transactions such as the one described in Scenario 1. The cost of establishing a NetBIOS session is usually under 50 milliseconds. The benefit of the non-persistent session server scheme is that it removes the ceiling on how many clients can be serviced using sessions. Another benefit is that the boundaries for the transaction execution and session coincide. This is goodness from an error-recovery viewpoint.

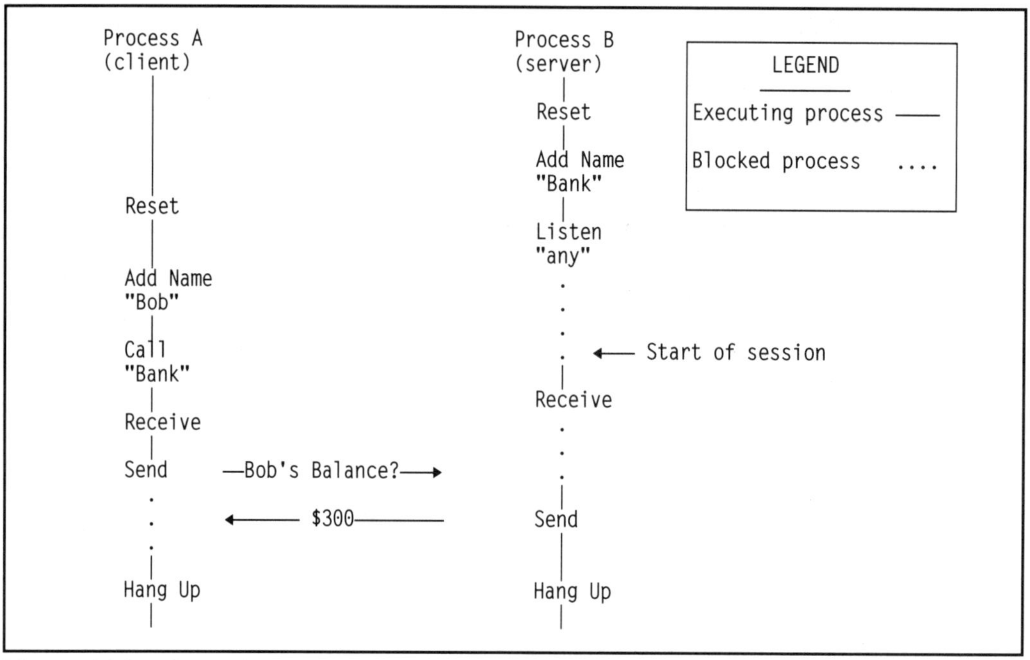

Figure 11-2. Scenario 1a: Simple Transaction Using a NetBIOS Session.

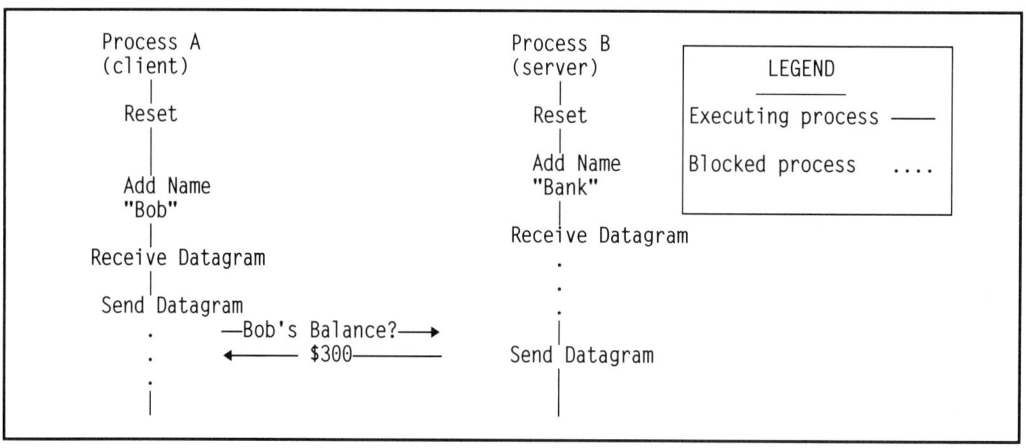

Figure 11-3. Scenario 1b: Simple Transaction Using NetBIOS Datagrams.

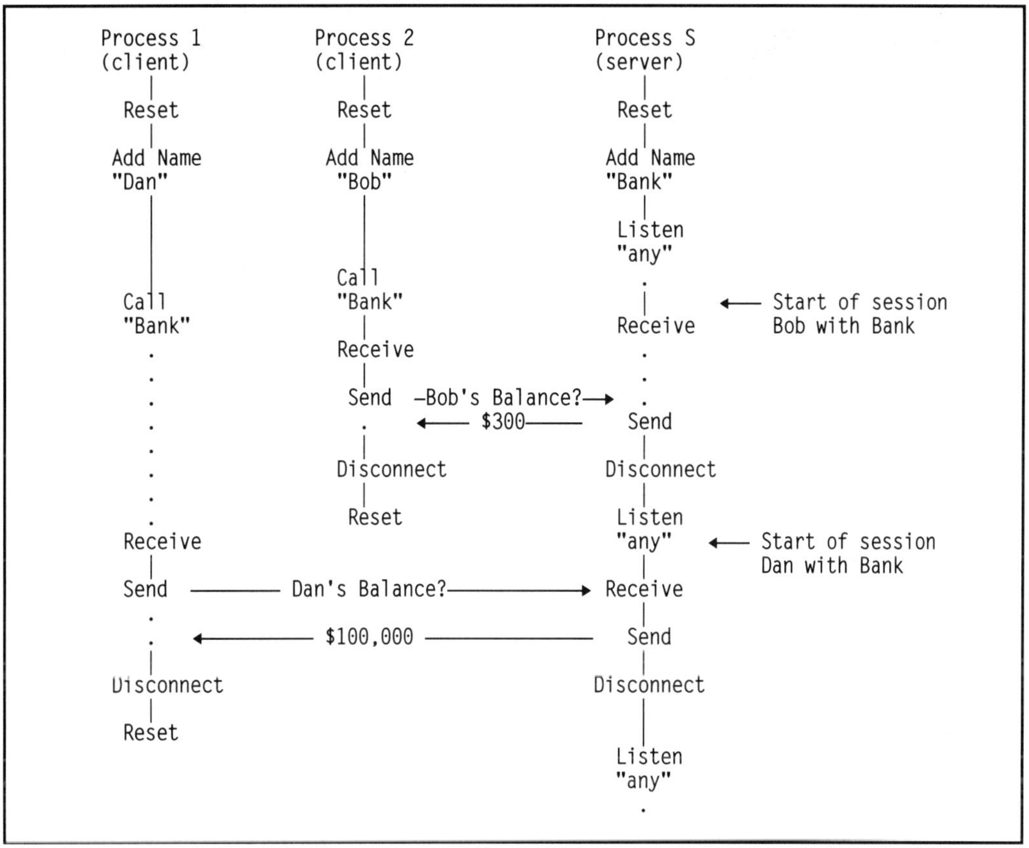

Figure 11-4. Scenario 2: Obtaining Services Using a Single NetBIOS Session.

The time-out values on the *call* command should be made large enough to keep the calling thread blocked until the server frees up. We expect that only the thread that issued the *call* command will block; other threads in the process can continue to do useful work. An application that attempts to *call* a name on the network that is registered, but for which there is no outstanding *Listen* will retry 12 times in 1/2 second intervals (i.e., the default time-out is six seconds). If no *Listen* response is obtained after this period, a "session open rejected" is returned. You can change the default values through the Communications Manager's Installation and Configuration facilities. You do that by modifying the TRANSMIT_TIMEOUT and TRANSMIT_COUNT parameters.

Scenario 3: Sending Bulk Data Over a NetBIOS Session

Scenario 3 shows how moving bulk data, such as a file transfer, may get implemented over a NetBIOS session (see Figure 11-5 on page 306). Initially, the server is blocked waiting for the client. The client starts the file transfer by telling the server that it is about to receive a file, and gives it the name of the file and its size. The server says "OK" and issues a *Receive* waiting on the first file segment to arrive. The file copy gets done through a series of exchanges. Eventually, the server finishes consuming the file and sends a message to the client saying the file got there OK after which both sides break their end of the session.

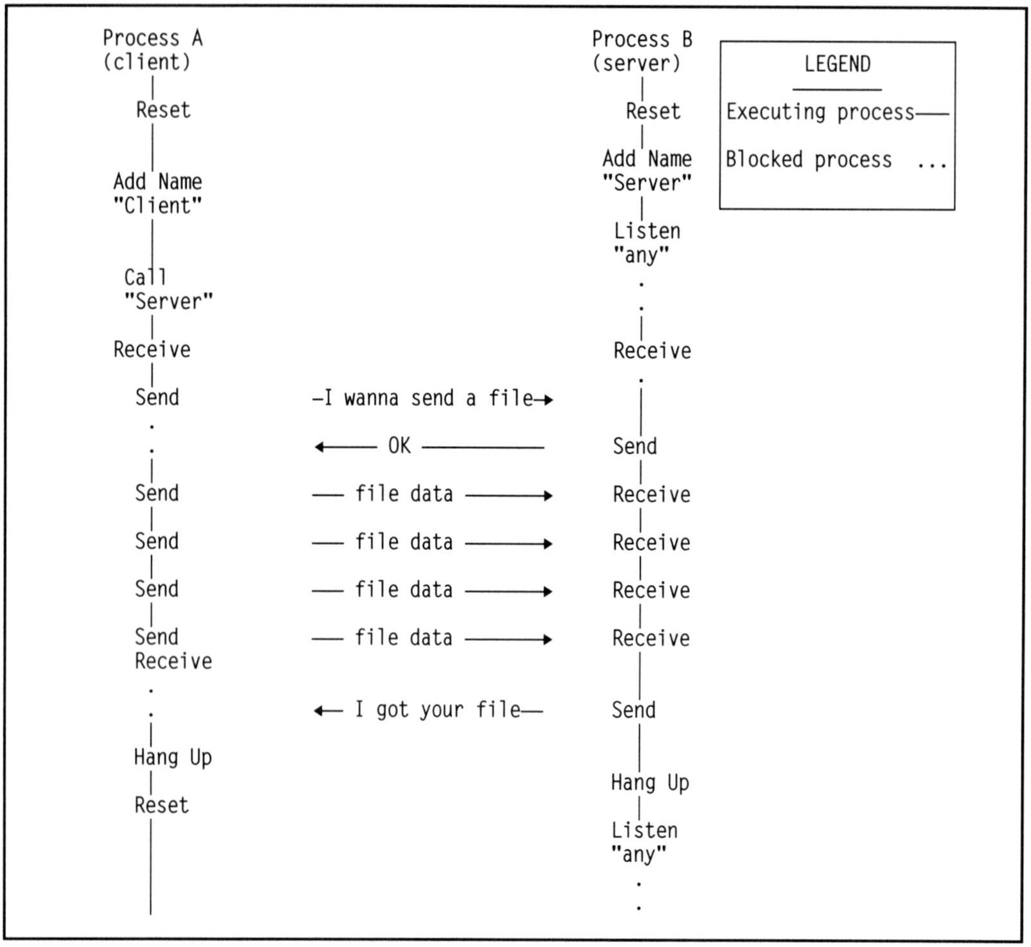

Figure 11-5. Scenario 3: Moving Bulk Data Over a NetBIOS Session.

Chapter 12

A Tutorial on APPC

This chapter presents a tutorial on APPC. Our focus is on APPC as a *peer-to-peer* communication protocol. When necessary, the prerequisite SNA background information is provided. The aim of this tutorial is to demystify the SNA jargon and make APPC perfectly understandable to the professional programmer.

Situating APPC

APPC provides an API for peer-to-peer communications within an SNA network (see Figure 12-1). Using APPC, an OS/2 EE program can converse through an SNA network with peers located anywhere in the world. These peers can run on PCs, RT PCs, AS/400s, S/38s, and S/370s, as well as on many non-IBM host platforms. Unlike NetBIOS or Named Pipes, APPC allows you to hook into an SNA backbone that interconnects many networks. Data and session protocol transparency is handled by APPC across the SNA internet. APPC also provides advanced services such as network security. IBM's SAA architecture for distributed transaction processing and remote database access builds entirely on an APPC communication base. What all this means is that APPC will most likely be your peer-to-peer protocol of choice if you are writing distributed applications across a network that includes mainframes from IBM or most other host vendors.

Do You Speak SNA?

One of the barriers to understanding APPC is the nearly unintelligible SNA jargon that surrounds it. Programmers need to understand this jargon in order to configure an APPC node and understand the mechanics of starting an SNA session. If you want to take advantage of the "intergalactic" connectivity that APPC offers, you'll have to learn how to configure an SNA node. In practice, what this means is figuring out how to answer a score of arcane questions about your application and all of its partners. These questions ask you to specify things like: the SNA base profile, the PU name, the LU profiles, session limits, the TP profiles, the conversation type, security, and the synchronization level. Worse yet, you will almost inevitably need to interface to system programmers from the host MIS group, and you will need to tell them what you need from VTAM and CICS on the host side of the interface. So welcome to the new partnership! In the next sections we will provide you with the information you need in order to play in this league.

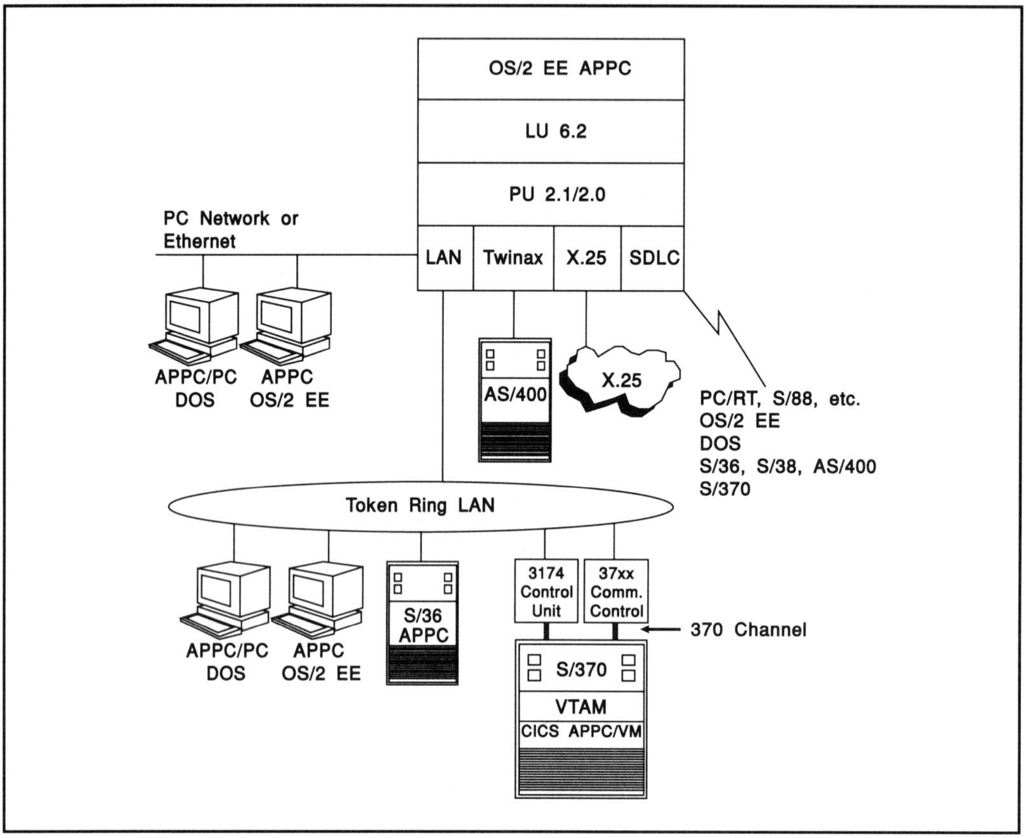

Figure 12-1. Examples of Connectivity Support Provided by OS/2 EE's APPC.

Demystifying the SNA Jargon

The purpose of this section is to introduce you to the SNA and APPC terminology, so as to make that jargon "perfectly clear."

What is a Transaction Program (TP)?

This is the logical network name that an application uses to communicate over the network. An application can define itself to APPC as multiple transaction programs (TPs). The primary goal of APPC is to provide the ability for transaction programs to communicate via conversations across the SNA network. The TP has a 64-byte name and an eight-byte identifier (the TP ID).

What is a Logical Unit (LU)?

This is the "socket" used by a Transaction Program to obtain access to an SNA network. The LU is the SNA software that accepts and executes the verbs from your programs. An LU manages the network on behalf of TPs and is responsible for the routing of data packets. Multiple TPs can use the services provided by one LU. The LU to which the transaction program issues APPC API calls is the *local* LU. The local LU communicates with *partner* LUs on other nodes. When Communications Manager is configured, your local and partner LUs are defined once for each machine. APPC uses a particular type of LU known as **LU 6.2**. This is SNA's strategic LU service for program-to-program communications. The older SNA LU types are built with the assumption that one LU represents an application program and its partner LUs represent dumb terminals or printers. With these older LUs, the application program is always the *primary* LU and has responsibility for error recovery. With LU 6.2, either partner can act as the primary and that role is negotiated as part of the session initiation process.

What is an SNA Session?

This is an SNA logical connection between two LUs across the network. Before TPs can talk to each other their LUs must be connected through a session. Sessions can be seen as providing the LU-to-LU links over which conversations can flow. In network protocol terms, sessions provide a reliable sequenced packet protocol service. The number of active sessions a local LU can have with a partner LU is configurable through the *session limits* parameter. *Parallel sessions* denote situations where more than one session is active between an LU pair, and are used to allow multiple conversations to take place concurrently between the same LU pair. Typically, sessions remain active even when there are no active conversations. This ensures that a session is available when a conversation requests it.

What is an APPC Conversation?

The actual exchange of information between two TPs is done over a conversation. Conversations are TP-to-TP links that are carried out over a session. Preferably, a conversation lasts only a short time, typically the time it takes to process a simple transaction. The idea is to have a series of conversations use the same session, one after the other. You can look at conversations as the mechanism to serially share sessions. However, only one conversation can be carried over a session at any one time. Conversations provide a way to avoid the overhead of establishing an SNA session for each network transaction (for our readers who are SNA experts, "its the cost of an

SNA bracket versus that of an SNA Bind"). Two TPs involved in a conversation are referred to as partners.

What is a Physical Unit (PU)?

This is a program on an SNA node that manages certain network resources on behalf of all the LUs on that node. A PU, for example, manages the connections of the node to adjacent nodes. The PU manages the physical data links on behalf of LUs that manage the sessions or *logical* needs between nodes. There needs to be one PU on each SNA node. PUs have types which distinguish a node's connection and routing capabilities. Your PU needs to be defined only once for each machine. Communications Manager provides **PU type 2.1** support for communications among peripheral nodes without any host involvement. PU 2.1 was designed to serve as the platform for LU 6.2's symmetrical form of peer-to-peer communications. It provides support for multiple links, multiple sessions, and parallel sessions between directly attached nodes (for example nodes on the same LAN). The more restrictive **PU type 2.0** may also be used for communication with host subarea nodes. A PU 2 node can only support a single active session, and it's partner can only be a host LU (i.e., a subarea node).

What is an APPC Verb?

Like NetBIOS, APPC uses a control block type of API. An APPC verb is equivalent to a NetBIOS command. Your program obtains APPC services by passing a verb record to the APPC API. Verb sequences are used to communicate with remote partner programs.

What is the Attach Manager?

The Attach Manager is a powerful service OS/2 EE provides for starting APPC Transaction Programs in response to remote conversation requests. This gives your programs the ability to load and execute programs on other network nodes. If the Attach Manager is not started, a node cannot accept any incoming APPC conversation requests. Through the Attach Manager's configuration services, you can specify which OS/2 process is to be started when a remote conversation request is received for a particular TP name. In addition, the Attach Manager can be configured on a per TP name basis to provide the following start-up services:

- It will pass remote arguments to your OS/2 process as if they were command line arguments.
- It will check the incoming user ID and password required to start the OS/2 process.
- It will handle conversation requests on behalf of busy processes. If you specify the *Queued Mode* at configuration time, Attach Manager will queue the requests for

the busy process in the order at which they arrive. If you specify *Non Queued Mode*, Attach Manager will start another instance of the process in response to a busy request.

- It can display a message window that informs an operator that a request has arrived to start a particular application. The operator can then choose to manually start the application. Applications configured in this mode are referred to as *Operator Started.*

How the Pieces Play Together

Sessions, Conversations, and LUs

The relationship between TPs, LUs, PUs, conversations, and sessions is depicted in Figure 12-2. The example shows a local workstation where TP C is involved in active conversations with the remote TPs: A and D. Remote TP B is also waiting for TP A to finish so that it can start its own conversation with TP C. Notice that the LU in the local workstation can handle more than one session; it is in active session with its partner LUs on workstations X and Y, simultaneously. Notice also that the session with the partner LU (in workstation X) is used to support multiple conversations in serial fashion.

Parallel Sessions and Parallel Conversations

Figure 12-3 demonstrates how *parallel sessions* between LUs can be used to provide concurrent conversations over the same LU pair. In this example, three conversations are being held concurrently over three parallel sessions between the local LU X and its partner LU Y.

Parallel sessions are an LU 6.2 feature that offers improved performance over single sessions. Work can now be queued against a pool of active sessions rather than waiting for a single session to free up. Parallel sessions are used to provide full-duplex communication channels (more on that later), high priority channels, and for balancing transmission loads. By using parallel sessions, you don't have to provide separate LUs for each session. This cuts down on your LU management overhead.

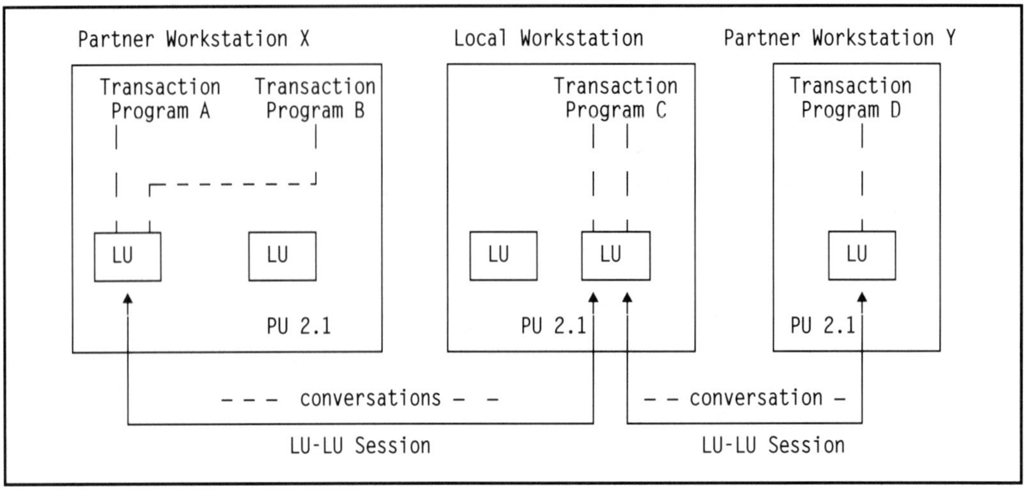

Figure 12-2. Example of a Local LU Communicating with Two Remote Partner LUs.

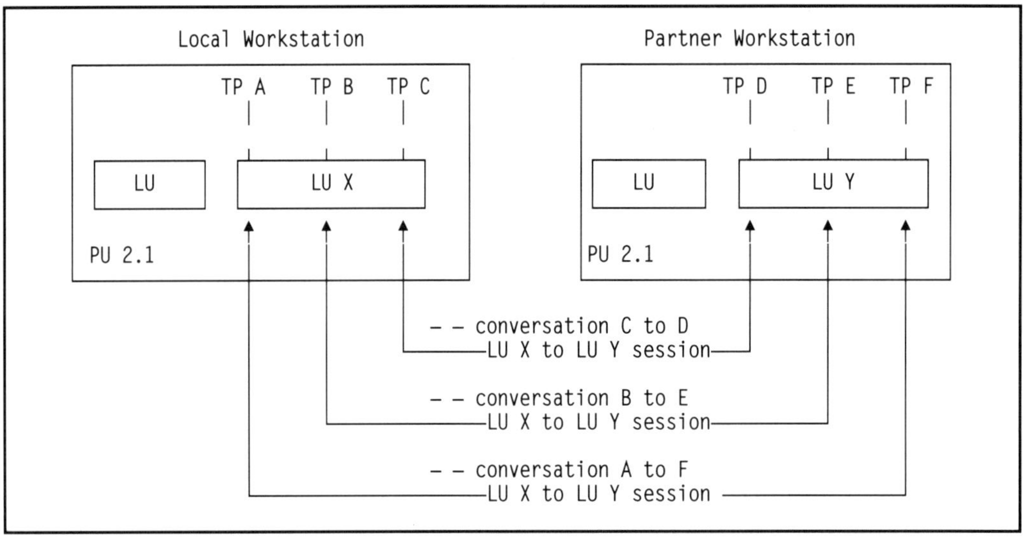

Figure 12-3. Example of a Parallel LU Sessions and Concurrent Conversations.

In Summary

An APPC network is made up of SNA nodes and links. A node has a PU, one or more LUs, and one or more TPs. LUs communicate through sessions, and TPs communicate through conversations over those sessions. Finally, your user program will consist of a series of verbs that are organized into conversations. The conversations are carried out with partner TPs over the network in accordance to the rules of the APPC protocol.

APPC's Verb Categories

APPC's verbs fall into three categories:

1. ***Control Verbs.*** These verbs start or end a transaction program.

2. ***Conversation Verbs.*** These verbs are used to exchange information between transaction programs. An APPC conversation may either be Basic or Mapped:

   - *Basic Conversations* require that you provide a two-byte length prefix at the start of all your exchange records. The benefit they provide is some amount of flexibility in terms of error-handling. The cost is that they are more complicated than Mapped Conversations and frequently require more parameters and data formatting. The error recovery, although more flexible, is less automatic than with Mapped Conversations. Basic Conversations are meant to be used by service TPs.
   - *Mapped Conversations* are intended for use by end-user programs written in high-level languages. With Mapped Conversations, APPC handles all the details of the underlying data stream used by LU 6.2, and provides a data mapping service that makes your programs more data independent. We will be using Mapped Conversations exclusively in this book.

3. ***Management or Operator Verbs.*** These verbs are used to manage sessions, links, and the APPC Attach Manager through API calls. These are the same functions that can manually be performed using an operator panel.

The APPC verb categories are shown in Table 12-1. Notice that there is a one-to-one relationship between the set of Mapped and Basic conversation verbs. The two sets of verbs are distinguished by the **MC_** prefix which stands for Mapped Conversation. The **GET_TYPE** command is a type-independent command that returns the conversation type that has been allocated.

Table 12-1. The APPC Verb Categories.

Control Verbs	Conversation Verbs		Management or Operator Verbs
	Basic	Mapped	
RECEIVE ALLOCATE TP STARTED TP ENDED	ALLOCATE CONFIRM CONFIRMED DEALLOCATE FLUSH GET ATTRIBUTES PREPARE TO RECEIVE RECEIVE AND POST RECEIVE AND WAIT RECEIVE IMMEDIATE REQUEST TO SEND SEND DATA SEND ERROR TEST RTS GET TYPE	MC ALLOCATE MC CONFIRM MC CONFIRMED MC DEALLOCATE MC FLUSH MC GET_ATTRIBUTES MC PREPARE TO RECEIVE MC RECEIVE AND POST MC RECEIVE AND WAIT MC RECEIVE IMMEDIATE MC REQUEST TO SEND MC SEND DATA MC SEND ERROR MC TEST RTS GET TYPE	CNOS DISPLAY START AM STOP AM CONNECT PHYSICAL LINK DEACTIVATE LOGICAL LINK DISCONNECT PHYSICAL LINK DEACTIVATE SESSION

We will now cover in some detail each of APPC's verb categories.

APPC's Control Verbs

These verbs are used to start or end a TP. For an application to start a conversation with a remote application, it must first create a TP. This is done by issuing a **TP_STARTED** command which returns a handle called the TP ID. An application can start multiple TPs each of which is identified by a respective TP ID handle. TPs created in this manner are referred to as locally initiated TPs. In order to establish a conversation, a partner TP needs to be remotely initiated through the Attach Manager. This kind of TP is called a remotely initiated TP. This is done by having the remote application issue **RECEIVE_ALLOCATE**, a new APPC verb that combines the following functions:

1. It handles remote TP initiation (for APPC/PC old-timers, this function is equivalent to a TP_INITIATE remote). The Attach Manager starts the application after it gets a remote invocation or displays a window that informs the operator to start the application.
2. It accepts (or rejects) the request to carry out a conversation. This means that when the command completes successfully, the TPs on both ends are linked in a conversation (for APPC/PC old timers this is equivalent to a GET_ALLOCATE).

The **RECEIVE_ALLOCATE** verb executes when it receives an **ALLOCATE** request from a remote TP and returns two handles: a TP ID and a Conversation ID. Thus, to start a TP and initiate a conversation one side issues **TP_STARTED** followed by **ALLOCATE** and the partner issues a **RECEIVE_ALLOCATE.** The partner side should have previously started the Attach Manager. The **TP_ENDED** verb is issued to return the TP resources to APPC. Table 12-2 provides a quick summary of APPC's Control Verbs:

Table 12-2. The APPC Control Verbs.

Verb Name	Verb Code	Function Description
RECEIVE ALLO-CATE	**0016 Hex**	This command establishes a new TP and conversation in response to an ALLOCATE issued by a partner TP. If no incoming ALLOCATE is present, the command waits for the amount of time configured in the TP Receive Timeout configuration panel field. You must configure a Remotely Attachable TP profile for each unique TP to be started by RECEIVE_ALLOCATE. APPC returns a TP ID and a Conversation ID.
TP STARTED	**0014 Hex**	This command tells APPC to reserve resources for a new TP initiated locally (meaning not from an incoming ALLOCATE). You do not have to configure a profile for this TP name. APPC returns a TP ID.
TP ENDED	**0013 Hex**	This command ends a TP and frees up its resources. APPC will then free all the conversations associated with this TP. You can tell APPC to terminate gracefully and wait for all active verbs to complete (this is called the "soft" option)

APPC's Conversation Verbs

In this section, we cover the verbs that allocate the conversation and actually do the talking. Table 12-3 provides a quick summary of APPC's Conversation Verbs. The explanations apply to both the Basic and Mapped Conversation modes. We will drop the use of the **MC_** prefix for Mapped in the remainder of this chapter. Our interest, of course, is in Mapped conversations. So unless otherwise stated, the discussion of verbs always assumes the Mapped conversation. Remember that the conversation mode is specified when it is first allocated, and from then on both sides have to issue either Basic or Mapped verbs and that no "mix and match" is allowed by APPC.

Table 12-3. The APPC Conversation Verbs.		
Verb Name	**Verb Code**	**Function Description**
ALLOCATE	**0001 Hex**	This command establishes a conversation between two TPs and creates an LU-to-LU session if one does not already exist. You must supply to this verb your local TP ID, the local name of your partner LU, and the TP name of your partner. You can also specify a password, the level of synchronization you need, and point to Program Initialization Parameters (PIP) you want passed to your partner. Finally, you can specify if you want the verb to return control to your program immediately or after a session is allocated or freed. APPC returns a conversation ID.
CONFIRM	**0003 Hex**	This command sends a confirmation request to a partner and awaits a reply. This is done to allow the two programs to synchronize their actions. This verb can only be used over conversations that are allocated with a synchronization level of CONFIRM.
CONFIRMED	**0004 Hex**	This command sends a confirmation reply to the partner TP. The local program can only issue this verb in response to a confirmation request. This verb can only be used over conversations that are allocated with a synchronization level of CONFIRM.
DEALLOCATE	**0005 Hex**	This command deallocates the specified conversation. The send buffer of the LU is flushed with this command. If your conversation is using the synchronization level CONFIRM then APPC will also send a CONFIRM as part of the deallocation (unless you specify otherwise).
FLUSH	**0006 hex**	This command flushes the send buffer of the local LU and sends all buffered information to the partner LU. This verb is very useful in speeding up the sending of local data. It circumvents APPC's normal buffering of send data (from send verbs) until it reaches a transmission threshold. You can also issue this verb immediately after an ALLOCATE to make sure the partner gets the connection request immediately.
PREPARE TO RECEIVE	**000A Hex**	This command changes a conversation from the Send to the Receive state in preparation for receiving data and it also causes the send buffer to be flushed. If the synchronization level is CONFIRM, APPC will send a CONFIRM directive to the partner requesting confirmation for this change of direction.
RECEIVE AND POST	**000D Hex**	This command causes APPC to return immediate control to the local program and post a semaphore when a sufficient amount of information is received for the specified conversation. APPC will place the received data in the specified buffer. The semaphore can either be a RAM or System semaphore and must be set using the OS/2 DosSemWait call prior to issuing this command. You cannot use this conversation until the command completes. But your program can wait on several semaphores to clear on different conversations. The information received can be data, status, a request for confirmation or a combination. APPC indicates the type of information received and the length of the data. It also tells you if there is more data coming, whether a confirmation is required and when it's your turn to send. The maximum number of bytes that can be received is 65,535.
RECEIVE AND WAIT	**000B Hex**	This command waits for information to arrive for the specified conversation. Otherwise it is similar to RECEIVE_AND_POST.

Table 12-3. The APPC Conversation Verbs.		
Verb Name	Verb Code	Function Description
RECEIVE IMME-DIATE	000C Hex	This command receives any currently available information for the specified conversation. Otherwise it is similar to RECEIVE_AND_WAIT.
REQUEST TO SEND	000E Hex	This command requests from the partner TP permission to enter the Send state. APPC places the conversation in the Send state when the SEND permission is received from the partner. This is obtained in the what_receive parameter through any of the receive verbs.
SEND DATA	000F Hex	This command sends the contents of a data buffer to the partner TP. The type parameter allows the program to combine sending data with certain other functions such as: FLUSH, CONFIRM, PREPARE_TO_RECEIVE, and DEALLOCATE. If you specify type = NONE, APPC will store data in the send buffer until it accumulates a sufficient amount of data for transmission. What constitutes a "sufficient" amount is a characteristic of the session allocated for that conversation. The number of bytes a local TP can send with this command is between 0 and 65,535.
SEND ERROR	0010 Hex	This command tells the partner TP that an error was detected. You can specify whether the error is in the data you just received or in the data you were about to send. For example, if an error gets encountered while doing a database transaction, then there may be no data to send to the partner. This command can also be used to reject a confirmation request.
TEST RTS	0012 Hex	This command tests whether the a REQUEST_TO_SEND was received from the partner TP.
GET ATTRIBUTES	0007 Hex	This command returns information such as the attributes of the specified conversation, the local and partner LU names, the level of processing synchronization and any user ID provided for security. It also returns the network name and the mode name. Many of the parameters returned are in EBCDIC. You can use the common CONVERT utility to translate them into ASCII.
GET TYPE (type independent)	0008 Hex	This command returns the conversation type: Basic or Mapped.

APPC's Management or Operator Verbs

With the exception of the **START_AM** command, you will probably not be issuing any of the Operator verbs from within your program. You should be aware of the existence of these verbs just in case you have some exceptional needs, such as writing an application that controls the network environment. Table 12-4 provides a very brief summary of APPC's Operator Verbs:

Table 12-4. The APPC Control or Operator Verbs.

Verb Name	Verb Code	Function Description
CNOS	**0015 Hex**	This command allows you to change the number of sessions that can exist between two LUs. You can also do this through the session limit panel when configuring APPC.
CONNECT PHYSICAL LINK	**0046 Hex**	This command allows you to connect a physical link.
DEACTIVATE LOGICAL LINK	**002C Hex**	This command allows you to discontinue the specified SNA link. You can do this gracefully and the command will wait for all sessions on that link to end. A possible use of this function is to end a deadlocked TP.
DEACTIVATE SESSION	**002E Hex**	This command is used to deactivate the specified LU 6.2 session. A possible use for this function is to end a deadlocked TP.
DISCONNECT PHYSICAL LINK	**0047 Hex**	This command discontinues a physical link and may be used to end a deadlocked TP.
DISPLAY	**001B Hex**	This command returns a wealth of SNA information and can be very useful if you are writing a network monitor program. You can obtain the following types of SNA information: global info (including version and release numbers, network name, node-ID, machine type, PU name etc.) LU 6.2 specific info, Attach Manager info, session info, TP info, link types info, and information about the SNA gateways on the network.
START AM	**0028 Hex**	This command starts the Attach Manager. Your node is now enabled to accept incoming allocation requests that can be matched with pending RECEIVE_ALLOCATEs.
STOP AM	**0029 Hex**	This command stops the Attach Manager. All incoming and queued allocates are rejected.

Common Services API

The OS/2 EE Common Services provide some useful protocol-independent services. They can be issued with any of the OS/2 EE Communications Manager protocols to obtain common services. Traditionally, these services are associated with SNA; this is why we include them in this APPC tutorial. Their control block structure, and method for calling the API, is very much like APPC's. APPC programs make heavy use of the **CONVERT** verb which translates character strings from ASCII to EBCDIC, and vice versa. This is because all the LU 6.2 control information that flows to a partner when a conversation is started must be in EBCDIC. This includes passwords, TP names, user IDs, and the mode name. Table 12-5 provides a brief summary of those services:

Table 12-5. The Communications Manager's Common Services API.

Verb Name	Verb Code	Function Description
SV_CONVERT	001A	This command allows you to convert an ASCII character string to EBCDIC and vice versa. To use this verb you specify the direction of the conversion and the conversion table: **Table A** converts uppercase strings. **Table AE** converts both character cases. **Table C** lets you create your own string conversion table.
SV_DEFINE_TRACE	001D Hex	This command allows you to specify the API verbs or events you want to trace.
SV_GET_CP_CONVERT_TABLE	0019 Hex	This command allows you to perform country code conversions on character strings. This is useful if the recipient of your data is using a different code page.
SV_LOG_MESSAGE	001F Hex	This command allows you to write a message into the message log. You may also specify that the message gets displayed as a popup.
SV_TRANSFER_MS_DATA	001C Hex	This command will build and send a network alert to Netview. The data is also logged in the Comm Mgr error log.
SV_SET_USER_LOG_QUEUE	004B Hex	This command allows you to specify an OS/2 user-created queue which can be notified of system and error messages. You can also select using filters the message types and number ranges you have an interest in.

Security and PIP Parameters

When a TP establishes a conversation with another TP located somewhere on an SNA network, it issues the **ALLOCATE** verb giving all the information needed to establish the connection. This includes the conversation type (Mapped or Basic), the synchronization level required (see next section), the security parameters required to access the remote TP and the *Program Initialization Parameters* or **PIP data**. In this section we discuss the security and PIP elements:

APPC Conversation Security

The **ALLOCATE** verb supports a security parameter that can be issued with the following options:

None Meaning that no conversation-level security is needed.

Same Meaning that the local program has already verified the User ID and password. The User ID information is still sent to the partner LU. This *already verified* capability is useful when multiple sites are participating in a distributed transaction and the remote LUs may be willing to accept the already verified status from another LU.

Pgm Meaning that the partner LU must validate the security parameters which include the User ID and password, both of which can be up to 10 EBCDIC characters long. You should right-pad both with EBCDIC blanks, if they are less than 10 characters. The security parameters are checked by the Attach Manager on the partner's machine and they have to match what was specified on the partner's Conversation Security menu. If the partner LU's profile specifies the password at the *session level*, then each conversation on that session uses the same password which gets verified with each incoming conversation request.

APPC PIP Data

Program Initialization Parameters, or PIP data, provide a mechanism for passing initialization parameters or environment setup information to a partner TP or operating system. For example, PIP data is used by APPC on the IBM S/36 for establishing the environment of the TPs it starts. The OS/2 EE version of APPC can send PIP data, but currently *does not* support the receipt of incoming PIP data.

APPC's Synchronization Services

Client-server transactions may require the update of resources that reside on multiple nodes. Synchronization capabilities are very important for such occasions. The APPC architecture specifies three levels of synchronization services:

None With this level, APPC provides no synchronization. You specify this level by allocating a conversation with **sync_level** = NONE.

Confirm This level allows application programs to agree that processing has been completed without errors. You specify this level by allocating a conversation with **sync_level** = CONFIRM. APPC will enforce confirmation exchanges and error reporting. An application can explicitly request that the partner TP confirm that the data sent so far was received and processed successfully. Applications can then issue a **CONFIRM** verb to request a confirmation from the partner. The partner can either respond with a **CONFIRMED**, indicating everything is OK, or with a **SEND_ERROR** which reports an error condition. You can also request a confirmation from a partner before a TP ends successfully by issuing a **DEALLOCATE** with **type** = SYNC_LEVEL.

Syncpoint This is an even more stringent level of synchronization which allows certain resources to be defined as LU protected. The LU is then responsible for *committing* the changes after a successful transaction; or *backing out* the changes if an error occurs during the processing of the transaction. Syncpoint protection addresses the problem of maintaining the integrity of the network transaction. Its full implementation requires a two-phase commit protocol with rollback and resynchronization capabilities.

OS/2 EE supports the first two levels of synchronization. Future releases will support the Syncpoint option. This is required to make distributed database updates work across multiple databases on a network. When it is fully implemented, it may become one of APPC's strongest selling points.

Peer-to-Peer Exchanges: The APPC Way

We cover here some of the APPC "features," which may confuse programmers more accustomed to a *free form* peer-to-peer protocol such as NetBIOS. The confusion clears up when you realize that APPC is designed to accommodate some of the needs of *transaction processing* at a communications level. The extra service APPC provides deals with issues like, "whose turn is it to send?" and "what to do in case of errors." Future releases of APPC will introduce more such features to be used primarily in distributed database management.

Taking Turns

The APPC protocol imposes a set of stringent rules for communications between partners at the session level. APPC has rules for how the permission to talk is granted. Even though the APPC communication links are full-duplex (i.e., bi-directional), the APPC protocol imposes and enforces a *logical half-duplex* protocol on both partners. This means that the partners take turns at sending and receiving. APPC does not support "anarchistic network behavior" such as broadcasts or datagrams. All exchanges are session-based and very much under the strict control of the protocol. In all fairness, the designers of APPC felt that the protocol should help the transaction partners maintain some kind of "law and order." All network applications, they reasoned, have to deal with issues like, "who gets to send data next?" and "who gets to do what in case of an error," and "how to avoid race conditions." Their conclusion was that if these rules were not built into the protocol, they would have to be reinvented for every application. Here is a list of session level rules APPC imposes:

- The partner that initiates the conversation goes first.
- Only one command can be outstanding at any one time.
- Partners take turns sending and receiving. Two APPC verbs are specifically designed to effect changes in the conversation direction: **REQUEST_TO_SEND**,

which requests permission to send and, **PREPARE_TO_RECEIVE**, which grants the partner permission to receive.
- The verbs that an APPC transaction can issue depend on the state of the conversation (more on that later).

Blocking and Flushing

APPC attempts to optimize performance by blocking a series of commands and then sending them as one communication message. This, in a sense, is a mixed blessing because things may not be where you may think they ought to be. To get around that, your application will have to explicitly issue commands that "flush" the buffer and cause the message to be delivered at the other end. You can use the **FLUSH** verb to force APPC to send the data in its buffers. If you want to ensure that the partner LU has received the information, issue a **CONFIRM** verb. The following receive verbs will cause a change of state which will implicitly cause data to flow to the partner LU: **PREPARE_TO_RECEIVE**, **RECEIVE_AND_WAIT**, and **RECEIVE_AND_POST**. The issuing of a **DEALLOCATE** verb at the end of a conversation will also flush the buffers.

APPC Conversation States

The verbs that an APPC transaction can issue at any one time (and for a particular conversation) depend on the state of the conversation. The state of a conversation can change as a result of the program (or its partner) issuing verbs. The detection of network errors may also cause changes in state. APPC will manage the state of a conversation and enforce that your program only issue the verbs that are correct for a particular conversation state. The state of the conversation is always defined from the local program's perspective. A conversation can be in one of the following states:

RESET This is the state of a conversation before a TP allocates it.

SEND While in this state, the program can send data, report errors, and request confirmations. Also an application needs to be in the Send state before it can issue a **DEALLOCATE** to terminate a conversation; this is because APPC notifies the partner TP that the conversation is terminated. If the application wants to exit and is not in the Send state, it can terminate the process. This causes APPC to deallocate the conversation automatically.

RECEIVE While in this state, the program can receive data and respond to a request for confirmation.

PENDING_POST This is the state entered after issuing a **RECEIVE_AND_POST**. In this state the program waits to receive data. Verbs can be issued to *other* conversations while waiting.

CONFIRM This is the state entered after a **CONFIRM** is received from the partner TP. The verbs that may be issued in this state are **CONFIRMED** or **SEND_ERROR**.

An OS/2 process can manage multiple conversations concurrently. This means that one TP may be in the Send state while another TP may be in the Receive state, etc.

The Anatomy of an APPC Program

A typical APPC program goes through the following sequence of operations:

1. ***Create the local TP***. This is done by issuing a TP_STARTED command which returns a TP ID. An application can start multiple TPs, each of which is identified by a respective handle. TPs created in this manner are referred to as locally initiated TPs.

2. ***Create the remotely initiated TP***. In order to establish a conversation, a partner TP needs to be remotely initiated through the Attach Manager. This kind of TP is called a remotely initiated TP. The remote application does that by issuing a RECEIVE_ALLOCATE verb. The Attach Manager should have been previously configured and started.

3. ***Allocate the conversation***. An ALLOCATE is issued to request a conversation with the remote application. A conversation ID is returned. This is followed by issuing a CONFIRM to force the conversation request to flow to the partner and to wait for a verification that the remote TP has accepted the conversation request. The incoming request causes the partner's Attach Manager to start the application directly or to display a window that instructs the operator to start the application. Once the application is started, the partner's previously issued RECEIVE_ALLOCATE verb executes and returns two handles: a TP ID and a Conversation ID. The two sides are now in conversation but the initiating TP is still blocked waiting for a confirmation.

4. ***Confirm the conversation***. The partner's application issues a RECEIVE_AND_WAIT as its first conversation verb (remember it starts out in the RECEIVE state). The RECEIVE command waits for either data or for status indicators. In this case, the command returns immediately with a *receive confirm* indicator which tells the partner that a confirm must be issued. The partner issues the CONFIRMED verb, which is what the local TP was waiting for. Now the two applications are in active conversation mode with the requesting TP still in the Send state and the partner TP in the Receive state.

5. ***Conduct network business***. This business will be conducted in an orderly logical half-duplex fashion. After the start of a conversation, the partner application is still in the Receive state and will typically issue another RECEIVE_AND_WAIT to obtain more data or status information. The initiating TP can then use SEND_DATA to send a buffer's worth of data. Every so often, a FLUSH should

be issued to force the data to be sent to the partner. A CONFIRM can be issued to flush the data and wait for the receipt of a CONFIRMED or SEND_ERROR indicator from the partner. A TP can implicitly relinquish the right to send, by issuing a RECEIVE verb, or it can do that explicitly by issuing a PREPARE_TO_RECEIVE. Either partner can request permission to send by issuing a REQUEST_TO_SEND verb.

6. ***Deallocate the conversation.*** A conversation can be deallocated from the Send state by issuing a DEALLOCATE verb. The partner receives a Deallocate indicator and may be asked to confirm the deallocation, or (in the case of deallocate ABEND) simply terminate.

7. ***Terminate the TPs.*** The two sides terminate their TPs by issuing TP_ENDED. If your process terminates at the same time as it stops using the network, then it can exit and let APPC issue a DEALLOCATE followed by a TP_ENDED on its behalf.

APPC SCENARIOS

The scenarios that follow will help demonstrate the use of APPC in typical peer-to-peer exchanges.

Scenario 1: A Simple Transaction Involving Two Processes

Scenario 1 presents the APPC version of the simple transaction:

```
What is Bob's Balance?  ------->
                        <-------    $300
```

We show two implementations of this simple transaction (or remote procedure call):

- *Without* the APPC confirmation services. (see Figure 12-5)
- *With* the APPC confirmation services (see Figure 12-4).

In both scenarios, we show the APPC conversation state before each verb is issued. In both scenarios, the client is the local TP and the server is the partner TP that is remotely invoked by an incoming conversation request.

Simple Transaction: Without Confirmation Services

This is how scenario 1 (see Figure 12-4) plays *without* confirmation services:

1. The client calls APPC with a TP_STARTED verb to start a Transaction Program (TP). APPC will return a TP ID which all subsequent verbs must use with this TP.

2. The client then requests a conversation by issuing an ALLOCATE verb. Notice that the sync_level parameter is set to NONE, meaning that no confirmation services are required. APPC returns a conversation ID and starts an LU-to-LU session if none is available. The actual request for a conversation is not yet sent because APPC blocks records into a logical record. This means that, so far, no information was passed between the client and server TPs.

3. The client issues a FLUSH verb to force the conversation request to flow to the partner.

4. The arrival of the conversation request causes the Attach Manager to start the server program.

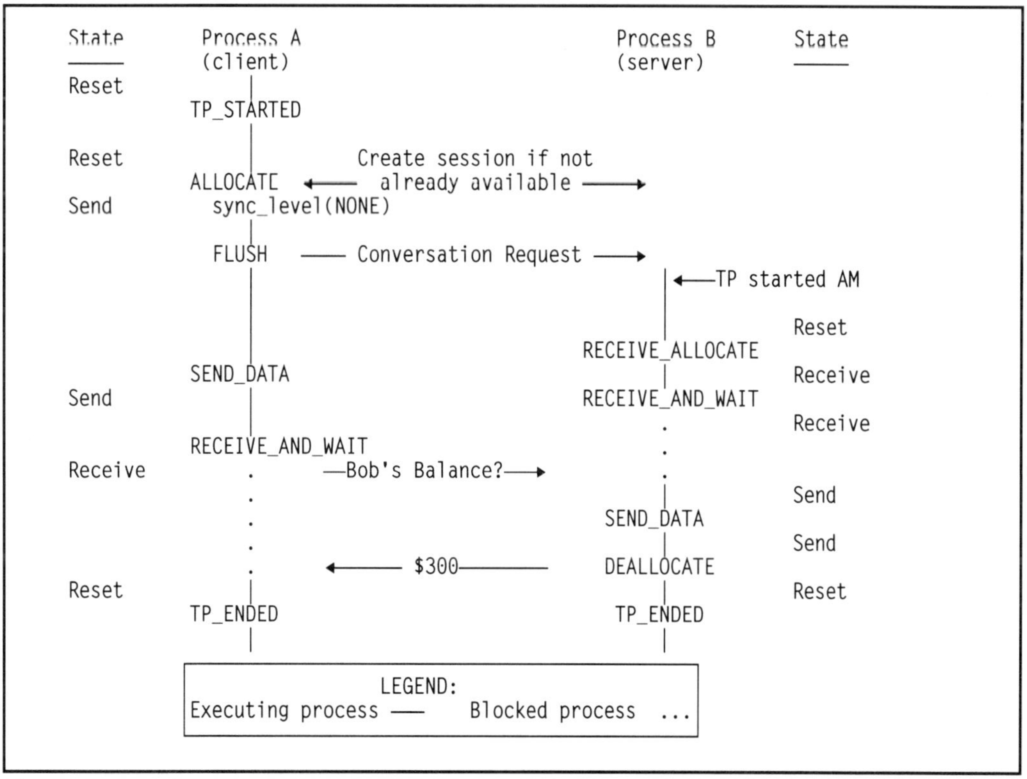

Figure 12-4. Scenario 1a: A Simple Transaction APPC with sync_level = None.

5. The server issues a RECEIVE_ALLOCATE verb which returns both a TP ID and Conversation ID. Now both sides have established their end of the conversation.

6. APPC starts the server in the Receive state. So the server issues a RECEIVE_AND_WAIT to find out what the client wants.

7. The client in the meantime has issued a SEND_DATA requesting Bob's balance, followed by RECEIVE_AND_WAIT which flushes the message and changes the state to Receive. The client is now blocked waiting for the reply to arrive.

8. The server sends back the reply, and since it is still in the Send state, it issues a DEALLOCATE followed by TP_ENDED to close the conversation and release the TP.

9. The client receives the reply and issues TP_ENDED to release its TP.

Simple Transaction: With Confirmation Services

We now demonstrate how scenario 1 plays *with* confirmation services (see Figure 12-5). Notice how APPC's confirmation services can be used to enhance the integrity of the implementation. Here are the differences:

1. The confirmation services are activated by issuing ALLOCATE, with sync_level parameter set to CONFIRM.

2. The client can now issue a CONFIRM to flush the buffer and cause the conversation request to flow to the server TP.

3. When the server TP issues RECEIVE_AND_WAIT, it gets an indication that a confirmation is required.

4. The server issues a CONFIRMED command which lets the client know that the conversation has succeeded. Notice that the server is still in the Receive state, which causes it to issue a second RECEIVE_AND_WAIT to find out what the client wants.

5. The client proceeds with the simple bank transaction just like it did in the previous implementation.

6. The DEALLOCATE verb makes use of the confirmation services. By setting the type parameter to SYNC_LEVEL, the server requests that the client confirm the receipt of the DEALLOCATE before issuing a TP_ENDED.

Scenario 2: Sending Bulk Data Over an APPC Conversation

Scenario 2 shows how moving bulk data, such as a file transfer, may get implemented over an APPC conversation (see Figure 12-6 on page 328). This is an area where

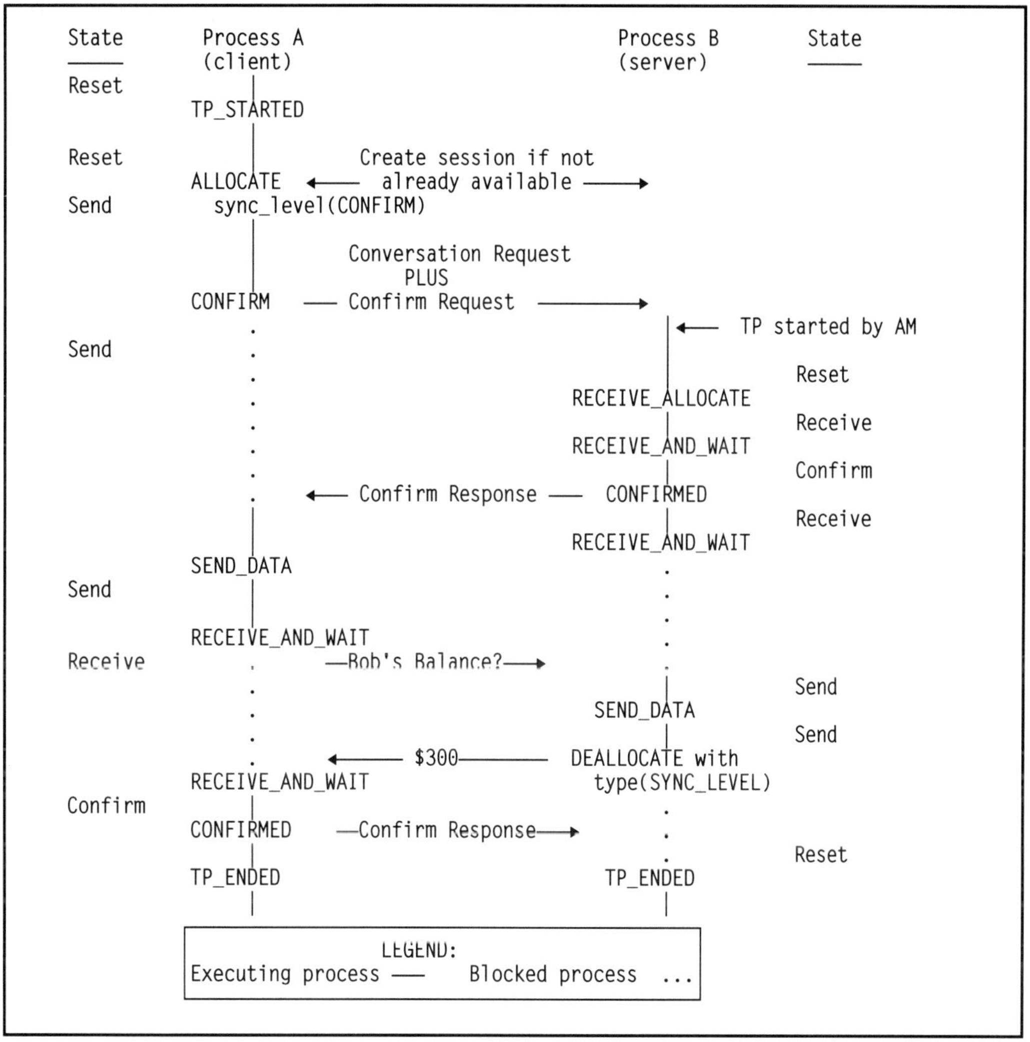

Figure 12-5. Scenario 1b: A Simple Transaction APPC with sync_level = CONFIRM.

APPC's blocking capabilities should favorably come into play. The client just sends logical records and APPC takes care of deciding when to send the accumulated records based on the network's buffering and transmission capabilities. Initially, the server is blocked waiting for the client.

The client starts the file transfer by telling the server that it is about to receive a file and gives it the name of the file and its size. The server says "OK" and issues a receive waiting on the first file segment to arrive. The file copy gets done through a series of message sends. Eventually, the server finishes consuming the file and sends a message to the client saying the file got there OK, after which both sides deallocate their end of the conversation.

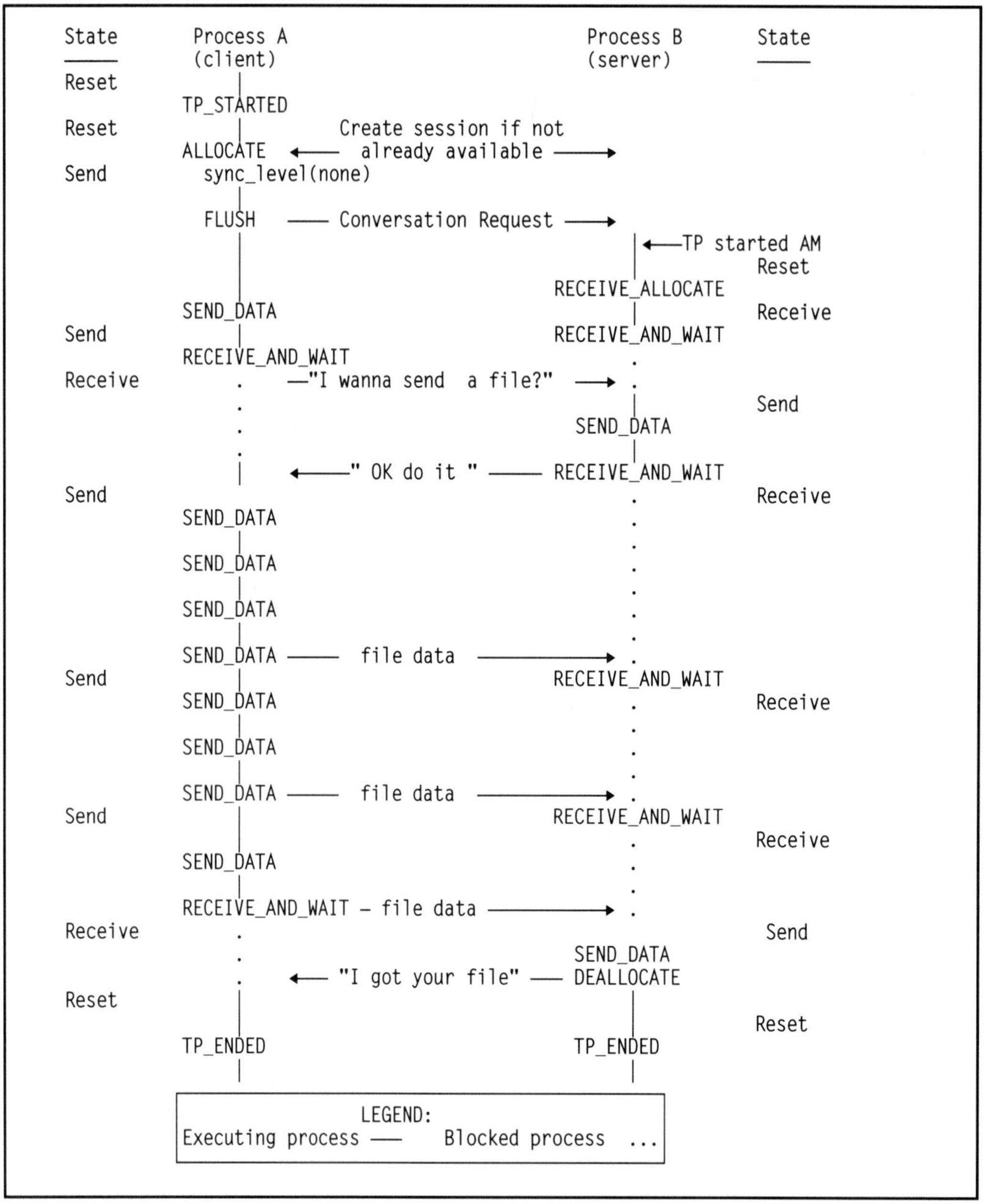

Figure 12-6. Scenario 2: Moving Bulk Data Over an APPC Conversation.

Chapter 13

FX Using NetBIOS

This chapter presents an implementation of the communication layer of the FX protocol using OS/2 EE's **NetBIOS** LAN protocol. The interface will be packaged as a Dynamic Link Library (FXNETB.DLL). The DLL will be created from **FXNETB.C** using the FX make file introduced in Chapter 9.

The NetBIOS communication DLL makes it possible to transfer files using FXREQ and FXSVR, the client-server programs developed in Chapter 9. Figure 13-1 shows how this all comes together. We will use this setup to collect benchmark numbers on the performance of NetBIOS by measuring the time it takes to exchange files between the client and the server.

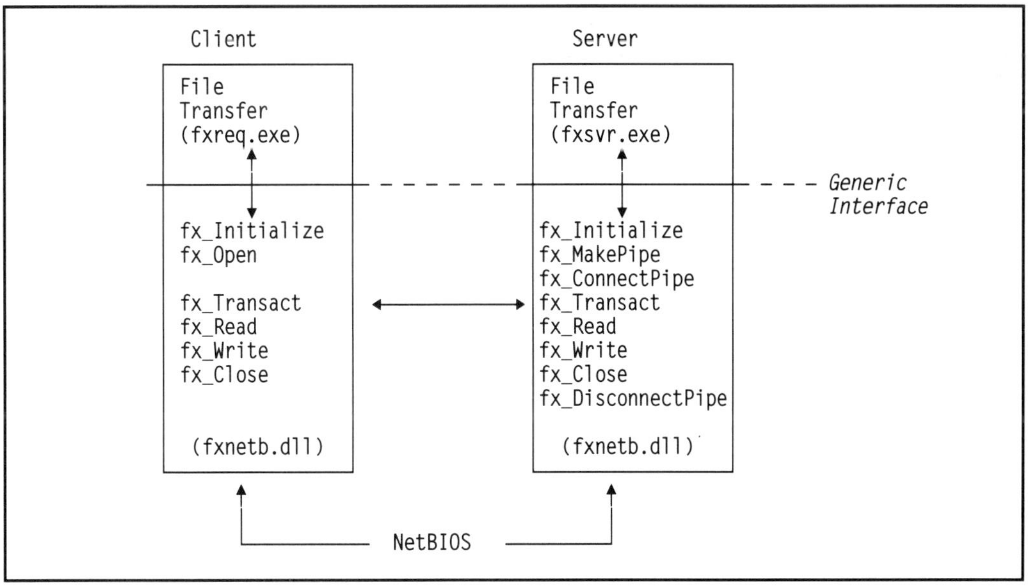

Figure 13-1. Implementing the FX Interface Using the NetBIOS DLL.

The plan for this chapter is to make use of whatever mechanisms are provided by the OS/2 EE's NetBIOS LAN protocol to implement the nine **FX** interface calls shown in Figure 13-1. Figure 13-2 demonstrates how each of the FX calls is implemented by the FXNETB.DLL using OS/2's NetBIOS LAN services. It also shows thc effect each call has on the partner transaction.

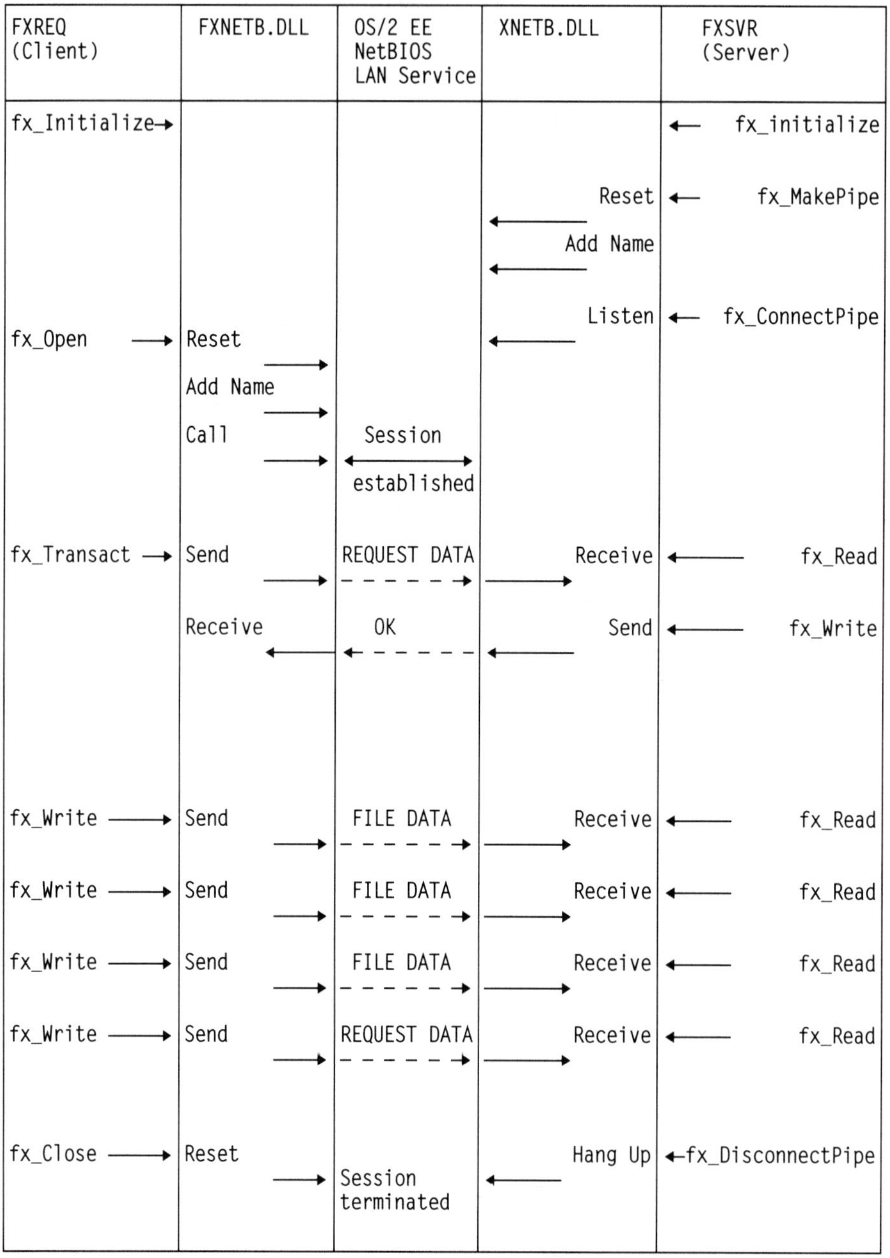

Figure 13-2. Sending a File Using the FXNETB.DLL.

PROGRAMMING NETBIOS

With the exception of Named Pipes, all the OS/2 EE LAN interfaces use a *command with a control block* style of programming that is popular in the communications world. NetBIOS uses a single control block, the Network Control Block or **NCB** (see Figure 13-3), for all of its commands. With a couple of exceptions, the fields in the NCB mean the same thing across all the NetBIOS commands. Different commands, of course, use different NCB fields based on the parameters required to perform an action. In this section, we describe the mechanics of programming NetBIOS's command interface. Once you understand the general principles that are described here, the rest of this chapter is a piece of cake.

How to Invoke a NetBIOS Command

The NetBIOS functions are defined by a set of commands or verbs. The verb to be executed is specified in an NCB which gets passed to an OS/2 API call. Thus, technically speaking, the NetBIOS API consists of a single OS/2 call. Here is how you submit a NetBIOS command in the OS/2 EE environment:

1. Allocate a 64-byte NCB control structure.
2. Zero out all 64 bytes of the NCB regardless of whether the fields are used or not. This prevents residual data from interfering with NetBIOS's operation.
3. Fill in the required NCB fields. This always includes the *command* field, which tells NetBIOS which command to execute. It also includes the relevant parameter fields for that command.
4. Invoke the OS/2 EE NetBIOS DLL (which handles the LAN adapter) by issuing the following API call:

   ```
   extern unsigned PASCAL FAR NETBIOS(char far *);
   ```

   where the parameter passed is the address of the NCB.
5. NetBIOS returns the control to the calling thread differently depending on whether the command is issued in *wait* or *no-wait* modes:

   wait The requesting thread is blocked until the command completes.

   no-wait Control is returned to the calling thread "at the earliest time possible, usually before the command completes." Note that each active no-wait command costs you an OS/2 thread. So if you have too many outstanding commands you may eventually run out of system resources.

   In either case, when the command completes, OS/2 places the appropriate return code in the NCB. In addition, OS/2 can invoke a post-routine when the command completes if the NCB specifies it. The NCB is owned by OS/2 until the command completes. The calling thread can reuse the NCB only after the command completes.

The Network Control Block (NCB)

NetBIOS is operated through the NCB. The nice thing about NetBIOS is that it only has one control block structure; and once you've understood its structure, all that remains for us to explain is which NCB fields get used for a particular command. We present the NCB structure and a definition of its fields in this reference section. The following is a C-language data structure that defines the NCB:

```
struct    network_control_block
 {
  BYTE      command;          /* Netbios command code                  */
  BYTE      retcode;          /* Return code                           */
  BYTE      lsn;              /* Local session number                  */
  BYTE      num;              /* Number of application name            */
  PBYTE     buffer_address;   /* Address of message buffer             */
  USHORT    length;           /* Length of message buffer (in bytes)   */
  BYTE      callname[16];     /* Destination name                      */
  BYTE      name[16];         /* Source name                           */
  BYTE      rto;              /* Receive timeout (units of 0.5 secs)   */
  BYTE      sto;              /* Send timeout  (units of 0.5 secs)     */
  PBYTE     post_address;     /* Address of post routine               */
  BYTE      lana_num;         /* Adapter number                        */
  BYTE      cmd_cplt;         /* Command status                        */
  BYTE      reserve[14];      /* Reserved (except RESET)               */
 };
```

Figure 13-3. NetBIOS Network Control Block (NCB) Type Definitions.

The following is a field-by-field description of the NCB:

command This field contains the NetBIOS command number. When the high-order bit of the command field is set to 1, the command executes in the no-wait mode. NetBIOS will queue a no-wait command and allow several commands to be pending at one time.

retcode This field contains the immediate return code from NetBIOS for both wait and no-wait commands. A zero return code indicates the command completed successfully. In the no-wait mode, NetBIOS first sets this field to X'FF' which means "don't touch the control block or data associated with this command; I'm still working on the command." Eventually, the return_code changes from X'FF' indicating that the command completed. If the value returned is zero, the command is successful.

lsn This field contains a handle that identifies the local session number. It is assigned by NetBIOS after a successful session is established. NetBIOS assigns session numbers between 1 and 254. This field is not used for datagram support.

num This field contains a handle that identifies a network name. It is returned by NetBIOS after an **ADD_NAME** or **ADD_GROUP_NAME** command is executed. This handle and not the name must be used with *all* the datagram commands and for the **RECEIVE_ANY** command. NetBIOS assigns name numbers between 2 and 254. Name number 1 is permanently assigned to NETBIOS_NAME_NUMBER_1 (which is 10 bytes of zeroes followed by the six byte burned-in adapter address).

buffer_address This field contains a pointer to the data buffer. The data buffers are supplied by the application program. (Note: the Reset command uses this field differently).

length This field indicates the length in bytes of the data buffer. For receive type commands, the field is updated by NetBIOS to indicate the number of bytes actually received. (Note: The Reset command uses this field differently).

callname This field contains the 16-byte network name of the remote application the program wants to communicate with. NetBIOS also allows you to send messages to names on your own adapter (this may be useful for testing software). The **CHAIN_SEND** command uses the first six bytes of the callname field to specify the second buffer in the chain. The first two bytes are the length of the buffer and the remaining four bytes point to the second data buffer's location in memory. (Note: The Reset command uses this field differently).

name This field contains the 16-byte network name of the local application. The NETBIOS_NAME_NUMBER_1 (which is 10 bytes of zeroes followed by the six byte node burned-in adapter address) may be used as a name. Any 16-byte combination can be used for the name with the following exceptions:

- The first character cannot be a binary zero or an asterisk "*".
- IBM reserves the values X'00' through X'1F' for the 16th character.
- IBM reserves the characters "IBM" as the first three characters of any name.

(Note: The Reset command uses this field differently).

rto This field is used by the **CALL** and **LISTEN** commands to specify the timeout period (in half-seconds) for all the **RECEIVE** commands associated with that session. The timeout specifies how long to wait for the command to complete before returning an error. The timeout value may be different for each session, but is fixed when the session is first established. The timeout period on the partner's side of the session may also be different. You can use the value X'00' to specify no timeout. (Note: The Reset command uses this field differently).

sto This field is used by the **CALL** and **LISTEN** commands to specify the timeout period (in half-seconds) for all the **SEND** commands associated with that session. The timeout specifies how long to wait for the command to complete before returning an error. The timeout value may be different for each session, but is fixed when the session is first established. The timeout period on the partner's side of the session may also be different. Send timeouts should be used with caution because they will end the session if they expire. You can use the value X'00' to specify no time-out. (Note: The Reset command uses this field differently).

post_address This field contains a pointer to a *post routine* that gets executed when the command completes. For OS/2, this is an ordinary procedure that returns control by issuing an ordinary C-language return. NetBIOS will only look at this field for no-wait commands, otherwise it gets ignored. If this field contains all zeros, the post routine will not be called by NetBIOS, and the application program must check the retcode field for a change from X'FF' for no-wait commands. (Note: The Reset command uses this field differently).

lana_num This field defines which LAN adapter should handle the command. In the case of IBM adapters, X'00' defines the primary adapter and X'01' defines the secondary adapter. (Note: The adapter must have the corresponding primary/alternate switch set correctly).

cmd_cplt This field is the same as the retcode field.

reserve This field contains 14 bytes reserved as a work area by NetBIOS.

FXNETB.C: THE NETBIOS FX DLL

The code we present in this section *does not* contain a main() procedure. The FX DLLs are simply functions that get linked to a (.EXE) file at runtime. The main() procedure is provided by the program that calls the DLL functions. This means **FXNETB.C** is not a separate program; it contains a list of functions that get packaged in a DLL.

FXNETB.C: General Stuff

The listing (see Figure 13-4) contains all the miscellaneous programming "stuff" that will be used by the FX procedures. This includes the usual declarations of constants, global variables, and forward declarations of functions. Notice that we've included, with the header material, all the OS/2 EE NetBIOS structures. The NCB was declared as C-language union to take care of all the deviations introduced by the **RESET** command.

The functions that are provided in this module fall into two categories: **FX** functions and *helper* functions. The helper functions, as usual, are used to provide common services for that module. In addition to the ubiquitous **print_error()**, we introduce seven general purpose NetBIOS helper functions. These functions are made general enough so that they can be reused "as is" in future programs. We will introduce the helper functions at the point where they first get used.

```
/*****************************************************************************/
/*  MODULE NAME: FXNETB  - NETBIOS communication.                            */
/*                                                                           */
/*  PROGRAM DESCRIPTION:  This module is a part of the FX file transfer      */
/*    programs.  Refer to the FXR.C program module for a program overview.   */
/*    This module implements the fx_* file transfer procedures using OS/2    */
/*    EE 1.2 NETBIOS.                                                        */
/*                                                                           */
/*****************************************************************************/
#include <stdio.h>                      /* For printf() & NULL               */
#include <stdlib.h>                     /* For conversion routines           */
#include <string.h>                     /* For string functions              */

#include <os2.h>

/*-------------------------------------------------------------------------*/
/* defines                                                                   */
/*-------------------------------------------------------------------------*/
                   /*-------------------------------------*/
                   /* return code defines                   */
                   /*-------------------------------------*/
#define FAILED     -1
#define GOOD        0
#define WARNING     1

                   /*-------------------------------------*/
                   /* NCB command code defines              */
                   /*-------------------------------------*/
#define   NB_CALL_WAIT                                 0x0010
#define   NB_LISTEN_WAIT                               0x0011
#define   NB_HANG_UP_WAIT                              0x0012
#define   NB_SEND_WAIT                                 0x0014
#define   NB_RECEIVE_WAIT                              0x0015
#define   NB_ADD_NAME_WAIT                             0x0030
#define   NB_RESET_WAIT                                0x0032

                   /*-------------------------------------*/
                   /* Netbios session resource  defines     */
                   /*-------------------------------------*/
#define LANA               0          /* lan adapter number                  */
#define NET_LSN            2          /* number of sessions                  */
#define NET_NCB            4          /* number of outstanding NCBs          */
#define NET_NAMES          2          /* number of names                     */
#define REQUEST_RESOURCES  0          /* request new resources               */
#define RELEASE_RESOURCES  1          /* release all resources               */

                   /*-------------------------------------*/
                   /* Netbios timeout defines               */
                   /*-------------------------------------*/
#define RECV_TIMEOUT    20            /* receive timeout in seconds          */
#define SEND_TIMEOUT    20            /* send timeout in seconds             */
```

Figure 13-4 (Part 1 of 4). FXNETB.C: General Header Stuff and print_error()

```
                    /*---------------------------------------*/
                    /* general structure for NCB commands   */
                    /*---------------------------------------*/
typedef struct
   { BYTE   command;                   /* Netbios command code          */
     BYTE   retcode;                   /* Return code                   */
     BYTE   lsn;                       /* Local session number          */
     BYTE   num;                       /* Number of application name    */
     PBYTE  buffer_address;            /* Address of message buffer     */
     USHORT length;                    /* length of message buffer      */
     BYTE   callname[16];              /* Destination name              */
     BYTE   name[16];                  /* Source name                   */
     BYTE   rto;                       /* Receive timeout               */
     BYTE   sto;                       /* Send timeout                  */
     PBYTE  post_address;              /* Address of post routine       */
     BYTE   lana_num;                  /* Adapter number                */
     BYTE   cmd_cplt;                  /* Command status                */
     BYTE   reserve[14];               /* Reserved (except RESET)       */
   } CMD_NCB;

                    /*---------------------------------------*/
                    /* reset NCB structure as used in DLL   */
                    /*---------------------------------------*/
typedef struct
   { BYTE   command;                   /* Netbios command code          */
     BYTE   retcode;                   /* Return code                   */
     BYTE   lsn;                       /* 0 = request 1= free resources */
     BYTE   num;                       /* Not Used                      */
     PBYTE  buffer_address;            /* Not Used                      */
     USHORT length;                    /* Not used                      */
     BYTE   req_sessions;              /* # of sessions requested       */
     BYTE   req_commands;              /* # of commands requested       */
     BYTE   req_names;                 /* # of names requested          */
     BYTE   req_name_one;              /* Name number one request       */
     BYTE   not_used2[12];             /* Not used                      */
     BYTE   act_sessions;              /* # of sessions obtained from DLL    */
     BYTE   act_commands;              /* # of commands obtained from DLL    */
     BYTE   act_names;                 /* # of names obtained from DLL       */
     BYTE   act_name_one;              /* Name number one response from DLL  */
     BYTE   not_used3[4];              /* Not used                      */
     BYTE   load_session;              /* Number of sessions at load from DLL*/
     BYTE   load_commands;             /* Number of commands at load from DLL*/
     BYTE   load_names;                /* Number of names at load from DLL   */
     BYTE   load_stations;             /* Number of stations at load from DLL*/
     BYTE   not_used4[2];              /* Not used                      */
     BYTE   load_remote_names;         /* Number of remote names from DLL    */
     BYTE   not_used5[5];              /* Not used                      */
     USHORT dd_id;                     /* Not used                      */
     BYTE   lana_num;                  /* Adapter number                */
     BYTE   not_used6;                 /* Not used                      */
     BYTE   reserve[14];               /* NCB error information         */
   } RESET_NCB;
typedef union
   { CMD_NCB   cmd_ncb;
     RESET_NCB reset_ncb;
   } NCB;
```

Figure 13-4 (Part 2 of 4). FXNETB.C: General Header Stuff and print_error()

```
/*-----------------------------------------------------------------------*/
/* forward declaration for functions in this module                      */
/*-----------------------------------------------------------------------*/
                    /*----------------------------------*/
                    /* communication functions          */
                    /*----------------------------------*/
USHORT fx_Initialize(PVOID *, PUSHORT);
USHORT fx_MakePipe(VOID);
USHORT fx_ConnectPipe(VOID);
USHORT fx_DisconnectPipe(VOID);
USHORT fx_Open(VOID);
USHORT fx_Write(PVOID, USHORT, PUSHORT);
USHORT fx_Read(PVOID,  USHORT, PUSHORT);
USHORT fx_Transact(PVOID, USHORT, PVOID, USHORT, PVOID);
USHORT fx_Close(VOID);
                    /*----------------------------------*/
                    /* netbios helper functions         */
                    /*----------------------------------*/
BYTE netbios_reset(BYTE);
BYTE netbios_reset(BYTE);
BYTE netbios_add_name(PCHAR);
BYTE netbios_call(PCHAR, PCHAR, PBYTE);
BYTE netbios_listen(PCHAR, PCHAR, PBYTE);
BYTE netbios_hang_up(BYTE);
BYTE netbios_send(PVOID, USHORT, BYTE);
BYTE netbios_recv(PVOID, USHORT, BYTE, PUSHORT);

                    /*----------------------------------*/
                    /* error display function           */
                    /*----------------------------------*/
VOID print_error(USHORT, PCHAR, PCHAR, USHORT);

                    /*----------------------------------*/
                    /* netbios dynamic link function    */
                    /*----------------------------------*/
extern unsigned PASCAL FAR NETBIOS (PVOID);

/*-----------------------------------------------------------------------*/
/* Configuration variables, initialized after fx_Initialize()           */
/* function call.                                                        */
/*-----------------------------------------------------------------------*/
CHAR   PipeName[128];
USHORT FileBufferSize;

/*-----------------------------------------------------------------------*/
/* global variables for this module.                                     */
/*-----------------------------------------------------------------------*/
BYTE    lsn;                        /* handle from DosOpen/DosMakeNmPipe  */
USHORT  rc;                         /* return code                        */
CHAR    server_name[17];            /* server name  for ncb name field    */
CHAR    requester_name[17];         /* requester name for ncb name field  */
USHORT  server;                     /* client/server indicator            */
NCB     ncb;                        /* network control block              */
```

Figure 13-4 (Part 3 of 4). FXNETB.C: General Header Stuff and print_error()

```
/*-----------------------------------------------------------------------*/
/* Error Display Routine                                                 */
/*-----------------------------------------------------------------------*/
VOID print_error(USHORT Error, PCHAR msg, PCHAR file, USHORT line)
{
 printf("NETBIOS Error %u (0x%x) detected while %s at line %u in file %s.\n",
        Error, Error, msg, line, file);
} /* end print_error */
```

Figure 13-4 (Part 4 of 4). FXNETB.C: General Header Stuff and print_error()

FXNETB.C: fx_Initialize()

The **fx_Initialize()** function (see Figure 13-5) reads a protocol-specific configuration file to obtain the parameters required to initialize the system. The name of the user specified configuration file for NetBIOS is: **fxnetb.cfg**. Here is an example of a such a file:

```
PIPE_NAME         = NETSVR
FILE_BUFFER_SIZE  = 512
```

Here's what these two parameters do:

PIPE_NAME This parameter is used to derive the network name of the client and server. The configuration file given above will result with a client machine called NETSVR.REQ and a server machine called NETSVR.SVR.

FILE_BUFFER_SIZE This parameter defines the size (in bytes) of the message buffer. This is the buffer we will use for reading and writing data to the disk and for exchanging messages across the LAN or the IPC. The memory space for this parameter will be dynamically allocated. The **fx_Initialize()** function returns a pointer to this buffer and its size to the application. One of the factors we will measure in our benchmarks is the effect of the message buffer size on performance.

No OS/2 calls are introduced in this function which was introduced in the FX protocol as a "catch-all" for performing protocol-specific start-up actions.

```
/*-----------------------------------------------------------------------*/
/* This function reads communication specific parameters and allocates a    */
/* buffer for communication.  A pointer to the buffer and the buffer size is */
/* returned.                                                                 */
/*-----------------------------------------------------------------------*/
USHORT fx_Initialize(PVOID *buffer_p , PUSHORT size)
{
  FILE    *config_file;                /* Input file control block           */
  CHAR     line[80];                   /* one line of config file            */

  printf("Reading configuration parameters.\n");
  /*-----------------------------------*/
  /* open the configuration file       */
  /*-----------------------------------*/
  if (NULL == (config_file = fopen("fxnetb.cfg","r")))
     {print_error(rc,"opening configuration file",__FILE__,__LINE__);
      return(FAILED);
     }
  else
     /*------------------------------------*/
     /* read the configuration parameters.  */
     /* The parameters are expected to be:  */
     /*     - in the form <name = value>     */
     /*     - if value is a string enclose   */
     /*       in double quotes               */
     /*     - in the order read below        */
     /*------------------------------------*/
     {
       fgets(line, sizeof(line), config_file);
       if (sscanf(line,"PIPE_NAME = %s ", PipeName) != 1)
          {print_error(rc,"reading PipeName from configuration",
                       __FILE__,__LINE__);
           return(FAILED);
          }
       printf("PIPE_NAME = %s \n", PipeName);

       fgets(line, sizeof(line), config_file);
       if (sscanf(line,"FILE_BUFFER_SIZE = %u ", &FileBufferSize) != 1)
          {print_error(rc,"reading FileBufferSize from configuration",
                       __FILE__,__LINE__);
           return(FAILED);
          }
       printf("FILE_BUFFER_SIZE = %u \n", FileBufferSize);
     } /* end if */

  fclose(config_file);
  /*-----------------------------------*/
  /* initialize server_name and        */
  /*   requester_name variable for use */
  /*   in ncb commands.                */
  /*-----------------------------------*/
  strcat(PipeName,"                 "); /* make pipe name >=16 char long       */

  strncpy(server_name, PipeName, 16);
  strncpy(&server_name[12], ".SVR", 4);

  strncpy(requester_name, PipeName, 16);
  strncpy(&requester_name[12], ".REQ", 4);
```

Figure 13-5 (Part 1 of 2). FXNETB.C: fx_Initialize().

```
   /*----------------------------------*/
   /* allocate buffer, return pointer     */
   /* and size                            */
   /*----------------------------------*/
   if ((*buffer_p = (void *)malloc(FileBufferSize)) == NULL)
      {print_error(rc,"allocating file buffer",__FILE__,__LINE__);
       return(FAILED);
      }
   *size = FileBufferSize;

   return(GOOD);
 } /* end fx_Initialize */
```

Figure 13-5 (Part 2 of 2). FXNETB.C: fx_Initialize().

FXNETB.C: fx_MakePipe()

The **fx_MakePipe()** function (see Figure 13-6) is used by the server side of an FX pipe to establish the pipe. We provide the function using NetBIOS as follows:

1. Issue a NetBIOS **RESET** command to allocate network resources to the process. The NetBIOS **RESET** command is executed by the **netbios_reset()** helper function listed in Figure 13-7.
2. Issue a NetBIOS **ADD NAME** to place the server's name on the network. The NetBIOS **ADD NAME** command is executed by the **netbios_add_name()** helper function listed in Figure 13-8.

```
/*---------------------------------------------------------------------------*/
/* This function establishes the server end of the communication pipe.       */
/*---------------------------------------------------------------------------*/
USHORT fx_MakePipe(VOID)
{
  /*----------------------------------*/
  /* remember that this is a server     */
  /*----------------------------------*/
  server = TRUE;

  /*----------------------------------*/
  /* perform netbios reset              */
  /*----------------------------------*/
  rc = netbios_reset(REQUEST_RESOURCES);
  if (rc)
     {print_error(rc,"resetting netbios",__FILE__,__LINE__);
      return(FAILED);
     }
```

Figure 13-6 (Part 1 of 2). FXNETB.C: MakePipe().

```
   /*-------------------------------------------*/
   /* perform netbios add name                  */
   /*-------------------------------------------*/
   rc = netbios_add_name(server_name);
   if (rc)
      {print_error(rc,"adding netbios name",__FILE__,__LINE__);
       return(FAILED);
      }

   return(GOOD);

} /* end fx_MakePipe */
```

Figure 13-6 (Part 2 of 2). FXNETB.C: MakePipe().

FXNETB.C: netbios_reset()

The NetBIOS **RESET** command can be used in one of two ways:

- To request resources from the NetBIOS pool.
- To release resources to the NetBIOS pool.

The **netbios_reset()** helper routine (see Figure 13-7) performs either reset, depending on the value of the *request_release* parameter that gets passed to it. Here is what **netbios_reset()** does:

1. It clears the NCB.
2. It fills in the NCB request fields for this command. The **RESET** command uses the **ncb.reset_ncb** type (whose typedef is given in Figure 13-4 on page 335). This is a special type of NCB used only by **RESET**, which requires a redefinition of the fields in order to specify the resources obtained from, or released to, the NetBIOS pool.
3. It issues a NetBIOS API call in wait mode.
4. It returns the *retcode* field contents.

```
/*----------------------------------------------------------------------*/
/* netbios reset helper routine                                         */
/*----------------------------------------------------------------------*/
BYTE
netbios_reset(BYTE request_release)
{
  memset(&ncb.reset_ncb, 0, sizeof(ncb.reset_ncb));/* set ncb to all zeros   */

  ncb.reset_ncb.command  = NB_RESET_WAIT;         /* command = reset         */
  ncb.reset_ncb.lana_num = LANA;                  /* lan adapter number      */
  ncb.reset_ncb.lsn = request_release;            /* 0=request, 1=release    */
  ncb.reset_ncb.req_sessions = NET_LSN;           /* number of sessions      */
  ncb.reset_ncb.req_commands = NET_NCB;           /* number of outstanding NCB*/
  ncb.reset_ncb.req_names    = NET_NAMES;         /* number of names         */

  NETBIOS(&ncb);                                  /* netbios call            */

  return(ncb.reset_ncb.retcode);
}
```

Figure 13-7. FXNETB.C: netbios_reset().

FXNETB.C: netbios_add_name()

The **netbios_add_name()** helper routine (see Figure 13-8) adds a specified name to the network. It does this by first clearing the NCB. Then it fills the NCB request fields for this command using a regular **ncb.cmd_ncb** type. Following that, a NetBIOS API call is issued in wait mode. Finally, the *retcode* field content is returned to the caller.

```
/*----------------------------------------------------------------------*/
/* netbios add name helper routine                                      */
/*----------------------------------------------------------------------*/
BYTE
netbios_add_name(PCHAR name)
{
  memset(&ncb.cmd_ncb, 0, sizeof(ncb.cmd_ncb));  /* set ncb to all zeros     */

  ncb.cmd_ncb.command  = NB_ADD_NAME_WAIT;       /* command = add name       */
  ncb.cmd_ncb.lana_num = LANA;                   /* lan adapter number       */
  strncpy(ncb.cmd_ncb.name, name, 16 );          /* copy 16 char name to ncb */

  NETBIOS(&ncb);                                 /* netbios call             */

  return(ncb.cmd_ncb.retcode);
}
```

Figure 13-8. FXNETB.C: netbios_add_name().

FXNETB.C: fx ConnectPipe()

The **fx_ConnectPipe()** function (see Figure 13-9) is used to establish a connection on the server side of an FX pipe. We provide the function with NetBIOS by issuing a

LISTEN command. This is done by calling **netbios_listen()**, the NetBIOS helper routine listed in Figure 13-10.

```
/*-------------------------------------------------------------------------*/
/* function to enable the server end of the communication pipe.            */
/*-------------------------------------------------------------------------*/
USHORT fx_ConnectPipe(VOID)
{
  /*-----------------------------------*/
  /* perform netbios listen            */
  /*-----------------------------------*/
  rc = netbios_listen(requester_name,  /* caller's name                  */
                      server_name,     /* this station's name            */
                      &lsn);           /* local session number returned  */
  if (rc)
     {print_error(rc,"performing a netbios listen",__FILE__,__LINE__);
      return(FAILED);
     }

  return(GOOD);
} /* end fx_ConnectPipe */
```

Figure 13-9. FXNETB.C: fx_ConnectPipe().

FXNETB.C: netbios_listen()

The **netbios_listen()** helper routine (see Figure 13-10) waits for a remote *caller_name* to call a local *station_name*. It does this by first clearing the NCB. Then it fills the NCB request fields for this command using a regular **ncb.cmd_ncb** type. Following that, a NetBIOS API call is issued in wait mode. The call completes when a call is received from the remote station. The session is then established. Finally, the *retcode* field content is returned to the caller as well as a pointer to the local session number field (*lsn*) returned by NetBIOS. The *lsn* contains a number that uniquely identifies the session.

```
/*---------------------------------------------------------------------------*/
/* netbios listen name helper routine                                        */
/*---------------------------------------------------------------------------*/
BYTE
netbios_listen(PCHAR caller_name, PCHAR station_name, PBYTE lsn)
{
  memset(&ncb.cmd_ncb, 0, sizeof(ncb.cmd_ncb)); /* set ncb to all zeros     */

  ncb.cmd_ncb.command  = NB_LISTEN_WAIT;        /* command = listen_wait    */
  ncb.cmd_ncb.lana_num = LANA;                  /* lan adapter number       */
  ncb.cmd_ncb.rto      = RECV_TIMEOUT<<1;       /* times 2 since in         */
  ncb.cmd_ncb.sto      = SEND_TIMEOUT<<1;       /* steps of 500 msecs       */
  strncpy(ncb.cmd_ncb.name, station_name, 16 ); /* local station name       */
  strncpy(ncb.cmd_ncb.callname, caller_name, 16);/* caller's name           */

  NETBIOS(&ncb);                                /* netbios call             */

  *lsn = ncb.cmd_ncb.lsn;
  return(ncb.cmd_ncb.retcode);
}
```

Figure 13-10. FXNETB.C: netbios_listen().

FXNETB.C: fx_DisconnectPipe()

The **fx_DisconnectPipe()** function (see Figure 13-11) is used to disconnect the server side of an FX pipe. We provide the function using NetBIOS by issuing a **HANG UP** command. This is done by calling **netbios_hang_up()**, the NetBIOS helper routine listed in Figure 13-12.

```
/*---------------------------------------------------------------------------*/
/* function to disable the server end of the communication pipe.             */
/*---------------------------------------------------------------------------*/
USHORT fx_DisconnectPipe(VOID)
{
  /*------------------------------*/
  /* perform netbios hangup       */
  /*------------------------------*/
  rc = netbios_hang_up(lsn);
  if (rc)
     {print_error(rc,"performing a netbios hang up",__FILE__,__LINE__);
      return(FAILED);
     }

  return(GOOD);
} /* end fx_DisconnectPipe */
```

Figure 13-11. FXNETB.C: fx_DisconnectPipe().

FXNETB.C: netbios_hang_up()

The **netbios_hang_up()** helper routine (see Figure 13-12) disconnects from a session identified by a *lsn* handle. It does this by first clearing the NCB. It then fills the NCB request fields for this command using a regular **ncb.cmd_ncb** type. Following that, a NetBIOS API call is issued in wait mode. Finally, the *retcode* field content is returned to the caller.

```
/*-----------------------------------------------------------------------*/
/* netbios hang up helper routine                                        */
/*-----------------------------------------------------------------------*/
BYTE
netbios_hang_up(BYTE lsn)
{
  memset(&ncb.cmd_ncb, 0, sizeof(ncb.cmd_ncb)); /* set ncb to all zeros     */
  ncb.cmd_ncb.command  = NB_HANG_UP_WAIT;       /* command = hang_up_wait   */
  ncb.cmd_ncb.lana_num = LANA;                  /* lan adapter number       */
  ncb.cmd_ncb.lsn      = lsn;                   /* local session number     */

  NETBIOS(&ncb);                                /* netbios call             */

  return(ncb.cmd_ncb.retcode);
}
```

Figure 13-12. FXNETB.C: netbios_hang_up().

FXNETB.C: fx_Open()

The **fx_Open()** function (see Figure 13-13) is used to establish the client side of an FX pipe. We provide the function using NetBIOS as follows:

1. We first issue a **RESET** command to obtain resources from the NetBIOS pool. This is done by invoking the **netbios_reset()** helper function listed in Figure 13-7 on page 342.
2. We then issue an **ADD NAME** command to add the client's name to the network. This is done by invoking the **netbios_add_name()** helper function listed in Figure 13-8 on page 342.
3. We then issue a **CALL** command to establish a session with the server. This is done by invoking the **netbios_call()** helper function listed in Figure 13-14 on page 347. (Note: The requester_name and server_name are both derived from the user-specified name in **fxnetb.cfg**).

```
/*-------------------------------------------------------------------------*/
/* function a requester uses to prepare a pipe for communication.          */
/*-------------------------------------------------------------------------*/
USHORT fx_Open(VOID)
{
  /*-------------------------------*/
  /* remember that this is not a server */
  /*-------------------------------*/
  server = FALSE;

  /*-------------------------------*/
  /* perform netbios reset         */
  /*-------------------------------*/
  rc = netbios_reset(REQUEST_RESOURCES);
  if (rc)
     {print_error(rc,"resetting netbios",__FILE__,__LINE__);
      return(FAILED);
     }

  /*-------------------------------*/
  /* perform netbios add name      */
  /*-------------------------------*/
  rc = netbios_add_name(requester_name);
  if (rc)
     {print_error(rc,"adding a netbios name",__FILE__,__LINE__);
      return(FAILED);
     }

  /*-------------------------------*/
  /* perform netbios call          */
  /*-------------------------------*/
  rc = netbios_call(server_name,      /* name being called             */
                    requester_name,   /* station name                  */
                    &lsn);            /* local station number returned */
  if (rc)
     {print_error(rc,"performing a netbios call",__FILE__,__LINE__);
      return(FAILED);
     }

  return(GOOD);
} /* end fx_Open */
```

Figure 13-13. FXNETB.C: fx_Open().

FXNETB.C: netbios_call()

The **netbios_call**() helper routine (see Figure 13-14 on page 347) issues a **CALL** command. The purpose is to establish a session between remote *callname* (which has an outstanding **LISTEN**) and a local *station_name*. This is done by first clearing the NCB. The NCB request fields for this command are then entered using a regular **ncb.cmd_ncb** type. Following that, a NetBIOS API call is issued in wait mode. The function completes when a session is established with the remote name. Finally, the *retcode* field content is returned to the caller, as well as a pointer to the local session number field (*lsn*) returned by NetBIOS. The *lsn* contains a number that uniquely identifies the session.

```
/*--------------------------------------------------------------------------*/
/* netbios call name helper routine                                         */
/*--------------------------------------------------------------------------*/
BYTE
netbios_call(PCHAR callname, PCHAR station_name, PBYTE lsn)
{
  memset(&ncb.cmd_ncb, 0, sizeof(ncb.cmd_ncb));  /* set ncb to all zeros     */

  ncb.cmd_ncb.command  = NB_CALL_WAIT;           /* command = call wait      */
  ncb.cmd_ncb.lana_num = LANA;                   /* lan adapter number       */
  ncb.cmd_ncb.rto      = RECV_TIMEOUT<<1;        /* times 2 since in         */
  ncb.cmd_ncb.sto      = SEND_TIMEOUT<<1;        /* steps of 500 msecs       */
  strncpy(ncb.cmd_ncb.name, station_name, 16 );  /* local station name       */
  strncpy(ncb.cmd_ncb.callname, callname, 16);   /* call name                */

  NETBIOS(&ncb);                                 /* netbios call             */

  *lsn = ncb.cmd_ncb.lsn;
  return(ncb.cmd_ncb.retcode);
}
```

Figure 13-14. FXNETB.C: netbios_call().

FXNETB.C: fx_Write()

The **fx_Write()** function (see Figure 13-15) is used to send information over an FX pipe. We provide this function using NetBIOS by invoking **netbios_send()**, helper function listed in Figure 13-16.

```
/*--------------------------------------------------------------------------*/
/* function both requester and server use to write to a pipe.               */
/*--------------------------------------------------------------------------*/
USHORT fx_Write(PVOID BufferArea, USHORT BufferLength, PUSHORT BytesWritten)
{
  /*------------------------------------*/
  /* perform netbios send               */
  /*------------------------------------*/
  rc = netbios_send(BufferArea,        /* buffer to send                    */
                    BufferLength,      /* length of buffer                  */
                    lsn);              /* session number                    */
  if (rc)
     {print_error(rc,"performing a netbios send",__FILE__,__LINE__);
      return(FAILED);
     }

  *BytesWritten = BufferLength;        /* success, all bytes sent           */
  return(GOOD);
} /* end fx_Write */
```

Figure 13-15. FXNETB.C: fx_Write().

FXNETB.C: netbios_send()

The **netbios_send()** helper routine (see Figure 13-16 on page 348) issues a **SEND** command. This is done by first clearing the NCB. The NCB request fields for this command are then entered using a regular **ncb.cmd_ncb** type. Following that, a NetBIOS API call is issued in wait mode. The function completes when the message is sent successfully. The *retcode* field content is returned to the caller.

```
/*---------------------------------------------------------------------------*/
/* netbios send helper routine                                              */
/*---------------------------------------------------------------------------*/
BYTE
netbios_send(PVOID buffer, USHORT length, BYTE lsn)
{
  memset(&ncb.cmd_ncb, 0, sizeof(ncb.cmd_ncb));  /* set ncb to all zeros     */

  ncb.cmd_ncb.command  = NB_SEND_WAIT;           /* command = send_wait      */
  ncb.cmd_ncb.lana_num = LANA;                   /* lan adapter number       */
  ncb.cmd_ncb.lsn      = lsn;                    /* local session number     */
  ncb.cmd_ncb.buffer_address = buffer;           /* address of buffer to send*/
  ncb.cmd_ncb.length   = length;                 /* length of send buffer    */

  NETBIOS(&ncb);                                 /* netbios call             */

  return(ncb.cmd_ncb.retcode);
}
```

Figure 13-16. FXNETB.C: netbios_send().

FXNETB.C: fx_Read()

The **fx_Read()** function (see Figure 13-17) is used to read information over an FX pipe. We provide this function using NetBIOS by invoking the **netbios_recv()** helper function listed in Figure 13-18.

```
/*---------------------------------------------------------------------*/
/* function both requester and server use to read from a pipe.         */
/*---------------------------------------------------------------------*/
USHORT fx_Read(PVOID BufferArea, USHORT BufferLength, PUSHORT BytesRead)
{
  /*------------------------------------*/
  /* perform netbios receive            */
  /*------------------------------------*/
  rc = netbios_recv(BufferArea,       /* buffer to send                 */
                    BufferLength,     /* length of buffer               */
                    lsn,              /* session number                 */
                    BytesRead);       /* number of bytes read returned  */

  if (rc)
     {print_error(rc,"performing a netbios receive",__FILE__,__LINE__);
      return(FAILED);
     }
  return(GOOD);
} /* end fx_Read */
```

Figure 13-17. FXNETB.C: fx_Read().

FXNETB.C: netbios_recv()

The **netbios_recv()** helper routine (see Figure 13-18) issues a **RECEIVE** command. This is done by first clearing the NCB. The NCB request fields for this command are then entered using a regular **ncb.cmd_ncb** type. Following that, a NetBIOS API call is issued in wait mode. The function completes when a message is successfully received. The *retcode* field content is returned to the caller.

```
/*---------------------------------------------------------------------*/
/* netbios receive helper routine                                      */
/*---------------------------------------------------------------------*/
BYTE
netbios_recv(PVOID buffer, USHORT length, BYTE lsn, PUSHORT bytes_received)
{
  memset(&ncb.cmd_ncb, 0, sizeof(ncb.cmd_ncb));  /* set ncb to all zeros     */

  ncb.cmd_ncb.command  = NB_RECEIVE_WAIT;        /* command = receive        */
  ncb.cmd_ncb.lana_num = LANA;                   /* lan adapter number       */
  ncb.cmd_ncb.lsn      = lsn;                    /* local session number     */
  ncb.cmd_ncb.length   = length;                 /* length of receive buffer */

  NETBIOS(&ncb);                                 /* netbios call             */

  *bytes_received = ncb.cmd_ncb.length;          /* length of data received  */
  return(ncb.cmd_ncb.retcode);
}
```

Figure 13-18. FXNETB.C: netbios_recv().

FXNETB.C: fx_Transact()

The **fx_Transact()** function (see Figure 13-19) sends a message and receives a reply over an FX pipe. This function is provided in NetBIOS by issuing a **SEND** command followed by a **RECEIVE** command. This is done by invoking **fx_write()** (see Figure 13-15 on page 347), followed by **fx_read()** (see Figure 13-17).

```
/*-----------------------------------------------------------------------*/
/* function requester uses to request a service.                         */
/*-----------------------------------------------------------------------*/
USHORT fx_Transact(PVOID InBufferArea,  USHORT InBufferLength,
                   PVOID OutBufferArea, USHORT OutBufferLength,
                   PUSHORT BytesRead)
{
  USHORT BytesWritten;

  rc = fx_Write(InBufferArea, InBufferLength, &BytesWritten);
  if (rc)
     {print_error(rc,"writing during a transaction",__FILE__,__LINE__);
      return(FAILED);
     }

  rc = fx_Read(OutBufferArea, OutBufferLength, BytesRead);
  if (rc)
     {print_error(rc,"reading during a transaction",__FILE__,__LINE__);
      return(FAILED);
     }

  return(GOOD);
} /* end fx_Transact */
```

Figure 13-19. FXNETB.C: fx_Transact().

FXNETB.C: fx_Close()

The **fx_Close()** function (see Figure 13-20) closes an FX pipe. In terms of NetBIOS, this means issuing a **RESET** command with the directive to RELEASE_RESOURCES. This function is only performed on the client side. On the Server side, the process is terminated by a Control-Break. OS/2 EE automatically issues a NetBIOS **RESET** on behalf of a terminating process which means that no action is required from our program.

```
/*------------------------------------------------------------------------*/
/* function requester uses to end communication with a server.            */
/*------------------------------------------------------------------------*/
USHORT fx_Close(VOID)
{
  if (!server)
     {
      /*--------------------------------*/
      /* perform netbios reset          */
      /*--------------------------------*/
      rc = netbios_reset(RELEASE_RESOURCES);
      if (rc)
         {print_error(rc,"resetting netbios",__FILE__,__LINE__);
          return(FAILED);
          }
     }

  return(GOOD);
} /* end fx_Close */
```

Figure 13-20. FXNETB.C: fx_Close().

Chapter 14

FX with APPC

This chapter presents an implementation of the communication layer of the FX protocol using OS/2 EE's **APPC** LAN protocol. The interface will be packaged as a Dynamic Link Library (FXAPPC.DLL). The DLL will be created from **FXAPPC.C** using the FX make file introduced in Chapter 9.

The APPC communication DLL makes it possible to transfer files using FXREQ and FXSVR, the client-server programs developed in Chapter 9. Figure 14-1 shows how this all comes together. We will use this setup to collect benchmark numbers on the performance of APPC by measuring the time it takes to exchange files between the client and the server.

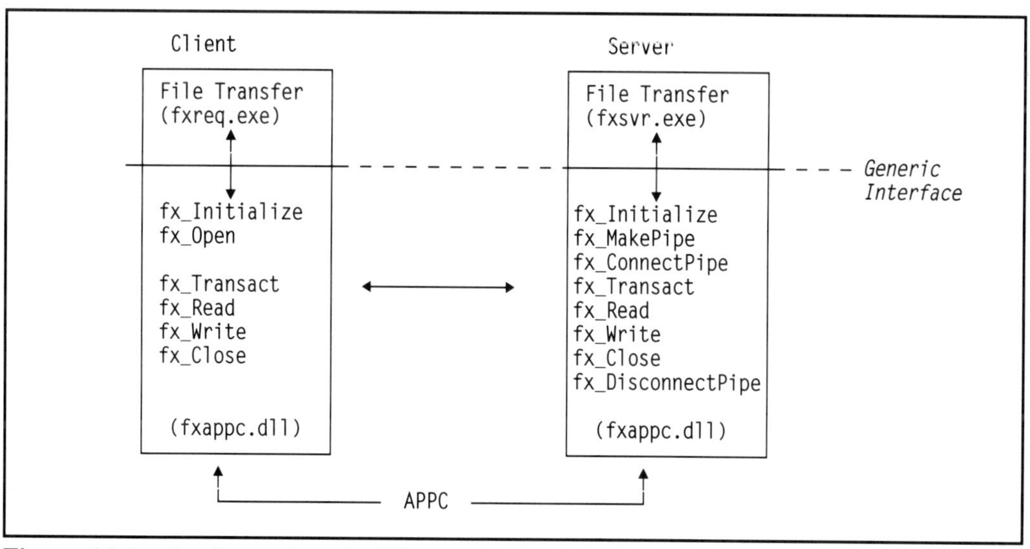

Figure 14-1. Implementing the FX Interface Using the FXAPPC.DLL.

The plan for this chapter is to make use of whatever mechanisms are provided by the OS/2 EE's APPC protocol to implement the nine **FX** interface calls shown in Figure 14-1. Figure 14-2 demonstrates how the FXAPPC.DLL is used to transfer a file and shows the effect each call has on the APPC partner transaction. Notice that the server program in the scenario is not started by the Attach Manager. We start from the command line like any other program. The scenario also demonstrates APPC's blocking feature. As was explained in the tutorials, blocking is used to lump together the data from many commands and send it over the network in one chunk.

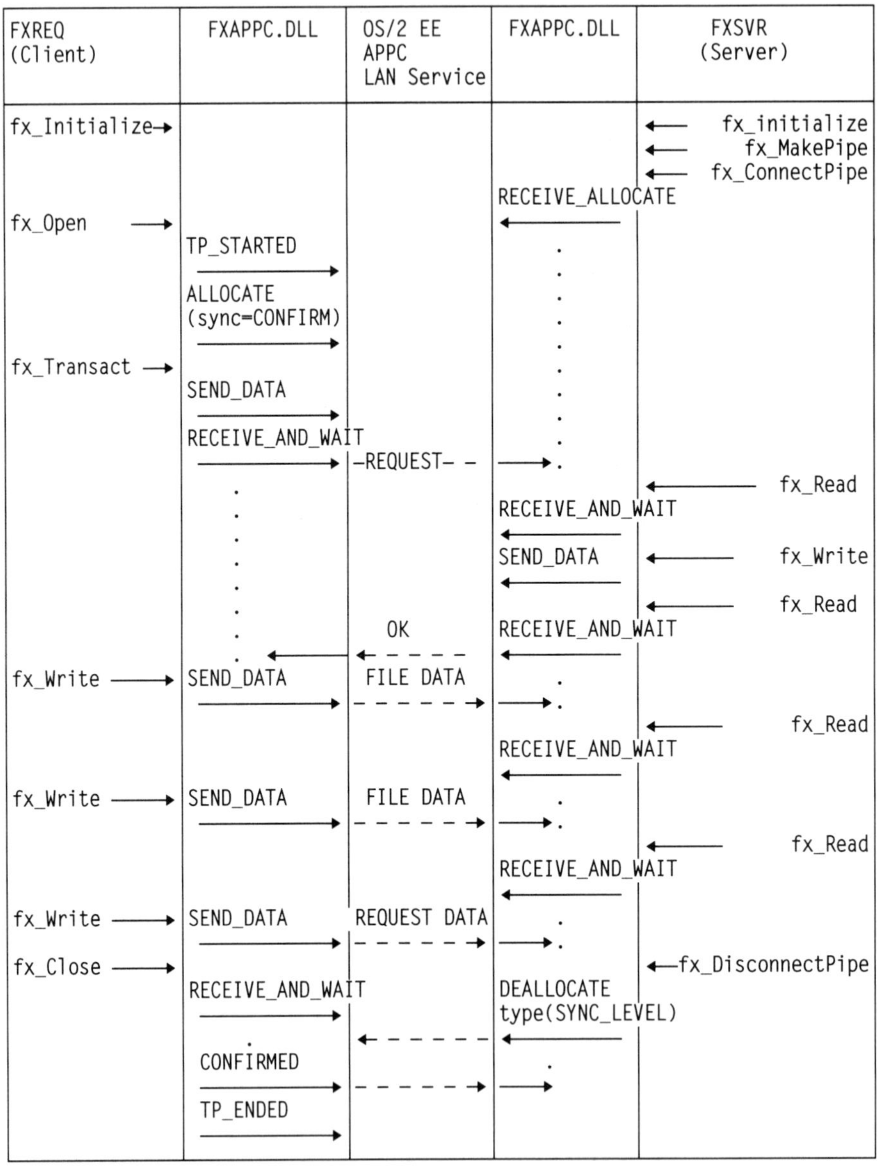

Figure 14-2. Sending a File Using the FXAPPC.DLL.

PROGRAMMING APPC

APPC, like NetBIOS, uses the *command with a control block* style of programming that is popular in the communications world. APPC calls its control blocks: **verb control blocks**. Unlike NetBIOS, APPC has a multiplicity of these verb control blocks. A program can request the various APPC commands by issuing the *verbs* described in the APPC tutorial, through their appropriate verb control block. The APPC service is provided by a single API call-return function.

How to Invoke an APPC "Verb"

Using APPC under OS/2 EE is not difficult. Here's how you do it:

1. Allocate a block of memory for your *verb control block* or preferably, simply declare it as a static variable. We provide the type definitions for the individual APPC *verb control blocks* and create the type **VCB** as the union of all the verb control block structures (see Figure 14-3). We declare the static variable **vcb** to be of type **VCB**. This will make using APPC a piece of cake.

2. APPC uses your stack. So make sure you have a stack size of at least 3 KBytes.

3. Initialize the fields in the verb control block to zeroes. This is a recommended practice for playing it safe.

4. Fill in the required fields in the verb control block. The first two bytes of every control block identify the APPC verb. Verb control block fields can contain pointers to associated data buffers. These associated buffers are unnamed read/write shared memory segments, created through the OS/2 **DosAllocSeg** API call. A shared segment can contain multiple data buffers but data cannot span across multiple segments. Once you allocate a data segment, reuse it each time you issue a verb with associated data buffers.

5. Issue the APPC API call:

   ```
   extern VOID pascal far APPC_C(PVOID);
   ```

   or call the *common services* API by issuing:

   ```
   extern VOID pascal far ACSSVC_C(PVOID);
   ```

   The *common services* perform services such as converting strings from ASCII to EBCDIC or for sending SNA alerts. Both calls take as their argument a pointer to the *control block*.

6. Wait for APPC to return. When it completes processing the verb it places the return parameters in the *control block*. Every verb contains a pair of fields where APPC returns the *return_code*.

   Note: You can use multiple threads to issue verbs. However, you can't issue multiple verbs simultaneously on a single **tp_ID**. If you do that, APPC will only process the first verb issued, and all the subsequent verbs receive a TP_BUSY primary return_code until the verb in progress completes.

Converting ASCII to EBCDIC

APPC requires that the control parameters use the EBCDIC character representation. This includes the net_name, all forms of LU names, the mode name, the tp_name, the user_ID, and the password. The data can be in any format that two partner programs agree on. Obviously, if you're moving data between a PC and an IBM host, somebody's going to have to do some translation. The **CONVERT** verb can be used to provide two-way conversions between ASCII and EBCDIC. We have an example of how this is done in the code that follows.

FXAPPC.C: THE APPC FX DLL

The code we present in this section *does not* contain a main() procedure. The FX DLLs are simply functions that get linked to a (.EXE) file at runtime. The main() procedure is provided by the program that calls the DLLs. This means **FXAPPC.C** is not a separate program; it contains a list of functions that get packaged as DLLs.

FXAPPC.C: General Stuff

The listing (see Figure 14-3) contains all the miscellaneous programming "stuff" that will be used by the FX procedures. This includes the usual declarations of constants, global variables, and forward declarations of functions. Notice that we've included the definitions of all the APPC verb control blocks. The **VCB** was declared as a C-language union that can accommodate all the different verb control block structures.

The functions that are provided in this module fall into two categories: **FX** functions and *helper* functions. The helper functions, as usual, are used to provide common services for that module. In addition to the ubiquitous **print_error()**, we introduce:

- Nine helper functions for executing APPC verbs
- One helper function for doing the conversion from ASCII to EBCDIC
- One helper function for displaying the APPC secondary return code

We made these APPC helper functions general enough so that you can use them "as is" in your programs. We introduce the *helper* functions at the point where they first get used in the code.

```
/*****************************************************************************/
/*  MODULE NAME: FXAPPC  - APPC communication.                               */
/*                                                                           */
/*  PROGRAM DESCRIPTION:  This module is a part of the FX file transfer     */
/*    programs.  Refer to the FXR.C program module for a program overview.  */
/*    This module implements the fx_* file transfer procedures using OS/2   */
/*    EE 1.1 APPC.                                                          */
/*                                                                           */
/*  PROCEDURES IN THIS MODULE:                                               */
/*                                                                           */
/*   Communication Functions                                                 */
/*   -----------------------                                                 */
/*     fx_Initialize(buffer_p, size);                                        */
/*     fx_MakePipe();                                                        */
/*     fx_ConnectPipe();                                                     */
/*     fx_DisconnectPipe();                                                  */
/*     fx_Open();                                                            */
/*     fx_Write(BufferArea, BufferLength, BytesWritten);                     */
/*     fx_Read(BufferArea, BufferLength, BytesRead);                         */
/*     fx_Transact(InBufferArea, InBufferLength,                             */
/*                 OutBufferArea, OutBufferLength, BytesRead);               */
/*     fx_Close();                                                           */
/*                                                                           */
/*   Signal Handler Function                                                 */
/*   -----------------------                                                 */
/*     signal_handler(argument, number);                                     */
/*                                                                           */
/*   APPC Helper Functions                                                   */
/*   ---------------------                                                   */
/*     convert_to_ebcdic(buffer, size, table);                               */
/*     display_secondary_rc();                                               */
/*     appc_mc_allocate(plu_alias, tp_name, mode_name, tp_id, conv_id);      */
/*     appc_mc_confirmed(conv_id, tp_id);                                    */
/*     appc_mc_deallocate(conv_id, tp_id);                                   */
/*     appc_mc_receive_and_wait(buffer, length, conv_id, tp_id[8],           */
/*                              what_rcvd, bytes_read)                       */
/*     appc_mc_request_to_send(conv_id, tp_id);                              */
/*     appc_mc_send_data(buffer, length, conv_id, tp_id, bytes_sent);        */
/*     appc_receive_allocate(tp_name, conv_id, tp_id);                       */
/*     appc_tp_started(lu_alias, tp_name, tp_id);                            */
/*     appc_tp_ended(tp_id);                                                 */
/*****************************************************************************/
#include <stdio.h>                    /* For printf() & NULL                 */
#include <stdlib.h>                   /* For conversion routines             */
#include <string.h>                   /* For string functions                */

#define INCL_DOSSIGNALS               /* for signal function declares        */
#include <os2.h>
```

Figure 14-3 (Part 1 of 9). FXAPPC.C: General Header Stuff and print_error()

```
/*------------------------------------------------------------------------*/
/* defines                                                                */
/*------------------------------------------------------------------------*/
                    /*-------------------------------------*/
                    /* return code defines                 */
                    /*-------------------------------------*/
#define FAILED      -1
#define GOOD         0
#define WARNING      1
                    /*-------------------------------------*/
                    /* DosAllocSeg flags                   */
                    /*-------------------------------------*/
#define GIVE_SEG_SHAREABLE  0x0001
#define GET_SEG_SHAREABLE   0x0002
#define DISCARDABLE         0x0004
#define RESIZEABLE          0x0008
                    /*-------------------------------------*/
                    /* APPC conversation states            */
                    /*-------------------------------------*/
#define APPC_RESET                 1
#define APPC_SEND                  2
#define APPC_RECEIVE               3
#define APPC_PENDING_POST          4
#define APPC_CONFIRM               5
#define APPC_CONFIRM_SEND          6
#define APPC_CONFIRM_DEALLOCATE    7
                    /*-------------------------------------*/
                    /* APPC verb parameter values          */
                    /*-------------------------------------*/
#define  AP_CONFIRM_SYNC_LEVEL              0x01
#define  AP_FLUSH                           0x01
#define  AP_MAPPED_CONVERSATION             0x01
#define  AP_NONE                            0x00
#define  AP_SYNC_LEVEL                      0x00
#define  AP_WHEN_SESSION_ALLOCATED          0x00

#define  AP_CONFIRM_WHAT_RECEIVED           0x0002
#define  AP_CONFIRM_DEALLOCATE              0x0004
#define  AP_CONFIRM_SEND                    0x0003
#define  AP_DATA                            0x0100
#define  AP_DATA_COMPLETE                   0x0200
#define  AP_DATA_INCOMPLETE                 0x0400
#define  AP_SEND                            0x0001

                    /*-------------------------------------*/
                    /* APPC operation codes                */
                    /*-------------------------------------*/
#define  AP_M_ALLOCATE                      0x0001
#define  AP_M_CONFIRMED                     0x0004
#define  AP_M_DEALLOCATE                    0x0005
#define  AP_M_RECEIVE_AND_WAIT              0x000B
#define  AP_M_REQUEST_TO_SEND               0x000E
#define  AP_M_SEND_DATA                     0x000F
```

Figure 14-3 (Part 2 of 9). FXAPPC.C: General Header Stuff and print_error()

```
#define  AP_RECEIVE_ALLOCATE                   0x0016
#define  AP_TP_ENDED                           0x0013
#define  AP_TP_STARTED                         0x0014
                   /*_________________________________*/
                   /* CM services parameter values     */
                   /*_________________________________*/
#define SV_A                                   0x01
#define SV_AE                                  0x00
#define SV_ASCII_TO_EBCDIC                     0x00
#define SV_EBCDIC_TO_ASCII                     0x01
                 /*_________________________________*/
                 /* CM services operation codes      */
                 /*_________________________________*/
#define SV_CONVERT                             0x001A

/*_____________________________________________________________________*/
/* type definitions for APPC control blocks                             */
/*_____________________________________________________________________*/
                   /*_________________________________*/
                   /* convert                          */
                   /*_________________________________*/
typedef struct
   { USHORT opcode;                   /* Verb operation code            */
     BYTE   opext;                    /* Verb extension code            */
     BYTE   reserv2;                  /* Reserved                       */
     USHORT primary_rc;               /* Primary RETURN_CODE            */
     ULONG  secondary_rc;             /* Secondary RETURN_CODE          */
     BYTE   direction;                /* DIRECTION                      */
                                      /*   SV_ASCII_TO_EBCDIC           */
                                      /*   SV_EBCDIC_TO_ASCII           */
     BYTE   char_set;                 /* CHARACTER_SET                  */
                                      /*   SV_AE                        */
                                      /*   SV_A                         */
                                      /*   SV_G                         */
     USHORT len;                      /* LENGTH                         */
     BYTE   far *source;              /* SOURCE_ADDR                    */
     BYTE   far *target;              /* TARGET_ADDR                    */
   } CONVERT;

                   /*_________________________________*/
                   /* mc_allocate                      */
                   /*_________________________________*/
typedef struct
   { USHORT opcode;                   /* Verb operation code            */
     BYTE   opext;                    /* Verb extension code            */
     BYTE   reserv2;                  /* Reserved                       */
     USHORT primary_rc;               /* Primary RETURN_CODE            */
     ULONG  secondary_rc;             /* Secondary RETURN_CODE          */
     BYTE   tp_id[8];                 /* TP_ID                          */
     ULONG  conv_id;                  /* CONV_ID                        */
     BYTE   reserv3;                  /* Reserved                       */
     BYTE   sync_level;               /* SYNC_LEVEL                     */
                                      /*    AP_NONE                     */
                                      /*    AP_CONFIRM                  */
```

Figure 14-3 (Part 3 of 9). FXAPPC.C: General Header Stuff and print_error()

```
        BYTE   reserv4[2];                /* Reserved                        */
        BYTE   rtn_ctl;                   /* RETURN_CONTROL                  */
                                          /*    AP_WHEN_SESSION_             */
                                          /*       ALLOCATED                 */
                                          /*    AP_IMMEDIATE                 */
                                          /*    AP_WHEN_SESSION_FREE         */
        BYTE   reserv5[9];                /* Reserved                        */
        BYTE   plu_alias[8];              /* PARTNER_LU_ALIAS                */
        BYTE   mode_name[8];              /* MODE_NAME                       */
        BYTE   tp_name[64];               /* TP_NAME                         */
        BYTE   security;                  /* SECURITY                        */
                                          /*    AP_NONE                      */
                                          /*    AP_SAME                      */
                                          /*    AP_PGM                       */
        BYTE   reserv6[11];               /* Reserved                        */
        BYTE   pwd[10];                   /* PASSWORD                        */
        BYTE   user_id[10];               /* USER_ID                         */
        USHORT pip_dlen;                  /* PIP_DATA_LENGTH                 */
                                          /*   (0 if no pip data)            */
        BYTE   far *pip_dptr;             /* PIP_DATA                        */
        BYTE   reserv7[26];               /* Reserved                        */
      } MC_ALLOCATE;

                   /*------------------------------------*/
                   /* mc_deallocate                      */
                   /*------------------------------------*/
    typedef struct
      {
        USHORT opcode;                    /* Verb operation code             */
        BYTE   opext;                     /* Verb extension code             */
        BYTE   reserv2;                   /* Reserved                        */
        USHORT primary_rc;                /* Primary RETURN_CODE             */
        ULONG  secondary_rc;              /* Secondary RETURN_CODE           */
        BYTE   tp_id[8];                  /* TP_ID                           */
        ULONG  conv_id;                   /* CONV_ID                         */
      } MC_CONFIRMED;

                   /*------------------------------------*/
                   /* mc_deallocate                      */
                   /*------------------------------------*/
    typedef struct
      { USHORT opcode;                    /* Verb operation code             */
        BYTE   opext;                     /* Verb extension code             */
        BYTE   reserv2;                   /* Reserved                        */
        USHORT primary_rc;                /* Primary RETURN_CODE             */
        ULONG  secondary_rc;              /* Secondary RETURN_CODE           */
        BYTE   tp_id[8];                  /* TP_ID                           */
        ULONG  conv_id;                   /* CONV_ID                         */
        BYTE   reserv3;                   /* Reserved                        */
        BYTE   dealloc_type;              /* TYPE                            */
                                          /*    AP_SYNC_LEVEL                */
                                          /*    AP_FLUSH                     */
                                          /*    AP_ABEND                     */
        BYTE   reserv4[2];                /* Reserved                        */
        BYTE   reserv5[4];                /* Reserved                        */
      } MC_DEALLOCATE;
```

Figure 14-3 (Part 4 of 9). FXAPPC.C: General Header Stuff and print_error()

```
                /*-----------------------------------*/
                /* mc_receive_and_wait               */
                /*-----------------------------------*/
typedef struct
   { USHORT opcode;                   /* Verb operation code              */
     BYTE   opext;                    /* Verb extension code              */
     BYTE   reserv2;                  /* Reserved                         */
     USHORT primary_rc;               /* Primary RETURN_CODE              */
     ULONG  secondary_rc;             /* Secondary RETURN_CODE            */
     BYTE   tp_id[8];                 /* TP_ID                            */
     ULONG  conv_id;                  /* CONV_ID                          */
     USHORT what_rcvd;                /* WHAT_RECEIVED                    */
                                      /*    AP_DATA_COMPLETE              */
                                      /*    AP_DATA_INCOMPLETE            */
                                      /*    AP_SEND                       */
                                      /*    AP_CONFIRM                    */
                                      /*    AP_CONFIRM_SEND               */
                                      /*    AP_CONFIRM_DEALLOCATE         */
     BYTE   reserv3;                  /* Reserved                         */
     BYTE   reserv4;                  /* Reserved                         */
     BYTE   rts_rcvd;                 /* REQUEST_TO_SEND_RECEIVED         */
                                      /*    AP_NO                         */
                                      /*    AP_YES                        */
     BYTE   reserv5;                  /* Reserved                         */
     USHORT max_len;                  /* MAX_LENGTH                       */
     USHORT dlen;                     /* DATA_LENGTH                      */
     BYTE   far *dptr;                /* DATA_PTR                         */
     BYTE   reserv6[5];               /* Reserved                         */
   } MC_RECEIVE_AND_WAIT;

                /*-----------------------------------*/
                /* mc_send_data                      */
                /*-----------------------------------*/
typedef struct
   { USHORT opcode;                   /* Verb operation code              */
     BYTE   opext;                    /* Verb extension code              */
     BYTE   reserv2;                  /* Reserved                         */
     USHORT primary_rc;               /* Primary RETURN_CODE              */
     ULONG  secondary_rc;             /* Secondary RETURN_CODE            */
     BYTE   tp_id[8];                 /* TP_ID                            */
     ULONG  conv_id;                  /* CONV_ID                          */
     BYTE   rts_rcvd;                 /* REQUEST_TO_SEND_RECEIVED         */
                                      /*    AP_NO                         */
                                      /*    AP_YES                        */
     BYTE   reserv3;                  /* Reserved                         */
     USHORT dlen;                     /* DATA_LENGTH                      */
     BYTE   far *dptr;                /* DATA address                     */
     BYTE   reserv4[2];               /* Reserved                         */
   } MC_SEND_DATA;
```

Figure 14-3 (Part 5 of 9). FXAPPC.C: General Header Stuff and print_error()

```
                /*----------------------------------*/
                /* receive_allocate control block    */
                /*----------------------------------*/
typedef struct
   { USHORT opcode;                    /* Verb operation code          */
     BYTE   opext;                     /* Verb extension code          */
     BYTE   reserv2;                   /* Reserved                     */
     USHORT primary_rc;                /* Primary RETURN_CODE          */
     ULONG  secondary_rc;              /* Secondary RETURN_CODE        */
     BYTE   tp_name[64];               /* TP_NAME                      */
     BYTE   tp_id[8];                  /* TP_ID                        */
     ULONG  conv_id;                   /* CONV_ID                      */
     BYTE   sync_level;                /* SYNC_LEVEL                   */
                                       /*    AP_NONE                   */
                                       /*    AP_CONFIRM                */
     BYTE   conv_type;                 /* CONVERSATION_TYPE            */
                                       /*    AP_BASIC_CONVERSATION     */
                                       /*    AP_MAPPED_CONVERSATION    */
     BYTE   user_id[10];               /* USER_ID                      */
     BYTE   lu_alias[8];               /* LU_ALIAS                     */
     BYTE   plu_alias[8];              /* PARTNER_LU_ALIAS             */
     BYTE   mode_name[8];              /* MODE_NAME                    */
     BYTE   reserv3[28];               /* Reserved                     */
   } RECEIVE_ALLOCATE;

                /*----------------------------------*/
                /* mc_request_to_send control block  */
                /*----------------------------------*/
typedef struct
   {
     USHORT opcode;                    /* Verb operation code          */
     BYTE   opext;                     /* Verb extension code          */
     BYTE   reserv2;                   /* Reserved                     */
     USHORT primary_rc;                /* Primary RETURN_CODE          */
     ULONG  secondary_rc;              /* Secondary RETURN_CODE        */
     BYTE   tp_id[8];                  /* TP_ID                        */
     ULONG  conv_id;                   /* CONV_ID                      */
   } MC_REQUEST_TO_SEND;

                /*----------------------------------*/
                /* tp_ended                          */
                /*----------------------------------*/
typedef struct
   { USHORT opcode;                    /* Verb operation code          */
     BYTE   opext;                     /* Verb extension code          */
     BYTE   reserv2;                   /* Reserved                     */
     USHORT primary_rc;                /* Primary RETURN_CODE          */
     ULONG  secondary_rc;              /* Secondary RETURN_CODE        */
     BYTE   tp_id[8];                  /* TP_ID                        */
     BYTE   reserv3;                   /* Reserved                     */
   } TP_ENDED;
```

Figure 14-3 (Part 6 of 9). FXAPPC.C: General Header Stuff and print_error()

```
                  /*________________________________*/
                  /* tp_started                     */
                  /*________________________________*/
typedef struct
  { USHORT  opcode;                   /* Verb operation code             */
    BYTE    opext;                    /* Verb extension code             */
    BYTE    reserv2;                  /* Reserved                        */
    USHORT  primary_rc;               /* Primary RETURN_CODE             */
    ULONG   secondary_rc;             /* Secondary RETURN_CODE           */
    BYTE    lu_alias[8];              /* LU_ALIAS                        */
                                      /*   or default LU                 */
    BYTE    tp_id[8];                 /* TP_ID                           */
    BYTE    tp_name[64];              /* TP_NAME                         */
  } TP_STARTED;
                  /*________________________________*/
                  /* union of all verb structures   */
                  /*________________________________*/
typedef union
  {
    MC_ALLOCATE          mc_alloc;     /* mc_allocate verb               */
    MC_CONFIRMED         mc_confirmed; /* mc_confirmed                   */
    MC_DEALLOCATE        mc_dealloc;   /* mc_dealloc                     */
    MC_RECEIVE_AND_WAIT  mc_recv_wait; /* mc_receive_and_wait verb       */
    MC_REQUEST_TO_SEND   mc_req_send;  /* mc_request_to_send verb        */
    MC_SEND_DATA         mc_send;      /* mc_send_data verb              */
    RECEIVE_ALLOCATE     recv_alloc;   /* receive_allocate               */
    TP_STARTED           tp_started;   /* tp_started verb                */
    TP_ENDED             tp_ended;     /* tp_ended verb                  */
  } VCB;

/*_____________________________________________________________________*/
/* forward declaration for functions in this module                    */
/*_____________________________________________________________________*/
                  /*________________________________*/
                  /* communication functions        */
                  /*________________________________*/
USHORT fx_Initialize(PVOID *, PUSHORT);
USHORT fx_MakePipe(VOID);
USHORT fx_ConnectPipe(VOID);
USHORT fx_DisconnectPipe(VOID);
USHORT fx_Open(VOID);
USHORT fx_Write(PVOID, USHORT, PUSHORT);
USHORT fx_Read(PVOID,  USHORT, PUSHORT);
USHORT fx_Transact(PVOID, USHORT, PVOID, USHORT, PVOID);
USHORT fx_Close(VOID);
```

Figure 14-3 (Part 7 of 9). FXAPPC.C: General Header Stuff and print_error()

```
                   /*-----------------------------------*/
                   /* APPC helper functions             */
                   /*-----------------------------------*/
USHORT appc_mc_allocate(PBYTE, PBYTE, PBYTE, PBYTE, PULONG);
USHORT appc_mc_confirmed(ULONG, PBYTE);
USHORT appc_mc_deallocate(ULONG, PBYTE);
USHORT appc_mc_receive_and_wait(PVOID, USHORT, ULONG, PBYTE, PUSHORT, PUSHORT);
USHORT appc_mc_request_to_send(ULONG, PBYTE);
USHORT appc_mc_send_data(PVOID, USHORT, ULONG, PBYTE, PUSHORT);
USHORT appc_receive_allocate(PBYTE, PULONG, PBYTE);
USHORT appc_tp_started(PBYTE, PBYTE, PBYTE);
USHORT appc_tp_ended(PBYTE);
USHORT convert_to_ebcdic(PVOID, USHORT, BYTE);
VOID   display_secondary_rc(VOID);

                   /*-----------------------------------*/
                   /* signal handler function           */
                   /*-----------------------------------*/
VOID far pascal signal_handler(USHORT, USHORT);
/*-----------------------------------------------------------------------*/
/* forward declaration for functions in other modules                    */
/*-----------------------------------------------------------------------*/
                   /*-----------------------------------*/
                   /* error display function            */
                   /*-----------------------------------*/
VOID print_error(USHORT, PCHAR, PCHAR, USHORT);
                   /*-----------------------------------*/
                   /* APPC  dynamic link function       */
                   /*-----------------------------------*/
extern VOID pascal far APPC_C(PVOID);
extern VOID pascal far ACSSVC_C(PVOID);

/*-----------------------------------------------------------------------*/
/* Configuration variables, initialized after fx_Initialize()            */
/* function call.                                                        */
/*-----------------------------------------------------------------------*/
CHAR   PipeName[128];
CHAR   ModeName[9];
USHORT FileBufferSize;
/*-----------------------------------------------------------------------*/
/* global variables for this module.                                     */
/*-----------------------------------------------------------------------*/
USHORT rc;                          /* return code                        */
CHAR   server_tp_name[64];          /* transaction program name (server)  */
CHAR   requester_tp_name[64];       /* transaction program name (requester)*/
CHAR   mode_name[8];                /* mode name                          */
CHAR   tp_id[8];                    /* transaction program id             */
ULONG  conv_id;                     /* conversation id                    */
SHORT  server;                      /* server/requester indicator         */
SHORT  appc_state;                  /* state of APPC conversation         */
USHORT bytes_read;                  /* how many bytes received            */
USHORT bytes_written;               /* how many bytes written             */
USHORT what_rcvd;                   /* what received verb field           */
VCB    vcb;                         /* control block for APPC verbs       */
```

Figure 14-3 (Part 8 of 9). FXAPPC.C: General Header Stuff and print_error()

```
/*--------------------------------------------------------------------------*/
/* Error Display Routine                                                    */
/*--------------------------------------------------------------------------*/
VOID print_error(USHORT Error, PCHAR msg, PCHAR file, USHORT line)
{
 printf("APPC Error %u (0x%x) detected while %s at line %u in file %s.\n",
        Error, Error, msg, line, file);
} /* end print_error */
/*--------------------------------------------------------------------------*/
/* display APPC secondary_rc                                                */
/*--------------------------------------------------------------------------*/
VOID
display_secondary_rc()
{
  printf("  APPC secondary rc = %lx\n", vcb.mc_alloc.secondary_rc);
}
```

Figure 14-3 (Part 9 of 9). FXAPPC.C: General Header Stuff and print_error()

FXAPPC.C: fx_Initialize()

The **fx_Initialize()** function (see Figure 14-4) reads a protocol-specific configuration file to obtain the parameters required to initialize the system. The name of the user-specified configuration file for APPC is: **fxappc.cfg**. Here is an example of such a file:

```
PIPE_NAME          = FILE
MODE_NAME          = MODE1
FILE_BUFFER_SIZE   = 4096
```

Here's what these parameters do:

PIPE_NAME This parameter is used to derive the network name of the client and server TPs. The client TP in the above example will be named FILEREQ and the server TP will be named FILESVR.

MODE_NAME This parameter defines the APPC mode.

FILE_BUFFER_SIZE This parameter defines the size (in bytes) of the message buffer. This is the buffer we will use for reading and writing data to the disk and for exchanging messages across the LAN or the IPC. The memory space for this parameter will be dynamically allocated. The fx_Initialize function returns a pointer to this buffer and its size to the application. One of the factors we will measure in our benchmarks is the effect of the message buffer size on performance.

The **fx_Initialize()** function acts as a FX protocol "catch-all" for performing protocol-specific start-up actions. The only thing strange in this code is the

convert_to_ebcdic() calls to the helper routine in Figure 14-5. Notice that different translation tables are specified depending on the parameter being translated. This is done to get the names in sync with the various APPC configuration profiles. Here's the rule of thumb to follow for selecting a translation table:

Table A Use this table for the net_name, LU_name and the mode_name. This table only does uppercase ASCII to EBCDIC conversions.

Table AE Use this table for the tp_name, user_ID and password. This table does both uppercase and lowercase ASCII to EBCDIC conversions.

This should help clear one more of APPC's great mysteries. Think about how useful this information could be in a game of Trivial Pursuit.

```
/*-----------------------------------------------------------------------*/
/* function to read communication specific parameters and allocate a buffer */
/* for communication.  A pointer to the buffer and the buffer size is     */
/* returned.                                                              */
/*-----------------------------------------------------------------------*/
USHORT fx_Initialize(PVOID *buffer_p , PUSHORT size)
{
  FILE    *config_file;               /* Input file control block        */
  CHAR    *error_rc;                  /* return code                     */
  USHORT   selector;                  /* selector for a file buffer      */
  CHAR     line[80];                  /* one line of config file         */
  CHAR     name[16];                  /* temp variable for creating tp names*/


  printf("Reading configuration parameters.\n");
  /*---------------------------------*/
  /* open the configuration file     */
  /*---------------------------------*/
  if (NULL == (config_file = fopen("fxappc.cfg","r")))
     {print_error(rc,"opening configuration file",__FILE__,__LINE__);
      return(FAILED);
     }
  else
     /*----------------------------------*/
     /* read the configuration parameters.  */
     /* The parameters are expected to be:  */
     /*     - in the form <name = value>    */
     /*     - if value is a string enclose  */
     /*       in double quotes              */
     /*     - in the order read below       */
     /*----------------------------------*/
     {
       fgets(line, sizeof(line), config_file);
       if (sscanf(line,"PIPE_NAME = %s ", PipeName) != 1)
          {print_error(rc,"reading PipeName from configuration",
                       __FILE__,__LINE__);
           return(FAILED);
          }
       printf("PIPE_NAME = %s \n", PipeName);
```

Figure 14-4 (Part 1 of 3). FXAPPC.C: fx_Initialize().

```
        fgets(line, sizeof(line), config_file);
        if (sscanf(line,"MODE_NAME = %s ", ModeName) != 1)
           {print_error(rc,"reading ModeName from configuration",
                       __FILE__,__LINE__);
            return(FAILED);
           }
        printf("MODE_NAME = %s \n", ModeName);

        fgets(line, sizeof(line), config_file);
        if (sscanf(line,"FILE_BUFFER_SIZE = %u ", &FileBufferSize) != 1)
           {print_error(rc,"reading FileBufferSize from configuration",
                       __FILE__,__LINE__);
            return(FAILED);
           }
        printf("FILE_BUFFER_SIZE = %u \n", FileBufferSize);
     } /* end if */

   fclose(config_file);

   /*--------------------------------------*/
   /* initialize server and requester      */
   /*    tp_names for use in APPC calls    */
   /*--------------------------------------*/
   strcpy(name, PipeName);                           /* make server tp name from */
   strcat(name, "SVR");                              /*    pipe name and "SVR"   */
   memset(server_tp_name, ' ',                       /* set tp_id to all blanks  */
          sizeof(server_tp_name));
   strncpy(server_tp_name, name, strlen(name));      /* copy all non zero chars  */
   rc = convert_to_ebcdic(server_tp_name,            /* convert to ebcdic        */
                          sizeof(server_tp_name),    /*  using table SV_AE       */
                          SV_AE);
   if (rc)
      {print_error(rc,"performing an ASCII to EBCDIC conversion",
                  __FILE__,__LINE__);
       display_secondary_rc();
       return(FAILED);
      }

   strcpy(name, PipeName);                           /* make req.   tp name from */
   strcat(name, "REQ");                              /*    pipe name and "REQ"   */
   memset(requester_tp_name, ' ',                    /* set tp_id to all blanks  */
          sizeof(requester_tp_name));
   strncpy(requester_tp_name, name, strlen(name));/* copy all non zero chars  */
   rc = convert_to_ebcdic(requester_tp_name,         /* convert to ebcdic        */
                          sizeof(requester_tp_name), /*  using table SV_AE       */
                          SV_AE);
   if (rc)
      {print_error(rc,"performing an ASCII to EBCDIC conversion",
                  __FILE__,__LINE__);
       display_secondary_rc();
       return(FAILED);
      }
```

Figure 14-4 (Part 2 of 3). FXAPPC.C: fx_Initialize().

```
     /*-------------------------------------*/
     /* initialize mode name for use in     */
     /*   APPC calls                        */
     /*-------------------------------------*/
     memset(mode_name, ' ',                           /* set  to all blanks       */
            sizeof(mode_name));
     strncpy(mode_name, ModeName, strlen(ModeName));/* copy all non zero chars  */
                                                      /* ModeName is from config. */
     rc = convert_to_ebcdic(mode_name,                /* convert to ebcdic        */
                            sizeof(mode_name),        /*  using table SV_A        */
                            SV_A);
     if (rc)
        {print_error(rc,"performing an ASCII to EBCDIC conversion",
                     __FILE__,__LINE__);
         display_secondary_rc();
         return(FAILED);
        }

     /*-------------------------------------*/
     /* allocate shareable buffer, return   */
     /* pointer to buffer and size          */
     /*-------------------------------------*/
     if (DosAllocSeg(FileBufferSize,       /* buffer size from configuration    */
                     &selector,            /* selector returned                 */
                     GIVE_SEG_SHAREABLE)) /* shareable, an APPC requirement*/
     if (rc)
        {print_error(rc,"allocating file buffer",__FILE__,__LINE__);
         return(FAILED);
        }

     *buffer_p = MAKEP(selector,0);        /* make a pointer from selector, 0   */
                                           /*  offset and return                */
     *size = FileBufferSize;               /* return buffer size                */

     return(GOOD);
   } /* end fx_Initialize */
```

Figure 14-4 (Part 3 of 3). FXAPPC.C: fx_Initialize().

FXAPPC.C: convert_to_ebcdic()

The **convert_to_ebcdic()** helper routine (see Figure 14-5) uses the Communications Manager's *common services* to perform the ASCII to EBCDIC conversion. The call is to **ACSSVC_C()**, the OS/2 EE supplied API for common services.

```
/*-----------------------------------------------------------------------*/
/* convert ASCII to EBCDIC helper routine                                */
/*-----------------------------------------------------------------------*/
USHORT
convert_to_ebcdic(PVOID buffer, USHORT size, BYTE table)
{
  CONVERT convert;                     /* structure for char conversion   */

  /*---------------------------------*
  /* convert a buffer in place       */
  /*---------------------------------*/
  memset(&convert, 0, sizeof(convert));        /* zero out control block  */
  convert.opcode    = SV_CONVERT;              /* CONVERT general service */
  convert.direction = SV_ASCII_TO_EBCDIC;      /* ASCII to EBCDIC         */
  convert.char_set  = table;                   /* conversion table        */
  convert.len       = size;                    /* size of area to convert */
  convert.source    = buffer;                  /* conversion source       */
  convert.target    = buffer;                  /* conversion target       */

  ACSSVC_C (&convert);                         /* invoke the service      */

  return(convert.primary_rc);
}
```

Figure 14-5. FXAPPC.C: convert_to_ebcdic().

FXAPPC.C: fx_MakePipe()

The **fx_MakePipe()** function (see Figure 14-6) is used by the server side of an FX pipe to establish its side of the pipe. In APPC there is not much to do, since most of the initialization is established through static configuration files and the Attach Manager. All this function does is initialize its state variable to Reset.

```
/*-----------------------------------------------------------------------*/
/* function to establish the server end of the communication pipe.       */
/*-----------------------------------------------------------------------*/
USHORT fx_MakePipe(VOID)
{
  /*---------------------------------*/
  /* set APPC state                  */
  /*---------------------------------*/
  appc_state = APPC_RESET;

  /*---------------------------------*/
  /* remember that this is a server  */
  /*---------------------------------*/
  server = TRUE;

  return(GOOD);
} /* end fx_MakePipe */
```

Figure 14-6. FXAPPC.C: MakePipe().

FXAPPC.C: fx_ConnectPipe()

The **fx_ConnectPipe()** function (see Figure 14-7) is used to establish a connection on the server side of an FX pipe. This function is provided using APPC by issuing a RECEIVE_ALLOCATE verb. The verb is executed by the helper routine **appc_receive_allocate()** listed in Figure 14-8. The state variable is now changed to Receive. The server is now waiting to hear from the outside world.

```
/*---------------------------------------------------------------------------*/
/* function to enable the server end of the communication pipe.             */
/*---------------------------------------------------------------------------*/
USHORT fx_ConnectPipe(VOID)
{
  /*-------------------------------*/
  /* perform APPC receive_allocate */
  /*-------------------------------*/
  rc = appc_receive_allocate(server_tp_name,     /* tp_name in EBCDIC        */
                             &conv_id,           /* conversation id returned */
                             tp_id);             /* tp_id returned           */
  if (rc)
     {print_error(rc,"performing an APPC receive_allocate", __FILE__,__LINE__);
      display_secondary_rc();
      return(FAILED);
     }

  /*-------------------------------*/
  /* set APPC state                */
  /*-------------------------------*/
  appc_state = APPC_RECEIVE;

  return(GOOD);
} /* end fx_ConnectPipe */
```

Figure 14-7. FXAPPC.C: fx_ConnectPipe().

FXAPPC.C: appc_receive_allocate()

The **appc_receive_allocate()** helper routine (see Figure 14-8) is in charge of issuing a RECEIVE_ALLOCATE verb. The call will wait for an incoming ALLOCATE request for the duration of the configured TP receive timeout. This verb takes as its input the server's TP name and returns a TP ID and a conversation ID when a successful conversation is established.

```
/*------------------------------------------------------------------------*/
/* APPC mc_receive_allocate helper routine                                */
/*------------------------------------------------------------------------*/
USHORT
appc_receive_allocate(BYTE   tp_name[64],       /* transaction pgm name     */
                      PULONG conv_id,           /* conversation id          */
                      BYTE   tp_id[8])          /* transaction pgm id       */
{
  memset(&vcb, 0, sizeof(vcb));                 /* zero out control block   */
  vcb.recv_alloc.opcode     =
           AP_RECEIVE_ALLOCATE;                 /* Set the APPC opcode      */
  memcpy(vcb.recv_alloc.tp_name, tp_name,
        sizeof(vcb.recv_alloc.tp_name));        /* tp_name in EBCDIC        */
  vcb.recv_alloc.sync_level =
           AP_CONFIRM_SYNC_LEVEL;               /* Confirm sync level       */

  APPC_C(&vcb);                                 /* Call APPC                */

  *conv_id = vcb.recv_alloc.conv_id;            /* Save the conversation_id */
  memcpy(tp_id, vcb.recv_alloc.tp_id,
        sizeof(vcb.recv_alloc.tp_id));          /* Save the tp_id           */

  return(vcb.recv_alloc.primary_rc);            /* return primary rc        */
}
```

Figure 14-8. FXAPPC.C: appc_receive_allocate().

FXAPPC.C: fx_DisconnectPipe()

The **fx_DisconnectPipe()** function (see Figure 14-9) is used to disconnect the server side of an FX pipe. A "graceful" implementation of this function is provided using APPC as follows:

- If we're not in the Receive state, we disconnect by simply calling the helper routine **appc_mc_deallocate()** see listing in Figure 14-10.
- If we're in the Receive state, we politely ask for permission to send by invoking the helper routine **appc_mc_request_to_send()**, see listing in Figure 14-11 on page 373. We then wait for an answer by invoking the helper routine **appc_mc_receive_and_wait()**, see listing in Figure 14-12 on page 374. If we don't obtain the permission to send, we return with an error. Otherwise, we do the deallocate by calling the helper routine **appc_mc_deallocate()** see listing in Figure 14-10.

FXAPPC.C: appc_mc_receive_and_wait()

The **appc_mc_receive_and_wait()** helper routine (see Figure 14-12) waits for information to arrive or receives it if it's already there. The *what_received* parameter indicates conversation status and whether data was received. The data itself is placed in the receive buffer. If all the data is received, *what_received* will indicate DATA_COMPLETE. If permission to send is requested, *what_received* will contain either YES or NO, depending on whether the partner wants to grant the permission or not. When the other side has nothing else to send and wants to turn the conversation around, *what_received* will contain a SEND indicator.

```
/*---------------------------------------------------------------------------*/
/* APPC mc_receive_and_wait helper routine                                   */
/*---------------------------------------------------------------------------*/
USHORT
appc_mc_receive_and_wait(PVOID buffer,         /* pointer to recv buffer   */
                         USHORT  length,       /* length of recv buffer    */
                         ULONG   conv_id,      /* conversation id          */
                         BYTE    tp_id[8],     /* transaction pgm id       */
                         PUSHORT what_rcvd,    /* what was received?       */
                         PUSHORT bytes_read)   /* number of bytes read     */
{
  memset(&vcb, 0, sizeof(vcb));                /* zero control block       */
  vcb.mc_recv_wait.opcode  =
          AP_M_RECEIVE_AND_WAIT;               /* MC_RECEIVE_AND_WAIT      */
  vcb.mc_recv_wait.opext   =
          AP_MAPPED_CONVERSATION;              /* Set MC ext. type         */
  vcb.mc_recv_wait.conv_id = conv_id;          /* Set Conversation_id      */
  memcpy(vcb.mc_recv_wait.tp_id, tp_id,        /* Set TP_id                */
         sizeof(vcb.mc_recv_wait.tp_id));
  vcb.mc_recv_wait.max_len = length;           /* Max length of buffer     */
  vcb.mc_recv_wait.dptr    = buffer;           /* Set data buffer pointer  */

  APPC_C(&vcb);                                /* Call APPC                */

  *what_rcvd  = vcb.mc_recv_wait.what_rcvd;    /* return what received     */
  *bytes_read = vcb.mc_recv_wait.dlen;         /* number of bytes read     */

  return(vcb.mc_recv_wait.primary_rc);         /* return primary rc        */
}
```

Figure 14-12. FXAPPC.C: appc_mc_receive_and_wait().

FXAPPC.C: fx_Open()

The **fx_Open()** function (see Figure 14-13) is used to establish the client side of an FX pipe. We provide the function using APPC by:

1. Doing a TP_START by calling the helper routine **appc_tp_started()**, see listing in Figure 14-14.
2. Doing an ALLOCATE by calling the helper routine **appc_mc_allocate()**, see Figure 14-15.
3. Set the state variable to Send.

```
/*---------------------------------------------------------------------------*/
/* function a requester uses to prepare a pipe for communication.            */
/*---------------------------------------------------------------------------*/
USHORT fx_Open(VOID)
{
  /*-----------------------------------*/
  /* set APPC state                    */
  /*-----------------------------------*/
  appc_state = APPC_RESET;

  /*-----------------------------------*/
  /* remember that this is not a server */
  /*-----------------------------------*/
  server = FALSE;

  /*-----------------------------------*/
  /* perform APPC tp_started           */
  /*-----------------------------------*/
  appc_tp_started("FILEREQ  ",                  /* LU_ALIAS                */
                  requester_tp_name,            /* TP_NAME                 */
                  tp_id);                       /* tp_id returned          */
  if (rc)
     {print_error(rc,"performing APPC tp_started", __FILE__,__LINE__);
      display_secondary_rc();
      return(FAILED);
     }

  /*-----------------------------------*/
  /* perform APPC mc_allocate          */
  /*-----------------------------------*/
  appc_mc_allocate("FILESVR  ",                 /* PLU_ALIAS               */
                   server_tp_name,              /* tp name                 */
                   mode_name,                   /* mode                    */
                   tp_id,                       /* tp id                   */
                   &conv_id);                   /* conversation id returned */
  if (rc)
     {print_error(rc,"performing APPC mc_allocate", __FILE__,__LINE__);
      display_secondary_rc();
      return(FAILED);
     }

  /*-----------------------------------*/
  /* set APPC state                    */
  /*-----------------------------------*/
  appc_state = APPC_SEND;

  return(GOOD);
} /* end fx_Open */
```

Figure 14-13. FXAPPC.C: fx_Open().

FXAPPC.C: appc_tp_started()

The **appc_tp_started()** helper routine, see Figure 14-14, notifies APPC that the program is requesting resources for initiating a TP. APPC responds by returning a TP ID.

```
/*----------------------------------------------------------------------------*/
/* APPC tp_started helper routine                                             */
/*----------------------------------------------------------------------------*/
USHORT
appc_tp_started(BYTE lu_alias[8],                /* logical unit alias      */
                BYTE tp_name[64],                /* transaction pgm name    */
                BYTE tp_id[8])                   /* transaction pgm id      */
{
  memset(&vcb, 0, sizeof(vcb));                  /* zero out control block  */
  vcb.tp_started.opcode = AP_TP_STARTED;         /* APPC verb - TP_STARTED  */
  memcpy(vcb.tp_started.lu_alias, lu_alias,
         sizeof(vcb.tp_started.lu_alias));       /* Set LU_ALIAS            */
  memcpy(vcb.tp_started.tp_name, tp_name,
         sizeof(vcb.tp_started.tp_name));        /* Set TP_NAME             */

  APPC_C (&vcb);                                 /* Call APPC               */

  memcpy (tp_id, vcb.tp_started.tp_id,           /* save tp_id              */
          sizeof(vcb.tp_started.tp_id));

  return(vcb.tp_started.primary_rc);             /* return primary rc       */
}
```

Figure 14-14. FXAPPC.C: appc_tp_started().

FXAPPC.C: appc_mc_allocate()

The **appc_mc_allocate()** helper routine, see Figure 14-15, is issued to tell APPC to start a mapped conversation with a partner TP. If successful, APPC returns the conversation ID.

```
/*-----------------------------------------------------------------------*/
/* APPC mc_allocate helper routine                                       */
/*-----------------------------------------------------------------------*/
USHORT
appc_mc_allocate(BYTE  plu_alias[8],        /* partner lu alias      */
                 BYTE  tp_name[64],         /* transaction pgm name  */
                 BYTE  mode_name[8],        /* mode name             */
                 BYTE  tp_id[8],            /* transaction pgm name  */
                 PULONG conv_id)            /* conversation id       */
{
  memset(&vcb, 0, sizeof(vcb));             /* zero out control block */
  vcb.mc_alloc.opcode     = AP_M_ALLOCATE;  /* Verb - MC_ALLOCATE    */
  vcb.mc_alloc.opext      =
          AP_MAPPED_CONVERSATION;           /* Mapped Conversation type */
  memcpy(vcb.mc_alloc.tp_id, tp_id,
       sizeof(vcb.mc_alloc.tp_id));         /* Set the TP_ID         */
  vcb.mc_alloc.sync_level =
          AP_CONFIRM_SYNC_LEVEL;            /* Sync level-confirm    */
  vcb.mc_alloc.rtn_ctl    =
          AP_WHEN_SESSION_ALLOCATED;        /* when to return        */
  vcb.mc_alloc.security   = AP_NONE;        /* No security           */
  memcpy(vcb.mc_alloc.plu_alias, plu_alias, 8); /* Set PLU_ALIAS     */
  memcpy(vcb.mc_alloc.tp_name, tp_name,
       sizeof(vcb.mc_alloc.tp_name));       /* Set TP_NAME           */
  memcpy(vcb.mc_alloc.mode_name, mode_name,
       sizeof(vcb.mc_alloc.mode_name));     /* Set MODE_NAME         */

  APPC_C(&vcb);                             /* Call APPC             */

  *conv_id = vcb.mc_alloc.conv_id;          /* return conversation id */

  return(vcb.mc_alloc.primary_rc);          /* return primary rc     */
}
```

Figure 14-15. FXAPPC.C: appc_mc_allocate().

FXAPPC.C: fx_Write()

The **fx_Write()** function (see Figure 14-16 on page 378) is used to send information over an FX pipe. We provide this function using APPC as follows:

- If we're *not* in the Receive state, we simply call the helper routine **appc_mc_send_data()**, see listing in Figure 14-17.
- If we're in the Receive state, we politely ask for permission to send by invoking the helper routine **appc_mc_request_to_send()**, see listing in Figure 14-11 on page 373. We then wait for an answer from the partner TP by invoking the helper routine **appc_mc_receive_and_wait()**, see listing in Figure 14-12 on page 374. If we don't obtain the permission to send, we return with an error. Otherwise, we initiate the send by calling the helper routine **appc_mc_send_data()**.

```
/*-----------------------------------------------------------------------*/
/* function both requester and server use to write to a pipe.           */
/*-----------------------------------------------------------------------*/
USHORT fx_Write(PVOID BufferArea, USHORT BufferLength, PUSHORT BytesWritten)
{
  /*-----------------------------------*/
  /* test state, change state if      */
  /*   necessary                      */
  /*-----------------------------------*/
  if (appc_state == APPC_RECEIVE)
     {
      rc = appc_mc_request_to_send(conv_id, tp_id);
      if (rc)
         {print_error(rc,"performing an APPC mc_request_to_send",
                      __FILE__,__LINE__);
          display_secondary_rc();
          return(FAILED);
         }

      /*-----------------------------------*/
      /* perform APPC mc_receive_and_wait    */
      /*   to see if mc_request_to_send was */
      /*   received by partner              */
      /*-----------------------------------*/
      rc = appc_mc_receive_and_wait(NULL,        /* no buffer               */
                                    0,           /* zero length buffer      */
                                    conv_id,     /* conversation id         */
                                    tp_id,       /* transaction program id  */
                                    &what_rcvd,  /* what was received?      */
                                    &bytes_read);/* how many bytes?         */
      if (rc)
         {print_error(rc,"performing APPC mc_receive_and_wait",
                      __FILE__,__LINE__);
          display_secondary_rc();
          return(FAILED);
         }

      if (what_rcvd  == AP_SEND)
         appc_state = APPC_SEND;
      else
         {print_error(0,"requesting SEND state", __FILE__,__LINE__);
          return(FAILED);
         }
     }
```

Figure 14-16 (Part 1 of 2). FXAPPC.C: fx_Write().

```
    /*-----------------------------------------*/
    /* perform APPC mc_send_data               */
    /*-----------------------------------------*/
    rc = appc_mc_send_data(BufferArea,            /* buffer address         */
                           BufferLength,          /* buffer length          */
                           conv_id,               /* conversation id        */
                           tp_id,                 /* transaction pgm id     */
                           BytesWritten);         /* number bytes sent      */
    if (rc)
       {print_error(rc,"performing an APPC mc_send_data", __FILE__,__LINE__);
        display_secondary_rc();
        return(FAILED);
       }

    return(GOOD);
  } /* end fx_Write */
```

Figure 14-16 (Part 2 of 2). FXAPPC.C: fx_Write().

FXAPPC.C: appc_mc_send_data()

The **appc_mc_send_data()** helper routine (see Figure 14-17) issues a SEND_DATA verb and returns the number of bytes actually sent.

```
/*---------------------------------------------------------------------------*/
/* APPC mc_send_data helper routine                                          */
/*---------------------------------------------------------------------------*/
USHORT
appc_mc_send_data(PVOID   buffer,             /* pointer to send buffer   */
                  USHORT  length,             /* length  of send buffer   */
                  ULONG   conv_id,            /* conversation id          */
                  BYTE    tp_id[8],           /* transaction pgm id       */
                  PUSHORT bytes_sent)         /* number of bytes sent     */
{
  memset(&vcb, 0, sizeof(vcb));               /* zero out control block   */
  vcb.mc_send.opcode   = AP_M_SEND_DATA;      /* MC_SEND_DATA opcode      */
  vcb.mc_send.opext    = AP_MAPPED_CONVERSATION; /* MC type extension     */
  vcb.mc_send.conv_id  = conv_id;             /* Set conversation_id      */
  memcpy(vcb.mc_send.tp_id, tp_id,
         sizeof(vcb.mc_send.tp_id));          /* Set tp_id                */
  vcb.mc_send.dlen     = length;              /* length of buffer to send */
  vcb.mc_send.dptr     = buffer;              /* Set pointer to data in   */
                                              /*    shared segment        */

  APPC_C(&vcb);                               /* Call APPC                */

  *bytes_sent = length;                       /* success, all bytes sent  */

  return(vcb.mc_send.primary_rc);             /* return primary rc        */
}
```

Figure 14-17. FXAPPC.C: appc_mc_send_data().

FXAPPC.C: fx_Read()

The **fx_Read()** function (see Figure 14-18) is used to read information over an FX pipe. We provide this function using APPC by invoking the helper routine **appc_mc_receive_and_wait()**, see listing in Figure 14-12 on page 374.

```
/*-------------------------------------------------------------------------*/
/* function both requester and server use to read from a pipe.            */
/*-------------------------------------------------------------------------*/
USHORT fx_Read(PVOID BufferArea, USHORT BufferLength, PUSHORT BytesRead)
{
  /*-----------------------------------*/
  /* perform APPC mc_receive_and_wait  */
  /*-----------------------------------*/
  rc = appc_mc_receive_and_wait(BufferArea,     /* buffer                 */
                                BufferLength,   /* length                 */
                                conv_id,        /* conversation id        */
                                tp_id,          /* transaction program id */
                                &what_rcvd,     /* what was received?     */
                                BytesRead);     /* how many bytes?        */
  if (rc)
     {print_error(rc,"performing APPC mc_receive_and_wait", __FILE__,__LINE__);
      display_secondary_rc();
      return(FAILED);
     }

  if (what_rcvd  != AP_DATA_COMPLETE)
     {print_error(0,"receiving data", __FILE__,__LINE__);
      return(FAILED);
     }

  /*-----------------------------------*/
  /* set APPC state                    */
  /*-----------------------------------*/
  appc_state = APPC_RECEIVE;

  return(GOOD);
} /* end fx_Read */
```

Figure 14-18. FXAPPC.C: fx_Read().

FXAPPC.C: fx_Transact()

The **fx_Transact()** function (see Figure 14-19) sends a message and receives a reply over an FX pipe. This function is provided by invoking **fx_write()** (see Figure 14-16 on page 378), followed by **fx_read()** (see Figure 14-18).

```
/*-----------------------------------------------------------------------*/
/* function requester uses to request a service.                         */
/*-----------------------------------------------------------------------*/
USHORT fx_Transact(PVOID   InBufferArea,  USHORT InBufferLength,
                   PVOID   OutBufferArea, USHORT OutBufferLength,
                   PUSHORT BytesRead)
{
  USHORT BytesWritten;

  rc = fx_Write(InBufferArea, InBufferLength, &BytesWritten);
  if (rc)
     {print_error(rc,"writing during a transaction",__FILE__,__LINE__);
      return(FAILED);
     }

  rc = fx_Read(OutBufferArea, OutBufferLength, BytesRead);
  if (rc)
     {print_error(rc,"reading during a transaction",__FILE__,__LINE__);
      return(FAILED);
     }

  return(GOOD);
} /* end fx_Transact */
```

Figure 14-19. FXAPPC.C: fx_Transact().

FXAPPC.C: fx_Close()

The **fx_Close()** function (see Figure 14-20) closes an FX pipe. This function will be performed differently depending on whether we're dealing with a client or a server. By design, the server does the DEALLOCATE, and the client confirms it. Also by design, the client's TP ends after the transaction while the server's TP will persist.

Here are the steps followed to close a *server*:

1. If we're not in the Send state, we disconnect by simply calling the helper routine **appc_mc_deallocate()**, see listing in Figure 14-10 on page 373.
2. Else, if we're in the Receive state, we politely ask our partner TP for permission to send by invoking the helper routine **appc_mc_request_to_send()**, see listing in Figure 14-11 on page 373. We then wait for an answer by invoking the helper routine **appc_mc_receive_and_wait()**, see listing in Figure 14-12 on page 374. If we don't obtain the permission to send, we return with an error. Otherwise, we do the deallocate.

Here are the steps followed to close a *client*:

1. Wait for the allocate confirm by invoking the helper routine **appc_mc_receive_and_wait()**, see listing in Figure 14-12 on page 374.
2. Check if *what_received* was an AP_CONFIRM_DEALLOCATE; if so, continue, otherwise return an error.

3. Issue a CONFIRMED, meaning that you confirm the deallocate that was issued by the server. You do this by invoking the helper routine **appc_mc_confirmed()**, see listing in Figure 14-21.
4. Issue a TP_ENDED by invoking the helper routine **appc_tp_ended()**, see listing in Figure 14-22.

```
/*---------------------------------------------------------------------*/
/* function reqester uses to end communication with a server.          */
/*---------------------------------------------------------------------*/
USHORT fx_Close(VOID)
{
  if (server)
     {
      /*---------------------------------*/
      /* test state, change state if     */
      /*   necessary                     */
      /*---------------------------------*/
      if (appc_state == APPC_RECEIVE)
         {
          rc = appc_mc_request_to_send(conv_id, tp_id);
          if (rc)
             {print_error(rc,"performing an APPC request_to_send",
                          __FILE__,__LINE__);
              display_secondary_rc();
              return(FAILED);
             }

          /*---------------------------------*/
          /* perform APPC mc_receive_and_wait */
          /*---------------------------------*/
          rc = appc_mc_receive_and_wait(NULL,        /* no buffer           */
                                        0,           /* zero length buffer  */
                                        conv_id,     /* conversation id     */
                                        tp_id,       /* transaction pgm id  */
                                        &what_rcvd,  /* what was received?  */
                                        &bytes_read);/* how many bytes?     */
          if (rc)
             {print_error(rc,"performing APPC mc_receive_and_wait",
                          __FILE__,__LINE__);
              display_secondary_rc();
              return(FAILED);
             }

          if (what_rcvd  == AP_SEND)
             appc_state = APPC_SEND;
          else
             {print_error(0,"requesting SEND state", __FILE__,__LINE__);
              return(FAILED);
             }
         }
```

Figure 14-20 (Part 1 of 3). FXAPPC.C: fx_Close().

```
        /*-----------------------------------------*/
        /* test state, if send state do the        */
        /*   deallocate                            */
        /*-----------------------------------------*/
        if (appc_state == APPC_SEND)
           {
            /*-----------------------------------------*/
            /* perform APPC deallocate                 */
            /*-----------------------------------------*/
            rc = appc_mc_deallocate(conv_id, tp_id);
            if (rc)
               {print_error(rc,"performing APPC mc_deallocate",
                                __FILE__,__LINE__);
                display_secondary_rc();
                return(FAILED);
                }

            /*-----------------------------------------*/
            /* set APPC state                          */
            /*-----------------------------------------*/
            appc_state = APPC_RESET;
           }

        }
   else
        {
        /*-----------------------------------------*/
        /* perform APPC mc_receive_and_wait        */
        /*-----------------------------------------*/
        rc = appc_mc_receive_and_wait(NULL,        /* no buffer              */
                                      0,           /* zero length buffer     */
                                      conv_id,     /* conversation id        */
                                      tp_id,       /* transaction program id */
                                      &what_rcvd,  /* what was received?     */
                                      &bytes_read);/* how many bytes?        */
        if (rc)
           {print_error(rc,"performing APPC mc_receive_and_wait",
                        __FILE__,__LINE__);
            display_secondary_rc();
            return(FAILED);
           }

        if (what_rcvd  == AP_CONFIRM_DEALLOCATE)
           appc_state = APPC_RESET;
        else
           {print_error(0,"deallocating partner LU", __FILE__,__LINE__);
            return(FAILED);
           }
```

Figure 14-20 (Part 2 of 3). FXAPPC.C: fx_Close().

```
      /*------------------------------------*/
      /* perform APPC mc_confirmed           */
      /*------------------------------------*/
      rc = appc_mc_confirmed(conv_id, tp_id);
      if (rc)
         {print_error(rc,"performing APPC mc_confirmed", __FILE__,__LINE__);
          display_secondary_rc();
          return(FAILED);
         }

     } /* end if server or requester*/
      /*------------------------------------*/
      /* perform APPC tp_ended               */
      /*------------------------------------*/
      rc = appc_tp_ended(tp_id);
      if (rc)
         {print_error(rc,"performing APPC tp_ended",__FILE__,__LINE__);
          display_secondary_rc();
          return(FAILED);
          }

   return(GOOD);
 } /* end fx_Close */
```

Figure 14-20 (Part 3 of 3). FXAPPC.C: fx_Close().

FXAPPC.C: appc_mc_confirmed()

The **appc_mc_confirmed()** helper routine (see Figure 14-21) sends a confirmation reply to the partner TP.

```
/*-----------------------------------------------------------------------*/
/* APPC mc_confirmed helper routine                                      */
/*-----------------------------------------------------------------------*/
USHORT
appc_mc_confirmed(ULONG conv_id,                    /* conversation id       */
                  BYTE  tp_id[8])                   /* transaction pgm id    */
{
  memset(&vcb, 0, sizeof(vcb));                     /* zero out control block */
  vcb.mc_confirmed.opcode = AP_M_CONFIRMED;         /* Verb=MC_CONFIRMED     */
  vcb.mc_confirmed.opext  =
           AP_MAPPED_CONVERSATION;                  /* Set MC ext. type      */
  vcb.mc_confirmed.conv_id= conv_id;                /* Set Conversation_id   */
  memcpy(vcb.mc_confirmed.tp_id, tp_id,
         sizeof(vcb.mc_confirmed.tp_id));           /* Set tp_id             */

  APPC_C(&vcb);                                     /* Call APPC             */

  return(vcb.mc_confirmed.primary_rc);              /* return primary rc     */
}
```

Figure 14-21. FXAPPC.C: appc_mc_confirmed().

FXAPPC.C: appc_tp_ended()

The **appc_tp_ended()** helper routine (see Figure 14-22) notifies APPC of the end of the identified TP. APPC will internally issue a DEALLOCATE to free all resources associated with the TP.

```
/*--------------------------------------------------------------------------*/
/* APPC tp_ended helper routine                                             */
/*--------------------------------------------------------------------------*/
USHORT
appc_tp_ended(BYTE tp_id[8])                     /* transaction pgm id      */
{
  memset(&vcb, 0, sizeof(vcb));                  /* zero out control block  */
  vcb.tp_ended.opcode = AP_TP_ENDED;             /* Verb - TP_ENDED         */
  memcpy(vcb.tp_ended.tp_id, tp_id,              /* set tp_id               */
         sizeof(vcb.tp_ended.tp_id));

  APPC_C(&vcb);                                  /* call APPC               */

  return(vcb.tp_ended.primary_rc);               /* return primary rc       */
}
```

Figure 14-22. FXAPPC.C: appc_tp_ended().

Chapter 15

FX Using the LAN Server and Remote Named Pipes

This chapter adds two more powerful network protocols to our repertoire of FX file transfer comparisons: Remote Named Pipes and the LAN Server. Both protocols build on top of NetBIOS and the LAN requester, and they both require that you install a copy of IBM's OS/2 LAN Server program on the server machine. In theory, both these programs should also work with Microsoft's LAN Manager. The purpose of this chapter is to make you aware that OS/2 can be extended into a full-fledged network operating system with programs like IBM's LAN Server or Microsoft's LAN Manager. You will also discover that the network operating system allows your stand-alone programs to work over the network without requiring any changes to your code. In other words, the network operating system makes the network transparent.

ABOUT NETWORK OPERATING SYSTEMS

The transparency feature that a network operating system provides makes it easy for you to develop network software. A typical network operating system also provides scores of network utilities which can make life on a network very enjoyable. "OS/2 EE LAN Requester and the IBM LAN Server" on page 60 contains a list of the benefits provided by IBM's LAN Server, and by extension, Microsoft's LAN Manager. These two products form the de facto standard for extending OS/2 and MS-DOS services to the network. But, there are no free lunches in life or operating systems, as we will see.

What are the Costs?

Here's what a network operating system ends up costing you:

- The dollar price of a new program. You need to purchase at least one copy of LAN Server for your server. This costs in the vicinity of $1000. On the other hand, peer-to-peer protocols like NetBIOS and APPC are bundled with OS/2 EE.

- More memory. LAN server adds two MBytes to the server and 100 KBytes to the requester.
- The loss of peer-to-peer symmetry. LAN Server is an asymmetrical protocol. You can only create a Named Pipe on a server machine. You can only offer to share subdirectories and printers on your server. If you want to make your protocols fully symmetrical, you need to install a full LAN Server on every machine. This is obviously an expensive solution. On the other hand, APPC and NetBIOS are fully symmetrical protocols.
- Some performance degradation (perhaps). We're introducing an extra layer on top of NetBIOS. We'll provide you the exact cost (if any) in performance when we present the comparative benchmark figures for FX in the next chapter.
- The logistics of installing and managing an additional program on the server. This always adds a certain level of complexity.

The bottom line is that a LAN Server is *not* the right protocol for you if each one of your clients can also be a server. In this case, you are better off with a plain peer-to-peer protocol like NetBIOS or APPC on top of which you can create your custom network services.

What are the Benefits?

On the other hand the LAN Server is good for the following situations:

- If your networks consist of many clients and few servers. This is the case where the services are centralized on a few high-powered superserver machines.
- If you have mixed networks of DOS and OS/2 clients. The LAN Server requester works with either DOS or OS/2. It extends the concept of Named Pipes to DOS requesters. In all fairness, NetBIOS also works well in mixed environments. However APPC takes up too much memory on DOS machines.
- If your networks require other LAN Manager services such as shared files, a print server and network management services. The LAN Server offers a myriad of network services such as: network management, configuration, resource management, security, audit trails, etc. Please review Chapter 3 for the full list of functions offered by the LAN Server.
- For networks that require an *open standard.* The Microsoft LAN Manager and the IBM LAN Server are de facto industry standards. The publication of their internal APIs makes them an *open* standard. Such a standard will make it easier to share distributed resources across operating systems (DOS, OS/2 and UNIX) and network platforms.

How Does it Work?

The key concept in a network operating system is *redirection.* The idea is that the call to any device controlled by the operating system can be *redirected* to the network. This simple idea makes it easy to create a virtual service space that extends over the network. The *binding* of the service with the server machine is performed by the operating system.

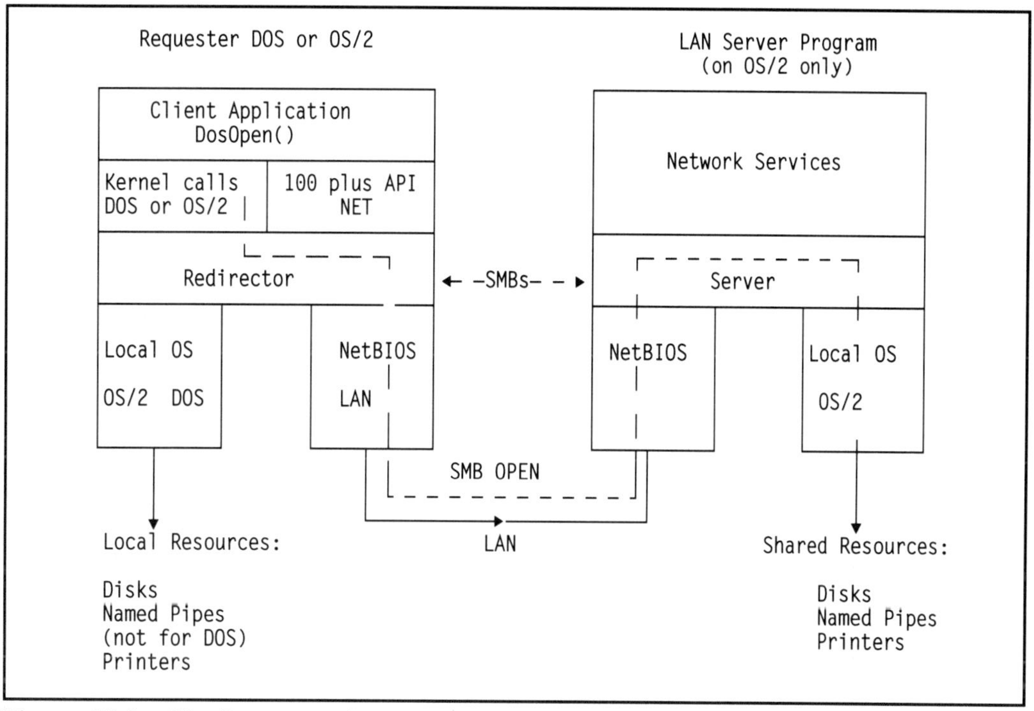

Figure 15-1. The Requester Server Protocol Used by LAN Server and LAN Manager.

What is a Redirector?

A *redirector* is a software component that intercepts system calls for remote resources, packages them, and sends them over the network for execution. It then unpackages the reply and returns the results to the caller. All this is done transparently at the API level. Figure 15-1 shows it all. The client workstation on the left is either running DOS or OS/2. On the right, we show a server workstation which runs the OS/2 LAN Server Program on top of OS/2. The LAN Server program is a client-server application. In addition to the full server element, it requires a redirector each of its clients. The redirector is packaged with the OS/2 EE (as the LAN Requester). 128 copies of a DOS requester are made available with the purchase of a single server.

So How Does a Redirector Work?

The redirector routes or *redirects* DOS or OS/2 system calls. For example, when you issue a call to open a file, named pipe, printer, or some other resource the redirector determines if the resource is local or remote. If the resource is local, it hands over the call to the local OS. If the resource is remote, it packages the request in an envelope called a **Server Message Block (SMB)** and ships it over the LAN using NetBIOS to the destination server. The SMB protocol consists of message exchanges conducted between servers and requester to perform network operating system functions. In the example in Figure 15-1 on page 389, the **DosOpen()** call is for a remote resource. So, it gets shipped over the network to the server, which accepts the call and reissues it to a local resource. When the server completes the open, it returns the results to the client redirector via an **SMB** reply message.

Local or Remote: It's All in the Name

How does the redirector know if the resource is local or remote? It infers it from the resource name. A fully qualified resource pathname includes the optional name of the machine on which it resides. The machine name is preceded by two backslashes (\\) in the pathname. This means that all you've got to do in your programs to access remote resources is call them using their fully qualified network name, and let the network operating system handle everything else.

Explicit Network API Calls

Figure 15-1 on page 389 also shows a category of **NET** API services that are available to your application. An application that makes NET calls as opposed to relying on simple redirection, is "network-aware." The network API services are extensive. They allow you to explicitly control, through programming interfaces, many of the Network Operating System functions. The API calls support alerts, network and resource management services, security, and access control. For more details, please review the descriptions in "OS/2 EE LAN Requester and the IBM LAN Server" on page 60.

FX USING REMOTE NAMED PIPES

This section is short and sweet. Our design objective is to create the FX DLLs that use *remote* Named Pipes. Well, the job couldn't be easier; it's just a question of changing the name of the pipe and running the program developed in Chapter 10. The code remains unchanged. This is a good example of a *network transparent program*. To make the program run on the network, just do the following:

1. Install a copy of the LAN Server on the server machine.
2. Change the name of the Named Pipe in the (.CFG) file for Named Pipes (in Chapter 10) to include a server name as part of the pipe name. This is done by preceding the pipe name with a (\\) followed by the server name.
3. The program will now run "as is" remotely; there is no need to even recompile it.

Now we have a version of FX that can run in the great network derby (see Chapter 16) as a remote Named Pipes DLL. Named Pipes, of course, build their network services on top of the *redirector*. Wouldn't it be nice if all our software projects were that simple?

FX USING THE LAN REQUESTER-SERVER

In this section, we demonstrate once more the power of *redirected* LAN services, with a program that makes direct use of the network operating system. Our design objective is to measure the file transfer performance of the LAN Server. We'll meet this objective by introducing a single program that replaces the FXREQ and FXSVR programs as well as the FX DLLs. This program performs the file transfer using a single OS/2 command: **DosCopy**. Requester magic working in tandem with the LAN Server will take care of all the details involved in the intercomputer file transfer. So what's left for us to do? We still have to issue the **DosCopy** and create (or mostly borrow) the code that measures the file transfer performance. Our program must be able to participate in the great network derby (in the next chapter) as the LAN Requester/Server champion. This means that it needs to be equipped with all the FX performance-measuring paraphernalia.

The FXLSCR.C Program

We present, in Figure 15-2, the listing of **FXLSVR.C**, the program which implements the file transfer using the LAN Server. The file is copied using the **DosCopy** from a local drive to a drive on the LAN Server machine. Unlike the other FX file transfer programs in this book, this one does not have a server peer component (actually it's built-in). Since it takes two parties to implement a protocol, and we can only control one of them, the requester, here's what we ended up doing:

1. We created a shared subdirectory on the server machine.
2. We wrote **FXLSVR.C** to implement the equivalent of a file COPY.
3. We ported all our timers and stopwatch procedures from the FX programs into **FXLSVR.C**. This program has been made an honest contender to run in the great FX derby as the LAN Server champion. We put all the hooks in the right places to measure and report the file transfer time. These are the same timing tools we used in all the other FX programs.

Except for the **DosCopy** feature, the **FXLSVR.C** program (see listing in Figure 15-2) is nothing more than the repackaging of FX timing and reporting functions. The listing contains the entire program. We don't even need a communication-specific DLL function. As a matter of fact, the code does not contain a single network API call. So how does the file get moved over the network? Where is the equivalent of the NetBIOS, APPC, or Named Pipes calls of the previous chapters? They've all been replaced by a simple *redirected* OS/2 call, **DosCopy**. One invocation of this call will cause the file to "auto-magically" get copied from one machine to the next. A description of this call follows.

DosCopy

This API call copies a file or subdirectory. The prototype for this call is:

```
DosCopy(PSZ    sourcefile,   /*Pointer to name of source file*/
        PSZ    targetfile,   /*Pointer to name of target     */
        USHORT options,      /*Copy over or append to target */
        ULONG  reserved);    /*Must be 0L                    */
```

The following is a description of the parameters:

- The ***sourcefile*** parameter points to the null terminated name of the file or directory to copy. No wild cards are permitted.
- The ***targetfile*** parameter points to the null terminated name of the file or directory that specifies the name of the destination. The path of the destination must be specified; you cannot just specify a drive.
- The ***options*** parameter specifies how the copy should be handled if a file already exists at the destination. Set this parameter to DCPY_EXISTING if you want to overwrite the destination file contents. Or set it to DCPY_APPEND if you want the data appended to the end of the destination file. If the destination file does not exist, a new file is created.

Now that we've explained the one OS/2 call, the **FXLSVR.C** code that follows is readable "as is." So we've left it all in one piece. If you get lost, you can always go back to main() to understand what the program does.

```
/*****************************************************************************/
/*  PROGRAM NAME: FXLSVR - File Transfer example using LAN SERVER and       */
/*                         LAN REQUESTER                                     */
/*                                                                           */
/*  PROGRAM DESCRIPTION:  This module uses the LAN Server program to         */
/*    implement a file transfer program.  The file transfer is accomplished */
/*    by using DosCopy to copy a file from a local drive to a redirected    */
/*    on the LAN Server machine.                                             */
/*                                                                           */
/*    A summary report is displayed showing how long it took to transfer    */
/*    the file.                                                              */
/*                                                                           */
/*  PROGRAM INVOCATION:                                                      */
/*                                                                           */
/*    FXLSVR direction file-name                                             */
/*                                                                           */
/*     where:                                                                */
/*         direction is either SEND or RECV.                                 */
/*                                                                           */
/*         file-name is the name of the file to transfer.  If a path is     */
/*                   specified the path must exist on the requester and     */
/*                   server machines.                                        */
/*                                                                           */
/*  EXAMPLE INVOCATIONS:                                                     */
/*                                                                           */
/*    FXLSVR  SEND MYFILE.TMP                                                */
/*    FXLSVR  RECV MYFILE.TMP                                                */
/*****************************************************************************/
#include <process.h>                /* For exit()                            */
#include <stdio.h>                  /* For printf() & NULL                   */
#include <stdlib.h>                 /* For printf                            */
#include <string.h>                 /* For printf                            */
#include <sys\types.h>              /* For time()                            */
#include <sys\timeb.h>              /* For time()                            */
#include <sys\stat.h>               /* For stat()                            */
#include <io.h>                     /* For file I/O                          */
#include <fcntl.h>                  /* For file I/O                          */
#include <sys\types.h>              /* For file I/O                          */

#include <os2.h>                    /* for types only                        */

#include "fxfer.h"
#include "fxreq.h"

/*---------------------------------------------------------------------------*/
/* Global variables, declares for this module                               */
/*---------------------------------------------------------------------------*/
CHAR rdr_drive[3];
CHAR rdr_file_name[128];
VOID read_config(VOID);
```

Figure 15-2 (Part 1 of 5). FXLSVR.C: File Transfer with LAN Sever.

```
/*---------------------------------------------------------------------------*/
/* Main routine. Performs a file transfer and calculates statistics.        */
/*---------------------------------------------------------------------------*/
VOID main(SHORT argc, PCHAR argv[], PCHAR envp[])
{
   /*---------------------------------*/
   /* get command line arguments      */
   /*---------------------------------*/
   if (get_args(argc, argv))
      { print_help();
        exit(FAILED);
      }

   /*---------------------------------*/
   /* initialize                      */
   /*---------------------------------*/
   read_config();

   /*---------------------------------*/
   /* perform the file transfer       */
   /*---------------------------------*/
   open_bgn_time = save_time();
   xfer_bgn_time = save_time();

   switch (service)
     {
      case FILE_SEND_TO_SERVER:      send_file();
                                     break;

      case FILE_RECEIVE_FROM_SERVER: receive_file();
                                     break;
     } /* end switch */

   close_bgn_time = save_time();
   end_time = save_time();

   /*---------------------------------*/
   /* print the statistics            */
   /*---------------------------------*/
   printf("File transfer completed.\n");
   file_size = get_file_size(file_name);
   print_statistics();

   exit(GOOD);
} /* end main */

/*---------------------------------------------------------------------------*/
/* Initialize program variables from command line.                          */
/*---------------------------------------------------------------------------*/
USHORT get_args(SHORT argc, PCHAR argv[])
{
   /*---------------------------------*/
   /* are there the right number of args? */
   /*---------------------------------*/
   if (argc != 3)
     return(FAILED);
```

Figure 15-2 (Part 2 of 5). FXLSVR.C: File Transfer with LAN Sever.

```
    /*_________________________________________*/
    /* send or receive?                        */
    /*_________________________________________*/
    if (strcmp("SEND", strupr(argv[1])) == 0)
      service = FILE_SEND_TO_SERVER;
    else
      if (strcmp("RECV", strupr(argv[1])) == 0)
        service = FILE_RECEIVE_FROM_SERVER;
      else return(FAILED);

    /*_________________________________________*/
    /* get the file name                       */
    /*_________________________________________*/
    strcpy(file_name, argv[2]);

    /*_________________________________________*/
    /* everything is OK!                       */
    /*_________________________________________*/
    return(GOOD);
} /* end eget_args */

/*_______________________________________________________________________________________*/
/* Read configuration data                                                               *
/*_______________________________________________________________________________________*/
VOID read_config(VOID)
{
  FILE    *config_file;                   /* Input file control block               */
  CHAR     line[80];                      /* one line of config file                */

  printf("Reading configuration parameters.\n");
  /*_________________________________________*/
  /* open the configuration file             */
  /*_________________________________________*/
  if (NULL == (config_file = fopen("fxlsvr.cfg","r")))
     {printf("\nError opening configuration file\n",__FILE__,__LINE__);
      exit(FAILED);
     }
  else
     /*_________________________________________*/
     /* read the configuration parameters.      */
     /* The parameters are expected to be:      */
     /*      - in the form <name = value>       */
     /*      - in the order read below          */
     /*_________________________________________*/
     {
      fgets(line, sizeof(line), config_file);
      if (sscanf(line,"REDIRECTED_DRIVE = %2s ", rdr_drive) != 1)
         {printf("\nError reading REDIRECTED_DRIVE from configuration file\n");
          exit(FAILED);
         }
     }
  fclose(config_file);
} /* end read_config */
```

Figure 15-2 (Part 3 of 5). FXLSVR.C: File Transfer with LAN Sever.

```
/*--------------------------------------------------------------------*/
/* Function to receive a file from the server.                        *
/*--------------------------------------------------------------------*/
VOID receive_file(VOID)
{ CHAR rdr_file_name[128];

  sprintf(rdr_file_name,"%s%s",rdr_drive,file_name);
  if (DosCopy(rdr_file_name, file_name, DCPY_EXISTING, 0L))
     {printf("\nError copying file from LAN Server\n");
      exit(FAILED);
     }
} /* end receive_file */

/*--------------------------------------------------------------------*/
/* Function to send a file to the server.                             */
/*--------------------------------------------------------------------*/
VOID send_file(VOID)
{
  sprintf(rdr_file_name,"%s%s",rdr_drive,file_name);
  if (DosCopy(file_name, rdr_file_name, DCPY_EXISTING, 0L))
     {printf("\nError copying file to LAN Server\n");
      exit(FAILED);
     }
} /* end send_file */

/*--------------------------------------------------------------------*/
/* Start timing an event.                                             */
/*--------------------------------------------------------------------*/
double save_time(VOID)
{
  ftime(&timebuff);
  return((double)timebuff.time+((double)timebuff.millitm)/(double)1000);
} /* end save_time */

/*--------------------------------------------------------------------*/
/* Get File Size                                                      */
/*--------------------------------------------------------------------*/
ULONG get_file_size(PCHAR name)
{
  int fhandle;
  unsigned long size;

  if (-1 == (fhandle = open(name, O_BINARY | O_RDONLY )))
     {printf("\nError opening file.\n");
      return(FAILED);
     }
  size = filelength(fhandle);
  close(fhandle);

  return(size);
} /* end get_file_size */
```

Figure 15-2 (Part 4 of 5). FXLSVR.C: File Transfer with LAN Sever.

```
/*-------------------------------------------------------------------*/
/* Print Statistics.                                                 */
/*-------------------------------------------------------------------*/
VOID print_statistics(VOID)
{
  if (service == FILE_SEND_TO_SERVER)
     printf("\n%s sent to the server.\n", file_name);
  else
     printf("\n%s received from the server.\n",file_name);

  printf("Communication link open time was %f seconds.\n",
          xfer_bgn_time-open_bgn_time);
  printf("%ld bytes transferred in %f seconds.\n",
          file_size, close_bgn_time-xfer_bgn_time);
  printf("The average transfer rate was %.2f kilobytes/second.\n",
          file_size/((close_bgn_time-xfer_bgn_time)*1000));
  printf("Communication link close time was %f seconds.\n",
          end_time-close_bgn_time);
} /* end print_statistics */

/*-------------------------------------------------------------------*/
/* Print Help.                                                       */
/*-------------------------------------------------------------------*/
VOID print_help(VOID)
{
  printf("\nIncorrect command invocation.  Enter as follows:\n");
  printf("\n");
  printf("FXLSVR direction file name                                \n");
  printf("                                                          \n");
  printf(" where:                                                   \n");
  printf("     direction is either SEND or RECV.                    \n");
  printf("                                                          \n");
  printf("     file-name is the name of the file to transfer.  If a \n");
  printf("               path is specified the path must exist on the \n");
  printf("               requester and server machines.             \n");
  printf("                                                          \n");
  printf("\n\n");
} /* end print_help */
```

Figure 15-2 (Part 5 of 5). FXLSVR.C: File Transfer with LAN Sever.

Chapter 16

The Great FX LAN Derby

In this chapter, we will run the races between the different protocol implementations of the FX file transfer. The first race compares the performance of local versus remote Named Pipes. This will give us a feel for the network overhead in interprocess communication. This is followed by a multiprotocol race that compares the network performance of NetBIOS, APPC, Named Pipes, and the LAN Server. This race is run varying the file sizes and message buffers. Finally, we present some *Sniffer* traces of the network exchanges. This is done to validate our benchmark numbers and give you some idea of what network protocol analyzers can do for you. Before declaring a winner, please take note of the disclaimer section. There are some big surprises in this race. In fact, the winner is the darkhorse of protocols when it comes to speed. But we're getting ahead of our story.

THE BLOBS ARE COMING

Images, video, voice, graphics, intelligent documents, and database snapshots are about to test the capabilities of our LANs for moving large data objects quickly. These large objects are affectionately called **BLOBs** which stands for Binary Large Objects. Client-Server applications, as they increasingly become multimedia, will be called upon to move these BLOBs quickly. The clients will capture and display BLOBs and send them to the servers for storage. Clients should be able to retrieve BLOBs from servers using ordinary transactions. If you think about it, the FX application is really a BLOB server. The FX benchmarks we present in this chapter may be the ultimate test of how well our leading LAN Protocols (NetBIOS, APPC, Named Pipes, and the LAN Server) compare when it comes to moving BLOBs.

"Lies, Damned Lies, and Benchmarks"

Yes, benchmarking is a tricky business where many factors can affect the overall network performance. When dealing with benchmarks, you should really make sure that you're comparing "apples to apples." Always make it a point to understand what factors are being measured. The numbers presented in this chapter should only be used to evaluate *relative* design trade-offs. All the measurements are of interest only in terms of the comparative information they convey. So, please don't get hung up on any absolute numbers.

What the FX Benchmarks Measure

Here's what the FX benchmarks help measure:

- Code complexity versus gains in performance.
- The effect of BLOB size on performance.
- The effect of message size on performance.
- What performance degradation can be expected when a peer process is run on a remote machine versus a local one?
- How well do each of Named Pipes, NetBIOS, APPC, and the LAN Server perform when it comes to moving BLOBs on the network.

What the FX Benchmarks Do Not Measure

Here's what the FX benchmarks do **not** measure or quantify:

- The performance of simple request/reply transactions used in Remote Procedure Calls.
- Protocol features such as broadcast, datagrams, security, etc.
- The overhead required to establish sessions. FX is equipped to do that, but we didn't record the results. You can try that yourself.
- Ease of installation and configuration.
- Network management.
- Connectivity to other networks and operating systems.

What Makes Our Benchmarks "Honest"

Now that we've recorded the disclaimer, let us tell you what's good about the FX benchmark:

- The code is *available*. It's all in this book. This means that you can see for yourself where we placed the measurement probes and how the results were derived. If you don't like something we did, just enter a change and see what the effects are.
- The protocols, with the exception of LAN Server, are all driven by a *common driver*. This is as close as it ever comes to creating a common test-bed.

- The relative results of the tests are easy to reproduce and duplicate. You should be looking at the test ratios independent of the hardware. Don't look at the absolute numbers. These can vary wildly with machine power, network bandwidth, network utilization and LAN adapters.
- The test results were validated with network Sniffer traces.
- The tests are representative of network *bulk transfer* situations. They test the buffering capabilities of the various protocols and how they chunk network transmissions.
- All the protocols that were measured are provided by the same vendor and (with the exception of LAN Server) are all part of the same product. This means we don't have an axe to grind.

WHAT EXACTLY ARE WE MEASURING?

The benchmark numbers we present in this chapter measure the data transfer times after a link is established. We do not include the time to initialize, open, and close a link. These are the areas where comparisons may be subject to controversy. However, you should try running the FX benchmarks yourself and get some numbers for the connect time and close time of each protocol.

We show on the left side of Figure 16-1 where the test starts and where it ends. The results are reported by FXREQ. Four protocol suites will be tested: Named Pipes, NetBIOS, APPC, and the LAN Server. The first three will be driven by FXREQ and FXSVR. The LAN Server protocol is driven by FXLSVR, which is a repackaged version of FXREQ's measurement probes.

LOCAL VERSUS REMOTE NAMED PIPES BENCHMARK

This benchmark first runs FXREQ and FXSVR on the same machine and then on separate machines attached by a 4 Mb/sec Token Ring LAN. What we're looking for is a measure of the overhead which the network introduces over local interprocess communications. Here are the results of moving a 100 KByte file using various buffer sizes. *The file exchanges always use RAM disk to remove the effects of the disk access from the measurements.*

Table 16-1. 100 KByte File Transfer: Local Named Pipes Vs Remote Named Pipes.

Protocol	Message Buffer Sizes			
	4 KByte Buffer	**16 KByte Buffer**	**32 Kbyte Buffer**	**64 KByte Buffer**
Named Pipes (Local)	158.7 KByte/sec	243.9 KByte/sec	291.1 KByte/sec	536.0 KByte/sec
Named Pipes (Remote)	103.9 KByte/sec	114.9 KByte/sec	123.5 KByte/sec	103.1 KByte/sec

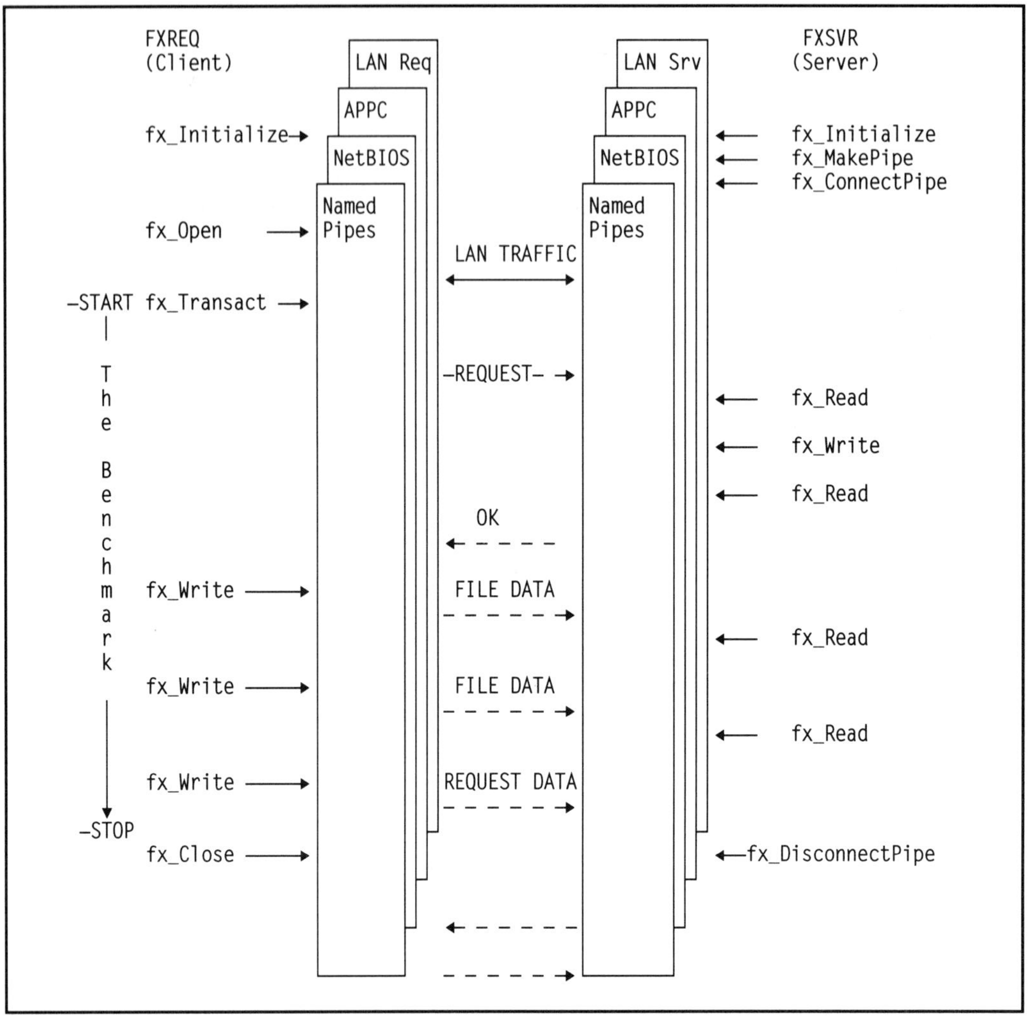

Figure 16-1. Benchmark is Between START and STOP.

Commentary

- Yes, the network does slow things down. If you're going to move a peer process to a remote machine, prepare yourself for a substantial performance degradation in the IPC.
- Yes, transfer buffer sizes matter when it comes to moving bulk data. The larger the buffer, the better off you are. However, with remote Named Pipes we seem to have hit a peak somewhere between a 32 KByte and 64 KByte message buffer size. Any idea why?

APPC, NETBIOS, NAMED PIPES, AND LAN SERVER

The second benchmark runs FXREQ and FXSVR on separate machines attached by a 4 Mb/sec Token Ring LAN. We'll be driving the different protocols by dynamically linking to their FX DLLs one protocol set at a time. This is done by copying the appropriate FX DLL (from the previous chapters) into the working subdirectory and running the tests. The exception is the LAN Server protocol, which is totally self-contained in FXLSVR.EXE and doesn't have a DLL. The benchmark consists of sending a file from FXREQ to FXSVR. *Here again, the file exchanges always use RAM disk to remove the effects of the disk access from the measurements.* We will conduct two variations of this benchmark:

- The first measures varying *message buffer* sizes.
- The second measures varying files sizes.

Varying the Message Buffer Sizes

We run the benchmark using four message buffer sizes: 4 KByte, 16 KByte, 32 KByte, and 64 KByte. The message size is varied by changing a parameter in the FX (.CFG) file. The file sent is 100 KBytes in size. The idea of this test is to measure how the different protocols perform when this message buffer factor is varied. Here are the averaged results of the runs:

Table 16-2. 100 KByte File Transfer Using: Named Pipes, APPC, NetBIOS, and LAN Server.

Protocol	Message Buffer Sizes			
	4 KByte Buffer	16 KByte Buffer	32 KByte Buffer	64 KByte Buffer
APPC	137.0 KByte/sec	152.5 KByte/sec	150.0 KByte/sec	141.0 KByte/sec
NetBIOS	117.6 KByte/sec	128.2 KByte/sec	128.2 KByte/sec	133.3 KByte/sec
Named Pipes	103.9 KByte/sec	114.9 KByte/sec	123.5 KByte/sec	103.1 KByte/sec
LAN Server	(see note)	(see note)	(see note)	114.9 KByte/sec

Note: In the case of the LAN Server program, the minimum allocation unit for the message buffer is 64 KBytes. This means we couldn't measure anything smaller.

Commentary

- It appears that when it comes to raw transfer speeds (excluding connect and disconnect time), APPC is superfast. Yes, APPC appears to be faster than both NetBIOS and Named Pipes. This is no optical illusion! Why? It looks like APPC's blocking algorithm is quite effective in bulk transfer situations.
- Yes, transfer buffer sizes matter when it comes to moving bulk data. However, there are points of diminishing returns. With APPC and Named Pipes, a peak is reached at some point after which increasing the buffer size leads to a degradation in performance.

Varying File Sizes

We run the benchmark and transfer files of three different sizes: 1 KByte, 10 KByte and 100 KByte. The idea is to measure how the different protocols perform when the file size factor is varied (also remember that all transfers are from RAM disk).

Note: The message size is 4 KByte, except for LAN Server which is 64 KByte.

Table 16-3. Varying File Sizes: Named Pipes, APPC, NetBIOS, and LAN Server.

Protocol	File Sizes		
	1 KByte File Size	10 KByte File Size	100 KByte File Size
APPC	11.1 KByte/sec	79.2 KByte/sec	137.0 KByte/sec
NetBIOS	16.7 KByte/sec	64.2 KByte/sec	117.6 KByte/sec
Named Pipes	14.3 KByte/sec	61.7 KByte/sec	103.9 KByte/sec
LAN Server	6.7 KByte/sec	44.7 KByte/sec	114.9 KByte/sec

Commentary

- Notice that APPC does not perform very well with small (1 KByte) files. This supports our hypothesis that its speed advantage with large files is due to its superior blocking techniques.
- In general, the larger the file to be moved, the better the effective transfer rates for all the protocols. They get to send more for the same amount of fixed overhead.

VALIDATING THE BENCHMARK WITH A SNIFFER

What's a Sniffer? It's a *Network Analyzer* made by Network General. A network analyzer is an indispensable tool for anyone doing serious LAN work (its our profession's microscope). It works by capturing all the frames it sees on the network in a buffer (you can filter the capture to what you're interested in seeing). Once a set of frames are in its buffer, this marvelous tool can display the information in hundreds of interesting ways. It can show you all the details at the byte stream level, or it can interpret the protocol for you. It can also show you conversational exchanges between two workstations and the elapsed time between packets. The purpose here is not to tell you all about the wonderful things Sniffers can do, we're just using the Sniffer to *validate* our benchmark results. Remember the old saying about *lies and benchmarks.*

What the Sniffer Sees?

We captured the Sniffer Traces for the 10 KByte file transfers of the previous section. We've included them here for your consideration. The traces displayed in this section are the summary reports of the network frames captured during a time interval. The summary corresponds to the topmost layer of protocol the Sniffer was able to decipher on a particular frame. Here is your guide to reading the summary Sniffer traces:

M — This is a marker that indicates the base time for all subsequent time measurements. The time on all the frames which follow is measured relative to the frame with the "M" marker.

number — The numbers in the first column identify the frame's position in the Sniffer's capture buffer. The numbers shown are not contiguous because we filtered out of the summary frames which did not contain protocol relevant information. We're only interested in APPC (SNA), NetBIOS (NET), and the SMB protocol (SMB) used by Named Pipes and the LAN Server.

Rel Time — This is the time elapsed in seconds measured relative to the frame marked with "M".

Size — This is the size in bytes of the frame. The size includes user data and all the communication headers which encapsulate it.

From Requester — This packet was sent by the requester (i.e., client). The Sniffer displays the results of the trace as a two-way communication handshake between the "Requester" and the "Server" machines.

From Server — This packet was sent by the "Server." This is the server end of the two-way exchange.

For more information on the Sniffer, refer to Network General's documentation.

APPC Sniff

```
SUMMARY Rel Time Size    From Requester              From Server

M    1   0.000   183  SNA C FMD ATTACH FILEMSVR
     3   0.016    29                               SNA R FMD
     5   0.052    36                               SNA C FMD user data
     7   0.084  1949  SNA C FMD user data
     9   0.093  1949  SNA C FMD user data
    11   0.103  1949  SNA C FMD user data
    13   0.113  1949  SNA C FMD user data
    15   0.122  1949  SNA C FMD user data
    17   0.128   616  SNA C FMD user data
```

Figure 16-2. APPC Sniff: 10 KByte File, Elapsed Time = 0.128 Secs.

Commentary

- According to the Sniffer trace above, it takes 0.128 seconds to transfer a 10 KByte file. This translates into a 78.1 KByte/s transfer rate.
- The equivalent result using FX timers is 79.2 KByte/s (see Table 16-3 on page 404). We're validated.

NetBIOS Sniff

```
SUMMARY Rel Time Size    From Requester               From Server

     1   -0.022   32  NET D=0E S=0E Session initialize
     3   -0.019   32                               NET D=0E S=0E Session confirm
M    5    0.000  163  NET D=0E S=0E Data, 131 bytes
     7    0.003   32                               NET D=0E S=0E Data ACK
     9    0.031   35                               NET D=0E S=0E Data, 3 bytes
    11    0.034   32  NET D=0E S=0E Data ACK
    13    0.050 1980  NET D=0E S=0E Data, 1948 bytes
    15    0.054   32                               NET D=0E S=0E Rcvd data
    17    0.063 1980  NET D=0E S=0E Data, 1948 bytes
    18    0.064  232  NET D=0E S=0E Data, 200 bytes
    21    0.068   32                               NET D=0E S=0E Data ACK
    23    0.087 1980  NET D=0E S=0E Data, 1948 bytes
    24    0.093 1980  NET D=0E S=0E Data, 1948 bytes
    26    0.095  232  NET D=0E S=0E Data, 200 bytes
    29    0.098   32                               NET D=0E S=0E Data ACK
    31    0.113 1867  NET D=0E S=0E Data, 1835 bytes
    33    0.117   32                               NET D=0E S=0E Send more now
    35    0.125 1867  NET D=0E S=0E Data, 1835 bytes
    37    0.129   32                               NET D=0E S=0E Data ACK
    39    0.135   41  NET D=0E S=0E Data, 9 bytes
    41    0.140   32                               NET D=0E S=0E Send more now
    43    0.143   41  NET D=0E S=0E Data, 9 bytes
    45    0.146   32                               NET D=0E S=0E Data ACK
    47    0.152  163  NET D=0E S=0E Data, 131 bytes
```

Figure 16-3. NetBIOS Sniff: 10 KByte File, Elapsed Time = 0.152 Secs.

Commentary

- According to the Sniffer trace above, it takes 0.152 seconds to transfer a 10 KByte file. This translates into a 65.8 KByte/s transfer rate.
- The equivalent result using FX timers is 64.2 KByte/s (see Table 16-3 on page 404). We're validated.

Named Pipe Sniff

```
SUMMARY Rel Time Size    From Requester              From Server

M    1    0.000   239  SMB C Transaction \PIPE\
     3    0.030    88                                SMB R Transaction
     5    0.034    35                                NET D=1F S=22 Data, 3 bytes
     7    0.037    32  NET D=22 S=1F Data ACK
     9    0.053  1980  SMB C F=4220 Write 4096 at 0
    11    0.063  1980  NET D=22 S=1F Data, 1948 bytes
    12    0.064   292  NET D=22 S=1F Data, 260 bytes
    15    0.071    79                                SMB R OK
    17    0.089  1980  SMB C F=4220 Write 4096 at 0
    19    0.099  1980  NET D=22 S=1F Data, 1948 bytes
    20    0.100   292  NET D=22 S=1F Data, 260 bytes
    23    0.107    79                                SMB R OK
    25    0.122  1927  SMB C F=4220 Write 1835 at 0
    27    0.128    79                                SMB R OK
    29    0.133   101  SMB C F=4220 Write 9 at 0
    31    0.138    79                                SMB R OK
    33    0.144   223  SMB C F=4220 Write 131 at 0
    35    0.149    79                                SMB R OK
    37    0.155    73  SMB C F=4220 Close
    39    0.162    67                                SMB R Closed
```

Figure 16-4. Named Pipe Sniff: 10 KByte File, Elapsed time = 0.162 Secs.

Commentary

- According to the Sniffer trace above, it takes 0.162 seconds to transfer a 10 KByte file. This translates into a 65.8 KByte/s transfer rate.
- The equivalent result using FX timers is 61.7 KByte/s (see Table 16-3 on page 404). We're validated.
- Notice how Named Pipes use the SMB protocol on top of NetBIOS.

LAN Server Sniff

```
SUMMARY Rel Time Size    From Requester              From Server

M    1   0.000    77  SMB C Get File Attributes
     3   0.010    87                             SMB R OK
     5   0.016    77  SMB C Get File Attributes
     7   0.027    87                             SMB R OK
     9   0.039   106  SMB C Open \10K.FIL
    11   0.065    97                             SMB R Opened F=2000
    17   0.105  1980  SMB C F=2000 Write Block Raw 10000 at 0
    19   0.116  1980  NET D=22 S=1F Data, 1948 bytes
    20   0.116   292  NET D=22 S=1F Data, 260 bytes
    23   0.121    32                             NET D=1F S=22 Data ACK
    25   0.126    69                             SMB R OK
    27   0.135  1980  NET D=22 S=1F Data, 1948 bytes
    29   0.146  1980  NET D=22 S=1F Data, 1948 bytes
    30   0.151  1980  NET D=22 S=1F Data, 1948 bytes
    32   0.153    92  NET D=22 S=1F Data, 60 bytes
    35   0.157    32                             NET D=1F S=22 Data ACK
    41   0.190    73  SMB C F=2000 Close
    43   0.199    67                             SMB R Closed
    45   0.206    95  SMB C Set File Attributes
    47   0.216    67                             SMB R OK
```

Figure 16-5. LAN Server Sniff: 10 KByte File, Elapsed Time = 0.216 Secs.

Commentary

- According to the Sniffer trace above, it takes 0.216 seconds to transfer a 10 KByte file. This translates into a 46.3 KByte/s transfer rate.
- The equivalent result using FX timers is 44.7 KByte/s (see Table 16-3 on page 404). We're validated.
- Notice how the LAN Server uses the SMB protocol on top of NetBIOS.

Part IV

The Database Manager

The chapters in Part IV teach you how to program the OS/2 EE Database Manager, the SQL Server component of the client-server platform. A SQL server provides the *heart* of both the Database and Transaction Server platforms. The effort you spend understanding what an SQL server can do for you is well worth it. There is no better productivity "enabler" available for writing robust distributed applications which involve shared data. What are the software structures that best take advantage of that power? To answer that question we go beyond the normal textbook expositions of SQL as a query tool or a decision-support language. Instead, we look at SQL as a key ingredient for building client-server, industrial-strength applications that run over networks. This means that Part IV will focus on issues such as:

- Transaction processing
- Referential Integrity
- Remote Procedure Calls
- Fine-tuning a production database
- The administration of a production database

Since we assume no prior knowledge on your part, we kick-off Part IV with a very complete three-chapter tutorial on the Database Manager's programming interfaces. As usual, we focus on the material that is of interest to C-language programmers. Following the tutorial, we run a set of command *scripts* that demonstrate the power of SQL and the special Database Administration Services that supplement it. These scripts are created and executed using **RSQL**, an "all-in-one" utility program which we develop in subsequent chapters of Part IV. To put it modestly, RSQL is a world-class hacker's tool for probing into the OS/2 EE Database Manager. You can use RSQL to run SQL command scripts, fine-tune the database, look at the system configuration parameters, run reports, measure performance, and invoke the Query Manager Callable Interface. There is nothing in the Database Manager that you can't get at with a simple RSQL script. In addition, the RSQL program itself serves as a template for production-quality SQL code. We will dissect the RSQL program and use it as an exhaustive example of how to write code for the OS/2 EE Database Manager.

Here is the roadmap we will follow in Part IV:

- In Chapter 17, "OS/2 Database Manager API Tutorial", we provide a tutorial on the Database Manager's SQL services. We introduce embedded SQL and cover all the static and dynamic SQL constructs.
- In Chapter 18, "Tutorial on the Database Administration Services", we provide a tutorial on the Database Administration Services. These are the services used to automate the maintenance, performance-tuning, and control of a database engine.
- In Chapter 19, "Tutorial on the Query Manager Callable Interface", we provide a tutorial on the Query Manager Callable Interface. This interface makes the Query Manager services available to your application through standard OS/2 EE API calls.
- In Chapter 20, "RSQL: The "All-In-One" Database Manager Utility", we introduce RSQL and use it to run various scripts that demonstrate the concepts covered in the tutorials.
- In Chapter 21, "RSQL: Programming Dynamic SQL", we use the RSQL program as an example of how to write Dynamic SQL code.
- In Chapter 22, "RSQL: Programming Query Manager", we use the RSQL program as an example of how to program the Query Manager Callable Interface.
- In Chapter 23, "RSQL: Programming the Database Administration API", we use the RSQL program as an example of how to program SQL extensions provided by the Database Administration Services.

Chapter 17

OS/2 Database Manager API Tutorial

This chapter starts out by presenting a taxonomy of the Database Manager's services. This will serve as your navigation map for the Database Manager's API services. Following the taxonomy, we present an in-depth tutorial on the Database Manager's SQL services. These are the key services provided by an SQL engine. The tutorial introduces embedded SQL and covers all the static and dynamic SQL constructs.

A TAXONOMY OF THE DATABASE MANAGER API SERVICES

The Database Manager API services (see Table 17-1 on page 412) fall into three broad categories: the SQL API, the Database Administration API, and the Query Manager Callable Interface. This section will give you a brief overview of the three main API categories and their respective subcategories.

1. **The SQL API:** The Database Manager is primarily a SQL language processor. It implements the SQL command set as defined by the ANSI standard and with some SAA superset extensions. The SQL command statements are either precompiled or dynamically created at run-time. SQL commands are not issued through the traditional OS/2 EE API call interface. Rather, they are treated like a separate language whose statements are *embedded* within a C-language program. You can think of it as a "language within a language." The SQL language statements are precompiled, during the program preparation process, before the program is submitted to a C-language compiler. The precompiler replaces the SQL statements with calls that are recognized by the C-language compiler. We will present the trade-offs of precompilation later in this chapter. In accordance with tradition, the taxonomy scheme employed in Table 17-1, further subdivides the SQL commands into four sub-categories:

   - ***Data Definition Language (DDL)*** consists of SQL commands that define database objects such as: tables, views, and indexes. The DDL is also used to define the integrity constraints on the objects created. This allows the

Table 17-1. A Taxonomy of the Database Manager's API Services.

SQL API	Database Administration API		Query Manager API
Data Definition Language CREATE DROP ALTER TABLE COMMENT ON **Data Manipulation Language** DELETE INSERT SELECT UPDATE **Data Control Language** COMMIT ROLLBACK GRANT REVOKE LOCK TABLE **Program Language Only** BEGIN DECLARE SECTION END DECLARE SECTION DECLARE CURSOR OPEN CLOSE FETCH PREPARE EXECUTE EXECUTE IMMEDIATE DESCRIBE INCLUDE WHENEVER SELECT INTO	**Environment Services** START DB MGR STOP DB MGR CREATE DB START USING DB STOP USING DB RESTART DB DROP DB CHANGE DB COMMENT MIGRATE DB CATALOG DB UNCATALOG DB CATALOG NODE UNCATALOG NODE OPEN DIRECTORY SCAN GET NEXT DIRECTORY ENTRY CLOSE DIRECTORY SCAN OPEN NODE DIRECTORY SCAN GET NEXT NODE ENTRY CLOSE NODE DIRECTORY SCAN INSTALL SIGNAL HANDLER INTERRUPT DB APPL REMOTE INTERFACE COLLECT DB STATUS GET NEXT DB STATUS BLOCK GET USER STATUS FREE DB STATUS RESOURCES **Application Services** BIND with options RETRIEVE MESSAGE	**General Utilities** BACKUP DB RESTORE DB EXPORT TABLE IMPORT TABLE RUNSTATS TABLE REORG TABLE GET ADMIN AUTHORIZATION **Configuration Services** RESET DB CONFIG FILE UPDATE DB CONFIG FILE RETURN COPY OF DB CONFIG FILE RESET DB MGR CONFIG FILE UPDATE DB MANAGER CONFIG FILE RETURN COPY OF DB MANAGER CONFIG **Generic Services** LOG ON LOG OFF	**Object Services** DISPLAY LIST RESET DEFINE TABLE EDIT TABLE RUN ERASE **Execution Control Services** START EXIT BEGIN WINDOW END WINDOW BEGIN WORK CANCEL WORK END WORK **Utilities** PRINT GET SET MESSAGE IMPORT TABLE EXPORT TABLE SAVE DATA AS CONVERT QUERY

Database Manager to ensure that the things users do to those objects are correct.

- ***Data Manipulation Language (DML)*** consists of SQL commands through which users can select, update, insert, or delete rows of information. These data access and manipulation functions are, of course, the principal reason for using the Database Manager.

- ***Data Control Language (DCL)*** consists of SQL commands that control the execution of other SQL commands. Controls must be provided to protect the database against a variety of possible internal and external threats. The controls manage the recovery, concurrency, security, and consistency aspects of a database. This includes controlling the execution of a transaction and undoing its effects if it fails. This also includes obtaining and releasing locks during the course of executing a transaction. Finally, the DCL provides commands for authorizing the access to tables, views, and database objects.
- ***Program Language Constructs*** consist of SQL commands that facilitate the interfacing of SQL to procedural languages such as C. These constructs allow C-language applications to share variables with the SQL sub-language and to mediate between SQL's set-orientation and the C-language's row-at-a-time limitation. The program language constructs provide the mechanism for a C program to prepare and execute SQL statements dynamically.

2. **The Database Administration API:** The Database Manager makes a rich set of database administration services available to your application through standard OS/2 EE API calls. These services complement the SQL language and make it possible for your programs to automate, view, and control almost every aspect of the database engine. Our taxonomy (see Table 17-1) further subdivides the database administration API into five subcategories of commands:

   - The ***Environment Services*** through which you can create and delete a database. Once a database is created, you can start or stop using it. These services also allow you to catalog databases and to maintain database directories.
   - The ***General Utilities*** through which you can write programs that automate and control the maintenance operations on individual databases. As an example, you can program an application to perform a database backup on a daily basis or to reorganize tables on a periodic basis to enhance performance.
   - The ***Application Services*** are useful in developing your programs.
   - The ***Generic Services*** are used to log on and log off.
   - The ***Configuration Services*** allow you to look at, or change the configuration parameters that effect database performance, the degree of concurrency, and resource utilization.

3. **The Query Manager Callable Interface API:** The Database Manager makes all the Query Manager services available to your application through standard OS/2 EE API calls. By using Query Manager's services for screens and panels, you are in essence taking advantage of a Presentation Manager-based user interface that has already been fully developed and debugged. You are also leveraging the familiarity users may already have with the Query Manager objects. The Query Manager Callable Interface allows C-programs to control Query Manager objects and take advantage of the Fourth-Generation (4-GL) language facilities Query Manager provides. Our taxonomy further divides the Query Manager API into the following three subcategories (see Table 17-1):

   - ***Object Services*** which are used to manipulate Query Manager objects. This includes running reports, displaying panels, providing an environment for performing actions on lists of objects, and providing a ready-made prompted interface for creating new objects. Query manager Panels can be designed to search for, retrieve, and update data from one or more tables. SQL commands can be entered and executed through prompted menus.

- ***Execution Control Services*** which are used to start Query Manager sessions and allow your application to control the unit of recovery and the foreground screen.
- ***Utilities*** which are used to format and print reports, to import and export files, to display messages, and to exchange variables with the Query Manager.

In the rest of this chapter, we explain the Database Manager's SQL services. We introduce embedded SQL and cover all the static and dynamic SQL constructs. In Chapter 18 we explain the Database Administration Services. In Chapter 19 we explain the Query Manager Callable Interface.

THE SQL API

Programming the SQL API is very different from the OS/2 EE call-based API model we've encountered so far in this book. Understanding what makes the SQL API different will prepare you for the anticipated "culture shock" of programming in SQL. We start out this section by first giving you a brief history of SQL and the benefits it provides. Then we explain the SQL sub-language model and tell you about the changes in "style" it requires from C programmers. We end the section with a brief description of the SQL verbs and what they each do.

The Origins of SQL

The Relational model of database management was developed at IBM's San Jose Research Lab in the early 1970s by E.F Codd. SQL was developed, also in San Jose, in the mid 1970s to serve as an "English-like" front-end query language to the System R Relational database prototype. Even though the SQL language is "English-like," it is firmly rooted in the solid mathematical foundation of set theory and predicate calculus. What this means is that SQL consists of a short list of powerful, yet highly-flexible, *verbs* which can be used to manipulate information collected in tables. Through SQL, you manipulate and control *sets* of records at a time. You tell the SQL Database Manager what data you need and it figures out how to get to the data. The Relational model frees you from having to concern yourself with the details of how the data is stored and makes the access to data purely logical. Using SQL statements, you only need to specify the tables, columns, and row qualifiers to get to any data item.

Oracle Corporation was the first company to offer a commercial version of SQL with its Oracle database in 1979. In the early 1980s, IBM came out with its own SQL products: SQL/DS and DB2. Today over 200 vendors offer SQL products on PCs, superminis, and mainframes. Most of these products are based on the SQL standard that the X3H2 Database Committee of ANSI started developing in 1982. The ANSI standard which was ratified in 1986 is very similar to IBM's DB2 dialect of SQL. The ANSI X3H2 committee is currently working on a specification of SQL extensions. The OS/2 EE Database Manager's SQL conforms to ANSI SQL and is nearly identical to its IBM mainframe brethren. This is not surprising considering that SQL is SAA's Database Access language and OS/2 EE has been designed from the ground up with SAA compatibility in mind.

The Benefits of SQL

SQL provides a number of advantages to system builders:

- It enforces the separation of data from code.
- It relies on the Relational model which is modular and versatile.
- It enforces a good methodology for data definition. Conveniently, the same language that is used to define the database is also used to manipulate it.
- It provides a high-level data manipulation language, thus enhancing productivity and cutting down on errors.
- It provides security.
- It provides good reliability features such as data validation, referential integrity, rollback (undo transaction), automatic locking, and deadlock detection and resolution in a multiuser LAN environment.
- It provides utilities for the import of files into and the export of files from database tables. Utilities are also provided for maintaining and fine-tuning the database.
- It provides an active data dictionary. The structure and organization of an SQL database is stored in the database itself.
- It brings to the PC world a database administration methodology and allows better communication between PC programmers and Database Administrators. Data is now better defined and documented in a PC environment.
- It can be embedded as a sub-language within the C-language.
- It provides a consistent language for programming with data. This raises programmer productivity and helps produce a more maintainable and easy to change system.
- It provides an excellent vehicle to specify product requirements in an unambiguous manner. This helps communications between customers, developers, and Database Administrators.
- It is supported as an SAA and ANSI standard.

By combining the SQL transaction discipline with the C-language, we can now create an OS/2 EE Server platform for the development of LAN-based Transaction-Processing.

"Them" vs. "Us"

When you first start using SQL in your programs, you are likely to experience acute "culture shock." Don't worry, it's only natural. Like "our C-programming subculture," SQL has its own strong subculture with folk heroes, gurus, and "set ways for doing things." These people have created some de facto standards for how SQL is to be used from within a programming language such as C. The bottom-line is that they want us to use their SQL sub-language "as is" within the C-language. Incidentally, they view this process as extending SQL with procedural capabilities. Here is the price a C programmer pays for this inter-cultural marriage:

- We have to use the (.SQC) extension for any source code file that contains embedded SQL statements.
- We have to run the (.SQC) source file through their precompiler, **SQLPREP**, to generate the (.C) source code file that our compiler understands.
- We have to locate the errors our compiler reports against the statement line numbers from the (.C) file. Then we need to locate and change the corresponding statement in the (.SQC) file.
- We have to have a running database with fully defined tables as part of the code preparation process. This means that you have to define and create your data tables before you can compile any code.
- We have to store the SQL plans prepared by the precompiler into a database.
- We have to look at the funny code their precompiler generates while debugging our code with CodeView.
- We have to match their data types to our C-language types. In many cases they don't exactly match.
- We have to learn a whole new vocabulary from the world of Database Administrators (DBAs) and SQL transaction processing.

Fortunately, there are benefits to be obtained from doing things their way:

- The SQL sub-language is almost independent of the programming language, compiler, and operating system used. This means that you can embed the same sub-language statements in C, Cobol, or Pascal with only a few minor changes. With some additional minor changes, the same sub-language program can easily be ported to SAA and other SQL engine platforms.
- We've retained the use of the C-language for writing procedural code. The alternative could have been letting "them" design a new procedural language for SQL, as some database vendors have done (wrongly in our opinion).
- The precompiler separates SQL processing from the C-language statements, which means that new SQL features can easily be introduced with minimum impact.
- We've gained the full power of SQL and the non-procedural discipline it entails.
- It is remarkably easy and productive to program in the SQL sub-language.

In the coming sections we help you overcome the SQL culture shock so that you can take full advantage of this powerful sub-language. And who knows, perhaps once you've gotten over the minor irritations, you may turn into an SQL true-believer and overcome the "us" vs "them" barrier.

Precompile With and Without Bind

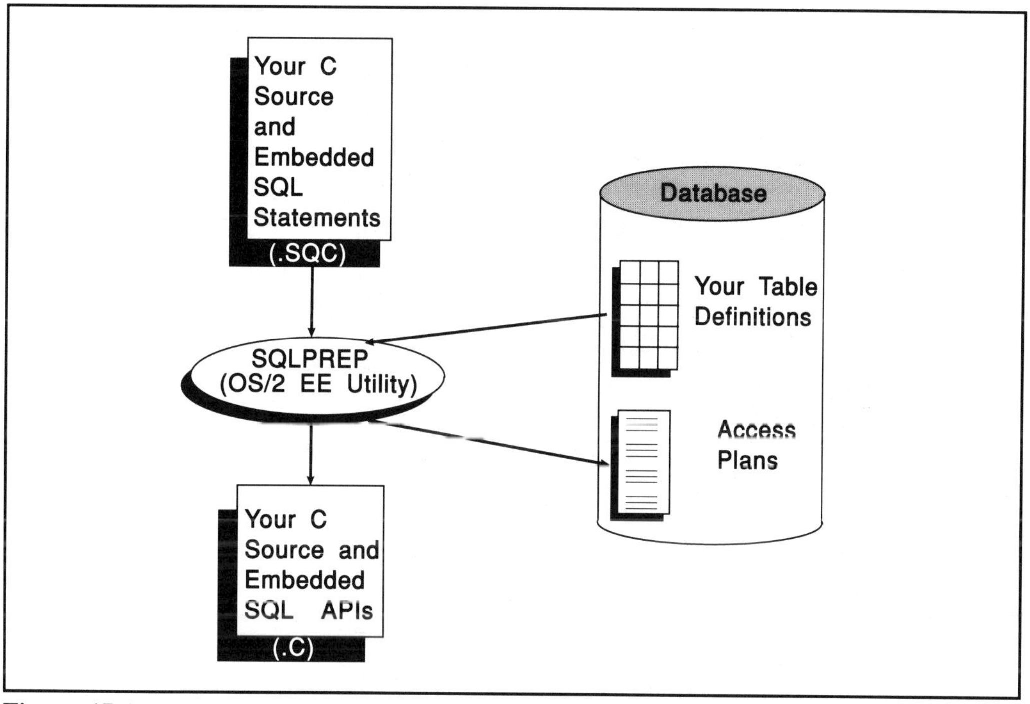

Figure 17-1. The SQL Precompile Process with Immediate Bind.

Embedded SQL: The Precompile and Bind Process

A SQL precompiler is a tool OS/2 EE provides for extending the C language with the power of the SQL data management language. The result is a powerful combination of SQL's non-procedural *set-at-a-time* constructs with the C-language's flexible procedural constructs. A precompiler processes your source code replacing SQL statements with C-language statements, and the result is "modified source" code that can be processed by the C/2 compiler.

A precompiler provides four functions:

- It manages the C-language variables that can be used directly inside SQL statements. These common variables are called *host-variables.*
- It checks the validity of SQL statements including the user's authority to issue such statements. This includes verifying that the table names and columns refer-

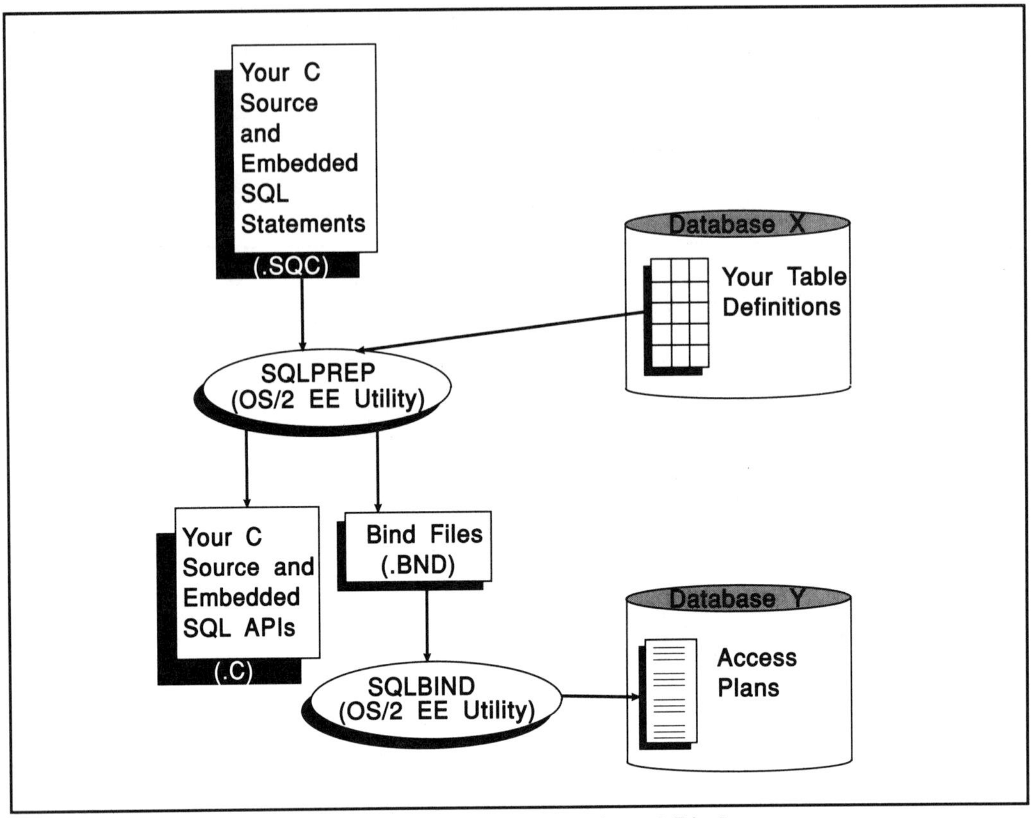

Figure 17-2. The SQL Precompile Process with Deferred Bind.

enced in your SQL statements actually exist and that their types are compatible with the host-variables declared in your programs.

- It generates a *modified source* C-language file. It does that by generating a (.C) file that can be compiled by a C-language compiler. The embedded SQL statements are changed into comments and the appropriate API calls are generated in their place. The precompiler takes as its input a (.SQC) file (see Figure 17-1 on page 417) containing your C-language source and embedded SQL statements.

- It builds *access plans* that tell the database engine how the SQL statement should be executed. These access plans use sophisticated heuristics that optimize the data access strategy based on the current state of the database. The access plans are stored as objects in the database. The process of storing the access plans is called *binding*. You can bind the plans during precompilation (see Figure 17-1 on page 417) or do it later through a separate bind utility (see Figure 17-2). If you to choose to defer the binding the precompiler will store the plans it creates in *bind files* with (.BND) extensions. You can bind the (.BND) files at a later time with the production database of your choice (see Figure 17-2) through either the **SQLBIND** utility or by issuing an OS/2 EE API call.

Embedded SQL: The Command Syntax

An embedded SQL statement or precompiler directive must start with the **EXEC SQL** key-word pair and end with a semi-colon ";". These bracketed statements will be processed by the precompiler and anything else in your source code will be passed through unchanged. An embedded SQL statement can span across multiple lines, as shown in the following example:

```
EXEC SQL CREATE TABLE JUNK (NAME        VARCHAR(16) NOT NULL,  -- SQL comment
                            PROFESSION  VARCHAR(20),           /* C   comment */
                            AGE         SMALLINT,              -- SQL comment
                            SALARY      DECIMAL(7,2));         /* C   comment */
```

Figure 17-3. Embedding SQL in the C-Language.

Embedded SQL: Static Vs Dynamic SQL Commands

- **Static SQL** statements are defined in your code and converted into an access plan by the precompiler at program preparation time. The SQL statement is known before your program is run. The database objects need to exist when precompiling static SQL statements. You can think of static SQL as being a compiled form of the SQL language. Static SQL is a performance enhancement feature.

- **Dynamic SQL** statements are created and issued at run-time. They offer maximum flexibility at the expense of execution speed. You can think of dynamic SQL as an interpretive form of the SQL language. The database objects need not exist when precompiling dynamic SQL statements. The compilation of dynamic SQL statements is done at run time and must be repeated every time the same statement gets executed again.

In this book, we will be using static SQL for writing highly optimized transaction programs, and dynamic SQL for writing general database programming utilities.

Embedded SQL: Error Handling

You may be wondering how error information gets passed from the embedded sub-language to C. This is done through a fixed-size global data structure called the **SQL Communications Area** or **SQLCA**. This is an SQL defined data structure that returns error return codes and warnings after the execution of each SQL statement or OS/2 EE Database Manger API call. We will develop some techniques for database error handling in later sections

Embedded SQL: Host Variables

The *host variable* is the primary mechanism the SQL sub-language provides for the exchange of data between a C-language application and embedded SQL statements. The idea is to get data from your program into the database and from the database into your program, where you can provide additional manipulation. Host variables are nothing more than C-language variables that are preceded by a colon ":" whenever they are placed inside an SQL statement. Here are some rules for using host variables from within C-language programs:

- Declare the host variables to the precompiler before referencing them in an SQL statement.
- You can have multiple precompiler host-variable declaration sections within one source file.
- From the C-language perspective, host variables can be local or global, and their storage class can be *extern*, *static*, or *auto*.
- From the precompiler perspective, host variables are global to a source file. This means a host variable must have a unique name within a source file, even if it is declared as a local C variable.
- Almost any C-language data type can be used as a host variable. Here are some of the features:
  - C pointers are supported.
  - C arrays are supported, provided that the array-size is explicitly declared.
  - C-language structures are acceptable host variables, but the embedded fields are not. For example, **structure_name.field_name** is not allowed; but **structure_name** is allowed.
  - C-language data type macros are not supported.
- You can initialize host variables; however, the SQL precompiler will not validate initialized data values.
- Your host variables must be of a data-type compatible with the SQL table column types to which they correspond. Table 17-2 provides a list of the main OS/2 EE SQL column types and their C-language host variable equivalents.

Embedded SQL: The SQL Descriptor Area (SQLDA)

In addition to host variables, the SQL sub-language provides a predefined C-language structure called the **SQLDA** through which a C-language program can exchange data with embedded SQL statements. The **SQLDA** is used mainly by Dynamic SQL programs that have no previous knowledge of the data types that are used in a SQL statement. Here are the three main uses of the **SQLDA**:

1. To return a description of the SQL command to an application program. This includes the name, length, and type of variables used by the Dynamic SQL statement. SQL provides two verbs for this purpose: **PREPARE** and **DESCRIBE**.
2. To pass data and to receive data from the SQL statements. You can use the **SQLDA** instead of host-variables where the C-language does not have a corre-

sponding column type, or for Dynamic SQL row fetches where the column data type is not known before-hand.

3. As a general purpose self-describing data buffer that is used in conjunction with the **Application Remote Interface** database services. This is the OS/2 EE service that allows clients to execute stored SQL procedures on remote servers. The **in_sqlda** structure is used to pass inbound parameters to the stored procedure, and the **out_sqlda** structure is used to return the results.

Embedded SQL: SQL Types and C-Language Data Types

Table 17-2. The Correspondence Between SQL Column-types and C-language Data Types.

Table Column SQL Data Type	SQL Type Number	SQL Type Description	You Can Use This C Data Structure
SMALLINT	**500**	16-bit, signed integer	short or short int
INTEGER	**496**	32-bit, signed integer	long or long int
FLOAT	**480**	8-byte floating point	double
DECIMAL(p,s)	**484**	Packed decimal	Not supported in C. Use double instead with some loss of precision.
CHAR(1)	**452**	1 character	char or unsigned char
CHAR(n)	**452**	n-byte char string	`char[n]` `1 <= n <= 254`
VARCHAR(n)	**460**	Variable length string (null terminated by SQL).	char[n] 1 <= n <= 4000

VARCHAR(n)	**448**	Variable length string (not-null terminated by SQL length indicator field used). Is used to store binary data. Declare column for BIT DATA.	`struct { short length;`
			`char data[n];`
			`} var_name;`
			`where 1 <= n <= 4000`

LONG VARCHAR(n)	**456**	Variable length string (not-null terminated by SQL length indicator field used). Is used to store bulk data such as text, code or images.	`struct { short length;`
			`char data[n];`
			`} var_name;`
			`where 1 <= n <= 32700`

DATE	**384**	10-byte char string	char[10]
TIME	**388**	8-byte char string	char[8]
TIMESTAMP	**392**	26-byte char string	char[26]
NULL	..	NULL indicator flag used to indicate NULL data in column.	short

The SQL Data Definition Language (DDL) Commands

The SQL Data Definition Language is used to define and maintain the user created database objects: tables, views, indexes, and access plans. The DDL is also used to define the *referential integrity* relationships between objects.

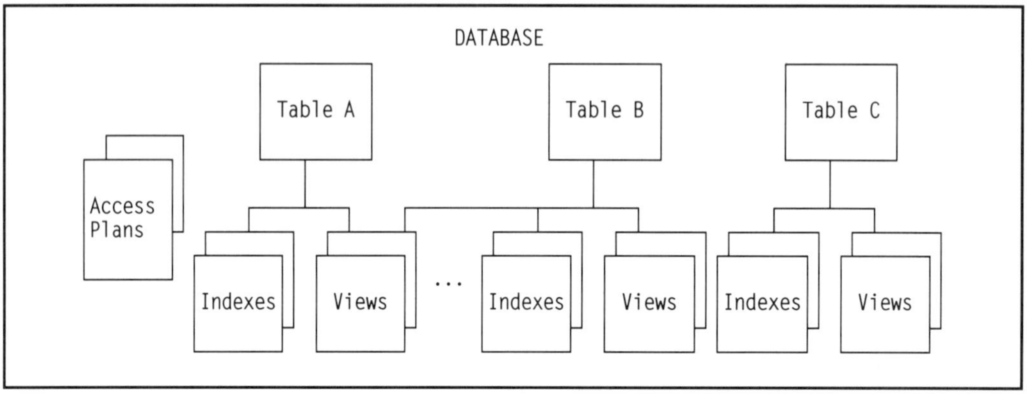

Figure 17-4. User Objects Within a Database Context.

Objects in General

Objects are things about which Database Manager retains information. Loosely speaking, a Database is an administrative entity that provides the context for a collection of related named objects such as tables, views, and indexes (see Figure 17-4). The Database context includes such things as: system catalogs, recovery logs, passwords, disk directories, and memory. User objects are always accessed from within the context of a database. What follows is a description of the user objects that are managed through the DDL.

The Table Object

A table object, also known as the *base* table, is the most basic database object. Like all major objects, a table has a name and an optional comment. Tables are defined as a series of *columns* each of which is identified by a name, a data type, and an optional comment. Each table is an unordered collection of rows, each of which has a fixed number of columns. Unlike the rows, columns in a table are ordered from left to right just as they appear in the **CREATE TABLE** command. Each column has a SQL data type (see Table 17-2 on page 421) which is used by the Database Manager to ensure that only data of the correct type gets put in the tables. In addition, you can specify the following optional *column constraints*:

- A column may be specified as NOT NULL, which causes the Database Manager to enforce that a value gets supplied for that column with every insert or update.

- A character column can be specified FOR BIT DATA to indicate that it contains binary non-textual information. In the default mode, the Database Manager assumes character columns to contain valid ASCII characters. The effect of FOR BIT DATA is not to translate the data when going to a machine with a different code page.
- A column may be identified as being part of a *primary key* or *foreign key* as part of the table definition. More on that when we discuss Referential constraints.

The View Object

Views provide "logical tables." These are tables that do not exist in physical storage but consist of data obtained through a query against one or more tables. Views do not contain data; instead they refer to data stored in base tables. A view is defined as a query against other base tables and/or other views. All that happens when a view is created is that the Database Manager stores the query under a named view object. The query itself is not issued. A view is a way of creating "windows" through which data in base tables can be viewed. These windows can be used to simplify the view of data, to reorder columns, or rename a table.

Views can also be used to enforce data security. For example, by creating a view you can restrict data access to certain rows and columns in the base tables. Views, like base tables, can be used to retrieve, update, or delete data. There are some exceptions for example: data from a view that is created by joining two tables cannot be inserted, updated, or deleted. A **join** is a query that combines information from two or more tables. A view may be created with the WITH CHECK OPTION constraint. This is a data integrity check that causes all data inserts and updates through that view to be checked for compatibility with the search condition of the view definition.

The Index Object

An index object consists of a set of pointers which are logically ordered by the values of a key. A *key* consists of one or more columns that identify one or more rows within a table. An index object provides a way for defining keys outside of the table definition. It also stores a pointer to the key values of each row in an indexed table. The pointers are stored in B-Tree format which speeds up row access and updates. You typically create indexes on frequently accessed columns to improve performance. One or more indexes may be defined on a table. Each index key consists of one or more columns, and, optionally, an attribute which specifies the order in which to access the rows (either ascending or descending). Typically, index keys are used in the following situations:

- To speed up the retrieval of data. If an index is present the Database Manager may use an *index scan* instead of the usual *table scan*. What this means is that an index B-Tree is searched for matches, instead of sequentially searching through every table row. The performance improvements in reading data have to be weighed against the costs of maintaining the index B-Tree during updates and inserts.

- To uniquely identify a table row. A *unique index* key defines exactly one row in a table and is used by Database Manager to enforce that each row in a table is unique (i.e., no two rows will have the same values in their unique index columns). This helps maintain the integrity of the information in a table. If you specify a Unique Index, then the database will make sure you do not create duplicate rows. This may help reflect real world situations where, for example, duplicate departments make no sense.
- To speed up the joining of tables by indexing the join columns.
- To speed up referential integrity checks.

Note: You're only involvement with indexes is to define them. After that, the Database Manager retains full control of when to use an index for retrieval. The Database Manager is also fully in charge of maintaining the indexes and keeping them synchronized with the underlying base tables.

Object Naming Conventions

User object names normally follow a two-level naming convention. A qualified name consists of authorization-id qualifier, followed by a period, followed by the name you assign to the object. The *authorization-id* identifies a database user and can be up to 8 characters long and cannot contain lowercase letters, the underscore character, or begin with numerals or the reserved words: IBM, SQL and SYS. The *object name* is the name you assign to the object. The object name does not have special character restrictions. Typically, you refer to an object through its unqualified name. The authorization-id is implied by the context. However, in multiuser situations you should use fully qualified names to keep track of which user owns which objects. An object gets assigned the authorization-id of the user that created it. Here's a "trivial pursuit" guide to the length of object names:

- The names of columns, correlations, cursors, indexes, tables, and views can be from 1 to 18 characters long.
- A fully qualified column name uses a three-level naming convention consisting of: the authorization-id, followed by a period, followed by the name of a table or view, followed by a period, and finally followed by the name of the column.
- The names of plans, constraints, and databases can only be up to eight characters long.
- A password consists of 4-8 characters.

Referential Relationships

The Database Manager provides, through *referential constraints*, a mechanism which ensures that cross-references between tables are always valid. What this means is that, if there is a reference to something, then that something should exist; otherwise the reference is invalid. The rules for referential integrity are specified as part of the **CREATE TABLE** statement through two sets of keys:

1. **Primary Key**. This is a key that uniquely identifies a single row within a table. The primary key consists of one or more columns none of which can be null. Each table can have only one primary key. A Unique Index is automatically created by the Database Manager for the primary key, which means you do not have to issue a separate CREATE UNIQUE INDEX command.

2. **Foreign Key**. This is a key that points to (or references) a primary key. The foreign key columns must match those of the primary key one for one. A foreign key establishes a referential link to a primary key. Each table (including the one with the primary key) can have one or more optional foreign keys.

A foreign key link to a primary key establishes a *referential constraint* between information stored in one or more tables. Through these referential constraints, the Database Manager will enforce, on your behalf, the integrity of dependent data (foreign key data) on parent data (primary key data). Referential constraints may be created between columns on the same table or in different tables. A table is *self-referencing* when it contains both the primary key and the foreign key.

The example in Figure 17-5 will help clarify these relationships. It shows 3 referential constraint links:

- The link between the dept_num foreign key on the EMPLOYEE table and the dept_num primary key on the DEPARTMENT table. In this link the EMPLOYEE is the *dependent* table and DEPARTMENT is the *parent* table.
- The link between the mgr_id foreign key and the empl_id primary key both of which are on the same EMPLOYEE table. This is an example of a *self-referencing* table.
- The link between the empl_id foreign key on the HOME_PHONE table and the empl_id primary key on the EMPLOYEE table. In this link the EMPLOYEE is the *parent* table and HOME_PHONE is the *dependent* table.

As you can see from the example, a table can be a parent, a dependent, or both, in an arbitrary number of referential constraints. The example also shows that a particular table can have multiple foreign keys but only a single primary key is allowed.

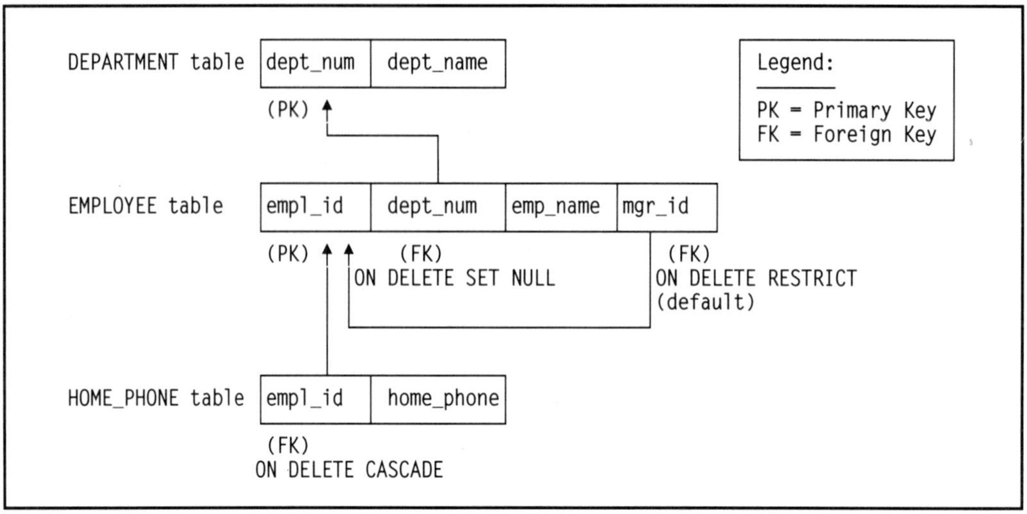

Figure 17-5. Referential Constraint Elements: Primary Keys and Foreign Keys.

Enforcing Referential Integrity

Once you've defined the relational constraints, here is what the Database Manager can do for you in terms of integrity checks:

- It will check for the existence of the primary keys when a table with foreign keys is first created.
- It will check for the existence of a primary key value that match the non-null value of the foreign key for every row that is inserted or updated in a dependent table.
- It will prevent the update of primary key data in the parent table if any dependent rows are found through matching foreign key values.
- It will enforce a user-specified rule on dependent rows when a row is deleted from the parent table. The action taken on dependent rows is specified in the *Delete Rule* for the foreign key and can be one of the following:

  RESTRICT meaning don't let the parent row get deleted if it has dependents. This is the default action.

  CASCADE meaning if the row gets deleted from the parent table, then delete the dependent rows too.

  SET NULL meaning if the row gets deleted from the parent table, then set to null the foreign key fields in the dependent rows.

An Example of Referential Integrity Rules Enforcement

The rules defined on the foreign keys in Figure 17-5 have the following effects:

- If a row is dropped from the DEPARTMENT table, then dept_num column is set to NULL for all the rows in the EMPLOYEE table which have employees that belong to the dept_num that is being dropped. This is in accordance with the ON DELETE SET NULL *delete rule* which in effect says "if the department is dropped, then set the dept_num value to an unknown for all the employees that belong to that department."

  Note: If we had chosen instead to impose the ON DELETE CASCADE rule, then all the employees in the dropped department would have gotten immediately "terminated" (by getting dropped from the EMPLOYEE table). So, setting the dept_num to NULL is a nice way of keeping the employees on the payroll until they get re-assigned to a new department!

- An attempt to drop a row from the EMPLOYEE table will cause the following to happen:

  1. First, a check is made to see if the empl_id in the row to be dropped is a manager; this is true for any row in the EMPLOYEE table has a mgr_id value equal to the empl id being dropped. If a match occurs, then the drop will fail because of the RESTRICT rule that has been placed on the foreign key. What the referential constraint rule is in effect saying is, "anybody is free to leave except managers" (perhaps they've been given tenure...).

  2. The delete succeeds if the employee is not a manager. In this case, the Database Manager will automatically delete the employee's home phone row from the HOME_PHONE table. This is in accordance with the CASCADE rule which says, "if an employee is no longer there, then there is no need for that employee's home phone number either."

The DDL and the User Objects

Table 17-3 provides a quick summary of the function each SQL DDL command provides. If you think of the SQL command as the "verb" that operates on an object, then ideally you should be able to apply each DDL verb to every object. Unfortunately, this is not the case. Here is a guide to the different verb/object combinations:

CREATE This verb breaks down into three SQL verbs: **CREATE TABLE**, **CREATE VIEW**, and **CREATE INDEX**. Each SQL verb has its own distinct syntax structure.

DROP This verb breaks down into four SQL verbs: **DROP TABLE**, **DROP VIEW**, **DROP INDEX** and **DROP PROGRAM**. The four verbs have an identical structure. It consists of the verb followed by the name of the object to be dropped. The **PROGRAM** object is another name for an access plan. You can delete an access plan through the SQL API, but an Access plan can only be created through the Precompile and Bind process described earlier.

ALTER This verb can be used only on **TABLE** objects. Other objects that need to be altered should be dropped and then re-created.

COMMENT ON This verb can be used on **TABLE** and **VIEW** objects as well as on the individual columns in a table or view object.

Table 17-3. The SQL Data Definition Language (DDL).

SQL Command	Description

CREATE TABLE	This command is used to define a base table. You need to provide a table name and define all table columns up to a maximum of 255 columns. Note that the maximum length of a row (not including LONG VARCHAR) is 4005 characters. Each column must have a unique name and a SQL data type. You can define a column as NOT NULL, if you want the Database Manager to enforce that a value is supplied for that column with every INSERT or UPDATE. A character column is to be specified FOR BIT DATA, if it is to contain binary data. You may specify referential constraints through the PRIMARY and FOREIGN key clauses. The REFERENCES keyword is used to identify the table on which the PRIMARY KEY resides. The Database Manager will check for the existence of the referenced PRIMARY KEY when creating the table. You can optionally include an ON DELETE rule with the FOREIGN KEY. Note: PRIMARY KEY or FOREIGN KEYs that consist of single columns may be specified as part of the column definition instead of via a separate key clause. The statements that follow will create the set of tables you previously encountered in the Referential Integrity example:
	`EXEC SQL CREATE TABLE department      /* primary KEY on column */`
	`          (dept_num    SMALLINT NOT NULL PRIMARY KEY,`
	`           dept_name   VARCHAR(20));`
	`EXEC SQL CREATE TABLE employee        /* separate KEY clauses  */`
	`          (empl_id     INT NOT NULL,`
	`           dept_num    SMALLINT REFERENCES department,`
	`           emp_name    VARCHAR(40) NOT NULL,`
	`           mgr_id      INT,`
	`           PRIMARY KEY (empl_id),`
	`           FOREIGN KEY mgr(mgr_id) REFERENCES employee);`
	`EXEC SQL CREATE TABLE home_phone         /* separate KEY clause*/`
	`          (empl_id     INT NOT NULL,    /* with rule          */`
	`           home_phone  CHAR(10),`
	`           FOREIGN KEY homenum(empl_id) REFERENCES employee`
	`                       ON DELETE CASCADE);`

Table 17-3. The SQL Data Definition Language (DDL).

SQL Command	Description
CREATE VIEW	This command defines a view. You provide the view name, the optional names of the columns in the view, and the SELECT query that defines the scope of the view. A view may be created from one or more base tables or views. You may specify an integrity check on the view with the optional: WITH CHECK OPTION which indicates that any updates or inserts to the view must be checked against the view definition, and rejected if they do not satisfy the view defining conditions. `Example: EXEC SQL CREATE VIEW managers (manager_name, department) AS SELECT emp_name,dept_num FROM employee WHERE empl_id = mgr_id WITH CHECK OPTION;`
CREATE INDEX	This command creates an index on a table. You provide an index name and specify the name of the table and the columns that constitute the index. You can optionally specify the index as being UNIQUE. The index is created by default in ascending order; you can change that to a descending order index by including the DESC keyword. `Example: EXEC SQL CREATE UNIQUE INDEX xhome_phone1 ON home_phone (empl_id DESC);`
DROP TABLE	This command is used to delete a table and all its dependent objects. You specify the name of the table you want dropped and it will be deleted from the catalog along with all its dependent indexes, views, primary keys, and foreign keys. Access plans that reference the table or its dependent objects are invalidated. `Example: EXEC SQL DROP TABLE home_phone;`
DROP VIEW	This command is used to delete a view and all its dependent objects. You specify the name of the view you want dropped and it will be deleted from the catalog along with any dependent views. Any access plans that reference the view or dependent views are invalidated. `Example: EXEC SQL DROP VIEW managers;`
DROP INDEX	This command is used to delete an index. You specify the name of the of the index you want dropped and it will be deleted from the catalog. Any access plans that reference that index are invalidated. `Example: EXEC SQL DROP INDEX xhome_phone1;`
DROP PROGRAM	This command is used to delete an access plan. You specify the name of the access plan you want dropped and it will be deleted from the catalog. `Example: EXEC SQL DROP PROGRAM xyz;`

Table 17-3. The SQL Data Definition Language (DDL).

SQL Command	Description

ALTER TABLE	This command allows you to add new columns or referential constraints to an existing table. New columns are added after the last column to the right of the table in order to maintain the order of the original columns unchanged. In this way, access plans created before the table is altered will remain valid. The format for the column attributes and referential constraints is similar to that of CREATE TABLE, except that you have specify the keyword ADD when adding new columns, and the keyword DROP to delete PRIMARY or FOREIGN keys. You do not need to include the ADD keyword when adding a new referential constraint.
	`Examples:`
	`EXEC SQL ALTER TABLE home_phone /* Add an address column */`
	`ADD address VARCHAR(100);`
	`EXEC SQL ALTER TABLE home_phone /* Drop homenum foreign key */`
	`DROP FOREIGN KEY homenum;`
	`EXEC SQL ALTER TABLE home_phone /* Add homenum foreign key */`
	`FOREIGN KEY homenum(empl_id) REFERENCES employee`
	`ON DELETE RESTRICT;`

COMMENT ON TABLE	This command adds or replaces comments in the catalog description of tables or views. The IS keyword is used to introduce a comment string that can be up to 254 characters long.
	`Example: EXEC SQL COMMENT ON TABLE home_phone`
	`IS 'This table employee home phone numbers';`

COMMENT ON COLUMN	This command adds or replaces comments in the catalog description of columns. The IS keyword is used to introduce a comment string that can be up to 254 characters long.
	`Example: EXEC SQL COMMENT ON COLUMN home_phone.empl_id`
	`IS 'This column serves as a foreign key';`

The SQL Data Manipulation Language (DML) Commands

The SQL Data Manipulation Language provides the verbs used for entering and manipulating data (after you've defined the database and created its tables, indexes and views). The **SELECT** verb is the heart of the SQL DML language and is used for retrieving information. The power of SELECT lies in its ability to construct complex queries with an infinite number of variations using a finite set of rules. The SELECT verb is recursive, meaning that the input of a SQL statement can be the output of a successive number of nested SELECTs. For example, nested SELECT subqueries can be embedded within the **INSERT**, **UPDATE**, **DELETE**, and **CREATE VIEW** SQL commands.

To do anything useful with SQL, you will need to fully master the SELECT command and understand its various subtleties. In the following sections, we start you off with the most rudimentary form of SELECT, and use it as a base from which we introduce progressively more sophisticated (and perhaps less used) features.

The "Minimal" SELECT

The SELECT verb in its most basic form consists of the **SELECT-FROM-WHERE** statement whose structure is shown below:

```
EXEC SQL
  DECLARE cursorname CURSOR FOR
    SELECT <selection_list>
    FROM   <table_list>
    WHERE  <search_condition> ;
```

- The **selection_list** is the comma-separated list of columns that you want to retrieve. An asterisk "*" can be used to obtain all the columns in a table without listing each column name. SELECT by default returns all the rows that match the query conditions including duplicate rows. The DISTINCT qualifier can be used to retrieve only the unique rows that match the query. The selection_list can also be used to perform arithmetic operations on data you select and to compute values for a group of rows based on column functions such as average or sum.

- The **table_list** is the comma-separated list of tables or views that are used in the query. The table_list also defines *correlated names*. These are shorthand alternate names for tables or views which are used when joining a table to itself or with subqueries that uses the same table name.

- The **search_condition** describes the rows in which you are interested and consists of one or more predicates. A *predicate* specifies a test that you want Database Manager to apply to each row of a table and evaluates to "true," "false," or "unknown." One or more predicates in a search can be combined by using parentheses or Boolean operators such as AND, OR, and NOT. When the predicates result in "true," it means that the SQL statement is to be applied to that row; "false" means no operation is required for that row. Predicates compare a column with a value, or a column with another column from the same table or from different tables. A *basic predicate* compares two values; a *quantified predicate* compares a value with a collection of values. All values specified in predicates must be of compatible types:

  - Numbers can only be compared with numbers. The Database Manager performs temporary conversions to match number types when necessary.
  - Strings can only be compared with strings.
  - Date and Time can only be compared with Date and Time types or string representations of Date and Time.

  Predicates use the familiar relational operators as well as a variety of special operators to specify the condition to be evaluated in the search. SELECT statements can also be embedded within certain predicates, and when used in this mode are called *subqueries*. The following is a list of the comparison operators that can be used in predicates:

Logic Operators These are the familiar relational operators: =, <>, <, >, <=, >=, NOT. These operators can be used to compare two expressions, or an expression with the result of a subquery. The NOT operator can be used to form the negative of any of the other operators.

IS NULL Is used in a predicate to test for NULL expressions.

BETWEEN...AND Is used in a predicate to compare a value with a range of values. The search condition is satisfied by any value that falls between the two specified values.

IN Is used in a predicate to test group membership. The group can be specified through a subquery or through lists of values in a statement.

LIKE Is used in a predicate to search for strings that match certain patterns. The special matching character "%" may be used for an unknown string of zero or more characters. The character "_" may be used as a pattern match for any single character.

EXISTS Is used in a predicate to test for the existence of certain rows. The predicate is true if the subquery returns one or more rows.

ALL Is used in predicates that involve subqueries. A predicate is true when the specified relationship is true for *all* rows returned by a subquery. It is also true if no rows are returned.

SOME or ANY Are used in predicates that involve subqueries. The predicate is true when the specified relationship is true for *at least one* row returned by a subquery.

The Ordering of Output Rows

A relational database has no explicit order. However, the output of a query can be sorted by applying the ORDER BY clause on the columns you want to order by. The output will follow the ascending order by default. You can over-ride the default by specifying the DESC keyword on descending order columns. You can name the columns to order by, or you can use a number. For example, ORDER BY 2 specifies that you want the results ordered by the second column as specified in the query.

Column Functions

Built-in functions and expressions are supported as part of the SELECT column-list statement. These functions operate on the aggregate values of a single column and produce a single result (nulls are not part of the calculation):

- SUM returns the sum of all the values in a column.
- AVG returns the average of all the values in a column.
- MAX returns the largest value in a column.
- MIN returns the smallest value in a column.
- COUNT returns the number of values in a column.

The special function COUNT(*) is provided to count all rows in a table without the elimination of duplicates.

Arithmetic Operations

You can use the SELECT column-list statement to perform arithmetic operations on the data you select before the data is presented to your program. This may be useful if you want to evaluate the effects of certain changes before updating the database. The following arithmetic operators are supported: +, -, *, and /.

Groups and Summaries

Summary rows can be obtained with GROUP BY and HAVING clauses which allow you to find out the characteristics of groups of rows as opposed to those of individual rows. The GROUP BY operator groups all rows that have the same value for a given column into a single row. The Database Manager then processes each group to produce a single-row result for the group. The SELECT clause when applied to groups is used in conjunction with functions that return a single value for a given column within a group. HAVING can be thought of a "WHERE clause for groups," and is used as a search condition for eliminating groups just as WHERE is used as a search condition for eliminating rows. This means HAVING can only be used in conjunction with GROUP BY.

JOIN

Is a powerful feature of relational databases that allows you to retrieve data from two or more tables by means of a single SELECT statement. The SELECT retrieves the requested information based on matching column values in the tables involved. The Database Manager supports joins that include up to 15 tables.

Subqueries

A subquery is a query within a query. These nested queries appear within the search condition of a WHERE or HAVING clause. A subquery may be used within a search condition for the INSERT, DELETE, and UPDATE SQL commands. A subquery may include search conditions of its own, and these search conditions may in turn include subqueries. The Database Manager first performs the innermost query and uses the results to execute the next outer SQL statement, etc. The subquery can either return a single value or a set of values. The set of values requires the use of the keywords IN, ALL, ANY, SOME, EXIST, and NOT EXIST.

Correlated Subqueries

Correlated Subqueries are special cases of subqueries where the inner SELECT executes once for each result row in the outer SELECT. You use a correlated subquery to search for some value that can be different for each row.

UNION, EXCEPT, and INTERSECT

These are set operations that can be applied on the result sets from different SELECT statements. The SELECT statements must have the same number of columns. The columns must have equivalent types none of which can be a LONG VARCHAR.

UNION Combines or "merges" the result tables of two SELECTs and eliminates duplicate rows.

EXCEPT Generates a result table consisting of all unique rows from the first SELECT statement that are not generated by the second SELECT statement.

INTERSECT Generates a result table consisting of unique rows that are common in the results of two SELECT statements.

The "Full-Featured" SELECT

The SELECT verb in its full-featured form consists of six clauses which with the exception of SELECT-FROM are all optional:

```
EXEC SQL
  DECLARE cursorname CURSOR FOR
    SELECT   <ALL or DISTINCT > <selection_list>
    FROM     <table_list>
    WHERE    <search_condition>
    GROUP BY <column_names>
    HAVING   <search_condition>
    ORDER BY <column_names> ;
```

The SELECT Statement and the SQL API

Here are the different ways the SELECT statement can appear in your code:

- Through a DECLARE CURSOR if the SELECT statement returns multiple rows.
- Through a SELECT INTO statement to retrieve one row of data.
- Through the PREPARE statement for a Dynamic SQL command. This also includes the processing of a cursor.
- Through a subquery that is part of the search condition of another SQL command such as INSERT, DELETE, or UPDATE.

What this means in terms of our code taxonomy scheme is that even though the multirow SELECT statement is the most important DML command, it can only be invoked through the DECLARE CURSOR which falls under Program Language Constructs SQL API category. The more constrained SELECT INTO call is also included under the Program Language Constructs, because it can only be issued through a programming language and has no interactive SQL equivalent. The taxonomy shown in Table 17-4 is therefore in line with the "purist" SQL division. It also shows the kinks introduced when bridging between the set-based tradition of SQL and our row-at-a-time procedural orientation.

Table 17-4. The SQL Data Manipulation Language (DML).

SQL Command	Description
SELECT	This command is used to retrieve rows from tables. The general format of the SELECT command was introduced earlier in this section. The SELECT can be embedded in SQL subqueries issued by INSERT, UPDATE, and DELETE. The direct execution of a multirow SELECT requires the DECLARE CURSOR construct. A single-row SELECT can be directly executed with the SELECT INTO verb (also see SQL Program Language Constructs).

Table 17-4. The SQL Data Manipulation Language (DML).

<table>
<tr><th>SQL Command</th><th>Description</th></tr>
<tr><td>INSERT</td><td>This command is used to add new rows to a table or a view. You can specify VALUES for a single column to be inserted, or you can include a SELECT statement in the INSERT statement that tells the Database Manager that the data for the new rows is contained in another table or view. In either case, you must supply a value for each non-null column.<pre>
Examples: EXEC SQL
            INSERT INTO home_phone (empl_id, home_phone)
            VALUES (905,'4082223333');
          EXEC SQL
            INSERT INTO home_phone
            VALUES (906,'4152224444');
          EXEC SQL
            INSERT INTO home_phone (empl_id)
              SELECT empl_id FROM employee
              WHERE dept_num = 40 ;
</pre></td></tr>
<tr><td>UPDATE</td><td>This command allows you to change data in a table. This is a set operation which in this case means one command will change the value of one or more columns in all the rows that satisfy the search condition of a WHERE clause.<pre>
Example: EXEC SQL   /* shows the use of host variables */
            UPDATE employee
              SET dept_num   = 333,
                  mgr_id   = :pgm_mgrid
              WHERE dept_num = :pgm_dept;
</pre></td></tr>
<tr><td>DELETE</td><td>This command allows you to remove entire rows from tables. This is a set operation which in this case means that one command will delete all the rows that satisfy the search condition of a WHERE clause. If you omit a WHERE clause all rows from that table will be deleted.<pre>
Examples: EXEC SQL
            DELETE FROM employee
              WHERE dept_num = 333;
          EXEC SQL   /* all rows are deleted from the table */
            DELETE FROM employee;
</pre></td></tr>
</table>

The SQL Data Control Language (DCL) Commands

The SQL Data Control Language (DCL) consists of verbs that perform transaction management, locking, and data access control. The DCL verbs control the execution of other SQL verbs in order to ensure the consistency and security of the database in multiuser environments. In this section, we discuss how the Database Manager provides data consistency, crash-recovery, data integrity, and security in a multiuser network environment. At the end of this lengthy introduction, we present the DCL verbs that are used in conjunction with those services.

Data Consistency

Refers to the capabilities of Database Manager for maintaining the quality and integrity of data in a multiuser environment. In a network environment requests for database services may be concurrently generated by remote clients. How does Database Manager protect your data from the inconsistencies that can be introduced in a multiuser environment? There are three kinds of inconsistencies that can happen during the concurrent execution of requests for database services: lost updates, dirty reads, and non-repeatable reads.

- A ***lost update*** is caused by two users who read the same record at about the same time and then each perform an update. Without the proper database consistency protection one of the updates is lost.
- ***Dirty reads*** occur when one user submits a transaction that updates a database but which subsequently gets undone or "rolled-back." If in the meantime a second user had read the same data before the roll-back, that user would be working with "dirty" data (i.e., it does not exist anymore). Obviously, this is an integrity violation.
- ***Non-repeatable reads*** occur when one user reads data that subsequently gets altered by another user. If the first user re-reads the data, the value read will be different than what was obtained the first time. The implication is that two or more read operations on the same data may yield different results (i.e., non-repeatable reads).

The Database Manager solves the problems of data consistency through two techniques: *transaction control* and *locking*.

Transaction Control

A *transaction* is the fundamental unit of recovery, consistency and concurrency in the OS/2 EE Database Manager. A "database" transaction consists of one or more related SQL commands that are treated as a single *unit of work*. Either all the commands within the unit of work fully complete, or the effects of every command get fully "undone." A transaction terminates with either a **COMMIT** verb which makes all the database changes permanent, or a **ROLLBACK** verb which cancels the changes and returns the database to its previous commit point state. Figure 17-6 shows the effects of a successful transaction and one that fails. The successful transaction transforms the system from an initial consistent state to a final consistent state. The unsuccessful transaction undoes its work and leaves the system in the previous consistent state (all the intermediate work gets rolled back). A transaction may be aborted by a user program that detects an error and then issues a rollback (suicide); or it may be aborted external events like a power-failure or a deadlock tie-breaker, in which case the system issues the rollback (murder).

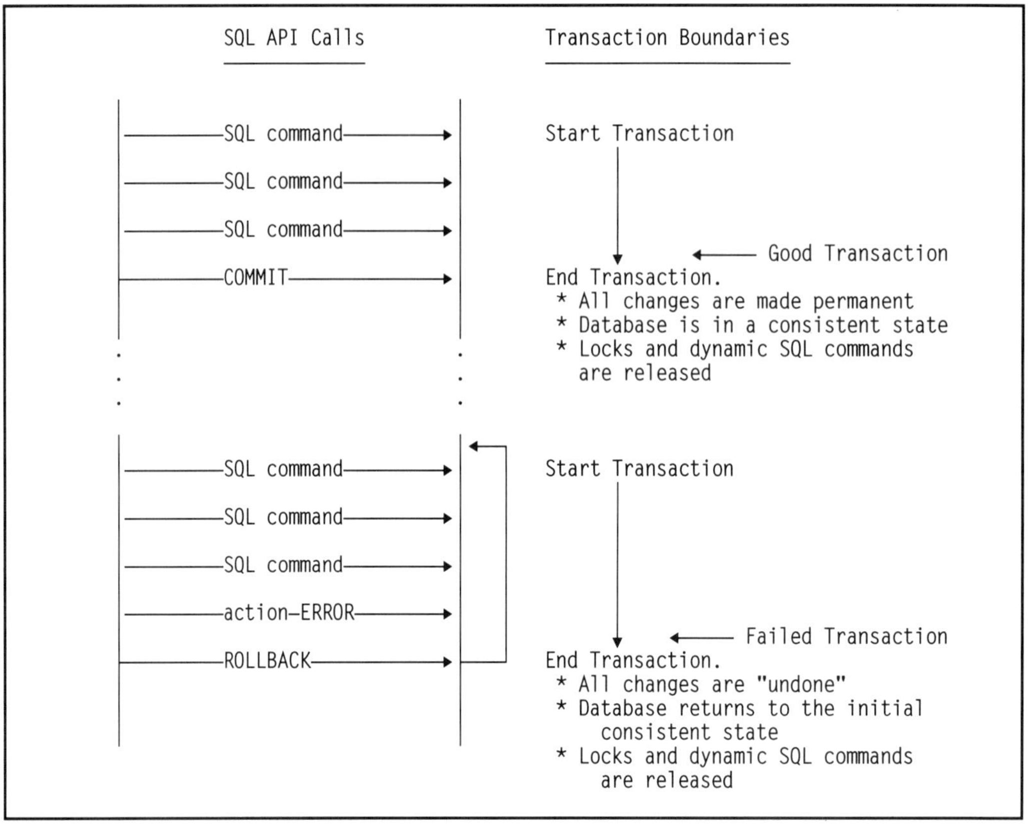

Figure 17-6. A transaction Groups a Sequence of SQL Commands as an Atomic Unit.

Transaction Logs and Crash Recovery

Crash recovery requires a clean termination of a program. We've seen how transactions provide "all or nothing" protection and ensure that either all of the requested services are performed or none are. Thus, a program terminates either producing the intended results or none at all. The Database Manager uses a write-ahead log technique in which before and after images of the transaction are kept on a log file. If the system crashes or the transaction gets aborted, the system can rollback the unsuccessful updates using the before and after image files.

Another technique called *roll forward* is used to recover a damaged database. This technique requires that all database updates be recorded on a log file that resides in a separate device. In case of a database disk crash, the logged updates are applied against the last backed-up copy of the database to provide a recovered database. The current release of the OS/2 EE Database Manager does not include a "roll forward" capability; however, IBM has stated that it intends to provide the function in a future release.

Transactions and Concurrency

In addition to being a *unit of recovery*, a transaction is also a *unit of consistency*. At the end of each transaction, the system releases all locks, cursors, and dynamically prepared SQL statements created or acquired during a transaction. An SQL application should always be broken down into a number of sequential transactions. In environments where many active transactions are accessing the database at the same time, the number and type of SQL commands that make up a transaction can dramatically affect the concurrency of a system. For this reason, transactions that execute in concurrent environments should be written at a much finer level of granularity while not compromising the consistency of the data. It is your responsibility to define, through transactions, the acceptable units of recovery and consistency for your application. It is the Database Manager's responsibility to automatically provide the right amount of locking to keep the database consistent (at the isolation level you specify) on transaction boundaries.

Note: Only one transaction at a time can be active on each process or remote application.

Locking

The Database Manager provides data consistency by introducing various locking techniques down to the row level. The effect of the various locks is to serialize, in one way or another, multiaccess to shared resources. Locking techniques have to provide a sufficient degree of *isolation* for users to maintain control over the data they are working on; without locking out other users for prolonged durations. This is a delicate balancing act.

The good news is that once you've structured your SQL application into transactions, the Database Manager will then automatically handle locks on your behalf. The Database Manager obtains the required locks at the start of a transaction and releases all locks when a transaction ends. It is never necessary for your programs to explicitly request locks. However, the **LOCK TABLE** verb gives you a way to override the Database Manager's rules for acquiring locks; but use it sparingly for it will have a negative effect on concurrency. Note that no corresponding verb is provided for explicitly locking individual table rows; only the Database Manager can do that. The only way you can effect row locking is by following the transaction discipline and, where possible, let your intentions be known so that you can help the Database Manager act smarter on behalf of your application. There are at least three ways through which you can let the Database Manager know of your intentions:

- You can specify FOR UPDATE OF in a SELECT clause. This states your intention to update a certain column at a later time.
- You can delay issuing the statements that acquire locks until the time when you actually need them. For example, you can delay issuing an OPEN CURSOR

command that contains a FOR UPDATE clause and increase the concurrency of your application.
- You can specify the required *isolation level* when precompiling or binding your application. The isolation level tells the Database Manager how much isolation from other processes your data requires.

Locking and Isolation Levels

Besides the exclusive lock required during an update, there are various levels of locking associated with database reads. This is an area where you're given the latitude to specify lesser levels of locking in exchange for higher levels of performance. The Database Manager allows you to specify one of three **isolation levels** or "degrees of isolation" required during database *reads*:

Read Repeatability: This is the level that provides the most isolation for your reads. In fact, you obtain the same amount of locking that is provided for updates. This level of locking may be required for non-browsing applications such as a financial report generator. With this level of isolation, any rows acquired by your transaction (for SELECT or UPDATE) cannot be altered (but they can be read) by another transaction. Your transaction will hold locks on any row it touches until it completes. This stringent level of isolation provides maximum protection and guarantees that you will get the same result from a SELECT statement throughout the duration of a transaction. The trade-off for this higher level of isolation is less overall concurrency.

Cursor Stability: This is the default level of isolation. It provides an intermediate level of locking where only the current row pointed to by a SQL cursor is locked, rather than all the rows involved in a query. This means other transactions can read or update rows that your transaction previously read. However, you retain exclusive locks for rows on which the cursor is currently positioned. With this more relaxed level of isolation, if you reissue the same SELECT statement at a later point in a transaction, you may get a different set of result rows each time. On the positive side, it enhances the overall level of concurrency in the system.

Uncommitted Read: This level provides the least amount of isolation. This is essentially an option to run without "read" locks, which therefore has minimum impact on transaction processing rates. Any application can read uncommitted data that may subsequently be rolled back. There are two situations where some protection is provided:

1. When the read cursor is for UPDATE.
2. When an application is about to drop the table.

This highly relaxed level of isolation may introduce some mysterious bugs into your programs and should be used only in "safe" situations, such as applications that browse only.

The Bottom Line: Using its *under-the-cover* locking schemes, the Database Manager guarantees that no program will have access to data that has been changed by another program but not yet committed, unless it is using the Uncommitted Read isolation level.

Deadlocks

Wherever there are locks, there looms the danger of *deadlocks*. This side-effect is caused when two transactions go after the same set of resources and each holds the resource the other needs to complete the job. The result is that both transactions get locked out and wait indefinitely. The Database Manager overcomes this problem by providing a deadlock detection and resolution mechanism. This is a background task that comes to life, at a user-specified wakeup interval, and looks for deadlocked transactions. If a deadlock is detected, the deadlock detector breaks it by declaring one transaction the "winner" and the other the "victim." The deadlock detector kills the victim's transaction (a -911 error code is returned), and in so doing releases all of its locks. The "winner" transaction resumes work where it left of. The "victim" transaction will need to be re-started by the application.

Authorization and Privileges

These are the mechanisms OS/2 EE provides to ensure that multiple users can share a database and retain control over their objects. Security of the database is handled at two levels:

- At the workstation level where OS/2 provides a *User Profile Management (UPM)* facility for handling the common security needs of all of its services. This includes the Communications Manager, the Database Manager, and the LAN Server program. For example, it does not make sense for you to define a user ID, password, and authentication process for each service you want to use; instead the UPM provides a single authentication system for the entire workstation.
- At the Database Manager level where SQL provides its own authorization subsystem which extends security to individual database objects. SQL provides a very granular level of security which defines the authority (or privilege) of a user to perform certain actions on certain objects.

User Profile Management (UPM) Services

When OS/2 EE is first installed, part of the installation procedure involves the automatic creation of the UPM facility for the workstation. The UPM provides a default *superuser* (defined as USERID) with a pre-defined password (defined as PASSWORD). The *superuser* or system administrator can do anything that involves security on any of the OS/2 EE components on that machine. For example, the *superuser* is automatically given a SYSADM authority which allows the user to perform every database operation the system supports. If you are interested in securing your database we suggest you do the following:

1. Log on to the UPM from the OS/2 Desktop as the *superuser*.
2. Add the user ID and password of your *administrator*.
3. Delete the *superuser* entry from the UPM. This will prevent anyone who has read this section of the book from taking full control of your machine.
4. Add to the UPM the authorization IDs and passwords of all the users of your database, including remote requesters.
5. Give the users a UPM authority of *user*. Only the UPM administrator can define a user to UPM.

Now your system is secure at the UPM level. Users and administrators will have to identify themselves through the LOGON command, which requires a valid UPM password and authorization ID.

The SQL Authorization Facility

The Database Manager's authorization subsystem provides the next level of defense after the UPM. It controls which objects and resources you can access or create, based on your authorization ID. Granting rights is done using the SQL **GRANT** command, and revoking rights is done through the SQL **REVOKE** command. The authorization subsystem maintains a system of privilege hierarchies (see Figure 17-7 on page 443) which closely parallel the object hierarchies you've already encountered. In order to perform any SQL operation, the user must have the appropriate authority for that operation. More specifically, the Database Manager provides three broad levels of control:

- Control at the system level. This level of control specifies the authority needed to create the system itself including the database.
- Control at the database level. This level of control specifies the authority needed to create objects within an existing database. It also specifies the authority required just to connect to a database.
- Control at the individual object level. This level of control specifies the authority to manipulate specific objects which exist within a database.

Authorization at the System Level

SYSADM This is the highest level of authority the Database Manager provides. This level of authority is needed to create a new database. In addition, only a user with this authority level can perform the following tasks:

- Create or drop a database.
- Catalog or uncatalog remote workstations and databases.

Protection Level:	*Protection services*	*Authority or "privilege"*
Workstation	Authority to log on to database "services" provided by the OS/2 User Profile Manager(UPM) →	User ID and password
Database Manager	Authority to create a database and control any Database Manager resource →	SYSADM
Individual Database	Authority to control a database →	DBADM
	Authority to connect to a database →	CONNECT
	Authority to create tables →	CREATETAB
	Authority to create plans →	BINDADD
Individual Object	Authority on a table, view, plan, or index →	CONTROL
	limited privileges on tables and views →	ALL ALTER (table only) DELETE INDEX (table only) INSERT REFERENCES(table only) SELECT UPDATE
	limited privileges on plans →	BIND EXECUTE

Figure 17-7. Authorization and Privilege Hierarchies.

- Migrate a database or reinstall the Database Manager.
- Change the database configuration file.
- Restore a database from backup.
- Grant or revoke the next highest level of authority: DBADM.

When the database is created, the creator is automatically given unlimited privileges to any database object; this is the DBADM level of authority. CONNECT, CREATETAB, and BINDADD privileges are automatically granted to the PUBLIC for the new database.

Authorization at the Database Level

DBADM This is the second highest level of authority. A user with this level of authority has unlimited privileges on any object within a specific database. Only users with DBADM (or SYSADM) authority can:

- Backup the database.
- Grant and revoke lower level privileges such as: CREATETAB, BINDADD, CONNECT, and CONTROL.

CREATETAB This level of authority enables a user to create tables in the database.

BINDADD This level of authority enables a user to create new access plans in the database.

CONNECT This level of authority enables a user to connect to the database.

Authorization at the Object Level

CONTROL This level of authority provides a user full control over a specific database object such as a table, access plan, or index. The creator of an object obtains automatic CONTROL privilege for that object. The creator of a view does not automatically receive CONTROL privileges, and can only have privileges on that view equal to those held for each of the tables referenced by the view. SYSADM and DBADM users have automatic CONTROL privileges on any database object.

Here is what each of the CONTROL privileges lets you do at the individual object level:

- With **table objects**, the CONTROL privilege allows you to reorganize the table and run statistics against it. In addition, it provides a full set of privileges on any table operations. These privileges can, in turn, be granted to other users of the table. Here is a breakdown of the more limited table privileges:

  ALTER Alter the base table and primary key definition.
  INSERT Insert rows into the table.
  UPDATE Change rows in the table.
  DELETE Delete rows from that table.
  SELECT Run selects against the table.
  INDEX Create indexes on that table. The creator of the index automatically gets CONTROL privileges on that index.
  REFERENCE Referential constraints which specify the table as the parent in a foreign key.
  ALL This is a short-hand keyword for all of the privileges on tables listed above.

- With **index objects**, the CONTROL privilege allows you to drop a specific index on a specific table.
- With **plan objects**, the CONTROL privilege allows you to rebind a specific plan, execute it, and drop it. In addition, you can grant to others the more limited privilege to:

  BIND This is the authority to rebind the plan.
  EXECUTE This is the authority to execute an existing plan.
- With **view objects**, the CONTROL privilege works differently depending on whether the view is:
  - **updatable**, in which case a user with CONTROL authority can drop the view or perform a full set of view operations, which can in turn be granted to other users. These operations are: SELECT, INSERT, UPDATE, or DELETE.
  - **not-updatable**, in which case a user with CONTROL authority can drop the view, but only perform or grant the SELECT operation.

The DCL SQL Commands

After this lengthy introduction to the SQL transaction management, locking, and authorization services, we are now positioned to introduce the verbs that participate in those functions. The DCL commands consist of a surprisingly small number of verbs as shown in Table 17-5. **COMMIT** and **ROLLBACK** provide transaction management. **LOCK TABLE** is used for explicit locking. The **GRANT** and **REVOKE** commands are used to interface to the SQL authorization services.

Table 17-5. The SQL Data Control Language (DCL).

SQL Command	Description

COMMIT	This command is used to terminate a transaction and make the changes to the database permanent. All the locks acquired by the transaction are released, except table locks for open cursors that are declared WITH HOLD. All open cursors not declared WITH HOLD are closed. All dynamically prepared SQL statements not associated with a WITH HOLD cursor are destroyed; likewise, prepared statements that reference open cursors defined WITH HOLD are retained. Database changes are automatically committed when an application terminates normally or when it issues a stop using the database.
	`Example: EXEC SQL`
	`COMMIT WORK;     /* The keyword WORK is optional */`

ROLLBACK	This command is used to terminate a transaction and "undo" any database changes that were made. All the locks acquired by the transaction are released, all open cursors are closed and all dynamically prepared statements are destroyed. If a program terminates abnormally, the Database Manager issues an automatic rollback.
	`Example: EXEC SQL`
	`ROLLBACK WORK;  /* The keyword WORK is optional */`

Table 17-5. The SQL Data Control Language (DCL).

<table>
<tr><th>SQL Command</th><th>Description</th></tr>
<tr><td>LOCK TABLE</td><td>This command allows you to acquire a shared or exclusive lock on the named table. A shared mode lock acquires the lock for the transaction which executes the command and only lets other transactions access the table for read-only operations. The exclusive mode lock prevents concurrent transactions from executing any operations on the identified table unless they are using the Uncommitted Read isolation level.
<pre>
Examples: EXEC SQL   /* Other programs are not   */
            LOCK TABLE employee /* allowed to read/update table*/
            IN EXCLUSIVE MODE;
          EXEC SQL   /* Other programs can read   */
            LOCK TABLE employee /* from table but not update   */
            IN SHARE MODE;
</pre></td></tr>
<tr><td>GRANT</td><td>This command grants authorization privileges to other users. Privileges are granted ON objects, TO specific authorization IDs, or PUBLIC meaning everybody. The privileges or authorizations are the ones we presented earlier in this chapter. The objects are: DATABASE, TABLE name, PROGRAM name, and INDEX name. The keyword TABLE is optional; if a name immediately follows the ON keyword, it is assumed to be a table or view.
<pre>
Examples: EXEC SQL   /* Granting a privilege to many   */
            GRANT CONNECT /* users, sales is a group name   */
            ON DATABASE TO Bob, Jeri, Sales;
          EXEC SQL   /* Granting many   */
            GRANT CREATETAB, BINDADD /* privileges to one user*/
            ON DATABASE TO Sandy;
          EXEC SQL   /* Granting a privilege   */
            GRANT EXECUTE /* to all users   */
            ON PROGRAM plan1 TO PUBLIC;
          EXEC SQL   /* Granting control privileges   */
            GRANT CONTROL /* on a table to all users   */
            ON TABLE employee TO PUBLIC;
          EXEC SQL   /* Granting all privileges on a   */
            GRANT ALL   /* table to a group of users   */
            ON TABLE salary TO managers;
</pre></td></tr>
<tr><td>REVOKE</td><td>This command revokes authorization privileges from users. Privileges are revoked ON objects, FROM specific authorization IDs, or PUBLIC meaning everybody. The privileges or authorizations are the ones we presented earlier in this chapter. The objects are: DATABASE, TABLE name, PROGRAM name, and INDEX name. The keyword TABLE is optional; if a name immediately follows the ON keyword, it is assumed to be a table or view.
<pre>
Examples: EXEC SQL   /* Increase security after   */
            REVOKE CONNECT /* creating a database   */
            ON DATABASE FROM PUBLIC;
          EXEC SQL   /* Revoking many   */
            REVOKE CREATETAB, BINDADD /* privileges to   */
            ON DATABASE FROM Sandy; /* a single user   */
          EXEC SQL   /* Revoking a table privilege */
            REVOKE SELECT
            ON TABLE salary FROM Sales;
          EXEC SQL   /* Revoking most privileges on*/
            REVOKE ALL   /* a table from a group name */
            ON TABLE salary FROM managers;
</pre></td></tr>
</table>

The SQL Program Language Constructs (PLC) Commands

The Program Language Constructs (PLC) consist of commands and constructs that facilitate the use of SQL with programming languages such as C. The PLC commands provide the following:

- Precompiler directives for declaring host variables.
- A precompiler directive for processing error codes.
- Cursor manipulation.
- The SELECT... INTO command for retrieving a single row.
- Dynamic SQL processing.

Precompiler Declarations

These directives tell the precompiler where to find host variables and "common" data structures to include. The **BEGIN DECLARE SECTION** and **END DECLARE SECTION** tell the precompiler where to find host variables. The **INCLUDE** command is used to declare the SQLCA and SQLDA data structures. As was previously described, the SQLCA conveys error information from the embedded SQL sub-language to the C program; the SQLDA is used for the passing self-describing data.

The Precompiler Directive for Processing Error Codes

The database Manager provides a **WHENEVER** directive that instructs the precompiler to generate source code that checks the SQLCA return codes and directs an application to a specified label. Essentially, you can instruct the precompiler to generate code for three types of conditions:

- **Errors**, which return a negative sqlcode.
- **Warnings**, which return a positive sqlcode.
- **Row not found**, which is an sqlcode of 100.

You can also tell the precompiler not to generate code by using the CONTINUE keyword.

Cursor Manipulation

A database *cursor*, like its famous cousin the familiar blip on the screen, is a pointing mechanism. The database cursor points to rows and enables procedural languages, such as C, to handle SQL queries that extract multiple rows called a *result set*. Using the cursor as a pointer, you can navigate from a C program through a set of rows, one row at a time, and pick out the information you need. Here is how a cursor works:

1. Issue a **DECLARE CURSOR** command to associate a cursor name with a particular SELECT statement. The cursor name is used by your program as a handle for that cursor-based SELECT.
2. Issue an **OPEN** command on that cursor, which conceptually causes the SELECT to execute and produce a result set. The cursor will be positioned before the first row.
3. Issue a **FETCH** command repeatedly on the opened cursor. Each fetch execution positions that cursor to the next row in the result set and then retrieves that row.
4. Issue an UPDATE or DELETE command with the keyword **CURRENT**, to update or delete a row on which the cursor is currently positioned.
5. Issue a **CLOSE** command, to close the cursor after you're done with processing the rows in the result set.

The SELECT... INTO for Retrieving a Single Row

The Database Manager provides a "non-cursored" version of the **SELECT** command which allows you to place the row contents directly **INTO** the specified host variables. You can only use this command to retrieve a single row of data. If more than one row is returned, it will result in an error condition. You'll find this command to be of limited use, since most queries generally produce "result sets" that consist of multiple rows of data. In addition, you cannot use this command with dynamic SQL which only supports the cursor-based SELECT.

Dynamic SQL Commands

Dynamic SQL commands provide maximum flexibility by piecing together SQL statements for execution at runtime. This flexibility comes at a price. Your programs must now handle dynamically prepared SQL statements whose fields and data types may vary with each call. You may also have to handle data types, tables, and table structures that are totally unknown at the time you write the program. The dynamic SQL statement is built up as a null-terminated ASCII string variable (up to 32765 characters). Your choice of method for dynamically preparing and executing the statement will depend on the nature of the command and how much information is available about host variables in the statement to be executed. The following four methods, presented in order of increasing complexity (and increased flexibility), illustrate how the dynamic SQL verbs are used:

- The simplest form of dynamic SQL execution is the **EXECUTE IMMEDIATE** command, which prepares and executes an SQL statement in a single operation. The statement to be executed cannot be a SELECT or contain any program variables or parameter markers.

- The second form of dynamic SQL execution separates the preparation of the command from its execution by using a two separate verbs: **PREPARE** and **EXECUTE**. With this method, you can place in your dynamic SQL statements a fixed number of place-holders for variables whose data types are fixed. These place-holders, also called *parameter markers*, are represented in an SQL statement by a question mark "?" for each program variable. A statement is prepared once and assigned a name. The name can then be executed multiple times using different parameter values each time. The separation of **PREPARE** from **EXECUTE** means that the access plan does not have to be recreated for each execution. This improves the performance in situations where the same statement gets repeatedly re-executed. This two-step execution also allows you to prepare multiple statements before any are executed. However, all statements must be prepared again once a transaction ends.

- The third form of dynamic SQL execution combines the **PREPARE** verb with a cursor mechanism. This method is used for the dynamic execution of SELECT statements whose columns are fixed and known at precompile time. Here's how to do it:

  1. Issue a **DECLARE CURSOR** on a string variable. Contrast this with static SQL where the full text of the select is declared as a cursor.
  2. Issue a **PREPARE** to assign the dynamically prepared select statement to the cursor which was previously declared on the string variable.
  3. Retrieve rows using the cursor verbs: **OPEN**, **FETCH** and **CLOSE**.
  4. You can reuse the cursor serially by issuing an **OPEN USING** with different parameters each time. This is done without "re-preparing" the select statement.

  The only limitation of this method is that you are required to know ahead of time the number of columns being fetched and their type. This is because the INTO clause expects a fixed number of host variables, whose types are declared at precompile time.

- This fourth method of dynamic SQL execution provides the greatest amount of flexibility. This is because it makes no assumptions on the types of SQL statements used or on the number of host variables and their data types. All of this is discovered at runtime by issuing a **PREPARE** in conjunction with a **SQLDA**. The Database Manager parses the statement to be prepared and places its description into the **SQLDA**. This includes a description of the data type, length, and name of each column in the statement. A **DESCRIBE** command is provided which places a description of a dynamic SQL statement into the **SQLDA** without precompiling it or creating an access plan. This provides a way of obtaining the type and description of a dynamic SQL statement before executing it. Using either of those verbs you have all the necessary information in the **SQLDA** to process the statement dynamically. Be warned, however, that a substantial amount of code is required to decipher all the SELECT parameters and their column names and types using the **SQLDA** as a descriptor.

The Program Language Constructs (PLC) SQL Commands

Now that you know all about cursors and dynamic SQL, we can describe the verbs that provide those functions. The PLC verbs and precompiler directives are briefly described in Table 17-6.

Table 17-6. The SQL Program Language Constructs (PLC).

<table>
<tr><th>SQL Command</th><th>Description</th></tr>
<tr><td>BEGIN DECLARE SECTION</td><td>This precompiler directive marks the beginning of a host variable declaration. This statement may appear in the application program wherever C-language variable declarations can. This statement must be paired with a END DECLARE SECTION statement and may not be nested. SQL statements cannot be included within the declare section. Variables referenced in SQL statements must first be declared in a declare section. Variable names must be unique both inside and outside the declare section.

Example: EXEC SQL BEGIN DECLARE SECTION;
double emplid; /* these host variable */
short vdeptnum; /* descriptions represent*/
char empname[41]=""; /* the columns of the */
double mgrid; /* EMPLOYEE table */
EXEC SQL END DECLARE SECTION;</td></tr>
<tr><td>END DECLARE SECTION</td><td>This precompiler directive marks the end of a host variable declare section (see BEGIN DECLARE SECTION above).</td></tr>
<tr><td>INCLUDE</td><td>This precompiler directive inserts declarations for a SQLCA or SQLDA into a source program. When your program is precompiled, the INCLUDE statement is replaced by source statements. Space is allocated for a sqlca variable; however, you must allocate space for the sqlda variable yourself. You can do that through the Database Manager provided macro, SQLDASIZE, which returns the SQLDA size in bytes.

Examples: EXEC SQL INCLUDE SQLCA; /* declares a variable */
/* sqlca of type SQLCA */
EXEC SQL INCLUDE SQLDA; /* declares a definition */
/* for a SQLDA struct */
struct sqlda far *sqlda = NULL;/* declare a pointer */
/* to a sqlda */
DosAllocSeg(/* obtain dynamic memory for SQLDA */
SQLDASIZE(10),/* macro for size of 10-element SQLDA */
&selector, /* address of segment selector */
PRIVATE); /* non-shared, non-discardable segment*/
sqlda = MAKEP(selector,0); /* convert to pointer */
/* and assign to sqlda */</td></tr>
<tr><td>WHENEVER</td><td>This precompiler directive specifies the action to take when a specified exception condition occurs. The exception can be: NOT FOUND, SQLERROR or SQLWARNING. The action can be GOTO a specified address, or CONTINUE.

Example: EXEC SQL WHENEVER SQLERROR GOTO error_handler;
error_handler: /* this is a C-language label */
printf("SQL error code = %ld \n",sqlca.sqlcode);</td></tr>
</table>

Table 17-6. The SQL Program Language Constructs (PLC).

SQL Command	Description

DECLARE CURSOR	This command associates a cursor name with the results of a SELECT statement. If the SELECT statement is not known at precompile time, the cursor can be declared against a statement-name and the SELECT gets prepared dynamically at runtime through PREPARE. Use the keyword HOLD if you do not want to "re-declare" the cursor at the end of a transaction.
	`Example 1: /* a cursor with a static SQL SELECT */`
	`EXEC SQL DECLARE cur1 CURSOR WITH HOLD FOR`
	`SELECT dept_num, dept_name /* example of a static */`
	`FROM department;           /* SQL cursor with HOLD */`
	`EXEC SQL OPEN CURSOR cur1;`
	`Example 2: /* a cursor with a dynamic fixed SELECT list */`
	`EXEC SQL BEGIN DECLARE SECTION;`
	`char   select_string[1000]; /* declare host var. */`
	`EXEC SQL END DECLARE SECTION;`
	`EXEC SQL DECLARE cur1`
	`CURSOR FOR name1; /* declare a cursor for name1 */`
	`.`
	`/*  later... build SELECT into select_string */`
	`EXEC SQL PREPARE name1`
	`FROM :select_string;/* assign SELECT to name1 */`
	`EXEC SQL OPEN cur1;  /* now you can go to work */`

OPEN	This command opens a cursor and causes the SELECT statement to be evaluated. The cursor is placed in the open state and positioned before the first row of its result set. The keyword USING can be used to introduce a list of host variables for the parameter markers of a prepared dynamic SQL statement. The keywords USING DESCRIPTOR may be also be used to supply the values of the parameter markers to a dynamic SQL statement through the SQLDA. The SQLDA must contain a description and value for each parameter. `Example:  EXEC SQL OPEN  cur1;         /* no parameter markers */`

FETCH	This command positions a cursor on the next row of its result table and fetches the row. If the INTO keyword is used, the row contents are placed into a list of host variables. If USING DESCRIPTOR is used, the row contents are placed inside the SQLDA.
	`Examples: EXEC SQL FETCH cur1 INTO        /* fetch a single row */`
	`INTO :vdeptnum, :vdeptname;/* using host vars.  */`
	`EXEC SQL FETCH cur1              /* fetch a single row */`
	`USING DESCRIPTOR :sqlda1;  /* using a SQLDA      */`

CLOSE	This command closes a cursor. The Database Manager will automatically close any open cursors when a program terminates. `Example:  EXEC SQL CLOSE cur1;`

Table 17-6. The SQL Program Language Constructs (PLC).

SQL Command	Description

PREPARE	This command dynamically creates an access plan for a SQL statement. The prepared statement is a named object, that persists only for the duration of the transaction where it gets created, unless it is associated with an open cursor defined WITH HOLD. To execute this command, you need to provide a name for the statement and the SQL string FROM which it gets prepared. You may optionally specify an INTO keyword followed by a SQLDA in which the Database Manager will return information about the prepared statement's structure. The dynamic SQL statement that gets prepared cannot contain host variables; however, it can contain parameter markers. The parameter markers have to be substituted one for one with host variables when an OPEN (for selects) or EXECUTE (for non-selects) gets issued.
	`Example: /* non-select dynamic SQL command (build then prepare)*/`
	`strcpy(stm, "INSERT INTO department VALUES(?,?)");`
	`EXEC SQL PREPARE dept_insert FROM :stm;`
	`Example: /*This is the select example that was used in DECLARE */`
	`/*CURSOR.  It is assigned to CURSOR name1            */`
	`EXEC SQL PREPARE name1 FROM :select_string;`

EXECUTE	This command executes a dynamically prepared non-SELECT SQL command. The keyword USING can be used to introduce a list of host variables for the parameter markers of a prepared dynamic SQL statement. The keywords USING DESCRIPTOR may be also be used to supply the values of the parameter markers to a dynamic SQL statement through the SQLDA. The SQLDA must contain for each parameter a description and a value.
	`Example: EXEC SQL`
	`EXECUTE dept_insert /* execute the previously      */`
	`USING :var1, :var2; /* PREPAREd dept_insert SQL    */`
	`/* command and substitutes    */`
	`/* markers with host variables */`

EXECUTE IMMEDIATE	This command prepares and executes a dynamically prepared non-SELECT SQL command. No parameter markers may be introduced. If the same SQL statement is to be executed multiple times, it is more efficient to use PREPARE and EXECUTE.
	`Example: strcpy(stm,"DELETE FROM department");/*build statement*/`
	`EXEC SQL EXECUTE IMMEDIATE :stm;     /*execute command*/`

DESCRIBE	This command returns information about a dynamically prepared SQL statement. You need to specify the name of the prepared SQL statement and the SQLDA where you want the information returned to. `Example:  EXEC SQL DESCRIBE dept_insert INTO :sqlda1;`

SELECT INTO	This static SQL command produces a result set consisting of at most one row, and assigns the values INTO a list of host variables. If no rows are returned, the command returns a +100 sqlcode and does not assign values to the host variables. If more than one row is returned, an error occurs.
	`Example:  EXEC SQL`
	`SELECT dept_num, dept_name`
	`INTO :var1, :var2;`
	`FROM department`
	`WHERE dept_num = 2500;`

Chapter 18

Tutorial on the Database Administration Services

This chapter provides the second part of the tutorial on the OS/2 EE Database Manager. This part of the tutorial covers the Database Administration API services.

THE DATABASE ADMINISTRATION API

These are the services used to automate the maintenance, performance tuning, and control of a database engine. The Database Administration API uses the call/return convention and is not part of the standard SQL sub-language. This is where you'll find all the database services that are particular to the OS/2 EE environment. Wherever possible, the OS/2 EE designers tried to maintain compatibility with the DB2 model for database administration services. In the sections that follow we provide a description of the functions for the Database Administration API services broken down according to the subdivisions shown in the figure below:

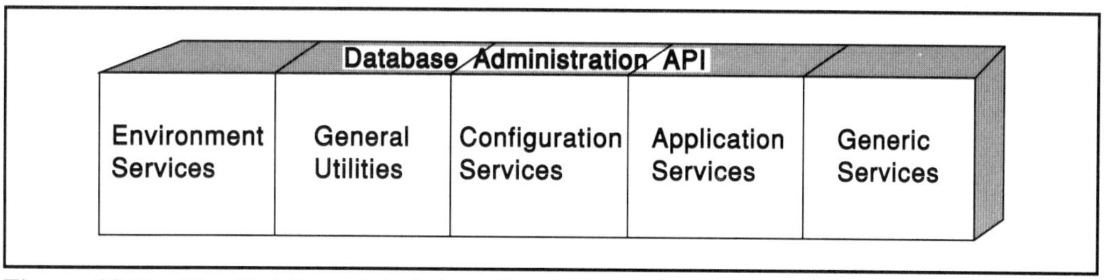

Figure 18-1. The Database Administration API Services.

Before plunging into the description of the services, we need to clarify two areas that are common to all of those services:

1. The naming convention used by the Database Administration API services.
2. The remote execution of Database Administration API services.

API Naming Convention

The OS/2 API services we've encountered so far, were endowed with luxuriously long and expressive names. Unfortunately, the Database Administration API does not carry on with this tradition. Instead, each function name is creatively packed with as much information as eight characters can provide. What follows is an explanation of the naming convention that may help you decipher, and perhaps even remember, some of the API names:

- Each API name has a maximum of eight characters.
- Each API name starts with **sql**.
- The fourth character in every name denotes the functional area to which the API call belongs, using the following convention:

  e for C-language specific Environment Services.
  u for C-language specific General Utilities.
  f for C-language specific Configuration Services.
  a for C-language specific Application Services.
  g for a Generic (language independent) version of the above services.

- The last four characters describe the function. This "four letter" limitation results in some strange sounding acronyms.

The C-language version of the service calls is optimized for the C-language. There is a C-language substitute call for almost every language-independent generic call. We recommend that you use the C-language specific version of the calls, since they are better suited for C programs. However, two commands **LOG ON** and **LOG OFF** have no C-language specific counterparts and can only be used in their generic form. There is one more catch. Both of these commands start with **upm** instead of **sql**. If you are planning on making your programs language independent you should, of course, consider using the generic commands instead of their C-language optimized counterparts.

Remote Execution of the API Services

With the SQL API calls that were presented in the previous chapter, any command that can be executed locally, can also be executed on a remote database with no changes to your code. This property makes the SQL API *transparent* to the database location. This means that SQL applications can be moved on a network without requiring any changes to your code; only the workstation directory and configuration files need to be modified. Unfortunately, this advanced level of network transparency does not carry over to the Database Administration Services API. This means that not all Database Administration Services can be executed remotely. In fact, some of the services are not even available to remote database requesters.

To complicate matters further, OS/2 and DOS database requesters were not "created equal." The DOS requesters have a more limited repertoire of Database Administration services than their OS/2 counterparts. To help you differentiate between the various remote capabilities, we added two columns to the description of the Database Administration API services. The entries in these columns indicate whether the service can execute in a transparent manner when issued from a remote DOS or OS/2 database requester.

When we say a service is *not remotely executable*, it can mean one of three things:

1. The API is not available to a remote requester.
2. The function is not applicable in a remote context.
3. The API can only execute on local resources.

In later chapters, we show you how to work around some of the remote service limitations.

DATABASE ADMINISTRATION API: ENVIRONMENT SERVICES

These are the API functions through which you can manipulate the Database Manager environment. The environment services fall into the following sub-categories:

- Start or stop the Database Manager.
- Database creation services.
- Database connection services.
- Database directory services.
- Interrupt handling.
- Database or user status collection.
- Remote Procedure Calls.

The table below classifies the Environment Services API commands according to the sub-category of service:

Table 18-1. The Environment Services API Commands, Broken Down by Function.	
Environment Service Type	**API Commands**
Start or Stop Database Manager	START DATABASE MANAGER and STOP DATABASE MANAGER
Database creation services	CREATE DATABASE, DROP DATABASE, MIGRATE DATA-BASE, and CHANGE DATABASE COMMENT
Database connection services	START USING DATABASE, STOP USING DATABASE, and RESTART DATABASE
Database directory services	CATALOG DATABASE, UNCATALOG DATABASE, OPEN DIRECTORY SCAN, GET NEXT DIRECTORY ENTRY, CLOSE DIRECTORY SCAN, CATALOG NODE, UNCATALOG NODE, OPEN NODE DIRECTORY SCAN, GET NEXT NODE ENTRY, and CLOSE NODE DIRECTORY SCAN
Interrupt handling	INSTALL SIGNAL HANDLER and INTERRUPT
Database or user status collection	COLLECT DATABASE STATUS, GET NEXT DATABASE STATUS BLOCK, GET USER STATUS, and FREE DATABASE STATUS RESOURCES
Remote procedure calls	DATABASE APPLICATION REMOTE INTERFACE

Most of these API services are straightforward and do not require an introduction. However, there are two areas which are not exactly "intuitive," and may benefit from a short introduction: database directory services and remote procedures.

Database Directory Services

Remote Data Services (RDS)

This is the component of the Database Manager that turns the OS/2 EE database engine into a networked database server. RDS uses the client-server distributed model with SQL messages passed between clients and servers over a network. With RDS, a workstation can be configured to be either:

- A stand-alone workstation.
- A database requester (DOS or OS/2).
- A database server.
- A database server/requester.

For the most part, the operation of the RDS is transparent to your programs. This transparency, however, comes at a price; you need to understand how to use and configure database directories. Part of the database directory services are executed automatically by the Database Manager, and the other part requires your explicit involvement. You can manipulate the directories that require your intervention either through a program that uses the directory services API, or manually through the Query Manager.

If your application will only run in stand-alone mode, meaning that it will only access a local database, the Database Manager will automatically maintain the database directories on your behalf, and you can skip over the rest of this section. On the other hand, if your application runs in either database requester or server mode, or if you will create databases on other machines and port them to a local machine through floppies, then read on.

The Database Directory Types

The purpose of the database directory services is to make the application as independent from the database location as possible. In order to achieve that, the Database Manager provides four types of database directories: system, volume, node, and DOS.

System This directory can be thought of as the master directory for a workstation. It contains an entry for each local or remote database that can be accessed from that workstation. This directory resides on the drive where the Database Services was installed. Each entry maintained in this directory consists of the following fields:

- The **database name** (up to 8 characters).
- An optional database **alias** (up to 8 characters), which can be used if the workstation needs to access more than one database with the same database name.
- The **disk drive** on which the database resides.
- The **product name and release number** for this database (up to 20 characters).
- An optional **comment** (up to 30 characters) associated with the database and the **code page** of the comment (for National Language Support).
- The database **entry type**, which denotes whether the database is *indirect* meaning it resides on this node or *remote*.
- The **node name** (up to 8 characters) on which the remote database resides. This item is required if the entry type specifies the database as being *remote*.

Volume This directory contains an entry for every database on a logical disk drive. This type of directory is maintained implicitly by the Database Manager each time a database is created or deleted on an OS/2 logical disk drive. An instance of this directory must exist on every OS/2 drive that contains one or more databases. Each entry maintained in this directory consists of the following fields:

- The **database name** (up to 8 characters).
- The **internal name** (up to 8 characters) that identifies the subdirectory off the root where the Database Manager stores the database objects.

- An optional **database alias** (up to 8 characters), which can be used if the workstation needs to access more than one database with the same database name.
- The **product name and release number** for this database (up to 20 characters).
- An optional **comment** (up to 30 characters) associated with the database and the **code page** of the comment (for National Language Support).
- The database **entry type**, which is always "home" for Volume directories, since the Volume directory keeps track of where the database is physically located.

Node This directory contains an entry for each remote workstation that can be accessed. The information contained in the directory is used by RDS to connect with the remote workstations. The connection information allows a database requester to establish an APPC session with the database server. Each entry maintained in this directory consists of the following fields:

- The **node name** (up to 8 characters) of a server workstation where a remote database resides.
- The **local LU** name (up to 8 characters) which identifies the local LU profile. This profile contains SNA information such as the LU session limit and the maximum number of TPs.
- The **partner LU name** (up to 8 characters) which identifies the partner LU profile. This profile contains SNA information such as conversation security, partner LU session limits, and the Data Link Controller type.
- The **mode name** (up to 8 characters) which identifies the SNA transmission service profile. This profile contains SNA information such as the RU size, the session limits, and the pacing limit.
- An optional **comment** (up to 30 characters) associated with the database and the code page of the comment (for National Language Support).

DOS This is the directory which resides on a *DOS database requester*. It provides the combined function of a System and Node directory. The connection information allows a DOS database requester to establish a NetBIOS communication session with the database server. Each entry maintained in this directory consists of the following fields:

- The **database name** (up to 8 characters).
- The optional database **alias** (up to 8 characters), which can be used if the workstation needs to access more than one database with the same database name.
- The **product name and release number** for this database (up to 20 characters).

- An optional **comment** (up to 30 characters) associated with the database and the code page of the comment (for National Language Support).
- The **node name** (up to 8 characters) of a server workstation where a remote database resides.
- The **adapter number** (0 or 1) used for the NetBIOS session.

Database Directories and RDS

Here is what each RDS configuration needs in terms of database directories:

- *A DOS requester* workstation must contain one DOS database directory.
- *An OS/2 EE database requester* workstation must contain one least one System directory and one Node directory.
- *An OS/2 EE database server* workstation must contain one System directory, and one Volume directory. An additional Volume directory is required for each logical drive on which a database is installed.
- *An OS/2 EE database server/requester* workstation must contain one System directory, one Node directory, and one Volume directory. An additional Volume directory is required for each logical drive on which a database is installed.

An Example

Figure 18-2 on page 460 shows a network configuration that consists of an OS/2 EE database requester on node WS1, and an OS/2 EE database server on node WS2. We first walk you through the configuration of the directories, on both the server and requester workstations, and then show how directories are used to establish connections to remote databases.

Configuring the Database Server in the Example

The System and Volume directory entries on the database server (see Figure 18-2 on page 460) are automatically created and initialized by the Database Manager when you create a new database. Let's walk through the process:

1. Use the **CREATE DATABASE** command to create databases DB1 and DB2 on disk drive C, and databases DB3 and DB4 on disk drive D.
2. The Database Manager automatically creates an OS/2 subdirectory (off the root) for each database. The directory names are supplied by the Database Manager using a naming convention which starts with SQL00001. The suffix in the name is incremented for each new database on a particular drive. Each table in a data-

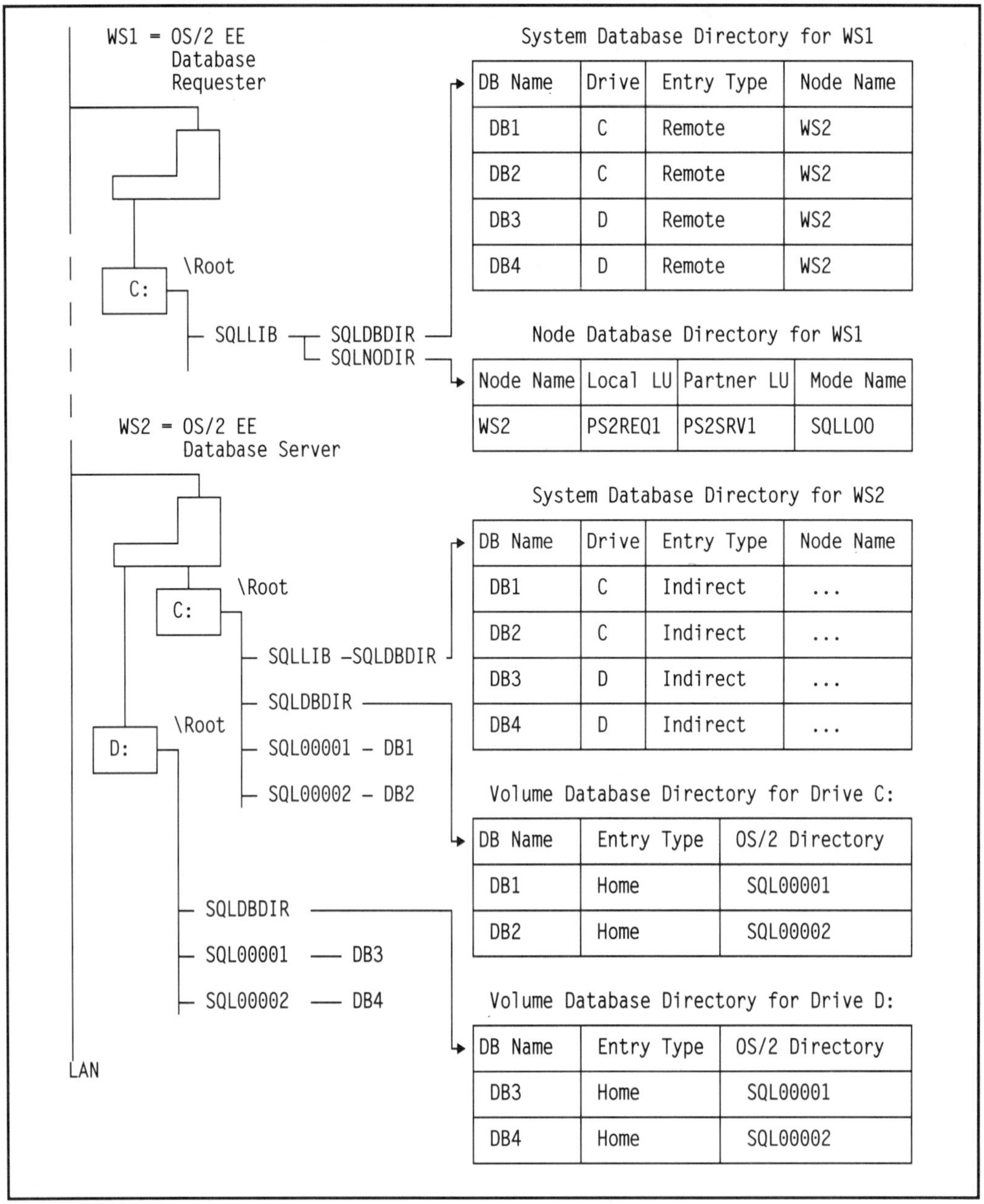

Figure 18-2. The Database Directories in an RDS Environment.

base is stored within the database subdirectory in its own (.DAT) file; the indexes for a table are stored in a (.INX) file.

3. The Database Manager automatically creates a Volume database directory for each of drives C and D. The Volume directory is initialized with a row for each database on that drive. Notice that the entry type for those databases is **home** because

this is the directory to which those databases belong. Also notice the correspondence between the logical database name you provide and the internal subdirectory name controlled by the Database Manager.

4. The Database Manager automatically creates a System Database directory for your machine and creates entries for all your newly created databases. Each database entry has an **indirect** type, meaning that the database resides on the WS2 machine.

Notice that the server in the example is self-sufficient when it comes to databases, and therefore does not need a Node directory.

Configuring the Database Requester in the Example

The Node and System directory entries on the database requester (see Figure 18-2 on page 460) must be provided by you. You can do this manually using the Query Manager, or by a program that uses the API services. In either case, the database directories have to exist and be properly initialized before your remote application can start using the database server. Let's walk through the process and introduce the information that needs to be provided:

1. Use the **CATALOG NODE** command to catalog the remote server node, WS2. In our example, there is only one entry, WS2, since all the remote databases reside on the same server. The APPC items identify the configuration profiles which APPC uses to establish the network connections. This information includes the Local LU, the Partner LU, and the mode profile of the SNA session. You may create and name your own APPC transmission service mode profile through configuration services or use the Database Manager provided SQL-LAN-ONLY-OPTION (**SQLLOO**) option.

   Note: The SQLLOO option is a high-performance APPC subset that only works on LANs. It is recommended that you use SQLLOO with LAN applications. However, you should be aware of two of SQLLOO's shortcomings:

   - It does not provide session security services.
   - It lacks the diagnostic features of APPC.

   The lack of security is not a problem, since database access control is provided by the **UPM** and the Database Manager's *authorization subsystem*. However, the lack of session diagnostics is a shortcoming. In the event of network problems, you may have to reestablish the session using the full APPC option to perform problem determination.

2. Use the **CATALOG DATABASE** command to catalog the remote databases DB1 through DB4 in the requester's System database directory. In this example, all the databases are cataloged as being of type **remote** and residing on node WS2.

Bringing the Requester and Server Together in the Example

Let's assume the requester workstation, WS1, needs to access data stored in DB3 on server WS2 (see Figure 18-2 on page 460). Here is a scenario that conceptually explains what takes place in this example:

1. The requester issues a **START USING DATABASE** specifying DB3 as the name of the database.

2. The RDS service on the requester searches for a DB3 entry in its **System Directory**. In our "ideal" example, a match is found. The directory entry identifies DB3 as being a remote database located on node WS2. The RDS then searches the **Node Directory** for a WS2 node which it finds, of course! The entry contains the information required to establish an APPC session.

3. The RDS then uses the Communications Manager to establish the connection between the requester and server.

4. Your user ID and password must be validated at both the requester and server workstations before the remote connection can be completed.

   Note: Attention APPC experts. An RDS TP on the database server is usually configured as non-queued and started by Attach Manager. The conversation type is basic. The conversation security is active. The Sync_level is set to NONE. If this information sounds confusing, you can either choose to ignore it or you can review the APPC tutorial.

5. At the other end of the APPC conversation, when the remote connection request arrives, the RDS service on the server searches for a DB3 entry in its **System Directory** and it, of course, finds one. The entry type "indirect" indicates that the database is local. The drive field identifies the database as being on the drive D.

6. The RDS on the server, then searches the D drive **Volume Directory** for a DB3 entry. Once again, an entry is found and the database connection can now be established.

7. The session remains active as long as the application does not issue a **STOP USING DATABASE** command.

8. The good news is that once you've got a connection, RDS will maintain *database consistency* across the communication link. What this means is that if a remote workstation or if the communications link fails during a database connection, APPC notifies RDS. RDS will then roll back the application's database transaction. RDS provides the same service for DOS requesters using NetBIOS.

9. You can use your remote connection to execute the full complement of SQL commands, remote procedures, and quite a few of the APIs that will be introduced in this chapter.

The Power of Remote Procedures

A Remote Procedure Call "For Database"

This an advanced database feature that uses a message service to trigger the execution of a remote procedure. The remote procedure typically executes a collection of pre-compiled SQL statements. The SQL statements can also accept parameters, so that a single procedure can be used over the network by multiple requesters using different input data. A variation of this service is known in the literature as *stored procedures*. The primary use of remote procedures (in all of its variations) is to support a class of performance-critical applications, known as On-line Transaction Processing or **OLTP**. These applications typically:

1. Receive a fixed set of inputs from remote requesters.
2. Perform multiple precompiled SQL commands against a **local** database.
3. Commit the work.
4. Return a fixed set of results.

The Remote Procedure Call serves as the foundation on which *Transaction Servers* are built. It reduces communications traffic, improves response times, and provides an object-oriented flavor of database service that is well suited for OLTP applications. The main drawback of remote procedures is that they provide less ad hoc flexibility than remote SQL.

A Client-Server for OLTP

The remote procedure call is an extension of the client-server model for transaction processing environments. You may recall that the client-server model splits an application into two parts: a client and a server. The client and server communicate requests and responses through messages. This simple construct allows intelligence to be easily distributed across a network and provides a framework for the design of loosely coupled network-based applications. Here is how this model has evolved to fit the needs of various distributed environments, including the more demanding needs of **OLTP** types of applications:

- With a *File Server*, the client passes requests for file data over a network. This is a very primitive form of service interface that typically necessitates many message exchanges over the network to find the required data.

- With a *Database Server*, the client passes SQL requests for information. This higher-level service interface allows the server to use its own processing power to find the required data. Only the final results of the search are returned over the network. The code that processes the SQL request and the data reside on the same machine. This results in a much more efficient use of distributed processing power than that provided by file servers.

- With a *Transaction Server*, the client invokes a remote procedure and passes it the parameters required to do a job. A single remote message triggers the execution of a collection of stored SQL statements. The result is an even greater reduction of network traffic and better performance. This approach also provides better *site autonomy*, since the remote modification of tables can only occur through locally executing programs. If the tables change, you don't need to recompile all your remote applications. In general, this implementation of client-server provides better distribution of intelligence, at the price of some loss of remote flexibility.

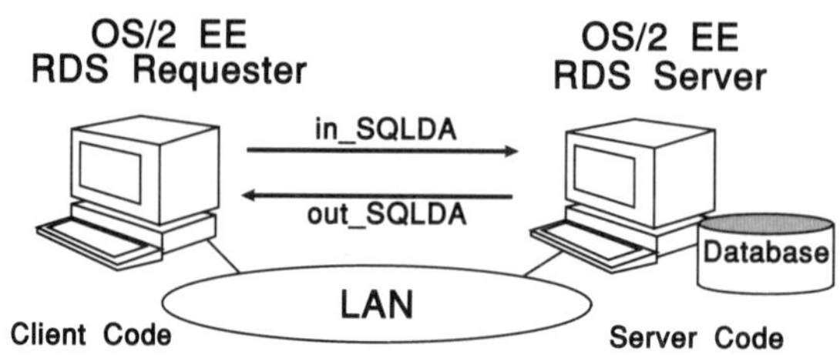

Figure 18-3. The Database Manager's Remote Procedure Call.

Benefits of the OS/2 EE Remote Procedures

As you may have surmised from your readings throughout this book, there are many ways to provide a Remote Procedure Call. The OS/2 EE Database Manager's **APPLICATION REMOTE INTERFACE** API provides an advanced implementation of a Remote Procedure Call for databases. The OS/2 EE implementation of remote calls contains many advanced features. Here are some of the highlights (also see Figure 18-3):

- The Remote Procedure Call is transparent to the location of the procedure. The stored procedure can reside in either a local or remote site.
- The Remote Procedure Call is optimized for the execution of a collection of SQL statements.
- The C-language is used to create the remote procedures as opposed to inventing a new transaction language.
- The remote procedures are implemented as DLLs, which provide an almost ideal package for such constructs.
- The remote parameters are passed over the network using self-describing data structures of type **SQLDA**. This choice of a container for passing data is consistent with the SQL programming paradigm.
- The reconstruction of the SQLDA at the remote location after it is sent over the network is a nice feature in its own right. It is also an attractive way of providing location transparency. It can provide this since the RDS handles the situation where the call may be local, in which case the SQLDA is shared through common memory and does not need to be reconstructed.

- The remote procedures can terminate after execution or remain active in memory. This choice of termination method allows remote procedures to provide both non-persistent simple transactions and persistent conversational programs.

How the Database Manager's Remote Procedure Call Works

Figure 18-4 presents a more detailed description of how the OS/2 EE Remote Procedure Call works.

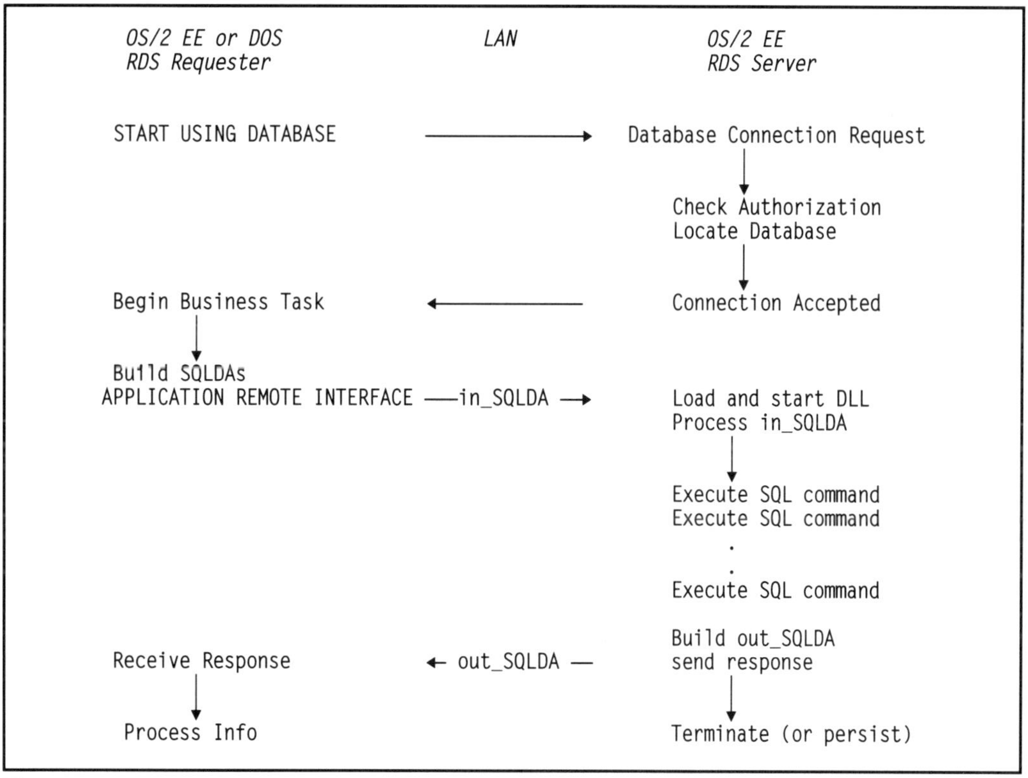

Figure 18-4. The Application Remote Interface's Remote Procedure Call.

The following explains what's going on in Figure 18-4:

The Client Side of the Call

The client must first issue a **START USING DATABASE** command to connect to the remote database. Once this is done, the client sets up two SQLDA structures. The information to be sent to the server is placed inside an in_SQLDA structure. The information returned from the server will be placed in the assigned out_SQLDA structure. The client then issues an **APPLICATION REMOTE INTERFACE** command to call a remote program on the server.

The SQLDA Exchange

The RDS on the client side automatically extracts the necessary information from the SQLDAs and transmits it to its RDS counterpart on the server. The RDS on the server side loads the server program requested by the remote call, and places the reconstructed SQLDA structures in its local memory. The server program must exist as an OS/2 Dynamic Link Library (.DLL) procedure. The remote call interface can also be used if the database is local. In this case, the RDS loads the .DLL and locally calls the procedure and makes available to it the SQLDAs through shared memory. This feature makes the remote call interface transparent to the location of the server application.

Invoking the Remote Procedure

The client can specify the name of the procedure to be run on the server in one of two ways:

1. By a single **funcname**. This causes a **funcname.dll** file to be loaded in memory. It is assumed that this file contains a function by the same name.
2. By the back-slash delimitation **dllname.dll\funcname**. In which case, the **dllname** is the name of the file to be loaded and **funcname** is the name of the function to be executed. A single (.DLL) file can contain multiple, remotely executable functions. Be sure to note that in this naming convention backslash does not indicate a subdirectory.

Executing the Remote Procedure

The remote procedure obtains its input data from the in_SQLDA. Each data item in the in_SQLDA has a SQL type, a length, and a pointer to the data in local memory. The remote procedure updates the database and places any results to be returned in the out_SQLDA. The RDS on the server returns the information to the RDS on the requester.

Terminating the Remote Procedure

Depending on the return code from the server application, the RDS will either:

- Retain the server application (.DLL) in memory. This mode is used for *persistent conversational programs* which require many calls and returns via the interface.

The return code from the server program code in such instances is: SQL_HOLD_PROC.

- Terminate the server application (.DLL) from memory and free all resources. This is used for simple transactions consisting of one call and one return after which the remote application terminates. The return code from the server program code in such instances is: SQLZ_DISCONNECT_PROC.

The Environment Services Commands

We are finally ready to present the individual API calls that constitute the Environment Services. These calls (see Table 18-2) are quite numerous. They provide the bulk of the Database Administration API services. Notice that we've added two columns to our normal description of the API functions to denote whether the function can transparently be executed on a RDS server from a remote DOS or OS/2 EE RDS requester.

Table 18-2. The Database Administration API: Environment Services Commands.

Function Call Name	Descriptive Name	Remote		Description
		DOS	OS/2	
sqlestar()	START DB MANAGER	No	Yes	This command starts the OS/2 EE Database Manager as a background process and allocates resources to it. This command has to first be issued before any application running on that workstation can access the Database Manager. The Communications Manager must be started before this command can be issued by remote RDS workstations.
sqlestdm()	STOP DB MANAGER	No	Yes	This command terminates the Database Manager background process and releases its resources. Unless explicitly stopped, the Database Manager will continue to be active, even if all the processes that were using it terminate. This call will fail if any applications are still connected to any of the databases under the Database Manager.
sqlecred()	CREATE DATABASE	No	No	This command creates a new database. You must specify the name of the database, the drive on which it will reside, an optional comment, and the code page for that comment. The Database Manager will create a subdirectory, off the root, for the new database and initialize the system tables and the recovery log. It will also automatically catalog the new database on the Volume and System database directories. The code page and country code of the creating application will get stored on the configuration file for this database.
sqledrpd()	DROP DATABASE	No	No	This command deletes all the tables in a database, and removes the entry for this database from both the Volume and System database directories. In addition, the disk subdirectory on which the database resides is deleted.
sqledchg()	CHANGE DB COMMENT	No	No	This command substitutes a new comment for an existing one for that database. It can only be executed on local directory entries.

Table 18-2. The Database Administration API: Environment Services Commands.				
Function Call Name	**Descriptive Name**	**Remote**		**Description**
		DOS	**OS/2**	
sqlemigd()	**MIGRATE DATABASE**	**Yes**	**Yes**	This command converts older database versions into Version 1.2 format. You must provide the password and name of the database to be migrated. The Database Manager will grant the initial user authorities.
sqlestrd()	**START USING DATABASE**	**Yes**	**Yes**	This command connects an application to a database. You must execute this command prior to performing any operations on a specific database. A process can be connected to only to one database at a time. Subsequent database accesses can be made by any thread within that process. If you are the first user connecting to the database, you can request exclusive use and prevent any subsequent users from accessing the database. If this function is called from a remote workstation, and the Database Manager is not started, an automatic START DATABASE MANAGER command gets issued before the remote request gets processed.
sqlestpd()	**STOP USING DATABASE**	**Yes**	**Yes**	This command disconnects an application from the database. A COMMIT is issued on behalf of any uncommitted transactions.
sqlerest()	**RESTART DATABASE**	**Yes**	**Yes**	This command recovers a database left in an inconsistent state during a previous session. This could happen, for example, as the result of a power failure or any other form of abnormal termination. You will typically issue this call after a START USING DATABASE fails and the sqlcode indicates that the database must be restarted. A second START USING DATABASE must be issued to connect to the database, after this command executes.
sqlecatd()	**CATALOG DATABASE**	**No**	**No**	This command creates an entry for a new database in the System database directory. The parameters you supply include the name of the database, an optional alias name, an optional comment, whether the database resides on this machine (indirect) or whether it is remote, the node name of the remote database, and finally, the drive on which this database resides. The new database can be located on the default drive, on other drives, on diskettes, or on a remote node.
sqleuncd()	**UNCATALOG DATABASE**	**No**	**No**	This command deletes a database entry from the system database directory. Home entries in the volume database directory must be deleted by using the DROP DATABASE command.

Table 18-2. The Database Administration API: Environment Services Commands.				
Function Call Name	Descriptive Name	Remote		Description
		DOS	OS/2	
sqlecatn()	CATALOG NODE	No	No	This command creates an entry in the Node database directory for the workstation (or node) on which a remote database resides. The entry contains the information required to establish a connection with the remote workstation. This information includes the name of the remote node, a comment, and the following APPC parameters: Local LU, Partner LU, and the mode profile of the SNA session. You may create and name your own APPC transmission service mode profile through configuration services. However, for LAN usage, it is recommended that you use the high-performance SQLLOO (SQL-LAN-ONLY-OPTION) default mode.
sqleuncn()	UNCAT-ALOG NODE	No	No	This command deletes an entry for a node name from the Node database directory.
sqledops()	OPEN DIRECTORY SCAN	No	No	This command retrieves all the entries of a database directory and places them in memory. You specify a Volume database directory by providing a drive name. The ASCII zero drive name returns the contents of the System database directory. The command returns the contents of the directory you specify, the number of entries, and a handle to be used with subsequent scan commands.
sqledgne()	GET NEXT DIRECTORY ENTRY	No	No	This command returns an entry from the database directory and points to the next entry after it. Most of the fields returned are common to both the System and Volume directories. However, a few of the fields are only valid for one or the other directory types.
sqledcls()	CLOSE DIRECTORY SCAN	No	No	This command frees the memory resource allocated by the OPEN DIRECTORY SCAN command.
sqlenops()	OPEN NODE DIRECTORY SCAN	No	No	This command retrieves all the entries of a Node database directory, places them in memory, returns the number of entries in the directory, and returns a handle to be used with subsequent scan commands.
sqlengne()	GET NEXT NODE DIRECTORY ENTRY	No	No	This command returns an entry from the Node database directory and points to the next entry after it.
sqlencls()	CLOSE NODE DIRECTORY SCAN	No	No	This command frees the memory resource allocated by the OPEN NODE DIRECTORY SCAN command.

Table 18-2. The Database Administration API: Environment Services Commands.				
Function Call Name	**Descriptive Name**	**Remote**		**Description**
		DOS	**OS/2**	
sqleisig()	**INSTALL SIGNAL HANDLER**	**No**	**No**	This command installs a simple interrupt handling routine for servicing the control interrupts that are generated when a user presses either the Ctrl + Break or the Ctrl + C key combinations. The interrupt handler resets the interrupt signal and then issues an INTERRUPT command that rolls back any active SQL transactions or commands. If you need a more elaborate signal-handler, then use DosSetSigHandler to create your own routine.
sqleintr()	**INTERRUPT**	**Yes**	**Yes**	This command allows an SQL request-in-progress to be halted and causes its effects to be rolled back. You cannot interrupt a transaction after a COMMIT or ROLLBACK command is issued. When this command is issued from a remote OS/2 EE requester, the Database Manager temporarily opens a parallel APPC session on which it issues the INTERRUPT. The session is closed after the command executes. When this command is issued from a DOS requester, it rolls back any in-progress transaction and disconnects the application from the database.
sqleproc()	**DATABASE APPLICATION REMOTE INTERFACE**	**Yes**	**Yes**	This command allows an application to execute a procedure stored at the location of a database. The remote procedure processes the results and returns the data to the application. This command reduces network traffic and improves the performance of network-based transactions. Your program will run in two parts. One part runs on the database requester and the other runs on the database server. The stored procedure on the server side runs within the same transaction as the procedure on the requester side. The program can be designed as a simple transaction (one call and one return) or as a conversational transaction (a set of calls and returns). The parameters you pass to this command are the name of the remote program, an in_sqlda which contains the name and memory addresses of variables that you want sent to the server program, and an out_sqlda where variables will be returned to your program. For remote calls, the Database Manager transmits and reconstructs the sqlda(s) including the data fields they point to. This means you can refer to host variables by name on both sides of the program. The server program must be written as a DLL.

Table 18-2. The Database Administration API: Environment Services Commands.				
Function Call Name	**Descriptive Name**	**Remote**		**Description**
		DOS	**OS/2**	
sqlestat()	**COLLECT DATABASE STATUS**	**No**	**Yes**	This command is used to collect a snapshot of the database activity at the time of the request. Status can be obtained at the system, database, or user level (for both local or remote users and databases). The command returns as system status the product ID, the release level, and the corrective level. For each database, it returns the last backup time, the number of current connects, the location of the database (local or remote), the drive where the database resides, the node name, and the type of database ("OS2 DBM" is the OS/2 EE reserved type). For each user, it returns the number of transactions since connect, the number of SQL calls made, the elapsed time since connect, the elapsed time of the current transaction, the authorization ID and authority level of the user, the transaction state, the lock state, and the node name.
sqlenext()	**GET NEXT DATABASE STATUS BLOCK**	**No**	**Yes**	This command returns the next database entry, from the results of a previous COLLECT DATABASE STATUS.
sqleuser()	**GET USER STATUS**	**No**	**Yes**	This command returns the status of all users connected to a specific database, from the results of a previous COLLECT DATABASE STATUS command.
sqlefree()	**FREE DATABASE STATUS RESOURCES**	**No**	**Yes**	This command frees the resources held by a previously issued COLLECT DATABASE STATUS command.

DATABASE ADMINISTRATION API: GENERAL UTILITIES

These are the API calls through which you can automate the management of database chores. Like a fancy sports car, a database needs to be maintained and serviced at regular intervals. A database needs to be backed up periodically. Its tables need to be physically reorganized on disk when the access performance becomes sluggish. The statistics maintained on the tables have to be refreshed after certain amounts of cumulative changes, to keep the plan heuristics in working order. Like car owners, database users tend to procrastinate when it comes to preventive maintenance. Many users of PC databases who do not have full time DBAs on their staffs, may not even be aware of the need to perform those maintenance chores. This is where the General Utilities APIs presented in this section will prove to be handy. They allow you to write programs that routinely perform the maintenance chores, and thereby help to offset the cost of ownership of a database system. The Utility commands fall into the following sub-categories:

- Backup and Restore database.
- Bulk Data Exchange.

- Performance Tuning.
- Authorization Status.

The chart below classifies the General Utilities API commands according to the sub-category of service:

Table 18-3. The General Utilities API Commands, Broken Down by Function.

Utility Service Type	API Commands
Backup and Restore Database	BACKUP DATABASE and RESTORE DATABASE
Bulk Data Exchange	EXPORT TABLE and IMPORT TABLE
Performance Tuning	RUNSTATS TABLE and REORGANIZE TABLE
Authorization Status	GET ADMIN AUTHORIZATION

The Utility Services Commands

We are now ready to present the individual API calls that constitute the Utility Services. These calls are described in Table 18-4. Notice that we've added two columns to our normal description of the API functions to denote whether the function can transparently be executed on a RDS server from a remote DOS or OS/2 EE RDS requester. Here are some rules that apply to the Utility API commands:

- With the exception of RUNSTATS and GET ADMIN AUTHORIZATION, you don't have to be connected to the database to use Utility commands. All the other Utility commands connect to the database through a separate OS/2 process.

- The BACKUP and RESTORE command use the standard OS/2 backup and restore services. The OS/2 services create their own Session and interact directly with the user if multiple diskette swaps are required. The space on the diskettes is automatically managed by OS/2.

- For Utility commands other than BACKUP and RESTORE, an error sqlcode is returned when diskette swapping is needed. Your application must provide the code to prompt the user for the next diskette. After the user places the next diskette in the drive, you will need to re-issue the Utility command with the **callerac** parameter set to 1 to continue the command.

  Note: The first time the command is invoked, the **callerac** parameter set to zero. If you want to abort the command set **callerac** to 2.

Table 18-4. The Database Administration API: General Utilities Commands.

Function Call Name	Descriptive Name	Remote		Description
		DOS	OS/2	
slquback()	BACKUP DATABASE	No	No	This command creates a backup copy of a database. You can specify through the API whether you want the entire database copied or just the incremental changes made since the last backup. You can apply incremental backups only after a full database copy is initially issued. You must provide the name of the database to back up and the drive on which the backup files are to be placed; the backup drive must be different from the drive on which the database resides. This command will fail if other applications are connected to the database. This command uses the standard OS/2 backup facility and starts its own OS/2 session and screen group. If multiple diskettes are required, the interaction with the user is done directly by the OS/2 utility.
sqludres()	RESTORE DATABASE	No	No	This command restores the contents of a previously backed up database. You have to provide the name of the database to restore, the drive to which it is to be restored and the drive on which the backup copy resides. This command will drop the database first and will fail if other applications are connected to the database. This command uses the standard OS/2 restore facility and starts its own OS/2 session and screen group. When a user interaction is required control returns to your application. Your appplication should look at the return code and determine whether to continue or terminate. You do this issuing another RESTORE DATABASE command, with the callerac flag set to either continue or terminate. The initial call must be issued with the callerac flag set to 0. If multiple diskettes are required the interaction with the user is done directly by the OS/2 utility and not through the callerac flag. This command is sometimes used to copy a database to another file system or workstation.
sqluexp()	EXPORT TABLE	Yes	Yes	This command copies data from a database table into an OS/2 file using one of several external file formats. You specify the data to be extracted by supplying an SQL SELECT statement. You must also supply the name of the file where you want the exported data to be copied to. The callerac flag repeat call facility, can be used to prompt the user for additional diskettes. You should supply the name of a message file where error, warning and informational messages can be placed by OS/2. The following exchange file formats are supported: **IXF** The internal Integrated eXchange Format (this format also exports the table DDL). **WSF** Lotus Worksheet formats. **DEL** ASCII Delimited, for exhanges with dBase. You should complete all database operations and release all locks before calling this API. This is best done by issuing STOP USING DATABASE.

Table 18-4. The Database Administration API: General Utilities Commands.				
Function Call Name	**Descriptive Name**	**Remote**		**Description**
		DOS	**OS/2**	
sqluimp()	**IMPORT TABLE**	**Yes**	**Yes**	This command copies data from an OS/2 file, using one of several file formats, to a database table. An INSERT, REPLACE, CREATE, or REPLACE_CREATE statement controls what to do with existing data in the specified table and column list. The data types in the file columns are converted into the data type of the corresponding SQL type, if possible. Minor incompatibilities are tolerated; for example, numeric data can be imported with a different numeric SQL type. You must also supply the name of the file which contains the data to be imported. The callerac flag repeat call facility can be used to prompt the user for additional diskettes. You should supply the name of a message file where error, warning, and informational messages can be placed by OS/2. The following exchange file formats are supported: **IXF** The internal Integrated eXchange Format (this format also exports the table DDL). **WSF** Lotus Worksheet formats. **DEL** ASCII Delimited, for exhanges with dBase. **ASC** ASCII non-delimited. Since the data for ASC files is non-delimited, you must specify through the dcoldata column structure positions of the input data. You should complete all database operations and release all locks before calling this command. The best way to do that is to issue a STOP USING DATABASE command first.
sqlureor()	**REOR-GANIZE TABLE**	**Yes**	**Yes**	This command reorganizes the physical storage for a base table. You typically issue this command when a table has become too fragmented due to many updates or deletes. You will know a table is fragmented and needs to be reorganized if the performance deteriorates. You can specify with this command how you want your tables physically ordered based on an index. To obtain the best results, reorganize the table using an index that is often used in queries. This command is fairly time-consuming (in the order of minutes). You should complete all database operations and release all locks before calling this command. The best way to do that is to issue a STOP USING DATABASE command first.

Table 18-4. The Database Administration API: General Utilities Commands.

Function Call Name	Descriptive Name	Remote		Description
		DOS	OS/2	
sqlustat()	**RUNSTATS TABLE**	**Yes**	**Yes**	This command updates statistics about the physical characteristics of a base table and/or its indexes. This command should be called when a table has had: • massive updates, inserts, or deletes. • after a table REORGANIZE command. • after creating a table index. The statistics tracked are the number of records and average record length. The optimizer uses this statistical information to determine optimal path lengths to tables when building the access plans. You must rebind any static SQL applications that use this table so that it can take full advantage of the updated statistics. You should be connected to the database and not have any outstanding locks before issuing this command.

sqluadau()	**GET ADMIN AUTHORIZATION**	**Yes**	**Yes**	This command returns the current user's database authority and privileges. The authorization list is returned in an array. A value of 1 indicates the user has the authority or privilege. This is a partial list of array elements:
				`Element  Authority`
				`0  SYSADM authority`
				`1  DBADM authority`
				`2  CREATETAB privilege`
				`3  BINDADD privilege`
				`4  CONNECT privilege`
				You should be connected to the database to use this command.

DATABASE ADMINISTRATION API: CONFIGURATION SERVICES

These are the API calls through which your applications can manipulate and view the configuration parameters that affect database performance.

Two Types of Configuration Files

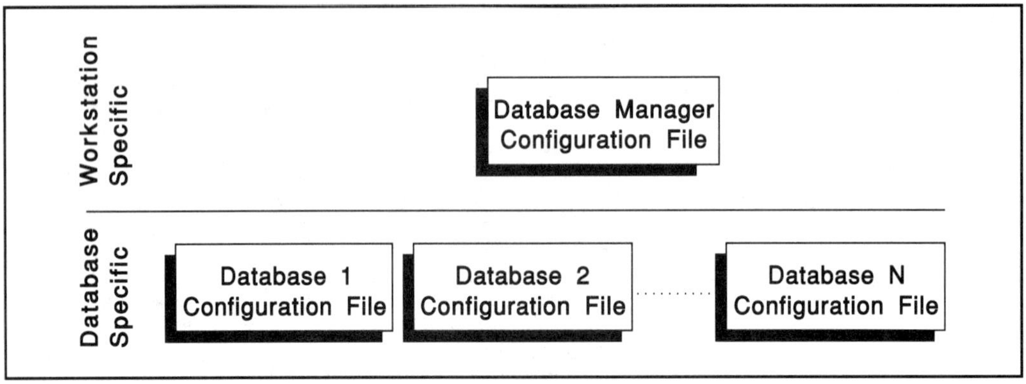

Figure 18-5. The Two Types of Configuration Files.

The Database Manager has two types of configuration files:

- **The Database Manager Configuration File** which contains configuration parameters that affect the overall performance of the Database Manager and its global resource requirements. This file also contains the database information specific to a workstation. The configuration parameters in this file can be grouped as follows:

  - Memory management
  - Concurrent databases
  - Workstation information

  There are a total of 10 configuration parameters, eight of which can be changed through the API services.

- **The Database Configuration File** which contains configuration parameters that affect the performance of an individual database and its resource requirements. Each database has its own configuration file which gets created when a **CREATE DATABASE** command is executed. The entries in this file can be changed to produce optimum performance depending on the type and activity of a database. The configuration parameters in this file can be grouped as follows:

  - Memory management
  - Lock management
  - File handle limits
  - Deadlock detection time
  - Log file management
  - Database information

  There are a total of 22 configuration parameters, 19 of which can be changed through the API services.

The Configuration Services Sub-categories

The Configuration Services API provide the commands to manipulate configuration information. These commands fall into the following sub-categories:

- Reset the configurations files to their system defaults.
- Update configuration file entries.
- Retrieve the values of configuration parameters from configuration files.

The chart below classifies the General Utilities API commands according to the sub-category of service:

Table 18-5. The Configuration Services API Commands, Broken Down by Function.

Configuration Service Type	API Commands
Reset Configuration	RESET DATABASE MANAGER CONFIGURATION FILE and RESET DATABASE CONFIGURATION FILE
Update Configuration	UPDATE DATABASE MANAGER CONFIGURATION FILE and UPDATE DATABASE CONFIGURATION FILE
Retrieve Configuration	RETURN COPY OF DATABASE MANAGER CONFIG FILE and RETURN COPY OF DATABASE CONFIGURATION FILE

The Configuration services API will rarely be used in general programs. Only programs that provide generalized database utilities will need to use this API service. Most users will use the Query Manager to manually manipulate the configuration file parameters. Serious database users need to fully understand how to use the configuration parameters to get the best performance out of their databases. We will use the Configuration Services API to introduce you to the configuration file parameters and to prepare you for one of those rare programs that uses the Configuration Services API.

The Database Manager Configuration File Parameters

Memory Management Parameters

sqlenseg This parameter specifies the total number of 64 KByte **shared segments** available to the Database Manager. The defaults are 20 segments for Stand-alone workstations, 50 segments for Database Server workstations and 1 segment for Database Requester workstations. At a minimum, you will need 6 segments for each additional activated database. The maximum number of shared segments is 802.

rqioblk This parameter specifies the maximum **I/O block size** in KBytes for requester workstations. This value can vary between 4 (default) and 64 KBytes. The I/O block is used to store a group of rows that have been transmitted from the server.

srvioblk This parameter specifies the maximum **I/O block size** in KBytes for Database Server workstations. This value can vary between 4 (default) and 64 KBytes. The server I/O block is used to store a group of rows that have been read from the database for transmission to a requester.

comheapsz This parameter specifies the total number of 64 KByte segments available for the **communication heap**. This is the dynamic memory used to allocate communication blocks. This value is always 0 for Stand-alone workstations. This value can range from 1 to 255 segments (default is 2) for Database Requester or Server workstations.

rsheapsz This parameter specifies the total number of 64 KByte segments available for the **Remote Data Services heap**. This is the dynamic memory used by RDS. This value is always 0 for Stand-alone workstations. This value can range from 1 to 255 segments (default is 2) for Database Requester or Server workstations.

numrc This parameter indicates the maximum number of **remote connections** to or from this workstation. This value is 0 for Database Stand-alone workstations. The defaults are 10 connections for Database Server workstations and 3 connections for Database Requester workstations. The maximum is 255 connections.

Concurrent Database Parameters

numdb This parameter specifies the maximum number of **concurrently active databases**. This value must be 0 for database requesters. The defaults are 3 databases for Stand-alone workstations and 8 databases for Database Server workstations. The maximum number of concurrently active databases is 8.

Workstation Information Parameters

nodetype This parameter contains the **workstation configuration**. It indicates whether the workstation was configured as a Database Server, Requester, or Stand-alone node. You can only change this parameter by reinstalling the system.

release This parameter contains the **release number** of the Database Manager software. You can only change this parameter by reinstalling the system.

nodename This parameter **names the workstation**. The name can be 1 to 8 characters long and must be null terminated. This parameter is not used by Stand-alone workstations.

The Database Configuration File Parameters

Memory Management Parameters

maxappls This parameter specifies the maximum **number of active** applications that can concurrently connect to the database. The default is 8 applications. The maximum is 117 applications. Remember that utilities require 1 connection.

buffpage This parameter specifies the number of 4 KByte pages used for a **buffer pool** for that database. A buffer pool is a memory cache where database records are read and changed. The data can be accessed much faster from RAM than from disk. This is the *single most important parameter* through which you can improve database performance (at the cost of buying more memory). The default is 16 pages. The maximum is 1500 pages.

sortheap This parameter specifies the maximum **number of private segments for sort buffers** per application. This is the dynamic buffer heap used for sort lists. The default is 2 segments. The allowable range is from 1 to 20 segments.

stmtheap This parameter specifies the maximum **storage heap used for compiling dynamic SQL statements**. The default for this value is 64 segments. The allowable range is from 8 to 255 segments.

Lock Management Parameters

locklist This parameter specifies the number of 4 KByte pages used for the **storage of locklists**. The size of this parameter affects the maximum number of locks available for all applications that are concurrently using a database. The default for this value is 8 pages. The allowable range is from 4 to 250 pages.

maxlocks This parameter specifies the maximum **percent of locklists** allowed per application. The range is from 1 to 100 percent.

File Handle Limit Parameters

maxfilop This parameter specifies the maximum **number of open database files** per application. The default is 20 files. The allowable range is from 2 to 235 files. The greater the value specified, the less frequently Database Manager must open and close files.

maxtotfilop This parameter specifies the maximum **number of open OS/2 files** per application. This includes all database and user files. The default is 255 files. The allowable range is from 25 to 32,700 files.

Deadlock Detection Time Parameters

dlchktime This parameter specifies the **time interval for checking deadlocks** in units of seconds. Increasing this parameter improves runtime performance but at the risk of freezing your applications for longer durations while a deadlock remains undetected. The default for this value is 10 seconds. The allowable range is from 1 to 600 seconds.

Log File Management Parameters

logfilsiz This parameter specifies the number of 4 KByte pages on disk used for the **circular recovery log files**. The size of this parameter affects the amount of changes to the database that can be done by active transactions. The changes a transaction makes to a database are written to the recovery log file where the records are kept until the transaction terminates. If there are many changes or many concurrent transactions, the log files can become full. When the primary log files becomes full, the overflow records are stored on secondary log files. The secondary log files are created empty but are extended by the size specified in **logfilsiz** when space is needed. They are truncated back to empty when space is no longer needed. The default for this value is 50 pages. The allowable range is from 15 to 4095 pages.

logprimary This parameter specifies the number of **primary log files**. These are the preallocated log files that are created when a database is created. The default for this value is 2 files. The allowable range is from 0 to 63 files. If you specify 0 for this parameter, more time will be required each time the database is opened, since the secondary log files will need to be extended.

logsecond This parameter specifies the number of **secondary log files**. These are empty log files that can be extended as needed when the primary log files run out of space. The default for this value is 3 files. The allowable range is from 0 to 63 files.

softmax This parameter specifies the maximum number of log records that can be written before a **soft checkpoint** is applied. A soft checkpoint establishes a pointer in the log at which recovery of a database is to begin. The recovery process will skip over old records (pre-checkpoint) and only process new records for recovery purposes. Making this number large extends the duration of a database restart in the event of failure; especially if the log file is very large. A smaller value for this parameter slows the run time of your transactions. The default value is 100 records. The allowable range is from 0 to 65,535 records. The value 0 indicates no soft checkpoints.

logpath This parameter specifies the **path of the current location of log files** on disk. The recovery log file is first created in the same directory as the database and this parameter is set to null. A null setting indicates the default path.

newlogpath This parameter specifies the **path of the new location of log files** on disk. When the **logpath** parameter is changed, the new path is temporarily stored in **newlogpath**. After all users stop using the database, the next START USING DATABASE command moves the log file to the new location and changes the **logpath** parameter to the new path, and sets **newlogpath** to null.

Database Information Parameters

sqlf_dets This parameter is used to enable or disable **copy protection**. When copy protection is enabled, a database cannot be used on a workstation other than the one on which it was created.

release This parameter contains the **release number** of the Database Manager system software. You can only change this parameter by reinstalling the system.

country This parameter contains the **country code** of the database. The Country Code affects among other things database TIME and DATA formats. You can only change this parameter by reinstalling the database.

code page This parameter contains the **code page** of the database. The codepage of a database affects the presentation of text. You can only change this parameter by reinstalling the database.

The Configuration Service Commands

We are now ready to present the individual API calls that constitute the Configuration Services. These calls are described in Table 18-6. Notice that we've added two columns to our normal description of the API functions to denote whether the function can be transparently executed on a RDS server from a remote DOS or OS/2 EE RDS requester. Here are some rules that apply to the Configuration Services API commands:

- The updates or resets to the Database Manager configuration files are not effective until all applications have completed and a **STOP DATABASE MANAGER** command has been performed. The changes are activated by the next **START DATABASE MANAGER** command.

- The updates or resets to the database configuration files are not effective until all applications have completed and a **STOP USING DATABASE** command has been performed. The changes are activated by the next **START USING DATABASE** command.

- If two applications modify the configuration files before the updates are made effective, the later update overrides the earlier one.
- The configuration parameters are updated or retrieved by passing an **array of items** to the API. Each item contains a number (the token) which identifies a parameter in the configuration file, and a pointer to a memory location for the parameter value to be returned or updated.

Table 18-6. The Database Administration API: Configuration Services Commands.

Function Call Name	Descriptive Name	Remote		Description
		DOS	OS/2	
sqlfrsys()	RESET DATABASE MANAGER CONFIG-URATION FILE	No	No	This command resets the Database Manager config file to the shipped parameter defaults. The default values will be based on the current node type.

sqlfxsys()	RETURN COPY OF DATABASE MANAGER CONFIG-URATION FILE	No	No	This command retrieves individual entries in the Database Manager config file. You must provide a count parameter that indicates the number of entries you want retrieved. You must also provide an array of elements for the returned entries. Each element in the array consists of a token and an address. The token is a number that identifies the parameter field. The address points to a variable which will receive the returned parameter. The following shows the token to DB Mgr config file parameter correspondence:
				`Token Field Nm.  Data Type Description`
				`  1   rqrioblk  SMALLINT  max requestr block`
				`  3   svrioblk  SMALLINT  max server block`
				`  5   sqlenseg  SMALLINT  max shared segs.`
				`  6   numdb     SMALLINT  max active DBs`
				`  7   nodename  CHAR[9]   workstation name`
				`  8   comheapsz SMALLINT  max comm heap size`
				`  9   rsheapsz  SMALLINT  max RDS heap size`
				` 10   numrc     SMALLINT  max connections`
				`100   nodetype  SMALLINT  node type (read)`
				`101   release   SMALLINT  DB release (read)`

sqlfusys()	UPDATE DATABASE MANAGER CONFIG-URATION FILE	No	No	This command allows individual entries in the Database Manager config files to be modified. You must provide a count of the number of parameters you want modified and an array of elements. Each element in the array contains a token number which identifies the field to be modified and an address that points to the new field value (see token description above).
sqlfrdbc()	RESET DB CONFIG FILE	No	No	This command resets the Database config file to the shipped parameter defaults.

Table 18-6. The Database Administration API: Configuration Services Commands.

Function Call Name	Descriptive Name	Remote		Description
		DOS	OS/2	
sqlfxdbc()	RETURN COPY OF DATABASE CONFIG-URATION FILE	No	No	This command retrieves individual entries in the Database config file. You must provide a count parameter that indicates the number of entries you want retrieved. You must also provide an array of elements for the returned entries. Each element in the array consists of a token and an address. The token is a number that identifies the parameter field. The address points to a variable which will receive the returned parameter. The following shows the token to the DB config file parameter correspondence: Token Field Nm. Data Type Description 1 locklist SMALLINT max locklist sz. 2 buffpage SMALLINT max buffer pool 3 maxfilop SMALLINT max DB files 5 softmax SMALLINT max soft checkpt 6 maxappls SMALLINT max active users 7 applheapsz SMALLINT application heap 8 dbheap SMALLINT database heap 9 dlchktime INTEGER deadlock chk ms 10 maxtotfilop SMALLINT max appl files 11 sortheap SMALLINT sort heap size 14 agentheap SMALLINT appl agent heap 15 maxlocks SMALLINT % of locklist 16 logprimary SMALLINT prim log files 17 logsecond SMALLINT sec log files 18 logfilsiz SMALLINT prim file size 19 stmtheap SMALLINT SQL stmt heap 20 newlogpath CHAR[248] changed log path 21 sqlf_dets SMALLINT copy protection 100 country SMALLINT country (read) 101 codepage SMALLINT DB codepage(rd.) 102 release SMALLINT DB release(read) 103 logpath CHAR[248] log path (read)
sqlfeudb()	UPDATE DATABASE CONFIG-URATION FILE	No	No	This command allows individual entries in the Database config files to be modified. You must provide a count of the number of parameters you want modified and an array of elements. Each element in the array contains a token number which identifies the field to be modified and an address that points to the new field value (see token description above).

DATABASE ADMINISTRATION API: APPLICATION SERVICES

There are two API calls that fall into the Application Services category: **BIND** and **RETRIEVE MESSAGE**. Neither of these two calls requires any new background information. We can go on to the description in Table 18-7 where, as previously noted, we added two columns to our normal description of the API functions to denote whether the function can transparently be executed on a RDS server from a remote DOS or OS/2 EE RDS requester.

Table 18-7. The Database Administration API: Application Services Commands.				
Function Call Name	**Descriptive Name**	**Remote**		**Description**
		DOS	**OS/2**	
sqlabndr()	**BIND with options**	**No**	**Yes**	This command calls the BIND utility from within an application program. This is the version of the BIND that supports isolation levels and other options. This command binds a precompiled application program to the database, and creates access plans that get stored in the database. You must provide the name of the (.BND) bind file or a file containing a list of bind file names. You can specify a path for these files. You should supply the name of a message file where error, warning, and informational messages can be placed by OS/2. You can also specify through a SQLOPT structure an array of bind options: **Option Token** **Description** **SQL_FORMAT_OPT** This option determines the format of the date and time fields: **SQL_FMT_1** IBM std. US **SQL_FMT_2** IBM std. Europe **SQL_FMT_3** ISO std. **SQL_FMT_4** Japan Industrial **etc.** **SQL_ISO_OPT** This option indicates the isolation level: **SQL_REP_READ** repeatable read **SQL_CUR_STAB** cursor stability **SQL_UNCOM_READ** uncommitted read **SQL_BLOCK_OPT** This option indicates the type of record blocking and the manner in which ambiguous cursors are treated: **SQL_BL_ALL** all cursors **SQL_BL_UNAMBIG** fetch-only cursors **SQL_NO_BL** no blocking **Note:** Record blocking can be used to decrease network traffic for applications that access a remote database.
sqlaintp()	**RETRIEVE MESSAGE**	**Yes**	**Yes**	This command returns the error message that corresponds to an error code in the SQLCODE field of the SQLCA. This is a very useful function for error handling. You provide a message buffer and specify the maximum line width of the message. The message will be broken down into a series of lines separated by CR/LF. A null is placed at the end of the message.

DATABASE ADMINISTRATION API: GENERIC SERVICES

We will make use of two API calls that fall into the Generic Services category: **LOG ON** and **LOG OFF**. These are the commands you need to interface with the User Profile Manager (UPM) that we introduced in the previous chapter. Neither of these two calls requires any new background information, and we can go on to the description of the commands in Table 18-8. Again, notice that we've added two columns to our normal description of the API functions to denote whether the function can transparently be executed on a RDS server from a remote DOS or OS/2 EE RDS requester.

Table 18-8. The Database Administration API: Generic Services Commands.

Function Call Name	Descriptive Name	Remote DOS	Remote OS/2	Description
upmglgn()	**LOG ON**	**Yes**	**Yes**	This command logs on the user to a specified node. You must supply a user ID, the password and the remote node name or domain. A remote type parameter specifies the type of remote node, as follows: **UPM_LOCAL** Identifies the node as the local workstation. In this case, the remote name parameter is ignored. **PM_DNODE** Identifies the remote node as an APPC node. **PM_DOMAIN** Identifies the remote node as the name of a LAN domain. The program issuing the logon must have been started by an authorized user. Valid indicators of the authority required to issue the logon are: **PM_CONFIG** The calling process must have been started by config.sys or from a process that was so started. **PM_ADMIN** The logged on local user for the calling session must have administrative authority. **PM_USER** The calling process does not require any additional authority. When logging on to a remote workstation, no logon actually occurs. The user ID and password are stored to be used for the next connection with the remote workstation.
upmglgff()	**LOG OFF**	**Yes**	**Yes**	This command disconnects the user from a session. A log on session remains active until you either issue this command or you turn off your workstation. To use this command, you must supply a user ID and the remote node name or domain, and the remote type parameter that was described in LOG ON.

Chapter 19

Tutorial on the Query Manager Callable Interface

This chapter provides the third part of the tutorial on the OS/2 EE Database Manager. This part of the tutorial covers the Query Manager Callable Interface whose main use in client-server architectures may be for **report servers**. A report server manages reports and executes them when a remote client requests it. Clients use transaction request mechanisms to invoke the execution of reports on the server. So in effect, executing a report becomes a long-winded transaction which operates on report objects. In this tutorial we first cover all the mechanics of the Query Manager Callable Interface and to entice you we introduce at the very end the concept of the report server.

A MARRIAGE OF CONVENIENCE

The Query Manager Callable Interface makes the Query Manager services available to your application through standard OS/2 EE API calls. By using Query Manager's services for screens and panels, you can add to your programs a Presentation Manager-based user interface that is already fully developed and debugged. You are also leveraging the familiarity that users may already have with the Query Manager objects, as well as adding to your programs a set of standard tools and decision support facilities.

With the Query Manager Callable Interface, you can now have your proverbial cake and eat it too. This means that C-language applications with their compiled code and powerful logic capabilities can now access the Fourth-Generation Language (4-GL) like environment of Query Manager with its ad hoc flexibility and tools. This marriage of convenience allows you to write production strength applications which also provide flexible ad hoc tools under program control.

Like all marriages of convenience, there is a small price to pay somewhere. In this case, the price is that you still have to use the Query Manager to create objects such as reports and queries. However, once these objects have been created, they can be brought under C-language program control through the Query Manager Callable Interface. This marriage could have been substantially stronger if it had provided a hook that allowed Query Manager objects to be dynamically created from a C-language environment. Wishful thinking aside, there is a lot of power available to your programs in this marriage, as it now stands. For example, packaged reports previously created through Query Manager can now be executed and printed under program control. After reading through this chapter, you will surely discover many uses for this marriage of services, that are particular to your environment and needs.

QUERY MANAGER OBJECTS AND FUNCTIONS

Before getting into the mechanics of the Query Manager Callable Interface, it may be useful to present a quick explanation of what the Query Manager provides in terms of services and special database objects. The focus of our presentation is on how to use those services and database objects from within C-language programs. This is not a tutorial on how the end-user interfaces with Query Manager.

What the Query Manager Does

As you may recall from Chapter 3, the Query Manager is the part of the Database Manager which provides an end-user interface to the database services. Three categories of end user services are provided:

Operations Support Tools: These are tools that are used to create, maintain, and update database objects and the database environment in general. Services that fall into these categories include table maintenance, reorganizing tables, running statistics against tables, the import or export of data, etc. Database environment services include the tools to create, backup, restore, catalog, and fine-tune a database.

Decision Support Tools: These are tools that are used to create ad hoc queries for retrieving data, and defining forms which specify how that data is to be presented in a final report format. The special database objects that Query Manager makes available for the creation of reports are: **Queries** and **Forms**.

Application Development Tools: These are 4-GL like tools through which you can develop simple end-user applications by defining and executing a set of Query Manager objects. No knowledge of the C-language is required to develop such applications, which makes them ideal for rapid-prototyping. However, the applications which can be developed do not have the robustness or the performance (they are interpretive) to handle complex screen navigations or run in multiuser environments. The special database objects that the Query Manager makes available for the creation of such applications are: **Panels**, **Menus**, and **Procedures**.

Query Manager Objects

In addition to supporting the familiar SQL objects such as Databases, Tables, Views, and Indexes, the Query Manager introduces its own set of objects namely: Queries, Forms, Panels, Menus, and Procedures (see Figure 19-1). Query Manager objects, like SQL objects, have names and are stored in the database. Unlike SQL objects, Query Manager objects can only be manipulated by a user using the Query Manager or by a program using the Query Manager Callable Interface.

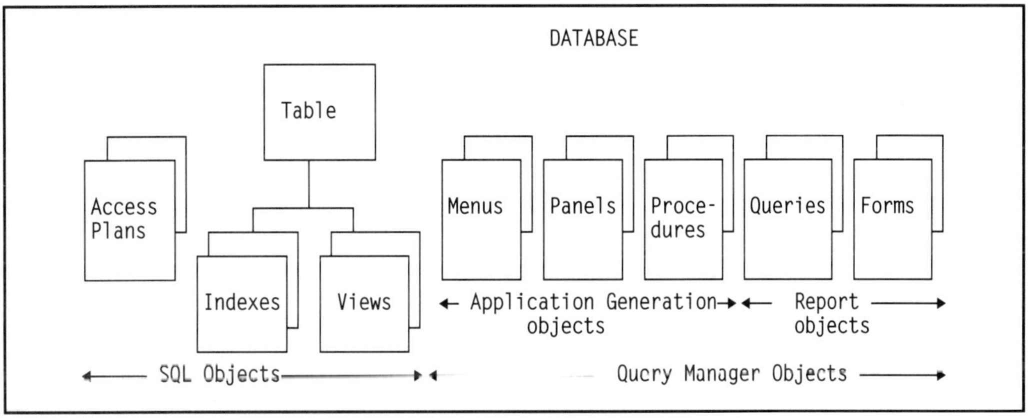

Figure 19-1. SQL and Query Manager Objects Within a Database Context.

Application Generation Objects

These are the objects used to create the 4-GL type of applications. Think of them as rapid-prototyping tools that can be used to put together a customized Presentation Manager front-end to the database. The following is a description of the objects that you can use to create such applications:

Menu This object is a special type of Presentation Manager screen which contains a customized list of items that can be selected. An application would typically start by displaying one or more menu screens that ask the user to select an object to be worked on.

Panel This object is a special type of Presentation Manager screen that contains a customized set of fill-in fields. These fields correspond to columns in SQL tables and are used for data entry or to display database information to the user. The panel displays one row of data at a time based on the selection criteria you define. For the selected row, the column data is automatically displayed in the corresponding field on the screen. You can customize an action bar and pull-down windows for a panel that specify the actions that can be performed. For each action, you can specify a Query Manager command to be executed.

Procedure This object customizes Query Manager command sequences. Procedures can invoke and execute various queries, panels, and menus. The Query Manager provides a simple command language that consists of a dozen or so instructions. These instructions provide: flow control (If, Then, Else), output (Say and Trace), and operators for assigning values, and doing algebraic, string, and logical operations. Query Manager commands may be issued from within procedures. Generally speaking, C programmers will not find the Query Manager procedures to be of much interest.

Report Objects

These are the objects used to create the report query and format the presentation of the results. Query Manager reports can be created in an ad hoc fashion by the end user. You can view this powerful capability as being a 4-GL tool for the creation of reports and decision support information. The following is a description of the objects that you can use to create such reports:

Query This object can be created either as a SQL query or as a prompted query. The SQL query consists of the familiar SQL SELECT statement, and it takes full advantage of the SQL language. Readers of this book will typically use SQL to create their queries. The prompted query is offered for those users who are not familiar with SQL. The Query Manager asks the user a series of questions and uses the answers to create an SQL query. This is a powerful ad hoc decision support tool that can be placed in the hands of a non-SQL literate end-user. Variables can be placed inside an SQL query, which can be helpful if you want to run the same report with different selection criteria. The variable should be provided at runtime through the Query Manager variable pool, or the user will be prompted through a pop-up menu to provide the non-existent value.

Form This object defines how the results of a query are presented. This includes the names of the columns to be displayed, the headings for the columns, the spacing between columns, the break order, and a myriad of other visual layout directives.

A Query Manager 4-GL Application

A Query Manager 4-GL application typically consists of a top procedure that does some initialization of global variables and passes control to a top menu. Through the top menu, the user chooses a major function to run. Based on the user's choice, the Menu may: run a Panel, run a procedure, or run another selection menu.

The Query Manager Variable Pool

Variables may be passed across objects (and to/from your C-programs) through the Query Manager **variable pool**. The following types of variables are stored in the pool:

- *Global variables* exist in the Query Manager pool from the time they are created until the time the Query Manager terminates.
- *Local Variables* exist in the pool from the time they are created until the object that created them ends.
- *System variables* such as current date and time are maintained by the Query Manager in its pool on behalf of all applications (more on that later).

These shared variables allow objects such as procedures, panels, menus, and queries to customize their runs based on external conditions. The **GET** and **SET** commands are used to copy Query Manager variables to and from local procedure or C-language variables.

The Query Manager Commands

The Query Manager provides a set of commands that perform actions on its objects such as queries, forms, menus, panels, and procedures. These commands can be issued:

- From Query Manager procedures.
- From within Query Manager menus, as menu actions.
- From within Query Manager panels, as panel actions.
- From the Query Manager Command Line.
- From within your C-language programs, through the Query Manager Callable Interface API.

The Query Manager commands are in the following object/action format:

verb object_type object_name

Table 19-1 shows the Query Manager Callable Interface commands that can be called by C programs. Later in this chapter, we explain each command in more detail.

Table 19-1. A Taxonomy of the Query Manager Callable Interface Commands.

Command Category	Query Manager Callable Interface Command
Object Manipulation Commands	DISPLAY, LIST, RESET, RUN, ERASE, DEFINE TABLE, EDIT TABLE.
Execution Control Commands	START, EXIT, BEGIN WINDOW, END WINDOW, BEGIN WORK, END WORK, CANCEL WORK.
General Utility Commands	GET, SET, MESSAGE, IMPORT TABLE, EXPORT TABLE, SAVE DATA AS, CONVERT QUERY, PRINT.

THE QUERY MANAGER USER INTERFACE

In this section, we present the Query Manager screen roadmap. You will need this information to help you understand how the Query Manager Callable Interface Commands hook up with existing menu structures. The Query Manager user interface presents itself as a set of hierarchically related menus (see Figure 19-2). A user navigates from menu to menu through object/action dialogs. These dialogs conform to the SAA Common User Access standard. This means the interface consists of choosing objects and the actions to be performed on those objects. Pop-up windows periodically appear in the body area of a menu to display status information or to prompt the user for additional information. Pull-down windows are used in conjunction with the action bar to present action choices.

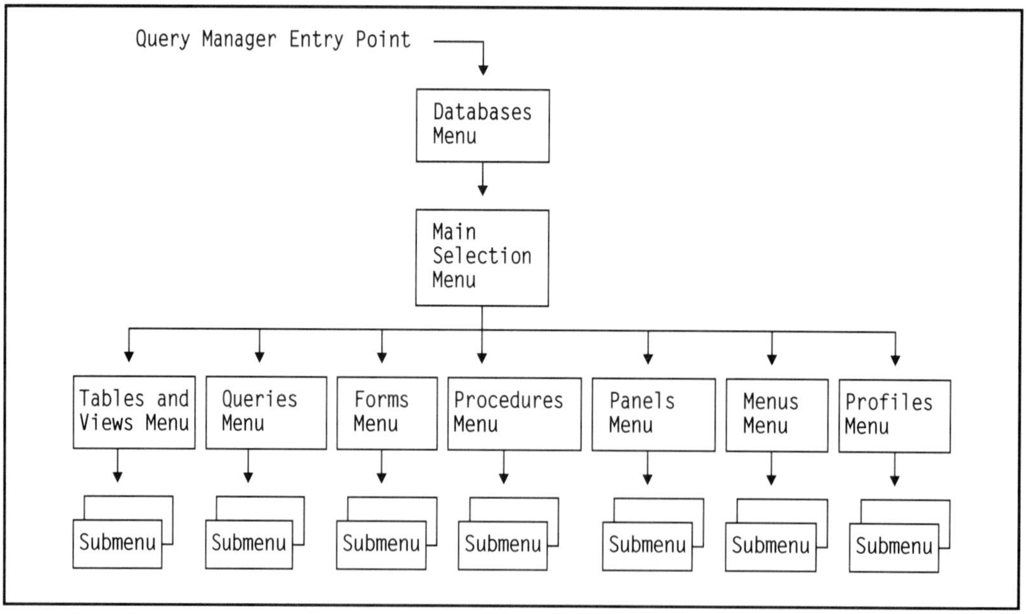

Figure 19-2. A Guide to the Query Manager Menu Map Hierarchy.

The root menu of the Query Manager is the **Databases Menu** (see Figure 19-3). This is the menu from which you select a database to work on. Next, you see the **Main Selection Menu**. This menu displays a choice of database object types (see Figure 19-4). When you pick an object type to work on, a menu displaying the list of objects in that category will appear. We will choose the Tables and Views object. Figure 19-5 shows the **Tables and Views Menu**. You can use this menu to pick a table (or view) to work on and then apply some action against it (see actions in Figure 19-6). We choose to create a new table as shown in Figure 19-7. This should give you a good idea of what the Query Manager can do.

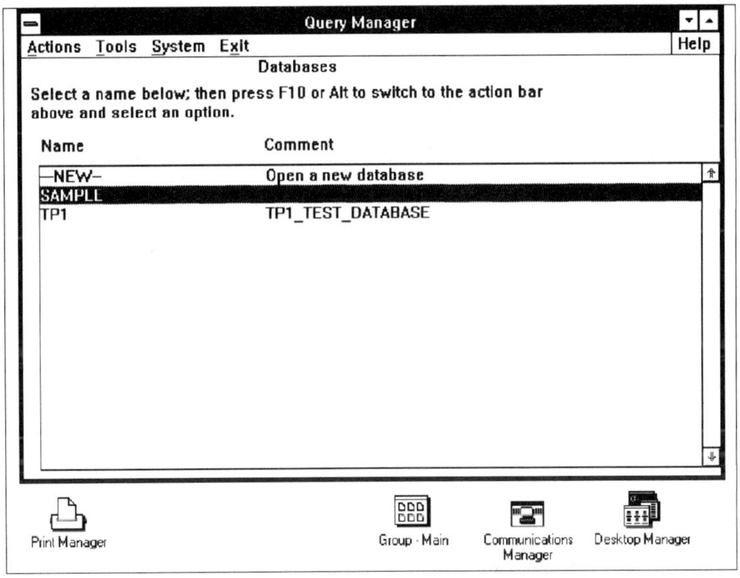

Figure 19-3. The Query Manager Databases Main Menu.

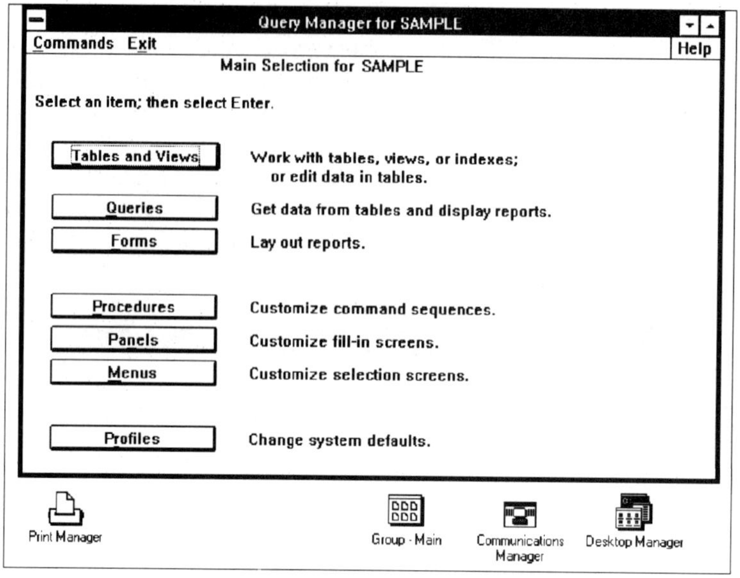

Figure 19-4. The Query Manager Main Selection Menu.

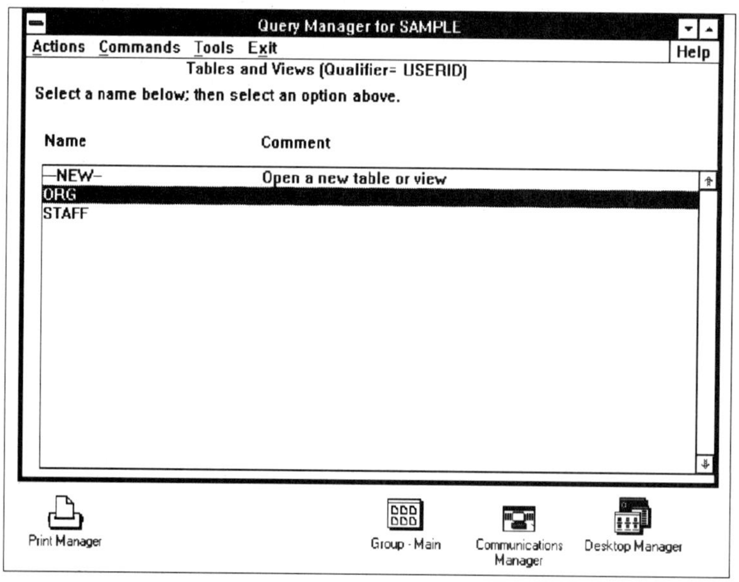

Figure 19-5. The Query Manager Tables and Views.

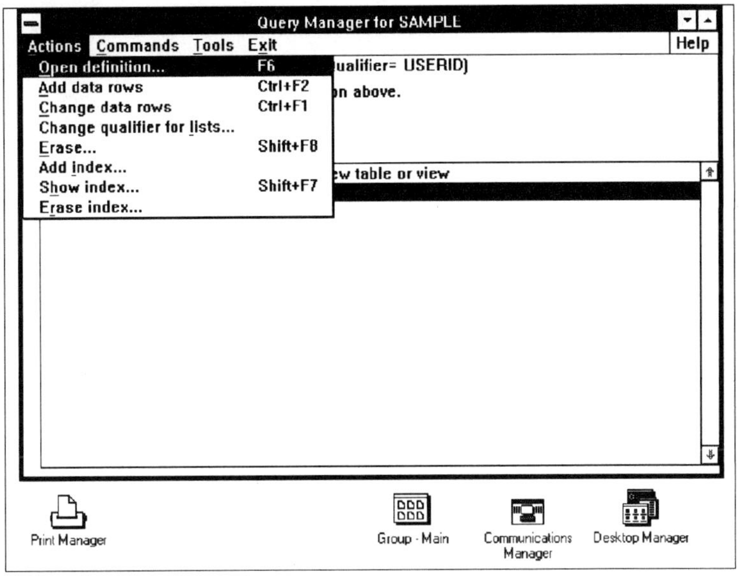

Figure 19-6. The Query Manager Tables and Views Actions.

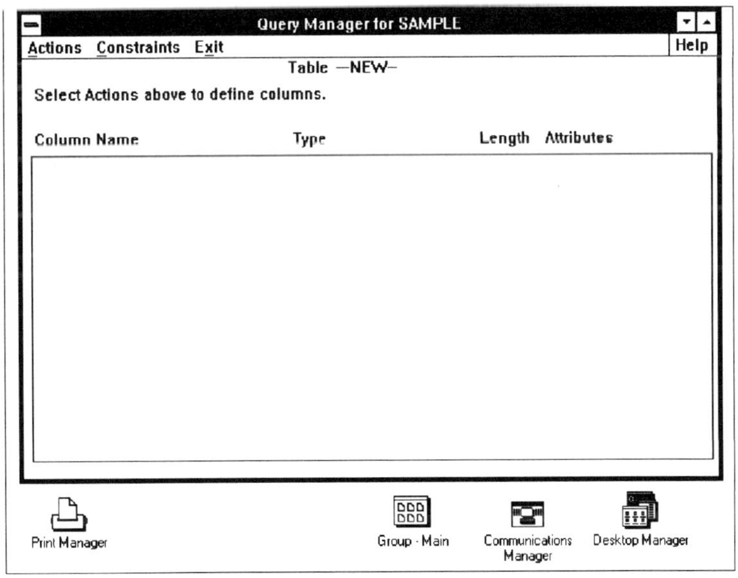

Figure 19-7. The Query Manager Tables and Views: Creating a New Table.

THE QUERY MANAGER INTERFACE API CALLS

The Query Manager Callable Interface allows your programs to pass commands and variables to the Query Manager through an API interface. This API is a standard call/return interface that consists of only two API calls:

dsqcic() This API call, also known as the *normal* call, is used to invoke Query Manager commands that do not require variables to be exchanged between the C-program and the Query Manager variable pools. The majority of the Query Manager verbs fall into this category.

dsqcice() This API call, also known as the *extended* call, is used to invoke Query Manager commands that require the exchange of variables between C-programs and the Query Manager variable pools. Only three Query Manager commands have this requirement: **START**, **SET**, and **GET**.

These two API calls follow the SAA Common Programming Interface (CPI) standard. The constructs used to pass the variables are meant to be language independent. We will describe those constructs in the programming chapters.

Your application invokes the Query Manager Callable Interface as follows:

1. Prepare the control blocks. These include a string that specifies the command to be executed, and a **DSQCOMM** structure that contains the return codes. Extended calls require six additional control blocks which specify the program variables for GET and SET, or session variables for START.
2. Issue the API call. This may be either a normal call or an extended call depending on the command that is being passed.
3. Control will return to your application when the processing of the command has been completed by the Query Manager. This may be quite a long time if the command is interactive.

THE MECHANICS OF THE CALLABLE INTERFACE

To use the Query Manager callable Interface you must:

- Issue a command to establish a session with the Query Manager.
- Pass the required sequence of commands to the Query Manager through API calls.
- Issue a command to terminate the session with the Query Manager.

Establishing a Session with Query Manager

A session with the Query Manager is initiated through the **START** command. A session can only be used by the process which starts it. The session gets automatically closed when the process terminates. Several Query Manager sessions may be run concurrently, one for each process that executes a **START** command. You may specify several parameters when starting a session, such as the database name and whether the session is batch or interactive. If you do not specify the name of a database, the Query Manager will prompt you for one as shown in Figure 19-8. Some of the more common Query Manager start parameters and their string lengths are described in Table 19-2.

Table 19-2. The START Parameters.

Parameter	Length	Description
DSQSCMD	**8**	Name of the (.CMD) command file to execute on start. If you do not provide one, the default QRWEXECZ.CMD will be executed.
DSQSMODE	**11**	Batch or Interactive display mode. In batch mode no screens are displayed.
DSQSPROF	**8**	Profile name. Profiles enable you to customize your use of the Query Manager. You can enter in the profile a default database name, a User ID, the buffer size for retrieving rows, printer options, data format options such as the currency symbol and the file formats for import/export.
DSQSDBNM	**8**	Database name
DSQSPOOL	**4**	Pool Size. The value for this variable is a string of digits between 0001 and 9999.
DSQSRUN	**27**	Name of procedure to run at start time.

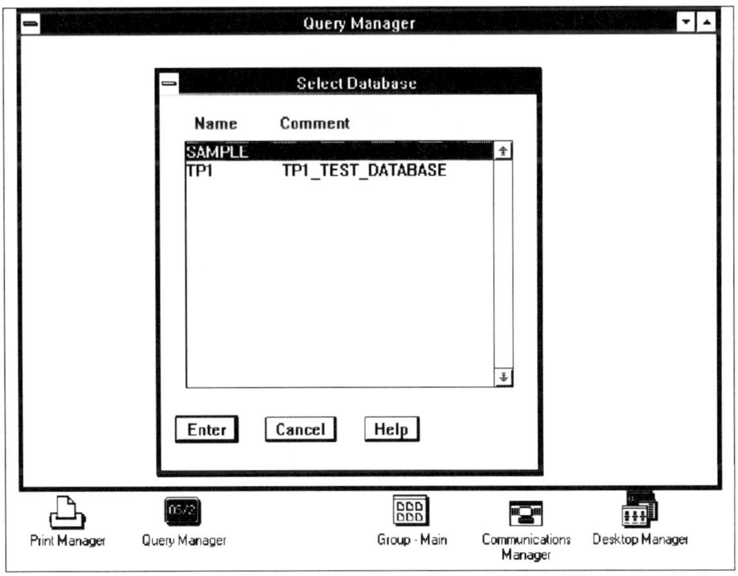

Figure 19-8. The Query Manager Start Command: Database Name Pop-up.

Controlling the Query Manager Execution Environment

The Query Manager Callable Interface provides a set of commands that enable you to manage the execution of a group of commands.

- The **BEGIN WORK** command is provided to group Query Manager commands into a database unit of work. The unit of work ends with either an **END WORK** command which commits the work, or a **CANCEL WORK** command which rolls back the work.
- The **BEGIN WINDOW** and **END WINDOW** commands are provided to keep Query Manager in the foreground window between commands. This prevents the foreground window from switching between your application and the Query Manager as each command is executed.

Displaying Query Manager Screens

Some of the Query Manager commands will take you into the Query Manager prompted menus at specific entry points. The end user will interact with the displayed object menu and any windows that are below it in the screen hierarchy. When the user exits from the prompted interface at the screen where the command entered, control is returned to the calling application. In other words, the entry screen and the exit screens for interactive commands are the same, and the end user can navigate through any functions on the entry screen and the sub-menus below it. The commands that allow entry into specific menus are:

- **DISPLAY**
- **LIST**
- **RESET**
- **DEFINE TABLE**
- **EDIT TABLE**

For example, issuing a **LIST TABLE (NAME=dept)** command takes you directly into a sub-menu for table objects, as shown in Figure 19-9. On the other hand, issuing a **LIST TABLES** command takes you one step higher in the Query Manager screen hierarchy and results in the display of all the tables that can be worked on, as shown in Figure 19-10. Issuing **LIST MAIN** command allows you to start even higher up in the hierarchy, as shown in Figure 19-11. The end user can, of course, traverse any menu below the entry point.

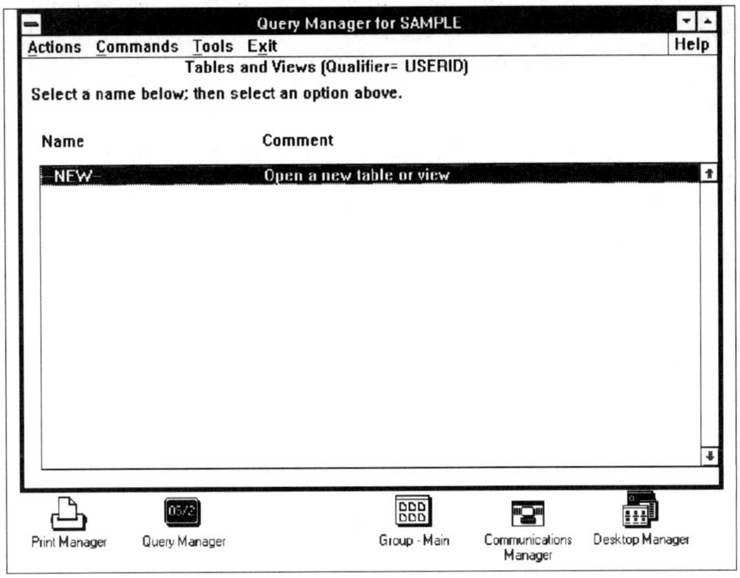

Figure 19-9. LIST TABLE (NAME=dept): Entry Point into the Query Manager.

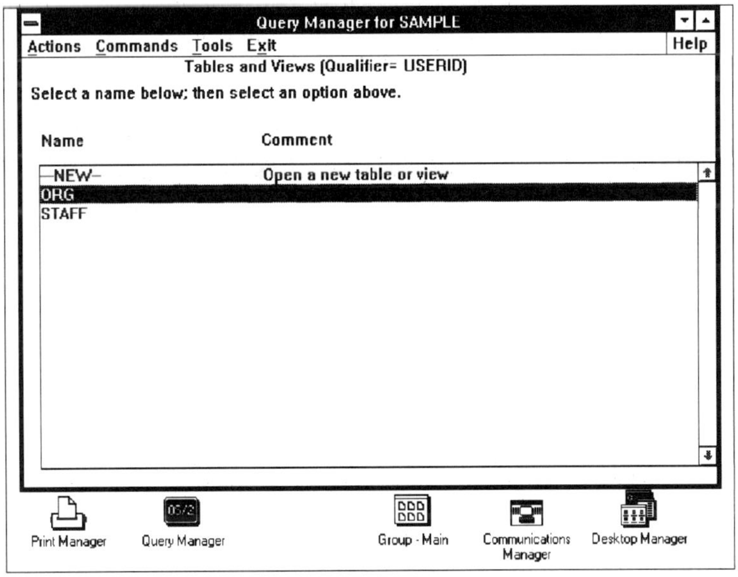

Figure 19-10. LIST TABLES: Entry Point into the Query Manager.

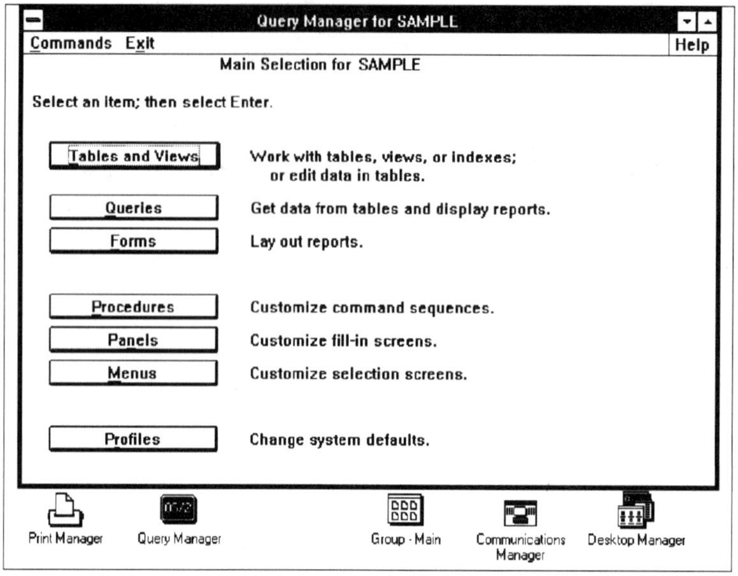

Figure 19-11. LIST MAIN: Entry Point into the Query Manager.

Running Reports

This is probably the most useful function provided by the Query Manager Callable Interface. A report is the combination of a query and a form that will be used to format the results of the query. The following commands support the creation and handling of reports:

- **RESET QUERY** and **RESET FORM** allow the user to interactively create a report and the form used to display it.
- **LIST QUERIES** and **LIST FORMS** provide a list of all the queries and forms stored in your database.
- **DISPLAY QUERY** and **DISPLAY FORM** allow you to edit interactively an existing query or form.
- **CONVERT QUERY** is used to convert a prompted Query into an SQL query which can be read by your program.
- **RUN QUERY** is used to run a query using a specific form.
- **SAVE DATA AS** is used to save the results of the report in a table.
- **PRINT REPORT** is used to print a report using a specified form.

THE QUERY MANAGER CALLABLE INTERFACE COMMANDS

This section describes the Query Manager Callable Interface commands. We explain what each command does and how it is used. The commands are presented under the same three categories described earlier.

Query Manager Execution Control Commands

Table 19-3. The Query Manager Callable Interface: Execution Control Commands.

Command	Description
START	This command starts a Query Manager Callable Interface session. You can use the extended function call to change the default session characteristics. You can specify any of the Query Manager start parameters, which were described in this section. `Example: START`
EXIT	This command ends a Query Manager Callable Interface session. `Example: EXIT`
BEGIN WINDOW	This command controls when Query Manager is displayed as the foreground window. Use this command to prevent the display from switching back to your application between commands. `Example: BEGIN WINDOW`
END WINDOW	This command returns the foreground window to the caller process. `Example: END WINDOW`
BEGIN WORK	This command starts a transaction or unit of work. All commands or statements that follow are treated as a single unit of recovery, and no permanent update to the database is made until an END WORK command is encountered. The IMPORT and EXPORT commands cannot be used between a BEGIN WORK and an END WORK command pair. Queries that contain SQL statements with COMMITs and ROLLBACKs can cause unpredictable results when used inside a BEGIN WORK/END WORK. `Example: BEGIN WORK`
END WORK	This command commits all work against the database since the last BEGIN WORK. `Example: END WORK`
CANCEL WORK	This command rolls back any changes to the database performed since the last BEGIN WORK. `Example: CANCEL WORK`

Query Manager Object Manipulation Commands

Table 19-4. The Query Manager Callable Interface: Object Manipulation Commands.

Command	Description

DISPLAY	This command opens an edit session for the definition of an existing Query Manager object. You need to provide the name of the object and the object type. Valid types are: FORM, MENU, PANEL, PROC, and QUERY. This command cannot be issued in Batch mode.
	`Examples: DISPLAY MENU friends`
	`          DISPLAY TABLE dept`

DEFINE TABLE	This command opens an edit session for the definition of a new or existing table or view. The Query Manager displays the table definition panel for that object. This command cannot be issued in Batch mode. The restrictions that apply to editing a table or view definition through Query Manager apply here too. For example, columns cannot be deleted from a previously saved table definition. `Example: DEFINE TABLE dept`
EDIT TABLE	This command starts a data entry or data edit session against a specified table. You must specify the table name, and you can optionally specify the edit MODE as being ADD or CHANGE. This command cannot be issued in Batch mode. `Example: EDIT TABLE dept (MODE = CHANGE)`
ERASE	This command drops an object from the database. You must name the object to be deleted and its type. Valid object types are: FORM, MENU, PANEL, PROC, QUERY, and TABLE. You can also optionally specify whether a confirmation is required through a CONFIRM clause. If a confirm is required, you cannot run this command in Batch mode. `Example: ERASE TABLE dept (CONFIRM = YES)`

LIST	This command displays either the main Query Manager selection menu (by specifying MAIN) or one of the object selection list windows. You can specify an object list selection by using the keywords: FORMS, MENUS, PANELS, PROCS, TABLES, and QUERIES. Or you can specify a specific object by naming an object through a NAME clause and specifying its type. Object types can be: FORM, MENU, PANEL, PROC, TABLE, and QUERY.
	`Examples: LIST MAIN`
	`          LIST TABLE (NAME=dept)`

RESET	This command displays an empty definition panel window for a new Query Manager object. You need to specify the type of object. Object types can be: FORM, MENU, PANEL, PROC, and QUERY. `Example: RESET PROC`

RUN	This command runs objects written using the Query Manager command language. Examples of such objects are: PROC, MENU and QUERY. You can run a QUERY interactively by specifying INTERACT = YES. If you specify the optional clause REPORT = YES, the Report panel is displayed using the default form or using a form name specified in a FORM clause.
	`Examples: RUN PROC prog1`
	`          RUN QUERY mydept (FORM= myform)`

Query Manager Utility Commands

<table>
<tr><th colspan="2">Table 19-5. The Query Manager Callable Interface: Utility Commands.</th></tr>
<tr><th>Command</th><th>Description</th></tr>
<tr><td>CONVERT QUERY</td><td>This command converts a SQL query object or a prompted query object into a global variable and stores it in the Query Manager variable pool. The query can either be a prompted query or an SQL query. If it is prompted, then it gets converted into an SQL statement with all comments removed and any variables substituted and then stores it. If the command encounters any variables which are not set, then it will prompt the user for the value of the variable. The CONVERT QUERY command sets the following Query Manager global variables:

DSQCQLNG A 1-byte character which indicates the original format of the query:
<code>1 = SQL query</code>
<code>3 = Prompted query</code>

DSQCQTYP A string up to 8 characters long set to the first token in the resulting statement.

DSQCQ001 A variable-length character string containing the converted query in SQL format.

DSQCL001 A 5-byte character string set to the length of DSQCQ001. For example, if DSQCQ001 is 52 bytes, then DSQCQ001 contains '00052'.

DSQCQCNT A 3-byte character string set to the number of converted SQL queries. The possible values are '000' and '001'.

<code>Example: CONVERT QUERY myquery</code></td></tr>
<tr><td>SAVE DATA AS</td><td>This command saves the results of a query containing a SELECT in a database table. If the table does not already exist, it will be created. The query is either a prompted query or an SQL SELECT. The query must have previously run using the RUN QUERY command. Some of the optional clauses are a COMMENT, CONFIRM, and REPLACE. The comment is placed with the table name and can be viewed through the table menu. REPLACE specifies whether to over-write existing data in the table. You are not allowed to overwrite data in a table that already contains data which is referred to from another table with existing data (i.e., it is a parent to a foreign key).

<code>Example: RUN QUERY mydept (FORM= myform)</code>
<code>SAVE DATA AS mytable (REPLACE= YES,</code>
<code>COMMENT = "Good stuff...")</code></td></tr>
</table>

Table 19-5. The Query Manager Callable Interface: Utility Commands.

Command	Description

IMPORT TABLE	This command copies data from an OS/2 file into a database table or view. You need to specify the table name, external file name, and a DATAFORMAT clause (which specifies the exchange format as IXF, WSF, DEL or ASC). The ASC format requires an additional FILESPEC descriptor (review the IMPORT command in previous chapter for more details). You can also specify through a REPLACE = YES or NO whether you want the current data in the table replaced. If REPLACE is set to YES, you are not allowed to import data into a table that already contains data which is referred to from another table with existing data (i.e., it is a parent to a foreign key). You can also optionally specify whether a confirmation is required through a CONFIRM =YES clause. If a confirm is required, you cannot run this command in Batch mode. Messages received during IMPORT processing are stored in a file named QRWIMPRT.LOG. This file is stored in the current subdirectory which by default is SQLLIB. This command should not be issued between BEGIN WORK and END WORK.
	`Example:`
	`IMPORT TABLE dept FROM filexyz.del (DATAFORMAT=DEL, CONFIRM=YES)`

EXPORT TABLE	This command copies a table or view to an OS/2 file. You need to specify the table name, file name, and a DATAFORMAT clause. The exchange format can be IXF, WSF or DEL (review the EXPORT command in previous chapter for more details). You can also optionally specify whether a confirmation is required through a CONFIRM clause. If a confirm is required, you cannot run this command in Batch mode. Messages received from the Database Manager during EXPORT processing are stored in the QRWEXPRT.LOG file. This file is stored in the current subdirectory (default is SQLLIB). This command should not be issued between BEGIN WORK and END WORK.
	`Example: EXPORT TABLE dept TO filexyz.del (DATAFORMAT=DEL,`
	`CONFIRM=YES)`

MESSAGE	This command displays a message text. You specify the message as a character string following the keyword, TEXT. You can also specify through the optional DISPLAY = ONLY clause whether the message is to be displayed, only if a Query Manager panel is on the screen. This command cannot run in Batch mode. `Example: MESSAGE (TEXT = 'Hi there' DISPLAY = ONLY)`

PRINT	This command prints Query Manager objects and reports. The format of the report is controlled by settings in the profile or by using explicit print parameters with this command. You can also specify the name of a form to be used with the report in an optional FORM clause. You must specify the name and type of object to be printed. Valid object types are: FORM, MENU, PANEL, PROC, and QUERY. A report is identified by the keyword REPORT, which uses the data from the last RUN QUERY. An optional FORM name can be specified.
	`Examples: RUN QUERY dept1`
	`PRINT REPORT ( FORM= myform)`
	
	`PRINT REPORT (PRINTER=LPT1, LENGTH=70, PAGENO=YES)`
	
	`PRINT REPORT (FILE=saverept.prt, PRINTTYPE=COMPRESSED,`
	`CONFIRM=NO)`
	`PRINT PANEL panel_name`

Table 19-5. The Query Manager Callable Interface: Utility Commands.	
Command	**Description**
GET	This command retrieves one or more values from the Query Manager variable pool and assigns them to C-language application variables. You need to provide the name of the Query Manager variable and specify whether it is CURRENT, GLOBAL, or LOCAL. You will also need to specify through the extended API call the addresses of the C-variables. `Example: GET CURRENT`
SET	This command copies one or more C-language variables to the Query Manager variable pool. You can specify the Query Manager variables as CURRENT, GLOBAL, or LOCAL. The C-language variables are specified through the extended API call that points to the addresses of the variables. `Example: SET GLOBAL`

THE REPORT SERVER

What is a Report Server?

Where there is data there are reports. As more data moves on to client-server platforms the question becomes how and where to run the reports. The trend in transaction-server architecture is to run both the the database and the transactions which operate on the data on the same server. This provides many advantages: improved performance, less network traffic (since both the code and the data reside on the same server machine), and the relatively central management and maintenance of the transaction code at the server. The transaction server concept can easily be extended to reports. A *report server* is a Transaction server which manages reports and executes them based on requests from remote clients. Clients can use any transaction request mechanism to invoke the execution of reports on the server. So in effect, a report becomes a long-winded transaction which operates on report objects.

Report Servers and OLTP

The architecture of the report server lends itself well to client-server On-line Transaction Processing (OLTP) environments which must guarantee deterministic response times (usually under 2 seconds). One of the vexing problems in such environments is how to service time-consuming reports while maintaining OLTP response times. By running both the transaction code and the report generation code on the same server we can enforce a two-level priority scheme which always executes reports at the lower priority. This translates into a requirement that the report should be executable from a programming language; which is precisely where the Query Manager Callable Interface comes into play.

How to Build a Report Server Using Query Manager

As was explained in this tutorial, the Query Manager provides elaborate user-friendly tools for the creation of reports. These include specifying the query, specifying the title and page layout of the report, formatting the report contents, labeling the columns, and providing complex summaries with business graphics. Once these reports are created they can be stored in the database and run and printed using a variety of formats. A winning report server strategy is one which can work with existing vendor tools. The user should be able to generate the report using a report-generation tool, but once the report is stored on the server it is run by the server code. This *once again* translates into the requirement that the report should be executable from a programming language, and again this is where the Query Manager Callable Interface comes into the picture.

As the tutorial points out the Query Manager Callable Interface provides an integrated environment where:

1. End-users can create new reports under program control (on a client machine). They can use all the fancy Query Manager facilities to create their reports.
2. The client program will export the created report and then ship it to the server with a transaction that involves a file transfer (this is similar to the FX protocol from Part II).
3. The server will import the report into the database.
4. The server can then run the report and print it based on any remote client's request. In essence, the report becomes a server-managed object.

It is easy to extend this scenario to trigger-initiated reports and all sorts of neat variations on the concept of automated server-managed reports. So yes Martha, there is a lot more to the Query Manager Callable Interface than first meets the eye!

Chapter 20

RSQL, the "All-In-One" Database Manager Utility

This chapter introduces **RSQL**, the "All-In-One" utility we will create for the OS/2 EE Database Manager. Think of **RSQL** as a Swiss Army Knife for the OS/2 EE Database Manager. You can use it to run SQL command scripts, fine-tune the database, look at the system configuration parameters, run reports, measure performance, and invoke the Query Manager Callable Interface. You'll find it to be the ultimate learning tool for familiarizing yourself with the Database Manager and observing its performance trade-offs. You may also discover, as we did, that playing with **RSQL** is a lot of fun. It's a great hacker's tool for the OS/2 EE Database Manager. There is nothing in the Database Manager that you can't get at with a simple **RSQL** script. This chapter teaches you how to use **RSQL** through scripts that demonstrate:

- The power of the SQL language.
- How to use the Database Manager's Administration Utilities.
- How to use the Query Manager Callable Interface.

These scripts mirror the material presented in the database tutorial chapters. Live examples will make those concepts more real and help demonstrate the power that is packed into the OS/2 EE Database Engine. Going through the scripts will also help you with the programming chapters that follow. These are the chapters where we dissect the **RSQL** program and use it as an exhaustive example of how to write code for the OS/2 EE Database Manager. So happy hacking and welcome to the world of scripts.

THE PLAN FOR THIS CHAPTER

We'll assume you've read the database tutorial chapters and absorbed every word of wisdom they contain. It's important that you start there because we won't be providing elaborate explanations in this chapter. Instead, we'll be running back-to-back **RSQL** scripts that demonstrate the concepts introduced in the tutorials. We'll try to present the scripts in the same order as the tutorial material. Here's the four-course menu of what we will be covering in this chapter:

- How to write an **RSQL** script.
- How to use **SQL**. We demonstrate with simple RSQL scripts the following SQL features:
  1. Simple Queries, Subqueries, and Multitable Queries (Joins).
  2. Database Inserts, Updates, and Deletes.
  3. Creating Tables, Indexes, and Views.
  4. Enforcing transactional units of recovery through COMMIT and ROLLBACK.
  5. Providing data integrity using Unique Indexes, Views, and Referential Integrity.
  6. Using Indexes to maximize performance.
  7. SQL security.
  8. The system catalogs.
- How to use the OS/2 EE **Database Administration** services. We demonstrate with simple RSQL scripts the following features:
  1. How to Export and Import "external" files.
  2. How to Create and Catalog a database.
  3. How to fine-tune database performance with Table Reorganizations and Runstats.
  4. How to Bind programs to the database.
  5. How to view and update the database and system configuration parameters.
  6. How to view the node and database directories.
  7. How to Backup and Restore a database.
- How to use the **Query Manager Callable Interface** for running reports and other Query Manager Services. These are also demonstrated using simple RSQL scripts.

CREATING AN RSQL SCRIPT

Creating an **RSQL** script is easy. Use an ASCII editor to create a script file of the commands you want to run. We'll call this file a *run* file. The following example demonstrates a simple script in a *run* file called **club.run**.

```
--
--      ***********   A simple example of an RSQL Script    ******************
--
--            /*** connect to the database in shared mode ***/
EXEC DBA:   STARTUSE club S;

--                    /*** display table data ***/
EXEC SQL:   SELECT village, country
            FROM vacations
            WHERE country = Mexico;

--                    /*** disconnect from the database ***/
EXEC DBA:   STOPUSE club;
```

Figure 20-1. A Simple RSQL Script File: CLUB.RUN.

The RSQL RUN File Format

As you can see from this simple example, writing an **RSQL** *script* isn't too difficult. Here's what you should know about writing a script file:

1. Comment lines starts with "--" in the first column, the ANSII standard for SQL comments. Comments cannot be placed inside commands.
2. Commands start with a two-word header that identifies the command type. The command types adhere to the classification scheme we introduced in the tutorial chapters:

   EXEC SQL: This is the header for SQL commands. The command that follows is the text for any valid dynamic SQL statement.

   EXEC DBA: This is the header for Database Administration commands. The command that follows can be almost any of the Database Administration commands described in the tutorial. The railroad diagrams in "Database Administration Commands" on page 967, describe how you can place these commands in your scripts.

   EXEC QM: This is the header for the Query Manager Callable Interface commands. The command that follows can be any of the Query Manager commands described in the tutorial. The railroad diagrams in "The RSQL Syntax for the Query Manager Callable Interface" on page 974, describe how you can place these commands in your scripts.

   EXEC DOS: This is the header for executing an OS/2 program from within an **RSQL** script. The header is followed by the name of an OS/2 program and its parameters.

3. Commands are separated from their parameters by at least 1 blank space or CR/LF (i.e., new-line).
4. A script is automatically committed to the database at the end of a successful run (that is when the **RSQL** program terminates). You can, of course, place your explicit commits anywhere within a script. Likewise, rollbacks may also be issued anywhere in the script.
5. You can specify through explicit directives whether **RSQL** should continue to execute the program after an error is encountered or whether it should terminate.
6. You can tell **RSQL** to pause execution through explicit pause directives. The execution is resumed by hitting any key.

RUN THE SCRIPT

The next step after creating the script is to run it. You do this by invoking **RSQL** at the OS/2 prompt as follows:

```
RSQL club.run answers.rsp
```

The syntax for invoking the program is:

```
RSQL   run   response
```

where *run* is file that contains the commands and *response* is the file where you want **RSQL** to put the results of a run.

VIEW THE RESPONSE FILE

The final step is to view the contents of the *response* file, **answers.rsp**, using any ASCII editor. For each command in the *run* file, **RSQL** will write the following to the *result* file:

- The input command text, including comments (from the *run* file).
- The results of running the command.
- The value of the SQLCA completion code.
- The time it took to execute the command.

This is what **answers.rsp** will contain after a successful run:

```
--
--        ***********   A simple example of an RSQL Script   ******************
--
--             /*** connect to the database in shared mode ***/
EXEC DBA:    STARTUSE club S;

 OK, sql_rcd = 0,        Execution time =     2.2200 secs

--                      /*** display table data ***/
EXEC SQL:    SELECT village, country
             FROM vacations
             WHERE country = Mexico;

 VILLAGE             COUNTRY
 ----------------    ------------
 CANCUN              MEXICO
 IXTAPA              MEXICO
 PLAYA BLANCA        MEXICO
 HUATULCO            MEXICO

 Total Number of Rows SELECTED = 4
 OK, sql_rcd = 0,        Execution time =     0.3600 secs

--                      /*** disconnect from the database ***/
EXEC DBA:    STOPUSE club;

 OK, sql_rcd = 0,        Execution time =     0.3700 secs
```

Figure 20-2. The Response File Created by: ANSWERS.RSP.

EXPLORING THE POWER OF SQL WITH SCRIPTS

The scripts that follow use the SAMPLE database supplied with the OS/2 EE Database Manager. SAMPLE is a database for a hypothetical marketing firm consisting of two tables:

- **ORG**, which contains information about the firm's structure. This includes department names, managers, and the divisions and locations of departments.
- **STAFF**, which contains information about the employees of this firm. This includes the number of years they've been employed, the department to which they belong, their salaries, etc.

Simple Queries: SELECT FROM

Our first script does the following:

1. It installs the SAMPLE database and fills it with data by executing the OS/2 EE supplied **sqlsampl.exe** program. It is placed in **\SQLLIB** at installation time.
2. It binds the **RSQL.BND** file to the newly created database.
3. It connects to the SAMPLE database.
4. It issues a SELECT with the wild card "*" for all columns. This will display all the rows and columns in the table.

```
--
--        ***********   A simple SQL Query Demonstration        ******************
--
--       /****************** Install the Sample Database *********************/
EXEC DOS:      sqlsampl.exe;

 Program completed with a return code of 0.
 OK,                        Execution time =     67.7800 secs

--       /************** BIND the rsql program to database  *******************/
EXEC DBA: BIND SAMPLE RSQL.BND ISO UNCOMMITTED_READ BLOCK_ALL PUBLIC;

 OK, sql_rcd = 0,        Execution time =     3.0000 secs

--       /************** connect to the database in shared mode ***************/
EXEC DBA:      STARTUSE sample S;

 OK, sql_rcd = 0,        Execution time =     1.7200 secs
```

Figure 20-3 (Part 1 of 3). Script 1: Demonstrating Simple SQL Queries.

```
--      /********* Display all rows and columns in  the ORG table ************/
EXEC SQL:      SELECT * FROM org;

 DEPTNUMB  DEPTNAME       MANAGER  DIVISION    LOCATION
 --------  -------------  -------  ----------  -------------
 10        Head Office    160      Corporate   New York
 15        New England    50       Eastern     Boston
 20        Mid Atlantic   10       Eastern     Washington
 38        South Atlantic 30       Eastern     Atlanta
 42        Great Lakes    100      Midwest     Chicago
 51        Plains         140      Midwest     Dallas
 66        Pacific        270      Western     San Francisco
 84        Mountain       290      Western     Denver

 Total Number of Rows SELECTED = 8
 OK, sql_rcd = 0,       Execution time =     0.4100 secs

--      /************ display all rows and columns in the STAFF table ********/
EXEC SQL:      SELECT *
               FROM staff;

 ID      NAME       DEPT   JOB    YEARS   SALARY    COMM
 ------  ---------  ------ -----  ------  --------  --------
 10      Sanders    20     Mgr    7       18357.50  NULL
 20      Pernal     20     Sales  8       18171.25    612.45
 30      Marenghi   38     Mgr    5       17506.75  NULL
 40      O'Brien    38     Sales  6       18006.00    846.55
 50      Hanes      15     Mgr    10      20659.80  NULL
 60      Quigley    38     Sales  NULL    16808.30    650.25
 70      Rothman    15     Sales  7       16502.83   1152.00
 80      James      20     Clerk  NULL    13504.60    128.20
 90      Koonitz    42     Sales  6       18001.75   1386.70
 100     Plotz      42     Mgr    7       18352.80  NULL
 110     Ngan       15     Clerk  5       12508.20    206.60
 120     Naughton   38     Clerk  NULL    12954.75    180.00
 130     Yamaguchi  42     Clerk  6       10505.90     75.60
 140     Fraye      51     Mgr    6       21150.00  NULL
 150     Williams   51     Sales  6       19456.50    637.65
 160     Molinare   10     Mgr    7       22959.20  NULL
 170     Kermisch   15     Clerk  4       12258.50    110.10
 180     Abrahams   38     Clerk  3       12009.75    236.50
 190     Sneider    20     Clerk  8       14252.75    126.50
 200     Scoutten   42     Clerk  NULL    11508.60     84.20
 210     Lu         10     Mgr    10      20010.00  NULL
 220     Smith      51     Sales  7       17654.50    992.80
 230     Lundquist  51     Clerk  3       13369.80    189.65
 240     Daniels    10     Mgr    5       19260.25  NULL
 250     Wheeler    51     Clerk  6       14460.00    513.30
 260     Jones      10     Mgr    12      21234.00  NULL
 270     Lea        66     Mgr    9       18555.50  NULL
 280     Wilson     66     Sales  9       18674.50    811.50
 290     Quill      84     Mgr    10      19818.00  NULL
```

Figure 20-3 (Part 2 of 3). Script 1: Demonstrating Simple SQL Queries.

```
300      Davis     84      Sales  5      15454.50    806.10
310      Graham    66      Sales  13     21000.00    200.30
320      Gonzales  66      Sales  4      16858.20    844.00
330      Burke     66      Clerk  1      10988.00     55.50
340      Edwards   84      Sales  7      17844.00   1285.00
350      Gafney    84      Clerk  5      13030.50    188.00

Total Number of Rows SELECTED = 35
OK, sql_rcd = 0,        Execution time =     0.2800 secs
```

Figure 20-3 (Part 3 of 3). Script 1: Demonstrating Simple SQL Queries.

Narrowing the Query: The WHERE Clause

The script below shows how "search conditions" are used in a WHERE clause, to help narrow down the SELECT (i.e., query) so that you can find exactly what you want. The search clauses use **predicate** logic which makes these clauses very powerful and flexible. Predicates can either compare two values or compare a value with a collection of values. The result of these comparisons is a condition of "true", "false", or "unknown" about a given row or a set of rows.

```
--      ***********   A Demonstration of the WHERE search clause *************
--
--      /*****  A simple relational predicate with no duplicate rows ********/
EXEC SQL:       SELECT DISTINCT *
                FROM org
                WHERE division = 'Eastern';

DEPTNUMB  DEPTNAME        MANAGER  DIVISION    LOCATION
--------  --------------  -------  ----------  -------------
15        New England     50       Eastern     Boston
20        Mid Atlantic    10       Eastern     Washington
38        South Atlantic  30       Eastern     Atlanta

Total Number of Rows SELECTED = 3
OK, sql_rcd = 0,        Execution time =     0.4000 secs
--      /******* Using AND to connect relational predicates      ***************/
EXEC SQL:       SELECT *
                FROM staff
                WHERE (job = 'Sales' AND years > 8)
                OR (job = 'Sales' AND comm >= 1200);

ID      NAME       DEPT    JOB    YEARS   SALARY     COMM
------  ---------  ------  -----  ------  --------   --------
90      Koonitz    42      Sales  6       18001.75   1386.70
280     Wilson     66      Sales  9       18674.50    811.50
310     Graham     66      Sales  13      21000.00    200.30
340     Edwards    84      Sales  7       17844.00   1285.00

Total Number of Rows SELECTED = 4
OK, sql_rcd = 0,        Execution time =     0.1900 secs
```

Figure 20-4 (Part 1 of 3). Script 2: Demonstrating Search Conditions with WHERE.

```
--        /**** Wild-card pattern-matching with the LIKE predicate      *********/
EXEC SQL:       SELECT id, name
                FROM staff
                WHERE name LIKE 'Lu%';

 ID      NAME
 ------  ---------
 210     Lu
 230     Lundquist

 Total Number of Rows SELECTED = 2
 OK, sql_rcd = 0,        Execution time =     0.1300 secs

--        /******  The BETWEEN predicate for comparing ranges of values  ******/
EXEC SQL:       SELECT id, name, salary
                FROM staff
                WHERE salary BETWEEN 20000 and 21000;

 ID      NAME       SALARY
 ------  ---------  --------
 50      Hanes      20659.80
 210     Lu         20010.00
 54      Graham     21000.00

 Total Number of Rows SELECTED = 3
 OK, sql_rcd = 0,        Execution time =     0.1200 secs

--        /******* The IN predicate for testing group membership      **********/
EXEC SQL:       SELECT id, name, dept
                FROM staff
                WHERE dept IN (66,84);

 ID      NAME       DEPT
 ------  ---------  ------
 270     Lea        66
 280     Wilson     66
 290     Quill      84
 300     Davis      84
 310     Graham     66
 320     Gonzales   66
 330     Burke      66
 340     Edwards    84
 350     Gafney     84

 Total Number of Rows SELECTED = 9
 OK, sql_rcd = 0,        Execution time =     0.1200 secs
```

Figure 20-4 (Part 2 of 3). Script 2: Demonstrating Search Conditions with WHERE.

```
--        /*******  The NULL predicate testing for NULL values       *********/
EXEC SQL:       SELECT id, name, dept
                FROM staff
                WHERE years IS NULL;

 ID      NAME       DEPT
 ------  ---------  ------
 60      Quigley    38
 80      James      20
 120     Naughton   38
 200     Scoutten   42

 Total Number of Rows SELECTED = 4
 OK, sql_rcd = 0,       Execution time =     0.0900 secs
```

Figure 20-4 (Part 3 of 3). Script 2: Demonstrating Search Conditions with WHERE.

Sorting the Query: the ORDER BY Clause

So far, the query results were not returned in any order. The script below shows how the **ORDER BY** clause is used to sort the query in some specified order.

```
--
--       **********   A Demonstration of the ORDER BY clause   ***************
--
--      /***********    The default sorting order is ascending (ASC)  ********/
EXEC SQL:       SELECT dept, name, id
                FROM staff
                WHERE (dept = 10 or dept = 20)
                ORDER BY dept, name;

 DEPT    NAME       ID
 ------  ---------  ------
 10      Daniels    240
 10      Joncs      260
 10      Lu         210
 10      Molinare   160
 20      James      80
 20      Pernal     20
 20      Sanders    10
 20      Sneider    190

 Total Number of Rows SELECTED = 8
 OK, sql_rcd = 0,       Execution time =     0.2800 secs
```

Figure 20-5 (Part 1 of 2). Script 3: Demonstrating the Ordering of Query Results with ORDER BY.

```
--      /********** You can over-ride the default by specifying (DESC)  ****/
EXEC SQL:     SELECT *
              FROM org
              ORDER BY division DESC, deptnumb DESC;

 DEPTNUMB  DEPTNAME        MANAGER  DIVISION     LOCATION
 --------  --------------  -------  ----------   -------------
 84        Mountain        290      Western      Denver
 66        Pacific         270      Western      San Francisco
 51        Plains          140      Midwest      Dallas
 42        Great Lakes     100      Midwest      Chicago
 38        South Atlantic  30       Eastern      Atlanta
 20        Mid Atlantic    10       Eastern      Washington
 15        New England     50       Eastern      Boston
 10        Head Office     160      Corporate    New York

 Total Number of Rows SELECTED = 8
 OK, sql_rcd = 0,        Execution time =     0.1900 secs
```

Figure 20-5 (Part 2 of 2). Script 3: Demonstrating the Ordering of Query Results with ORDER BY.

Simple Nested Queries

The script below shows how SELECT statements can be nested within one another. The **subquery** is an "inner" SELECT statement nested in the WHERE or HAVING clause of the "outer" SELECT statement. The results of the subquery are fed to the "outer" SELECT. If the subquery returns more than one value, you must use the keywords, IN, ALL, ANY, SOME, or EXISTS in the WHERE clause. The subquery table does not have to be the same as the "outer" query table.

```
--
--      ********** A Demonstration of Simple Nested Queries *************
--
--      /********   The inner SELECT returns a single value     *************/
EXEC SQL:   SELECT name, job, years, salary, comm
            FROM staff
            WHERE job='Sales'
            AND   salary > (SELECT AVG(salary) FROM staff where job='Mgr');

 NAME       JOB    YEARS  SALARY     COMM
 ---------  -----  ------ --------   --------
 Graham     Sales  13     21000.00   200.30

 Total Number of Rows SELECTED = 1
 OK, sql_rcd = 0,        Execution time =     0.2700 secs
```

Figure 20-6 (Part 1 of 2). Script 4: Demonstrating Nested Queries.

```
--       /********    The inner SELECT returns multiple values     *************/
EXEC SQL:    SELECT name, job, years, salary, comm
             FROM staff
             WHERE job='Sales'
             AND   years  > ALL
             (SELECT years FROM staff where job='Mgr');

 NAME        JOB    YEARS   SALARY    COMM
 ---------   -----  ------  --------  --------
 Graham      Sales  13      21000.00    200.30

 Total Number of Rows SELECTED = 1
 OK, sql_rcd = 0,        Execution time =     0.2200 secs

--       /********  Different tables involved in inner and outer query     *****/
EXEC SQL:    SELECT name, job, years, salary, comm
             FROM staff
             WHERE job='Sales'
             AND dept IN
             (SELECT deptnumb FROM org WHERE division = 'Eastern')
             ORDER BY years;

 NAME        JOB    YEARS   SALARY    COMM
 ---------   -----  ------  --------  --------
 O'Brien     Sales  6       18006.00    846.55
 Rothman     Sales  7       16502.83   1152.00
 Pernal      Sales  8       18171.25    612.45
 Quigley     Sales  NULL    16808.30    650.25

 Total Number of Rows SELECTED = 4
 OK, sql_rcd = 0,        Execution time =     0.8800 secs
```

Figure 20-6 (Part 2 of 2). Script 4: Demonstrating Nested Queries.

Compound Nested Queries

The script below demonstrates queries which contain multiple subqueries. The subqueries can be at the same level (and tied together by AND or OR), or they can be nested into other subqueries. SELECT statements with multiple subqueries are known as **Compound Queries**.

```
--
--       ********** A Demonstration of Compound Nested Queries ***********
--

--      /************   Two subqueries at the same level     *****************/
EXEC SQL:   SELECT name, job, years, salary, comm
            FROM staff
            WHERE job='Sales'
            AND (salary + comm) >
                (SELECT MIN(salary) FROM staff where job='Mgr')
            AND dept IN
                (SELECT deptnumb FROM org WHERE division = 'Eastern')
            ORDER BY job, salary;

 NAME       JOB    YEARS   SALARY     COMM
 ---------  -----  ------  --------   --------
 Rothman    Sales  7       16502.83   1152.00
 O'Brien    Sales  6       18006.00    846.55
 Pernal     Sales  8       18171.25    612.45

 Total Number of Rows SELECTED = 3

 OK, sql_rcd = 0,         Execution time =     0.7200 secs

--      /********    A subquery inside another subquery          *************/
EXEC SQL:   SELECT name, job, years, salary, comm
            FROM staff
            WHERE job='Sales'
            AND   years  > ALL
            (SELECT years FROM staff where job='Mgr'
            AND dept IN
                (SELECT deptnumb FROM org WHERE division = 'Eastern'))
            ORDER BY years;

 NAME       JOB    YEARS   SALARY     COMM
 ---------  -----  ------  --------   --------
 Graham     Sales  13      21000.00    200.30

 Total Number of Rows SELECTED = 1
 OK, sql_rcd = 0,         Execution time =     0.5300 secs
```

Figure 20-7. Script 5: Demonstrating Compound Nested Queries.

Correlated Subqueries

The script below demonstrates a special kind of nested query, where the subquery is run once for each row in the outer query. These two queries are **correlated**, in the sense that the inner query requires information from the outer query. To find the highest paid employee per job category: for each job category a subquery identifies the maximum salary and an outer query identifies the employee that earns it.

```
--
--      ***********   A Demonstration of Correlated Subqueries    ************
--
--      /************ Inner query runs once for each job category  ***********/
EXEC SQL:   SELECT name, job, years, salary, comm
            FROM staff s
            WHERE salary =
                  (SELECT MAX(SALARY) FROM staff WHERE job= s.job)
            ORDER BY job, salary;

 NAME       JOB    YEARS   SALARY     COMM
 ---------  -----  ------  --------   --------
 Wheeler    Clerk  6       14460.00     513.30
 Molinare   Mgr    7       22959.20   NULL
 Graham     Sales  13      21000.00     200.30

 Total Number of Rows SELECTED = 3
 OK, sql_rcd = 0,        Execution time =     1.3000 secs
```

Figure 20-8. Script 6: A Demonstration of Correlated Subqueries.

Merging Query Results with Set Operators

The script below demonstrates how the results from two or more autonomous SELECT statements can be merged using the following set operators:

UNION Combines the results of two queries

EXCEPT Picks out all the rows from the first query that do not appear in the second query.

INTERSECT Picks out all the rows in the first query that also appear in the second query.

The corresponding columns in the SELECT statements need not have the same name but they must have equivalent data types. Do not use a column name after ORDER BY, instead use a column number.

```
--
--      *****************   A Demonstration of set operators *****************
--
--      /*********   Merging two Queries with the INTERSECT set operator *****/
EXEC SQL:   SELECT name, job
            FROM staff WHERE job = 'Sales'
            INTERSECT
            SELECT name, job
            FROM staff WHERE years > 10;
 1          2
 ---------  -----
 Graham     Sales
 Total Number of Rows SELECTED = 1
 OK, sql_rcd = 0,        Execution time =     0.4000 secs
```

Figure 20-9 (Part 1 of 2). Script 8: Merging Result Tables Using Set Operators.

```
--      /*********   Merging two Queries with the EXCEPT  set operator *****/
EXEC SQL:   SELECT name, job
            FROM staff WHERE job = 'Sales'
            EXCEPT
            SELECT name, job
            FROM staff WHERE years > 10
            ORDER by 1;

 1          2
 ---------  -----
 Davis      Sales
 Edwards    Sales
 Gonzales   Sales
 Koonitz    Sales
 O'Brien    Sales
 Pernal     Sales
 Quigley    Sales
 Rothman    Sales
 Smith      Sales
 Williams   Sales
 Wilson     Sales

 Total Number of Rows SELECTED = 11
 OK, sql_rcd = 0,        Execution time =     0.5000 secs

--      /*********   Merging two Queries with the UNION set operator    *******/
EXEC SQL:   SELECT name, job
            FROM staff WHERE job = 'Sales'
            UNION
            SELECT name, job
            FROM staff WHERE years > 10
            ORDER by 1;

 1          2
 ---------  -----
 Davis      Sales
 Edwards    Sales
 Gonzales   Sales
 Graham     Sales
 Jones      Mgr
 Koonitz    Sales
 O'Brien    Sales
 Pernal     Sales
 Quigley    Sales
 Rothman    Sales
 Smith      Sales
 Williams   Sales
 Wilson     Sales

 Total Number of Rows SELECTED = 13
 OK, sql_rcd = 0,        Execution time =     0.3400 secs
```

Figure 20-9 (Part 2 of 2). Script 8: Merging Result Tables Using Set Operators.

Multitable Queries (Joins)

The previous scripts have demonstrated the retrieval of data from one table. Many times, the data you want will not always be in one table. A single SELECT can be used to retrieve data from more than one table through a process called **join**. To join two or more tables, you specify the table names in the FROM clause and the connection between them in the WHERE clause (this is called the **join predicate**). A join predicate based on the equality relationship is called an **equijoin**. If you use columns from different tables that have the same name, you must qualify the name of the columns to show which table they come from. We will qualify all column names involved in joins to better document the query. Theoretically, up to 15 tables can participate in a very slow **multijoin**.

```
--
--       ****************  A Demonstration of Joins    *********************
--
--      /*********   Two-table equijoin using fully qualified names    *******/
EXEC SQL:   SELECT org.deptname, org.location, staff.name, staff.salary
            FROM staff, org
            WHERE org.manager = staff.id
            ORDER BY org.deptname;

 DEPTNAME        LOCATION        NAME       SALARY
 --------------  -------------  ---------  --------
 Great Lakes     Chicago         Plotz      18352.80
 Head Office     New York        Molinare   22959.20
 Mid Atlantic    Washington      Sanders    18357.50
 Mountain        Denver          Quill      19818.00
 New England     Boston          Hanes      20659.80
 Pacific         San Francisco  Lea        18555.50
 Plains          Dallas          Fraye      21150.00
 South Atlantic  Atlanta         Marenghi   17506.75

 Total Number of Rows SELECTED = 8
 OK, sql_rcd = 0,        Execution time =     0.6900 secs

--      /*********   Two-table equijoin using correlation names      *********/
EXEC SQL:   SELECT o.deptname, o.location, s.name, s.salary
            FROM staff s, org o
            WHERE o.manager = s.id
            ORDER BY o.deptname;

 DEPTNAME        LOCATION        NAME       SALARY
 --------------  -------------  ---------  --------
 Great Lakes     Chicago         Plotz      18352.80
 Head Office     New York        Molinare   22959.20
 Mid Atlantic    Washington      Sanders    18357.50
 Mountain        Denver          Quill      19818.00
 New England     Boston          Hanes      20659.80
 Pacific         San Francisco  Lea        18555.50
 Plains          Dallas          Fraye      21150.00
 South Atlantic  Atlanta         Marenghi   17506.75

 Total Number of Rows SELECTED = 8
 OK, sql_rcd = 0,        Execution time =     0.6500 secs
```

Figure 20-10. Script 7: Demonstrating Joins.

Creating Tables, Inserts, Updates, and Deletes

The script below gets into "the meat and potatoes" of SQL. It shows how to create a table, put some data in it, update the data, and delete some of the data. These are all your basic every day SQL operations. The table we'll be creating, NEWSTAFF, is a carbon copy of the STAFF table. We'll be inserting data one row at a time and through a subquery.

```
--
--      ************  Creating Tables, Inserts, Updates and Deletes ********
--

--      /*************     Create the staff table's twin        ****************/
EXEC SQL:   CREATE TABLE newstaff
                        (id         SMALLINT NOT NULL,
                         name       VARCHAR(9),
                         dept       SMALLINT,
                         job        CHAR(5),
                         years      SMALLINT,
                         salary     DECIMAL(7,2),
                         comm       DECIMAL(7,2));

 OK, sql_rcd = 0,        Execution time =     1.3100 secs

--      /*************     Insert into newstaff two rows        ****************/
EXEC SQL:   INSERT INTO newstaff
            VALUES (500, 'Bob' , 99, 'Nerds', 5, 45000.00, 0 );

 OK, sql_rcd = 0,        Execution time =     0.0600 secs

EXEC SQL:   INSERT INTO newstaff
            VALUES (501, 'Dan', 99, 'Nerds', 4, 42000.00, 0 );

 OK, sql_rcd = 0,        Execution time =     0.0600 secs

--      /*************     Use a subquery to insert rows from staff **********/
EXEC SQL:   INSERT INTO newstaff
            SELECT * from staff where job= 'Sales' and salary > 18000;

 OK, sql_rcd = 0,        Execution time =     0.1800 secs

--      /*************     commit the work done so far               **********/
EXEC SQL:   COMMIT;

 OK, sql_rcd = 0,        Execution time =     0.1000 secs
```

Figure 20-11 (Part 1 of 2). Script 9: Creating Tables, Inserts, Updates, and Deletes.

```
--      /*************      Let's see what we've got so far           **********/
EXEC SQL:   SELECT * from newstaff
            ORDER BY salary DESC;

 ID      NAME        DEPT    JOB    YEARS   SALARY     COMM
 ------  ---------  ------  -----  ------  --------  --------
 500     Bob         99      Nerds  5       45000.00     00.00
 501     Dan         99      Nerds  4       42000.00     00.00
 310     Graham      66      Sales  13      21000.00    200.30
 150     Williams    51      Sales  6       19456.50    637.65
 280     Wilson      66      Sales  9       18674.50    811.50
 20      Pernal      20      Sales  8       18171.25    612.45
 40      O'Brien     38      Sales  6       18006.00    846.55
 90      Koonitz     42      Sales  6       18001.75   1386.70

 Total Number of Rows SELECTED = 8
 OK, sql_rcd = 0,        Execution time =     0.5100 secs

--      /*************      Let's give ourselves a good raise...      **********/
EXEC SQL:   UPDATE newstaff
            SET salary = salary * 1.8
            WHERE job = 'Nerds';

 OK, sql_rcd = 0,        Execution time =     0.0900 secs

--      /*************      Things look better now...                 **********/
EXEC SQL:   SELECT * from newstaff
            WHERE salary + comm > 21000
            ORDER BY salary DESC;

 ID      NAME        DEPT    JOB    YEARS   SALARY     COMM
 ------  ---------  ------  -----  ------  --------  --------
 500     Bob         99      Nerds  5       81000.00     00.00
 501     Dan         99      Nerds  4       75600.00     00.00
 310     Graham      66      Sales  13      21000.00    200.30

 Total Number of Rows SELECTED = 3
 OK, sql_rcd = 0,        Execution time =     0.2500 secs

--      /*************      Here's How delete works                   **********/
EXEC SQL:   DELETE  from newstaff
            WHERE job = 'Sales';

 OK, sql_rcd = 0,        Execution time =     0.1000 secs

--      /*************      Let's see what happened                   **********/
EXEC SQL:   SELECT * from newstaff
            ORDER BY salary DESC;

 ID      NAME        DEPT    JOB    YEARS   SALARY     COMM
 ------  ---------  ------  -----  ------  --------  --------
 500     Bob         99      Nerds  5       81000.00     00.00
 501     Dan         99      Nerds  4       75600.00     00.00

 Total Number of Rows SELECTED = 2
 OK, sql_rcd = 0,        Execution time =     0.1900 secs
```

Figure 20-11 (Part 2 of 2). Script 9: Creating Tables, Inserts, Updates, and Deletes.

Data Integrity Scripts

Data integrity is concerned with the correctness and consistency of data in a database. The scripts that follow demonstrate some of the mechanisms provided by the OS/2 EE Database Manager to help enforce the validity of the data entrusted to it. The following data integrity mechanisms will be demonstrated through scripts: Transaction recovery, the NOT NULL constraint, Entity Integrity, Views with check option, and Referential Integrity.

Transactional Units of Recovery: COMMIT and ROLLBACK

A transaction is a sequence of one or more SQL statements that get treated as an atomic unit of work. Either all the statements execute successfully, or none of the statements execute. The script below demonstrates the use of the SQL transaction processing.

```
--
--       ************  A Demonstration of SQL Transactions         ********
--
--       /*************     Start a Unit of Recovery              ***************/
EXEC SQL:   COMMIT;

 OK, sql_rcd = 0,        Execution time =     0.1200 secs

--       /*************     Let's see what we've got to start     ***************/
EXEC SQL:   SELECT * from newstaff;

 ID      NAME       DEPT    JOB    YEARS   SALARY     COMM
 ------  ---------  ------  -----  ------  --------   --------
 500     Bob        99      Nerds  5       81000.00      00.00
 501     Dan        99      Nerds  4       75600.00      00.00

 Total Number of Rows SELECTED = 2
 OK, sql_rcd = 0,        Execution time =     0.0900 secs

--       /*************     Delete all rows in table              ***************/
EXEC SQL:   DELETE  from newstaff;

 OK, sql_rcd = 0,        Execution time =     0.0600 secs

--       /*************     Undo the transaction                  ***************/
EXEC SQL:   ROLLBACK;

 OK, sql_rcd = 0,        Execution time =     0.1200 secs
```

Figure 20-12 (Part 1 of 2). Script 10: Transactional Units of Recovery: COMMIT and ROLLBACK.

```
--      /*************     Magic we're back where we started    ***************/
EXEC SQL:   SELECT * from newstaff;

 ID      NAME        DEPT    JOB    YEARS   SALARY     COMM
 ------  ---------   ------  -----  ------  --------   --------
 500     Bob         99      Nerds  5       81000.00     00.00
 501     Dan         99      Nerds  4       75600.00     00.00

 Total Number of Rows SELECTED = 2
 OK, sql_rcd = 0,         Execution time =     0.1500 secs
```

Figure 20-12 (Part 2 of 2). Script 10: Transactional Units of Recovery: COMMIT and ROLLBACK.

The No Nulls Constraint

This is the simplest data integrity constraint. You can require that a column should always contain a value by specifying it as **NOT NULL**. The Database Manager will automatically enforce that constraint on your behalf. This simple concept is demonstrated in the script below:

```
--
--     *****************     Data Integrity with NO NULLS    *****************
--

--      /**** Here's one way to insert missing values in regular columns *****/
EXEC SQL:   INSERT INTO newstaff (id, name, dept, job)
            VALUES (506, 'Ray', 99, 'Nerds');

 OK, sql_rcd = 0,         Execution time =     0.0600 secs

--      /**** Here's another way to insert missing values in regular columns */
EXEC SQL:   INSERT INTO newstaff
            VALUES (507, 'Dan', 99, 'Nerds',NULL, NULL, NULL);

 OK, sql_rcd = 0,         Execution time =     0.0700 secs

--      /*************     Let's see what we got                      **********/
EXEC SQL:   SELECT * from newstaff
            ORDER BY salary DESC;

 ID      NAME        DEPT    JOB    YEARS   SALARY     COMM
 ------  ---------   ------  -----  ------  --------   --------
 506     Ray         99      Nerds  NULL    NULL       NULL
 507     Dan         99      Nerds  NULL    NULL       NULL
 500     Bob         99      Nerds  5       81000.00     00.00
 501     Dan         99      Nerds  4       75600.00     00.00

 Total Number of Rows SELECTED = 4
 OK, sql_rcd = 0,         Execution time =     0.1900 secs
```

Figure 20-13 (Part 1 of 2). Script 11: Data Integrity with NO NULLS.

```
--      /**** Watch what happens if we insert into a NOT NULL column    *******/
EXEC SQL:   INSERT INTO newstaff
            VALUES (NULL, 'Joe', 99, 'Nerds',1, 30000.00, 0.0);

 ERROR, sql_code = -407
 SQL0407N  Assignment of a null value to a NOT NULL column "ID" was attempted on
 UPDATE or INSERT.

--      /*************      Let's get rid of the garbage data         **********/
EXEC SQL:   ROLLBACK;
```

Figure 20-13 (Part 2 of 2). Script 11: Data Integrity with NO NULLS.

Entity Integrity

The Entity Integrity constraint ensures that each row in a table is unique. This is done to reflect real-world situations where we deal with unique entities. You can specify, through **primary keys** or **unique indexes**, that each row in a table uniquely identify the "entity" represented by that row. The Database Manager will prevent rows with duplicate primary keys from being entered accidentally. The script shown below demonstrates this concept.

```
--
--      **************** Data Integrity with  Unique keys *****************
--
--      /**** Let's try inserting a duplicate record into NEWSTAFF  **********/
EXEC SQL:   INSERT INTO newstaff
            VALUES (501, 'Dan', 99, 'Nerds', 4, 75600.00, 0 );

 OK, sql_rcd = 0,        Execution time =     0.0900 secs

--      /**** As you can see we're not protected against duplicates     **********/
EXEC SQL:   SELECT * from newstaff
            ORDER BY id;

 ID     NAME      DEPT   JOB    YEARS  SALARY    COMM
 ------ --------- ------ -----  ------ --------  --------
 500    Bob       99     Nerds  5      81000.00     00.00
 501    Dan       99     Nerds  4      75600.00     00.00
 501    Dan       99     Nerds  4      75600.00     00.00

 Total Number of Rows SELECTED = 3
 OK, sql_rcd = 0,        Execution time =     0.2400 secs

--      /*************      Let's get rid of this entry               **********/
EXEC SQL:   ROLLBACK;

 OK, sql_rcd = 0,        Execution time =     0.0900 secs
```

Figure 20-14 (Part 1 of 2). Script 12: Data Integrity with Unique Keys.

```
--       /****** Let's protect ourselves: add a unique index on id     **********/
EXEC SQL:   CREATE UNIQUE INDEX xid ON newstaff (id);

 OK, sql_rcd = 0,        Execution time =     2.1000 secs

--       /******* Let's see if "entity integrity" really works?       **********/
EXEC SQL:   INSERT INTO newstaff
            VALUES (501, 'Dan', 99, 'Nerds', 4, 42000.00, 0 );

 ERROR, sql_code = -803
 SQL0803N  One or more values in the INSERT or UPDATE statement are not valid
 because they would produce duplicate rows for a table with a unique index.
```

Figure 20-14 (Part 2 of 2). Script 12: Data Integrity with Unique Keys.

Using Views with Check Option and Validity Checks

The **Validity check constraint** restricts the values that can appear in a column. When a table is created each column is assigned a SQL data type, and the Database Manager automatically ensures that only data of the specified type is introduced in a column. But what about restricting the set of legal values of the same column type? The Database Manager provides a **check** option with views, which automatically enforces that each INSERT and UPDATE meets the search criteria (domain restrictions) in the view definition. This search criteria can be used to further restrict the set of values that can appear in a column. The script that follows demonstrates this concept.

```
--
--       ********** Data Integrity using Views with Check Option ************
--

--       /****** Create a View PROTECT_STAFF with CHECK option           **********/
EXEC SQL:   CREATE VIEW  protect_staff
                         AS SELECT * FROM newstaff
                         WHERE job = 'Nerds' OR job= 'Sales'
                         WITH CHECK OPTION;

 OK, sql_rcd = 0,        Execution time =     2.2200 secs

--       /****** Let's see what's in this view so far                    **********/
EXEC SQL:   SELECT * FROM protect_staff;

 ID      NAME       DEPT    JOB    YEARS    SALARY     COMM
 ------  ---------  ------  -----  ------  --------   --------
 500     Bob        99      Nerds  5        81000.00     00.00
 501     Dan        99      Nerds  4        75600.00     00.00

 Total Number of Rows SELECTED = 2
 OK, sql_rcd = 0,        Execution time =     0.5400 secs
```

Figure 20-15 (Part 1 of 2). Script 13: Data Integrity Using Views with Check Option.

```
--      /****** Let's put some more data in PROTECT_STAFF          **********/
EXEC SQL:   INSERT INTO protect_staff
            SELECT * from staff where job= 'Sales' and salary > 20000;

 OK, sql_rcd = 0,        Execution time =     0.4700 secs

--      /**** Now let's insert another well paid nerd              **********/
EXEC SQL:   INSERT INTO protect_staff
            VALUES (508, 'Joe', 99, 'Nerds',4, 99000.00, 0.0);

 OK, sql_rcd = 0,        Execution time =     0.1200 secs

--      /**** Watch what happens if we violate the CHECK and insert a Mgr ****/
EXEC SQL:   INSERT INTO protect_staff
            VALUES (603, 'Sam', 99, 'Mgr',4, 89000.00, 0.0);

 ERROR, sql_code = -161
 SQL0161N  The resulting row of the INSERT or UPDATE does not conform to the
 view definition.
```

Figure 20-15 (Part 2 of 2). Script 13: Data Integrity Using Views with Check Option.

Referential Integrity

Referential Integrity is a powerful data integrity feature which ensures that cross-references *between* tables are always valid. This is done by enforcing that **foreign key** values match existing values in **primary keys**. For example, the Database Manager can automatically enforce a relation such as "no employee gets assigned to a department that does not exist." As we explained in the tutorial, see "Referential Relationships" on page 424, this is done through the magic of the parent/child relationships between **primary keys** and **foreign keys**. Support for foreign keys takes the form of clauses in the CREATE TABLE or ALTER TABLE SQL commands. In the script that follows, we create such a parent/child dependency:

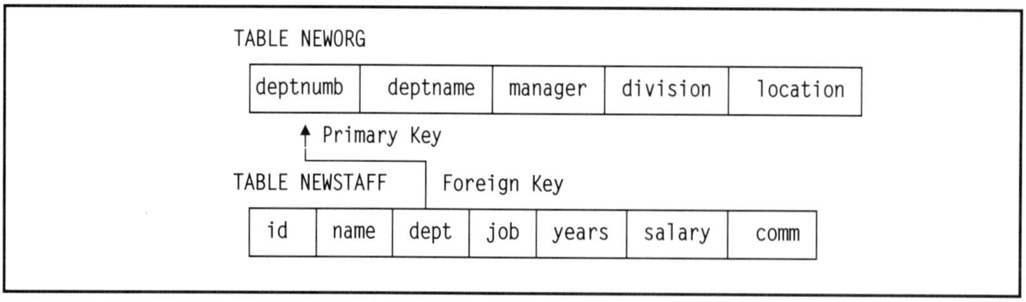

Figure 20-16. The Foreign Key/Primary Key Reference Used in Script.

We then show you what happens when this dependency is violated. The violation we demonstrate is an insert in table NEWSTAFF for a department that is not in table NEWORG. You will get to watch first-hand the wrath of the Database Manager when it detects such violations.

```
--
--      ******** Enforcing Data Integrity with Referential Integrity *******
--

--      /*************     Create the org table's cousin      ***************/
EXEC SQL:   CREATE TABLE neworg
                         (deptnumb   SMALLINT NOT NULL PRIMARY KEY,
                          deptname   VARCHAR(14),
                          manager    SMALLINT,
                          division   VARCHAR(10),
                          location   VARCHAR(13));

 OK, sql_rcd = 0,        Execution time =     3.9400 secs

--      /*************     Let's put some data in it          ***************/
EXEC SQL:   INSERT INTO neworg
            VALUES (99, 'Software', NULL, 'Oceanview','Hawaii');

 OK, sql_rcd = 0,        Execution time =     0.1500 secs

EXEC SQL:   INSERT INTO neworg
            VALUES (90, 'Multimedia', NULL, 'Oceanview','Tahiti');

 OK, sql_rcd = 0,        Execution time =     0.0700 secs

--      /*************   Let's start with nerds only in the table   **********/
EXEC SQL:   DELETE FROM newstaff
            WHERE job <> 'Nerds';

 OK, sql_rcd = 0,        Execution time =     0.3100 secs

--      /*************     Let's see what we've got so far    ***************/
EXEC SQL:   SELECT * from neworg;

 DEPTNUMB  DEPTNAME        MANAGER  DIVISION    LOCATION
 --------  --------------  -------  ----------  -------------
 99        Software        NULL     Oceanview   Hawaii
 90        Multimedia      NULL     Oceanview   Tahiti

 Total Number of Rows SELECTED = 2
 OK, sql_rcd = 0,        Execution time =     0.0600 secs

EXEC SQL:   SELECT * from newstaff;

 ID      NAME       DEPT    JOB    YEARS   SALARY     COMM
 ------  ---------  ------  -----  ------  --------   --------
 500     Bob        99      Nerds  5       81000.00      00.00
 501     Dan        99      Nerds  4       75600.00      00.00
 508     Joe        99      Nerds  4       99000.00      00.00

 Total Number of Rows SELECTED = 3
 OK, sql_rcd = 0,        Execution time =     0.1500 secs
```

Figure 20-17 (Part 1 of 2). Script 14: Data Integrity with Referential Integrity.

```
--      /**** Make the dept column a foreign key to primary key in neworg  ***/
EXEC SQL:    ALTER TABLE newstaff
             FOREIGN KEY keyname1(dept) REFERENCES neworg
             ON DELETE RESTRICT;

 OK, sql_rcd = 0,        Execution time =     1.1200 secs

--      /**** Insert  data for a valid department               *************/
EXEC SQL:    INSERT INTO newstaff
             VALUES (605, 'Newhire', 99, 'Nerds',0, 29000.00, 0.0);

 OK, sql_rcd = 0,        Execution time =     0.1200 secs

--      /**** Insert  data for a valid department               *************/
EXEC SQL:    INSERT INTO newstaff
             VALUES (607, 'Newhire', 90, 'Nerds',0, 29000.00, 0.0);

 OK, sql_rcd = 0,        Execution time =     0.1300 secs

--      /**** Watch what happens with a non-valid department (not in NEWORG) */
EXEC SQL:    INSERT INTO newstaff
             VALUES (609, 'Newhire', 20, 'Sales',0, 29000.00, 0.0);

 ERROR, sql_code = -530
 SQL0530N  The insert or update value of FOREIGN KEY "KEYNAME1" is not equal to
 some value of the primary key of the parent table.
```

Figure 20-17 (Part 2 of 2). Script 14: Data Integrity with Referential Integrity.

Enforcing DELETE Rules using Referential Integrity

The Referential Integrity clauses can specify how to treat rows in dependent tables if a parent row is deleted. The question is what to do with the orphan rows? For each foreign key it is possible to specify one of three "delete rules:"

1. **The RESTRICT rule**, which tells the Database Manager to prevent the deletion of the parent row if that row has any children (this is the default rule).
2. **The SET NULL rule**, which tells the Database Manager to automatically set the foreign key values to Nulls in all the child rows when the parent row gets deleted.
3. **The CASCADE rule**, which tells the Database Manager to automatically delete all orphan rows when the parent row gets deleted.

The script below demonstrates how to specify those rules and shows their effects when a delete is attempted for a parent row with dependents.

```
--
--      ******** Enforcing Delete Rules with Referential Integrity   *******
--
--      /****** Observe how the default RESTRICT rule protects dependents ****/
EXEC SQL:   DELETE FROM neworg
            WHERE location = 'Tahiti';

 ERROR, sql_code = -532
 SQL0532N  A parent row cannot be deleted because the relationship "KEYNAME1"
 restricts the deletion.

--      /*************      Let's see what data is in our tables      **********/
EXEC SQL:   SELECT * from neworg;

 DEPTNUMB  DEPTNAME        MANAGER  DIVISION    LOCATION
 --------  --------------  -------  ----------  -------------
 99        Software        NULL     Oceanview   Hawaii
 90        Multimedia      NULL     Oceanview   Tahiti

 Total Number of Rows SELECTED = 2
 OK, sql_rcd = 0,        Execution time =     0.1600 secs

EXEC SQL:   SELECT * from newstaff;

 ID      NAME       DEPT    JOB    YEARS   SALARY    COMM
 ------  ---------  ------  -----  ------  --------  --------
 500     Bob        99      Nerds  5       81000.00     00.00
 501     Dan        99      Nerds  4       75600.00     00.00
 605     Newhire    99      Nerds  0       29000.00     00.00
 508     Joe        99      Nerds  4       99000.00     00.00
 607     Newhire    90      Nerds  0       29000.00     00.00

 Total Number of Rows SELECTED = 5
 OK, sql_rcd = 0,        Execution time =     0.1800 secs

--      /**** DROP the referential constraint                   ***************/
EXEC SQL:   ALTER TABLE newstaff
            DROP FOREIGN KEY keyname1;

 OK, sql_rcd = 0,        Execution time =     0.2500 secs

--      /**** Let's change the referential constraint to SET NULLs  **********/
EXEC SQL:   ALTER TABLE newstaff
            FOREIGN KEY keyname1(dept) REFERENCES neworg
            ON DELETE SET NULL;

 OK, sql_rcd = 0,        Execution time =     0.4100 secs

--      /***** Commit the change                                      **********/
EXEC SQL:   COMMIT;

 OK, sql_rcd = 0,        Execution time =     0.1200 secs
```

Figure 20-18 (Part 1 of 3). Script 15: The Delete Rules Using Referential Integrity.

```
--      /**** Let's see what  referential integrity does for us now     *****/
EXEC SQL:   DELETE FROM neworg
            WHERE location = 'Tahiti';

 OK, sql_rcd = 0,        Execution time =     0.2200 secs

--      /****  The Tahiti department is dropped (this is the parent row)  ****/
EXEC SQL:   SELECT * from neworg;

 DEPTNUMB  DEPTNAME        MANAGER  DIVISION    LOCATION
 --------  --------------  -------  ----------  -------------
 99        Software        NULL     Oceanview   Hawaii

 Total Number of Rows SELECTED = 1
 OK, sql_rcd = 0,        Execution time =     0.0900 secs

--      /****  The Tahiti department in child rows is set to NULL         ****/
EXEC SQL:   SELECT * from newstaff;

 ID      NAME       DEPT    JOB    YEARS   SALARY     COMM
 ------  ---------  ------  -----  ------  --------   --------
 500     Bob        99      Nerds  5       81000.00      00.00
 501     Dan        99      Nerds  4       75600.00      00.00
 605     Newhire    99      Nerds  0       29000.00      00.00
 508     Joe        99      Nerds  4       99000.00      00.00
 607     Newhire    NULL    Nerds  0       29000.00      00.00

 Total Number of Rows SELECTED = 5
 OK, sql_rcd = 0,        Execution time =     0.1200 secs

--      /*************      Let's get back our data            ***************/
EXEC SQL:   ROLLBACK;

 OK, sql_rcd = 0,        Execution time =     0.1300 secs

--      /**** DROP the referential constraint                     ***************/
EXEC SQL:   ALTER TABLE newstaff
            DROP FOREIGN KEY keyname1;

 OK, sql_rcd = 0,        Execution time =     0.2200 secs

--      /**** Let's change the referential rule to CASCADE        **************/
EXEC SQL:   ALTER TABLE newstaff
            FOREIGN KEY keyname1(dept) REFERENCES neworg
            ON DELETE CASCADE;

 OK, sql_rcd = 0,        Execution time =     0.3700 secs

--      /***** Commit the change                                       **********/
EXEC SQL:   COMMIT;

 OK, sql_rcd = 0,        Execution time =     0.1600 secs
```

Figure 20-18 (Part 2 of 3). Script 15: The Delete Rules Using Referential Integrity.

```
--      /**** Let's see what  referential integrity will do for us now  *****/
EXEC SQL:   DELETE FROM neworg
            WHERE location = 'Hawaii';

 OK, sql_rcd = 0,        Execution time =     0.2200 secs

--      /***** The parent department for Hawaii is gone...      *************/
EXEC SQL:   SELECT * from neworg;

 DEPTNUMB DEPTNAME        MANAGER DIVISION    LOCATION
 -------- --------------- ------- ----------  -------------
 90       Multimedia      NULL    Oceanview   Tahiti

 Total Number of Rows SELECTED = 1
 OK, sql_rcd = 0,        Execution time =     0.1300 secs

--      /***** All the Hawaii employees (the child rows) are gone also  *****//
EXEC SQL:   SELECT * from newstaff;

 ID     NAME       DEPT    JOB    YEARS   SALARY     COMM
 ------ ---------  ------  -----  ------  --------   --------
 607    Newhire    90      Nerds  0       29000.00     00.00

 Total Number of Rows SELECTED = 1
 OK, sql_rcd = 0,        Execution time =     0.1200 secs

--      /*************     Let's bring back our data, we made the point  ******/
EXEC SQL:   ROLLBACK;
 OK, sql_rcd = 0,        Execution time =     0.1600 secs
```

Figure 20-18 (Part 3 of 3). Script 15: The Delete Rules Using Referential Integrity.

Enforcing Cascaded DELETEs Using Referential Integrity

The RESTRICT rule is a "single-level" rule which only affects the parent row in a Referential relationship. The SET NULL rule is a two-level rule whose impact stops with the child table. The CASCADE rule, however, is a "multilevel" rule whose effects ripple throughout all the descendant tables. The tables below will be used to demonstrate these concepts:

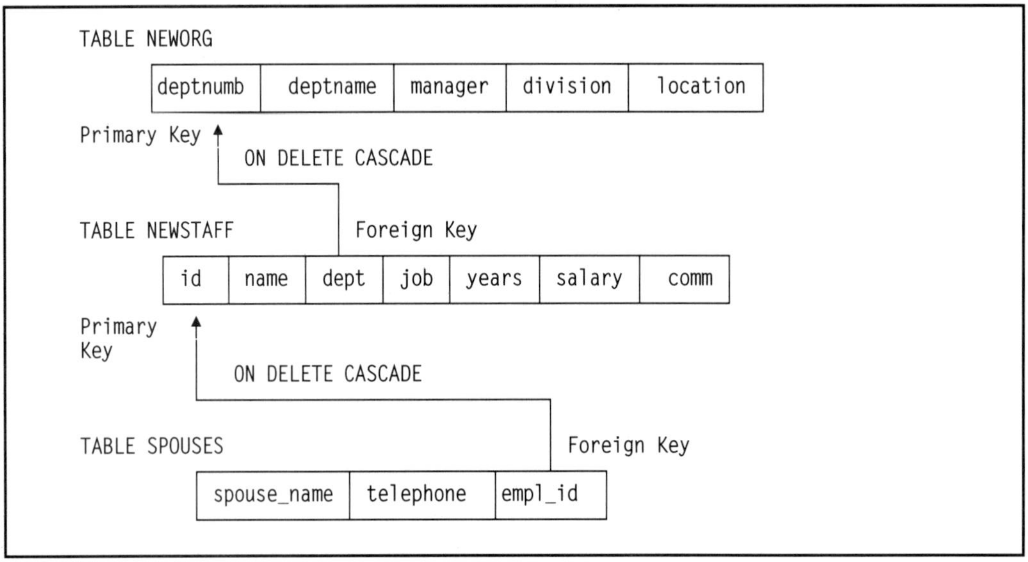

Figure 20-19. The "Delete Rules" Used in the Script.

In the sadistic script that follows, we first create the relationships between the tables shown above. We then close down a department in one of our paradise islands and watch its unfortunate effects on the workers and their spouses.

```
--
--      ******** Cascaded  Delete Rules with Referential Integrity   *******
--
--      /*************     Create the spouses table            ****************/
EXEC SQL:   CREATE TABLE spouses
                      (spouse_name  VARCHAR(20),
                       telephone    VARCHAR(10),
                       empl_id      SMALLINT,
                       FOREIGN KEY  homenum(empl_id) REFERENCES newstaff
                       ON DELETE CASCADE);

 OK, sql_rcd = 0,        Execution time =     1.1200 secs

--      /*************     Insert some data in spouses         ****************/
EXEC SQL:   INSERT INTO spouses
            VALUES ('Michiko','4152223333',501);

 OK, sql_rcd = 0,        Execution time =     0.2900 secs
EXEC SQL:   INSERT INTO spouses
            VALUES ('Jeri','4154445555',500);

 OK, sql_rcd = 0,        Execution time =     0.0900 secs
```

Figure 20-20 (Part 1 of 3). Script 16: Cascaded Deletes Using Referential Integrity.

```
--      /*************      Let's take stock of what we've got  ***************/
EXEC SQL:   SELECT * FROM neworg;

 DEPTNUMB  DEPTNAME        MANAGER  DIVISION    LOCATION
 --------  --------------  -------  ----------  -------------
 99        Software        NULL     Oceanview   Hawaii
 90        Multimedia      NULL     Oceanview   Tahiti

 Total Number of Rows SELECTED = 2

 OK, sql_rcd = 0,        Execution time =     0.4500 secs

EXEC SQL:   SELECT * FROM newstaff;

 ID      NAME       DEPT    JOB    YEARS   SALARY    COMM
 ------  ---------  ------  -----  ------  --------  --------
 500     Bob        99      Nerds  5       81000.00     00.00
 501     Dan        99      Nerds  4       75600.00     00.00
 605     Newhire    99      Nerds  0       29000.00     00.00
 508     Joe        99      Nerds  4       99000.00     00.00
 607     Newhire    90      Nerds  0       29000.00     00.00

 Total Number of Rows SELECTED = 5

 OK, sql_rcd = 0,        Execution time =     0.3900 secs

EXEC SQL:   SELECT * FROM spouses;

 SPOUSE_NAME           TELEPHONE   EMPL_ID
 --------------------  ----------  -------
 Michiko               4152223333  501
 Jeri                  4154445555  500

 Total Number of Rows SELECTED = 2

 OK, sql_rcd = 0,        Execution time =     0.1200 secs

--      /****** Watch this cruel and unusual punishment: No more Hawaii ******/
EXEC SQL:   DELETE  FROM neworg
            WHERE location='Hawai';

 OK, sql_rcd = 0,        Execution time =     0.4000 secs

--      /*************      Let's see the damage this has created    ***********/
EXEC SQL:   SELECT * FROM neworg;

 DEPTNUMB  DEPTNAME        MANAGER  DIVISION    LOCATION
 --------  --------------  -------  ----------  -------------
 90        Multimedia      NULL     Oceanview   Tahiti

 Total Number of Rows SELECTED = 1

 OK, sql_rcd = 0,        Execution time =     0.0700 secs
```

Figure 20-20 (Part 2 of 3). Script 16: Cascaded Deletes Using Referential Integrity.

```
EXEC SQL:   SELECT * FROM newstaff;

 ID      NAME       DEPT    JOB    YEARS   SALARY    COMM
 ------  ---------  ------  -----  ------  --------  --------
 607     Newhire    90      Nerds  0       29000.00     00.00

 Total Number of Rows SELECTED = 1

 OK, sql_rcd = 0,        Execution time =     0.1000 secs

EXEC SQL:   SELECT * FROM spouses;

 SPOUSE_NAME           TELEPHONE   EMPL_ID
 --------------------  ----------  -------

 Total Number of Rows SELECTED = 0

 OK, sql_rcd = 0,        Execution time =     0.0600 secs

--      /*************   Let's bring back our data, we made the point  ******/
EXEC SQL:   ROLLBACK;

 OK, sql_rcd = 0,        Execution time =     0.7200 secs
```

Figure 20-20 (Part 3 of 3). Script 16: Cascaded Deletes Using Referential Integrity.

Using Indexes to Maximize Performance

An index is an SQL structure that provides rapid access to table data. The purpose of this script is to give you a feel for the performance improvements you can obtain by using indexes. In order to get some meaningful numbers, we'll create a table that contains 10,000 rows, and measure the effects of a SELECT with and without an index. We're going to borrow the table definitions and data for this script from the TP1 chapters that come later in this book. You should be seeing some *dramatic* improvements in performance when we introduce the query with the index.

```
--
--      ******** A demonstration of how indexes affect performance    *******
--

--      /*************     Create a bank accounts table called ACCT **********/
EXEC SQL: CREATE TABLE ACCT  (ACCT_NUM    INT      NOT NULL,
                              NAME        CHAR(20) NOT NULL,
                              BRANCH_ID   SMALLINT NOT NULL,
                              BALANCE     INT      NOT NULL,
                              ADDRESS     CHAR(30) NOT NULL,
                              TEMP        CHAR(40) NOT NULL);

 OK, sql_rcd = 0,        Execution time =     0.6600 secs
```

Figure 20-21 (Part 1 of 3). Script 17: Using Indexes to Maximize Performance.

```
--      /*************     Commit the work done so far              **********/
EXEC SQL:        COMMIT;

 OK, sql_rcd = 0,        Execution time =     0.1000 secs

--      /************* Let's fill the ACCT table with 10,000 records *********/
EXEC DBA: IMPORT sample  c:\acct.del   REPLACE DEL ACCT;

 No messages in msgfile.msg
 OK, sql_rcd = 0,        Execution time =   241.3100 secs

--      /*************     Commit the work done so far              **********/
EXEC SQL:        COMMIT;

 OK, sql_rcd = 0,        Execution time =     0.3200 secs

--      /************* Let's make sure the ACCT table has 10,000 rows ********/
EXEC SQL:        SELECT COUNT(*) FROM ACCT;

 1
 -----------
 10000

 Total Number of Rows SELECTED = 1
 OK, sql_rcd = 0,        Execution time =    10.4100 secs

--      /************* Perform a Query On that table with no Indexes   *******/
EXEC SQL:        SELECT * acct_num, name, branch_id, balance
                 FROM ACCT
                 WHERE ACCT_NUM
                 BETWEEN 7000 and 7001
                 ORDER BY ACCT_NUM;

 ACCT_NUM     NAME                  BRANCH_ID  BALANCE
 -----------  --------------------  ---------  -----------
 7000         <--20 BYTE STRING-->  74         1000
 7001         <--20 BYTE STRING-->  46         1000

 Total Number of Rows SELECTED = 2
 OK, sql_rcd = 0,        Execution time =     7.9000 secs

--      /*************       Create an Index on that table        ************/
EXEC SQL: CREATE INDEX ACCTINDX ON ACCT(ACCT_NUM);

 OK, sql_rcd = 0,        Execution time =    31.8700 secs

--      /*************     Commit the work done so far            ************/
EXEC SQL:        COMMIT;

 OK, sql_rcd = 0,        Execution time =     0.0700 secs

--      /************* disconnect from to free all buffers        ************/
EXEC DBA:        STOPUSE sample;

 OK, sql_rcd = 0,        Execution time =     2.2200 secs
```

Figure 20-21 (Part 2 of 3). Script 17: Using Indexes to Maximize Performance.

```
--      /************* Reconnect  with a clean slate                   ************/
EXEC DBA:       STARTUSE sample S;

 OK, sql_rcd = 0,        Execution time =     2.1900 secs

--      /************* Perform the same query with an index.  Is it faster? **/
EXEC SQL:       SELECT * acct_num, name, branch_id, balance
                FROM ACCT
                WHERE ACCT_NUM
                BETWEEN 7000  and 7001
                ORDER BY ACCT_NUM;

 ACCT_NUM     NAME                 BRANCH_ID  BALANCE
 -----------  -------------------- ---------  -----------
 7000         <--20 BYTE STRING--> 74         1000
 7001         <--20 BYTE STRING--> 46         1000

 Total Number of Rows SELECTED = 2
 OK, sql_rcd = 0,        Execution time =     0.8400 secs
```

Figure 20-21 (Part 3 of 3). Script 17: Using Indexes to Maximize Performance.

SQL Security

With SQL making access to the data so easy, it becomes important for a Database Manager to provide access protection. You can define the overall framework for securing your data using the SQL language. The enforcement of the security then becomes the responsibility of the Database Manager. As we explained in the tutorial, database security is based on the interplay of three concepts: *users*, *database objects*, and *access* privileges. The **privileges** define the actions that a *user* can perform on a given *database object*. The script assumes you've read the UPM and SQL security tutorial in "Authorization and Privileges" on page 441. The UPM for our machine is setup with an *administrator* called "Jeri" and two *users*: "Dan" and "Bob." The script shows some of the things "Jeri" can do for "Dan," a trusted knowledge worker, and "Bob" an occasional consumer of information.

```
--
--      ******** A Script for exploring SQL Security      *****************
--
--     /****  Jeri grants CONNECT privileges to Bob and Dan        ************/
     EXEC SQL:  GRANT CONNECT ON DATABASE TO Dan, Bob;

 OK, sql_rcd = 0,        Execution time =     0.2200 secs

--     /****  Jeri can grant many privileges in one statement      ************/
     EXEC SQL:  GRANT CREATETAB, BINDADD ON DATABASE TO Dan;

 OK, sql_rcd = 0,        Execution time =     0.0300 secs
```

Figure 20-22 (Part 1 of 2). Script 18: A "Brief" Introduction to SQL Security.

```
--     /****  Jeri can grant privileges to all users with PUBLIC  ************/
     EXEC SQL:  GRANT EXECUTE ON PROGRAM rsql TO PUBLIC;

 OK, sql_rcd = 0,         Execution time =     0.4100 secs

--     /****  Jeri grants some query privileges to Bob            ************/
     EXEC SQL:  GRANT SELECT  ON TABLE newstaff TO Bob;

 OK, sql_rcd = 0,         Execution time =     0.2800 secs

--     /****  Jeri grants a lot more privileges to Dan           ************/
     EXEC SQL:  GRANT ALL ON TABLE newstaff TO Dan;

 OK, sql_rcd = 0,         Execution time =     0.0700 secs

EXEC SQL:  GRANT INSERT, UPDATE, DELETE ON TABLE neworg TO Dan;

 OK, sql_rcd = 0,         Execution time =     0.0600 secs

--     /****     What Jeri "gives" she can take back            ***********/
     EXEC SQL:  REVOKE CONNECT ON DATABASE FROM PUBLIC;

 OK, sql_rcd = 0,         Execution time =     0.1200 secs

EXEC SQL:  REVOKE INSERT  ON TABLE neworg FROM Dan;

 OK, sql_rcd = 0,         Execution time =     0.9100 secs
```

Figure 20-22 (Part 2 of 2). Script 18: A "Brief" Introduction to SQL Security.

The System Catalogs

The Database Manager, like most Relational databases, is self-describing. It automatically maintains information about its own structure in the database. These self-describing tables, collectively known as the **catalog tables**, can be accessed (but not modified) through standard queries. This means you can ask the Database Manager to describe its own tables where it maintains its structures for views, columns, privileges, plans, ownership, user comments, and all sorts of useful systemic information. Database tools can use this information very advantageously. All the catalog tables have the same user ID, **SYSIBM**. We introduce the catalog tables in the script below.

```
--
--      ******** A Script for exploring the System Catalog Tables **********
--
--      /************* List name and time-stamp of all system tables *********/
EXEC SQL:       SELECT creator, name, type, colcount, ctime
                FROM SYSIBM.SYSTABLES
                WHERE CREATOR = 'SYSIBM'  ORDER BY ctime;

 CREATOR   NAME                TYPE  COLCOUNT  CTIME
 --------  ------------------  ----  --------  --------------------------
 SYSIBM    SYSTABLES           T     20        1990-04-19-20.36.33.930000
 SYSIBM    SYSCOLUMNS          T     16        1990-04-19-20.36.34.870000
 SYSIBM    SYSINDEXES          T     13        1990-04-19-20.36.35.150000
 SYSIBM    SYSVIEWS            T     5         1990-04-19-20.36.35.400000
 SYSIBM    SYSVIEWDEP          T     6         1990-04-19-20.36.35.650000
 SYSIBM    SYSPLAN             T     11        1990-04-19-20.36.35.840000
 SYSIBM    SYSPLANDEP          T     7         1990-04-19-20.36.36.000000
 SYSIBM    SYSSECTION          T     5         1990-04-19-20.36.36.310000
 SYSIBM    SYSSTMT             T     6         1990-04-19-20.36.36.430000
 SYSIBM    SYSDBAUTH           T     6         1990-04-19-20.36.36.590000
 SYSIBM    SYSPLANAUTH         T     7         1990-04-19-20.36.36.750000
 SYSIBM    SYSTABAUTH          T     13        1990-04-19-20.36.37.590000
 SYSIBM    SYSINDEXAUTH        T     5         1990-04-19-20.36.37.780000
 SYSIBM    SYSRELS             T     11        1990-04-19-20.36.38.250000

 Total Number of Rows SELECTED = 14
 OK, sql_rcd = 0,        Execution time =     0.7300 secs

--      /************* List all the tables we created in this chapter ********/
EXEC SQL:       SELECT creator, name, type, colcount, ctime
                FROM SYSIBM.SYSTABLES
                WHERE CREATOR = USER
                AND type = 'T'  ORDER BY ctime;

 CREATOR   NAME                TYPE  COLCOUNT  CTIME
 --------  ------------------  ----  --------  --------------------------
 JERI      ORG                 T     5         1990-04-19-20.37.07.090000
 JERI      STAFF               T     7         1990-04-19-20.37.09.000000
 JERI      NEWSTAFF            T     7         1990-04-19-20.37.31.560000
 JERI      NEWORG              T     5         1990-04-19-20.37.44.430000
 JERI      ACCT                T     6         1990-04-19-20.38.00.710000

 Total Number of Rows SELECTED = 6
 OK, sql_rcd = 0,        Execution time =     0.4300 secs

--      /************* List all the views  we created in this chapter ********/
EXEC SQL:       SELECT creator, name, type, colcount, ctime
                FROM SYSIBM.SYSTABLES
                WHERE CREATOR = USER
                AND type = 'V';

 CREATOR   NAME                TYPE  COLCOUNT  CTIME
 --------  ------------------  ----  --------  --------------------------
 JERI      PROTECT_STAFF       V     7         1990-04-19-20.37.41.180000

 Total Number of Rows SELECTED = 1
 OK, sql_rcd = 0,        Execution time =     0.3100 secs
```

Figure 20-23 (Part 1 of 2). Script 19: An Introduction to the Catalog Tables.

```
--      /************* List all the users and their authorizations    ********/
EXEC SQL:       SELECT *
                FROM SYSIBM.SYSDBAUTH;

 GRANTOR   GRANTEE   DBADMAUTH  CREATETABAUTH  BINDADDAUTH  CONNECTAUTH
 --------  --------  ---------  -------------  -----------  -----------
 SYSIBM    JERI      Y          Y              Y            Y
 SYSIBM    PUBLIC    N          Y              Y            N
 JERI      DAN       N          Y              Y            Y
 JERI      BOB       N          N              N            Y

 Total Number of Rows SELECTED = 4
 OK, sql_rcd = 0,         Execution time =     0.1200 secs

--      /************* List all the access plans that have been compiled *****/
EXEC SQL:       SELECT name, creator, valid, isolation, block
                FROM SYSIBM.SYSPLAN
                WHERE CREATOR = USER;

 NAME      CREATOR   VALID  ISOLATION  BLOCK
 --------  --------  -----  ---------  -----
 RSQL      JERI      Y      U          B

 Total Number of Rows SELECTED = 1
 OK, sql_rcd = 0,         Execution time =     0.1900 secs

--      /************* List all the referential relationships we created *****/
EXEC SQL:       SELECT  tbname, relname, reftbname, deleterule, updaterule
                FROM SYSIBM.SYSRELS
                WHERE CREATOR = USER;

 TBNAME              RELNAME   REFTBNAME           DELETERULE  UPDATERULE
 ------------------  --------  ------------------  ----------  ----------
 NEWSTAFF            KEYNAME1  NEWORG              R           R

 Total Number of Rows SELECTED = 1
 OK, sql_rcd = 0,         Execution time =     0.7200 secs
```

Figure 20-23 (Part 2 of 2). Script 19: An Introduction to the Catalog Tables.

EXPLORING THE DATABASE ADMINISTRATION COMMANDS WITH SCRIPTS

The scripts that follow demonstrate the versatility of RSQL as a system administrator's tool. Be sure to reference the railroad diagrams in "Database Administration Commands" on page 967, which describe how those commands are used.

How to Fine-Tune a Database Using RUNSTATs and REORGs

The script below shows how to fine-tune the performance of your database using **RUNSTATs** and **REORGs**. A great deal of the credit for the improved performance of relational databases goes to the *optimizer*. As we explained in the tutorial, the optimizer is an expert at determining the minimum number of disk accesses for getting to the requested data. The information at the optimizer's disposal for making such decisions consists of statistics stored in the system catalog. Based on those statistics, the optimizer will decide whether to use an index or to sequentially scan an entire table. The OS/2 EE Database Manager gives you control of when these table statistics are generated. You should refresh those statistics after significant changes have occurred to the database, such as: the import of a large number of data records, the restructuring of tables, threshold points in the steady growth of a database, and after an index is added or deleted. You should rebind your static SQL programs after a refresh of statistics so that the applications can take the new statistics into account.

The **REORG** command reorganizes the physical storage of a base table. You typically issue this command when a table has become too fragmented due to many updates or deletes. You will know a table is fragmented and needs to be reorganized if the performance deteriorates. This command is fairly time-consuming (in the order of minutes). You should complete all database operations and release all locks before executing this command. Our script will apply a REORG and RUNSTATs on the ACCT table. We will then re-run the query in "Using Indexes to Maximize Performance" on page 536 to see if the performance improved any.

```
--
--      ******** How to fine-tune performance with RUNSTATS and REORG ******
--
--    /***************   Commit the work done so far                  *********/
EXEC SQL:       COMMIT;

 OK, sql_rcd = 0,        Execution time =     0.0000 secs

--    /***************   Disconnect from the database                 *********/
EXEC DBA:       STOPUSE sample;

 OK, sql_rcd = 0,        Execution time =     1.4400 secs

-- /*** update the Database Config to increase available log file space    ****/
EXEC DBA: UPDATE_DB_CFG SAMPLE  LOGFILSIZ   = 100,
                                LOGPRIMARY  = 2,
                                LOGSECOND   = 20;

 OK, sql_rcd = 0,        Execution time =     0.9700 secs

--      /************** connect to the database     **************************/
EXEC DBA:      STARTUSE sample S;

 OK, sql_rcd = 0,        Execution time =     9.3500 secs

--    /*************     REORG the ACCT table using index ACCTINDX   *********/
EXEC DBA:       REORG sample jeri.acct jeri.acctindx;

 OK, sql_rcd = 0,        Execution time =   205.7200 secs
```

Figure 20-24 (Part 1 of 2). Script 20: How to Fine-Tune Performance with RUNSTATS and REORG.

```
--    /*************      "-1" means no row statistics gathered        *********/
EXEC SQL:         SELECT creator, name, card
                  FROM SYSIBM.SYSTABLES
                  WHERE name ='ACCT';

 CREATOR   NAME                CARD
 --------  ------------------  -----------
 JERI      ACCT                -1

 Total Number of Rows SELECTED = 1
 OK, sql_rcd = 0,        Execution time =     0.1900 secs

--    /*************      RUNSTAT refreshes the statistics on table ACCT  *****/
EXEC DBA:         RUNSTATS jeri.acct;

 OK, sql_rcd = 0,        Execution time =   123.8800 secs

--    /*************      View the row statistics after RUNSTATs       *********/
EXEC SQL:         SELECT creator, name, card
                  FROM SYSIBM.SYSTABLES
                  WHERE name ='ACCT';

 CREATOR   NAME                CARD
 --------  ------------------  -----------
 JERI      ACCT                10000

 Total Number of Rows SELECTED = 1
 OK, sql_rcd = 0,        Execution time =     0.1900 secs

--      /*** Perform the same query as in script 17.  Is it faster?       *****/
EXEC SQL:         SELECT * acct_num, name, branch_id, balance
                  FROM ACCT
                  WHERE ACCT_NUM
                  BETWEEN 7000 and 7001
                  ORDER BY ACCT_NUM;

 ACCT_NUM     NAME                  BRANCH_ID  BALANCE
 -----------  --------------------  ---------  -----------
 7000         <--20 BYTE STRING >   74         1000
 7001         <--20 BYTE STRING-->  46         1000

 Total Number of Rows SELECTED = 2
 OK, sql_rcd = 0,        Execution time =     0.2100 secs
```

Figure 20-24 (Part 2 of 2). Script 20: How to Fine-Tune Performance with RUNSTATS and REORG.

The Database and Database Manager Configuration Files

The OS/2 EE Database Manager maintains system configuration information about the Database Manager and the individual databases in configuration files. The information contained in those files was explained in the tutorials ("Database Administration API: Configuration Services" on page 475). The script below demonstrates the database environment for our scripts. We also display the user and database status information maintained by the OS/2 EE Database Manager. Finally, we display the authority information kept by OS/2 EE for the current user. There is a lot of information out there! Perhaps you'll find some of it useful.

```
--
--      ******** Viewing and Updating the System Configuration Files  ******
--
--    /***************   Commit the work done so far                      *********/
EXEC SQL:      COMMIT;

 OK, sql_rcd = 0,        Execution time =     0.1300 secs

--    /***************   Show SAMPLE's database configuration             *********/
EXEC DBA:      SHOW_DB_CFG sample;

 Database Configuration for Database sample
 ============================================

 Configuration Parameter          Current  Parm.      Parm.      Parm.
 Description                      Value    Units      Range      Default
 -------------------------------- -------- ---------- ---------- -------
 Max. Active Applications                8 Appl.      1-117          8
 Max. DB Files Open/Application         20 files      2-235         20
 Max. Files Open/Application           255 files      25-32700     255
 Buffer Pool Size                       16 4K pages     (1)         16
 Time Interval for Deadlocks         10000 millisecs. 1-600 sec.    10
 Max. Storage for Locklists              8 4K pages   4-250          8
 Max. percent locklist/appl.            22 percent    1-100         22
 Default Application Heap                3 segments   2-20           3
 Application Agent Heap                  2 segments   2-85           3
 Sort List Heap                          2 segments   1-20           2
 Database Heap                           1 segments   1-45           1
 SQL Statement Heap                     64 segments                 64
 Log File Size                         100 4K pages   15-255        50
 Primary Log Files                       2 files      0-63           2
 Secondary Log Files                    20 files      0-63           3
 Log Records/soft checkpoint           100 records    0-65535      100

 Current Log Location = C:\SQL00002\
 New Log Location     =
 Copy Protection      =    1
 Country              =    1
 Code Page            =  850
 Release              =  512

 OK, sql_rcd = 0,        Execution time =     0.4700 secs

--    /***************   Show the Database Manager's configuration        *********/
EXEC DBA:      SHOW_DM_CFG;

 Database Manager Configuration
 ==============================

 Configuration Parameter          Current  Parm.      Parm.      Parm.
 Description                      Value    Units      Range      Default
 -------------------------------- -------- ---------- ---------- -------
 Max. Shared Segments                  200 Segments   7-802      20/50   (1)
 Max. Concurrently Active apps.          8 Number     1-8        3/8     (1)
 Max. Requestor I/O Block Size        4096 bytes      4k-64k     0/0/4   (2)
```

Figure 20-25 (Part 1 of 3). Script 21: Looking Inside the Configuration Files.

```
Max. Server   I/O Block Size        4096   bytes      4k-64k     0/4/4/0 (2)
Communication Heap Size                2   Segments   1-255      2
Remote Data Services Heap size         2   Segments   1-255      2
Max. Remote Connections               10   Number     1-255      10      (3)

Node Type     =       1
Node Name     =  DBSVR01
Release Level =    512

(1) - Stand-alone/Server
(2) - Stand-alone/Server/Requester-Server/Requester
(3) - Server

OK, sql_rcd = 0,        Execution time =     0.1800 secs

--    /***************   Up the number of allowable databases       *********/
EXEC DBA:      UPDATE_DM_CFG   NUMDB      = 8 ;

OK, sql_rcd = 0,        Execution time =     0.6500 secs

--    /***************  What is the current ID authorized to do?     *********/
EXEC DBA:      GET_ADMIN;

Authorization type                Authorized? (0=NO, 1=YES)
------------------                -------------------------
System Administrator                        1
Database Administrator                      1
Create Tables                               1
Bind new Programs                           1
Access current database                     1
Group System Administrator                  1
Group Database Administrator                1
Group Create Tables                         1
Group Bind new Programs                     1
Group Access current database               1

OK, sql_rcd = 0,        Execution time =     0.2800 secs

--    /***************  Collect system, database, and user status    *********/
EXEC DBA:      COLLECT_STATUS sample;

System Status
-------------
 Current Normalized time          = 640525779 seconds elapsed from 1-1-1970
 Time Zone Displacement           = -1 seconds different from UTC
 Product name                     = IBM OS/2 Database Services
 Component Identification         = 566933603
 Release Level                    = 1.20
 Correct Service Level            = WR04053_
```

Figure 20-25 (Part 2 of 3). Script 21: Looking Inside the Configuration Files.

```
Database Status
---------------
 Normalized time of last backup   = 0 seconds elapsed from 1-1-1970
 Time Zone Displacement           = 0 seconds different from UTC
 Number of connects               = 1
 Database alias                   = SAMPLE
 Database Name                    = SAMPLE
 Location                         = L
 Database drive                   = C:
 Node Name                        =
 Database Type                    = OS2 DBM

User Status
-----------
 Transactions since connect       = 5
 Requests since connect           = 23
 Requests current transaction     = 0
 Elapsed time since connect       = 343 seconds
 Elapsed time, current transaction = 2 seconds
 Authorization ID                 = JERI
 Node Name                        =  DBSVR01
 Authority Level                  = 7967
 Transaction State                = S
 Lock State                       = N

OK, sql_rcd = 0,        Execution time =      1.0400 secs
```

Figure 20-25 (Part 3 of 3). Script 21: Looking Inside the Configuration Files.

Creating a Database and Viewing the Directories

In the script that follows we look at the contents of the **System**, **Volume** and **Node** directories. You may recall from the tutorial ("Database Directory Services" on page 456) that OS/2 EE uses a distributed directory strategy which involves keeping on every RDS machine information about local database objects as well as information about how to get to remote databases. Here is a refresher on database directories:

System This is the master directory for a workstation. It contains an entry for each local or remote database that can be accessed from that workstation.

Volume This is a directory which contains an entry for every database on a logical disk drive. This directory gets updated automatically by the Database Manager each time a database is created or deleted on an OS/2 logical disk drive. This directory must exist on every OS/2 drive that contains one or more databases.

Node This is a directory which contains an entry for each remote database site that can be accessed. The information in this directory is used by RDS to connect with the remote workstations.

```
--
--        ******** Viewing the Node, System, and Volume Directories     ******
--
--   /***************   Show the contents of the SYSTEM directory   *********/
EXEC DBA:       SHOW_DB_DIR 0;

 Database Directory for Drive 0:
 ================================

 Alias    Name     Drive Directory Node     Comment                        Type
 -------- -------- ----- --------- -------- ------------------------------ ----
 TP1      TP1      C:                       TP1_Test_Database              0
 CLUB     CLUB     D:                       Club_Med_Database              0
 SAMPLE   SAMPLE   C:                       Sample Database                0

 OK, sql_rcd = 0,        Execution time =     0.1500 secs

--   /***************   Show the VOLUME directory for drive C:      *********/
EXEC DBA:       SHOW_DB_DIR C;

 Database Directory for Drive C:
 ================================

 Alias    Name     Drive Directory Node     Comment                        Type
 -------- -------- ----- --------- -------- ------------------------------ ----
 TP1      TP1      C:    SQL00002           TP1_Test_Database              2
 SAMPLE   SAMPLE   C:    SQL00001           Sample Database                2

 OK, sql_rcd = 0,        Execution time =     0.1900 secs

--   /***************   Show the NODE directory for this machine    *********/
EXEC DBA:       SHOW_NODE_DIR;

 Node Directory
 ==============

 Node      Local LU  Partner LU  Mode      Comment
 --------  --------  ----------  --------  ------------------------------
 DBSVR03   LU1       LU2         SQLLOO    RDS_SERVER_03

 OK, sql_rcd = 0,        Execution time =     0.3200 secs

--   /***************   Disconnect from the sample database         *********/
EXEC DBA:       STOPUSE sample;

 OK, sql_rcd = 0,        Execution time =     2.1800 secs

--   /***************   Create a database called NEW_DB1 on drive C: *********/
EXEC DBA:       CREATE_DB new_db1 C This_is_a_test;

 OK, sql_rcd = 0,        Execution time =    51.4700 secs
```

Figure 20-26 (Part 1 of 2). Script 22: Creating a DB and Viewing the Directories.

```
--    /***************   Show the contents of the SYSTEM directory    *********/
EXEC DBA:        SHOW_DB_DIR 0;

 Database Directory for Drive 0:
 ================================

 Alias     Name      Drive Directory Node      Comment                         Type
 --------  --------  ----- --------- --------  ------------------------------  ----
 NEW_DB1   NEW_DB1   C:                         This_is_a_test                  0
 TP1       TP1       C:                         TP1_Test_Database               0
 CLUB      CLUB      D:                         Club_Med_Database               0
 SAMPLE    SAMPLE    C:                         Sample Database                 0

 OK, sql_rcd = 0,        Execution time =     0.2500 secs

--      /*************   Let's get rid of the junk databases          *********/
EXEC DBA:       DROP_DB new_dbl;

 OK, sql_rcd = 0,        Execution time =     3.1800 secs
```

Figure 20-26 (Part 2 of 2). **Script 22: Creating a DB and Viewing the Directories.**

How to Backup and Restore a Database

The script below shows how RSQL can be used to perform routine maintenance tasks on a database.

```
--
--      ******** A Script for how to Backup and Restore a database *********
--
--    /***************   To make things go faster...                  *********/
EXEC SQL:       DROP TABLE ACCT;

 OK, sql_rcd = 0,        Execution time =     5.6000 secs

--    /***************   Disconnect from the sample database          *********/
EXEC DBA:       STOPUSE sample;

 OK, sql_rcd = 0,        Execution time =     1.4700 secs

--    /***************   Backup "ALL" the database to the A:  drive   *********/
EXEC DBA:       BACKUP sample ALL A;

 OK, sql_rcd = 0,        Execution time =   263.7200 secs

--    /***************   Delete the sample database from the system   *********/
EXEC DBA:       DROP_DB  sample;

 OK, sql_rcd = 0,        Execution time =     4.3100 secs

--    /***************   Let's restore it from the backup A: to  C:   *********/
EXEC DBA:       RESTORE sample C  A;

 OK, sql_rcd = 0,        Execution time =   122.1300 secs
```

Figure 20-27 (Part 1 of 2). **Script 23: How to Backup and Restore a Database.**

```
-- bind the rsql program
--     /***************   BIND the RSQL  program                        *********/
EXEC DBA: BIND sample rsql.bnd ISO UNCOMMITTED_READ BLOCK_ALL USERID;

 OK, sql_rcd = 0,        Execution time =     3.3700 secs

--      /************* Reconnect  to database sample                   *********/
EXEC DBA:       STARTUSE sample S;

 OK, sql_rcd = 0,        Execution time =     1.8800 secs

--      /************* Let's see if it still works                     *********/
EXEC SQL:       SELECT * FROM neworg;

 DEPTNUMB  DEPTNAME        MANAGER  DIVISION    LOCATION
 --------  --------------  -------  ----------  -------------
 99        Software        NULL     Oceanview   Hawai
 90        Multimedia      NULL     Oceanview   Tahiti

 Total Number of Rows SELECTED = 2
 OK, sql_rcd = 0,        Execution time =     0.4000 secs
```

Figure 20-27 (Part 2 of 2). Script 23: How to Backup and Restore a Database.

QUERY MANAGER CALLABLE INTERFACE SCRIPTS

You can execute any of the Query Manager Callable Interface commands through RSQL scripts. The script that follows demonstrates the general principle. Please reference the railroad diagrams in "The RSQL Syntax for the Query Manager Callable Interface" on page 974 for an explanation of how these commands are used in RSQL scripts. The commands shown in this script will appear very cryptic if you haven't already gone through the Query Manager Callable Interface tutorial.

```
--      ******** Playing with the Query Manager Callable Interface    ******
--
--     /***************   Disconnect from the sample database          *********/
EXEC DBA:   STOPUSE sample;

 OK, sql_rcd = 0,        Execution time =     1.8800 secs

--     /***************   Start Query Manager                          *********/
EXEC QM: START DSQSMODE = INTERACTIVE, DSQDSPLY = IMMEDIATE;

 OK, qm_rcd = 0,        Execution time =    25.6300 secs

--     /*************** Begin Query Manager Window                      *********/
EXEC QM: BEGIN WINDOW;

 OK, qm_rcd = 0,        Execution time =     0.0000 secs
```

Figure 20-28 (Part 1 of 3). Script 24: Query Manager Callable Interface Script.

```
-- Query Manager Define Table Screen
EXEC QM: DEFINE TABLE;

 OK, qm_rcd = 0,        Execution time =    43.6900 secs

--    /*************** Query Manager LIST                              *********/
EXEC QM: LIST TABLES;

 OK, qm_rcd = 0,        Execution time =     1.9600 secs

--    /*************** Query Manager MESSAGE                           *********/
EXEC QM: MESSAGE (TEXT= 'Hello World!' DISPLAY=IMMED);

 OK, qm_rcd = 0,        Execution time =     4.5300 secs

--    /*************** set a variable CHAR value                       *********/
EXEC QM: SET LOCAL CHAR MYTEMP1 = YES1;

 OK, qm_rcd = 0,        Execution time =     0.0300 secs

--    /*************** get a variable CHAR value                       *********/
EXEC QM: GET LOCAL CHAR MYTEMP1;

 OK, qm_rcd = 0,        Execution time =     0.0600 secs

--    /*************** set a variable FINT value                       *********/
EXEC QM: SET LOCAL CHAR MYTEMP2 = 1001;

 OK, qm_rcd = 0,        Execution time =     0.0400 secs

--    /*************** get a variable FINT value                       *********/
EXEC QM: GET LOCAL CHAR MYTEMP2;

     MYTEMP2 = 1001

 OK, qm_rcd = 0,        Execution time =     0.0600 secs

--    /*************** run a query                                     *********/
EXEC QM: RUN QUERY SEL_ORG;

 OK, qm_rcd = 0,        Execution time =     2.8100 secs

--    /*************** get FINT system variable                        *********/
EXEC QM: GET GLOBAL CHAR DSQAROWS, DSQSQLEC;

     DSQAROWS = 8
     DSQSQLEC = 0

 OK, qm_rcd = 0,        Execution time =     0.0600 secs

--    /*************** get CHAR system variable                        *********/
EXEC QM: GET GLOBAL CHAR DSQAAUTH, DSQADBNM;

     DSQAAUTH = USERID
     DSQADBNM =

 OK, qm_rcd = 0,        Execution time =     0.0600 secs
```

Figure 20-28 (Part 2 of 3). Script 24: Query Manager Callable Interface Script.

```
--    /*************** End   Query Manager Window                    *********/
EXEC QM: END WINDOW;

--    /*************** exit Query Manager                             *********/
EXEC QM: EXIT;
```

Figure 20-28 (Part 3 of 3). Script 24: Query Manager Callable Interface Script.

Chapter 21

RSQL: Programming Dynamic SQL

This is the first of a three chapter series that examines the inner workings of the **RSQL.SQC** program. You've already seen in the last chapter how **RSQL**, the "all-in-one" database utility, was used to explore almost every aspect of the OS/2 EE Database Manager. As expected, this "all-in-one" capability comes at a price: a long journey into the **RSQL** code lies ahead. This is the bad news! The good news is that by the time you finish this long journey, which spans across three chapters, you will have accomplished the following:

- You will learn how to precompile and build a Database Manager program.
- You will learn how to program dynamic SQL.
- You will learn how to program the OS/2 EE Database Administration commands.
- You will learn how to program the Query Manager Callable Interface.
- You will have completed 80% of the journey towards your accreditation as an OS/2 EE Database Manager "programming guru."
- You will experience absolute ecstasy once you've gone through the whole thing and come out alive!

With this cheerful preview of wonderful things to come, let us now tell you how this three-chapter series is organized:

- The first chapter in the series introduces the main outline of the RSQL code, and covers the following areas:

    1. **RSQL.MAK**, the *make* file for the RSQL program.
    2. **RSQL.H**, the common header file for the RSQL program.
    3. The **main()** procedure of the RSQL program.
    4. The command handlers for the execution of **dynamic SQL** statements.
    5. The command handler for the execution of OS/2 programs from RSQL.
    6. The internals of the **SQLDA** and **SQLCA** data structures.
    7. The *common* procedures used by RSQL to read input commands, decode the parameters, measure performance, and perform error handling.

- The second chapter in the series examines the workings of the RSQL code which executes the **Query Manager Callable Interface** commands.

- The third chapter in the series examines the RSQL code which executes the **Database Administration Services**.

The RSQL code breaks nicely into three distinct functional areas: **Dynamic SQL**, **Query Manager Callable Interface**, and **Database Administration services**. The first chapter contains common procedures that you may occasionally need to reference from the other two chapters. This minor inconvenience is incurred to keep RSQL whole, so that at the end of the exercise, you will have a single general purpose "all-in-one" utility.

THE RSQL.MAK MAKE FILE

The **RSQL.MAK** make file demonstrates the process used to build a Database Manager program. Here are the points of interest:

- The database services require several new libraries: **sql_dyn** for dynamic sql services, **sql_stat** for static sql services, and **dsqci** for the Query Manager Callable Interface services. In addition, the **upm** library is needed for the User Profile Management.
- The precompiler and binder require the name of an existing database on the machine where you are compiling the program.
- The **.sqc** inference rule was introduced to precompile and bind your (.SQC) source code. If you're not clear on what this means, please review “Precompile With and Without Bind” on page 417
- The precompiler, **SQLPREP**, is run with the following options:

  /B This option is used to defer the binding. We do that to create (.BND) files. We provide an explicit BIND by running **sqlbind** separately.

  /FISO This option specifies the use of the International Standards Organization (ISO) format for date (yyyy-mm-dd) and time (hh.mm.ss) in the access plans.

  /ICS This option specifies the locking isolation level as being **Cursor Stability**; for a review of what this means refer to “Locking and Isolation Levels” on page 440.

- The modified (.C) file generated by the precompiler and binder is run through the C compiler and linker to produce executable code.

```
#************************   MACROS ***********************************

cflags=-AL -c -DLINT_ARGS -FPc -G2s -nologo -Od -W3 -Zip
lflags=/ST:30000/SE:1024/A:16/CO/NOD/L/PACKCODE/MAP
exe_libs= sql_dyn sql_stat os2 llibcep upm dsqci
database=SAMPLE

#************************  INFERENCE RULES *************************
.SUFFIXES: .sqc

.obj.exe:
      echo linking   $** to create $*.exe
      link $**,,, $(exe_libs) $(lflags), $*.def ;  >>err.lst;

.c.obj:
      echo compiling $*.c
      cl $(cflags) $*.c  >>err.lst

.sqc.c:
      echo preparing $*.sqc
      sqlprep $*.sqc $(database) /B /FISO /ICS >> err.lst
      echo binding   $*.bnd
      sqlbind $*.bnd $(database) >> err.lst

#************************  BUILD STATEMENTS  ************************
all: erase rsql.exe

erase:
     if exist err.lst erase err.lst

rsql.exe                  :  rsql.obj    # SQL executable module
rsql.c       rsql.obj     :  rsql.sqc    # SQL source module
```

Figure 21-1. The RSQL.MAK MAKE File.

RSQL.SQC main() Listing

RSQL is fairly straightforward; the program reads a command from a *run* file, executes it, and returns the output in a *response* file. RSQL executes the entire repertoire of OS/2 Database Manager commands, with two exceptions: static SQL commands and stored procedure calls, which are both fully covered in **Part V**. We start the journey into the RSQL code with the **main()** function (see listing in Figure 21-2), which of course serves as the outline for the **RSQL.SQC** program. The first few statements are the usual *includes* for the various C library header files. Like any good OS/2 program, RSQL includes header material from **OS2.H** which serves as the "master file" for a set of IBM- and Microsoft-provided include files that contain definitions for specific groups of OS/2 functions. The following conditional include flags are enabled:

```
#define INCL_DOSMEMMGR
#define INCL_DOSPROCESS
```

These flags indicate that RSQL will be using OS/2's memory management and tasking services.

Following the OS/2 header file are header files specific to the OS/2 EE Database Manager. We're including the OS/2 EE-supplied header files for the SQL services, Database Administration services, the User Profile Management, the Query Manager Callable Interface, and the header files for SQL data structures and return codes. The final header file to be included is **RSQL.H**, listed in Figure 21-14. This file contains RSQL's forward function declarations, the definitions of constants and data types, and the program's global variables.

The **main()** function's code follows. It serves as RSQL's executive. Here is how **main()** controls the execution of the RSQL application:

- It first invokes **initialize_rsql()**, listed in Figure 21-3. This procedure registers **exit_proc()**, also listed in Figure 21-3 as the Exit List function for RSQL. The sole purpose of this exit function is to close the *response* file in case of program failure. (This will save the results of the RSQL commands that executed before disaster struck.)

- It then invokes **check_args_and_prepare_files()**, also listed in Figure 21-3. This function accepts two user supplied program input parameters:

  - The name of the *run* file. This is the file that contains the script of RSQL commands you want executed.
  - The name of the *response* file. This is the file where you want RSQL to place the results of an execution run.

  These two files are opened and RSQL is now initialized and ready to perform its run.

- The RSQL *run* file is executed as a do loop which terminates when all the commands in *run* have been executed. Here is how the loop goes about doing its thing:

  1. A command is read from the *run* file. The command type and number is decoded by **get_command()**, listed in Figure 21-4.
  2. The timer is started. The timer code is listed in Figure 21-6.
  3. Each command is executed by the appropriate command handler. Here is a guide to where you can find these command handlers:
     - The command handler for immediate dynamic SQL commands is **sql_immediate()**, listed in Figure 21-7.
     - The command handler for varying-list dynamic SQL SELECTs is **sql_select()**, listed in Figure 21-9.
     - The command handler which executes OS/2 programs from within RSQL is **dos_exec()**, listed in Figure 21-11.
     - The top-level command handler for the Query Manager Callable Interface is **qm_exec()**. The code for that handler and its assistants is provided in Chapter 22, "RSQL: Programming Query Manager" on page 595.
     - The top-level command handler for the Database Administration Commands is **dba_exec()**. The code for that handler and its numerous assist-

ants is provided in Chapter 23, "RSQL: Programming the Database Administration API" on page 617.

4. The timer is stopped. The elapsed time for the execution of the command is saved (the timer procedures are listed in Figure 21-6).
5. The results of the execution of the command, including the elapsed time, are recorded in the *response* file by our results handler. The name of the our results handler is **record_command_results()** and its code listing can be found in Figure 21-13.

- When there are no commands left to process in the *run* file, the program exits the loop and the function **terminate_program()**, listed in Figure 21-3, is invoked to close all open files.

```
/*************************************************************************/
/*  PROGRAM NAME:  RSQL.SQC    -- Run SQL program                        */
/*                                                                       */
/*  DESCRIPTION:  This program allows a user to run a batch file consisting  */
/*    of SQL and Database Administrator commands against an OS2/EE database. */
/*    The script is submitted to RSQL in a command file and the results      */
/*    appear in a response file.  RSQL runs as an OS2 task and does not      */
/*    require the services of Query Manager.                                 */
/*                                                                       */
/*  PROGRAM INVOCATION:                                                  */
/*                                                                       */
/*    rsql cmd_file resp_file                                            */
/*                                                                       */
/*         cmd_file  = run file that contains the user script            */
/*         resp_file = response file that contains the output            */
/*************************************************************************/
#include <process.h>                        /* For exit()                 */
#include <stdio.h>                          /* For printf() & NULL        */
#include <stdlib.h>                         /* For printf                 */
#include <string.h>                         /* For printf                 */
#include <sys\types.h>                      /* For time()                 */
#include <sys\timeb.h>                      /* For time()                 */
#include <sys\stat.h>                       /* For stat()                 */
#include <io.h>                             /* For file I/O               */
#include <conio.h>                          /* For getch and kbhit        */
#include <fcntl.h>                          /* For file I/O               */

#define INCL_DOSMEMMGR
#define INCL_DOSPROCESS
#include <os2.h>

#include <sqlca.h>                          /* For sqlca                  */
#include <sql.h>                            /* For error msg retrieval    */
#include <sqlcodes.h>                       /* For SQL return code constants */
#include <sqlenv.h>                         /* For environment functions  */
#include <sqlutil.h>                        /* For utility functions      */
#include <dsqcommc.h>                       /* For QM callable interface  */
#include <upm.h>                            /* For logon/logoff functions */
struct   sqlca sqlca;                       /* For DB mgr return codes    */

#include "rsql.h"
```

Figure 21-2 (Part 1 of 3). RSQL.SQC main().

```
/*---------------------------------------------------------------------------*/
/* Main function.                                                            */
/*---------------------------------------------------------------------------*/
VOID main(USHORT argc, PCHAR argv[])
{
  SHORT cmd_type;
  SHORT ch;

  initialize_rsql();

  check_args_and_prepare_files(argc, argv);

  /*----------------------------------------*/
  /* Process commands one at a time         */
  /*----------------------------------------*/
  while (!feof(cmd_stream))
   {
    /*----------------------------------------*/
    /* get next command                       */
    /*----------------------------------------*/
    cmd_type = get_command(parm_buf);

    /*----------------------------------------*/
    /* Initialize Timer                       */
    /*----------------------------------------*/
    reset_timer();
    start_timer();

    /*----------------------------------------*/
    /* Execute the command.                   */
    /*----------------------------------------*/
    switch (cmd_type)
    {                 /*----------------------------------*/
                      /*   Dynamic SQL commands           */
                      /*----------------------------------*/
      case CMD_SQL_IMMEDIATE      : rcd = sql_immediate(parm_buf);     break;
      case CMD_SQL_SELECT         : rcd = sql_select(parm_buf);        break;
                      /*----------------------------------*/
                      /*   Execute an OS/2 program        */
                      /*----------------------------------*/
      case CMD_DOS                : rcd = dos_exec(parm_buf);          break;
                      /*----------------------------------*/
                      /* Query Manager Callable Interface */
                      /*----------------------------------*/
      case CMD_QM                 : rcd = qm_exec(parm_buf);           break;
                      /*----------------------------------*/
                      /* Database Administration Commands */
                      /*----------------------------------*/
      case CMD_DBA                : rcd = dba_exec(parm_buf);          break;
                      /*----------------------------------*/
                      /*  RSQL execution controls         */
                      /*----------------------------------*/
      case CMD_DBA_CONTINUE_ON_ERROR : rcd = RECORD_NOTHING;
                                       continue_on_error = TRUE;       break;
      case CMD_DBA_STOP_ON_ERROR     : rcd = RECORD_NOTHING;
                                       continue_on_error = FALSE;      break;
```

Figure 21-2 (Part 2 of 3). RSQL.SQC main().

```
        case CMD_DBA_PAUSE              : rcd = RECORD_NOTHING;
                                          printf("\nPausing! Press any key "
                                                 "to continue...");
                                          while (!kbhit());
                                          ch = getch();
                                          break;
        case CMD_SYNTAX_ERROR           : rcd = RECORD_ERR_MSG;          break;
        case CMD_NO_CMD                 : rcd = RECORD_NOTHING;          break;

        default: break;
      } /* endswitch */
      /*-----------------------------------------*/
      /* Stop the timer, record the results,     */
      /* terminate command processing if error   */
      /*-----------------------------------------*/
      stop_timer();
      if (record_command_results(rcd)  == TERMINATE)
         break;

    }/* endwhile not eof */

  terminate_program();
} /* end main */
```

Figure 21-2 (Part 3 of 3). RSQL.SQC main().

RSQL.SQC: Listing of Top Level Functions

The functions listed in this section are the non-command handler functions called by RSQL's **main()** procedure. The listing for those functions is provided in Figure 21-3. Collectively, these top level functions initialize RSQL, open its *run* and *response* files, and then close those files when the program either terminates normally or abnormally. This ensures that you will always know what last happened by looking at the contents of the *response* file, even if the RSQL program terminates abnormally. You should find no surprises in the code that follows:

```
/*--------------------------------------------------------------------------*/
/* perform required program initialization                                  */
/*--------------------------------------------------------------------------*/
VOID initialize_rsql(VOID)
{
  /*------------------------------------------*/
  /* Enable the exit list procedure           */
  /*------------------------------------------*/
   DosExitList(1,                             /* 1 = Add to exit list        */
               (PFNEXITLIST) exit_proc);      /* pointer to procedure        */
} /* end initialize_rsql */
```

Figure 21-3 (Part 1 of 3). RSQL.SQC Listing of Top Level Functions.

```
/*-----------------------------------------------------------------------*/
/* Check for the right number of program arguments and open files.       */
/*-----------------------------------------------------------------------*/
VOID check_args_and_prepare_files(USHORT argc, PCHAR argv[])
{
  /*-----------------------------------*/
  /* Are the required parameters there?    */
  /*-----------------------------------*/
  if (argc < 3)
  {  fprintf(stderr,"\nCalling syntax is: rsql run_file resp_file");
     exit(1);
  }  /* endif */
  /*-----------------------------------*/
  /* Open the RUN and RESPONSE files.      */
  /*-----------------------------------*/
  if (NULL == (cmd_stream = fopen(argv[1], "r")))
  {  printf("\nError opening the RUN file :  %s", argv[1]);
     exit(1);
  }  /* endif */

  if (NULL == (out_stream = fopen(argv[2], "w")))
  {  printf("\nError opening the RESPONSE file :  %s", argv[2]);
     exit(1);
  }  /* endif */
} /* end check_args_and_prepare_files */

/*-----------------------------------------------------------------------*/
/* Clean up and terminate the program.                                   */
/*-----------------------------------------------------------------------*/
VOID terminate_program(VOID)
{
  fclose(cmd_stream);
  fclose(out_stream);
} /* end terminate_program */

/*-----------------------------------------------------------------------*/
/*  This procedure displays how the program terminated and performs cleanup  */
/*  if abnormal termination.                                             */
/*-----------------------------------------------------------------------*/
VOID FAR exit_proc(USHORT term_code)
{
                      /*-------------------*/
                      /*Determine cause     */
                      /*-------------------*/
   switch (term_code)
    {  case  0  :
              printf("\n**program terminated normally**\n");
              break;
       case  1  :
              printf("\n**program terminated by hard error**\n");
              break;
       case  2  :
              fclose(cmd_stream);
              fclose(out_stream);
              printf("\n**program terminated by a trap**\n ");
              break;
```

Figure 21-3 (Part 2 of 3). RSQL.SQC Listing of Top Level Functions.

```
        case  3  :
              fclose(cmd_stream);
              fclose(out_stream);
              printf("\n**program terminated by a DosKillProcess**\n");
              break;
       default :
                   printf("\n**unknown program termination**\n");
     } /* end switch */

                        /*________________________*/
                        /* Allow next exit list*/
                        /*________________________*/
     DosExitList(3,                                /* 3 allows next exit to run */
                 (void far *) 0);                  /* null pointer              */
   } /* end exit_proc */
```

Figure 21-3 (Part 3 of 3). RSQL.SQC Listing of Top Level Functions.

The get_command() Function

The **get_command()** procedure (see Figure 21-4) retrieves a command from the *run* file and provides a first-level parsing of the command and its parameters. This information is used by **main()** to dispatch the appropriate command handler. The **get_command()** procedure will format the commands so that they can be directly executed. The extracted parameters are placed in a global **parm_str** variable. Most of the parameters will need further parsing, but this will be done by the individual command handlers.

The following is a step-by-step summary of what **get_command()** does:

1. It reads a command from the *run* file. The C-language **fscanf()** is used to read in a string of characters from the *run* file until a ";" terminator is found. The string of characters may span across multiple lines in the *run* file, in the case of multi-line commands.

2. It writes the command line in the *response* file. This way you'll be able to see command/response pairs when viewing the results of a run.

3. It removes comment lines from the command.

4. It parses the first four tokens of a command to determine the type of the command.

5. It performs the following command and parameter preparation based on the type of command that is parsed:

   - For *SQL commands*, the "EXEC SQL:" header and the Carriage-Return and Line-Feed characters are stripped off the command string. In addition, the third token in the header is decoded to determine whether this is an SQL SELECT command. Based on the decode, the procedure either returns a

CMD_SQL_SELECT or a CMD_SQL_IMMEDIATE. The **parm_str** variable will contain the SQL command to be executed.

- For *DOS commands*, the "EXEC DOS:" header is stripped off the command string. The **parm_str** variable will contain the name of the OS/2 program to be executed, followed by a NULL, followed by any parameters to be passed to the **DosExecPgm** API call.

- For *QM commands*, the "EXEC QM:" header is stripped off the command string. The **parm_str** variable will contain the Query Manager command string to be executed.

- For *DBA commands*, the "EXEC DBA:" header is stripped off the command string. A **cmds** array is searched for a Database Administration command name that matches this command. If a match is found, a command number and the maximum number of parameters for this command is retrieved from the array. The **parm_str** variable will contain the command parameters in their input string format. In addition, the entries from the **cmds** array for this command are placed in the **parms** data structure. As you will see later, **parms** serves as a *global blackboard* which maintains context for the Database Administration command that is currently being executed. The definition of **parms** is given in RSQL.H (see Figure 21-14).

The **get_command()** procedure does not introduce any new OS/2 programming constructs. It's just straight C code that is part of the overhead required for making RSQL end-user friendly.

```
/*--------------------------------------------------------------------*/
/*  This procedure determines the command type                        */
/*--------------------------------------------------------------------*/
SHORT get_command(PCHAR parm_str)
{ char  cmd[MAX_CMD_SIZE];            /* temp buffer for cmd processing   */
  char  token1[5];                    /* token to receive EXEC            */
  char  token2[5];                    /* token to receive DBA: or SQL:    */
  char  token3[25];                   /* token to receive cmd name        */
  char  token4[MAX_CMD_SIZE];         /* token to receive parms           */

  /*-----------------------------------*/
  /* Initialize cmds table             */
  /*-----------------------------------*/
  typedef struct
  { CHAR      cmd_name[40];           /* cmd name                         */
    CHAR      cmd_num;                /* numerical representation of cmd  */
    USHORT    num_parms;              /* number of parms for this command */
  } CMD_TYPE;
  static CMD_TYPE cmds[] =
  {/*<--- cmd_name ---><-- cmd_num ------------------><-- num_parms -->*/
   {"BACKUP",          CMD_DBA_BACKUP                ,  3              },
   {"BIND",            CMD_DBA_BIND                  ,  6              },
   {"CATALOG_DB",      CMD_DBA_CATALOG_DB            ,  6              },
```

Figure 21-4 (Part 1 of 4). RSQL.SQC Listing of the get_command() Function.

```
     {"CATALOG_NODE",      CMD_DBA_CATALOG_NODE        , 5              },
     {"COLLECT_STATUS",    CMD_DBA_COLLECT_STATUS      , 1              },
     {"CONTINUE_ON_ERROR",CMD_DBA_CONTINUE_ON_ERROR    , 0              },
     {"CREATE_DB",         CMD_DBA_CREATE_DB           , 3              },
     {"DROP_DB",           CMD_DBA_DROP_DB             , 1              },
     {"EXPORT",            CMD_DBA_EXPORT              , 4              },
     {"GET_ADMIN",         CMD_DBA_GET_ADMIN           , 0              },
     {"IMPORT",            CMD_DBA_IMPORT              , 5              },
     {"LOGOFF",            CMD_DBA_LOGOFF              , 3              },
     {"LOGON",             CMD_DBA_LOGON               , 5              },
     {"PAUSE",             CMD_DBA_PAUSE               , 0              },
     {"REORG",             CMD_DBA_REORG               , 3              },
     {"RESET_DM_CFG",      CMD_DBA_RESET_DM_CFG        , 0              },
     {"RESET_DB_CFG",      CMD_DBA_RESET_DB_CFG        , 1              },
     {"RESTORE",           CMD_DBA_RESTORE             , 3              },
     {"RUNSTATS",          CMD_DBA_RUNSTATS            , 1              },
     {"SHOW_DB_CFG",       CMD_DBA_SHOW_DB_CFG         , 1              },
     {"SHOW_DB_DIR",       CMD_DBA_SHOW_DB_DIR         , 1              },
     {"SHOW_DM_CFG",       CMD_DBA_SHOW_DM_CFG         , 0              },
     {"SHOW_NODE_DIR",     CMD_DBA_SHOW_NODE_DIR       , 0              },
     {"STARTDM",           CMD_DBA_STARTDM             , 0              },
     {"STARTUSE",          CMD_DBA_STARTUSE            , 2              },
     {"STOPDM",            CMD_DBA_STOPDM              , 0              },
     {"STOP_ON_ERROR",     CMD_DBA_STOP_ON_ERROR       , 0              },
     {"STOPUSE",           CMD_DBA_STOPUSE             , 0              },
     {"UNCATALOG_DB",      CMD_DBA_UNCATALOG_DB        , 1              },
     {"UNCATALOG_NODE",    CMD_DBA_UNCATALOG_NODE      , 1              },
     {"UPDATE_DB_CFG",     CMD_DBA_UPDATE_DB_CFG       , 2              },
     {"UPDATE_DM_CFG",     CMD_DBA_UPDATE_DM_CFG       , 0              } };
    SHORT      cmd_not_found;              /* True if a match is found        */
    USHORT     i;                          /* loop index variable             */
    PCHAR      char_ptr;                   /* used to remove CRLF from SQL stmts*/

    /*------------------------------------------*/
    /* Read a command from the RUN file         */
    /*------------------------------------------*/
    num_parms = fscanf(cmd_stream," %[^;]%*c ", cmd);
    if (num_parms == EOF)
       return(CMD_NO_CMD);                               /* empty file        */
    strcat(cmd,";");                                     /* maintain cmd delim. */

    /*------------------------------------------*/
    /* Echo command to the response file        */
    /*------------------------------------------*/
    fprintf(out_stream,"%s\n", cmd);

    /*------------------------------------------*/
    /* Remove any comment lines                 */
    /*------------------------------------------*/
    while ((cmd[0] == '-') && (cmd[1] == '-'))
      {
       num_parms = sscanf(cmd,"%*[^\n]\n%[^;]%*c",cmd); /* remove comment line */
       if (num_parms == EOF)
          return (CMD_NO_CMD);                           /* ";" within a comment*/
       strcat(cmd,";");                                  /* maintain cmd delim. */
      }
```

Figure 21-4 (Part 2 of 4). RSQL.SQC Listing of the get_command() Function.

```
/*-------------------------------------------*/
/* parse the command, make some validity    */
/* checks                                    */
/*-------------------------------------------*/
num_parms = sscanf(cmd," %4s %4s %24s %[^;]", token1, token2, token3, token4);

if (num_parms == 3)                      /* no parms, parse accordingly */
   {
     num_parms = sscanf(cmd, " %4s %4s %24[^;]", token1, token2, token3);
     strcpy(token4,"");
   }

if ( (num_parms < 3)              ||
     (strcmp(token1,"EXEC") != 0) ||
     ((strcmp(token2,"DBA:" ) != 0) && (strcmp(token2,"DOS:" ) != 0) &&
      (strcmp(token2,"QM:" ) != 0) && (strcmp(token2,"SQL:" ) != 0)) )
   {
     sprintf(err_msg,
     "\nSYNTAX ERROR: Expected EXEC SQL: or EXEC DBA: etc..."
     " to begin a command.");
     return(CMD_SYNTAX_ERROR);
   }
/*-------------------------------------------*/
/* SQL CMD, return command type,             */
/* remove EXEC SQL:                          */
/*-------------------------------------------*/
if (strcmp(token2,"SQL:" ) == 0)
   {
    char_ptr = strpbrk(token4,"\n\r");              /* remove CRLF chars   */
    while (char_ptr != NULL)
      {
        char_ptr[0] = ' ';
        char_ptr = strpbrk(char_ptr,"\n\r");
      }

    sprintf(parm_str, "%s %s", token3, token4);     /* return the cmd for  */
    if (strcmp(strupr(token3),"SELECT" ) == 0)      /*    processing       */
        return(CMD_SQL_SELECT);
    else
        return(CMD_SQL_IMMEDIATE);
   } /* end if */

/*-------------------------------------------*/
/* DOS CMD, return command type,             */
/* remove EXEC DOS:                          */
/*-------------------------------------------*/
if (strcmp(token2,"DOS:" ) == 0)
   {
    sprintf(parm_str, "%s%c%s", token3, 0, token4);  /* return the cmd for  */
                                                     /*   in the form for   */
                                                     /*   DosExecPgm        */
    return(CMD_DOS);
   } /* end if */
```

Figure 21-4 (Part 3 of 4). RSQL.SQC Listing of the get_command() Function.

```
/*---------------------------------------*/
/* QM CMD, return command type,          */
/* remove EXEC QM:                       */
/*---------------------------------------*/
if (strcmp(token2,"QM:" ) == 0)
   {
    sprintf(parm_str, "%s %s", token3, token4);
    return(CMD_QM);
   } /* end if */

/*---------------------------------------*/
/* DBA CMD, return command type,         */
/* remove "EXEC DBA: cmd_name"           */
/*---------------------------------------*/
i = 0 ;
cmd_not_found = TRUE ;

while ( cmd_not_found && (i < CMD_LAST_CMD))
{
  cmd_not_found = strcmp(cmds[i].cmd_name,token3);
  if (!cmd_not_found)
     break;
  else
     i++;
}

if (cmd_not_found )
{
  sprintf(err_msg,
  "\nSYNTAX ERROR: Unknown Command. ");
  return(CMD_SYNTAX_ERROR);
}

if ((cmds[i].cmd_num ==CMD_DBA_CONTINUE_ON_ERROR) ||
    (cmds[i].cmd_num ==CMD_DBA_STOP_ON_ERROR) ||
    (cmds[i].cmd_num ==CMD_DBA_PAUSE))
{
  return(cmds[i].cmd_num);
} /* endif */

sprintf(parm_str, "%s", token4);
strcpy(parms.cmd_name,cmds[i].cmd_name);
parms.cmd_num = cmds[i].cmd_num;
parms.num_parms = cmds[i].num_parms;
return(CMD_DBA);
} /* end get_command */
```

Figure 21-4 (Part 4 of 4). RSQL.SQC Listing of the get_command() Function.

The Timer Functions

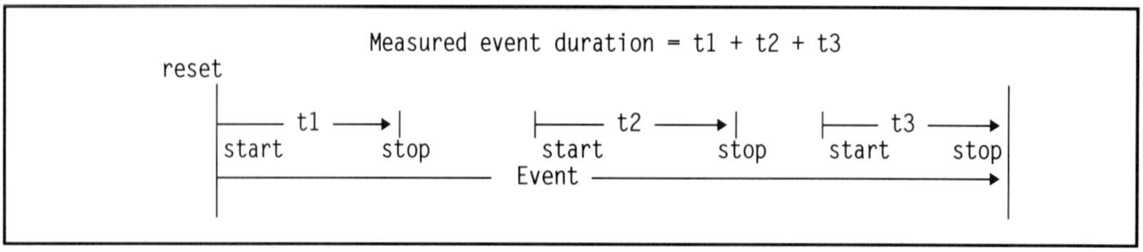

Figure 21-5. Playing with the RSQL Timer Functions.

This section contains the listing for three very straightforward procedures that are used to measure the execution time of an RSQL command. The **reset_timer()** function initializes the timer variables. You can then use **start_timer()** and **stop_timer()** calls to start and stop time measurements. This allows us to refine our command performance measurements by pausing the timers during processing intervals that are not part of the command performance.

```
/*----------------------------------------------------------------------*/
/*  This procedure initializes the time variables.                      */
/*----------------------------------------------------------------------*/
VOID   reset_timer(VOID)
{
  event_time = 0.0 ;
  start_time = 0.0 ;
  end_time   = 0.0 ;
} /* end reset_time */

/*----------------------------------------------------------------------*/
/*  This procedure records the time at the start of an interval         */
/*----------------------------------------------------------------------*/
VOID   start_timer(VOID)
{
  ftime(&timebuff);
  start_time = (double)timebuff.time+((double)timebuff.millitm)/(double)1000;
} /* end start_time */

/*----------------------------------------------------------------------*/
/*  This procedure records the time at the end of an interval           */
/*  and calculates the elapsed time for an event.                       */
/*----------------------------------------------------------------------*/
VOID   stop_timer(VOID)
{
  ftime(&timebuff);
  end_time = (double)timebuff.time+((double)timebuff.millitm)/(double)1000;
  event_time = event_time  + (end_time - start_time);
} /* end stop_time */
```

Figure 21-6. RSQL.SQC Listing of the Timer Functions.

The Dynamic SQL Command Handler: sql_immediate()

The **sql_immediate()** function (see Figure 21-7) presents a gentle introduction to SQL programming. The function itself packs a lot of power. It can directly execute any SQL command with the exception of the SELECT command. Before you go on, please make sure you understand the dynamic SQL material in the tutorial ("Dynamic SQL Commands" on page 448).

The dynamic SQL statement to be executed is loaded into a character-string host variable. This is done by declaring the **cmd** pointer to be a host variable using:

- **BEGIN DECLARE SECTION**
- **END DECLARE SECTION**

The host variable is then assigned to point at the **cmd_sql** input parameter, which in turn points to **parm_str**, which contains the SQL command obtained from the *run* file by **get_command()**. The **EXECUTE IMMEDIATE** command is then used to prepare and execute the SQL statement in a single operation.

The SQL command's return code is contained in **sqlca**, a global variable of type SQLCA declared at the start of the program. The constant, RECORD_SQLCA, is returned by the procedure to indicate that the sqlca results should be processed. The processing of **sqlca** is performed by **record_command_results()**, listed in Figure 21-13.

```
/*---------------------------------------------------------------------*/
/* This procedure executes an sql command dynamically.                  */
/*---------------------------------------------------------------------*/
SHORT sql_immediate(PCHAR cmd_sql)
{
  /*-------------------------------------*/
  /* Declare cmd to DBM                  */
  /*-------------------------------------*/
  EXEC SQL BEGIN DECLARE SECTION;
      char         * cmd;                         /* command buffer   */
  EXEC SQL END DECLARE SECTION;
  cmd = cmd_sql;

  /*-------------------------------------*/
  /* Execute cmd                         */
  /*-------------------------------------*/
  EXEC SQL EXECUTE IMMEDIATE  :cmd;

  return (RECORD_SQLCA);
}/* end sql_immediate */
```

Figure 21-7. RSQL.SQC Listing of the Dynamic SQL sql_immediate() Function.

The Dynamic SQL Command Handler: sql_select()

If the last section was the "gentle" introduction to SQL programming, then this section is its "brutal" counterpart. The varying-list SELECT is definitely the most difficult form of SQL programming. When you're done with this command handler everything else will seem easy.

The **sql_select()** procedure gets invoked when **main()** discovers that it has a SELECT command to execute. The SELECT statement in an RSQL *run* file is of the **varying-list** variety. What this means is that no assumptions can be made about the number of columns in the SELECT statements or their data types. All of this is to be discovered at runtime by using a **PREPARE** in conjunction with a variable of type **SQLDA**. If you haven't yet done so, please make sure you go through the tutorial on the dynamic SQL commands, which starts with "Dynamic SQL Commands" on page 448.

The **sql_select()** procedure, listed in Figure 21-9, processes a SQL SELECT statement dynamically. The helper procedure **print_format_row()** (see Figure 21-10) formats the output of the result file. This two-level hierarchy will help you better navigate through the code.

The SQLDA Structure

The varying-list SELECT is one of the few SQL commands that require an intimate knowledge of the SQLDA. The definition of a SQLDA type is repeated in Figure 21-8 for quick reference.

```
struct SQLDA
{
   BYTE          sqldaid[8];          /* Eye catcher = 'SQLDA   '        */
   LONG          sqldabc;             /* SQLDA size in bytes = 16+44*sqln */
   SHORT         sqln;                /* Number of SQLVAR elements       */
   SHORT         sqld;                /* # of used SQLVAR elements       */
   struct sqlvar
   {
      SHORT          sqltype;         /* Variable data type              */
      SHORT          sqllen;          /* Variable data length            */
      BYTE          *sqldata;         /* Pointer to variable data value  */
      SHORT         *sqlind;          /* Pointer to Null indicator       */
      struct sqlname                  /* Variable Name                   */
      {
         SHORT           length;      /* Name length [1..30]             */
         BYTE            data[30];    /* Variable or Column name         */
      } sqlname;
   } sqlvar[SQLVAR_NUM];
};
```

Figure 21-8. The SQLDA Structure.

Executing Varying-list SELECT: A Step-by-Step Overview

The following is a step-by-step recipe of how **sql_select()** executes a varying-list SELECT:

1. A static **sqlca** variable is declared in the include file RSQL.H (see Figure 21-14).

2. A static **sqlda** variable is also declared in the RSQL.H.

3. The SQL SELECT statement to be executed is loaded into a character-string host variable. This is done by declaring the **cmd** pointer to be a host variable through the SQL **BEGIN DECLARE SECTION** and **END DECLARE SECTION** statements. The host variable is then assigned to point at the **cmd_sql** input parameter, which in turn points to **parm_str**, which contains the SQL command obtained from the *run* file by **get_command()**.

4. The **sqlda** header fields are initialized. The SQLVAR_NUM constant is 255, the maximum number of columns in a SELECT.

5. The SELECT statement is PREPARED by issuing the following command:

   ```
   EXEC SQL PREPARE st INTO :sqlda FROM :cmd sql;
   ```

   where **st** is the name assigned to the statement in **cmd_sql**. Later, this statement name will be associated with a cursor.

6. The Database Manager parses the contents of **cmd_sql** and returns the description in the **sqlda**. The number of column elements in the SELECT is returned in the **sqld** field. Each column is represented by an array element of **sqlvar**. The Database Manager fills a description of the column **sqltype** and **sqllen**. In addition, it returns the name of the column and the length of the name.

7. The information returned in the **sqlda** is used to allocate the storage needed to hold a row of retrieved data and the null indicators. Since this is the first time **sql_select()** finds out about the data types, it will allocate the storage dynamically for each item in the select list and store the pointers to data areas in the **sqlda**. Notice how the **sqlda** is being used as a global black-board where all the relevant information is stored as the execution of the statement progresses.

8. At this point, there is enough information in the **sqlda** to format the names of the column headings of the result file. This is done by issuing two calls to the **print_format_row()** helper function:

   - The first invocation of **print_format_row()** passes the SET_TABS_WIDTH parameter, which tells **print_format_row()** to calculate start position in a line, of each table column that is part of the SELECT query. This information is calculated once for each query and stored in a data structure.

- The second invocation of **print_format_row()** passes PRINT_COLUMNS parameter, which tells **print_format_row()** to write a line to the *response* file containing the name of each table column that is part of the SELECT query.

9. A cursor named **cur** is then declared for the **st** statement name by invoking the command:

```
EXEC SQL DECLARE cur CURSOR FOR st;
```

   At this point, the SELECT statement is associated with a cursor.

10. The cursor is then opened by invoking:

```
EXEC SQL OPEN cur;
```

11. We are now ready to retrieve all the rows of data that meet the SELECT conditions. This is done by repeatedly executing the fetch command until all the rows in the result-set have been retrieved.

12. The repeated fetches are done in a loop by issuing:

```
EXEC SQL FETCH cur USING DESCRIPTOR :sqlda;
```

   The results of the fetch are placed in the **sqlda**. The **print_format_row()** helper function is called with the PRINT_SELECTED_ROW option, which extracts the data out of the **sqlda** and writes it to the *response* file. The code in the loop also keeps track of the number of rows read. A column heading is written to the *response* file after a specified number of rows have been read to make the final report more readable.

13. After all the rows have been read, the cursor is closed by issuing the command:

```
EXEC SQL CLOSE cur;
```

14. At this point, the number of rows read is written to the *response* file.

15. The command processor terminates normally by returning the RECORD_SQLCA parameter. Abnormal terminations return RECORD_ERR_MSG. In all cases, the return codes from running the SQL command is contained in the **sqlca**, a global variable. The **record_command_results()** processes the **sqlca** results (see Figure 21-13).

This concludes the main logic of the code which processes the **varying-list** SELECT. We still have to look at the **print_format_row()** code in the next section to understand the intricacies of information passing using the **sqlda**.

Note: The **start_timer()** and **stop_timer()** functions are used repeatedly by **sql_select()** to bracket time measurements. In order to provide a fair measure of the command execution time, we disable the counter during a write to the *response* file, or while allocating dynamic memory.

```
/*-----------------------------------------------------------------------*/
/* This procedure executes an sql command dynamically.                   */
/*-----------------------------------------------------------------------*/
SHORT sql_select(PCHAR cmd)
{
  SHORT  index, i ;                    /* for counting                  */
  SHORT  num_of_rows;                  /* number of rows selected       */
  SHORT  num_brk;                      /* number of rows since break    */
  SHORT  byte_count;                   /* number of bytes to allocate   */

  /*---------------------*/
  /* Declare cmd to DBM  */
  /*---------------------*/
  EXEC SQL BEGIN DECLARE SECTION ;
   char          *  cmd_sql;           /* command buffer                */
  EXEC SQL END DECLARE SECTION ;

  cmd_sql     = cmd;
  num_of_rows = 0;
  num brk     = 0;

  /*------------------------------------------*/
  /* Initialize the sqlda                     */
  /*------------------------------------------*/
  strncpy( sqlda.sqldaid, "SQLDA   ", 8) ;
  sqlda.sqldabc =  (long ) sizeof(sqlda);
  sqlda.sqln = SQLVAR_NUM;
  sqlda.sqld = 0 ;

  /*------------------------------------------*/
  /* Prepare cmd                              */
  /*------------------------------------------*/
  EXEC SQL PREPARE st INTO :sqlda FROM :cmd_sql;
  if (SQLCODE != 0)
     return(RECORD_SQLCA);

  /*------------------------------------------*/
  /* Stop  timer                              */
  /*------------------------------------------*/
  stop_timer();

  /*------------------------------------------*/
  /*Allocate space for select variables       */
  /*------------------------------------------*/
  for (index=0; index< sqlda.sqld; index++)
    {
     if ((sqlda.sqlvar[index].sqltype ==SQL_TYP_DECIMAL) ||
         (sqlda.sqlvar[index].sqltype ==SQL_TYP_NDECIMAL)    )
      byte_count = ( LOBYTE(sqlda.sqlvar[index].sqllen) + 2 ) / 2;
     else byte_count = sqlda.sqlvar[index].sqllen;
```

Figure 21-9 (Part 1 of 3). RSQL.SQC Listing of the Dynamic SQL sql_select().

```
        sqlda.sqlvar[index].sqldata = (unsigned char *) malloc(byte_count);
        if ( sqlda.sqlvar[index].sqldata == NULL )
        { fprintf(out_stream,
          "\nOut of dynamic memory while space for select column %d",index + 1);
          return(RECORD_ERR_MSG);
        }

        /*-----------------------------------------*/
        /*Allocate space for null indicators     */
        /*-----------------------------------------*/
        if ( sqlda.sqlvar[index].sqltype & 1 )                     /*  odd   */
        { sqlda.sqlvar[index].sqlind =  (short *) malloc(2) ;
          if ( sqlda.sqlvar[index].sqldata == NULL )
          {
            fprintf(out_stream,
            "\nOut of dynamic memory while space for NULL  column %d",index +1);
            return(RECORD_ERR_MSG);
          }/* end if NULL */
         } /* end if odd */
       } /* end for */

     rcd = print_format_row(SET_TABS_WIDTH);
     if (rcd != 0 )
        return(RECORD_ERR_MSG);

     rcd = print_format_row(PRINT_COLUMNS);
     if (rcd != 0 )
        return(RECORD_ERR_MSG);

     /*------------------------------------------*/
     /* Start timer                              */
     /*------------------------------------------*/
     start_timer();

     EXEC SQL DECLARE cur CURSOR FOR st ;
     if (SQLCODE != 0)
        return(RECORD_SQLCA);

     EXEC SQL OPEN cur ;
     if (SQLCODE != 0)
        return(RECORD_SQLCA);

     /*------------------------------------------*/
     /*Handle data one row at a time             */
     /*------------------------------------------*/
     EXEC SQL FETCH cur USING DESCRIPTOR :sqlda ;
     if ((SQLCODE != 0) && (SQLCODE != SQL_RC_W100))
        return(RECORD_SQLCA);
```

Figure 21-9 (Part 2 of 3). RSQL.SQC Listing of the Dynamic SQL sql_select().

```
while ( SQLCODE == 01 )
{
  stop_timer();
  num_of_rows++;
  if (num_brk++ > BREAK_SEP)
  {

    for (i=0; i < BREAK_ROWS ; i++)
      fputs("\n",out_stream);

    print_format_row(PRINT_COLUMNS);
    num_brk = 0;
  }
  rcd =   print_format_row(PRINT_SELECTED_ROW);
  if (rcd != 0 )
     return(RECORD_ERR_MSG);
  else
  {
     start_timer();
     EXEC SQL FETCH cur USING DESCRIPTOR :sqlda ;
     if ((SQLCODE != 0) && (SQLCODE != SQL_RC_W100))
        return(RECORD_SQLCA);
  }/* end else*/
}/*end while */

EXEC SQL CLOSE cur ;
if (SQLCODE != 0)
   return(RECORD_SQLCA);

/*--------------------------------------------*/
/* Stop timer                                 */
/*--------------------------------------------*/
stop_timer();
fprintf(out_stream,"\n\n Total Number of Rows SELECTED = %d\n",num_of_rows);

/*--------------------------------------------*/
/* Free space for select variables            */
/*--------------------------------------------*/
for (index=0; index< sqlda.sqld; index++)
  {
   free(sqlda.sqlvar[index].sqldata);

   /*-----------------------------------------*/
   /*Free space for null indicators           */
   /*-----------------------------------------*/
   if ( sqlda.sqlvar[index].sqltype & 1 )                /*  odd   */
   {
     free(sqlda.sqlvar[index].sqlind);
    } /* end if odd */
  } /* end for */

 return(RECORD_SQLCA);
}/* end sql_select */
```

Figure 21-9 (Part 3 of 3). RSQL.SQC Listing of the Dynamic SQL sql_select().

The Helper Function for Dynamic SELECT: print_format_row()

The **print_format_row()** function, listed in Figure 21-10, is used to format the results of a dynamic SELECT query and write them to the *response* file. Essentially, what we are doing is creating a pretty output format of the query results (at a minimum, this is something a human being could comfortably read). The function is told through an invocation parameter to perform one of three actions:

SET_TABS_WIDTH: This action causes the width of each SELECT field to be calculated. The displacement or **tab** of each field within an output line is calculated and stored.

PRINT_COLUMNS: This action causes the underscored column headings to be written to the *response* file.

PRINT_SELECTED_ROW: This action causes one row of SELECT data to be formatted and written to the *response* file.

The **print_format_row()** obtains its information from the **sqlda**. It writes the formatted output it generates directly to the *response* file. The function maintains its internal data in a static structure of type **FLD_TYPE**, which contains the tab location and maximum width for each column that is part of a SELECT statement. A call requesting the SET_TABS_WIDTH action must be issued first, for each execution of a SELECT query. A call requesting PRINT_ROW must be issued for each row fetched. The PRINT_COLUMNS request is issued at whatever row interval you feel is most visually pleasing to see the column headings for the report.

What the SET_TABS_WIDTH Action Does

For each field in the SELECT statement (as stored in the sqlda), do the following:

1. Record the length of the column's name and the length of the data field from the **sqlda**, and assign them to the variables: **col_name_width** and **col_fld_width**.
2. If the field is a non-string SQL type, then over-write the **col_fld_width** variable with the string-representation width of that type. This is what the switch is all about.
3. Store the larger of **col_name_width** or **col_fld_width** in the width field of the array **FLD_TYPE**.
4. Calculate the tab position by adding the field width just calculated to the tab displacement of the previous field and the length of the column separator. Store the calculated tab value in tab position field of the array of **FLD_TYPE**.

What the PRINT COLUMNS Action Does

This is a simple function to perform:

1. The column names are concatenated in a buffer using the information in the array of **FLD_TYPE**.
2. The buffer is then written to the *response* file.
3. The buffer is then cleared.
4. A row of underscores for the column names is assembled in the buffer also using the information in the array of **FLD_TYPE**.
5. The buffer is then written to the *response* file.

What the PRINT_SELECTED_ROW Action Does

For each field in the SELECT statement (i.e., sqlda), do the following:

1. Test if the field is null; if so, write the string "NULL" in the **temp** character string variable.
2. If the field is not NULL, format the string-representation of the output value of the field and write it to the **temp** variable. As you can see, there are three types of formatting conversions:

    - The SQL character types do not require any formatting and are simply copied "as is" using the strncpy() call.

    - The SQL data types that have C-language equivalents are formatted using sprintf().

    - The SQL data types for which there are no C-language equivalents are formatted through "brute force" code. We do whatever it takes to convert the data into a string-format representation, and it may not be pretty.

3. The contents of **temp** are copied into the output buffer using the positional information in the array of **FLD_TYPE**.

When all the fields have been processed, the buffer is then written to the *response* file.

```
/*------------------------------------------------------------------------*/
/*  This procedure performs requested format actions:                     */
/*                                                                        */
/*  SET_TABS_WIDTH calculates the tab position for each field in a Query  */
/*  PRINT_COLUMNS  formats one row of columns using the tabs and sqlda    */
/*  PRINT_SELECTED_ROW formats one SELECT row using the tabs and sqlda    */
/*------------------------------------------------------------------------*/
SHORT print_format_row(USHORT action)
{
  #define      MAX_FLDS     50              /* for this exercise            */
  SHORT        index, i, y;                 /* for counting                 */
  CHAR         row[MAX_LINE_SIZE+1];        /* row to be printed            */
  CHAR         temp[MAX_LINE_SIZE+10];      /* temp buffer                  */
  CHAR         temp1[100];                  /* second temp buffer           */
  typedef struct
  {
   SHORT     tab_pos;                       /* column position              */
   SHORT     max_width;                     /* max_width str width of type  */
  }   FLD_TYPE;
  static FLD_TYPE    field[MAX_FLDS];       /* contains the field descriptors*/

  SHORT          col_name_width;            /* width of col name            */
  SHORT          col_fld_width;             /* width of col fld             */

  static SHORT   max_num_flds;              /* number of printable columns  */
  SHORT          null_not_found;            /* a flag                       */
  USHORT         top, precision, scale ;    /* for decimal flds             */
  SHORT          bottom, point;             /* for decimal flds             */
  SHORT          len;                       /* for decimal flds             */
  UCHAR          *ptr ;                     /* for decimal flds             */
  BOOL           output_blank;              /* for decimal flds             */

  /*-----------------------------------*/
  /* Initialize                        */
  /*-----------------------------------*/
  memset(row,' ',sizeof(row));
  row[sizeof(row) + 1] = '\0';
  i = 0 ;
  rcd = GOOD;

  /*-----------------------------------*/
  /* Do action                         */
  /*-----------------------------------*/
  switch (action)
  { case SET_TABS_WIDTH :
         field[0].tab_pos = 1;              /* Start   with column 1        */
         for (index=0; index< sqlda.sqld; index++)
           {
             col_name_width = sqlda.sqlvar[index].sqlname.length;
             col_fld_width  = sqlda.sqlvar[index].sqllen;

             switch (sqlda.sqlvar[index].sqltype)
             {
               case SQL_TYP_INTEGER:
               case SQL_TYP_NINTEGER:
               case SQL_TYP_FLOAT:
               case SQL_TYP_NFLOAT:
                                   col_fld_width = 11;
                                   break ;
```

Figure 21-10 (Part 1 of 6). RSQL.SQC Listing of the Dynamic SQL Helper Functions.

```
            case SQL_TYP_SMALL:
            case SQL_TYP_NSMALL:
                           col_fld_width = 6;
                           break ;
            case SQL_TYP_DECIMAL:
            case SQL_TYP_NDECIMAL:
                           col_fld_width =
                              LOBYTE(sqlda.sqlvar[index].sqllen) + 1;
                                         /* precision + decimal point */
                           break ;
            case SQL_TYP_DATE:
            case SQL_TYP_NDATE:
                           col_fld_width = 10;
                           break ;
            case SQL_TYP_TIME:
            case SQL_TYP_NTIME:
                           col_fld_width = 8;
                           break ;
            case SQL_TYP_STAMP:
            case SQL_TYP_NSTAMP:
                           col_fld_width = 26;
                           break ;
            default :                /* string type                    */
                           break;
          } /* endswitch */

          /*----------------------------------------*/
          /* Use the larger of col_name or col_fld   */
          /*----------------------------------------*/
          if (col_name_width > col_fld_width)
                field[index].max_width =  col_name_width;
          else
                field[index].max_width =  col_fld_width;
          /*----------------------------------------*/
          /* Update tab field 1 space between columns*/
          /*----------------------------------------*/
          field[index + 1].tab_pos = field[index].tab_pos +
                                     field[index].max_width +
                                     COL_SEP ;
          /*----------------------------------------*/
          /*Check limits                             */
          /*----------------------------------------*/
          if (field[index + 1].tab_pos >  MAX_LINE_SIZE)
          { max_num_flds =  index;
            break;                   /* out of for loop                */
          }
          else
            max_num_flds = index + 1;

          if ( max_num_flds > MAX_FLDS)
            break;                   /* out of for loop                */

        } /* end for */

      break; /* end of action SET_TABS_WIDTH */
```

Figure 21-10 (Part 2 of 6). RSQL.SQC Listing of the Dynamic SQL Helper Functions.

```
case PRINT_COLUMNS :
     /*-----------------------------------------------*/
     /* Print column names                            */
     /*-----------------------------------------------*/
     for (index=0; index< max_num_flds; index++ )
          memcpy(&row[field[index].tab_pos],
                 sqlda.sqlvar[index].sqlname.data,
                 sqlda.sqlvar[index].sqlname.length);
     fprintf(out_stream,"\n%s",row);

     /*-----------------------------------------------*/
     /* Clear row buffer                              */
     /*-----------------------------------------------*/
     memset(row,' ',sizeof(row));
     row[sizeof(row) + 1] = '\0';

     /*-----------------------------------------------*/
     /* Underline  names                              */
     /*-----------------------------------------------*/
     row[sizeof(row) + 1] = '\0';
     for (index=0; index< max_num_flds; index++)
     {
       memset(temp,'-',field[index].max_width);
       memcpy(&row[field[index].tab_pos],
                 temp,field[index].max_width);
     } /* end for */
     fprintf(out_stream,"\n%s",row);
     break;

case PRINT_SELECTED_ROW:
     for (index=0; index< max_num_flds ; index++)
       {
         /*-----------------------------------------------*/
         /* Initialize                                    */
         /*-----------------------------------------------*/
         null_not_found = TRUE;

         /*-----------------------------------------------*/
         /* Is it null?                                   */
         /*-----------------------------------------------*/
         if (sqlda.sqlvar[index].sqltype & 1)
         {
            if (* (sqlda.sqlvar[index].sqlind) ==  -1  )
            {
             sprintf(temp,"NULL");
             null_not_found = FALSE;
            }
```

Figure 21-10 (Part 3 of 6). RSQL.SQC Listing of the Dynamic SQL Helper Functions.

```
         else
         {
           if (* (sqlda.sqlvar[index].sqlind) !=  0  )
              {
               sprintf(err_msg,
               "\n Truncated field  col = %d ",
               index + 1);
               rcd = FAILED;
               break;
              }
         } /* end if */
      } /* end if */

      /*----------------------------------------------*/
      /* Is not NULL field                            */
      /*----------------------------------------------*/
      if (null_not_found)
      {
        switch (sqlda.sqlvar[index].sqltype)
        {
          case SQL_TYP_INTEGER:
          case SQL_TYP_NINTEGER:
               sprintf(temp,"%ld", *(PLONG)sqlda.sqlvar[index].sqldata);
               break ;
          case SQL_TYP_SMALL:
          case SQL_TYP_NSMALL:
               sprintf(temp,"%d", *(PSHORT)sqlda.sqlvar[index].sqldata);
               break ;
          case SQL_TYP_DECIMAL:
          case SQL_TYP_NDECIMAL:
               len = sqlda.sqlvar[index].sqllen ;
               ptr = sqlda.sqlvar[index].sqldata;
               sprintf(temp,"");
               scale     = HIBYTE(len);
               precision = LOBYTE(len);
               y    = ( precision + 2 ) / 2 ;    /* total number bytes */
               point = precision - scale ;
               bottom = *(ptr + y  -   1) & 0x000F ;           /* sign */
               if ( (bottom == 0x000D) || (bottom == 0x000B) )
                       strcat(temp,"-") ;
               output_blank = TRUE;
               for (i = 0; i < y ; i++  )
                 {
                   top = *(ptr + i ) & 0x00F0 ;
                   top = (top >> 4 ) ;
                   bottom = *(ptr + i) & 0x000F ;
                   if ( point-- == 0 )
                      strcat(temp,".") ;

                   if ( ((output_blank) && (top != 0)) || (point <= 1) )
                      output_blank = FALSE;
                   if (output_blank)
                      strcat(temp," ") ;
                   else
                      {
                       sprintf(temp1,"%d", top ) ;
                       strcat(temp,temp1) ;
                      }
```

Figure 21-10 (Part 4 of 6). RSQL.SQC Listing of the Dynamic SQL Helper Functions.

```
                    /*________________________________*/
                    /* Ignore bottom of last          */
                    /* half byte because its the sign */
                    /*________________________________*/
                    if ( i < (y - 1) )
                    { /* sign half byte ? */
                          if ( point-- == 0 )
                             strcat(temp,".") ;

                          if ( ((output_blank) && (bottom != 0))
                             || (point <= 1) )
                             output_blank = FALSE;
                          if (output_blank)
                             strcat(temp," ") ;
                          else
                             {
                              sprintf(temp1,"%d", bottom ) ;
                              strcat(temp,temp1) ;
                             }
                    }/* end if */
                  } /* end for */
                if ( scale == 0 )
                     strcat(temp,".") ;
                break ;
            case SQL_TYP_FLOAT:                              /* double */
            case SQL_TYP_NFLOAT:
                sprintf(temp,"%e", *(float *)sqlda.sqlvar[index].sqldata);
                break ;
            case SQL_TYP_CHAR:          /* fixed length character string */
            case SQL_TYP_NCHAR:
                strncpy(temp,
                        sqlda.sqlvar[index].sqldata,
                        sqlda.sqlvar[index].sqllen);
                temp[sqlda.sqlvar[index].sqllen] = '\0';     /*terminate */
                break ;
            case SQL_TYP_VARCHAR:     /* varying length character string */
            case SQL_TYP_NVARCHAR:
            case SQL_TYP_LONG:   /* long varying length character string */
            case SQL_TYP_NLONG:
                strncpy(temp,
                        sqlda.sqlvar[index].sqldata + 2,
                        (SHORT)*sqlda.sqlvar[index].sqldata);
                temp[(SHORT)*sqlda.sqlvar[index].sqldata]
                                     = '\0';                 /*terminate */
                break ;
            case SQL_TYP_DATE:                                 /* date */
            case SQL_TYP_NDATE:
                strncpy(temp,
                        sqlda.sqlvar[index].sqldata,
                        10);
                temp[10] = '\0';                             /*terminate */
                break ;
            case SQL_TYP_TIME:                                 /* time */
            case SQL_TYP_NTIME:
                strncpy(temp,
                        sqlda.sqlvar[index].sqldata,
                        8);
                temp[8] = '\0';                              /*terminate */
                break ;
```

Figure 21-10 (Part 5 of 6). RSQL.SQC Listing of the Dynamic SQL Helper Functions.

```
            case SQL_TYP_STAMP:                              /* timestamp */
            case SQL_TYP_NSTAMP:
                 strncpy(temp,
                         sqlda.sqlvar[index].sqldata,
                         26);
                 temp[26] = '\0';                            /*terminate */
                 break ;
            case SQL_TYP_LSTR:  /* varying length string, 1-byte length */
            case SQL_TYP_NLSTR:
                 strncpy(temp,
                         sqlda.sqlvar[index].sqldata + 1,
                         sqlda.sqlvar[index].sqllen);
                 temp[sqlda.sqlvar[index].sqllen] = '\0';    /*terminate */
                 break ;
            case SQL_TYP_CSTR: /* null terminated varying length string */
            case SQL_TYP_NCSTR:
                 sprintf(temp,"%s",sqlda.sqlvar[index].sqldata + 2);
                 break ;
            default:
                 sprintf(err_msg,
                 "\n Unknown type col = %d type = %d",
                 index + 1,sqlda.sqlvar[index].sqltype);
                 rcd = FAILED;
                 break;
          }  /* endswitch type*/
        } /* if null_not_found */

        if (rcd == FAILED)
          break;                                /* break out of for loop */
        if (strlen(temp) <= field[index].max_width)
          memcpy(&row[field[index].tab_pos],
                 temp,
                 strlen(temp) );
        else
        { sprintf(err_msg,
          "\n Field too long col = %d value  = %s",
            (index + 1) ,temp);
          rcd = FAILED;
          break;                                /* break out of for loop */
        }
      } /* end for */

     /*----------------------------------------*/
     /*Print selected row                      */
     /*----------------------------------------*/
     fputs("\n",out_stream);
     fputs(row,out_stream);
     break;
  } /* endswitch  action */

  return (rcd);

} /* end print_format_row */
```

Figure 21-10 (Part 6 of 6). RSQL.SQC Listing of the Dynamic SQL Helper Functions.

The dos_exec() Command Handler

The **dos_exec()** command handler (see listing in Figure 21-11) executes an external program from the within an RSQL program. This is a very uncomplicated command handler since all it does is turn around and issue an OS/2 **DosExecPgm** API call (this was previously covered in "DosExecPgm" on page 182).

The parameters required by **DosExecPgm** are passed to **dos_exec()** in the correct format. The input parameter, **cmd_dos** contains the name of the child program to be executed and its parameters. This is a the string **get_command()** prepared in the **parm_str** variable, from the reading an EXEC DOS command in the *run* file. The string is already in the format required by **DosExecPgm**. It contains the program name, a NULL, the program arguments (separated by spaces), followed by a double NULL termination. A command line string may look like this:

```
"program.exe\0arg1 arg2 arg3 ...argN\0\0"
```

The child program is run synchronously to the RSQL parent process, which means RSQL waits for the child process to terminate, and then obtains the child's result code. Since this is a synchronous call, the **RESULTCODES** structure **codeTerminate** field contains the Terminate code for the child process, and the **codeResult** field contains the Exit code.

```
SHORT dos_exec(PCHAR cmd_dos)
{
        /*----------------------------------------*/
        /* Execute the program                    */
        /*----------------------------------------*/
  api_rcd = DosExecPgm(object_name,     /* failing object if progam fails*/
                 sizeof(object_name), /* the object size              */
                 0,                   /* sync.  program execution     */
                 cmd_dos,             /* program name and parameters  */
                 NULL,                /* inherit environment          */
                 &ExecResult,         /* termination reason code      */
                 cmd_dos);            /* program name                 */
  if (api_rcd)
     {sprintf(err_msg,
             "\n ERROR: DosExecProgram API call failed with a %d return code",
             api_rcd);
      return(RECORD_DOS_EXEC_RESULTS);
     }
```

Figure 21-11 (Part 1 of 2). RSQL.SQC Listing of the dos_exec() Function.

```
      /*──────────────────────────────────────*/
      /* Format the return codes               */
      /*──────────────────────────────────────*/
   switch (ExecResult.codeTerminate)
     {  case  0  :
              sprintf(err_msg, "\n Program completed with a return code of %d.",
                      ExecResult.codeResult);
              api_rcd = ExecResult.codeResult;
              break;

        case  1  :
              sprintf(err_msg, "\n Program terminated by hard error.");
              api_rcd = ExecResult.codeTerminate;
              break;

        case  2  :
              sprintf(err_msg, "\n Program terminated by a TRAP.");
              api_rcd = ExecResult.codeTerminate;
              break;

        case  3  :
              sprintf(err_msg, "\n Program terminated by a DosKill Process.");
              api_rcd = ExecResult.codeTerminate;
              break;

       default :
              sprintf(err_msg, "\n Unknown Program termination code.");
              api_rcd = ExecResult.codeTerminate;
     } /* end switch */
     return(RECORD_DOS_EXEC_RESULTS);
 } /* end exec_dos */
```

Figure 21-11 (Part 2 of 2). RSQL.SQC Listing of the dos_exec() Function.

The Results Processor: record_command_results()

RSQL introduces an all-purpose return-code processor to handle the diversity and variety in Database Manager API styles. The **record_command_results**() procedure (see listing in Figure 21-13) records the command return codes in the *response* file along with the elapsed time for the execution of a command. Commands can fail because of a syntax error, a bad error code from an api call, or a non-zero return code in the **SQLCA** or **QMCA**. Depending on the action required, an error message, API return code, or all of the SQLCA information is respectively written to the *response* file along with a user-friendly error message that describes what happened. The following is the list of actions and their effects:

RECORD_NOTHING: This action causes two blank lines to be entered in the *response* file.

RECORD_DOS_EXEC_RESULTS: This action causes return codes of an OS/2 program that executed under RSQL, to be recorded. The execution time of the program is also recorded.

RECORD_SQLCA: This action causes the results of the execution of a SQL command to be recorded. The return codes and the execution time are written to the *response* file. If a failure is detected in the **sqlcode**, the error or warning message is recorded along with the contents of the **sqlca** (more on that below).

RECORD_QM_RESULTS: This action causes the results of the execution of a Query Manager Callable Interface Command to be recorded. The return codes and the execution time are written to the *response* file. The return codes are obtained by reading the **dsq_return_code** and the **qmca.dsq_reason_code** of the **QMCA** structure. The **QMCA** is discussed in the next chapter.

RECORD_API_RCD: This action causes the results of the execution of a Database Administration API call to be recorded. The return codes and the execution time are written to the *response* file.

RECORD_ERR_MSG: This action causes a general error message to be recorded in the *response* file.

In addition, the error handlers also decide, based on the return codes and the state of the **continue_on_error** directive, whether to CONTINUE or TERMINATE the program.

SQL Error Handling: The SQLCA and the sqlaintp()

This is what the **SQLCA** structure looks like:

```
/* SQL Communication Area - SQLCA */
struct sqlca
{
   unsigned char  sqlcaid[8];        /* Eyecatcher = 'SQLCA   '        */
   long           sqlcabc;           /* SQLCA size in bytes            */
   long           sqlcode;           /* SQL return code                */
   short          sqlerrml;          /* Length for SQLERRMC            */
   unsigned char  sqlerrmc[70];      /* Error message tokens           */
   unsigned char  sqlerrp[8];        /* Diagnostic information         */
   long           sqlerrd[6];        /* Diagnostic information         */
   unsigned char  sqlwarn[8];        /* Warning flags                  */
   unsigned char  sqlext[8];         /* Reserved                       */
};
```

Figure 21-12. SQLCA Structure.

You will notice in the listing (on Figure 21-13), that the **RECORD_SQLCA** action results in a flurry of code. What we're trying to do is provide you with a dump of the **sqlca** contents when an error occurs. Perhaps this information may mean something to you, so we've included it in the *response* file output. There are two gems in that piece of code that deserve your attention:

- The **sqlcode** field, which contains the command return code. A zero return code is OK. A positive return code indicates a warning. A negative return code indicates a serious error.
- The **sqlaintp()** call. This is the famous **RETRIEVE MESSAGE** application service, provided by the Database Administration API. This command returns the error message text that corresponds to the error code in the **sqlcode** field of the SQLCA. You must provide a message buffer and specify the maximum line width of the message. The returned message will be broken down into a series of lines separated by CR/LF, with a null indicating the end of message.

```
/*----------------------------------------------------------------------*/
/*  This procedure records the command results along with the elapsed time  */
/*  of execution of a command.                                           */
/*----------------------------------------------------------------------*/
SHORT record_command_results(SHORT rcd)
{
 CHAR              display_msg[1000];       /* temporary buffer         */
 CHAR              msgbuf[512];             /* rcd explanation          */
 SHORT             index;                   /* for counting             */
 CHAR              temp[20];                /* char buffer              */
 CHAR             *err_line;                /* a line of error info.    */

 switch (rcd)
    {
     case RECORD_NOTHING :
          fprintf(out_stream, "\n\n");
          return(CONTINUE); break;

     case RECORD_DOS_EXEC_RESULTS :
          if (api_rcd == 0)
           /*-----------------------------------*/
           /* If success...                     */
           /*-----------------------------------*/
           { fprintf(out_stream, " %s", err_msg);
            fprintf(out_stream,
            "\n OK,                    "
            "Execution time = %10.4lf secs\n\n\n",
            (double)event_time) ;
            return(CONTINUE);
           }
          else
           { /*-----------------------------------*/
            /* Otherwise ...                      */
            /*-----------------------------------*/
            fprintf(out_stream, " %s", err_msg);
            fprintf(out_stream,
            "\n ERROR,                 "
            "Execution time = %10.4lf secs\n\n\n",
            (double)event_time) ;
            if (continue_on_error)
               return(CONTINUE);
            else
               return(TERMINATE);
          }
          break;
```

Figure 21-13 (Part 1 of 5). RSQL.SQC Listing of record_command_results()

```
case RECORD_SQLCA   :
     if (sqlca.sqlcode == 0)
      /*--------------------------------------------*/
      /* If success...                              */
      /*--------------------------------------------*/
     {
       fprintf(out_stream,
       "\n OK, sql_rcd = %ld,          "
       "Execution time = %10.4lf secs\n\n\n",
       sqlca.sqlcode,(double)event_time) ;
       return(CONTINUE);
     }
     else
     {
      /*--------------------------------------------*/
      /* Otherwise ...                              */
      /*--------------------------------------------*/
      if (sqlca.sqlcode >  0)
         sprintf(display_msg,
         "\n WARNING, sql_code = %ld,    Execution time = %10.4lf secs",
         sqlca.sqlcode,(double)event_time) ;
      else
         sprintf(display_msg,
         "\n ERROR, sql_code = %ld\n",
         sqlca.sqlcode) ;
      /*--------------------------------------------*/
      /* RETRIEVE ERROR MESSAGE                     */
      /*--------------------------------------------*/
      rcd = sqlaintp(msgbuf,                 /* buffer for msg text */
                     512,                    /* buffer size         */
                     79,                     /* line width          */
                     &sqlca);                /* SQLCA               */

      if (rcd < 0)                           /* message retrieve err*/
        sprintf(msgbuf,"\n SQLAINTP ERROR. Return code = %d \n",rcd);

      err_line = strtok(msgbuf,"\n");
      while (err_line != NULL)
         {
          sprintf(display_msg,"%s\n %s", display_msg, err_line);
          err_line = strtok(NULL,"\n");
         }
      strcat(display_msg,"\n\n ------ ADDITIONAL SQLCA info --------");
      fputs(display_msg,out_stream);

      /*--------------------------------------------*/
      /* Display SQLCA  sqlerrmc                    */
      /*--------------------------------------------*/
      if(sqlca.sqlerrml)
      {
       sqlca.sqlerrmc[sqlca.sqlerrml] = '\0';          /* NULL terminate */
       while ( sqlca.sqlerrml-- )
       {
          if (sqlca.sqlerrmc[sqlca.sqlerrml] == 0xFF)     /* remove FFs */
            sqlca.sqlerrmc[sqlca.sqlerrml] = ' ';
       }
       fprintf(out_stream,"\n SQLERRMC's:  %s",sqlca.sqlerrmc);
      }
```

Figure 21-13 (Part 2 of 5). RSQL.SQC Listing of record_command_results()

```
        /*-------------------------------------------*/
        /* Display SQLCA sqlerrp                     */
        /*-------------------------------------------*/
        sprintf(display_msg,"\n SQLERRP: ") ;
        for(index=0;index<8;index++)
        {
         sprintf(temp,"%c", sqlca.sqlerrp[index]) ;
         strcat(display_msg,temp);
        }
        fputs(display_msg,out_stream);

        /*-------------------------------------------*/
        /* Display SQLCA sqlerrd                     */
        /*-------------------------------------------*/
        sprintf(display_msg,"\n SQLERRD: ") ;
        for(index=0;index<6;index++)
        {
         sprintf(temp,"%10ld",sqlca.sqlerrd[index]) ;
         strcat(display_msg,temp);
        }
        fputs(display_msg,out_stream);

        /*-------------------------------------------*/
        /* Display SQLCA Warnings                    */
        /*-------------------------------------------*/
        sprintf(display_msg,"\n Warning Indicators: ") ;
        for(index=0;index<5;index++)
        {
         sprintf(temp,"%c",sqlca.sqlwarn[index]) ;
         strcat(display_msg,temp);
        }
        fprintf(out_stream,"%s\n\n\n",temp);

        if (continue_on_error)
           return(CONTINUE);
        else
           return(TERMINATE);
       } /*else otherwise*/
  case RECORD_QM_RESULTS :
       if (qmca.dsq_return_code == DSQ_SUCCESS)
          {
            fprintf(out_stream,
            "\n OK, qm_rcd = %ld,          "
            "Execution time = %10.4lf secs\n\n\n",
            qmca.dsq_reason_code,(double)event_time) ;
            return(CONTINUE);
          }
```

Figure 21-13 (Part 3 of 5). RSQL.SQC Listing of record_command_results()

```
        if (qmca.dsq_return_code == DSQ_WARNING)
           {
              fprintf(out_stream,
              "\n WARNING, qm_rcd = %ld,          "
              "Execution time = %10.4lf secs\n\n\n",
              qmca.dsq_reason_code,(double)event_time) ;
              if (continue_on_error)
                 return(CONTINUE);
              else
                 return(TERMINATE);
           }

        if (qmca.dsq_return_code == DSQ_FAILURE)
           {
              fprintf(out_stream,
              "\n ERROR, qm_rcd = %ld,          "
              "Execution time = %10.4lf secs\n\n\n",
              qmca.dsq_reason_code,(double)event_time) ;
              if (continue_on_error)
                 return(CONTINUE);
              else
                 return(TERMINATE);
           }

        if (qmca.dsq_return_code == DSQ_SEVERE)
           {
              fprintf(out_stream,
              "\n SEVERE ERROR, qm_rcd = %ld,          "
              "Execution time = %10.4lf secs\n\n\n",
              qmca.dsq_reason_code,(double)event_time) ;
              if (continue_on_error)
                 return(CONTINUE);
              else
                 return(TERMINATE);
           }
        break;

     case RECORD_API_RCD :
        if (api_rcd == 0)
         /*-----------------------------------------------*/
         /* If success...                                 */
         /*-----------------------------------------------*/
         {
          fprintf(out_stream,
          "\n OK, api_rcd = %ld,          "
          " Execution time = %10.4lf secs\n\n\n",
          api_rcd,(double)event_time) ;
          return(CONTINUE);
         }
```

Figure 21-13 (Part 4 of 5). RSQL.SQC Listing of record_command_results()

```
          else
           {
            /*________________________________________*/
            /* Otherwise ...                          */
            /*________________________________________*/
            fprintf(out_stream,
                    "\n API for command %s failed with "
                    "a return code of %d.\n\n\n",
                    parms.cmd_name, api_rcd);
            if (continue_on_error)
               return(CONTINUE);
            else
               return(TERMINATE);

          }
          break;

     case RECORD_ERR_MSG  :
          fprintf(out_stream, " %s\n\n\n", err_msg);
          return(TERMINATE);
     }
} /* end record_command_results */
```

Figure 21-13 (Part 5 of 5). RSQL.SQC Listing of record_command_results()

RSQL.H Include File

```
/*________________________________________________________________________*/
/*  INCLUDE FILE NAME: RSQL.H - declarations for RSQL program            */
/*________________________________________________________________________*/
/*________________________________________________________________________*/
/* defines                                                                */
/*________________________________________________________________________*/
                  /*__________________________________*/
                  /* Constants used as command values  */
                  /*__________________________________*/
#define CMD_SYNTAX_ERROR         (-1)
#define CMD_NO_CMD                 0
#define CMD_SQL_IMMEDIATE          1
#define CMD_SQL_SELECT             2
#define CMD_DOS                    3
#define CMD_QM                     4
#define CMD_DBA                    5
#define CMD_DBA_BACKUP             5
#define CMD_DBA_BIND               6
#define CMD_DBA_CATALOG_DB         7
#define CMD_DBA_CATALOG_NODE       8
#define CMD_DBA_COLLECT_STATUS     9
#define CMD_DBA_CONTINUE_ON_ERROR 10
#define CMD_DBA_CREATE_DB         11
```

Figure 21-14 (Part 1 of 6). RSQL.H Include File.

```
#define CMD_DBA_DROP_DB          12
#define CMD_DBA_EXPORT           13
#define CMD_DBA_GET_ADMIN        14
#define CMD_DBA_IMPORT           15
#define CMD_DBA_LOGOFF           16
#define CMD_DBA_LOGON            17
#define CMD_DBA_PAUSE            18
#define CMD_DBA_REORG            19
#define CMD_DBA_RESET_DM_CFG     20
#define CMD_DBA_RESET_DB_CFG     21
#define CMD_DBA_RESTORE          22
#define CMD_DBA_RUNSTATS         23
#define CMD_DBA_SHOW_DB_CFG      24
#define CMD_DBA_SHOW_DB_DIR      25
#define CMD_DBA_SHOW_DM_CFG      26
#define CMD_DBA_SHOW_NODE_DIR    27
#define CMD_DBA_STARTDM          28
#define CMD_DBA_STARTUSE         29
#define CMD_DBA_STOPDM           30
#define CMD_DBA_STOP_ON_ERROR    31
#define CMD_DBA_STOPUSE          32
#define CMD_DBA_UNCATALOG_DB     33
#define CMD_DBA_UNCATALOG_NODE   34
#define CMD_DBA_UPDATE_DB_CFG    35
#define CMD_DBA_UPDATE_DM_CFG    36
#define CMD_LAST_CMD             37
                   /*------------------------------------*/
                   /* Constants used as return codes     */
                   /*------------------------------------*/
#define TRUE                      1
#define FALSE                     0
#define YES                       1
#define NO                        0
#define GOOD                      0
#define FAILED                   (-1)
#define CONTINUE                  0
#define TERMINATE                (-1)
#define RECORD_NOTHING            0
#define RECORD_SQLCA              1
#define RECORD_API_RCD            2
#define RECORD_ERR_MSG            3
#define RECORD_DOS_EXEC_RESULTS   4
#define RECORD_QM_RESULTS         5

#define         RESTART     -1015          /* database needs restart        */
                   /*------------------------------------*/
                   /* Parsing delimiter                  */
                   /*------------------------------------*/
#define DLM                       " \n"

                   /*------------------------------------*/
                   /* Row Formatting Parameters          */
                   /*------------------------------------*/
#define       SET_TABS_WIDTH       1
#define       PRINT_COLUMNS        2
#define       PRINT_SELECTED_ROW   3
```

Figure 21-14 (Part 2 of 6). RSQL.H Include File.

```
                /*------------------------------------------------*/
                /* Other Constants                                */
                /*------------------------------------------------*/
#define MAX_CMD_SIZE            1500
#define MAX_LINE_SIZE            220
#define COL_SEP                    2
#define BREAK_SEP                 40
#define BREAK_ROWS                 1

                /*------------------------------------------------*/
                /* SQLDA                                          */
                /*------------------------------------------------*/
#define SQLVAR_NUM             255      /* max number of columns in SELECT   */
struct sqlda
{
   BYTE          sqldaid[8];            /* Eye catcher = 'SQLDA   '          */
   LONG          sqldabc;               /* SQLDA size in bytes = 16+44*sqln  */
   SHORT         sqln;                  /* Number of SQLVAR elements         */
   SHORT         sqld;                  /* # of used SQLVAR elements         */
   struct sqlvar
   {  SHORT          sqltype;           /* Variable data type                */
      SHORT          sqllen;            /* Variable data length              */
      BYTE          *sqldata;           /* Pointer to variable data value    */
      SHORT         *sqlind;            /* Pointer to Null indicator         */
      struct sqlname                    /* Variable Name                     */
      {  SHORT          length;         /* Name length [1..30]               */
         BYTE           data[30];       /* Variable or Column name           */
      }  sqlname;
   } sqlvar[SQLVAR_NUM];
};
struct sqlda      sqlda;                /* declare a static sqlda variable   */
struct sqlca      sqlca;                /* declare a static sqlca variable   */

                /*------------------------------------------------*/
                /* DBM/Database configuration                     */
                /*------------------------------------------------*/
typedef struct
  {
    SHORT       locklist;                  /* Max. Storage for Locklists     */
    SHORT       buffpage;                  /* Buffer Pool Size               */
    SHORT       maxfilop;                  /* Max. DB Files Open/Appl,       */
    SHORT       softmax;                   /* Log Records/soft checkpoint    */
    SHORT       maxappls;                  /* Max. Active Applications       */
    SHORT       applheapsz;                /* Default Application Heap       */
    SHORT       dbheap;                    /* Database Heap                  */
    LONG        dlchktime;                 /* Time Interval for Deadlocks    */
    SHORT       maxtotfilop;               /* Max. Files Open/Application    */
    SHORT       sortheap;                  /* Sort List Heap                 */
    SHORT       agentheap;                 /* Application Agent Heap         */
    SHORT       maxlocks;                  /* Max. percent locklist/appl.    */
    SHORT       logprimary;                /* Primary Log Files              */
    SHORT       logsecond;                 /* Secondary Log Files            */
    SHORT       logfilsiz;                 /* Log File Size                  */
    SHORT       stmtheap;                  /* SQL Statement Heap             */
    CHAR        newlogpath[248];           /* New Log Location               */
    SHORT       dets;                      /* Copy Protection                */
    SHORT       country;                   /* Country                        */
```

Figure 21-14 (Part 3 of 6). RSQL.H Include File.

```
      SHORT      codepage;                /* Code Page                       */
      SHORT      release;                 /* Release                         */
      CHAR       logpath[248];            /* Current Log Location            */
    } DBCFG;
  DBCFG dbcfg;                      /* variable for database configuration   */
  typedef struct
    {
      SHORT      nodetype;                /* node type (remote/indirect)     */
      SHORT      rqrioblk;                /* requester I/O block size        */
      SHORT      svrioblk;                /* Server I/O block size           */
      SHORT      sqlenseg;                /* Database segments               */
      SHORT      numdb;                   /* number of active databases      */
      CHAR       nname[9];                /* node name                       */
      SHORT      comheapsz;               /* communication heap size         */
      SHORT      rsheapsz;                /* Remote Data Services heap       */
      SHORT      numrc;                   /* number of remote connections    */
      SHORT      release;                 /* release number                  */
    } DMCFG;
  DMCFG dmcfg;                      /* variable for database manager config. */
                    /*______________________________________*/
                    /* command parameters structure         */
                    /*______________________________________*/
  typedef struct
      {
        CHAR     cmd_name[40];        /* Cmd name                            */
        CHAR     cmd_num;             /* Numerical representation of cmd     */
        USHORT   num_parms;           /* Number of parms for this command    */
      }   parms_type;
  parms_type           parms;         /* Variable that contains parameters*/

  typedef struct
  {
   USHORT          token;                /* which field to return         */
   CHAR           *ptrvalue;             /* where to put field info       */
  }  CONFG_ENTRY_TYPE;

  /*______________________________________________________________________*/
  /* Global variables                                                     */
  /*______________________________________________________________________*/
                    /*______________________________________*/
                    /* timing                               */
                    /*______________________________________*/
  struct   timeb timebuff;                 /* Timer buffer                  */
  double         start_time = 0.0;         /* Start of command time        */
  double         end_time   = 0.0;         /* End of command time          */
  double         event_time = 0.0;         /* Elapsed time                 */

                    /*______________________________________*/
                    /* buffers and misc. variables          */
                    /*______________________________________*/
  CHAR           err_msg[512];             /* for errors                   */
  CHAR           parm_buf[MAX_CMD_SIZE];   /* buffer for processing cmds   */
  SHORT          rcd;                      /* general return code variable */
  SHORT          api_rcd;                  /* api return code variable     */
  BOOL           continue_on_error;        /* error stop/continue indicator*/
                                           /*  FALSE = stop on error,      */
                                           /*  TRUE  = continue on error   */
```

Figure 21-14 (Part 4 of 6). RSQL.H Include File.

```
                    /*---------------------------------*/
                    /* file variables                  */
                    /*---------------------------------*/
USHORT          num_parms;                  /* # parms returned from fscanf */
FILE            *cmd_stream;                /* CMD file handle              */
FILE            *out_stream;                /* RESPONSE  file handle        */
static CHAR     msgfile[]="msgfile.msg";    /* msgfile name                 */

                    /*---------------------------------*/
                    /* variables for DosExecPgm        */
                    /*---------------------------------*/
CHAR object_name[13];                   /* buffer for failure name          */
RESULTCODES ExecResult;                 /* structure for child proc. results */

                    /*---------------------------------*/
                    /* variables for QM callable ifc.  */
                    /*---------------------------------*/
struct dsqcomm qmca;                    /* comm. area for QM callable ifc.  */
LONG var_name_lens[10];                 /* array for var. name lengths      */
CHAR var_names[100];                    /* array for variable names         */
LONG var_value_lens[10];                /* array for var. value length      */

typedef union                           /* typedef for two value types      */
   { CHAR char_values[256];
     LONG fint_values[64];
   } VALUES;
VALUES var_values;                      /* array for variable values        */

CHAR var_types[] = "CHAR";              /* variable type string             */
CHAR qm_cmd[MAX_CMD_SIZE];              /* QM command string                */

/*------------------------------------------------------------------------*/
/* Forward declarations of procedures                                      */
/*------------------------------------------------------------------------*/
                    /*---------------------------------*/
                    /* file variables                  */
                    /*---------------------------------*/
VOID initialize_rsql(VOID);
VOID check_args_and_prepare_files(USHORT argc, PCHAR argv[]);
VOID terminate_program(VOID);

                    /*---------------------------------*/
                    /* command/parm parsing functions  */
                    /*---------------------------------*/
SHORT get_command(PCHAR cmd);
SHORT decode_parm_string(PCHAR parm, PSHORT parm_num);
SHORT decode_dmcfg_string(PCHAR parm, PSHORT parm_num,
                          PCHAR *parm_val_ptr, PSHORT parm_val_type);
SHORT decode_dbcfg_string(PCHAR parm, PSHORT parm_num,
                          PCHAR *parm_val_ptr, PSHORT parm_val_type);

                    /*---------------------------------*/
                    /* EXEC SQL functions              */
                    /*---------------------------------*/
SHORT sql_immediate(PCHAR cmd_sql);
SHORT sql_select(PCHAR cmd);
```

Figure 21-14 (Part 5 of 6). RSQL.H Include File.

```
                   /*------------------------------------*/
                   /* EXEC DBA functions                 */
                   /*------------------------------------*/
SHORT dba_exec(PCHAR parms);
SHORT dba_backup(PCHAR parms);
SHORT dba_bind(PCHAR parms);
SHORT dba_catalog_db(PCHAR parms);
SHORT dba_catalog_node(PCHAR parms);
SHORT dba_collect_status(PCHAR parms);
SHORT dba_create_db(PCHAR parms);
SHORT dba_drop_db(PCHAR parms);
SHORT dba_export(PCHAR parms);
SHORT dba_get_admin(VOID);
SHORT dba_import(PCHAR parms);
SHORT dba_logoff(PCHAR parms);
SHORT dba_logon(PCHAR parms);
SHORT dba_reorg(PCHAR parms);
SHORT dba_reset_dm_cfg(VOID);
SHORT dba_reset_db_cfg(PCHAR parms);
SHORT dba_restore(PCHAR parms);
SHORT dba_runstats(PCHAR parms);
SHORT dba_show_db_cfg(PCHAR parms);
SHORT dba_show_db_dir(PCHAR parms);
SHORT dba_show_dm_cfg(VOID);
SHORT dba_show_node_dir(VOID);
SHORT dba_startdm(VOID);
SHORT dba_startuse(PCHAR parms);
SHORT dba_stopdm(VOID);
SHORT dba_stopuse(VOID);
SHORT dba_uncatalog_db(PCHAR parms);
SHORT dba_uncatalog_node(PCHAR parms);
SHORT dba_update_db_cfg(PCHAR parms);
SHORT dba_update_dm_cfg(PCHAR parms);
                   /*------------------------------------*/
                   /* EXEC DOS function                  */
                   /*------------------------------------*/
SHORT dos_exec(PCHAR cmd_dos);
                   /*------------------------------------*/
                   /* EXEC QM callable Interface         */
                   /*------------------------------------*/
SHORT qm_exec(PCHAR parm_str);
SHORT qm_simple(VOID);
SHORT qm_start_set(PCHAR parm_str);
SHORT qm_get(PCHAR parm_str);
                   /*------------------------------------*/
                   /* helper functions                   */
                   /*------------------------------------*/
SHORT merge_file(FILE *dest_stream, char  * merge_file_name);
SHORT record_command_results(SHORT rcd);
VOID  reset_timer(VOID);
VOID  start_timer(VOID);
VOID  stop_timer(VOID);
SHORT print_format_row(USHORT action);
VOID  FAR exit_proc(USHORT term_code);
```

Figure 21-14 (Part 6 of 6). RSQL.H Include File.

Chapter 22

RSQL: Programming Query Manager

This is the second of the three chapter series that examines the inner workings of the **RSQL.SQC** program. In this chapter, we walk through the command handlers that execute the Query Manager Callable Interface. The plan for this chapter is to first introduce the description of the data structures and API calls that are used to program the Query Manager Callable Interface. Following that, we resume our examination of **RSQL.SQC**, where we left off in the last chapter. As you'll soon see, the only hard thing in this chapter is getting used to the SAA CPI conventions for passing parameters. Once you get a hang of how that works, the rest is all straight C code. However, this chapter has two hard-prerequisites:

- Chapter 19, "Tutorial on the Query Manager Callable Interface"
- Chapter 21, "RSQL: Programming Dynamic SQL"

Without first going through this pre-requisite reading, it may feel like you've entered a movie theatre half-way through the feature show.

THE NORMAL AND EXTENDED API CALLS

The Query Manager Callable Interface allows your programs to pass commands and variables to the Query Manager through an API interface. As we previously pointed out in the tutorial (see Chapter 19), the API consists of only two calls:

- **dsqcic()**, the *normal* Query Manager call.
- **dsqcice()**, the *extended* Query Manager call.

These two API calls follow the SAA Common Programming Interface (CPI) standard. The constructs used to pass the variables are designed to be language independent. You invoke the Query Manager's API services as follows:

1. Prepare the control blocks. These include a string that specifies the command to be executed and a **DSQCOMM** structure that contains the return codes. Extended calls require six additional control parameters in order to specify the program vari-

ables for GET and SET, or session variables for START. The control structures are presented later in this section.

2. Issue the API call. This may be either a normal call or an extended call depending on the command that is being processed.
3. Process the Query Manager return codes. The Query Manager returns control to your application when it's completed processing the command. This may be quite a long time if the command is interactive.

The Normal Query Manager Call: dsqcic()

This API call, also known as the *normal* call, is used to process Query Manager commands that do not require variables to be exchanged between the C-program and the Query Manager variable pools. The majority of the Query Manager verbs fall into this category. The prototype for this call is:

```
dsqcic(DSQCOMM   * qmca,                  /* communication area         */
       PLONG       command_length,        /* length of command          */
       PCHAR       qm_cmd);               /* command string             */
```

A description of the parameters follows:

- The ***qmca*** parameter points to the **DSQCOMM** structure, described in the section on "The Query Manager Control Block: DSQCOMM" on page 597.
- The ***command_length*** parameter points to a 4-byte integer that contains the length of the command string. The maximum command string length is 256 characters.
- The ***qm_cmd*** parameter points to a string containing the Query Manager command to be processed.

The Extended Query Manager Call: dsqcice()

This API call, also known as the *extended* call, is used to process Query Manager commands that require the exchange of variables between C-programs and the Query Manager variable pools. Only three Query Manager commands have this requirement: **START**, **SET**, and **GET**. The prototype for this call is:

```
dsqcice(DSQCOMM   * qmca,                 /* communication area         */
        PLONG       command_length,       /* length of command          */
        PCHAR       qm_cmd,               /* command string             */
        PLONG       parm_num,             /* number of variables        */
        PLONG       var_name_lens,        /* name lengths               */
        PCHAR       var_names,            /* variable names             */
        PLONG       var_value_lens,       /* variable value lengths     */
        void      * var_values,           /* variable values            */
        PCHAR       var_types);           /* type  = {FINT || CHAR}     */
```

A description of the parameters follows:

- The ***qmca*** parameter points to the **DSQCOMM** structure, described in "The Query Manager Control Block: DSQCOMM" on page 597.
- The ***command_length*** parameter points to a 4-byte integer that contains the length of the command string. The maximum command string length is 256 characters.
- The ***qm_cmd*** parameter points to a string containing the Query Manager command to be processed.
- The ***parm_num*** parameter points to a 4-byte integer that contains the number of variable names exchanged in this Query Manager command.
- The ***var_name_lens*** parameter points to an array of 4-byte integers. This array contains the lengths (in bytes) of the Query Manager variable names.
- The ***var_names*** parameter points to a character string containing the names of the Query Manager variables back-to-back. The lengths described in the previous parameter are used to determine the actual offset of each name in the character string.
- The ***var_value_lens*** parameter points to an array of 4-byte integers containing the lengths of the application variable values.
- The ***var_values*** parameter points to an array containing the variables, back-to-back. These values are all of the same type. The supported types are character strings or 4-byte signed integers. For SET or START, this array contains the values that are moved to the Query Manager variable pool. For GET, the values received are copied into the array.
- The ***var_types*** parameter points to a 4-character string that describes the data type of the variables in this call. Valid values are:
  CHAR The variables are all character strings.
  FINT The variables are all 4-byte signed integers.

If all this reads like pure gibberish don't despair! It will all become "perfectly clear" when we come to the code that uses this API later in the chapter.

The Query Manager Control Block: DSQCOMM

Each session that's started with the Query Manager Callable Interface is required to allocate a 256-byte variable of type **DSQCOMM** which serves as an anchor block for that session. All subsequent calls for that session must pass that anchor block, which essentially provides two functions:

- It receives from Query Manager Callable Interface a return code, reason code Error ID, and Message ID information, for a completed command.
- It provides a working storage area to the Query Manager Callable Interface.

The type definition for a **DSQCOMM** structure is shown in Figure 22-1:

```
typedef struct DSQCOMM
  {
    ULONG        dsq_return_code;          /* function return code        */
    ULONG        dsq_instance_id;          /* instance id for this session */
    UCHAR        dsq_reserve1[32];         /* reserved space              */
    ULONG        dsq_reason_code;          /* function reason code        */
    ULONG        dsq_error_id;             /* function error id for OS/2  */
                                           /* and Query Manager errors    */
    void     far *dsq_window_handle;       /* application switch handle   */
    UCHAR        dsq_message_id[8];        /* completion message id       */
    UCHAR        dsq_q_message_id[8];      /* query message id            */
    UCHAR        dsq_start_parm_error[8];  /* name of start parm in error */
    UCHAR        dsq_cancel_ind[1];        /* command canceled by         */
                                           /* Control-Break (1=yes,0=no)  */
    UCHAR        dsq_reserve2[23];         /* reserved space              */
    UCHAR        dsq_reserve3[156];        /* reserved space              */
  } ;
```

Figure 22-1. The DSQCOMM Structure.

The **return code** is always one of the following values:

```
#define DSQ_SUCCESS              0
#define DSQ_WARNING              4
#define DSQ_FAILURE              8
#define DSQ_SEVERE               16
```

Along with the return code, the Query Manager Callable Interface returns a **reason code** and an **Error ID** which further explain the outcome of the call.

Note: The Query Manager variable, **DSQCIMSG**, contains the message text of the error. Of course, this assumes you're able to GET the variable out of the Query Manager's pool after an error.

The Query Manager Command Router: qm_exec()

We are now ready to resume our examination of the **RSQL.SQC** program. This time we will focus on the code that handles the Query Manager commands. You may recall from the last chapter that **main()** invokes the **get_command()** function in order to fetch and decode a *run* file command. When **get_command()** encounters a Query Manager command it strips the **EXEC QM:** header from the command string. It then returns control to **main()**, which in turn passes the command string to the Query Manager command handler, **qm_exec()**.

The topic of this chapter is to look at what happens after **qm_exec()** gets called. So let's start by looking at **qm_exec()** (see listing in Figure 22-2). Here's what **qm_exec()** does in life:

1. It first parses the command string to determine which command to run.

2. It then invokes the appropriate command handler and passes it the command parameters. The choice of command handlers is:

   - **qm_simple()** for the execution of normal commands (see listing in Figure 22-3).

   - **qm_start_set()** for the execution of START or SET commands. These commands require the extended API call (see listing in Figure 22-4).

   - **qm_get()** for the execution of the GET command. This command requires the extended API call (see listing in Figure 22-5).

3. It returns control to **main()** and passes back the return code.

Parsing the RSQL Query Manager Command

Even though the command parsing is straight C code, it may be helpful to clarify what's going on. The job of **qm_exec()** is to parse the command and determine which command handler to invoke. The command string is parsed by **sscanf()**, which is told to look for four tokens in the command string. The first three tokens can be terminated by either a space, " ", or a semi-colon, ";". The fourth token can only be terminated by a semi-colon, ";". The examples that follow demonstrate how this parsing works:

Parsing a Simple Command

The **parm_str** in this example contains the PRINT REPORT command shown below:

```
PRINT REPORT (FILE=saverept.prt, PRINTTYPE=COMPRESSED, CONFIRM=NO);
```

After running **parm_str** through **sscanf()**, this is what the different variables will contain:

```
token1     = "PRINT"
token2     = "REPORT"
token3     = "(FILE=saverept.prt,"
token4     = "PRINTTYPE=COMPRESSED, CONFIRM=NO)"
num_parms  = 4
```

The contents of **token1** are then converted to upper-case and a string comparison is made against the key-words: START, GET, and SET. Our example doesn't match any of those key-words, which leads **qm_exec()** to take the following actions:

1. The original command string contents are copied into the **qm_cmd** variable.
2. The **qm_simple()** command handler is invoked.

Parsing a SET Command

The **parm_str** in this example contains the SET command shown below:

```
SET GLOBAL CHAR table = dept, employee = Susan;
```

After running **parm_str** through **sscanf()**, this is what the different variables will contain:

```
token1     = "SET"
token2     = "GLOBAL"
token3     = "CHAR"
token4     = "table = dept, employee = Susan"
num_parms  = 4
```

This example is not as lucky as the previous one; a match is found with the key-word, SET. This leads **qm_exec()** to take the following actions:

1. The **qm_cmd** variable is formatted as a string consisting of token1 and token2. In our example, this is: "SET GLOBAL".
2. The **var_types** variable is formatted as the upper-case value of token3. In our example, this is: "CHAR".
3. The contents of token4 are copied into the **parm_str** variable. In our example, this is: "table = dept, employee = Susan".
4. The **qm_start_set(parm_str)** command handler is invoked and passed **parm_str** as an argument. As you will see later, the helper function has some more parsing to do.

Parsing a START Command

The **parm_str** in this example contains the START command shown below:

```
START DSQDBNM=DEMO DSQMODE=INTERACTIVE;
```

After running **parm_str** through **sscanf()**, this is what the different variables will contain:

```
token1     = "START"
token2     = "DSQDBNM=DEMO"
token3     = "DSQMODE=INTERACTIVE"
token4     = ""
num_parms  = 3
```

In this example, a match is found with the key-word, START. This leads **qm_exec()** to take the following actions:

1. The **qm_cmd** variable is formatted as a string consisting of token1. In this case: "START"
2. The "CHAR" string is copied into **var_types** variable.
3. The **parm_str** variable will contain: "DSQDBNM=DEMO DSQMODE=INTERACTIVE".
4. The **qm_start_set(parm_str)** command handler is invoked and passed **parm_str** as an argument. As you will see later, the helper function has some more parsing to do.

Parsing a GET Command

In this example, the **parm_str** contains the GET command shown below:

```
GET GLOBAL CHAR table, employee;
```

After running **parm_str** through **sscanf()**, this is what the different variables will contain:

```
token1     = "GET"
token2     = "GLOBAL"
token3     = "CHAR"
token4     = "table, employee"
num_parms  = 4
```

In this example, a match is found with the key-word, GET. This leads **qm_exec()** to take the following actions:

1. The **qm_cmd** variable is formatted as a string consisting of token1 and token2. In our example, this is: "GET GLOBAL."
2. The **var_types** variable is formatted as the upper-case value of token3. In our example, this is: "CHAR."
3. The contents of token4 are copied into the **parm_str** variable. In our example, this is: "table, employee."
4. The **qm_get(parm_str)** command handler is invoked and passed **parm_str** as an argument. As you will see later, the helper function has some more parsing to do.

```
/*------------------------------------------------------------------*/
/*  Query Manager Callable interface                                */
/*------------------------------------------------------------------*/
SHORT qm_exec(PCHAR parm_str)
{
  CHAR token1[12];
  CHAR token2[12];
  CHAR token3[12];
  CHAR token4[MAX_CMD_SIZE];
  SHORT num_parms;

  /*--------------------------------*/
  /* parse EXEC QM: command         */
  /*--------------------------------*/
  strcat(parm_str,";");                           /* add a delimiter     */
  num_parms = sscanf(parm_str, " %[^ ;] %[^ ;] %[^ ;] %[^;]",
                          token1, token2, token3, token4);

  switch (num_parms)
    {
     case 0: sprintf(err_msg,
                     "\nSYNTAX ERROR: Invalid command.");
             return(RECORD_ERR_MSG);
             break;
     case 1: sscanf(parm_str, " %[^;]", token1);
             strcpy(token2,"");
             strcpy(token3,"");
             strcpy(token4,"");
             break;
     case 2: sscanf(parm_str, " %s %[^;]", token1, token2);
             strcpy(token3,"");
             strcpy(token4,"");
             break;
     case 3: sscanf(parm_str, " %s %s %[^;]", token1, token2, token3);
             strcpy(token4,"");
             break;
    default : break;
   } /* end switch */

  strcpy(token1,strupr(token1));

  /*--------------------------------*/
  /* START command                  */
  /*--------------------------------*/
  if (strcmp(token1,"START") == 0)
    {
     strcpy(qm_cmd, token1);
     sprintf(parm_str,"%s %s %s", token2, token3, token4);
     strcpy(var_types, "CHAR");
     return(qm_start_set(parm_str));
    }
```

Figure 22-2 (Part 1 of 2). RSQL.SQC: qm_exec() the Query Manager Command Router.

```
/*--------------------------------------*/
/* GET   command                        */
/*--------------------------------------*/
if (strcmp(token1,"GET") == 0)
   {
    sprintf(qm_cmd, "%s %s", token1, token2);        /* concat scope to cmd */
    strcpy(var_types, strupr(token3));
    strcpy(parm_str, token4);
    return(qm_get(parm_str));
   }

/*--------------------------------------*/
/* SET   command                        */
/*--------------------------------------*/
if (strcmp(token1,"SET") == 0)
   {
    sprintf(qm_cmd, "%s %s", token1, token2);        /* concat scope to cmd */
    strcpy(var_types, strupr(token3));
    strcpy(parm_str, token4);
    return(qm_start_set(parm_str));
   }

/*--------------------------------------*/
/* other QM command                     */
/*--------------------------------------*/
sprintf(qm_cmd, "%s %s %s %s", token1, token2, token3, token4);
return(qm_simple());
} /* end qm_exec */
```

Figure 22-2 (Part 2 of 2). RSQL.SQC: qm_exec() the Query Manager Command Router.

The Normal QM Command Handler: qm_simple()

This is the command handler that processes "simple" Query Manager commands. Remember, we defined "simple" as those commands which do not exchange variables with the Query Manager pool. The parameters in the command are passed in the same string as the command itself. The RSQL syntax diagram for these commands is shown below. As you can see from the railroad diagram, almost the entire repertoire of Query Manager commands can be executed by this handler.

```
                                                       ┌──────,──────┐
                                                       ▼             │
▶▶── EXEC QM: ──┬─ BEGIN WINDOW ──┬────────────────────┴─ cmd-parms ─┴──▶◀
                ├─ BEGIN WORK ────┤
                ├─ CANCEL WORK ───┤
                ├─ CONVERT QUERY ─┤
                ├─ DEFINE TABLE ──┤
                ├─ DISPLAY ───────┤
                ├─ EDIT TABLE ────┤
                ├─ END WINDOW ────┤
                ├─ END WORK ──────┤
                ├─ ERASE ─────────┤
                ├─ EXIT ──────────┤
                ├─ EXPORT TABLE ──┤
                ├─ GET ───────────┤
                ├─ IMPORT TABLE ──┤
                ├─ LIST ──────────┤
                ├─ MESSAGE ───────┤
                ├─ PRINT ─────────┤
                ├─ RESET ─────────┤
                ├─ RUN ───────────┤
                └─ SAVE ──────────┘
```

The **qm_simple()** code, listed in Figure 22-3, presents a very straightforward interface. The contents of the **qm_cmd** variable are submitted to the Query Manager Callable Interface using the normal API that we covered in the section, "The Normal Query Manager Call: dsqcic()" on page 596.

Continuing with the PRINT REPORT Example

We now continue where we left off with "Parsing a Simple Command" on page 599. When **qm_simple()** is invoked, here is what the variables contain:

```
qm_cmd =  PRINT REPORT (FILE=saverept.prt, PRINTTYPE=COMPRESSED, CONFIRM=NO)
```

The **qm_cmd** gets submitted as is, to **dsqcic()**. The results of the call are returned in the **qmca** variable. This is the control block we described in "The Query Manager Control Block: DSQCOMM" on page 597. The contents of the **dsqcom** will be analyzed by the common return code handler we introduced in the previous chapter, see "The Results Processor: record_command_results()" on page 583.

```
/*----------------------------------------------------------------------*/
/*  Query Manager Callable interface (all commands except GET, SET, START)  */
/*----------------------------------------------------------------------*/
SHORT qm_simple(VOID)
{
  LONG   command_length;                      /* temp var. for cmd length*/

  /*------------------------------------*/
  /* make QM callable interface call    */
  /*------------------------------------*/
  command_length = strlen(qm_cmd) + 1;
  dsqcic (&qmca,                              /* communication area      */
          &command_length,                    /* length of command       */
          qm_cmd);                            /* command string          */

  return(RECORD_QM_RESULTS);
} /* end qm_simple */
```

Figure 22-3. The Normal QM Command Handler: qm_simple().

The Extended Command Handler: qm_start_set()

This command handler handles the Query Manager **START** and **SET** commands. The RSQL syntax diagram for these commands is shown below:

```
                                          ┌──────────,──────────┐
                                          ▼                     │
▶▶──EXEC QM: START ───────────────────────┬─ DSQSCMD   = string ─┤──▶◀
                                          ├─ DSQSMODE  = string ─┤
                                          ├─ DSQSPROF  = string ─┤
                                          ├─ DSQSDBNM  = string ─┤
                                          ├─ DSQSQUAL  = string ─┤
                                          ├─ DSQSPOOL  = string ─┤
                                          ├─ DSQSRUN   = string ─┤
                                          └─ DSQDSPLY  = string ─┘

                                          ┌──────────,──────────┐
                                          ▼                     │
▶▶── EXEC QM: SET ───┬─ GLOBAL ──┬───┬─ CHAR ─┬─ var-name  = string ─┴──▶◀
                     ├─ LOCAL ───┤   └─ FINT ─┘
                     └─ CURRENT ─┘
```

As you can see from the diagram, both commands can set variables in the Query Manager pool. The **qm_start_set()** code is listed in Figure 22-4. You can see from the listing that both of these commands are passed to the Query Manager through the extended API call that was described in “The Extended Query Manager Call: dsqcice()” on page 596.

We promised you earlier that we would make this API become "perfectly clear." This is the section where we hope to fulfill this promise. The plan is to walk through the API call for the START example. At the end of this exercise, you'll either be more confused, or things will be "perfectly clear." If it's still not "perfectly clear," then we invite you to walk through the SET example. If things are still not "perfectly clear" after that, then stay tuned to receive more instructions.

Continuing with the START Example

We now continue where we left off "Parsing a START Command" on page 600. When **qm_start_set()** is invoked, here is what the different variables contain:

```
qm_cmd    =    "START"
var_types =    "CHAR"
parm_str  =    "DSQDBNM=DEMO DSQMODE=INTERACTIVE"
```

The question is how do we deal with the variables in the **parm_str**? The answer is that we have to repackage the contents of **parm_str** into the 6-variable representation we described in "The Extended Query Manager Call: dsqcice()" on page 596. One of those parameters, **var_types**, is already known; the parameters are of type "CHAR". The packaging of the remaining 5 variables is what the do-loop, in the middle of the listing on Figure 22-4, is all about. Let's walk through the loop once:

1. We first terminate **parm_str** with a ";", so it should look like this:

```
parm_str  =    "DSQDBNM=DEMO DSQMODE=INTERACTIVE;"
```

2. Here are the results of running **parm_str** through **sscanf()**:

```
var_name             =    "DSQDBNM"
char_var_value       =    "DEMO"
&delimiter           =    ","
parm_str             =    "DSQMODE=INTERACTIVE"
rcd                  =    4
```

3. These values are stuffed into our 5 parameter variables, which should now contain the following:

```
varnames             =    "DSQDBNM"
var_name_lens[0]     =    7
var_values.char_values =  "DEMO"
var_value_lens[0]    =    4
parm_num             =    1  ←— This is done last
```

The second (and final) iteration through the loop produces the following:

1. We first terminate **parm_str** with a ";", so it should look like this:

```
parm_str  =    "DSQMODE=INTERACTIVE;"
```

2. Running **parm_str** through **sscanf()** produces the following:

```
var_name                    =    "DSQMODE"
char_var_value              =    "INTERACTIVE"
&delimiter                  =    ";"
parm_str                    =    ""
rcd                         =     3
```

3. These values are stuffed into our 5 parameter variables, which should now contain the following:

```
varnames                    =    "DSQDBNMDSQMODE"
var_name_lens[1]            =    7
var_values.char_values      =    "DEMOINTERACTIVE"
var_value_lens[1]           =    11
parm_num                    =    2     ←— this is done last
```

These are the 5 parameters that get passed to **dsqcice()** along with:

```
qm_cmd                  =       "START"
var_types               =       "CHAR"
```

Notice that the results of the call are returned in the **qmca** variable. This is the control block we described in "The Query Manager Control Block: DSQCOMM" on page 597. The contents of the **dsqcom** will be analyzed by the common return code handler we introduced in the previous chapter, see "The Results Processor: record_command_results()" on page 583.

If you feel we've made the **sqlcice()** API "perfectly clear," then you are invited to skip over the example that follows.

Continuing with the SET Example

We now continue where we left of with "Parsing a SET Command" on page 600. When **qm_start_set()** is invoked, here is what the different variables contain:

```
qm_cmd     =     "SET GLOBAL"
var_types  =     "CHAR"
parm_str   =     "table = dept, employee = Susan"
```

The task at hand is to repackage the contents of **parm_str**, into the 6-variable representation we described in "The Extended Query Manager Call: dsqcice()" on page 596. One of those parameters, **var_types**, is ready to go; we know the parameters are of type "CHAR". The packaging of the remaining 5 variables is what the do-loop, in the middle of Figure 22-4, is all about. Let's walk through the loop once:

1. We first terminate **parm_str** with a ";", so it should look like this:

```
parm_str  =    "table = dept, employee = Susan;"
```

2. We now run **parm_str** through **sscanf()** which produces the following:

```
var_name                    =   "table"
char_var_value              =   "dept"
&delimiter                  =   ","
parm_str                    =   "employee = Susan"
rcd                         =   4
```

3. These values are stuffed into our 5 parameter variables, which should now contain the following:

```
varnames                    =   "table"
var_name_lens[0]            =   5
var_values.char_values      =   "dept"
var_value_lens[0]           =   4
parm_num                    =   1     ←— This is done last
```

The second (and final) iteration through the loop produces the following:

1. We terminate **parm_str** with a ";", so it should look like this:

```
parm_str  =    "employee = Susan;"
```

2. We put **parm_str** through **sscanf()**, which produces the following results:

```
var_name                    =   "employee"
char_var_value              =   "Susan"
&delimiter                  =   ";"
parm_str                    =   ""
rcd                         =    3
```

3. These values are stuffed into our 5 parameter variables, which should now contain the following:

```
varnames                    =   "tableemployee"
var_name_lens[1]            =   8
var_values.char_values      =   "deptSusan"
var_value_lens[1]           =   5
parm_num                    =   2    ←— this is done last
```

These are the 5 parameters that get passed to **dsqcice()** along with:

```
qm_cmd                    =    "SET GLOBAL"
var_types                 =    "CHAR"
```

Notice that the results of the call are returned in the **qmca** variable. This is the control block we described in the section on the "The Query Manager Control Block: DSQCOMM" on page 597. The contents of the **dsqcom** will be analyzed by the common return code handler that we introduced in the previous chapter, see "The Results Processor: record_command_results()" on page 583.

Note: If the extended API hasn't become "perfectly clear" by now, let's move on to the next section. This is an API that has to grow on you with time and repetition.

```
/*------------------------------------------------------------------*/
/*  Query Manager Callable interface (SET, START commands)          */
/*------------------------------------------------------------------*/
SHORT qm_start_set(PCHAR parm_str)
{
  SHORT  rcd;                              /* return code temp var    */
  LONG   parm_num;                         /* parm counter/index      */
  CHAR   delimiter;                        /* config parm delimiter   */
  CHAR   var_name[9];                      /* temp variable parm name */
  CHAR   char_var_value[28];               /* temp variable parm val. */
  LONG   fint_var_value;                   /* temp variable parm val. */
  LONG   command_length;                   /* temp var. for cmd length*/

  /*-----------------------------------------*/
  /* get the parm strings and their values   */
  /*   to form the start parameters          */
  /*-----------------------------------------*/
  var_names[0] = '\0';
  var_values.char_values[0] = '\0';
  parm_num=0;

  do
   { /*                                        */
     /* get a parm name                        */
     /*----------------------------------------*/
     strcat(parm_str,";");                       /* add a delimiter   */
     if (strcmp(var_types,"CHAR") == 0)
        /*-------------------------------------*/
        /* read a character string             */
        /*-------------------------------------*/
        rcd = sscanf(parm_str, " %11s = %27[^ ,;]%*[^,;]%c%[^;]",
                          var_name, char_var_value,
                          &delimiter, parm_str);
     else
        /*-------------------------------------*/
        /* read a FINT (long integer)          */
        /*-------------------------------------*/
        rcd = sscanf(parm_str, " %11s = %ld%*[^,;]%c%[^;]",
                          var_name, fint_var_value,
                          &delimiter, parm_str);
```

Figure 22-4 (Part 1 of 2). The Extended Command Handler: qm_start_set().

```
        /*-----------------------------------------------*/
        /* check if syntax was correct                   */
        /*-----------------------------------------------*/
        if ( ((delimiter == ';') && (rcd != 3)) ||
             ((delimiter == ',') && (rcd != 4)) ||
             ((delimiter != ',') && (delimiter != ';')) )
           {sprintf(err_msg, "\nSYNTAX ERROR: Invalid configuration parameter %s.",
                    var_name);
            return(RECORD_ERR_MSG);
           }
        strcat(var_names, var_name);                 /* add to name array    */
        var_name_lens[parm_num] = strlen(var_name);  /* length of var name   */

        if (strcmp(var_types,"CHAR") == 0)
           {
            strcat(var_values.char_values, char_var_value);/* add to value array*/
            var_value_lens[parm_num] = strlen(char_var_value);/* len of var val */
           }
        else
           {
            var_values.fint_values[parm_num]
                                     = fint_var_value;  /* add to value array   */
            var_value_lens[parm_num] = 4;               /* len of var val       */
           }

        ++parm_num;                                     /* increment num of parm*/
      } while (delimiter != ';'); /* enddo */

     /*-----------------------------------------------*/
     /* make QM callable interface call               */
     /*-----------------------------------------------*/
     command_length = strlen(qm_cmd) + 1;
     dsqcice(&qmca,                                  /* communication area      */
             &command_length,                        /* length of command       */
             qm_cmd,                                 /* command string          */
             &parm_num,                              /* number of parms         */
             var_name_lens,                          /* start var. name lengths */
             var_names,                              /* start variable names    */
             var_value_lens,                         /* start var. value length */
             var_values.char_values,                 /* start variable values   */
             var_types);                             /* start variable types    */

     return(RECORD_QM_RESULTS);
   } /* end qm_start_set */
```

Figure 22-4 (Part 2 of 2). The Extended Command Handler: qm_start_set().

The Extended Query Manager Command Handler: qm_get()

This command handler handles the Query Manager **GET** command. The RSQL syntax diagram for this command is shown below:

```
                                                  ┌──────────,─────────┐
                                                  ▼                    │
▶▶──EXEC QM: - GET ──┬─ GLOBAL ──┬──┬─ CHAR ─┬──┴─ var-name ──────────┴──▶◀
                     ├─ LOCAL ───┤  └─ FINT ─┘
                     └─ CURRENT ─┘
```

As you can see from the diagram, this command extracts named variables from the Query Manager pool. The **qm_get()** code is listed in Figure 22-5. You can see from the listing that both of these commands are passed to the Query Manager through the extended API call that was described in "The Extended Query Manager Call: dsqcice()" on page 596. We promised you then that in due time this API would become "perfectly clear." This is the section where this is going to happen. The plan is to submit the GET example to the API and walk one more time through a command handler.

Continuing with the GET Example

We now continue where we left of with "Parsing a GET Command" on page 601. When **qm_get()** is invoked, this is what the different variables contain:

```
qm_cmd    =    "GET GLOBAL"
var_types =    "CHAR"
parm_str  =    "table, employee"
```

The task at hand is to repackage the contents of **parm_str** into the 6-variable representation that we described in the section on the "The Extended Query Manager Call: dsqcice()" on page 596. One of those parameters, **var_types**, is ready to go; we know the parameters are of type "CHAR". The packaging of the remaining 5 variables is what the do-loop, in the middle of Figure 22-5, is all about. Let's walk through the loop once:

1. We first terminate **parm_str** with a ";", so it should look like this:

```
parm_str  =    "table, employee;"
```

2. When we put **parm_str** through **sscanf()** these are the results:

```
var_name          =    "table"
&delimiter        =    ","
parm_str          =    "employee"
rcd               =    3
```

3. These values are stuffed into our 5 parameter variables, which should now contain the following:

```
varnames                 =    "table"
var_name_lens[0]         =    5
var_values.char_values   =    ""    ← what we're looking for
var_value_lens[0]        =    0     ← we don't know yet for CHAR
parm_num                 =    1     ← this is done last
```

The second (and final) iteration through the loop produces the following:

1. We first terminate **parm_str** with a ";", so it should look like this:

```
parm_str  =     "employee;"
```

2. We put **parm_str** through **sscanf()** which produces the following:

```
var_name                 =    "employee"
&delimiter               =    ";"
parm_str                 =    ""
rcd                      =     2
```

3. These values are stuffed into our 5 parameter variables, which should now contain the following:

```
varnames                 =    "tableemployee"
var_name_lens[1]         =    8
var_values.char_values   =    ""    ← what we're looking for
var_value_lens[1]        =    0     ← we don't know yet for CHAR
parm_num                 =    2     ← this is done last
```

These are the 5 parameters that get passed to **dsqcice()** along with:

```
qm_cmd                   =    "GET GLOBAL"
var_types                =    "CHAR"
```

There is a subtle point worth noting in Figure 22-5. The **dsqcice()** call gets issued twice for "CHAR" **var_types**, and only once for "FINT" **var_types**. Why? Because the length of "FINT" variables is always 4-bytes. However, there is no way of knowing a priori how long the "CHAR" strings will be. So we issue the first call to return the length of the variables we're interested in. After issuing our first **dsqcice()** call, our parameter values contain the following:

```
qm_cmd                   =    "GET GLOBAL"
var_types                =    "CHAR"
varnames                 =    "tableemployee"
var_name_lens[0]         =    5
var_name_lens[1]         =    8
var_values.char_values   =    ""    ← what we're still looking for
var_value_lens[0]        =    4     ← that's what first call returns
var_value_lens[1]        =    5     ← that's what first call returns
parm_num                 =    2
```

After issuing the **dsqcice()** with the parameter values shown above, here is what the final outcome looks like:

```
qm_cmd                   =    "GET GLOBAL"
var_types                =    "CHAR"
varnames                 =    "tableemployee"
var_name_lens[0]         =    5
var_name_lens[1]         =    8
var_values.char_values   =    "deptSusan" ←  returned by second call
var_value_lens[0]        =    4
var_value_lens[1]        =    5
parm_num                 =    2
```

The results of the call are returned in the **qmca** variable. This is the control block we described in the section on the "The Query Manager Control Block: DSQCOMM" on page 597. The contents of the **dsqcom** will be analyzed by the common return code handler we introduced in the previous chapter, see "The Results Processor: record_command_results()" on page 583.

But we're not done yet! The final step is to format the values returned, in a way that is humanly readable. The formatted values returned by **GET** are then written to the *response* file.

We're done; but is it "perfectly clear?"

```
/*------------------------------------------------------------------*/
/*  Query Manager Callable interface (SET, START commands)          */
/*------------------------------------------------------------------*/
SHORT qm_get(PCHAR parm_str)
{
  SHORT  i;                              /* loop index             */
  SHORT  rcd;                            /* return code temp var   */
  LONG   parm_num;                       /* parm counter/index     */
  CHAR   delimiter;                      /* config parm delimiter  */
  CHAR   var_name[9];                    /* temp variable parm name */
  CHAR   char_var_value[32];             /* temp variable parm value*/
  CHAR   fint_var_value;                 /* temp variable parm value*/
  LONG   command_length;                 /* temp var. for cmd length*/
  CHAR  *var_name_ptr;                   /* pointer to var name     */
  CHAR  *var_value_ptr;                  /* pointer to var value    */
```

Figure 22-5 (Part 1 of 3). The Extended Query Manager Handler: qm_get().

```
/*---------------------------------------------*/
/* get the parm strings and their values        */
/*   to form the start parameters               */
/*---------------------------------------------*/
var_names[0] = '\0';
var_values.char_values[0] = '\0';
parm_num=0;

do
 {
   /*-------------------------------------------*/
   /* get a parm name                           */
   /*-------------------------------------------*/
   strcat(parm_str,";");                                /* add a delimiter   */
   rcd = sscanf(parm_str, " %11[^ ,;]%*[^,;]%c%[^;]",
                         var_name, &delimiter, parm_str);

   if ( ((delimiter == ';') && (rcd != 2)) ||
        ((delimiter == ',') && (rcd != 3)) ||
        ((delimiter != ',') && (delimiter != ';')) )
      {sprintf(err_msg,
              "\nSYNTAX ERROR: Invalid configuration parameter %s.",
              var_name);
       return(RECORD_ERR_MSG);
      }

   strcat(var_names, var_name);                      /* add to name array   */
   var_name_lens[parm_num] = strlen(var_name);       /* length of var name  */
   if (strcmp(var_types,"CHAR") == 0)
       var_value_lens[parm_num] = 0;                 /* set to zero         */
   else
       var_value_lens[parm_num] = 4;                 /* set to FINT length  */

   ++parm_num;                                       /* increment num of parm*/
 } while (delimiter != ';'); /* enddo */
/*---------------------------------------------*/
/* make QM callable interface call to           */
/* retrieve variable lengths                    */
/*---------------------------------------------*/
command_length = strlen(qm_cmd) + 1;
if (strcmp(var_types,"CHAR") == 0)
   {
    dsqcice(&qmca,                               /* communication area    */
            &command_length,                     /* length of command     */
            qm_cmd,                              /* command string        */
            &parm_num,                           /* number of parms       */
            var_name_lens,                       /* var. name lengths     */
            var_names,                           /* variable names        */
            var_value_lens,                      /* var. value length     */
            var_values.char_values,              /* variable values       */
            var_types);                          /* variable types        */

    if (qmca.dsq_return_code > DSQ_WARNING)
       return(RECORD_QM_RESULTS);
   }
```

Figure 22-5 (Part 2 of 3). The Extended Query Manager Handler: qm_get().

```
    /*-------------------------------------------*/
    /* make QM callable interface call to        */
    /* retrieve variable values                  */
    /*-------------------------------------------*/
    dsqcice(&qmca,                                   /* communication area      */
            &command_length,                         /* length of command       */
            qm_cmd,                                  /* command string          */
            &parm_num,                               /* number of parms         */
            var_name_lens,                           /* start var. name lengths */
            var_names,                               /* start variable names    */
            var_value_lens,                          /* start var. value length */
            var_values.char_values,                  /* start variable values   */
            var_types);                              /* start variable types    */

    if (qmca.dsq_return_code != DSQ_SUCCESS)
     return(RECORD_QM_RESULTS);

    /*-------------------------------------------*/
    /* print the values                          */
    /*-------------------------------------------*/
    var_name_ptr  = var_names;
    var_value_ptr = var_values.char_values;
    for (i=0; i < parm_num; i++ )
       {
         strncpy(var_name,  var_name_ptr,  var_name_lens[i] );
         var_name[var_name_lens[i]] = '\0';

         if (strcmp(var_types,"CHAR") == 0)
            {
             strncpy(char_var_value, var_value_ptr, var_value_lens[i]);
             char_var_value[var_value_lens[i]] = '\0';
             fprintf(out_stream, "\n     %s = %s", var_name, char_var_value);
            }
         else
            {
             memcpy(&fint_var_value, var_value_ptr, var_value_lens[i]);
             fprintf(out_stream, "\n     %s = %ld", var_name, fint_var_value);
            }
         var_name_ptr  = var_name_ptr  + var_name_lens[i];
         var_value_ptr = var_value_ptr + var_value_lens[i];
       } /* endfor */
    fprintf(out_stream, "\n");

    return(RECORD_QM_RESULTS);
  } /* end qm_get */
```

Figure 22-5 (Part 3 of 3). The Extended Query Manager Handler: qm_get().

Chapter 23

RSQL: Programming the Database Administration API

This is the third of a three chapter series that examines the inner workings of the **RSQL.SQC** program. In this chapter, we walk through the command handlers that execute the Database Administration services. This chapter has two hard-prerequisites:

- Chapter 18, "Tutorial on the Database Administration Services".
- Chapter 21, "RSQL: Programming Dynamic SQL".

The presentation of the Database Administration services closely mirrors the exposition in the tutorial chapter. The command handlers follow to the letter the taxonomy scheme that was presented in the tutorial. This means that for almost every command described in the tutorial, there is a command-handler in this chapter which serves as its coding template. Of course, the command handlers are not isolated programming examples. They are articulated by RSQL into a powerful OS/2 EE database administration tool. The database administration tool is the third, and final component of RSQL's "all-in-one" database services.

HOW TO READ THE CODE IN THIS CHAPTER

This chapter looks at what happens after the **RSQL.SQC**'s **main()** procedure invokes **dba_exec()**, the dispatcher for Database Administration command handlers. The **dba_exec()** function will serve as the "jumping off" point for the code in this chapter. But before "jumping off" into new code, let's quickly review what **main()**'s already done for us in terms of command parsing. You may recall from Chapter 21 that **main()** invokes the **get_command()** function when it needs to fetch and decode a command from the *run* file. Here's what **get_command()** does when it finds a Database Administration command:

1. It looks up a command number which corresponds to the command name, and inserts the value in the **parms**'s structure **num** field.

2. It obtains the minimum number of parameters from the look-up table that the command expects, and inserts that number in the **parms**'s structure **num_parms** field.
3. It strips off the command string, the **"EXEC DBA:"** header, and the command name that follows it.
4. It returns control to **main()**.

The **main()** procedure then turns around and invokes the Database Administration's command router, **dba_exec()**, and passes it the command string. Now the ball is in the court of the Database Administration command handlers that make up the bulk of the code in this chapter. Here is how these handlers go about conducting their business:

- The **dba_exec()** function's sole purpose in life is to route the commands it receives from **main()** to the appropriate command handler and pass it a command parameter string where necessary (see listing in Figure 23-1).
- The command handlers are the real workers. They sometimes have helpers, which are mainly used for decoding parameters.
- The command handlers will do their own parameter parsing using the C function, **sscanf()**.
- The command handlers are functionally organized along the same categories that were introduced in the Database Administration Tutorial chapter. However, a command handler may, in some cases, perform more than one related Database Administration API call.
- The code for the command handlers was designed to be intuitive and self-contained. Each parameter used by an API call is defined inside the command handler code or in the text that surrounds it. This includes the type definitions of the relevant structures. The benefit of this approach is that we do not have to provide API prototype descriptions in an already very long chapter. You should also consult the command descriptions in the Database Administration Tutorial chapter whenever something is not "perfectly clear."
- When the command handler is done doing its thing, it returns control to **dba_exec()** and passes it a return code which is either: RECORD_SQLCA, RECORD_API_RCD, CMD_SYNTAX_ERROR, or RECORD_ERR_MSG. This return code is in turn passed to **main()**, which in turn passes it to the common return code handler, "The Results Processor: record_command_results()" on page 583, which analyzes the **sqlca** and writes the results to *response* file.
- There are many command handlers and this accounts for the bulk of the material in this chapter. However, if you do not feel like doing a lot of reading you can always selectively go to the command handler you're interested in without having to read the rest of the code in the chapter.

THE DATABASE ADMINISTRATION COMMAND ROUTER: DBA_EXEC()

The **dba_exec()** (see listing in Figure 23-1) acts as the central dispatcher for calls to the Database Administration command handlers. The function knows which handler to call by switching on the **cmd_num** field of the **parms** variable. This is the field in which **get_command()** places the command number to be executed. The parameter in **parm_buf** is passed as required. When the command handler has completed its job, it passes back a return code which in turn gets passed back to **main()**.

```
/*-------------------------------------------------------------------*/
/*  Dispatch Database Administration Command Handler                 */
/*-------------------------------------------------------------------*/
SHORT dba_exec(PCHAR parm_buf)
{
    /*--------------------------------------*/
    /* Execute the command.                 */
    /*--------------------------------------*/
    switch (parms.cmd_num)
    {     /*-------------------------*/
          /* Environment Services    */
          /*-------------------------*/
      case CMD_DBA_STARTDM        : rcd = dba_startdm();              break;
      case CMD_DBA_STOPDM         : rcd = dba_stopdm();               break;
      case CMD_DBA_CREATE_DB      : rcd = dba_create_db(parm_buf);    break;
      case CMD_DBA_STARTUSE       : rcd = dba_startuse(parm_buf);     break;
      case CMD_DBA_STOPUSE        : rcd = dba_stopuse();              break;
      case CMD_DBA_DROP_DB        : rcd = dba_drop_db(parm_buf);      break;
      case CMD_DBA_CATALOG_DB     : rcd = dba_catalog_db(parm_buf);   break;
      case CMD_DBA_UNCATALOG_DB   : rcd = dba_uncatalog_db(parm_buf); break;
      case CMD_DBA_CATALOG_NODE   : rcd = dba_catalog_node(parm_buf); break;
      case CMD_DBA_UNCATALOG_NODE : rcd = dba_uncatalog_node(parm_buf);break;
      case CMD_DBA_SHOW_DB_DIR    : rcd = dba_show_db_dir(parm_buf);  break;
      case CMD_DBA_SHOW_NODE_DIR  : rcd = dba_show_node_dir();        break;
      case CMD_DBA_COLLECT_STATUS : rcd = dba_collect_status(parm_buf);break;
          /*-------------------------*/
          /* General Utilities       */
          /*-------------------------*/
      case CMD_DBA_BACKUP         : rcd = dba_backup(parm_buf);       break;
      case CMD_DBA_RESTORE        : rcd = dba_restore(parm_buf);      break;
      case CMD_DBA_EXPORT         : rcd = dba_export(parm_buf);       break;
      case CMD_DBA_IMPORT         : rcd = dba_import(parm_buf);       break;
      case CMD_DBA_RUNSTATS       : rcd = dba_runstats(parm_buf);     break;
      case CMD_DBA_REORG          : rcd = dba_reorg(parm_buf);        break;
      case CMD_DBA_GET_ADMIN      : rcd = dba_get_admin();            break;
          /*-------------------------*/
          /* Configuration Services  */
          /*-------------------------*/
      case CMD_DBA_RESET_DB_CFG   : rcd = dba_reset_db_cfg(parm_buf); break;
      case CMD_DBA_UPDATE_DB_CFG  : rcd = dba_update_db_cfg(parm_buf); break;
      case CMD_DBA_SHOW_DB_CFG    : rcd = dba_show_db_cfg(parm_buf);  break;
      case CMD_DBA_RESET_DM_CFG   : rcd = dba_reset_dm_cfg();         break;
      case CMD_DBA_UPDATE_DM_CFG  : rcd = dba_update_dm_cfg(parm_buf); break;
      case CMD_DBA_SHOW_DM_CFG    : rcd = dba_show_dm_cfg();          break;
          /*-------------------------*/
          /* Application Services    */
          /*-------------------------*/
      case CMD_DBA_BIND           : rcd = dba_bind(parm_buf);         break;
```

Figure 23-1 (Part 1 of 2). RSQL.SQC's DB Administration Command Router: dba_exec().

```
        /*─────────────────────────────*/
        /* Generic Services             */
        /*─────────────────────────────*/
      case CMD_DBA_LOGON        : rcd = dba_logon(parm_buf);      break;
      case CMD_DBA_LOGOFF       : rcd = dba_logoff(parm_buf);     break;

      default: RECORD_NOTHING;           break;
    } /* endswitch */

    return(rcd);
} /* end dba_exec */
```

Figure 23-1 (Part 2 of 2). RSQL.SQC's DB Administration Command Router: dba_exec().

RSQL.SQC: ENVIRONMENT SERVICES COMMAND HANDLERS

Start Database Manager: dba_startdm()

The **dba_startdm()** command handler, whose code is listed in Figure 23-2, executes the RSQL command:

```
▸▸─EXEC DBA: STARTDM ──────────────────────────────────────────────▸◂
```

This command handler simply executes a **sqlestar()** API call.

```
/*──────────────────────────────────────────────────────────────────────*/
/*  execute the STARTDM DBA function                                    */
/*──────────────────────────────────────────────────────────────────────*/
SHORT dba_startdm(VOID)
{
  /*──────────────────────────────────*/
  /* call the START DBM API           */
  /*──────────────────────────────────*/
  api_rcd = sqlestar();                        /* no SQLCA            */

  return(RECORD_API_RCD);
} /* end dba_start_dm */
```

Figure 23-2. Start Database Manager Command Handler: dba_startdm().

Stop Database Manager: dba_stopdm()

The **dba_stopdm()** command handler, whose code is listed in Figure 23-3, executes the RSQL command:

```
▸▸─EXEC DBA: STOPDM ───────────────────────────────────────────────▸◂
```

This command handler simply executes a **sqlestop()** API call.

```
/*------------------------------------------------------------------------*/
/*  execute the STOPDM DBA function                                       */
/*------------------------------------------------------------------------*/
SHORT dba_stopdm(VOID)
{
  /*------------------------------------*/
  /* call the STOP DBM API              */
  /*------------------------------------*/
  sqlestop(&sqlca);                              /* SQLCA              */

  return(RECORD_SQLCA);
} /* end dba_stopdm */
```

Figure 23-3. Stop Database Manager Command Handler: dba_stopdm().

Create Database: dba_create_db()

The **dba_create_db()** command handler, whose code is listed in Figure 23-4, executes the RSQL command:

```
▸▸-EXEC DBA: CREATE_DB- database_name — drive - comment ——————————▸◂
```

This command handler decodes its parameters and then executes a **sqlecred()** API call.

```
/*------------------------------------------------------------------------*/
/*  execute the CREATE_DATABASE DBA function                              */
/*------------------------------------------------------------------------*/
SHORT dba_create_db(PCHAR parm_str)
{
  BYTE   database_name[9];            /* Database name, null terminated   */
  UCHAR  db_drive;                    /* Drive on which DB resides e.g. C */
  CHAR   comment[31];                 /* Comment on DB, null terminated   */

  /*------------------------------------*/
  /* get the parm strings               */
  /*------------------------------------*/
  if (sscanf(parm_str, " %8s %c %30s ", database_name, &db_drive, comment)
            != parms.num_parms)
     {
      sprintf(err_msg, "\nSYNTAX ERROR: invalid parameters");
      return(RECORD_ERR_MSG);
     }
```

Figure 23-4 (Part 1 of 2). Create Database Command Handler: dba_create_db().

```
  /*-----------------------------------------*/
  /* call the CREATE_DATABASE API            */
  /*-----------------------------------------*/
  sqlecred(database_name,                            /* database           */
           db_drive,                                 /* database drive     */
           comment,                                  /* comment            */
           0,                                        /* comment code page  */
           &sqlca);                                  /* SQLCA              */
  return(RECORD_SQLCA);
} /* end dba_create_database */
```

Figure 23-4 (Part 2 of 2). Create Database Command Handler: dba_create_db().

Start Use Database: dba_startuse()

The **dba_startuse()** command handler, whose code is listed in Figure 23-5, executes the RSQL command:

```
►►-EXEC DBA: STARTUSE —database_name ─┬─ S ─┬──────────────────►◄
                                      └─ X ─┘
```

where "S" designates the shared use of the database, and "X" designates exclusive use.

The only strange thing in the command handler code is what happens if the **sqlestrd()** call fails and returns a RESTART code in the **sqlca**. As you may remember from the tutorial, this is the Database Manager's way of telling you that the last time the database was used, it was left in an inconsistent state by an abnormal termination or a power outage. When that happens, don't worry, just issue a **sqlerest()** restart command. This will rollback any unfinished work and return the database to its last consistent state. Once that's done, re-issue the start command, and off you go.

Note: This command handler also installs a signal handler for trapping Ctrl+Break. This is done once at start-up time, so that you can safely interrupt an RSQL program at any time by hitting Ctrl + Break.

```
/*---------------------------------------------------------------------------*/
/*  execute the STARTUSE DBA function                                        */
/*---------------------------------------------------------------------------*/
SHORT dba_startuse(PCHAR parm_str)
{
  BYTE      database_name[9];            /* Database name, null terminated   */
  CHAR      share_mode;                  /* Share mode for STARTUSE          */
```

Figure 23-5 (Part 1 of 2). Start Use Database Command Handler: dba_startuse().

```
    /*-----------------------------------------------*/
    /* get the parm strings                          */
    /*-----------------------------------------------*/
    if (sscanf(parm_str, " %8s %c ", database_name, &share_mode
              ) != parms.num_parms)
       {
        sprintf(err_msg, "\nSYNTAX ERROR: invalid parameters.");
        return(RECORD_ERR_MSG);
       }

    /*-----------------------------------------------*/
    /* call the START USING DB API                   */
    /*-----------------------------------------------*/
    sqlestrd(database_name,                          /* database             */
             share_mode,                             /* share mode           */
             &sqlca);                                /* SQLCA                */
    if (sqlca.sqlcode == RESTART)                    /* if start db func     */
    {                                                /* fails, call restart */
    /*-----------------------------------------------*/
    /* call the RESTART DB API                       */
    /*-----------------------------------------------*/
    sqlerest(database_name,                          /* database             */
             &sqlca);                                /* SQLCA                */

    if (sqlca.sqlcode != 0)
       return(RECORD_SQLCA);                         /* restart failed, exit*/
    else
    /*-----------------------------------------------*/
    /* call the START USING DB API (again)           */
    /*-----------------------------------------------*/
    sqlestrd(database_name,                          /* database             */
             share_mode,                             /* share mode           */
             &sqlca);                                /* SQLCA                */
    }

    if (sqlca.sqlcode != 0)
       return(RECORD_SQLCA);                         /* second start use     */
                                                     /* failed, record SQLCA*/
    sqleisig(&sqlca);                                /* handle Ctrl + Break */
                                                     /* signal handler      */
    return(RECORD_SQLCA);
  } /* end dba_startuse */
```

Figure 23-5 (Part 2 of 2). Start Use Database Command Handler: dba_startuse().

Stop Use Database: dba_stopuse()

The **dba_stopuse()** command handler, whose code is listed in Figure 23-6, executes the RSQL command:

```
▸▸-EXEC DBA: STOPUSE ----------------------------------------▸◂
```

This command handler simply executes a **sqlestpd()** API call.

```
/*---------------------------------------------------------------------*/
/*  execute the STOPUSE DBA function                                   */
/*---------------------------------------------------------------------*/
SHORT dba_stopuse(VOID)
{
  /*-----------------------------------------*/
  /* call the STOP USING DB API              */
  /*-----------------------------------------*/
  sqlestpd(&sqlca);                               /* SQLCA              */

  return(RECORD_SQLCA);
} /* end dba_stopuse */
```

Figure 23-6. Stop Use Database Command Handler: dba_stopuse().

Drop Database: dba_drop_db()

The **dba_drop_db**() command handler, whose code is listed in Figure 23-7, executes the RSQL command:

```
▸▸-EXEC DBA: DROP_DB — database_name ——————————————————————▸◂
```

This command handler decodes its parameters and then executes a **sqledrpd**() API call.

```
/*---------------------------------------------------------------------*/
/*  execute the DROP_DB  DBA function                                  */
/*---------------------------------------------------------------------*/
SHORT dba_drop_db(PCHAR parm_str)
{
  BYTE      database_name[9];         /* Database name, null terminated   */

  /*-----------------------------------------*/
  /* get the parm strings                    */
  /*-----------------------------------------*/
  if (sscanf(parm_str, " %8s ", database_name) != parms.num_parms)
     {
      sprintf(err_msg, "\nSYNTAX ERROR: invalid parameters");
      return(RECORD_ERR_MSG);
     }

  /*-----------------------------------------*/
  /* call the DROP_DATABASE API              */
  /*-----------------------------------------*/
  sqledrpd(database_name,                         /* database           */
           &sqlca);                               /* SQLCA              */
  return(RECORD_SQLCA);
} /* end dba_drop_db */
```

Figure 23-7. Drop Database Command Handler: dba_drop_db().

Catalog Database: dba_catalog_db()

The **dba_catalog_db()** command handler, whose code is listed in Figure 23-8, executes the RSQL command:

```
▶▶-EXEC DBA: CATALOG_DB- database_name - alias ─┬─ LOCAL ─┬─ ──────▶
                                                └─ REMOTE ┘
▶── node_name ─────── drive ─────── comment ──────────────▶◀
```

This is the first time we use the helper function, **decode_parm_str()**, whose code is listed in Figure 23-9. We pass a string to the helper and it returns the database number representation of that string. For example, "LOCAL" translates to 0, and "REMOTE" translates to 1. The handler then uses the decoded parameters to issue a **sqlecatd()** API call.

```
/*-------------------------------------------------------------------------*/
/*  execute the CATALOG_DB DBA function                                    */
/*-------------------------------------------------------------------------*/
SHORT dba_catalog_db(PCHAR parm_str)
{
  BYTE      database_name[9];          /* Database name, null terminated    */
  CHAR      database_alias[9];         /* alias id for a database           */
  UCHAR     db_drive;                  /* Drive on which DB resides e.g. C  */
  CHAR      node_name[9];              /* node name for a database          */
  CHAR      comment[31];               /* Comment on DB, null terminated    */
  SHORT     database_location;         /* db location 0=local, 1=remote     */
  CHAR      database_location_parm[9]; /* local/remote database string      */

  /*------------------------------------*/
  /* get the parm strings               */
  /*------------------------------------*/
  if (sscanf(parm_str, " %8s %8s %8s %c %8s %31s ",
                     database_name, database_alias, database_location_parm,
                      &db_drive, node_name, comment)
                  != parms.num_parms)
     {
      sprintf(err_msg, "\nSYNTAX ERROR: invalid parameters.");
      return(RECORD_ERR_MSG);
     }
  /*------------------------------------*/
  /* decode the parms                 . */
  /*------------------------------------*/
  if ( decode_parm_string(database_location_parm, &database_location) )
     {
      sprintf(err_msg, "\nSYNTAX ERROR: invalid parameter.");
      return(RECORD_ERR_MSG);
     }
```

Figure 23-8 (Part 1 of 2). Catalog Database Command Handler: dba_catalog_db().

```
/*---------------------------------------------------------*/
/* call the CATALOG API                                    */
/*---------------------------------------------------------*/
sqlecatd(database_name,                  /* database          */
         database_alias,                 /* database alias    */
         database_location,              /* database location */
         node_name,                      /* node name         */
         db_drive,                       /* database drive    */
         comment,                        /* comment           */
         0,                              /* current code page */
         &sqlca);                        /* SQLCA             */
return(RECORD_SQLCA);
} /* end dba_catalog_db */
```

Figure 23-8 (Part 2 of 2). Catalog Database Command Handler: dba_catalog_db().

The Helper Function: decode_parm_string()

The **decode_parm_string()** helper function takes a character string as an input, and returns the Database Manager's numeric value for that string. This is done through a look-up table, created as a static C structure which gets initialized with strings and their corresponding numeric values. You may find this structure to be a useful reference of non-string parameters used by the Database Manager.

```
/*--------------------------------------------------------------------------*/
/*  This procedure converts a parameter string into a value.                */
/*--------------------------------------------------------------------------*/
SHORT decode_parm_string(PCHAR parm, PSHORT parm_num)
{
  SHORT      parm_not_found;          /* True if a match is found        */
  USHORT     i;                       /* loop index variable             */

  /*-------------------------------------------*/
  /* Initialize cmds table                     */
  /*-------------------------------------------*/
  typedef struct
  {
    CHAR      parm_str[40];           /* cmd name                        */
    SHORT     parm_num;               /* numerical representation of cmd */
  }   PARM_TYPE;

  #define PARM_COUNT     22
  static PARM_TYPE parms[PARM_COUNT] =
  {/*<--- parm_str --------->|<-- parm_num------------------->*/
   {"ALL",                 0                             },
   {"INCREMENTAL",         1                             },
   {"LOCAL",               '0'                           },
   {"REMOTE",              '1'                           },
   {"REPEATABLE_READ",     SQL_REP_READ                  },
```

Figure 23-9 (Part 1 of 2). The Helper Procedure: decode_parm_string().

```
    {"CURSOR_STABILITY",        SQL_CURSOR_STAB              },
    {"UNCOMMITTED_READ",        SQL_UNCOM_READ               },
    {"BLOCK_UNAMBIG",           SQL_BL_UNAMBIG               },
    {"BLOCK_ALL",               SQL_BL_ALL                   },
    {"NO_BLOCKING",             SQL_NO_BL                    },
    {"DEF",                     SQL_FMT_0                    },
    {"USA",                     SQL_FMT_1                    },
    {"EUR",                     SQL_FMT_2                    },
    {"ISO",                     SQL_FMT_3                    },
    {"JIS",                     SQL_FMT_4                    },
    {"LOC",                     SQL_FMT_5                    },
    {"UPM_LOCAL",               UPM_LOCAL                    },
    {"UPM_DNODE",               UPM_DNODE                    },
    {"UPM_DOMAIN",              UPM_DOMAIN                   },
    {"UPM_CONFIG",              UPM_CONFIG                   },
    {"UPM_ADMIN",               UPM_ADMIN                    },
    {"UPM_USER",                UPM_USER                     }
   };
   /*----------------------------------------*/
   /* decode the parm string                 */
   /*----------------------------------------*/
   i = 0 ;
   parm_not_found = TRUE ;

   while ( parm_not_found && (i < PARM_COUNT))
   {
     parm_not_found = strcmp(parms[i].parm_str,parm);
     if (!parm_not_found)
        break;
     else
        i++;
   }
   if (parm_not_found )
      { sprintf(err_msg,
          "\nSYNTAX ERROR: Unknown parameter string. ");
       return(CMD_SYNTAX_ERROR);
      }
   else
      { *parm_num = parms[i].parm_num;
       return(GOOD);
      }
 } /* end decode_parm_string */
```

Figure 23-9 (Part 2 of 2). The Helper Procedure: decode_parm_string().

Uncatalog Database : dba_uncatalog_db()

The **dba_uncatalog_db()** command handler, whose code is listed in Figure 23-10, executes the RSQL command:

```
▸▸-EXEC DBA: UNCATALOG_DB- database_name ------------------▸◂
```

This command handler decodes its parameters and then executes a **sqleuncd()** API call.

```
/*------------------------------------------------------------------------*/
/*  execute the UNCATALOG_DB DBA function                                 */
/*------------------------------------------------------------------------*/
SHORT dba_uncatalog_db(PCHAR parm_str)
{
  BYTE      database_name[9];           /* Database name, null terminated    */
  /*----------------------------------------*/
  /* get the parm strings                   */
  /*----------------------------------------*/
  if (sscanf(parm_str, " %8s ", database_name
          ) != parms.num_parms)
     {
      sprintf(err_msg, "\nSYNTAX ERROR: invalid parameters.");
      return(RECORD_ERR_MSG);
     }
  /*----------------------------------------*/
  /* call the START USING DB API            */
  /*----------------------------------------*/
  sqleuncd(database_name,                              /* database            */
          &sqlca);                                     /* SQLCA               */
  return(RECORD_SQLCA);
} /* end dba_uncatalog_db */
```

Figure 23-10. Uncatalog Database Command Handler: dba_uncatalog_db().

Catalog Node: dba_catalog_node()

The **dba_catalog_node()** command handler, whose code is listed in Figure 23-11, executes the RSQL command:

```
▸▸-EXEC DBA: CATALOG_NODE- node_name —— local_lu — remote_lu ————————▸

▸———————— mode —— comment ——————————————————————————————————————————▸◂
```

This command handler decodes its parameters and then executes a **sqlecatn()** API call.

```
/*------------------------------------------------------------------------*/
/*  execute the CATALOG_NODE DBA function                                 */
/*------------------------------------------------------------------------*/
SHORT dba_catalog_node(PCHAR parm_str)
{
  CHAR      node_name[9];               /* node name for a database        */
  CHAR      local_lu[9];                /* name of APPC local LU           */
  CHAR      remote_lu[9];               /* name of APPC remote LU          */
  CHAR      mode[9];                    /* name of APPC mode               */
  CHAR      comment[31];                /* Comment on DB, null terminated  */
```

Figure 23-11 (Part 1 of 2). Catalog Node Command Handler: dba_catalog_node().

```
  /*---------------------------------------------------------*/
  /* get the parm strings                                    */
  /*---------------------------------------------------------*/
  if (sscanf(parm_str, " %8s %8s %8s %8s %31s ",
                       node_name, local_lu, remote_lu,mode, comment)
                    != parms.num_parms)
    {
     sprintf(err_msg, "\nSYNTAX ERROR: invalid parameters.");
     return(RECORD_ERR_MSG);
    }

  /*---------------------------------------------------------*/
  /* call the CATALOG API                                    */
  /*---------------------------------------------------------*/
  sqlecatn(node_name,                              /* nodename            */
           local_lu,                               /* APPC local LU       */
           remote_lu,                              /* APPC remote LU      */
           mode,                                   /* APPC mode           */
           comment,                                /* comment for node dir*/
           0,                                      /* current code page   */
           &sqlca);                                /* SQLCA               */
  return(RECORD_SQLCA);
} /* end dba_catalog_node */
```

Figure 23-11 (Part 2 of 2). Catalog Node Command Handler: dba_catalog_node().

Uncatalog Node: dba_uncatalog_node()

The **dba_uncatalog_node()** command handler, whose code is listed in Figure 23-12, executes the RSQL command:

```
▸▸—EXEC DBA: UNCATALOG_NODE— nodename ————————————————————————▸◂
```

This command handler decodes its parameters and then executes a **sqleuncn()** API call.

```
/*---------------------------------------------------------------------*/
/*  execute the UNCATALOG_NODE DBA function                            */
/*---------------------------------------------------------------------*/
SHORT dba_uncatalog_node(PCHAR parm_str)
{
  CHAR      node_name[9];             /* node name for a database       */

  /*---------------------------------------------------------*/
  /* get the parm strings                                    */
  /*---------------------------------------------------------*/
  if (sscanf(parm_str, " %8s ", node_name
            ) != parms.num_parms)
    {
     sprintf(err_msg, "\nSYNTAX ERROR: invalid parameters.");
     return(RECORD_ERR_MSG);
    }
```

Figure 23-12 (Part 1 of 2). Uncatalog Node Command Handler: dba_uncatalog_node().

```
    /*______________________________________________*/
    /* call the START USING DB API                  */
    /*______________________________________________*/
    sqleuncn(node_name,                               /* node name          */
             &sqlca);                                 /* SQLCA              */
    return(RECORD_SQLCA);
  } /* end dba_uncatalog_node */
```

Figure 23-12 (Part 2 of 2). Uncatalog Node Command Handler: dba_uncatalog_node().

Show Database Directory: dba_show_db_dir()

The **dba_show_db_dir()** command handler, whose code is listed in Figure 23-13, executes the RSQL command:

```
▸▸─EXEC DBA: SHOW_DB_DIR ──────── db_drive ──────────────────────▸◂
```

The command handler does the following:

1. It obtains the number of database directory entries by issuing the open directory call **sqledops()**.
2. It then goes into a loop fetching one directory entry at a time by issuing repeatedly, the **sqledgne()**, get next entry API call.
3. Finally, it issues a **sqledcls()** API call to close the session with the database directory.

```
/*____________________________________________________________________________*/
/*  execute the SHOW_DB_DIR DBA function                                      */
/*____________________________________________________________________________*/
SHORT dba_show_db_dir(PCHAR parm_str)
{
  USHORT          dir_handle;                 /* db directory handle     */
  USHORT          dir_count;                  /* num of directory items  */

  typedef struct
  {
   CHAR           alias[8];                   /* Alias name              */
   CHAR           dbname[8];                  /* Database name           */
   CHAR           drive[2];                   /* Drive 'd:'              */
   CHAR           intname[8];                 /* Database subdirectory   */
   CHAR           nodename[8];                /* Node name               */
   CHAR           dbtype[20];                 /* Release information     */
   CHAR           comment[30];                /* Comment                 */
   SHORT          com_codepage;               /* Code page of comment    */
   CHAR           type;                       /* Entry type defines above*/
  } DIR_ENTRY_TYPE;
  DIR_ENTRY_TYPE *dir_entry;                  /* directory entry returned*/

  UCHAR           db_drive;                   /* drive dir, "0" =home dir*/
```

Figure 23-13 (Part 1 of 2). Show DB Directory Handler: dba_show_db_dir().

```
/*------------------------------------------*/
/* get the parm strings                     */
/*------------------------------------------*/
if (sscanf(parm_str, " %c ", &db_drive ) != parms.num_parms)
   { sprintf(err_msg, "\nSYNTAX ERROR: invalid parameters.");
     return(RECORD_ERR_MSG);
   }
/*------------------------------------------*/
/* call the OPEN DB DIRECTORY API           */
/*------------------------------------------*/
sqledops(db_drive,                          /* database drive      */
         &dir_handle,                       /* directory handle    */
         &dir_count,                        /* number of entries   */
         &sqlca);                           /* SQLCA               */

if (sqlca.sqlcode != 0)
    return(RECORD_SQLCA);                   /* open failed         */
/*------------------------------------------*/
/* print a header                           */
/*------------------------------------------*/
fprintf(out_stream,
"\n Database Directory for Drive %c:"
"\n ================================"
"\n\n Alias    Name     Drive Directory Node     "
"Comment                   Type"
"\n -------- -------- ----- --------- -------- "
"------------------------------ ----", db_drive);
while( dir_count-- )
{ /*------------------------------------------*/
  /* call the GET NEXT DIRECTORY ENTRY API    */
  /*------------------------------------------*/
sqledgne(dir_handle,                        /* directory handle    */
         (struct sqledinfo **)&dir_entry,   /* directory item      */
         &sqlca);                           /* SQLCA               */
if (sqlca.sqlcode != 0)
    break;                                  /* read failed         */
fprintf(out_stream, "\n %8.8s %8.8s %2.2s    %8.8s  %8.8s %30.30s %c",
        dir_entry->alias, dir_entry->dbname, dir_entry->drive,
        dir_cntry->intnamc, dir_cntry->nodename,
        dir_entry->comment, dir_entry->type);
} /* end while */
fprintf(out_stream,"\n");
/*------------------------------------------*/
/* call the CLOSE DB DIRECTORY API          */
/*------------------------------------------*/
sqledcls(dir_handle,                        /* directory handle    */
         &sqlca);                           /* SQLCA               */
return(RECORD_SQLCA);
} /* end dba_show_db_dir */
```

Figure 23-13 (Part 2 of 2). Show DB Directory Handler: dba_show_db_dir().

Show Node Directory: dba_show_node_dir()

The **dba_show_node_dir()** command handler, whose code is listed in Figure 23-14, executes the RSQL command:

```
▸▸-EXEC DBA: SHOW_NODE_DIR ──────────────────────────────▸◂
```

The command handler does the following:

1. It first obtains the number of node directory entries by issuing the open directory call **sqlenops()**.
2. It then goes into a loop fetching one directory entry at a time by issuing repeatedly, the **sqlengne()**, get next entry API call.
3. It issues a **sqlencls()** API call to close the session with the node directory.

```
/*-----------------------------------------------------------------------*/
/*  execute the SHOW_NODE_DIR DBA function                               */
/*-----------------------------------------------------------------------*/
SHORT dba_show_node_dir(VOID)
{
  typedef struct
  {  UCHAR    nodename[8];                           /* Node name         */
     UCHAR    local_lu[8];                           /* Local_lu name     */
     UCHAR    partner_lu[8];                         /* Partner_lu name   */
     UCHAR    mode[8];                               /* Mode              */
     UCHAR    comment[30];                           /* Comment           */
     USHORT   com_codepage;                          /* Comment code page */
     unsigned char reserved[SQL_NRESERVE_SZ];        /* Reserved          */
  } sqleninfo;
  struct sqleninfo *node_dir_entry;
  USHORT node_dir_handle;
  USHORT node_dir_count;
  /*-----------------------------------*/
  /* call the OPEN NODE DIRECTORY API  */
  /*-----------------------------------*/
  sqlenops(&node_dir_handle,                         /* node dir  handle  */
           &node_dir_count,                          /* node dir  entries */
           &sqlca);                                  /* SQLCA             */
  if (sqlca.sqlcode != 0)
     return(RECORD_SQLCA);                           /* open failed       */

  /*-----------------------------------*/
  /* print a header                    */
  /*-----------------------------------*/
  fprintf(out_stream,
          "\n Node Directory"
          "\n =============="
          "\n\n Node      Local LU  Partner LU  Mode      Comment"
          "\n --------  --------  ----------  --------"
          "   ----------------------------");

  while( node_dir_count-- )
  {  /*-----------------------------------------*/
     /* call the OPEN DB DIRECTORY ENTRY API    */
     /*-----------------------------------------*/
  sqlengne(node_dir_handle,                          /* directory handle  */
           (struct sqleninfo **)&node_dir_entry,     /* directory item    */
           &sqlca);                                  /* SQLCA             */
  if (sqlca.sqlcode != 0)
      break;                                         /* read failed       */
```

Figure 23-14 (Part 1 of 2). Show Node Directory Handler: dba_show_node_dir().

```
    fprintf(out_stream,
            "\n %8.8s  %8.8s  %8.8s    %8.8s  %30.30s",
            node_dir_entry->nodename, node_dir_entry->local_lu,
            node_dir_entry->partner_lu, node_dir_entry->mode,
            node_dir_entry->comment);
    } /* end while */
    fprintf(out_stream,"\n");
    /*-----------------------------------------------*/
    /* call the CLOSE DB DIRECTORY API               */
    /*-----------------------------------------------*/
    sqlencls(node_dir_handle,                       /* directory handle    */
             &sqlca);                               /* SQLCA               */
    return(RECORD_SQLCA);
  } /* end dba_show_node_dir */
```

Figure 23-14 (Part 2 of 2). Show Node Directory Handler: dba_show_node_dir().

Collect Database Status: dba_collect_status()

The **dba_collect_status()** command handler, whose code is listed in Figure 23-15, executes the RSQL command:

```
▶▶─EXEC DBA: COLLECT_STATUS ── database_name ─────────────────────▶◀
```

Here's what this command handler does:

1. It first obtains the system and database status (for the named database) by issuing the **sqlestat()** API call. The system status information is obtained using the data structure:

```
typedef struct    /* System Status data structure */
{   ULONG  current_time;                /* Current time                */
    LONG   time_zone_disp;              /* Time zone of current time   */
    UCHAR  product_name[30];            /* Product name                */
    UCHAR  component_id[9];             /* Component Id                */
    UCHAR  reserved;                    /* Reserved byte               */
    UCHAR  release_lvl[4];              /* Release level               */
    UCHAR  corr_serv_lvl[8];            /* Corrective service level    */
} sqlesystat;
```

2. It also obtains the database status information through the same call, using the data structure:

```
typedef struct    /* Database Status data structure */
{   ULONG  backup_time;                  /* Last backup time          */
    LONG   time_zone_disp;               /* Time zone of backup time  */
    USHORT connects;                     /* Number of current users   */
    UCHAR  db_alias[8];                  /* Alias name                */
    UCHAR  db_name[8];                   /* Database name             */
    UCHAR  location;                     /* 'L' = Local, 'R' = Remote */
    UCHAR  reserved;                     /* Reserved byte             */
    UCHAR  drive[2];                     /* Drive containing database */
    UCHAR  node[8];                      /* Node containing database  */
    UCHAR  db_type[20];                  /* Type of database ="OS2 DBM" */
}  sqledbstat;
```

3. If users are found to be connected to the database, then the command handler does the following:
   a. It allocates a dynamic memory area large enough to hold the status entries for all the users that are connected to the database.
   b. It issues the API call, **sqleuser()**, to read into memory the status entries of all the connected users.
   c. It goes through a loop which reads from memory one user status entry at a time, formats it, and writes the output to the *response* file.
   d. It frees the dynamic memory which was previously allocated.
4. The user information is obtained through the following data structure:

```
typedef struct sqleusrstat  /* User Status data structure */
{   ULONG  con_trans;                    /* Transactions since connect  */
    ULONG  con_reqs;                     /* Requests since connect      */
    ULONG  cur_reqs;                     /* Requests current transact   */
    ULONG  connect_time;                 /* Time since connect          */
    ULONG  trans_time;                   /* Time since current transact */
    UCHAR  authid[8];                    /* User's Id                   */
    UCHAR  node[8];                      /* Nodename of connected user  */
    USHORT authority_lvl;                /* User's authority level      */
    UCHAR  trans_state;                  /* Transaction state           */
    UCHAR  lock_state;                   /* Transaction lock state      */
} sqleusrstat;
```

5. All three data structures are defined in the OS/2 EE provided **sqlenv.h** include file.
6. It frees resources by issuing the **sqlefree()** API call.

```
/*-------------------------------------------------------------------------*/
/*  execute the COLLECT_STATUS DBA function                                 */
/*-------------------------------------------------------------------------*/
SHORT dba_collect_status(PCHAR parm_str)
{
  typedef struct
     { struct sqlesystat   system_status;     /* system status variable      */
       struct sqledbstat   database_status;   /* db   status variable        */
     } status;
  status              stat;                   /* system/db status            */
  typedef struct
     { struct sqleusrstat  user_status[1];    /* user status variable        */
     } user_stat;
  user_stat  *user_stat_ptr;                  /* user status variable        */
  USHORT status_blocks_remaining;
  USHORT index;
  SEL    selector;
  BYTE   database_name[9];                    /* Database name, null term.   */
  /*--------------------------------*/
  /* get the parm strings           */
  /*--------------------------------*/
  if (sscanf(parm_str, " %8s ", database_name) != parms.num_parms)
     { sprintf(err_msg, "\nSYNTAX ERROR: invalid parameters.");
       return(RECORD_ERR_MSG);
     }
  /*--------------------------------*/
  /* call the COLLECT STATUS API    */
  /*--------------------------------*/
  sqlestat(SQL_OPSTAT_ALL,                 /* Collect System and DB status    */
           SQL_OBJECT_DATABASE,            /* The DB status is for specific DB*/
           strlen(database_name) + 1,      /* Length of the DB name           */
           database_name,                  /* DB name                         */
           &status_blocks_remaining,       /* We're only getting one DB entry */
           (UCHAR *)&stat,                 /* buffer pointer to status struct */
           &sqlca);                        /* SQLCA                           */
  if (sqlca.sqlcode != 0 )
     return(RECORD_SQLCA);
  /*--------------------------------*/
  /* record system status           */
  /*--------------------------------*/
  fprintf(out_stream,
  "\n System Status "
  "\n ------------- "
  "\n  Current Normalized time         = %lu seconds elapsed from 1-1-1970"
  "\n  Time Zone Displacement          = %ld seconds different from UTC"
  "\n  Product name                    = %30.30s"
  "\n  Component Identification        = %9.9s"
  "\n  Release Level                   = %4.4s"
  "\n  Correct Service Level           = %8.8s\n",
  stat.system_status.current_time, stat.system_status.time_zone_disp,
  stat.system_status.product_name, stat.system_status.component_id,
  stat.system_status.release_lvl,  stat.system_status.corr_serv_lvl);
```

Figure 23-15 (Part 1 of 3). Collect Database Status Handler: dba_collect_status().

```
/*----------------------------------------------------------*/
/* record database status                                   */
/*----------------------------------------------------------*/
fprintf(out_stream,
"\n Database Status "
"\n --------------- "
"\n  Normalized time of last backup    = %lu seconds elapsed from 1-1-1970"
"\n  Time Zone Displacement            = %ld seconds different from UTC"
"\n  Number of connects                = %u"
"\n  Database alias                    = %8.8s"
"\n  Database Name                     = %8.8s"
"\n  Location                          = %c"
"\n  Database drive                    = %2.2s"
"\n  Node Name                         = %8.8s"
"\n  Database Type                     = %20.20s\n",
stat.database_status.backup_time, stat.database_status.time_zone_disp,
stat.database_status.connects,    stat.database_status.db_alias,
stat.database_status.db_name,     stat.database_status.location,
stat.database_status.drive,       stat.database_status.node,
stat.database_status.db_type);
/*----------------------------------------------------------*/
/* get user status                                          */
/*----------------------------------------------------------*/
if (stat.database_status.connects == 0)
   fprintf(out_stream,
   "\n Database Status "
   "\n --------------- "
   "\n No users connected to the database \n");
else
   {
    DosAllocSeg(stat.database_status.connects
                 * sizeof(struct sqleusrstat),     /* size            */
                &selector,                         /* selector        */
                0);                                /* flags           */
    user_stat_ptr = MAKEP(selector,0);

    sqleuser(strlen(database_name) + 1,            /* length of DB name  */
             database_name,                        /* database name      */
             (UCHAR *)user_stat_ptr,               /* buffer pointer     */
             &sqlca);                              /* SQLCA              */
    if (sqlca.sqlcode != 0 )
       return(RECORD_SQLCA);
    /*----------------------------------------------------------*/
    /* record user status                                       */
    /*----------------------------------------------------------*/
    for (index=0; index < stat.database_status.connects; index++)
       {
        fprintf(out_stream,
        "\n User Status "
        "\n ----------- "
        "\n  Transactions since connect        = %lu"
        "\n  Requests since connect            = %lu"
        "\n  Requests current transaction      = %lu"
        "\n  Elapsed time since connect        = %lu seconds"
        "\n  Elapsed time, current transaction = %lu seconds"
        "\n  Authorization ID                  = %8.8s"
        "\n  Node Name                         = %8.8s"
```

Figure 23-15 (Part 2 of 3). Collect Database Status Handler: dba_collect_status().

```
            "\n  Authority Level                    = %u"
            "\n  Transaction State                  = %c"
            "\n  Lock State                         = %c\n",
            user_stat_ptr->user_status[index].con_trans,
            user_stat_ptr->user_status[index].con_reqs,
            user_stat_ptr->user_status[index].cur_reqs,
            user_stat_ptr->user_status[index].connect_time,
            user_stat_ptr->user_status[index].trans_time,
            user_stat_ptr->user_status[index].authid,
            user_stat_ptr->user_status[index].node,
            user_stat_ptr->user_status[index].authority_lvl,
            user_stat_ptr->user_status[index].trans_state,
            user_stat_ptr->user_status[index].lock_state);
         } /* end while */
         DosFreeSeg(selector);
      } /* end else */
      /*------------------------------------------------*/
      /* call the FREE DB STATUS RESOURCES              */
      /*------------------------------------------------*/
      sqlefree(&sqlca);
      if (sqlca.sqlcode != 0 )
         return(RECORD_SQLCA);

   return(RECORD_SQLCA);
} /* end dba_collect_status */
```

Figure 23-15 (Part 3 of 3). Collect Database Status Handler: dba_collect_status().

RSQL.SQC: GENERAL UTILITIES COMMAND HANDLERS

Backup Database: dba_backup()

The **dba_backup()** command handler, whose code is listed in Figure 23-16, executes the RSQL command:

```
▸▸-EXEC DBA: BACKUP —— database_name ——┬—INCREMENTAL—┬— drive ——▸◂
                                       └— ALL ———————┘
```

The "ALL" option is used to backup an entire database. The "INCREMENTAL" option is used to back up the changes made since the last backup, and is therefore much faster. The database must be backed up once with the "ALL" option, before an "INCREMENTAL" backup can be issued. The handler issues a **sqluback()** API call to backup the database.

```
/*-----------------------------------------------------------------------*/
/*  execute the BACKUP DBA function                                      */
/*-----------------------------------------------------------------------*/
SHORT dba_backup(PCHAR parm_str)
{
  BYTE     database_name[9];        /* Database name, null terminated    */
  SHORT    type_of_backup;          /* A = 0, I = 1                      */
  UCHAR    bk_drive;                /* Drive where backup resides e.g D  */
  CHAR     type_of_backup_parm[12]; /* from user command                 */

  /*-------------------------------------*/
  /* get the parm strings                */
  /*-------------------------------------*/
  if (sscanf(parm_str, " %8s %11s %c ",
                   database_name, type_of_backup_parm, &bk_drive)
                   != parms.num_parms)
     {
      sprintf(err_msg, "\nSYNTAX ERROR: invalid parameters.");
      return(RECORD_ERR_MSG);
     }

  if (decode_parm_string(type_of_backup_parm, &type_of_backup))
     {
      sprintf(err_msg, "\nSYNTAX ERROR: invalid parameter.");
      return(RECORD_ERR_MSG);
     }

  /*-------------------------------------*/
  /* call the BACKUP API                 */
  /*-------------------------------------*/
  sqluback(database_name,                       /* database           */
           type_of_backup,                      /* type, Changes or all*/
           bk_drive,                            /* backup drive       */
           &sqlca);                             /* SQLCA              */
  return(RECORD_SQLCA);
 } /* end dba_backup */
```

Figure 23-16. Backup Database Command Handler: dba_backup().

Restore Database: dba_restore()

The **dba_restore()** command handler, whose code is listed in Figure 23-17, executes the RSQL command:

```
▸▸—EXEC DBA: RESTORE — database_name — db_drive — bk_drive ————————▸◂
```

This command handler decodes its parameters and then executes a **sqludres()** API call.

```
/*-----------------------------------------------------------------------*/
/*  execute the RESTORE DBA function                                     */
/*-----------------------------------------------------------------------*/
SHORT dba_restore(PCHAR parm_str)
{
  BYTE      database_name[9];          /* Database name, null terminated   */
  UCHAR     db_drive;                  /* Drive on which DB resides e.g. C */
  UCHAR     bk_drive;                  /* Drive where backup resides e.g D */
  /*-----------------------------------------*/
  /* get the parm strings                    */
  /*-----------------------------------------*/
  if (sscanf(parm_str, " %8s %c %c ",
             database_name, &db_drive, &bk_drive
            ) != parms.num_parms)
     {
      sprintf(err_msg, "\nSYNTAX ERROR: invalid parameters.");
      return(RECORD_ERR_MSG);
     }

  /*-----------------------------------------*/
  /* call the RESET DATABASE CONFIG API      */
  /*-----------------------------------------*/
  sqludres(database_name,                          /* database          */
           db_drive,                               /* database drive    */
           bk_drive,                               /* backup drive      */
           0,                                      /* caller action     */
           &sqlca);                                /* SQLCA             */
  return(RECORD_SQLCA);
} /* end dba_restore */
```

Figure 23-17. Restore Database Command Handler: dba_restore().

Export Table: dba_export()

The **dba_export()** command handler, whose code is listed in Figure 23-18, executes the RSQL command:

```
▸▸─EXEC DBA: EXPORT ── database_name ─ datafile ─┬─ DEL ─┬─ tname ─▸◂
                                                 ├─ WSF ─┤
                                                 └─ IXF ─┘
```

where **datafile** is the path-name of the OS/2 file which will receive the exported data, and **tname** is the fully qualified name of a table or view from which the data is extracted.

Here is what this command handler does:

1. It parses the parameters in the usual manner.
2. It sets the **dcoldata** parameter to NULL. This tells Database Manager to use the same names for the output columns as those in the database table columns.
3. It uses the table name to format a SELECT statement which it places in the *data* field of the **tcolstrg** parameter.
4. It specifies a **msgfile** parameter which points to the name and path of an OS/2 file where additional error messages will be written to by the Database Manager.

5. It issues the **sqluexp()** API call.
6. It calls the **merge_file()** helper function (see Figure 23-19) to append the contents of the **msgfile** returned by OS/2 EE to the *response* file.

```
/*-------------------------------------------------------------------------*/
/*  execute the EXPORT DBA function                                        */
/*-------------------------------------------------------------------------*/
SHORT dba_export(PCHAR parm_str)
{
  static struct   sqldcol  *dcoldata = NULL;      /* dcoldata              */
  typedef struct
  {
   SHORT          length;                         /* string length         */
   CHAR           data[100];                      /* string of data        */
  } NUM_STR_TYPE;
  NUM_STR_TYPE    tcolstrg;                       /* tcolstrg              */
  BYTE           database_name[9];       /* Database name, null terminated   */
  CHAR           datafile[80];           /* Path name of file, null terminat. */
  CHAR           exchange_format[4];     /* ASC, DEL etc., null terminated   */
  CHAR           table_name[29];         /* fully qualif., null terminated   */

  /*--------------------------------------*/
  /* get the parm strings                 */
  /*--------------------------------------*/
  if (sscanf(parm_str, " %8s %80s %3s %28s ",
                     database_name,datafile, exchange_format, table_name)
                  != parms.num_parms)
    {
     sprintf(err_msg, "\nSYNTAX ERROR: invalid parameters.");
     return(RECORD_ERR_MSG);
    }

  sprintf(tcolstrg.data,"SELECT * FROM %s", table_name);
  tcolstrg.length = strlen(tcolstrg.data);
  /*--------------------------------------*/
  /* call the EXPORT API                  */
  /*--------------------------------------*/
  sqluexp(database_name,                              /* database          */
          datafile,                                   /* datafile          */
          dcoldata,                                   /* dcoldata          */
          (struct sqlchar *)&tcolstrg,                /* tcolstrg          */
          exchange_format,                            /* filetype          */
          NULL,                                       /* filetmod          */
          msgfile,                                    /* message file      */
          0,                                          /* caller action     */
          &sqlca);                                    /* SQLCA             */
  merge_file(out_stream,msgfile);
  return(RECORD_SQLCA);
} /* end dba_export */
```

Figure 23-18. Export Table Command Handler: dba_export().

The Helper Procedure: merge file()

```
/*------------------------------------------------------------------------*/
/*  This procedure copies the contents of a file into another.            */
/*  The file to be copied must exist.  It will be merged and then erased. */
/*  The destination file must be already open and will be left that way.  */
/*------------------------------------------------------------------------*/
SHORT merge_file(FILE *dest_stream, char  * merge_file_name)
{ FILE          *merge_stream;                /* merge file handle        */
  CHAR          in_line[256];                 /* store a line             */
  /*----------------------------------------*/
  /* Open to_be_merged file                 */
  /*----------------------------------------*/
  if (NULL == (merge_stream = fopen(merge_file_name, "r")))
    { fprintf(dest_stream,"\n No messages in %s\n",merge_file_name);
      return(GOOD);
    }
  else
    { /*----------------------------------------*/
      /* Copy contents...                       */
      /*----------------------------------------*/
      while (!feof(merge_stream))
      {
       if (NULL == fgets(in_line,sizeof(in_line), merge_stream))
         break;
       else
         fputs(in_line,dest_stream);
      }  /* endwhile */
    } /* end if */
  /*----------------------------------------*/
  /* Close file and erase contents          */
  /*----------------------------------------*/
  fclose(merge_stream);
  merge_stream = fopen(merge_file_name, "w+");  /* this opens the file and */
  fclose(merge_stream);                         /* destroys its contents   */
  return(GOOD);
} /* end merge_file */
```

Figure 23-19. The Helper Procedure: merge file().

Import Table: dba_import()

The **dba_import()** command handler, whose code is listed in Figure 23-20, executes the RSQL command:

```
>>-EXEC DBA: IMPORT --- database_name ----------------- datafile --------->

>---------------- INSERT -----------------+------- DEL ---+------- tname ---------><
              |-- REPLACE-----------------|     |- ASC ---|
              |-- CREATE -----------------|     |- WSF ---|
              +-- REPLACE_CREATE ---------+     +- IXF ---+
```

where **datafile** is the path-name of the OS/2 file which contains the data to be imported, and **tname** is the fully qualified name of a table or a view which can be updated and which is to be the recipient of the data.

Here is what this command handler does:

1. It parses the parameters in the usual manner.
2. It sets the **dcoldata** parameter to NULL. This will let the Database Manager choose the columns in the same order as they appear in the datafile.
3. It formats a string which specifies how the data is to be imported. The choices are: INSERT, REPLACE, CREATE, and REPLACE_CREATE. This string is placed in the **data** field of the **tcolstrg** parameter.
4. It specifies a **msgfile** parameter which points to the name and path of an OS/2 file where additional error messages will be written to by the API handler.
5. It issues the **sqluimp()** API call.
6. It calls the **merge_file** helper function (see Figure 23-19 on page 641) to append the contents of the returned **msgfile** to the *response* file.

```
/*-------------------------------------------------------------------*/
/*  execute the IMPORT DBA function                                  */
/*-------------------------------------------------------------------*/
SHORT dba_import(PCHAR parm_str)
{
  static struct   sqldcol  *dcoldata = NULL;     /* dcoldata          */
  typedef struct
  { SHORT         length;                        /* string length     */
    CHAR          data[100];                     /* string of data    */
  } NUM_STR_TYPE;
  NUM_STR_TYPE    tcolstrg;                      /* tcolstrg          */
  BYTE            database_name[9];              /* Database name, null term*/
  CHAR            import_verb[9];                /* REPLACE etc, null term. */
  CHAR            table_name[29];                /* Qualified and null term.*/
  CHAR            datafile[80];                  /* Path name, null term.   */
  CHAR            exchange_format[4];            /* ASC, DEL etc., null term*/
  /*---------------------------------*/
  /* get the parm strings            */
  /*---------------------------------*/
  if (sscanf(parm_str, " %8s %80s %8s %3s %28s ",
                     database_name, datafile, import_verb, exchange_format,
                     table_name)
                  != parms.num_parms)
     {sprintf(err_msg, "\nSYNTAX ERROR: invalid parameters.");
      return(RECORD_ERR_MSG);
     }
  sprintf(tcolstrg.data,"%s INTO %s", import_verb, table_name);
  tcolstrg.length = strlen(tcolstrg.data);
```

Figure 23-20 (Part 1 of 2). Import Table Command Handler: dba_import().

```
   /*--------------------------------------------*/
   /* call the IMPORT API                         */
   /*--------------------------------------------*/
   sqluimp(database_name,                          /* database       */
           datafile,                               /* datafile       */
           dcoldata,                               /* dcoldata       */
           (struct sqlchar *)&tcolstrg,            /* tcolstrg       */
           exchange_format,                        /* filetype       */
           NULL,                                   /* filetmod       */
           msgfile,                                /* message file   */
           0,                                      /* caller action  */
           &sqlca);                                /* SQLCA          */
   merge_file(out_stream,msgfile);
   return(RECORD_SQLCA);
} /* end dba_import */
```

Figure 23-20 (Part 2 of 2). Import Table Command Handler: dba_import().

RUNSTATS: dba_runstats()

The **dba_runstats()** command handler, whose code is listed in Figure 23-21, executes the RSQL command:

```
▸▸─EXEC DBA: RUNSTATS── tname ──────────────────────────▸◂
```

This command handler decodes its parameters and then executes a **sqlustat()** API call. The handler, through its parameters, specifies that statistics are to be generated on the table as well as all of its indexes. Make sure to read the comments that are associated with the API parameters in the code below.

```
/*------------------------------------------------------------------*/
/*  execute the RUNSTATS DBA function                               */
/*------------------------------------------------------------------*/
SHORT dba_runstats(PCHAR parm_str)
{
  CHAR          table_name[29];       /* fully qualif., null terminated   */

  /*--------------------------------------------*/
  /* get the parm strings                        */
  /*--------------------------------------------*/
  if (sscanf(parm_str, " %28s ", table_name
          ) != parms.num_parms)
     {
      sprintf(err_msg, "\nSYNTAX ERROR: invalid parameters.");
      return(RECORD_ERR_MSG);
     }
```

Figure 23-21 (Part 1 of 2). RUNSTATS Command Handler: dba_runstats().

```
  /*-------------------------------------------------------*/
  /* call the RUNSTATS API                                  */
  /*-------------------------------------------------------*/
  sqlustat(table_name,          /* name of the table              */
           0,                   /* run statistics on all indexes  */
           NULL,                /* empty index list because all is chosen*/
           'B',                 /* run stats on both table and indexes   */
           'R',                 /* read-only access to others during cmd.*/
           &sqlca);             /* SQLCA                          */
  return(RECORD_SQLCA);
} /* end dba_runstats */
```

Figure 23-21 (Part 2 of 2). RUNSTATS Command Handler: dba_runstats().

REORG Table: dba_reorg()

The **dba_rerog()** command handler, whose code is listed in Figure 23-22, executes the RSQL command:

```
►►-EXEC DBA: REORG ---- database_name -- tname ---- tindex ------------►◄
```

where **tindex** is the fully qualified index name to be used in the reorganization. Rows will be physically ordered according to this index. A NULL may be entered if no index is to be used for the reorganization. The command handler decodes its parameters and then executes a **sqlureor()** API call.

```
/*----------------------------------------------------------------------*/
/*  execute the REORG DBA function                                      */
/*----------------------------------------------------------------------*/
SHORT dba_reorg(PCHAR parm_str)
{
  BYTE          database_name[9];           /* Database name, null term*/
  CHAR          table_name[29];             /* Qualified and null term.*/
  CHAR          index_name[29];             /* Qualified and null term.*/

  /*-------------------------------------------------------*/
  /* get the parm strings                                   */
  /*-------------------------------------------------------*/
  if (sscanf(parm_str, " %8s %28s %28s ",
                     database_name, table_name, index_name)
                  != parms.num_parms)
     {
      sprintf(err_msg, "\nSYNTAX ERROR: invalid parameters.");
      return(RECORD_ERR_MSG);
     }
```

Figure 23-22 (Part 1 of 2). REORG Table Command Handler: dba_reorg().

```
/*-------------------------------------------------------*/
/* call the REORG  API                                   */
/*-------------------------------------------------------*/
sqlureor(database_name,                              /* database           */
         table_name,                                 /* table_name         */
         index_name,                                 /* index_name         */
         NULL,                                       /* temp file path     */
         &sqlca);                                    /* SQLCA              */
return(RECORD_SQLCA);
} /* dba_reorg */
```

Figure 23-22 (Part 2 of 2). REORG Table Command Handler: dba_reorg().

Get Admin Authorization: dba_get_admin()

The **dba_get_admin()** command handler, whose code is listed in Figure 23-23, executes the RSQL command:

```
▸▸-EXEC DBA: GET_ADMIN ------------------------------------------▸◂
```

The handler issues the **sqluadau()** API call and the authorization list is returned in an OS/2 EE defined structure. This OS/2 EE-provided structure is included in **sqlaprep.h** and reproduced below:

```
typedef struct      /* System Status data structure */
{   USHORT      sql_authorizations_len;   /* User provided length of struct  */
    USHORT      sql_sysadm_auth;          /* System Administrator? 0=No 1=Yes*/
    USHORT      sql_dbadm_auth;           /* DB Administrator auth?0=No 1=Yes*/
    USHORT      sql_createtab_auth;       /* Create table auth?    0=No 1=Yes*/
    USHORT      sql_bindadd_auth;         /* BindAdd auth?         0=No 1=Yes*/
    USHORT      sql_connect_auth;         /* Connect auth?         0=No 1=Yes*/
    USHORT      sql_sysadm_grp_auth;      /* Group Sysadm auth?    0=No 1=Yes*/
    USHORT      sql_dbadm_grp_auth;       /* Group DB admin  auth? 0=No 1=Yes*/
    USHORT      sql_createtab_grp_auth;   /* Group Create table?   0=No 1=Yes*/
    USHORT      sql_bindadd_grp_auth;     /* Group BindAdd?        0=No 1=Yes*/
    USHORT      sql_connect_grp_auth;     /* Group Connect?        0=No 1=Yes*/
} sql_authorizations;
```

```
/*-------------------------------------------------------------------*/
/*  execute the GET_ADMIN DBA function                               */
/*-------------------------------------------------------------------*/
SHORT dba_get_admin(VOID)
{
  struct sql_authorizations  author_list;
  /*----------------------------------*/
  /* call the GET_ADMIN API           */
  /*----------------------------------*/
  author_list.sql_authorizations_len = sizeof(author_list);
  sqluadau(&author_list,                        /* authorization list  */
           &sqlca);                             /* SQLCA               */
  if (sqlca.sqlcode != 0 )
     return(RECORD_SQLCA);
  /*----------------------------------*/
  /* record authorizations            */
  /*----------------------------------*/
  fprintf(out_stream,"\n Authorization type         Authorized? (0=NO, 1=YES)"
                     "\n ------------------         -------------------------"
                     "\n System Administrator                 %d"
                     "\n Database Administrator               %d"
                     "\n Create Tables                        %d"
                     "\n Bind new Programs                    %d",
  author_list.sql_sysadm_auth,      author_list.sql_dbadm_auth,
  author_list.sql_createtab_auth,   author_list.sql_bindadd_auth);
  fprintf(out_stream,"\n Access current database              %d"
                     "\n Group System Administrator           %d"
                     "\n Group Database Administrator         %d"
                     "\n Group Create Tables                  %d"
                     "\n Group Bind new Programs              %d"
                     "\n Group Access current database        %d\n",
  author_list.sql_connect_auth,    author_list.sql_sysadm_grp_auth,
  author_list.sql_dbadm_grp_auth,   author_list.sql_createtab_grp_auth,
  author_list.sql_bindadd_grp_auth, author_list.sql_connect_grp_auth);

  return(RECORD_SQLCA);
} /* end dba_get_admin */
```

Figure 23-23. Get Admin Authorization Handler: dba_get_admin().

RSQL.SQC: CONFIGURATION SERVICES COMMAND HANDLERS

Reset Database Configuration: dba_reset_db_cfg()

The **reset_db_cfg()** command handler, whose code is listed in Figure 23-24, executes the RSQL command:

```
▸▸-EXEC DBA: RESET_DB_CFG - database_name ----------------------▸◂
```

This command handler decodes its parameters and then executes a **sqlfrdbc()** API call.

```
/*------------------------------------------------------------------*/
/*  execute the RESET_DB_CFG DBA function                           */
/*------------------------------------------------------------------*/
SHORT dba_reset_db_cfg(PCHAR parm_str)
{ BYTE            database_name[9];          /* Database name, null term*/

  if (sscanf(parm_str, " %8s ", database_name) != parms.num_parms)
     { sprintf(err_msg, "\nSYNTAX ERROR: invalid parameters.");
       return(RECORD_ERR_MSG);
     }
  /*------------------------------------*/
  /* call the RESET DATABASE CONFIG API */
  /*------------------------------------*/
  sqlfrdbc(database_name,                      /* database          */
           &sqlca);                            /* SQLCA             */
  return(RECORD_SQLCA);
} /* end dba_reset_db_cfg */
```

Figure 23-24. Reset Database Configuration Command Handler: dba_reset_db_cfg().

Update Database Configuration: dba_update_db_cfg()

The **dba_update_db_cfg()** command handler, whose code is listed in Figure 23-25, executes the RSQL command:

```
                                                ┌──────────,──────────┐
                                                ▼                     │
►►-EXEC DBA: UPDATE_DB_CFG — database_name ─┬─ MAXAPPLS    = value  ─┴─►◄
                                            ├─ MAXFILOP    = value  ─┤
                                            ├─ MAXTOTFILOP= value   ─┤
                                            ├─ BUFFPAGE    = value  ─┤
                                            ├─ DLCHKTIME   = value  ─┤
                                            ├─ LOCKLIST    = value  ─┤
                                            ├─ MAXLOCKS    = value  ─┤
                                            ├─ APPLHEAPSZ  = value  ─┤
                                            ├─ AGENTHEAP   = value  ─┤
                                            ├─ SORTHEAP    = value  ─┤
                                            ├─ DBHEAP      = value  ─┤
                                            ├─ STMTHEAP    = value  ─┤
                                            ├─ LOGFILSIZ   = string ─┤
                                            ├─ LOGPRIMARY  = value  ─┤
                                            ├─ LOGSECOND   = value  ─┤
                                            ├─ SOFTMAX     = value  ─┤
                                            ├─ NEWLOGPATH  = string ─┤
                                            └─ DETS        = value  ─┘
```

These parameters are all explained in the "Database Administration API: Configuration Services" on page 475. The command handler first parses the database name. After that, its job is to create an entry for each of the configuration parameters specified in the RSQL command in a **db_cfg_array** of type **CONFG_ENTRY_TYPE**. This type is defined in RSQL.H and reproduced below for your convenience:

```
typedef struct
{
 USHORT         token;                    /* which field to return        */
 CHAR          *ptrvalue;                 /* where to put field info      */
}  CONFG_ENTRY_TYPE;
```

The command handler parses the configuration parameters by iterating through a loop once for each parameter that is passed to it. This is what happens during each loop iteration:

1. The parameter name is parsed into the **parm_name** variable.
2. The helper routine **decode_dbcfg_string()** (see listing in Figure 23-26) is invoked and passed the parameter name. This routine takes the parameter name and looks up a Database Manager defined (in **sqlutil.h**) token constant for it. It then returns the token number, a pointer to a global variable, and the data type of that variable.
3. The command handler uses the returned type to parse the value on the right of the equal sign and convert it to the appropriate type. It does this by creating "on the fly" a type-specific **format_string**, which it then uses in conjunction with **sscanf()** to extract the parameter value and assign it to the global variable that the **ptrvalue** field in the array points to.

At the end of the loop, the command handler knows how many configuration items need to be updated and, for each item, it has created an entry in the **db_cfg_array**. The handler is now ready to issue the update database configuration API call **sqlfudb()**.

```
/*-------------------------------------------------------------------------*/
/*  execute the UPDATE_DB_CFG DBA function                                 */
/*-------------------------------------------------------------------------*/
SHORT dba_update_db_cfg(PCHAR parm_str)
{
  CHAR   parm_name[12];                      /* config token name       */
  SHORT  rcd;                                /* return code temp var    */
  USHORT index;                              /* array index             */
  USHORT parm_val_type;                      /* config parm type        */
  CONFG_ENTRY_TYPE db_cfg_array[18];         /* array of token and item */
                                             /*     parameters          */
  CHAR   format_string[40];                  /* format string for sscanf*/
  CHAR   delimiter;                          /* config parm delimiter   */
  BYTE   database_name[9];                   /* Database name, null term*/
  /*---------------------------------------*/
  /* get the database name                 */
  /*---------------------------------------*/
  strcat(parm_str,";");                               /* add a delimiter   */
  if (sscanf(parm_str, " %8s %[^;] ", database_name, parm_str
            ) != parms.num_parms)
     {
      sprintf(err_msg, "\nSYNTAX ERROR: invalid parameters.");
      return(RECORD_ERR_MSG);
     }
  index=0;
```

Figure 23-25 (Part 1 of 3). Update DB Config Handler: dba_update_db_cfg().

```
/*-----------------------------------------*/
/* get the parm strings and their values   */
/*   to form the configuration array       */
/*-----------------------------------------*/
do
{  /*-----------------------------------------*/
   /* get a parm name                         */
   /*-----------------------------------------*/
   strcat(parm_str,";");                          /* add a delimiter   */
   if (sscanf(parm_str, " %11s = %[^;] ", parm_name, parm_str) != 2)
      {sprintf(err_msg, "\nSYNTAX ERROR: invalid parameters.");
       return(RECORD_ERR_MSG);
      }
   strcat(parm_str,";");                          /* add a delimiter   */
   /*-----------------------------------------*/
   /* convert to a parm number, value_ptr,    */
   /*    and value_type                       */
   /*-----------------------------------------*/
   if (decode_dbcfg_string(parm_name, &db_cfg_array[index].token,
                           &db_cfg_array[index].ptrvalue, &parm_val_type))
      {sprintf(err_msg,
               "\nSYNTAX ERROR: Invalid configuration parameter %s.",
               parm_name);
       return(RECORD_ERR_MSG);
      }
   /*-----------------------------------------*/
   /* Create a format template for variable   */
   /*-----------------------------------------*/
   switch (parm_val_type)
     { case SQL_TYP_SMALL:                        /* small integer(SHORT)*/
            strcpy(format_string, " %d%*[^,;]%c%[^;]");
            break;
       case SQL_TYP_INTEGER:                      /* integer (LONG)      */
            strcpy(format_string, " %ld%*[^,;]%c%[^;]");
            break;
       case SQL_TYP_CSTR:                         /* c string            */
            strcpy(format_string, " %[^ ,;]%*[^,;]%c%[^;]");
            break;
     } /* endswitch */
   /*-----------------------------------------*/
   /* Read the variable and convert it        */
   /*-----------------------------------------*/
   rcd = sscanf(parm_str, format_string,
                db_cfg_array[index].ptrvalue, &delimiter, parm_str);

   if ( ((delimiter == ';') && (rcd != 2)) ||
        ((delimiter == ',') && (rcd != 3)) ||
        ((delimiter != ',') && (delimiter != ';')) )
      {sprintf(err_msg,
               "\nSYNTAX ERROR: Invalid configuration parameter %s.",
               parm_name);
       return(RECORD_ERR_MSG);
      }
   ++index;                                       /* increment array index*/
 } while (delimiter != ';'); /* enddo */
```

Figure 23-25 (Part 2 of 3). Update DB Config Handler: dba_update_db_cfg().

```
/*---------------------------------------------*/
/* call the UPDATE DB CONFIG API               */
/*---------------------------------------------*/
sqlfudb(database_name,                           /* database name     */
        index,                                   /* number of items   */
        (struct sqlfupd   *)db_cfg_array,        /* list of items     */
        &sqlca);                                 /* SQLCA             */

return(RECORD_SQLCA);
} /* end dba_update_db_cfg */
```

Figure 23-25 (Part 3 of 3). Update DB Config Handler: dba_update_db_cfg().

The Helper Procedure: decode_dbcfg_string()

```
/*-------------------------------------------------------------------------*/
/*  This procedure converts a parameter string into a value and a pointer  */
/*  to a variable and a type for update database manager configuration.   */
/*-------------------------------------------------------------------------*/
SHORT decode_dbcfg_string(PCHAR  parm, PSHORT parm_num, PCHAR *parm_val_ptr,
                          PSHORT parm_val_type)
{ /*-----------------------------------------*/
  /* Initialize cmds table                   */
  /*-----------------------------------------*/
  typedef struct
  {
    CHAR      parm_str[40];            /* cmd name                        */
    SHORT     parm_num;                /* numerical representation of cmd */
    PCHAR     parm_val_ptr;            /* parameter value pointer         */
    SHORT     parm_val_type;           /* parameter value pointer         */
  }   PARM_TYPE;

  #define DBCFG_COUNT     18
  static PARM_TYPE parms[DBCFG_COUNT] =
  {/*<-parm_str><- parm_num------><-- parm_val_ptr---------><-parm_val_type>*/
{"LOCKLIST",    SQLF_DBTN_LOCKLIST,    (CHAR *)&dbcfg.locklist,   SQL_TYP_SMALL},
{"BUFFPAGE",    SQLF_DBTN_BUFFPAGE,    (CHAR *)&dbcfg.buffpage,   SQL_TYP_SMALL},
{"MAXFILOP",    SQLF_DBTN_MAXFILOP,    (CHAR *)&dbcfg.maxfilop,   SQL_TYP_SMALL},
{"SOFTMAX",     SQLF_DBTN_SOFTMAX,     (CHAR *)&dbcfg.softmax,    SQL_TYP_SMALL},
{"MAXAPPLS",    SQLF_DBTN_MAXAPPLS,    (CHAR *)&dbcfg.maxappls,   SQL_TYP_SMALL},
{"APPLHEAPSZ" ,SQLF_DBTN_APPLHEAPSZ, (CHAR *)&dbcfg.applheapsz, SQL_TYP_SMALL},
{"DBHEAP",      SQLF_DBTN_DBHEAP,      (CHAR *)&dbcfg.dbheap,     SQL_TYP_SMALL},
{"DLCHKTIME",   SQLF_DBTN_DLCHKTIME,   (CHAR *)&dbcfg.dlchktime,SQL_TYP_INTEGER},
{"MAXTOTFILOP",SQLF_DBTN_MAXTOTFILOP,(CHAR *)&dbcfg.maxtotfilop,SQL_TYP_SMALL},
{"SORTHEAP",    SQLF_DBTN_SORTHEAP,    (CHAR *)&dbcfg.sortheap,   SQL_TYP_SMALL},
{"AGENTHEAP",   SQLF_DBTN_AGENTHEAP,   (CHAR *)&dbcfg.agentheap,  SQL_TYP_SMALL},
{"MAXLOCKS",    SQLF_DBTN_MAXLOCKS,    (CHAR *)&dbcfg.maxlocks,   SQL_TYP_SMALL},
{"LOGPRIMARY", SQLF_DBTN_LOGPRIMARY, (CHAR *)&dbcfg.logprimary, SQL_TYP_SMALL},
{"LOGSECOND",   SQLF_DBTN_LOGSECOND,   (CHAR *)&dbcfg.logsecond,  SQL_TYP_SMALL},
```

Figure 23-26 (Part 1 of 2). The Helper Procedure: decode_dbcfg_string().

```
{"LOGFILSIZ",  SQLF_DBTN_LOGFILSIZ,  (CHAR *)&dbcfg.logfilsiz,  SQL_TYP_SMALL},
{"STMTHEAP",   SQLF_DBTN_STMTHEAP,   (CHAR *)&dbcfg.stmtheap,   SQL_TYP_SMALL},
{"NEWLOGPATH", SQLF_DBTN_NEWLOGPATH, (CHAR *) dbcfg.newlogpath, SQL_TYP_CSTR },
{"DETS",       SQLF_DBTN_DETS,       (CHAR *)&dbcfg.dets,       SQL_TYP_SMALL}
  };
  SHORT     parm_not_found;           /* True if a match is found         */
  USHORT    i;                        /* loop index variable              */

  /*------------------------------------------*/
  /* decode the parm string                   */
  /*------------------------------------------*/
  i = 0 ;
  parm_not_found = TRUE ;

  while ( parm_not_found && (i < DBCFG_COUNT))
  {
    parm_not_found = strcmp(parms[i].parm_str,parm);
    if (!parm_not_found)
       break;
    else
       i++;
  }

  if (parm_not_found )
     {
      sprintf(err_msg,
        "\nSYNTAX ERROR: Unknown Configuration parameter string. ");
      return(FAILED);
     }
  else
     {
      *parm_num      = parms[i].parm_num;
      *parm_val_ptr  = parms[i].parm_val_ptr;
      *parm_val_type = parms[i].parm_val_type;
      return(GOOD);
     }
} /* end decode_dbcfg_string */
```

Figure 23-26 (Part 2 of 2). The Helper Procedure: decode_dbcfg_string().

Show Database Configuration: dba_show_db_cfg()

The **dba_show_db_cfg()** command handler, whose code is listed in Figure 23-27, executes the RSQL command:

```
▸▸-EXEC DBA: SHOW_DB_CFG — database_name ——————————————————▸◂
```

This command handler will format and write all the configuration parameters to the *response* file for the specified database. This is how it does that:

1. A static C array of type CONFG_ENTRY_TYPE is initialized with an entry for each database parameter. You've already encountered this type in the previous section:

```
typedef struct
{
 USHORT         token;                      /* which field to return        */
 CHAR          *ptrvalue;                   /* where to put field info      */
}  CONFG_ENTRY_TYPE;
```

2. Each array entry is initialized to contain a token number (remember these are defined by OS/2 EE in **sqlutil.h**) and a pointer to a variable which will receive the value of the parameter. These variables are all part of a structure defined in RSQL.H.
3. The **sqlfxdbc**() API is called and told to go and fetch all 22 database parameters and put the results in the variables the **db_cfg_array** points to.
4. Finally, the results are formatted and inserted in the *response* file. If you are not clear on what those 22 parameters do, please make sure to refer to the tutorial in "Database Administration API: Configuration Services" on page 475.

```
/*-------------------------------------------------------------------------*/
/*  execute the SHOW_DB_CFG DBA function                                   */
/*-------------------------------------------------------------------------*/
SHORT dba_show_db_cfg(PCHAR parm_str)
{
 static CONFIG_ENTRY_TYPE db_cfg_array[] =        /* array of token and items*/
   {/*<--- token ------------><-- pointer ------------------>*/
    {SQLF_DBTN_LOCKLIST     , (CHAR *)&dbcfg.locklist       },
    {SQLF_DBTN_BUFFPAGE     , (CHAR *)&dbcfg.buffpage       },
    {SQLF_DBTN_MAXFILOP     , (CHAR *)&dbcfg.maxfilop       },
    {SQLF_DBTN_SOFTMAX      , (CHAR *)&dbcfg.softmax        },
    {SQLF_DBTN_MAXAPPLS     , (CHAR *)&dbcfg.maxappls       },
    {SQLF_DBTN_APPLHEAPSZ   , (CHAR *)&dbcfg.applheapsz     },
    {SQLF_DBTN_DBHEAP       , (CHAR *)&dbcfg.dbheap         },
    {SQLF_DBTN_DLCHKTIME    , (CHAR *)&dbcfg.dlchktime      },
    {SQLF_DBTN_MAXTOTFILOP  , (CHAR *)&dbcfg.maxtotfilop    },
    {SQLF_DBTN_SORTHEAP     , (CHAR *)&dbcfg.sortheap       },
    {SQLF_DBTN_AGENTHEAP    , (CHAR *)&dbcfg.agentheap      },
    {SQLF_DBTN_MAXLOCKS     , (CHAR *)&dbcfg.maxlocks       },
    {SQLF_DBTN_LOGPRIMARY   , (CHAR *)&dbcfg.logprimary     },
    {SQLF_DBTN_LOGSECOND    , (CHAR *)&dbcfg.logsecond      },
    {SQLF_DBTN_LOGFILSIZ    , (CHAR *)&dbcfg.logfilsiz      },
    {SQLF_DBTN_STMTHEAP     , (CHAR *)&dbcfg.stmtheap       },
    {SQLF_DBTN_NEWLOGPATH   , (CHAR *) dbcfg.newlogpath     },
    {SQLF_DBTN_DETS         , (CHAR *)&dbcfg.dets           },
    {SQLF_DBTN_COUNTRY      , (CHAR *)&dbcfg.country        },
    {SQLF_DBTN_CODEPAGE     , (CHAR *)&dbcfg.codepage       },
    {SQLF_DBTN_RELEASE      , (CHAR *)&dbcfg.release        },
    {SQLF_DBTN_LOGPATH      , (CHAR *) dbcfg.logpath        }
   };
 BYTE    database_name[9];                       /* Database dame, null term*/
```

Figure 23-27 (Part 1 of 3). Show DB Config Command Handler: dba_show_db_cfg().

```
/*-----------------------------------------------*/
/* get the parm strings                          */
/*-----------------------------------------------*/
if (sscanf(parm_str, " %8s ", database_name
          ) != parms.num_parms)
   {
    sprintf(err_msg, "\nSYNTAX ERROR: invalid parameters.");
    return(RECORD_ERR_MSG);
   }
/*-----------------------------------------------*/
/* call the GET DB CONFIG API                    */
/*-----------------------------------------------*/
sqlfxdb(database_name,                          /* database          */
        22,                                     /* num of fields reqd */
        (struct sqlfupd   *)db_cfg_array,       /* array of cfg items */
        &sqlca);                                /* SQLCA             */
if (sqlca.sqlcode != 0)
  return(RECORD_SQLCA);                         /* command failed    */
/*-----------------------------------------------*/
/* record the results                            */
/*-----------------------------------------------*/
fprintf(out_stream,
"\n Database Configuration for Database %s"
"\n ==============================================="
"\n\n Configuration Parameter          Current  Parm.      Parm.      Parm."
"\n Description                      Value    Units      Range      Default"
"\n ------------------------------- -------- ---------- ---------- -------",
database_name);
fprintf(out_stream,
"\n Max. Active Applications         %5d   Appl.      1-117          8"
"\n Max. DB Files Open/Application   %5d   files      2-235         20"
"\n Max. Files Open/Application      %5d   files      25-32700     255"
"\n Buffer Pool Size                 %5d   4K pages     (1)         16"
"\n Time Interval for Deadlocks   %91d   millisecs. 1-600 sec.    10",
dbcfg.maxappls, dbcfg.maxfilop, dbcfg.maxtotfilop,
dbcfg.buffpage, dbcfg.dlchktime);
fprintf(out_stream,
"\n Max. Storage for Locklists       %5d   4K pages   4-250          8"
"\n Max. percent locklist/appl.      %5d   percent    1-100         22"
"\n Default Application Heap         %5d   segments   2-20           3"
"\n Application Agent Heap           %5d   segments   2-85           3"
"\n Sort List Heap                   %5d   segments   1-20           2"
"\n Database Heap                    %5d   segments   1-45           1"
"\n SQL Statement Heap               %5d   segments                 64",
dbcfg.locklist, dbcfg.maxlocks, dbcfg.applheapsz, dbcfg.agentheap,
dbcfg.sortheap, dbcfg.dbheap, dbcfg.stmtheap);
fprintf(out_stream,
"\n Log File Size                    %5d   4K pages   15-255        50"
"\n Primary Log Files                %5d   files      0-63           2"
"\n Secondary Log Files              %5d   files      0-63           3"
"\n Log Records/soft checkpoint      %5d   records    0-65535      100",
dbcfg.logfilsiz, dbcfg.logprimary, dbcfg.logsecond, dbcfg.softmax);
```

Figure 23-27 (Part 2 of 3). Show DB Config Command Handler: dba_show_db_cfg().

```
    fprintf(out_stream,
    "\n\n Current Log Location = %-80.80s"
    "\n New Log Location     = %-80.80s"
    "\n Copy Protection      = %5d"
    "\n Country              = %5d"
    "\n Code Page            = %5d"
    "\n Release              = %5d\n",
    dbcfg.logpath, dbcfg.newlogpath, dbcfg.dets, dbcfg.country,
    dbcfg.codepage, dbcfg.release);

    return(RECORD_SQLCA);
  } /* end dba_show_db_cfg */
```

Figure 23-27 (Part 3 of 3). Show DB Config Command Handler: dba_show_db_cfg().

Reset Database Mgr Configuration: dba_reset_dm_cfg()

The **dba_reset_dm_cfg()** command handler, whose code is listed in Figure 23-28, executes the RSQL command:

```
►►─EXEC DBA: RESET_DM_CFG ──────────────────────────────────►◄
```

This command handler simply issues an **sqlfrsys()** API call.

```
/*──────────────────────────────────────────────────────────────────*/
/*  execute the RESET_DM_CFG DBA function                           */
/*──────────────────────────────────────────────────────────────────*/
SHORT dba_reset_dm_cfg(VOID)
{
  sqlfrsys(&sqlca);                              /* SQLCA            */
  return(RECORD_SQLCA);
} /* end dba_reset_dm_cfg */
```

Figure 23-28. Reset Database Mgr Config Handler: dba_reset_dm_cfg().

Update Database Mgr Configuration: dba_update_dm_cfg()

The **dba_update_dm_cfg()** command handler, whose code is listed in Figure 23-29, executes the RSQL command:

```
                                        ┌──────────────,───────────────┐
                                        ▼                              │
►►─EXEC DBA: UPDATE_DM_CFG ─────────────┬─ RQRIOBLK   = value  ────────┴─►◄
                                        ├─ SVRIOBLK   = value  ─┤
                                        ├─ SQLENSEG   = value  ─┤
                                        ├─ NUMDB      = value  ─┤
                                        ├─ NNAME      = string ─┤
                                        ├─ COMHEAPSZ  = value  ─┤
                                        ├─ RSHEAPSZ   = value  ─┤
                                        └─ NUMRC      = value  ─┘
```

This command handler is like "Update Database Configuration: dba_update_db_cfg()" on page 647. The API uses the same "array of tokens and pointers" mechanism to pass the values of the parameters to be updated. The different tokens are obtained by calling the helper routine **decode_dmcfg_string()** (see listing in Figure 23-30). This helper routine works just like **decode_dbcfg_string()**, but uses a different internal look-up table for its tokens. The API call **sqlfisys()** is issued instead of **sqlfudb()**.

```
/*------------------------------------------------------------------------*/
/*  execute the UPDATE_DM_CFG DBA function                                */
/*------------------------------------------------------------------------*/
SHORT dba_update_dm_cfg(PCHAR parm_str)
{ CHAR   parm_name[12];                   /* config token name       */
  SHORT  rcd;                             /* return code temp var    */
  USHORT index;                           /* array index             */
  USHORT parm_val_type;                   /* config parm type        */
  CONFG_ENTRY_TYPE dm_cfg_array[8];       /* configuration array     */
  CHAR   format_string[40];               /* format string for sscanf*/
  CHAR   delimiter;                       /* config parm delimiter   */
  /*------------------------------------------*/
  /* get the parm strings and their values    */
  /*------------------------------------------*/
  index=0;
  do
   { /*------------------------------------------*/
     /* get a parm name                          */
     /*                                          */
     strcat(parm_str,";");                       /* add a delimiter   */
     if (sscanf(parm_str, " %11s = %[^;] ", parm_name, parm_str) != 2)
        {sprintf(err_msg, "\nSYNTAX ERROR: invalid parameters.");
         return(RECORD_ERR_MSG);
        }
     strcat(parm_str,";");                       /* add a delimiter   */
     /*------------------------------------------*/
     /* convert to a parm number, value_ptr,     */
     /*    and value_type                        */
     /*------------------------------------------*/
     if (decode_dmcfg_string(parm_name, &dm_cfg_array[index].token,
                        &dm_cfg_array[index].ptrvalue, &parm_val_type))
        {sprintf(err_msg,
                 "\nSYNTAX ERROR: Invalid configuration parameter %s.",
                 parm_name);
         return(RECORD_ERR_MSG);
        }
```

Figure 23-29 (Part 1 of 2). Update DB Mgr Config Handler: dba_update_dm_cfg().

```
        /*-----------------------------------------*/
        /* customize the format parameters         */
        /*-----------------------------------------*/
        switch (parm_val_type)
          { case SQL_TYP_SMALL:                            /* small integer(SHORT)*/
                 strcpy(format_string, " %d%*[^,;]%c%[^;]");
                 break;
            case SQL_TYP_INTEGER:                          /* integer (LONG)      */
                 strcpy(format_string, " %ld%*[^,;]%c%[^;]");
                 break;
            case SQL_TYP_CSTR:                             /* c string            */
                 strcpy(format_string, " %[^ ,;]%*[^,;]%c%[^;]");
                 break;
          } /* endswitch */
        /*-------------------------------*/
        /* Parse the values              */
        /*-------------------------------*/
        rcd = sscanf(parm_str, format_string,
                    dm_cfg_array[index].ptrvalue, &delimiter, parm_str);
        if ( ((delimiter == ';') && (rcd != 2)) ||
             ((delimiter == ',') && (rcd != 3)) ||
             ((delimiter != ',') && (delimiter != ';')) )
           {sprintf(err_msg,
                    "\nSYNTAX ERROR: Invalid configuration parameter %s.",
                    parm_name);
            return(RECORD_ERR_MSG);
           }
          ++index;                                         /* increment array index*/
      } while (delimiter != ';'); /* enddo */

      /*-----------------------------------------*/
      /* call the UPDATE DM CONFIG API           */
      /*-----------------------------------------*/
      sqlfusys(index,                                      /* number of items     */
               (struct sqlfupd   *)dm_cfg_array,           /* list of items       */
               &sqlca);                                    /* SQLCA               */

      return(RECORD_SQLCA);

    } /* end dba_update_dm_cfg */
```

Figure 23-29 (Part 2 of 2). Update DB Mgr Config Handler: dba_update_dm_cfg().

The Helper Procedure: decode_dmcfg_string()

```
/*-------------------------------------------------------------------------*/
/*  This procedure converts a parameter string into a value and a pointer   */
/*  to a variable and a type for update database manager configuration.    */
/*-------------------------------------------------------------------------*/
SHORT decode_dmcfg_string(PCHAR  parm, PSHORT parm_num, PCHAR *parm_val_ptr,
                          PSHORT parm_val_type)
{
  /*--------------------------------------*/
  /* Initialize cmds table                 */
  /*--------------------------------------*/
  typedef struct
  {
    CHAR      parm_str[40];            /* cmd name                           */
    SHORT     parm_num;                /* numerical representation of cmd    */
    PCHAR     parm_val_ptr;            /* parameter value pointer            */
    SHORT     parm_val_type;           /* parameter value pointer            */
  }  PARM_TYPE;
  #define DMCFG_COUNT     8
  static PARM_TYPE parms[DMCFG_COUNT] =
  {/*<-parm_str><- parm_num------><-- parm_val_ptr---------><-parm_val_type>*/
   {"RQRIOBLK", SQLF_KTN_RQRIOBLK, (CHAR *)&dmcfg.rqrioblk,   SQL_TYP_SMALL},
   {"SVRIOBLK", SQLF_KTN_SVRIOBLK, (CHAR *)&dmcfg.svrioblk,   SQL_TYP_SMALL},
   {"SQLENSEG", SQLF_KTN_SQLENSEG, (CHAR *)&dmcfg.sqlenseg,   SQL_TYP_SMALL},
   {"NUMDB",    SQLF_KTN_NUMDB,    (CHAR *)&dmcfg.numdb,      SQL_TYP_SMALL},
   {"NNAME",    SQLF_KTN_NNAME,    (CHAR *) dmcfg.nname,      SQL_TYP_CSTR },
   {"COMHEAPSZ",SQLF_KTN_COMHEAPSZ,(CHAR *)&dmcfg.comheapsz,  SQL_TYP_SMALL},
   {"RSHEAPSZ", SQLF_KTN_RSHEAPSZ, (CHAR *)&dmcfg.rsheapsz,   SQL_TYP_SMALL},
   {"NUMRC",    SQLF_KTN_NUMRC,    (CHAR *)&dmcfg.numrc,      SQL_TYP_SMALL}
  };

  SHORT      parm_not_found;            /* True if a match is found         */
  USHORT     i;                         /* loop index variable              */

  /*------------------------------------*/
  /* decode the parm string              */
  /*------------------------------------*/
  i = 0 ;
  parm_not_found = TRUE ;

  while ( parm_not_found && (i < DMCFG_COUNT))
  {
    parm_not_found = strcmp(parms[i].parm_str,parm);
    if (!parm_not_found)
       break;
    else
       i++;
  }

  if (parm_not_found )
     {
      sprintf(err_msg,
        "\nSYNTAX ERROR: Unknown Configuration parameter string. ");
      return(FAILED);
     }
```

Figure 23-30 (Part 1 of 2). The Helper Procedure: decode_dmcfg_string().

```
      else
        {
         *parm_num      = parms[i].parm_num;
         *parm_val_ptr  = parms[i].parm_val_ptr;
         *parm_val_type = parms[i].parm_val_type;
         return(GOOD);
        }
    } /* end decode_dmcfg_string */
```

Figure 23-30 (Part 2 of 2). The Helper Procedure: decode_dmcfg_string().

Show Database Mgr Configuration: dba_show_dm_cfg()

The **dba_show_dm_cfg()** command handler, whose code is listed in Figure 23-31, executes the RSQL command:

```
▸▸─EXEC DBA: SHOW_DM_CFG ──────────────────────────────────────▸◂
```

This command handler works just like "Show Database Configuration: dba_show_db_cfg()" on page 651, with the following exceptions:

- The **sqlfxsys()** API call is issued instead of **sqlfxdbc()**.
- The results are formatted differently, which is to be expected since we're displaying 10 Database Manager-related parameters instead of 22 Database-related parameters.

```
/*─────────────────────────────────────────────────────────────────*/
/*  execute the SHOW_DM_CFG DBA function                           */
/*─────────────────────────────────────────────────────────────────*/
SHORT dba_show_dm_cfg(VOID)
{
 static CONFIG_ENTRY_TYPE dm_cfg_array[] =        /* array of token and items*/
   {/*<--- token ------------><-- pointer ------------------->*/
    {SQLF_KTN_NODETYPE      , (CHAR *)&dmcfg.nodetype       },
    {SQLF_KTN_RQRIOBLK      , (CHAR *)&dmcfg.rqrioblk       },
    {SQLF_KTN_SVRIOBLK      , (CHAR *)&dmcfg.svrioblk       },
    {SQLF_KTN_SQLENSEG      , (CHAR *)&dmcfg.sqlenseg       },
    {SQLF_KTN_NUMDB         , (CHAR *)&dmcfg.numdb          },
    {SQLF_KTN_NNAME         , (CHAR *) dmcfg.nname          },
    {SQLF_KTN_COMHEAPSZ     , (CHAR *)&dmcfg.comheapsz      },
    {SQLF_KTN_RSHEAPSZ      , (CHAR *)&dmcfg.rsheapsz       },
    {SQLF_KTN_NUMRC         , (CHAR *)&dmcfg.numrc          },
    {SQLF_KTN_RELEASE       , (CHAR *)&dmcfg.release        },
   };
```

Figure 23-31 (Part 1 of 2). Show DB Mgr Config Handler: dba_show_dm_cfg().

```
     /*________________________________________*/
     /* call the GET DM CONFIG API             */
     /*________________________________________*/
     sqlfxsys(10,                                    /* num of fields reqd. */
              (struct sqlfupd   *)dm_cfg_array,      /* array of cfg items  */
              &sqlca);                               /* SQLCA               */

     if (sqlca.sqlcode != 0)
       return(RECORD_SQLCA);                         /* command failed      */
     /*________________________________________*/
     /* record the results                     */
     /*________________________________________*/
     fprintf(out_stream,
     "\n Database Manager Configuration"
     "\n =============================="
     "\n\n Configuration Parameter         Current  Parm.      Parm.      Parm."
     "\n Description                      Value    Units      Range      Default"
     "\n ------------------------------- -------- ---------- ---------- -------"
     );
     fprintf(out_stream,
     "\n Max. Shared Segments             %5d   Segments   7-802      20/50   (1)"
     "\n Max. Concurrently Active apps.   %5d   Number     1-8        3/8     (1)"
     "\n Max. Requestor I/O Block Size    %5d   bytes      4k-64k     0/0/4   (2)"
     "\n Max. Server   I/O Block Size     %5d   bytes      4k-64k     0/4/4/0 (2)"
     "\n Communication Heap Size          %5d   Segments   1-255      2",
     dmcfg.sqlenseg, dmcfg.numdb, dmcfg.rqrioblk, dmcfg.svrioblk, dmcfg.comheapsz);
     fprintf(out_stream,
     "\n Remote Data Services Heap size   %5d   Segments   1-255      2 "
     "\n Max. Remote Connections          %5d   Number     1-255      10      (3)"
     "\n\n Node Type     = %8d"
     "\n Node Name     = %8.8s"
     "\n Release Level = %5d"
     "\n\n (1) - Stand-alone/Server"
     "\n (2) - Stand-alone/Server/Requester-Server/Requester"
     "\n (3) - Server\n",
     dmcfg.rsheapsz, dmcfg.numrc, dmcfg.nodetype, dmcfg.nname, dmcfg.release);
     return(RECORD_SQLCA);
   } /* end dba_show_dm_cfg */
```

Figure 23-31 (Part 2 of 2). Show DB Mgr Config Handler: dba_show_dm_cfg().

RSQL.SQC: APPLICATION SERVICES COMMAND HANDLERS

BIND: dba_bind()

The **dba_bind()** command handler, whose code is listed in Figure 23-32, executes the RSQL command:

```
>>-EXEC DBA: BIND ---- database_name ---- pgm_name --+-ISO-+-------->
                                                     +-USA-+
                                                     +-DEF-+
                                                     +-EUR-+
                                                     +-JIS-+
                                                     +-LOC-+

>---------+- REPEATABLE_READ ---+-+- NO_BLOCKING ---+-- user_id ------><
          +- CURSOR_STABILITY --+ +- BLOCK_ALL -----+
          +- UNCOMMITTED_READ --+ +- BLOCK_UNAMBIG -+
```

These parameters are all explained in the tutorial in Chapter 18. We're only interested here in how the command handler conveys that information using the **sqlabndr()** API call. This is done as follows:

1. The parameters are parsed in the usual manner.
2. The parameters that need to be converted from strings to numbers are passed to **decode_parm_string()** which does its usual magic.
3. The next step is to fill-in the contents of **bind_options**, a structure of type SQLOPT. This structure has a fixed header portion and a variable array of elements. The BIND API has four options, so we set the header's *allocated* field to four. We allocate an array of four option elements, and place in each element the option type and a pointer to the option value. The four option types are:

   SQL_FRMT_OPT This option defines the date-time format, such as ISO or USA.

   SQL_ISO_OPT This option defines the isolation level of the program, such as Read Repeatability or Cursor Stability.

   SQL_BLOCK_OPT This option defines the blocking, such as BLOCK_ALL.

   SQL_GRANT_OPT This option defines the grant ID.

4. The **sqlabndr()** call is then issued to do the BIND.
5. The **merge_file()** helper function is called (see Figure 23-19 on page 641) to append the contents of the **msgfile** to the *response* file.

```
/*------------------------------------------------------------------------*/
/*  execute the BIND DBA function                                          */
/*------------------------------------------------------------------------*/
SHORT dba_bind(PCHAR parm_str)
{
  typedef struct                         /* options structure for binder    */
  {
     struct sqloptheader                 /* Header for sqlopt structur      */
     {
        ULONG allocated;                 /* Number of options allocated     */
        ULONG used;                      /* Number of options used          */
     }  header;
     struct sqlbindopt                   /* Array of bind options           */
     {
        ULONG type;                      /* Type of bind option             */
        ULONG val;                       /* Value of bind option            */
     }  option[4];
  } SQLOPT;

  SQLOPT bind_options;                   /* variable for binder options     */
  USHORT date_time_option;               /* temp variable for option value  */
  USHORT isolation_level_option;         /* temp variable for option value  */
  USHORT blocking_option;                /* temp variable for option value  */
  BYTE   database_name[9];               /* Database name, null terminated  */
  CHAR   pgm_name[80];                   /* Path name bind file, null term. */
  CHAR   date_time_format[4];            /* ISO, DEF, USA etc. null term.   */
  CHAR   isolation_level[17];            /* isolation level for bind        */
  CHAR   blocking_type[14];              /* type of blocking for bind       */
  struct
  {  SHORT  length;
     BYTE   data[9];
  }  grant_id;                           /* grant id for bind               */

  /*-----------------------------------*/
  /* get the parm strings              */
  /*-----------------------------------*/
  strcpy(grant_id,"        ");           /* fill grant_id with blanks       */
  if (sscanf(parm_str, " %8s %80s %4s %17s %14s %8s ",
                     database_name, pgm_name, date_time_format,
                     isolation_level, blocking_type, grant_id.data)
                  != parms.num_parms)
     {
      sprintf(err_msg, "\nSYNTAX ERROR: invalid parameters.");
      return(RECORD_ERR_MSG);
     }

  grant_id.length = strlen(grant_id.data);     /* calculate grant id length */

  /*-----------------------------------*/
  /* decode the parms, set up options struc. */
  /*-----------------------------------*/
  if ( decode_parm_string(date_time_format, &date_time_option) ||
       decode_parm_string(isolation_level,  &isolation_level_option) ||
       decode_parm_string(blocking_type,    &blocking_option) )
     {
      sprintf(err_msg, "\nSYNTAX ERROR: invalid parameter.");
      return(RECORD_ERR_MSG);
     }
```

Figure 23-32 (Part 1 of 2). Bind Command Handler: dba_bind().

```
    bind_options.header.allocated = 4;
    bind_options.header.used      = 4;
    bind_options.option[0].type   = SQL_FRMT_OPT;
    bind_options.option[0].val    = (LONG)date_time_option;
    bind_options.option[1].type   = SQL_ISO_OPT;
    bind_options.option[1].val    = (LONG)isolation_level_option;
    bind_options.option[2].type   = SQL_BLOCK_OPT;
    bind_options.option[2].val    = (LONG)blocking_option;
    bind_options.option[3].type   = SQL_GRANT_OPT;
    bind_options.option[3].val    = (LONG)&grant_id;

    /*-----------------------------------------*/
    /* call the bind API                       */
    /*-----------------------------------------*/
    sqlabndr(pgm_name,                            /* name of program to BIND  */
             database_name,                       /* database name            */
             msgfile,                             /* message file name        */
             (struct sqlopt *)&bind_options,      /* options structure        */
             &sqlca);                             /* SQLCA                    */
    merge_file(out_stream,msgfile);
    return(RECORD_SQLCA);
  } /* end dba_bind */
```

Figure 23-32 (Part 2 of 2). Bind Command Handler: dba_bind().

RSQL.SQC: GENERIC SERVICES COMMAND HANDLERS

LOG ON: dba_logon()

The **dba_logon()** command handler, whose code is listed in Figure 23-33, executes the RSQL command:

```
►►─EXEC DBA: LOGON ─── userid ── password ── remotename ──────────────►◄

►──────────┬─ UPM_LOCAL ──┬────┬─ UPM_CONFIG ─┬─────────────────────────►◄
           ├─ UPM_DNODE ──┤    ├─ UPM_ADMIN ──┤
           └─ UPM_DOMAIN ─┘    └─ UPM_USER ───┘
```

This command handler parses its parameters and issues a **upmelgn()** API call.

```
/*---------------------------------------------------------------------*/
/*  execute the LOGON DBA function                                     */
/*---------------------------------------------------------------------*/
SHORT dba_logon(PCHAR parm_str)
{ CHAR  password[9];              /* Current password, null terminat. */
  CHAR  userid[9];                /* logon ID                         */
  CHAR  remote_name[9];           /* name of a remote node            */
  SHORT remote_type;              /* logon type                       */
  SHORT authority_check;          /* authority required for logon     */
  CHAR  remote_type_parm[11];     /* logon type                       */
  CHAR  authority_check_parm[11]; /* authority required for logon     */
  /*------------------------------------------*/
  /* get the parm strings                     */
  /*------------------------------------------*/
  if (sscanf(parm_str, " %8s %8s %8s %10s %10s  ",
                     userid, password, remote_name, remote_type_parm,
                     authority_check_parm)
                  != parms.num_parms)
     {sprintf(err_msg, "\nSYNTAX ERROR: invalid parameters.");
      return(RECORD_ERR_MSG);
     }

  if ( decode_parm_string(remote_type_parm,     &remote_type) ||
       decode_parm_string(authority_check_parm, &authority_check) )
     {sprintf(err_msg, "\nSYNTAX ERROR: invalid parameter.");
      return(RECORD_ERR_MSG);
     }
  /*------------------------------------------*/
  /* call the LOGON  API                      */
  /*------------------------------------------*/
  api_rcd = upmelgn (userid,                     /* userid          */
                     password,                   /* password        */
                     remote_name,                /* remotename      */
                     remote_type,                /* remote type     */
                     authority_check);           /* authority_check */
  return(RECORD_API_RCD);
} /* end dba_logon */
```

Figure 23-33. LOG ON Command Handler: dba_logon().

LOG OFF: dba_logoff()

The **dba_logoff()** command handler, whose code is listed in Figure 23-34, executes the RSQL command:

```
▸▸–EXEC DBA: LOGOFF — userid — remotename ──┬─ UPM_LOCAL  ─┬──────▸◂
                                            ├─ UPM_DNODE  ─┤
                                            └─ UPM_DOMAIN ─┘
```

This command handler parses its parameters and issues a **upmelgff()** API call.

```
/*----------------------------------------------------------------------*/
/*  execute the LOGOFF DBA function                                     */
/*----------------------------------------------------------------------*/
SHORT dba_logoff(PCHAR parm_str)
{
  CHAR  userid[9];                  /* logon ID                         */
  CHAR  remote_name[9];             /* name of a remote node            */
  SHORT remote_type;                /* logon type                       */
  CHAR  remote_type_parm[11];       /* logon type                       */

  /*----------------------------------*/
  /* get the parm strings             */
  /*----------------------------------*/
  if (sscanf(parm_str, " %8s %8s %10s ",
                     userid, remote_name, remote_type_parm)
                  != parms.num_parms)
     {
      sprintf(err_msg, "\nSYNTAX ERROR: invalid parameters.");
      return(RECORD_ERR_MSG);
     }
  if (decode_parm_string(remote_type_parm, &remote_type))
     {
      sprintf(err_msg, "\nSYNTAX ERROR: invalid parameter.");
      return(RECORD_ERR_MSG);
     }

  /*----------------------------------*/
  /* call the LOGOFF API              */
  /*----------------------------------*/
  api_rcd = upmelgff(userid,                      /* userid         */
                   remote_name,                   /* remotename     */
                   remote_type);                  /* remote type    */
  return(RECORD_API_RCD);
} /* end dba_logoff */
```

Figure 23-34. LOG OFF Command Handler: dba_logoff().

Part V

Why Transaction Servers Are Best for OLTP

The chapters in Part V introduce you to the issues of On-line Transaction Processing (*OLTP*) client-server computing by developing and running the famous TP1 benchmark for OLTP. The recent TP1 Database Benchmark Wars, conducted as if they were major Olympic Game events, captured a great deal of attention in the industry and a large number of column-inches in the press. But benchmarking can contribute more than just comparing the maximum performances of various vendors' database engines. In Part V, we will introduce a new TP1 Olympic event. We will conduct TP1 races that measure the performance of different client-server architectures. Instead of telling you which is the world's fastest database server, we will show *what really matters in client-server design* using the TP1 benchmark:

- How slow is Dynamic SQL?
- Which is faster, a Transaction Server or a Database Server?
- What is the effect of CPU speed?
- What is the effect of the database cache?
- What is the effect of the *network* on transaction performance?
- Are Named Pipes really faster than APPC?
- How well does OS/2 EE's *Application Remote Interface* perform on APPC and its streamlined cousin SQLLOO?

The answers to these questions will help you make the right design trade-offs in the client-server applications you create. In order to avoid refueling the benchmark wars (and, of course, to create a common testbed for our evaluation), we limited our tests to a single database product, the OS/2 EE Database Manager. This allows us to study architectural issues which have an effect on performance, while maintaining other things equal. Our tests differ radically from the previous TP1 benchmarks in that we focus on *relative* performance measurements of client-server architectures instead of on maximum raw performance. This difference leads us, for example, to purposely run our tests on commonly available 80386 type machines and on a 4 MBit/s Token Ring. We chose not to run the tests on "super-servers" from IBM or Compaq since we are deliberately not trying to test OS/2 EE's maximum performance or how it compares with other vendor products.

The major programming effort in Part V is to develop a *Transaction Benchmark Kit* for the Database Manager using **TP1**, the industry's best-known OLTP benchmark. Our toolkit will include the old favorites: MULTI, RSQL, and Named Pipes. It will also include a multiuser Transaction Server kernel and a set of specially designed TP1 database programs that demonstrate the techniques and performance trade-offs in networked client-server software. We will provide four flavors of the TP1 benchmark:

1. A *Database Server* flavor that uses Static SQL and OS/2 EE's Remote Data Services.
2. A *Database Server* flavor that uses Dynamic SQL and OS/2 EE's Remote Data Services.
3. A *Transaction Server* flavor that uses the standard stored procedures for Remote Data Services: the **Application Remote Interface**. The TP1 transaction is coded in Static SQL.
4. A *Transaction Server* flavor that uses Named Pipes and a "do-it-yourself" version of "stored procedures." The TP1 transaction is coded in Static SQL.

The toolkit is an excellent learning aid, which you can use to compare the performance of the various client-server alternatives. It is especially good at measuring the performance of remote services on a network server.

Here is the roadmap we will follow in Part V:

- In Chapter 24, "A Transaction Benchmark Kit for the Database Manager", we introduce the *Transaction Benchmark Kit* for the Database Manager. This chapter covers OLTP benchmark considerations and provides toolkit components for creating and loading a TP1 database.
- In Chapter 25, "The Static SQL Database Server TP1", we develop a *Database Server* version of TP1 that uses static SQL and can be run either on the same machine as the server or on a remote machine using **Remote Data Services** (RDS).
- In Chapter 26, "The Application Remote Interface Transaction Server TP1", we develop a *Transaction Server* version of TP1, where the communications is provided by the **Application Remote Interface** services. This is the Database Manager's implementation of remote procedures over an APPC (SQLLOO) LAN.
- In Chapter 27, "The Named Pipes Transaction Server TP1", we develop a *Transaction Server* version of TP1, which includes a "do-it-yourself" remote Named Pipes server.
- In Chapter 28, "The Dynamic SQL Database Server TP1", we develop a *Database Server* version of TP1 that uses Dynamic SQL. We expect this version to be the poorest performer of the bunch. We've included it in the series so that we can gather some empirical measurements on performance trade-offs between static SQL and the more flexible but much slower Dynamic SQL.
- In Chapter 29, "Transaction Servers Are Best for OLTP", we present a summary of the TP1 benchmark results and some observations on the design of OLTP applications using the client-server model.

Chapter 24

A Transaction Benchmark Kit for the Database Manager

This chapter starts us on a new journey, which takes us into the world of benchmarks designed to measure the power of transaction servers. With SQL database servers becoming commodity items, benchmarks have become a powerful marketing tool for differentiating the SQL Ferraris from the Volkswagens. This is called "benchmarketing." We will introduce you to **TP1**, the industry's best-known benchmark for On-line Transaction Processing or **OLTP**. This is the benchmark that can make or break a company in the lucrative OLTP market. TP1 has become the universal test of SQL engine "machismo." It defines a contest in which all can participate, from the largest mainframe database engines to OS/2 EE running on a PS/2. The unit of measure in this race is the dollar price of a transaction per second or **tps**. The server that provides the lowest-priced **tps** wins!

THE TP1 BENCHMARK MARATHON SERIES

Our journey spans over six chapters and will take us straight into the heart of TP1. We will do this by writing our *own* version of a TP1 toolkit for the OS2/EE Database Manager. This toolkit includes the old favorites: MULTI, RSQL, and Named Pipes. It will also include a set of specially designed TP1 database programs that demonstrate the techniques and performance trade-offs in networked client-server software. Here's how this six-chapter marathon is organized:

- The first chapter in the series introduces the benchmark kit and covers the following areas:

    1. OLTP benchmark considerations and the definition of the TP1 benchmark.
    2. The constituents of our TP1 benchmark kit and how it departs from the standard.
    3. The toolkit components for creating and loading the TP1 database
    4. The *make* file for our benchmark programs.

- The second chapter in the series provides a *Database Server* version of the TP1 transaction that uses static SQL and can be run either on the same machine as the server or on a remote machine using **Remote Data Services** (RDS). The TP1 transaction performance will be measured using the following configurations:

  1. On a local versus remote database server.
  2. On a slower server versus a faster server.
  3. On the same server but using different buffer pool sizes.
  4. On standard APPC versus the SQLLOO APPC subset.
  5. On the HPFS versus FAT OS/2 file systems.

- The third chapter in the series provides a *Transaction Server* version of the TP1 transaction, where the communications is provided by the **Application Remote Interface** services. This is the Database Manager's implementation of remote procedures over an APPC LAN. We will, of course, measure the performance of this TP1 flavor.

- The fourth chapter in the series provides a *Transaction Server* version of the TP1 transaction, which is invoked through a do-it-yourself remote Named Pipe communication mechanism. We will, of course, also measure the performance of this TP1 flavor.

- The fifth chapter in the series provides a *Database Server* version of the TP1 transaction, which is implemented using Dynamic SQL. We expect this transaction to be the worst performer of the bunch. We've included it in the series so that we can gather some empirical measurements on performance trade-offs between static SQL and the more flexible, but supposedly much slower, Dynamic SQL.

- The sixth chapter in the series presents a summary of the test results.

Note: The performance numbers we produce should only be used to compare different transaction coding techniques or hardware configurations, with all other things being equal. They are not meant to serve as absolute performance benchmark numbers to be quoted.

WHAT YOU WILL LEARN FROM THIS MARATHON

At the end of this TP1 benchmarking exercise you will have acquired the following new database skills:

- How to design and develop working models of Database Servers and Transaction Servers.
- How to write a Static SQL program.
- How to write remote SQL procedures and transactions.
- How to create complete database systems from the ground up.
- How to fine-tune a database.

- An understanding of the performance trade-offs of the various transaction processing techniques.
- An introduction to the design of OLTP applications.

OLTP BENCHMARK CONSIDERATIONS

OLTP applications are designed to support multiple users submitting their transactions against a large database. A typical OLTP application is characterized by the repeated execution of a set of predefined transactions by a number of simultaneous users. Transaction atomicity and record-level locking are mandatory requirements. The important issues for designers of OLTP applications are throughput, response time, and number of concurrent users. OLTP tests exercise virtually every system facility including the database hardware and software, the server's operating system and CPU, the data communications network, and the client-server message exchanges. A well-designed OLTP test that takes all these factors into account may very well be *the ultimate system benchmark.* The following is a list of what should be measured and reported in an OLTP benchmark:

- **Throughput:** This is the rate at which the OLTP system can process transactions. The unit of measure is stated in terms of transactions per second (**tps**). As users are added, the system reaches a maximum throughput which then starts to drop as more users are added. A target in the design of a good OLTP system is to maintain a stable throughput as more users are added.
- **Response Time:** This is the elapsed time a user experiences from the time a transaction is submitted until a response is returned. Response time should grow linearly (as opposed to exponentially) as users are added to the system.
- **Concurrent Users:** The number of users concurrently using the system is an important consideration in OLTP systems. Throughput and response times are meaningful when measured as a function of number of users. The performance of the system at peak times should be of considerable interest to OLTP developers.
- **The exact definition of a transaction:** For a **tps** measure to be meaningful it is important to agree on what exactly we mean by a transaction. What constitutes a *transaction*, of course, varies from application to application. A transaction that reserves an airline seat is obviously different from a manufacturing shop floor transaction. A benchmark needs to specify at an exact level a "generic" transaction which performs a representative set of SQL commands. The specification must include the actual SQL commands and how the commit, logging, and locking are to be applied.
- **System Steady State Verification:** A system reaches "steady state" when its performance remains constant from that point on. The system performance may vary by 20% or more before it reaches a steady state. This variance may be attributed to many factors, including buffers that fill up and the swapping of pages from memory to disk as the system load increases. Benchmark results must be reported at the steady state conditions.
- **Cost per transaction:** The system cost is used to normalize **tps** test results across widely differing systems. It requires reporting cost per **tps**. This is neces-

sary so that if an abnormally large system is used to obtain a high **tps** rating, it will be reflected in a poor cost-per-tps figure. As you may expect, it will not be easy to come up with an objective measure of system cost.

- **The Test Environment:** A benchmark must specify the system's hardware and software configuration. The hardware configuration must include the speed of the processor, the amount of memory, the size of the buffer pool, the speed of the disks, and the type of disk controller. It is also important to specify the communications environment (LANs or TP lines including bandwidth and loading factors) and the type of front-end client (a terminal or workstation).
- **Full Disclosure:** There is a substantial agreement within the benchmark community that some form of "full disclosure" should be made part of the standard. This will provide an added check on the work of an auditor and will allow an end user to replicate a vendor's test results.

A HISTORY OF TP1

TP1 was first specified in **Datamation** ("A Measure of Transaction Processing Power," April 1, 1985, pp 112-118) in an article submitted by 24 computer professionals active in transaction processing. The purpose of the article was: *"to record the folklore we use to measure system performance"*. Traditional measures of computer performance such as MIPS, MFLOPS, and Whetstones focus on CPU speed and don't capture the features that make one transaction processing system faster or cheaper than another. The TP1 Datamation benchmark was published to fill this void. The Datamation benchmark, also known as **DebitCredit** and **ET1** in some circles, was further refined and firmed up over the years. The following are some of the key milestones in this refinement process:

1. In February 1987, Tandem Computers published the results of an extensive series of tests using DebitCredit to measure the performance of NonStop SQL (Gray, Jim. "NonStop SQL Benchmark White Paper," February 1987). These tests were audited by Codd and Date and became the new basis for the industry's de facto standard.

2. In late 1988, a Transaction Processing Council (TPC) was formed to develop a formal OLTP benchmark based on the DebitCredit de facto standard. The council is made up of over 30 members representing the major database vendors. As of this writing, the council is recommending to split DebitCredit into two separate standards:

   ET1 Also known as "Benchmark A," ET1 is based on the original DebitCredit transaction definition. An ET1 server is front-ended with block-mode terminals, which submit their transactions to the server via X.25 lines. The management of the terminal-network is part of the server's overhead.

   TP1 Also known as "Benchmark B," TP1 is also based on the original DebitCredit transaction definition. However, the TP1 does not use a terminal-network. Instead, TP1 replaces the front-end clients with one or more "transaction generators" which produce back-to-back transactions. The transaction generators may run on the same system as the server and deliver their transactions directly through shared memory; or, they may reside on separate client machines and deliver their transactions to the server via a LAN. TP1 is generally considered to be the less demanding version of DebitCredit.

3. In June 1989, Ashton-Tate/Microsoft published an extensive benchmark study of their OS/2 SQL Server using the TP1 definition of DebitCredit ("SQL Server Benchmarking Kit", Microsoft part number 098-11955). The publication of their benchmark kit further helped refine the TP1 definition. The audit of the Microsoft TP1 benchmark was carried out by Richard Finkelstein and Colin White, both independent industry experts specializing in SQL performance.

WHAT IS TP1?

The TP1 transaction models a hypothetical debit/credit banking application. It defines a standard transaction called the *DebitCredit* transaction, a standard database, a scaling method for larger systems, and a measure of throughput and price performance of the resulting system.

The TP1 Database

The TP1 database consists of four tables and a set of rules that define their contents and sizes. The four tables are:

- A table of bank accounts.
- A table of tellers.
- A table of bank branches.
- A history table containing a record of all the transactions.

The benchmark specifies an automatic scaling of the three key tables: account, tellers, and branches. A **1-tps** system supports a database with 100,000 accounts, 100 tellers, and 10 branches. A system which runs at a higher **tps** rate is required to scale its database linearly. For example, a **100-tps** system has a database which is 100 times larger than that of a **1-tps** system. For such a system, the accounts table should use 10 million account records, which translates into at least 1 GByte of disk space. The history table should be able to hold 90 days of transaction history. This innocent looking provision may turn out to be a tough requirement to meet.

The Definition of the TP1 Transaction

The TP1 transaction is deceptively simple and quite general. The transaction simulates an online teller who enters a debit/credit transaction. This is how the transaction executes:

1. A screen message containing a teller-generated deposit/withdrawal transaction is received from a teller terminal (or workstation).
2. An account record is randomly retrieved, updated, and rewritten to reflect the transaction.
3. The teller record is retrieved and updated to reflect the transaction.
4. A branch totals record is retrieved and updated to reflect the transaction.
5. A record is written to the history table to record the transaction.
6. A screen message is formatted and sent to the teller terminal (or workstation).

Each terminal generates a transaction every 100 seconds which implies 100 terminals for each reported **tps**. The more popular alternative is to have the transaction driver simulate the terminal message load.

How the TP1 Response-Time is Measured

The transaction response time (as shown in Figure 24-1) is measured as the wall-clock time between the send and the completion of the receive in the Transaction Generator system.

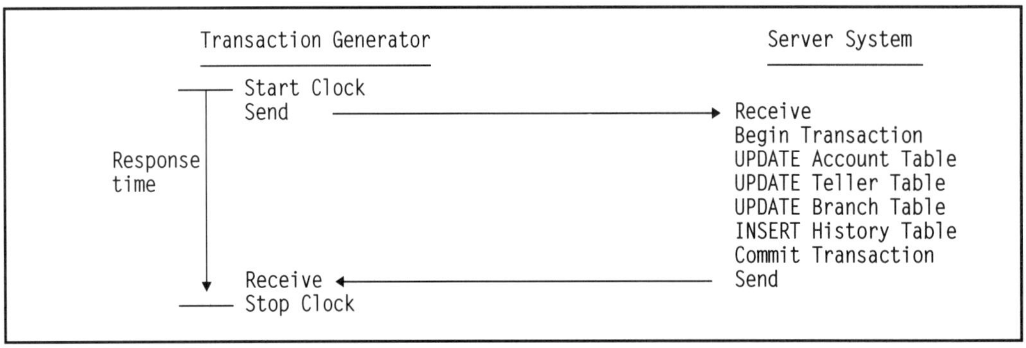

Figure 24-1. Measuring the Response-Time of a TP1 Transaction.

The TP1 Constraints

Here is a list of the constraints that must be met by the system:

- Each TP1 transaction must **randomly** generate the account branch and teller numbers, and at least 15% of the transactions must be inter-branch. The random generation of numbers is usually sufficient to meet this requirement (especially with a large database).
- All the tables must be protected by a fine granularity of **locking and logging**.
- The OLTP system under test should be observed over ten-minute windows.
- Ninety-five percent of the transactions must provide a response time of less than one second. A system that can run 1 transaction per second giving less than one second response times to 95% of all transactions, is classified as a **1-tps** system.

Price/Performance of TP1

The price/performance of a TP1 server is measured in **dollars per tps**. A **1-tps** system is defined as a system which can run 1 TP1 transaction per second with less than one second response times for 95% of all transactions. As was mentioned earlier, the "cost" of a transaction can be quite tricky to measure. The cost formula TP1 prescribes, is the *"five-year cost of ownership of the computing facility."* This is further defined as the five-year capital cost of vendor supplied hardware and software in the computer room. It does not include expenditures for terminals (or client PCs), communications, application development, or operations. It does, however, include installation and maintenance charges, without specifying what type of maintenance support should be included: full on-site or just remote? Should price discounts be disallowed? By the admission of the original TP1 authors, the cost measure they specified is *"typically a fifth of the total cost of ownership of a system."*

Note: PCs would benefit from the disclosure of the full cost of ownership in TP1 tests as opposed to the simplified cost version. The cost of ownership of PC-based systems tends to be very small compared to conventional host-based systems.

THE TP1 BENCHMARK KIT FOR DATABASE MANAGER

TP1 is a difficult and demanding benchmark to install and run. Depending on the available tools, it can take anywhere from a day to several months to install, configure, and build a TP1 test system. The good news is that the TP1 toolkit we will develop in Part V is a world-class hacker's tool. It is powerful, flexible, and a pleasure to experiment with.

Build Your TP1 Test System in One Afternoon

You should be able to build a custom TP1 test system in less than half a day; and once you've got a system up and running, you'll find yourself mesmerized by its user interface and the interactive control knobs it provides. After all, the user interface is provided by none other than **MULTI**, our old friend that puts you at the controls! However, we're getting ahead of our story. Let's first describe our benchmarking toolkit.

What Does the TP1 Kit Provide?

We've put together a very flexible toolkit that allows you to mix and match pieces to your heart's content. And if that's not enough, you can always modify and recompile the source code to create any variation you may fancy. The benchmark toolkit brings together many of the programs that were previously developed in this book, and integrates them with the new TP1 programs that we develop in this six-chapter series. The essence of good architecture is to build on top of existing foundations. We will now tell you how we do it.

RSQL

RSQL, our old friend, is used to create the TP1 tables, load the tables with data, bind the transaction programs to the database, add indexes to the tables, run statistics against the tables, log on to the database, and change the database configuration parameters. We provide samples of RSQL run files that perform these tasks. You can, of course, modify any of these run files to run the benchmarks with the system environment of your choice.

TP1.MAK

This is the *make* file with which we build the different flavors of TP1 transaction programs that we will develop in this series.

TP1LOAD.SQC

This is a new program we will create to load TP1 tables with the data as specified in the standard. This includes generating the random numbers and representative data. This program will also scale the database to the size you specify through a **tps** scaling parameter. This program will also serve as a gentle introduction to static SQL programming.

Four TP1 Transaction Flavors

The toolkit provides four flavors of TP1 transactions. These are all new programs, which we will develop in Part V:

1. The **SQLTP1.SQC** program provides a static SQL transaction. Instances of this transaction can be executed against either a local or remote database engine.
2. The **SQLTP1RI.SQC** program provides a client application that submits its TP1 transactions using the *Application Remote Interface*. The Transaction Server code is provided by **SQLTP1DL.SQC**. It is packaged as a **DLL**.
3. The **SQLTP1RQ.C** program provides a client application that submits its TP1 transactions using Named Pipes. The Transaction Server code is provided by **SQLTP1SV.SQC**.
4. The **SQLTP1DY.SQC** program provides a Dynamic SQL flavor of a TP1 transaction.

The MULTI Process Driver Program

MULTI is another dear old friend that we use to execute multiple instances (or processes) of the TP1 programs. Through MULTI, you can start and stop the benchmark runs, you can start or stop the transaction processes, you can specify the process priorities, and you can literally watch the TP1s execute, each in their little MULTI window. MULTI displays the total number of transactions executed per process, as well as the number of transactions that ran under the response time threshold which you specify through the MULTI configuration file.

Figure 24-2 shows a MULTI screen for a four-process TP1 run. You can read the following information off this screen:

- Four **SQLTP1** processes were run concurrently for 600 seconds (10 minutes).
- During this period, a total of 3307 TP1 transactions ran successfully.
- A total of 3278 (add the TXNS in the four windows) TP1 transactions ran below the user-specified response time threshold.

This machine may be classified as being in the 5.5 TP1 range (3278 divided by 600).

Note: To add more TP1 drivers, simply run the MULTI program on more networked client machines. MULTI becomes an incremental TP1 driver with some very powerful control knobs and displays.

```
                    Multiprocess Execution Example

 Use arrow keys to move the cursor.  Use + and - keys to change field values.
 Press R to start running, S to stop, or C to clear the count.
 Press ESC to terminate the program.

┌SQLTP1.EXE─────────┐┌SQLTP1.EXE─────────┐┌SQLTP1.EXE─────────┐┌SQLTP1.EXE─────────┐
│                   ││                   ││                   ││                   │
│Count = 822        ││Count = 824        ││Count = 826        ││Count = 835        │
│TXNS  = 814        ││TXNS  = 817        ││TXNS  = 818        ││TXNS  = 829        │
│Priority  = RG     ││Priority  = RG     ││Priority  = RG     ││Priority  = RG     │
│Level     = 0      ││Level     = 0      ││Level     = 0      ││Level     = 0      │
│Semaphore = CLEAR  ││Semaphore = CLEAR  ││Semaphore = CLEAR  ││Semaphore = CLEAR  │
│                   ││                   ││                   ││                   │
│Ready              ││Ready              ││Ready              ││Ready              │
└───────────────────┘└───────────────────┘└───────────────────┘└───────────────────┘
┌EXECUTION STATUS─────────────────────────┐┌SYSTEM INFORMATION───────────────────────┐
│                                         ││                                         │
│Stop Time     = 600.0            sec     ││Maximum Wait       = 3          sec      │
│Elapsed Time  = 600.0            sec     ││Minimum Time Slice = 32         ms       │
│Total Count   = 3307                     ││Maximum Time Slice = 248        ms       │
│Run Status    = STOPPED                  ││Dynamic Variation  = ACTIVE              │
│                                         ││                                         │
└─────────────────────────────────────────┘└─────────────────────────────────────────┘
```

Figure 24-2. A MULTI Screen of a Four-Process TP1 Run.

TP1: To Cheat or Not to Cheat?

To produce correct results, the TP1 benchmark specification must be strictly followed. The TP1 toolkit lets you control the benchmark environment at a very granular level. It lets you decide what level of adherence you're going to abide by when running the benchmark. The benchmark runs that you will see in this book follow a very lax interpretation of the benchmark rules. Which is another way of saying *we will do a little bit of cheating*. Why?

Remember, our focus is on the relative performance measurements of client-server architectures. We are *purposely not measuring maximum raw performance* so as not to get embroiled in the controversial benchmark wars. This difference leads us to purposely run our tests on commonly available 80386 type machines and 4 MBit/s Token Ring. We also chose to run a lax interpretation of TP1 (as you will soon see) that gives us a consistent set of performance numbers. We chose not to run the tests on "super-servers" from IBM or Compaq since we are deliberately not trying to test OS/2 EE's maximum performance or how it compares with other vendor products. So, please don't quote absolute numbers!

Having made this disclaimer, we are quick to point out that the toolkit provides a very credible set of tools for doing some very serious benchmark work, if you can afford the right hardware platform. By that we mean lots of memory, many client machines on a network, a heavy-duty OS/2 EE "super-server" machine with SCSI disk drives, and lots of disk space for the 60-day history table. For your information, we've included a list of "common shortcuts" (this is another polite word for cheating). This is what people in the business warn you to look for when evaluating *other* people's benchmark results (see Table 24-1).

Table 24-1. TP1: To Cheat or Not to Cheat?

TP1 Requirements	Common "Shortcuts"	What You Can do With the Toolkit
Database Scaling	None	Yes. Specify the required tps level.
Some user interface	None	Yes. We have MULTI screens.
Open Benchmark Code	Not Available	Source and executable code is available and fully documented in this book.
Network Support	None	3 versions of networked TP1s: • Remote SQL (static and dynamic) using RDS • Remote Applications over APPC/SQLLOO • Named Pipes
Single History table	Multiple tables	Single table
1-second response time	Not Measured	Yes. We provide two numbers: 1) total transactions; 2) total transactions under a user-specified response time.
95 percent of transactions under 1 second	Not Measured	100 percent of transactions which are under toolkit specified response time.
Random Account Numbers	Not Provided	Yes
90-day History	No provisions	Yes, if you provide enough disk space.
Error-checking	None	SQL return codes. Will check if account is non-existent.
Frequent checkpoints	Not activated	Under user control using RSQL.
Granular locks	None	Under user control using RSQL's Bind options. (i.e., toolkit).
Steady State Response	Not measured	Under user control through MULTI.

CREATING THE TP1 DATABASE

Creating a database is the first step in the development of a database program. Without a database you can't even compile the program. RSQL makes the process of database creation easy. You can see that for yourself by looking at Figure 24-3, which contains the results of a simple RSQL run that creates a **TP1** database consisting of four tables:

ACCT This table contains an entry for each customer account record.
BRANCH This table contains an entry for each branch office of that bank.
TELLER This table contains an entry for each tellers in all of the branch offices.
HISTORY This table contains an entry for each TP1 transaction executed against the database.

```
--                        Create TP1 Database
-- =========================================================================
-- logon
EXEC DBA: LOGON USERID PASSWORD DBSVRO3 UPM_LOCAL UPM_USER;
 OK, api_rcd = 0,          Execution time =     0.0000 secs

-- create a database called TP1
EXEC DBA: CREATE_DB TP1 C TP1_TEST_DATABASE;
 OK, sql_rcd = 0,        Execution time =    52.5000 secs

-- bind the rsql program
EXEC DBA: BIND TP1 RSQL.BND ISO REPEATABLE_READ BLOCK_ALL PUBLIC;
 OK, sql_rcd = 0,        Execution time =    14.5000 secs

-- connect to the database
EXEC DBA: STARTUSE TP1 S;
 OK, sql_rcd = 0,        Execution time =     2.1900 secs

-- create tables
EXEC SQL: CREATE TABLE ACCT(ACCT_NUM      INT      NOT NULL,
                            NAME          CHAR(20) NOT NULL,
                            BRANCH_ID     SMALLINT NOT NULL,
                            BALANCE       INT      NOT NULL,
                            ADDRESS       CHAR(30) NOT NULL,
                            TEMP          CHAR(40) NOT NULL);
 OK, sql_rcd = 0,        Execution time =     1.2200 secs

EXEC SQL: CREATE TABLE BRANCH(BRANCH_ID   SMALLINT NOT NULL,
                              BRANCH_NAME CHAR(20) NOT NULL,
                              BALANCE     INT      NOT NULL,
                              AREA_CODE   CHAR(4)  NOT NULL,
                              ADDRESS     CHAR(30) NOT NULL,
                              TEMP        CHAR(40) NOT NULL);
 OK, sql_rcd = 0,        Execution time =     0.5600 secs

EXEC SQL: CREATE TABLE TELLER(TELLER_ID   SMALLINT NOT NULL,
                              TELLER_NAME CHAR(20) NOT NULL,
                              BRANCH_ID   SMALLINT NOT NULL,
                              BALANCE     INTEGER  NOT NULL,
                              TELLER_CODE CHAR(2)  NOT NULL,
                              ADDRESS     CHAR(30) NOT NULL,
                              TEMP        CHAR(40) NOT NULL);
 OK, sql_rcd = 0,        Execution time =     0.5600 secs

EXEC SQL: CREATE TABLE HISTORY(ACCT_NUM   INTEGER  NOT NULL,
                              TELLER_ID   SMALLINT NOT NULL,
                              BRANCH_ID   SMALLINT NOT NULL,
                              BALANCE     INTEGER  NOT NULL,
                              DELTA       INTEGER  NOT NULL,
                              PID         INTEGER  NOT NULL,
                              TRANSID     INTEGER  NOT NULL,
                              ACCTNAME    CHAR(20) NOT NULL,
                              TEMP        CHAR(6)  NOT NULL);
 OK, sql_rcd = 0,        Execution time =     0.6000 secs

-- commit the tables
EXEC SQL: COMMIT;
 OK, sql_rcd = 0,        Execution time =     0.0300 secs
```

Figure 24-3 (Part 1 of 2). Creating a TP1 Database Using RSQL.

```
-- disconnect from the database
EXEC DBA: STOPUSE TP1;
 OK, sql_rcd = 0,        Execution time =     1.9700 secs

-- logoff
EXEC DBA: LOGOFF USERID DBSVRO3 UPM_LOCAL;
 OK, api_rcd = 0,          Execution time =     0.0000 secs
```

Figure 24-3 (Part 2 of 2). Creating a TP1 Database Using RSQL.

THE TP1.MAK MAKE FILE

Now that we have a database, we can use it to precompile SQL programs against it. The **TP1.MAK** *make* file (see Figure 24-4) will be used to create seven new database programs which will be offered as part of the TP1 benchmark kit. These programs will be explained in great detail in this chapter and in the TP1 chapters that follow.

The TP1 make file does not introduce any new constructs. However, notice that the **.def.lib** and **.obj.dll** inference rules are used to create a dynamic link library (.DLL). This is for **sqltp1dl.sqc**, the server part of the Remote Application Interface version of the TP1 program. You may remember from the tutorial (see "The Power of Remote Procedures" on page 463) that a Remote Application Server must exist as an OS/2 Dynamic Link Library (.DLL). The process for the creation of DLLs was explained in "Packaging FX Using Dynamic Link Libraries" on page 233.

```
#** MACROS *****************************************************************
cflags=-c -Alfu -DLINT_ARGS -G2s -Zp -W3 -Od -Zi -nologo
lflags=/ST:15000/SE:1024/A:16/CO/NOD/NOI/L/PACKCODE
exe_libs= sql_dyn sql_stat llibcep  os2 acs
dll_libs= sql_dyn sql_stat llibcdll os2
DATABASE=TP1

#** INFERENCE RULES ********************************************************
.SUFFIXES: .lib .def .sqc

.obj.exe:
      echo LINKING      $** to create $*.exe
      link $**,,nul, $(exe_libs) $(lflags),;  >>err.lst;

.obj.dll:
      echo LINKING      $* to create $*.dll
      LINK $*,$*.dll,nul, $(dll_libs) $(lflags),$*.def; >>err.lst;
```

Figure 24-4 (Part 1 of 2). The TP1.MAK MAKE File.

```
.c.obj:
      echo COMPILING    $*.c
      cl $(cflags) $*.c  >>err.lst

.sqc.c:
      echo PRECOMPILING $*.sqc for database $(DATABASE)
      sqlprep  $*.sqc $(DATABASE) /b  >>err.lst
      echo BINDING      $*.bnd to  database $(DATABASE)
      sqlbind  $*.bnd $(DATABASE)  >>err.lst

.def.lib:
      echo CREATING     $*.lib import library
      implib $*.lib $*.def >>err.lst

#** BUILD STATEMENTS ********************************************************

all: erase tp1load.exe sqltp1.exe sqltp1ri.exe sqltp1dl.dll \
           sqltp1rq.exe sqltp1sv.exe sqltp1dy.exe launcher.exe

erase:
     if exist err.lst erase err.lst

tp1load.exe:             tp1load.obj               # Load TP1 tables
tp1load.c tp1load.obj:   tp1load.sqc

sqltp1.exe:              sqltp1.obj                # TP1 transaction using
sqltp1.c sqltp1.obj:     sqltp1.sqc                # embedded SQL

sqltp1ri.exe:            sqltp1ri.obj              # TP1 transaction using
sqltp1ri.obj:            sqltp1ri.c                # remote interface req

sqltp1dl.dll:            sqltp1dl.obj sqltp1dl.def # TP1 transaction DLL for
sqltp1dl.c sqltp1dl.obj: sqltp1dl.sqc              # interface server

sqltp1sv.exe:            sqltp1sv.obj              # TP1 transaction using
sqltp1sv.c sqltp1sv.obj: sqltp1sv.sqc              # named pipe server

launcher.exe:            launcher.obj              # Named Pipe server
launcher.obj:            launcher.c                # launcher

sqltp1rq.exe:            sqltp1rq.obj              # TP1 transaction using
sqltp1rq.obj:            sqltp1rq.c                # named pipe requester

sqltp1dy.exe:            sqltp1dy.obj              # TP1 transaction using
sqltp1dy.c sqltp1dy.obj: sqltp1dy.sqc              # dynamic sql
```

Figure 24-4 (Part 2 of 2). The TP1.MAK MAKE File.

TP1LOAD.SQC: A PROGRAM FOR LOADING TP1 DATABASE TABLES

In this section, we introduce **TP1LOAD.SQC**, a program whose sole function is to load data into the three newly created TP1 database tables. This program shows how to write code using static SQL. As you will soon appreciate, static SQL is both powerful and simple. The following is a step-by-step description of what the **TP1LOAD.SQC** program (see listing in Figure 24-5) does:

1. The program starts by including the C-language, OS/2 and OS/2 EE header files that are needed for system services. Notice that the **sqlenv.h** file is included to obtain the Database Administration's Environment services.

2. A structure of type **SQLCA** is created by issuing the directive:

```
EXEC SQL INCLUDE SQLCA;
```

3. The host variables that will be used to exchange data between SQL and the C program are declared. As you can see, it's OK to initialize host variables.

4. The **main()** program obtains the tps argument that defines the size of the database to be built. The database of a 1-tps system is defined as:

```
100,000 Accounts
    100 Tellers
     10 Branches
```

   The program will create a database whose size is a multiple of the 1-tps numbers shown above. The scaling factor is provided by the tps parameter that gets passed to the program. If no argument is passed, the default is to create a 1-tps database. Make sure you have enough disk space to accommodate the tps number you provide.

5. The **sqlestrd()** API call is issued to connect to the TP1 database in shared mode.

6. The **ACCT** table data is generated one row at a time and placed into host variables. The information is passed directly to the database through an embedded SQL INSERT statement with host variables containing the data to be placed into the named table columns. Notice the following:

   - The **ACCT** table contains (tps*100,000) rows.
   - Each row is 100 bytes long and represents a customer's bank account. It contains the account number, the account balance, the customer's name and address, and the branch_id. The account records have account numbers from 1 to (tps*100,000).
   - The branch_id is a random number from 1 to (tps*10). The TP1 benchmark requires that the selection of the accounts used for a given transaction be truly random to test the non-cached performance of the database. To accomplish this effect, we generate the branch_id field as a pseudo random number based on an input seed.
   - We commit to the database after every 10,000 inserts to prevent our logs from overflowing.

7. The **TELLER** table data is generated one row at a time and the SQL INSERT command is used to write the contents of the host variables to the database. Notice the following:

- The **TELLER** table contains (tps*100) rows.
- Each row is 100 bytes long and represents a bank teller in a branch office. It contains the teller_id, the teller name, the branch_id, the teller balance, a teller code of "ab" and the address strings.
- The branch_id is a random number from 1 to (tps*10).
- The teller_id's are generated sequentially and range from 1 to (tps*100).

8. The **BRANCH** table data is generated one row at-a-time and the SQL INSERT command is used to write the contents of the host variables to the database. Notice the following:

   - The **BRANCH** table contains (tps*10) rows.
   - Each row is 100 bytes long and represents a bank branch office. It contains the branch_id, the branch name and address strings, and the branch balance.
   - The branch numbers are generated sequentially and range from 1 to (tps*10).

9. The program issues a **sqlestpd()** API call to disconnect from the TP1 database. We're done!

```
/****************************************************************************/
/*  PROGRAM NAME:  TP1LOAD.SQC -- LOAD TP1 table data                      */
/*                                                                          */
/*  DESCRIPTION:  This program inserts data into the ACCOUNT,              */
/*    TELLER, and BRANCH tables to prepare the database for running the    */
/*    TP1 benchmark.                                                        */
/*                                                                          */
/*  PROGRAM INVOCATION:   tp1load                                           */
/*                                                                          */
/****************************************************************************/
#include <stdio.h>                          /* For printf() & NULL          */
#include <stdlib.h>                         /* For printf                   */
#include <sqlenv.h>                         /* For environment functions    */
#include <os2.h>                            /* for OS/2 types               */

EXEC SQL INCLUDE SQLCA;

                  /*--------------------------------*/
                  /* Host variables for SQL calls   */
                  /*--------------------------------*/
EXEC SQL BEGIN DECLARE SECTION;
   char  name[21]    = "<--20 BYTE STRING-->";
   char  address[31] = "<------ 30 BYTE STRING ------>";
   char  temp[41]    =  "<---------- 40 BYTE STRING ---------->";
   long  acct_num;
   short branch_id;
   short teller_id;
EXEC SQL END DECLARE SECTION;
```

Figure 24-5 (Part 1 of 4). The TP1LOAD.SQC program.

```
/*------------------------------------------------------------------------*/
/* Main function.                                                         */
/*------------------------------------------------------------------------*/
SHORT main(USHORT argc, PCHAR argv[])
{
 USHORT   tps;                                   /* number of tps        */

  /*----------------------------------------*/
  /* Get number of tps from arguments       */
  /*----------------------------------------*/

 if (argc != 2)
   printf ("\nThe default 1-tps database will be built...");
 else
   tps  = atoi(argv[2]);                   /* get tps value              */

  /*----------------------------------------*/
  /* Initialize random number generator     */
  /*----------------------------------------*/
 srand(37);                                /* seed = 37 for random numbers  */

  /*----------------------------------------*/
  /* Connect to the TP1 database            */
  /*----------------------------------------*/
 printf("\nConnecting to TP1 database");
 sqlestrd( "TP1", SQL_USE_SHR, &sqlca);
 if (sqlca.sqlcode)
     { printf("\nERROR during connect, sqlcode= %d\n",sqlca.sqlcode);
       exit(1);
     }
  /*-----------------------------------------------*/
  /* Load ACCOUNT table data                       */
  /*-----------------------------------------------*/
 printf ("\nInserting Data into ACCT Table....");

 for (acct_num=1; acct_num <= tps*100000; acct_num++)
     {
      branch_id = rand();
      branch_id = branch_id % tps*10;

      /*----------------------------------------*/
      /* Insert one row into table              */
      /*----------------------------------------*/
      EXEC SQL
      INSERT INTO ACCT (ACCT_NUM, NAME, BRANCH_ID, BALANCE, ADDRESS, TEMP)
      VALUES ( :acct_num, :name, :branch_id, 1000, :address, :temp );

      if (sqlca.sqlcode)
         { printf("\nError on Insert number %ld, sqlcode= %ld\n",
                   acct_num, sqlca.sqlcode);
           exit(1);
         }
```

Figure 24-5 (Part 2 of 4). The TP1LOAD.SQC program.

```
        /*---------------------------------------------*/
        /* Commit after every 10,000 rows inserted   */
        /*---------------------------------------------*/
        if ((acct_num % 10000)==0)
        {
          EXEC SQL COMMIT;
          if (sqlca.sqlcode)
             { printf("\nError on Commit, sqlcode= %ld\n", sqlca.sqlcode);
               exit(1);
             }
          printf("\n %8ld accounts created",acct_num);
        } /* end if */
       } /* end for */
    /*-------------------------------------------------------*/
    /* Load TELLER  table data                               */
    /*-------------------------------------------------------*/
    printf ("\nInserting Data into TELLER Table....");

    for (teller_id = 1; teller_id <= tps*100; teller_id++)
        {
         branch_id = rand();
         branch_id = branch_id % tps*10 ;
         /*--------------------------------------------*/
         /* Insert one row into table                 */
         /*--------------------------------------------*/
         EXEC SQL
         INSERT INTO TELLER (TELLER_ID, TELLER_NAME, BRANCH_ID, BALANCE,
                             TELLER_CODE, ADDRESS, TEMP)
         VALUES ( :teller_id, :name, :branch_id, 1000, 'ab', :address, :temp );

         if (sqlca.sqlcode)
            { printf("\nError on Insert number %d, sqlcode= %ld\n",
                     teller_id, sqlca.sqlcode);
              exit(1);
            }
        } /* end for */

    EXEC SQL COMMIT;
    if (sqlca.sqlcode)
       { printf("\nError on Commit, sqlcode= %ld\n", sqlca.sqlcode);
         exit(1);
       }
    printf("\n %8d teller entries created", teller_id-1);
```

Figure 24-5 (Part 3 of 4). The TP1LOAD.SQC program.

```
 /*----------------------------------------------------------*/
 /* Load BRANCH  table data                                  */
 /*----------------------------------------------------------*/
printf ("\nInserting Data into BRANCH Table....");

for (branch_id = 1; branch_id <= tps*10; branch_id++)
   {
     /*------------------------------------------------*/
     /* Insert one row into table                      */
     /*------------------------------------------------*/
     EXEC SQL
     INSERT INTO BRANCH (BRANCH_ID, BRANCH_NAME, BALANCE,
                         AREA_CODE, ADDRESS, TEMP)
     VALUES ( :branch_id, :name, 1000, 'abcd', :address, :temp );
     if (sqlca.sqlcode)
        { printf("\nError on Insert number %d, sqlcode= %ld\n",
                 branch_id, sqlca.sqlcode);
          exit(1);
        }
   }/* end for */

EXEC SQL COMMIT;
if (sqlca.sqlcode)
   { printf("\nError on Commit, sqlcode= %ld\n", sqlca.sqlcode);
     exit(1);
   }
printf("\n %8d branch entries created", branch_id-1);

 /*----------------------------------------------------------*/
 /* Disconnect from the database                             */
 /*----------------------------------------------------------*/
printf ("\nDisconnecting from TP1 database");
sqlestpd(&sqlca);
if (sqlca.sqlcode)
   { printf("\nError on Disconnect from database, sqlcode= %ld\n",
             sqlca.sqlcode);
     exit(1);
   }
printf("\nTP1 database created successfully.\n");

return(0);
} /* end main */
```

Figure 24-5 (Part 4 of 4). The TP1LOAD.SQC program.

LOADING THE TP1 DATABASE

Now that we've got a program that can generate TP1 data, let's run it. We'll run the program using RSQL because there are some additional tasks that need to be taken care of when loading such large amounts of data. Figure 24-6 shows what some of those additional tasks are. It contains the results of an RSQL run that is used to load the database tables with TP1 data. Let's go through this run step-by-step to get some idea what typically needs to be done in conjunction with loading large amounts of data in tables:

1. Logon to the database.

2. BIND **TP1LOAD** program to the database.

3. Execute the **TP1LOAD** program using the RSQL "DOS EXEC:" command. This is the C program we developed in the previous section to load the TP1 tables.

4. Create the indexes on the TP1 tables. Why is this done here instead of at table create time? The answer is that it is much faster to do inserts without an index. The **TP1LOAD** program already takes 1412 seconds (about 23 minutes) to run. If the TP1 tables had indexes, that program would have literally taken hours to run. So what we do instead is create the indexes after the bulk data is loaded.

5. Run statistics against the tables, so that the Database Manager optimizer has the right information for the execution of its plans.

```
--                          Load TP1 Table Data
-- ===========================================================================
EXEC DBA: CONTINUE_ON_ERROR;

-- logon
EXEC DBA: LOGON USERID PASSWORD DBSVR03 UPM_LOCAL UPM_USER;
 OK, api_rcd = 0,          Execution time =     0.0000 secs

-- bind the tpl load tables program
EXEC DBA: BIND TP1 TP1LOAD.BND ISO REPEATABLE_READ BLOCK_ALL PUBLIC;
 OK, sql_rcd = 0,          Execution time =     6.1200 secs

-- use a program to load table data
EXEC DOS: TP1LOAD.EXE;
 Program completed with a return code of 0.
 OK,                       Execution time =  1412.9100 secs

-- connect to the database
EXEC DBA: STARTUSE TP1 S;
 OK, sql_rcd = 0,          Execution time =     2.1300 secs

-- create table indices
EXEC SQL: CREATE INDEX ACCTINDX ON ACCT(ACCT_NUM);
 OK, sql_rcd = 0,          Execution time =   319.6200 secs

EXEC SQL: CREATE INDEX BRANINDX ON BRANCH(BRANCH_ID);
 OK, sql_rcd = 0,          Execution time =     1.1000 secs

EXEC SQL: CREATE INDEX TELLINDX ON TELLER(TELLER_ID);
 OK, sql_rcd = 0,          Execution time =     3.7200 secs

EXEC SQL: COMMIT;
 OK, sql_rcd = 0,          Execution time =     0.0900 secs

-- perform runstats on the tables
EXEC DBA: RUNSTATS USERID.ACCT;
 OK, sql_rcd = 0,          Execution time =   969.0300 secs

EXEC DBA: RUNSTATS USERID.BRANCH;
 OK, sql_rcd = 0,          Execution time =     1.5300 secs
```

Figure 24-6 (Part 1 of 2). Loading a TP1 Database with Data Using RSQL.

```
EXEC DBA: RUNSTATS USERID.TELLER;
 OK, sql_rcd = 0,        Execution time =    10.7500 secs

-- connect to the database
EXEC DBA: STOPUSE TP1;
 OK, sql_rcd = 0,        Execution time =     1.8700 secs

-- logoff
EXEC DBA: LOGOFF USERID DBSVRO3 UPM_LOCAL;
 OK, api_rcd = 0,         Execution time =     0.0000 secs
```

Figure 24-6 (Part 2 of 2). Loading a TP1 Database with Data Using RSQL.

WHERE DO WE GO FROM HERE?

This concludes our presentation of the common tools that the **SQLTP1** benchmarking toolkit offers. To summarize, these tools include:

- **RSQL** run files.
- **TP1.MAK**, the common *make* file for building TP1 transactions.
- **TP1LOAD.SQC**, the static SQL-based program for loading the TP1 tables.
- **MULTI**, which can run TP1 transactions as processes and display their results.

So, where do we go from here? The next step is to create our four flavors of TP1 transactions and measure their performance. We will be developing one transaction flavor per chapter. The first transaction will be the longest, since this is where all the common procedures are described. In subsequent chapters, we will be using some of those common procedures. Instead of repeating their code, we will refer you to the chapter where the code was first described. This way, the remaining chapters will become progressively shorter, and we will maintain our focus on the new concepts being introduced.

Chapter 25

The Static SQL Database Server TP1

This is the second of a six-chapter series, in which we develop a TP1 Benchmark toolkit for the OS/2 EE Database Manager. This chapter provides a static SQL *Database Server* version of the TP1 transaction. The code that implements this transaction is provided in the **SQLTP1.SQC** program. Instances of this transaction can be executed against either a local or remote database engine. The TP1 transaction performance will be measured using the following configurations:

1. On a local versus remote Database Server.
2. On a slower server versus a faster Database Server machine.
3. On the same Database Server but using different buffer pool sizes.

We also introduce the results of tests we conducted to measure *side effects* on TP1 performance which are caused by:

- A slow disk versus a fast disk on the database server.
- HPFS versus FAT file systems.
- Vanilla APPC versus SQLLOO APPC.

These tests are filled with surprises! This chapter has two hard prerequisites:

- The SQL tutorial.
- The first chapter in the Benchmark Series.

In addition, you should review the **MULTI** chapter in Part II, and you should be familiar with **RSQL** at the user level.

THE STATIC SQL VERSION OF TP1

We have a database, we have the data, so let's create the program that does the TP1. The **SQLTP1.SQC** program is designed to run as a **MULTI** process. This means **MULTI** will create the process, pass it the parameters, and tell it when to start or stop executing TP1 transactions. When the process is told to start executing TP1s, it will go into a continuous loop submitting TP1 transactions against the database, and displaying the running count of the results. Two counts are displayed in each of the four process windows:

- The total number of transactions executed.
- The total number of transactions executed with a response time that is equal to or less than the specified threshold.

The user specifies the transaction threshold as a parameter to be passed to the process at start-up time. Another parameter that is specified is the seed for the random number generator that the process will use to generate its TP1 requests. The **tps** scaling factor for the database is also passed and it will also be used to generate the random number.

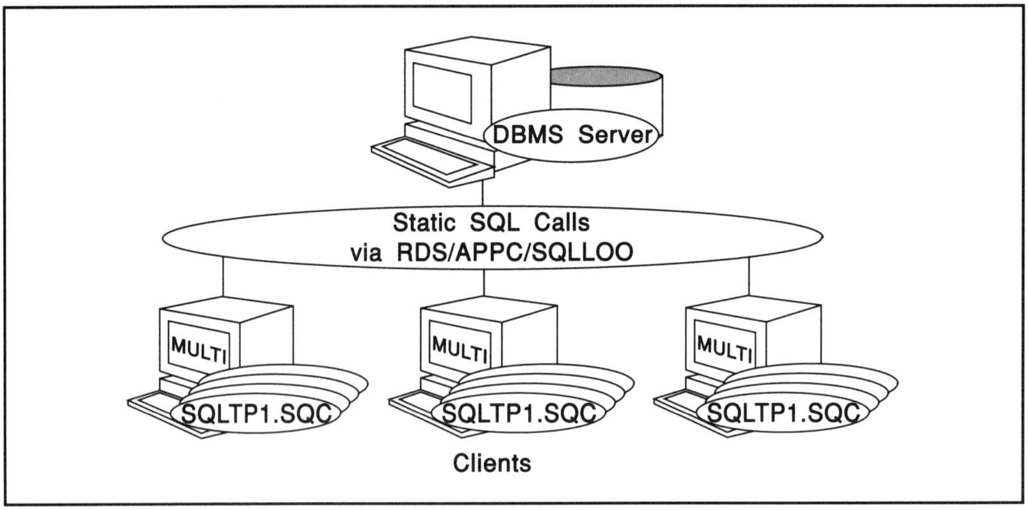

Figure 25-1. A 12-Client Static SQL TP1 Database Server.

LOCAL AND REMOTE TP1 CONFIGURATIONS

The TP1 transactions execute as static SQL statements against a database. This database may be either local or remote. The location of the database is totally transparent to the code. If the database is remote, then the **Remote Data Services (RDS)** component of the Database Manager will pass the SQL statement to the remote database using APPC/SQLLOO.

Each instance of **MULTI** can run four **SQLTP1.SQC** processes. If you need more TP1 generators, simply add more **MULTI** client workstations. Figure 25-1 shows you how to create a 12-client TP1 system. You can scale this configuration in any direction depending on your budget considerations. We will be scaling our experiments downward to a four-client TP1 system and we'll throw in a network! We'll then run benchmarks against the local and remote database configurations to understand the overhead that **RDS** introduces.

WALKING THROUGH THE SQLTP1.SQC CODE

SQLTP1.SQC: The main() Procedure

In this section, we present the **main()** procedure of the **SQLTP1** program whose code listing is shown in Figure 25-2. The following is a step-by-step description of what this code does:

1. The program starts by including the C-language, OS/2 and OS/2 EE header files that are needed for system services. Our current interest is on the OS/2 EE header files for the Database Services:

   sqlca.h This include file provides the type definition of a **SQLCA** structure. We have to create a variable of that type in the program, which the Database Manager uses to return error information.

   sql.h This include file contains the text of SQL error messages.

   sqlcodes.h This include file contains SQL constant definitions.

   sqlenv.h This include file contains the function prototypes and type definitions for the Database Administration's Environment API services.

2. We then include two of our program header files:

   const.h You've already encountered this include file when we developed **MULTI**. It contains **MULTI**-related constants and structures. The listing for this file is provided in Figure 25-11.

   sqltp1.h This include file contains the forward declarations, type definitions, and global variables for all the TP1 transaction programs. The listing for this file is provided in Figure 25-10.

3. The **EXEC SQL WHENEVER** statements that follow indicate that we will do our own error detection in-line.

4. We then declare our host variables.

5. The **main()** program follows, and you can see that it's not going to be a monster. Here's what **main()** does:

   - It invokes **get_args()**, listed in Figure 25-4, to obtain the arguments **MULTI** passes it when it invokes the program. **MULTI** gets these arguments from reading the **MULTI.CFG** file.

   - It invokes **initialize_multi_ipc()**, listed in Figure 25-5, to perform all the interprocess communication chores required from a process that runs under **MULTI**'s control.

- It invokes **initialize_task()**, listed in Figure 25-6, to connect to the database, install a signal handler, and do all kinds of one-time housekeeping in preparation for the *big TP1 loop*.
- It invokes **execute_task()**, listed in Figure 25-7. This is the home of the *big TP1 loop*, which forever executes TP1 transactions. **MULTI** can at any time pause and resume the execution of TP1 transactions through semaphores. The TP1 transaction is executed by the helper routine, **tp1_transaction()**, whose code is listed in Figure 25-8.

```
/******************************************************************************/
/*  PROGRAM NAME: SQLTP1 - A process program that MULTI starts               */
/*                                                                            */
/*  PROGRAM DESCRIPTION:  This program is run as a child task of MULTI.      */
/*      It executes static SQL TP1 Transactions as part of a DB benchmark.   */
/******************************************************************************/
#include <process.h>                    /* For exit()                         */
#include <string.h>                     /* For printf                         */
#include <sys\types.h>                  /* For time()                         */
#include <sys\timeb.h>                  /* For time()                         */
#include <sys\stat.h>                   /* For stat()                         */
#include <stdlib.h>                     /* For atoi                           */
#include <stdio.h>                      /* For sprintf, printf                */
#define INCL_VIO                        /* include VIO calls                  */
#define INCL_DOSSEMAPHORES              /* include semaphore api calls        */
#define INCL_DOSMEMMGR                  /* include segment   api calls        */
#define INCL_ERRORS                     /* include error definitions          */
#include <os2.h>

#include <sqlca.h>                      /* sqlca                              */
#include <sql.h>                        /* error msg. retrieval               */
#include <sqlcodes.h>                   /* SQL return code constants          */
#include <sqlenv.h>                     /* environment functions and          */
#include "const.h"                      /* constants for multi                */
#include "sqltp1.h"                     /* tp1 program vars, declares,etc.    */

struct sqlca sqlca;
EXEC SQL WHENEVER SQLERROR CONTINUE;
EXEC SQL WHENEVER SQLWARNING CONTINUE;
EXEC SQL WHENEVER NOT FOUND CONTINUE;
EXEC SQL BEGIN DECLARE SECTION;
 long  acct_num;
 short branch_id;
 short teller_id;
 long  balance;
 long  delta         = 100;
 char  acct_name[20] = "<--20 BYTE STRING-->";
EXEC SQL END   DECLARE SECTION;
```

Figure 25-2 (Part 1 of 2). SQLTP1.SQC: The main() Procedure.

```
/*-------------------------------------------------------------------*/
/* Main routine.                                                     */
/*-------------------------------------------------------------------*/
VOID main(USHORT argc, PCHAR argv[])
{
  get_args(argc, argv);              /* get program arguments          */

  initialize_multi_ipc();            /* Init MULTI semaphores/shared memory*/

  initialize_task();                 /* perform one time intializations  */

  execute_task();                    /* Issue TP1s in a loop            */
} /* end main */
```

Figure 25-2 (Part 2 of 2). SQLTP1.SQC: The main() Procedure.

SQLTP1.SQC: The get_args() Function

In this section, we present the **get_args()** function, whose code listing is shown in Figure 25-4. This function obtains the arguments that **MULTI** passes to the program when it invokes it. **MULTI** gets those arguments from reading the **MULTI.CFG** file, an example of which is shown below:

```
PROGRAM_TYPE     = PROCESS
STOP_TIME_MS     = 600000
TASK_NAME        = SQLTP1.EXE 0 17 2.0 1;
TASK_NAME        = SQLTP1.EXE 1 23 2.0 1;
TASK_NAME        = SQLTP1.EXE 2 29 2.0 1;
TASK_NAME        = SQLTP1.EXE 3 57 2.0 1;
```

Figure 25-3. A MULTI.CFG File for Running Four TP1 Processes.

The arguments appear right after the program's name. The **get_args()** function expects four parameters:

- A process number, which determines which **MULTI** window this process will use to display its output.
- A seed value for the random number generator.
- A threshold value which indicates the required TP1 response time. All transactions whose response time is less or equal to this threshold will be counted in the window's **TXNS** field.
- A *tps scale value* which indicates the scaling factor used for building the TP1 database was built. This number will be used in conjunction with the random number generated to calculate a random account number.

```
/*--------------------------------------------------------------------------*/
/* Get program arguments.  Arguments are 1) process_number, 2) seed_value,  */
/* 3) threshold  4) tps                                                     */
/*--------------------------------------------------------------------------*/
VOID get_args(USHORT argc, PCHAR argv[])
{
  /*----------------------------------*/
  /* validate and get arguments       */
  /*----------------------------------*/
  if (argc != 5)
     { print_error(0, "reading command arguments",
                   __FILE__,__LINE__);
       exit(FAILED);
     }

  process_number = atoi(argv[1]);           /* get process number           */
  if ((process_number < 0) || (process_number > 3))
     { print_error(0, "reading process number", __FILE__,__LINE__);
       exit(FAILED);
     }

  seed_value = atoi(argv[2]);               /* get seed value               */
  threshold  = atof(argv[3]);               /* get threshold value          */
  tps        = atoi(argv[4]);               /* get tps scale factor         */

} /* end get_args */
```

Figure 25-4. SQLTP1.SQC: The get_args() Function.

SQLTP1.SQC: The initialize_multi_ipc() Function

In this section, we present the **initialize_multi_ipc()** function, whose code listing is shown in Figure 25-5. This function does all the interprocess communication chores required from a process that runs under **MULTI**'s control. If the code looks unfamiliar, then please review the chapter in Part II on **MULTI** and its child processes. Briefly, a **MULTI** child process execution is controlled by two global semaphores:

- The **RUN**x semaphore which controls when this individual task can run.
- The **RUNALL** semaphore which controls when all the child tasks under MULTI can run. When this semaphore clears all processes that are enabled can start participating in a TP1 benchmark run.

This function also obtains a pointer to the shared memory array in which it will write its count results.

```
/*-----------------------------------------------------------------------*/
/* initialize semaphores and shared memory for communication between this */
/* process and the MULTI process.                                         */
/*-----------------------------------------------------------------------*/
VOID initialize_multi_ipc(VOID)
{
  CHAR sem_name[30];
  /*----------------------------------*/
  /* open and initialize the semaphores */
  /*----------------------------------*/
  sprintf(sem_name,"\\SEM\\RUN%d", process_number);
  if (rc = DosOpenSem(&sem_handle,          /* handle to semaphore returned */
                      sem_name))            /* ASCIIZ name of semaphore     */
     { print_error(rc,"during DosCreateSem", __FILE__,__LINE__);
       exit(FAILED);
     }

  sprintf(sem_name,"\\SEM\\RUNALL");
  if (rc = DosOpenSem(&control_sem_handle,  /* handle to semaphore returned */
                      sem_name))            /* ASCIIZ name of semaphore     */
     { print_error(rc,"during DosCreateSem", __FILE__,__LINE__);
       exit(FAILED);
     }
  /*----------------------------------*/
  /* get a shared segment for the count */
  /*   values                           */
  /*----------------------------------*/
  sprintf(name,"\\SHAREMEM\\TASK");
  rc = DosGetShrSeg( name, &selector);
  if (rc)
     {print_error(rc,"allocating count buffer",__FILE__,__LINE__);
      exit(FAILED);
     }
  count_ptr = MAKEP(sclcctor,0);        /* create a pointer to file buffer    */
} /* end initialize_multi_ipc */
```

Figure 25-5. SQLTP1.SQC: The initialize_multi_ipc() Function.

SQLTP1.SQC: The initialize_task() Function

In this section, we present the **initialize_task()** function, whose code listing is shown in Figure 25-6. This function does the following task-specific one-time chores:

1. It connects to the TP1 database.
2. It installs a signal handler that intercepts CTRL + Break and gracefully terminates the program.
3. It adds a TXNS field to the task's window. This is where the count is displayed for TP1 transactions which meet the response time threshold.
4. It seeds the random number generator.

```
/*------------------------------------------------------------------------*/
/* Perform onetime initializations for the task such as database connects.  */
/*------------------------------------------------------------------------*/
VOID  initialize_task(VOID)
{
  /*--------------------------------------------*/
  /* connect to the database, restart if necessary  */
  /*--------------------------------------------*/
  sqlestrd("TP1", 'S', &sqlca);

  if (sqlca.sqlcode == SQLE_RC_DB_RESTART)
     sqlerest("TP1", &sqlca);

  if (sqlca.sqlcode)
     { sprintf(error_string,"connnecting to the database, sqlca.sqlcode = %ld",
               sqlca.sqlcode);
       print_error(0, error_string, __FILE__,__LINE__);
       exit(FAILED);
     }
  /*-------------------------------*/
  /* install database signal handler     */
  /*-------------------------------*/
  sqleisig(&sqlca);
  if (sqlca.sqlcode)
     { sprintf(error_string,"installing signal handler, sqlca.sqlcode = %ld",
               sqlca.sqlcode);
       print_error(0, error_string, __FILE__,__LINE__);
       exit(FAILED);
     }
  /*-------------------------------*/
  /* add transaction count field         */
  /*-------------------------------*/
  write_str("TXNS  = ", FIELD_TEXT_ATTR,
           (process_number * 20) + 2, 10); /* calculate display location    */
                                           /*  based on process number      */
  /*-------------------------------*/
  /* initialize random number generator  */
  /*-------------------------------*/
  srand(seed_value);
} /* end initialize_task */
```

Figure 25-6. SQLTP1.SQC: The initialize_task() Function.

SQLTP1.SQC: The execute_task() Function

In this section, we present the **execute_task**() function, whose code listing is shown in Figure 25-7. This function provides the control loop for executing TP1 transactions. Here is how it works:

1. It waits on the **RUN**x sempaphore through which **MULTI** controls the execution of a particular task. When this semaphore clears, the task can move to the next step.
2. It waits on the **RUNALL** semaphore through which **MULTI** synchronizes the execution of all its child tasks. When this semaphore clears, all the enabled processes can start participating in a TP1 benchmark run.
3. It starts the timer and obtains two random numbers.

4. It invokes the helper procedure **tp1_transaction()** to execute a TP1 transaction (see Figure 25-8).
5. It calculates the elapsed time.
6. It increments the result counters and displays the new results in the **MULTI** process window. Note that the display is a critical resource protected by a semaphore. The task waits on the semaphore to clear. When that happens it sets the semaphore, writes the counts to the process display window, and then clears the semaphore.

As you can see, this control procedure does the typical stuff expected from a program executing under **MULTI**. There is no new material here.

```
/*-------------------------------------------------------------------------*/
/* Task routine. This routine continuously 1) requests a semaphore,        */
/*   2) increments and displays a count, 3) clears the semaphore.  The user */
/*   can disable counting by setting the semaphore from the display panel.  */
/*-------------------------------------------------------------------------*/
VOID execute_task(VOID)
{
  CHAR   count_str[10];

  count_ptr->count[process_number] = 0;

  /*-----------------------------------*/
  /* display process status            */
  /*-----------------------------------*/
  write_str("Ready        ", PANEL_STATUS_ATTR,
            (process_number * 20) + 2, 15); /* calculate display location   *//
                                            /*  based on thread number      */

  /*-----------------------------------*/
  /* continuous count loop             */
  /*-----------------------------------*/
  while (TRUE)
    { /*-----------------------------------*/
      /* wait for control sem to clear     */
      /*-----------------------------------*/
      rc = DosSemWait(control_sem_handle,   /* semaphore handle             */
                      -1L);                 /* infinite timeout             */
      if (rc && (rc != ERROR_INTERRUPT))    /* if error but not interrupted *//
        { print_error(rc,"during DosSemWait", __FILE__,__LINE__);
          exit(FAILED);
        }
      /*-----------------------------------*/
      /* request the semaphore             */
      /*-----------------------------------*/
      if (rc = DosSemRequest(sem_handle,    /* semaphore handle             */
                             -1L))          /* infinite timeout             */
        { print_error(rc,"during DosSemRequest", __FILE__,__LINE__);
          exit(FAILED);
        }
```

Figure 25-7 (Part 1 of 2). SQLTP1.SQC: The execute_task() Function.

```
        /*________________________________________*/
        /* execute a TP1 transaction              */
        /*________________________________________*/
        reset_timer();
        start_timer();

        random1 =  rand();
        random2 =  rand();
        if ( tp1_transaction( ) )
           exit(FAILED);

        stop_timer();

        /*________________________________________*/
        /* increment the count                    */
        /*________________________________________*/
        rc = DosSemWait(control_sem_handle, 0L);  /* don't wait if not clear   */
        if (rc == 0)
           {  ++(count_ptr->count[process_number]);

              if (event_time <= threshold)
                 ++(count_ptr->count[process_number + 4]);
           }
        /*________________________________________*/
        /* display the count value                */
        /*________________________________________*/
        sprintf(count_str, "%-7lu", count_ptr->count[process_number]);
        write_str(count_str, OUTPUT_FIELD_ATTR,    /* calculate display location*//
                  (process_number * 20) + 10,  9);/*  based on thread number   */

        sprintf(count_str, "%-7lu", count_ptr->count[process_number + 4]);
        write_str(count_str, OUTPUT_FIELD_ATTR,
                  (process_number * 20) + 10, 10);/* calculate display location*//
                                                   /*  based on thread number   */
        /*________________________________________*/
        /* clear the semaphore                    */
        /*________________________________________*/
        if (rc = DosSemClear(sem_handle))
           { print_error(rc,"during DosSemClear", __FILE__,__LINE__);
             exit(FAILED);
           }
      }/* end while */
   } /* end execute_task */
```

Figure 25-7 (Part 2 of 2). SQLTP1.SQC: The execute_task() Function.

SQLTP1.SQC: The tp1_transaction() Function

In this section, we present the **tp1_transaction()** function, whose code listing is shown in Figure 25-8. This is the function that does the "real TP1 work." So, let's take a close look at what it does:

1. It generates a set of random numbers, for the account number, the teller ID, and the branch ID. This simulates a real world random event as required by the TP1 specification.

2. It retrieves the balance for that random account from the ACCT table and adds some money to it. We're going to be generous with everybody! This operation demonstrates the use of the cursor in a static SQL context. Let's see how it works:

   - The **DECLARE CURSOR** command associates CURSOR1 with the **SELECT** statement. From now on, CURSOR1 can be used as a handle for that **SELECT** statement.

   - The **OPEN** command on CURSOR1 causes the **SELECT** to execute and produces a "result set"; hopefully, there will be only one account returned. The cursor will be positioned before the first row.

   - The **FETCH** command positions that cursor to the first row in the "result set," and then retrieves that row and puts the result **INTO** the host variable, **balance**.

   - The **UPDATE** with the keyword **CURRENT**, updates the row on which the cursor is currently positioned. We credit this account with the contents of the host variable, **delta**.

   - The **CLOSE** command is issued to close the cursor. We've done our first TP1 update, to the ACCT table. Three more to go.

3. It updates the balance for a random teller in the TELLER table. This is a "simple" non-cursored SQL **UPDATE**.

4. It updates the balance for a random branch in the BRANCH table. This is also a "simple" non-cursored SQL **UPDATE**.

5. It inserts a record for that transaction into the HISTORY table using a SQL **INSERT**. Again, this is straightforward; we just have to be sure that the host variables and literals in the list of **VALUES** map to the list of named columns.

6. It issues a **COMMIT**, so that the TP1 is recorded for posterity in the database, making all parties slightly richer. It's a bit like printing money, isn't it?

7. Congratulations, we've just completed the first of our TP1 flavors!

```
/*---------------------------------------------------------------------------*/
/* function for TP1 transaction                                              */
/*---------------------------------------------------------------------------*/
SHORT APIENTRY tpl_transaction(VOID)
{
  CHAR   msgbuf[512];
      /*------------------------------------*/
      /* generate some random data          */
      /*------------------------------------*/
  acct_num = (random1 * random2) % (tps*1000001) + 1;/* generate account num */
  teller_id= (short)(random1 % (tps*100) + 1;       /* generate teller id   */
  branch_id= (short)(random2 % (tps*10) + 1;        /* generate branch id   */
      /*------------------------------------*/
      /* get the current balance from ACCT  */
      /*------------------------------------*/
  EXEC SQL DECLARE CURSOR1 CURSOR FOR
           SELECT BALANCE FROM ACCT WHERE ACCT_NUM = :acct_num
           FOR UPDATE OF BALANCE;
  EXEC SQL OPEN CURSOR1;
  if (sqlca.sqlcode != 0)
     { sqlaintp(msgbuf, sizeof(msgbuf), 80, &sqlca);
       printf("%s\n",msgbuf);
       print_error((SHORT)sqlca.sqlcode, "during SQL OPEN",
                   __FILE__, __LINE__);
       return(FAILED);
     }
  EXEC SQL FETCH CURSOR1 INTO :balance;
  if (sqlca.sqlcode != 0)
     { sqlaintp(msgbuf, sizeof(msgbuf), 80, &sqlca);
       printf("%s\n",msgbuf);
       print_error((SHORT)sqlca.sqlcode, "during SQL FETCH",
                   __FILE__, __LINE__);
       return(FAILED);
     }
      /*--------------------------------------*/
      /* Credit the balance in the ACCT table */
      /*--------------------------------------*/
  EXEC SQL UPDATE ACCT
           SET BALANCE = BALANCE + :delta
           WHERE CURRENT OF CURSOR1;
  if (sqlca.sqlcode != 0)
     { sqlaintp(msgbuf, sizeof(msgbuf), 80, &sqlca);
       printf("%s\n",msgbuf);
       print_error((SHORT)sqlca.sqlcode, "during SQL UPDATE",
                   __FILE__,__LINE__);
       return(FAILED);
     }
  EXEC SQL CLOSE CURSOR1;
  if (sqlca.sqlcode != 0)
     { sqlaintp(msgbuf, sizeof(msgbuf), 80, &sqlca);
       printf("%s\n",msgbuf);
       print_error((SHORT)sqlca.sqlcode, "during SQL CLOSE",
                   __FILE__,__LINE__);
       return(FAILED);
     }
```

Figure 25-8 (Part 1 of 2). SQLTP1.SQC: The tp1_transaction() Function.

```
     /*------------------------------------*/
     /* Update the TELLER table's balance   */
     /*------------------------------------*/
   EXEC SQL UPDATE TELLER
            SET BALANCE = BALANCE + :delta
            WHERE TELLER_ID = :teller_id;
   if (sqlca.sqlcode != 0)
      { sqlaintp(msgbuf, sizeof(msgbuf), 80, &sqlca);
        printf("%s\n",msgbuf);
        print_error((SHORT)sqlca.sqlcode, "during SQL UPDATE",
                     __FILE__,__LINE__);
        return(FAILED);
      }

     /*------------------------------------*/
     /* Update the BRANCH table's balance   */
     /*------------------------------------*/
   EXEC SQL UPDATE BRANCH
            SET BALANCE = BALANCE + :delta
            WHERE BRANCH_ID = :branch_id;
   if (sqlca.sqlcode != 0)
      { sqlaintp(msgbuf, sizeof(msgbuf), 80, &sqlca);
        printf("%s\n",msgbuf);
        print_error((SHORT)sqlca.sqlcode, "during SQL UPDATE",
                     __FILE__,__LINE__);
        return(FAILED);
      }
     /*------------------------------------*/
     /* Insert transaction in HISTORY table */
     /*------------------------------------*/
   EXEC SQL INSERT
            INTO HISTORY(ACCT_NUM, TELLER_ID, BRANCH_ID, BALANCE,
                         DELTA, PID, TRANSID, ACCTNAME, TEMP)
            VALUES(:acct_num, :teller_id, :branch_id, :balance,
                   :delta, 1, 3, :acct_name, 'hist  ');
   if (sqlca.sqlcode != 0)
      { sqlaintp(msgbuf, sizeof(msgbuf), 80, &sqlca);
        printf("%s\n",msgbuf);
        print_error((SHORT)sqlca.sqlcode, "during SQL INSERT",
                     __FILE__,__LINE__);
        return(FAILED);
      }
     /*------------------------------------*/
     /* Commit the transaction to database  */
     /*------------------------------------*/
   EXEC SQL COMMIT;
   if (sqlca.sqlcode != 0)
      { sqlaintp(msgbuf, sizeof(msgbuf), 80, &sqlca);
        printf("%s\n",msgbuf);
        print_error((SHORT)sqlca.sqlcode, "during SQL COMMIT",
                     __FILE__, __LINE__);
        return(FAILED);
      }
   return(GOOD);
} /* end tp1_transaction */
```

Figure 25-8 (Part 2 of 2). SQLTP1.SQC: The tp1_transaction() Function.

Helper Functions

In this section, we present the helper functions whose code is listed in Figure 25-9. These are just our standard timer and print error functions that you've already seen throughout this book.

```
/*-----------------------------------------------------------------------*/
/*  This procedure initializes the time variables.                       */
/*-----------------------------------------------------------------------*/
VOID   reset_timer(VOID)
{ event_time = 0.0 ;
  start_time = 0.0 ;
  end_time   = 0.0 ;
} /* end reset_time */

/*-----------------------------------------------------------------------*/
/*  This procedure records the time at the start of an interval          */
/*-----------------------------------------------------------------------*/
VOID   start_timer(VOID)
{ ftime(&timebuff);
  start_time = (double)timebuff.time+((double)timebuff.millitm)/(double)1000;
} /* end start_time */

/*-----------------------------------------------------------------------*/
/*  This procedure records the time at the end of an interval            */
/*  and calculates the elapsed time for an event.                        */
/*-----------------------------------------------------------------------*/
VOID   stop_timer(VOID)
{ ftime(&timebuff);
  end_time = (double)timebuff.time+((double)timebuff.millitm)/(double)1000;
  event_time = event_time  + (end_time - start_time);
} /* end stop_time */
.
/*-----------------------------------------------------------------------*/
/* write a character string to the screen.                               */
/*-----------------------------------------------------------------------*/
VOID write_str(PCHAR charstr, CHAR attribute, USHORT x, USHORT y)
{ if (rc = VioWrtCharStrAtt(charstr,    /* character string              */
                      strlen(charstr),/* number of times                 */
                      y, x,           /* screen position                 */
                      &attribute,     /* attribute                       */
                      0))             /* reserved                        */
     print_error(rc,"during VioWrtCharStrAtt",__FILE__,__LINE__);
} /* end write_str */
/*-----------------------------------------------------------------------*/
/* Error Display Routine                                                 */
/*-----------------------------------------------------------------------*/
VOID print_error(USHORT Error, PCHAR msg, PCHAR file, USHORT line)
{if (Error == 0)
   printf("Error detected while %s at line %d in file %s.\n", msg,line,file);
 else
   printf("Error %d detected while %s at line %d in file %s.\n",
   Error,msg,line,file);
} /* end print_error */
```

Figure 25-9. SQLTP1.SQC: Helper Functions.

SQLTP1.H Include File

In this section, we present the **sqltp1.h** include file, whose code is listed in Figure 25-10. Again, this is just your garden variety C include file, with all the forward function declarations, type definitions, and global variables.

```
/*****************************************************************************/
/*  INCLUDE NAME: SQLTP1 - declarations for TP1 task programs               */
/*****************************************************************************/
/*-------------------------------------------------------------------------*/
/* Forward declarations of procedures in this module                        */
/*-------------------------------------------------------------------------*/
                    /*-----------------------------------*/
                    /* top level routines                */
                    /*-----------------------------------*/
VOID get_args(USHORT argc, PCHAR argv[]);
VOID initialize_multi_ipc(VOID);
VOID initialize_task(VOID);
VOID execute_task(VOID);
SHORT APIENTRY tp1_transaction(VOID);

                    /*-----------------------------------*/
                    /* VIO call helper functions         */
                    /*-----------------------------------*/
VOID write_str(PCHAR, CHAR, USHORT, USHORT);

                    /*-----------------------------------*/
                    /* timer routines                    */
                    /*-----------------------------------*/
VOID  reset_timer(VOID);
VOID  start_timer(VOID);
VOID  stop_timer(VOID);

                    /*-----------------------------------*/
                    /* Error display routine             */
                    /*-----------------------------------*/
VOID print_error(USHORT, PCHAR, PCHAR, USHORT);

/*-------------------------------------------------------------------------*/
/* Global variables/type definitions for this module                        */
/*-------------------------------------------------------------------------*/
                    /*-----------------------------------*/
                    /* for program parameters            */
                    /*-----------------------------------*/
USHORT process_number;                /* number of this process          */
USHORT seed_value;                    /* initial seed for random number gen*/
double threshold;                     /* time thresholds for TP1 txns    */
USHORT tps;                           /* the tps database scaling factor */
```

Figure 25-10 (Part 1 of 2). SQLTP1.H Include File.

```
                    /*------------------------------------*/
                    /* for multi IPC                      */
                    /*------------------------------------*/
HSEM   sem_handle;                      /* handle for task semaphore         */
HSEM   control_sem_handle;              /* handle for global control sem.    */
typedef struct
        { ULONG count[8];
        } COUNT;
COUNT   *count_ptr;                     /* structure for count variables     */

                    /*------------------------------------*/
                    /* for task execution                 */
                    /*------------------------------------*/
USHORT random1, random2;

                    /*------------------------------------*/
                    /* global variables for timing        */
                    /*------------------------------------*/
struct   timeb  timebuff;                   /* Timer buffer                  */
double          start_time = 0.0;           /* Start of command time         */
double          end_time   = 0.0;           /* End of command time           */
double          event_time = 0.0;           /* Elapsed time                  */

                    /*------------------------------------*/
                    /* misc variables                     */
                    /*------------------------------------*/
CHAR     name[80];                     /* variable for building ascii names  */
USHORT   selector;                     /* variable for selector values       */
USHORT rc;                              /* return code variable              */
CHAR   error_string[80];
```

Figure 25-10 (Part 2 of 2). SQLTP1.H Include File.

CONST.H Include File

In this section, we present the **const.h** include file, whose code is listed in Figure 25-11. This file is the same one used by all the **MULTI** child programs. It contains the screen constants and other constant declarations used to make the program pretty.

```
/*****************************************************************************/
/*  INCLUDE NAME: CONST - constants for MULTI and related programs          */
/*****************************************************************************/
/*--------------------------------------------------------------------------*/
/* defines                                                                   */
/*--------------------------------------------------------------------------*/
                   /*-----------------------------------*/
                   /* box characters                    */
                   /*-----------------------------------*/
#define HORIZONTAL_LINE "─"
#define VERTICAL_LINE   "│"
#define BOX_UL_CORNER   "┌"
#define BOX_UR_CORNER   "┐"
#define BOX_LL_CORNER   "└"
#define BOX_LR_CORNER   "┘"
#define BLANK           " "
                   /*-----------------------------------*/
                   /* foreground color values           */
                   /*-----------------------------------*/
#define BLACK               0x00
#define BLUE                0x01
#define GREEN               0x02
#define CYAN                0x03
#define RED                 0x04
#define MAGENTA             0x05
#define BROWN               0x06
#define LT_GRAY             0x07
#define GRAY                0x08
#define LT_BLUE             0x09
#define LT_GREEN            0x0A
#define LT_CYAN             0x0B
#define LT_RED              0x0C
#define LT_MAGENTA          0x0D
#define YELLOW              0x0E
#define WHITE               0x0F
                   /*-----------------------------------*/
                   /* background color values           */
                   /*-----------------------------------*/
#define BGND_BLACK          0x00
#define BGND_BLUE           0x10
#define BGND_GREEN          0x20
#define BGND_TURQ           0x30
#define BGND_RED            0x40
#define BGND_MAGENTA        0x50
#define BGND_BROWN          0x60
#define BGND_LT_GRAY        0x70
#define BGND_GRAY           0x80
#define BGND_LT_BLUE        0x90
#define BGND_LT_GREEN       0xA0
#define BGND_LT_CYAN        0xB0
#define BGND_LT_RED         0xC0
#define BGND_LT_MAGENTA     0xD0
#define BGND_YELLOW         0xE0
#define BGND_WHITE          0xF0
```

Figure 25-11 (Part 1 of 3). CONST.H Include File.

```
                    /*-----------------------------------------*/
                    /* panel color attributes                  */
                    /*-----------------------------------------*/
#define BOX_ATTR            ((CHAR)CYAN    | BGND_BLACK)
#define BOX_TITLE_ATTR      ((CHAR)GREEN   | BGND_BLACK)
#define FIELD_TEXT_ATTR     ((CHAR)BROWN   | BGND_BLACK)
#define IO_FIELD_ATTR       ((CHAR)LT_GRAY | BGND_BLACK)
#define OUTPUT_FIELD_ATTR   ((CHAR)WHITE   | BGND_BLACK)
#define CURSOR_FIELD_ATTR   ((CHAR)BLACK   | BGND_LT_GRAY)
#define PANEL_TITLE_ATTR    ((CHAR)YELLOW  | BGND_BLACK)
#define PANEL_HELP_ATTR     ((CHAR)LT_RED  | BGND_BLACK)
#define PANEL_STATUS_ATTR   ((CHAR)RED     | BGND_BLACK)
                    /*-----------------------------------------*/
                    /* key definitions                         */
                    /*-----------------------------------------*/
#define UP_ARROW            (256 + 72)
#define DOWN_ARROW          (256 + 80)
#define LEFT_ARROW          (256 + 75)
#define RIGHT_ARROW         (256 + 77)
#define PLUS_KEY            '+'
#define MINUS_KEY           '-'
#define ESC_KEY             27
                    /*-----------------------------------------*/
                    /* panel field limits                      */
                    /*-----------------------------------------*/
#define FIELD_X_MAX         3
#define FIELD_Y_MAX         2
                    /*-----------------------------------------*/
                    /* task field values                       */
                    /*-----------------------------------------*/
#define PRIORITY            0
#define LEVEL               1
#define SEMAPHORE           2
                    /*-----------------------------------------*/
                    /* function return values                  */
                    /*-----------------------------------------*/
#define GOOD                0
#define WARNING             1
#define FAILED             -1
                    /*-----------------------------------------*/
                    /* program terminate flag                  */
                    /*-----------------------------------------*/
#define CONTINUE            0
#define TERMINATE           1
                    /*-----------------------------------------*/
                    /* program types                           */
                    /*-----------------------------------------*/
#define THREADS             0
#define PROCESSES           1
                    /*-----------------------------------------*/
                    /* semaphore types                         */
                    /*-----------------------------------------*/
#define EXCLUSIVE           0
#define NONEXCLUSIVE        1
                    /*-----------------------------------------*/
                    /* update_value direction flags            */
                    /*-----------------------------------------*/
#define DECREMENT           0
#define INCREMENT           1
```

Figure 25-11 (Part 2 of 3). CONST.H Include File.

```
                        /*---------------------------------------*/
                        /* task execution states                 */
                        /*---------------------------------------*/
#define SUSPENDED                0
#define RUNNING                  1
                        /*---------------------------------------*/
                        /* semaphore states                      */
                        /*---------------------------------------*/
#define CLEAR                    0
#define SET                      1
                        /*---------------------------------------*/
                        /* thread priorities                     */
                        /*---------------------------------------*/
#define BACKGROUND               1
#define REGULAR                  2
#define TIME_CRITICAL            3
#define FIXED_HIGH               4
```

Figure 25-11 (Part 3 of 3). CONST.H Include File.

RUNNING FOUR TP1 BENCHMARK TESTS USING SQLTP1.SQC

Now that we've got some code, let's run some benchmarks to see how well this TP1 flavor performs. We will run three local TP1 benchmark tests and one remote one:

- The **local** benchmark tests measure performance as a function of improved server hardware (see Figure 25-13 on page 708).
  1. A PS/2 Mod-70 with a 16-MHz clock and a 500 KByte RAM buffer.
  2. A PS/2 Mod-80 with a 20-MHz clock and a 500 KByte RAM buffer.
  3. A PS/2 Mod-80 with a 20-MHz clock and a 1000-KByte RAM buffer.
- The remote benchmark uses for its server, a PS/2 Mod-80 with a 20-MHz clock and a 1000-KByte memory buffer. The clients run on a PS/2 Mod 70 with a 16-MHz clock (see Figure 25-14 on page 708).

All four benchmarks use the same software configuration; a four-process **MULTI** whose configuration file is shown below:

```
PROGRAM_TYPE     = PROCESS
STOP_TIME_MS     = 600000
TASK_NAME        = SQLTP1.EXE 0 17 2.0 1;
TASK_NAME        = SQLTP1.EXE 1 23 2.0 1;
TASK_NAME        = SQLTP1.EXE 2 29 2.0 1;
TASK_NAME        = SQLTP1.EXE 3 57 2.0 1;
```

Figure 25-12. A MULTI.CFG File for Running Four TP1 Processes.

As you can see from the configuration file the benchmarks are set up to run for 10-minute tests (i.e., 600,000 milliseconds). The response time threshold is set to 2.0 seconds, and a 1-tps database size is specified.

Note: Our liberal interpretation of TP1 uses a 2-second response threshold and a 1-tps database. However, on the plus side we're measuring 100% transaction completions as opposed to the 95% threshold required by the benchmark.

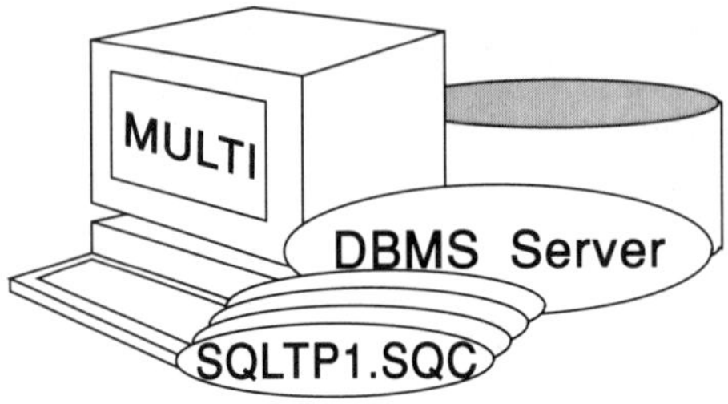

Test 1 16-MHz PS/2 Mod-70, 500 KByte RAM buffer

Test 2 20-MHz PS/2 Mod-80, 500 KByte RAM buffer

Test 3 20-MHz PS/2 Mod-80, 1000-KByte RAM buffer

Figure 25-13. Local Static SQL TP1 Benchmark Configurations.

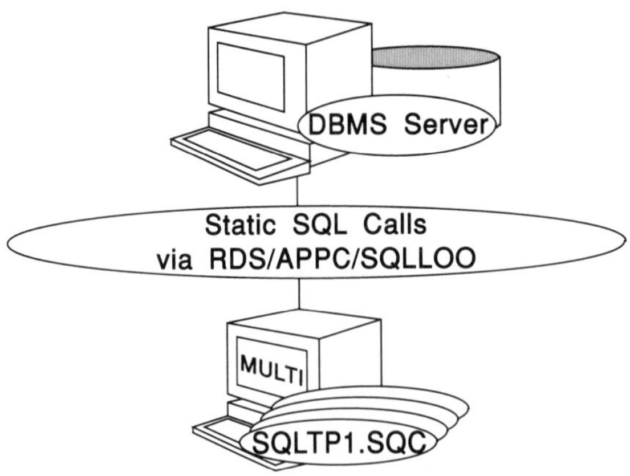

Test 4 Client: 16-MHz PS/2 Mod-70

Server: 20-MHz PS/2 Mod-80, 1000-KByte RAM buffer

LAN: 4 Mb/s Token Ring (APPC/SQLLOO/RDS)

Figure 25-14. Remote Static SQL TP1 Benchmark Configurations.

Running SQLTP1 Against a Local Database (Benchmark1)

The configuration for this benchmark is a four-client MULTI running against a local database. The test is run on a PS/2 Mod-70 with a 16-MHz clock and a 500 KByte RAM buffer (*BufPage parameter*). The database is already loaded for a 1-tps database scale. The following RSQL run is used to set up the 500 KByte buffer (we're allocating 128 4k-pages) and prepare the database for Benchmark1.

```
--                    Change TP1 Database Configuration
-- ========================================================================
-- logon
EXEC DBA: LOGON USERID PASSWORD DBSVRO3 UPM_LOCAL UPM_USER;
 OK, api_rcd = 0,          Execution time =     0.0000 secs

-- update the Database Configuration for database for a 500k buffer
EXEC DBA: UPDATE_DB_CFG TP1      MAXAPPLS    = 8,
                                 DLCHKTIME   = 10000,
                                 BUFFPAGE    = 128,
                                 LOGFILSIZ   = 50,
                                 LOGPRIMARY  = 2,
                                 LOGSECOND   = 20;
 OK, sql_rcd = 0,        Execution time =     1.3700 secs

-- Show the database configuration for database TP1
EXEC DBA: SHOW_DB_CFG TP1;

 Database Configuration for Database TP1
 ==============================================

 Configuration Parameter          Current Parm.      Parm.      Parm.
 Description                      Value   Units      Range      Default
 -------------------------------- ------- ---------- ---------- -------
 Max. Active Applications               8 Appl.      1-117            8
 Max. DB Files Open/Application        20 files      2-235           20
 Max. Files Open/Application          255 files      25-32700       255
 Buffer Pool Size                     128 4K pages     (1)           16
 Time Interval for Deadlocks        10000 millisecs. 1-600 sec.      10
 Max. Storage for Locklists             8 4K pages   4-250            8
 Max. percent locklist/appl.           22 percent    1-100           22
 Default Application Heap               3 segments   2-20             3
 Application Agent Heap                 2 segments   2-85             3
 Sort List Heap                         2 segments   1-20             2
 Database Heap                          1 segments   1-45             1
 SQL Statement Heap                    64 segments                   64
 Log File Size                         50 4K pages   15-255          50
 Primary Log Files                      2 files      0-63             2
 Secondary Log Files                   20 files      0-63             3
 Log Records/soft checkpoint          100 records    0-65535        100

 Current Log Location = C:\SQL00003\
 New Log Location     =
 Copy Protection      =    1
 Country              =    1
 Code Page            =  437
 Release              =  512
 OK, sql_rcd = 0,        Execution time =     0.3700 secs
```

Figure 25-15 (Part 1 of 2). Preparing the Database for Benchmark1.

```
-- bind the tp1 program
EXEC DBA: BIND TP1 SQLTP1.BND ISO REPEATABLE_READ BLOCK_ALL PUBLIC;
 OK, sql_rcd = 0,         Execution time =    14.5000 secs

-- delete all of the history data
EXEC SQL: DELETE FROM HISTORY;
 WARNING, sql_code = 100,    Execution time =     0.9700 secs
 SQL0100W  No row was found for FETCH, UPDATE or DELETE; or the result of a
 query is an empty table.

-- commit the changes
EXEC SQL: COMMIT;
 OK, sql_rcd = 0,         Execution time =     0.0300 secs

-- disconnect
EXEC DBA: STOPUSE TP1;
 OK, sql_rcd = 0,         Execution time =     0.7900 secs

-- logoff
EXEC DBA: LOGOFF USERID DBSVR03 UPM_LOCAL;
 OK, api_rcd = 0,           Execution time =     0.0000 secs
```

Figure 25-15 (Part 2 of 2). Preparing the Database for Benchmark1.

```
                    Multiprocess Execution Example

 Use arrow keys to move the cursor.  Use + and - keys to change field values.
 Press R to start running, S to stop, or C to clear the count.
 Press ESC to terminate the program.

-SQLTP1.EXE-         -SQLTP1.EXE-         -SQLTP1.EXE-         -SQLTP1.EXE-
 Count = 725          Count = 729          Count = 715          Count = 717
 TXNS  = 718          TXNS  = 723          TXNS  = 708          TXNS  = 711
 Priority  = RG       Priority  = RG       Priority  = RG       Priority  = RG
 Level     = 0        Level     = 0        Level     = 0        Level     = 0
 Semaphore = CLEAR    Semaphore = CLEAR    Semaphore = CLEAR    Semaphore = CLEAR

 Ready                Ready                Ready                Ready

-EXECUTION STATUS-                        -SYSTEM INFORMATION-
 Stop Time     = 600.0          sec        Maximum Wait       = 3        sec
 Elapsed Time  = 600.0          sec        Minimum Time Slice = 32       ms
 Total Count   = 2886                      Maximum Time Slice = 248      ms
 Run Status    = STOPPED                   Dynamic Variation  = ACTIVE
```

Figure 25-16. Benchmark1: Four-Client TP1 on Local DB Server (16 Mhz Mod 70, 0.5MB bufPage).

Benchmark1 Results: The MULTI screen capture in Figure 25-16 shows the results of a 10-minute test. During this period a total of 2886 TP1 transactions ran successfully. However, only (718 + 723 + 708 + 711 = 2860) transactions had a response time under the 2-second threshold. Using the liberal interpretation of TP1 introduced earlier, this machine is in the *4.7 TP1* range.

Running SQLTP1 Against a Local Database (Benchmark2)

The configuration for this benchmark is a four-client MULTI running against a local database. The test will is run on a PS/2 Mod-80 with a 20-MHz clock and a 500 KByte buffer. What we've done is upgraded the server machine to a PS/2 Mod-80, and left everything else the same. We assume the database is already loaded for a 1-tps database scale. The 500 KByte buffer configuration is the same as in the previous benchmark.

```
                        Multiprocess Execution Example

  Use arrow keys to move the cursor.  Use + and - keys to change field values.
  Press R to start running, S to stop, or C to clear the count.
  Press ESC to terminate the program.

-SQLTP1.EXE-          -SQLTP1.EXE-          -SQLTP1.EXE-          -SQLTP1.EXE-
 Count = 825           Count = 823           Count = 805           Count = 818
 TXNS  = 819           TXNS  = 817           TXNS  = 799           TXNS  = 813
 Priority  = RG        Priority  = RG        Priority  = RG        Priority  = RG
 Level     = 0         Level     = 0         Level     = 0         Level     = 0
 Semaphore = CLEAR     Semaphore = CLEAR     Semaphore = CLEAR     Semaphore = CLEAR

 Ready                 Ready                 Ready                 Ready

-EXECUTION STATUS-                          -SYSTEM INFORMATION-
 Stop Time      = 600.0          sec         Maximum Wait       = 3        sec
 Elapsed Time   = 600.0          sec         Minimum Time Slice = 32       ms
 Total Count    = 3271                       Maximum Time Slice = 248      ms
 Run Status     = STOPPED                    Dynamic Variation  = ACTIVE
```

Figure 25-17. Benchmark2: Four-Client TP1 on Local DB Server (20 Mhz Mod 80, 0.5MB bufPage).

Benchmark2 Results: The MULTI screen capture in Figure 25-17 shows the results of a 10-minute test. During this period, a total of 3271 TP1 transactions ran successfully. However, only (819 + 817 + 799 + 813 = 3248) transactions had a response time under the 2-second threshold. Using the liberal interpretation of TP1 introduced earlier, this machine is therefore in the *5.4 TP1* range.

Running SQLTP1 Against a Local Database (Benchmark3)

The configuration for this benchmark is a four-client MULTI running against a local database. The test is run on a PS/2 Mod-80 with a 20-MHz clock and a 1000-KByte buffer. What we've done is upgraded the buffer on the server machine to 1000 KBytes and left everything else the same. We assume the database is already loaded for a 1-tps database scale.

```
                      Multiprocess Execution Example

 Use arrow keys to move the cursor.  Use + and - keys to change field values.
 Press R to start running, S to stop, or C to clear the count.
 Press ESC to terminate the program.

-SQLTP1.EXE-         -SQLTP1.EXE-         -SQLTP1.EXE-         -SQLTP1.EXE-

 Count = 822          Count = 824          Count = 826          Count = 835
 TXNS  = 814          TXNS  = 817          TXNS  = 818          TXNS  = 829
 Priority  = RG       Priority  = RG       Priority  = RG       Priority  = RG
 Level     = 0        Level     = 0        Level     = 0        Level     = 0
 Semaphore = CLEAR    Semaphore = CLEAR    Semaphore = CLEAR    Semaphore = CLEAR

 Ready                Ready                Ready                Ready

-EXECUTION STATUS-                         -SYSTEM INFORMATION-

 Stop Time     = 600.0          sec         Maximum Wait       = 3        sec
 Elapsed Time  = 600.0          sec         Minimum Time Slice = 32       ms
 Total Count   = 3307                       Maximum Time Slice = 248      ms
 Run Status    = STOPPED                    Dynamic Variation  = ACTIVE
```

Figure 25-18. Benchmark3: Four-Client TP1 on Local DB Server (20 Mhz Mod 80, 1 MB bufPage).

Benchmark3 Results: This MULTI screen in Figure 25-18 shows the results of a 10-minute test. During this period, a total of 3307 TP1 transactions ran successfully. However, only (814 + 817 + 818 + 829 = 3278) transactions had a response time under the 2-second threshold. Using the liberal interpretation of TP1 we introduced earlier, this machine is therefore in the *5.5 TP1* range. The results show a very slight improvement in performance with the 500 KByte buffer increase.

Running SQLTP1 Against a Remote Database (Benchmark4)

The configuration for this benchmark is a four-client MULTI running against a remote database. The test is run on a PS/2 Mod-80 database server with a 20-MHz clock and a 1000-KByte buffer. The client machine is a PS/2 Mod-70 with a 16-MHz clock. We're effectively working with the same database set up as in Benchmark3, but we've offloaded the clients to a separate machine, and in so doing introduced the *network* factor. We use APPC's SQLLOO option (more on that later). We assume the database is already loaded for a 1-tps database scale.

```
                    Multiprocess Execution Example

 Use arrow keys to move the cursor.  Use + and - keys to change field values.
 Press R to start running, S to stop, or C to clear the count.
 Press ESC to terminate the program.

-SQLTP1.EXE-            -SQLTP1.EXE-            -SQLTP1.EXE-            -SQLTP1.EXE-

Count = 415             Count = 418             Count = 414             Count = 419
TXNS  = 411             TXNS  = 414             TXNS  = 408             TXNS  = 414
Priority  = RG          Priority  = RG          Priority  = RG          Priority  = RG
Level     = 0           Level     = 0           Level     = 0           Level     = 0
Semaphore = CLEAR       Semaphore = CLEAR       Semaphore = CLEAR       Semaphore = CLEAR

Ready                   Ready                   Ready                   Ready

-EXECUTION STATUS-                              -SYSTEM INFORMATION-

Stop Time      = 600.0          sec             Maximum Wait       = 3         sec
Elapsed Time   = 600.0          sec             Minimum Time Slice = 32        ms
Total Count    = 1666                           Maximum Time Slice = 248       ms
Run Status     - STOPPED                        Dynamic Variation  - ACTIVE
```

Figure 25-19. Benchmark4: Four-Client TP1 on Remote DB Server (20 Mhz Mod 80, 1 MB bufPage).

Benchmark4 Results: The MULTI screen capture in Figure 25-19 shows the results of a 10-minute test. During this period, a total of 1666 TP1 transactions ran successfully. However, only (411 + 414 + 408 + 414 = 1465) transactions had a response time under the 2-second threshold. Using the liberal interpretation of TP1 we introduced earlier, this machine is therefore in the *2.7 TP1* range. This number indicates that the Remote Data Service component introduces a significant performance overhead. In this implementation, each SQL statement is sent over the network using APPC in the SQLLOO mode.

MORE BENCHMARKS AND MORE SURPRISES

In this section, we discuss the implications of the results of the benchmarks that were run in this chapter. We also introduce the results of tests we conducted to measure *side effects* on TP1 performance which are caused by:

- A slow disk versus a fast disk on the database machine.
- HPFS versus FAT file systems.
- Vanilla APPC versus SQLLOO APPC.

These areas are filled with surprises and interesting observations.

Server Speed: Could 4 Mhz Make a Difference?

The results of the tests strongly suggest that SQL servers are very CPU-intensive. We were able to improve the performance by 18% (from *4.7 TP1* to *5.4 TP1*) by just going from a 16 Mhz 80386 machine (Benchmark1) to a 20 Mhz 80386 machine (Benchmark2). Just think of the TP1 performance gains you could achieve by going to a 33 Mhz 80386, or better yet a 33 Mhz 80486 "super server." *10 TP1s* (or more) is not an inconceivable number for OS/2 EE on such servers.

More RAM Buffer is Always Better, Right?

Wrong! The 500 KByte increment in buffer space introduced by Benchmark3, had a surprisingly minor effect on performance (from *5.4 TP1* to *5.5 TP1*). Nothing to get very excited over. So, yes, you need the buffer (we started with 500 KBytes) but in this benchmark *more is not necessarily better.* We must have hit a knee where our "more is better" curve went flat. So think about where this flattening effect may occur for your application before you go out and buy an extra 10 MBytes of RAM buffer for your database.

Surely a Faster Disk Will Help?

We then tried a much faster disk drive. After all, the data must be stored either in RAM or on disk. The result was also surprising: **no** performance improvement was registered. What all this probably means is that 500 KBytes is the optimum cache size for our database (in this specific application). So, neither the faster disk nor the extra RAM were able to improve on an already optimum situation (what a great marketing line).

When "High Performance" Means "Slower"

We first ran the benchmarks on OS/2's High Performance File System (**HPFS**) which we had installed on our machines. Later, just to check on how much slower the performance would be, we ran the benchmarks on OS/2's other file system: the venerable **FAT**. Guess which file system turned out to be slower? The "high performance" one. Yes, HPFS registered *4 TP1s* for Benchmark3 versus FAT's *5.5 TP1s.* What's going on here? Our guess is that TP1s are made up of very small record seeks. It may be that HPFS is not too comfortable with those situations. HPFS, on the other hand, will probably do very well in a situation that involves larger records and gigantic files. We also think that the randomized access against very large files (dozens of MBytes), required by the TP1 benchmark, is interfering with HPFS's sophisticated look-ahead access schemes.

SQLLOO: Now We Know Why It's There

The SQL-LAN-ONLY-OPTION (**SQLLOO**) option is a high-performance APPC subset that only works on LANs. In the tutorial, we recommended that you use SQLLOO instead of vanilla APPC with your database LAN applications. Here's why: The vanilla APPC version of Benchmark4 ran a dismal *0.8 TP1s* versus the *2.7 TP1s* of its SQLLOO cousin. With numbers like that, we now understand why there is a SQLLOO option.

Better Numbers Yet to Come...

The benchmarks that were run in this chapter used the "vintage" static SQL *Database Server* implementation of TP1. In later chapters, we demonstrate how Remote Procedure Calls on *Transaction Servers* can significantly improve the TP1 numbers for network servers.

A Philosophical Note

When we ran the great LAN derby, we brought to your attention the lament from the computer industry that: *"There are lies, damned lies, and benchmarks"*. On the other hand, the numbers we're uncovering in this chapter, and the chapters that follow, show that benchmarks are a great *investigative reporting* tool. We've put all those tools in your hands, which means that you can keep us honest, and in the process you can also go about making your own discoveries. And, yes, there are a lot more investigations to be made. You will see some interesting cases in the chapters that follow.

Chapter 26

The Application Remote Interface Transaction Server TP1

This is the third of a six chapter series, in which we develop a TP1 Benchmark toolkit for the OS/2 EE Database Manager. This chapter provides the **Application Remote Interface** *Transaction Server* version of TP1. This is the Database Manager's implementation of remote procedures over an APPC LAN with the high-performance SQLLOO mode.

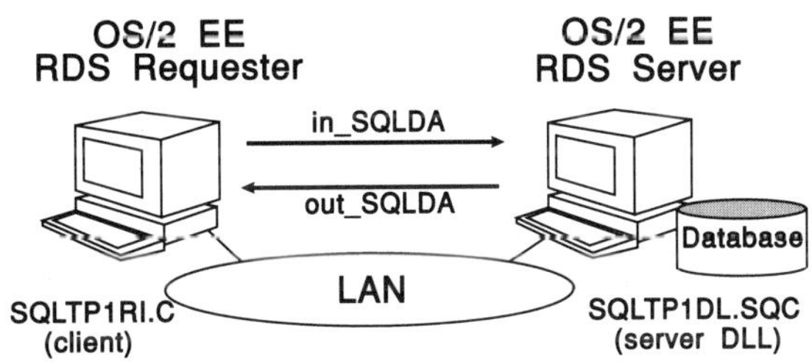

Figure 26-1. The Database Manager's Remote Procedure Call Implementation of TP1.

The plan for this chapter is to split the **SQLTP1.SQC** program that you saw in the last chapter into two programs:

1. The **SQLTP1RI.C** client program which drives the TP1s and interacts with **MULTI**.

2. The **SQLTP1DL.SQC** server program which executes the TP1 transaction against the database. This program's code is packaged as a **DLL**.

The client and server programs communicate through the Remote Procedure Call mechanism provided by the **Application Remote Interface**. The client and server programs can execute in the same machine or on separate machines connected by a LAN (see Figure 26-1). The TP1 transaction performance will be measured using both configurations.

WHAT YOU WILL LEARN

This chapter serves as an elaborate example of how to use the mechanics of the **Application Remote Interface**. On the client side of the code, you will learn how to set up the **SQLDAs** and issue the Remote Procedure Call. On the server side, you will learn how to write a remote procedure DLL, and you will see how this DLL obtains its parameters and sends back its response. This chapter has the following prerequisites:

- The SQL Tutorial chapter.
- The Database Administration Tutorial chapter, with special emphasis on the section, "The Power of Remote Procedures" on page 463.
- The first two chapters in the TP1 Benchmark Series. Much of the code in this chapter is identical to code you've already seen in **SQLTP1.SQC**. This common code will not be repeated. Instead, we will refer you to the appropriate **SQLTP1.SQC** listings where the common code is first introduced.

In addition, you should review the **MULTI** chapter in Part II, and you should be familiar with **RSQL** at the user level.

THE APPLICATION REMOTE INTERFACE TP1

The Application Remote Interface provides a Remote Procedure Call extension of the client-server model for *Transaction Server* environments. You may recall that the client-server model splits an application into two parts: a client and a server. The client and server communicate requests and responses through messages. This simple construct allows intelligence to be easily distributed across a network and provides a framework for the design of loosely coupled networked based applications. A client uses the **Application Remote Interface** API to trigger the execution of a TP1 remote procedure on a server machine and passes it the parameters required to do a job. The server procedure is a DLL that executes the TP1 as a collection of static SQL statements. The Remote Procedure Call is transparent to the location of the stored procedure, which can reside in either a local or remote site.

Transaction Servers are designed to reduce network traffic, improve response times, and provide a more object-oriented database service that is well suited for **OLTP** applications. This approach also provides improved *site autonomy*. As an example, if your tables change, you don't need to recompile all your client applications. Your changes are localized to the server's procedures. Here is how we divide the TP1 task between the client and the server:

- The **SQLTP1RI.C** client program runs as a **MULTI** process. This means **MULTI** will create the process, pass it the parameters, and tell it when to start or stop executing. The client goes into an endless loop which repeatedly issues requests for the execution of a TP1 transaction on the server side. The loop, of course, runs under the control of **MULTI**. The request to execute the TP1 is done by invoking the **Application Remote Interface** API. The information to be sent to the server is placed inside a **in_SQLDA** structure. It consists of three variables: **random1**, **random2**, and **tps**. When a failure occurs the server will return a message in the **out_SQLDA** structure. Success consists of a SQLCA return code of zero (the remote SQLCA gets returned). The client will display running counts of transaction execution results in its process window.

- The server **SQLTP1DL.SQC** program is packaged as a **DLL**. When a remote request is received, the RDS on the server side loads the **SQLTP1DL.DLL** server program, and places the SQLDA structures in its local memory. The server program then simply executes a TP1 using static SQL code. The random numbers for the account, teller, and branch are generated from the three parameters received in the SQLDA. The RDS on the server returns the information to the RDS on the requester. The return code from the server program is SQL_HOLD_PROC, which tells RDS to keep this instance of the server program active in memory.

TP1 CONFIGURATIONS

The location of the TP1 server procedure is transparent to the client code. If the server is remote, then the **Remote Data Services** (RDS) component of the Database Manager will invoke the remote procedure on the server using APPC/SQLLOO. Each instance of **MULTI** can run up to four **SQLTP1RI.C** client processes. If you need more TP1 generators, simply add more workstations that run **MULTI**. Figure 26-2 shows an example of a 12-client remote driver system.

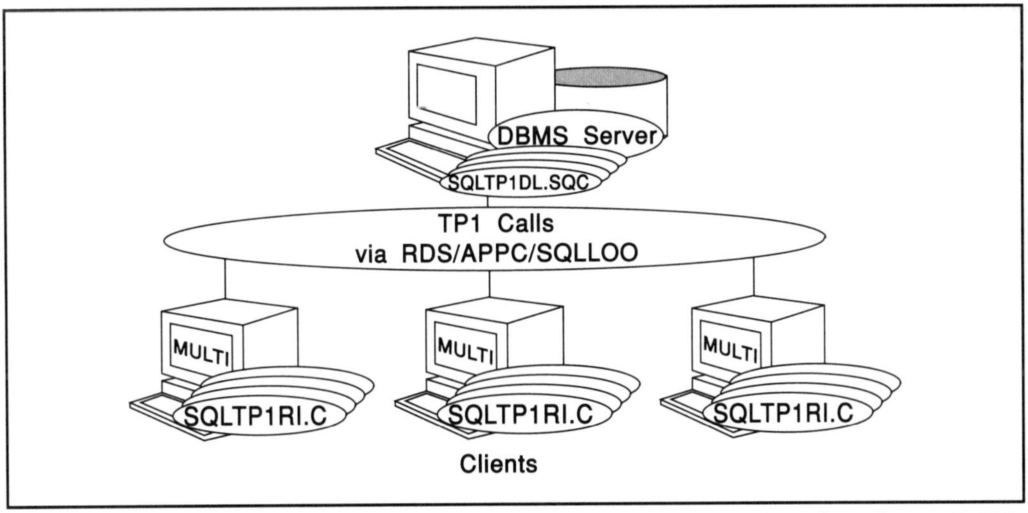

Figure 26-2. 12-Client TP1 Driver Using the Application Remote Interface Over a LAN.

You can scale this configuration in either direction depending on your budget considerations. As usual, we will be scaling our experiments to a four-client TP1 system and a network. We'll then run a benchmark using a remote client-server configuration. We can also run TP1 transactions against a local machine. This is done mainly for calibration purposes, so that you can get a feel for the network overhead.

WALKING THROUGH THE SQLTP1RI.C REQUESTER

SQLTP1RI.C: The main() Procedure

In this section, we present the **main()** procedure of the **SQLTP1RI.C** requester program whose code listing is shown in Figure 26-3 on page 721. You will find that much of the code is identical to the **SQLTP1.SQC** code from the previous chapter. This is not surprising since both programs have a front-end which interacts with **MULTI**. The difference is that the code presented here does *not* execute the TP1 transaction directly. Instead, it issues a remote procedure call to the server through the **Application Remote Interface**. What you will learn that's new and exciting is how to issue this call. We will not repeat the code and explanations that deal with the interaction with **MULTI**. Instead, we will point you to the appropriate sections in the previous chapter. We only introduce code listings that do something new. The following is a step-by-step description of what **main()** does:

1. The program starts by including the C-language, OS/2, and OS/2 EE header files that are needed for system services. These are identical to the header files that were discussed in the previous chapter, since much of what we do is interact with **MULTI**.

2. The following program header files are included:

   const.h This is the same header file that was used in **SQLTP1.SQC** in the previous chapter. Its listing can be found in Figure 25-11 on page 705.
   sqltp1.h This is the same header file that was used in **SQLTP1.SQC** in the previous chapter. Its listing can be found in Figure 25-10 on page 703.

3. A structure of type **SQLCA** is declared.

4. Two structures of type **SQLDA** are declared. These structures are used to exchange parameters between the client and server.

5. The **main()** program follows and, as you can see, it's almost a carbon copy of **SQLTP1.SQC**'s **main()**. However, there are also some key differences which will be the focus of our presentation. Here's what **main()** does:

   - It invokes the previously encountered **get_args()** function, whose listing can be found in the previous chapter in Figure 25-4 on page 694. This function obtains the arguments **MULTI** passes to the program. **MULTI**, of course, gets these arguments from reading the **MULTI.CFG** file.

- It invokes the previously encountered **initialize_multi_ipc()** function, whose listing can be found in the previous chapter in Figure 25-5 on page 695. This function performs all the interprocess communication chores required from a process that runs under **MULTI**'s control.

- It invokes the previously encountered **initialize_task()** function, whose listing can be found in the previous chapter in Figure 25-6 on page 696. This function connects to the database, installs a signal handler, and does all kinds of one-time housekeeping chores in preparation for the **big loop**.

- It invokes **initialize_sqldas()**, a new function (see listing in Figure 26-5 on page 724). This function initializes the **SQLDA** structures that the **Application Remote Interface** uses as carriers for remote parameters. We will be explaining what this all means when we get to that section.

- It invokes the previously encountered **execute_task()** function, listed in Figure 25-7 on page 697. This is the home of the **big loop**, which forever executes TP1 transactions. **MULTI** can pause and resume (at any time) the execution of TP1 transactions through semaphores.

  Note: This is where we part company in a major way with the code in the previous chapter. The TP1 transaction is *not* directly executed by the helper routine, **tp1_transaction()**. Instead, this function (see listing in Figure 26-6) merely issues a remote call to a server procedure through the **Application Remote Interface**. The server procedure executes the TP1. This is one of the key differences between *Transaction Servers* and *Database Servers*.

```
/****************************************************************************/
/*  PROGRAM NAME: SQLTP1RI.C - A process program that MULTI starts          */
/*                                                                          */
/*  PROGRAM DESCRIPTION:  This program is run as a child task of MULTI.     */
/*  This code provides the requester for an Application Remote Interface TP1 */
/****************************************************************************/
#include <process.h>                  /* For exit()                         */
#include <string.h>                   /* For printf                         */
#include <sys\types.h>                /* For time()                         */
#include <sys\timeb.h>                /* For time()                         */
#include <sys\stat.h>                 /* For stat()                         */
#include <stdlib.h>                   /* For atoi                           */
#include <stdio.h>                    /* For sprintf, printf                */
#define INCL_VIO                      /* include VIO calls                  */
#define INCL_DOSSEMAPHORES            /* include semaphore api calls        */
#define INCL_DOSMEMMGR                /* include segment   api calls        */
#define INCL_ERRORS                   /* include error definitions          */
#include <os2.h>
```

Figure 26-3 (Part 1 of 2). SQLTP1RI.C: The main() Procedure.

```
#include <sqlca.h>                  /* sqlca                             */
#include <sqlda.h>                  /* sqlda                             */
#include <sql.h>                    /* error msg. retrieval              */
#include <sqlcodes.h>               /* SQL return code constants         */
#include <sqlenv.h>                 /* environment functions and         */

#include "const.h"                  /* constants for multi               */
#include "sqltpl.h"                 /* tpl program vars, declares,etc.   */

struct sqlca sqlca;
struct sqlda *sqlda_in;                  /* input sqlda for sqleproc     */
struct sqlda *sqlda_out;                 /* output sqlda for sqleproc    */
CHAR   msgbuf[512];                      /* msg buffer for sqleintp      */
CHAR   ri_msgbuf[512];                   /* msg buffer for remote ifc    */
VOID initialize_sqldas(VOID);

/*--------------------------------------------------------------------*/
/* Main routine.                                                      */
/*--------------------------------------------------------------------*/
VOID main(USHORT argc, PCHAR argv[])
{
  get_args(argc, argv);            /*  get program arguments             */

  initialize_multi_ipc();          /*  Init MULTI semaphores/shared memory*/

  initialize_task();               /*  perform one time intializations   */

  initialize_sqldas();             /*  prepare for APPLICATION REMOTE IFC */

  execute_task();                  /*  Remote Procedure Call  loop       */

} /* end main */
```

Figure 26-3 (Part 2 of 2). SQLTP1RI.C: The main() Procedure.

SQLTP1RI.C: The initialize_sqldas() Procedure

In this section, we present the **initialize_sqldas()** procedure, whose code listing is shown in Figure 26-5. The remote parameters are passed over the network using self-describing data structures of type **SQLDA**. This choice of a container for passing data is consistent with the SQL programming paradigm. The Database Manager's Remote Data Services (RDS) takes care of reconstructing of the SQLDA at the remote location after it is sent over the network. The RDS also takes care of situations where the call is local. In such cases, the SQLDAs are exchanged through shared memory. The code in this section takes care of all this SQLDA handling. For your quick reference, we repeat the SQLDA type definition in Figure 26-4.

```
struct SQLDA
{
   BYTE           sqldaid[8];          /* Eye catcher = 'SQLDA   '          */
   LONG           sqldabc;             /* SQLDA size in bytes = 16+44*sqln  */
   SHORT          sqln;                /* Number of SQLVAR elements         */
   SHORT          sqld;                /* # of used SQLVAR elements         */
   struct sqlvar
   {
      SHORT          sqltype;          /* Variable data type                */
      SHORT          sqllen;           /* Variable data length              */
      BYTE          *sqldata;          /* Pointer to variable data value    */
      SHORT         *sqlind;           /* Pointer to Null indicator         */
      struct sqlname                   /* Variable Name                     */
      {
         SHORT          length;        /* Name length [1..30]               */
         BYTE           data[30];      /* Variable or Column name           */
      } sqlname;
   } sqlvar[SQLVAR_NUM];
};
```

Figure 26-4. The SQLDA Structure.

Here is what the **initialize_sqldas()** function does:

1. It allocates memory for two SQLDA structures:

   sqlda_in This structure is sized to contain the three parameters to be sent to the server.

   sqlda_out This structure is sized to contain the single parameter the server returns.

   The size of the SQLDAs is automatically calculated using the OS/2 EE supplied macro, SQLDASIZE.

2. It places the three parameters to be sent to the server inside the **sqlda_in**: **random1**, **random2**, and **tps**. Each of these parameters is described in a SQLDA field of type **sqlvar**. From Figure 26-4, you can see that **sqlvar** requires the following information for each parameter passed:

   - The parameter's SQL data type.
   - The parameter's length in bytes.
   - A pointer to the variable which contains the parameter.
   - A pointer to Null indicator which is applicable for this type of SQLDA usage.
   - The name and name length of the parameter.

3. It specifies, to the **sqlda_out**, the name of the variable where the response from the server is to be placed. The variable **ri_msgbuf** is used to receive messages from the server (mostly error messages). This buffer will only be checked when the SQLCA returns an error. Again, all the information describing **ri_msgbuf** has to be provided in a **sqlvar** element of the **sqlda_out** variable.

4. In summary, we're sending three variables of type *short* to the server, and getting back from the server a single variable of type *array of characters*. The code in this section shows how to prepare the SQLDAs that will be used for the Remote Procedure Call.

```
/*-----------------------------------------------------------------------------------*/
/* Perform onetime initializations for the sqldas                                    */
/*-----------------------------------------------------------------------------------*/
VOID  initialize_sqldas(VOID)
{
  /*---------------------------------*/
  /* Allocate sqldas and fill headers    */
  /*---------------------------------*/
  sqlda_in = (struct sqlda *)malloc(SQLDASIZE(3));
  sqlda_in->sqldabc = 148;
  sqlda_in->sqln    = 3;
  sqlda_in->sqld    = 3;

  sqlda_out = (struct sqlda *)malloc(SQLDASIZE(1));
  sqlda_out->sqldabc = 60;
  sqlda_out->sqln    = 1;
  sqlda_out->sqld    = 1;
  /*---------------------------------*/
  /* initialize 3 parameters in sqlda_in */
  /*---------------------------------*/

              /*--------------------*/
              /* random1 parm       */
              /*--------------------*/
  sqlda_in->sqlvar[0].sqltype        = SQL_TYP_SMALL;
  sqlda_in->sqlvar[0].sqllen         = SQL_SMALL_LENGTH;
  sqlda_in->sqlvar[0].sqldata        = (UCHAR *)&random1;
  sqlda_in->sqlvar[0].sqlind         = NULL;
  sqlda_in->sqlvar[0].sqlname.length  = strlen("RANDOM1");
  strcpy(sqlda_in->sqlvar[0].sqlname.data,"RANDOM1");

              /*--------------------*/
              /* random2 parm       */
              /*--------------------*/
  sqlda_in->sqlvar[1].sqltype        = SQL_TYP_SMALL;
  sqlda_in->sqlvar[1].sqllen         = SQL_SMALL_LENGTH;
  sqlda_in->sqlvar[1].sqldata        = (UCHAR *)&random2;
  sqlda_in->sqlvar[1].sqlind         = NULL;
  sqlda_in->sqlvar[1].sqlname.length  = strlen("RANDOM2");
  strcpy(sqlda_in->sqlvar[1].sqlname.data,"RANDOM2");

              /*--------------------*/
              /* tps parm           */
              /*--------------------*/
  sqlda_in->sqlvar[2].sqltype        = SQL_TYP_SMALL;
  sqlda_in->sqlvar[2].sqllen         = SQL_SMALL_LENGTH;
  sqlda_in->sqlvar[2].sqldata        = (UCHAR *)&tps;
  sqlda_in->sqlvar[2].sqlind         = NULL;
  sqlda_in->sqlvar[2].sqlname.length  = strlen("TPS");
  strcpy(sqlda_in->sqlvar[2].sqlname.data,"TPS");
```

Figure 26-5 (Part 1 of 2). SQLTP1RI.C: The initialize_sqldas() Procedure.

```
    /*-----------------------------------*/
    /* initialize 1 parameter in sqlda_out */
    /*-----------------------------------*/
                 /*-------------------*/
                 /* ri_msgbuf parm    */
                 /*-------------------*/
    sqlda_out->sqlvar[0].sqltype        = SQL_TYP_CSTR;
    sqlda_out->sqlvar[0].sqllen         = sizeof(ri_msgbuf);
    sqlda_out->sqlvar[0].sqldata        = ri_msgbuf;
    sqlda_out->sqlvar[0].sqlind         = NULL;
    sqlda_out->sqlvar[0].sqlname.length = strlen("RI_MSGBUF");
    strcpy(sqlda_out->sqlvar[0].sqlname.data,"RI_MSGBUF");

  } /* end initialize_sqldas */
```

Figure 26-5 (Part 2 of 2). SQLTP1RI.C: The initialize_sqldas() Procedure.

SQLTP1RI.C: The tp1_transaction() Procedure

In this section, we present the **tp1_transaction()** procedure, whose code listing is shown in Figure 26-6. This procedure, unlike its counterpart in the previous chapter, does not perform the actual TP1 transaction. Instead, it invokes a procedure on the server (that executes the TP1) through the **Application Remote Interface**.

The remote call is performed by the OS/2 EE **sqleproc()** API, which is described below. The **sqlca.sqlcode** is non-zero if the call fails. Failure in this case also includes any SQL failure detected in the remote procedure. When the code detects such a failure, it issues a **sqlaintp()** to print the message text of the SQL return code. In addition, the contents of **ri_msgbuf** will be printed. This variable contains the text of an error message created at the server. Notice how conveniently it got mapped into the local address space through the remote SQLDA magic!

sqleproc()

This Database Environment Service API call is known as the **Application Remote Interface**. It allows a DOS or OS/2 EE RDS requester application to execute a DLL procedure stored at the location of a database. This command reduces network traffic and improves the performance of network-based transactions. The stored procedure can be designed as a simple transaction (one call and return) or as a conversational transaction (a set of calls and returns). The prototype for this call is:

```
sqleproc(PCHAR       funcname,       /* The remote procedure name    */
         PCHAR       data_area,      /* Variable length data area    */
         SQLDA      *in_SQLDA,       /* Pointer to input SQLDA       */
         SQLDA      *out_SQLDA,      /* Pointer to output SQLDA      */
         SQLCA      *sqlca);         /* Pointer to SQLCA             */
```

A description of the parameters follows:

- The ***funcname*** parameter points to the name of the procedure to be run on the server. This can be specified in one of two ways:
    1. By a **funcname** with no extensions. This causes a **funcname.dll** file to be loaded into memory. It is assumed that this file contains a function by the same name.
    2. By the back-slash delimitation **dllname.dll\funcname**. In this case, the **dllname** is the name of the file to be loaded, and **funcname** is the name of the function to be executed. A single (.DLL) file can contain multiple remotely executable functions. In this naming convention backslash does *not* indicate a subdirectory. For example: "**sqltp1dl.dll\tp1_transaction**" is read as the function **tp1_transaction** which is found in the **sqltp1dl.dll** (.DLL) file.

- The ***data_area*** parameter points to a variable length data area. This data area is used to pass information to the server routine. The first two bytes contain the length of the next **n** bytes. Set this parameter to NULL if you're not going to use it.

- The ***in_SQLDA*** parameter points to the input SQLDA, which is used to pass data to the remote procedure. This structure is defined in Figure 26-4 on page 723.

- The ***out_SQLDA*** parameter points to the output SQLDA, where variables will be returned to your program. This structure is defined in Figure 26-4 on page 723. If the call is remote, the Database Manager transmits the sqldas over the network and reconstructs them in the server's memory, including the data fields they point to. This means that you can refer to host variables by name on both sides of the program.

- The ***sqlca*** parameter points to the SQLCA.

```
/*-----------------------------------------------------------------*/
/* function for TP1 transaction                                    */
/*-----------------------------------------------------------------*/
SHORT APIENTRY tpl_transaction(VOID)
{
  /*-------------------------------*/
  /* call remote transaction       */
  /*-------------------------------*/
  sqleproc("sqltpldl.dll\\tpl_transaction", NULL,
           sqlda_in, sqlda_out, &sqlca);
```

Figure 26-6 (Part 1 of 2). SQLTP1RI.C: The tp1_transaction() Procedure.

```
      if (sqlca.sqlcode != 0)
         {
           sqlaintp(msgbuf, sizeof(msgbuf), 80, &sqlca);
           printf("%s\n",msgbuf);
           printf("%s\n",ri_msgbuf);
           return(FAILED);
         }

      return(GOOD);
   } /* end tpl_transaction */
```

Figure 26-6 (Part 2 of 2). SQLTP1RI.C: The tp1_transaction() Procedure.

WALKING THROUGH THE SQLTP1DL.SQC SERVER

SQLTP1DL.SQC: The tp1_transaction() Remote Procedure

In this section, we present the **tp1_transaction()** procedure whose code listing is shown in Figure 26-8. This procedure is part of the **SQLTP1DL.DLL**. This is what the RDS does when an **Application Remote Interface** call is received on the *server* side for a **tp1_transaction()** function which is part of the **SQLTP1DL.DLL**:

- It constructs a copy in local memory of the SQLDA structures that were sent.
- It loads the DLL, **SQLTP1DL.DLL**, from disk.
- It calls the function **tp1_transaction()**, and passes it the reconstructed SQLDA parameters.
- When the function completes, it returns the information to the requester.

So, what does a DLL for remote procedures look like? Let's take a look at what's in Figure 26-8:

1. Notice that there is no **main()** function in this code.

2. The familiar include files, WHENEVER directives, and host variable declarations are all present.

3. The forward declarations of the functions in the DLL follows. Only the first of these two functions, **tp1_transaction()** is "exported" to the outside world. This also happens to be a function that can be invoked through the **APPLICATION REMOTE INTERFACE**. Here is how this function is declared:

   ```
   SHORT APIENTRY tpl_transaction(struct sqlchar *parms,
                                  struct sqlda  *sqlda_in,
                                  struct sqlda  *sqlda_out,
                                  struct sqlca  *sqlca_in);
   ```

   Notice the correspondence between this function's parameters and those of "sqleproc()" on page 725.

4. The **tp1_transaction()** is exported i.e., made known to the outside world through the (.DEF) file **SQLTP1DL.DEF**.

```
LIBRARY SQLTP1DL INITINSTANCE
DESCRIPTION 'TP1 transaction routine'
PROTMODE
EXPORTS TP1_TRANSACTION
DATA MULTIPLE
```

Figure 26-7. The Definition File: SQLTP1DL.DEF.

5. The code for the TP1 transaction, with a few minor exceptions, is identical to the static SQL implementation of TP1 which was described in the last chapter (see Figure 25-8). Here are the exceptions:

   a. The random numbers are obtained through **sqlda_in**. These are the parameters the client sends to the server through the RDS mechanism.
   b. When an error occurs, the sqlca is copied over to **sqlca_in**. The contents of **sqlca_in** are shipped over the network by RDS and placed into the client's **sqlca**.
   c. When an error occurs, the **format_error()** function (see Figure 26-9) is passed the name of the file and line number where the error occurred, a pointer to a parameter in **sqlda_out**, and the sqlca's **sqlcode** value. The **format_error()** function takes all this information and formats an error message. The **sqlda_out**, including its message parameter, is then copied by RDS over the network and into the client's **sqlda_out**, where it magically updates the value of the client's **ri_msgbuf** variable. (see Figure 26-5 on page 724).
   d. The sqlca is copied over to **sqlca_in**. The contents of **sqlca_in** are shipped over the network by RDS and placed into the client's **sqlca**.
   e. The constant code **SQLZ_HOLD_PROC** is returned, which tells RDS not to terminate the DLL.

6. Congratulations, we've just completed the second of our TP1 flavors!

```
/*****************************************************************************/
/*  PROGRAM NAME: TP1DLL - A DLL for the TP1 transaction                     */
/*                                                                           */
/*  PROGRAM DESCRIPTION:  This program is invoked as a result of a           */
/*    sqleproc database manager API.                                         */
/*                                                                           */
/*****************************************************************************/
#include <process.h>                  /* For exit()                          */
#include <string.h>                   /* For printf                          */
#include <sys\types.h>                /* For time()                          */
#include <sys\timeb.h>                /* For time()                          */
#include <sys\stat.h>                 /* For stat()                          */
#include <stdlib.h>                   /* For atoi                            */
#include <stdio.h>                    /* For sprintf, printf                 */

#define INCL_VIO                      /* include VIO calls                   */
#define INCL_DOSSEMAPHORES            /* include semaphore api calls         */
#define INCL_DOSMEMMGR                /* include segment   api calls         */
#include <os2.h>

#include <sqlca.h>                    /* sqlca                               */
#include <sqlda.h>                    /* sqlda                               */
#include <sql.h>                      /* error msg. retrieval                */
#include <sqlcodes.h>                 /* SQL return code constants           */
#include <sqlenv.h>                   /* environment functions and           */
#include <sqlutil.h>                  /* for sqlchar structure               */

/*___________________________________________________________________________*/
/* database includes, defines, etc.                                          */
/*___________________________________________________________________________*/
struct sqlca sqlca;

EXEC SQL WHENEVER SQLERROR CONTINUE;
EXEC SQL WHENEVER SQLWARNING CONTINUE;
EXEC SQL WHENEVER NOT FOUND CONTINUE;

EXEC SQL BEGIN DECLARE SECTION;
 long  acct_num;
 short branch_id;
 short teller_id;
 long  balance;
 long  delta          = 100;
 char  acct_name[20] = "<--20 BYTE STRING-->";
EXEC SQL END   DECLARE SECTION;
/*___________________________________________________________________________*/
/* function forward declarations                                             */
/*___________________________________________________________________________*/
SHORT APIENTRY tpl_transaction(struct sqlchar *parms,
                               struct sqlda   *sqlda_in,
                               struct sqlda   *sqlda_out,
                               struct sqlca   *sqlca_in);

VOID format_error(PCHAR msgbuf, USHORT Error, PCHAR msg,
                  PCHAR file, USHORT line);
```

Figure 26-8 (Part 1 of 4). SQLTP1DL.SQC: The tp1_transaction() Remote Procedure.

```
/*-----------------------------------------------------------------------*/
/* function for TP1 transaction                                          */
/*-----------------------------------------------------------------------*/
SHORT APIENTRY tp1_transaction(struct sqlchar *parms,
                               struct sqlda   *sqlda_in,
                               struct sqlda   *sqlda_out,
                               struct sqlca   *sqlca_in)
{
  USHORT  random1, random2, tps ;           /* local variables          */

      /*--------------------------------------*/
      /* Extract parms from SQLDA             */
      /*--------------------------------------*/
  random1  = *(sqlda_in->sqlvar[0].sqldata);
  random2  = *(sqlda_in->sqlvar[1].sqldata);
  tps      = *(sqlda_in->sqlvar[2].sqldata);

      /*--------------------------------------*/
      /* generate some random data            */
      /*--------------------------------------*/
  acct_num = (random1 * random2) % (tps*100000l) + 1;/* generate account num. */
  teller_id= (short)(random1 % (tps*100)) + 1;      /* generate teller id    */
  branch_id= (short)(random2 % (tps*10)) + 1;       /* generate branch id    */

      /*--------------------------------------*/
      /* get the current balance from ACCT    */
      /*--------------------------------------*/
  EXEC SQL DECLARE CURSOR1 CURSOR FOR
           SELECT BALANCE FROM ACCT WHERE ACCT_NUM = :acct_num
           FOR UPDATE OF BALANCE;

  EXEC SQL OPEN CURSOR1;
  if (sqlca.sqlcode != 0)
     { format_error(sqlda_out->sqlvar[0].sqldata, (SHORT)sqlca.sqlcode,
                    "during SQL OPEN", __FILE__, __LINE__);
       memcpy(sqlca_in, &sqlca, sizeof(struct sqlca)); /* return the sqlca    */
       return(SQLZ_HOLD_PROC);
     }

  EXEC SQL FETCH CURSOR1 INTO :balance;
  if (sqlca.sqlcode != 0)
     { format_error(sqlda_out->sqlvar[0].sqldata, (SHORT)sqlca.sqlcode,
                    "during SQL FETCH", __FILE__, __LINE__);
       memcpy(sqlca_in, &sqlca, sizeof(struct sqlca)); /* return the sqlca    */
       return(SQLZ_HOLD_PROC);
     }
```

Figure 26-8 (Part 2 of 4). SQLTP1DL.SQC: The tp1_transaction() Remote Procedure.

```
    /*------------------------------------------*/
    /* Credit the balance in the ACCT table */
    /*------------------------------------------*/
EXEC SQL UPDATE ACCT
         SET BALANCE = BALANCE + :delta
         WHERE CURRENT OF CURSOR1;
if (sqlca.sqlcode != 0)
   { format_error(sqlda_out->sqlvar[0].sqldata, (SHORT)sqlca.sqlcode,
                  "during SQL UPDATE", __FILE__,__LINE__);
     memcpy(sqlca_in, &sqlca, sizeof(struct sqlca)); /* return the sqlca    */
     return(SQLZ_HOLD_PROC);
   }

EXEC SQL CLOSE CURSOR1;
if (sqlca.sqlcode != 0)
   { format_error(sqlda_out->sqlvar[0].sqldata, (SHORT)sqlca.sqlcode,
                  "during SQL CLOSE", __FILE__,__LINE__);
     memcpy(sqlca_in, &sqlca, sizeof(struct sqlca)); /* return the sqlca    */
     return(SQLZ_HOLD_PROC);
   }

    /*------------------------------------------*/
    /* Update the TELLER table's balance   */
    /*------------------------------------------*/
EXEC SQL UPDATE TELLER
         SET BALANCE = BALANCE + :delta
         WHERE TELLER_ID = :teller_id;
if (sqlca.sqlcode != 0)
   { format_error(sqlda_out->sqlvar[0].sqldata, (SHORT)sqlca.sqlcode,
                  "during SQL UPDATE", __FILE__,__LINE__);
     memcpy(sqlca_in, &sqlca, sizeof(struct sqlca)); /* return the sqlca    */
     return(SQLZ_HOLD_PROC);
   }

    /*------------------------------------------*/
    /* Update the BRANCH table's balance   */
    /*------------------------------------------*/
EXEC SQL UPDATE BRANCH
         SET BALANCE = BALANCE + :delta
         WHERE BRANCH_ID = :branch_id;
if (sqlca.sqlcode != 0)
   { format_error(sqlda_out->sqlvar[0].sqldata, (SHORT)sqlca.sqlcode,
                  "during SQL UPDATE", __FILE__,__LINE__);
     memcpy(sqlca_in, &sqlca, sizeof(struct sqlca)); /* return the sqlca    */
     return(SQLZ_HOLD_PROC);
   }
```

Figure 26-8 (Part 3 of 4). SQLTP1DL.SQC: The tp1_transaction() Remote Procedure.

```
    /*______________________________________*/
    /* Insert transaction in HISTORY table */
    /*______________________________________*/
  EXEC SQL INSERT
           INTO HISTORY(ACCT_NUM, TELLER_ID, BRANCH_ID, BALANCE,
                        DELTA, PID, TRANSID, ACCTNAME, TEMP)
           VALUES(:acct_num, :teller_id, :branch_id, :balance,
                  :delta, 1, 3, :acct_name, 'hist  ');
  if (sqlca.sqlcode != 0)
     { format_error(sqlda_out->sqlvar[0].sqldata, (SHORT)sqlca.sqlcode,
                    "during SQL INSERT", __FILE__,__LINE__);
       memcpy(sqlca_in, &sqlca, sizeof(struct sqlca)); /* return the sqlca    */
       return(SQLZ_HOLD_PROC);
     }

    /*______________________________________*/
    /* Commit the transaction to database  */
    /*______________________________________*/
  EXEC SQL COMMIT;
  if (sqlca.sqlcode != 0)
     { format_error(sqlda_out->sqlvar[0].sqldata, (SHORT)sqlca.sqlcode,
                    "during SQL COMMIT", __FILE__, __LINE__);
       memcpy(sqlca_in, &sqlca, sizeof(struct sqlca)); /* return the sqlca    */
       return(SQLZ_HOLD_PROC);
     }

   memcpy(sqlca_in, &sqlca, sizeof(struct sqlca));    /* return the sqlca    */
   return(SQLZ_HOLD_PROC);

} /* end tpl_transaction */
```

Figure 26-8 (Part 4 of 4). SQLTP1DL.SQC: The tp1_transaction() Remote Procedure.

SQLTP1DL.SQC: The format_error() Helper Procedure

This section contains the code for the **format_error()** helper procedure, which essentially formats an error message from the parameters that are passed to it. This is the error message that will magically end up in the client's **ri_msgbuf**.

```
/*______________________________________________________________________*/
/* Error Routine                                                        */
/*______________________________________________________________________*/
VOID format_error(PCHAR msgbuf, USHORT Error, PCHAR msg,
                  PCHAR file, USHORT line)
{
    sprintf(msgbuf,"Error %d detected while %s at line %d in file %s.\n",
         Error, msg, line, file);
} /* end format_error */
```

Figure 26-9. SQLTP1DL.SQC: The format_error() Helper Procedure.

RUNNING TWO TP1 BENCHMARK TESTS USING THE APPLICATION REMOTE INTERFACE

Now that we've got some code, let's run some benchmarks to see how well this TP1 flavor performs. We will run two TP1 benchmark tests:

1. A **local** benchmark test where the client and servers are on the same machine. The machine is a PS/2 Mod-80 with a 20-MHz clock and a 1000-KByte buffer pool (see Figure 26-11).
2. A **remote** benchmark test where the clients and servers are on different machines. The client machine is a PS/2 Mod 70 with a 16-MHz clock. The server machine is a PS/2 Mod-80 with a 20-MHz clock and a 1000-KByte buffer pool (see Figure 26-12).

The two benchmarks use the same software configuration, a four-process **MULTI** whose configuration file is shown below:

```
PROGRAM_TYPE     = PROCESS
STOP_TIME_MS     = 600000
TASK_NAME        = SQLTP1RI.EXE 0 17 2.0 1;
TASK_NAME        = SQLTP1RI.EXE 1 23 2.0 1;
TASK_NAME        = SQLTP1RI.EXE 2 29 2.0 1;
TASK_NAME        = SQLTP1RI.EXE 3 57 2.0 1;
```

Figure 26-10. A MULTI.CFG File for Running Four TP1 Processes.

The benchmarks are set up to run for 10-minute tests (i.e., 600,000 milliseconds). The response time threshold is set to 2.0 seconds, and a 1-tps database size is specified.

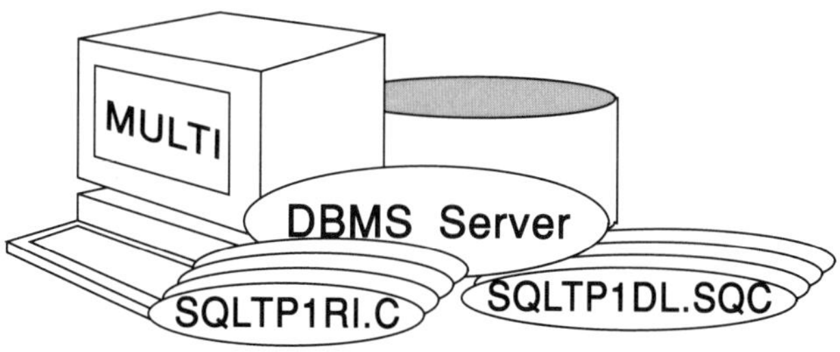

Test 1 20-MHz PS/2 Mod-80, 1000-KByte buffer pool

Figure 26-11. The Application Remote Interface Local Benchmark Configuration.

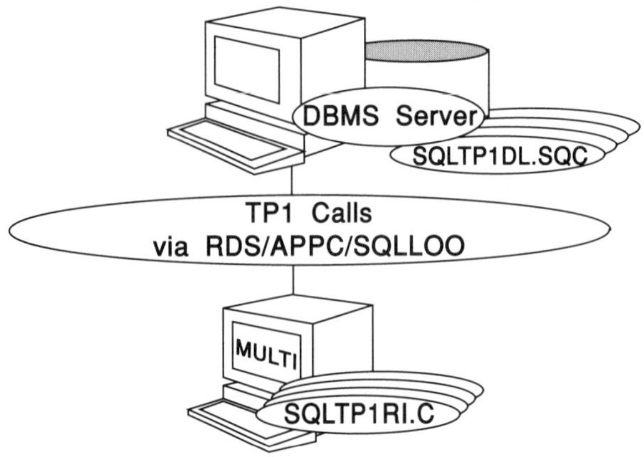

Test 2 Client: PS/2 Mod-70 16 MHz

Server: 20 Mhz PS/2 Mod-80, 1000-KByte buffer pool

LAN: 4 Mb/s Token Ring (APPC/SQLLOO/RDS)

Figure 26-12. The Application Remote Interface Remote Benchmark Configuration.

Running the Application Remote TP1 Locally (Benchmark1)

The configuration for this benchmark is a four-client MULTI running against a local database. The test is run on a PS/2 Mod-80 with a 20-MHz clock and a 1000-KByte buffer pool. We assume the database is already loaded for a 1-tps database scale. The following RSQL run is used to set up the 1000-KByte buffer configuration and prepare the database for the benchmark1 run.

```
--                     Change TP1 Database Configuration
-- =========================================================================
-- logon
EXEC DBA: LOGON USERID PASSWORD DBSVR03 UPM_LOCAL UPM_USER;
 OK, api_rcd = 0,          Execution time =     0.0000 secs

-- update the Database Configuration for database for a 500k buffer
EXEC DBA: UPDATE_DB_CFG TP1      MAXAPPLS    = 8,
                                 DLCHKTIME   = 10000,
                                 BUFFPAGE    = 256,
                                 LOGFILSIZ   = 50,
                                 LOGPRIMARY  = 2,
                                 LOGSECOND   = 20;
 OK, sql_rcd = 0,        Execution time =     1.3700 secs
```

Figure 26-13 (Part 1 of 2). Preparing the Database for Benchmark1.

```
-- Show the database configuration for database TP1
EXEC DBA: SHOW_DB_CFG TP1;

 Database Configuration for Database TP1
 ==============================================
 Configuration Parameter          Current  Parm.       Parm.       Parm.
 Description                      Value    Units       Range       Default
 -------------------------------- -------- ----------  ----------  -------
 Max. Active Applications                8  Appl.       1-117           8
 Max. DB Files Open/Application         20  files       2-235          20
 Max. Files Open/Application           255  files       25-32700      255
 Buffer Pool Size                      256  4K pages      (1)          16
 Time Interval for Deadlocks         10000  millisecs.  1-600 sec.     10
 Max. Storage for Locklists              8  4K pages    4-250           8
 Max. percent locklist/appl.            22  percent     1-100          22
 Default Application Heap                3  segments    2-20            3
 Application Agent Heap                  2  segments    2-85            3
 Sort List Heap                          2  segments    1-20            2
 Database Heap                           1  segments    1-45            1
 SQL Statement Heap                     64  segments                   64
 Log File Size                          50  4K pages    15-255         50
 Primary Log Files                       2  files       0-63            2
 Secondary Log Files                    20  files       0-63            3
 Log Records/soft checkpoint           100  records     0-65535       100

 Current Log Location = C:\SQL00003\
 New Log Location     =
 Copy Protection      =    1
 Country              =    1
 Code Page            =  437
 Release              =  512
 OK, sql_rcd = 0,        Execution time =     0.3700 secs

-- bind the tp1 program
EXEC DBA: BIND TP1 SQLTP1DL.BND ISO REPEATABLE_READ BLOCK_ALL PUBLIC;
 OK, sql_rcd = 0,        Execution time =    14.5000 secs

-- delete all of the history data
EXEC SQL: DELETE FROM HISTORY;
 WARNING, sql_code = 100,    Execution time =     0.9700 secs
 SQL0100W  No row was found for FETCH, UPDATE or DELETE; or the result of a
 query is an empty table.

-- commit the changes
EXEC SQL: COMMIT;
 OK, sql_rcd = 0,        Execution time =     0.0300 secs

-- disconnect
EXEC DBA: STOPUSE TP1;
 OK, sql_rcd = 0,        Execution time =     0.7900 secs
```

Figure 26-13 (Part 2 of 2). Preparing the Database for Benchmark1.

```
                    Multiprocess Execution Example

Use arrow keys to move the cursor.  Use + and - keys to change field values.
Press R to start running, S to stop, or C to clear the count.
Press ESC to terminate the program.

-SQLTP1RI.EXE-------  -SQLTP1RI.EXE-------  -SQLTP1RI.EXE-------  -SQLTP1RI.EXE-------
Count = 756           Count = 783           Count = 766           Count = 781
TXNS  = 750           TXNS  = 774           TXNS  = 756           TXNS  = 771
Priority  = RG        Priority  = RG        Priority  = RG        Priority  = RG
Level     = 0         Level     = 0         Level     = 0         Level     = 0
Semaphore = CLEAR     Semaphore = CLEAR     Semaphore = CLEAR     Semaphore = CLEAR

Ready                 Ready                 Ready                 Ready

-EXECUTION STATUS-----------------------  -SYSTEM INFORMATION---------------------
Stop Time     = 600.0         sec         Maximum Wait       = 3          sec
Elapsed Time  = 600.0         sec         Minimum Time Slice = 32         ms
Total Count   = 3086                      Maximum Time Slice = 248        ms
Run Status    = STOPPED                   Dynamic Variation  = ACTIVE
```

Figure 26-14. The Results of a Four-Process TP1 Run Against Local Procedures.

Benchmark1 Result: The MULTI screen capture in Figure 26-14, shows the results of a 10-minute test. During this period, a total of 3086 TP1 transactions ran successfully. However, only (750 + 774 + 756 + 771 = 3051) transactions had a response time that was under the 2-second threshold. Using the liberal interpretation of TP1 introduced in the previous chapter, this machine is therefore in the *5.1 TP1* range.

Commentary: This number demonstrates that using remote procedures locally does not improve performance over the straight SQL implementation of the previous chapter. In fact, the performance is worse (5.1 TP1s versus 5.5 TP1s).

Running the Application Remote TP1 Remotely (Benchmark2)

The configuration for this benchmark is a four-client MULTI running against a remote database. The database runs on a PS/2 Mod-80 with a 20-MHz clock and a 1000-KByte buffer pool.

```
                      Multiprocess Execution Example

 Use arrow keys to move the cursor.  Use + and - keys to change field values.
 Press R to start running, S to stop, or C to clear the count.
 Press ESC to terminate the program.

-SQLTP1RI.EXE-        -SQLTP1RI.EXE-        -SQLTP1RI.EXE-        -SQLTP1RI.EXE-

 Count = 705           Count = 707           Count = 713           Count = 711
 TXNS  = 697           TXNS  = 698           TXNS  = 705           TXNS  = 704
 Priority  = RG        Priority  = RG        Priority  = RG        Priority  = RG
 Level     = 0         Level     = 0         Level     = 0         Level     = 0
 Semaphore = CLEAR     Semaphore = CLEAR     Semaphore = CLEAR     Semaphore = CLEAR

 Ready                 Ready                 Ready                 Ready

-EXECUTION STATUS-                          -SYSTEM INFORMATION-

 Stop Time     = 600.0          sec          Maximum Wait       = 3        sec
 Elapsed Time  = 600.0          sec          Minimum Time Slice = 32       ms
 Total Count   = 2836                        Maximum Time Slice = 248      ms
 Run Status    = STOPPED                     Dynamic Variation  = ACTIVE
```

Figure 26-15. The Results of a Four-Process TP1 Run Against Remote Procedures.

Benchmark2 Result: The MULTI screen capture in Figure 26-15, shows the results of a 10-minute test. During this period, a total of 2836 TP1 transactions ran successfully. However, only (697 + 698 + 705 + 704 = 2804) transactions had a response time that was under the 2 second threshold. Using the liberal interpretation of TP1 introduced in the previous chapters, this machine is therefore in the *4.7 TP1* range.

Commentary: This result demonstrates a very significant performance gain over the remote SQL as used in the previous chapter (4.7 TP1 versus 2.7 TP1). This improvement is directly attributed to the reduced network utilization of stored procedures. A single message exchange takes place, as opposed to an exchange for each SQL statement in the transaction.

Chapter 27

The Named Pipes Transaction Server TP1

This is the fourth of a six-chapter series, in which we develop a TP1 Benchmark toolkit for the OS/2 EE Database Manager. This chapter provides a "do-it-yourself" *Transaction Server* version of TP1 using Named Pipes. The TP1 client drivers run under **MULTI** and issue requests to the server via Named Pipes (see Figure 27-1). The server receives the request from a client, executes a TP1, and returns the results to the client via a Named Pipe. The TP1 server maintains a pool of TP1 server processes. All the TP1 processes on a machine are known by the same pipe "name." However, each server process controls its own instance of that Named Pipe. So, what we've essentially put together is a multiuser server machine on a Named Pipes platform.

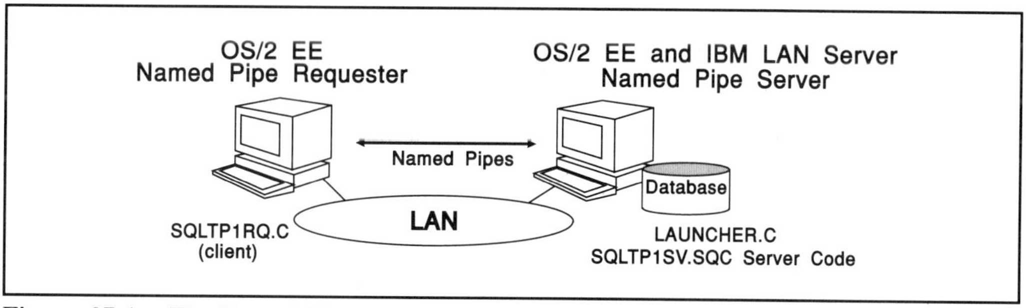

Figure 27-1. The Named Pipes Remote Program Execution Implementation of TP1.

The Named Pipes TP1 *Transaction Server* is similar to the **Application Remote Interface** from the previous chapter. However, the two approaches differ significantly in the following areas:

- In the Named Pipes approach, clients and servers communicate using Named Pipes over NetBIOS. In the **Application Remote Interface** approach, clients and servers communicate using RDS over APPC or APPC/SQLLOO.

- The server element in the Named Pipes approach is a remote process at the end of a Named Pipe. In the **Application Remote Interface** approach, the server element is a "well-known" procedure loaded as a DLL.
- The Named Pipes approach requires a running copy of the IBM **LAN Server program** on the server. With the **LAN Server Program**, you also get a file server, print server, and a general purpose Network Operating System. The **Application Remote Interface** approach requires an RDS requester (i.e., OS/2 EE) on every client.
- The Named Pipes approach can be used in any client-server situation. The **Application Remote Interface** approach is optimized for SQL-based remote procedures.

This chapter splits the original **SQLTP1.SQC** program (see Chapter 25) into three programs:

1. The **SQLTP1RQ.C** client program, which drives TP1s and runs under **MULTI** control.
2. The **SQLTP1SV.SQC** server program, which executes the TP1 transactions against the database.
3. The **LAUNCHER.C** program, which starts "n" process instances of the **SQLTP1SV.SQC** program on the server machine.

WHAT YOU WILL LEARN

This chapter serves as an elaborate example of how "custom" servers can be put together using the building blocks provided in this book. The TP1 example developed here applies to any client-server program that uses Named Pipes. This chapter has the following prerequisites:

- The Tutorial chapter on Named Pipes in Part II.
- The Named Pipes implementation of **FX** in Parts II and III.
- The SQL Tutorial chapter.
- The first two chapters in the TP1 Benchmark Series. Much of the code in this chapter is identical to code you've already seen in **SQLTP1.SQC**. This common code will not be repeated. Instead, we will refer you to the appropriate **SQLTP1.SQC** listings where the common code is first introduced.
- You should review the **MULTI** chapters in Part II, and you should be familiar with **RSQL** at the user level.

THE NAMED PIPES VERSION OF TP1

This application serves as another example of how the client-server model extends to transaction processing environments. The client and server processes in this application communicate requests and responses through messages via the Named Pipes Interprocess Communication (IPC). Named Pipes makes the location of the server program transparent to the code. A server program can be moved from a local machine to a remote machine by simply preceding the pipe name with the name of a server machine. The arrival of a message at the *Transaction Server* triggers the execution of a TP1 transaction. A server process executes the TP1 as a collection of static SQL statements.

Why are we using processes instead of threads? This is because the Database Manager allows only one open database connection per process. Since we want the TP1 transactions to execute concurrently, we will start a separate process for each concurrent database connection. The number of server processes to be started is a parameter which gets passed to the **LAUNCHER** program. Here is how we divide the TP1 task between the clients and servers:

- The **SQLTP1RQ.C** client program runs as a **MULTI** process. This means **MULTI** will create the process, pass it the parameters, and tell it when to start or stop executing. The client goes into an endless loop that repeatedly issues requests for the execution of a TP1 transaction on the server side. The loop, of course, runs under the control of **MULTI**. The request to execute the TP1 is done by invoking a **DosCallNmPipe**. This API call is ideal for non-persistent sessions which consist of a single request-reply message exchange. Here is what happens during such an exchange:

    1. A session is opened with the server pipe.
    2. A message is sent to the server consisting of three variables: **random1**, **random2**, and **tps**.
    3. A reply is received from the server indicating success or failure of the TP1 execution.
    4. The pipe is closed.

- The **SQLTP1SV.SQC** server program creates a Named Pipe, and then blocks waiting for a request to come in. When a request comes in, the server reads the two random numbers and tps count that were sent by the client, and generates random numbers for the account, teller, and branch. The server program then executes a TP1 transaction using static SQL and returns an error message over the pipe in case of failure. Otherwise, an empty message is returned. The server process then disconnects the pipe instance with that particular client and reissues a **DosConnectNmPipe**, which blocks the server process until the next request for work arrives.

TP1 CONFIGURATIONS

The location of the TP1 server process is transparent to the client code. The MULTI configuration file contains an optional server name field for remote configurations. The Named Pipes IPC determines whether the server is local or remote from its name, and handles all the transport mechanics accordingly. Each instance of **MULTI** can run up to four **SQLTP1RI.C** client processes. If you need more TP1 generators, simply add more workstations that run **MULTI**. Figure 27-2 shows an example of a 12-client remote driver system. You can scale this configuration in either direction depending on your budget considerations. We will be scaling our experiments downward, of course, to a four-client TP1 system. We'll then run a benchmark using a remote client-server configuration. We will also run TP1 transactions against a local machine, mainly to get a feel for the network overhead. We are especially interested in how the Named Pipes remote TP1 measures up to its **Application Remote Interface** counterpart.

WALKING THROUGH THE SQLTP1RQ.C REQUESTER

SQLTP1RQ.C: The main() Procedure

In this section, we present the **main()** procedure of the **SQLTP1RQ.C** requester program whose code listing is shown in Figure 27-3. You will find that much of the code is identical to the original **SQLTP1.SQC** code, from Chapter 25. This is not surprising since both programs have a front-end which interacts with **MULTI**. The difference is that the code presented here does *not* execute the TP1 transaction directly. Instead, it issues a request to a TP1 server process via a Named Pipe. What you will learn that's "new and exciting," is how to issue this call using the **DosCallNmPipe** API call. We will not repeat the code and explanations that deal with the interaction with **MULTI**. Instead, we will point you to the appropriate sections in the previous chapters. We only introduce code listings that do something new. The following is a step-by-step description of what **main()** does:

1. The program starts by including the C-language, OS/2 and OS/2 EE header files that are needed for system services. These are identical to the header files that were discussed in the previous chapters, since much of what we do is interact with **MULTI**.

2. The following program header files are included:

   const.h This is the same header file that was used in the previous chapters. Its listing can be found in Figure 25-11 on page 705.

   sqltp1.h This is the same header file that was used in the previous chapters. Its listing can be found in Figure 25-10 on page 703.

3. The **main()** program follows and, as you can see, it's almost a carbon copy of **SQLTP1.SQC**'s **main()**. However, there are also some key differences on which we will focus our presentation. Here's what **main()** does:

   - It invokes the **get_args()** function, which is listed in Figure 27-5. This function obtains the arguments **MULTI** passes to the program. It is similar to the

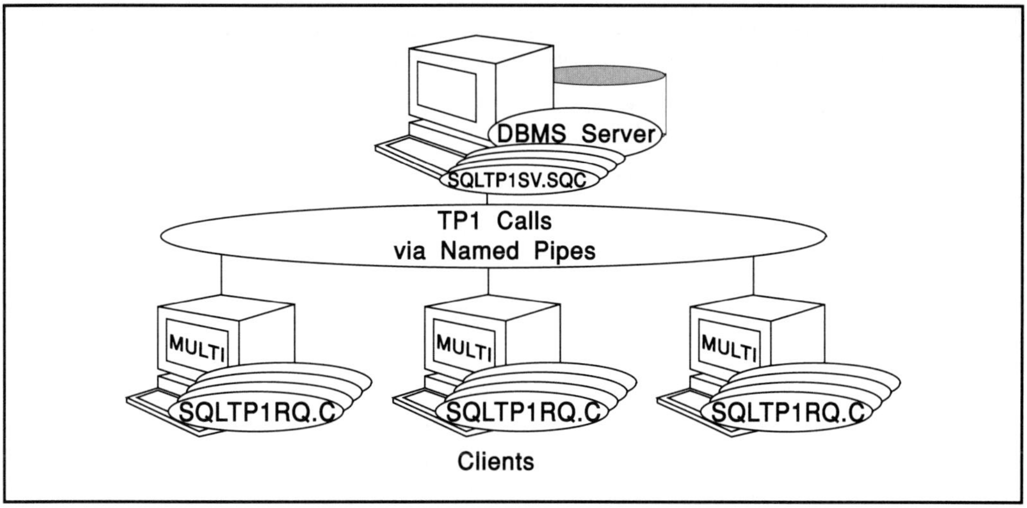

Figure 27-2. 12-client TP1 Driver Using Remote Named Pipes Over a LAN.

get_args() function we encountered in the previous chapters with the exception that the name of a remote server can be specified as an input parameter to the program. This name is then concatenated to the pipe name when the client and server execute on different machines. **MULTI**, of course, gets these arguments from reading the **MULTI.CFG** file.

- It invokes the previously encountered **initialize_multi_ipc()** function, whose listing can be found in Chapter 25 in Figure 25-5 on page 695. This function performs all the interprocess communication chores required from a process that runs under **MULTI**'s control.

- It invokes the **initialize_task()** function, whose listing can be found in Figure 27-6. This function does one-time housekeeping chores in preparation for the *big loop*. It is similar to the previously encountered **initialize_task** functions with the exception that it does *not* connect to the database or install a signal handler.

- It invokes the previously encountered **execute_task()** function, listed in Figure 25-7 on page 697. This is the home of the *big loop*, which forever requests TP1 transactions. **MULTI** can pause at any time and resume the execution of TP1 transactions through semaphores.

  Note: This is where we part company in a major way with the code in Chapter 25. The TP1 transaction is *not* directly executed by the helper routine, **tp1_transaction()**. Instead, this function (see listing in Figure 27-7) merely sends a request to execute a TP1 to a server process through the **DosCallNmPipe** API call. The server process executes the TP1.

```
/*****************************************************************************/
/*  PROGRAM NAME: SQLTP1RQ - A process program that MULTI starts            */
/*                                                                           */
/*  PROGRAM DESCRIPTION:  This program is run as a child task of MULTI      */
/*   This code provides the driver side of a Named Pipe TP1 application.    */
/*                                                                           */
/*****************************************************************************/
#include <process.h>                /* For exit()                            */
#include <string.h>                 /* For printf                            */
#include <sys\types.h>              /* For time()                            */
#include <sys\timeb.h>              /* For time()                            */
#include <sys\stat.h>               /* For stat()                            */
#include <stdlib.h>                 /* For atoi                              */
#include <stdio.h>                  /* For sprintf, printf                   */

#define INCL_VIO                    /* include VIO calls                     */
#define INCL_DOSSEMAPHORES          /* include semaphore api calls           */
#define INCL_DOSMEMMGR              /* include segment   api calls           */
#define INCL_DOSNMPIPES             /* include named pipe api calls          */
#define INCL_ERRORS                 /* include error definitions             */
#include <os2.h>

#include "const.h"                  /* constants for multi                   */
#include "sqltp1.h"                 /* tp1 program vars, declares,etc.       */

/*--------------------------------------------------------------------------*/
/* includes, defines, etc. for task function                                 */
/*--------------------------------------------------------------------------*/
CHAR   input_msgbuf[512];                /* msg buffer for receiving txn  */
CHAR   output_msgbuf[512];               /* msg buffer for sending resp.  */

USHORT pipe_handle;
CHAR   pipe_name[] = "\\PIPE\\TP1";
CHAR   server_pipe_name[25];
USHORT bytes_read;
USHORT bytes_written;

/*--------------------------------------------------------------------------*/
/* Main routine.                                                             */
/*--------------------------------------------------------------------------*/
VOID main(USHORT argc, PCHAR argv[])
{
  get_args(argc, argv);            /*  get program arguments                 */

  initialize_multi_ipc();          /*  Init MULTI semaphores/shared memory*/

  initialize_task();               /*  perform one time intializations       */

  execute_task();                  /*  Remote Procedure Call  loop           */

} /* end main */
```

Figure 27-3. SQLTP1RQ.C: The main() Procedure.

SQLTP1RQ.C: The get_args() Procedure

In this section, we present the **get_args()** function, whose code listing is shown in Figure 27-5. This function obtains the arguments **MULTI** passes to the program when MULTI invokes it. **MULTI** itself gets these arguments from reading the **MULTI.CFG** file, an example of which is shown below:

```
PROGRAM_TYPE     = PROCESS
STOP_TIME_MS     = 600000
TASK_NAME        = SQLTP1RQ.EXE 0 17 2.0 1 \\RemoteServerName;
TASK_NAME        = SQLTP1RQ.EXE 1 23 2.0 1 \\RemoteServerName;
TASK_NAME        = SQLTP1RQ.EXE 2 29 2.0 1 \\RemoteServerName;
TASK_NAME        = SQLTP1RQ.EXE 3 57 2.0 1 \\RemoteServerName;
```

Figure 27-4. A MULTI.CFG File for Running Four TP1 Processes.

The arguments appear right after the program's name. The **get_args()** function requires the first four parameters, which are identical to the parameters from the previous chapters. The fifth parameter is *optional*. It indicates the **network name** of a remote server machine. Don't forget to enter the double-backslash in front of the name.

```
/*-----------------------------------------------------------------------------*/
/* Get program arguments.  Argument are 1) process_number, 2) seed_value,      */
/* 3) threshold, 4) tps count, 5) server_name (optional)                       */
/*-----------------------------------------------------------------------------*/
VOID get_args(USHORT argc, PCHAR argv[])
{
  /*-----------------------------------*/
  /* validate and get arguments        */
  /*-----------------------------------*/
  if (argc < 5)
     { print_error(0, "reading command arguments",
                   __FILE__,__LINE__);
       exit(FAILED);
     }

  process_number = atoi(argv[1]);          /* get process number           */
  if ((process_number < 0) || (process_number > 3))
     { print_error(0, "reading process number", __FILE__,__LINE__);
       exit(FAILED);
     }

  seed_value = atoi(argv[2]);              /* get seed value               */
  threshold  = atof(argv[3]);              /* get threshold value          */
  tps        = atoi(argv[4]);              /* get tps scale                */

  if (argc > 5)
      sprintf(server_pipe_name,"%s%s",     /* remote pipe with server name */
          argv[5],pipe_name);
  else
      sprintf(server_pipe_name,"%s",       /* local pipe                   */
          pipe_name);

} /* end get_args */
```

Figure 27-5. SQLTP1RQ.C: The get_args() Procedure.

SQLTP1RQ.C: The initialize_task() Function

In this section, we present the **initialize_task()** function, whose code listing is shown in Figure 27-6. This function does the following task-specific one-time chores:

1. It adds a TXNS field to the task's window. This is where the count is displayed for TP1 transactions which meet the response time threshold.

2. It seeds the random number generator.

```
/*------------------------------------------------------------------------*/
/* Perform onetime initializations for the task such as database connects. */
/*------------------------------------------------------------------------*/
VOID  initialize_task(VOID)
{
  /*-------------------------------*/
  /* add transaction count field   */
  /*-------------------------------*/
  write_str("TXNS  = ", FIELD_TEXT_ATTR,
           (process_number * 20) + 2, 10); /* calculate display location    */
                                           /*  based on thread number       */

  /*-------------------------------*/
  /* initialize random number generator */
  /*-------------------------------*/
  srand(seed_value);

} /* end initialize_task */
```

Figure 27-6. SQLTP1RQ.C: The initialize_task() Function.

SQLTP1RQ.C: The tp1_transaction() Function

In this section, we present the **tp1_transaction()** function, whose code listing is shown in Figure 27-7. This procedure, unlike its counterpart in Chapter 25, does not perform the actual TP1 transaction. Instead, it calls a process on the server through the **DosCallNmPipe** API which executes the TP1. This is the first time we encounter this Named Pipe API call, so it will be described below. The **DosCallNmPipe** is used to connect to the server process, send a request, receive a reply and disconnect. The message sent is placed in the **input_msgbuf**. It consists of three parameters: **random1**, **random2**, and **tps**. When the server process receives this message, it executes a TP1; and if all goes well, it returns in the **output_msgbuf** an empty string. Otherwise, it returns a message describing what failed.

DosCallNmPipe

The **DosCallNmPipe** API call opens a Named Pipe, writes to it, reads from it, and closes it, all in one operation. This call combines in a single operation: **DosOpen**, **DosSetNmpHandState**, **DosTransactNmPipe**, and a **DosClose**. This aggregate call is the preferred way to code "non-persistent" connections that get established and terminated just to issue a single request/reply. The aggregate call is simpler to read and also generates less network traffic. This is because the acknowledgements are piggybacked with returned data, resulting in increased efficiency. The prototype for this call is:

```
DosCallNmPipe(PSZ          Name,          /* Name of pipe \\serv\pipe\name */
              PBYTE        InBuf,         /* Read buffer address           */
              USHORT       InLen,         /* Read buffer length            */
              PBYTE        OutBuf,        /* Write buffer address          */
              USHORT       OutLength,     /* Write buffer length           */
              PUSHORT      BytesRead,     /* Actual number of Bytes read   */
              PUSHORT      TimeOut);      /* In milliseconds               */
```

A description of the parameters follows:

- The ***Name*** parameter points to a null-terminated string that contains the name of the Named Pipe to be opened. Named Pipes are named **\PIPE\PipeName**, where **\PIPE** is the name of a virtual subdirectory in memory.
- The ***InBuf*** parameter points to the input buffer (where the message is received).
- The ***InLen*** parameter specifies the size in bytes of the input buffer.
- The ***OutBuf*** parameter points to the buffer containing the data to be written to the pipe.
- The ***OutLength*** parameter specifies the size in bytes of the output buffer.
- The ***BytesRead*** parameter points to a variable that receives the actual number of bytes read into the input buffer.
- The ***TimeOut*** parameter specifies in milliseconds the amount of time OS/2 should wait for the pipe to become available.

```
/*------------------------------------------------------------------------*/
/* function for TP1 transaction                                           */
/*------------------------------------------------------------------------*/
SHORT APIENTRY tp1_transaction(VOID)
{
  sprintf(input_msgbuf,"\\RANDOM1=%u \\RANDOM2=%u \\TPS=%u",
                       random1, random2, tps);

  rc = DosCallNmPipe(server_pipe_name,          /* name of the pipe        */
                     input_msgbuf,              /* input  msg              */
                     strlen(input_msgbuf) + 1,  /* input  msg size         */
                     output_msgbuf,             /* output msg              */
                     sizeof(output_msgbuf),     /* output msg max size     */
                     &bytes_read,               /* output msg actual size  */
                     -1L);                      /* timeout (wait forever)  */
  if (rc)
     { print_error(rc,"during DosCallNmPipe", __FILE__,__LINE__);
       exit(FAILED);
     }
```

Figure 27-7 (Part 1 of 2). SQLTP1RQ.SQC: The tp1_transaction() Procedure.

```
    if (strcmp(output_msgbuf,"") != 0)
      {
        printf("%s\n",output_msgbuf);
        return(FAILED);
      }

    return(GOOD);
  } /* end tp1_transaction */
```

Figure 27-7 (Part 2 of 2). SQLTP1RQ.SQC: The tp1_transaction() Procedure.

WALKING THROUGH THE SQLTP1SV.SQC SERVER

SQLTP1SV.SQC: The main() Procedure

In this section, we present the **main()** procedure of the TP1 server for the Named Pipes benchmark. Here's an overview of what this server code does:

1. It accepts client requests to perform a TP1 transaction.
2. It obtains the input parameters to perform the TP1.
3. It executes the TP1.
4. It returns the results.
5. It disconnects from the client and waits for the next request to come in.

The following is a step-by-step description of what **main()** does:

1. The program starts by including the C-language, OS/2, and OS/2 EE header files that are needed for system services. These are identical to the header files that were discussed in the previous chapters.

2. A structure of type SQLCA is declared.

3. The SQL WHENEVER directions are issued.

4. The SQL host variables are declared.

5. The **main()** program follows and, as you can see, it's very similar to the TP1 back-end part of the programs we've already encountered. We will focus our presentation on what's new and different. As you will soon find out, there is nothing in this program that you did not previously encounter elsewhere in this book. This may be a sign of progress. Here's what **main()** does:

   - It invokes a slimmed-down version of the previously encountered **initialize_task()** function. We provide the listing of this slim version in Figure 27-9. This function connects to the database and installs a signal handler.

   - It invokes **initialize_pipe()**, a new function listed in Figure 27-10. This function creates a Named Pipe for this process. All the server processes use the

same pipe name. This means that when a pipe is created, the process obtains a handle for a pipe instance with that common name. We will explain what this all means when we get to that section.

- It invokes a slimmed-down version of the previously encountered **execute_task()** function. The code for this slim version is in Figure 27-11. This function is the home of the *big loop*, which forever executes TP1 transactions. The difference is that it is not under **MULTI** control. The loop ends when the process gets killed by its parent, the **LAUNCHER** program.
- The TP1 transaction is executed by the helper routine, **tp1_transaction()**. This is a straight implementation of a TP1 using static SQL. We've listed this helper procedure (see listing in Figure 27-12) because it handles errors slightly differently from the TP1 code in the previous chapters.

```
/*****************************************************************************/
/*  PROGRAM NAME: SQLTP1SV.SQC                                               */
/*                                                                           */
/*  PROGRAM DESCRIPTION:  This program is run as a child task of the LAUNCHER*/
/*    program and executes the TP1 transaction using Named Pipes to          */
/*    communicate with a client.                                             */
/*    This code provides the server side of a Name Pipe TP1                  */
/*                                                                           */
/*****************************************************************************/
#include <process.h>                    /* For exit()                        */
#include <string.h>                     /* For printf                        */
#include <sys\types.h>                  /* For time()                        */
#include <sys\timeb.h>                  /* For time()                        */
#include <sys\stat.h>                   /* For stat()                        */
#include <stdlib.h>                     /* For atoi                          */
#include <stdio.h>                      /* For sprintf, printf               */

#define INCL_VIO                        /* include VIO calls                 */
#define INCL_DOSSEMAPHORES              /* include semaphore api calls       */
#define INCL_DOSMEMMGR                  /* include segment   api calls       */
#define INCL_DOSNMPIPES                 /* include named pipe api calls      */
#define INCL_ERRORS                     /* include error definitions         */
#include <os2.h>
#include <sqlca.h>                      /* sqlca                             */
#include <sql.h>                        /* error msg. retrieval              */
#include <sqlcodes.h>                   /* SQL return code constants         */
#include <sqlenv.h>                     /* environment functions and         */

                   /*_________________________________*/
                   /* forward declarations of procedures */
                   /*_________________________________*/
VOID initialize_task(VOID);
VOID initialize_pipe(VOID);
VOID execute_task(VOID);
SHORT APIENTRY tp1_transaction(VOID);
VOID print_error(USHORT, PCHAR, PCHAR, USHORT);
VOID format_error(PCHAR msgbuf, USHORT Error, PCHAR msg,
                  PCHAR file, USHORT line);
```

Figure 27-8 (Part 1 of 2). SQLTP1SV.SQC: The main() Procedure.

```
                    /*------------------------------------*/
                    /* constant definitions               */
                    /*------------------------------------*/
#define GOOD                0
#define FAILED             -1
                    /*------------------------------------*/
                    /* variables                          */
                    /*------------------------------------*/
USHORT seed_value;                  /* initial seed for random number gen*/
double threshold;                   /* time thresholds for TP1 txns     */
USHORT tps;                         /* the tps scale, input from client  */
USHORT random1, random2;            /* inputs from client                */
CHAR   input_msgbuf[512];           /* msg buffer for receiving txn      */
CHAR   output_msgbuf[512];          /* msg buffer for sending resp.      */
USHORT rc;                          /* return code variable              */
CHAR   error_string[80];            /* error string container            */

USHORT pipe_handle;
CHAR   pipe_name[] = "\\PIPE\\TP1";
USHORT bytes_read;
USHORT bytes_written;

struct sqlca sqlca;

EXEC SQL WHENEVER SQLERROR CONTINUE;
EXEC SQL WHENEVER SQLWARNING CONTINUE;
EXEC SQL WHENEVER NOT FOUND CONTINUE;

EXEC SQL BEGIN DECLARE SECTION;
 long  acct_num;
 short branch_id;
 short teller_id;
 long  balance;
 long  delta          = 100;
 char  acct_name[20] = "<--20 BYTE STRING-->";
EXEC SQL END   DECLARE SECTION;

/*-------------------------------------------------------------------*/
/* Main routine.                                                     */
/*-------------------------------------------------------------------*/
VOID main(USHORT argc, PCHAR argv[])
{
  initialize_task();                /* perform database connect etc. */

  initialize_pipe();                /* create Named Pipe             */

  execute_task();                   /* Loop executing TP1s           */

} /* end main */
```

Figure 27-8 (Part 2 of 2). SQLTP1SV.SQC: The main() Procedure.

SQLTP1SV.SQC: The initialize_task() Procedure

In this section, we present the **initialize_task()** procedure whose code is listed in Figure 27-9. This function does the following task-specific one-time chores:

1. It connects to the TP1 database.

2. It installs a signal handler that intercepts CTRL + Break, and gracefully terminates the program.

```
/*-------------------------------------------------------------------------*/
/* Perform onetime initializations for the task such as database connects. */
/*-------------------------------------------------------------------------*/
VOID  initialize_task(VOID)
{
  /*-----------------------------------*/
  /* connect to the database, restart if */
  /*    necessary                       */
  /*-----------------------------------*/
  sqlestrd("TP1", 'S', &sqlca);

  if (sqlca.sqlcode == SQLE_RC_DB_RESTART)
     sqlerest("TP1", &sqlca);

  if (sqlca.sqlcode)
     { sprintf(error_string,"connnecting to the database, sqlca.sqlcode = %ld",
               sqlca.sqlcode);
       print_error(0, error_string, __FILE__,__LINE__);
       exit(FAILED);
     }
  /*-----------------------------------*/
  /* install database signal handler    */
  /*-----------------------------------*/
  sqleisig(&sqlca);
  if (sqlca.sqlcode)
     { sprintf(error_string,"installing signal handler, sqlca.sqlcode = %ld",
               sqlca.sqlcode);
       print_error(0, error_string, __FILE__,__LINE__);
       exit(FAILED);
     }
} /* end initialize_task */
```

Figure 27-9. SQLTP1SV.SQC: The initialize_task() Procedure.

SQLTP1SV.SQC: The initialize_pipe() Procedure

In this section, we present the **initialize_pipe()** procedure whose code is listed in Figure 27-10. This function simply issues a **DosMakeNmPipe** API call. This API is fully described in "DosMakeNmPipe" on page 271. Here are some points worth noting:

- The **PIPE_OPENMODE** parameter is specified for the following pipe attributes:

  1. Data is sent over LAN after each write (no blocking)
  2. Either the server or the client can send data (duplex)

- The **PIPEMODE** parameter is specified for the following pipe attributes:

  1. The pipe will operate in message stream mode.
  2. An instance count of 128 is specified. The maximum is 254 instances. Any attempts to make a pipe will fail if the maximum number of allowed instances

already exists. This parameter is looked at only when the first instance of a pipe is created (OS/2 ignores it after that). When multiple instances are allowed, multiple clients can simultaneously issue DosOpen to the same pipe name and get handles to distinct pipe instances.

```
/*---------------------------------------------------------------------------*/
/* Perform onetime initializations for the  Named Pipe                       */
/*---------------------------------------------------------------------------*/
VOID  initialize_pipe(VOID)
{
 #define PIPE_OPENMODE      0x4002     /* no write-behind allowed, duplex    */
 #define PIPEMODE           0x0580     /* message pipe, 128 instances        */
 #define TIMEOUT            0L         /* wait forever timeout value         */

 rc = DosMakeNmPipe(pipe_name,         /* PipeName                           */
                    &pipe_handle,      /* pipe handle returned               */
                    PIPE_OPENMODE,
                    PIPEMODE,
                    512,               /* Output buffer size in bytes        */
                    512,               /* Input  buffer size in bytes        */
                    TIMEOUT);
 if (rc)
    {print_error(rc,"Making a named pipe",__FILE__,__LINE__);
     exit(FAILED);
    }
} /* end initialize_pipes */
```

Figure 27-10. SQLTP1SV.SQC: The initialize_pipe() Procedure.

SQLTP1SV.SQC: The execute_task() Procedure

In this section, we present the **execute_task()** procedure whose code is listed in Figure 27-11. This code executes as a loop which ends only when the task is killed by its parent, the **LAUNCHER** program. Here is what this loop does:

1. It issues the **DosConnectNmPipe** API call and waits for a client to open this pipe instance. The process is blocked waiting for that to happen. This API call is described in "DosConnectNmPipe" on page 273.
2. It issues a **DosRead** API call to receive a message from the client on this Named Pipe instance. This API call is described in "DosRead" on page 281.
3. It receives and decodes three parameters from the client: **random1**, **random2**, and **tps**.
4. It executes a TP1 transaction by invoking the **tp1_transaction()** helper function.
5. It issues a **DosWrite** API call to send a reply message to the client on this Named Pipe instance. This API call is described in "DosWrite" on page 280.
6. It issues a **DosDisConnectNmPipe** API call to disconnect from the client. This API call is described in "DosDisConnectNmPipe" on page 274.

```
/*-----------------------------------------------------------------------------*/
/* Task routine. This routine continuously 1) waits for a remote request      */
/*   2) reads the incoming parameters,  3) invokes the TP1 helper procedure */
/*   4) sends back response  5) disconnects from client                        */
/*-----------------------------------------------------------------------------*/
VOID execute_task(VOID)
{
  /*------------------------------------*/
  /* continuous TP1 loop                */
  /*------------------------------------*/
  while (TRUE)
    {
      /*------------------------------------*/
      /* execute a TP1 transaction          */
      /*------------------------------------*/
      rc = DosConnectNmPipe(pipe_handle);
      if (rc)
         {print_error(rc,"Connecting to pipe",__FILE__,__LINE__);
          exit(FAILED);
         }

      rc = DosRead(pipe_handle,
                   input_msgbuf,
                   sizeof(input_msgbuf),
                   &bytes_read);
      if (rc)
         {print_error(rc,"Reading from pipe",__FILE__,__LINE__);
          exit(FAILED);
         }

      if (sscanf(input_msgbuf,"\\RANDOM1=%u \\RANDOM2=%u \\TPS=%u",
              &random1, &random2, &tps) != 3)
         {print_error(rc,"Reading TP1 Parameters",__FILE__,__LINE__);
          exit(FAILED);
         }
      if ( tp1_transaction() )
         exit(FAILED);

      rc = DosWrite(pipe_handle,
                    output_msgbuf,
                    strlen(output_msgbuf) + 1,
                    &bytes_written);
      if (rc)
         {print_error(rc,"Writing to pipe",__FILE__,__LINE__);
          exit(FAILED);
         }

      rc = DosDisConnectNmPipe(pipe_handle);
      if (rc)
         {print_error(rc,"Disconnecting from Pipe",__FILE__,__LINE__);
          exit(FAILED);
         }

    }/* end while */
 } /* end execute_task */
```

Figure 27-11. SQLTP1SV.SQC: The execute_task() Procedure.

SQLTP1SV.SQC: The tp1_transaction() Procedure

In this section, we present the **tp1_transaction()** procedure whose code is listed in Figure 27-12. There is nothing new in this code; it is the standard static SQL implementation of a TP1 which was described in the previous two chapters.

```
/*----------------------------------------------------------------------------*/
/* function for TP1 transaction                                               */
/*----------------------------------------------------------------------------*/
SHORT APIENTRY tpl_transaction(VOID)
{
      /*------------------------------------*/
      /* generate some random data          */
      /*------------------------------------*/
  acct_num = (random1 * random2) % (tps*1000001) + 1;/* generate account number */
  teller_id= (short)(random1 % (tps*100)) + 1;      /* generate teller id      */
  branch_id= (short)(random2 % (tps*10)) + 1;       /* generate branch id      */

      /*------------------------------------*/
      /* get the current balance from ACCT  */
      /*------------------------------------*/
  EXEC SQL DECLARE CURSOR1 CURSOR FOR
           SELECT BALANCE FROM ACCT WHERE ACCT_NUM = :acct_num
           FOR UPDATE OF BALANCE;

  EXEC SQL OPEN CURSOR1;
  if (sqlca.sqlcode != 0)
     { format_error(output_msgbuf, (SHORT)sqlca.sqlcode,
                    "during SQL OPEN", __FILE__, __LINE__);
       return(GOOD);
     }

  EXEC SQL FETCH CURSOR1 INTO :balance;
  if (sqlca.sqlcode != 0)
     { format_error(output_msgbuf, (SHORT)sqlca.sqlcode,
                    "during SQL FETCH", __FILE__, __LINE__);
       return(GOOD);
     }
      /*------------------------------------*/
      /* Credit the balance in the ACCT table */
      /*------------------------------------*/
  EXEC SQL UPDATE ACCT
           SET BALANCE = BALANCE + :delta
           WHERE CURRENT OF CURSOR1;
  if (sqlca.sqlcode != 0)
     { format_error(output_msgbuf, (SHORT)sqlca.sqlcode,
                    "during SQL UPDATE", __FILE__,__LINE__);
       return(GOOD);
     }

  EXEC SQL CLOSE CURSOR1;
  if (sqlca.sqlcode != 0)
     { format_error(output_msgbuf, (SHORT)sqlca.sqlcode,
                    "during SQL CLOSE", __FILE__,__LINE__);
       return(GOOD);
     }
```

Figure 27-12 (Part 1 of 2). SQLTP1SV.SQC: The execute_task() Procedure.

```
      /*————————————————————————————————————*/
      /* Update the TELLER table's balance  */
      /*————————————————————————————————————*/
   EXEC SQL UPDATE TELLER
            SET BALANCE = BALANCE + :delta
            WHERE TELLER_ID = :teller_id;
   if (sqlca.sqlcode != 0)
      { format_error(output_msgbuf, (SHORT)sqlca.sqlcode,
                     "during SQL UPDATE", __FILE__,__LINE__);
        return(GOOD);
      }

      /*————————————————————————————————————*/
      /* Update the BRANCH table's balance  */
      /*————————————————————————————————————*/
   EXEC SQL UPDATE BRANCH
            SET BALANCE = BALANCE + :delta
            WHERE BRANCH_ID = :branch_id;
   if (sqlca.sqlcode != 0)
      { format_error(output_msgbuf, (SHORT)sqlca.sqlcode,
                     "during SQL UPDATE", __FILE__,__LINE__);
        return(GOOD);
      }
      /*————————————————————————————————————*/
      /* Insert transaction in HISTORY table */
      /*————————————————————————————————————*/
   EXEC SQL INSERT
            INTO HISTORY(ACCT_NUM, TELLER_ID, BRANCH_ID, BALANCE,
                         DELTA, PID, TRANSID, ACCTNAME, TEMP)
            VALUES(:acct_num, :teller_id, :branch_id, :balance,
                   :delta, 1, 3, :acct_name, 'hist    ');
   if (sqlca.sqlcode != 0)
      { format_error(output_msgbuf, (SHORT)sqlca.sqlcode,
                     "during SQL INSERT", __FILE__,__LINE__);
        return(GOOD);
      }
      /*————————————————————————————————————*/
      /* Commit the transaction to database  */
      /*————————————————————————————————————*/
   EXEC SQL COMMIT;
   if (sqlca.sqlcode != 0)
      { format_error(output_msgbuf, (SHORT)sqlca.sqlcode,
                     "during SQL COMMIT", __FILE__, __LINE__);
        return(GOOD);
      }

   output_msgbuf[0] = '\0';                  /* no errors                  */
   return(GOOD);
} /* end tp1_transaction */
```

Figure 27-12 (Part 2 of 2). SQLTP1SV.SQC: The execute_task() Procedure.

SQLTP1SV.SQC: format_error() and print_error()

In this section, we present the **format_error()** and the **print_error()** helper functions. There are, of course, no surprises in this code.

```
/*--------------------------------------------------------------------*/
/* Error Format Routine                                               */
/*--------------------------------------------------------------------*/
VOID format_error(PCHAR msgbuf, USHORT Error, PCHAR msg,
                  PCHAR file, USHORT line)
{
    sprintf(msgbuf,"Error %d detected while %s at line %d in file %s.\n",
         Error, msg, line, file);
} /* end format_error */
```

Figure 27-13. SQLTP1SV.SQC: The format_error() Helper Function.

```
/*--------------------------------------------------------------------*/
/* Error Display Routine                                              */
/*--------------------------------------------------------------------*/
VOID print_error(USHORT Error, PCHAR msg, PCHAR file, USHORT line)
{
 if (Error == 0)
    printf("Error detected while %s at line %d in file %s.\n",
           msg, line, file);
 else
    printf("Error %d detected while %s at line %d in file %s.\n",
         Error, msg, line, file);
} /* end print_error */
```

Figure 27-14. SQLTP1SV.SQC: The print_error() Helper Function.

WALKING THROUGH THE LAUNCHER.C CODE

In this section, we present the code for a stand-alone program, **LAUNCHER.C**, whose sole function in life is to start child processes. We will be using this program to "launch" several TP1 server processes. If you want to be extra generous, you can start one server process for each concurrent client. For example, if you have six concurrent clients, you could issue:

```
LAUNCHER  sqltp1sv 6
```

This creates a six-server process pool. The TP1 benchmark will run moderately well with a pool consisting of a single server process, but you won't be getting the maximum throughput from such a benchmark. Here is what the **LAUNCHER.C** program does:

1. It reads two input arguments:
   - The name of the program you want to "launch"
   - The number of instances of that program you want to start.
2. It issues a **DosExecPgm** API call once for each instance of that program requested. The instances created are child processes of the **LAUNCHER** program.
3. It blocks waiting for any key to be hit.

4. It kills all the child processes it created. This is so you don't have to reboot your machine.

Congratulations, we've just completed the final piece of code that makes up the third flavor of our TP1 benchmark!

```
/*****************************************************************************/
/*  PROGRAM NAME: LAUNCHER                                                   */
/*                                                                           */
/*  PROGRAM DESCRIPTION:  This simple program is used to launch              */
/*    multiple instances of a child process.  The user specifies the         */
/*    name of the program to launch and the number of instances.             */
/*    This program is used as part of the TP1 toolkit to start multiple     */
/*    instances of a named pipe server program.  One server process          */
/*    instance is needed for each concurrent client                          */
/*                                                                           */
/*****************************************************************************/
#include <process.h>                  /* For exit()                          */
#include <stdio.h>                    /* For printf() & NULL                 */
#include <conio.h>                    /* For getch()                         */
#include <stdlib.h>                   /* For printf                          */
#include <string.h>                   /* For printf                          */
#define  INCL_BASE
#include <os2.h>

#define GOOD                 0
#define FAILED              -1

/*-------------------------------------------------------------------------*/
/* Main routine.                                                           */
/*-------------------------------------------------------------------------*/
VOID main(USHORT argc, PCHAR argv[], PCHAR envp[])
{ UCHAR       program_name[128];                /* includes path            */
  UCHAR       object_name[128];                 /* buffer for fail object   */
  RESULTCODES   ExecResult;                     /* defined by OS/2          */
  UCHAR       rc;                               /* return code              */
  UINT        i;                                /* counter                  */
  UINT        instances;                        /* number of child processes*/
  USHORT      processid[100];                   /* process ids to terminate */
  /*-----------------------------------*/
  /* Get input parameters              */
  /*-----------------------------------*/
  if (argc != 3)
  { printf("Enter command as follows: LAUNCHER program-name instances \n");
    exit(FAILED);
  }

  sprintf(program_name,"%s.exe", argv[1]);
  instances      = atoi(argv[2]);
```

Figure 27-15 (Part 1 of 2). The LAUNCHER.C Code.

```
    /*-----------------------------------------------------*/
    /* start the processes                                 */
    /*-----------------------------------------------------*/
    for (i=0; i<instances; ++i)
    {
        rc = DosExecPgm(object_name,          /* failing object if program fails*/
                        sizeof(object_name),/* the object size               */
                        2,                    /* async. program execution      */
                        0L,                   /* no program parameters         */
                        0L,                   /* no inherit environment        */
                        &ExecResult,          /* child process id              */
                        program_name);        /* program name                  */
        if (rc)
        { printf("Error rc = %u, while creating  process instance = %u \n",
                  rc, instances);
          exit(FAILED);
        }
        printf("process instance %u started successfully \n", i + 1);
        processid[i] = ExecResult.codeTerminate;     /* save process id        */
    } /* end for */

    /*-----------------------------------------------------*/
    /* Wait for user request                               */
    /*-----------------------------------------------------*/
    printf("Hit any key to kill all server processes \n");
    getch();

    /*-----------------------------------------------------*/
    /* Kill all the processes                              */
    /*-----------------------------------------------------*/
    for (i=0; i<instances; ++i)
    {
        rc = DosKillProcess(1,                        /* only kill one process */
                            processid[i]);            /* process handle        */
        if (rc)
        { printf("Error killing process instance = %u \n",  instances);
          exit(FAILED);
        }
    }
    exit(GOOD);
  } /* end main */
```

Figure 27-15 (Part 2 of 2). The LAUNCHER.C Code.

RUNNING TWO TP1 BENCHMARK TESTS USING NAMED PIPES

Now that we've got some code, let's run some benchmarks to see how well this TP1 flavor performs. We will run two TP1 benchmark tests:

1. A **local** benchmark test where the client and servers are on the same machine. The machine is a PS/2 Mod-80 with a 20-MHz clock and a 1000-KByte buffer pool (see Figure 27-18).

2. A **remote** benchmark test where the clients and servers are on different machines. The client machine is a PS/2 Mod 70 with a 16-MHz clock. The server machine

is a PS/2 Mod-80 with a 20-MHz clock and a 1000-KByte buffer pool (see Figure 27-19).

The two benchmarks use identical four-process software configurations. The **MULTI** configuration file used for the local test is:

```
PROGRAM_TYPE     = PROCESS
STOP_TIME_MS     = 600000
TASK_NAME        = SQLTP1RQ.EXE 0 17 2.0  1;
TASK_NAME        = SQLTP1RQ.EXE 1 23 2.0  1;
TASK_NAME        = SQLTP1RQ.EXE 2 29 2.0  1;
TASK_NAME        = SQLTP1RQ.EXE 3 57 2.0  1;
```

Figure 27-16. A MULTI.CFG file for Running Four TP1 Processes Locally.

The **MULTI** configuration file used for the remote test is:

```
PROGRAM_TYPE     = PROCESS
STOP_TIME_MS     = 600000
TASK_NAME        = SQLTP1RQ.EXE 0 17 2.0  1 \\LSVR03;
TASK_NAME        = SQLTP1RQ.EXE 1 23 2.0  1 \\LSVR03;
TASK_NAME        = SQLTP1RQ.EXE 2 29 2.0  1 \\LSVR03;
TASK_NAME        = SQLTP1RQ.EXE 3 57 2.0  1 \\LSVR03;
```

Figure 27-17. A MULTI.CFG File for Running Four TP1 Processes Remotely.

The benchmarks are set up to run for 10-minute tests (i.e., 600,000 milliseconds). The response time threshold is set to 2.0 seconds, and a 1-tps database size is specified.

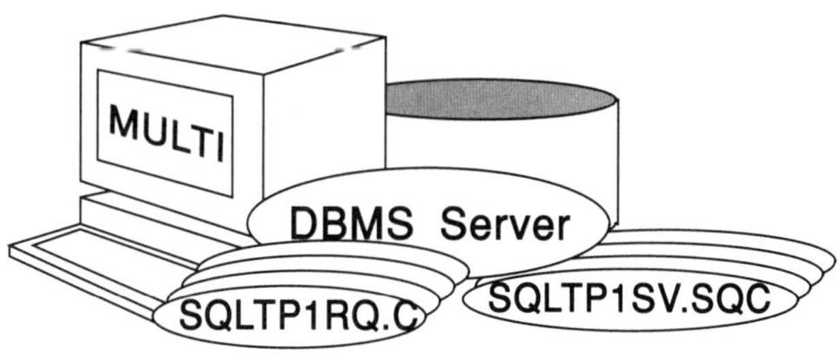

Test 1 20-MHz PS/2 Mod-80, 1000-KByte buffer pool

Figure 27-18. The Named Pipes Local Benchmark Configuration.

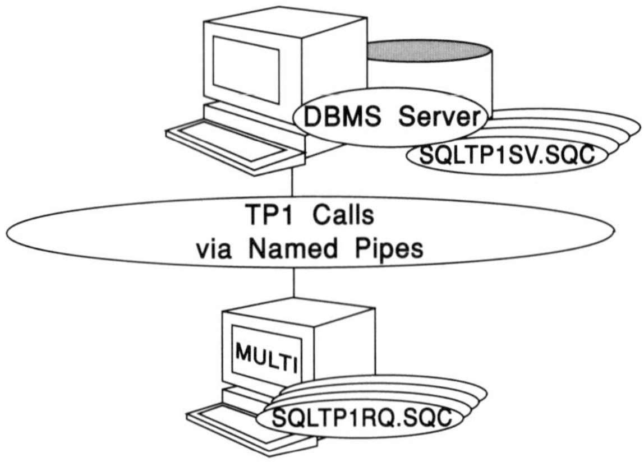

Test 2 Client: PS/2 Mod-70 16 MHz

Server: PS/2 Mod-80, 20-MHz 1000-KByte buffer pool

LAN: 4 Mb/s Token Ring (Named Pipes/Netbios)

Figure 27-19. The Named Pipes Remote Benchmark Configuration.

Running the Named Pipes Remote TP1 Locally (Benchmark1)

The configuration for this benchmark is a four-client MULTI running against a local database. The test is run on a PS/2 Mod-80 with a 20-MHz clock and a 1000-KByte buffer pool. We assume the database is already loaded for a 1-tps database scale. The following RSQL run is used to set up the 1000-KByte buffer configuration and prepare the database for the benchmark1 run.

```
--                  Change TP1 Database Configuration
-- ===========================================================================
-- logon
EXEC DBA: LOGON USERID PASSWORD DBSVR03 UPM_LOCAL UPM_USER;
 OK, api_rcd = 0,          Execution time =     0.0000 secs

-- update the Database Configuration for database for a 500k buffer
EXEC DBA: UPDATE_DB_CFG TP1     MAXAPPLS    = 8,
                                DLCHKTIME   = 10000,
                                BUFFPAGE    = 256,
                                LOGFILSIZ   = 50,
                                LOGPRIMARY  = 2,
                                LOGSECOND   = 20;
 OK, sql_rcd = 0,        Execution time =     1.3700 secs
```

Figure 27-20 (Part 1 of 2). Preparing the Database for Benchmark1.

```
-- Show the database configuration for database TP1
EXEC DBA: SHOW_DB_CFG TP1;

 Database Configuration for Database TP1
 =============================================
 Configuration Parameter          Current  Parm.      Parm.      Parm.
 Description                      Value    Units      Range      Default
 -------------------------------- -------- ---------- ---------- -------
 Max. Active Applications               8  Appl.      1-117           8
 Max. DB Files Open/Application        20  files      2-235          20
 Max. Files Open/Application          255  files      25-32700      255
 Buffer Pool Size                     256  4K pages     (1)          16
 Time Interval for Deadlocks        10000  millisecs. 1-600 sec.     10
 Max. Storage for Locklists             8  4K pages   4-250           8
 Max. percent locklist/appl.           22  percent    1-100          22
 Default Application Heap               3  segments   2-20            3
 Application Agent Heap                 2  segments   2-85            3
 Sort List Heap                         2  segments   1-20            2
 Database Heap                          1  segments   1-45            1
 SQL Statement Heap                    64  segments                  64
 Log File Size                         50  4K pages   15-255         50
 Primary Log Files                      2  files      0-63            2
 Secondary Log Files                   20  files      0-63            3
 Log Records/soft checkpoint          100  records    0-65535       100

 Current Log Location = C:\SQL00003\
 New Log Location     =
 Copy Protection      =    1
 Country              =    1
 Code Page            =  437
 Release              =  512
 OK, sql_rcd = 0,        Execution time =     0.3700 secs

-- bind the tp1 program
EXEC DBA: BIND TP1 SQLTP1SV.BND ISO REPEATABLE_READ BLOCK_ALL PUBLIC;
 OK, sql_rcd = 0,        Execution time =    14.5000 secs

-- delete all of the history data
EXEC SQL: DELETE FROM HISTORY;
 WARNING, sql_code = 100,    Execution time =     0.9700 secs
 SQL0100W  No row was found for FETCH, UPDATE or DELETE; or the result of a
 query is an empty table.

-- commit the changes
EXEC SQL: COMMIT;
 OK, sql_rcd = 0,        Execution time =     0.0300 secs

-- disconnect
EXEC DBA: STOPUSE TP1;
 OK, sql_rcd = 0,        Execution time =     0.7900 secs
```

Figure 27-20 (Part 2 of 2). Preparing the Database for Benchmark1.

```
                     Multiprocess Execution Example

 Use arrow keys to move the cursor.  Use + and - keys to change field values.
 Press R to start running, S to stop, or C to clear the count.
 Press ESC to terminate the program.

-SQLTP1RQ.EXE-        -SQLTP1RQ.EXE-        -SQLTP1RQ.EXE-        -SQLTP1RQ.EXE-

 Count = 722           Count = 751           Count = 755           Count = 749
 TXNS  = 712           TXNS  = 742           TXNS  = 748           TXNS  = 740
 Priority  = RG        Priority  = RG        Priority  = RG        Priority  = RG
 Level     = 0         Level     = 0         Level     = 0         Level     = 0
 Semaphore = CLEAR     Semaphore = CLEAR     Semaphore = CLEAR     Semaphore = CLEAR

 Ready                 Ready                 Ready                 Ready

-EXECUTION STATUS-                          -SYSTEM INFORMATION-

 Stop Time     = 600.0        sec            Maximum Wait       = 3       sec
 Elapsed Time  = 600.0        sec            Minimum Time Slice = 32      ms
 Total Count   = 2977                        Maximum Time Slice = 248     ms
 Run Status    = STOPPED                     Dynamic Variation  = ACTIVE
```

Figure 27-21. The Results of a Four-Process TP1 Run Against a Local Named Pipes Server.

Benchmark1 results: The MULTI screen in Figure 27-21 shows the results of a 10-minute test. During this period, a total of 2977 TP1 transactions ran successfully. However, only (712 + 742 + 748 + 740 = 2942) transactions had a response time under the 2-second threshold. Using the liberal interpretation of TP1 introduced in the previous chapters, this machine is therefore in the *4.9 TP1* range.

Commentary: This result shows a slight degradation in performance compared to both the local SQL version of TP1 and the local Application Remote Interface version of TP1. Why? Perhaps we could attribute this degradation to the interprocess communication overhead introduced by Named Pipes.

Running the Named Pipes Remote TP1 Remotely (Benchmark2)

The configuration for this benchmark is a four-client MULTI running against a remote database. The database is on a PS/2 Mod-80 with a 20-MHz clock and a 1000-KByte buffer.

```
                     Multiprocess Execution Example

Use arrow keys to move the cursor.  Use + and - keys to change field values.
Press R to start running, S to stop, or C to clear the count.
Press ESC to terminate the program.

-SQLTP1RQ.EXE-        -SQLTP1RQ.EXE-        -SQLTP1RQ.EXE-        -SQLTP1RQ.EXE-

Count = 761           Count = 762           Count = 779           Count = 782
TXNS  = 754           TXNS  = 755           TXNS  = 772           TXNS  = 774
Priority  = RG        Priority  = RG        Priority  = RG        Priority  = RG
Level     = 0         Level     = 0         Level     = 0         Level     = 0
Semaphore = CLEAR     Semaphore = CLEAR     Semaphore = CLEAR     Semaphore = CLEAR

Ready                 Ready                 Ready                 Ready

-EXECUTION STATUS-                          -SYSTEM INFORMATION-

Stop Time     = 600.0        sec            Maximum Wait       = 3       sec
Elapsed Time  = 600.0        sec            Minimum Time Slice = 32      ms
Total Count   = 3084                        Maximum Time Slice = 248     ms
Run Status    = STOPPED                     Dynamic Variation  = ACTIVE
```

Figure 27-22. The Results of a Four-Process TP1 Run Against a Remote Named Pipes Server.

Benchmark2 Results: The MULTI screen in Figure 27-22 shows the results of a 10-minute test. During this period, a total of 3084 TP1 transactions ran successfully. However, only (754 + 755 + 772 + 774 = 3055) transactions had a response time that was under the 2-second threshold. Using the liberal interpretation of TP1 introduced in the previous chapters, this machine is in the *5.1 TP1* range.

Commentary: Like the Application Remote Interface version of TP1, this result shows a substantial improvement in performance over the remote SQL version of TP1. In fact, this is the best remote performance we've seen in all of the remote benchmarks. This improvement is attributed to the better network utilization inherent in the stored procedures approach. A single message exchange takes place as opposed to an exchange for each SQL statement in the transaction. However, the results also show that Named Pipes' **DosCallNmPipe** utilizes the network very effectively.

Why does the remote version of the Named Pipes TP1 outperform its local version (*5.1 TP1s* versus *4.9 TP1s*)? What happened to the network overhead? A possible explanation is that the overhead introduced by the network is offset by the off-loading of the four client processes from the server machine.

Chapter 28

The Dynamic SQL Database Server TP1

This is the fifth chapter of the TP1 Benchmark Series. In this chapter, we develop a Dynamic SQL version of a TP1 transaction. Why would anybody want to run a TP1 benchmark on a *Database Server* using the notoriously slow Dynamic SQL? We do this to obtain a precise measure of *"just how slow is slow?"* Dynamic SQL commands provide maximum flexibility by preparing SQL statements for execution at runtime. You can think of dynamic SQL as an interpretive form of the SQL language. The database objects need not exist when precompiling dynamic SQL statements. The compilation of dynamic SQL statements is done at run time and must be repeated every time the same statement is executed. This flexibility comes at the expense of execution speed. However, there are many situations where the flexibility of Dynamic SQL outweighs its poor performance. The Dynamic SQL TP1 benchmark will give you information you can use for making *trade-offs between performance and flexibility.*

WHAT YOU WILL LEARN

The **SQLTP1DY.SQC** program we develop in this chapter is the Dynamic SQL version of the original **SQLTP1.SQC** program of Chapter 25. All we need to do in this chapter is code the Dynamic SQL version of the **tp1_transaction**() procedure and we'll have our final TP1 flavor. This chapter has the following prerequisites:

- The SQL Tutorial chapter.
- The **RSQL** chapter on Programming Dynamic SQL. We'll assume you're an old hand at this kind of programming.
- The first two chapters in the TP1 Benchmark Series. Much of the code in this chapter is identical to code you've already seen in **SQLTP1.SQC**. This common code will not be repeated. Instead, we will refer you to the appropriate **SQLTP1.SQC** listings where the common code is first introduced.
- You should review the **MULTI** chapters in Part II, and you should be familiar with **RSQL** at the user level.

THE DYNAMIC SQL VERSION OF TP1

The **SQLTP1DY.SQC** program is designed to run as a **MULTI** process. This means **MULTI** will create the process, pass it the parameters, and tell it when to start or stop executing TP1 transactions. When the process is told to start executing TP1s, it will go into a continuous loop submitting TP1 transactions against the database, and displaying the running count of the results.

LOCAL AND REMOTE TP1 CONFIGURATIONS

The TP1 transactions execute as Dynamic SQL statements against a database. This database may be either local or remote. The location of the database is totally transparent to the code. If the database is remote, then the **Remote Data Services** (RDS) component of the Database Manager will pass the SQL statement to the remote database using APPC/SQLLOO.

Each instance of **MULTI** can run four **SQLTP1DY.SQC** processes. If you need more TP1 generators, simply add more **MULTI** client workstations. Figure 28-1 shows you how to create a 12-client TP1 system. You can scale this configuration in any direction depending on your budget considerations. As usual, we will be scaling our experiments downward to a four-client TP1 system. We'll then run benchmarks against the local and remote database configurations to understand the overhead **RDS** introduces. The idea behind this dynamic benchmark is not to obtain numbers you can "write home about." Rather, the idea is to get a feel for how slow Dynamic SQL really is so that we can make intelligent design decisions on when to use it in our programs.

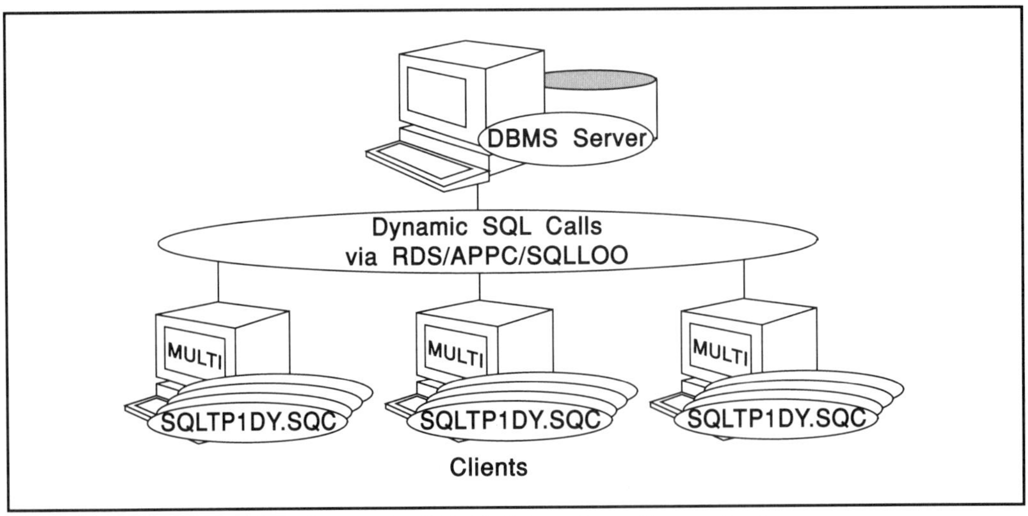

Figure 28-1. A 12-Client Dynamic SQL TP1 Database Server System.

WALKING THROUGH THE SQLTP1DY.SQC CODE

SQLTP1DY.SQC: The main() Procedure

In this section, we present the **main()** procedure of the **SQLTP1DY.SQC** Dynamic SQL TP1 program whose code listing is shown in Figure 28-2. You will find that much of the code is identical to the original **SQLTP1.SQC** code, from Chapter 25. This is not surprising since both programs are structurally identical. They both consist of a front-end which interacts with **MULTI** and of a back-end which uses the Database Manager's SQL API services.

The difference is that the code presented in this chapter performs the TP1 transactions using *Dynamic* SQL instead of *Static* SQL. What you will learn that's "new and exciting" is how to issue the TP1 SQL calls using Dynamic SQL statements. We will not repeat the code and explanations that you've already encountered **SQLTP1.SQC** program. Instead, we will refer you to the appropriate sections in Chapter 25. We only introduce code listings that do something new. The following is a step-by-step description of what **main()** does:

1. The program starts by including the C-language, OS/2, and OS/2 EE header files that are needed for system services. These are identical to the header files that were discussed in the previous chapters, since much of what we do is interact with **MULTI**.

2. The following program header files are included:

   const.h This is the same header file that was used in the previous chapters. Its listing can be found in Figure 25-11 on page 705.
   sqltp1.h This is the same header file that was used in the previous chapters. Its listing can be found in Figure 25-10 on page 703.

3. A structure of type SQLCA is declared.

4. The SQL WHENEVER directions are issued.

5. The SQL host variables are declared. This is where the fun starts. You will notice that most of the SQL statements used for the TP1 are declared as host variable strings. For example:

```
char  ins_hist[240]  = "INSERT \
                        INTO HISTORY(ACCT_NUM, TELLER_ID, BRANCH_ID, BALANCE, \
                                     DELTA, PID, TRANSID, ACCTNAME, TEMP) \
                        VALUES(?, ?, ?, ?, ?, 1, 3, ?, 'hist  ')";
```

   What are the question marks "**?**" in the middle of the SQL statement? These are *parameter markers*, or place-holders for variables whose data types are fixed but whose values are unknown at the time the code is created. A Dynamic SQL statement is prepared once with these place-holders and assigned a name. The name can then be executed multiple times using different parameter values each time.

6. The **main()** program follows and, as you can see, it's a carbon copy of **SQLTP1.SQC**'s **main()**. The key difference is in the helper function which executes the Dynamic SQL TP1. Here's what **main()** does:

   - It invokes the previously encountered **get_args()** function from Chapter 25. The listing for this function can be found in Figure 25-4 on page 694. This function obtains the arguments **MULTI** passes to the program. **MULTI**, of course, gets these arguments from reading the **MULTI.CFG** file.
   - It invokes the previously encountered **initialize_multi_ipc()** function, whose listing can be found in Chapter 25 in Figure 25-5 on page 695. This function performs all the interprocess communication chores required from a process that runs under **MULTI**'s control.
   - It invokes the previously encountered **initialize_task()** function, whose listing can be found in Chapter 25 in Figure 25-6 on page 696. This function connects to the database, installs a signal handler, and does all kinds of one-time housekeeping chores in preparation for the *big loop*.
   - It invokes the previously encountered **execute_task()** function listed in Figure 25-7 on page 697. This is the home of the *big loop*, which forever requests TP1 transactions. **MULTI** can at any time pause and resume the execution of TP1 transactions through semaphores. The TP1 transaction is executed by the helper routine, **tp1_transaction()**.

   Note: This is where we part company in a major way with the code in Chapter 25. The **tp1_transaction()** presented in this chapter (see listing in Figure 28-3) uses Dynamic SQL instead of static SQL. So, all we need to do now is see how this is done and we'll be finished with the SQL benchmark code, at least as far as this book is concerned.

```
/*****************************************************************************/
/*  PROGRAM NAME: SQLTP1DY - A process program that MULTI starts            */
/*                                                                           */
/*  PROGRAM DESCRIPTION:  This program is run as a child task of the MULTI  */
/*    program.   It executes the TP1 Benchmark program using Dynamic SQL    */
/*                                                                           */
/*****************************************************************************/
#include <process.h>                  /* For exit()                          */
#include <string.h>                   /* For printf                          */
#include <sys\types.h>                /* For time()                          */
#include <sys\timeb.h>                /* For time()                          */
#include <sys\stat.h>                 /* For stat()                          */
#include <stdlib.h>                   /* For atoi                            */
#include <stdio.h>                    /* For sprintf, printf                 */
```

Figure 28-2 (Part 1 of 3). SQLTP1DY.SQC: The main() Procedure.

```
#define INCL_VIO                          /* include VIO calls              */
#define INCL_DOSSEMAPHORES                /* include semaphore api calls    */
#define INCL_DOSMEMMGR                    /* include segment   api calls    */
#define INCL_ERRORS                       /* include error definitions      */
#include <os2.h>

#include <sqlca.h>                        /* sqlca                          */
#include <sql.h>                          /* error msg. retrieval           */
#include <sqlcodes.h>                     /* SQL return code constants      */
#include <sqlenv.h>                       /* environment functions and      */

#include "const.h"                        /* constants for multi            */
#include "sqltp1.h"                       /* tpl program vars, declares,etc.   */

/*_____________________________________________________________________________*/
/* database includes, defines, etc. for task function                          */
/*_____________________________________________________________________________*/
struct sqlca sqlca;

EXEC SQL WHENEVER SQLERROR CONTINUE;
EXEC SQL WHENEVER SQLWARNING CONTINUE;
EXEC SQL WHENEVER NOT FOUND CONTINUE;

EXEC SQL BEGIN DECLARE SECTION;
 long  acct_num;
 short branch_id;
 short teller_id;
 long  balance;
 long  delta          = 100;
 char  acct_name[20] = "<--20 BYTE STRING-->";
                  /*_________________________________*/
                  /* SQL statements for dynamic SQL  */
                  /*_________________________________*/
 char  sel_bal[120]   = "SELECT BALANCE FROM ACCT WHERE ACCT_NUM = ? \
                         FOR UPDATE OF BALANCE";

 char  upd_acct[120]  = "UPDATE ACCT \
                         SET BALANCE = BALANCE + ? \
                         WHERE CURRENT OF CURSOR1";

 char  upd_teller[120]= "UPDATE TELLER \
                         SET BALANCE = BALANCE + ? \
                         WHERE TELLER_ID = ?";

 char  upd_branch[120]= "UPDATE BRANCH \
                         SET BALANCE = BALANCE + ? \
                         WHERE BRANCH_ID = ?";

 char  ins_hist[240]  = "INSERT \
                         INTO HISTORY(ACCT_NUM, TELLER_ID, BRANCH_ID, BALANCE, \
                                      DELTA, PID, TRANSID, ACCTNAME, TEMP) \
                         VALUES(?, ?, ?, ?, ?, 1, 3, ?, 'hist  ')";

 char  sql_commit[8]  = "COMMIT";

EXEC SQL END   DECLARE SECTION;
```

Figure 28-2 (Part 2 of 3). SQLTP1DY.SQC: The main() Procedure.

```
/*--------------------------------------------------------------------*/
/* Main routine.                                                      */
/*--------------------------------------------------------------------*/
VOID main(USHORT argc, PCHAR argv[])
{
  get_args(argc, argv);             /*  get program arguments         */

  initialize_multi_ipc();           /*  Init MULTI semaphores/shared memory*/

  initialize_task();                /*  perform one time intializations   */

  execute_task();                   /*  Remote Procedure Call  loop       */

} /* end main */
```

Figure 28-2 (Part 3 of 3). SQLTP1DY.SQC: The main() Procedure.

SQLTP1DY.SQC: The tp1_transaction() Procedure

In this section, we present the Dynamic SQL **tp1_transaction()** procedure whose code is listed in Figure 28-3. This procedure executes the Dynamic SQL command strings, which were previously declared and intialized as the host variables. As you should know by now, the SQL statements that make up a TP1 transaction are known ahead of time. We also know, ahead of time, the SQL types of the data that is used in a TP1 transaction. The only thing we don't know is the actual run-time values for that data. What all this means is that we're much better off in terms of what we know in this chapter than was the case in the **RSQL** Dynamic SQL chapter. None of the statements we'll be executing here are as difficult as the varying-list SELECT we encountered in **RSQL**. We're *not* even going to be using a **SQLDA**. Here's how Dynamic SQL handles situations where much of the SQL statement is known at compile time:

- The part of the SQL statement we know is placed in a null-terminated string and declared as a host variable.
- The things we don't know at compile time are represented by "?" place-holders.
- We will provide the values that go into the place-holders when the statement is prepared and executed at run-time.
- Since all of our SQL command strings contain *parameter markers*, we have to separate the preparation of the SQL command from its execution. This is done using two verbs: **PREPARE** and **EXECUTE**.
- When a statement is prepared, it is assigned a name. We assign the names, **S1** through **S5**, for our five SQL statements when we **PREPARE** them. For example:

  ```
  EXEC SQL PREPARE S1 FROM :sel_bal;
  ```

  The statement above assigns the prepared **sel_bal** command to **S1**, which can then be executed multiple times using different parameter values each time.
- The **sel_bal** host variable was previously declared and initialized with the SQL statement:

```
char  sel_bal[120]   = "SELECT BALANCE FROM ACCT WHERE ACCT_NUM = ? \
                        FOR UPDATE OF BALANCE";
```

Our first Dynamic SQL command is a SELECT. This command requires, in addition to a **PREPARE** and **EXECUTE**, the declaration and use of a cursor. This is similar to what we did for static SQL. Here's how we read and update the TP1 ACCT table using Dynamic SQL:

1. The **DECLARE CURSOR** command is issued to make CURSOR1 a cursor for S1. Contrast this with static SQL where the full text of the select is declared as a cursor.
2. The SELECT is used to retrieve a row using the cursor verbs: **OPEN** and **FETCH**.
   - The **OPEN** verb with the **USING** clause substitutes the value in the host variable **acct_num** for the place-holder in the SELECT statement.
   - The **FETCH** verb with the **INTO** clause places the row in the host variable string **balance**.
3. To update the balance in the ACCT table, we **PREPARE S2** from the contents of **upd_acct** command string:

```
char  upd_acct[120]  = "UPDATE ACCT \
                        SET BALANCE = BALANCE + ? \
                        WHERE CURRENT OF CURSOR1";
```

4. We **EXECUTE** S2 to perform the actual update using the still open CURSOR1 and the appropriate run-time variables that are provided through the **USING** clause.
5. We **CLOSE** the cursor since the balance in the ACCT table has been updated.

The remaining two TP1 updates to the TELLER and BRANCH tables and the insert into HISTORY table are handled by simple **PREPARE** and **EXECUTE** commands. No cursor is needed. The simplest and last TP1 Dynamic SQL command to execute is COMMIT. Since this command has no place-holders, it can be executed with a single **EXECUTE IMMEDIATE** command as opposed to the two-step **PREPARE** and **EXECUTE**.

Congratulations, we have just completed the code for our fourth and final flavor of the TP1 transaction. Now let's run the benchmark on this flavor and see how it performs compared to its peers.

```
/*-------------------------------------------------------------------------*/
/* function for TP1 transaction                                            */
/*-------------------------------------------------------------------------*/
SHORT APIENTRY tp1_transaction(VOID)
{
  CHAR   msgbuf[512];

      /*---------------------------------------*/
      /* generate some random data             */
      /*---------------------------------------*/
  acct_num = (random1 * random2) % (tps*100000l) + 1;/* generate acct number */
  teller_id= (short)(random1 % (tps*100)) + 1;       /* generate teller id   */
  branch_id= (short)(random2 % (tps*10)) + 1;        /* generate branch id   */

      /*---------------------------------------*/
      /* get the current balance from ACCT     */
      /*---------------------------------------*/
  EXEC SQL PREPARE S1 FROM :sel_bal;
  if (sqlca.sqlcode != 0)
     {
       sqlaintp(msgbuf, sizeof(msgbuf), 80, &sqlca);
       printf("%s\n",msgbuf);
       print_error((SHORT)sqlca.sqlcode, "preparing SQL statement S1",
                   __FILE__, __LINE__);
       return(FAILED);
     }

  EXEC SQL DECLARE CURSOR1 CURSOR FOR S1;

  EXEC SQL OPEN CURSOR1 USING :acct_num;
  if (sqlca.sqlcode != 0)
     {
       sqlaintp(msgbuf, sizeof(msgbuf), 80, &sqlca);
       printf("%s\n",msgbuf);
       print_error((SHORT)sqlca.sqlcode, "during SQL OPEN",
                   __FILE__, __LINE__);
       return(FAILED);
     }

  EXEC SQL FETCH CURSOR1 INTO :balance;
  if (sqlca.sqlcode != 0)
     {
       sqlaintp(msgbuf, sizeof(msgbuf), 80, &sqlca);
       printf("%s\n",msgbuf);
       print_error((SHORT)sqlca.sqlcode, "during SQL FETCH",
                   __FILE__, __LINE__);
       return(FAILED);
     }
```

Figure 28-3 (Part 1 of 4). SQLTP1DY.SQC: The tp1_transaction() Procedure.

```
    /*----------------------------------------*/
    /* Credit the balance in the ACCT table */
    /*----------------------------------------*/
EXEC SQL PREPARE S2 FROM :upd_acct;
if (sqlca.sqlcode != 0)
   {
     sqlaintp(msgbuf, sizeof(msgbuf), 80, &sqlca);
     printf("%s\n",msgbuf);
     print_error((SHORT)sqlca.sqlcode, "preparing SQL statement S2",
                 __FILE__, __LINE__);
     return(FAILED);
   }

EXEC SQL EXECUTE S2 USING :delta;
if (sqlca.sqlcode != 0)
   {
     sqlaintp(msgbuf, sizeof(msgbuf), 80, &sqlca);
     printf("%s\n",msgbuf);
     print_error((SHORT)sqlca.sqlcode, "during SQL UPDATE",
                 __FILE__,__LINE__);
     return(FAILED);
   }

EXEC SQL CLOSE CURSOR1;
if (sqlca.sqlcode != 0)
   {
     sqlaintp(msgbuf, sizeof(msgbuf), 80, &sqlca);
     printf("%s\n",msgbuf);
     print_error((SHORT)sqlca.sqlcode, "during SQL CLOSE",
                 __FILE__,__LINE__);
     return(FAILED);
   }

    /*--------------------------------------*/
    /* Update the TELLER table's balance    */
    /*--------------------------------------*/
EXEC SQL PREPARE S3 FROM :upd_teller;
if (sqlca.sqlcode != 0)
   {
     sqlaintp(msgbuf, sizeof(msgbuf), 80, &sqlca);
     printf("%s\n",msgbuf);
     print_error((SHORT)sqlca.sqlcode, "preparing SQL statement S3",
                 __FILE__, __LINE__);
     return(FAILED);
   }

EXEC SQL EXECUTE S3 USING :delta, :teller_id;
if (sqlca.sqlcode != 0)
   {
     sqlaintp(msgbuf, sizeof(msgbuf), 80, &sqlca);
     printf("%s\n",msgbuf);
     print_error((SHORT)sqlca.sqlcode, "during SQL UPDATE",
                  __FILE__,__LINE__);
     return(FAILED);
   }
```

Figure 28-3 (Part 2 of 4). SQLTP1DY.SQC: The tp1_transaction() Procedure.

```
    /*------------------------------------*/
    /* Update the BRANCH table's balance  */
    /*------------------------------------*/
EXEC SQL PREPARE S4 FROM :upd_branch;
if (sqlca.sqlcode != 0)
   {
     sqlaintp(msgbuf, sizeof(msgbuf), 80, &sqlca);
     printf("%s\n",msgbuf);
     print_error((SHORT)sqlca.sqlcode, "preparing SQL statement S4",
                 __FILE__, __LINE__);
     return(FAILED);
   }

EXEC SQL EXECUTE S4 USING :delta, :branch_id;
if (sqlca.sqlcode != 0)
   {
     sqlaintp(msgbuf, sizeof(msgbuf), 80, &sqlca);
     printf("%s\n",msgbuf);
     print_error((SHORT)sqlca.sqlcode, "during SQL UPDATE",
                 __FILE__,__LINE__);
     return(FAILED);
   }

    /*------------------------------------*/
    /* Insert transaction in HISTORY table */
    /*------------------------------------*/
EXEC SQL PREPARE S5 FROM  :ins_hist;
if (sqlca.sqlcode != 0)
   {
     sqlaintp(msgbuf, sizeof(msgbuf), 80, &sqlca);
     printf("%s\n",msgbuf);
     print_error((SHORT)sqlca.sqlcode, "preparing SQL statement S5",
                 __FILE__, __LINE__);
     return(FAILED);
   }

EXEC SQL EXECUTE S5 USING :acct_num, :teller_id, :branch_id, :balance,
                          :delta, :acct_name;
if (sqlca.sqlcode != 0)
   {
     sqlaintp(msgbuf, sizeof(msgbuf), 80, &sqlca);
     printf("%s\n",msgbuf);
     print_error((SHORT)sqlca.sqlcode, "during SQL INSERT",
                 __FILE__,__LINE__);
     return(FAILED);
   }
```

Figure 28-3 (Part 3 of 4). SQLTP1DY.SQC: The tp1_transaction() Procedure.

```
        /*----------------------------------------*/
        /* Commit the transaction to database   */
        /*----------------------------------------*/
    EXEC SQL EXECUTE IMMEDIATE :sql_commit;
    if (sqlca.sqlcode != 0)
       {
         sqlaintp(msgbuf, sizeof(msgbuf), 80, &sqlca);
         printf("%s\n",msgbuf);
         print_error((SHORT)sqlca.sqlcode, "during SQL COMMIT",
                     __FILE__, __LINE__);
         return(FAILED);
       }

    return(GOOD);
  } /* end tpl_transaction */
```

Figure 28-3 (Part 4 of 4). SQLTP1DY.SQC: The tp1_transaction() Procedure.

RUNNING TWO TP1 BENCHMARK TESTS USING DYNAMIC SQL

Now that we've got some code, let's run some benchmarks to see how well this TP1 flavor performs. We will run two TP1 benchmark tests:

1. A **local** benchmark test where the client and servers are on the same machine. The machine is a PS/2 Mod-80 with a 20-MHz clock and a 1000-KByte buffer pool (see Figure 28-5).

2. A **remote** benchmark test where the clients and servers are on different machines. The client machine is a PS/2 Mod 70 with a 16-MHz clock. The server machine is a PS/2 Mod-80 with a 20-MHz clock and a 1000-KByte buffer pool (see Figure 28-6).

The two benchmarks use identical four-process software configurations. The **MULTI** configuration file used for both tests is:

```
PROGRAM_TYPE     = PROCESS
STOP_TIME_MS     = 600000
TASK_NAME        = SQLTP1DY.EXE 0 17 2.0  1;
TASK_NAME        = SQLTP1DY.EXE 1 23 2.0  1;
TASK_NAME        = SQLTP1DY.EXE 2 29 2.0  1;
TASK_NAME        = SQLTP1DY.EXE 3 57 2.0  1;
```

Figure 28-4. A MULTI.CFG File for Running Four TP1 Processes using Dynamic SQL.

The benchmarks are set up to run for 10-minute tests (i.e., 600,000 milliseconds). The response time threshold is set to 2.0 seconds, and a 1-tps database size is specified.

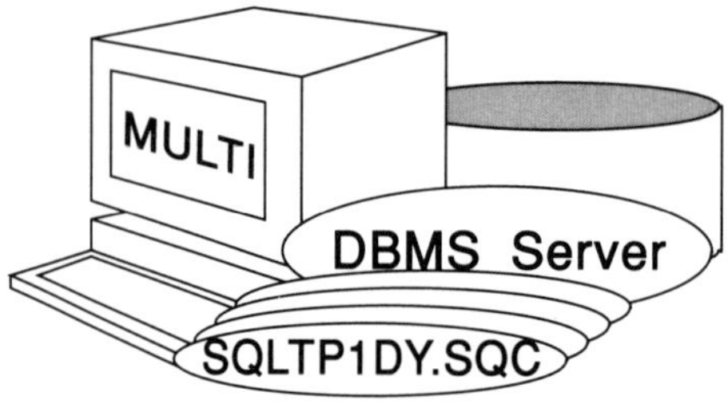

Test 1 20 MHz PS/2 Mod-80, 1000-KByte buffer pool

Figure 28-5. The Dynamic SQL TP1: Local Benchmark Configuration.

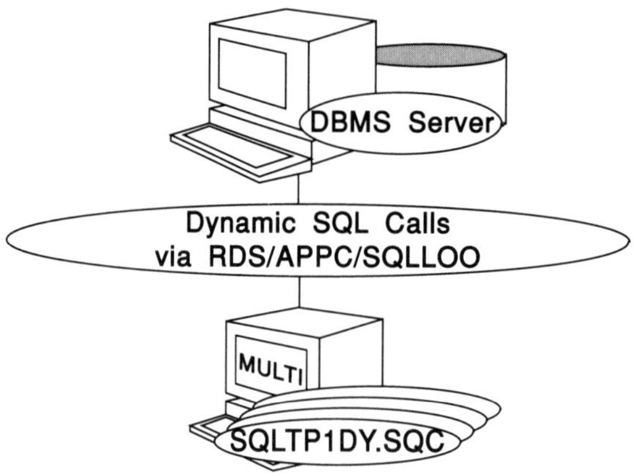

Test 2 Client: PS/2 Mod-70 16 MHz

Server: 20-MHz PS/2 Mod-80, 1000-KByte buffer pool

LAN: 4 Mb/s Token Ring/ APPC/SQLLOO/RDS

Figure 28-6. The Dynamic SQL TP1: Remote Benchmark Configuration.

Running the Dynamic SQL TP1 Locally (Benchmark1)

The configuration for this benchmark is a four-client MULTI running against a local database. The test is run on a PS/2 Mod-80 with a 20-MHz clock and a 1000-KByte buffer pool. We assume the database is already loaded for a 1-tps database scale. The following RSQL run is used to set up the 1000-KByte buffer configuration and prepare the database for the benchmark1 run.

```
--                    Change TP1 Database Configuration
-- ==========================================================================
-- logon
EXEC DBA: LOGON USERID PASSWORD DBSVRO3 UPM_LOCAL UPM_USER;
 OK, api_rcd = 0,          Execution time =     0.0000 secs

-- update the Database Configuration for database for a 500k buffer
EXEC DBA: UPDATE_DB_CFG TP1      MAXAPPLS    = 8,
                                 DLCHKTIME   = 10000,
                                 BUFFPAGE    = 256,
                                 LOGFILSIZ   = 50,
                                 LOGPRIMARY  = 2,
                                 LOGSECOND   = 20;
 OK, sql_rcd = 0,        Execution time =     1.3700 secs

-- Show the database configuration for database TP1
EXEC DBA: SHOW_DB_CFG TP1;

 Database Configuration for Database TP1
 =============================================
 Configuration Parameter           Current  Parm.      Parm.      Parm.
 Description                       Value    Units      Range      Default
 -------------------------------- -------- ---------- ---------- -------
 Max. Active Applications                8  Appl.      1-117          8
 Max. DB Files Open/Application         20  files      2-235         20
 Max. Files Open/Application           255  files      25-32700     255
 Buffer Pool Size                      256  4K pages     (1)         16
 Time Interval for Deadlocks         10000  millisecs. 1-600 sec.    10
 Max. Storage for Locklists              8  4K pages   4-250          8
 Max. percent locklist/appl.            22  percent    1-100         22
 Default Application Heap                3  segments   2-20           3
 Application Agent Heap                  2  segments   2-85           3
 Sort List Heap                          2  segments   1-20           2
 Database Heap                           1  segments   1-45           1
 SQL Statement Heap                     64  segments                 64
 Log File Size                          50  4K pages   15-255        50
 Primary Log Files                       2  files      0-63           2
 Secondary Log Files                    20  files      0-63           3
 Log Records/soft checkpoint           100  records    0-65535      100

 Current Log Location = C:\SQL00003\
 New Log Location     =
 Copy Protection      =    1
 Country              =    1
 Code Page            =  437
 Release              =  512
 OK, sql_rcd = 0,        Execution time =     0.3700 secs

-- bind the tp1 program
EXEC DBA: BIND TP1 SQLTP1DY.BND ISO REPEATABLE_READ BLOCK_ALL PUBLIC;
 OK, sql_rcd = 0,        Execution time =    14.5000 secs

-- delete all of the history data
EXEC SQL: DELETE FROM HISTORY;
 WARNING, sql_code = 100,    Execution time =     0.9700 secs
 SQL0100W  No row was found for FETCH, UPDATE or DELETE; or the result of a
 query is an empty table.
```

Figure 28-7 (Part 1 of 2). Preparing the Database for Benchmark1.

```
-- commit the changes
EXEC SQL: COMMIT;
 OK, sql_rcd = 0,        Execution time =     0.0300 secs

-- disconnect
EXEC DBA: STOPUSE TP1;
 OK, sql_rcd = 0,        Execution time =     0.7900 secs
```

Figure 28-7 (Part 2 of 2). Preparing the Database for Benchmark1.

```
                        Multiprocess Execution Example

  Use arrow keys to move the cursor.  Use + and - keys to change field values.
  Press R to start running, S to stop, or C to clear the count.
  Press ESC to terminate the program.

-SQLTP1DY.EXE-------  -SQLTP1DY.EXE-------  -SQLTP1DY.EXE-------  -SQLTP1DY.EXE-------

 Count = 250           Count = 246           Count = 253           Count = 256
 TXNS  = 71            TXNS  = 58            TXNS  = 78            TXNS  = 85
 Priority  = RG        Priority  = RG        Priority  = RG        Priority  = RG
 Level     = 0         Level     = 0         Level     = 0         Level     = 0
 Semaphore = CLEAR     Semaphore = CLEAR     Semaphore = CLEAR     Semaphore = CLEAR

 Ready                 Ready                 Ready                 Ready

-EXECUTION STATUS-----------------------  -SYSTEM INFORMATION---------------------

 Stop Time     = 600.0          sec        Maximum Wait        = 3          sec
 Elapsed Time  = 600.0          sec        Minimum Time Slice = 32          ms
 Total Count   = 1005                      Maximum Time Slice = 248         ms
 Run Status    = STOPPED                   Dynamic Variation  = ACTIVE
```

Figure 28-8. The Results of a Four-Process Dynamic SQL TP1 with a Local Database.

Benchmark1 Results

The MULTI screen capture in Figure 28-8 shows the results of a 10-minute test. During this period a total of 1005 TP1 transactions ran successfully. However, only (71 + 58 + 78 + 85 = 292) transactions had a response time that was under the 2-second threshold. Using the liberal interpretation of TP1 from the previous chapters, this machine is in the *0.5 TP1* range.

Commentary: How often is it that you can put an exact price tag on flexibility? We have it: Dynamic SQL is roughly 10 times slower than Static SQL. This is the high price you pay for flexibility. Do you need it?

Running the Dynamic SQL TP1 Remotely (Benchmark2)

The configuration for this benchmark is a four-client MULTI running against a remote database. The Database will be run on a PS/2 Mod-80 with a 20-MHz clock and a 1000-KByte buffer pool.

```
                      Multiprocess Execution Example

 Use arrow keys to move the cursor.  Use + and - keys to change field values.
 Press R to start running, S to stop, or C to clear the count.
 Press ESC to terminate the program.

-SQLTP1DY.EXE-        -SQLTP1DY.EXE-        -SQLTP1DY.EXE-        -SQLTP1DY.EXE-

 Count = 144           Count = 145           Count = 144           Count = 145
 TXNS  = 0             TXNS  = 0             TXNS  = 0             TXNS  = 0
 Priority  = RG        Priority  = RG        Priority  = RG        Priority  = RG
 Level     = 0         Level     = 0         Level     = 0         Level     = 0
 Semaphore = CLEAR     Semaphore = CLEAR     Semaphore = CLEAR     Semaphore = CLEAR

 Ready                 Ready                 Ready                 Ready

-EXECUTION STATUS-                          -SYSTEM INFORMATION-

 Stop Time      = 600.0          sec         Maximum Wait       = 3        sec
 Elapsed Time   = 600.0          sec         Minimum Time Slice = 32       ms
 Total Count    = 578                        Maximum Time Slice = 248      ms
 Run Status     = STOPPED                    Dynamic Variation  = ACTIVE
```

Figure 28-9. The Results of a Four-Process Dynamic SQL TP1 Run Against a Remote Database.

Benchmark2 Results

The MULTI screen capture in Figure 28-9 shows the results of a 10-minute test. During this period a total of 578 TP1 transactions ran successfully. However, only (0 + 0 + 0 + 0 = 0) transactions had a response time that was under the 2-second threshold. This machine is therefore in the *0 TP1* range.

Commentary: This is another dramatic illustration of *"how slow is slow"* when it comes to Dynamic SQL. You will need to think at least twice before submitting dynamic SQL statements over the network.

Chapter 29

Transaction Servers Are Best for OLTP

This is the final chapter of our OLTP benchmark series. We will present a summary of the TP1 Benchmark results so that you can have it all in one place for easy reference. We will also inject some further commentary on how the *network* and the *message-passing mechanism* affect the performance of client-server systems.

Database Servers

With a database server, the client passes SQL requests as messages to a database server. Only the final results of the data search are returned over the network. The code that processes the SQL request and the data reside on the same machine. This allows the server to use its own processing power to find the requested data, rather than pass all the records back to a client and let it find its own data. With this approach, the server code is shrink-wrapped by the vendor, but you need to write the client application. The requests a client sends over the network can be *Dynamic* SQL, *Static* SQL, or both.

So what can we say about Database Servers?

The results of the benchmarks from the previous chapters (see Table 29-1) lead to some interesting general observations about *Database Servers*:

- The network slows them down significantly.
- Dynamic SQL is very slow over the network. You should use static SQL if you do not need all the flexibility dynamic SQL provides.
- Invest in a "super server" machine if you can afford one.
- If you're going to use RDS and APPC, make sure to use the SQLLOO option.

Table 29-1. Database Server Benchmark Results.		
Benchmark	**Description**	**TP1 Rating**
Chapter 25/Benchmark1 **(see page 709)**	Stand-alone Static SQL Server PS/2 Mod-70, 16-MHz 500 KByte RAM buffer	4.7
Chapter 25/Benchmark2 **(see page 711)**	Stand-alone Static SQL Server PS/2 Mod-80, 20-MHz 500 KByte RAM buffer	5.4
Chapter 25/Benchmark3 **(see page 712)**	Stand-alone Static SQL Server PS/2 Mod-80, 20-MHz 1000-KByte RAM buffer	5.5
Chapter 25/Benchmark4 **(see page 712)**	Network Static SQL Server with APPC's SQLLOO option over a 4 Mb/s Token Ring (Server same as above)	2.7
Chapter 25/Additional Benchmark **(see page 715)**	Network Static SQL Server Same as Benchmark4 but uses standard APPC instead of the SQLLOO option. (Server same as above)	0.8
Chapter 28/Benchmark1 **(see page 776)**	Stand-alone Dynamic SQL Server (Server same as above)	0.5
Chapter 28/Benchmark2 **(see page 779)**	Network Dynamic SQL Server with SQLLOO over 4 Mb/s Token Ring (Server same as above)	0.0

Transaction Servers

With a transaction server, the client invokes "remote procedures" that reside on a server which also contains an SQL database engine. The remote procedures on the server execute a group of SQL statements (i.e., transactions). The SQL statements either all succeed or fail as a unit. You create your client-server applications by writing the code for both the server transactions and the client component which usually includes a graphical user interface. These OLTP type of applications tend to be mission-critical with 1-3 second response-time requirements (100% of the time). OLTP applications also require tight controls over the security and integrity of the database. The communication overhead in this approach is kept to a minimum. The exchange consists of a single request/reply (as opposed to multiple SQL statements). In the previous chapters we benchmarked two types of *Transaction Servers* using:

- Named Pipes
- The Application Remote Interface.

Table 29-2. Transaction Server Benchmark Results.		
Benchmark	**Description**	**TP1 Rating**
Chapter 26/Benchmark1 (see page 734)	Stand-alone Transaction Server RPC= Application Remote Interface PS/2 Mod-80, 20-MHz 1000-KByte RAM buffer	5.1
Chapter 27/Benchmark1 (see page 760)	Stand-alone Transaction Server RPC= Named Pipes (Server same as above)	4.9
Chapter 26/Benchmark2 (see page 736)	Network Transaction Server RPC= Application Remote Interface with SQLLOO version of APPC 4 Mb/s Token Ring (Server same as above)	4.7
Chapter 27/Benchmark2 (see page 762)	Network Transaction Server RPC= Named Pipes Named Pipes over NetBIOS 4 Mb/s Token Ring (Server same as above)	5.1

Note: RPC= Remote Procedure Call.

So what can we say about Transaction Servers?

The results (see Table 29-2) lead to some interesting observations about *Transaction Servers*:

- They are super fast on the network. In some cases, they are as fast as if the transaction executed on the same machine.
- Invest in a "super server" machine if you can afford one.
- If you're going to use RDS and APPC, make sure you use the SQLLOO option.

Conclusion: Transaction Servers are Fastest

Database Servers Versus Transaction Servers: the winner is...

Table 29-3. Server Network Performance Comparison			
LAN Database Servers		**LAN Transaction Servers**	
Dynamic SQL SQLLOO (APPC)	**Static SQL SQLLOO (APPC)**	**Application Remote Interface SQLLOO (APPC)**	**Roll-Your-Own Named Pipes NetBIOS**
0 TP1s	2.7 TP1s	4.7 TP1s	5.1 TP1s

The network performance comparison chart (see Table 29-3) shows that Transaction servers are super fast on the network, much faster than database servers (5.1 TP1s and 4.7 TP1s versus 2.7 TP1s for the Static SQL Database Server). These results demonstrate that Transaction Servers are the way to go for OLTP systems where the transactions can be pre-coded. The significant performance gain is directly attributed to the reduced network utilization of stored procedures. A single message exchange takes place as opposed to an exchange for each SQL statement in the transaction. The Named Pipes Transaction Server (5.1 TP1s) provides the best remote performance on the network. The Application Remote Interface also provides a respectable network performance (4.7 TP1s). Transaction Servers allow you to centrally manage (on the server) your transaction code. This provides an object-oriented flavor to network services. Security is also enhanced.

On the negative side Transaction Servers are not as *flexible* as Database Servers. They are not suitable for running ad hoc queries.

As a closing observation, life and client-server architectures are full of interesting trade-offs where the maxim *there is no free lunch* always seems to be with us. Our TP1 benchmarks served to make that observation painfully obvious!

Part VI

Presentation Services for Clients

This part of the book focuses on the design client applications. What all client applications have in common is that they request the services of a server and accept the results. What makes client applications different is how those requests are triggered and what user interface, if any, is needed. At one end of the spectrum, *simple* clients like robots, testers, or daemon programs generate server requests without having a human user in the loop. In the middle spectrum are applications in which client requests are human generated, but without the need for an elaborate graphical user interface. Examples of these middle-of-the-road clients are human requests assisted by automatic teller machines (ATMs), barcode readers, or touch-tone telephones. At the other end of the spectrum, all the requests to the server result from a human interacting with an elaborate graphical user interface (*GUI*, pronounced "gooey").

In this book, we will focus on GUI clients because they are a superset of all the client types. GUIs present many new opportunities. They allow us to move user interfaces from the dumb terminals (the "green uglies") to graphic dialogs, color, and the presentation of information in multimedia.

The design of *human computer* dialogs is one of the most time-consuming and least understood elements of client-server application development. It is relatively easy for an intelligent robot to generate a simple transaction. On the other hand, human driven dialogs that generate transactions are more intricate, ad hoc, and complex. This makes them much more difficult to design, build, and test. Ironically, this is a subject which receives minimal attention in proportion to all the headaches it creates. These headaches only get worse in distributed client-server environments, and the graphical world of Presentation Manager, and MS-Windows,

Part VI is about creating highly graphic front-ends to transaction servers. We will explain the principles of GUI design using IBM's Common User Access (CUA) Object/Action model. We will then introduce the tools that allow us to develop GUIs in record time. Tools allow your front-end code to be ported to multiple GUI platforms (such as PM and MS-Windows). This is a desirable feature in this age of rapidly shifting GUI trends and fads. GUI tools also help make your code more maintainable, thereby reducing the cost of software ownership. To make the discussion of

GUIs more concrete, we will create an interactive front-end client application using the Presentation Manager and Dialog Manager window services. The Dialog Manager is a little-known GUI tool that is bundled with the OS/2 Software Development Toolkit. This is the same toolkit that is required to develop Presentation Manager programs. The nice thing about the Dialog Manager is that it's practically free. *It doesn't require a runtime license fee* for the programs you develop on top of it. This is a very big advantage for the creators of low-cost client-server applications. Arcadia Technology offers a version of Dialog Manager which generates Windows 3.0 code (a runtime license is required).

Our approach is to use a GUI tool such as the Dialog Manager to create the bulk of our Presentation Manager (or MS-Windows) applications. We will program directly to the Presentation Manager from the Dialog Manager when we need to produce specialized graphic effects. Most importantly, we will demonstrate how this graphic environment can be used as a front-end for networked database transactions.

In Part VI, we will focus on issues such as:

- What are the elements of a human computer dialog?
- What is CUA, and why should professional programmers care?
- How do you evaluate Graphical User Interface (GUI) tools?
- What are dialog objects?
- What is the best way to write event-driven C programs in which the user is at the controls?
- What is Dialog Manager?
- How do you read a Presentation Manager Program?
- How to get the best of Dialog Manager and Presentation Manager?
- What are the architectural and conceptual models that can be used in the front-end environment?

Since we assume no prior knowledge on your part, we kick off Part VI with tutorials on CUA, GUI tools, and the Dialog Manager. We then introduce the Presentation Manager, with the goal of making you PM literate. We're not going to cover PM's 900 plus API calls. Instead, we'll focus on how to read a Presentation Manager program. We then show you how to drop into the Presentation Manager from the Dialog Manager. This is like writing in C and dropping into assembler when you need special things done.

Here is the road map we will follow in Part VI:

- In Chapter 30, "The CUA Standard for Graphical User Interfaces", we start our discussion of graphical user interfaces by introducing the CUA standard. CUA provides some extensive insights on the principles of human computer dialogs. We will cover some of the CUA principles for human computer dialogs.
- In Chapter 31, "A Taxonomy of GUI Tools", we explain what to look for in the area of GUI tools. Picking the right GUI tool is essential for doing serious client-server development work.

- In Chapter 32, "The Dialog Manager: A GUI Tool", we provide a tutorial on how to create screen objects using the Dialog Manager. We will show you how to create elaborate Presentation Manager screens without writing one line of PM code.
- In Chapter 33, "Programming the Dialog Manager", we provide a tutorial on the Dialog Manager's programming interface. You will learn how to manipulate the Dialog Manager objects from within your C-language programs. Programming the Dialog Manager is easy. It consists of learning 12 verbs.
- In Chapter 34, "The Presentation Manager", we provide a crash course in Presentation Manager "literacy." We focus on the structure of a PM program and on understanding the PM programming paradigm. At the end of this chapter, you should be able to read a PM program and follow its logic.
- In Chapter 35, "PM and DM: Two to Tango", we explain how Dialog Manager programs can drop into the Presentation Manager. This marriage (of convenience?) allows us to develop, structure, and maintain the bulk of our dialog code using the high productivity environment that DM provides, and then drop into PM whenever we need to develop some fancy graphic presentation that is beyond the scope of DM.

Chapter 30

The CUA Standard for Graphical User Interfaces

The real revolution in client-server architecture is in the graphic front-end. Ninety-nine percent of the multiuser database applications in the world today consist of dumb terminals attached to a host DBMS. These applications do not exploit the intuitive power of graphics. Moving the client code to PCs using the client-server technology makes it possible to front-end databases with the full power of a graphical user interface (**GUI**). This chapter starts off our investigation of graphical user interfaces for client-server by introducing the CUA model.

CUA PRINCIPLES FOR HUMAN COMPUTER DIALOG

Until recently, the design of dialogs between humans and machines was pure art and intuition. There were probably as many theories of *human computer* dialog as the number of computer users. There were also, unfortunately, many variants of sadistic command-driven user interfaces that were very successful at turning off large numbers of potential computer users. To those users who persisted, the name of the game was how to beat the computer by memorizing endless sets of commands and all the kinky ways in which they could be used.

The friendly *look and feel* of the Xerox Star and Apple Macintosh GUIs demonstrated that it was possible to introduce some method and kindness in the design of user interfaces. IBM's **Common User Access (CUA)** architecture, as described in the **CUA Advanced Interface Design Guide**, is probably the most complete attempt to codify the principles of interface design and common presentation techniques.

CUA Credo: The User is at the Controls

CUA is built on the following design concepts:

- The dialog should present the user with a consistent interface. The goal of CUA is to provide users with a familiar *look and feel* across applications. This consistency is especially needed in a multitasking desktop where the user can, at any time, switch back and forth between different applications.

- The user controls the dialog, not the computer. Users should be able to perform tasks in any sequence they choose. The computer should never ignore the user. Your client applications should always keep the user informed and provide immediate feedback. During operations of uncertain durations, be sure to display progress messages or status indicators.
- The dialog should incorporate familiar metaphors and represent them visually wherever possible. Metaphors help the user create a conceptual image of the subject and associate the interface with previous world knowledge. Examples of metaphors are: business forms, work folders, or desktops. An entire application can be designed around a single metaphor.
- The interface should be intuitive. Users want to concentrate on solutions and not on how the computer operates.
- The interface should *conform in a reasonable manner* to the user's expectations. The more natural that the interface seems to the user, the more it recedes from the user's consciousness and lets the user focus on the task itself.
- The interface should not rely on the user's memory. Controls should be visible and concrete. The user should be asked to *point-and-select* rather than recall commands. Point-and-select implies recognition rather than memorization.
- The interface should be forgiving of user errors. Users should feel comfortable *learning by exploring*. User actions that are potentially destructive should require confirmation. A cancel action should always take a user one logical step backwards in a dialog.

CUA and Object-Action Design

In a typical dialog, the first major hurdle for the user is getting started. CUA simplifies this hurdle by defining an object-action processing sequence for all applications. Users select certain objects, and then select the actions to be performed on these objects. This approach gives the users a feeling of freedom. They can select objects in any order, and they can then browse through an application's action choices to identify the action they want to apply. The object-action approach follows a *Noun-Verb* model. The user says "Here's an object (the noun) and apply this action (the verb) on it."

Why object-action as opposed to action-object? Objects are *things* that need to be manipulated; they are metaphors for real things in life. There are typically more things in life than actions on things. When an object is selected, your interface code can easily tailor the list of allowable actions and display them to the user.

You can reinforce the parallel between objects on the screen and real-life concepts through the use of icons (i.e., small pictures). CUA prescribes a consistent approach to option selections and entry fields. This is done through the use of metaphors such as check box controls, radio buttons, list boxes, combo boxes, and multiple-line entry fields. Actions are selected through the use of an action bar, pull-down menus, or action buttons.

CUA's Consistent Presentation

In a multitasking environment, many applications can share the screen. How? By having applications interact with parts of the screen, called *windows*, rather than with the entire screen. The user can then control the size and placement of these windows on the screen. CUA defines four types of windows that together provide a consistent application model:

- **Primary Windows:** These are windows that present the user with object choices, an action-bar, and pull-down menus. Every application has a primary window which is the main focal point of the user's activity. Primary windows persist throughout the life of an application. Primary windows can be moved and scaled by a user. A primary window can be minimized into an icon which represents a running application. When an icon is opened, its window is restored in the same position occupied before it was closed.
- **Secondary Windows:** These are windows that contain objects and action choices that are supportive of the primary window. Secondary windows can also be used to conduct parallel dialogs with users. For example, a help secondary window allows the user to carry out a parallel dialog independent of the window from which the help was requested. Secondary windows should be used to display dialog information which may require scrolling. Secondary windows can be moved and scaled by a user, and they are almost identical in appearance to primary windows.
- **Dialog Boxes:** These are windows that support dialogs. They are typically used to obtain or display additional information. They can be moved but not sized. There are two types of dialog boxes: modal and modeless. *Modal* boxes are used for serial dialogs, which must be completed before the user can resume an activity in the primary window. *Modeless* dialog boxes are available concurrently with the primary application. Modeless dialogs are used for displaying parallel (or non-modal) dialogs.
- **Message Boxes:** These are windows that convey unexpected information and errors to the user. They can also be used to ask questions. CUA defines three standard icons to help the user understand what action needs to be taken when a message is displayed: information, warning, and error. Message boxes can be moved but not sized.

CUA's Help Subsystem

Users can get contextual help at any time in CUA by pressing the F1 key. CUA also defines an extensive help subsystem with a Help Index and Extended Help to guide users through an application. Extended help provides information on the contents of the window from which the user requests help. The indexed help is even more extensive; it presents an alphabetized list of help topics to the user. The user can pick a help topic from the index and browse through the corresponding help screens. *Hypertext* links may be used within help windows to provide further information about highlighted words or phrases. The CUA help subsystem also makes help choices available through the action bar.

CUA's Advanced Features

Advanced CUA extensions provided by products such as **Office Vision** gives the user the freedom to carry out some functions without pull-down menus. A mouse is used to *drag* an object and *drop* it on its target. This is called *direct object manipulation*, a technique which allows objects to have actions directly performed on them. For example, using a mouse, a user can *drag* a file from one directory to another to move or copy it. Direct manipulation frees the user from language and makes applications more graphic. It provides a good fit with object-orientation and is especially well suited for applications such as graphic editors that require What-You-See-Is-What-You-Get *WYSIWYG* capabilities. Currently, some of the pitfalls associated with direct manipulation are:

- It is difficult to provide contextual help for actions.
- Some actions are impossible to specify with any precision.
- Actions with more than two objects are difficult.
- Some of the graphic metaphors are *overly stretched* and may end up confusing the user.
- Icons drawn by amateurs may not be recognizable to the user.
- The desktop can get cluttered very quickly with all sorts of graphic objects and parallel dialogs.
- Highly iconic interfaces make inflexible database front-ends. The current Relational paradigm for database is centered around alphanumeric data tables. The most flexible front-end to such a database is a tabular view of rows and columns of alphanumeric information. Custom graphics, however, can be hand-tailored to create very visual database front-ends that are application-specific.

CUA: Present Versus Future

Ever more advanced graphic objects can be envisioned that directly negotiate their interaction with each other through *object protocols*. Future applications will be built by creating ensembles of object capsules that work together in *task-force* mode. The user will be able to directly customize such ensembles through desktop meta-controls. The "unofficial" message we're trying to convey is that CUA is a moving target. CUA provides an acceptable *least common denominator* for a certain level of technology. You can be sure that CUA will not remain static in the age of multimedia and motion picture displays. The CUA project will always attempt to define a consistent presentation paradigm using a snapshot of the most economically available advanced technology at a juncture in time.

CUA '89 and "CUA 3"

The current CUA paradigm, also known as **CUA '89**, is a window-based graphic paradigm that is adequately supported by the current versions of Presentation Manager and MS-Windows 3.0. The *workplace* model, also known as **CUA 3**, extends the graphical model with direct object manipulation, object containers, and interobject communications. The *workplace* provides a visual space (think of it as a container) where related objects and programs can be brought together to perform a task. The desktop can contain multiple workplaces running concurrently. Both CUA models are described in the SAA **Common User Access Advanced Guide** (SC26-4582), published in June, 1989. The workplace model was included in the guide "to help you prepare for the evolution of CUA."

Which CUA Should I Write Code For?

The decision for commercial software designers is whether to be at the "bleeding edge" of display technology and invest a fortune in "groundbreaking" new user interface code and tools; or whether to use the current interface paradigm which, today, is CUA '89. Consider, when making your choice, that the user interface code has never been known to be a trivial development effort. It can easily chew up 70% of an application's development budget. Staying within the current paradigm provides the following benefits:

- A wide platform base with Fortune 500 acceptance.
- A well-supported graphical user interface technology.
- A common "look and feel" with Microsoft Windows.
- A wide selection of GUI tools.
- A level of stability which protects developers from being at the continual mercy of shifting Graphical User Interface *fashions.*
- A low development cost.

The approach we take in this book is to use the technology that gives us Presentation Manager screens for the least effort using IBM's *current* CUA paradigm. We prefer to let the IBMs and the Apples of the world educate the public at large as to what constitutes the next *common view* and, hopefully, a new generation of GUI tools will be available to help us develop software quickly and economically for this new common view.

The Dialog Manager is an example of a *current vintage* CUA-compatible GUI tool. We will use it to create and maintain some *very respectable* CUA applications quickly and at a very low development cost. The Dialog Manager has by no means the most state-of-the-art user interface, but it is solidly in the CUA '89 mainstream and is very suitable for creating front-end clients for database servers and OLTP. If you're willing to invest in some Presentation Manager programming effort, you can quickly extend the Dialog Manager with your own repertoire of *avantgarde* presentation objects. In the next chapter we will cover GUI tools. You will find that most of the GUI tools are capable of creating CUA '89 compliant interfaces. However, very few of them support the advanced capabilities of CUA 3.

Chapter 31

A Taxonomy of GUI Tools

A good client-server platform should be able to support the greatest number of GUI front-end clients. We feel the easiest way to achieve this goal is to build your client applications using a GUI tool and let the tool-vendor worry about porting the code to multiple GUI platforms such as PM, Windows 3.0, Motif, OPEN LOOK, and Macintosh. GUI tools also create more maintainable code and shorten the development cycle. There are dozens of excellent tools on the market, and it will be worth your while to do some comparison shopping. To help you with your evaluation of graphic tools, we will first point out some of the pitfalls to avoid in a tool. We then introduce a classification scheme that will help you sort through the paradigms on which the different tools are based. We feel that it is very important to use the right tool for the job, and that it pays to research the matter.

WHAT TO LOOK FOR IN A TOOL

We looked at tools from the point of view of what would be best for a C (or C++ when it is available) programmer. The discussion refers to PM, since this book uses OS/2, but *the concepts apply equally to Windows 3.0*. Here's a list of requirements we compiled when we did our comparison shopping:

- ***C or C++ should be in control, not the tool.*** In general, the non-presentation aspects of the client code should be done outside the GUI tool environment using a procedural language such as C or C++. The program should call the tool and not vice versa. We prefer to code the client initialization, LAN communications, and Remote Procedure Calls using C (or C++), as opposed to doing it from within the specialized and vendor-specific environment of a GUI tool.
- ***The tool should let you drop into PM from within it.*** This is an important requirement because PM will always contain new graphic constructs which a tool does not "yet" provide.
- ***The tool should be able to access C global variables.*** If not, we'll have to create protocols to copy everything back and forth. It's a headache.

- ***The tool should generate separate objects not in-line code.*** It is important to be able to maintain dialog objects separate from the code. This makes the objects more reusable and maintainable. It makes it easier to support other *national* languages. Tools that generate tons of in-line PM code should be shunned. You have to read, maintain, and manage that code. It is not a flexible environment and the code that is produced is hard to maintain and change.
- ***The tool should be fast.*** Some of the tools on the market are general purpose but interpretive. That's slow.
- ***The tool's runtime should be small.*** Some of the tools on the market require runtimes in excess of 1.5 MBytes. This is in addition to OS/2 and whatever code you write. Be careful; this added memory goes into client workstations which we would prefer to keep "skinny."
- ***No runtime license charges, please.*** Some of the best tools on the market require a runtime charge of over $150 per workstation on which they run. This adds to the cost of the client, to say nothing of how difficult it is to administer those charges on a LAN workstation basis. Remember, the competition to LAN workstations using client-server architectures is the $500 dumb terminal attached to a time-sharing minicomputer.
- ***Low-cost development package.*** Some of those tools cost over $7000 per developer software package. If you have a large team of programmers, this can quickly eat into your profits. However, if the tool *really* improves productivity, paying $7000 is a steal.
- ***Enforcement of CUA.*** The last thing you want to worry about is keeping up with the hundreds of little rules your application needs to adhere to in order to be CUA compatible. Let the tool do it for you.
- ***Multiple-GUI platform support.*** Pick a tool which allows your code to run on multiple GUI platforms, or at least the most popular ones. Today this means Windows 3.0, and PM if you need multitasking.
- ***Other value-added benefits.*** A long list comes to mind: a WYSIWYG screen painter, multimedia support, audio/image capture and playback, libraries of screen objects, clip-art, etc.

WHICH TOOL?

The Dialog Manager tool that comes with the OS/2 Programmer Toolkit comes pretty close to fulfilling the requirements list described above, and it is a better than average tool for creating OLTP front-ends. So, we will use it in the next few chapters to demonstrate how a GUI tool can help speed up the client application development process. But, what about the future? What will you need to create direct manipulation objects? What about multimedia? If you have such requirements today, you are better off with a more advanced tool than Dialog Manager. The GUI Tool Taxonomy which follows is to help you get a feel for what tools can do for you.

WHY ARE GUI TOOLS TAKING OFF?

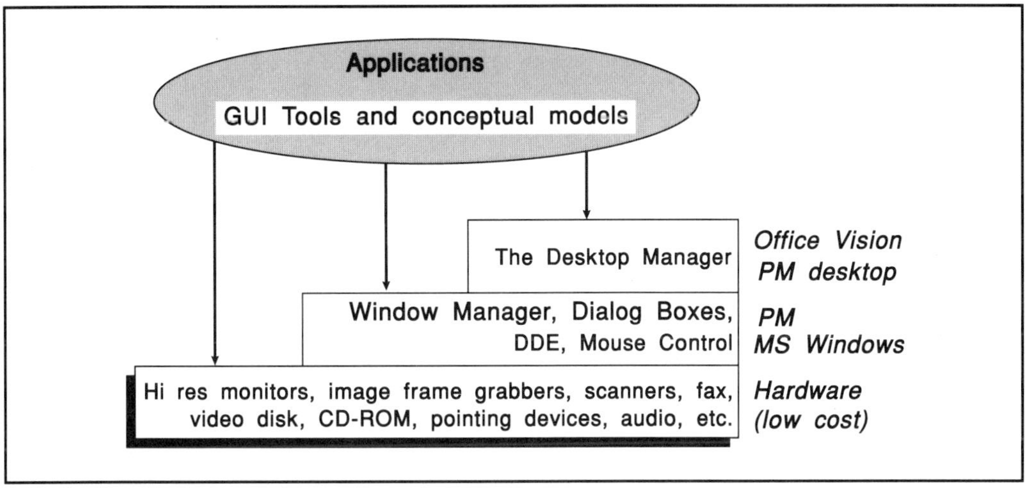

Figure 31-1. The Graphic Layers.

Graphical User Interface (GUI) tools are an exciting growth area whose time has come. Here's why:

- The graphic capability of PCs is improving in quantum leaps and it is now in the affordable price range. We're seeing more color and sharper screen resolutions at lower costs. PCs can attach to all kinds of image frame grabbers and scanners. Mass data storage for graphic objects is economically available with CD-ROMs and optical disks. What this all means is that the hardware for supporting multimedia is becoming available at the right prices.

- The base software platform to support GUIs is in place (see Figure 31-1). PM and Microsoft Windows are now available on a large installed base of PCs. This base platform provides graphic primitives, a window manager, icons, and data exchange facilities.

- The technology for GUI software to coexist on desktops is coming together. Standard desktops (such as OfficeVision) are defining how to start applications and how these applications should communicate using DDE, the clipboard, and "drag and drop" direct manipulation techniques. A rudimentary object model is enforced so that the applications appear to work together naturally, even when they are provided by different vendors.

A new generation of tools is focused on facilitating the design of screen objects that represent the user's activities. The emphasis is now on the relationship between objects and how they react to manipulation from the user and from other objects. Vendors are beginning to provide libraries of objects which an application designer can use to "plug and play." Another hot area of vendor activity is in the WYSIWYG screen layout editors to create graphic applications. Finally, we believe that all the pieces are here for tool providers to focus on making it easy to create graphic multimedia applications.

A TAXONOMY OF GUI TOOLS

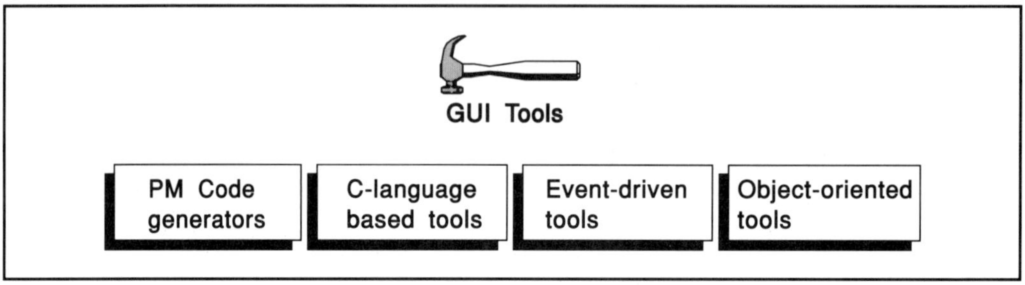

Figure 31-2. A Taxonomy of Graphic User Interface Tools.

There is currently an explosion of GUI PM tool offerings on the market. Many of these tools are the embodiment of many years of research in programming paradigms for graphic front-ends. They all promise to make you more productive in generating PM applications. Instead of reviewing all the tools on the market, we present in this section a classification scheme for tools based on the software paradigm they build on. As shown in Figure 31-2, we divide the GUI tools into four categories: inline code generator tools, C-language based tools, event-driven tools, and object-oriented tools. These categories are explained in the sections which follow.

Tools That Generate PM Code Outlines

The tools in this category generate PM code which you can include in your C-language programs. These tools usually provide a WYSIWYG editor with which you can lay out screens consisting of regular PM window classes. The tool then produces PM code including: (.C) files, (.H) files, (.RC) files, (.DEF) files, and the *make* file. The code creates the PM main() loop and provides skeleton window and dialog procedures. You can then edit the source code files created by the tool to add whatever code is required by your application. In addition, you must write the code which services many of the low-level PM constructs. For example, you have to provide the code which services: scroll-bars, action selections, information in list boxes, variables, help, display messages, etc. These are all low-level constructs that you would normally expect a tool to handle on your behalf.

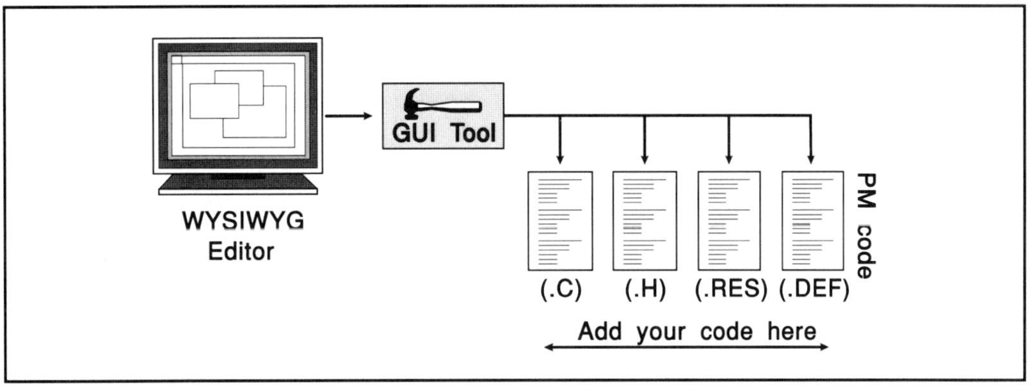

Figure 31-3. Tools That Generate PM Code Outlines.

Benefits: These tools are great for learning PM. They can be very useful if you plan to stay within the PM environment and your applications are kept small. These tools usually handle a lot of the CUA layout rules on behalf of your application. A final advantage is that tools of this kind are not too expensive (under $1000) and do not require a runtime license for the code they produce.

Costs: These tools provide a jump-start into PM, but eventually leave you inside the PM environment. You have to deal with all the low-level PM constructs instead of focusing on the logic of your application. You will essentially be maintaining and debugging a PM program. You cannot use this kind of tool for the direct manipulation of objects using "drag and drop" techniques, DDE is not supported, and you are mostly limited to creating PM dialog forms.

C-Language Based Tools

Tools in this category allow you to manipulate *external* display objects directly from within your C programs. It is business as usual for C programmers. You specify in your C programs which objects to display and when. Your interface to screen objects is through the familiar API method. You display objects and wait for events to happen. There are no control loops or event handlers or PM calls. The tool takes care of all these details. So, how do you specify your screen objects and their behavior? This is done outside your code. Dialog Manager, for example, lets you create display objects through the tag language. Other tools allow you to specify display objects and their layout through WYSIWYG editors (see Figure 31-4). One of the key areas which differentiate these tools is how data is exchanged with the screen objects and how the user selections (and actions) are returned to the C program.

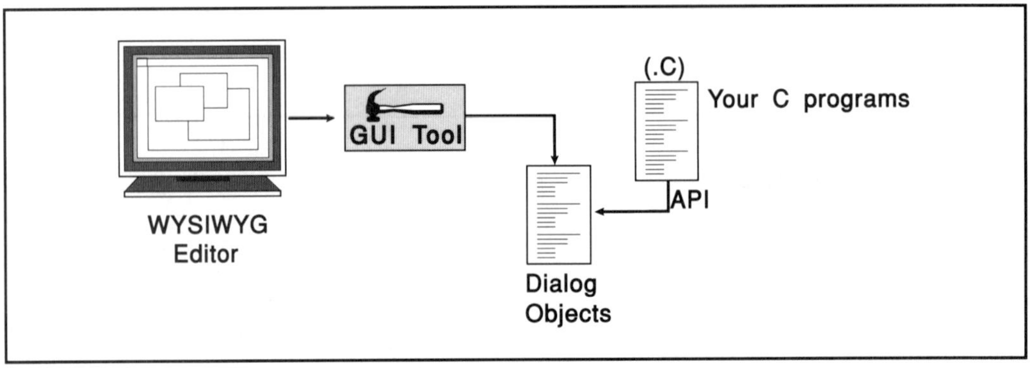

Figure 31-4. C-language Based Tools.

Benefits: It is business as usual for C programmers with the benefit that there is a clean separation of the C code from the screen objects. Screen objects are created and managed outside of the code. This helps program maintenance and allows the developer to focus on the logic of the visual elements independently of the code. You can impose by choice an event-driven methodology on your code. For more details on the benefits provided by tools of this type, please refer to "What Does DM Bring to the Party?" on page 872.

Costs: You're limited by the constructs which can be described using tags or the WYSIWYG editor. These constructs tend to be PM dialog-type forms. To fully exploit the power of PM, you must write PM code.

Event-Driven Tools

These tools build on the event-driven programming paradigm. They provide a full-fledged, event-driven environment where you can create your events and code the responses to them. They require that you plan your application event by event. For each event, you must supply the appropriate response. A WYSIWYG editor is usually provided by the tool vendor to define the windows and dialog boxes in your application. Some vendors call these event-driven tools: "programming with forms."

The WYSIWYG editor allows you to associate event names with various window components. An event can be a push button selection, a keyboard input, a mouse click in graphic areas which are made mouse-sensitive (*hot-spots*), etc. The editor will generate a core script (or outline) of object definitions and the stimulus events they produce (usually in an English-like proprietary tool language).

You can then add to the core script the action statements which describe your responses to the various events (see Figure 31-5). Most of the action statements will be coded in the language supplied by the tool vendor. You need to do that in order to take advantage of the libraries of "canned" actions that are typically supplied with the tool. However, most vendors will allow you to call C-language functions (packaged in

DLLs) from within your action statements. The source code for the script is eventually compiled into runtime files. The event-driven code executes when the end user performs actions like pushing buttons.

Two factors differentiate vendors in the "Event-driven" tool market:

- ***The scripting environment.*** The script is really an outliner for the program. A whole environment can be built around this outliner. Here are some examples of what the best of breed tools provide:
  - The text outline is used to navigate through the program. The WYSIWYG screen objects are displayed side-by-side with the outline code. A very complete browsing environment is provided. Different conceptual views of the outline are provided.
  - A debugging environment based on the outline. You should be able to run the program, set break-points and view the output from within the outline.
  - A code library and versioning system.

  The scope of the event-triggers. What is the level of granularity of the event-triggers? What information do they convey? How are event-triggers managed?

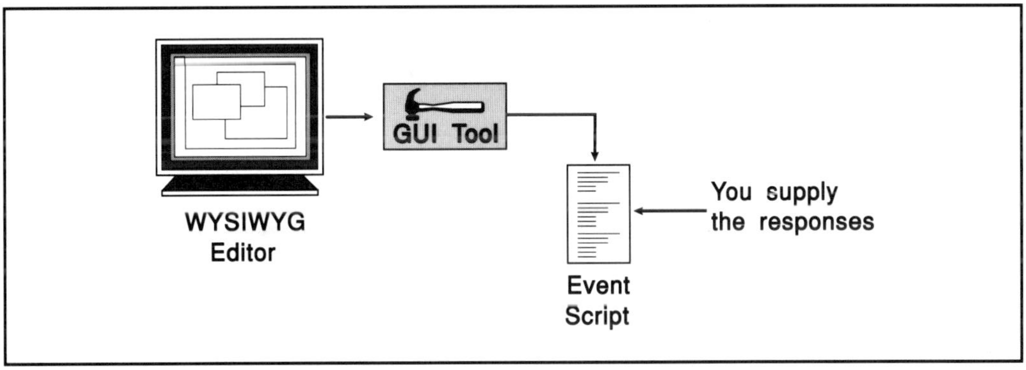

Figure 31-5. Event-Driven Tools.

Benefits: An event-driven program is a collection of responses to various kinds of inputs and stimuli. This is an elegant paradigm for organizing reactive user interface programs. Once a core script is put together, you can reuse parts of it with minor modifications for new applications. The control of events is organized via forms (or panels) which preserves the logic of the application.

Costs: You need to learn a new language and environment which is typically proprietary. Most of your front-end programming will be done using the vendor tool language instead of the C-language. All the screens required for an application get compiled into a single file which could become unmanageable for major applications. The constructs provided by the vendor will typically lag behind what PM provides. This means you'll still have to program in PM and C whenever you need to create user interfaces that go beyond the PM dialog style. The development environment for such tools is expensive (in the vicinity of $5000 for the better tools). These tools typically require a runtime license (of $150 or more per workstation). The runtime can also be a memory hog (1 MByte, or more in some cases).

Object-Oriented Tools

These tools probably provide the only "clean" way to build and maintain complex *direct manipulation* style user interfaces. Object-oriented tools use object-oriented language features to provide powerful libraries of reusable code and the "glue" that makes it all work together. You can then use this code "as is" or customize it to provide your own display constructs. The power of this code is that it describes not only the object's structure but also its behavior and its interface to other objects. The notion of independent interacting objects seems to naturally represent objects that can be directly manipulated on a screen.

Like the other tools, object-tools also come with WYSIWYG layout editors. These editors typically allow you to create screens from a library of predefined display classes. A *class* encapsulates (or brings together) data structures and the procedures that manipulate these structures (also called *methods*). Methods are invoked by sending messages. The bottom line is that when you create an object of a particular class, you automatically *inherit* all its methods and attributes. You can create your own composite subclasses from multiple parent classes and inherit their combined behaviors.

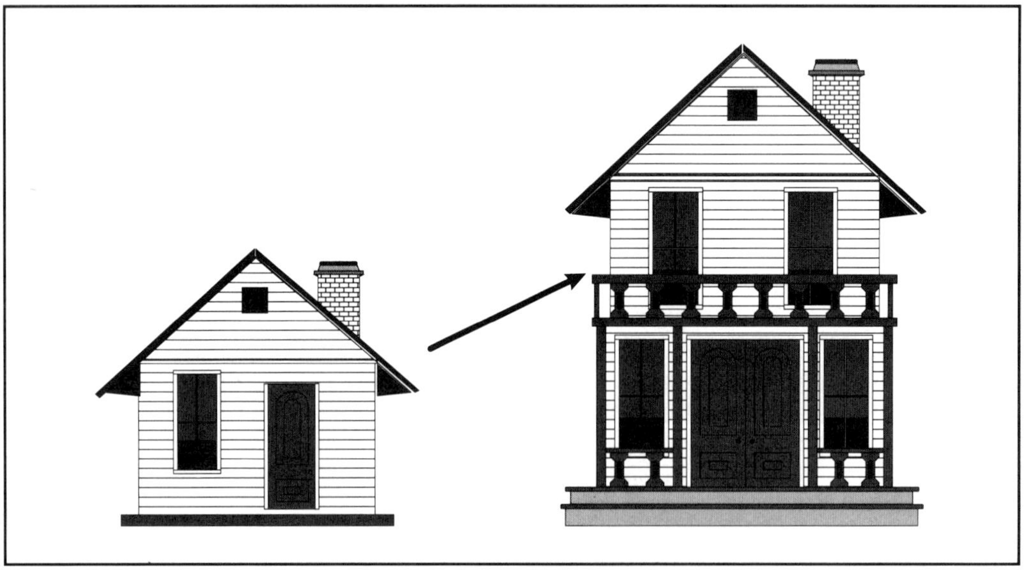

Figure 31-6. Subclassing with Single-Inheritance: Start with a House and Create a Mansion.

Figure 31-6 demonstrates *single-inheritance* subclassing. You take an existing class, such as house, and by adding your own methods create a "mansion" class. Figure 31-7 on page 803 demonstrates *multiple-inheritance*. This process allows you to create new classes by mix and matching the attributes of several parent classes. The figure shows how a motorcycle class can be created from the parent classes: car and bicycle.

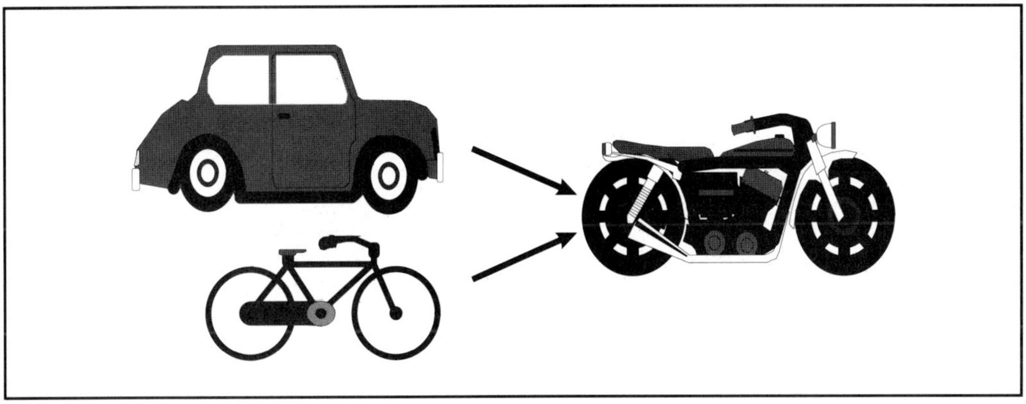

Figure 31-7. Subclassing with Multiple-Inheritance: Start with a Car and Bicycle and Create a Motorcycle.

Typically, you will use existing vendor classes and customize your own subclasses using the following object-oriented techniques:

- By inheriting *all* the class methods of a parent and augmenting them by adding some of your own.
- By inheriting *some* of the methods of a parent and overriding some of the methods with your own.
- By *combining* class attributes and methods of more than one parent class through multiple-inheritance.

The result is that you can mix and match objects to your heart's content using libraries of vendor-provided visual classes. The vendor is happy because even though you get all the effects of the objects, you never get to see a line of the vendor's code. It's all encapsulated in the objects. This is a classic win-win situation.

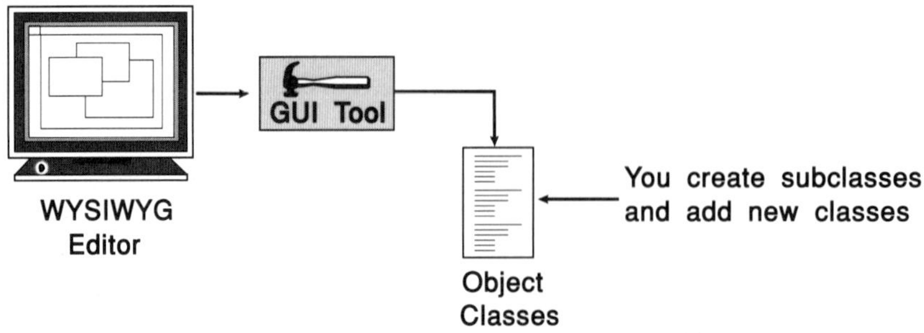

Figure 31-8. Object-Oriented Tools.

Benefits: You will be using the vendor's extensive libraries of debugged code. This gives you a lot of power for very little additional code. Typically, an object-based debugging environment is provided to allow you to place break-points on messages and look at the object's state. The environment typically supplies object-browsing tools which display class family trees. Objects can send messages directly to other objects instead of indirectly through an event loop. The object discipline makes you write your programs as a collection of reusable objects. Inheritance and method "overriding" capabilities encourage you to flexibly reuse existing code. This means that your programs will be highly maintainable and reusable. Because objects are self-contained, you can add features by adding new objects with a minimal change to existing code.

Costs: An object environment *really* requires an object-oriented language like C++ or Smalltalk. Most vendors today provide their own home-made object language on top of PM (they're all waiting for C++). If you can afford to wait, you may be better off starting with C++ rather than with a proprietary object language and environment. The major obstacle to most programmers in adopting object programming is the *steep learning curve*. It may take you up to six months to become proficient with an object-based environment and the vendor's class library. Much of this time will be invested in trying to understand what may appear to be a frighteningly large collection of vendor-supplied classes. Most beginners feel overwhelmed by hundreds of new classes, each with its own name, purpose, and messages. However, the consolation is that you can start out with a few classes and build your class knowledge base gradually (understanding how an individual class works is usually not difficult). Another problem is that you may still have to drop into C and PM occasionally to create graphic classes which cannot be subclassed from vendor libraries. Lastly, today's object-based tools are expensive. The best of the breed sell their development environment for $7000 (as we mentioned earlier, this money is well spent if the tool is good). A runtime license (of over $150 per workstation) is also required. The runtime can also be a memory hog (1 MByte, or more in some cases).

Chapter 32

The Dialog Manager: A GUI Tool

This chapter presents a tutorial on how to create screen objects using the Dialog Manager, a Graphical User Interface (GUI) tool. You will learn how to create elaborate Presentation Manager screens without writing one line of PM code. What makes all this possible is the Dialog Manager's powerful *markup* language for describing "dialog objects."

DIALOG OBJECTS AND C PROGRAMS

One of the major advantages of using the Dialog Manager is that it provides a clean separation of code from the dialog objects. This division is not unlike the way SQL separates the data objects from the C language. In the case of the Dialog Manager, the separation is between screen objects and the C-language. Figure 32-1 demonstrates this concept pictorially:

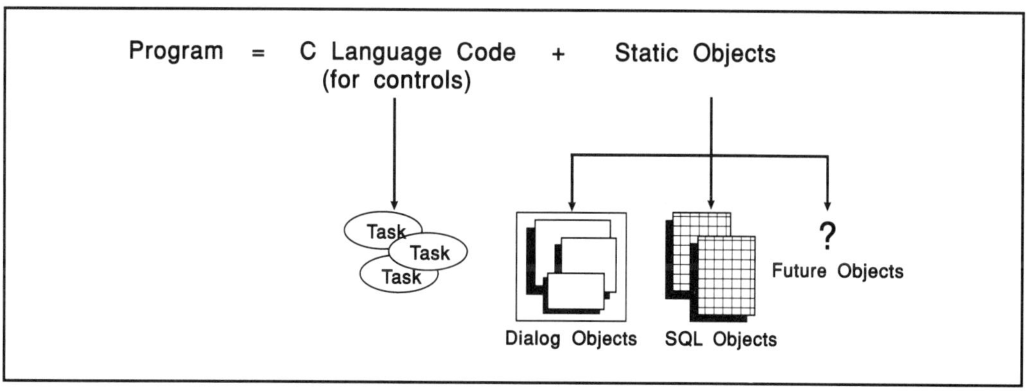

Figure 32-1. Code + Dialog Objects + SQL Objects + ...

Here are some of the benefits provided by the separation of Dialog objects from C-language code:

- **A lower cost of software ownership**. This is because the application is easier to maintain. The C-language code will be more structured, less massive, and easier to read. The division between the application logic and the screen objects will be enforced throughout the life of the application. Screen changes have a minimal impact on code. Screens can be reused and maintained in separate libraries.
- **Improved time to market**. This is because the application is easier to develop. Less code is required. The screens can be developed quickly and rapid prototyping techniques can be used for gathering customer requirements. The detailed control logic can be added when the requirements are better understood.
- **National Language Support**. This translates into widening the market for your applications. The separation of the code from the screen objects makes it easy to translate the application and help screens into different foreign languages. The translation can be done without recompiling your C-language programs. It is very important to think of national language support when dealing with applications that are front-end intensive.

So, all we're doing here is extending some sound software engineering practices into the area of front-end application design. This topic should be no more controversial than accepting SQL for the separation of data from C-language programs.

DIALOG MANAGER: THEORY OF OPERATION

In this section, we explain how the Dialog Manager works by walking you through a four-step application development process. Figure 32-2 provides the overall view of this four-step process. The detailed explanation follows:

Step One: Identify the Dialog Sequences and Objects

A dialog is the interaction between a person and a computer. You identify the elements needed to create a dialog by answering questions such as:

- What is the background and knowledge of your users?
- What are the parallel functions (or activities)?
- What objects go in the primary window?
- What subobjects need to be supported?
- What are the attributes associated with object and subobject types?
- Which actions can be taken with which objects? Which actions require additional information?
- What are the secondary dialogs created by an object-action selection?
- What are the responses to object-action selections? Which responses take a long time to execute? What C-language code is required?
- What are the input fields, output fields, selection boxes, and command buttons for each dialog window?
- What are the validity checks required for input data?

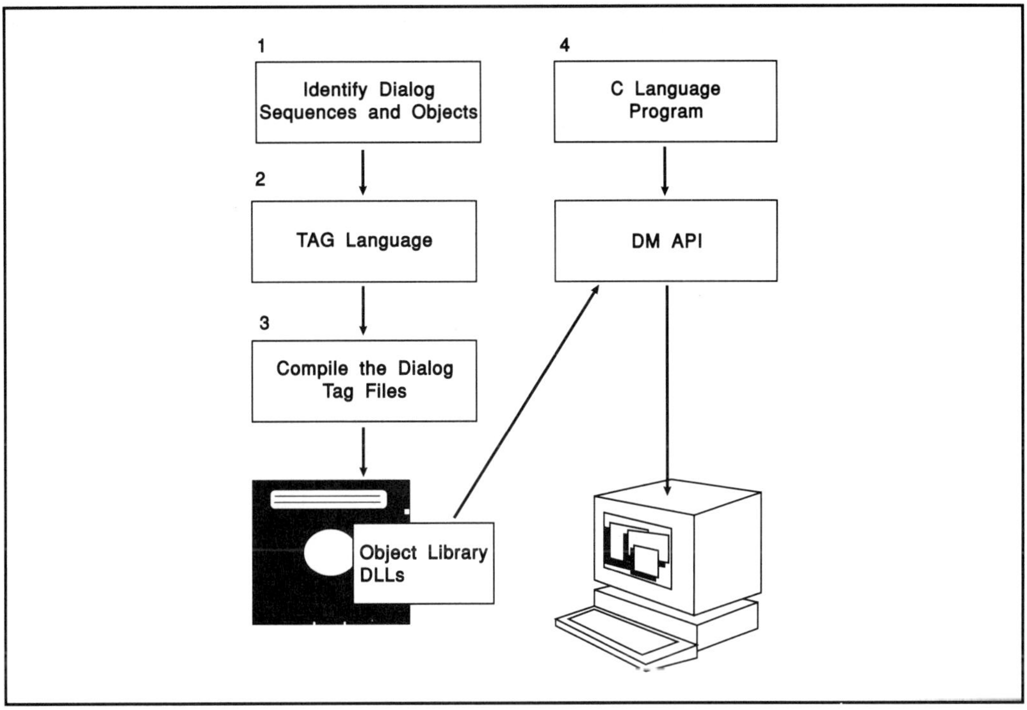

Figure 32-2. Dialog Manager Development Versus Runtime.

- What messages are needed to notify the user of notable events and errors in the dialog?
- What level of context help is required?
- What graphic constructs are required?

It is unlikely that any design will turn out right the first time. Prototyping and direct user involvement will undoubtedly be required.

Step Two: Create the Dialog Objects

The next step after you've identified the dialog elements is to use the tag language and a text-editor to write tag files that describe the panels and their contents. The Dialog Tag Language (DTL) is a programming markup language that is based on the **Standard Generalized Markup Language** (SGML). You use the DTL to define dialog objects such as:

- Primary and pop-up panels.
- Help panels.
- Variable pools.
- Messages.
- Commands.

Step Three: Compile the Dialog Tag Files

The next step in developing a Dialog Manager application, is to compile the tag source file using the Dialog Tag Language compiler. The compiler converts the tag files into a format that is usable by your DM application. In addition to processing the file, the compiler also checks and verifies the syntax of your markup. After compilation, the elements you defined in your source file are stored within libraries. The compiler output for dialog objects is placed in files with (.DTL) extensions. The help text is placed in files with (.HLP) extensions. For example, to compile a dialog named EXAMPLE.DLG, you enter from the OS/2 command prompt:

```
DTLC  EXAMPLE.DLG
```

The compiler creates EXAMPLE.DTL and EXAMPLE.HLP. DM also provides a display utility that you can use to display application panels and messages on your screen after they have been compiled. You can invoke the display utility by entering the following command at the OS/2 command prompt:

```
DMDISPLY
```

You then select the library that contains the objects you want to view. We explain the details of the Dialog Tag Language later in this chapter.

Step Four: Develop Your C-language Program

A C-language program in this case consists of a set of calls to the Dialog Manager plus the code that executes the tasks the user requests. For example, a travel agency program may consist of calls to the Dialog Manager to display panels that request input from the user, and to get the values the user enters in the panels. The program will take this input and generate a transaction against a database that may result in a reply that gets displayed to the user. The C-language program interacts with the Dialog Manager runtime services through an API which consists of 12 verbs. Using these verbs, your application can display panels and messages, manage variables, and control the flow of the dialog. The verbs can be grouped into the following four categories:

- **Display Services**, which display and remove panels, pop-up windows, and messages.
- **Control Services**, which begin and end a Dialog Manager application.
- **Variable Services**, which communicate information between the Dialog Manager and your C code. From the C-language you can define, copy, and delete shared variables.
- **Library Services**, which allow your application to specify a library or a list of libraries to be searched for panels. Libraries are used to store related groups of

panels. This can simplify the access, retrieval, and distribution of panels in the runtime environment.

These verbs will be explained more fully in the next chapter.

WHAT DOES A TAG LANGUAGE DO?

The **Dialog Tag Language (DTL)** is a tag-based markup language which is similar to IBM Publishing Systems' **BookMaster**. *Markup* is a term associated with document description. In the old days, typesetters used *marked-up* instructions to show how a document should be set in type. Today, it means the information that is added to a document to enable a system to process it. The Dialog Tag Language extends this *markup* paradigm to describe the characteristics of screen objects, their various interrelationships, and the processing actions they can perform. DTL tags specify the structure of each dialog element and the events they generate. Here are some of the benefits DTL markups provide:

- They are easy to use and somewhat easy to remember.
- They allow panels to be quickly changed without having to tediously line up titles and fields.
- They make it easier to maintain an application by separating the screens from the code.
- They provide consistency when many programmers are working on the same application.
- They allow you to easily prototype an application before developing the code.
- They make you think, early in the design, in terms of the structure of the various dialog objects and their interrelationships.
- They enforce some of the guidelines defined by the Systems Application Architecture Common User Access (CUA). This means that you do not have to be familiar with the hundreds of CUA guidelines, in order to create CUA-compliant applications.
- They make it easy to support "national" languages through special translation options.

Here are some of the negatives associated with DTLs:

- They may limit your artistic expression.
- They don't take full advantage of PM graphics.
- They don't support the direct manipulation of objects with mouse "drags."
- They create dialogs that are mostly modal.
- They require learning a new, non-visual tag language.

In the sections that follow, we provide an introduction to DTL and show you by example how to create some of the more common dialog objects. We will show you in later chapters how to get around some of the DTL limitations by dropping into PM from a Dialog Manager program.

CREATING DIALOG OBJECTS USING TAGS

In this section, we show you how to create Presentation Manager screens using the Dialog Manager's tag language. We start by showing you all the structural elements that go into a Dialog Manager object file. We then explain each structural element and provide examples of the screens they create.

The Anatomy of a Dialog Object File

Figure 32-3 on page 811 is a conceptual representation a dialog object file. You can think of this as a self describing object file which contains the following elements:

1. **A Document type**. This is a one-line tag that specifies the document type. Currently only the *dm system* type of markup document is supported.
2. **Variable Class Declarations**. The "types" of the variables you will be creating have to be defined explicitly in a variable class table. Here is what you can define using tag constructs:
   - The display width.
   - The data type.
   - The translations or transformations to be applied during input or output.
   - The validation checks to be applied on input.
3. **Variable Declarations**. Variables are used to obtain data from a screen dialog and pass it to a C-language application for processing and to write information from the application into output areas on the screens. Variables are also used to communicate information between tag objects. The result is that programs, panels, and messages can all use dialog variables to reference the same data. The Dialog Manager provides the mechanisms for "binding" C-language variables with the tag language. These variables communicate information between your runtime program and the screen dialogs. This means your C variables can be associated with input and output fields on a screen. Dialog manager supports individual variables or arrays of variables. Variables belong to classes that are specified in variable class tables.
4. **Command Definitions**. The Dialog Manager lets you associate executable commands with action bar pull-down choices, selection fields, or function keys. A number of built-in commands are provided by the Dialog Manager. Additionally, you can define your own application supported commands and you can override the standard Dialog Manager commands.
5. **Message Definitions**. These are custom messages that can be displayed in Presentation Manager windows when the tag logic requires it. You can specify the text of a message and its type. The type determines whether the message gets displayed in a notification, warning, or error window.
6. **Window Panel Descriptions**. These are the panels that will appear in the in Presentation Manager primary and popup windows. The Dialog Manager provides extensive tag language support for the design of the content and structure of CUA-compliant windows. Using the tag language, you can specify the window

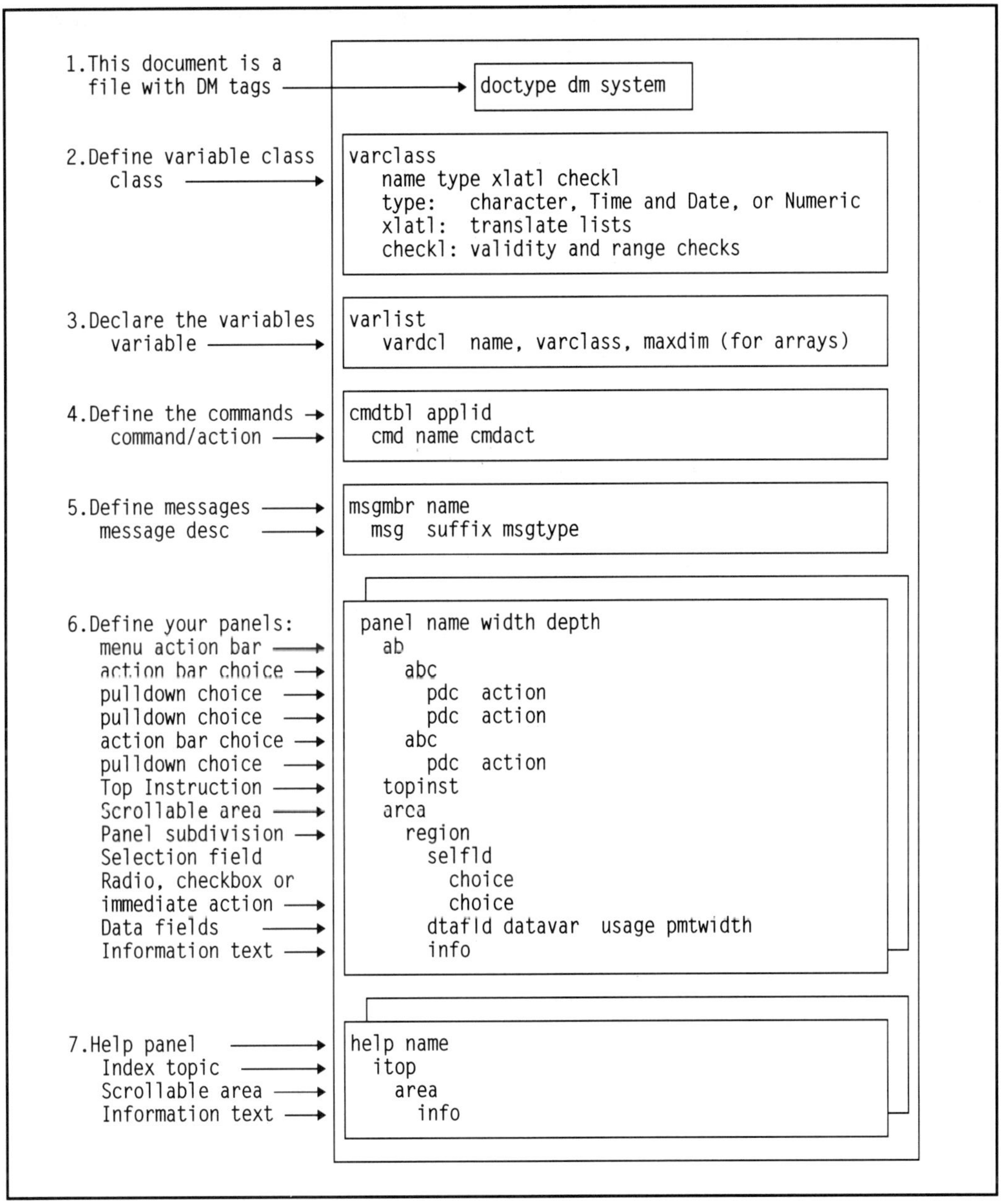

Figure 32-3. The Dialog Objects.

title, the action bar area, the panel body area, and the function key area. The panel body may include panel usage instructions, input/output fields, and selection fields. Input fields are the data areas from which you obtain information from the user. You can also obtain information through selection fields where choices are made. Output fields are areas on a panel where a program provides information to the user. Additionally, you can divide a single panel body area into multiple regions that each contain interactive fields. Scrollable fields are also supported, and can be used to navigate through arrays of information.

7. **Window Help Panels**. These are custom panels that will be displayed in Presentation Manager help windows in response to user requests for assistance. Through the tag language, you can create context-specific help at the panel or field level. You can also create an index of help topics and an application tutorial. Hypertext-like links can be placed inside your help text.

Tag Syntax Conventions

The DTL tags act as control words. The control words are enclosed within a set of delimiter symbols. **Start tags**, which initiate text interpretation, are preceded by the start tag open delimiter "<" and followed by the close delimiter ">". **End tags**, which explicitly end text interpretation, are preceded by the end tag open delimiter "</" and followed by the close delimiter ">". For example, the DTL tags used for defining the beginning and end of an application panel are the PANEL tag and its matching end tag, which look like this:

```
<panel>
</panel>
```

Many DTL start tags contain attributes and values that define various physical and functional characteristics of the dialog objects. For example, the PANEL tag has a required NAME attribute that you must specify in order for the compiler to identify the panel. In the example below, the PANEL tag has the NAME value *mypanel*:

```
<panel name=mypanel>
</panel>
```

The PANEL tag also has two optional attributes, DEPTH and WIDTH. These specify the dimensions of the PM window the panel appears in:

```
<panel name=mypanel depth=30 width=50>
</panel>
```

Values for some of the tag attributes are predetermined or obtained by default. A special type of markup is defined for providing directives to the tag compiler. This special markup uses the open delimiter "!" and is followed by the close delimiter ">". Here is an example of how you declare a document:

```
<!doctype dm system>
```

Comments use the special markup, but they must also be preceded and followed by two "-". Here's an example:

```
<!-- This is line 1 of a comment --
  -- This is line 2 of a comment -->
```

Defining Action Bars and Pull-down Menus

The best way to demonstrate the tag language is by example. Our first example creates a panel with an action bar. CUA recommends that application panels intended for display within primary windows contain an action bar. The action bar is a way to organize and group commands. The commands are made accessible when you need them and kept out of the way at other times. Here's how it works:

- The visible action bar (or menu) presents a top-level view of the choice of command categories available for this primary window.
- Each action bar choice is associated with a group of related actions that appear in a pull-down menu of command choices when the user selects an action bar choice. When they are not needed, pull-down menus stay out of sight so as not to occupy the "prime real estate" which makes up the primary window.
- When the user selects a command from the pull-down menu, it will result in some action on the contents of the panel (objects).

The tags you can use to create an action bar and its pull-down menus are:

AB The **Action Bar** tag starts the definition of an action menu. An AB end tag is required to bracket it.

ABC The **Action Bar Choice** tag defines each of the choices on the action bar.

M The **Mnemonic** tag allows you to specify a mnemonic character for an action bar choice or pull-down choice.

PDC The **Pull-Down Choice** tag allows you to define the choices on the pull-down menus.

ACTION The **Action** tag is coded within the PDC. It specifies what action is to be taken when a pull-down choice is selected.

PDSEP The **Pull-Down Separator** tag creates a horizontal divider line in a pull-down menu. It is used to visually separate groups of choices.

Figure 32-4 shows the tag language markup that was used to create the Presentation Manager screen shown in Figure 32-5.

```
<!doctype dm system>
<!---------------------------------------------------------------->
<!-- Example 1: Creating a menu action bar using DM             -->
<!---------------------------------------------------------------->
<!------------------------------------------->
<!-- Define a panel named EXAMPLE1          -->
<!------------------------------------------->
<panel name=EXAMPLE1 width=70 depth=20 >Action Menu Example
  <ab>
    <abc><m>Actions
      <pdc><m>Create
      <pdc><m>Update...
      <pdsep>
      <pdc><m>Save
      <pdc>S<m>end
      <pdc><m>Destroy...
    <abc><m>View
      <pdc>Sort by <m>Name...
      <pdc>Sort by <m>Data...
    <abc>E<m>xit
      <pdc>E<m>xit Sample Program...
    <abc><m>Help
      <pdc><m>Help for help...
      <pdc><m>Extended help...
      <pdc>Help <m>index...
  </ab>
</panel>
```

Figure 32-4. Creating an Action Bar Menu with Tags.

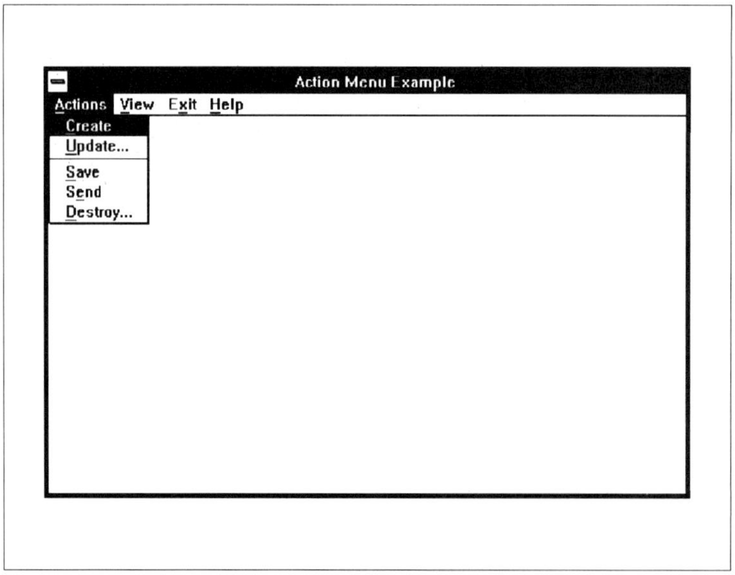

Figure 32-5. Action Bar and Pull-Down Menu.

Notice that no action is associated with the menu choices in the Figure 32-4. We need to specify actions to make our tag objects active. We do that by manipulating variables and executing commands in response to a tag selection. In the next few sections, we'll add to our tag repertoire how to create variables and variable classes, and how to define commands. We'll then revisit the menu example, and make it do something when a menu choice is made.

Defining Variable Classes

A variable class is defined with the **VARCLASS** tag. This tag has three attributes:

NAME This required attribute specifies the name by which this class will be referenced.

TYPE This required attribute specifies the type of data and its length. The data can be of the following types:

- **Character variables**. For example, 'CHAR 900' specifies a variable that can have a maximum length of 900 single-byte characters. DBCS is used to denote double-byte characters. ANY will enable your application for either DBCS or CHAR.

- **Time and Date variables**. The supported types are: **ITIME** stored as HHMM, **SDTTIME** stored as HHMMSS, **IDATE** stored as YYMMDD, and **STDDATE** stored as YYYYMMDD. The Dialog Manager displays time and date using the country code for your application and it will automatically perform the conversions to and from the internal representation. For example, for the U.S. country code format then **STDTIME** '122014' is automatically displayed as '12:20:14'.

- **Numeric Variables**. These variables ensure that a valid number is entered. When you use the **NUMERIC** type, you specify the total number of digits and the number of fractional digits. For example, 'NUMERIC 6 2' specifies a total of 6 digits, 2 of which are to the right of a decimal point. You can use the optional **THS** attribute to specify that the number is displayed or entered with the thousands separators. Dialog Manager will also handle negative numbers. For example, an internal format 'NUMERIC 7 2' may be '-99550.20. When it is displayed using the U.S country code format with 'THS=YES', it will look like '-99,550.20'.

MSG This is an optional attribute which specifies the message to be displayed if data that fails the validity check is entered.

Tagging Data Translation Options within a Variable Class

You can specify a data translation option within a variable class definition. This is done by embedding a Translate List tag **XLATL** and its required end tag within the VARCLASS. XLATL provides a useful means of translating a displayed value into a different internal value and vice versa. You can specify different translation options by the value you assign to the FORMAT attribute of the XLATL tag. Here's a sampling of the translate options provided:

UPPER This option converts a value to uppercase.

STRIP This option will remove leading and trailing blanks from a value.

CLASS This option allows you to create your own translations through a "user hook."

Tagging Validity Check Options within a Variable Class

You can also add validity checks to a variable class definition. This is done by embedding a Check List tag, **CHECKL**, and its required end tag within the VARCLASS tag. **CHECKL** automatically validates the data entered by the user after translation. Multiple check lists may be defined. All checks must pass for the data to be successfully accepted. You can specify the various validity checks by the value you assign to the TYPE attribute of the CHECKL tag. Here's a sampling of the validity checks provided:

RANGE This option checks that a value is within a numeric range. The lower bound of the range is specified by PARM1 and its upper bound by PARM2. These attributes can be up to 31 digits. They may contain a decimal point and they can be preceded by a plus or minus sign.

ALPHA This option limits the characters allowed to A-Z, a-z, and the space character.

CHARACTER This option allows you to specify a list of characters that are either allowed or not allowed in the data the user enters. The PARM1 attribute is assigned to EQ (equal) or NE (not equal) and the PARM2 attributes specifies a list of allowable or excluded characters. For example: 'AF123456789'.

VALUES This option allows you to check a user entry against a list of values. The value the user enters must match one or none of the values specified in the list. The PARM1 attribute is assigned to EQ or NE. The PARM2 value specifies the list of values. For example, PARM1=NE PARM2='Bob Dan' will check that the entered value is neither Dan nor Bob.

CLASS This option allows you to create your own custom checks through a "user hook."

Defining Variables

Dialog Manager variables are declared within variable lists. A variable list starts with a **VARLIST** tag and ends with a required end tag. Individual variables are declared using the variable declaration tag, **VARDCL**. This tag has three attributes, one of which is optional:

NAME This required attribute specifies the name of the variable.

TYPE This required attribute specifies the type of data and its length plus any translations and checks to perform on that data.

MAXDIM This optional attribute defines the dimension of an array variable.

Defining Commands

Commands specify dialog actions in response to a user selection, pull-down choice, or entry. You can create your own application-specific commands and register them in an application command table, or you can use the Dialog Manager built-in commands. The following is a brief description of the more popular built-in commands:

ENTER This command initiates the processing of the current panel.

EXHELP This command displays the help text for an entire panel.

HELP This command displays context-sensitive help at the field level.

HELPHELP This command displays a panel describing how to use help.

INDEX This command displays the help index panel.

EXIT This command requests that the current function be ended.

CANCEL This command requests that the panel be removed.

ACTIONS This commands toggles between the action bar and the panel fields.

PASSTHRU This command passes the command and any parameters to the C-language application through the ZCMD system variable.

SETVERB This command passes the command and any parameters to the C-language application. The command is placed in the ZVERB variable and the parameters are placed in the ZCMD variable.

BACKWARD, FORWARD, LEFT, RIGHT These commands are for navigating in a scrollable area.

You can create your own Dialog commands by declaring them within a command table that is defined within a **CMDTBL** tag and a required end tag. An APPLID four-character attribute is required to identify the command table. Individual commands are declared using a **CMD** tag and its required NAME attribute, immediately followed by a command action tag, **CMDACT**. An end tag is not required. The **CMDACT** tag has two attributes: ACTION and class. You must provide one these two attributes for each command:

ACTION This attribute allows you to specify a Dialog Manager set of actions for the command.

CLASS This attribute names a Presentation Manager class that processes the command. You have to code this class in your C-language program. This command is quite useful because it directly calls one of your procedures as opposed to simply returning control to your application.

An Example of Variables and Commands

Figure 32-6 shows a beefed-up version of Example 1, where we now do something in response to an action-bar selection. This example is not very exciting, but it does demonstrate how to use the new tag constructs for variable classes, variables, and commands.

```
<!doctype dm system>
<!--------------------------------------------------------------->
<!-- Example 1: Creating a menu action bar using DM             -->
<!--------------------------------------------------------------->

<!------------------------------------------->
<!-- Define a varclass named charl          -->
<!------------------------------------------->
<varclass  name=charl     type='charl'>
<xlatl format=upper>
</xlatl>
<checkl>
  <checki type=chars parml=eq parm2='123456789'>
</checkl>
<!------------------------------------------->
<!-- Define a variable choice of class charl  -->
<!------------------------------------------->
<vardcl  name=choice    varclass=charl>
```

Figure 32-6 (Part 1 of 2). Creating an Action Bar Menu with Tags.

```
<!------------------------------------------->
<!-- Define: A Command Table               -->
<!------------------------------------------->
<cmdtbl applid=mine>
  <cmd name=MYCMD>MYCMD
    <cmdact class='mycmdclass'
    parm='Hi there. Please process me'>
</cmdtbl>
<!------------------------------------------->
<!-- Define a panel named EXAMPLE1         -->
<!------------------------------------------->
<panel name=EXAMPLE1 width=70 depth=20 >Action Menu Example
  <ab>
    <abc><m>Actions
      <pdc><m>Create
        <action setvar=choice value=1>
        <action run=MYCMD>
      <pdc><m>Update...
        <action setvar=choice value=2>
        <action run=PASSTHRU>
      <pdsep>
      <pdc><m>Save
        <action setvar=choice value=3>
        <action run=ENTER>
      <pdc>S<m>end
        <action setvar=choice value=4>
        <action run=ENTER>
      <pdc><m>Destroy...
        <action setvar=choice value=5>
        <action run=ENTER>
    <abc><m>View
      <pdc>Sort by <m>Name...
        <action run=ENTER>
      <pdc>Sort by <m>Data...
        <action run=ENTER>
    <abc>E<m>xit
      <pdc>E<m>xit Sample Program...
        <action run=EXIT>
    <abc><m>Help
      <pdc help=PANHLP><m>Help for help...
        <action run=HELPHELP>
      <pdc help=PANHLP><m>Extended help...
        <action run=EXHELP>
      <pdc help=PANHLP>Help <m>index...
        <action run=INDEX>
  </ab>
</panel>
```

Figure 32-6 (Part 2 of 2). Creating an Action Bar Menu with Tags.

Defining an Icon

An icon is a picture that is used to represent an application. The icon is displayed on the Presentation Manager desktop when the application's primary window is minimized. An icon is also used to start an application from the desktop. The **ICON** tag defines an icon source file. This tag requires an end tag and two attributes:

NAME This attribute defines the name given to this icon resource.

SOURCE This attribute defines the name of a source file (.ICO) that contains the bitmap for this icon. You create this file using an icon editor. The compiler creates a dialog element from the information in the source file.

Here's an example of how this tag is used:

```
<icon name=CLUB source=CLUB>
```

Figure 32-7 shows how an icon is used to represent an application. Notice how the Club Med icon we created represents the application both in the application start list and on the desktop as a started instance of the application that is minimized.

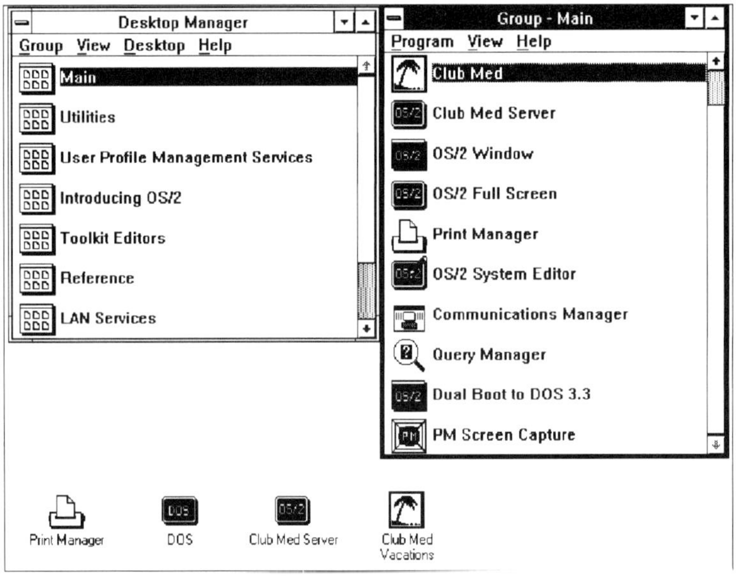

Figure 32-7. A Demonstration of How an Icon is Used to Represent an Application.

Defining Selection Buttons

Selection fields allow the user to select from a group of choices. You can specify using the tag language **radio buttons** for single choice selections, **Check-boxes** for multiple choice selections, and **push buttons** for immediate action selections. You create these selection objects by declaring them within a select field tag, **SELFLD**, and its required end tag. The **SELFLD** has a TYPE attribute which specifies the type of selection button. Your TYPE attribute choices are:

SINGLE Specifies single choice fields that appear as radio buttons. A radio button shows up as a circle and choice text. Radio button choices are combined to show users a fixed set of choices that are mutually exclusive.

MULTI Specifies multiple-choice fields that appear as check-boxes. Check-boxes are not mutually exclusive. They act like switches that are used to set Yes/No or On/Off type of choices.

ACTION Specifies a push button control. Push buttons, like action bars, are used to specify immediate actions. Action bars should only be used in Primary windows while push buttons are usually associated with Dialog and Message windows. Object-action dialogs let users think in terms of a two-stage process: "This is what I want done; now do it." The "do it" part is provided by push buttons and action bars (i.e., menus). A push button is a rounded-corner rectangle, which encloses text that describes the action which occurs when the button is selected.

Individual choices are declared using a **CHOICE** tag and its two required attributes:

CHECKVAR This attribute defines a variable which is used in conjunction with the MATCH attribute to preselect a choice, and to return which choice was selected by the user. Single choice fields all use the same check variable. With multiple-choice fields a unique check variable is defined for each choice.

MATCH This attribute defines the value that goes into CHECKVAR to preselect a choice or to indicate which choice was made.

In addition, you must specify for each choice item a string of descriptive text not to exceed 40 bytes.

Defining Top and Bottom Instructions

Top instructions define text that tells the user how to interact with the panel. Bottom instructions appear at the bottom of a panel and tell the user how to continue with an application. These instructions are coded using the **TOPINST** and **BOTINST** tags, neither of which require an end tag.

Defining Scrollable Areas

The **AREA** tag and its required end tag defines a scrollable portion of a panel. Dialog Manager will automatically place vertical or horizontal scroll bars to bring into view the contents of the area contents that are not visible. Help panels always have a visible vertical scroll (but no horizontal scroll bar). You can use the MARGINW attribute to increase the margin on the left side of a scrollable area. The default margin is one-character wide.

Defining Panel Regions

The **REGION** and its required end tag is very useful for more finely defining how information is grouped and arranged on a panel. The DIR, direction attribute specifies whether the elements within a region are arranged vertically (the default) or horizontally (HORIZ).

Defining Panel Dividers

The **DIVIDER** tag defines a blank or solid line divider within a region. This directive helps the Dialog Manager group panel elements within a region. The direction of the divider line is determined by the direction of the region it is coded within. In a vertical region, the line is horizontal; in a horizontal region, the line is vertical. The separator tag uses the following three attributes:

TYPE This attribute specifies the type of divider line. NONE, the default, specifies a blank line; SOLID specifies a solid line.

GAP This attribute set to NO creates a divider line that crosses from one side of the enclosing region to the other. When set to YES, the default, a 1-character unit gap is created at each end of the divider line.

GUTTER This attribute specifies the size (in character units) of any additional space you want added on either side of the divider line.

Defining Data Fields

Information is exchanged in a dialog through the use of interactive data fields. A data field is defined using the **DTAFLD** tag and its required end tag. Here are some of the more important attributes that can be specified within a data field tag:

HELP This optional attribute specifies the name of the help panel associated with that field.

DATAVAR This required attribute specifies the variable name that contains the field data.

USAGE This optional attribute specifies whether the field is for input-only (IN), output-only (OUT), or both (BOTH). The default is BOTH.

REQUIRED This optional attribute specifies if the field requires input (YES). The default is NO. A MSG attribute may be used to specify the ID of a message that gets displayed when the user does not complete a required entry.

ENTWIDTH This optional attribute defines the data field size.

PMTWIDTH This optional attribute specifies the width of the prompt field. Otherwise, the default is the width of the prompt text.

AUTOCLR This optional attribute specifies whether the field will be cleared on input of new data. The contents of an auto-clear field are erased when the user types the first character in the field. The default is NO.

ALIGN This optional attribute specifies the alignment of the variable value within a field. The default is START for left-justified. Other choices are END and CENTER.

PMTLOC This optional attribute specifies whether the prompt text is to be placed BEFORE (in front) or ABOVE the data field. The default is BEFORE.

DISPLAY This optional attribute specifies whether the data is displayed in the field when the user types it. The default is YES.

PROMPT This optional field specifies the prompt text for that field.

A related tag is **DATAFLDD**, which defines descriptive text that is placed to the right of a data field. This optional tag is used to explain what the user can enter in a field.

An Example: Selection Buttons, Areas, Regions, and Data Fields

Figure 32-8 demonstrates how the tag concepts we just introduced are used to create a take-out pizza ordering *form*. A form is a type of screen used to collect information. Forms are frequently used for OLTP type high-volume repetitive tasks. The screen shown in Figure 32-9 is an example of what you can do with Areas, Regions, Selector Buttons, and Data Field tags.

```
<!doctype dm system>
<!--------------------------------------------------------------->
<!-- Example 2: Creating a Pizza Take-out Pizza Order Screen      -->
<!--------------------------------------------------------------->
<!------------------------------------------->
<!-- Define  varclass                      -->
<!------------------------------------------->
<varclass  name=char1     type='char1'>
<varclass  name=char2     type='char2'>
<varclass  name=char8     type='char8'>
<varclass  name=char20    type='char20'>

<!------------------------------------------->
<!-- Define variables                      -->
<!------------------------------------------->
<varlist>
  <vardcl  name= size      varclass=char1>
  <vardcl  name= garlic    varclass=char1>
  <vardcl  name= pesto     varclass=char1>
  <vardcl  name= ham       varclass=char1>
  <vardcl  name= beef      varclass=char1>
  <vardcl  name= sausage   varclass=char1>
  <vardcl  name= pepperoni varclass=char1>
  <vardcl  name= salami    varclass=char1>
  <vardcl  name= tomato    varclass=char1>
  <vardcl  name= olives    varclass=char1>
  <vardcl  name= anch      varclass=char1>
  <vardcl  name= name      varclass=char20>
  <vardcl  name= tele      varclass=char8>
  <vardcl  name= by        varclass=char2>
</varlist>

<!------------------------------------------->
<!-- Define a panel named EXAMPLE2         -->
<!------------------------------------------->
<panel name=EXAMPLE2 width=70 depth=20 >Pizza Ordering Example
 <area>
  <topinst> Select Pizza Size and check additional items:
       <selfld dir=horiz selwidth=12>Pizza Size:
          <choice checkvar=size match=S>Small
          <choice checkvar=size match=M>Medium
          <choice checkvar=size match=L>Large
          <choice checkvar=size match=H>Huge
       </selfld>
  <divider gutter=3 type=solid>
       <selfld type=multi dir=horiz selwidth=12>Additionals:
          <choice checkvar=garlic>Garlic
          <choice checkvar=pesto>Pesto
          <choice checkvar=ham>Ham
          <choice checkvar=beef>Beef
          <choice checkvar=sausage>Sausage
       </selfld>
```

Figure 32-8 (Part 1 of 2). A Take-out Pizza Ordering Example.

```
    <divider>
         <selfld type=multi dir=horiz selwidth=12>
            <choice checkvar=pepperoni>Pepperoni
            <choice checkvar=salami>Salami
            <choice checkvar=tomato>Tomatoes
            <choice checkvar=olives>Olives
            <choice checkvar=anch>Anchovies
         </selfld>
    <divider gutter=3 type=solid>
         <dtacol pmtwidth=11 entwidth=20 deswidth=24
           <dtafld datavar=name>Name
             <dtafldd>Customer's last name
           <dtafld datavar=tele>Telephone
             <dtafldd>home or work
           <dtafld datavar=by>by:
             <dtafldd>your initials here
    <divider gutter=2>
    <region dir=horiz>
         <divider gutter=10>
         <selfld type=action>
           <choice>OK
             <action run=ENTER>
    <divider gutter=5>
         <selfld type=action>
           <choice>CANCEL
             <action run=CANCEL>
    <divider gutter=5>
         <selfld type=action>
           <choice>HELP
             <action run=EXHELP>
    </region>
   </area>
  </panel>
```

Figure 32-8 (Part 2 of 2). A Take-out Pizza Ordering Example.

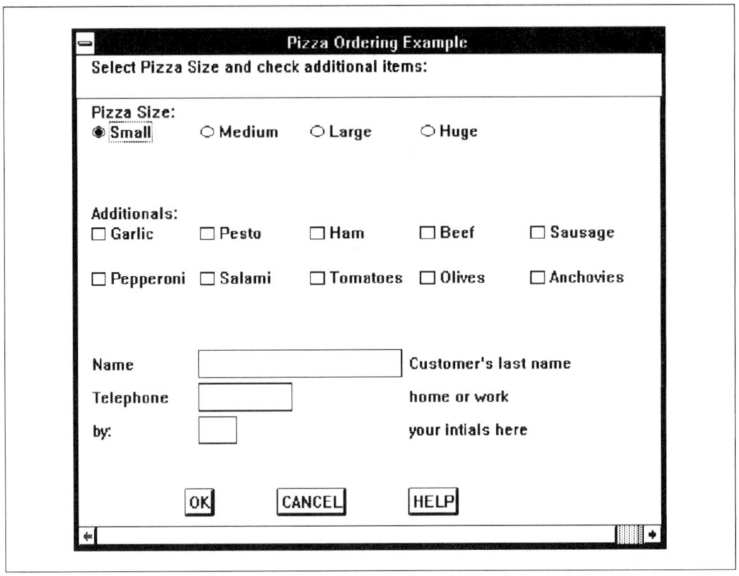

Figure 32-9. The Take-out Pizza Order Screen.

Selection Lists

An important dialog requirement for database front-ends is the ability to display a list of rows and allow a user to select and highlight one or more rows from the list. The **SELLST** tag defines a scrollable list from which the user can select choices. The items displayed in the selection lists are defined by an array variable in an embedded **SELCOL** tag. Here are some of the more important attributes that can be specified within a SELLST tag:

HELP This optional attribute specifies the name of the help panel associated with that list.

SELVAR This optional attribute specifies the name of a variable that indicates the index of the array items preselected by the application and/or selected by the user. This variable must be an array if MULTI selections are enabled. When control returns to the C application, this variable will contain "ones" for the list elements that were selected by the user.

TYPE This optional attribute specifies whether the list is single-choice (SINGLE) or multiple-choice (MULTI). The default is SINGLE.

TOPROW This optional attribute specifies the index of the array items that appears at the top of the list window when the panel is first displayed. The default is 1.

MINROWS This optional attribute specifies the minimum number of rows that the list window can be sized to. The default is 1.

MAXROWS This optional attribute specifies the maximum number of rows that the list window can be sized to. The default is 32.

MINWIDTH This optional attribute specifies the minimum width in character units that the list window can be sized to. The default is 8.

MAXWIDTH This optional attribute specifies the maximum width in character units that the list window can be sized to. The default is 64.

NUMROWS This optional attribute specifies the number of items in the selection list. This number will be reflected in the vertical scroll-bar position. If the value is not specified, the Dialog Manager assumes that the number of rows is equal to the number of elements in the array variable.

The **SELCOL** tag defines the array of column data. It has two attributes:

DATAVAR This required attribute specifies the name of the array variable that contains the list items.

VARCLASS This optional attribute is used to override the variable class for the previously declared array variable.

An Example of a Selection List

Figure 32-10 demonstrates the selection list tags. The tags are a subset of those used in the Club Med application in **Part VII**. Notice how the "%" is used to assign a specific value to a variable. To distinguish a variable name from a specific value you must enclose the variable name in quotes and precede it with "%". The screen created by this tag definition is shown in Figure 32-11.

```
<!doctype dm system>
<!----------------------------------------------------------------->
<!-- Example 3: A demonstration of a selection list             -->
<!----------------------------------------------------------------->
<!-------------------------------------------->
<!-- Define  varclass                       -->
<!-------------------------------------------->
<varclass name=char32 type='char 32'>
<varclass name=char72 type='char 72'>

<!-------------------------------------------->
<!-- Define variables                       -->
<!-------------------------------------------->
<varlist>
  <vardcl name=clubst1  varclass=char32>
  <vardcl name=clubst2  varclass=char32>
  <vardcl name=clubs    varclass=char72  maxdim=40>
  <vardcl name=clubnum  varclass=int>
  <vardcl name=clubmax  varclass=int>
</varlist>

<!-------------------------------------------->
<!--  CLUB MED VACATIONS panel              -->
<!-------------------------------------------->
<panel name=clubs width=78 depth=26>Club Med Vacations
  <ab>
    <abc><m>Actions
       .
       .
  </ab>
  <Topinst>Select a club then choose an action.
  <region dir=horiz>
    <divider gutter=5>
    <region dir=vert>
      <region dir=horiz>
        <dtafld datavar=clubst1 usage=out pmtwidth=0>
        <divider gutter=10>
        <dtafld datavar=clubst2 usage=out pmtwidth=0>
      </region>
      <sellst name=clubs selvar=clubnum numrows='%clubmax' maxwidth=64>
        <selcol datavar=clubs>
      </sellst>
    </region>
  </region>
</panel>
```

Figure 32-10. A Demonstration of a Selection List.

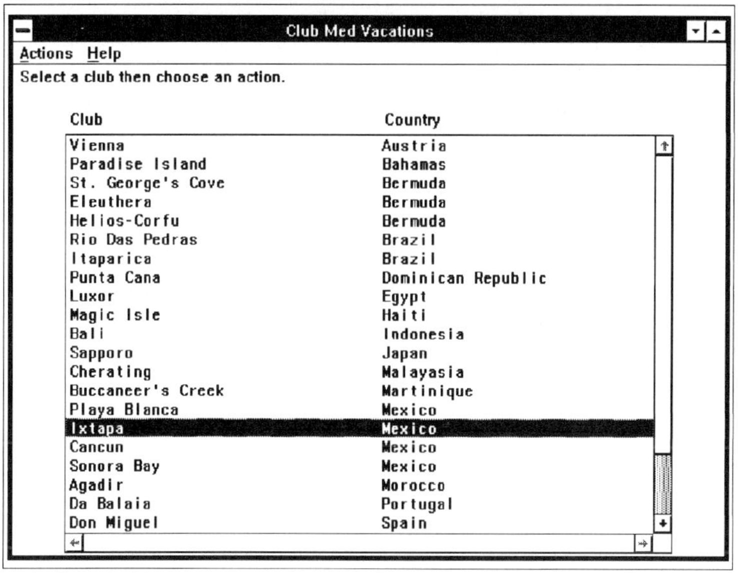

Figure 32-11. A Demonstration of a Selection List.

Defining List Fields

A list field is used to display data in column format and to allow users to enter data in column rows. The list provides automatic scrolling. A list field can contain one or more columns of data from array variables, where each column can be input only, output only, or input/output. List fields are defined using the **LSTFLD** tag. The **LSTCOL** tag is used to define one or more columns of data within a list field. Here are some of the more important attributes that can be specified within a LSTFLD tag:

HELP This optional attribute specifies the name of the help panel associated with that list.

MODVAR This optional attribute specifies the name of a variable that indicates which rows in the file have been modified.

RULES This optional attribute specifies the line grid pattern within the window. NONE, the default specifies no grid; HORIZ specifies horizontal lines; VERT specifies vertical lines; BOTH specifies a full grid.

TOPROW, MINROWS, MAXROWS, MINWIDTH, MAXWIDTH, NUMROWS
These attributes are identical to those defined for SELLST (see “Selection Lists” on page 826).

The **LSTCOL** tag defines a column within a LSTFLD. Here are some of the most used attributes:

DATAVAR This required attribute specifies the name of the array variable that contains the list items.

VARCLASS This optional attribute is used to override the variable class for the previously declared array variable.

USAGE This optional attribute specifies whether the field is for input-only (IN), output-only (OUT), or both (BOTH). The default is BOTH.

REQUIRED This optional attribute specifies if the field requires input (YES). The default is NO. A MSG attribute may be used to specify the ID of a message that gets displayed when the user does not complete a required entry.

AUTOCLR This optional attribute specifies whether the field will be cleared on input of new data. The contents of an auto-clear field are erased when the user types the first character in the field. The default is NO.

ALIGN This optional attribute specifies the alignment of the variable value within a field. The default is START for left-justified. Other choices are END and CENTER.

COLWIDTH This optional attribute specifies the boundary of the column width. If it is not specified, the default is the lesser of 25 or the data size.

In addition to these attributes, you can also specify the text for the title of a column.

Defining Information Regions

You can define information regions within your panels using the **INFO** tag. These are regions where you can display static text using tags to format the presentation. We will define some of those tags when we discuss HELP panels.

An Example of a List Field and Information Region

Figure 32-12 demonstrates the list field tags. The tags are a subset of those used in the Club Med application where they are used to list the "Additional Party Members." Figure 32-13 shows how the list field appears on a screen.

```
<!doctype dm system>
<!----------------------------------------------------------------->
<!-- Example 4: A demonstration of list fields                  -->
<!----------------------------------------------------------------->
<!--------------------------------------------->
<!-- Define  varclass                        -->
<!--------------------------------------------->
<varclass name=alpha32   type='char 32'>
<varclass name=number3   type='char 3'>

<!--------------------------------------------->
<!-- Define variables                        -->
<!--------------------------------------------->
<varlist>
  <vardcl name=lnamem   varclass=alpha32 maxdim=10>
  <vardcl name=fnamem   varclass=alpha32 maxdim=10>
  <vardcl name=agem     varclass=number3 maxdim=10>
</varlist>

<!--------------------------------------------->
<!--  CLUB MED CONFIRMATION panel            -->
<!--------------------------------------------->
<panel name=resvcnfm>Confirm Club Med Reservations
  <area>
       .
       .
       .
       .
      <info width=75>
      <lines>

Additional Party Members:
      </lines>
      </info>
      <lstfld name=lstfld1 toprow=1 numrows=10
        minrows=1 maxrows=10 minwidth=75 maxwidth=75 rules=both>
        <lstcol datavar=lnamem  usage=out  colwidth=27>LAST NAME
        <lstcol datavar=fnamem  usage=out  colwidth=27>FIRST NAME
        <lstcol datavar=agem    usage=out  colwidth=4 align=end>AGE
      </lstfld>
       .
       .
       .
  </area>
</panel>
```

Figure 32-12. A Demonstration of a List Field.

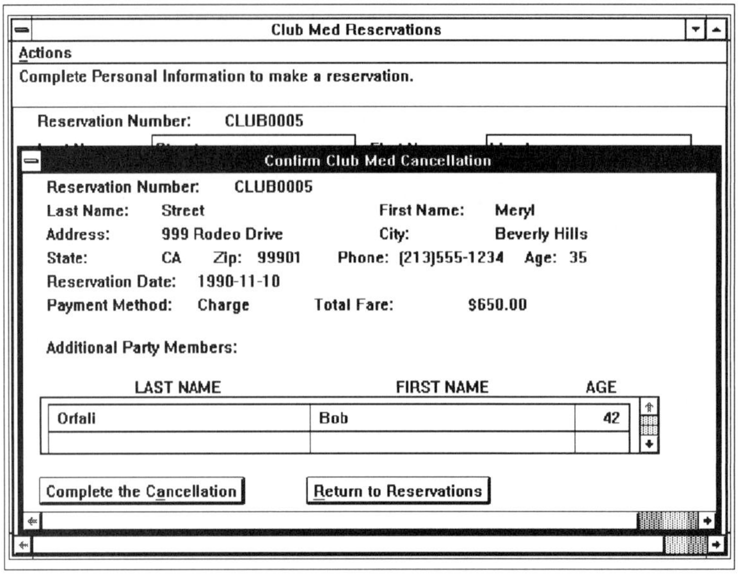

Figure 32-13. A Demonstration of a List Field for Additional Party Members.

Defining a User Control

The **UC** tag allows you to create custom Presentation Manager (PM) objects. This is how you can extend the Dialog Manager graphics with your own PM code or "class." The code for this new class is registered with Presentation Manager at runtime. The new objects you create are called user controls. We will provide code that demonstrates how to create such objects in later chapters. This section defines the tag language that supports this construct. Here is a list of the more important attributes that are supported by the UC tag:

NAME This optional attribute defines the user control name.

HELP This optional attribute specifies the name of the help panel associated with that list.

CLASS This required attribute specifies the name of the PM window class to which the user control belongs.

PRMDATA This optional attribute allows you to pass a 253-byte parameter string to the PM window class procedure. This string is non-translatable. A translatable string can be passed using a control-text field.

MINWIDTH, MAXWIDTH, MINDEPTH, MAXDEPTH These attributes collectively define the size of the UC area. The maximum area 512 by 512 character units.

An Example of User Controls

Figure 32-14 demonstrates how user controls are used to create your own PM objects within Dialog Manager panels. The user objects displayed in the control areas are PM bitmaps and a PM metafile. We'll be looking at the PM code that creates those objects in a later chapter. The purpose of this example is to demonstrate how the user control tags work. Figure 32-15 shows the how these objects appear on a screen.

```
<!doctype dm system>
<!------------------------------------------------------------------->
<!-- Example 5: A demonstration of User Controls                  -->
<!------------------------------------------------------------------->
<varclass name=alpha32   type='char 32'>
<!--------------------------------------------->
<!-- Define variables                        -->
<!--------------------------------------------->
<varlist>
  <vardcl name=metafile varclass=char32>
  <vardcl name=bmp1file varclass=char32>
  <vardcl name=bmp2file varclass=char32>
  <vardcl name=bmp3file varclass=char32>
  <vardcl name=bmp4file varclass=char32>
  <vardcl name=bmp5file varclass=char32>
  <vardcl name=bmp6file varclass=char32>
</varlist>
<!--------------------------------------------->
<!--  CLUB MED VACATION GRAPHIC              -->
<!--------------------------------------------->
<panel name=clubgrph>Club Med Vacation
  <region dir=horiz>
    <divider gutter=5>
    <region dir=vert>
      <uc class=METAFILE PRMDATA='%metafile'
         mindepth=10 maxdepth=45 minwidth=8 maxwidth=150>
      <divider>
      <region dir=horiz>
        <divider gutter=15>
        <uc class=BITMAP PRMDATA='%bmp1file'
            minwidth=6 maxwidth=6 mindepth=3 maxdepth=3>
        <divider>
        <uc class=BITMAP PRMDATA='%bmp2file'
            minwidth=6 maxwidth=6 mindepth=3 maxdepth=3>
        <divider>
        <uc class=BITMAP PRMDATA='%bmp3file'
            minwidth=6 maxwidth=6 mindepth=3 maxdepth=3>
        <divider>
        <uc class=BITMAP PRMDATA='%bmp4file'
            minwidth=6 maxwidth=6 mindepth=3 maxdepth=3>
        <divider>
        <uc class=BITMAP PRMDATA='%bmp5file'
            minwidth=6 maxwidth=6 mindepth=3 maxdepth=3>
```

Figure 32-14 (Part 1 of 2). A Demonstration of User Controls.

```
        <divider>
        <uc class=BITMAP PRMDATA='%bmp6file'
            minwidth=6 maxwidth=6 mindepth=3 maxdepth=3>
      </region>
    </region>
  </region>
</panel>
```

Figure 32-14 (Part 2 of 2). A Demonstration of User Controls.

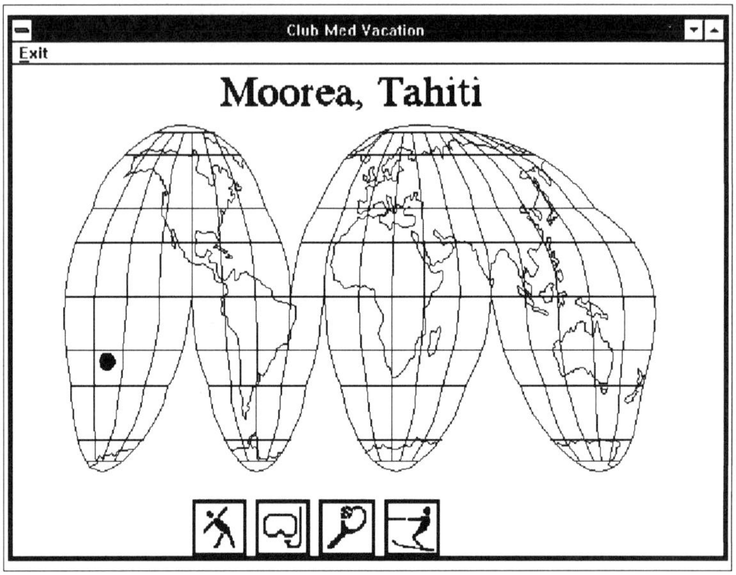

Figure 32-15. A Demonstration of PM Objects Drawn in User Control Areas.

Defining Help

The Dialog Manager provides a comprehensive help system which is based on the SAA model. Dialog Manager provides the framework of the help system and it's up to the application developer to supply the help text and panels. Here's the general outline of this help framework:

Extended Help: This is help that covers an entire panel. You supply the name of the help panel as part of the panel definition. For example:

```
<panel name=clubs width=78 depth=26 help=clubs>Club Med Vacations
```

The user can request extended help from the help pull-down menu or by requesting help on an item (by pressing the F1 key) which does not have an associated help panel.

Context Help: This is help for a specific Dialog Object within an application panel. You can associate a help panel with almost all the dialog tags that were covered in this chapter. If the item does not have a help panel defined, DM displays the extended help associated with the panel. Here's an example of a field-specific help:

```
<dtafld name=fname datavar=fname usage=both required=yes
 pmtwidth=12 entwidth=20 help=resfld>First Name:
```

Help Index: The help index provides a list of all help topics in the application. To create a topic index, use the **ITOP** tag when defining your help panel. The help index can be selected from the help pull-down menu.

Help for Help: This level of help provides general information about how to use or access the various types of help. The help for help can be selected from the help pull-down menu.

Hypertext Help: When defining the text for a help panel, you can use the **RP** tag to identify words for which you want to provide additional information. When you click your mouse on the highlighted phrases, additional help material will appear in a window.

The Main Help Window

Dialog Manager supplies the main help panel which contains an action bar with three choices:

Services The choices in this pull-down menu lets you search for an expression, print something you're interested in, leave "bookmarks" of paths you've already explored, and copy information to files.

Options The choices in this pull-down menu provide a hypertext-like navigation environment for selecting and branching into help topics.

Help The choices in this pull-down menu provide help about help.

Figure 32-16, Figure 32-17, and Figure 32-18 show the extended SAA help services that are provided as part of the help facilities of Dialog Manager. As you can see, the Dialog Manager tries to make sure that your user gets complete help coverage at every level. All you've got to do is write the help panels that are specific to your application and provide the linkages to the appropriate objects that need help coverage.

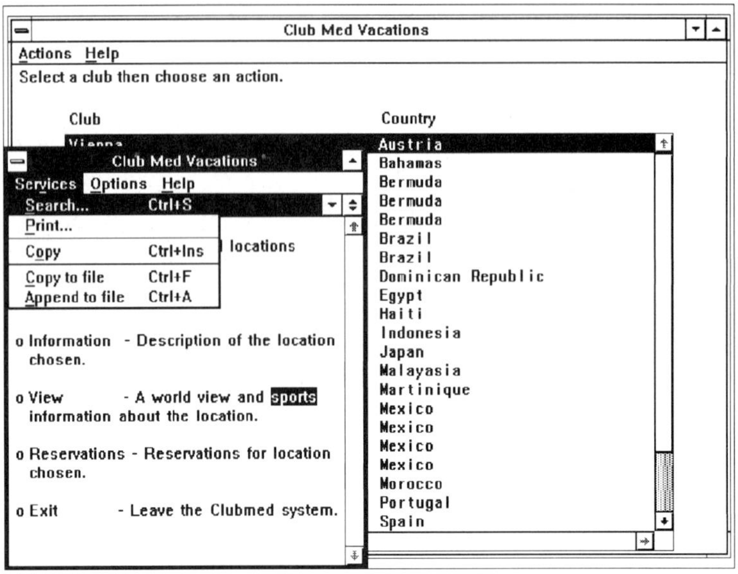

Figure 32-16. The Choice of Help Services.

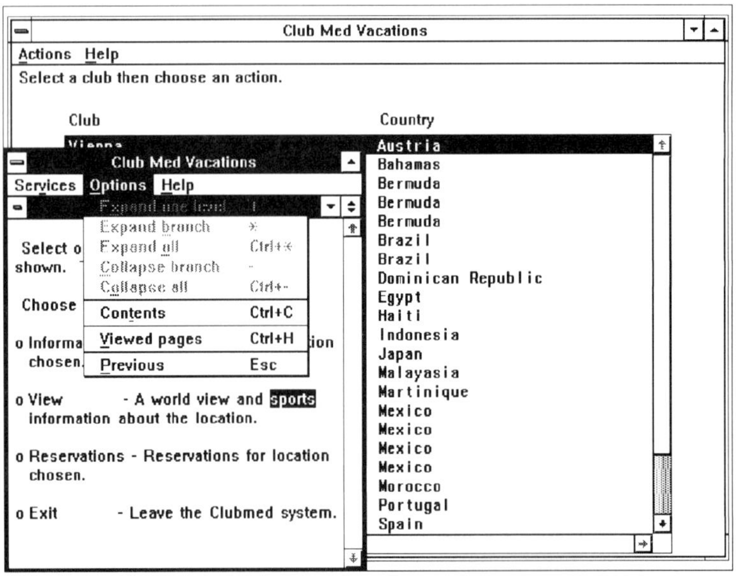

Figure 32-17. The Choice of Help Navigation Options.

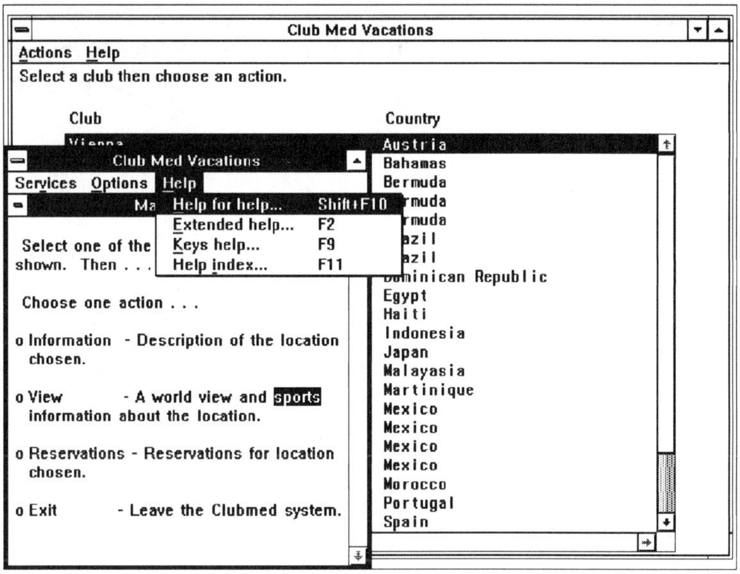

Figure 32-18. The SAA-CUA Help Hierarchy.

Creating Help Panels

The **HELP** tag and its required end tag define a help panel. All the other tags that make-up a help panel are coded between these two tags. You must code an **AREA** start and end tag within every help panel. Finally, you must code an **INFO** region for the text of your help panel. The Dialog Manager provides a very rich set of tag constructs which can be embedded within the **INFO** region of both application and help panels. Here is a small sample of what those tags can do:

Paragraph The **P** tag defines a paragraph start.

Lines The **LINES** tag defines text that will not be formatted.

Hypertext The reference phrase tag, **RP**, specifies a link to additional help text.

Heading The **Hn** tag allows you to define hierarchies of information, based on topics and subtopics.

Note The **NT** tag allows you to define notes that can also appear in note windows.

Caution The **CAUTION** tag allows you to define alert statements.

Warning The **WARNING** tag allows you to define warning statements.

Lists You can define simple lists with the **SL** tag, unordered lists with the **UL** tag, and ordered lists with the **OL** tag. The **PARML** tag allows you to define a list of terms and their descriptions. It creates text that is very similar to what you are now reading.

An Example of Application Help

Figure 32-19 demonstrates how help panels are created using the tag language. Figure 32-20 on page 839 shows how the extended help for a panel appears on a screen. Notice that "sports" is highlighted. This is a "hypertext" word (or phrase) on which you can click the mouse and obtain more information on that topic. Figure 32-21 on page 840 shows field-specific help. It is displayed when a user places the mouse pointer within a field and presses F1.

```
<!doctype dm system>
<!------------------------------------------------------------------->
<!-- Example 6: A demonstration of Help Panels                   -->
<!------------------------------------------------------------------->
<!------------------------------------------->
<!--  CLUB MED VACATIONS - Help For a Panel   -->
<!------------------------------------------->
<help name=clubs> Main panel
<itop roots='clubs' > Clubmed Help
<area >
  <info>
  <p> Select one of the Clubmed locations shown.  Then . . .
  <p> Choose one action . . .
  <ul>
    <li>Information  - Description of the location chosen.
    <li>View         - A world view and <rp help=sports>sports</rp> information
                       about the location.
    <li>Reservations - Reservations for location chosen.
    <li>Exit         - Leave the Clubmed system.
  </ul>
  </info>
</area>
</help>
```

Figure 32-19 (Part 1 of 2). A Demonstration of Help.

```
<!------------------------------------------->
<!--  CLUB MED VACATIONS - field help panel  -->
<!------------------------------------------->
<help name=resfld> Reservation Field
<area >
  <info>
  <p> Your personal information must be filled in before the reservation
      can be submitted. Complete the following before making the reservation:
  <ul compact>
    <li>Last Name
    <li>First Name
    <li>Street Address
    <li>City
    <li>State
    <li>Zip Code
    <li>Telephone Number
    <li>Age
  </ul>
  <note>Party member information can be filled in as required. </note>
  </info>
</area>
</help>
</panel>
```

Figure 32-19 (Part 2 of 2). A Demonstration of Help.

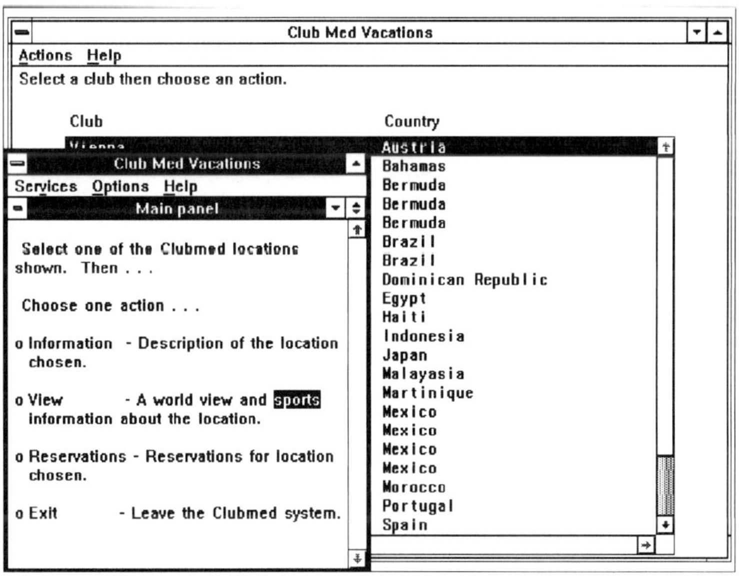

Figure 32-20. A Demonstration of Panel Help (i.e., Extended Help).

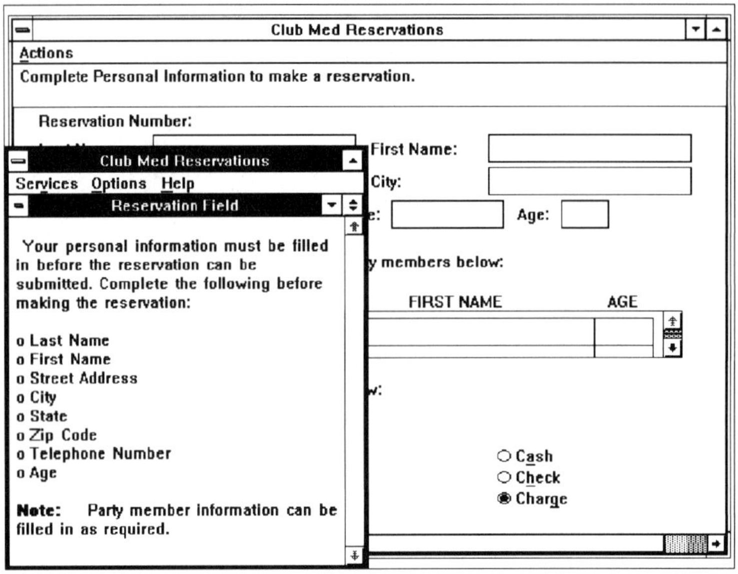

Figure 32-21. A Demonstration of Field-Specific Help.

Chapter 33

Programming the Dialog Manager

This chapter presents a tutorial on the Dialog Manager's programming interface. You will learn how to manipulate the Dialog Manager objects that were defined in the previous chapter from within your C-language programs. Programming the Dialog Manager is easy. It consists of learning 12 verbs that are issued through two API calls. The plan for this chapter is to first go over the verbs, then the two API calls, and finally write a Dialog Manager version of the famous "Hello World" program.

DIALOG MANAGER PROGRAMMING

The Dialog Manager builds on top of the graphic capabilities of PM (or Windows 3.0 using the Arcadia CUA Workbench). Dialog Manager displays the user-defined panels (see previous chapter) in the client area of a PM window. Dialog Manager applications (unlike the event-driven PM applications) are procedural in nature. Referring to Figure 33-1 on page 842, Dialog Manager applications use the services of the Dialog Manager *layer*, which in turn uses the services of the Presentation Manager *layer*. Dialog Manager applications are thus one layer removed from the Presentation Manager's message queues and polling loop mechanisms. The Dialog Manager service layer handles all the user interaction on behalf of your C-language application. Your application does not need to monitor the mouse and keystroke events as they occur; it only has to handle application-specific events (as defined in the tag language).

DM, C, AND THE USER: WHO'S IN CONTROL?

Any time you have a marriage of languages or programming environments the following questions need to be answered:

- Who is in control when the program starts?
- How are shared variables declared?
- How is control passed back and forth between the two environments?
- What is the API?

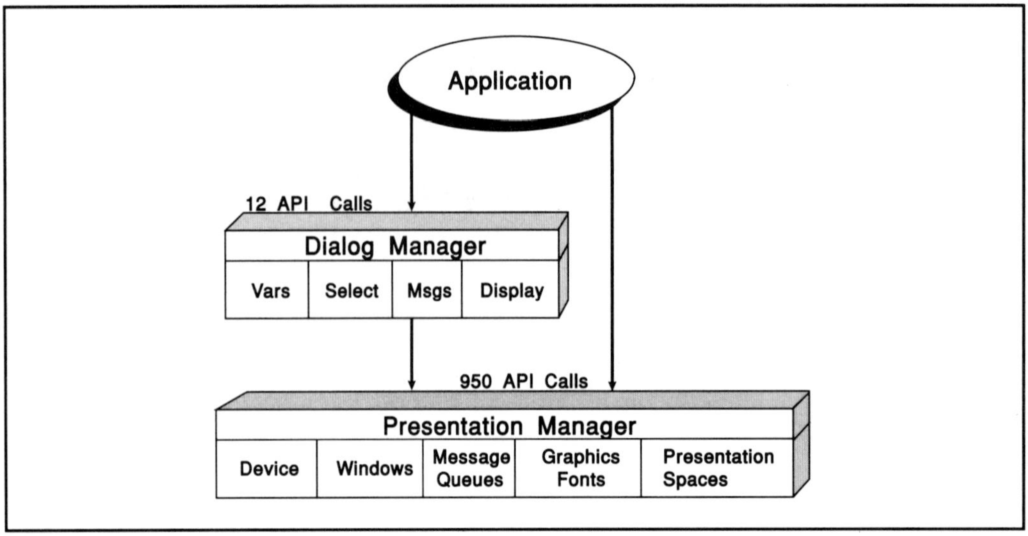

Figure 33-1. Dialog Manager and Presentation Manager Interaction.

In the case of the Dialog Manager, we have the additional complication of having a user in the loop who, as required by CUA, is "always in control." So, we have to answer the following additional questions:

- When does Dialog Manager pass control to the user?
- When does the user return control to the Dialog Manager?
- When does Dialog Manager pass the user's request to the C program?

Figure 33-2 shows, by example, how the control gets passed between your C program, the Dialog Manager, and the user. The little boxes on the far right indicate the panels which appear on the screen. The dotted line indicates the C program is blocked. The example covers most of the situations encountered in a typical dialog. Here's a step-by-step explanation of the interactions shown in Figure 33-2 on page 843:

1. **Initialize the Dialog Manager**. The front-end program starts with the C-language program in control. You initiate an instance of DM and its resource pool by issuing a DMOPEN verb. Notice that the control immediately returns to the C application and the user is not in the loop.
2. **Bind the shared variables**. The C-language program issues multiple VDEFINE verbs to bind all the shared variables that will be used by both C and DM. The user is still out of the loop.
3. **Display the primary window**. The C-language issues the first DISPLAY verb to present the user with a primary window. Dialog Manager will place the "club" panel in the primary window. The user is now in the loop and in control. The user can interact with the panel by entering information in the input fields or making selections as described in the panel's definition. The Dialog Manager validates and processes user input according to the rules specified in the tags. When the user submits an action for processing, the Dialog Manager stores the contents

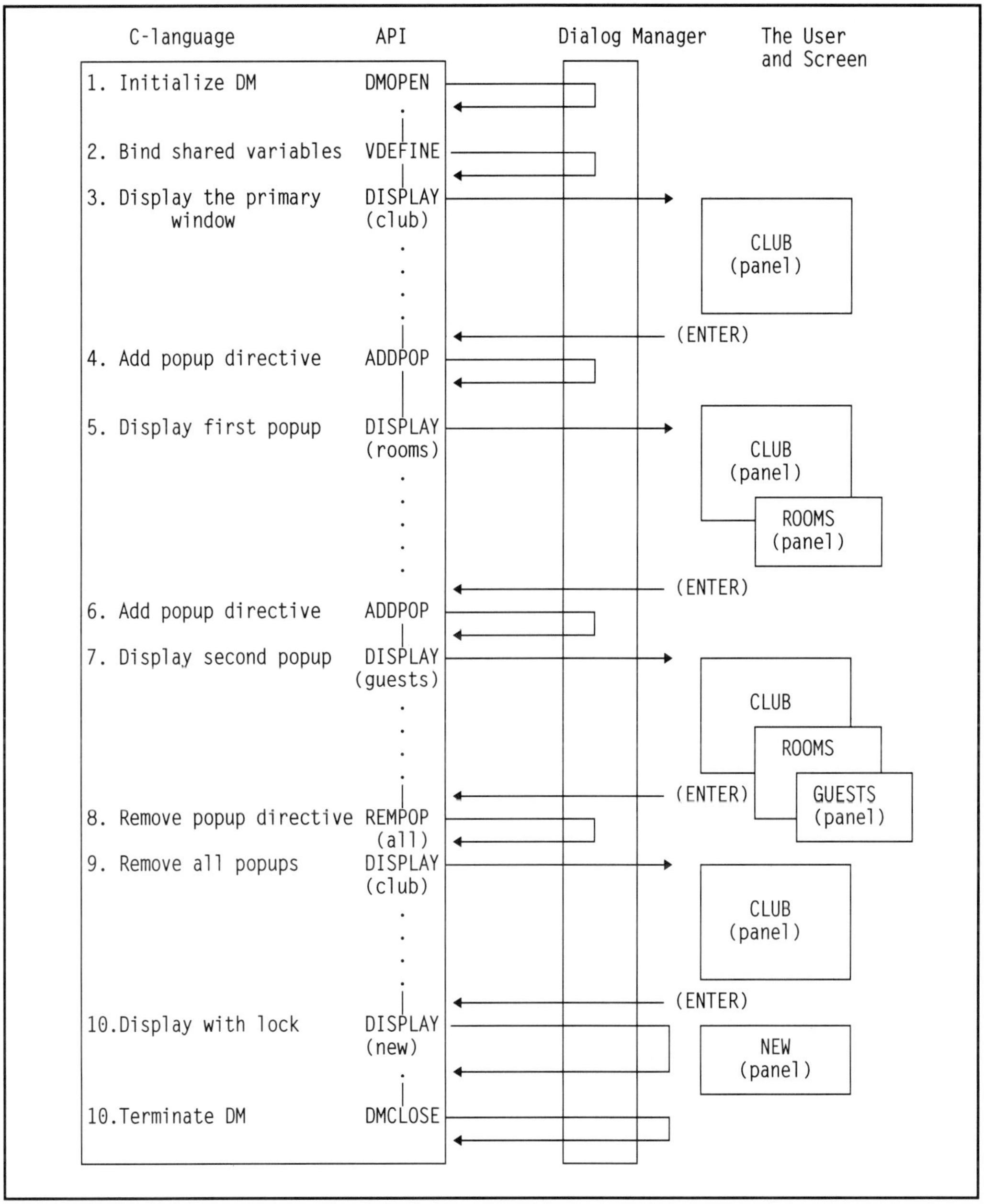

Figure 33-2. Who's in Control and When?

of the input field in dialog variables and returns control to the C-language program.

4. **Add popup directive**. The ADDPOP verb instructs the Dialog Manager to display the next panel on top of the existing panel. The user is not in the loop.

5. **Display first popup**. The DISPLAY verb causes the "rooms" panel to be displayed on top of the existing panel. The user is in the loop again and interacts with this secondary window.
6. **Add popup directive**. The ADDPOP verb instructs the Dialog Manager to display the panel on top of the existing panel.
7. **Display next popup**. The next DISPLAY verb causes the "guests" panel to be displayed on top of the existing panels. The user can now interact with this top-level window.
8. **Remove popup directive**. The REMPOP verb instructs Dialog Manager to remove the popups from the screen when the next DISPLAY is issued. The "all" parameter instructs it to remove all the popups.
9. **Display and remove all popups**. DISPLAY causes the popups to be removed.
10. **Display with lock**. The DISPLAY verb is issued with the "lock" parameter set. This causes a panel to be displayed, but without relinquishing control to the user. Instead, the control returns immediately to the C-language program once the panel is visible.
11. **Terminate DM**. The DMCLOSE verb causes this instance of the Dialog Manager to be terminated.

THE DIALOG VERBS

The dialog services consist of 12 verbs through which your application can control the flow of the tag-defined objects. The verbs are placed in a control block and issued through one of two API calls. The Dialog Manager API is similar in style to the Query Manager Callable Interface, which is not too surprising considering that they are both SAA "common programming interfaces." The following table shows the dialog service categories to which specific verbs belong:

Table 33-1. The Categories of Dialog Verbs.

Dialog Service Category	Verbs or Commands
Control	DMOPEN, DMCLOSE, FORCEXIT
Display	DISPLAY, ADDPOP, REMPOP
Variable	VDEFINE, VCOPY, VDELETE, VREPLACE, VRESET
Library	LIBDEF

The Control Service Verbs

The Control verbs establish or end communication with the Dialog Manager run-time and control the flow of the dialog. The FORCEXIT verb, which is used as a signal from an external thread to a DM thread, can be issued without a prior DMOPEN. The rest of the DM verbs need to be bracketed by DMOPEN and DMCLOSE verbs. Table 33-2 provides a brief description of the DM control verbs.

<table>
<tr><th colspan="2">Table 33-2. The Dialog Manager Control Verbs.</th></tr>
<tr><th>Verb</th><th>Description</th></tr>
<tr><td>DMOPEN</td><td>This verb establishes communications with the Dialog Manager. This is the first Dialog verb you issue to establish a dialog. Three parameters are used with a DMOPEN:
APPLID This four-byte name identifies the command table.
INSTID This ID can be used to associate subsequent DMOPENs with an open dialog session.
UNIQUE Creates an exclusive dialog.
Example:
<code>"DMOPEN APPLID(mine) UNIQUE"</code></td></tr>
<tr><td>DMCLOSE</td><td>This verb completes a set of dialog services and releases the dialog resources. After the last DMCLOSE, an application cannot issue any calls to DM unless a new dialog is started with a DMOPEN.
Example:
<code>"DMCLOSE"</code></td></tr>
<tr><td>FORCEXIT</td><td>This verb is used to inform a Dialog Manager thread (foreground) that a background thread has finished executing a long job. Your application will typically start a background thread to perform a non-display (background) task of uncertain duration. The background thread issues this verb to inform the foreground when it has completed the task. The foreground thread can then display the results of the operation.
Example:
<code>"FORCEXIT"</code></td></tr>
</table>

The Display Service Verbs

Display verbs display panels in primary and popup windows. As a result of one display call, many user interactions can occur. The Dialog Manager will automatically process user interactions, such as moving, sizing, and scrolling. It can also validate the input. You get all this service by simply issuing a DISPLAY verb which lets the Dialog Manager (with the help of your tag instructions) go to work on your behalf. The first panel displayed appears in a primary window. Subsequent panels can either be displayed in a primary window (by replacing the previous primary window panel) or as popup windows. Popups are modal windows that cannot be resized by the user. Up to six levels of popups can be displayed. DM does not support the CUA concept of secondary windows. Popups are the equivalent of CUA dialog boxes. Table 33-3 provides a brief description of the DM display verbs.

Table 33-3. The Dialog Manager Display Verbs.

Verb	Description

ADDPOP	This verb causes the subsequent panel DISPLAYed to appear in a popup window. Another ADDPOP call creates a separate (nested) popup window. The number of separate popup windows using nested ADDPOP calls is limited to six. At least one DISPLAY verb must be issued to create the primary window prior to issuing any ADDPOP calls. Two successive ADDPOP calls cannot be issued without an intervening DISPLAY or REMPOP call. When a popup window is on the screen, the user can interact with only the top-level popup window. Explicit user action is required to remove the popup window. The user can move the popup window but cannot size it.
	
	`Example:`
	`"ADDPOP"`

REMPOP	This verb removes the popup window created by an ADDPOP call. The REMPOP ALL call removes all the popup windows
	
	`Example:`
	`"REMPOP ALL"`

DISPLAY	This verb is used to display a panel in either a primary or popup window and control the interaction with the user until the user submits the panel for processing. This is done through one of the following DM commands: ENTER, EXIT, CANCEL, PASSTHRU, or SETVERB. The DISPLAY verb takes five parameters:
	
	PANEL the tag name of the panel to be displayed.
	MSG a tag created message to be displayed.
	CURSOR the field where the cursor will be displayed.
	LOCK immediate return after a panel is displayed.
	ALARM beep when the panel is displayed.
	
	`Example:`
	`"DISPLAY PANEL(pizza) CURSOR(beef) LOCK ALARM"`

The Variable Service Verbs

An important concept in the Dialog Manager is the dialog variable pool. The variables contained in the dialog variable pool are used by a DM application to get data to and from panels, place data in messages, and dynamically define command actions. A dialog variable pool is created by Dialog Manager when a DMOPEN verb is issued. It will contain application variables that were defined using the Dialog Tag Language and a number of system variables which DM controls. All system variable names begin with the letter "Z". An example of a system variable is ZAPPLID, which the Dialog Manager sets to the current application ID.

How are the variables in the DM pool made available to your C-language program? There are two ways of doing this:

1. You can use the VDEFINE verb to explicitly "bind" your C-language variables with DM variables. The two variables will then have the same value (i.e., they are associated) until a VDELETE is issued.
2. You can use the VCOPY verb to assign the value of a DM variable to a C-language variable and the VREPLACE verb to assign a C-variable to a DM

pool variable. All the variables in the DM pool can be cleared by issuing a VRESET verb

Table 33-4 provides a brief description of the DM Variable service verbs.

Table 33-4. The Dialog Manager Variable Verbs.

Verb	Description

VDEFINE	This verb is used to associate a DM variable name created using tags with a C-language variable. The two variables will have the same value until a VDELETE verb is issued. This verb takes three parameters:
	
	name-list This is the name of the DM pool variable
	FORMAT This is the data-type; i.e., CHAR, HEX, BINSTR (null term string), FIXED (int), FIXEDU (unsigned int).
	DIM This is the number of bytes in a string.
	
	`Example:`
	`"VDEFINE clubs    FORMAT(BINSTR) DIM(40)"`

VCOPY	This verb is used to assign a DM pool variable to a C-language variable. The only parameter required is the name of the of the pool variable. The C-variable is passed as part of the API call
	
	`Example:`
	`"VCOPY clubs"`

VREPLACE	This verb is used to assign a C-language variable to a DM pool variable. The only parameter required is the name of the of the pool variable. The C-variable is passed as part of the API call
	
	`Example:`
	`"VREPLACE clubs"`

VRESET	This verb is used to reset all the variables in the DM pool to empty. No parameters are required.
	
	`Example:`
	`"VRESET"`

VDELETE	This verb is used to remove associations that were created using VDEFINE from the DM variable pool. You can specify removing the associations for a particular set of variables or all associations by using an asterisk.
	
	`Example:`
	`"VDELETE *"`

The Library Service Verbs

A DM application must tell the DM system where to find the files containing the panels to be displayed and the help screens. DM provides a single verb LIBDEF to define your libraries. There are two ways to use LIBDEF:

1. By placing LIBDEF commands in a **library definition file** with an entry for each file which contains dialog objects. For example, the library definition file for the **club** application ID is named **club**lib.app and it contains the following LIBDEF statements:

```
LIBDEF LIBRARY LIBLIST(clubpan.dtl)
LIBDEF HELP    LIBLIST(clubpan.hlp)
```

When you issue the DMOPEN verb, one of the parameters you can pass is the four-character application ID. DM will use this parameter to locate a (xxxxlib.APP) file that contains your definitions.

2. By issuing LIBDEF verbs from your programs. This method allows you to define a set of libraries **dynamically**. This means that you can change your dialog libraries at run time, if you so desire. The format of the LIBDEF verb is the same as in the application library definition file.

Table 33-5 provides a brief description of the DM library service verbs.

Table 33-5. The Dialog Manager Library Verbs.

Verb	Description

LIBDEF	This verb defines the DM object files used by an application. There are three parameters associated with this verb:
	lib-type This parameter is either LIBRARY or HELP.
	LIBRLIST This parameter contains library file names.
	condition This parameter is set to UNCOND (default) when you don't care if a previous library was defined. COND means you care and the verb fails if a previous LIBDEF was issued.
	`Example:`
	`"LIBDEF LIBRARY LIBLIST(clubpan.dtl)"`

The Normal and Extended DM API Calls

The 12 Dialog Manager verbs are executed using one of two API calls:

- **ISPCI()**, the *normal* Dialog Manager API call.
- **ISPCI2()**, the *extended* Dialog Manager API call.

These two API calls follow the SAA Common Programming Interface (CPI) standard. The constructs used to pass the variables are designed to be language independent. You invoke the Dialog Manager's API services as follows:

1. Prepare the control blocks. These include a string that specifies the command to be executed and a **DMCOMMBLOCK** structure that contains the return codes and identifies the instance ID and dialog pool that DM is currently using. Extended calls require two additional parameters in order to specify the program variables used by the VCOPY, VREPLACE and VDEFINE verbs. The control structures are presented later in this section.
2. Issue the API call. This may be either a normal call or an extended call, depending on the command that is being processed.

3. Process the Dialog Manager return codes. The Dialog Manager returns control to your application when it's completed processing the command. This may take quite a long time if the command is interactive.

The Normal Dialog Manager Call: ISPCI()

This API call, also known as the *normal* call, is used to process Dialog Manager commands that do not require variables to be exchanged between the C-program and the Dialog Manager variable pools. The majority of the Dialog Manager verbs fall into this category. The prototype for this call is:

```
ISPCI(DMCOMMBLOCK   * dmcomm,              /* communication area          */
      LONG            buflen,              /* length of command           */
      PCHAR           buffer);             /* command string              */
```

A description of the parameters follows:

- The first parameter points to the **DMCOMMBLOCK** structure, described in the section on "The Dialog Manager Control Block: DMCOMMBLOCK" on page 850.
- The second parameter contains the length of the command string.
- The third parameter points to a string containing the Dialog Manager command to be processed.

The Extended Dialog Manager Call: ISPCI2()

This API call, also known as the *extended* call, is used to process Dialog Manager commands that require the exchange of variables between C-programs and the Dialog Manager variable pools. Only three Dialog Manager commands have this requirement: VCOPY, VREPLACE, and VDEFINE. The prototype for this call is:

```
ISPCI2(DMCOMMBLOCK   * dmcomm,              /* communication area          */
       LONG            buflen,              /* length of command           */
       PCHAR           buffer,              /* command string              */
       PLONG           parm1,               /* ptr to length of C variables */
       void          * parm2);              /* ptr to array of C variables  */
```

A description of the parameters follows:

- The first parameter points to the **DMCOMMBLOCK** structure, described in the section on "The Dialog Manager Control Block: DMCOMMBLOCK" on page 850.
- The second parameter contains the length of the command string.
- The third parameter points to a string containing the Dialog Manager command to be processed.
- The fourth parameter points to the size of the C variable(s) being passed.

- The fifth parameter points to the C variable(s) being passed.

The Dialog Manager Control Block: DMCOMMBLOCK

Each DMOPEN session started with the Dialog Manager is required to allocate a 128-byte variable of type **DMCOMMBLOCK**. This variable serves as an anchor for that session. All subsequent calls for that session must pass the same variable, which essentially provides three functions:

- It receives an instance identifier for the DMOPEN from Dialog Manager. This identifier must be used in the control block with subsequent calls.
- It receives from Dialog Manager a return code, reason code Error information, and the OS/2 return code for a completed command.
- It provides a working storage area to the Dialog Manager.

The type definition for a **DMCOMMBLOCK** structure is shown in Figure 33-3:

```
typedef struct DMCOMMBLOCK
  {
    ULONG        ReturnCode;              /* Dialog Manager Return Code */
    ULONG        ReasonCode;              /* Dialog Manager Reason Code */
    UCHAR        InstanceID [8];          /* Instance Identifier        */
    ULONG        OS2ReturnCode;           /* OS/2 Return Code           */
    DMERRORINFO *ErrorInfo[6];            /* Trace  of last 6 errors    */
    char         Filler [60];             /* Used by DM -- don't modify */
  } ;
```

Figure 33-3. The DSQCOMM Structure.

The **DMERRORINFO** is an array that contains error information on the last six errors that may have occurred during the API call. You may find it useful; here's its type declaration:

```
typedef struct DMERRORINFO
  {
    ULONG        ReasonCode;              /* Dialog Manager Reason Code */
    ULONG        OS2ReturnCode;           /* OS/2 Return Code           */
  } ;
```

Figure 33-4. The DMERRORINFO Structure.

Along with the return code the Dialog Manager API returns a **reason code** and an **Error ID**, which further explain the outcome of the call.

"HELLO WORLD FROM DM"

This section shows you the steps necessary to develop a simple DM application. In the next chapter, we will develop an identical version of "Hello World from PM" by programming directly to PM. You will then be in a position to compare the two programming approaches.

The Output

Figure 33-5 is a screen capture of the output produced by this program.

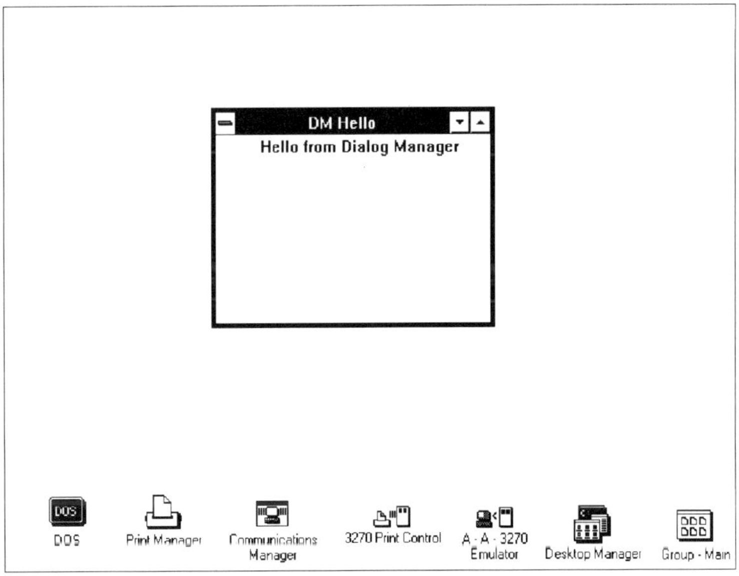

Figure 33-5. The Output of Hello World Using DM.

The Dialog Tag Language

Figure 33-6 shows the Dialog Tag Language that produces the window shown in Figure 33-5.

```
<!doctype dm system>

<panel name=hellodm depth=10 width=30>DM Hello
  <info width=30>
    <h1>Hello from Dialog Manager
  </info>
</panel>
```

Figure 33-6. The HELLODM.GML File.

The C Program: HELLODM.C

Figure 33-7 demonstrates the C-language program for "Hello from DM." The **ispcast.h** include file, which is part of the toolkit, contains the declarations for the DM structures. The program uses three DM verbs:

1. A DMOPEN to start communications with DM.
2. A DISPLAY to display the panel.
3. A DMCLOSE to close the communications with DM.

The APPLID "hi" that is passed by the DMOPEN is used by DM to locate a library definition file named **hilib.app**. This file contains the single statement:

```
LIBDEF LIBRARY LIBLIST(hellodm.dtl)
```

The hellodm.dtl file contains the compiled output of the tag panels.

```
/*****************************************************************************/
/*  PROGRAM NAME: HELLODM - a Dialog Manager hello example                   */
/*                                                                           */
/*  PROGRAM DESCRIPTION:  This program demonstrates a simple DM program      */
/*                        which only displays hello.                         */
/*  PROGRAM INVOCATION:   HELLODM                                            */
/*****************************************************************************/
#include <string.h>
#include <ispcast.h>
#include <os2.h>
DMCOMMBLOCK dmcomm;
CHAR        dm_command[64];

VOID main(VOID)
{
  strcpy(dm_command,"DMOPEN APPLID(hi)");
  ISPCI(&dmcomm, strlen(dm_command), dm_command);

  strcpy(dm_command,"DISPLAY PANEL(HELLODM)");
  ISPCI(&dmcomm, strlen(dm_command), dm_command);

  strcpy(dm_command,"DMCLOSE");
  ISPCI(&dmcomm, strlen(dm_command), dm_command);

} /* end main */
```

Figure 33-7. The HELLODM.C Listing.

Chapter 34

The Presentation Manager

This chapter provides a crash course in Presentation Manager "literacy." We will not be covering PM's 900 plus API calls. Instead, we will focus on the structure of a PM program and on understanding the PM (and Windows 3.0) programming paradigm. At the end of this chapter, you should be able to read a PM program and follow its logic. This is a very important prerequisite for the chapters that follow, where we will be introducing some of PM's more advanced functions. To give you a feel for what it takes to program in PM, we will present the PM version of "Hello World."

WHAT MAKES PM PROGRAMS SO DIFFERENT?

The Reactive Event-Driven Paradigm

PM programs are mostly reactive. They spend most of their time in an "idle" state waiting for events to happen. When an event such as a keypress or a mouse click occurs PM routes the input to the appropriate procedure in your code in the form of messages. The procedure can then choose to either react to the event or just return it to PM and let it handle it. If the procedure needs to display information in a window, it calls PM to do so. After making the appropriate response, the procedure returns to its idle state waiting for the next event. So, the first thing we can say about a PM program is that it is made up of a collection of lazy, event-driven procedures that wait for work to find them. No self-respecting PM procedure ever goes out of its way to look for work.

The Heart of PM: "Everything is a Window"

How does PM associate procedures with events? It does that through the magic of windows. Windows in PM are more than just the familiar overlapping rectangles that appear on a screen. A window is an "object." It becomes "an object that knows what

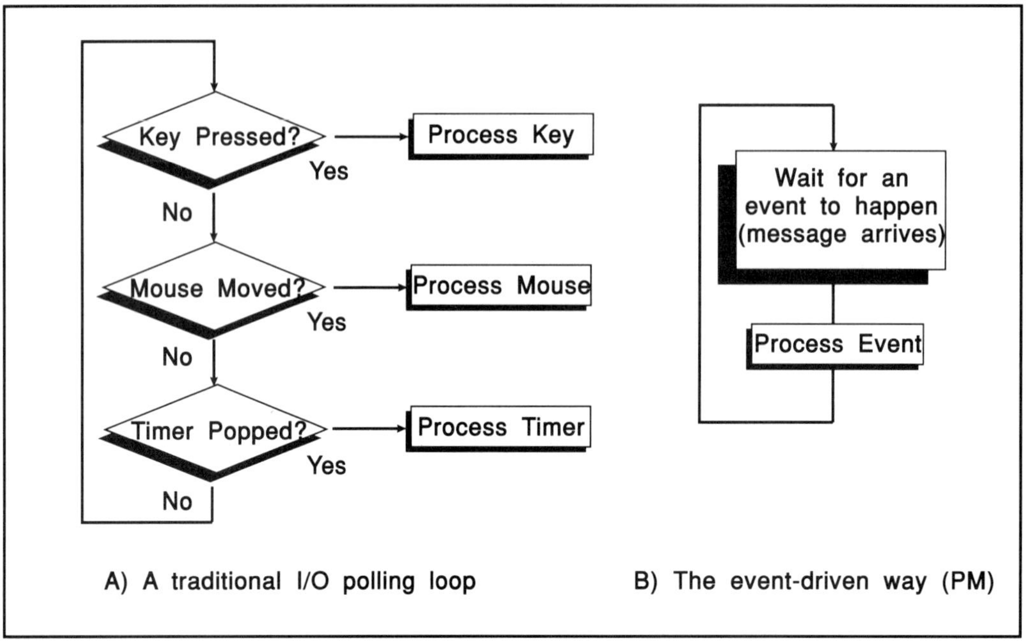

Figure 34-1. I/O Polling Loops Versus PM's Event-Driven Processing.

to do" when it teams up with an event handler procedure (more on that later). A PM program is conceptually a number of windows and the stuff that makes them know what to do. Some windows look like the traditional rectangular areas typically called windows. On the other hand, structures that are not "window-like" such as scroll bars, buttons, and menus, are also considered to be windows in PM. A window may or may not be visible on the screen. Most PM applications create at least one "traditional" window called the main window, which is typically visible and represents the application to the outside world. Here is a quick guide to PM's window terminology:

- A **frame window** provides a border and serves as a base for constructing composite windows, such as the main window or a dialog window. Think of the frame window as a "border" which contains an assembly of child windows which act as an ensemble. Frames provide the visual unity that gives the window its "look and feel" to end-users.
- A **main window** or "standard window" is a frame window which contains control windows such as a title bar, an action bar, and a scroll bar. Every main window includes a client window area. This is the area where an application does all its work. Figure 34-2 shows four "standard" windows. The "standard window" corresponds to a CUA primary window.
- A **dialog window** is a frame window that contains one or more control windows that are used primarily to prompt the user for input. The dialog window corresponds to a CUA dialog box.
- A **message window** is a frame window that an application uses to display a message. It is equivalent to a CUA message box.

- A **client window** is the area in the window where the application displays its information. The insides of the four windows in Figure 34-2 are client areas. Every main window typically has a client window. What is displayed in the client window is entirely application specific. The frame window receives events from the control windows that surround the client window and passes them to the client window. The application program provides the event-handler procedures that service these events.
- A **control window** is used in conjunction with another window to provide control structures. PM provides several pre-defined control windows such as: push buttons, entry fields, list boxes, check boxes, menus, scroll bars, combo boxes, and multiple line editors (MLEs).

An application may consist of several main windows, dialog windows, and all the child windows associated with them.

Window Lineage

Every window has a parent window. A window is positioned relative to the coordinates of its parent. When a parent window is hidden, so are its children. When the parent moves, its children move with it. Children are always drawn on top of the parent, and they get "clipped" if they go past the parent's borders. Windows that have the same parent are called siblings. In PM, just like in real life, a parent can have several children, each of which has its own children, and so on.

Figure 34-2 visually demonstrates the window hierarchy depicted in Figure 34-3. WIN1 and WIN2 are sibling "standard windows" that have a common parent: the PM desktop. WIN1a is the child of WIN1, and WIN2a is the child of WIN2; both children are "standard windows." While this four-window hierarchy is "visually" quite obvious, what is not as obvious is that each "standard window" has its own set of child windows. Figure 34-4 shows the standard window's offspring. It's quite a prolific tribe, isn't it?

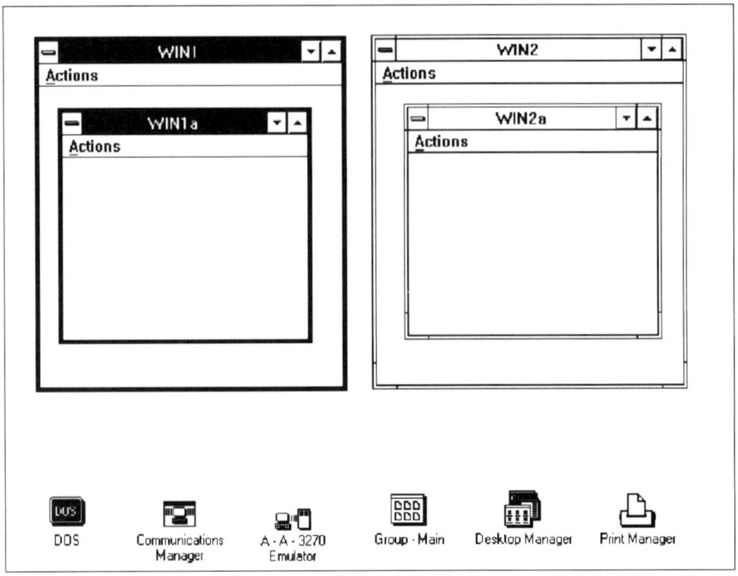

Figure 34-2. Four "Standard Windows:" Two Main Siblings with One Child Each.

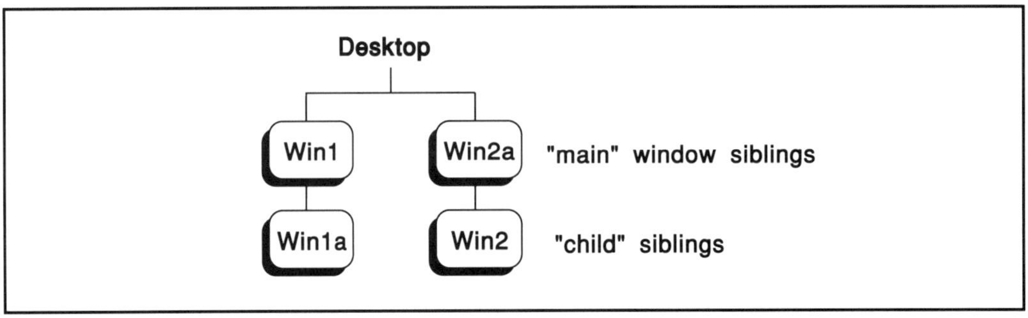

Figure 34-3. The Four-Window Family Tree.

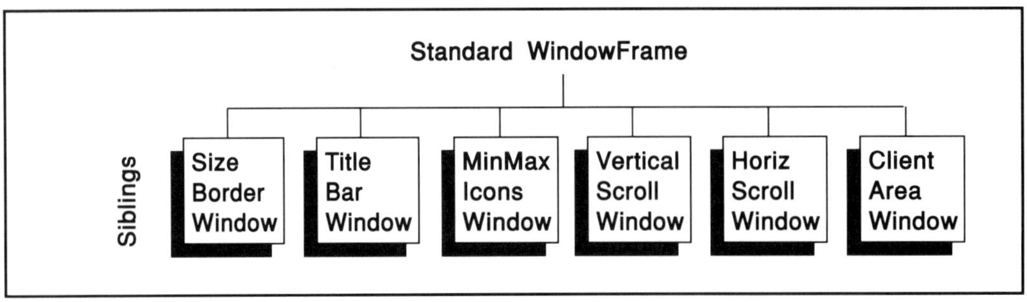

Figure 34-4. Inside a "Standard Window."

The concept of *parenting* should not be confused with PM's concept of *ownership*. In PM, a window can "own" other windows. An owner window is the recipient of all messages for the windows that it owns. Note that parents do not necessarily "own" their children.

The Brains of the Window: Classes and Procedures

The "smart" element that defines a window's behavior is the **window class**. This is the element that knows "what to do." Every window belongs to a window class which determines the style of the window, and specifies the event-driven procedure that will handle the messages for the window. In PM terminology, these event-driven procedures are called **window procedures**. The window procedures are at the heart of programming in PM. They are responsible for all aspects of a window including:

- How the window appears.
- How the window behaves and responds to state changes.
- How the window handles user input.

All user interaction with the window is passed as messages to its window procedure. When an application creates a window, it must specify a window class. The "class" tells PM which window procedure gets to process the messages generated by some window activity. Multiple windows can belong to the same class. This means that the window procedure can handle events from more than one window. A good programming practice is to make the window procedure code reentrant, since it may be called from several sources simultaneously.

PM supplies a number of built-in windows that have their own window procedures in preregistered "public" window classes. These built-in windows can be used to give your applications a "common look" which, by no coincidence, is very CUA-like. Examples of the built-in window classes are: scrollbar, menu, button, frame, entry field, list box, combo box, and the MLE. These classes are window procedures for the predefined PM windows, which we presented in the previous section.

PM's Message-Based Nervous System

If windows are the heart of PM, and window procedures its brain; then *messages are its nervous system*. Typically, dozens of messages will be circulating around the PM system. A message can contain information, the request for information, or a request for an action.

Even though OS/2 is a true multitasking operating system, PM applications must share the computer's keyboard, mouse, and screen. OS/2 places input events into PM's single system queue (see Figure 34-5 on page 858), which has a capacity for handling in the vicinity of 60 keystrokes or mouse clicks. Messages are read off the system queue by the PM message router on a first-in, first-out basis. The PM input router

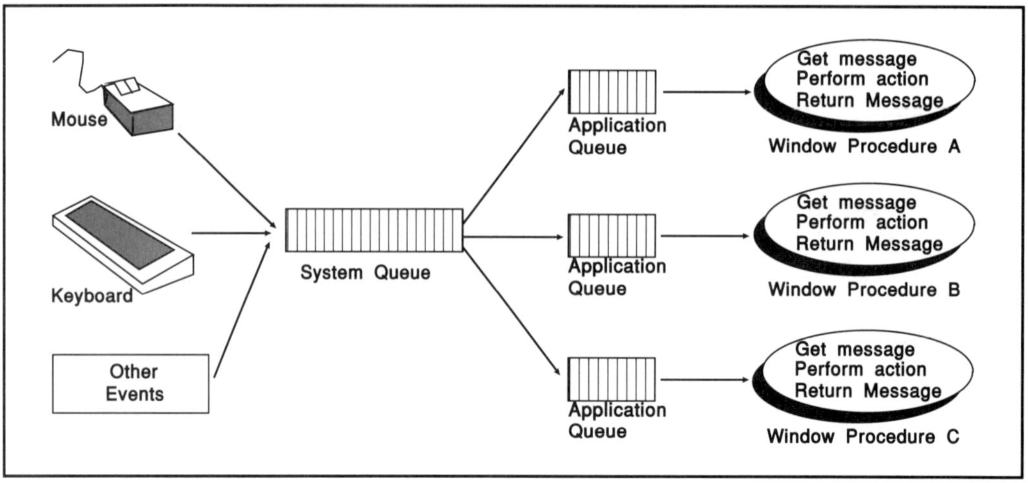

Figure 34-5. PM's System Queue and the Window Procedure Queues.

converts the system input information into a message for the application that controls the window where the event was generated. The router can communicate the message to the application in one of two ways:

- By **posting** the message to the application's message queue. This is done for messages that do not require immediate action. Every PM application needs at least one message queue to receive input from the keyboard or mouse. An application can create one message queue per thread. A window is associated with the message queue of the thread which creates it. A single queue can, of course, handle more than one window. An application thread can retrieve and process the message from its queue at the appropriate time.
- By **sending** the message directly to the application's window procedure. This is done when PM requires immediate action from the application. The window procedure can carry out the request or pass the unprocessed messages to a default window procedure provided by PM.

The window procedure handles both queued and non-queued messages in the same manner. It doesn't care how the message got to it.

The PM Message Etiquette

A message will not be presented to an application until the previous message has been processed. Since the majority of an application's time is spent waiting for a message to arrive, PM will allow during the interim other applications to process their respective messages. This is a form of cooperative multitasking using message processing to schedule applications. An ill-behaved application can slow down or even stop PM, if it starts a time-consuming task while processing a PM message. There is a rule-of-thumb that says *messages must be processed within 0.1 seconds.* More on that later.

The PM Message Structure

PM can generate about 100 general purpose messages, and 150 special-purpose messages which serve special control windows. You can also create your own application-specific messages for communicating between windows. A PM message is always addressed to a particular window and each message contains the following information:

- **A window handle:** This parameter identifies the window for which a message is destined. This parameter is useful because most message queues and window procedures handle more than one window. Your code can use the handle to determine the window for which this is addressed.
- **A message ID:** This is an integer value that uniquely identifies the message.
- **Two message parameters:** Each message parameter is a 32-bit value that specifies either the data or the data's address for that message. An application will process the message parameters based on the message ID.

Table 34-1 provides a brief sampling of some of the more common PM system messages:

Table 34-1. Examples of Some Commonly Used PM Messages.

PM Message	Description
WM_CREATE	This message notifies a window procedure that its window is about to be made visible on the screen (this is creation time). This gives the window procedure a chance to do some processing before the window is displayed on the screen for the first time.
WM_PAINT	This message tells a window procedure that its window needs repainting.
WM_ERASEBACKGROUND	This message gives a window procedure an opportunity to paint the window background in some preferred color. Returning TRUE causes PM to paint the background itself, using the default color: CLR_BACKGROUND.
WM_SIZE	This message tells a window procedure that the window is being resized. Both the old and new dimensions are passed in the message parameters.
WM_CHAR	This message tells a window procedure that a key was pressed or released.
WM_MOUSEMOVE	This message tells a window procedure (or a mouse capture handler) that the mouse pointer has moved. It supplies the new mouse coordinates relative to the receiving window.
WM_BUTTON1DOWN	This message tells a window procedure (or a mouse capture handler) that the mouse button has been depressed. It supplies the mouse coordinates where that happened.
WM_COMMAND	This message tells a window procedure that one of the control windows in its frame has a significant action to report. These messages are typically originated by push buttons and pull-down menu selections.

Table 34-1. Examples of Some Commonly Used PM Messages.

PM Message	Description
WM_CONTROL	This message tells a window procedure that one of the control windows in its frame has a significant control event to report. These messages are typically originated by radio buttons, check boxes, MLEs and entry fields.
WM_HELP	This message tells a window procedure that a help button (or the F1 key) was entered. We can make use of this message to consolidate help related processing.
WM_DESTROY	This message tells a window procedure that its window is about to be destroyed.
WM_CLOSE	This message tells a window procedure that the window is about to be closed.
WM_QUIT	This message marks the end of message processing for a window queue. It does not get dispatched to the window procedure.

So What Does a PM Programmer Do?

A PM application will, at the very minimum, define one new window and one new window procedure. Commercial PM programs will typically consist of hundreds of "custom" window procedures that are developed to meet an application's requirements. For each window the PM programmer will:

- Define the window attributes.
- Identify the window input messages that the procedure will process. The rest of the messages are passed on to PM's default message handlers.
- Write the window procedure that handles the responses to the input messages that are of interest.
- Document the output messages created by the window procedure.

In a nutshell, a PM program consists of many window procedures that act on anything they're interested in and leave the rest for OS/2 to handle.

Putting it all Together

Here's how the concepts we've introduced so far come together:

- The combination of the window and the window procedure is the PM version of an object-like architecture. The window procedure defines the class to which the window belongs.
- The window procedure receives messages on behalf of its window and responds appropriately.

- The PM windows have a genealogy. Each window must have a parent and the parent-child relationships determine how windows are positioned and moved on the screen.
- Messages are used in PM for conveying information and events between windows. Transmitting a message to a window is in effect making a call to its window procedure.
- Messages may be sent directly to a window procedure or they may be posted on a message queue. The receiver of the message can't tell the difference.
- PM makes available a number of predefined windows and their message procedures (public classes) in DLLs. These windows help create the CUA "common look."
- Programming in PM consists mostly of defining windows and then coding their window procedures.

RESOURCES AND TOOLS

Resources are "things" that are created separately from your programs using specialized tools. Here are some reasons for using resources in PM:

1. Changes may be made to the resources without recompiling your source code. An example is National language-specific data.
2. PM makes specialized tools to create resources available in the OS/2 Toolkit. Without tools these resources would be very difficult to create.
3. Multiple instances of your application can share resources without reloading them into memory.

A PM resource starts out as a file that is managed independently from your program. It contains: data, bitmaps, or other independently created resources that your program will use. These resources get added to your program's (.EXE) or are placed in DLLs. They usually end up in the read-only data segments of your programs. The items in resource files are loaded in memory using specialized PM API calls.

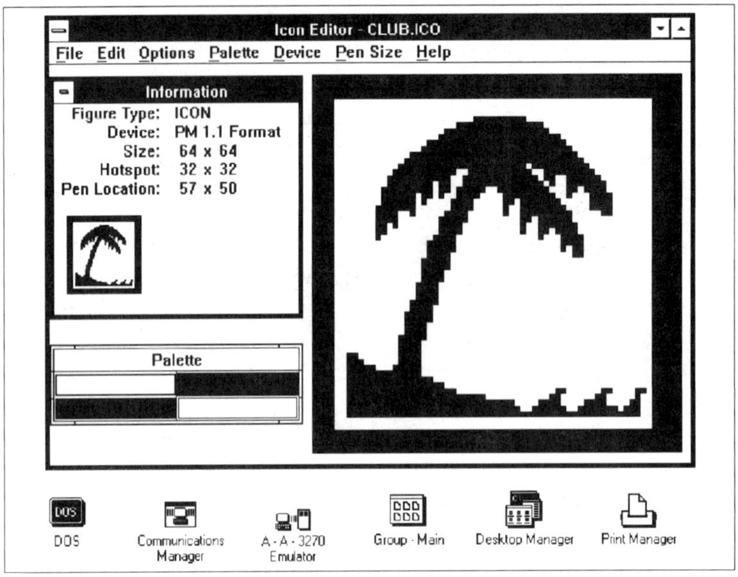

Figure 34-6. Using the Icon Editor to Create the Club Med Font.

Here are some of the tools PM makes available for the creation of specialized resources:

ICONEDIT.EXE This is an icon editor that is used to create the following resource files: bitmaps (.BMP), icons (.ICO), and pointers (.PNT). Figure 34-6 shows the icon editor screen capture.

FONTEDIT.EXE This is a font editor that is used to create your own font files (.FNT). Note that PM comes with a number of built-in fonts that can be used with your applications.

DIALOG.EXE This WYSIWYG editor is used to create dialog boxes that use PM's built-in control windows.

RC.EXE This is a resource compiler. After you create the resource, you declare them in a resource definition file (.DEF) and then compile them using the RC utility. The resources then get added to your executable file. In other words, RC binds the resources to the (.EXE) file created by LINK.

THE ANATOMY OF A PM PROGRAM

A PM program consists of a main() procedure and a set of window procedures. The main() procedure allocates global data, does initialization, and creates the PM objects. It then goes into a loop waiting for messages to be placed on its queue. When it finds a message, it dispatches it to the appropriate window procedure. When a special

WM_QUIT message is received, main() cleans up after itself and terminates the program.

All PM programs use more or less the same main() template which consists of about 40 lines of code. PM programmers usually paste this setup code into a source file when writing a new program. The heart of a PM application is its window procedures. This is the code that controls the attributes of a window and responds to the messages it generates. Figure 34-7 presents the structure of a PM program. Here's a step-by-step description:

1. ***Connect to PM***. Issue a WinInitialize call to obtain an anchor block handle from PM. This handle is used with subsequent commands.

2. ***Load the resources***. This is a good place to load the separate resources you created using the PM tools. These separate resources can be text strings, text files, binary files containing graphics, or other separate pieces of information. PM provides several specialized API calls for loading resources, such as: WinLoadString, WinLoadPtr, WinLoadDlg, WinLoadMenu, etc.

3. ***Create the message queue***. Issue the WinCreateMsgQueue call to create your application's message queue and obtain a handle for it. You can specify the queue size through a parameter. The default size is 10 messages. The queue is the primary mechanism by which your application communicates with PM.

4. ***Register the window classes***. You must issue a WinRegisterClass call for every window class before creating one or more instances of a window. This call registers the window class and its associated window procedure with PM.

5. ***Create and display the main windows***. First, create all the windows that are direct children of the PM desktop. These are the most "senior" windows in your application. Issue a WinCreateStdWindow call to create a "standard" window. This call returns two handles, one that identifies the frame of the standard window, and one that identifies its client area.

6. ***Create and display the child windows***. Now that you've obtained the handles of the parent windows, you can create child windows using WinCreateStdWindow or WinCreateWindow. Continue this process until you've created all the descendant windows for your application. You may also want to issue WinSetWindowPos calls to position the windows on your desktop. Remember, the child windows always get displayed on top of their parent window. Child windows are positioned relative to the lower-left corner of the parent window.

7. ***Enter the message dispatch loop***. At this point, your PM program is ready to receive messages and do some work. The main program enters a "while" loop issuing WinGetMsg calls to obtain messages from PM and then turns around and issues WinDispatchMsg calls to call the appropriate window procedure via PM. The program will remain in this loop until the WinGetMsg call receives a WM_QUIT message. An application can terminate its own loop by posting a WM_QUIT message to its queue.

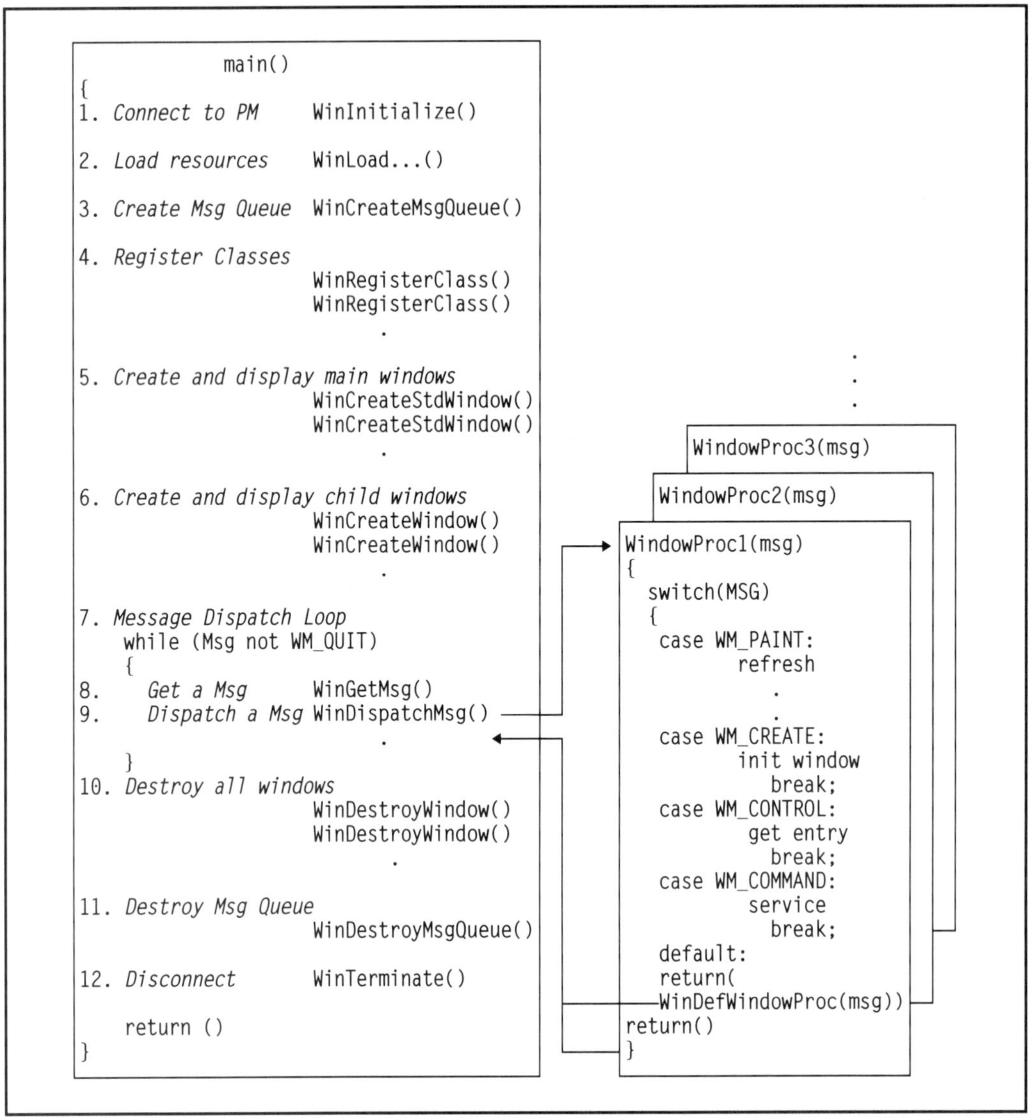

Figure 34-7. The Anatomy of a PM Program.

8. ***Get a message***. A WinGetMsg call retrieves a message from the application queue. If there are no messages in the queue the WinGetMsg call blocks until a message arrives.

9. ***Dispatch a message***. A WinDispatchMsg will call the appropriate window procedure via PM and pass it the message to be processed. Notice in the figure that control is now passed to a window procedure. The window procedure's code is straightforward. It consists of a switch statement with a case for each message type the procedure intends to process. The real work of a PM application is done within the case statements. The messages that are not of interest to the window

procedure, end up in the default section of the switch statement. Notice that the default consists of handing the message over to WinDefWindowProc. This is a PM-supplied window procedure that handles all the messages that your window procedure is not interested in processing.

10. ***Destroy all windows***. A well-behaved PM application cleans up after itself when it drops out of the loop. The WinDestroyWindow call releases the window's resources.

11. ***Destroy the message queue***. The WinDestroyMsgQueue is issued to release the queue.

12. ***Disconnect from PM***. The WinTerminate call disconnects the application from PM.

"HELLO WORLD FROM PM"

This section shows you the steps necessary to develop a simple PM application. We're going to code the PM version of the world famous "Hello World" application. The code will display "Hello from Presentation Manager" on the screen.

The Display

Figure 34-8 is a screen capture of the output produced by this program.

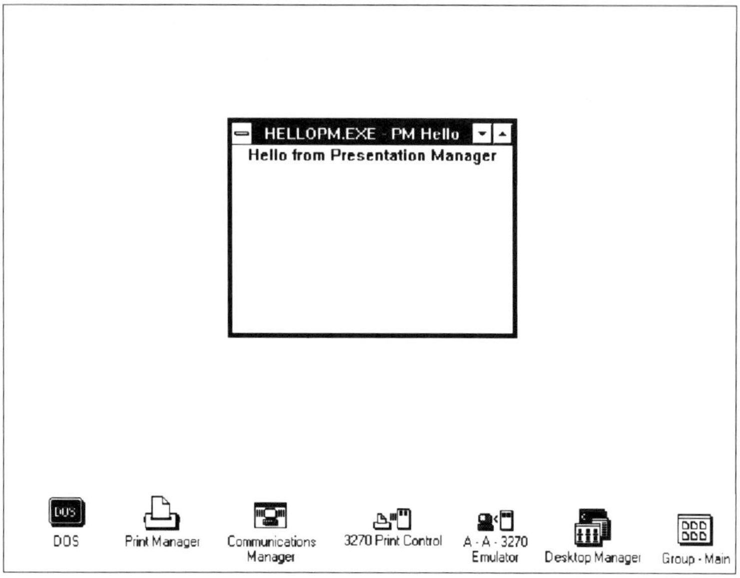

Figure 34-8. The Output of Hello World Using PM.

The HELLOPM.C Program

Figure 34-9 shows the listing for the program that created "Hello from PM." Like all PM programs, this program consists of a **main()** procedure that provides the initialization and setup and the window procedures. The code for the **main()** procedure is straightforward. Here is what it does:

1. It declares the global variables.
2. It connects to PM and creates the application queue.
3. It registers a window class called "helloWindow" and associates it with the window procedure: **HelloWindowProc()**. It tells PM that the window is resizable.
4. It sets the flags for all the child control windows and options that will appear in the window's frame.
5. It issues the call to create a standard window with the control options that are specified.
6. It positions the window on the desktop.
7. It executes the message loop until WM_QUIT is issued.
8. It terminates PM and releases resources.

The code for the window procedure, **HelloWindowProc()**, is also straightforward. It consists of a switch statement which processes only three messages: WM_ERASEBACKGROUND, WM_PAINT, and WM_CLOSE. The rest of the message types are of no interest and get returned to PM's default handler window procedure. The bulk of the code is used to process the WM_PAINT message. Here's how this message gets processed:

1. A WinBeginPaint call is issued to obtain a presentation space handle from PM.
2. A WinDrawText call is issued to display the text. Notice how the different attribute options.
3. A WinEndPaint call is issued to release the presentation space.

This may seem like a lot of work just to issue a simple "Hello World." In fairness to PM, a lot of this code consists of the standard **main()** template. PM also provides many window features that are not included in your standard "Hello World" programs. However, so does DM, and writing a DM application is a lot simpler. In the next chapter, we'll show you how to combine PM with DM and make them each do what they do best.

```
/*************************************************************************/
/*  PROGRAM NAME: HELLOPM - a Presentation Manager hello example         */
/*                                                                        */
/*  PROGRAM DESCRIPTION:  This program demonstrates a simple PM program   */
/*                        which only displays hello.                      */
/*                                                                        */
/*  PROGRAM INVOCATION:   HELLOPM                                         */
/*************************************************************************/
#include <string.h>
#define INCL_WIN                          /* include Win calls           */
#define INCL_GPI                          /* include Gpi calls           */
#include <os2.h>                          /* PM header file              */

/*-----------------------------------------------------------------------*/
/* global variables and declares                                         */
/*-----------------------------------------------------------------------*/
HAB  hab;                            /* PM anchor block handle      */
CHAR szHello[] = "Hello from Presentation Manager";

MRESULT EXPENTRY HelloWindowProc(HWND hwnd, USHORT msg, MPARAM mp1, MPARAM mp2);

/*-----------------------------------------------------------------------*/
/* Main routine.                                                         */
/*-----------------------------------------------------------------------*/
void cdecl main()
{
  HMQ  hmq;                               /* Message queue handle        */
  HWND hwndClient;                        /* Client area window handle   */
  HWND hwndFrame;                         /* Frame window handle         */
  QMSG qmsg;                              /* Message from message queue  */
  ULONG flCreate;                         /* Window creation control flags*/

  hab = WinInitialize( NULL );            /* Initialize PM               */
  hmq = WinCreateMsgQueue( hab, 0 );      /* Create a message queue      */

  WinRegisterClass(                       /* Register window class       */
     hab,                                 /* Anchor block handle         */
     "HelloWindow",                       /* Window class name           */
     HelloWindowProc,                     /* Address of window procedure */
     CS_SIZEREDRAW,                       /* Class style                 */
     0);                                  /* No extra window words       */

  flCreate = FCF_TITLEBAR | FCF_SYSMENU | /* Set frame control flags     */
             FCF_SIZEBORDER | FCF_MINMAX |
             FCF_SHELLPOSITION | FCF_TASKLIST | FCF_PALETTE_NORMAL;
```

Figure 34-9 (Part 1 of 3). The HELLOPM.C Listing.

```
    hwndFrame = WinCreateStdWindow(
                HWND_DESKTOP,                    /* Desktop window is parent     */
                0L,                              /* No frame styles              */
                &flCreate,                       /* Frame control flag           */
                "HelloWindow",                   /* Client window class name     */
                " - PM Hello",                   /* Window title text            */
                0L,                              /* No special class style       */
                NULL,                            /* Resource is in .EXE file     */
                255,                             /* Frame window identifier      */
                &hwndClient);                    /* Client window handle         */

    WinSetWindowPos(hwndFrame, HWND_TOP, 230, 150, 250, 185,
                    SWP_SIZE | SWP_MOVE | SWP_ACTIVATE | SWP_SHOW);

    /*-----------------------------------*/
    /* Get and dispatch messages         */
    /*-----------------------------------*/
    while( WinGetMsg( hab, &qmsg, NULL, 0, 0 ) )
      WinDispatchMsg( hab, &qmsg );

    WinDestroyWindow( hwndFrame );               /* Destroy the window           */
    WinDestroyMsgQueue( hmq );                   /* Destroy the queue            */
    WinTerminate( hab );                         /* terminate                    */
  }

  /*-------------------------------------------------------------------------*/
  /* Window Procedure                                                        */
  /*-------------------------------------------------------------------------*/
  MRESULT EXPENTRY HelloWindowProc( HWND hwnd, USHORT msg,
                                    MPARAM mp1, MPARAM mp2 )
  {
    HPS    hps;                                  /* Presentation Space handle    */
    RECTL  rc;                                   /* Rectangle coordinates        */

    switch( msg )
    {
      case WM_ERASEBACKGROUND:
        /*-----------------------------------*/
        /* cause window background to be     */
        /* painted in SYSCLR_WINDOW          */
        /*-----------------------------------*/
        return (MRESULT)( TRUE );

      case WM_PAINT:
        /*-----------------------------------*/
        /* paint the window                  */
        /*-----------------------------------*/
        hps = WinBeginPaint( hwnd, NULL, &rc ); /* Create a presentation space */
        WinDrawText(hps,                         /* presentation space           */
                    -1,szHello,                  /* string, calculate strlen     */
                    &rc,                         /* rectangle from WinBeginPaint*/
                    CLR_DARKBLUE,SYSCLR_WINDOW,  /* Fore/Background colors       */
                    DT_TOP | DT_CENTER);         /* string placement in rect.    */
        WinEndPaint( hps );
        break;
```

Figure 34-9 (Part 2 of 3). The HELLOPM.C Listing.

```
        case WM_CLOSE:
          /*--------------------------------*/
          /* cause the application to end   */
          /*--------------------------------*/
          WinPostMsg( hwnd, WM_QUIT, 0L, 0L );
          break;

        default:
          /*--------------------------------*/
          /* unknown messages to default    */
          /*--------------------------------*/
          return WinDefWindowProc( hwnd, msg, mp1, mp2 );
      }
      return FALSE;
    }
```

Figure 34-9 (Part 3 of 3). The HELLOPM.C Listing.

Chapter 35

PM and DM: Two to Tango

This chapter proposes a marriage between DM and PM. So, we will start out with an explanation of what DM, a GUI tool, brings to the party. We then explain the mechanics which allow Dialog Manager programs to drop into the Presentation Manager. The result is like using a high-level language with the hooks in place to drop into assembler whenever you need to. This marriage of convenience allows us to develop, structure, and maintain the bulk of our dialog code using the high productivity environment a GUI tool provides, and then drop into PM whenever we need to develop some fancy graphic presentation that is beyond the scope of what the tool provides.

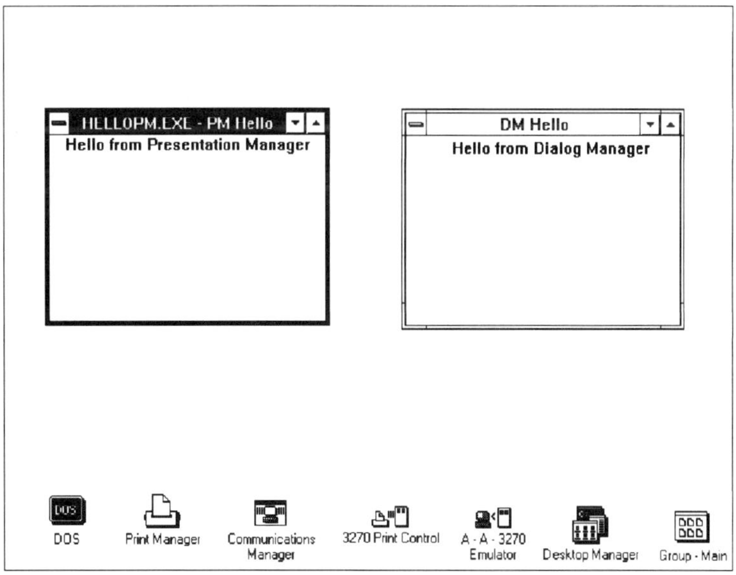

Figure 35-1. "Hello World from PM" and "Hello World from DM."

What Does DM Bring to the Party?

Figure 35-1 makes a very graphic point: we have two identical "Hellos," one of which took much less code to produce. This is because we used thc Dialog Manager, a GUI tool, to create the display (see the previous chapters). Performing the same job with substantially less code is only the tip of the productivity iceberg. The real productivity gains show up when you consider the "other" things a tool like Dialog Manager can do for you. Here's a list of value-added benefits that can be obtained by using Dialog Manager:

- It allows you to create PM screens and dialogs quickly (once you learn the tag language). DM manages the control loop and all the low-level PM stuff. You get to specify the screen objects and how they behave.

- It allows you to specify rules for field-entry validation. The user input is automatically validated at runtime according to the rules you specify (through the tag language).

- It allows you to bind C-language variables (such as arrays) to the screen areas where they get automatically displayed and updated. For example, the Dialog Manager may display the contents of a C-language array as a scrollable selection listbox and return the user-selected items to your program.

- It provides automatic scrolling which includes the display of scrolling lists and the scrollbar itself.

- It creates windows and window classes, and provides a subclassed environment for your code to create its own PM constructs.

- It creates CUA conforming screens.

- It provides extensive facilities for the creation of CUA conforming help windows. The help windows can be associated with individual fields for context-based help. You can also lace your help text with "hypertext-like" references to other help topics. The help facility also allows you to easily create an alphabetized index of help topics which refer to your various help panels.

- It allows you to specify messages and the conditions which trigger their display. The messages will be displayed in message windows using the appropriate CUA icons. Messages are maintained separately from the code which makes it convenient to translate into other National languages.

- It is easy to maintain a Dialog Manager application. The screen descriptions and the rules that describe the screen behavior (including how it reacts to user actions) are in tag files that are maintained separately from the C-language code. The tags impose a structure on screen objects which makes it easy to reuse object parts.

- It is easy to change a Dialog Manager application. Most of the changes that affect the screen will not require a recompile of your C-language code. The panel library allows you to specify at runtime what panels are needed as opposed to compiling all the screens required for an application.

- It is easy to provide National Language Support. Everything the user sees is in tag files, which can easily be translated into different languages.
- It is easy to provide rapid-prototype systems using tags with very little C-language code behind them. These systems can be used to gather user requirements. The beauty is that the screens in the prototype do not have to be re-implemented once they work. In addition, the user gets to see the interface during all stages of development.

Unequal Competition

Yes, this is a very unequal race. With Dialog Manager, an average C programmer can produce a PM application ten times faster than an advanced PM programmer. Most importantly, the cost of ownership of a large PM application is substantially lowered if it is coded using Dialog Manager. Just think about how you would manage a 100 panel PM application without Dialog Manager or some equivalent GUI tool?

What about the added cost? Well, DM is practically *free*. It is bundled with the OS/2 Toolkit and there are no runtime license charges for distributing DM. In this sense, it's a bargain! You can count on IBM support for DM for at least another five years. It's like any other product that is in the OS/2 Toolkit.

The Arcadia CUA Workbench from Arcadia Technologies Inc. supports a WYSIWYG screen painter that allows developers to design the layout of Dialog Manager panels. The Arcadia tool generates tag files which are portable to Windows 3.0 or PM. You will need to purchase the Windows 3.0 DM runtime from Arcadia.

So Where's the Bad News?

On the other hand, you also heard us say that "there are no free lunches in life or in software systems"; so where's the catch when it comes to DM or any GUI tool for that matter?

- No GUI tool will ever totally harness the awesome power that is packaged in PM. It is simply the most powerful graphic system ever provided on a personal computer.
- GUI tools will always lag behind PM when it comes to offering new functions.
- PM is addictive. "Real" programmers will never totally give it up. Look at what it took to move us from assembler into C.

A Marriage of Convenience

So, we propose a compromise, a marriage of convenience. We code the bulk of our "garden variety" database dialog panels in DM and drop into PM whenever we need some special graphic effects. When you think about it, almost all the information inside a database is textual or numeric. A front-end system like DM can easily take care of generating 90% of database front-end dialogs. The remaining 10% will be done using PM directly.

DM AND PM: HOW THEY COME TOGETHER?

The Dialog Manager provides a very convenient method for dropping into PM: the **User Control**. A User Control allows you to create your own PM constructs within a Dialog Manager panel. You define the User Control area on the panel using the UC tag. You then write your own PM window procedure to support the User Control area. User Controls can be used to track a mouse, handle input, or draw complicated pictures. It's all done by the PM code you supply. Figure 35-2 takes you through the steps involved in writing a User Control:

1. ***Define the User Control area in your tag file using the UC tag***. Create a UC tag area for each User Control on your panel. In the example, we reserve an area (window) that's six by six characters and we assign it a window class name, "BITMAP".

2. ***Register the window class in your C code***. We do this by issuing a WinRegisterClass API call for each class we define. These calls should be issued when you first start your program. Remember that each window class requires a window procedure. In the example, we register the window procedure BitMapProc() for the BITMAP class.

3. ***Write a window procedure for each window class***. This is where all the PM action takes place. This window procedure is like a PM window procedure. You cannot issue direct DM calls from within the window procedure.

4. ***Interact with DM through messages***. Your window procedure can interact with DM through DM defined messages. For example, it can issue a CM_END_DISPLAY message to tell DM to remove a panel and return control to the user. Or DM may issue CM_UPDATE_CONTROL to notify the window procedure that its panel is being displayed or redisplayed.

5. ***Interact with PM through messages***. Your window procedure also handles the PM messages as required by your application.

6. ***Return any messages that are not processed to DM***. The window procedure should return any messages it does not process to DM instead of PM. To pass all messages not processed back to DM, we first call WinQueryClassInfo to obtain the address of the window procedure for the DM_USER_CONTROL class. We

then pass control back to this window procedure by calling it. (Note to PM experts: our window procedure is subclassed from the DM_USER_CONTROL class).

Tag file:

```
1.      <uc class=BITMAP PRMDATA='%bmp1file'
            minwidth=6 maxwidth=6 mindepth=6 maxdepth=6>
```

main():

```
2.  WinRegisterClass((HAB)NULL,"BITMAP", BitMapProc,
               CCTL_UC_CLASS_STYLE, CCTL_UC_EXTRA_BYTES);
```

Window Procedure:

```
3. extern MRESULT EXPENTRY BitMapProc(HWND hwnd, USHORT msg,
                                      MPARAM mp1, MPARAM mp2)
    {
     switch(msg)
     {
4.     case CM_UPDATE_CONTROL:
            WinInvalidateRect(hwnd, NULL, TRUE);
            break;

       case CM_FREE_CTL_RESOURCES:
            /*--------------------------------------*/
            /* Terminate and free resources         */
            /*--------------------------------------*/
            break;

5.     case WM_PAINT:
            /*--------------------------------------*/
            /* display bitmap                       */
            /*--------------------------------------*/
            break;

6.     default:
            WinQueryClassInfo((HAB)NULL,
                              "DM_USER_CONTROL",
                              &classInfo);
            returnValue =
              (*classInfo.pfnWindowProc)(hwnd, msg, mp1, mp2);
            break;

     } /* end switch */
     return returnValue;
    }
```

Figure 35-2. The Anatomy of a DM/PM Program.

Part VII

The Grand Finale, Club Med Client-Server Application

We will end the book with a fun program that connects front-end clients with a back-end *Transaction Server*. This is the adventurous grand finale that brings together all the elements developed in this book. The project of Part VII is to take you through the complete design and implementation of a client-server application. To pick on a fun topic, we will develop an Online Transaction Program (OLTP) that provides a fictitious reservation system for Club Med. Here are some highlights of what Part VII provides:

- A methodology that helps you design, rapidly prototype, develop and document client-server applications.
- A multithreaded, event-driven GUI client.
- A multiuser transaction server. The server is Named Pipes based and supports the movement of Binary Large Objects (BLOBs) between the clients and the server.
- Advanced graphic constructs for the display of Bitmaps, Metafiles, and MLEs.
- A working client-server application.

Here is the road map we will follow in Part VII:

- In Chapter 36, "Designing the Club Med Application", we start the three-chapter Grand Finale, which consists of writing a complete Club Med client-server program. This chapter introduces the Club Med application and database, and develops a methodology for dissecting and designing client-server programs.
- Chapter 37, "The Club Med Client", provides the code and the tag objects for the front-end of the Club Med application. This chapter also provides an architectural foundation for the creation of PM-DM based front-ends for OLTP.
- Chapter 38, "The Club Med Server", provides the code that implements the *back-end* of the Club Med application. This is essentially a transaction server engine which receives requests for work from networked clients using Named Pipes.

Chapter 36

Designing the Club Med Application

This is the first of a three-chapter "grand finale" that brings together all the building blocks developed in this book into a single client-server application: Club Med. We will develop an Online Transaction Program (OLTP) that provides a "fictitious" reservation system for Club Med.

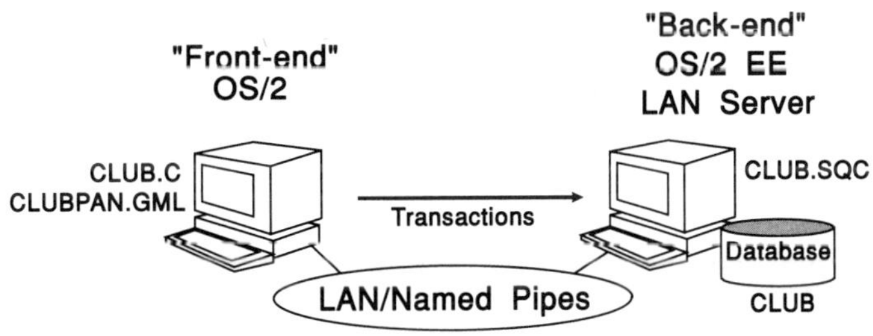

Figure 36-1. Club Med Client and Server.

Club Med is a "classical" GUI front-end client-server application (see Figure 36-1). The DM/PM client provides the "front-end" of the application. The client code is provided by CLUB.C in conjunction with the CLUBPAN.GML Dialog Tag file. The server executes the "back-end" transactions. The server code is provided by the CLUB.SQC program and a CLUB database which uses the OS/2 EE Database Manager. The server also runs the IBM LAN Server program, which provides Named Pipe support and acts as a file server. The client and the server communicate using Named Pipes and the LAN Server's file services. Transactions are submitted over Named Pipes and large files are moved over the network using the LAN Server's redirector.

You can see that this application provides "the whole works." Here's the plan for presenting all this information:

- The current chapter, the first of the three-chapter series, starts you off by presenting a framework on how to dissect and analyze client-server applications. We will use this framework to present an overall view of the client-server application, starting with what the end user sees. This overall view includes a description of the internal logic of the application and its major interfaces and interprocess protocols. It also includes RSQL *run* file used to create the CLUB database and the *Make* file which builds the Club Med client and server programs.
- The second chapter in the series, Chapter 37, "The Club Med Client", presents the front-end client. This is an important chapter which demonstrates how to create an event-driven client using a PM/DM based methodology.
- The third and last chapter in the series, Chapter 38, "The Club Med Server", shows you how to create a multiuser transaction server. We provide the code for database transactions which use SQL. We also include the code for the Named Pipes and LAN server based client-server exchanges.

HOW TO DEVELOP A CLIENT-SERVER PROGRAM

Client-Server systems are complex by nature. They are made up of peer programs that run on separate machines. The human in the distributed loop can be a source of added complications. Humans make lots of errors, do unexpected things, and typically require lots of information from diverse sources. The Club Med application we present in this chapter is a working client-server program. We will be spending most of our time "reverse engineering" this program and analyzing how it works. But before we start doing that, we will first take a look at what it takes to design a new client-server application from the ground up.

Where Does the Design Start?

The design of traditional applications usually starts with the data. Client-Server applications, on the other hand, ideally have two starting points: the screen and the data (unless the data for a business process is already in place). The screen and data designs come together at the transaction level. The transaction maps the screen to the database and vice versa. One way to avoid a "chicken and egg" situation from developing between the data and the screens is to use the rapid prototyping method described below. Rapid prototyping allows you to develop your system incrementally. You start with the client and work your way iteratively towards the server. You always move in small steps, constantly refining the design as you go along. Make sure to involve your end user during all the stages of the interface design.

The user interface and the objects which make it up permeate the entire application and determine its shape. The design of the application starts from what the user sees on the screen and works its way towards the server and the database structure. What the user sees in a CUA application are windows containing objects which react to user input and actions. The objects are manipulated according to the requirements of the business process. So, the first order of the day is to identify the objects and the sequence of operations on them. The design process then starts with scenarios of how an application is typically used in the business environment.

Rapid Prototyping is Essential

Client-Server applications which use PC front-ends are by nature graphic-intensive (particularly the new applications). Prototyping the user interface is essential. Prototypes are used to identify with your customer's participation, the application's requirements. Prototyping is an iterative activity with many false starts. Here is how the typical prototype evolves:

1. ***Identify the window flow.*** How is the application invoked from the desktop? How many windows will run concurrently? What are the initial window sizes? Where will they be placed?

2. ***Define your object-types.*** What are the main object types in the application? What subobjects do they contain? What are the attributes of the objects? What functions should they have?

3. ***Work on the detailed window contents.*** What are the menu selection items? What actions apply to each object? What input and output fields are required? What push buttons and control buttons are needed? What level of help is needed?

4. ***Develop dry run scenarios.*** You can create your screen objects using Dialog Manager. A simple skeleton program can be used to navigate through different screens without causing anything real to happen. Use the scenarios to validate the user interface. The scenarios should also help you identify the major event-driven interactions.

5. ***Define your database tables.*** You are now in a position to take a first stab at defining the database objects which correspond to the visual objects you just created. Iterate on this step until you get it right. Many trade-offs are involved.

6. ***Publish the client-server messages.*** Messages are the methods by which the clients execute transactions on servers. Define the major transactions and the request/reply messages associated with them. Will file transfers be required?

7. ***Develop your code one object-type at a time.*** Write the SQL code for each transaction. Do that one object-type at a time. There are typically many transactions per object-type. Validate the user interface and the performance of the system with your customer.

8. ***From prototype to working system.*** A working system is the sum of all the objects it contains. Since you are developing your system incrementally, you will have a full working system when you've coded your last object-type.

This prototype-based approach to design eliminates the need for lengthy specifications. More importantly, this approach allows the customer to participate in the specification of the product and its stepwise refinement. The approach also lends itself well to the design of distributed applications, since you can refine and fine-tune the distribution of function as you learn more about your system's real-life behavior.

HOW TO DISSECT A CLIENT-SERVER APPLICATION

In the section, we will dive deeper into the design of client-server systems by analyzing in some detail a system that works. This reverse engineering is like *learning anatomy by dissecting a frog*. We already have a working client-server program, Club Med, and we want to understand how it works. The assumption is that the program was designed using the eight-point methodology described in "How to Develop a Client-Server Program" on page 880. For the rest of this chapter, you should think of yourself as being in the following role model:

- Club Med has contracted you to finish writing their club reservation system.
- This is your first day on the job.
- You are trying to size up what part of the system was completed and what remains to be done.
- You need a method to organize your thinking and conceptually understand the prototype code that was given to you.
- A working model of the prototype is available for you to experiment with.

Where do you start? We will develop a method to help you analyze an existing client-server system. We will then demonstrate this method by explaining how the Club Med Program works. The idea is to extend our knowledge of how to design client-server applications. Here are the main highlights of the proposed method:

1. ***Start with what the user sees***. A client-server system can be thought of as a client-driven event system. The server is in a sense passively waiting on requests from clients. The client in turn is driven by the user who is at the "controls" within the confines of the business process. User actions and screen transitions are typically the source of transactions. Information required upon entering a screen may also be the source of a transaction. Object/action intersections almost always lead to the generation of a transaction. There is also a high probability that events such as data entry and action dialogs will generate transactions. The best way to analyze these transaction-generating sources is to walk through scenarios of how the application is used. Each scenario tells a story by traversing one of the paths that an end user might take in an application. The scenario described in "Club Med: What the User Sees" on page 883 is a good example of this process.

2. ***Look at the transaction message formats***. The messages provide the only coupling between the clients and the server. The publication of the messages advertises to the world what a server does. A message typically has a "command" field

and a data field. The data field contains the command parameters. In our scheme of things, we divide transactions (or commands) into two broad categories based on the type of responses they produce:

a. *Request/reply transactions*. These are transactions that generate short replies. These, are usually updates, inserts, deletes, or single-row queries against database objects.
b. *Bulk Response transactions*. These are transactions that generate one or more result files. Think of a result file as bulk data (a BLOB). Result files may "result" from a multirow SELECT, or from the request for a metafile or bitmap.

The messages to the Club Med transaction server are described in "The Club Med Transactions" on page 891. The description includes the response generated and what the transaction does to the database.

3. ***Look at the database table definitions***. The SQL CREATE TABLE statements provide very complete documentation of data types and the relationships between tables (such as referential integrity constraints). If you want to get fancy, you can develop an Entity-Relationship model of your data (we don't). We provide the table definitions for the CLUB database in "The CLUB Database" on page 894.

4. ***Walk through a system scenario***. Such a scenario should follow a transaction from its source through its execution. Identify the protocols that link the different elements. Blow up this scenario in areas that require more detail. We provide such a scenario in "Club Med: A System Scenario" on page 895.

5. ***Look at the Make file***. You'll get a description of all the program elements in one place. We provide the Make file for Club Med in "The Club Med Make File" on page 898. This file builds both the client and server programs. It also identifies the tag language files and those which contain embedded SQL statements.

CLUB MED: WHAT THE USER SEES

Since we already have a working Club Med application, some of the actual screen captures will be used to introduce you to the application and show you how it is typically used. You should follow the scenario described below by walking through the screen captures that correspond to the text (starting with Figure 36-2). We annotate the scenario with some juicy tidbits on what goes on "behind the scenes" or, to be more exact, "behind the glass" of the screen:

1. **Start the application from the OS/2 desktop**. Notice the now famous Club Med icon. (See screen capture Figure 36-2).

2. **Select a Club**. A well-behaved CUA application first selects an object (a club in this case). ***Behind the scenes:*** the client workstation first obtains the list of clubs

from the server. The result is returned in a file which is copied into a shared array and displayed inside a DM selection list. The name of the transaction that does all this work is *get_club_names*. (See screen capture Figure 36-3).

3. **Select an Action**. A well-behaved CUA application then selects an action to be applied on the chosen club "object." The action selected is a request for "information" on this club's facilities. ***Behind the scenes:*** the object/action combination determines the transaction that is sent to the server. In this case, the transaction is *get_club_graphics* for IXTAPA. It results in the return of a metafile which displays the club's location on a map of the world, and several bitmaps which display icons of the sports offered in the IXTAPA club. (See screen capture Figure 36-5).

4. **Find out all about Club Med's village in Ixtapa**. You can see in iconic form all the sports offered. ***Behind the scenes:*** the graphics are created using PM User Controls. Each sport icon is a User Control where a bitmap is displayed. The map of the world is a User Control in which a metafile is displayed. Ixtapa is located on the West Coast of Mexico. (See screen capture Figure 36-5).

5. **Obtain a text description of Ixtapa**. Another action choice allows you to get a text file of information on Ixtapa. ***Behind the scenes:*** this object/action selection results in a *get_club description* transaction to the server. This will result in loading a text file into a PM Multi Line Editor (MLE) control. The MLE is a very sophisticated PM control window that allows users to edit or view multiple lines of text (it has a built-in text editor). The MLE panel is another example of a User Control into PM. (See screen capture Figure 36-6).

6. **The "Make a Reservation" Dialog**. We skipped a few screens, but the end result of selecting a club and choosing the "Make A Reservation" action is the dialog window which obtains information on the lucky vacationers, "Bob and Meryl." ***Behind the scenes:*** all the dialog objects for this screen are created using DM tags. (See screen capture Figure 36-7).

7. **Submit the reservation**. Pick the action "Make A Reservation" on the object displayed in the panel. ***Behind the scenes:*** nothing gets submitted to the server yet! (See screen capture Figure 36-8).

8. **Confirm the reservation**. We're not done yet. Look at the information on the panel; if you like what you see, hit the complete button; otherwise cancel. ***Behind the scenes:*** the *add_reservation* transaction is submitted to the server. (See screen capture Figure 36-9).

9. **View reservations list**. You can always view a list of clients (also objects) who have reservations and perform actions on them. ***Behind the scenes:*** the transaction *find_all_reservations* is submitted to the server to obtain this list. (See screen capture Figure 36-10).

10. **Cancel Bob and Meryl's reservation**. It was a mistake, of course. ***Behind the scenes:*** the *find_reservation* transaction is issued to obtain all the information on

"Bob and Meryl." When the complete button is pushed, a *cancel_reservation* transaction is issued and no more "Bob and Meryl" after that. (See screen capture Figure 36-11).

11. **Error detection**. This is what appears on the screen when the user does not provide required information. ***Behind the scenes:*** the DM message facility is used for that. No C code is required. (See screen capture Figure 36-12).

12. **Context Help**. Help is available everywhere. Hit F1 for context help; or select the general help from the action bar. Help for the Club Med Vacations panel is displayed. ***Behind the scenes:*** the DM message facility takes care of all the help. No C code is required. The CUA help model is used. (See screen capture Figure 36-13).

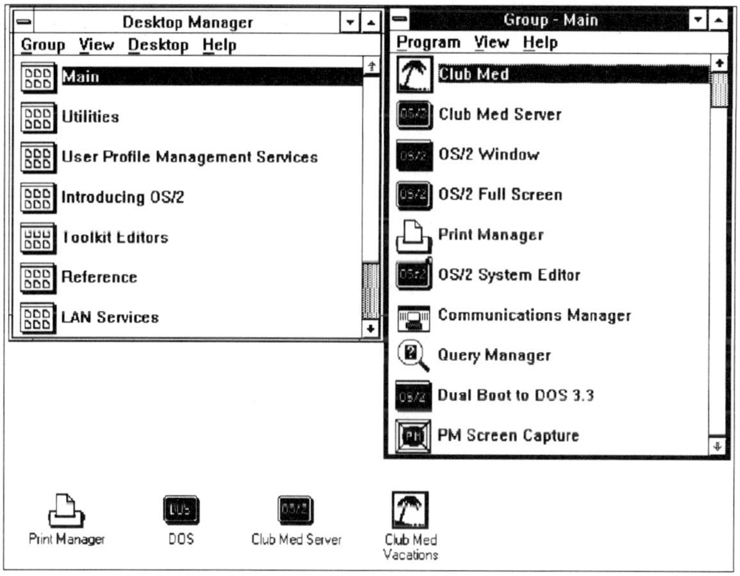

Figure 36-2. Double Click on Club Med to Start the Application.

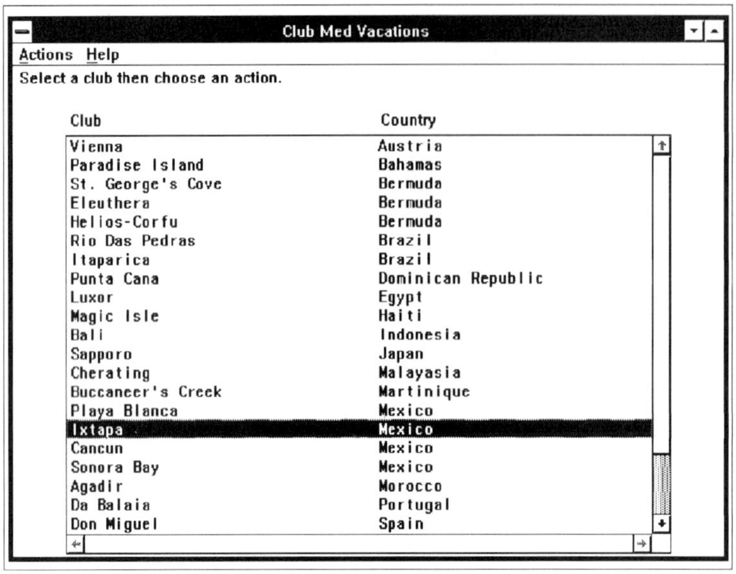

Figure 36-3. Select a Club (an Object in CUA Parlance).

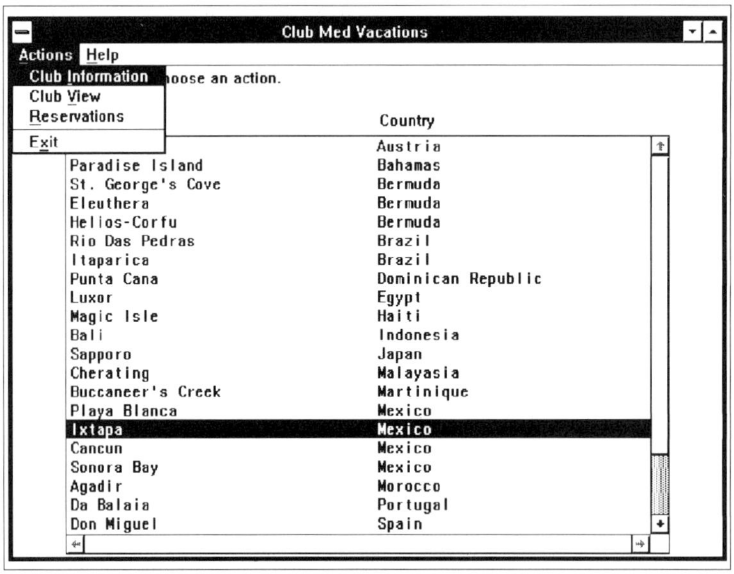

Figure 36-4. Select an Action Against this Club.

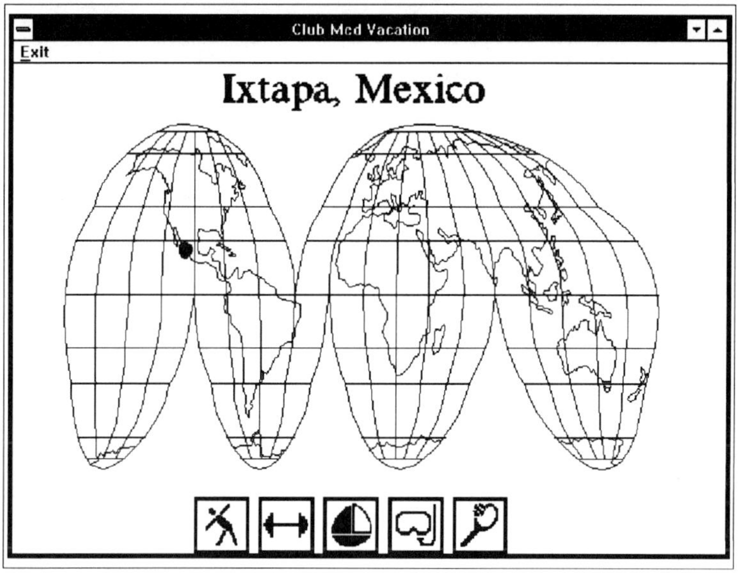

Figure 36-5. The Result of the Object/Action Selection.

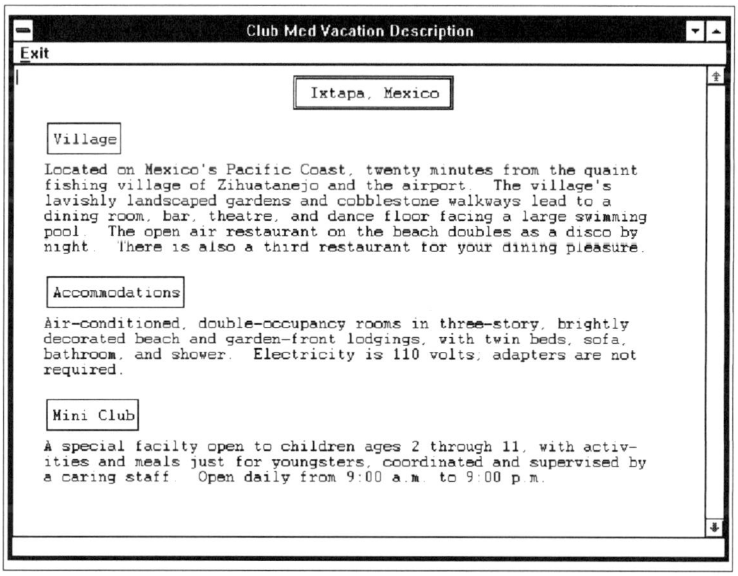

Figure 36-6. Text Information on Ixtapa Using an MLE User Control.

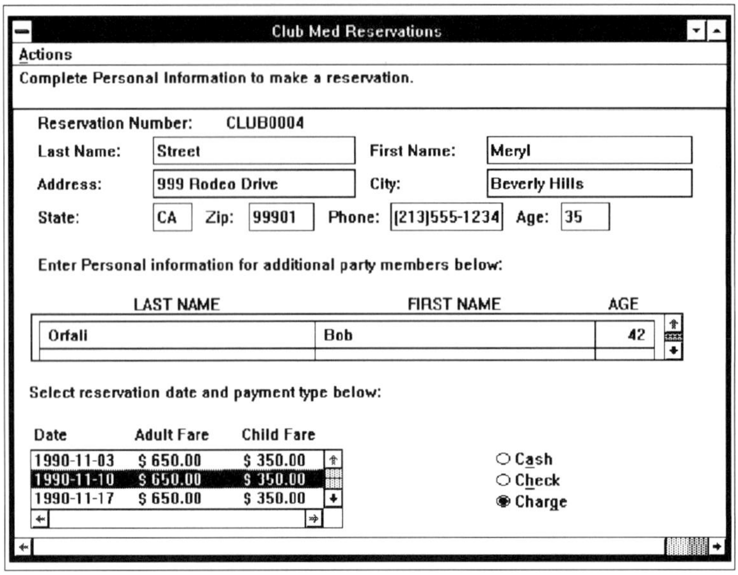

Figure 36-7. Reservation Data.

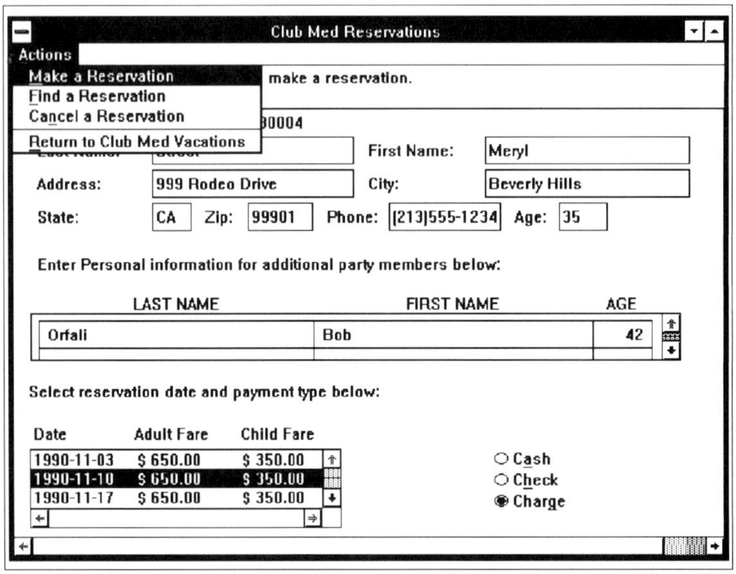

Figure 36-8. Submit the Reservation.

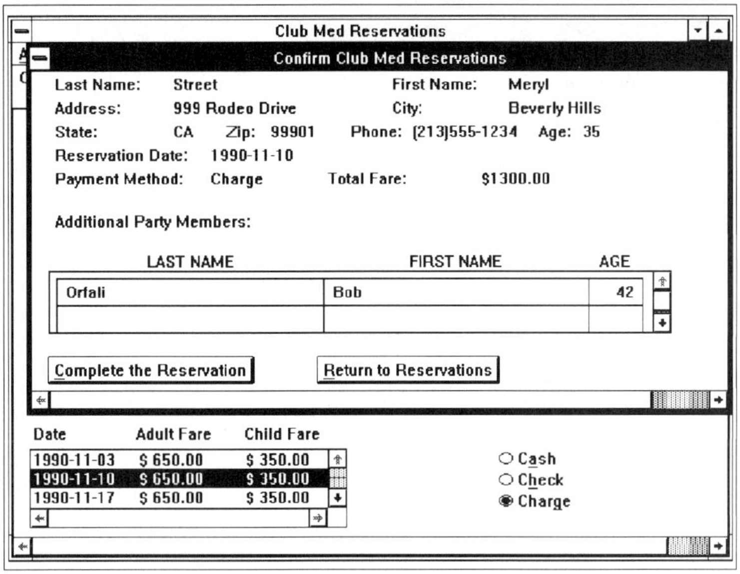

Figure 36-9. One Last Confirmation.

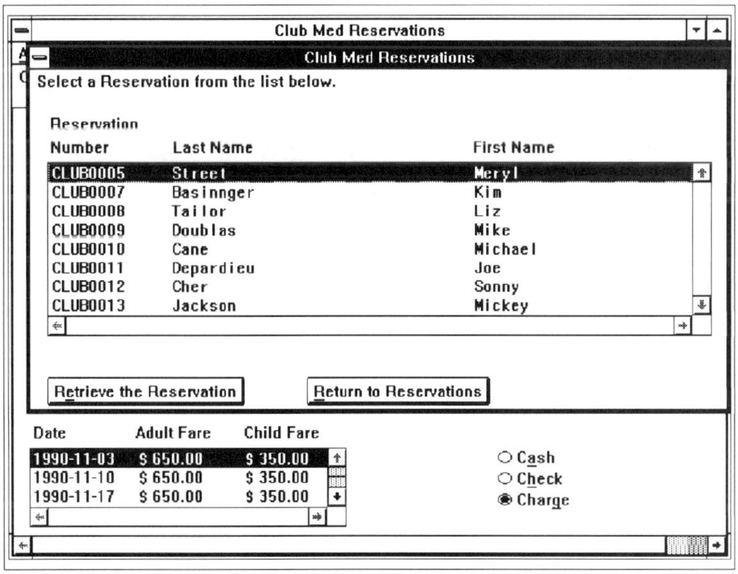

Figure 36-10. Display the Reservation List for Ixtapa.

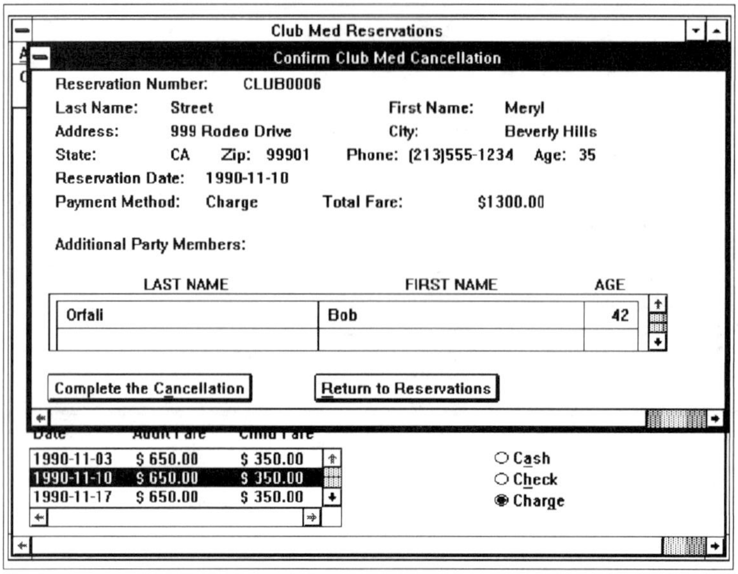

Figure 36-11. Cancel "Bob and Meryl."

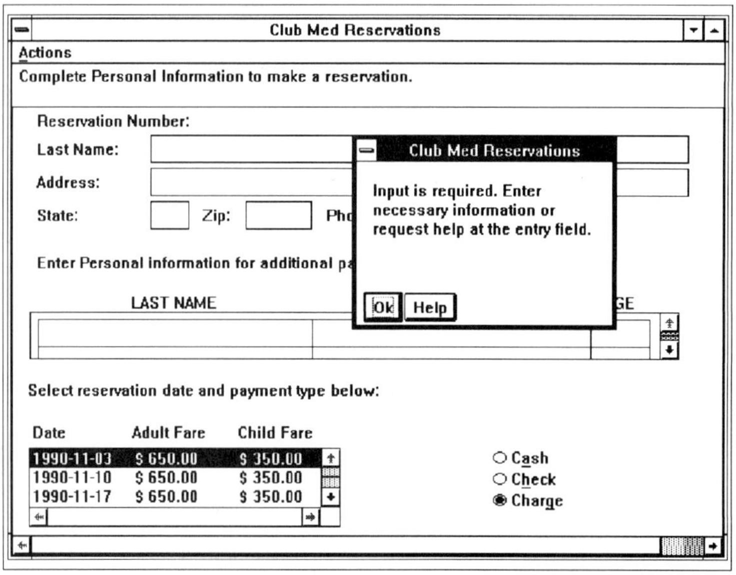

Figure 36-12. Error Handling using DM's Built-in Messages.

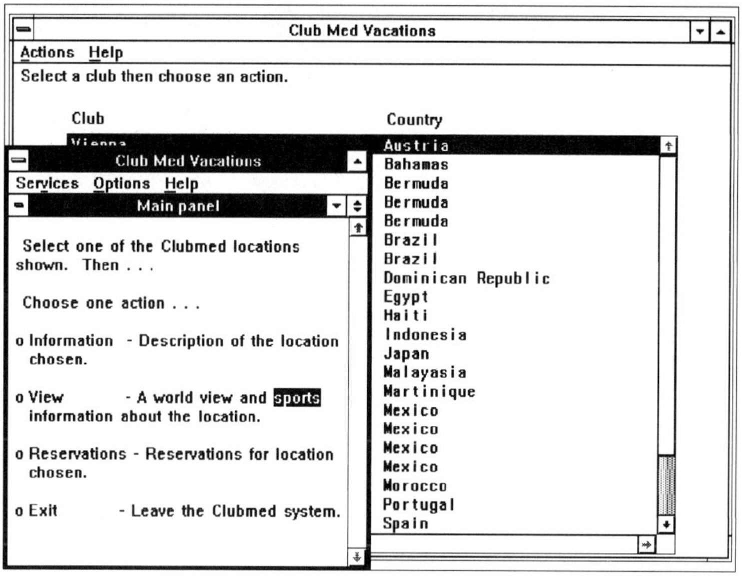

Figure 36-13. Built-In Help using DM.

THE CLUB MED TRANSACTIONS

The Club Med client generates eight simple transactions. Their description follows:

Table 36-1. The Club Med Transactions.

```
                      Transaction 1:  GET_CLUB_NAMES

Description: This transaction obtains the list of club names.

Input Msg:      ——  "TRANSACTION_ID= 1" ——→   |
                                          SELECT from CLUBS
Process:                                  generate response file
                                          COMMIT
                                              |
                                              ↓
Response Msg   ←——  "TXN_COMPLETION = SUCCESS  RESPONSE_FILE = file_name"
```

Table 36-1. The Club Med Transactions.

```
                         Transaction 2:  GET_CLUB_GRAPHICS

Description: This transaction obtains the name of a metafile and the name
             of all the sport bitmaps associated with a club. This info is
             displayed in the panel that has the map and sport icons.

Input Msg:     —— "TRANSACTION_ID= 2 CLUB=name" → |
                                             SELECT from CLUBS
                                             SELECT from ACTIVITIES
Process:                                     generate response file
                                             COMMIT
                                                  |
                                                  ↓
Response Msg  ←—— "TXN_COMPLETION = SUCCESS  RESPONSE_FILE = file_name"
```

```
                         Transaction 3:  GET_CLUB_DESCRIPTION

Description: This transaction obtains the name and path of a file containing
             a textual description of the specified Club Med.  This
             is the information file which gets displayed in the MLE.

Input Msg:     —— "TRANSACTION_ID= 3 CLUB=name" → |
                                             SELECT from CLUBS
Process:                                     generate response file
                                             COMMIT
                                                  |
                                                  ↓
Response Msg  ←—— "TXN_COMPLETION = SUCCESS  RESPONSE_FILE = file_name"
```

```
                         Transaction 4:  GET_CLUB_PRICES

Description: This transaction obtains a price list for a club.  The list
             contains the week number, the price for adults and the price
             for children.

Input Msg:     —— "TRANSACTION_ID= 4 CLUB=name" → |
                                             SELECT from PRICES
Process:                                     generate response file
                                             COMMIT
                                                  |
                                                  ↓
Response Msg  ←—— "TXN_COMPLETION = SUCCESS  RESPONSE_FILE = file_name"
```

Table 36-1. The Club Med Transactions.

```
                         Transaction 5:  FIND_ALL_RESERV

Description: This transaction obtains a list of the names of people
             who have confirmed reservations for this club.

Input Msg:      —— "TRANSACTION_ID= 5 CLUB=name" ——▸ |
                                                 SELECT from RESERVATIONS
Process:                                         generate response file
                                                 COMMIT
                                                     |
                                                     ▾
Response Msg  ◂—— "TXN_COMPLETION = SUCCESS  RESPONSE_FILE = file_name"

                         Transaction 6:  FIND_RESERVATION

Description: This transaction obtains all the reservation information
             associated with a particular reservation number.

Input Msg       — "TRANSACTION_ID= 6 RESERV_NO=number"—▸
                                                     |
                                                 SELECT from RESERVATIONS
Process:                                         generate response file
                                                 COMMIT
                                                     |
                                                     ▾
Response Msg  ◂—— "TXN_COMPLETION = SUCCESS  RESPONSE_FILE = file_name"

                         Transaction 7:  ADD_RESERVATION

Description: This transaction tells creates  a reservation.  The club
             and weekdate are identified in the message.  The file
             contains all the information on accompanying party
             members, telephone number, method of payment, address etc.

Input Msg    — "TRANSACTION_ID= 7 CLUB=club WEEKDATE=date FILENAME=name —▸
                                                     |
Process:                                         INSERT into RESERVATIONS
                                                 COMMIT
                                                     |
                                                     ▾
Response Msg  ◂—"TXN_COMPLETION = SUCCESS
                     RESPONSE_FILE = NONE RESERV_NO=number" ——
```

Table 36-1. The Club Med Transactions.

```
                    Transaction 8:  CANCEL_RESERVATION
                    ----------------------------------
Description: This transaction cancels a reservation identified
             by a reservation number.

Input Msg    — "TRANSACTION_ID= 8 CLUB=club RESERV_NO=number →
                                                  |
                                         DELETE from RESERVATIONS
Process:                                 COMMIT
                                                  |
                                                  ↓
Response Msg  ←"TXN_COMPLETION = SUCCESS RESPONSE_FILE = NONE" ——
```

The CLUB Database

Figure 36-14 presents the RSQL *run* script that is used to create the Club Med database. The database consists of four tables. These tables are loaded with data from import files.

```
-- create a database called club
EXEC DBA: CREATE_DB CLUB D TEST_DATABASE;

-- bind the rsql program
EXEC DBA: BIND CLUB \ZBK\RSQL\RSQL.BND ISO REPEATABLE_READ BLOCK_ALL PUBLIC;

EXEC DBA: STARTUSE CLUB S;

EXEC SQL: CREATE TABLE CLUBS(        CLUB          CHAR(32) NOT NULL,
                                     COUNTRY       CHAR(32) NOT NULL,
                                     PICTURE       CHAR(20) NOT NULL,
                                     DESCRIPTION   CHAR(20) NOT NULL );
EXEC SQL: CREATE UNIQUE INDEX CLUBSX1 ON CLUBS(CLUB);

EXEC SQL: CREATE TABLE ACTIVITIES(   CLUB       CHAR(32) NOT NULL,
                                     ACTIVITY   CHAR(20) NOT NULL);

EXEC SQL: CREATE TABLE PRICES(       CLUB          CHAR(32) NOT NULL,
                                     WEEK_DATE     DATE     NOT NULL,
                                     ADULT_PRICE   CHAR(8)  NOT NULL,
                                     CHILD_PRICE   CHAR(8)  NOT NULL );
EXEC SQL: CREATE UNIQUE INDEX PRICESX1 ON PRICES(CLUB, WEEK_DATE);
```

Figure 36-14 (Part 1 of 2). Create a 4-Table DB Called CLUB and Import Data.

```
EXEC SQL: CREATE TABLE RESERVATIONS( CLUB           CHAR(32) NOT NULL,
                                     WEEK_DATE      DATE     NOT NULL,
                                     LAST_NAME      CHAR(32) NOT NULL,
                                     FIRST_NAME     CHAR(32) NOT NULL,
                                     AGE            CHAR(3)  NOT NULL,
                                     PARTY_MEMBER   CHAR(1)  NOT NULL,
                                     RESERV_NO      CHAR(9)  NOT NULL,
                                     PAYMENT_METHOD CHAR(9),
                                     PHONE_NO       CHAR(20),
                                     ADDRESS        CHAR(32),
                                     CITY           CHAR(32),
                                     STATE          CHAR(2),
                                     ZIP            CHAR(10));
EXEC SQL: CREATE INDEX RESERVX1 ON RESERVATIONS(CLUB, WEEK_DATE);

EXEC SQL: COMMIT;

-- disconnect from the database for export
   EXEC DBA: STOPUSE CLUB;

-- import table data
EXEC DBA: IMPORT CLUB D:\ZBK\CLUB\CLUBS.DEL    REPLACE DEL CLUBS;
EXEC DBA: IMPORT CLUB D:\ZBK\CLUB\ACTIVITY.DEL REPLACE DEL ACTIVITIES;
EXEC DBA: IMPORT CLUB D:\ZBK\CLUB\PRICES.DEL   REPLACE DEL PRICES;
```

Figure 36-14 (Part 2 of 2). Create a 4-Table DB Called CLUB and Import Data.

CLUB MED: A SYSTEM SCENARIO

We now walk you through the first few screens of the Club Med application and show a scenario of what happens at the process-to-process level. Figure 36-15 graphically demonstrates the cooperative nature of a client-server application. We show all the activity that takes place on both the client and server to perform the first two screen selections in "Club Med: What the User Sees" on page 883. Here's a step-by-step description of the scenario in Figure 36-15:

1. ***DMOPEN***. This steps starts DM from the C program.

2. ***VDEFINE***. This step "binds" the C and DM shared variables.

3. ***Register UCs***. This step registers the PM User Controls. The application contains PM code that handles an MLE, bitmaps, and metafiles.

4. ***Perform the transaction***. A *get_club_names* transaction is invoked on the server using DosCallNmPipe.

5. ***Process the reply***. The server obtains the list of clubs from the CLUB database and places the result file in a shared subdirectory on the LAN Server. The name of this response file is part of the reply message.

6. ***Read the response file***. The client copies the contents of the response file into a C-array, which is also a shared DM variable.

7. ***Split the program into two threads.*** The main client thread starts a new thread called *perform_action()*. The function of this new thread is to handle transactions with the server. The main thread can now dedicate itself to interactions with the user. So, we've effectively split CLUB.C program into a "front-end thread" which exclusively interacts with the user, and a "back-end thread" which exclusively interacts with the server. This means the user can still be at the controls while long jobs are executing over the network. This satisfies the PM requirement of not blocking the system queue, and the CUA requirement that the system must always be responsive to the user. The back-end thread blocks on a semaphore waiting for work.

8. ***Display the clubs panel.*** This is the initial panel for the application. The display the user sees is the screen capture shown in Figure 36-3 on page 886. The selection list of clubs shown was obtained from the CLUB database by the *get_club names* transaction. The panel itself is a DM object whose behavior and appearance is described using the tag language.

9. ***User picks an object/action.*** The C application is blocked waiting for an event from the user. The user can scroll through the list of clubs and look at action bar choices using pull-down menus. All this is automatically handled by DM. The user selects the object ***Ixtapa*** and the action ***View***. Here is how this event was defined in the tag definitions:

   ```
   <pdc>Club <m>View
     <action setvar=function value='get_club_graphics'>
     <action setvar=panel value='clubgrph'>
     <action run=ENTER>
   ```

   Function, a shared variable, is assigned "get_club_graphics". *Panel*, another shared variable, is assigned "clubgrph". What we're doing is specifying in the tags the name of the transaction and next panel to be executed as a result of this specific choice. This information is passed to the CLUB.C program through the shared variables. The program will execute these instructions.

   Note: What we've effectively created is an event-driven client. The events and the triggering instructions are coded in the tag language along with the object definitions. This is a very flexible feature which can be used to change the flow of control without recompiling your code. Its also very good for prototyping. You can specify the next panels without the transactions, and the code will sequence through the panels. The transactions are then introduced when the requirements are stable.

10. ***Clear the semaphore.*** The front-end thread has a user event to process. The event contains a request to perform a server transaction. The front-end thread passes on that job to the back-end thread by clearing a semaphore.

11. ***Get Club Graphics.*** The back-end thread wakes up and goes to work. Its instructions are to submit for execution a *get_club_graphics* transaction. It does that by preparing the request message and sending it over the LAN to the server

using DosCallNmPipe. The server wakes up and issues SQL SELECTs against the CLUBS and ACTIVITIES tables. It creates a response file with the name of the bitmaps and a metafile. These files are then obtained using LAN Server's file services.

12. ***Meanwhile back at the ranch.*** The front-end thread is also active. It issued an ADDPOP followed by a DISPLAY wait panel. The effect of these two calls is to place a busy message popup on the user's screen, telling the user "Processing, Please wait!" The user can cancel the job (or program in this case) or wait. The front-end thread will block waiting to hear from either the user or the back-end thread. The user can unblock the thread by entering a command, but how does the back-end thread reactivate the blocked front-end thread? With FORCEXIT (see step below).

13. ***FORCEXIT.*** When the long-winded back-end thread obtains the results of the transaction it submitted, it issues a FORCEXIT DM command which causes the blocked front-end thread to wake up and go to work.

14. ***DISPLAY clubgrph panel.*** The front-end thread issues a DISPLAY command to display "clubgrph" panel. This is in accordance with the instructions it got from the event (via the tags) which triggered it. The screen now contains the famous graphic display of the world map with Ixtapa in it (see Figure 36-5 on page 887). The map of the world and the bitmaps below it are provided by the User Control PM code we wrote to supplement DM's services.

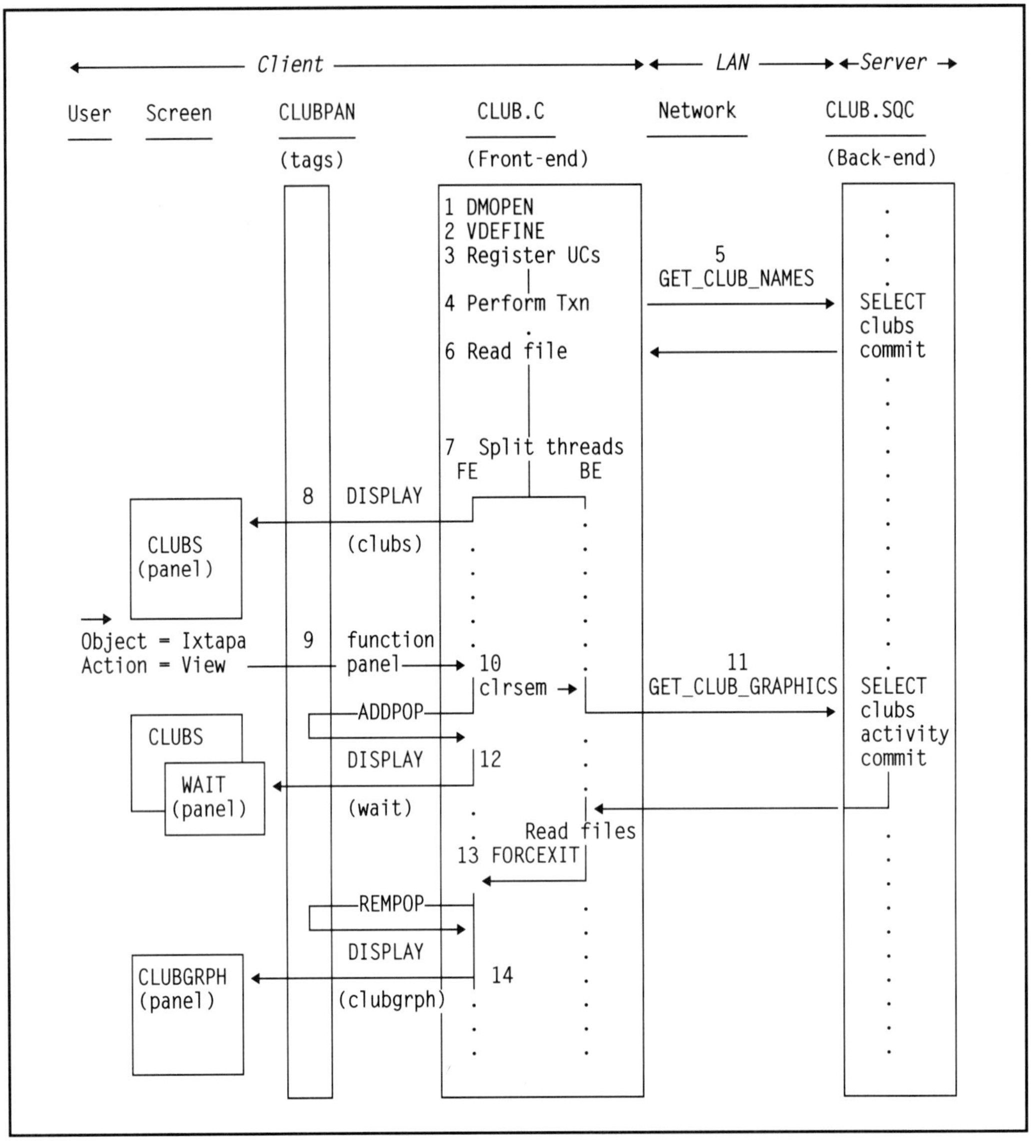

Figure 36-15. The Inter-program Cooperation Required to Display Two Panels.

THE CLUB MED MAKE FILE

Figure 36-16 on page 899 presents CLUB.MAK, the make file used to create both the client and server parts of the Club Med application. Notice that we've introduced a tag compiler. Otherwise, everything else should be familiar.

```
applid=club
cflags=-u -W3 -DLINT_ARGS -d -c -Alfu -G2s -Od -Zipe -nologo
lflags=/ST:40000/CO/NOD
linklibs=os2 llibcmt c_isp sql_dyn sql_stat
errfile=err.lst
DATABASE=club
#** INFERENCE RULES ***********************************************************
FFIXES: .c .obj .gml .dtl .hlp .sqc

.obj.exe:
      echo LINKING      $*.exe
      link $(lflags) $**, $*.exe,nul,$(linklibs),$*.def;  >>$(errfile)

.c.obj:
      echo COMPILING    $*.c
      cl $(cflags) $*.c  >>$(errfile)

.sqc.c:
      echo PRECOMPILING $*.sqc for database $(DATABASE)
      sqlprep  $*.sqc $(DATABASE) /b /FISO >>err.lst
      echo BINDING      $*.bnd to  database $(DATABASE)
      sqlbind  $*.bnd $(DATABASE)  >>err.lst

.gml.dtl:
     if exist $*.dtl del *.dtl
     if exist $*cmds.dtl del *.dtl
     @echo Compiling    $*.gml
     -2dtlc $* /comp    >>$(errfile)

#** BUILD STATEMENTS **********************************************************
all: erase club.exe clubpan.dtl clubsvr.exe
#--------- client program ---------------------------------------------------
club.exe:                     club.obj userctls.obj dmfont.obj
club.obj:                     club.c club.h
clubpan.dtl clubcmds.dtl:     clubpan.gml
#--------- client program dialog manager user controls ---------------------
userctls.obj:                 userctls.c
#--------- server program ---------------------------------------------------
clubsvr.exe:                  clubsvr.obj          # club server program
clubsvr.c clubsvr.obj:        clubsvr.sqc          #
```

Figure 36-16. Make File for all CLUB MED Programs.

Chapter 37

The Club Med Client

This is the second of a three-chapter series on the Club Med client-server application. This chapter provides the code and tag-based objects that make up the front-end of the Club Med application. This is also the chapter where we demonstrate how to create event-driven Graphical User Interfaces (GUIs) for On-line Transaction Processing (OLTP) using PM and DM. Here are the highlights of what this chapter provides:

- A flexible event-driven client that uses a tag-based protocol for its event-triggers. Event-related instructions tell the C program which transaction (if any) to execute on the server and the name of the next panel to display on the client.
- A two-thread design that allows the client to respond to the user in the foreground, while a lengthy transaction is executing in the background.
- A client-server exchange protocol that uses Named Pipes and the LAN Server.
- Three PM-based User Controls for MLEs, Bitmaps, and Metafiles.

In short, this chapter shows you how to create elaborate graphic front-ends for On-line Transaction Processing (OLTP) systems.

THE CLUB MED CLIENT COMPONENTS

As shown in Figure 37-1 on page 902, the client code consists of three components:

1. **The tags which specify screen objects and event-triggers**. CLUBPAN.GML is the tag file which specifies the contents of the windows used in the Club Med application, and the event-triggers which will be passed to the C program when the user performs certain tag specified actions.
2. **The event-handler code**. The CLUB.C C-language program provides the code which initializes the client and reacts to user events. An event typically triggers a set of activities such as submitting a transaction to the server and displaying a new window. To maintain a reactive interface with the user while a transaction is executing in the background, we split the CLUB.C code into two concurrent threads:

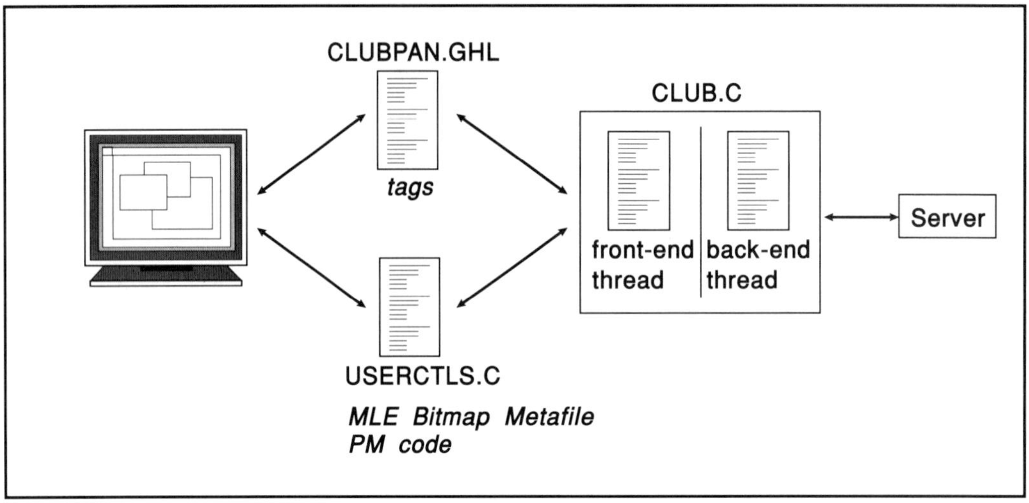

Figure 37-1. The Components of the Club Med Client Code.

- The *front-end thread*, which handles all the interactions with the user through PM/DM.
- The *back-end thread*, which handles all the interactions with the server using Named Pipes and the LAN Server redirector.

The CLUB.C program includes two header files: CLUB.H and CLUBTXNS.H.

3. **The PM User Controls**. The USERCTLS.C module provides PM code which adds three new classes to Dialog Manager's graphic repertoire:
   - A Bitmap user control.
   - A Metafile user control.
   - A Multi Line Editor (MLE) user control.

   The PM user control code is registered by CLUB.C as part of the client initialization routine. After that, the code gets invoked by PM/DM interactions.

The rest of this chapter is spent walking through the code for each of the three components.

CLUBPAN.GML: SCREEN AND EVENT TAGS

The power of the tag language is that it allows us to maintain the definition of the screen objects and event-triggers separately from the C-language code. The DM tag language was explained in great detail in Chapter 32, "The Dialog Manager: A GUI Tool" on page 805. So what remains to be done is to provide you with the source code for the tags and a brief description of the objects they contain.

The Club Med Panels

The panel definitions specify the contents of a PM window. The windows can be main windows, dialog windows, message windows, or help windows. A panel is identified by its name. The panels are in a sense object containers. At runtime, the CLUB.C program tells DM, through an API call, which panel to display in a window or popup window. Table 37-1 presents the list of panels CLUBPAN.GML provides along with a brief explanation of what each panel does.

Table 37-1. The Club Med Panels Created in CLUBPAN.GML.

Panel Name	Description
CLUBS	This panel displays a selection list of clubs. The user selects a club from the list to obtain information or to make reservations. Figure 36-3 on page 886 shows a screen capture of this panel. The tags which create the panel are shown in Figure 37-4.
CLUBGRPH	This panel displays bitmaps and metafile graphics for the selected club. Figure 36-5 on page 887 shows a screen capture of this panel. The tags which create the panel are shown in Figure 37-5.
CLUBINFO	This panel uses an MLE to display a text file which contains the description of a selected club. Figure 36-6 on page 887 shows a screen capture of this panel. The tags which create the panel are shown in Figure 37-6.
RESV	This panel is used to make, cancel, or find a reservation for a selected club. Figure 36-7 on page 888 shows a screen capture of this panel. The tags which create the panel are shown in Figure 37-7.
RESVALL	This panel displays a list of all the reservations made for a selected club. Figure 36-10 on page 889 shows a screen capture of this panel. The tags which create the panel are shown in Figure 37-8.
RESVCNFM	This panel is used to confirm a reservation before it gets submitted. Figure 36-9 on page 889 shows a screen capture of this panel. The tags which create the panel are shown in Figure 37-9.
RESVCAN	This panel is used to confirm a cancellation before it gets submitted. Figure 36-11 on page 890 shows a screen capture of this panel. The tags which create the panel are shown in Figure 37-10.
EXIT	This panel is used to confirm that the user wishes to exit the Club Med reservation program. The tags which create the panel are shown in Figure 37-11.
WAIT	This panel is used to display a busy message to the user. The tags which create the panel are shown in Figure 37-12.

In addition, the tag file contains three help panels. The screen capture for the CLUBS help panel is shown in Figure 36-13 on page 891. The screen capture for the RESFLD help panel is shown in Figure 32-21 on page 840. The tags which create the help panels are shown in Figure 37-13.

The Event Triggers

Panels also provide a context for associating event triggers with the panel's visual objects. First, *what are event-triggers?* They are triggers that return control to your main program when the user invokes an action (through a pull-down menu or a command button). DM provides many hooks for associating information with event-triggers. Your C program can then process the event which caused the trigger and act on the information which is returned to it.

Why Tag-Based Event-triggers?

The capability to associate tag-based information with the event triggers opens up some interesting architectural possibilities. Why not put all the control flow information in the tags and have the tags drive the C-program entirely? The tags can tell the program which procedure or transaction to execute, which panel to display next, etc. So, an important design issue is: how much intelligence should be put in the trigger source versus the C program which processes the triggers? We chose to put as much control information as possible in the trigger source. Here's why:

- It creates a very flexible tag-driven event-based front-end.
- It is allows you to create rapid prototyping systems. The control logic or screen objects can easily be changed (in the tags) without recompiling the C code.
- It provides clear documentation. The triggers are documented along with the display panels. This makes it easy to understand the associations between screen actions and event-triggers.

A Protocol for Event-triggers

The ideal is to create a trigger source which "calls back" the C program (CLUB.C) and tells it which transaction to invoke on the server, which panel to display next, and whether there is a popup to add or remove from the screen. We will approximate this ideal using a simple tag-based protocol and shared variables. The example below shows how to create an event-trigger and associate it with the *"Make a Reservation"* pull-down menu choice:

```
<abc><m>Actions
  <pdc><m>Make a Reservation
    <action setvar=function value='confirm_reservation'>
    <action setvar=panel    value='resvcnfm'>
    <action setvar=addpop   value='addpop'>
    <action run=ENTER>
```

Here's what this all means:

function This variable contains the name of the transaction which is to be executed by CLUB.C. Of course, CLUB.C merely packages a transaction request and sends it to the server. The transaction gets executed at the server. In the example above, the transaction name to be executed on the server is *confirm_reservation.*

panel This variable contains the tag language name of the next panel to be displayed. In the example above, the name of the next panel is *resvcnfm.*

addpop, rempop These two variables indicate whether an addpop or rempop directive is to be issued prior to displaying the panels. In the example above, an *addpop* directive is specified, meaning that the panel will be displayed in a dialog window.

The run ENTER instruction returns the control to the C program.

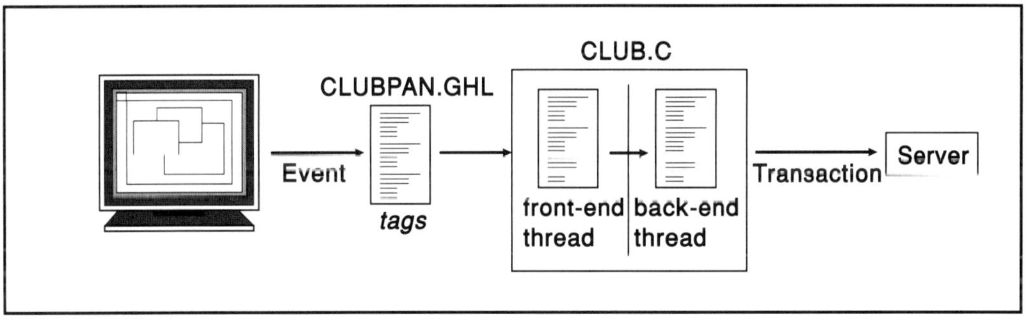

Figure 37-2. Event-Driven Transaction Triggers.

Figure 37-2 shows how a user event triggers a remote transaction on the server. This simple "trigger" protocol effectively allows you to associate a remote procedure call (i.e., transaction invocation) with an action tag. The remote procedure is triggered when the user selects that action. This means that the "tags contain the controls" and that the CLUB.C program simply acts as a "conduit" to the server. So, we've essentially created a tag-based event-driven client.

WALKING THROUGH CLUBPAN.GML

In this section we break down the listing of CLUBPAN.GML into subsections which correspond to panel objects and other structural components. This is done merely as a convenience to help you locate objects quickly.

CLUBPAN.GML: Variable and Icon Declarations

```
<!doctype dm system>

<!--========================================================================-->
<!--  Declarations for CLUBMED application                                  -->
<!--========================================================================-->
<!--************************************************************************-->
<!--  Variable Class Declarations                                           -->
<!--************************************************************************-->
<varclass name=alpha32   type='char 32'>
<varclass name=alpha2    type='char 2'>
<varclass name=number3   type='char 3'>
<varclass name=number5   type='char 5'>
<varclass name=number9   type='char 9'>
<varclass name=number20  type='char 20'>

<varclass name=bool type='numeric 1'>
<varclass name=int  type='numeric 2'>
<varclass name=char8  type='char  8'>
<varclass name=char9  type='char  9'>
<varclass name=char10 type='char 10'>
<varclass name=char12 type='char 12'>
<varclass name=char13 type='char 13'>
<varclass name=char14 type='char 14'>
<varclass name=char32 type='char 32'>
<varclass name=char40 type='char 40'>
<varclass name=char72 type='char 72'>
<varclass name=char90 type='char 90'>

<!--************************************************************************-->
<!--  Variable Declarations                                                 -->
<!--************************************************************************-->
<varlist>
 <vardcl name=true     varclass=bool>
 <vardcl name=function varclass=char40>
 <vardcl name=rempop   varclass=char12>
 <vardcl name=addpop   varclass=char8>
 <vardcl name=panel    varclass=char8>
 <vardcl name=canaval  varclass=bool>

 <vardcl name=pricest  varclass=char72>
 <vardcl name=prices   varclass=char72  maxdim=52>
 <vardcl name=pricnum  varclass=int>
 <vardcl name=pricmax  varclass=int>
 <vardcl name=clubst1  varclass=char32>
 <vardcl name=clubst2  varclass=char32>
 <vardcl name=clubs    varclass=char72  maxdim=40>
 <vardcl name=clubnum  varclass=int>
 <vardcl name=clubmax  varclass=int>
 <vardcl name=reservt1 varclass=char32>
 <vardcl name=reservt2 varclass=char32>
 <vardcl name=reservt3 varclass=char32>
 <vardcl name=reservt4 varclass=char32>
 <vardcl name=reserv   varclass=char90  maxdim=40>
 <vardcl name=resvnum  varclass=int>
```

Figure 37-3 (Part 1 of 2). CLUBPAN.GML: The Variable and Icon Declarations.

```
    <vardcl name=resvmax  varclass=int>
    <vardcl name=pmemmax  varclass=int>

    <vardcl name=metafile varclass=char32>
    <vardcl name=textfile varclass=char32>
    <vardcl name=bmp1file varclass=char32>
    <vardcl name=bmp2file varclass=char32>
    <vardcl name=bmp3file varclass=char32>
    <vardcl name=bmp4file varclass=char32>
    <vardcl name=bmp5file varclass=char32>
    <vardcl name=bmp6file varclass=char32>

    <vardcl name=resvno   varclass=number9>
    <vardcl name=fname    varclass=alpha32>
    <vardcl name=lname    varclass=alpha32>
    <vardcl name=age      varclass=number3>
    <vardcl name=phone    varclass=number20>
    <vardcl name=address  varclass=alpha32>
    <vardcl name=city     varclass=alpha32>
    <vardcl name=state    varclass=alpha2>
    <vardcl name=zip      varclass=number9>
    <vardcl name=lnamem   varclass=alpha32 maxdim=10>
    <vardcl name=fnamem   varclass=alpha32 maxdim=10>
    <vardcl name=agem     varclass=number3 maxdim=10>
    <vardcl name=fare     varclass=number9>
    <vardcl name=paymeth  varclass=char9>
    <vardcl name=weekdate varclass=char10>
   </varlist>

   <!--**********************************************************************-->
   <!--  ICON Declarations                                                   -->
   <!--**********************************************************************-->
   <icon name=CLUB source=CLUB>
```

Figure 37-3 (Part 2 of 2). CLUBPAN.GML: The Variable and Icon Declarations.

CLUBPAN.GML: The CLUBS Panel

```
<!--=========================================================================-->
<!--  Panels for CLUBMED application                                         -->
<!--=========================================================================-->
<!--*************************************************************************-->
<!--  CLUB MED VACATIONS - This panel allows a user to select a club         -->
<!--    for information and to make reservations.                            -->
<!--*************************************************************************-->
<panel name=clubs width=78 depth=26 help=clubs>Club Med Vacations
  <ab>
    <abc><m>Actions
      <pdc>Club <m>Information
        <action setvar=function value='get_club_description'>
        <action setvar=panel    value='clubinfo'>
        <action run=ENTER>
      <pdc>Club <m>View
        <action setvar=function value='get_club_graphics'>
        <action setvar=panel    value='clubgrph'>
        <action run=ENTER>
      <pdc><m>Reservations
        <action setvar=function value='get_club_prices'>
        <action setvar=panel  value='resv'>
        <action setvar=canaval value=0>
        <action run=ENTER>
      <pdsep>
      <pdc>E<m>xit
        <action run=EXIT>
    <abc><m>Help
      <pdc><m>Help for Help
        <action run=helphelp>
      <pdc><m>Extended Help
        <action run=exhelp>
      <pdc><m>Keys Help
        <action run=keys>
      <pdc>Help <m>Index
        <action run=index>
  </ab>
  <Topinst>Select a club then choose an action.
  <region dir=horiz>
    <divider gutter=5>
    <region dir=vert>
      <region dir=horiz>
        <dtafld datavar=clubst1 usage=out pmtwidth=0>
        <divider gutter=6>
        <dtafld datavar=clubst2 usage=out pmtwidth=0>
      </region>
      <sellst name=clubs selvar=clubnum numrows='%clubmax' maxwidth=64>
        <selcol datavar=clubs>
      </sellst>
    </region>
  </region>
  <uc class='DMFONT' prmdata=CLUBS>10.System Monospaced
</panel>
```

Figure 37-4. CLUBPAN.GML: The CLUBS Panel.

CLUBPAN.GML: The CLUBGRPH Panel

```
<!--*************************************************************************-->
<!--  CLUB MED VACATION GRAPHIC - This panel show bitmaps and metafile      -->
<!--    graphics for the club selected.                                     -->
<!--*************************************************************************-->
<panel name=clubgrph>Club Med Vacation
  <ab>
    <abc><m>Exit
      <pdc><m>Return to Club Med Vacations
        <action setvar=function value='get_club_names'>
        <action setvar=panel    value='clubs'>
        <action run=ENTER>
  </ab>
  <region dir=horiz>
    <divider gutter=5>
    <region dir=vert>
      <uc class=METAFILE PRMDATA='%metafile'
         mindepth=10 maxdepth=45 minwidth=8 maxwidth=150>
      <divider>
      <region dir=horiz>
        <divider gutter=15>
        <uc class=BITMAP PRMDATA='%bmp1file'
            minwidth=6 maxwidth=6 mindepth=3 maxdepth=3>
        <divider>
        <uc class=BITMAP PRMDATA='%bmp2file'
            minwidth=6 maxwidth=6 mindepth=3 maxdepth=3>
        <divider>
        <uc class=BITMAP PRMDATA='%bmp3file'
            minwidth=6 maxwidth=6 mindepth=3 maxdepth=3>
        <divider>
        <uc class=BITMAP PRMDATA='%bmp4file'
            minwidth=6 maxwidth=6 mindepth=3 maxdepth=3>
        <divider>
        <uc class=BITMAP PRMDATA='%bmp5file'
            minwidth=6 maxwidth=6 mindepth=3 maxdepth=3>
        <divider>
        <uc class=BITMAP PRMDATA='%bmp6file'
            minwidth=6 maxwidth=6 mindepth=3 maxdepth=3>
      </region>
    </region>
  </region>
</panel>
```

Figure 37-5. CLUBPAN.GML: The CLUBGRPH Panel.

CLUBPAN.GML: The CLUBINFO Panel

```
<!--***********************************************************************-->
<!--  CLUB MED VACATION TEXT    - This panel show text about the various    -->
<!--    features of the club selected.                                      -->
<!--***********************************************************************-->
<panel name=clubinfo>Club Med Vacation Description
  <ab>
    <abc><m>Exit
      <pdc><m>Return to Club Med Vacations
        <action setvar=function value='get_club_names'>
        <action setvar=panel    value='clubs'>
        <action run=ENTER>
  </ab>
  <uc class=MLE prmdata='%textfile'
      mindepth=10 maxdepth=25 minwidth=8 maxwidth=100>8.Courier
</panel>
```

Figure 37-6. CLUBPAN.GML: The CLUBINFO Panel.

CLUBPAN.GML: The RESV Panel

```
<!--***********************************************************************-->
<!--  CLUB MED RESERVATIONS - This panel is used to make/cancel/find        -->
<!--    reservations                                                        -->
<!--***********************************************************************-->
<panel name=resv>Club Med Reservations
  <ab>
    <abc><m>Actions
      <pdc><m>Make a Reservation
        <action setvar=function value='confirm_reservation'>
        <action setvar=panel    value='resvcnfm'>
        <action setvar=addpop   value='addpop'>
        <action run=ENTER>
      <pdc><m>Find a Reservation
        <action setvar=function value='find_all_reserv'>
        <action setvar=panel    value='resvall'>
        <action setvar=addpop   value='addpop'>
        <action run=CANCEL>
      <pdc availvar=canaval>Ca<m>ncel a Reservation
        <action setvar=panel    value='resvcan'>
        <action setvar=addpop   value='addpop'>
        <action setvar=canaval value=0>
        <action run=ENTER>
      <pdsep>
      <pdc><m>Return to Club Med Vacations
        <action setvar=function value='get_club_names'>
        <action setvar=panel    value='clubs'>
        <action run=CANCEL>
  </ab>
```

Figure 37-7 (Part 1 of 3). CLUBPAN.GML: The RESV Panel.

```
<Topinst>Complete Personal Information to make a reservation.
</topinst>
<area>
  <region dir=horiz>
    <divider type=none gutter=1>
    <region dir=vert>
      <dtafld name=resvno datavar=resvno usage=out
       pmtwidth=20>Reservation Number:
      <region dir=horiz>
        <dtafld name=lname datavar=lname usage=both required=yes
         pmtwidth=12 entwidth=20 help=resfld>Last Name:
        <dtafld name=fname datavar=fname usage=both required=yes
         pmtwidth=12 entwidth=20 help=resfld>First Name:
      </region>
      <region dir=horiz>
        <dtafld name= address datavar=address usage=both required=yes
         pmtwidth=12 entwidth=20 help=resfld>Address:
         <dtafld name=city datavar=city usage=both required=yes
           pmtwidth=12 entwidth=20 help=resfld>City:
      </region>
      <region dir=horiz>
         <dtafld name=state datavar=state usage=both required=yes
           pmtwidth=12 help=resfld>State:
         <dtafld name=zip datavar=zip usage=both required=yes
           pmtwidth=4 entwidth=5 help=resfld>Zip:
         <dtafld name=phone datavar=phone usage=both required=yes
           pmtwidth=6 entwidth=10 help=resfld>Phone:
         <dtafld name=age datavar=age usage=both required=yes
           pmtwidth=4 help=resfld>Age:
      </region>
      <info width=75>
      <lines>

Enter Personal information for additional party members below:
      </lines>
      </info>
      <lstfld name=lstfld1 toprow=1 numrows=10 minrows=1 maxrows=1
             minwidth=75 maxwidth=75 rules=both >
        <lstcol datavar=lnamem  usage=both colwidth=27>LAST NAME
        <lstcol datavar=fnamem  usage=both colwidth=27>FIRST NAME
        <lstcol datavar=agem    usage=both colwidth=4 align=end>AGE
      </lstfld>
    </region>
  </region>
  <info width=70>
  <lines>

Select reservation date and payment type below:
  </lines>
  </info>
  <dtafld datavar=pricest usage=out entwidth=60 pmtwidth=0>
  <region dir=horiz>
    <sellst selvar=pricnum numrows='%pricmax'
     minrows=2 maxrows=52 maxwidth=32>
       <selcol datavar=prices>
    </sellst>
```

Figure 37-7 (Part 2 of 3). CLUBPAN.GML: The RESV Panel.

```
        <divider type=none gutter=15>
        <selfld type=single selwidth=10 dir=vert>
          <choice checkvar=paymeth match='Cash'>C<m>ash
            <action setvar=paymeth value='Cash'>
          <choice checkvar=paymeth match='Check'>C<m>heck
            <action setvar=paymeth value='Check'>
          <choice checkvar=paymeth match='Charge'>Char<m>ge
            <action setvar=paymeth value='Charge'>
        </selfld>
      </region>
    </area>
  </panel>
```

Figure 37-7 (Part 3 of 3). CLUBPAN.GML: The RESV Panel.

CLUBPAN.GML: The RESVALL Panel

```
<!--************************************************************************-->
<!--  CLUB MED ALL RESERVATIONS - This panel is used to display a list of   -->
<!--    all existing reservations                                           -->
<!--************************************************************************-->
<panel name=resvall>Club Med Reservations
  <Topinst>Select a Reservation from the list below.
  </topinst>
  <region dir=horiz>
    <divider gutter=1>
    <region dir=vert>
      <dtafld datavar=reservt1 usage=out entwidth=10 pmtwidth=0>
      <region dir=horiz>
        <dtafld datavar=reservt2 usage=out entwidth=10 pmtwidth=0>
        <dtafld datavar=reservt3 usage=out entwidth=29 pmtwidth=0>
        <dtafld datavar=reservt4 usage=out entwidth=29 pmtwidth=0>
      </region>
        <sellst name=reserv selvar=resvnum numrows='%resvmax'
         minrows=5 maxrows=40 maxwidth=70>
          <selcol datavar=reserv>
        </sellst>
        <divider>
        <region dir=horiz>
          <selfld type=action>
            <choice>R<m>etrieve the Reservation
              <action setvar=function value='find_reservation'>
              <action setvar=panel  value='resv'>
              <action setvar=rempop value='rempop'>
              <action setvar=canaval value=1>
              <action run=Enter>
          </selfld>
```

Figure 37-8 (Part 1 of 2). CLUBPAN.GML: The RESVALL Panel.

```
          <divider gutter=5>
          <selfld type=action>
            <choice><m>Return to Reservations
              <action setvar=panel  value='resv'>
              <action setvar=rempop value='rempop'>
              <action run=cancel>
          </selfld>
        </region>
    </region>
  </region>
  <uc class='DMFONT' prmdata=RESERV>10.System Monospaced
</panel>
```

Figure 37-8 (Part 2 of 2). CLUBPAN.GML: The RESVALL Panel.

CLUBPAN.GML: The RESVCNFM Panel

```
<!--************************************************************************-->
<!--  CLUB MED CONFIRMATION - This panel is used to confirm a reservation   -->
<!--                                                                        -->
<!--************************************************************************-->
<panel name=resvcnfm>Confirm Club Med Reservations
  <area>
    <region dir=horiz>
      <divider type=none gutter=1>
      <region>
        <region dir=horiz>
          <dtafld name=lname datavar=lname usage=out
           pmtwidth=12 entwidth=20>Last Name:
          <dtafld name=fname datavar=fname usage=out
           pmtwidth=12 entwidth=20>First Name:
        </region>
        <region dir=horiz>
          <dtafld name= address datavar=address usage=out
           pmtwidth=12 entwidth=20>Address:
          <dtafld name=city datavar=city usage=out
            pmtwidth=12 entwidth=20>City:
        </region>
        <region dir=horiz>
          <dtafld name=state datavar=state usage=out
            pmtwidth=12>State:
          <dtafld name=zip datavar=zip usage=out
            pmtwidth=4 entwidth=5>Zip:
          <dtafld name=phone datavar=phone usage=out
            pmtwidth=6 entwidth=10>Phone:
          <dtafld name=age datavar=age usage=out
            pmtwidth=4>Age:
        </region>
```

Figure 37-9 (Part 1 of 2). CLUBPAN.GML: The RESVCNFM Panel.

```
          <dtafld name=weekdate datavar=weekdate usage=out
            pmtwidth=16 entwidth=10>Reservation Date:
          <region dir=horiz>
            <dtafld name=paymeth datavar=paymeth usage=out
              pmtwidth=16>Payment Method:
            <dtafld name=fare datavar=fare usage=out
              pmtwidth=16 entwidth=8>Total Fare:
          </region>
        <info width=75>
        <lines>

Additional Party Members:
        </lines>
        </info>
        <lstfld name=lstfld1 toprow=1 numrows=10
          minrows=1 maxrows=10 minwidth=75 maxwidth=75 rules=both>
          <lstcol datavar=lnamem  usage=out  colwidth=27>LAST NAME
          <lstcol datavar=fnamem  usage=out  colwidth=27>FIRST NAME
          <lstcol datavar=agem    usage=out  colwidth=4 align=end>AGE
        </lstfld>
      </region>
    </region>
    <divider>
    <region dir=horiz>
      <selfld type=action>
        <choice><m>Complete the Reservation
          <action setvar=function value='add_reservation'>
          <action setvar=panel  value='resv'>
          <action setvar=rempop value='rempop'>
          <action run=Enter>
      </selfld>
      <divider gutter=5>
      <selfld type=action>
        <choice><m>Return to Reservations
          <action setvar=panel  value='resv'>
          <action setvar=rempop value='rempop'>
          <action run=Cancel>
      </selfld>
    </region>
  </area>
</panel>
```

Figure 37-9 (Part 2 of 2). CLUBPAN.GML: The RESVCNFM Panel.

CLUBPAN.GML: The RESVCAN Panel

```
<!--**************************************************************************-->
<!--  CLUB MED CANCELLATIONS - This panel is used to confirm a cancellation -->
<!--                                                                        -->
<!--**************************************************************************-->
<panel name=resvcan depth=19>Confirm Club Med Cancellation
  <area>
    <region dir=horiz>
```

Figure 37-10 (Part 1 of 3). CLUBPAN.GML: The RESVCAN Panel.

```
        <divider type=none gutter=1>
        <region>
          <dtafld name=resvno datavar=resvno usage=out
           pmtwidth=20>Reservation Number:
          <region dir=horiz>
            <dtafld name=lname datavar=lname usage=out
             pmtwidth=12 entwidth=20>Last Name:
            <dtafld name=fname datavar=fname usage=out
             pmtwidth=12 entwidth=20>First Name:
          </region>
          <region dir=horiz>
            <dtafld name= address datavar=address usage=out
             pmtwidth=12 entwidth=20>Address:
            <dtafld name=city datavar=city usage=out
              pmtwidth=12 entwidth=20>City:
          </region>
          <region dir=horiz>
            <dtafld name=state datavar=state usage=out
              pmtwidth=12>State:
            <dtafld name=zip datavar=zip usage=out
              pmtwidth=4 entwidth=5>Zip:
            <dtafld name=phone datavar=phone usage=out
              pmtwidth=6 entwidth=10>Phone:
            <dtafld name=age datavar=age usage=out
              pmtwidth=4>Age:
          </region>
          <dtafld name=weekdate datavar=weekdate usage=out
            pmtwidth=16 entwidth=10>Reservation Date:
          <region dir=horiz>
            <dtafld name=paymeth datavar=paymeth usage=out
              pmtwidth=16>Payment Method:
            <dtafld name=fare datavar=fare usage=out
              pmtwidth=16 entwidth=5>Total Fare:
          </region>
        <info width=75>
        <lines>

  Additional Party Members:
        </lines>
        </info>
        <lstfld name=lstfld1 toprow=1 numrows=10
          minrows=1 maxrows=10 minwidth=75 maxwidth=75 rules=both>
          <lstcol datavar=lnamem  usage=out  colwidth=27>LAST NAME
          <lstcol datavar=fnamem  usage=out  colwidth=27>FIRST NAME
          <lstcol datavar=agem    usage=out  colwidth=4 align=end>AGE
        </lstfld>
       </region>
     </region>
     <divider>
     <region dir=horiz>
      <selfld type=action>
        <choice>Complete the C<m>ancellation
          <action setvar=function value='cancel_reservation'>
          <action setvar=panel  value='resv'>
          <action setvar=rempop value='rempop'>
          <action run=Enter>
      </selfld>
```

Figure 37-10 (Part 2 of 3). CLUBPAN.GML: The RESVCAN Panel.

```
      <divider gutter=5>
      <selfld type=action>
        <choice><m>Return to Reservations
          <action setvar=panel  value='resv'>
          <action setvar=rempop value='rempop'>
          <action run=Cancel>
      </selfld>
     </region>
    </area>
  </panel>
```

Figure 37-10 (Part 3 of 3). CLUBPAN.GML: The RESVCAN Panel.

CLUBPAN.GML: The EXIT Panel

```
<!--************************************************************************-->
<!--  PROGRAM EXIT - This panel confirms that the users wishes to exit the  -->
<!--                 program.                                               -->
<!--************************************************************************-->
<panel name=exit width=45 depth=6>Program Exit Verification
  <region>
    <info>
    <lines>

  You have chosen to exit the Clubmed program.
  Do you wish to exit?
    </lines>
    </info>
  </region>
  <region dir=horiz>
    <divider type=none gutter=7>
    <selfld type=action selwidth=10 dir=horiz>
      <choice><m>Yes
       <action setvar=function value='terminate'>
       <action run=ENTER>
      </choice>
    </selfld>
    <divider gutter=2>
    <selfld type=action selwidth=10 dir=horiz>
      <choice><m>No
       <action setvar=rempop   value='rempop'>
       <action run=CANCEL>
      </choice>
    </selfld>
  </region>
</panel>
```

Figure 37-11. CLUBPAN.GML: The EXIT Panel.

CLUBPAN.GML: The WAIT Panel

```
<!--************************************************************************-->
<!--  Message POPUP to display busy                                         -->
<!--************************************************************************-->
<panel name=wait depth=3 width=25>Processing
  <info>
  <p>Processing...Please wait!
  </info>
</panel>
```

Figure 37-12. CLUBPAN.GML: The WAIT Panel.

CLUBPAN.GML: The Help Panels

```
<!--************************************************************************-->
<!--  CLUB MED VACATIONS - help panel                                       -->
<!--************************************************************************-->
<help name=clubs> Main panel
<itop roots='clubs' > Clubmed Help
<area >
  <info>
  <p> Select one of the Clubmed locations shown.  Then . . .
  <p> Choose one action . . .
  <ul>
    <li>Information  - Description of the location chosen.
    <li>View         - A world view and <rp help=sports>sports</rp> information
                       about the location.
    <li>Reservations - Reservations for location chosen.
    <li>Exit         - Leave the Clubmed system.
  </ul>
  </info>
</area>
</help>
```

Figure 37-13 (Part 1 of 2). CLUBPAN.GML: The Help Panels.

```
<!--*************************************************************************-->
<!--  CLUB MED VACATIONS - help panel                                        -->
<!--*************************************************************************-->
<help name=resfld> Reservation Field
<area >
  <info>
  <p> Your personal information must be filled in before the reservation
      can be submitted. Complete the following before making the reservation:
  <ul compact>
    <li>Last Name
    <li>First Name
    <li>Street Address
    <li>City
    <li>State
    <li>Zip Code
    <li>Telephone Number
    <li>Age
  </ul>
  <note>Party member information can be filled in as required. </note>
  </info>
</area>
</help>

<!--*************************************************************************-->
<!--  CLUB MED SPORTS - help panel                                           -->
<!--*************************************************************************-->
<help name=sports> Sports
<area >
  <info>
  <p><warning>Some sports require skill certification. </warning>
  </info>
</area>
</help>
```

Figure 37-13 (Part 2 of 2). CLUBPAN.GML: The Help Panels.

WALKING THROUGH THE CLUB.C CLIENT PROGRAM

The CLUB.C program initializes the client application and then goes into a loop waiting for events to happen. When an event occurs, it gets processed by the appropriate event-handler. The program is split into two concurrent threads to ensure that the application's front-end can maintain its interface with the user while a previous event is executing on the back-end server. The CLUB.C program should be easy to follow since it does not introduce any new programming constructs. Instead, it brings together many familiar constructs such as: threads, Named Pipes, the LAN Server, the Dialog Manager, and Presentation Manager. The end result is an event-driven front-end client.

CLUB.C: The main() Procedure

In this section, we present the **main()** procedure of the Club Med client program, whose code listing is shown in Figure 37-14. The following is a step-by-step description of what this code does:

1. The program starts by including the C-language, OS/2, and Dialog Manager header files.

2. We then include two of our program header files:

   club.h This file is a garden variety C header file which defines variables, constants and structures. It also provides forward declarations for all the procedures used in the code.

   clubtxns.h This include file contains constants which identify the transaction number. This file is also included with the server program.

   The listing for both header files is provided in Figure 37-19.

3. The **main()** program follows, and you can see it's not going to be a "piece of cake." Here's what **main()** does:

   - The first four procedures invoked initialize the program and define variables which are shared between DM and CLUB.C. The listings for all four procedures are provided in Figure 37-15.

   - It invokes the **register_user_cntls()** function, listed in Figure 37-20, to register the PM user controls.

   - It invokes **interact_with_user()** function, listed in Figure 37-16. This function is the event-driven loop which interacts with the user and then services the events generated. The actual work is performed by:

     a. The application functions listed in Figure 37-17.
     b. The DM service routines listed in Figure 37-17.
     c. The PM User Controls described in "Walking through USERCTLS.C" on page 935.

```
/*****************************************************************************/
/*  PROGRAM NAME: CLUB    - a Dialog Manager application example            */
/*                                                                           */
/*  PROGRAM DESCRIPTION:  This program demonstrates how to use dialog       */
/*                        manager as an application front end.              */
/*                                                                           */
/*  PROGRAM INVOCATION:   CLUB                                              */
/*****************************************************************************/
#include <mt\stdio.h>
#include <mt\stdlib.h>
#include <mt\string.h>
#include <mt\process.h>
```

Figure 37-14 (Part 1 of 2). CLUB.C: The main() Procedure.

```
#define  INCL_BASE
#define  INCL_WIN
#include <os2.h>
#include <ispcast.h>
#include <ispuser.h>

#include "club.h"
#include "clubtxns.h"

/*------------------------------------------------------------------*/
/* Main routine.                                                    */
/*------------------------------------------------------------------*/
VOID
main(VOID)
{
  initialize_DM();                    /* Initialize Dialog Manager        */

  read_config();                      /* Read Application Configuration   */

  vdefine_DM_variables();             /* define "system" Dialog Manager vars*/

  vdefine_application_variables();    /* define application vars to DM    */

  register_user_cntls();              /* tell PM about our user controls  */

  interact_with_user();               /* start a conversation with the user */

} /* end main */
```

Figure 37-14 (Part 2 of 2). CLUB.C: The main() Procedure.

CLUB.C: The Initialization Functions

In this section, we present (see listings in Figure 37-15) four of the initialization functions called by main() before it starts interacting with the user. These are described below:

1. The **initialize_DM()** function tells DM to use the CLUB tag library.

2. The **read_config()** function reads the name of the shared drive from a "club.cfg" file (provided by the file server) and the network name of the transaction server's Named Pipe (this is the name of the machine followed by the pipe name).

3. The **vdefine_DM_variables()** function "binds" the DM system variables with the CLUB.C variables. The system variables are used to exchange system information. Examples: *zverb* returns the name of the DM "run" command selected by the user; *zcurfld* is used to place the cursor on a particular field, etc.

4. The **vdefine_application_variables()** function is used to "bind" the variables from CLUB.C with the DM variables we defined in CLUBPAN.GML. These are the variables used to display information on the screen, to capture user input, and to return event-trigger information.

The DM functions are provided by calling the DM helper routines see "CLUB.C: The DM Helper Routines" on page 930. If you have trouble following any of the DM specific functions, please review Chapter 33.

```
/*-------------------------------------------------------------------*/
/* initialize Dialog Manager                                          */
/*-------------------------------------------------------------------*/
VOID initialize_DM(VOID)
{
  dmService("DMOPEN APPLID(CLUB)");
} /* end initialize_DM */

/*-------------------------------------------------------------------*/
/* read configuration information from CLUB.CFG                       */
/*-------------------------------------------------------------------*/
VOID read_config(VOID)
{
  CHAR config_file_name[80];
                   /*------------------------------*/
                   /* configuration file variables */
                   /*------------------------------*/
  FILE    *config_file;             /* Input file control block      */
  CHAR     line[80];                /* one line of config file       */

  /*-------------------------------*/
  /* determine config file name    */
  /*-------------------------------*/
  strcpy(config_file_name, "club.cfg");

  /*-------------------------------*/
  /* open the configuration file   */
  /*-------------------------------*/
  if (NULL == (config_file = fopen(config_file_name,"r")))
     display_app_error("Error opening configuration file.");

   fgets(line, sizeof(line), config_file);
   if (sscanf(line,"DATAFILE_DRIVE_PATH = %s ", datafile_drive_path) != 1)
      display_app_error("Error reading datafile_drive_path from config. file.");

   fgets(line, sizeof(line), config_file);
   if (sscanf(line,"PIPE_NAME = %s ", PipeName) != 1)
      display_app_error("Error reading PipeName from configuration file.");

   fgets(line, sizeof(line), config_file);
   if (sscanf(line,"COMPUTER_NAME = %s ", ComputerName) == EOF)
      strcpy(ComputerName,"");

  strcpy(RemotePipeName, ComputerName);
  strcat(RemotePipeName, PipeName);

  /*-------------------------------*/
  /* all done with the config file */
  /*-------------------------------*/
  fclose(config_file);

} /* end read_config */
```

Figure 37-15 (Part 1 of 4). CLUB.C: The Initialization Functions.

```
/*-------------------------------------------------------------------------*/
/* VDEFINE Dialog Manager System variables                                 */
/*-------------------------------------------------------------------------*/
VOID vdefine_DM_variables(VOID)
{
  len[0] = strlen(zwinicon) + 1;
  dmService2("VDEFINE zwinicon FORMAT(BINSTR)", len, zwinicon);
  len[0] = 8;
  dmService2("VDEFINE ZVERB FORMAT(CHAR)", len, zverb);
  len[0] = sizeof(fkaType);
  dmService2("VDEFINE(fkaType) FORMAT(FIXED)", len, &fkaType);
  len[0] = sizeof(zcurfld);
  dmService2("VDEFINE zcurfld FORMAT(CHAR)", len, zcurfld);
} /* end vdefine_DM_variables */

/*-------------------------------------------------------------------------*/
/* VDEFINE application variable used in Dialog Manager panels.             */
/*-------------------------------------------------------------------------*/
VOID vdefine_application_variables(VOID)
{
  len[0] = sizeof(BOOL);
  dmService2("VDEFINE TRUE FORMAT(FIXEDU)", len, &true);
  len[0] = sizeof(select[0]);
  dmService2("VDEFINE select FORMAT(BINSTR) DIM(20)", len, select);
  len[0] = sizeof(action_str);
  dmService2("VDEFINE function FORMAT(BINSTR)", len, action_str);
  len[0] = sizeof(panel_id);
  dmService2("VDEFINE panel    FORMAT(BINSTR)", len, panel_id);
  len[0] = sizeof(addpop_str);
  dmService2("VDEFINE addpop   FORMAT(BINSTR)", len, addpop_str);
  len[0] = sizeof(rempop_str);
  dmService2("VDEFINE rempop   FORMAT(BINSTR)", len, rempop_str);

  len[0] = sizeof(clubstl);
  dmService2("VDEFINE clubstl   FORMAT(BINSTR)", len, clubstl);
  len[0] = sizeof(clubst2);
  dmService2("VDEFINE clubst2   FORMAT(BINSTR)", len, clubst2);
  len[0] = CLUBDATAWIDTH;
  dmService2("VDEFINE clubs    FORMAT(BINSTR) DIM(40)", len, clubs);
  len[0] = sizeof(clubmax);
  dmService2("VDEFINE clubmax   FORMAT(FIXEDU)", len, &clubmax);
  len[0] = sizeof(clubnum);
  dmService2("VDEFINE clubnum   FORMAT(FIXEDU)", len, &clubnum);

  len[0] = sizeof(pricest);
  dmService2("VDEFINE pricest   FORMAT(BINSTR)", len, pricest);
  len[0] = PRICEDATAWIDTH;
  dmService2("VDEFINE prices   FORMAT(BINSTR) DIM(52)", len, prices);
  len[0] = sizeof(pricmax);
  dmService2("VDEFINE pricmax   FORMAT(FIXEDU)", len, &pricmax);
  len[0] = sizeof(pricnum);
  dmService2("VDEFINE pricnum   FORMAT(FIXEDU)", len, &pricnum);
```

Figure 37-15 (Part 2 of 4). CLUB.C: The Initialization Functions.

```
len[0] = sizeof(reservt1);
dmService2("VDEFINE reservt1   FORMAT(BINSTR)", len, reservt1);
len[0] = sizeof(reservt2);
dmService2("VDEFINE reservt2   FORMAT(BINSTR)", len, reservt2);
len[0] = sizeof(reservt3);
dmService2("VDEFINE reservt3   FORMAT(BINSTR)", len, reservt3);
len[0] = sizeof(reservt4);
dmService2("VDEFINE reservt4   FORMAT(BINSTR)", len, reservt4);
len[0] = RESERVDATAWIDTH;
dmService2("VDEFINE reserv   FORMAT(BINSTR) DIM(40)", len, reserv);
len[0] = sizeof(resvmax);
dmService2("VDEFINE resvmax   FORMAT(FIXEDU)", len, &resvmax);
len[0] = sizeof(resvnum);
dmService2("VDEFINE resvnum   FORMAT(FIXEDU)", len, &resvnum);

len[0] = sizeof(text_file_name);
dmService2("VDEFINE textfile   FORMAT(BINSTR)", len, text_file_name);

len[0] = sizeof(meta_file_name);
dmService2("VDEFINE metafile   FORMAT(BINSTR)", len, meta_file_name);

len[0] = sizeof(bmap_file_name[0]);
dmService2("VDEFINE bmp1file   FORMAT(BINSTR)", len, bmap_file_name[0]);
len[0] = sizeof(bmap_file_name[1]);
dmService2("VDEFINE bmp2file   FORMAT(BINSTR)", len, bmap_file_name[1]);
len[0] = sizeof(bmap_file_name[2]);
dmService2("VDEFINE bmp3file   FORMAT(BINSTR)", len, bmap_file_name[2]);
len[0] = sizeof(bmap_file_name[3]);
dmService2("VDEFINE bmp4file   FORMAT(BINSTR)", len, bmap_file_name[3]);
len[0] = sizeof(bmap_file_name[4]);
dmService2("VDEFINE bmp5file   FORMAT(BINSTR)", len, bmap_file_name[4]);
len[0] = sizeof(bmap_file_name[5]);
dmService2("VDEFINE bmp6file   FORMAT(BINSTR)", len, bmap_file_name[5]);

len[0] = sizeof(reserv_no);
dmService2("VDEFINE resvno  FORMAT(BINSTR)", len, reserv_no  );
len[0] = sizeof(first_name);
dmService2("VDEFINE fname   FORMAT(BINSTR)", len, first_name   );
len[0] = sizeof(last_name);
dmService2("VDEFINE lname   FORMAT(BINSTR)", len, last_name   );
len[0] = sizeof(age);
dmService2("VDEFINE age      FORMAT(BINSTR)", len, age  );
len[0] = sizeof(address);
dmService2("VDEFINE address FORMAT(BINSTR)", len, address );
len[0] = sizeof(city);
dmService2("VDEFINE city    FORMAT(BINSTR)", len, city    );
len[0] = sizeof(state);
dmService2("VDEFINE state   FORMAT(BINSTR)", len, state   );
len[0] = sizeof(zip);
dmService2("VDEFINE zip     FORMAT(BINSTR)", len, zip     );
len[0] = sizeof(phone_no);
dmService2("VDEFINE phone   FORMAT(BINSTR)", len, phone_no);

len[0] = sizeof(first_namem[0]);
dmService2("VDEFINE fnamem   FORMAT(BINSTR) DIM(10)", len, first_namem);
len[0] = sizeof(last_namem[0]);
dmService2("VDEFINE lnamem   FORMAT(BINSTR) DIM(10)", len, last_namem);
len[0] = sizeof(agem[0]);
dmService2("VDEFINE agem     FORMAT(BINSTR) DIM(10)", len, agem  );
```

Figure 37-15 (Part 3 of 4). CLUB.C: The Initialization Functions.

```
    len[0] = sizeof(payment_method);
    dmService2("VDEFINE paymeth   FORMAT(BINSTR)", len, payment_method);

    len[0] = sizeof(week_date);
    dmService2("VDEFINE weekdate FORMAT(BINSTR)", len, week_date);
    len[0] = sizeof(total_fare);
    dmService2("VDEFINE fare FORMAT(BINSTR)", len, total_fare);
} /* end vdefine_application_variables */
```

Figure 37-15 (Part 4 of 4). CLUB.C: The Initialization Functions.

CLUB.C: The interact_with_user Function

In this section, we present the **interact_with_user()** function, whose code listing is shown in Figure 37-16. Here is what this function does:

1. It invokes **perform_action()** to set up the first display the user will see when the client program first comes up. The perform_action() function operates on four variables which are normally set by the tag-based event-trigger mechanism described in "The Event Triggers" on page 904. In the initial invocation, which we're presently looking at, the function displays whatever the four variables are initialized to, in Figure 37-19:

   - *action_str* contains "GET_CLUB_NAMES".
   - *panel_id*. contains "clubs".
   - *rempop_str* and *addpop_str* both contain empty strings.

   So we're telling **perform_action()** to run the "GET_CLUB_NAMES" transaction and then display the "clubs" panel on the screen. This is how we start the dialog with the user; after that, the user controls the flow of the dialog.

2. The *back-end* thread is started. This is the thread that handles all the interaction with the server machine. Notice that this simply means running the **perform_action()** function concurrently with the main() thread (i.e., "front-end" thread).

3. The "front-end" thread enters a do forever loop. This is an event-driven loop that reacts to user requests (i.e., event-triggers). Here's what happens when an event is triggered:

   a. A trigger-event which specifies a server transaction will cause the *start_txn_sem_handle* semaphore to clear. This will wake up the back-end thread and cause it to execute whatever transaction the event-trigger specifies. Meanwhile, the front-end thread will display a "wait" panel.
   b. When the transaction completes (or if no transaction is requested), the next panel specified by the event-trigger is displayed after the specified ADDPOP or REMPOP directive is issued.
   c. An "EXIT" trigger-event causes the exit pop-up to be displayed. The program terminates when the user returns a confirmation.

The event loop was explained more graphically in "Club Med: A System Scenario" on page 895. Make sure to review this system scenario before plunging into the code.

```
/*--------------------------------------------------------------------------*/
/* Interact with user via Dialog Manager, call database function as required.*/
/*--------------------------------------------------------------------------*/
VOID interact_with_user(VOID)
{
  /*------------------------------------*/
  /* execute the first transaction      */
  /*------------------------------------*/
  perform_force_exit = FALSE;
  perform_action(&perform_force_exit);
  if (strcmp(error_string,"") != 0)
     { display_app_error(error_string);
       exit(FAILED);
     }

  /*------------------------------------*/
  /* start a thread for subsequent txns */
  /*------------------------------------*/
  perform_force_exit = TRUE;
  DosSemSet(start_txn_sem_handle);
  _beginthread(perform_action,          /* name of function         */
               thread_stack,            /* thread stack             */
               THREAD_STACK_SIZE,       /* thread stack size        */
               &perform_force_exit);    /* action to perform        */

  /*------------------------------------*/
  /* enter panel processing loop        */
  /*------------------------------------*/
  while (TRUE)
     {
       /*------------------------------------*/
       /* display the panel                  */
       /*------------------------------------*/
       sprintf(dmServiceBuffer,"DISPLAY PANEL(%s) CURSOR(%s)",panel_id,curfld);
       dmService(dmServiceBuffer);
       if (strcmp(action_str,"TERMINATE") == 0)
          terminate_application();

       /*------------------------------------*/
       /* exit verification                  */
       /*------------------------------------*/
       if (strcmp(zverb,"EXIT    ") == 0)
          {
           sprintf(dmServiceBuffer,"ADDPOP");
           dmService(dmServiceBuffer);
           sprintf(dmServiceBuffer,"DISPLAY PANEL(EXIT)");
           dmService(dmServiceBuffer);
           strcpy(zverb,"");
          }
```

Figure 37-16 (Part 1 of 2). CLUB.C: The interact_with_user() Function.

```
         /*_________________________________________*/
         /* execute function specified in GML       */
         /*_________________________________________*/
         if (strcmp(action_str,"")!=0)
            {
              DosSemClear(start_txn_sem_handle);
              dmService("ADDPOP");
              dmService("DISPLAY panel(wait)");
              if (strcmp(action_str,"TERMINATE") == 0)
                 terminate_application();
              dmService("rempop");
              if (strcmp(error_string,"") != 0)
                 display_app_error(error_string);
              strcpy(action_str,"");
            } /* endif */

         /*_________________________________________*/
         /* execute REMPOP from GML if any          */
         /*_________________________________________*/
         if (strcmp(strupr(rempop_str),"") != 0)
            { dmService(rempop_str);
              strcpy(rempop_str,"");
            }

         /*_________________________________________*/
         /* execute ADDPOP from GML if any          */
         /*_________________________________________*/
         if (strcmp(strupr(addpop_str),"") != 0)
            { dmService(addpop_str);
              strcpy(addpop_str,"");
            }
      } /* end while */
   } /* end interact_with_user */
```

Figure 37-16 (Part 2 of 2). CLUB.C: The interact_with_user() Function.

CLUB.C: The Application Functions

In this section (see code listings in Figure 37-17), we present the functions which do most of the work:

- The **terminate_application()** function simply issues a DMCLOSE verb.
- The **perform_action()** function is our "back-end" thread. It spends most of its time blocked on the *start_txn_sem_handle* semaphore waiting for work. It unblocks when an event-trigger is received which requires the execution of a transaction on the server. Here's what it does:

  1. It compares the name of the transaction it receives in *action_str* against a lookup table. The table looks up the "id" of the transaction to be performed on the remote server.
  2. It calls the procedure which services that particular transaction on the client side. The Club Med application supports nine transactions. Because of space limitations, we're only providing the code for one representative transaction. The code for the rest of the transactions is on the program diskette.

3. It sets the *start_txn_sem_handle* semaphore.
4. It issues a "FORECEXIT" command if the caller so requested. This command will break the "front-end" thread out of any display service (usually a wait panel) and allow it to continue processing.

- The **get_club_names** function will serve as our representative client transaction requester. Here is what it does:

1. It prepares a transaction request message.
2. It invokes the **execute_transaction()** function, which submits the transaction to the server.
3. It checks the reply message from the server and, if necessary, copies the rows returned (in a result file) into an array in memory. This is the *clubs* array which is a shared DM variable. The contents of *clubs* will be displayed on the screen in a scrollable selection list (see Figure 36-3 on page 886).
4. It closes the response file and deletes it from disk.

- The **execute_transaction()** function performs the following actions:

1. It issues a **DosCallNmPipe**, which connects to a Name Pipe on the server, sends a transaction request message, receives the reply message, and closes the pipe. (The DosCallNmPipe function is described in "DosCallNmPipe " on page 746).
2. It parses the reply message and copies the response parameters into the appropriate variables.
3. It checks for a response file reply parameter. If it finds one, it opens the response file and obtains a handle for it.

```
/*-------------------------------------------------------------------*/
/* terminate application                                             */
/*-------------------------------------------------------------------*/
VOID terminate_application(VOID)
{
  dmService("DMCLOSE");
  exit(GOOD);
} /* end terminate_application */

/*-------------------------------------------------------------------*/
/* determine which routine was selected within the GML and execute   */
/*-------------------------------------------------------------------*/
VOID perform_action(PUSHORT perform_force_exit)
{
  typedef struct
  {
    CHAR     action_str[41];          /* action name string          */
    USHORT   action_id;               /* action numerical ID         */
  }  ACTION;
```

Figure 37-17 (Part 1 of 4). CLUB.C: The Application Functions.

```
    static ACTION actions[] =
    {/*<--- action_str ----------------->< -- action_id ------------------->*/
     {"GET_CLUB_NAMES",                     GET_CLUB_NAMES                  },
     {"GET_CLUB_GRAPHICS",                  GET_CLUB_GRAPHICS               },
     {"GET_CLUB_DESCRIPTION",               GET_CLUB_DESCRIPTION            },
     {"GET_CLUB_PRICES",                    GET_CLUB_PRICES                 },
     {"FIND_ALL_RESERV",                    FIND_ALL_RESERV                 },
     {"FIND_RESERVATION",                   FIND_RESERVATION                },
     {"ADD_RESERVATION",                    ADD_RESERVATION                 },
     {"CANCEL_RESERVATION",                 CANCEL_RESERVATION              },
     {"CONFIRM_RESERVATION",                CONFIRM_RESERVATION             },
     {"",                                   0                               }
    };
    USHORT i;

    while (TRUE)
    {
      DosSemWait(start_txn_sem_handle, -1L);
      /*________________________________________*/
      /* find ACTION id                         */
      /*________________________________________*/
      i = 0 ;

      while (strcmp(actions[i].action_str, "") != 0)
      {
        if (strcmp(actions[i].action_str, strupr(action_str)) == 0)
           break;
        else
           ++i;
      }

      switch(actions[i].action_id)
        {
         case GET_CLUB_NAMES       :   get_club_names();        break;
         case GET_CLUB_GRAPHICS    :   get_club_graphics();     break;
         case GET_CLUB_DESCRIPTION :   get_club_description();  break;
         case GET_CLUB_PRICES      :   get_club_prices();       break;
         case FIND_ALL_RESERV      :   find_all_reserv();       break;
         case FIND_RESERVATION     :   find_reservation();      break;
         case ADD_RESERVATION      :   add_reservation();       break;
         case CANCEL_RESERVATION   :   cancel_reservation();    break;
         case CONFIRM_RESERVATION  :   confirm_reservation();   break;
         default:                                               break;
        } /* endswitch */

        DosSemSet(start_txn_sem_handle);
        if (*perform_force_exit)
           dmService("FORCEXIT");
        else
           return;
      } /* endwhile */
  } /* end perform_action */
```

Figure 37-17 (Part 2 of 4). CLUB.C: The Application Functions.

```
/*--------------------------------------------------------------------------*/
/* get the club names from the database                                     */
/*--------------------------------------------------------------------------*/
SHORT get_club_names(VOID)
{
 sprintf(input_msgbuf, "TRANSACTION_ID=%d", GET_CLUB_NAMES);

 if (execute_transaction() == GOOD)
    { for (i=0;i< MAXCLUBS; i++)
       { if (fgets(clubs[i],CLUBDATAWIDTH,rsp_file) == 0) break;
         clubs[i][strlen(clubs[i])-1] = '\0';       /* remove CR              */
       }
      clubmax = i;
      clubnum = 1;
    }
 else return(FAILED);

 fclose(rsp_file);
 remove(rsp_file_path_name);
 return(GOOD);
} /* end get_club_names */

/*--------------------------------------------------------------------------*/
/* execute DosCallNMPipe                                                    */
/*--------------------------------------------------------------------------*/
SHORT  execute_transaction(VOID)
{
  rc = DosCallNmPipe(RemotePipeName,              /* name of CLUBSVR pipe     */
                 input_msgbuf,                   /* input buffer             */
                 strlen(input_msgbuf) + 1,       /* input buffer size        */
                 output_msgbuf,                  /* output buffer            */
                 sizeof(output_msgbuf),          /* output buffer size       */
                 &PipeBytesRead,                 /* number of response bytes */
                 PIPE_TIMEOUT);                  /* timout fir this call     */
  if (rc)
     {format_app_error(error_string,rc,"executing DosCallNmPipe",
                       __FILE__,__LINE__);
      return(FAILED);
     }
 strcat(output_msgbuf,";");
 sscanf(output_msgbuf, "TXN_COMPLETION = %s RESPONSE_FILE = %[^ ;] %[^;]",
        completion, file_name, rsp_parms);
 if (strcmp(completion,"SUCCESS") == 0)
    {
     if (strcmp(file_name,"NONE") != 0)
        { sprintf(rsp_file_path_name, "%s\\%s", datafile_drive_path, file_name);
          if ((rsp_file = fopen(rsp_file_path_name,"r")) == NULL)
              return(FAILED);
        } /* endif */
    }
 else
    { sprintf(error_string,"TRANSACTION FAILURE: \nMESSAGE: %s \nRESPONSE: %s",
                          input_msgbuf,output_msgbuf);
      return(FAILED);
    } /* endif */
 return(GOOD);
} /* end execute_transaction */
```

Figure 37-17 (Part 3 of 4). CLUB.C: The Application Functions.

```
            See program diskettes for the following functions:

SHORT get_club_graphics(VOID)          { ... }
SHORT get_club_description(VOID)       { ... }
SHORT get_club_prices(VOID)            { ... }
SHORT find_all_reserv(VOID)            { ... }
SHORT find_reservation(VOID)           { ... }
SHORT add_reservation(VOID)            { ... }
SHORT cancel_reservation(VOID)         { ... }
SHORT confirm_reservation(VOID)        { ... }

SHORT get_club_name(VOID)              { ... }
SHORT get_date_price(VOID)             { ... }
SHORT get_reserv_no(VOID)              { ... }
SHORT write_resv_data_to_file(VOID)    { ... }
SHORT init_reservation_data(VOID)      { ... }
```

Figure 37-17 (Part 4 of 4). CLUB.C: The Application Functions.

CLUB.C: The DM Helper Routines

In this section (see listing Figure 37-18), we present the helper functions used in the code. Most of the "help" consists of simplifying the DM function calls. If you have trouble following any of the DM specific functions, please review Chapter 33.

```
/*-------------------------------------------------------------------------*/
/* call Dialog Manager (no application variable in the call)               */
/*-------------------------------------------------------------------------*/
VOID
dmService(PCHAR service)
{
  ISPCI(&dmcomm, (long)strlen(service), service);
  if (    (dmcomm.ReturnCode > 0)       && (dmcomm.ReasonCode != 401700)
      && (dmcomm.ReasonCode != 801700) && (dmcomm.ReasonCode != 801705))
      display_dm_error(service);
}

/*-------------------------------------------------------------------------*/
/* call Dialog Manager (application variable pointer and its length required)*/
/*-------------------------------------------------------------------------*/
VOID
dmService2(PCHAR service, PLONG len, PVOID vars )
{
  ISPCI2(&dmcomm, (long)strlen(service), service, len, vars);
  if (dmcomm.ReturnCode > 0) display_dm_error(service);
}
```

Figure 37-18 (Part 1 of 2). CLUB.C: The DM Helper Routines.

```
/*-----------------------------------------------------------------------------*/
/* DM Error found, display error and terminate the application                 */
/*-----------------------------------------------------------------------------*/
VOID display_dm_error(PCHAR msg)
{
  CHAR        errorBoxMessage[256];
  CHAR        errorInfo[40];
  USHORT      i;

  sprintf(errorBoxMessage, "\"%s\" failed. \n   ReasonCode = %lu ",
      msg, dmcomm.ReasonCode);
  i = 0;
  do {
       if (dmcomm.ErrorInfo[i].ReasonCode != 0)
          {
            sprintf(errorInfo, "\n   ErrorInfo[%d].ReasonCode = %lu ",
                   i, dmcomm.ErrorInfo[i].ReasonCode);
            strcat(errorBoxMessage, errorInfo);
          }
       if (dmcomm.ErrorInfo[i].OS2ReturnCode != 0)
          {
            sprintf(errorInfo, "\n   ErrorInfo[%d].OS2ReturnCode = %lu ",
                   i, dmcomm.ErrorInfo[i].OS2ReturnCode);
            strcat(errorBoxMessage, errorInfo);
          }
       ++i;
     } while ( ( (dmcomm.ErrorInfo[i].ReasonCode != 0)
                || (dmcomm.ErrorInfo[i].OS2ReturnCode != 0))
               && (i < DMCOMMBLOCK_ERROR_INFO_COUNT)
              );   /* end do */

  WinMessageBox(HWND_DESKTOP, HWND_DESKTOP, errorBoxMessage,
    "                         Dialog Manager Error                          ", 0,
    (MB_ENTER | MB_CUACRITICAL | MB_MOVEABLE));
  ISPCI(&dmcomm, 7L, "DMCLOSE");
  exit(FAILED);
}

/*-----------------------------------------------------------------------------*/
/* Application error found, format the error for later display                 */
/*-----------------------------------------------------------------------------*/
VOID format_app_error(PCHAR ErrorString, USHORT Error, PCHAR msg,
                      PCHAR file, USHORT line)
{
  sprintf(ErrorString,"Error %d detected while %s at line %d in file %s.\n",
         Error, msg, line, file);
}

/*-----------------------------------------------------------------------------*/
/* Display application error string and terminate the application              */
/*-----------------------------------------------------------------------------*/
VOID display_app_error(PCHAR ErrorString)
{
  WinMessageBox(HWND_DESKTOP, HWND_DESKTOP, ErrorString,
    "                         Application Error                             ", 0,
    (MB_ENTER | MB_CUACRITICAL | MB_MOVEABLE));
  ISPCI(&dmcomm, 7L, "DMCLOSE");
  exit(FAILED);
}
```

Figure 37-18 (Part 2 of 2). CLUB.C: The DM Helper Routines.

THE INCLUDE FILES: CLUB.H AND CLUBTXNS.H

This section presents two garden variety type of include files: **club.h** and **clubtxns.h**. The first file is specific to the client. The second file is used by both the client and server applications.

```
/*****************************************************************************/
/*  INCLUDE NAME: CLUB.H declarations for CLUB client program               */
/*****************************************************************************/
/*-------------------------------------------------------------------------*/
/* Defines                                                                  */
/*-------------------------------------------------------------------------*/
                  /*-------------------------------------*/
                  /* Bitmap IDs                           */
                  /*-------------------------------------*/
#define  ID_BITMAP1               1
#define  ID_BITMAP2               2
                  /*-------------------------------------*/
                  /* misc. defines                        */
                  /*-------------------------------------*/
#define  GOOD                     0
#define  FAILED                   1
#define  PIPE_TIMEOUT          10000L          /* 10 seconds                 */
                  /*-------------------------------------*/
                  /* misc. defines                        */
                  /*-------------------------------------*/
#define  MAXCLUBS             40
#define  CLUBDATAWIDTH        73
#define  MAXPRICES            52
#define  PRICEDATAWIDTH       73
#define  MAXRESERV            40
#define  RESERVDATAWIDTH      91
#define  MAXPARTYMEMBERS      10
#define  FILENAMEWIDTH        32
#define  MAXBITMAPS            6

/*-------------------------------------------------------------------------*/
/* Global variables/type definitions for this module                        */
/*-------------------------------------------------------------------------*/
                  /*-------------------------------------*/
                  /* DM system variables                  */
                  /*-------------------------------------*/
CHAR        zverb[9];
CHAR        zwinicon[9] = "CLUB";
CHAR        zcurfld[8];
int         fkaType     = 0;
```

Figure 37-19 (Part 1 of 4). The Include files: CLUB.H and CLUBTXNS.H.

```
                    /*______________________________________*/
                    /* variables for DM calls               */
                    /*______________________________________*/
CHAR        dmServiceBuffer[512];
DMCOMMBLOCK dmcomm;
long        buflen;
long        len[10];

CHAR        action_str[41]   = "GET_CLUB_NAMES";
CHAR        rempop_str[13]   = "";
CHAR        addpop_str[9]    = "";
CHAR        panel_id[9]      = "clubs";
CHAR        curfld[9]        = "" ;

                    /*______________________________________*/
                    /* application variables                */
                    /*______________________________________*/
CHAR         select[10][41] = {"1","2","3","4","5","6","7","8","9","10"};
BOOL         true = TRUE;
CHAR         input_msgbuf[1024];      /* transaction buffer                */
CHAR         output_msgbuf[1024];     /* transaction response buffer       */
CHAR         PipeName[128];           /* name of the club server named pipe */
CHAR         ComputerName[128];       /* computer name for club server     */
CHAR         RemotePipeName[128];     /* computer name for club server     */
USHORT       PipeBytesRead;           /* number of bytes read from pipe    */
USHORT       PipeBytesWritten;        /* number of bytes written to pipe   */
USHORT       PipeHandle;              /* handle from DosOpen or DosMakeNmPipe*/
USHORT       rc;                      /* return code                       */
USHORT       ActionTaken;             /* DosOpen action                    */
CHAR         datafile_drive_path[64]; /* path for data file                */
FILE        *rsp_file;
FILE        *msg_file;
ULONG        start_txn_sem    = 0;
HSEM         start_txn_sem_handle    = &start_txn_sem;
USHORT       perform_force_exit;
SHORT        i;
CHAR         completion[10];
CHAR         file_name[FILENAMEWIDTH];
CHAR         msg_file_path_name[128];
CHAR         rsp_file_path_name[128];
CHAR         error_string[1024];
CHAR         rsp_parms[1024];
#define      THREAD_STACK_SIZE 10240
BYTE         thread_stack[THREAD_STACK_SIZE]; /* thread stack              */
TID          thread_id;                       /* thread stack              */

                    /*______________________________________*/
                    /* variables for DM variable pool       */
                    /*______________________________________*/
CHAR         clubst1[]  = " Club";
CHAR         clubst2[]  = "Country";
CHAR         clubs[MAXCLUBS][CLUBDATAWIDTH]; /* array for club data        */
USHORT       clubmax;                        /* number of array items      */
USHORT       clubnum;                        /* item selected by user      */
```

Figure 37-19 (Part 2 of 4). The Include files: CLUB.H and CLUBTXNS.H.

```
CHAR        pricest[] = " Date              Adult Fare      Child Fare";
CHAR        prices[MAXPRICES][PRICEDATAWIDTH];/* array for prices data     */
USHORT      pricmax;                        /* number of array items       */
USHORT      pricnum;                        /* item selected by user       */

CHAR        reservt1[] = " Reservation ";
CHAR        reservt2[] = " Number";
CHAR        reservt3[] = "Last Name";
CHAR        reservt4[] = "First Name";
CHAR        reserv[MAXRESERV][RESERVDATAWIDTH];/* array for reserv. data     */
USHORT      resvmax;                        /* number of array items       */
USHORT      resvnum;                        /* item selected by user       */

CHAR        text_file_name[FILENAMEWIDTH] = "textdesc.txt";
CHAR        meta_file_name[FILENAMEWIDTH] = "metafile.met";
CHAR        bmap_file_name[6][FILENAMEWIDTH]={"bmp1file.bmp", "bmp2file.bmp",
                                  "bmp3file.bmp", "bmp4file.bmp",
                                  "bmp5file.bmp", "bmp6file.bmp"};
CHAR        club_name[32];
CHAR        week_date[27];
CHAR        reserv_no[10];
CHAR        first_name[33];
CHAR        last_name[33];
CHAR        age[4];
CHAR        address[33];
CHAR        phone_no[21];
CHAR        city[33];
CHAR        state[3];
CHAR        zip[10];
CHAR        last_namem[MAXPARTYMEMBERS][33];
CHAR        first_namem[MAXPARTYMEMBERS][33];
CHAR        agem[MAXPARTYMEMBERS][4];
CHAR        adult_fare[8];
CHAR        child_fare[8];
CHAR        total_fare[8];
CHAR        payment_method[10] = "Charge   ";

/*-----------------------------------------------------------------------*/
/* Forward declarations of procedures in this module                     */
/*-----------------------------------------------------------------------*/
                 /*------------------------------*/
                 /* top level routines           */
                 /*------------------------------*/
VOID  initialize_DM(VOID);
VOID  read_config(VOID);
VOID  vdefine_DM_variables(VOID);
VOID  vdefine_application_variables(VOID);
extern BOOL register_user_cntls(VOID);
VOID  interact_with_user(VOID);
VOID  terminate_application(VOID);

                 /*------------------------------*/
                 /* application routines         */
                 /*------------------------------*/
VOID  perform_action(PUSHORT);
SHORT get_club_names(VOID);
```

Figure 37-19 (Part 3 of 4). The Include files: CLUB.H and CLUBTXNS.H.

```
SHORT get_club_graphics(VOID);
SHORT get_club_description(VOID);
SHORT get_club_prices(VOID);
SHORT find_all_reserv(VOID);
SHORT find_reservation(VOID);
SHORT add_reservation(VOID);
SHORT cancel_reservation(VOID);
SHORT confirm_reservation(VOID);
SHORT execute_transaction(VOID);
SHORT get_club_name(VOID);
SHORT get_date_price(VOID);
SHORT get_reserv_no(VOID);
SHORT write_resv_data_to_file(VOID);
SHORT init_reservation_data(VOID);

                  /*-----------------------------------------*/
                  /* helper routines                         */
                  /*-----------------------------------------*/
VOID  dmService(PCHAR);
VOID  dmService2(PCHAR, PLONG, PVOID);
VOID  display_dm_error(PCHAR);
VOID  display_app_error(PCHAR);
VOID  format_app_error(PCHAR, USHORT, PCHAR, PCHAR, USHORT);
/*********************************************************************/
/*  INCLUDE NAME: CLUBTXNS.H common client/server declarations       */
/*********************************************************************/
                  /*-----------------------------------------*/
                  /* Transaction IDs                         */
                  /*-----------------------------------------*/
#define  GET_CLUB_NAMES         1
#define  GET_CLUB_GRAPHICS      2
#define  GET_CLUB_DESCRIPTION   3
#define  GET_CLUB_PRICES        4
#define  FIND_ALL_RESERV        5
#define  FIND_RESERVATION       6
#define  ADD_RESERVATION        7
#define  CANCEL_RESERVATION     8
#define  GET_MESSAGE_FILENAME   9
#define  CONFIRM_RESERVATION   10
```

Figure 37-19 (Part 4 of 4). The Include files: CLUB.H and CLUBTXNS.H.

WALKING THROUGH USERCTLS.C

In this section, we will walk through the PM client code module which registers and implements three user control classes: BITMAP, METAFILE, and MLE. User controls (or UCs) are used to augment DM's graphic repertoire by writing PM code to create your own DM classes. This mechanism was explained in Chapter 35, "PM and DM: Two to Tango". Here's the plan we will follow in walking through the USERCTLS.C module:

1. We first briefly explain the concepts of Bitmaps, Metafiles, and MLEs as used in PM.
2. In "The DM Messages used in the User Controls" on page 937, we explain the DM created PM messages. These messages trigger all the processing that is provided by the user control code.

3. In "USERCTLS.C: Registering the User Controls" on page 938, we present the header information associated with the UCs and the procedure which registers the three UC classes.
4. In "USERCTLS.C: The BitMap_Proc()" on page 940, we present the code for the BITMAP UC.
5. In "USERCTLS.C: The Metafile_Proc()" on page 944, we present the code for the METAFILE UC.
6. In "USERCTLS.C: The MLE_Proc()" on page 947, we present the code for the MLE UC.

What is a PM Bitmap?

A bitmap is an array of bits that represents an image. Depending on the colors and shades desired, each pixel in the image can be represented in: 1, 4, 8, or 24 bits. Bitmaps are used to store and display images in the following contexts:

- You can copy an image from a video display into a bitmap.
- You can scan an image into a bitmap file.
- You can load a bitmap from a file into memory.
- You can draw bitmapped images on the screen.
- You can use the powerful GpiBitBlt "bit blip" function to do all kinds of interesting manipulations and transformations on bitmaps.
- Bitmaps can be used to create graphic objects which are impossible to create using GPI draw primitives. Icons, pointers, and fill patterns are typically bitmaps.
- You can exchange bitmaps with other applications using the clipboard.

Bitmaps are device-dependent constructs; the output will look different on different devices. OS/2 publishes a bitmap file format which can be used to exchange bitmap graphic information between applications.

What is a PM Metafile?

A metafile stores an image as a series of GPI draw statements called *graphic orders*, which can redraw a picture very quickly. Compared to bitmaps, metafiles provide a very compact store of graphic objects. Metafiles use vector graphics as opposed to raster graphics. Metafiles are device independent and can be attached to devices with superior graphic displays and resolutions. Metafiles can be used to store and display images in the following contexts:

- You can draw complex images in a metafile and save the metafile in a file on disk.
- You can load the metafile from a disk file into an application where it can be played.
- You can display, print, or plot a metafile.

- You can edit a metafile. A metafile can be decomposed into individual graphic elements, edited, and then reassembled.
- You can exchange metafiles with other applications using the clipboard.

OS/2 considers a metafile to be a device just like a printer or plotter.

What is a PM Multiple-Line Entry Field (MLE)?

The PM MLE is a very sophisticated control window which allows users to edit and view multiple lines of text. An MLE essentially provides all the features of a simple text editor and makes them readily available to your application. Here's a list of some of the MLE's more important features:

- You can import text from a buffer into an MLE, and export text from an MLE into a buffer using a variety of exchange formats.
- You can edit, delete, insert, search, and replace text in an MLE.
- You can query the number of lines of text in an MLE.
- You can cut, copy, and paste text from an MLE into the clipboard and from the clipboard into the MLE.
- You can control the style of an MLE. You can draw a border, add vertical and horizontal scroll bars, and control word-wrapping, line length, colors, and the font. You can also prevent the user from entering text in an MLE.

The MLE will notify your application of any notable events.

The DM Messages used in the User Controls

Table 37-2 provides a brief sampling of some of the more common DM defined PM messages. The DM-defined PM message is the main mechanism used for exchanges between DM and the UC code. This makes sense, when you consider that the UC code is primarily a PM window procedure.

Table 37-2. Examples of Some Commonly Used DM-Defined PM Messages.

DM Message	Description
CM_UPDATE_CONTROL	This message is sent by DM to the user control to notify it that the panel in which it is located is about to be displayed or redisplayed. The user control uses this message to perform any processing needed before the panel is displayed or "redisplayed." (DM maintains a cache of three panels, and "redisplayed" means that the panel is being restored from the cache).
CM_GET_UC_PARM_AND_TEXT	The user control sends this message to itself when it needs access to the parameters that are passed to the user control class using the PRMDATA attribute of the UC tag.

Table 37-2. Examples of Some Commonly Used DM-Defined PM Messages.

DM Message	Description
CM_FREE_CTL_RESOURCES	This message is sent by DM to the user control to notify it to free any system resources such as memory or file handles.

USERCTLS.C: Registering the User Controls

We're now ready to start dissecting the PM code in the USERCTLS.C module. We will start with the listing in Figure 37-20 which contains the following:

1. The include files needed by the UCs. Notice that we've included two DM-specific header files: **ispuser.h** and **isperror.h**.
2. The constants and typdefs needed by the UCs. Most of the strange-looking variables are PM defined types required for bitmaps and metafiles. We'll see that later.
3. The code for the **register_user_cntls()** function. You must register a window class for each UC using PM's WinRegisterClass function. Notice that for MLEs, we combine (bitwise OR) the class style constants to create a class which combines a UC with the PM MLE control. Prior to registering the MLE class, we issued a WinQueryClassInfo call to obtain the PM MLE class information. We combined the information returned by that call with the UC style to create our hybrid class. More on that later. The extra bytes in the UC are required by DM. Otherwise, this is an ordinary class registration.

```
/*****************************************************************************/
/* USERCTLS    - User controls for the Club Med application.  There are     */
/*               three controls: BITMAP, METAFILE, and MLE.                  */
/*                                                                           */
/* GML examples:                                                             */
/* ------------                                                              */
/*                                                                           */
/*  <uc class=BITMAP prmdata='%filename'                                     */
/*       minwidth=6 maxwidth=6 mindepth=3 maxdepth=3>                        */
/*                                                                           */
/*  <uc class=METAFILE prmdata='%filename'                                   */
/*       mindepth=10 maxdepth=45 minwidth=8 maxwidth=150>                    */
/*                                                                           */
/*  <uc class=MLE prmdata='%filename'                                        */
/*       mindepth=10 maxdepth=25 minwidth=8 maxwidth=100>10.Courier          */
/*                                                                           */
/*****************************************************************************/
```

Figure 37-20 (Part 1 of 3). Registering the PM User Controls.

```
#include <stdlib.h>
#include <string.h>
#include <memory.h>
#include <stdio.h>
#include <malloc.h>
#include <sys\types.h>
#include <sys\stat.h>

#define  INCL_WIN
#define  INCL_BITMAPFILEFORMAT
#define  INCL_GPI
#include <os2.h>
#include <ispuser.h>
#include <isperror.h>

/*-----------------------------------------------------------------------*/
/* Variables for this module                                             */
/*-----------------------------------------------------------------------*/
                  /*------------------------------------*/
                  /* variables for drawing metafiles    */
                  /*------------------------------------*/
HDC     hdc;                          /* device context handle            */
HPS     hps;                          /* Presentation space handle        */
HMF     hmf;                          /* Metafile handle                  */
SIZEL   Size = {0,0};
LONG    alOptions[] = {0L,            /* PMF_SEGBASE                      */
                LT_ORIGINALVIEW,      /* PMF_LOADTYPE                     */
                RS_DEFAULT,           /* PMF_RESOLVE                      */
                LC_LOADDISC,          /* PMF_LCIDS                        */
                RES_DEFAULT,          /* PMF_RESET                        */
                SUP_DEFAULT,          /* PMF_SUPPRESS                     */
                CTAB_REPLACE,         /* PMF_COLORTABLES                  */
                CREA_DEFAULT,         /* PMF_COLORREALIZABLE              */
               };

MATRIXLF matlfXform   = {MAKEFIXED(1, 0x4000), MAKEFIXED(0, 0     ),   0L,
                         MAKEFIXED(0, 0     ), MAKEFIXED(1, 0x8000),   0L,
                         0L,                   0L
                         };

                  /*------------------------------------*/
                  /* variables for drawing bitmaps      */
                  /*------------------------------------*/
HDC     hdcMem;                       /* Memory device context handle     */
HPS     hpsMem;                       /* Presentation space handle        */
HBITMAP hbmMem;                       /* Bit maps held in a resource file */
POINTL  bmarray [5];                  /* bit map src, dst pointers        */

PBITMAPFILEHEADER bm_header_ptr;      /* pointer to bitmap header in memory */
PBITMAPINFOHEADER bm_info_ptr;        /* pointer to bitmap info   in memory */
PBYTE             bm_data_ptr;        /* pointer to bitmap pels   in memory */

PSZ         dcdatablk[9] = {(PSZ)0 ,(PSZ)"DISPLAY"    /* for device context   */
                           ,(PSZ)0 ,(PSZ)0 ,(PSZ)0
                           ,(PSZ)0 ,(PSZ)0 ,(PSZ)0
                           ,(PSZ)0 };
```

Figure 37-20 (Part 2 of 3). Registering the PM User Controls.

```
/*---------------------------------------------------------------------*/
/* Forward declarations of procedures in this module                   */
/*---------------------------------------------------------------------*/
extern BOOL register_user_cntls(VOID);
extern MRESULT EXPENTRY Metafile_Proc(HWND, USHORT, MPARAM, MPARAM);
extern MRESULT EXPENTRY MLE_Proc(HWND, USHORT, MPARAM, MPARAM);
extern MRESULT EXPENTRY BitMap_Proc(HWND, USHORT, MPARAM, MPARAM);

/*---------------------------------------------------------------------*/
/* Registration Routine for user controls                              */
/*---------------------------------------------------------------------*/
extern BOOL register_user_cntls()
{
  CLASSINFO classInfo;

  WinQueryClassInfo((HAB) NULL, WC_MLE, &classInfo);
  WinRegisterClass((HAB) NULL, "MLE", MLE_Proc,
         ( CS_PUBLIC & (classInfo.flClassStyle | CCTL_UC_CLASS_STYLE)),
         (classInfo.cbWindowData + CCTL_UC_EXTRA_BYTES));

  WinRegisterClass((HAB)NULL,"METAFILE", Metafile_Proc,
                  CCTL_UC_CLASS_STYLE, CCTL_UC_EXTRA_BYTES);

  WinRegisterClass((HAB)NULL,"BITMAP", BitMap_Proc,
                 CCTL_UC_CLASS_STYLE, CCTL_UC_EXTRA_BYTES);

} /* end Register_user_cntls */
```

Figure 37-20 (Part 3 of 3). Registering the PM User Controls.

USERCTLS.C: The BitMap_Proc()

In this section, we present the PM window procedure which performs the BITMAP UC function (see listing in Figure 37-21). This procedure loads a bitmap from a file into memory and then displays it in the UC window area. As you will soon see, this innocent function turns out to be quite contrived. The story follows:

When a panel is first displayed or redisplayed, each UC it contains will receive a CM_UPDATE_CONTROL message. Our UC uses the occasion to issue a WinInvalidateRect call. This causes PM to send the window a WM_PAINT message requesting it to repaint its contents. This is how the WM_PAINT message is processed by the UC:

1. The UC sends a CM_GET_UC_PARM_AND_TEXT message to itself to obtain the name of the OS/2 file which contains the bitmap to be displayed. Remember, the file name is passed as a UC parameter.
2. The UC displays an "hourglass" window to let the user know that something is happening. The loading of the bitmap can be time consuming depending on the size of the bitmap file.
3. The UC obtains the size of the bitmap file in bytes, allocates a memory buffer large enough to contain the bitmap and its header, and then loads the bitmap file contents into the buffer.

4. The UC associates a device context and presentation space with a bitmap structure and provides it with a pointer to the memory buffer.
5. The UC obtains the location and size of the UC's screen area. It then uses "bit blip" to copy and display the bitmap into that screen area.
6. The UC returns control to DM. This is because it is a subclass of a DM-provided window procedure.

You can obtain the rest of the gory details by reading the code in which we comment every step of the process.

The CM_FREE_CTL_RESOURCES is always received last. It causes the UC to release the presentation space and device context it created. Other than that, congratulations! You've just walked through the most difficult of the three UCs.

```
/*-----------------------------------------------------------------*/
/* Function for User Control BITMAP                                */
/*-----------------------------------------------------------------*/
extern MRESULT EXPENTRY BitMap_Proc(HWND hwnd, USHORT msg,
                                    MPARAM mp1, MPARAM mp2)
{
  CLASSINFO     classInfo;
  MRESULT       returnValue;
  MRESULT       WinRC;

  cmGetUCParmAndTextParm getUCParmAndTextParm;
  char     fname[32];

  HPS     hps;
  RECTL   PaintArea;
  SIZEL   bmSize;

  int          return_code;
  FILE         *file;
  struct stat StatBuff;

  returnValue = 0;

  switch(msg)
  {
    case CM_UPDATE_CONTROL:
         WinInvalidateRect(hwnd, NULL, TRUE);
         break;

    case WM_PAINT:
         /*--------------------------------------*/
         /* get bitmap file name                 */
         /*--------------------------------------*/
         memset(&getUCParmAndTextParm, 0, sizeof(getUCParmAndTextParm));
         getUCParmAndTextParm.MessageParmSize =
             sizeof(getUCParmAndTextParm);
         WinRC = WinSendMsg(hwnd, CM_GET_UC_PARM_AND_TEXT,
                            &getUCParmAndTextParm, NULL);
         strcpy(fname, getUCParmAndTextParm.ReturnControlPrmdataPtr);
```

Figure 37-21 (Part 1 of 4). The PM Bitmap Control Function: BitMap_Proc().

```
/*-----------------------------------------*/
/* Open the bitmap file                    */
/*-----------------------------------------*/
file = fopen( fname, "rb" );
if ( file != NULL )
{
  /*-----------------------------------------*/
  /* set pointer to hourglass                */
  /*-----------------------------------------*/
  WinSetPointer(HWND_DESKTOP,
              WinQuerySysPointer(HWND_DESKTOP, SPTR_WAIT, FALSE));
  /*-----------------------------------------*/
  /* Obtain the size of the file (i.e.bitmap)*/
  /*-----------------------------------------*/
  return_code = stat( fname, &StatBuff);
  /*-----------------------------------------*/
  /* Allocate memory buffer for the bitmap   */
  /*-----------------------------------------*/
  bm_header_ptr = (PBITMAPFILEHEADER)malloc( (size_t)StatBuff.st_size );
  if ( bm_header_ptr == NULL )
     WinMessageBox( HWND_DESKTOP, HWND_DESKTOP,
                    "Can't allocate storage", "BITMAP",
                    1, MB_OK );

  /*-----------------------------------------*/
  /* Copy bitmap file contents into memory   */
  /*-----------------------------------------*/
  fread( (PVOID)bm_header_ptr, sizeof(CHAR),
         (size_t)StatBuff.st_size, file );
  fclose( file );

  /*-----------------------------------------*/
  /* make pointers to bitmap info header     */
  /* and pel data portions of the buffer     */
  /*-----------------------------------------*/
  bm_info_ptr = MAKEP(SELECTOROF(bm_header_ptr),
                      OFFSETOF(bm_header_ptr)
                      + (sizeof(BITMAPFILEHEADER)
                         - sizeof(BITMAPINFOHEADER))  );
  bm_data_ptr = MAKEP(SELECTOROF(bm_header_ptr),
                      OFFSETOF(bm_header_ptr) + bm_header_ptr->offBits);

  bmSize.cx = bm_header_ptr->bmp.cx;
  bmSize.cy = bm_header_ptr->bmp.cy;

  /*-----------------------------------------*/
  /* remove any old bitmaps                  */
  /*-----------------------------------------*/
  if (hbmMem)
     {
      GpiSetBitmap (hpsMem, (HBITMAP)NULL);
      GpiDeleteBitmap(hbmMem);
      GpiAssociate( hpsMem, (HDC)NULL );
      GpiDestroyPS( hpsMem );
      DevCloseDC( hdcMem );
      hbmMem = (HBITMAP)NULL;
     }
```

Figure 37-21 (Part 2 of 4). The PM Bitmap Control Function: BitMap_Proc().

```
/*-------------------------------------------------*/
/* Create a memory Device Context                  */
/*-------------------------------------------------*/
hdcMem  = DevOpenDC((HAB)NULL, OD_MEMORY, "*", 8L,
                 (PDEVOPENDATA)dcdatablk, (HDC)NULL);
/*-------------------------------------------------*/
/* Create a memory Presentation Space (PS) */
/*-------------------------------------------------*/
hpsMem  = GpiCreatePS((HAB)NULL, hdcMem, &bmSize,
                 (LONG) PU_PELS | GPIT_NORMAL | GPIA_ASSOC);
/*-------------------------------------------------*/
/* Create a memory Bitmap                          */
/*-------------------------------------------------*/
hbmMem  = GpiCreateBitmap(hpsMem, bm_info_ptr, (ULONG)0,
                 (PBYTE)NULL, (PBITMAPINFO)NULL);
/*-------------------------------------------------*/
/* Associate Bitmap with Presentation Space*/
/*-------------------------------------------------*/
GpiSetBitmap(hpsMem, hbmMem);

/*-------------------------------------------------*/
/* Copy buffer pel data into bitmap                */
/*-------------------------------------------------*/

GpiSetBitmapBits(hpsMem,                /* memory presentation space*/
                 0L,                    /* starting row              */
                 (LONG)bm_info_ptr->cy, /* ending row                */
                 bm_data_ptr,           /* pointer to bit map data   */
                 (PBITMAPINFO)bm_info_ptr); /* pointer to bit info   */

/*-------------------------------------------------*/
/* Free buffer memory                              */
/*-------------------------------------------------*/
free(bm_header_ptr);

/*-------------------------------------------------*/
/* Determine size of UC screen area                */
/*-------------------------------------------------*/
hps = WinBeginPaint( hwnd, (HPS)NULL, &PaintArea );

/*-------------------------------------------------*/
/* set bitmap sizes (source and target)    */
/*-------------------------------------------------*/
bmarray[2].x = 0;
bmarray[2].y = 0;
bmarray[3].x = bmSize.cx;
bmarray[3].y = bmSize.cy;

bmarray[0].x = PaintArea.xLeft;
bmarray[0].y = PaintArea.yBottom;
bmarray[1].x = PaintArea.xRight;
bmarray[1].y = PaintArea.yTop;
```

Figure 37-21 (Part 3 of 4). The PM Bitmap Control Function: BitMap_Proc().

```
            /*-------------------------------------------*/
            /* bit blit  copy from Source to UC area    */
            /*-------------------------------------------*/
            GpiBitBlt(hps, hpsMem, 4L, (PPOINTL)bmarray,
                    (LONG) ROP_SRCCOPY, (LONG) BBO_IGNORE);
            WinEndPaint( hps );

            /*-------------------------------------------*/
            /* return hourglass pointer to normal        */
            /*-------------------------------------------*/
            WinSetPointer(HWND_DESKTOP, WinQuerySysPointer(HWND_DESKTOP,
                                              SPTR_ARROW, FALSE));
          } /* endif */
            /*-------------------------------------------*/
            /* return to DM: "subclass"  requirement     */
            /*-------------------------------------------*/

          WinQueryClassInfo((HAB)NULL, "DM_USER_CONTROL", &classInfo);
          return (*classInfo.pfnWindowProc)(hwnd, msg, mp1, mp2);
          break;

      case CM_FREE_CTL_RESOURCES:
          GpiSetBitmap (hpsMem, (HBITMAP)NULL);
          GpiDeleteBitmap(hbmMem);
          GpiAssociate( hpsMem, (HDC)NULL );
          GpiDestroyPS( hpsMem );
          DevCloseDC( hdcMem );
          hbmMem = (HBITMAP)NULL;
          break;

      default:
          WinQueryClassInfo((HAB)NULL, "DM_USER_CONTROL", &classInfo);
          returnValue = (*classInfo.pfnWindowProc)(hwnd, msg, mp1, mp2);
          break;

    } /* end switch */
    return returnValue;
 }
```

Figure 37-21 (Part 4 of 4). The PM Bitmap Control Function: BitMap_Proc().

USERCTLS.C: The Metafile_Proc()

This section presents the PM window procedure which performs the METAFILE UC function (see listing in Figure 37-22) This procedure loads a metafile from a file into memory and then displays it in the UC window area. The story follows:

When a panel is first displayed or redisplayed, each UC it contains will receive a CM_UPDATE_CONTROL message. Our UC will check to see if this is a first display versus a redisplay. If it is a first display, the UC has a keen interest in the message which it will process as follows:

1. The UC sends a CM_GET_UC_PARM_AND_TEXT message to itself to obtain the name of the OS/2 file which contains the metafile to be displayed. Remember, the file name is passed as a UC parameter.

2. The UC creates a metafile Device Context and associates it to a Presentation Space.
3. The UC then loads the metafile from a file to the Presentation Space.

The message which invariably follows is a PM WM_PAINT. Here is how it is processed:

1. The UC displays an "hourglass" window to let the user know that something is happening.
2. The UC zooms out the metafile (i.e., scales it down) and then displays it into the presentation space specified by the handle. The display options are set in *alOptions* (see Figure 37-20 on page 938). Mostly, we end up using the metafile's color table.
3. The UC returns control to DM. This is because it is a subclass of a DM-provided window procedure.

You can obtain the rest of the gory details by reading the code in which we comment every step of the process.

```
/*----------------------------------------------------------------------*/
/* Function for User Control METAFILE                                   */
/*----------------------------------------------------------------------*/
extern MRESULT EXPENTRY Metafile_Proc(HWND hwnd, USHORT msg,
                                      MPARAM mp1, MPARAM mp2)
{
  CLASSINFO     classInfo;
  MRESULT       returnValue;
  MRESULT       WinRC;
  LONG          SegCount;
  BOOL          Success;
  CHAR          metafile_desc[256];

  cmGetUCParmAndTextParm getUCParmAndTextParm;
  cmUpdateControlParmPtr updateControlParmPtr;
  char    fname[32];

  returnValue = 0;

  switch(msg)
  {
```

Figure 37-22 (Part 1 of 3). The PM Metafile Control Function: Metafile_Proc().

```
case CM_UPDATE_CONTROL:

     updateControlParmPtr = (cmUpdateControlParmPtr) mp1;

       /*----------------------------------------*/
       /* Is it the first CM_UPDATE_CONTROL?      */
       /*----------------------------------------*/
     if (updateControlParmPtr->SetInitialState)
     { /*----------------------------------------*/
       /* get file name                           */
       /*----------------------------------------*/
       memset(&getUCParmAndTextParm, 0, sizeof(getUCParmAndTextParm));
       getUCParmAndTextParm.MessageParmSize =
           sizeof(getUCParmAndTextParm);
       WinRC = WinSendMsg(hwnd, CM_GET_UC_PARM_AND_TEXT,
                          &getUCParmAndTextParm, NULL);
       strcpy(fname, getUCParmAndTextParm.ReturnControlPrmdataPtr);

       /*----------------------------------------*/
       /* Create Device Context and Presentation  */
       /*----------------------------------------*/
       hdc  = WinOpenWindowDC(hwnd);
       hps  = GpiCreatePS( (HAB)NULL, hdc, &Size,
                      (LONG) PU_LOENGLISH | GPIT_NORMAL | GPIA_ASSOC);
       /*----------------------------------------*/
       /* Load Metafile from file                 */
       /*----------------------------------------*/
       hmf = GpiLoadMetaFile( (HAB)NULL, fname);
     }
     break;

case WM_PAINT:
     /*----------------------------------------*/
     /* set pointer to hourglass                */
     /*----------------------------------------*/
     WinSetPointer(HWND_DESKTOP,
                WinQuerySysPointer(HWND_DESKTOP, SPTR_WAIT, FALSE));

     /*----------------------------------------*/
     /* zoom out to scale down the image        */
     /*----------------------------------------*/
     Success = GpiSetDefaultViewMatrix(hps, 8L, &matlfXform,
                                   TRANSFORM_REPLACE);
     /*----------------------------------------*/
     /* Play the metafile using alOptions       */
     /*----------------------------------------*/
     hps = WinBeginPaint( hwnd, hps, NULL );
     GpiPlayMetaFile(hps, hmf, 8L, alOptions, &SegCount,
                (LONG)sizeof(metafile_desc), metafile_desc);
     WinEndPaint( hps );

     /*----------------------------------------*/
     /* return hourglass pointer to normal      */
     /*----------------------------------------*/
     WinSetPointer(HWND_DESKTOP, WinQuerySysPointer(HWND_DESKTOP,
                                           SPTR_ARROW, FALSE));
```

Figure 37-22 (Part 2 of 3). The PM Metafile Control Function: Metafile_Proc().

```
        /*---------------------------------------*/
        /* return to DM: "subclass" requirement  */
        /*---------------------------------------*/
        WinQueryClassInfo((HAB)NULL, "DM_USER_CONTROL", &classInfo);
        return (*classInfo.pfnWindowProc)(hwnd, msg, mp1, mp2);
        break;

    case CM_FREE_CTL_RESOURCES:
        GpiDeleteMetaFile(hmf);
        GpiAssociate( hps, (HDC)NULL );
        GpiDestroyPS( hps );
        hdc = (HDC)NULL;
        break;

    default:
        WinQueryClassInfo((HAB)NULL, "DM_USER_CONTROL", &classInfo);
        returnValue = (*classInfo.pfnWindowProc)(hwnd, msg, mp1, mp2);
        break;

  } /* end switch */
  return returnValue;
}
```

Figure 37-22 (Part 3 of 3). The PM Metafile Control Function: Metafile_Proc().

USERCTLS.C: The MLE_Proc()

This section presents the PM window procedure which performs the MLE UC function (see listing in Figure 37-23). This procedure loads a file of text information into memory and then imports it into an MLE control where the information gets displayed. The MLE is inside the UC area. The story follows:

The first message we process is the PM WM_CREATE message. Why? The reason is that when we registered the MLE UC (in in Figure 37-20 on page 938), we specified that it consisted of a PM MLE class within a DM user control. So, in effect we're letting PM create the MLE for us. When PM is about ready to do so, it notifies us with a WM_CREATE message. So what does the UC do with this message?

1. It modifies the style of the MLE and makes it "read only." It also adds a vertical scroll bar and requests that a border be placed around it. Notice that the UC can do all this, because the *mp2* parameter in the message that it just received points to a structure which contains all the style information that will be used to create the MLE.
2. It then returns the message to PM for processing. This is because this message was received from PM and not DM.

When a panel is first displayed, each UC it contains will receive a CM_UPDATE_CONTROL message from DM. Our MLE UC is no exception. If this panel is being displayed for the first time, as opposed to being redisplayed, our UC has a keen interest in the message. Here's what it does with it:

1. The UC sends a CM_GET_UC_PARM_AND_TEXT message to itself to obtain the name of the OS/2 file which contains the MLE to be displayed, and the font name and size. These are all UC parameters.
2. The UC sets the font for this MLE based on the instructions received in the tags.
3. The UC allocates a buffer in memory and copies into it the contents of the MLE text file.
4. The UC then sends a series of messages to the MLE window. The first message, MLM_DELETE, tells the MLE to clear its contents. The second message, MLM_SETIMPORTEXPORT, tells the MLE to set the import/export buffer to point to the very beginning. The third message, MLM_IMPORT, tells the MLE to copy the contents of the buffer into the MLE.

OK, we're almost done. There is one more detail you should be aware of: notice how the return is handled in the default case. Why the dual return paths? It's a very simple explanation. If the message received is greater than the *WM_USER* constant, it belongs to DM, so we return it to DM. Otherwise, it belongs to PM, and we return it to PM. The reason that we're getting so much interaction from PM in this UC is because the MLE was created as an ordinary PM class combined with the UC.

```
/*----------------------------------------------------------------------------*/
/* Function for User Control Class MLE                                        */
/*----------------------------------------------------------------------------*/
extern MRESULT EXPENTRY MLE_Proc(HWND  hwnd, USHORT msg,
                                 PVOID mp1,  PVOID  mp2)
{
  CLASSINFO    classInfo;
  MRESULT      returnValue;
  MRESULT      WinRC;

  char fname[32];
  cmGetUCParmAndTextParm getUCParmAndTextParm;
  cmUpdateControlParmPtr updateControlParmPtr;

  PCREATESTRUCT create_struct_ptr;

  int         return_code;
  CHAR        *Buffer;
  IPT         ipt;
  FILE        *Stream;
  CHAR        szMsg[256];
  CHAR        szFontName[32];
  struct stat StatBuff;

  returnValue = 0;
```

Figure 37-23 (Part 1 of 4). The PM MLE Control Function: MLE_Proc().

```
switch (msg)
{
  case WM_CREATE:
       /*--------------------------------------------*/
       /* modify window style, let PM create MLE     */
       /*--------------------------------------------*/
       create_struct_ptr = (PCREATESTRUCT)mp2;
       create_struct_ptr->flStyle = create_struct_ptr->flStyle |
                                    MLS_READONLY | MLS_VSCROLL | MLS_BORDER;

       WinQueryClassInfo((HAB) NULL, WC_MLE, &classInfo);
       returnValue =  (*classInfo.pfnWindowProc)
                      (hwnd, msg, mp1, mp2);
       break;

  case CM_UPDATE_CONTROL:
       updateControlParmPtr = (cmUpdateControlParmPtr) mp1;

         /*--------------------------------------------*/
         /* Is it the first CM_UPDATE_CONTROL?         */
         /*--------------------------------------------*/
       if (updateControlParmPtr->SetInitialState)
       {
         /*--------------------------------------------*/
         /* get file name for loading into the MLE     */
         /*--------------------------------------------*/
         memset(&getUCParmAndTextParm, 0, sizeof(getUCParmAndTextParm));
         getUCParmAndTextParm.MessageParmSize =
             sizeof(getUCParmAndTextParm);

         WinSendMsg(hwnd, CM_GET_UC_PARM_AND_TEXT,
             &getUCParmAndTextParm, NULL);

         /* 'prmdata' value is name of file to load into MLE */
         strcpy(fname,      getUCParmAndTextParm.ReturnControlPrmdataPtr);

         /*--------------------------------------------*/
         /* set font for the MLE                       */
         /*--------------------------------------------*/
         if (getUCParmAndTextParm.ReturnControlTextPtr != NULL)
            {
             strcpy(szFontName, getUCParmAndTextParm.ReturnControlTextPtr);
             WinSetPresParam( hwnd,
                              PP_FONTNAMESIZE,
                              (LONG)strlen( szFontName ) + 11,
                              (PVOID)szFontName );
            }
```

Figure 37-23 (Part 2 of 4). The PM MLE Control Function: MLE_Proc().

```
        /*-----------------------------------------*/
        /* Open file and read data into a buffer   */
        /*-----------------------------------------*/
        Stream = fopen( fname, "rb" );
        if ( Stream == NULL )
           {
            sprintf( szMsg, "Can't open the file < %s >", fname);
            WinMessageBox( HWND_DESKTOP,
                           HWND_DESKTOP,
                           szMsg,
                           "MLE",
                           1,
                           MB_OK );
           } /* endif */

        return_code = stat( fname, &StatBuff);
        Buffer = (CHAR *)malloc( (size_t)StatBuff.st_size );
        if ( Buffer == NULL )
           WinMessageBox( HWND_DESKTOP,
                          HWND_DESKTOP,
                          "Can't allocate storage",
                          "MLE",
                          1,
                          MB_OK );

        fread( (void *)Buffer,
               sizeof(CHAR),
               (size_t)StatBuff.st_size,
               Stream );
        fclose( Stream );

        /*-----------------------------------------*/
        /* import buffer data into the MLE Control */
        /*    - clear the buffer                   */
        /*    - import from location 0 (beginning) */
        /*    - import the data                    */
        /*    - make the MLE read only             */
        /*-----------------------------------------*/
        ipt = 0;    /* delete buffer data */
        WinSendMsg(hwnd, MLM_DELETE, (MPARAM)ipt, MPFROMLONG((ULONG)100000));
        ipt = 0;    /* Import from the beginning  */
        WinRC = WinSendMsg(hwnd, MLM_SETIMPORTEXPORT, (MPARAM)Buffer,
                           MPFROMLONG( (LONG)StatBuff.st_size-1 ) );
        WinRC= WinSendMsg(hwnd, MLM_IMPORT, (MPARAM)&ipt,
                          MPFROMLONG( (ULONG)StatBuff.st_size-1 ) );
        WinRC= WinSendMsg(hwnd, MLM_SETREADONLY, (MPARAM)TRUE, NULL);
      } /* end if */
      break;
```

Figure 37-23 (Part 3 of 4). The PM MLE Control Function: MLE_Proc().

```
      default:
           /*-------------------------------------------*/
           /* pass other messages to the right class   */
           /*-------------------------------------------*/
           if (msg>=WM_USER)
             WinQueryClassInfo((HAB) NULL, "DM_USER_CONTROL", &classInfo);
           else
             WinQueryClassInfo((HAB) NULL, WC_MLE, &classInfo);

           returnValue =  (*classInfo.pfnWindowProc) (hwnd, msg, mp1, mp2);
           break;
    } /* end switch */

    return returnValue;
  } /* end DM_MLE_Proc */
```

Figure 37-23 (Part 4 of 4). The PM MLE Control Function: MLE_Proc().

Chapter 38

The Club Med Server

This is the third and last of a three-chapter series on the Club Med client-server application. This chapter walks you through the transaction server code. We show you how to create a multiuser transaction server which uses Named Pipes, the IBM LAN Server, and the OS/2 EE Database Manager. The program demonstrates how a transaction is processed using the CLUB database and how the results are returned to the PM-DM front-end client. We start out this chapter with a short discussion on the design of transaction servers.

WHAT'S A CLUB MED TRANSACTION SERVER

The Club Med transaction server is simply a dedicated computer on the network which provides code that executes transactions on a database. The transaction code and the database reside on the same machine. The multiuser capabilities are provided by creating multiple instances of the transaction server process. The client invokes the execution of transactions on the server through request messages sent over the network using Named Pipes. For each request, a reply message is returned using the same Named Pipe instance. Large result files are returned via the IBM Lan Server.

Does this all sound like "deja vu?" It should. The program we will be walking through in this chapter is just a revisit of the TP1 implementation described in Chapter 27. The only difference is that we replaced the TP1 transaction with Club Med-specific transactions. We're also introducing the concept of returning a large result file as part of the execution of a transaction. The simple TP1 DebitCredit transaction consists of a simple request-reply message exchange and does not contain the notion of a large response file.

The good news then is that since you've already seen it all, we expect the walk through the server end of the Club Med application to be fairly brisk. To keep the code well focused and reasonable in size, we're only presenting one transaction: *get_club_names*. The other eight server transactions are available on the program diskette together with their client counterparts.

THE CLUB TRANSACTION SERVER ELEMENTS

The purpose of this section is to get you acquainted with the different components of the Club Med Transaction Server and show you how they play together. You should first review "Club Med: A System Scenario" on page 895 to get the big picture of how the client and server interact at the system level.

Why is a Multiuser Server Needed?

You clearly don't want your clients to depend on a single server process. If you do so, you run the risk of having a client hog all the system's resources and starve out its fellow clients. A server should be designed to provide the best overall performance for all of its clients. This means that your server processes must provide a certain level of multitasking and support more than one client at the same time.

What Does a Multiuser Server Need?

Now, that we've introduced the notion of a multitasking server instead of a serially reusable server, we open up a flood gate of new requirements, all of which have to do with sharing the server's resources. Let's go down the list of what is needed:

1. ***Multisession peer-to-peer communications:*** We obviously can't have a single communication session, since it will quickly become the serially reusable bottleneck. So we need a protocol which supports multiple concurrent sessions. How many? It depends on whether your sessions are persistent or non-persistent. If they're persistent, you will need one session per client. If they're non-persistent, you can create a pool of reusable sessions. We will take the non-persistent design approach, which allows us to provide service on demand and play the law of statistical averages. This means we'll be providing fewer sessions than the number of clients, which means a client may occasionally wait on a reusable session to free up. Of course, we do not place an upper limit on the number of clients that our server pool will support. The concept of dynamic allocation of connections when needed makes the network easier to manage than with static session allocations. The Named Pipes protocol allows us to create a single Named Pipe with multiple instances. The Named Pipe transaction services such as **DosCallNmPipe** make it easy to create non-persistent service calls.

2. ***Multitasking Transaction Server Processes:*** The transaction server process interfaces with the client and executes the SQL transactions. *Why is it a process and not a thread?* Because the OS/2 Database Manager allows only a single database connection per process. *How many processes are needed?* As many as the number of concurrent sessions you have chosen to support. In our design, each transaction server process will own one Named Pipe instance and one connection to the Database Manager.

3. ***Shared Access to Data:*** Our server needs to protect the integrity of shared data while allowing concurrent access to the data. No problem! Our transaction server is built on top of the OS/2 EE Database Manager which is a multiuser SQL server engine.

4. ***Shared File Access:*** Our server needs to support the return of large result files to its clients. These result files may contain multiple table rows or large objects (BLOBs) such as bitmaps, metafiles, text files, or image frames. How are these objects passed to the client? The servers produce the large file objects and return their name and location to the clients as part of the reply message. The clients can then either directly manipulate the files or copy them over. A file server, such as the IBM LAN Server program, is needed to provide multiple client and server processes network access to a shared file system.

How are the Transaction Processes Started and Killed?

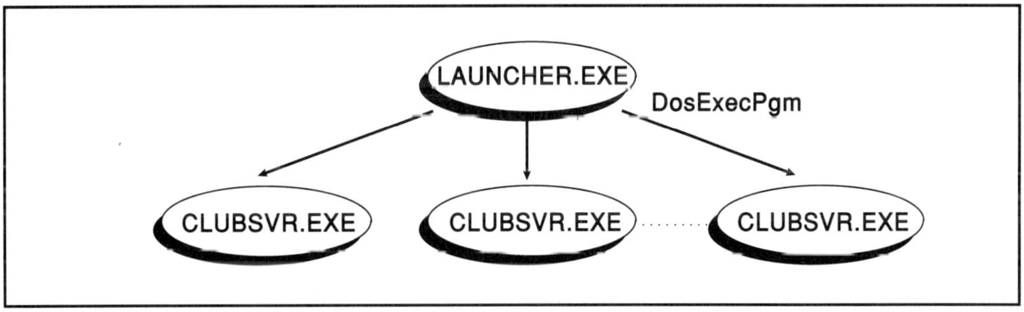

Figure 38-1. Launcher Starts "N" Instances of the Transaction Server Program.

This is an area that can get really wild. There are many schemes for starting processes dynamically to match incoming client requests. Each scheme introduces its own set of interesting heuristics. However, remember that it takes time to create a process. Do you want that to happen when a request comes in? You may be better off priming a static number of processes. If the processes take up too much space in memory, share some of the functions using DLLs. Occasionally, you may have to fine-tune your server by adding or removing some transaction processes.

Our aim in this chapter is to provide you with a bare bones process launcher program that provides the basic function. You can then take that code and modify it to suit your requirements. The good news is that we already have such a program: the one for the TP1 transaction server LAUNCHER developed in Chapter 27. We will use this program to start "n" process instances of the Club Med transaction server program (see Figure 38-1). The launcher program takes, as input parameters, the name of the process to be launched and the number of times to "clone" it. For example, to start three concurrent Club Med transaction server processes issue:

```
LAUNCHER  clubsvr 3
```

where *clubsvr* is the name of Club Med transaction server program we will be developing in this chapter. After it creates the three processes, the launcher blocks itself and waits for any key to be hit on the server machine. A key hit wakes up the launcher and causes it to kill all the processes it created and then terminate the server application.

The Transaction Server and the Database Server

Figure 38-2 shows the elements of the Club Med transaction server. The server machine contains both the transaction server processes and the OS/2 EE Database Manager. The transaction server processes are instances of the CLUBSVR program, whose code we will shortly be walking through. Each CLUBSVR process creates an instance of a Named Pipe and connects to the CLUB database. Clients submit their transactions by issuing DosCallNmPipe calls. This call will be handed automatically to the first available server process. If no server process is available, the clients will queue their requests until one frees up. All this queuing is provided by Named Pipes automatically. Remember, all the clients use instances of the *same* Named Pipe.

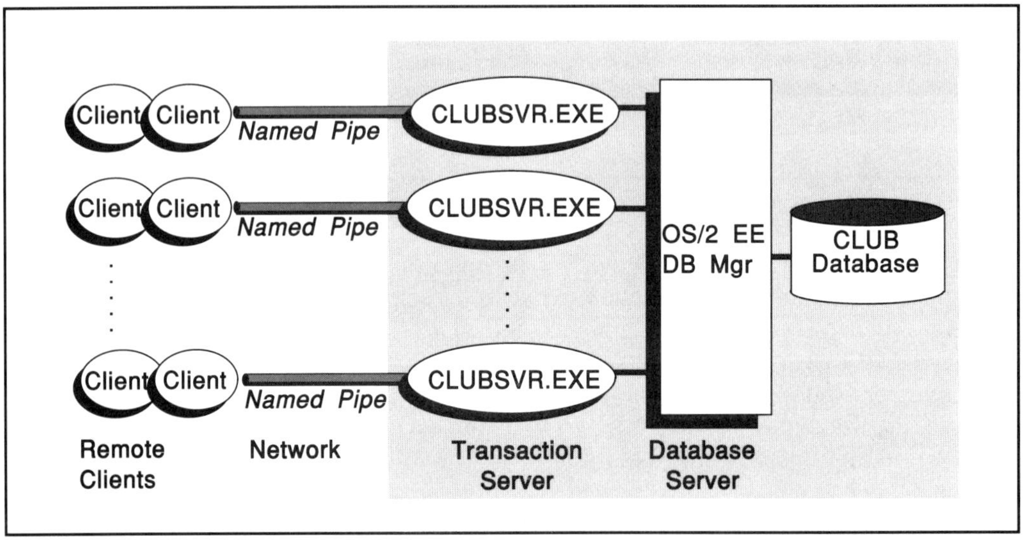

Figure 38-2. The Transaction Server Processes and the Database Server.

The Transaction Server and the File Server

Figure 38-3 shows another element of our Club Med server: the file server. The file server is the IBM PC LAN program which is also installed on the server machine. The server processes create response files on the file servers, which clients can then directly access over the network using the OS/2 LAN Requester.

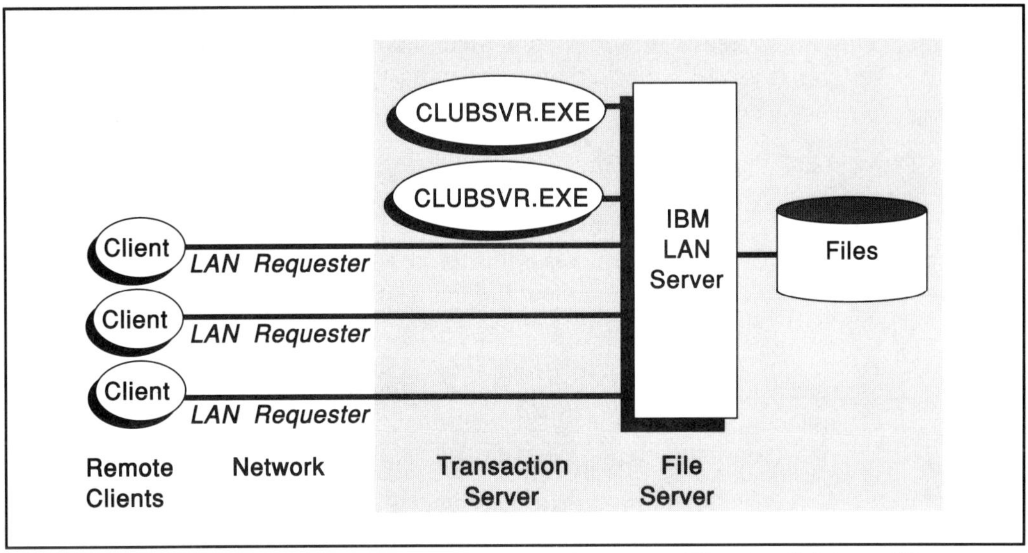

Figure 38-3. Using a File Server to Make Large Response Files Available to Clients.

CLUBSVR.SQC: THE TRANSACTION SERVER

Now that we know how the pieces play together, we are ready to introduce the element which customizes the Club Med transaction server: the CLUBSVR.SQC program (see listing in Figure 38-4). This is a program that is designed to run Club Med-specific transactions. The transactions operate on data stored in the CLUB database. Transactions are triggered by messages sent by remote clients using Named Pipes.

The core of the CLUBSVR.SQC program is identical to "Walking through the SQLTP1SV.SQC Server" on page 748. In fact, we just copied many of the procedures. So, what is it that makes CLUBSVR.SQC special? Here's the list of what's value-added and new:

- ***The transaction dispatcher:*** This new piece of code provided by the **dispatch_transaction()** function is a switch which invokes the appropriate transaction handler procedure. The switch dispatches a handler procedure based on the "transaction id" field value it reads from the incoming request message. TP1 did not require a switch because its server was only capable of executing a single transaction: TP1.

- ***Club Med-specific transactions:*** The Club Med server executes the eight transactions described in "The Club Med Transactions" on page 891. These transactions are, of course, all new and specific to the club application. The SQL code for the *get_club_names* transaction is supplied in the listing. The code for the remaining transactions is on the program diskette.

- ***The response file mechanism:*** The TP1 server did not return large objects to the client. This is an area where the Club Med server provides a value-added function. The response file mechanism is demonstrated in the **get_club_names()** listing. It's very simple:

  1. Transactions that generate multirow responses create a client-specific response file. The server is responsible for naming the file and assigning unique names.
  2. The transaction handler writes the results of a query into the response file one row at a time. This is done as part of the SQL cursor loop.
  3. The formatting of the rows in the response file is based on a common format known to both the client and the server.
  4. The transaction handler closes the response file when the last row is fetched.
  5. The transaction handler returns the name of the response file to the client as part of the transaction reply message (see "The Club Med Transactions" on page 891).
  6. The client can access the response file using the LAN requester. The file can be directly manipulated or copied over the network.
  7. The client is responsible for deleting the response file from the shared subdirectory.

Except for the three items described above, you should find no surprises in the code. We've left it all in one chunk because it requires no further explanation.

```
/******************************************************************************/
/*  PROGRAM NAME: CLUBSVR.SQC                                                 */
/*                                                                            */
/*  PROGRAM DESCRIPTION:  This program is run as a child task of the LAUNCHER*/
/*    program and executes the CLUB Server transactions using Named Pipes    */
/*    to communicate with a client.                                           */
/*                                                                            */
/******************************************************************************/
#include <mt\process.h>              /* For exit()                            */
#include <mt\string.h>               /* For printf                            */
#include <mt\sys\types.h>            /* For time()                            */
#include <mt\sys\timeb.h>            /* For time()                            */
#include <mt\sys\stat.h>             /* For stat()                            */
#include <mt\stdlib.h>               /* For atoi                              */
#include <mt\stdio.h>                /* For sprintf, printf                   */
#include <mt\io.h>                   /* For mktemp                            */
```

Figure 38-4 (Part 1 of 9). CLUBSVR.SQC: The Transaction Server Program.

```
#define INCL_DOSPROCESS              /* for DosGetPID                     */
#define INCL_DOSNMPIPES              /* include named pipe api calls      */
#define INCL_ERRORS                  /* include error definitions         */
#include <os2.h>

#include <sqlca.h>                   /* sqlca                             */
#include <sql.h>                     /* error msg. retrieval              */
#include <sqlcodes.h>                /* SQL return code constants         */
#include <sqlenv.h>                  /* environment functions and         */

#include "clubtxns.h"

                   /*---------------------------------------*/
                   /* forward declarations of functions     */
                   /*---------------------------------------*/
VOID read_config(VOID);
VOID initialize_task(VOID);
VOID initialize_pipe(VOID);
VOID execute_task(VOID);

SHORT dispatch_transaction(VOID);
SHORT get_club_names(VOID);
SHORT get_club_graphics(VOID);
SHORT get_club_description(VOID);
SHORT get_club_prices(VOID);
SHORT find_all_reserv(VOID);
SHORT find_reservation(VOID);
SHORT add_reservation(VOID);
SHORT cancel_reservation(VOID);
SHORT generate_message_filename(VOID);
SHORT open_response_file(VOID);
SHORT open_message_file(PCHAR);
SHORT unknown_transaction(VOID);

VOID print_error(USHORT, PCHAR, PCHAR, USHORT);
VOID format_error(PCHAR msgbuf, LONG Error, PCHAR msg,
                  PCHAR file, USHORT line);
                   /*---------------------------------------*/
                   /* constant definitions                  */
                   /*---------------------------------------*/
#define GOOD              0
#define FAILED           -1
                   /*---------------------------------------*/
                   /* variables                             */
                   /*---------------------------------------*/
CHAR    input_msgbuf[1024];         /* msg buffer for receiving txn      */
CHAR    txn_parms[512];             /* transaction parms from input msg  */
CHAR    output_msgbuf[1024];        /* msg buffer for sending resp.      */
CHAR    error_msgbuf[1024];         /* msg buffer for formatting errors  */
USHORT  rc;                         /* return code variable              */
CHAR    error_string[80];           /* error string container            */
SHORT   txn_id;                     /* transaction identifier            */
PCHAR   fn_template="FLXXXXXX";     /* template for generated file name  */
CHAR    file_name[13];              /* generated file name               */
CHAR    response_file_name[13];     /* generated file name with ext      */
CHAR    message_file_name[13];      /* message file name                 */
PIDINFO pidinfo;                    /* for generating temp. file name    */
```

Figure 38-4 (Part 2 of 9). CLUBSVR.SQC: The Transaction Server Program.

```
USHORT  filenum;                        /* for generating temp. file name    */
FILE    *rsp_file;
FILE    *msg_file;

USHORT pipe_handle;
CHAR   pipe_name[] = "\\PIPE\\CLUB";
USHORT bytes_read;
USHORT bytes_written;

struct sqlca sqlca;

EXEC SQL WHENEVER SQLERROR CONTINUE;
EXEC SQL WHENEVER SQLWARNING CONTINUE;
EXEC SQL WHENEVER NOT FOUND CONTINUE;

                   /*________________________________*/
                   /* SQL Host variables              */
                   /*________________________________*/
EXEC SQL BEGIN DECLARE SECTION;
 char      club[33];
 char      country[33];
 char      activity[21];
 char      picture[21];
 char      description[21];
 char      adult_price[9];
 char      child_price[9];
 char      week_date[11];
 char      last_name[33];
 char      first_name[33];
 char      age[4];
 char      party_member[2];
 char      reserv_no[10];
 char      phone_no[21];
 char      address[33];
 char      city[33];
 char      state[3];
 char      zip[11];
 char      payment_method[10];
EXEC SQL END   DECLARE SECTION;

/*______________________________________________________________________*/
/* Main routine.                                                         */
/*______________________________________________________________________*/
VOID main(USHORT argc, PCHAR argv[])
{
  initialize_task();                    /* perform database connect etc. */

  initialize_pipe();                    /* create Named Pipe             */

  execute_task();                       /* Loop executing TPls           */

} /* end main */
```

Figure 38-4 (Part 3 of 9). CLUBSVR.SQC: The Transaction Server Program.

```
/*--------------------------------------------------------------------------*/
/* Perform onetime initializations for the task such as database connects.  */
/*--------------------------------------------------------------------------*/
VOID  initialize_task(VOID)
{
  /*------------------------------------*/
  /* connect to the database, restart if */
  /*    necessary                       */
  /*------------------------------------*/
  sqlestrd("CLUB", 'S', &sqlca);

  if (sqlca.sqlcode == SQLE_RC_DB_RESTART)
     sqlerest("CLUB", &sqlca);

  if (sqlca.sqlcode)
     { sprintf(error_string,"connnecting to the database, sqlca.sqlcode = %ld",
               sqlca.sqlcode);
       print_error(0, error_string, __FILE__,__LINE__);
       exit(FAILED);
     }

  /*------------------------------------*/
  /* get PID for file name generation   */
  /*------------------------------------*/
  DosGetPID(&pidinfo);

  /*------------------------------------*/
  /* install database signal handler    */
  /*------------------------------------*/
  sqleisig(&sqlca);
  if (sqlca.sqlcode)
     { sprintf(error_string,"installing signal handler, sqlca.sqlcode = %ld",
               sqlca.sqlcode);
       print_error(0, error_string, __FILE__,__LINE__);
       exit(FAILED);
     }

} /* end initialize_task */

/*--------------------------------------------------------------------------*/
/* Perform onetime initialization  for the  Named Pipe                      */
/*--------------------------------------------------------------------------*/
VOID  initialize_pipe(VOID)
{

 #define PIPE_OPENMODE      0x4002    /* no write-behind allowed, duplex    */
 #define PIPEMODE           0x0580    /* message pipe, 128  instances       */
 #define TIMEOUT            0L        /* wait forever timeout value         */
```

Figure 38-4 (Part 4 of 9). CLUBSVR.SQC: The Transaction Server Program.

```
    rc = DosMakeNmPipe(pipe_name,          /* PipeName                          */
                       &pipe_handle,       /* pipe handle returned              */
                       PIPE_OPENMODE,
                       PIPEMODE,
                       512,                /* Output buffer size in bytes       */
                       512,                /* Input  buffer size in bytes       */
                       TIMEOUT);
    if (rc)
       {print_error(rc,"Making a named pipe",__FILE__,__LINE__);
        exit(FAILED);
       }
   } /* end initialize_pipes */

   /*--------------------------------------------------------------------------*/
   /* Task routine. This routine continuously 1) waits for a remote request    */
   /*   2) reads the incoming parameters,  3) invokes the transaction dispatcher*/
   /*   4) sends back response  5) disconnects from client                     */
   /*--------------------------------------------------------------------------*/
   VOID execute_task(VOID)
   {
     /*-----------------------------------*/
     /* continuous loop                   */
     /*-----------------------------------*/
     while (TRUE)
       {
         /*-----------------------------------*/
         /* execute a transaction             */
         /*-----------------------------------*/
         rc = DosConnectNmPipe(pipe_handle);
         if (rc)
            {print_error(rc,"Connecting to pipe",__FILE__,__LINE__);
             exit(FAILED);
            }

         rc = DosRead(pipe_handle,
                      input_msgbuf,
                      sizeof(input_msgbuf),
                      &bytes_read);
         if (rc)
            {print_error(rc,"Reading from pipe",__FILE__,__LINE__);
             exit(FAILED);
            }

         if ( dispatch_transaction() )
            exit(FAILED);

         rc = DosWrite(pipe_handle,
                       output_msgbuf,
                       strlen(output_msgbuf) + 1,
                       &bytes_written);
         if (rc)
            {print_error(rc,"Writing to pipe",__FILE__,__LINE__);
             exit(FAILED);
            }
```

Figure 38-4 (Part 5 of 9). CLUBSVR.SQC: The Transaction Server Program.

```
        rc = DosDisConnectNmPipe(pipe_handle);
        if (rc)
           {print_error(rc,"Disconnecting from Pipe",__FILE__,__LINE__);
            exit(FAILED);
           }
     }/* end while */
} /* end execute_task */

/*----------------------------------------------------------------------*/
/* function to dispatch a transaction                                   */
/*----------------------------------------------------------------------*/
SHORT dispatch_transaction(VOID)
{
  strcat(input_msgbuf, ";");
  sscanf(input_msgbuf, "TRANSACTION_ID=%d %[^;]", &txn_id, txn_parms);

  switch (txn_id)
  { case GET_CLUB_NAMES       :  get_club_names();            break;
    case GET_CLUB_GRAPHICS    :  get_club_graphics();         break;
    case GET_CLUB_DESCRIPTION :  get_club_description();      break;
    case GET_CLUB_PRICES      :  get_club_prices();           break;
    case FIND_ALL_RESERV      :  find_all_reserv();           break;
    case FIND_RESERVATION     :  find_reservation();          break;
    case ADD_RESERVATION      :  add_reservation();           break;
    case CANCEL_RESERVATION   :  cancel_reservation();        break;
    case GET_MESSAGE_FILENAME :  generate_message_filename(); break;
    default                   :  unknown_transaction();       break;
  } /* endswitch */

  return(GOOD);
} /* end dispatch_transaction */

/*----------------------------------------------------------------------*/
/* execute get_club_names    transaction                                */
/*----------------------------------------------------------------------*/
SHORT get_club_names(VOID)
{
   if (open_response_file())
      return(FAILED);

   /*-----------------------------------*/
   /* Select clubs and countries        */
   /*-----------------------------------*/
   EXEC SQL DECLARE CLUB_SEL CURSOR FOR
            SELECT DISTINCT CLUB, COUNTRY
            FROM CLUBS
            ORDER BY COUNTRY;

   /*-----------------------------------*/
   /* Open the cursor                   */
   /*-----------------------------------*/
   EXEC SQL OPEN CLUB_SEL;
   if (SQLCODE)
      { format_error(output_msgbuf, SQLCODE,"opening cursor",__FILE__,__LINE__);
        return(FAILED);
      }
```

Figure 38-4 (Part 6 of 9). CLUBSVR.SQC: The Transaction Server Program.

```
    /*------------------------------------*/
    /* Get row data                       */
    /*------------------------------------*/
    while (TRUE)
    { EXEC SQL FETCH CLUB_SEL
               INTO :club, :country;

      if ((SQLCODE!=0) && (SQLCODE != 100))
         { format_error(output_msgbuf, SQLCODE,"fetching data",__FILE__,__LINE__);
           return(FAILED);
         }

      if (SQLCODE == 100) break;

      /*------------------------------------*/
      /* Write row to response file         */
      /*------------------------------------*/
       if (!fprintf(rsp_file,"%32s  %32s\n", club, country))
         { format_error(output_msgbuf, 0L,"writing to response file",
                        __FILE__,__LINE__);
           return(FAILED);
         }
    } /* end while */

    /*------------------------------------*/
    /* Close the cursor                   */
    /*------------------------------------*/
    EXEC SQL CLOSE CLUB_SEL;
    if (SQLCODE)
       { format_error(output_msgbuf, SQLCODE,"closing cursor",__FILE__,__LINE__);
         return(FAILED);
       }

    /*------------------------------------*/
    /* Set the message, close response file*/
    /*------------------------------------*/
    sprintf(output_msgbuf,
           "TXN_COMPLETION = SUCCESS RESPONSE_FILE = %s", response_file_name);
    fclose (rsp_file);
    rsp_file = NULL;
    return(GOOD);
}/* end get_club_names */


          See program diskette for the following functions:

SHORT get_club_graphics(VOID)        { ... }
SHORT get_club_description(VOID)     { ... }
SHORT get_club_prices(VOID)          { ... }
SHORT find_all_reserv(VOID)          { ... }
SHORT find_reservation(VOID)         { ... }
SHORT add_reservation(VOID)          { ... }
SHORT cancel_reservation(VOID)       { ... }
SHORT generate_message_filename(VOID) { ... }
SHORT unknown_transaction(VOID)      { ... }
```

Figure 38-4 (Part 7 of 9). CLUBSVR.SQC: The Transaction Server Program.

```
/*-----------------------------------------------------------------------------*/
/* open a response file                                                        */
/*-----------------------------------------------------------------------------*/
SHORT open_response_file(VOID)
{
  sprintf(response_file_name,"R%5.5d%2.2d.TMP", pidinfo.pid, filenum % 99);
  if (NULL == (rsp_file = fopen(response_file_name,"w")))
     {format_error(output_msgbuf, (LONG)rsp_file,"opening response file",
                   __FILE__,__LINE__);
      return(FAILED);
     }
  return(GOOD);
} /* end open_response_file */

/*-----------------------------------------------------------------------------*/
/* open a message file                                                         */
/*-----------------------------------------------------------------------------*/
SHORT open_message_file(PCHAR message_file_name)
{
  if (NULL == (msg_file = fopen(message_file_name,"r")))
     {format_error(output_msgbuf, (LONG)rsp_file,"opening message file",
                   __FILE__,__LINE__);
      return(FAILED);
     }
  return(GOOD);
} /* end open_message_file */

/*-----------------------------------------------------------------------------*/
/* Error Format Routine                                                        */
/*-----------------------------------------------------------------------------*/
VOID format_error(PCHAR msgbuf, LONG Error, PCHAR msg,
                  PCHAR file, USHORT line)
{
  CHAR sql_msgbuf[256];

  if (rsp_file != NULL)
     { fclose (rsp_file);
       rsp_file = NULL;
     }
  if (SQLCODE)
  { sqlaintp(sql_msgbuf,                         /* buffer for msg text */
             sizeof(sql_msgbuf),                 /* buffer size         */
             80,                                 /* line width          */
             &sqlca);                            /* SQLCA               */
  } /* endif */
  sprintf(msgbuf, "TXN_COMPLETION = FAILED RESPONSE_FILE = NONE\n"
                  "Error %ld detected while %s at line %d in file %s.\n%s\n",
                   Error, msg, line, file, sql_msgbuf);
} /* end format_error */
```

Figure 38-4 (Part 8 of 9). CLUBSVR.SQC: The Transaction Server Program.

```
/*-----------------------------------------------------------------------*/
/* Error Display Routine                                                 */
/*-----------------------------------------------------------------------*/
VOID print_error(USHORT Error, PCHAR msg, PCHAR file, USHORT line)
{
 if (Error == 0)
    printf("Error detected while %s at line %d in file %s.\n",
           msg, line, file);
 else
    printf("Error %d detected while %s at line %d in file %s.\n",
          Error, msg, line, file);
} /* end print_error */
```

Figure 38-4 (Part 9 of 9). CLUBSVR.SQC: The Transaction Server Program.

CONGRATULATIONS AND GOODBYE

This is where the Club Med Grand Finale all comes together. This is also where the book comes to an end. If you've made it so far, congratulations; it was a long journey. We hope you got out of it what you were looking for. The future is with "downsized" client-server applications which run on PC LANs. OS/2 EE, in one form or another, provides most of the major components you will need to build mission-critical applications on PCs. We hope this lengthy introduction to client-server has shown you what elements are required to build such systems. Now that you know what to look for, you can shop around for the pieces.

As we said in the introduction, you may want to look at other vendor offerings for the missing "system" components or for extensions that suit your particular needs. The IBM solution is the *de facto* standard for extensions and is an excellent base for comparison shopping. Now that you've mastered SQL using OS/2 EE and the examples in this book, you may decide to switch database engines to SQL Server, Oracle or Gupta's SQLBase. For database front-end tools, you may prefer to use Borland, Sybase or Ingres tools. You may want to develop your own graphic interface using Gupta's SQLWindows, Choreographer or Easel. Client-Server is synonymous with "mix and match." Have fun!

Appendix A

RSQL Command Syntax

DATABASE ADMINISTRATION COMMANDS

```
BACKUP:
▸▸─EXEC DBA: BACKUP ── database_name ──┬─INCREMENTAL─┬─ drive  ───▸◂
                                       └─ ALL ───────┘

                     database_name -- char[9] no blanks
                     ALL           -- backup entire database
                     INCREMENTAL   -- backup only incremental changes
                     drive         -- name of drive on which to backup
```

Figure A-1 (Part 1 of 8). The RSQL Syntax for DBA Commands Presented in Alphabetical Order.

```
BIND:
►►─EXEC DBA: BIND ──── database_name ──── pgm_name ─┬─ISO─┬──────────►
                                                     ├─USA─┤
                                                     ├─DEF─┤
                                                     ├─EUR─┤
                                                     ├─JIS─┤
                                                     └─LOC─┘

►──────────┬─ REPEATABLE_READ ──┬─┬─ NO_BLOCKING ───┬─ user_id ─────►◄
           ├─ CURSOR_STABILITY ─┤ ├─ BLOCK_ALL ─────┤
           └─ UNCOMMITTED_READ ─┘ └─ BLOCK_UNAMBIG ─┘

                 database_name -- char[9] no blanks
                 pgm_name      -- The name and path of a bind file
                                  or the name and path of a file
                                  containing a list of bind file names.
                                  The name of the list file must
                                  be preceded by an ampersand.

                 One of the following date/time formats:
                 ISO           -- date/time = yyyy-mm-dd  hh.mm.ss
                 USA           -- date/time = mm.dd/yyyy  hh:mm xM
                 DEF           -- date/time from country code
                 EUR           -- date/time = dd.mm.yyyy  hh.mm.ss
                 JIS           -- date/time = yyyy-mm-dd  hh:mm:ss
                 LOC           -- Local form

                 One of the following locking Isolation Levels:
                 REPEATABLE_READ
                 CURSOR_STABILITY
                 UNCOMMITTED_READ

                 One of the following record blocking types:
                 NO_BLOCKING
                 BLOCK_ALL
                 BLOCK_UNAMBIG

                 grant_id      -- id with execute/bind privileges

Catalog Database:
►►─EXEC DBA: CATALOG_DB─ database_name ─ alias ─┬─ LOCAL ──┬──────────►
                                                └─ REMOTE ─┘

►── node_name ──────── drive ──────── comment ────────────────────►◄

                 database_name -- char[9] no blanks
                 alias         -- char[9] no blanks
                 Specify if the database is local or remote:
                 LOCAL         -- Local database
                 REMOTE        -- Remote database

                 node_name     -- char[9] no blanks,name of node on
                                  which remote database resides.
                 drive         -- drive on which database reside
                 comment       -- This is the comment that gets
                                  associated with the database
                                  char[31] no blanks
```

Figure A-1 (Part 2 of 8). The RSQL Syntax for DBA Commands Presented in Alphabetical Order.

```
Catalog Node:
▸▸-EXEC DBA: CATALOG_NODE- node_name ── local_lu ─ remote_lu ──────▸

 ▸────── mode ── comment ───────────────────────────────────▸◂

                        node_name     -- char[9] no blanks
                        local_lu      -- char[9] no blanks
                        remote_lu     -- char[9] no blanks
                        mode          -- char[9] no blanks
                        comment       -- comment for node directory entry.

Collect Status:
▸▸-EXEC DBA: COLLECT_STATUS ─ database_name ────────────────▸◂
                        database_name -- char[9] no blanks


Continue On Error:
▸▸-EXEC DBA: CONTINUE_ON_ERROR ──────────────────────────────▸◂

Create Database:
▸▸-EXEC DBA: CREATE_DB- database_name ─ drive - comment ──────▸◂

                        drive         -- drive on which database reside
                        comment       -- This is the comment that gets
                                         associated with the database
                                         char[31] no blanks

Drop Database:
▸▸-EXEC DBA: DROP_DB ─ database_name ────────────────────────▸◂

                        database_name -- char[9] no blanks
Export:
▸▸-EXEC DBA: EXPORT ── database_name ─ datafile ─┬─ DEL ─┬─ tname ─▸◂
                                                 ├─ WSF ─┤
                                                 └─ IXF ─┘

                        database_name -- char[9] no blanks
                        datafile      -- This is the path and name of the
                                         OS/2 file which will receive the
                                         exported data.

                        One of the following interchange file formats
                        is chosen:
                        DEL           -- Delimited ASCII  (dBase)
                        WSF           -- Work-sheet format (Lotus)
                        IXF           -- OS/2 DB manager format

                        tname         -- The fully qualified name of a
                                         table or view

Get Administrative Authority:
▸▸-EXEC DBA: GET_ADMIN ──────────────────────────────────────▸◂
```

Figure A-1 (Part 3 of 8). The RSQL Syntax for DBA Commands Presented in Alphabetical Order.

```
Import:
▶▶─EXEC DBA: IMPORT ── database_name ─────────── datafile ──────▶

▶───────┬── INSERT ──────────┬──────┬─ DEL ─┬────── tname ────────▶◀
        ├── REPLACE──────────┤      ├─ ASC ─┤
        ├── CREATE ──────────┤      ├─ WSF ─┤
        └─ REPLACE_CREATE ───┘      └─ IXF ─┘

                        database_name  -- char[9] no blanks
                        password       -- char[9] no blanks
                        datafile       -- This is the path and name of the
                                          OS/2 file containing the data to
                                          be imported.

                        One of the following control parameters is
                        specified to detemine the disposition of existing
                        table data:
                        INSERT         -- add data to table
                        REPLACE        -- delete all rows then add new data
                        CREATE         -- create and add only with IXF
                        REPLACE_CREATE -- replace create and add, IXF only

                        One of the following interchange file formats
                        is chosen:
                        DEL           -- Delimited ASCII  (dBase)
                        ASC           -- Non delimited ASCII import only
                        WSF           -- Work-sheet format (Lotus)
                        IXF           -- OS/2 DB manager format

                        tname         -- The fully qualified name of a
                                         table or non-read-only view
Install Signal Handler:
▶▶─EXEC DBA: INSTALL_SIG ──────────────────────────────────────────▶◀

Interrupt:
▶▶─EXEC DBA: INTERRUPT ────────────────────────────────────────────▶◀

Logoff:
▶▶─EXEC DBA: LOGOFF ── userid ─ remotename ───┬─ UPM_LOCAL ──┬────▶◀
                                              ├─ UPM_DNODE ──┤
                                              └─ UPM_DOMAIN ─┘
                        userid        -- char[9] no blanks
                        remotename    -- char[9] no blanks

                        One of the following remote types is used:
                        UPM_LOCAL     -- local node
                        UPM_DNODE     -- LU 6.2 node
                        UPM_DOMAIN    -- domain name
```

Figure A-1 (Part 4 of 8). The RSQL Syntax for DBA Commands Presented in Alphabetical Order.

```
Logon:
▶▶─EXEC DBA: LOGON ── userid ─ password ─ remotename ──────────▶◀

▶──────── UPM_LOCAL ──────── UPM_CONFIG ───────────────────────▶◀
        ├ UPM_DNODE ─┤    ├ UPM_ADMIN ─┤
        └ UPM_DOMAIN ┘    └ UPM_USER  ─┘

                  userid        -- char[9] no blanks
                  password      -- char[9] no blanks
                  remotename    -- char[9] no blanks

                  One of the following remote types is used:
                  UPM_LOCAL     -- local node
                  UPM_DNODE     -- LU 6.2 node
                  UPM_DOMAIN    -- domain name

                  One of the following authority indicators:
                  UPM_CONFIG    -- started from config.sys
                  UPM_ADMIN     -- local user has Administrative authority
                  UPM_USER      -- no additional authority required

Pause RSQL directive
▶▶─EXEC DBA: PAUSE          ───────────────────────────────────▶◀

REORG Table:
▶▶─EXEC DBA: REORG ── database_name ─ tname ── tindex ─────────▶◀

                  database_name -- char[9] no blanks
                  tname         -- fully qualified table name to reorg
                  tindex        -- fully qualified index name to
                                   be used in reorg. Rows are
                                   physically ordered according to
                                   this index. Enter NULL if no index

RESET Database Manager Configuration:
▶▶─EXEC DBA: RESET_DM_CFG ─────────────────────────────────────▶◀

RESET Database Configuration:
▶▶─EXEC DBA: RESET_DB_CFG ─ database_name ─────────────────────▶◀
                  database_name -- char[9] no blanks

RESTORE Database:
▶▶─EXEC DBA: RESTORE ─ database_name ─ db_drive ─ bk_drive ────▶◀

                  database_name -- char[9] no blanks
                  db_drive      -- drive on which database reside
                  bk_drive      -- drive on which backup resides

Run Statistics on a Table:
▶▶─EXEC DBA: RUNSTATS── tname ─────────────────────────────────▶◀

                  tname         -- fully qualified table
                                   name to reorg.

Show Database Configuration:
▶▶─EXEC DBA: SHOW_DB_CFG ─ database_name ──────────────────────▶◀

                  database_name -- char[9] no blanks
```

Figure A-1 (Part 5 of 8). The RSQL Syntax for DBA Commands Presented in Alphabetical Order.

```
Show Database Directory:
►►─EXEC DBA: SHOW_DB_DIR ──────── db_drive ──────────────────────────────►◄

                   db_drive      -- drive on which database reside
                                    '0' = system database

Show Database Manager Configuration:
►►─EXEC DBA: SHOW_DM_CFG ────────────────────────────────────────────────►◄

Show Node Directory:
►►─EXEC DBA: SHOW_NODE_DIR ──────────────────────────────────────────────►◄

Show Database Status:
►►─EXEC DBA: SHOW_STATUS ────────────────────────────────────────────────►◄

Start Database Manager:
►►─EXEC DBA: STARTDM ────────────────────────────────────────────────────►◄

Start Use Database (connect):
►►─EXEC DBA: STARTUSE ─database_name ─┬─ S ─┬────────────────────────────►◄
                                      └─ X ─┘

                   database_name -- char[9] no blanks
                   S             -- shared mode use of database
                   X             -- exclusive mode use of database

Stop Database Manager:
►►─EXEC DBA: STOPDM ─────────────────────────────────────────────────────►◄

Stop On Error:
►►─EXEC DBA: STOP_ON_ERROR ──────────────────────────────────────────────►◄

Stop Use Database (disconnect):
►►─EXEC DBA: STOPUSE ────────────────────────────────────────────────────►◄

Uncatalog Database:
►►─EXEC DBA: UNCATALOG_DB─ database_name ────────────────────────────────►◄
                   database_name -- char[9] no blanks

Uncatalog Node:
►►─EXEC DBA: UNCATALOG_NODE─ nodename ───────────────────────────────────►◄
                   nodename      -- char[9] no blanks
```

Figure A-1 (Part 6 of 8). The RSQL Syntax for DBA Commands Presented in Alphabetical Order.

Update Database Configuration:

```
                                             ┌──────────,──────────────┐
                                             ↓                         │
▸▸─EXEC DBA: UPDATE_DB_CFG — database_name ─┬─ MAXAPPLS    =  value  ─┬─▸◂
                                             ├─ MAXFILOP    =  value  ─┤
                                             ├─ MAXTOTFILOP=  value  ─┤
                                             ├─ BUFFPAGE    =  value  ─┤
                                             ├─ DLCHKTIME   =  value  ─┤
                                             ├─ LOCKLIST    =  value  ─┤
                                             ├─ MAXLOCKS    =  value  ─┤
                                             ├─ APPLHEAPSZ  =  value  ─┤
                                             ├─ AGENTHEAP   =  value  ─┤
                                             ├─ SORTHEAP    =  value  ─┤
                                             ├─ DBHEAP      =  value  ─┤
                                             ├─ STMTHEAP    =  value  ─┤
                                             ├─ LOGFILSIZ   =  string ─┤
                                             ├─ LOGPRIMARY  =  value  ─┤
                                             ├─ LOGSECOND   =  value  ─┤
                                             ├─ SOFTMAX     =  value  ─┤
                                             ├─ NEWLOGPATH  =  string ─┤
                                             └─ DETS        =  value  ─┘

                    database_name -- char[9] no blanks
```

Update Database Configuration(cont.):

The parameters can have the following values:

Token Name	Config Parameter Description	Units	Range	Default
MAXAPPLS	Max. Active Applications	Appl.	1-117	8
MAXFILOP	Max. DB Files Open/Application	files	2-235	20
MAXTOTFILOP	Max. Files Open/Application	files	25-32700	255
BUFFPAGE	Buffer Pool Size	4K pages	(1)	16
DLCHKTIME	Time Interval for Deadlocks	millisec.	1-600 sec.	10
LOCKLIST	Max. Storage for Locklists	4K pages	4-250	8
MAXLOCKS	Max. percent locklist/appl.	percent	1-100	22
APPLHEAPSZ	Default Application Heap	segments	2-20	3
AGENTHEAP	Application Agent Heap	segments	2-85	3
SORTHEAP	Sort List Heap	segments	1-20	2
DBHEAP	Database Heap	segments	1-45	1
STMTHEAP	SQL Statement Heap	segments		64
LOGFILSIZ	Log File Size	4K pages	15-255	50
LOGPRIMARY	Primary Log Files	files	0-63	2
LOGSECOND	Secondary Log Files	files	0-63	3
SOFTMAX	Log Records/soft checkpoint	records	0-65535	100
NEWLOGPATH	New Log Location	path string		
DETS	Copy Protection		0-1	

Figure A-1 (Part 7 of 8). The RSQL Syntax for DBA Commands Presented in Alphabetical Order.

```
Update Database Manager Configuration:

                                        ┌──────────,──────────┐
                                        ▼                     │
▸▸─EXEC DBA: UPDATE_DM_CFG ─────────────┬─ RQRIOBLK   = value ─┴─▸◂
                                        ├─ SVRIOBLK   = value ─┤
                                        ├─ SQLENSEG   = value ─┤
                                        ├─ NUMDB      = value ─┤
                                        ├─ NNAME      = string ┤
                                        ├─ COMHEAPSZ  = value ─┤
                                        ├─ RSHEAPSZ   = value ─┤
                                        └─ NUMRC      = value ─┘

    where the parameters can have the following values:

    Token Name  Description                       Units     Range   Default
    ──────────  ────────────────────────────────  ────────  ──────  ──────────
    RQRIOBLK    Max. Reqestor I/O Block Size      bytes     4-64K   0/0/4   (2)
    SVRIOBLK    Max. Server   I/O Block Size      bytes     4-64K   0/4/4/0 (2)
    SQLENSEG    Max. Shared Segments              Segments  7-802   20/50   (1)
    NUMDB       Max. Concurrently Active apps.    Number    1-8     3/8     (1)
    COMHEAPSZ   Communication Heap Size           Segments  1-255   2
    RSHEAPSZ    Remote Data Services Heap size    Segments  1-255   2
    NUMRC       Max. Remote Connections           Number    1-255   10      (3)
    NNAME       Node Name                         String

     (1) - Stand-alone/Server
     (2) - Stand-alone/Server/Requester-Server/Requester
     (3) - Server
```

Figure A-1 (Part 8 of 8). The RSQL Syntax for DBA Commands Presented in Alphabetical Order.

THE RSQL SYNTAX FOR THE QUERY MANAGER CALLABLE INTERFACE

```
Start Query Manager:

                                        ┌──────────,──────────┐
                                        ▼                     │
▸▸─EXEC QM: START ──────────────────────┬─ DSQSCMD   = string ─┴─▸◂
                                        ├─ DSQSMODE  = string ─┤
                                        ├─ DSQSPROF  = string ─┤
                                        ├─ DSQSDBNM  = string ─┤
                                        ├─ DSQSQUAL  = string ─┤
                                        ├─ DSQSPOOL  = string ─┤
                                        ├─ DSQSRUN   = string ─┤
                                        └─ DSQDSPLY  = string ─┘
```

Figure A-2 (Part 1 of 2). The RSQL Syntax for the Query Manager Callable Interface.

```
Set Query Manager Variables:

                                                        ┌──────────,──────────┐
                                                        ↓                     │
▸▸─EXEC QM: ─ SET ──┬─ GLOBAL ──┬─┬─ CHAR ─┬─┴─ var-name   = string ─┴─▸◂
                    ├─ LOCAL ───┤ └─ FINT ─┘
                    └─ CURRENT ─┘

Get Query Manager Variables:

                                                        ┌──────────,──────────┐
                                                        ↓                     │
▸▸─EXEC QM: ─ GET ──┬─ GLOBAL ──┬─┬─ CHAR ─┬─┴─ var-name ──────────┴─▸◂
                    ├─ LOCAL ───┤ └─ FINT ─┘
                    └─ CURRENT ─┘

Execute the Query Manager Simple Command Set:

                                                        ┌──────────,──────────┐
                                                        ↓                     │
▸▸─EXEC QM: ─┬─ BEGIN WINDOW ──┬────────────────────────┴─ cmd-parms ──────┴─▸◂
             ├─ BEGIN WORK ────┤
             ├─ CANCEL WORK ───┤
             ├─ CONVERT QUERY ─┤
             ├─ DEFINE TABLE ──┤
             ├─ DISPLAY ───────┤
             ├─ EDIT TABLE ────┤
             ├─ END WINDOW ────┤
             ├─ END WORK ──────┤
             ├─ ERASE ─────────┤
             ├─ EXIT ──────────┤
             ├─ EXPORT TABLE ──┤
             ├─ GET ───────────┤
             ├─ IMPORT TABLE ──┤
             ├─ LIST ──────────┤
             ├─ MESSAGE ───────┤
             ├─ PRINT ─────────┤
             ├─ RESET ─────────┤
             ├─ RUN ───────────┤
             └─ SAVE ──────────┘
```

Figure A-2 (Part 2 of 2). The RSQL Syntax for the Query Manager Callable Interface.

Index

A

B

C

D

E

F

G

H

I

O

P

Q

R

S

T

Ordering Sample Program Diskettes

As a convenience and learning aid you may order diskettes containing the current version of the programs contained in "Client-Server Programming With OS/2 Extended Edition". The source files are shipped on an unsupported, as-is basis. Neither the Authors nor Van Nostrand Reinhold assume any liability with respect to the use, accuracy, or fitness of information contained within the diskettes.

Send the order form with payment to:

Client-Server Programs
124-H Blossom Hill Road, Box 600
San Jose, Ca. 95123

"Client-Server Programming with OS/2 EE" Diskette Offer

Name______________________________ Company____________________________

Address____________________________ City________________ State_______

Country____ Zip________

2 - 5 1/4" 1.2 MByte diskettes
Quantity ____________@$29.95 Total: $________________

2 - 3 1/2" 1.4 MByte diskettes
Quantity ____________@$29.95 Total: $________________

California residents, add 6.5%
Santa Clara County, Ca. residents add 7% Tax: $________________

____U.S. Orders - $2.50
____Foreign Orders - $5.00
____Overnight Delivery - $11.00 (U.S. only) Shipping & Handling: $________________

_____ Check or Money order enclosed.
Make Payable to "Client-Server Programs"
Overnight delivery orders must be accompanied by a money order. Total Order Amount $________________

Overnight deliveries mailed within two business days.
Allow 4-6 weeks delivery within the U.S. if not overnight delivery.

Ordering Sample Program Diskettes

As a convenience and learning aid you may order diskettes containing the current version of the programs contained in "Client-Server Programming With OS/2 Extended Edition". The source files are shipped on an unsupported, as-is basis. Neither the Authors nor Van Nostrand Reinhold assume any liability with respect to the use, accuracy, or fitness of information contained within the diskettes.

Send the order form with payment to:

Client-Server Programs
124-H Blossom Hill Road, Box 600
San Jose, Ca. 95123

"Client-Server Programming with OS/2 EE" Diskette Offer

Name____________________ Company____________________

Address____________________ City____________ State________

Country______________________________ Zip________

2 - 5 1/4" 1.2 MByte diskettes
Quantity __________@$29.95 Total: $____________

2 - 3 1/2" 1.4 MByte diskettes
Quantity __________@$29.95 Total: $____________

California residents, add 6.5%
Santa Clara County, Ca. residents add 7% Tax: $____________

____U.S. Orders - $2.50
____Foreign Orders - $5.00
____Overnight Delivery - $11.00 (U.S. only) Shipping & Handling: $____________

_____ Check or Money order enclosed.
Make Payable to "Client-Server Programs"
Overnight delivery orders must be accompanied by a money order. Total Order Amount $____________

Overnight deliveries mailed within two business days.
Allow 4-6 weeks delivery within the U.S. if not overnight delivery.